A Survey and Study of Each Book
From Genesis to Revelation
COMPLETE IN ONE VOLUME !

EXPLORE THE BOOK

J. Sidlow Baxter

ZONDERVAN PUBLISHING HOUSE OF THE ZONDERVAN CORPORATION
GRAND RAPIDS, MICHIGAN 49506

EXPLORE THE BOOK

Copyright by J. Sidlow Baxter

First published U.S.A. 1960

No part to be reproduced without permission

Library of Congress Catalog Card Number 60-50187

First printing (6 vols. in 1)   1966
Seventeenth printing   1980
ISBN 0-310-20620-0

Printed in the United States of America

DEDICATION

These studies are dedicated with deep gratitude and affectionate esteem to my beloved, saintly, and now elderly friend,

JAMES ARTHUR YOXALL, ESQ.,
of Ashton-under-Lyne
and Stalybridge;

my spiritual "father" and gifted teacher in the precious things of Christ; the inspirer of many heavenward aspirings within me, the one who first planted in my youthful heart a zest for Bible study; who has always been to me the ideal Christian gentleman, the choicest of preachers, and, above all, a kindly, experienced older friend ever brimming over with the sanctifying love of the Lord Jesus.

FOREWORD

THE BULK of the instalments which comprise this Bible Course were originally delivered as my Thursday evening Bible Lectures in Charlotte Chapel, Edinburgh. That accounts for their conversational mode of address in parts. They were not written as essays, but were designed for public utterance, and I have thought it wise to leave them in their first form, believing that there are certain practical advantages in so doing. I would ask that this be noted leniently, especially if the exacting eyes of some literary connoisseur or dilettante should wander over them in their now-printed fixity. Moreover, I must plead that as these studies were first prepared to be spoken, without thought of later publication, I have in various parts indulged a preacher's rather than a writer's liberty in appropriating from the writings of others. I can only hope that sheer admiration may not have betrayed me too near the dreaded boundary-line of plagiarism. If it has, then I am relieved to feel certain that it can only be with authors who are no longer with us. I can never be too grateful to dear old (and, to many, old-fashioned) John Kitto, and to John Urquhart and A. T. Pierson, and Sir Robert Anderson, and G. Campbell Morgan, and others of the same evangelical tradition. They were all masters in their own day and in their own way. To them all, and to that incomparable composite work, the *Pulpit Commentary*, I here acknowledge my repeated indebtedness, and pay my tribute to them all. This Bible Course as a whole, however, is solidly the product of my own independent study, and I gladly accept responsibility for it, believing that in every part it genuinely honours the Bible as the inspired Word of God. May God graciously crown it with a ministry of usefulness to many who live and labour for His dear Son, our Lord and Saviour.

J. S. B.

CONTENTS OF VOLUME ONE

	PAGE
INTRODUCTION	9
PRELIMINARY	15
THE BOOK OF GENESIS Studies 1, 2, 3, 4	21
THE BOOK OF EXODUS Studies 5, 6, 7, 8	73
THE BOOK OF LEVITICUS Studies 9, 10, 11, 12	111
THE BOOK OF NUMBERS Studies 13, 14, 15, 16	155
THE BOOK OF DEUTERONOMY Studies 17, 18, 19	207
THE BOOK OF JOSHUA Studies 20, 21, 22, 23	235

THE BIBLE

"Within this wondrous volume lies
The mystery of mysteries;
Happiest they of human race
To whom their God has given grace
To read, to fear, to hope, to pray,
To lift the latch, to find the way;
And better had they ne'er been born
Who read to doubt, or read to scorn."

SIR WALTER SCOTT.

INTRODUCTION

No MAN's education is complete if he does not know the Bible No Christian minister is really qualified for the ministry of the Christian Church without a thorough study of the Bible. No Christian worker can be fully effective without a ready knowledge of the Bible. No Christian believer can live the Christian life to the full without an adequate grasp of the Bible.

Our Purpose

Our purpose in this present course of Bible study is to give *a grounding in the Scriptures*. Let us be frank and clear at the outset. If we really want to know the word of God better, this course of study will help us. Our effort has been to maintain the same standard of thoroughness throughout. We would emphasise, however, that it is no use reading the following studies *instead of* the Bible. To do that would be to miss the purpose altogether. What we are after is that *the Bible itself* shall be read, part by part, each part several times over, and the present scheme of studies used *along with* this. However carefully the following lessons are read, if they are read *without* the parallel study of the Bible itself, the real fascination of Bible study will be missed. Our hope is that some who have not yet studied their way right through the Bible will resolve on devoting such and such hours of their available time each week to beginning at Genesis and gradually exploring the whole Bible, book by book, as directed by this Bible study course, and using the help which is here provided at each stage.

With all too many Christians today the tendency is to read the Bible just to pick up a few good points or suggestions for addressing meetings or preparing sermons, or to pick out a few nice bits to help with the Christian life. This is bad. It results in scrappiness. It engenders superficiality both mentally and spiritually. The word of God was never meant merely for these hurried consultations. We need to study and to know the written word of God as a whole, for such study and knowledge gives depth and richness and fulness to *all* our public ministry, and stabilises our whole Christian experience. Moreover, I would remind fellow-preachers that the greatest sermons usually come when we are not looking for sermons but are studying the word of God for the sake of its own vital truth.

Now this present course of Bible study is not meant merely to yield suggestions for addresses and sermons—though it will probably do that again and again if really studied along with the Bible. It is meant to give a practical grip on the Bible as a whole. We do well to realise that those sermons or books which most stir us at the time of hearing or reading often leave us little that is of permanent value, while, on the other hand, those that teach us most may not be so immediately stirring. Quite apart from any superficial interest of the moment, such as preparing messages or seeking guidance in some crisis, we should determine to get a worthy grasp of God's book; for to know it well gives a quality to our Christian service which nothing else can, and stands us in good stead throughout our life. Every Christian minister and worker should be a specialist in the Bible.

Our Method

We ought to say a few words here about our *method*. The Bible is such an endless book, and there are so many ways of studying it, that as we launch forth into this course of studies we are reminded of the sailor who, when asked where he sailed, said: "Sir, I am restricted to the ocean!" Like a great ocean, the wonderful contents of the Bible are before us, but we do not want to be merely sailing anywhere—or we shall get nowhere! We need the chart and compass of a settled method so that we may navigate these glorious seas without unprofitable digressions to the right hand or to the left.

Much depends on our method of study. According to choice, we may study the books of the Bible spiritually, historically, typically, topically, prophetically, dispensationally, analytically, biographically, critically, devotionally, or in other ways. The method which we adopt in this present series is that which we may call *interpretative*. We shall study the books of the Bible interpretatively; that is, we shall seek to get hold of the controlling thought, the outstanding meaning and message of each book, and then see it in relation to the other books of Scripture. The importance of this kind of study will be obvious at once; for unless we grasp the *significance* of what is written we miss that which is of first concern. Moreover, this progressive, interpretative study of the Scriptures is really a necessary basis and preliminary to all the other kinds of study which we have mentioned.

Following this method, then, and with a view to determining the essential message of each book, as we take each of the different books in turn we shall set forth its *STRUCTURE*, by means of an analysis; its main movements in the form of a *SYNOPSIS*; and its special features by way of *SUGGESTION* for further study. We shall let each book tell us its secret and open its heart to us. We shall resolutely guard against forcing any artificial outline on any book of Scripture. To sacrifice exactness for the sake of smart alliteration is an impertinence when dealing with Divinely inspired writings. There are Bible teachers today, of a certain type, who excel in ingenious "skeletons." But an erroneous analysis, however adroitly drawn up, obscures the real and vital message of a book. As we proceed with our studies we shall see how often a book or passage lights up with new force or beauty when a true analysis is made of it.

It may be thought strange at first, perhaps, that we give some books fuller treatment and more detailed analysis than others. We would point out, therefore, that this variation is in accord with our purpose. The relative importance of things must not be gauged simply by the page-space which they occupy. As the one small diamond outvalues the large square of plate-glass, and as the epochal event of one day may dwarf the ordinary doings of decades, so in the Scriptures, while everything has its due place, there are things which stand out, as did Saul among the sons of Israel, head and shoulders above their fellows. Each part is important; but some parts are especially so.

Therefore our aim is to deal with each book or part in just such a way as will most effectively lay bare its special significance, and thus contribute most effectively toward a practical hold on the message of the Bible in its entirety. It is for this reason that we have given fuller treatment to the five books of Moses, which are the foundation of all else. It is for this reason, also, that we deal more in detail with a book like Leviticus, the words and symbols and types and ideas of which are interwoven with all that follows, right to the end of the Apocalypse, whereas we give comparatively brief treatment to 1 and 2 Chronicles, the contents of which, being historical, need to be grouped rather than minutely expounded. Our purpose is not that of a Commentary, in which the books, chapters, paragraphs and verses are successively annotated. Let it be borne in mind throughout that we are after the main meanings and special significances, with a view to getting the broad scope and comprehensive message of the whole.

Our Approach

A right *approach* to the Bible is of utmost importance. There is a movement today to popularise the Bible simply as *literature*. It is our careful opinion that such a movement has in it more of harm than of good. Amid the wonderful *diversity* of the Scriptures there is an even more wonderful *unity*. The sixty-six books are not simply a collection of writings; they are one book—one in the progressiveness of the revelation which they collectively unfold, one in the harmony of the structure which they collectively constitute, one in the spiritual unity of the message which they collectively declare. The Bible *as a whole* claims to be the word of God; and its claim is substantiated both by the nature of its contents and the history of its influence. If, then, this book is the word of *GOD* it cannot be read simply as literature! —not without forcing the mind to an artificial or evasive or dishonest attitude which must prove harmful. In the studies which we here commence we approach the Bible as being in its totality *the Word of God*; and in all our studying of it, therefore, we are seeking to learn, under the illumination of the Holy Spirit, the mind and the truth and the will of *God*.

In our study of the Bible, also, we need ever to guard against becoming so engrossed in the fascination of the *subject* that we lose sight of the *object*. As we have said, in these studies we want to get hold of the big, broad meanings in the wonderful old Book: but unless the meanings get hold of *us* our study will have failed of its vital objective. Our Lord Jesus Himself has taught us that *HE* is the focal theme of all the Scriptures; and everywhere, therefore, we want to see beyond the *written* word, to Him who is the *living* Word. And we want to see Him in such a way as causes us to love and trust Him the more. Dr. Jowett tells of a tourist who was travelling through some of Scotland's loveliest scenery, but who was so absorbed in his guide book that he never saw the loveliness through which he was passing. There can be Bible study of that sort, too. Our great object is to know the true God, to become more like Christ, and to be more fully possessed by the Holy Spirit. True Bible study will encompass that object, for the inspired pages of Holy writ live and thrill and glow with the presence of God!

Let us therefore come to the Scriptures very *reverently*, realising that they are inbreathed by the Holy Spirit, and that He, the Holy Spirit, "the Spirit of wisdom and unveiling" in the knowledge of God (Eph. i. 18), must be our Teacher. Let our prayer be: "Open Thou mine eyes, that I may behold wondrous things out of Thy law" (Ps. cxix. 18). And let the dominating motive in all our study of God's word be, in the words of Colossians i. 10: "*That ye might walk worthy of the Lord unto all pleasing, being fruitful in every good work, and increasing in the knowledge of God.*"

This is the greatest book on earth,
    Unparalleled it stands;
Its author God, its truth Divine,
Inspired in every word and line,
    Tho' writ by human hands.

This is the living rock of truth
    Which all assaults defies.
O'er every stormy blast of time
It towers with majesty sublime;
    It lives, and never dies.

This is the volume of the Cross;
    Its saving truth is sure;
Its doctrine pure, its history true,
Its Gospel old, yet ever new,
    Shall evermore endure.

PRELIMINARY

The Bible as a Whole

WITH THE aforementioned method and motive clearly in our minds, we now open our Bible to explore this wonderful old Book of Books as far as the self-imposed limits of our present study-scheme will allow us. But before we actually make a start with Genesis, it will be helpful for us to take an anticipative view of the Bible as a whole.

Our Bible consists of sixty-six component parts. These are divided into two distinctive major collections, the Old Covenant scriptures and the New Covenant scriptures; or, as we commonly name them, the Old and New Testaments. But each of these two Testaments, the one consisting of thirty-nine books, the other of twenty-seven, is found to be arranged in certain clearly homogeneous groups; and in this connection careful investigation reveals the presence of a marvellous Divine design running through the whole.

THE OLD TESTAMENT

The First Seventeen

Take the Old Testament first. We start with Genesis, Exodus, Leviticus, Numbers and Deuteronomy. These obviously constitute a fivefold unity which marks them off at once as a separate group. They are all from one pen, that of Moses. They are all historical. They have always been known as the Five Books of Moses or the Pentateuch. Note, then, their number and their nature. As to their number, they are *five*. As to their nature, they are *historical*.

Next we find Joshua, Judges, Ruth, 1 Samuel, 2 Samuel, 1 Kings, 2 Kings, 1 Chronicles, 2 Chronicles, Ezra, Nehemiah, Esther. We instinctively stop at Esther, without going on to the Book of Job, because we are conscious that with Job we come to a very different kind of literature. Joshua to Esther are the twelve which make up the second main group of books in the Old Testament. Note the number and nature again. As to their number, they are *twelve*. As to their nature, they are again *historical*.

So, then, the first stretch of our Old Testament consists of *seventeen historical* books, falling into a natural sub-division of five and twelve. And there is a further sub-division in the twelve; for the first nine (Joshua to 2 Chronicles) are records of Israel's *occupancy* of Canaan, while the last three (Ezra, Nehemiah, Esther) concern the period after the *expulsion* from the land, and the repatriation of the "Remnant". Thus the seventeen historical books are really sub-divided into five (pre-Canaan), nine (in Canaan), and three (post-Exile).

The Middle Five

Next we find Job, Psalms, Proverbs, Ecclesiastes and the Song of Solomon. We need no telling to make another break at the end of the Song of Solomon, for immediately following it is the Book of the Prophet Isaiah, which obviously introduces another and quite different set of writings, i.e. those of the prophets. There is no doubt about it—Job, Psalms, Proverbs, Ecclesiastes and the Song of Solomon belong together and make up the third distinctive Old Testament group. All the preceding seventeen, as we have noted, are found to be historical; but these further five are not historical; they are individual and experiential. All of the foregoing seventeen historical books are national; but these five are not national, they are personal, and they deal mainly with the problems of the individual human heart. Moreover, the preceding seventeen are all written in prose, whereas these further five are not prose; they are poetry. So then, mark their number and their nature. As to their number, they are *five*. As to their nature, they are *experiential*.

The Remaining Seventeen

Finally, we come to another stretch of seventeen. This time it is the prophetical books: Isaiah, Jeremiah, Lamentations, Ezekiel, Daniel, Hosea, Joel, Amos, Obadiah, Jonah, Micah, Nahum, Habakkuk, Zephaniah, Haggai, Zechariah, Malachi. Obviously these seventeen belong together just as clearly as do the seventeen historical books. And just as we found the seventeen historical books sub-dividing themselves into five (Moses) and twelve (Joshua to Esther), so do we find it with these seventeen prophetical books. The first five are rightly termed the "*Major* Prophets", while the remaining twelve, which were always classed together as one book in the Jewish canon of the Old Testament (see Acts vii. 42), are known as the "*Minor* Prophets".

That this is no artificial distinction a moment's reflection will show. It is in Isaiah, Jeremiah, Ezekiel and Daniel that we find the basic ethical features of all Old Testament prophecy and the comprehensive scheme of Messianic prediction. In Isaiah the coming Messiah is seen both as the suffering Saviour and as the victorious Sovereign who reigns in world empire. In Jeremiah, where we also have Jehovah's full case against Israel, He is the righteous "Branch" of David and the ultimate Restorer of the judged and dispersed people. In Ezekiel, looking beyond intermediate judgments, we see Him as the perfect Shepherd-King in whose glorious reign the ideal temple of the future is erected. In Daniel, who gives us the most particularised programme of times and events in their successive order, we see the Messiah "cut off" without throne or kingdom, yet standing up at last as universal Emperor on the ruins of the crashed Gentile world-system.

The twelve "minor" prophets, though they amplify various aspects, do not determine the main shape of Messianic prophecy; they conform to the general frame already formed for us in Isaiah, Jeremiah, Ezekiel and Daniel.

Nor let it be thought that the poetic dirge, "Lamentations", is merely an addendum to Jeremiah. Not only does it have the marks of independence and separateness, but it also has a positional significance which we should not fail to note. It is the centre-point of the "major" prophets. That is, it divides Isaiah and Jeremiah on the one hand from Ezekiel and Daniel on the other. In other words, it intersects between the greatest two of the *pre*-exile prophets and the greatest two of the *post*-exile prophets. And it belongs there properly, for besides dividing them *positionally* it divides them *historically*. It monumentalises that toweringly and tragically significant event, which separates the pre-exile from the post-exile prophets, namely the destruction of Jerusalem, the abortion of the Davidic dynasty, and the scattering of the covenant people in a world-wide dispersion from which even yet, after 2,500 years, they have not been regathered, although providentially preserved as a distinct people.

Moreover, as the last twelve of the seventeen *historical* books further sub-divide themselves into nine and three, the first nine being *pre*-exilic, and the remaining three (Ezra, Nehemiah, Esther) being *post*-exilic, so is it with these twelve "minor" prophets, i.e. the first nine are all *pre*-exilic, while the remaining three (Haggai, Zechariah, Malachi) are *post*-exilic; and these two terminal trios, the last three *historical* books and the last three *prophetical*, have a reciprocal correspondence with each other.

Thus the thirty-nine books of our Old Testament fall into this orderly grouping of seventeen historical, five experiential, and seventeen prophetical, with both the seventeens sub-grouped into five and nine and three, and the five books which deal with the individual human heart placed right between the two seventeens, at the very heart of the Old Testament.

Is this accident or design? Think of it: over thirty writers contributed to the Old Testament, spaced out over twelve hundred years, writing in different places, to different parties, for different purposes, and little dreaming that their writings, besides being preserved through generations, were eventually to be compiled into that systematic plurality in unity which we now find in the Old Testament. When one reflects on this, surely one cannot be charged with fancifulness for thinking that behind the human writers there must have been a controlling divine design.

THE NEW TESTAMENT

Gospels and Acts

We turn to the New Testament now; and here we find equal order, with equally evident design. First we have Matthew, Mark, Luke, John, Acts. These are the only historical books of the New Testament, and are foundational to everything which follows, and therefore stand together. Note their number and their nature. As to their number, they are *five*. As to their nature, they are *historical*.

Christian Church Epistles

Next comes a group which just as plainly coheres as one subsidiary whole. It is that group of epistles which are all addressed to *Christian Churches*: Romans, 1 Corinthians, 2 Corinthians, Galatians, Ephesians, Philippians, Colossians, 1 and 2 Thessalonians. Note their number and their nature. As to their number, they are *nine*. As to their nature, they are *doctrinal*.

Pastoral Epistles

Then come four epistles which are another little group in themselves, namely, 1 Timothy, 2 Timothy, Titus, Philemon. These four are not written to Christian churches. They are *pastoral and personal*.

Hebrew Christian Epistles

Finally, we have another group of nine, that is, Hebrews, James, 1 Peter, 2 Peter, 1 and 2 and 3 John, Jude, Revelation (which is really an epistle of our Lord Himself: see the opening verse). These nine are not addressed to Christian churches as the other nine are; and indeed there is nothing in any of them about the Church mystical either. The first of them (Hebrews) is obviously addressed to the Hebrew nation as such. James, likewise, is addressed to "the twelve tribes which are scattered abroad". And Peter addresses his writing to "the sojourners of the Dispersion" (i.e., the Jews of the Dispersion). There is no need to go into further details to show that these nine epistles, Hebrews to the Apocalypse, are distinctively Hebrew in their standpoint and atmosphere, and they are rightly called the "Hebrew Christian Epistles".

A Wonderful Archway

Thus our New Testament consists of five historical books, making a solid, fivefold slab of basic fact beneath our feet; then, rising up on each side, like two beautifully wrought pillars, the nine Christian Church Epistles and the nine Hebrew Christian Epistles; and these two wonderful pillars are connected and arched by the four Pastoral Epistles, the whole making a wonderful archway of truth into the Church of Christ and the Kingdom of God, and reaching its high vertex in that transcendent epitome of

Christian truth, "Great is the mystery of godliness, God was manifest in the flesh, justified in the Spirit, seen of angels, preached unto the Gentiles, believed on in the world, received up into glory". Yes, by its literary structure, the New Testament is a wonderful *archway* into saving truth and everlasting blessedness.

The comparative and contrastive parallels between the two ninefold groups of epistles is a study all in itself. Both groups start with a great doctrinal treatise, Romans and Hebrews respectively. Both groups end with an eschatological unveiling, 1 and 2 Thessalonians in the one case, and the book of the Revelation in the other. Romans, at the beginning of the first group, shows us that salvation in Christ is the *only* way. Hebrews, at the beginning of the second group, shows us that salvation through Christ is the *better* way. In Thessalonians, at the end of the first group, we see the second coming of Christ especially in relation to the *Church*. In Revelation at the end of the second group, we see the second coming of Christ especially in relation to *Israel* and the *nations*. And so on; for we might elaborate this much further.

This presence of plan and design does not only pertain to the Bible in this general sense; it runs through all the different book-groups considered separately; and the more we follow it through in detail, so the more wonderful it becomes, until all possibility of its being mere coincidence is eliminated by overwhelming abundance of evidence that this is indeed the word of the living God.

NEW TESTAMENT

EXPERIENCE : DOCTRINE		
9	4	9
CHRISTIAN CHURCH EPISTLES	PASTORAL AND PERSONAL	HEBREW CHRISTIAN EPISTLES

NEW TESTAMENT HISTORY				
5 HISTORIC FOUNDATIONS				
MATTHEW	MARK	LUKE	JOHN	ACTS

OLD TESTAMENT

HISTORY (17)			EXPERIENCE	PROPHECY (17)		
BASIC LAW 5	PRE-EXILE RECORDS 9	POST EXILE 3	FIVE INNER LIFE	BASIC PROPHECY 5	PRE-EXILE PROPHETS 9	POST EXILE 3
MOSES	CANAAN	ANNALS	HEART	MAJOR	& TWELVE MINOR

THE BOOK OF GENESIS (1)

Lesson Number 1

NOTE :—For this first study read the whole Book of Genesis through once or twice.

AUTHORSHIP OF THE PENTATEUCH

Again and again in these studies we shall briefly but carefully consider questions of authorship relating to different parts of Scripture. In the long-drawn-out battle between theological " Modernism " and evangelical conservatism, the biggest (as it was the first) of Bible authorship controversies has been about the authorship of the Pentateuch. Is it *Mosaic*, or a *mosaic*?

To attempt a commensurate review here is beyond our scope. Perhaps, however, it is scarcely needful; for a point is now reached historically where the controversy may be seen in comprehensive silhouette, and results may be safely judged. We believe it fair to say that the main arguments for the Mosaic authorship remain unshaken; those for composite and later authorship are now largely fallen to pieces. This is forcibly indicated in the following quotation from Sir Charles Marston.

" It is quite possible that portions of some of the books of the Old Testament are derived from earlier documents. But to suppose that a cut-and-dried method could be found of isolating them, which nevertheless was entirely useless for our contemporary literature, imposed a considerable strain on anyone's credulity. It raised questions as to how and when the original books of the Old Testament were written; and above all it raised questions of the literary facilities possessed by the Israelites from the time of Moses onwards. The critical methods met these questions by assuming that the Hebrews were more or less illiterate. The assumption has completely broken down. It will be seen, from the archaeological evidence . . . that the Israelites had, from the time of Moses onwards, at least three alphabetical scripts. First, what is known as the Sinai Hebrew; next, what is known as the Phoenician Hebrew; and lastly, after the captivity in Babylon, what is known as the Assyrian Hebrew. Those facts entirely change the whole literary problem. Oral transmission becomes inadmissible. And the theory of the institution and adoption of the Mosaic ritual many centuries after the time of Moses, becomes grotesque and absurd, in the light of what we now know of his time.

" So J., E. and P., the supposed authors of the Pentateuch, are becoming mere phantom scribes and fetishes of the imagination. They have made Old Testament study unattractive, they have wasted our time, and they have warped and confused our judgments on outside evidence. It has been assumed that they possessed some sort of prescriptive right and authority superior to the Sacred Text. In the clearer light that Science is casting, these shadows that have dimmed our days of study and devotion are silently stealing away."

THE BOOK OF GENESIS (1)

ALTHOUGH, in the sweep of its revelation, the Bible carries our minds back to patriarchal and primeval and even pre-Adamite eras of the earth, the Bible itself did not begin to be written until the time of Moses. As an *historical* revelation its commencement coincides with the third chapter of Exodus, which records the communication of God through the burning bush of Horeb, and synchronises with the eightieth year of Moses. All that precedes this chapter was already *past* when the writing of our Bible began; and all that is recorded in the foregoing chapters is designed to lead up to the great new movement in human history, and the wonderful new unfolding of Divine revelation, which here begins.

Genesis and the entire Bible.

The Bible is not the *earliest* revelation of God. Its own pages clearly convey that the first human pair and the antediluvians and the post-Flood patriarchs received Divine revelations; and it is not improbable that these were in some degree committed to written form. In Genesis we have a synopsis of all former revelation, sufficient to constitute a working introduction to the further revelation of God communicated to us in the Bible.

Moreover, besides being introductory, Genesis is *explanatory*. The other writings of the Bible are inseparably bound up with it inasmuch as it gives us the origin and initial explanation of all that follows. The major themes of Scripture may be compared to great rivers, ever deepening and broadening as they flow; and it is true to say that all these rivers have their rise in the watershed of Genesis. Or, to use an equally appropriate figure, as the massive trunk and widespreading branches of the oak are in the acorn, so, by implication and anticipation, all Scripture is in Genesis. Here we have in germ all that is later developed. It has been truly said that "the roots of all subsequent revelation are planted deep in Genesis, and whoever would truly comprehend that revelation must begin here."

Genesis and the Pentateuch.

The Bible opens with the Pentateuch, or five books of Moses, the name "Pentateuch" (Greek—*pente*, five; and *teuchos*, book) having come down from the Septuagint Version of the Old Testament (the translation of the Old Testament into Greek, which is said to have been made by seventy Alexandrian Jews about the third century B.C., and is called the Septuagint Version from *septuaginta*, the Latin for seventy). There is good reason, however, for believing that before ever the Septuagint Version was made the writings of Moses were recognised as fivefold. The Jews called them "the Law" or "the five fifths of the Law" or simply "the fifths." It is probable that originally the whole was one, divided into five sections, each having as its title its first word or words.

There is a spiritual *completeness* about the Pentateuch. Its five parts not only give us a consecutive history covering the first two thousand five hundred years of human history; they constitute a progressive spiritual unity, setting forth, in their main features, what has been described as "the order of the experience of the people of God in all ages."

In Genesis we have *ruin* through the sin of man. In Exodus we have *redemption* through the blood of the Lamb and the Spirit of power. In Leviticus we have *communion* on the ground of atonement. In Numbers we have *direction* during pilgrimage, by the overruling will of God. In Deuteronomy we have the double truth of renewed and completed *instruction*, and the pilgrim people brought to the pre-determined *destination*. Is not this truly "the order of the experience of the people of God in all ages"?

But besides this, these first five books of the Old Testament give us most unmistakably a progressive fivefold revelation of God in His relationship with His people. In Genesis we see the *sovereignty* of God in creation and in election (in the choosing of Abraham, Isaac, Jacob, and their descendants; and in covenanting the land of Canaan to them as their predestined inheritance). In Exodus we see the redeeming *power* of God in His deliverance of Israel from Egypt, "with a mighty hand and with an outstretched arm." In Leviticus we see the *holiness* of God in His insistence on the separation and sanctification of His redeemed people. In Numbers we see the *"goodness and severity"* of God, —severity toward the unbelieving generation which came up from Egypt but never entered the covenanted inheritance, and goodness toward their children, in providing, protecting, and preserving, till Canaan was occupied. In Deuteronomy we see the *faithfulness* of God,—faithful to His purpose, His promise, His people, in bringing the redeemed to the promised possession. Thus—

THE HUMAN SIDE

Genesis.	Ruin—through the sin of man.
Exodus.	Redemption—by "blood" and "power."
Leviticus.	Communion—on the ground of atonement.
Numbers.	Direction—guidance by the will of God.
Deuteronomy.	Destination—through the faithfulness of God.

THE DIVINE SIDE

Genesis.	Divine sovereignty—in creation and election.
Exodus.	Divine power—in redemption and emancipation.
Leviticus.	Divine holiness—in separation and sanctification.
Numbers.	Divine goodness and severity—judging, caring.
Deuteronomy.	Divine faithfulness—in discipline and destination.

Thus it is seen that these five parts of the Pentateuch are full of purpose and progress. They are the Bible in miniature.

Genesis and the Apocalypse

It is important to recognise the relationship between Genesis and the last book of Scripture. There is a correspondence between them which at once suggests itself as being both a *proof* and a *product* of the fact that the Bible is a *completed* revelation. There is no adequate understanding of either of them without the other; but taken together they are mutually completive. There is no going back beyond the one, and no going forward beyond the other; nor is there in either case any *need* to do so. In broad outline and majestic language Genesis answers the question: "How did all begin?" In broad outline and majestic language Revelation answers the question: "How will all issue?" All that lies between them is development from the one to the other.

Note the *similarities* between Genesis and the Apocalypse. In both we have a new beginning, and a new order. In both we have the tree of life, the river, the bride, the walk of God with man; and in both paradises we have the same moral and spiritual ideals. God has never abandoned the Eden ideal for man; and although in the end the garden has given place to the city, the Eden ideal of holiness finally triumphs.

Mark the *contrasts* between the one book and the other. In Genesis we see the first paradise *closed* (iii. 23); in Revelation we see the new paradise *opened* (xxi. 25). In Genesis we see *dis*-possession through human sin (iii. 24); in Revelation we see *re*possession through Divine grace (xxi. 24). In Genesis we see the "curse" imposed (iii. 17); in Revelation we see the "curse" removed (xxii. 3). In Genesis we see access to the tree of life disinherited, in Adam (iii. 24); in Revelation we see access to the tree of life *re*inherited, in Christ (xxii. 14). In Genesis we see the beginning of sorrow and death (iii. 16–19); in Revelation we read "there shall be no more death, neither sorrow" (xxi. 4). In Genesis we are shown a garden, into which defilement entered (iii. 6–7); in Revelation we are shown a city, of which it is written: "There shall in no wise enter into it any thing that defileth" (xxi. 27). In Genesis we see man's dominion broken, in the fall of the first man, Adam (iii. 19); in Revelation we see man's dominion restored, in the rule of the New Man, Christ (xxii. 5). In Genesis we see the evil triumph of the Serpent (iii. 13); in Revelation we see the ultimate triumph of the Lamb (xx. 10; xxii. 3). In Genesis we see the walk of God with man interrupted (iii. 8–10); in Revelation we see the walk of God with man resumed, and a great voice says from heaven, "Behold the tabernacle of God is with men, and He will dwell with them . . ." (xxi. 3).

Note the *completions* of the one book in the other. The Garden, in Genesis, gives place to the City, in the Apocalypse; and the one man has become the race. In Genesis we see human sin in its beginnings; in the Apocalypse we see it in its full and final developments, in the Harlot, the False Prophet, the Beast, and the Dragon. In Genesis we see sin causing *physical* death, on earth; in the Apocalypse we see sin issuing in the dread darkness of the "*second* death," in the beyond. In Genesis we have the *sentence* passed on Satan; in the Apocalypse we have the sentence *executed*. In Genesis we are given the *first promise* of a coming

Saviour and salvation; in the Apocalypse we see that promise in its final and glorious *fulfilment*. Genesis causes *anticipation*; the Apocalypse effects *realisation*. Genesis is the *foundation* stone of the Bible; the Apocalypse is the *capstone*.

THE STRUCTURE OF GENESIS

As we have said, all that goes before the third chapter of Exodus was already past when the writing of the Bible began. Let us stand, then, at that third chapter of Exodus and look back over what is recorded in Genesis, getting the main lines of perspective. It will be readily seen that Genesis is in two major divisions. All Bible students agree that the call and response of Abram constitute a quite new departure in the narrative, and mark off the two main parts of the book—the first part covering chapters one to eleven, and the second part chapters twelve to fifty.

This being so, we see how each part is arranged according to a significant fourfold plan. In the first part we have four outstanding *events*—the Creation, the Fall, the Flood, the Babel crisis. In the second part we have four outstanding *persons*—Abraham, Isaac, Jacob, Joseph. The entire contents of Genesis are arranged around and in relation to these four pivotal events in the one part, and these four pivotal figures in the other.

Seeing the pivotal events and figures of Genesis thus thrown into relief, we quickly perceive also the unifying idea running through what is recorded; and this gives us the principal significance of the book as a whole. Standing right at the beginning of the sixty-six books, Genesis would bring us to our knees in reverent obeisance before God as it exhibits to our eyes, and thunders in our ears, that truth which is to be learned before all others, in our dealings with God, in our interpretation of history, and in our study of Divine revelation, namely—*THE DIVINE SOVEREIGNTY*.

Looking back over the four great events of part one, and the four great figures of part two, we see that they constitute an impressive demonstration of the Divine sovereignty. In the first of the four *events*, we have the Divine sovereignty in *the physical creation*. In the second we have the Divine sovereignty in *human probation.* In the third we have the Divine sovereignty in *historical retribution.* In the fourth we have the Divine sovereignty in *racial distribution.* In these four great events we see the sovereignty of the Creator in His eternal priority, His moral authority, His judicial severity, and His governmental supremacy.

Turning to the second part of Genesis, we see the sovereignty of God in *regeneration.* The process of regeneration here outlined stands in sharp contrast to the process of *degeneration* in the first part of the book. From Adam to Abraham we see the course of *degeneration*: first, in the individual—Adam; then in the family —Cain and his descendants; then in the nations—the antediluvian civilisation; and then persisting throughout the race, as such, at Babel. Then there comes a new departure. We see the process of *regeneration* operating: first, in the individual—Abraham, Isaac, Jacob; then in the family—the sons of Jacob; then in the nation—Israel; all with a view to the ultimate regeneration of the race. In Abraham, Isaac, and Jacob we see Divine sovereignty in *election.* Abraham, although the youngest son, is chosen in preference to his two elder brothers. Isaac is chosen in preference to Ishmael, the elder son of Abraham. Jacob, although second to Esau, is chosen in preference to his brother. Running through it all we see the principle of Divine *election.* God chooses whom He will, in sovereign grace. Then, in the wonderful biography of Joseph, we see the sovereignty of God in *direction,*— in the overruling and infallible directing of all happenings, however seemingly contrary, to the predetermined end.

In the case of Abraham we see this sovereign election expressed by a supernatural *call*; for it is clear that God had directly intervened (see Gen. xii. 1–3).

In the case of Isaac, we see it expressed by a supernatural *birth.* Abraham had said, "Oh, that Ishmael might live before Thee!" (xvii. 18). But no! When Abraham is 100, and Sarah 90, the miracle-babe Isaac comes to them.

In the case of Jacob it is shown in supernatural *care.* First God saves him from Esau's knife; then meets him at Bethel; prospers him despite Laban's guile; saves him from the revengeful ire of his brother who comes to meet him with a band of four hundred men; and so it goes on, until at last when Jacob is dying, he blesses young Manasseh and Ephraim, "The Angel which redeemed me from all evil, bless the lads."

Finally, in Joseph, we see the Divine sovereignty in direction, exhibited in supernatural *control*, making all happenings to contribute to the predestined issue.

Thus, in these four men, we see a fourfold development— (1) supernatural call, (2) supernatural birth, (3) supernatural care, (4) supernatural control.

And so in this first book of Scripture we find that by marking the pivotal events and figures we come to understand the significance of the writing as a whole; and we may set the facts down as follows.

THE BOOK OF GENESIS

THE DIVINE SOVEREIGNTY—IN CREATION, HISTORY AND REDEMPTION

I. PRIMEVAL HISTORY (i.–xi.)

Four Outstanding Events

THE CREATION—Divine sovereignty in the physical creation.
God's eternal priority.
THE FALL—Divine sovereignty in human probation.
God's moral authority.
THE FLOOD—Divine sovereignty in historical retribution.
God's judicial severity.
THE BABEL CRISIS—Divine sovereignty in racial distribution.
God's governmental supremacy.

II. PATRIARCHAL HISTORY (xii.–l.).

Four Outstanding Persons

ABRAHAM—Divine sovereignty in election.
Supernatural *call*.
ISAAC—Divine sovereignty in election.
Supernatural *birth*.
JACOB—Divine sovereignty in election.
Supernatural *care*.
JOSEPH—Divine sovereignty in direction.
Supernatural *control*.

THE BOOK OF GENESIS (2)

Lesson Number 2

NOTE :—For this second study read thoroughly again (making **notes** of any impressive points) Genesis, chapters i. to xi.

In anticipation of our remarks concerning the geographical extent of the Flood, we would give a word of counsel. As we study our English Bible we should ever remember that we are dealing with a translation, not the original. A true understanding of the word used in the original may greatly affect our interpretation in many an instance. This need not discourage those who do not know Hebrew or Greek, for in these days wonderful facilities are provided. Without a doubt the greatest of these is Strong's Exhaustive Concordance, which, by a very easy system of reference, gives not only every occurrence of every word in the English, but also the Hebrew or Greek word so translated, also the English pronunciation, and every other English word, too, by which the same Hebrew or Greek word is translated in our English Bible—not to mention other excellent features. It is a possession beyond price to the Bible student. We cannot too highly recommend it. The looking up and following through of words used in the original is as enlightening as it is fascinating.

J. S. B.

THE BOOK OF GENESIS (2)

WE HAVE seen, in our first study, that the dominant idea in this Book of Genesis is *the sovereignty of God.* We have noted, also, that the book falls into two main parts. In the first part (i.–xi.) we have four outstanding *events*—the Creation, the Fall, the Flood, the Babel dispersion. In the second part (xii.–l.) we have four outstanding *persons*—Abraham, Isaac, Jacob, Joseph. We now briefly review the four super-events of part one.

The Creation

First, then, we go back to chapters i. and ii., to that transcendent initial event, *the Creation.* In the opening verse of the book we read: "In the beginning God created the heaven and the earth." This is not a human theory: it is a Divine "testimony." In Psalm xciii. 5 we read: "Thy testimonies are very sure." The word of God testifies concerning truths which are above the unaided intelligence of man, and beyond the farthest reach of human investigation. Genesis i. 1 is the first such "testimony." There is a polarity of difference between a theory and a "testimony" or "witness." A theory deals with the *interpretation* of facts. A witness deals with *the facts themselves.* It is vital to realize that this opening verse of Scripture is not merely the first postulate of a human philosophy, but the first testimony of a Divine revelation. It is the first great truth which God would have man to know: and man could not know it apart from the Divine testimony. We accept it as such, believing with the psalmist that "the testimony of Jehovah is sure, making wise the simple" (Ps. xix. 7).

This initial testimony of our faithful Creator stands sublime in its simplicity. There is no definition of God, no description of creation, and no declaration of date. Positive and complete in itself, it yet leaves room for all subsequent development in Scripture and all discovery by Science. It is axiomatic. As geometry is built upon certain axiomatic truths, so the one foundation axiom of the Bible is laid down in its first sentence.

It is fashionable today to profess disbelief in miracles. Accept this first sentence of Scripture, and there will be little difficulty in accepting all the miracles that follow; for the less are included in the greater. Note, also, that in this first, basal pronouncement of Scripture there is a denial of all the principal false philosophies which men have propounded.

"In the beginning *God*"—that denies Atheism with its doctrine of *no* God.

"In the beginning God"—that denies Polytheism with its doctrine of *many* gods.

"In the beginning *God created*"—that denies Fatalism with its doctrine of *chance*.

"In the beginning *God created*"—that denies Evolution with its doctrine of infinite *becoming*.

"God created *heaven and earth*"—that denies Pantheism which makes God and the universe identical.

"God created *heaven and earth*"—that denies Materialism which asserts the eternity of matter.

Thus, this first "testimony" of Jehovah is not only a declaration of Divine truth, but a repudiation of human error.

But what of verse 2—"And the earth was without form, and void; and darkness was upon the face of the deep"? Does this describe the first condition of the earth after its creation? And what of the six "days" which follow in this first chapter? Do they describe the *process* of the original creation? We need to think and speak very clearly here, for there is much misunderstanding. If the Bible is the inspired word of God, nothing can be more important than to understand rightly its teaching as to the origin of things. Yet the fact is, alas, that no chapters in the Bible have been more misunderstood and misrepresented than these first two chapters of Genesis. It is quite correct to say that in these two chapters we have a record of "creation" (for we have the original creation of the universe stated in chapter i. 1, and the subsequent creation of the present animal order in verse 21, and the creation of man in verse 27); yet the statement needs qualifying and explaining.

A discrimination must be made (the Bible certainly makes it) between the original creation of the earth and its subsequent *reconstruction* with a view to its becoming the habitation of *man*. It cannot be too strongly emphasised that the six "days" in this first chapter of Genesis do *not* describe the original creation of the earth. Those who suppose or assert this are obliged to treat the six "days" as vast periods of time, so as to square Genesis with what modern science has shown us concerning the vast antiquity of our earth. Yet in all truth they fail thus to reconcile Genesis and geology; and what is worse, they involve the Scripture itself in unresolvable self-contradictions. We do not purpose to go into all that just here, but we submit a brief addendum on the matter at the end of this present study.

That second verse, which says that the earth was "waste and void," does not, as the many think, describe the first condition of the earth after its creation. It alludes to a cataclysm which desolated the earth later. Verses 1 and 2 have no logical connection. There is a break between them, the duration of which is not known. Undoubtedly verse 2 should read, "And the earth *became* (not just 'was') without form and void . . ." The same Hebrew word here used is so rendered in chapter ii. 7—"Man *became* a living soul" (not to mention many other such instances, in some of which the rendering is, "it came to pass"). Modern geology furnishes data proving the immense age of our globe. Genesis has no controversy with geology on that score. Between the first two verses of Genesis there is ample scope for all the geologic eras. None can say what lapse of ages lies between them.

So, then, the first verse of Genesis simply states the fact of the original creation, and leaves it there, in the dateless past. Then verse 2 tells of a chaos which came to this earth later. And then *the six "days" which follow describe the re-formation of the earth with a view to its becoming the habitation of man.* What brought about the cataclysm which laid the earth "waste and void" we do not know with any certainty. Scripture does seem to give certain veiled indications that it had to do with a pre-Adamite rebellion and judgment of Lucifer and associated angel-beings (see Isa. xiv. 9–17; Jer. iv. 23–7; Ezek. xxviii. 12–18, where the language certainly transcends any merely local or temporal limits). It is not within our present purpose to go into these things here. What we do re-emphasise is that these six "days" in the first chapter of Genesis do *not* describe the original creation. Nowhere in Scripture are they said to be an account of the original creation. During the first four days no creative act is recorded. It is only when we come to the animals and man that the Hebrew word for "create" is used (verses 21 and 27). In a word, these six days give the account of a *new* beginning; but they are not the *first* beginning. When once this is clearly appreciated the supposed conflict between Genesis and geology dies away.

Our final remarks here about these six "days" must be to point out the *process* and the *progress* and the *purpose* which they exhibit. From the very first we find the earth swathed about by "the Spirit of Elohim" (i. 2); and at each stage of the reconstruction we read that "God *said*." Thus we have the *will* of God, expressed by the *word* of God, and executed by the *Spirit* of God. Such is the process here exhibited. And this process expresses itself in an orderly six-fold *progress* culminating in man. In man we see the crowning *purpose* of the whole.

Man the Crown

In chapter ii *the creation and first condition of Adam* are described. There are four movements—production, provision, probation, progression. The act of *production* is narrated in verse 7. Man is formed of "the dust of the ground," yet he is inbreathed of God with the "breath of lives." Behold his littleness and his loftiness!—his earthliness and heavenliness! Next, in verses 8–14, we see the Divine *provision* for man. It was provision in perfection and profusion. Next, in verses 15–17, we see man placed under *probation*. Man's liberty was to be conditioned by loyalty. Amid many provisions there was just one prohibition. This constituted the point of probation. Finally, note the *progression* as indicated in verses 18–25. Point by point there is forward movement. This is seen in the relation between man and the animals; in the calling forth of the latent faculty of speech; and supremely in the provision of Eve for that deeper need of Adam, and in that perfect first marriage-bliss of Eden. Thus there is *production* in the likeness of God; *provision* for the body, *probation* for the mind, and *progression* to the point of heart-satisfaction. In these four movements we see the *MAN*, the *SERVANT*, the *KING*, the *HUSBAND*.

The Fall

That sin, with all its attendant sufferings, exists throughout our world is plain to all. How did it get in? The Scripture explanation is given in Genesis iii. It is not our purpose here to *vindicate* the Scripture explanation against the contrary opinions of men. We are touching on it expositorily, not controversially. We accept the Scripture explanation; and there are three things which make up the account—(i) the tempting, (ii) the yielding, (iii) the results.

As for *the tempting* (verses 1–6), we note first that temptation was permitted. It is not easy to see how it could have been otherwise in the educating of a rational and volitional being such as man. The real tragedy is that there was a tempter. The fact that man was under the simple probation mentioned in chapter ii. 17 made him liable to temptation. But, mark, the tempter could *only* tempt. There *need not* have been sin. And there was *no reason* to yield. We note, too, that the temptation was introduced to Eve in solitariness. This is Satan's common method. And again, the temptation was connected with the beautiful: its real character was concealed. There was also a gradual growth in the strength of the temptation. First, God's word is merely questioned (verse 1). Then it is flatly contradicted (verse 4). And then, as the tempted one foolishly continues to listen, the very motive behind God's word is maligned (verse 5).

As for *the yielding* (verse 6), we see that Satan first captured the ear, then the eye, then the inward desire, and finally the will. Eve allowed her ear to listen to the tempter. Then she allowed her eye to feed on the object of temptation. Then she allowed desire to run away with the will. Compare verse 6 with 1 John ii. 16. "When the woman saw that the tree was good for food"—*the lust of the flesh.* "And that it was pleasant to the eyes"—*the lust of the eyes.* "And a tree to be desired to make one wise"—*the pride of life.* The first temptation, in Eden, and all the myriad temptations by which men and women have been lured into sin ever since, are fundamentally identical. And the tempter's great purpose is ever to divorce the will of man more and more from the will of God. It is important to note that God had made it as easy as could be to resist such temptation. Adam and Eve had been forewarned concerning the thing which Satan sought

to make them do. See chapter ii. 17 with iii. 3. The command was
plain. The warning was emphatic. Obedience was easy, for God
had surrounded them with abundant satisfactions, and given them
the most distinguished place in His earth creation. Finally, it
is well to compare the Genesis account of the yielding with
1 Timothy ii. 14. Eve was "beguiled," but Adam was not. His
was a clear choice, so it would seem, to be one with Eve in her
fall.

As for *the results* (verses 7–24), note the following points. Satan
had said that their eyes would be opened and that they should
know good and evil (verse 5). There was a mocking fulfilment
now. Their eyes *were* "opened"!—and they "knew"!—but what
an eye-opening, and what a knowing!—"The eyes of them both
were opened, and they knew that they were naked." There was
innocency no longer. That was the first result. We note now
the first appearance of *shame*—"They sewed fig leaves together,
and made themselves aprons." Thank God for the sense of
shame which He has put in human nature! It has saved mankind
from many evils. A sense of shame—that was the second result.
But note also that there was evidently a change in *the human
body*. In Romans viii. 3 we read that Christ came "in the likeness of sinful flesh." That cannot mean that our Lord's human
nature was in any way infected by sin. How then was He in
the likeness of *sinful* flesh? The answer is that although our
Lord was absolutely sinless He did not have about His body
the pristine glory, the original glory of unfallen man, in Eden.
The inference is that before the Fall there was a radiant glory
about the bodies of Adam and Eve which was itself their
resplendent covering. We are told that the very skin of Moses'
face shone after his forty days of communion with God on Sinai.
What then must have been the shining beauty of that as yet
sinless pair in lovely Eden? Bathed in the glory-light of that
unsullied communion with God, their whole bodies must have
shone. But immediately upon the Fall that glory departed, and
"they knew that they were naked." That was the third result.

Nor was that all. There was a tragic *inward* change. There
suddenly sprang into consciousness a strange war within where
all had hitherto been love and joy and peace. There came the
terror of a newly-awakened faculty—the faculty of *conscience*.
Thus, with the first sin came the first *fear*: Adam and his wife

fled from God and tried to hide from Him! That was the fourth result—and note that there does not seem to have been any humble contrition, even when the sin was exposed before God. There had come about a spiritual alienation of man from God. The reign of spiritual death had set in. And besides all this, man is now expelled from the Garden wherein is the Tree of Life; the ground is cursed; the Serpent is cursed; man is given the headship over woman; and God provides clothes for Adam and Eve. Yet, amid judgment, God remembers mercy, and the first great promise of the coming Saviour is given in verse 15. The full music is to be developed as time goes on and as the Scripture revelation unfolds; but here in Genesis iii. 15 the first few notes are struck, in the promise that the "seed of the woman" should break the head of the serpent.

The Flood

If there is one period of history more than another about which we could wish for fuller information, it is the antediluvian, the period between the Fall and the Flood. The Genesis narrative is severely reticent, and that for a plain reason. Sixteen hundred years are packed into two pages, so that, whatever else we may or may not see, we may not miss the significant connection between the Fall and the Flood. The inspired writer omits all that is not vital to his purpose. Biblical narrative is never concerned with the mere lapse of time, but with the moral significance of events. There is an almost dramatic development from the Fall to the Flood. Let us mark it clearly. In chapter iii. we have the Fall. In chapter iv. we have Cain and the Cain line—"the sons of men." In chapter v. we have Seth and the Seth line— "the sons of God." In chapter vi. the two lines cross, with tragic moral results. In chapter vii. judgment falls—the Flood. This dramatic sequence, once seen, can never be forgotten. The separation of the two lines was vital. Their confusion was fatal. The resultant moral condition was appalling. The corruption was extreme. Divine intervention became unavoidable. Retribution was inevitable. The Flood came, both as an act of judgment and as a moral salvage measure. This is the first great Bible lesson on the indispensability of separation and no-compromise. The Divine insistence all the way through is that the spiritual seed shall "come out and be separate."

There are those who have held that "the sons of God" spoken of in chapter vi. were fallen angels, that is, the "angels which kept not their first estate, but left their own habitation," who are referred to in Jude 6. The late Dr. E. W. Bullinger, that able but all-too-often fanciful and unreliable exegete, sponsors this idea. A little reflection will show how preposterous it is. The angels are spirit beings. They are sexless, and therefore are not capable either of sensuous experience or of sexual processes: nor are they capable of reproduction. As for the suggestion that these evil angels somehow took human bodies to themselves and thus became capable of sex functions, it is sheer absurdity, as anyone can see. Both on psychological and physiological grounds it is unthinkable. We all know what an exquisitely delicate, sensitive, intricate inter-reaction there is between the human body and the human mind or soul. This is because soul and body came into being together and are mysteriously united *in one human personality*. Thus it is that the sensations of the body become experiences of the mind. Now if angels merely took bodies, and indwelt them for the time being, their doing so could not have made them in the slightest degree able to experience the sensations of those bodies, for the angels and those bodies were not united in one personality, as is the case with the human mind and body. Indeed, the bodies could not have been bodies of flesh and blood, for without being inhabited by the human spirit the human flesh-and-blood body dies. When our Lord Jesus came into this world to be our Saviour, He did not merely take to Himself a human body and inhabit it for the time being. That would not have made Him human. That would not have been real incarnation. The Son of God not only took a human body, He took to Himself our human *nature*; and to do this He had to be *born*. If, then, these "sons of God" in Genesis were the fallen angels, the only way they could have become human and have married and have had children (vi. 1, 4) is by their having undergone a real human *birth*—that is, by their having been incarnated and born of human mothers but without human fathers! To think that this happened is preposterous. Bullinger asserts that "sons of God" is a description only used of those who are *direct* creations of God—that is, of the angels, of the first man, Adam (Luke iii. 38), and of those in the present dispensation who are a "new creation" in Christ (2 Cor. v. 17;

Rom. viii. 14, etc.): but he surely forgets verses like Isaiah xliii. 6 and xlv. 11, where the expression "My sons" is equivalent to "Sons of God." Let us dismiss completely from our minds, then, the strange idea that these "sons of God" in Genesis were the fallen angels, who left "their first estate" in order to cohabit with women of the earth. Besides the objections which we have already raised to it, surely the impression which Scripture conveys to us is that the fall of these angels—like that of Satan—occurred before ever man was created upon the earth.

Was the Flood in Noah's day universal? As to the *fact* of the Flood, the testimony of universal tradition and of twentieth-century archaeology have put that finally beyond doubt: but was the Flood *universal*? To discuss this question adequately would require space far exceeding the limits of our present purpose; but there are two or three basically important facts which we cannot leave unmentioned. First, let us clearly understand that it is not vital to the inspiration of the Scriptures to maintain that the Noachian Flood was universal. That expression "the earth," which comes so often in the Biblical account, does not bind us to this, for the Hebrew word (*eretz*) which is translated as "earth" frequently means one country or locality merely. For instance, in the Divine call to Abram, "Get thee out of thy country," the word is *eretz*; and in very many other places *eretz* is given as "land." Similarly, the Hebrew word (*har*) which is translated as "mountain" (vii. 20) is a word of variable connotation. It may mean little more than hillocks, or uplands, as well as mountains proper. It is the word which is used again and again in the title, "Mount Zion." Clearly, we are not intended to picture Noah and the Ark as borne aloft above Alps and Himalayas, where through sheer weight the waters would become part of the everlasting snows and ice, where the Ark, in fact, would have become buried in ice for several thousands of feet, and where, even if such ice-burial could have been somehow overcome, life in the Ark would have been impossible apart from some miraculous system of "central heating"! There is a legitimate and idiomatic use of hyperbole in the Hebrew language of the Old Testament, just as there is in the English of today. When the cricket spectator tells us that the batsman sent the ball spinning "miles away" we appreciate the meaning at once. Even so, when Moses speaks of cities "fenced up to heaven"

(Deut. ix. 1) we recognise legitimate hyperbole; and similarly, when he says that the waters of the Flood covered all the hills that were "under the whole heaven" (Gen. vii. 19) we recognise the same hyperbolic usage as in Deuteronomy ii. 25, where the very same expression, "under the whole heaven," occurs with an obviously limited connotation. As a matter of fact the depth of the waters is given to us in Genesis vii. 20; and hyperbolisms must always be read in the light of literal statements and figures. (See our note concerning Strong's Exhaustive Concordance, preceding this present study.) Much more might be said along this line, but we have said enough to show that the inspiration of the Scripture is not at the mercy of our proving that the Flood was universal.

Another word which we must add is that the Noachian Flood must not be confounded with *the prehistoric flood* of which our geologists speak. All round the crust of this planet there are the marks of a vast flood; but these are not such as could have been left by an inundation of such short duration as that in Noah's day, even if that in Noah's day was universal. The flood to which geology bears witness is that of Genesis i. 2. It is to this, also, that 2 Peter iii. 5 refers.

And we note, finally, that when the whole Adamic race was destroyed, there was one man and his family who "found grace" in the sight of God. "Noah was a righteous man, and pure in his generations; and Noah walked with God." This man and his family were spared: and this man, be it noted, was the *vital* man. He was the tenth man from Adam *in the Messianic line*, from which the world's Saviour was to come in "the fulness of the time." Satan may do his worst, and man may sink to his lowest, and judgment may fall to the utmost; but the ultimate purpose of Jehovah cannot be thwarted. It moves on, and will yet triumph in a "new heavens and a new earth" wherein shall be righteousness and undimmed glory.

The Babal Dispersion

We must not think of the pre-Flood age as one of primitive crudity. The indications are that it was the most remarkable civilisation our race has ever known. Human longevity in that era, uniformity of language, nearness to the original Divine revelation, and the freer communication between God and men—think what these must have meant. We get significant hints as to the arts and industries of that time in Genesis iv. 20–4. But that first civilisation, with its accumulations of knowledge and experience, its treasures of art and literature, its agriculture and industries, is now gone, and the Adamic race is to have a new start in Noah and his three sons with their families.

Marked restraints are now imposed. The duration of human life is now greatly curtailed. The length of a generation is much shorter. The soil takes more toil now and gives less in return; and "flesh" is therefore now included in man's diet. A restraint of "fear" towards man, also, has to be put upon the beasts. The restraint of the death-penalty is put upon the slaying of man by man (which "violence" had become rife in the pre-Flood days: vi. 11, 13). Amid these restraints the faithfulness of God stands out in the sign of the rainbow. The Divine promise was necessary. It gave man an assured hope for the future.

But there was another restraint to be imposed, namely, *the confusion of tongues* (xi. 1–9). The essential fact to grasp is that the pluralising of human language was a culminating restraint-measure. It was precipitated by a human confederacy to establish a big racial centre, with a high astral tower. We must not attribute to those long-ago builders the stupidity of imagining that they could build a tower right up to heaven. In chapter xi. 4 the words *"may reach"* are in italics, indicating that they do not come in the original. The verse does not really relate to the height of the tower. What it says is, *"And his top with the heavens"*, that is, with an astronomical planisphere, Zodiac pictures, and drawings of the constellations—just such as we find in the ancient temples of Esneh and Denderah in Egypt. Perhaps we ought to give the late Lieut.-Gen. Chesney's corroboration of this. After describing other discoveries among the ruins of Babylon, he says: "About five miles S.W. of Hillah, the most remarkable of all the ruins, the *Birs Nimroud* of the Arabs, rises to a height of 153 feet above the plain from a base covering a square of 400 feet, or almost four acres. It was constructed of kiln-dried bricks in seven stages to correspond with the planets to which they were dedicated: the lowermost black, the colour of Saturn; the next orange, for Jupiter; the third red, for Mars; and so on. These stages were surmounted by a lofty tower, on the summit of which, we are told, were the signs of the Zodiac and other astronomical figures; thus having (as it should have been translated) *a representation of the heavens*, instead of 'a top which reached unto heaven.'" We ourselves would not go so far as to claim that these are the remains of the original tower; but beyond a doubt they illustrate its nature and dimensions.

The Babel crisis probably occurred some three hundred years after the Flood. In chapter x. 25 we are told that it was in Peleg's days that "the earth was divided" (as happened at the confusion of tongues: xi. 9). Peleg died 340 years after the Flood, as can easily be reckoned in chapter xi. 10–19. The Babel tower was designed to hand down antediluvian traditions. Its wrongness lay in the fact that its builders were defying the Divine command to spread abroad and replenish the earth. "Let us make us a name!" exclaim the builders. "Let us not be scattered abroad upon the face of the whole earth." Dr. Alfred Edersheim comments: "Such words breathe the spirit of 'Babylon' in all ages. Assuredly their meaning is 'Let us rebel!'—for not only would the Divine purpose of peopling the earth have thus been frustrated, but such a world-empire would have been a defiance to God and to the kingdom of God, even as its motive was pride and ambition."

We cannot stay here to discuss the greatness of Babel, the capital of Nimrod's kingdom; but from this time onward Babel, or Babylon, becomes the symbol-city of "this present evil world," energised, as it is, by the arch-rebel, Satan. The utter destruction of the historic Babylon, which duly happened in fulfilment of predictions like that in Isaiah xiii. 19–22, is one of the wonders of Biblical prophecy. But Babylon lives on in "mystery" form, as we find in the Book of the Revelation; and the destruction of the *historic* Babylon typifies the coming crash of the "*mystery*" Babylon and the present world system.

NOTE. It occurs to us to mention that those who may be interested in a further consideration of those "sons of God" in Genesis vi will find a much fuller treatment of the subject in the last chapter of the author's book, *Studies in Problem Texts*.

ADDENDUM TO LESSON 2

Genesis i. 2, and the six "days"

It is supposed by many that the words, "without form, and void," in Genesis i. 2, describe the first condition of the earth after its creation, and that the six "days" of chapter i. are therefore the six successive stages of the original creation-process; but the more one examines this the less tenable it becomes.

To begin with, *it occasions needless conflict between Scripture and Science.* According to reckoning based on Bible chronology, the race of Adam did not appear on this earth until six or seven thousand years ago; but modern geology has now shown beyond doubt that the earth existed immense ages before then. How are we to account, then, for that vast period of the earth's existence before the time when, according to the Bible, the Adamic race first appeared? If we say there is no break between the first two verses of Genesis, and that the words, "without form, and void," in verse 2, describe the first condition of the earth at its creation, away back beyond all the geologic ages, then, of course, the only way we can fit in the vast expanse of time between the creation of the earth and the comparatively recent appearance of man is to say that the six "days" of Genesis i. were six great *ages*, and that man appeared somewhere in the sixth.

But this lands us in a difficulty. These great ages, we are assured, would cover tens of thousands of years each, which means that man, if created somewhere in the sixth, must have been at least some thousands of years old at the time when, according to Genesis, Adam was in Eden; whereas the clear teaching of Genesis is that even as late as the birth of Seth, Adam was only 130 years old (Gen. v. 3). So, then, on this score alone, if we are to accept the plain words of Scripture, yet at the same time avoid hopeless disagreement with the well-established findings of modern geology, we simply cannot hold that Genesis i. 2 describes the original state of the earth at its creation. Genesis and geology are reconciled, however, when we see that between verses 1 and 2 there is a gap sufficient to cover all the geologic ages, and that the six "days" describe, not the original creation of the earth, but its reconstruction, ages later, to become the habitation of man.

This geological difficulty increases upon further consideration. Vegetable remains from pre-Adamite ages are found in the earth's strata, as also are fossils of animals which had eyes. It is noteworthy that in the six days of Genesis no beings having eyes were created until after the fourth day, when the sun was caused to shine on the earth. *How shall we explain these pre-Adamite vegetables, and these animals having eyes ?* If we deny the break between the first two verses of Genesis, and say that the words "without form, and void" describe the earth at its original creation, we are shut up to three expedients, each of which is untenable.

First, we may say that the six days were six ordinary days of twenty-four hours each, *immediately following* the creation of the earth in its waste and void condition. But in that case Genesis is made to teach that the earth is only six or seven thousand years old (seeing that man was created on the sixth of those days, and the human race is only six or seven thousand years old), and at once geology parts company with Scripture.

Second, we may say that the six days were six ordinary days, but *not* immediately following the original creation of the earth in its waste and void condition. But in that case, during the vast period between the original creation of the earth and those six days of only a few thousand years ago, the earth must have *remained* in its condition of chaos and emptiness and darkness; and this again puts us at war with geology; for how can we account for that pre-Adamite vegetation, and the animals having eyes, in that dense, ages-long chaos and darkness?

Third, we may say that the six days were immense ages which followed upon the earth's original creation in its waste and void condition. But in that case the beginning of the present order of the animals and man is carried thousands and thousands of years farther back than any fair dealing with the language of Scripture allows.

If, however, we reject these three expedients, recognising that there is a break between the first two verses of Genesis, so that verse 1 refers to the original creation, and verse 2 refers to a desolation which occurred later, all such difficulty is removed. There is ample and intelligent play for all geological discoveries, and at the same time we do justice to the language of Scripture.

Still further, to say that verse 2 describes the state of the earth as originally created seems *incompatible with the wording of Genesis concerning the third and fourth days.* We read that on the third day God said: "Let the earth bring forth grass, the herb yielding seed, the fruit tree yielding fruit after its kind whose seed is in itself upon the earth." The wording here does not imply any creative act. The word "create" is not used. It is simply "bring forth." The life-germs of vegetation were already in the earth. Now if the earth was created "without form, and void," it is surely very difficult to account for this latent vegetation, unless we are thorough-going evolutionists holding the absurd idea that matter can produce life. Whether we say that the six days were six ordinary days of twenty-four hours each or six long ages, this difficulty remains. But the difficulty disappears as soon as we recognise that this second verse of Genesis refers to the wreck of an anterior creation in which both vegetable and animal life flourished. The "Scofield" Reference Bible well says on this point: "It is by no means necessary to suppose that the life-germ of seeds perished in the catastrophic judgment which overthrew the primitive order. With the restoration of dry land and light the earth would 'bring forth' as described. It was *animal* life which perished, the traces of which remain as fossils. Relegate fossils to the primitive creation, and no conflict of science with the Genesis cosmogony remains."

So with the fourth day: "God made two great lights." No creative act is here implied. The word "create" is not used. The Hebrew word translated as "made" does not involve origination. Sun, moon, stars were already there. How shall we explain this? If the second verse of Genesis adverts to the original creation, then there are difficulties right and left. We cannot say that the six days were ordinary days of twenty-four hours each, for that brings down the creation of the sun and moon and stars to the time when Adam was created, some six or seven thousand years ago, merely, and thus puts us hopelessly wrong on the age of the solar and sidereal systems. Yet neither can we say that the six days were long ages, for that would make the vegetation which thrived through that sunless *third* age an enigma. No such problem remains, however, when we see that although the first verse of Genesis refers to the original creation, the second verse refers to a subsequent disruption. Needless opposition to science is removed, and at the same time we pay a proper respect to the language of Scripture.

But now, quite apart from geological considerations, surely the Bible itself makes quite plain that the words "without form, and void" do not refer to the earth's first condition. Turn to Isaiah xlv. 18 —"Thus saith Jehovah that created the heavens, God Himself that formed the earth and made it: He hath established it: He created it not in vain, He formed it to be inhabited." The Hebrew word here translated "in vain" is that which is translated "without form" in Genesis i. 2. Isaiah xlv. 18 says that God did *not* create the earth "without form." Surely such a statement is conclusive. The prophet's argument is that the Jehovah of Israel is the Elohim of the creation: He did not create the *earth* a desolation, nor was the desolation of *Israel* the design of His providence, but the outcome of Israel's sin; and as the desolated earth was restored, so would a repentant Israel be restored. The reference to Genesis is incidental but none the less conclusive. God "did *not* create" the earth "without form"; therefore it must have become so at a *later* time. This at once implies that between the first two verses of Genesis there is an indefinite interval.

Besides this, the very wording of Genesis i. 2 gives evidence that it does not refer to the earth as it was originally. As we have already mentioned (in Lesson 2), the word "was," in our English version, should be "became." Undoubtedly, we should read it: "And the earth *became* waste and empty." Again and again, in the Old Testament, the same Hebrew verb is translated as "became," or even as "it came to pass." This is the verb in Genesis ii. 7—"Man *became* a living soul." Surely, then, when we read in Genesis i. 2, that "the earth *became* without form, and void," we are to understand that this desolation befell the earth at some point of time *after* its original creation, and that the six "days" which now follow on from verse 3 describe, not the original creation, but a process of *reconstruction*.

An ancillary argument to the same effect may also be drawn from the two Hebrew words which are here translated as "without form" and "void." The two Hebrew words are *tohu* and *bohu*; and it is noteworthy that the only two other places where the double expression occurs in Scripture are prophetic passages depicting terrible divine judgments. The first is Isaiah xxxiv. 11, where the two Hebrew words are translated "confusion" and "emptiness." The second is Jeremiah iv. 23, where the translation, like that in Genesis, is "without form" and "void." Examination of the context shows that, in the first passage *certainly*, and in the second *probably*, the prophet is describing calamity which envelops *the whole earth*. The prophets, of course, knew full well that the double expression, *tohu and bohu*, was used in the opening lines of Genesis; and since they now use the same expression to describe colossal crises of Divine retribution and desolation, is there not strong suggestion that they understood the occurrence of the expression in Genesis i. 2 similarly to indicate judgment and destruction, and *not* to refer to the earth's first condition after its original creation?

It is noteworthy, too, that the six days of Genesis i. are nowhere said in Scripture to be an account of the original creation. On the other hand, a careful differentiation is observed. During the first four of the six days no creative act is recorded. We are not told that God "created" the light. What is light? It is not a substance: it is the effect of ethereal vibrations; and modern science has shown how accurate are the words used in Genesis about it. We are not told that God "created" the waters: He "*divided*" them. We are not told that God "created" the "land," but that, having gathered the waters, He let the land "*appear*." We are not told that God "created" new vegetation, but that He said, "*Let the earth bring forth*." The Hebrew word for "create" is not once used until we come to the fifth and sixth days, when *sentient* life is introduced, in the creation of the animals and man. The Hebrew word for "create" is *bara*, and there are only three places in the first chapter of Genesis where it occurs— in verse 1, to describe the original act of creation; in verse 21, where we have the creation of the "living creatures" other than man; in verse 27, where we have the creation of man. Thus, there is not one place in these six days where the word "create" is used of mere matter —of the earth itself.

Now all this leads to a further important point. That is, it settles *the question as to whether the six "days" were ordinary days, or long ages*. When once we recognise the break between the first two verses of Genesis we can dispense with the artifice of forcing the six days to mean six geological ages. It is regrettable that some of our leading evangelical expositors should have resorted to this expedient. They have done so—with good motive, no doubt—to escape certain supposed geological difficulties. Apart from this these six days would have continued to be understood simply as six ordinary days of twenty-four hours each. There is certainly no *Scriptural* warrant for making them into periods; though, of course, those who adopt the period theory now try to make out that there *is*. What, then, are their pleas?

First, they say that the word "day" is frequently used in Scripture to mean a period. To this the answer is clear. Where the word is so used, its symbolic meaning is so plain that it can scarcely be misunderstood; and, further, the word is never so used when a *number* of days are being recorded—whether it be the hundred and fifty days of the Flood (Gen. viii. 3), or the forty days that Moses spent on the Mount (Exod. xxiv. 18) or the three days that Jonah was inside the great fish (Jonah i. 17), or the six days in which the Lord made heaven and earth (Exod. xx. 11), or other numbers of days.

Second, they say that ordinary days cannot be meant because the sun was only placed in relation to our earth on the fourth day. Again the answer is clear. Not only was there *light* before the fourth day, but we read, in connection with the very first day, "And God called the light *day*, and the darkness He called *night*" (i. 5). Sir Robert Anderson, who tried to uphold the period theory, was obliged to admit that "*this passage clearly indicates our ordinary day.*" Besides, men of science now know that the sun is not the only source of light.

Third, they say that the *seventh* day still continues (because the words, "the evening and the morning," are not used of it as of the other six), and that if the seventh day be thus a long period, then so must be the preceding six. But again the answer is clear. The words, "the evening and the morning" do not describe the *close* of each day. If they were meant to do that, the order would be inverted to "the morning and the evening." They rather describe the *commencement* of each day (and the Jews still reckon their days to commence from six o'clock in the evening). After describing each day's proceedings, the inspired writer goes back to the beginning of the day, to number it—"the evening and the morning were the first day," and so on. Those who argue that the seventh day still continues point us to Hebrews iv. 9—"There *remaineth* therefore a Sabbath rest to the people of God"—which is supposed to confirm their theory. But in all truth it is no confirmation at all, for it certainly does not teach or even suggest that God's seventh-day rest in Genesis still continues. On the contrary, it merely says "God *did* rest (not *does* rest) on the seventh day"; and our Lord's own word is "My Father *worketh* (not resteth) *even until now*, and I work" (John v. 17, R.V.)! The simple truth about that Hebrews passage is that there are *three* rests there mentioned—(1) God's seventh-day rest in Genesis: see chapter iv. 4,

(2) the Canaan rest which God provided for Israel: see chapter iii. 11, iv. 8, R.V.), and (3) the spiritual rest which is provided for ourselves in Christ, and of which the other two were types: see chapter iv. 9–11. Now it is this *third* "rest" which "*remaineth*" (not God's seventh-day rest in Genesis) as verses 8 and 9 make absolutely clear.

Thus fall to pieces the efforts to supply Scripture support for making the six days of Genesis i. into six long periods. Mr. Sydney Collett has well said, "Four things are mentioned in connection with these days —viz. there was *light* and there was *darkness*, there was *evening* and there was *morning*; and I contend that in the absence of any inspired word to the contrary, we are bound by all known phenomena to regard such words as defining natural days as we know them, of twenty-four hours, one part of which was dark and the other part light. It is to be feared that the period theory expositors scarcely realise what the consequences would have been had those days of Genesis i. really been long periods, as they suggest; for, taking a very moderate estimate, each day is supposed to have occupied a period representing ten million years of our time. Now let it be carefully noted that, according to the Scriptures, those 'days' had only two divisions—viz. darkness and light, intersected by evening and morning i.e. the part that was called 'day' was *all light*, and that part which was called 'night' was *all darkness*. There is no escape from this. So that, according to the most recent of estimates, each 'day' must have consisted of about five million years of unbroken darkness, followed by about five million years of unbroken light! Now, seeing that the trees and shrubs and grass were made on the third day, and the fowls and other living creatures on the fifth day, one naturally asks what became of these things after they were created, for it is certain that no vegetable creation could possibly live—much less animal life— through five million years of unbroken light, any more than it could survive a similar period of unbroken darkness. And yet, if we accept the period theory, this is what we should have to believe took place!" There are other grotesque problems, also, involved in the period theory, but we must leave them. Let it be settled in our minds that between the first two verses of Genesis there is a break sufficient to cover all the geologic ages, and that the six days of the earth's reconstruction to become the abode of man were six days of twenty-four hours each. We shall thus maintain a harmony both with Scripture and Science. The six days of Genesis i describe a *new* beginning; but they are not the *first* beginning. That vast, remote act by which the universe began is summarised in the one brief, august, initial sentence—"In the beginning God created the heaven and the earth."

THE BOOK OF GENESIS (3)

Lesson Number 3

NOTE :—For this third study read again Genesis, chapters vi. to ix. and xxxvii. to l.

"To constitute one thing the type of another, something more is wanted than mere resemblance. The former must not only resemble the latter, but must have been designed to resemble the latter. It must have been so designed in its original institution. It must have been designed as something preparatory to the latter. The type as well as the antitype must have been pre-ordained ; and they must have been pre-ordained as constituent parts of the same general scheme of Divine providence. It is this previous design and this pre-ordained connection (together, of course, with the resemblance) which constitute the relation of type and antitype."

BISHOP MARSH, *Lectures*.

THE BOOK OF GENESIS (3)

THE TYPE-TEACHING OF GENESIS

(a) Old Testament Types in General

IT IS a fact that in no little degree the Old Testament Scriptures are permeated by latent typical meanings. Instances of their typical content are cited again and again in the New Testament, the following being specimens:

Persons
> "Adam . . . is a figure (*tupos* = type) of Him that was to come."—Rom. v. 14.
> "Melchizedek . . . made like unto (*aphomoioō* = made to resemble) the Son of God."—Heb. vii. 3.

Objects
> "That rock (of which the Israelites drank: see Exod. xvii.) was Christ."—1 Cor. x. 4.
> "The first Tabernacle . . . was a figure (*parabolē* = a parable or comparison)."—Heb. ix. 8-9.

Events
> "Noah . . . saved by water: the like figure (*antitupos* = antitype) even baptism, doth now save us."—1 Pet. iii. 21.
> "Abraham . . . received him (Isaac) from the dead, in a figure (*parabolē* = a simile)."—Heb. xi. 19.

But besides these and other similar instances, in which particular persons, objects, and events are said to be types, or figures, there are passages in the New Testament which equally clearly assert the *general* presence of types and symbols in the Old Testament Scriptures. Note the following:

"Now these things (see context) were our examples (lit:—
types for us)."—I Cor. x. 6.

"All these things happened unto them for ensamples (*tupoi*=
types)."—I Cor. x. II.

"The Law . . . a shadow (dark outline or silhouette) of . . .
things to come."—Heb. x. I.

Still further, there are other chapters, passages, and verses, in
the New Testament, which, while they do not actually assert the
fact of Old Testament typology, unmistakably *imply* it. We
think, for example, of our Lord's great discourse on the Manna,
in John vi.; Paul's contrastive exposition of the two ministrations—the "Letter" versus the "Spirit," in 2 Corinthians iii.–iv.;
the argument based upon Ishmael and Isaac, in Galatians iv.;
the Melchizedek and Aaronic passages in the epistle to the
Hebrews; our Lord's words about the Brazen Serpent; His
reference to Jonah's three days in the great fish; and the various
New Testament references to Christ as the Passover, the Firstfruits, the Mercy Seat, and the Lamb. Who can read the many
such passages without seeing in them the implication of Old
Testament typology?

Indeed, quite apart from this unanswerable New Testament
warrant for our belief in the typology of the Old Testament, such
are the circumstantial data in some cases that we could not fail
to perceive the presence of typical meanings, the similitudes
being far too clear and numerous to be merely coincidence. For
example, we are nowhere told that Joseph is a type of Christ,
yet who can read that wonderful Old Testament record, in the
light of New Testament history, without recognising in Joseph
—beloved, humiliated, exalted (not to mention the variety of
contributory details)—one of the clearest and fullest types of
Christ anywhere in the Scriptures?

Notwithstanding such circumstantial data, however, it is well
to be clear on this point, that the one all-sufficient authority for
Old Testament typology is the clear warrant of the New Testament—a warrant which, as we have shown, is clearly there. We
hold that the writers of the New Testament, like those of the
Old, were men inspired by the Spirit of God; and because of this
their word has a unique authority with us.

Values of Typology.

Now the presence of this latent typical content invests the Old Testament Scriptures with a wonderful new wealth of meaning; and it is regrettable, therefore, that the study of types has fallen into considerable disfavour in some quarters, because allegorical and mystical interpretations have been carried to foolish extravagances which are without any New Testament warrant whatever. Studied with good sense and a careful eye to New Testament teaching, the typology of the Old Testament is a priceless treasure-mine to the Bible student, and should on no account be neglected.

Besides this, the typology of the Old Testament furnishes a grand proof of its Divine inspiration. If this typical import does indeed inhere, how unanswerably it argues superhuman wisdom and foreknowledge!—for not only do the Old Testament types exhibit the consummate skill of the Divine Workman, they are a form of *prophecy*, forepicturing persons and things which were yet to be, and revealing the Divine anticipation of all future events. Indeed, they are the most wonderful kind of prophecy, for they give a colour and fulness and vividness of presentation which cannot be given in direct, unfigurative prediction.

Principles of Interpretation.

In our interpretation and application of types there are two precautions which should always be borne in mind. First: no doctrine or theory should ever be built upon a type or types independently of direct teaching elsewhere in Scripture. Types are meant to amplify and vivify doctrine, but not to originate it. They are illuminative but not foundational. Their purpose is to illustrate, not to formulate.

This is obvious in the very nature of the case, for if they are types, then they are not originals, but representations of things other than themselves; and unless the realities which they typify existed, the types themselves could not exist. Thus, types are dependent, and must not be used independently to authenticate doctrine.

Some time ago a preacher was heard advocating an elaborate theory, that at the Second Coming of Christ the saints must pass through successive heavens to undergo a process of purification before being presented at the throne of God, the whole theory being construed from a passage of somewhat doubtful import in Leviticus. That kind of thing is wrong and should be avoided.

Second: the parallelism between type and antitype should not be pressed to fanciful extremes. Types, it would seem, are not meant to be exact replicas of those things which they typify, but to enrich and illumine our understanding of the more essential features in the antitype. When the interpretation of types is carried into insignificant minutiae it degenerates into imaginative allegorising, which has many dangers.

Definition and Classification.

A type may be said to be any person, object, event, act, or institution Divinely adapted to represent some spiritual reality, or to prefigure some person or truth to be later revealed. Or, to put it another way—God has been pleased to invest certain persons, objects, events, acts, institutions, with a prefigurative meaning, so that besides having a real relationship with their own times they have had a significance reaching far forward into the future. (The word "institutions" in the above definitions covers all rules, rites, ceremonies, organisations, offices, times, places, instruments, implements, structures, furniture, robes, forms, colours, and numbers, which may be invested with a typical value.)

It is thus seen that types fall into four classes—persons, objects, events, institutions. It may be wise, also, to add here that no Old Testament person, object, event, or institution should be dogmatically asserted to be a type without clear New Testament warrant. It has been well said that types which are not thus authenticated have merely the authority of analogy and congruity.

(b) Types in Genesis

The foregoing remarks about Old Testament typology in general are made for two reasons—(1) it is well that while we are still in the early stages of this Bible Course we should have clear ideas regarding the presence and purpose of types; and (2) the book of Genesis, which we are now studying, is singularly rich in types. We submit, below, a catalogue of the more prominent types found in Genesis; and it will be seen that this first book of Scripture is specially marked by the prevalence of typical *persons*.

Persons.

Adam—type of Christ.
Eve—type of the Church.
Cain and Abel—carnal *v.* spiritual.
Enoch—the coming Translation.
Flood-survivors—the Church.
Lot—type of worldly believer.
Melchizedek—type of Christ.
Hagar and Sarah—Law *v.* Grace.
Ishmael and Isaac—Flesh *v.* Spirit.
Abraham—the Father (xxii. and xxiv.).
Isaac—Christ (xxii. and xxiv., etc.).
The Servant—the Spirit (xxiv.).
Rebekah—the Church (xxiv.).
Joseph—type of Christ.
Asenath—type of the Church.

Objects, Events, etc.

The Sun—type of Christ.
The Moon—type of the Church.
The Stars—type of saints.
The Six days—regeneration.
The Sabbath—spiritual rest.
Coats (iii. 21)—imputed righteousness.
Abel's lamb—type of Calvary.
The Flood—type of Judgment.
The Flood—regeneration (1 Pet. iii. 21).
The Ark—type of Christ.
The raven—the old nature.
The dove—the new nature.
Sodom Fire—final Judgment.
Ram (xxii.)—Christ our Substitute.
Egypt—type of the "World."

All of these are deep wells of truth; truth which, when it is brought to the surface, is as clear and fresh as it is deep and hidden. We recommend a careful consideration of them. Meanwhile we here pick out just two of them for brief treatment, as examples.

SPECIMEN TYPES IN GENESIS

(1) The Flood Survivors—a Type of the Church

Noah and those who were saved with him in the Ark are remarkably typical of Christian believers, and of the Church as a whole, in seven outstanding ways. (See Gen. vi.–ix.)

1. *Chosen.*

They were made party to a covenant (vi. 18). This covenant, in which they were chosen to salvation, was made 120 years before the Flood came, as it would seem from chapter vi. 3 with vi. 8.

Even so, Christian believers are a chosen people. "God hath from the beginning chosen you to salvation" (2 Thess. ii. 13). "He hath chosen us in Christ before the foundation of the world" (Eph. i. 4).

2. *Called.*

The Ark was entered in response to a Divine call. "The Lord said unto Noah: Come thou and all thy house into the Ark" (Gen. vii. 1).

Similarly, the true people of Christ, besides being eternally chosen in Him, are brought into their vital union with Christ by a Divine call. Thus we read in Romans viii. 30, "Moreover, whom He (God) did predestinate, them He also called." And in 1 Corinthians i. 9, we read, "God is faithful, by whom ye were called into the fellowship of His Son."

3. *Believers.*

Noah built the Ark, and entered it with his family, because he believed God (vii. 4 with vii. 7). See also Hebrews xi.—"By faith Noah . . . prepared an Ark."

So the people of Christ are distinctively *believers.* See Hebrews x. 39—"We are of them who believe to the saving of the soul"; (and many other passages). Note: Noah's faith made him *obedient* (Gen. vi. 22; vii. 5). So is it with the Christian (1 Pet. i. 22; Rom. xvi. 26; etc.). Noah's faith also brought him *imputed righteousness* (Heb. xi. 7 with Gen. vii. 1). So is it with the faith of the Christian believer (Rom. v. 1; x. 4).

4. *Separated.*

The Ark which effected salvation also involved separation. Noah was already separated from his wicked generation, in the spirit and tenor of his life. His entering the Ark was the outward culmination of it.

Christians also are a separated people. "They are not of the world" (John xvii. 16); "A people for God's own possession" (1 Pet. ii. 9, R.V.); and accordingly we are exhorted to make our separation a practical and obvious thing,—"Wherefore come out from among them, and be ye separate, saith the Lord" (2 Cor. vi. 17).

5. *Sealed.*

Besides being told that "they went in" to the Ark, we are told that "the Lord shut him in" (Gen. vii. 16). Thus were the occupants of the Ark inviolably sealed by God Himself unto the day of salvation after the Flood.

So are Christian believers sealed. "After that ye believed, ye were sealed with that Holy Spirit of promise" (Eph. i. 13). "Ye are sealed unto the day of redemption" (Eph. iv. 30). "He which stablisheth us with you in Christ, and hath anointed us, is God, who also hath sealed us" (2 Cor. i. 22).

6. *Risen.*

The higher the Flood prevailed the more the Ark rose above it. When the guilty world was beneath the Flood of judgment and death, those in the Ark were risen above it and were alive! (Gen. vii. 17-19). Thus in a remarkable figure the Ark meant life out of death.

This has its counterpart in the experience of the Christian. "The Ark was . . . the like figure whereunto baptism doth also now save us *by the resurrection of Jesus Christ*" (1 Pet. iii. 21). "Risen with Christ" (Col. iii. 1).

7. *Rewarded.*

They not only survived the Flood, they became the possessors of a new world (Gen. viii. 15-19). So is it to be with the redeemed in Christ. "We, according to His promise, look for new heavens and a new earth, wherein dwelleth righteousness" (2 Pet. iii. 13). See also Rev. xxi. 1–4.

Note the outstanding facts about Noah's occupation of the new world: (1) Fragrant fellowship (viii. 20); (2) The "curse" stayed (viii. 21); (3) A perpetual covenant (ix. 12, etc.). Even so is it in the "new heaven and new earth" for which Christian believers look (Rev. vii. 15–17; xxii. 3–5, with iv. 3).

(2) Joseph—a Type of Christ

A more intriguing story than that of Joseph was never written. What makes it the more wonderful is that it is true. The supposition that it is a mythological post-Mosaic invention has now been flung to the rubbish-heap of discredited modernist presumptions, by the spade of the archæologist. The story is true: and one cannot read it thoughtfully without exclaiming, "Truth is stranger than fiction!" It has been truly said that while we are nowhere specifically notified that Joseph was a type of Christ, "the analogies are too numerous to be accidental."

The life of Joseph runs in three periods. We see him first as the beloved son, supreme in the regard of his father; then as the suffering servant, rejected by his brethren; and, finally, as the exalted saviour, lifted high over all in princely splendour and administrative authority. Thus, in this triple way, Joseph becomes the most complete single type of Christ anywhere in the Bible.

The Beloved Son.

1. *Pre-eminent in the love of the father.*—See xxxvii. 3. "Israel loved Joseph more than all his children." So is Christ the well-beloved Son in whom the Divine Father specially delights. See Matt. iii. 17; Col. i. 13 (R.V.).

2. *Pre-eminent in filial honour.*—See xxxvii. 3. The tunic of distinction and heirship was the outward attestation of the father's regard. See John v. 37 (which probably refers to Voice and Dove at Baptism): John v. 36; iii. 35.

3. *Pre-eminent in the Divine purposes.*—This is clearly revealed in Joseph's dreams which were prophetic, as Jacob himself perceived (xxxvii. 5–11). So is it with Christ. In Him God "framed the ages" (Heb. i. 2). Also Eph. i. 9–10.

4. *Pre-eminent as the father's messenger.*—See xxxvii. 13–14. "I will send thee unto them . . ." So is Christ the pre-eminent Messenger of the Father. See Isaiah xlii. 1; Luke iv. 18 ("He hath sent Me"); Heb. i. 1–2.

The Rejected Servant.

1. *Hated.* Joseph was hated by his brethren. Alas, this is also true of Christ. Almost the same words are used of both. Compare xxxvii. 4 with John xv. 24; xxxvii. 8 with Luke xix. 14; xxxvii. 18 with Matt. xxvi. 3–4; xxxvii. 19–20 with Matt. xxi. 38; xxxvii. 11 with Matt. xxvii. 18.

2. *Sold.* Joseph was sold by his brethren for twenty pieces of silver (xxxvii. 27–28) to Gentiles. Christ was sold for thirty pieces of silver (Matt. xxvii. 9) and delivered to the Gentiles. Joseph was stripped of his "coat." (See Matt. xxvii. 28.)

3. *Suffering.* How Joseph must have suffered! Compare xxxvii. 23–4 with xlii. 21. See Joseph in the slave-market, then under temptation (xxxix. 7–12), in further adversity (xxxix. 20). All this has its counterpart in the gracious Antitype.

4. *Dead (in intent and figure).* About twenty years elapsed between the selling of Joseph and the re-union. He was accounted dead (xxvii. 31–4; xlii. 13 and 38; xliv. 20). So Christ, in actuality, suffered death for our sakes.

The Exalted Saviour.

1. *Exalted as the wisdom and power of God to salvation.* See xli. 38–9, and Joseph's new name (xli. 45). Becomes the world's bread-supplier (xli. 57). Administrator of affairs (xli. 40 with xlvii. 14–26). So Christ (1 Cor. i. 24; Acts v. 31; John vi. 51; v. 22).

2. *Exalted to the right hand of the throne.* See xli. 39–44. So is Christ exalted to right hand of Majesty on high (Eph. i. 20–1; Heb. i. 3). Joseph given Gentile bride (xli. 45). So bride of Christ, the Church, during this age (Rom. xi. 25; Eph. iii. 6).

3. *Exalted among his own brethren.* See xlii. 6; xliii. 26. Revealed to penitent brethren after sin brought home to them (xlv). Becomes special succourer of Israel (xlvii. 11–12). Consummates wonderful Divine plan (xlv. 5–9). Becomes (virtually) resurrected

(xlv. 28). All this paralleled in Antitype (Rev. i. 7; Jer. xxiii. 5–6;
Eph. i. 9–10; Rev. i. 18).

4. *Exalted to an everlasting pre-eminence.* See xlix. 26. He was
"separate from his brethren" in *character*, as records show. Scripture levels not one charge against Joseph, although more space
is given to him than any other in Genesis. His exaltation was
both a vindication and a reward. So with Christ. "He humbled
Himself . . . wherefore God also hath highly exalted Him, etc."
(Phil. ii. 5–11).

THE BOOK OF GENESIS (4)

Lesson Number 4

NOTE :—For this fourth study in Genesis re-read chapters xii. to l. Make notes of any striking bits or special thoughts in connection with the four outstanding characters, Abraham, Isaac, Jacob, Joseph.

" The scientific method is applicable to Scripture. First we trace scattered facts and truths, and then gather them up and arrange them. Like things are put together under a common designation, a process, based on similarities of nature and feature, attributes and characteristics, structure and relations, with a view to discovering what general law pervades them all, and supplies a broad basis for inference and deduction. This, the Baconian method of inductive philosophy which revolutionized scientific study is the true principle in Scripture research."

ARTHUR T. PIERSON, D.D.

THE BOOK OF GENESIS (4)

WE HERE reach our fourth and final study in the Book of Genesis. Thus far we have not given separate consideration to the four pivotal persons—Abraham, Isaac, Jacob, and Joseph, around whom the whole of the narrative revolves in the second part of the book (xii.–l.): but in this present study they come under review, though as part of a larger theme. We here give a final example of the type-teaching of Genesis, and then make certain closing suggestions about the further study of the book.

THE SEVEN GREAT MEN OF GENESIS

The principal personalities which are brought successively before us in the Book of Genesis all have a typical significance. That this is so seems clearly shown by New Testament references such as that in which Paul speaks of Ishmael and Isaac as representing the two covenants (Gal. iv. 22–7), and at the same time representing the two natures—that which is "after the flesh," and that which is "after the Spirit" (Gal. iv. 29). The priest-king Melchizedek is another example (Heb. vii.); and the first man of all, Adam, is declared to be a "figure (type) of Him that was to come" (Rom. v. 14).

Turning, then, to the main figures in Genesis, we observe that not only are some of them types of *persons* (as, for instance, Isaac and Joseph are types of Christ), but when viewed collectively they typify *progressive stages of spiritual experience*.

It goes almost without saying that the first man, Adam, besides being (in his relationships) a type of Christ, is (in his fallen state) a type of the natural man, or of unregenerate human nature. Again and again in the New Testament he is thus alluded to (Rom. vi. 6; Eph. iv. 22; Col. iii. 9). Now one of the leading purports of Genesis seems to be that of showing us all that which springs from the first Adam—all that which *can* spring from him, both of good and ill, both by nature and through the influence of Divine grace. This corresponds with the work of God's Spirit in our own hearts. The Holy Spirit first shows us what we are in Adam—what we are in ourselves, by nature, with a view to creating a sense of need, so that as the prodigal first "came to himself" and then came to the father, we also might know ourselves, and seek God. So then, in Genesis, we are first shown that which is in Adam, and that which naturally and normally springs from him.

If we want to know the awful capabilities of evil which are within Adamic human nature, we only need to trace the Cain line through its records of godless culture, earthly-mindedness, vanity, violence, and rebellion against God.

If we would know what can come from the same human material when under the renewing and transforming power of Divine grace, we need to follow the line of *the men of faith.*

There are seven such men in Genesis, standing out in unmistakable prominence. They are Abel, Enoch, Noah, Abraham, Isaac, Jacob, Joseph. That these seven do indeed have a peculiar prominence and significance is indicated by the fact that, under the guidance of the inspiring Spirit, the writer of the epistle to the Hebrews picks them out, as distinct from all others, for inclusion in that classic New Testament catalogue of Old Testament worthies, Hebrews xi. Let us note the *outstanding* characteristics of these men.

Abel.

What is the marked characteristic of Abel? His name, his choice of occupation, his sacrifice, and the reflective comments of the New Testament concerning him, together mark him out as being distinctively and representatively *the man of spiritual desire.*

Cain, the man of earthly desire, is the first-born. Abel, the man of spiritual desire, comes afterwards. The order is ever thus. "That is not first which is spiritual, but that which is natural; and afterward that which is spiritual" (1 Cor. xv. 46). The name "Cain" means *possession,* pointing, as did Cain's life, to hopes fixed on earthly things. The name "Abel" means *exhalation* (or vapour), speaking of ascent to higher regions.

Cain was a "tiller of the ground"—with earthward interests and holdings. Abel was a "keeper of sheep"—the tent-dwelling pilgrim, desiring something beyond. Cain goes "out from the presence of the Lord," and busies himself with "cities" and with works "in brass and iron." Abel reaches after better things (Heb. xi. 16), seeking rest in God; suffering and dying in hope of the "better resurrection." Cain, ignoring sin and the Fall, is all for a religion of self-culture, offering the fruit of that which is under a curse. Abel, the man of spiritual aspiration, offers a sacrifice which is at once a confession of sin, and the expression of strong desire for fellowship with God on the ground of forgiveness through sacrifice and faith. Abel is *the man of spiritual desire.*

Enoch.

Next comes Enoch. What is the distinguishing characteristic here? Enoch is forever immortalised as the man who "walked with God." But what is the inner meaning of his walk with God, so far as the man himself is concerned. *Why* did Enoch walk with God? There was no compulsion about it. There was no *need* for him to walk with God, whether he wished to do so or not. The inner truth is that behind the *walk* was the *will.* There was a blending of Enoch's will with the will of God. It was this that made the walk possible. "Can two walk together except they be agreed?" (Amos iii. 3). Enoch put from him all controversy with the will of God, and accepted it in preference to his own.

But if behind the walk was the will, behind the will was the activity of that strange and vital faculty in human nature which we call *choice.* While it is true that God and Enoch walked together in a wonderful fellowship, yet the basic truth is not that God walked with Enoch, but (as indeed Genesis puts it) that "Enoch walked with God." It was not God going Enoch's way, but Enoch going God's way. Behind this walk with God was Enoch's full and final *choice* of God's will and way. His name means *dedicated.* Enoch is the man who chooses God's way— *the man of spiritual choice.*

Noah.

And now comes Noah. As a type-figure among the seven outstanding men of Genesis, the special significance attaching to Noah is unmistakable. From the New Testament we learn that

Noah's experience of being "saved through water" is a typical anticipation of *regeneration*, of which Christian baptism is the symbol (1 Pet. iii. 21).

Of Noah, as well as of Enoch, it is written that he "walked with God"; but the type-emphasis is shifted a further stage forward in the account of Noah, so that now, consequent upon the spiritual *choice* indicated in the words "Noah walked with God," we see spiritual *renewal*, typified in Noah's passing through the waters of the Flood. First, in chapter six, we see Noah, the man of spiritual choice, still on the ground of the old world. Then, in chapter seven, we see him separated from the old world, in the ark (Christ), and by the water (regeneration). Then, in chapters eight and nine, we see him going forth into a new life in a new world—which speaks of newness of life through regeneration. Thus, in Noah, we see, typically, *spiritual renewal*.

Abraham, Isaac, Jacob, Joseph.

We come now to the post-Flood patriarchs, and to save space we group them together, though there is much we should like to have said about them separately. These four, following the typifying of regeneration, in Noah, exhibit, in a typical way, the qualities and characteristics of the regenerate life. They show us those forms of life which are known after regeneration.

In ABRAHAM we see *the life of faith*. He stands out as the supreme exemplar of the faith-life. In him we see the man of faith going forth, trusting in the Divine guidance, believing the Divine promises, receiving Divine assurances, inheriting the Divine blessing, undergoing sharp testings, and—despite occasional failures—being "accounted righteous" through faith, and being called "the friend of God."

In ISAAC we see *the life of sonship*. The Genesis account clearly puts the emphasis upon Isaac's unique sonship. He is the son of special promise, of special birth, of special preciousness, the only son of his mother, and the only heir of his father, the son at whose weaning a great feast is made, and through whom the promises are to be realised, and for whom a special bride must be chosen. In Isaac, then, dwelling in the land of inheritance, biding by the wells of water, with many joys and few conflicts, we see the typified privileges and joys of sonship.

In JACOB we see *the life of service.* Jacob is that life which (as at his birth) "takes hold with the hand." Jacob is the worker throughout, busy with his hands. Here is untiring service. There are mistakes in method and manner, yet there is blessing, for at heart the motive is good. The busy worker would even help God to work the Divine purposes out the more expeditiously, until God has to touch His servant's thigh, and teach him, also, to be a prince in prayer. Yet Jacob is spiritual at heart, as all his words show. Esau will give up the birthright for meat. Jacob will give up his meat for the birthright, if by any means he might obtain the inheritance. Here, then, in Jacob, is eager activity, work, service.

Finally, in JOSEPH, the finest and highest type of regenerate life is set forth. The biographical sketches of the Bible are un-flatteringly true to fact, yet although more space is devoted to Joseph than to any other single subject in Genesis, in all the record God does not speak one word of reproof against Joseph. In him we see *the life of suffering and glory.* Here faith and son-ship and service are blended in something deeper and grander, issuing in complete rule over the world and the flesh. Here Egypt (type of the world and the sense-life), which had been a snare to Abraham and Isaac, is completely ruled. Here is "the fellow-ship of His sufferings and the power of His resurrection." Here is the character of the regenerate made "perfect through suffer-ings." Here is suffering and reigning with Christ, and being "glorified together"!

These, then, are the marked characteristics exhibited by the seven outstanding men of Genesis.

> Abel—spiritual desire.
> Enoch—spiritual choice.
> Noah—spiritual renewal.
> Abraham—the life of faith.
> Isaac—the life of sonship.
> Jacob—the life of service.
> Joseph—the life of suffering and glory.

Is there not clear and wonderful typical teaching here? Note the progressive order. First comes spiritual *desire,* then spiritual *choice,* then spiritual *renewal.* After this we see life lived by a new principle—that of *faith*. Then faith brings the sense of *sonship*, out of which grows *service*. Finally, we have the deeper depths and higher heights of fellowship with the life of God, in *suffering* and *glory*. Obviously, this is the *true* order, and must not be altered.

Truly there is fascinating type-teaching here! Let these seven characters be studied in this light, and they become rich with suggestions that fill out our ideas of the great truths which they typify. This is the genius of typology. Truths of which we should have a very limited apprehension if they were only communicated to us by plain didactic language, are made to live and grow before us when we see them in the picturesque and vivid setting of type and symbol.

For instance, if we were merely told in so many words that there must be spiritual desire and choice and renewal, followed by faith, sonship, service, suffering and glory, how limited would our idea of these things be! But when we see them illustrated and exemplified in the living and fascinating characters of these seven men, our understanding of the truths thus typified is incalculably enriched.

Of course, it must be clearly realised that we are here viewing these seven men *typically*, and not biographically. Because Noah here typifies, in a unique way, spiritual renewal, this must not be taken to imply that Abel and Enoch, who went before him, were *not* spiritually renewed men! And because Abraham here typifies, in a unique way, the life of faith, this must not be taken to imply that the three before him and the three after him were not men of faith! All the seven were men spiritually renewed, men of faith. Each of the seven, considered *individually*, shows his experience, in measure, of the whole seven-fold truth set forth by all the seven *collectively*. Yet each of the seven is nevertheless marked by the one outstanding characteristic, which invests him with a special *typical* significance, and gives him his place in the completed type constituted by all the seven together.

Finally, let it be our prayer that *we* may be men and women of spiritual desire, spiritual choice, and spiritual renewal, walking by faith, realising our heavenly sonship, serving the Lord from a sense of filial devotion, knowing "the fellowship of His suffering," and ever rejoicing in the prospect of glory yet to be!

CONCLUDING SUGGESTIONS

The Book of Genesis should also be studied *biographically*. It is rich in human characters. Study, for instance, the seven great men before-mentioned, noting the dominant feature or determining crisis in the recorded history of each—Abel the worshipper, Enoch the walker, Noah the worker, Abraham the wanderer, Isaac the watcher, Jacob the wrestler, Joseph the waiter. What character studies are Esau, Lot, Cain!—illustrating, respectively, "the lust of the flesh, and the lust of the eyes, and the pride of life" (1 John ii. 16). Nimrod, Sarah, Laban, Judah, and others, well repay study.

Genesis should be specially studied *spiritually*. No book of the Old Testament is richer in spiritual values. Here is a life-time of rewarding study in itself! Its spiritual teachings fall into two categories—(1) truths to enlighten the mind; (2) lessons to regulate the life. As to the former, we may mention—the presence and gracious purposes of God in human history; the presence and evil purposes of a personal devil; the origin and progress of sin in the human race; the depravity of fallen human nature; the Divine prevision and provision; the ministry of angels; the Divine sovereignty and condescension; these being but a few of many tremendous truths. As for the *lessons* which abound here—to cite only one of many fruitful instances—what illuminating spiritual lessons we find in the records pertaining to the rise and progress of faith in the soul of Abraham! Take, for instance, the very first records concerning him—chapter xii. 4 to xiii. 4. See here (1) faith *responding* (xii. 4–9); then faith *receding* (xii. 10–20); then faith *returning* (xiii. 1–4). The lessons associated with these early experiences of the pilgrim believer are important beyond expression.

Then, again, Genesis should be studied *prophetically*. The whole of subsequent revelation and history is really the unfolding of the prophecies in this first book of Scripture. Here are great prophecies, concerning *Christ* (iii. 14–15), concerning the *Earth* (iii. 17–18; viii. 21–2), concerning the *Race* (ix. 25–27), concerning *Israel* (xiii. 14–17; xxii. 15–18), concerning other nations and tribes (xvii. 19–20; xxv. 23; xlviii. 17–20; xlix. 1–28). In the light of many wonderful fulfilments these prophecies constitute unanswerable evidence of the superhuman origin of the Scriptures.

Genesis should be studied *dispensationally*. In His dealings with mankind, it has pleased God to adopt different methods suited to different times. These periods are conveniently termed "dispensations." A dispensation has been defined as "a period of time during which man is tested in respect of obedience to some *specific* revelation of the will of God." Seven such are distinguished in the Scriptures; and four of these we find in Genesis. They have been well expressed as: (1) the period of *Innocence*, in which God tested man; (2) that of *Conscience*, in which God suffered man; (3) that of human *Government*, in which God restrained man; (4) that of *Promise*, in which God wrought for man.

There are other ways of studying Genesis, such as geographically, critically, textually; but the above-mentioned supply enough suggestion to occupy us profitably for a long while.

PAUSE HERE!—AND TEST YOUR STUDY THUS FAR

1. What are the main groups of books in the Old Testament? (Give number and nature of each.)
2. What are the main groups of books in the New Testament? (Give number and nature of each.)
3. What are the progressive truths which run through the Pentateuch?
4. What are the similarities and contrasts between Genesis and the Apocalypse?
5. What is the structure of Genesis, and how does it suggest the principal lesson of the book?
6. What is our authority for asserting the presence of types in the Old Testament? What is a type? Define and classify.
7. What are the grounds for saying that the six days of Genesis describe the re-formation of the earth, and not its original creation?
8. What were the main results of the Fall?
9. Were the "sons of God" in Genesis vi. the fallen angels? If not, why not?
10. What suggestions are there that the Noachian Flood may not have been universal?
11. When did the Babel crisis probably occur? What were its main significances?
12. Who are the seven outstanding "men of faith" in Genesis? And what may they be said progressively to typify?

THE BOOK OF EXODUS (1)

Lesson Number 5

NOTE:—For this study read the whole book of Exodus through
once or twice, and the first eighteen chapters a third time.

THE BOOK OF EXODUS

THE DIVINE POWER, HOLINESS, AND WISDOM

I. THE EXODUS (i.–xviii.).

PROJECTED—i.–iv.
OBSTRUCTED—v.–xi.
EFFECTED—xii.–xviii.

II. THE LAW (xix.–xxiv.).

"COMMANDMENTS"—(Moral).
"JUDGMENTS"—(Social).
"ORDINANCES"—(Religious).

III. THE TABERNACLE (xxv.–xl.).

DESIGNED—xxv.–xxxi.
DELAYED—xxxii.–xxxiv.
COMPLETED—xxxv.–xl.

THE BOOK OF EXODUS (1)

WE TURN now to the second book of Scripture, namely, Exodus; and we have good reason to approach our study of it with real eagerness, for never was there a more striking or vital record written for our learning.

It is here that we see the outgoing of Israel from Egypt—an entire race of people suddenly and forever flinging away the shackles of a generations-long servitude, and migrating to a new country and a new corporate life. It is here that we have the giving of the Law, and the enunciating of the Mosaic Covenant. It is here that we see the erecting of that marvellously symbolical structure, the Tabernacle. It is here that Moses grows up before us and goes forth to his mighty task. It is here that we mark the transition of the Israelites from being merely a plurality of kindred tribes into one nation, Divinely adopted, constituted, and conditioned, as such, at Sinai.

Is there in all history a more amazing spectacle than the Exodus?—a more august and solemn revelation of God than at Sinai?—a more significant piece of architecture than the Israelite Tabernacle?—a greater human figure than the man Moses?— a more influential national epoch than the founding of the Israel theocracy? All these are found in this second book of Scripture. It is the *fons et origo*—the very fount and origin of the national life, law, and organised religion of Israel.

The title "Exodus," which means "outgoing," accurately conveys the main subject of the book; but two other subjects are associated with the Exodus, as being the direct outcome of it, and complimentary to it, namely, the *Law*, and the *Tabernacle*. The book quite naturally divides thus—

1. THE EXODUS—i.–xviii.

2. THE LAW—xix.–xxiv.

3. THE TABERNACLE—xxv.–xl.

Each of the three main divisions of the book breaks up into three further subsidiary parts—(see preceding diagram on p. 74).

The Divine Power, Holiness, Wisdom.

This threefold plan at once suggests the principal significance of the book. Observe, first, the teaching here concerning *GOD*. In the Exodus (i.–xviii.) we see the *power* of God. In the Law (xix.–xxiv.) we see the *holiness* of God. In the Tabernacle (xxv.–xl.) we see the *wisdom* of God. We have seen that the outstanding message of Genesis is the Divine sovereignty. How fitting that now, in this Book of Exodus, we should see the Divine power and holiness and wisdom outstandingly exhibited to us!

Life, Law and Love.

Note, also, the teaching here regarding *ISRAEL*. In the Exodus we see Israel being brought to a new *condition*—of freedom. In the Law we see Israel being brought to a new *constitution* —that of the theocracy. In the Tabernacle we see Israel being brought to a new *conception*—of worship, and of God. By the Exodus they are brought *out*—to new liberty. By the Law they are brought *under*—a new government. By the Tabernacle they are brought *into*—a new fellowship.

These things speak to the people of God, in all times, of the basic principles underlying the Divine dealings with us. Here, in the Exodus, the Law, and the Tabernacle, is redemption, reconstruction, reconciliation. Here is life, law, love. The Exodus leads to a new and fuller *life*. Sinai conditions the new life by the one perfect *law*. The Tabernacle leads to the sublime *love* behind both.

Liberty, Responsibility, Privilege.

Fundamentally, the problem with which the various philosophies of life seek to deal is that of human freedom, responsibility, and privilege. Liberty without law is licence. Responsibility without freedom is bondage. Liberty and responsibility together, without privilege—without rewards and punishments—lack motive and meaning. Here, in the Exodus, the Law, and the Tabernacle, we see these three things—in the Exodus, *liberty*; in the Law, *responsibility*; in the Tabernacle, *privilege*.

Thus in these three parts of this book—historical, legislative, ecclesiastical—we are touching wonderful teaching. Let us now explore part one. It opens up as follows—

I. THE EXODUS (i.–xviii.).

PROJECTED—THROUGH MOSES (i.–iv.).

How necessitated—
   (a) Israel's expansion in Egypt (i. 1–12).
   (b) Israel's oppression by Egypt (i. 13–22).
How anticipated—
   (a) Moses' preparation in Egypt (ii. 1–15).
   (b) Moses' preparation in Midian (ii. 16–25).
How precipitated—
   (a) The New Message from God (iii. 1–iv. 17).
   (b) The New Mission of Moses (iv. 18–31).

OBSTRUCTED—BY PHARAOH (v.–xi.).

The eight requests—
   v. 1–3; vii. 10; vii. 15–18; viii. 1–4; viii. 20–3; ix. 1–4;
   ix. 13–19; x. 1–6.
The eight refusals—
   v. 2; vii. 13; vii. 22–3; viii. 15, 19; viii. 32; ix. 7, 12;
   ix. 34–5; x. 11, 20, 27.
The ten requitals—
   vii. 20; viii. 6; viii. 16; viii. 24; ix. 3; ix. 10; ix. 22;
   x. 12; x. 21; xi. 5.

EFFECTED—BY JEHOVAH (xii.–xviii.).

Goshen to Red Sea—
   (a) The Passover and memorials (xii. 1–xiii. 16).
   (b) The Leading out of Israel (xiii. 17–22).
Through Red Sea—
   (a) Egyptian pursuit of Israel (xiv. 1–12).
   (b) Israel saved: pursuers dead (xiv. 13–31).
Red Sea to Sinai—
   (a) One month: to Desert (xv. 1–xvi. 1).
   (b) Two weeks: to Sinai (xvi. 1–xviii. 27).

In these three movements the three great actors in this drama of ancient history are emphasised respectively—ISRAEL, EGYPT, GOD.

THE EXODUS—AND ISRAEL

Think what the Exodus meant for Israel. It meant four things specially. First, it marked the beginning of a new *LIFE*. In chapter xii. 2, we read: "This month (Nisan) shall be unto you the beginning of months: it shall be the first month of the year to you." April becomes January. The new life is marked by the beginning of a new calendar. They are to reckon anew from this event which marks their birth as a nation.

Second, the Exodus meant the beginning of a new *LIBERTY*. As the great host came forth from Egypt Moses thus addressed them: "Remember this day in which ye came out from Egypt, out of the house of bondage; for by strength of hand the Lord brought you out from this place" (xiii. 3). That grim word "bondage" was to be associated with Egypt for ever afterward in the memory of Israel. Egypt was distinctively "the house of bondage." But at the Exodus Israel went out to liberty.

Third, the Exodus meant the beginning of a new *FELLOW-SHIP*. This is symbolised in the "feast" which was instituted in connection with the Passover. "This day shall be unto you for a memorial; and ye shall keep it a feast to the Lord throughout your generations" (xii. 14). In the Old Testament the feast is ever the symbol of fellowship (see xxiv. 11).

Fourth, the Exodus marked the beginning of a new *ASSURANCE*. When God announced His purpose to bring about the Exodus, He thus addressed the people through Moses: "I will take you to Me for a people, and I will be to you a God: and ye shall know that I am the Lord your God, which bringeth you out from under the burdens of the Egyptians. And I will bring you into the land concerning the which I did swear to give it to Abraham, to Isaac, and to Jacob; and I will give it you for an heritage: I am the Lord" (vi. 7–8).

All this has its counterpart in the Gospel of Christ. Luke tells us that when Moses and Elijah appeared with Christ on the Mount of the Transfiguration they "spake of His decease (lit.— 'His Exodus') which He should accomplish at Jerusalem." Christ is the Leader of an Exodus far greater than that under Moses. The exodus under Moses is indeed a *type* of that which Christ has wrought for us, as we see from 1 Corinthians v. 7–8—"For even Christ our Passover is sacrificed for us." As the Exodus under Moses meant a new life, a new liberty, a new fellowship, and a new assurance for Israel, so the Gospel of Christ means all this to the believer.

THE EXODUS—AND EGYPT

Think what the Exodus meant in relation to Egypt. It meant three things specially. First, it was the first big-scale exposure of the falsity of idolatry. The primal revelation of Himself, and of Divine truth, which God had given to the early fathers of the race, had been more and more obscured or perverted as time had elapsed, through the perverted mind and will of fallen man; and systems of idolatry had grown up (Joshua xxiv. 2, 14, 15), man having made all manner of gods for himself. Egypt at the time of the Exodus was probably the greatest kingdom on earth, and its gods were considered correspondingly great. When God would call out the people of Israel to their new life and their intended national mission of restoring the knowledge of the one true God, He would, at the same time, expose the falsity of all man-concocted deities. Thus we find God saying: "Against all the gods of Egypt I will execute judgment: I am the Lord" (xii. 12) (see also Num. xxxiii. 4). This smash-up of Egypt's gods not only compelled even the magicians of Egypt to confess: "This is the finger of God (i.e., of the *true* God)," but, being so conspicuous, it was a lesson to all the nations of that day (xv. 14–15; xviii. 11; and see Joshua ix. 9). It duly impressed, also, the minds of the Israelites; and we hear them singing, from the farther bank of the Red Sea: "Who is like unto Thee, O Lord, among the gods?"

Second, the overthrow of Egypt demonstrates the uselessness, sin, and folly of attempting to resist Jehovah, the God of Israel, the one true God. At the beginning of the contest Pharaoh contemptuously asked: "Who is Jehovah, that I should obey Him?" The Exodus was designed to answer that question in a way which should be a lesson to all men for all time. Indeed, God announced to Pharaoh, through Moses: "In very deed for this cause have I raised thee up, for to show in thee My power, and that My Name may be declared throughout the earth" (ix. 16).

Third, it is to be remembered that all the principal features of the Exodus possess a typical import, and that in line with this, Egypt, the scene of the Exodus, is a type of "the world," in the morally evil sense. Egypt is a type of the world (1) in its material wealth and power (Heb. xi. 26); (2) in its fleshly wisdom and false religion (Exod. viii. 7, etc.; 1 Kings iv. 30); (3) in its despotic prince, Pharaoh, who himself is a figure of Satan; (4) in its organisation on the principles of force, human aggrandisement, ambition, and pleasure; (5) in its persecution of the people of God (Deut. iv. 20); (6) in its overthrow by Divine judgment (xii. 29; xv. 4–7). In the plagues, the smiting of the firstborn, and the drowning of the Egyptian host, we see the final tribulation, judgment and destruction of the present world-system.

THE EXODUS—AND GOD

Supremely, the Exodus was an expression of the Divine power. It was as such that it made its outstanding impact on the Hebrew mind. It became for ever afterwards, to Israel, the standard of God's power to deliver His people. Scores of times it is thus referred to in the Old Testament, Micah vii. 15 being representative—"According to the days of thy coming out of the land of Egypt will I show unto him marvellous things." Note the "according to," indicating the unit of measurement.

That the Exodus should thus become the Old Testament unit of measurement is no surprising thing when we consider what a complex marvel it was. It was (1) a marvel of *judgment*—in the miraculous plagues, the smiting of the firstborn, and the over-whelming of the Egyptian host in the sea; (2) a marvel of *grace* —in the exempting of the blood-marked dwellings, and the delivering of the Israelites; (3) a marvel of *might*—in the clearing of a way through the Red Sea; (4) a marvel of *guidance*—in the pillar of cloud and of fire; (5) a marvel of *provision*—in the miraculous supplying of food and drink; (6) a marvel of *faithfulness*—in the Divine honouring of the Abrahamic covenant and the further covenant with the nation at Sinai; (7) a marvel of *condescension*—as seen in the Tabernacle, by means of which the infinite, holy God abode, in a special way, among His redeemed people.

It is an interesting point, in the *comparative* study of the Scriptures, to note the change-over from this Old Testament standard to a new unit of measurement in the New Testament. The New Testament standard of God's power to deliver His people is seen in Ephesians i. 19–21:

"That ye may know . . . what is the exceeding greatness of His power to us-ward who believe, according to the working of His mighty power which He wrought in Christ when He raised Him from the dead, and set Him at His own right hand in the heavenlies, far above all principality and power and might and dominion and every name that is named, not only in this age, but also in that which is to come."

The Old Testament unit of measurement is thus superseded by the greater manifestation of the Divine power through Christ.

In comparing the new standard with that of the Old Testament, however, it is instructive to observe that the New Testament standard repeats the seven wonderful characteristics marked in the Exodus. Like the Exodus, it is (1) a marvel of *judgment*— in the judicial dealing of God with human sin, at Calvary, and in the overthrow of Satan, with the "principalities and powers" of evil; (2) a marvel of *grace*—in the exempting of the blood-sealed believer from judgment and punishment, on the ground of identification with the Cross; (3) a marvel of *might*—in the raising up of Christ from the dead and His exaltation as Prince and Saviour far above all the powers of heaven and earth and hell; (4) a marvel of guidance—in the giving and ministry of the Holy Spirit as the new pillar of cloud and fire; (5) a marvel of *provision*—in the blessing of the believer with "all spiritual blessings in the heavenlies in Christ," and the supplying of all need "according to God's riches, in glory, by Christ Jesus"; (6) a marvel of *faithfulness*—in the further developing of the Abrahamic covenant, through Christ, in whom all kindreds of the earth are blessed, in the honouring of the later covenant through Moses, which disobedient Israel had broken, and in the revelation of the New Covenant, in Christ's blood; (7) a marvel of *condescension*—in the abiding of the Holy Spirit within the believer, transforming the human personality into a "temple of the living God."

THE EXODUS—AND THE GOSPEL

Finally—as already noted—the Exodus under Moses is a graphic type of that greater exodus in Christ: it is meant to speak to us of this; and it is well, therefore, to fix in mind the points of comparison and contrast.

Main Points of Comparison.
1. The Exodus brought a mighty emancipation for Israel. The Gospel brings deliverance from the guilt and penalty and bondage of sin.
2. The Exodus centred in the Passover and the slain lamb. The Gospel centres in the great passover of Calvary and "the Lamb slain from the foundation of the world."
3. The Exodus became for ever afterwards commemorated in the Passover Feast. So "Christ our Passover is sacrificed for us; therefore let us keep the feast" (1 Cor. v. 7).

Main Points of Contrast.
1. (In means.) The sheltering blood, in the Exodus, was merely that of an animal. In the Gospel it is "the precious blood of Christ." In the one case *many* lambs are slain; in the other, One for all.
2. (In extent.) The Exodus was national and therefore limited. The Gospel is universal, its characteristic word of address being "whosoever."
3. (In effects.) The one was deliverance from physical bondage; the other is from spiritual. The one deliverance was temporal; the other is eternal. The one opened up the way to an earthly Canaan; the other to a heavenly.

THE BOOK OF EXODUS (2)

Lesson Number 6

NOTE :—For this study read three times over chapters xix. to xxiv.

II. THE LAW (xix.–xxiv.)

"COMMANDMENTS" (governing *Moral* Life—xix.–xx.).

The terms of the Sinai Covenant submitted (xix. 3–6).
The terms of the Sinai Covenant accepted (xix. 7–8).
The two parties to the Covenant meet—(1) Israel (xix. 9–17).
The two parties to the Covenant meet—(2) God (xix. 18–25).
The ten commands—spiritual basis of Covenant (xx. 1–17).
The earthen altar—outward symbol of Covenant (xx. 18–26).

"JUDGMENTS" (governing *Social* Life—xxi.–xxiii.).

Concerning masters and servants (xxi. 1–11).
Concerning physical injuries (xxi. 12–36).
Concerning property rights (xxii. 1–15).
Concerning various evil practices (xxii. 16–xxiii. 9).
Concerning national Sabbaths and Feasts (xxiii. 10–19).
Concerning national relationships (xxiii. 20–33).

"ORDINANCES" (governing *Religious* Life—xxiv.).

NOTE: The "Ordinances" (which are contained in the instructions regarding the Tabernacle), really begin in the next chapter (xxv.). We include them here to set off the threefold nature of the Law, and because they also were part of the Divine communications to Moses during the forty days in the Mount, mentioned at the end of the present section (xxiv. 12–18).

THE BOOK OF EXODUS (2)

THE LAW (xix.–xxiv.)

THE SECOND of the three main parts of Exodus runs from the beginning of chapter xix. to the end of chapter xxiv. It is occupied with the giving of the Law, and the enunciating of the Mosaic Covenant. The Law is in three parts—"Commandments," "Judgments," "Ordinances." (See across.)

There are certain important considerations which we must bear in mind if we would truly understand the giving of the Law, marking, as it does, that new relationship between God and Israel which we speak of as the Mosaic Covenant.

HOW THE LAW CAME IN

First, the Mosaic Covenant, strictly speaking, is not a new covenant, but a development in and of the Abrahamic Covenant. The subject of the Covenant is thus introduced to Israel at Sinai:

"Ye have seen what I did unto the Egyptians, and how I bare you on eagles' wings, and brought you unto Myself. Now, therefore, if ye will obey My voice indeed, and keep My covenant, then ye shall be a peculiar treasure unto Me above all people; for all the earth is Mine. And ye shall be unto Me a kingdom of priests, and an holy nation" (Exod. xix. 4–6).

What is meant here by "My covenant"? It is referred to without explanation, as something known already by Israel. We can only know by turning back to earlier occurrences of that word "covenant." We find it twice before this in Exodus. First, in chapter ii. 24 we read: "God heard their groaning, and God remembered His covenant with Abraham, with Isaac, and with Jacob." Then in chapter vi. 4–5 we read: "I have established My covenant with them (Abraham, Isaac, Jacob), to give them the land of Canaan. . . . I have also heard the groaning of the Children of Israel, whom the Egyptians keep in bondage, and I have remembered My covenant." In both these references the word "remembered" looks back to the Abrahamic Covenant, and specially, therefore, to Genesis xv. and xvii., in which chapters we have the seal (xv. 17–18) and sign (xvii. 10) of the Abrahamic covenant. Between Genesis xvii. and Exodus ii. 24 there is no mention whatever of any other Divine covenant. Thus it is perfectly clear that when God says to Israel, at Sinai, "Keep My covenant," the reference is to the Abrahamic covenant.

Now the giving of the Law at Sinai, and the forming of the Mosaic covenant, are often misunderstood because their relationship with the Abrahamic covenant is not clearly grasped. There are two basically important facts to realise about the Abrahamic covenant—(1) the ground of Abraham's acceptance was his *faith* (Gen. xv. 6); and (2) Abraham's part in the keeping of the covenant was simply a sincere continuance in faith and uprightness,—"Walk before Me, and be thou perfect (sincere, upright), and I will make My covenant between Me and thee" (Gen. xvii. 1–2). When the keeping of the covenant was again enjoined at Sinai, the giving of the Law did not intend a change-over from this faith-basis of the Abrahamic covenant to a works-basis. Knowing the heart of fallen man, God did not now impose the keeping of the moral law as a new basis of acceptance. Nay, going with the commandments, in the Sinai elaboration of the Abrahamic covenant, was the provision of the "ordinances" which pointed to the atonement of Christ, and showed the real basis of acceptance through faith. Canaan was to be possessed, and the nation still to be blessed, on the promise-and-faith basis. The reason why the Mosaic covenant brought Israel under "the curse of the law," instead of into fuller benediction, lay in the wrong reaction of the people themselves to it ; for, as the narrative apparently indicates, and as Israel's subsequent history confirms, the Hebrew people themselves seem from the first to have shifted the emphasis from the faith-basis to that of acceptance on a works-basis, so that for ever afterward, in the words of Paul, they were "going about to establish their own righteousness" (Rom. x. 3). See their self-confident response at Sinai—"All the people answered together, and said : All that the Lord hath spoken we will do" (Exod. xix. 8); "And they said : All that the Lord hath said we will do, and be obedient" (Exod. xxiv. 7). Surely there is grave presumption in this self-confident vow.

In sovereign wisdom, and knowing the end from the beginning, God forbearingly received the people on their own standing, gave them the Law, and promised abundant blessing upon their obedience: but in the light of Israel's wrong attitude, at and after Sinai, we can see how their experience under the Mosaic Covenant developed into the saddest tragedy in Hebrew history.

WHY THE LAW WAS GIVEN

If, then, the giving of the Law was not meant to displace the faith-basis of the Abrahamic Covenant, why was the Law given? It was given for three reasons.

1. *To provide a standard of righteousness.* Whereas periodic oral communications were sufficient in the Divine dealings with Abraham and the first fathers of the Hebrew race, it became necessary, now that the people were constituted a nation and a theocracy, to furnish a written and permanent standard of morality, expressing the Divine ideal for character and conduct (Deut. iv. 8; Ps. xix. 7-9; cxix. 142).

2. *To expose and identify sin.* As solid objects become black when silhouetted against a bright background, so sin—unrecognised as such in the comparative obscureness of fallen man's perverted conscience—becomes at once shown up and sharply marked off against the light of the Law. Thus, we find Paul saying: "The Law entered that the offence might abound (or become obvious)" (Rom. v. 20); "By the Law is the knowledge of sin" (Rom. iii. 20); "I had not known sin but by the Law" (Rom. vii. 7); "It (the Law) was added because of transgressions"—i.e., that sin might be exposed as offence against God (Gal. iii. 19).

3. *To reveal the Divine holiness.* It was absolutely indispensable that the unique privileges conferred upon the elect nation, for the fulfilling of its high vocation, should be safeguarded by a reverential recognition of the inviolate holiness of God, lest privilege should lead to presumption. It is not without significance that the Biblical revelation, considered as a whole, presents first the *power* of God (as seen specially in the Creation, the Flood, the Babel dispersion, the overthrow of Sodom, the Exodus); then the *holiness* of God (as

seen specially in the Mosaic Law and the subsequent Divine dealings with Israel); and *then* the *love* of God (as seen specially in the Gospel of Christ);—the truth being at once suggested that the revelation of the *love* of God must be safeguarded by a due recognition of His awful power and holiness.

The characteristic word for God, on the lips of Jesus, is "Father"; but let it be remembered that *not until* Christ came, as the crowning revelation of God, was the Divine fatherhood given prominence. The truth of the Divine fatherhood is not safe for man without earlier revelation of the Divine power and holiness. One of the faults of certain modern theology is the mental divorcing of the Divine love from the Divine power and holiness.

The symbol of holiness is fire. Thus the Law is given amid fire on Sinai (xix. 18; xxiv. 17), and with strictest prohibitions (xix. 10–13, 21–5). Israel ever realised that the Law enshrined a God of awful holiness (Deut. xxviii. 58; xxxiii. 2; Ps. lxviii. 17; Heb. xii. 18 and 29). As an expression of the Divine holiness, the Law given through Moses is unapproachable. In the "Commandments"—especially when spiritually interpreted, as Christ interpreted them (Matt. v. 21–8),—we see the holiness of God in its sublimity. In the "Judgments," with their intolerance of all wrongdoing and compromise, we see the holiness of God in its awful severity. In the "Ordinances," with their exhaustive prescriptions covering Israel's worship, we see the holiness of God in its utter inviolateness. The God of Sinai is a holy God; and truly, in His holiness, "our God is a consuming fire"!

THE LAW AND THE ABRAHAMIC COVENANT

A further question now arises, namely: What then, really, is the relationship between the Law of Moses and the covenant through Abraham?

1. The Law was *added to* the Abrahamic Covenant. "It was added because of (i.e.—to mark) transgressions till the Seed should come to whom the promise was made" (Gal. iii. 19). This, in itself, shows that the Law was not meant to delete the faith-feature of the Abrahamic Covenant. It came by

way of insertion, not deletion. It was meant to mark an addition not a subtraction.

2. The Law *does not disannul* the Abrahamic covenant. "The covenant that was confirmed before of God, in (to) Christ, the Law, which was four hundred and thirty years after, cannot disannul, that it should make the promise of none effect. For if the inheritance be of the Law, it is no more of promise; but God gave it to Abraham by promise" (Gal. iii. 17–18).

3. The Law, as wrongly accepted by Israel, passed its death-sentence on guilt, and thus inflicted a curse *which held back the blessing* of the Abrahamic Covenant: but in Christ the curse was removed, that the Abrahamic blessing might be released to faith. "Christ hath redeemed us from the curse of the Law . . . that the blessing of Abraham might come on the Gentiles through Jesus Christ, that we might receive the promise of the Spirit through faith" (Gal. iii. 13–14).

THE LAW AND THE HISTORY OF ISRAEL

Israel, as a *nation*, broke the Law and the Mosaic Covenant (see 1 Kings xix. 10; 2 Kings xvii. 15; xviii. 12; Ps. lxxviii. 37; Jer. xi. 10; xxxi. 32; Ezek. xvi. 59; Hos. viii. 1; Heb. viii. 9, etc.). But what do we really imply by this? Do we mean, simply, that the individuals who composed the nation failed to measure up to the requirements of the ten commandments, and that it was for this reason alone that the captivities and exile took place? No, for have we not seen that when God gave the ten "Commandments" He also gave the "Ordinances" which pointed to Christ, and showed the true ground of acceptance, through vicarious atonement, and by faith?

It is of vital importance to understand how the word "law" is used in the Old Testament. First, it is used just once or twice to denote the ten "Commandments" (Exod. xxiv. 12; see R.V.). Second, it is used of individual "judgments" and "ordinances" —"This is the law of the burnt-offering," etc. (Lev. vi. 9, 14, 25; xxiv. 22, etc.). Third, it is used by far the most commonly to denote the whole of the Mosaic economy, comprising "Commandments," "Judgments" and "Ordinances" alike. This, its general use, is shown with absolute conclusiveness in such passages as

Deuteronomy iv. 8, 44–5; Joshua viii. 34; 1 Kings ii. 3; Daniel ix. 11–13; Malachi iv. 4.

Now when it is asserted that Israel broke the Law, and thus violated the Covenant, it is not meant simply that individual Israelites, few or many, broke the ten "Commandments," but that the nation as a whole fell foul of the major obligations of the Covenant contained in the "Judgments" and the "Ordinances." The following are notable instances:

1. Israel was to keep a Sabbatic year every seventh year, and the Jubilee Sabbatic year every fiftieth, when all slaves were to be freed, and all debts cancelled. See Leviticus xxv. for interesting details and promised blessings. The Sabbaths were covenant "signs" between God and Israel (Exod. xxxi. 13). In them the land was to be rested, in grateful acknowledgment of the Divine ownership and goodness; and wonderful blessing was to attend their due observance. Yet from the first Israel disobeyed. Where is there anywhere in Scripture any record of Israel's keeping these Sabbaths? (see Jer. xxxiv. 8–22). It was because of Israel's unfaithfulness here that the seventy years of desolation came as a long Sabbath of judgment (see the remarkable connection between Jer. xxv. 11 and 2 Chron. xxxvi. 21; and then read Lev. xxvi. 32–5 as explaining both).

2. Israel was not to make any covenant with the surrounding nations, but was to be completely separate—and that for benign reasons. (see Exod. xxiii. 24–33; xxxiv. 12–17; Deut. vii. 1–6, etc.). Yet from the first we find Israel defaulting here (see Joshua ix. 14–16; Judges ii. 2; iii. 5–6; and many similar references).

3. Israel was to shun idolatry and the use of religious images (Exod. xx. 2–5; Deut. iv. 12–20; xvii. 2–7). Yet from the first Israel disobeyed (see Judges ii. 11–23; Jer. ii. 28; xi. 10; and the awful account in 2 Kings xvii. 17–23).

Other examples of Israel's grievous default might be given as, for instance, failure in the matter of Passover observance (2 Chron. xxx. 5), the weekly Sabbath (Ezek. xx. 13), and Tithing (Mal. iii. 8).

It was in these ways that Israel, as a nation, broke the Law, violated the Covenant, and fell foul of the high calling of God.

THE LAW AND THE GOSPEL

Finally, a brief word about the Law in relation to the Gospel of Christ. The Law is done away, in Christ, in three ways.

1. The performing of the "*Commandments*" as a condition of personal justification is emphatically and conclusively done away; for "Christ is the end of the Law for righteousness to every one that believeth" (Rom. x. 4). Although all of the Ten Commandments, except the fourth, are included in the ethics of the New Testament, they are included as independent principles, and not as part of the Mosaic system. The keeping of them is not *obligatory to* salvation, but the spontaneous *result of* salvation.

2. The performing of the "*Ordinances*" of the Law, as a way of acceptance with God, is now superseded, inasmuch as the religious ordinances of the Mosaic dispensation were but the types and shadows of which Christ is the fulfilment and substance (Col. ii. 17; Heb. ix. 22–x. 18).

3. The Law, as a *Dispensation*, or method of Divine dealing, is now done away, inasmuch as the Gospel introduces a new dispensation for Israel and Gentiles alike. The old dispensation was that of "the Letter"—*an outward command*. The new dispensation is that of "the Spirit"—*an inward power* (see 2 Cor. iii.–iv.). The one was an objective code. The other is a subjective change. The one was a condemning ethic. The other is a transforming dynamic. "What the Law could not do, in that it was weak through the flesh, God sending His own Son in the likeness of sinful flesh, and for sin, condemned sin in the flesh; that the righteousness of the Law might be fulfilled in us who walk not after the flesh but after the Spirit" (Rom. viii. 3–4).

THE BOOK OF EXODUS (3)

Lesson Number 7

NOTE:—For this seventh lesson read again chapters xxv. to xxxiv.; and, of course, turn to them again and again to compare the details given in the lesson with the Scripture references.

MEASUREMENTS OF TABERNACLE

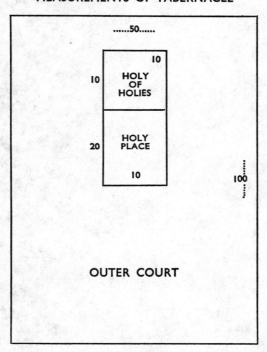

NOTE:—The figures in this simple diagram are the measurements in cubits. In the actual structure the Outer Court was larger in proportion than is shown here, and the "Holy Place" rather longer.

THE BOOK OF EXODUS (3)
THE TABERNACLE (xxv.–xl.)

THE THIRD of the three main parts of Exodus covers chapters xxv. to xl., where the book ends. It is occupied with the construction and appointments of the Tabernacle. First, the pattern of the Tabernacle is given to Moses during his forty days in the Mount (xxv.–xxxi.). Then, in the episode of the golden calf, we see the execution of the plan temporarily suspended through Israel's lapse into idolatry (xxxii.–xxxiv.), during which interval a temporary substitute for the Tabernacle is provided in a tent pitched "without the Camp" (xxxiii. 7). Finally, the Tabernacle is completed and erected (exactly one year after the Exodus— xl. 2), and the glory of the Divine presence descends upon it (xxxv.–xl.). The chapters thus naturally break up into three groups (for fuller analysis see end of lesson):

THE TABERNACLE DESIGNED (xxv.–xxxi.)
THE TABERNACLE DELAYED (xxxii.–xxxiv.)
THE TABERNACLE COMPLETED (xxxv.–xl.)

The Scriptures devote more room to the description of the Tabernacle and its appurtenances than to any other single subject. Its details are described with noticeable particularity; and no less than seven times in Scripture we find reference to God's solemn charge to Moses that he should make all things according to the "pattern" which was shown to him "in the Mount" (Exod. xxv. 9, 40; xxvi. 30; xxvii. 8; Num. viii. 4; Acts vii. 44; Heb. viii. 5). Must there not be some special meaning behind this? There must; and there is. The Tabernacle was not designed with a view to any merely architectural impressiveness. It was designed to be a symbolical and typical expression of wonderful spiritual truth; and herein lies its significance.

To attempt anything like an exhaustive elucidation of the Tabernacle, with its many symbolical and typical meanings, is quite outside the scope of our present study. In the first place, it would require a book all to itself; and, in the second place, so many books have now been written about the Tabernacle that lengthy expatiation here is uncalled for. Our purpose is to deal with the subject summarily, yet in suchwise as to help towards a clear perception of its latent treasures.

What, then, are the principal features pertaining to the Tabernacle? They are four—

> The Structure;
> The Furniture;
> The Priesthood;
> The Offerings.

The last-mentioned of these four, however—the system of offerings—is a subject all in itself, and is given special treatment in the book of Leviticus to which we shall come later. Let us briefly consider here, therefore, the other three—the Structure, the Furniture, the Priesthood.

THE STRUCTURE

The structure, all told, was in three parts—the Outer Court, the Holy Place, the Holy of Holies. The one entrance to the Outer Court was called the "gate" (xxvii. 16). The one entrance to the Holy Place was called the "door" (xxvi. 36). The one entrance to the Holy of Holies was called the "veil" (xxvi. 31).

The Outer Court

The Outer Court was a large, oblong, rectangular enclosure with the two longer sides facing north and south, and the two shorter facing east and west. The two longer sides were 100 cubits each, and the two shorter were 50 cubits each. As a cubit is approximately eighteen inches, the Outer Court was therefore about 150 by 75 feet. Its construction was very simple from an architectural point of view, the four sides consisting of "pillars" equally spaced from each other, with curtains hung upon them and filling the spaces between them—twenty "pillars" to each of the longer sides, and ten to each of the shorter, making sixty pillars in all, erected at intervals of five cubits, and each pillar being five cubits, or seven and a half feet high. At the top, these pillars had each a capital overlaid with silver, also silver hooks and rods which connected the pillars, and to which the hangings were attached. At the base, the pillars were shod with sockets of brass, while ropes and pins were also used to give the structure firmness. The hangings which composed the screen were made of "fine linen." The entire circumference of the Outer Court was (100 + 100 + 50 + 50 = 300) three hundred cubits, or about four hundred and fifty feet.

The Sanctuary

The sanctuary or dwelling-place itself, consisting of the Holy Place and the Holy of Holies, was, like the Outer Court, rectangular and oblong, being thirty cubits long by ten cubits wide. As with the Outer Court, the two sides running lengthwise faced north and south, while the two ends, or smaller sides, faced east and west. A veil divided the Tabernacle into its two parts, the Holy Place being twenty cubits long, or two-thirds the length of the whole, and the Holy of Holies taking the remaining ten cubits, and both apartments being ten cubits wide, the uniform width of the structure. Unlike the Outer Court, the walls of the Tabernacle were completely of wood—not merely of pillars standing apart from each other—the pillars being in close contact, and bound together by transverse rods or bolts passing through rings fixed on the pillars for this purpose. Four large and beautiful curtains covered the whole structure above, roofing it in and thus making it a "dwelling."

For fuller treatment of the many interesting details, the student is advised to consult some standard Bible Dictionary. For our present purpose the simple diagram on page 94 must be sufficient. Further, it goes almost without saying that there is considerable symbolical and typical import in the materials and parts of the Tabernacle structure, into which we cannot go here; and for an interpretation of all this we refer the student to the good books on this subject which are obtainable at small cost through any evangelical publisher. We must content ourselves here by speaking about one part only of the Tabernacle structure, and even about that part very briefly, though it is perhaps the most interesting part of all—the Holy of Holies. (See the diagram above-mentioned: preceding present chapter.)

The Holy of Holies

There are three intensely interesting things about the Holy of Holies which impress us right away. First, we note its *dimensions*. It measured 10 × 10 × 10 cubits. That is to say, its breadth and length and height were each an exact ten cubits, and were therefore all equal with each other. Thus, the Holy of Holies was a *cube*. Later, when the Tabernacle gave place to the magnificent Temple built by Solomon, the Holy of Holies was made *twenty* cubits long; but the breadth and height were similarly doubled (1 Kings vi. 20), so that it had now become 20 × 20 × 20 cubits. Turning right over to the last two chapters of the Bible, we find that the heavenly city is described as being similarly foursquare—"The city lieth foursquare . . . the length and the breadth and the height of it are equal" (Rev. xxi. 16). What is the symbolism behind this use of the cube? Dr. A. T. Pierson tells us that among the Hebrews the cube was the old-time symbol of perfection, because of its absoluteness of symmetry. Every side of a cube is a perfect square, and each of the six sides is exactly equal with all the others. Turn the cube about any way we will, it is still the same in appearance—just as high and deep and broad. Thus we have a symbol of perfection. The Holy of Holies must be a cube, speaking at once, and before all else, of the infinite perfection of Israel's God. The heavenly city must be represented as a cube, indicating the glorious perfection of that city yet to be, "whose builder and maker is God." Is it not this significance of the cube which Paul has in mind when he speaks of "the *breadth* and *length* and *depth* and *height*" of "the love of Christ which passeth knowledge"? (Eph. iii. 18). O the wonder of that perfect love!—and, still more, of a heart-felt experience of it!

Second, note the *purpose* served by the Holy of Holies. It was to be a dwelling-place for God among His people. Have we grasped the wonder and significance of this? The Tabernacle in the wilderness was God's *first* dwelling-place on earth. He had *walked* with Adam in Eden; He had *spoken* to the Patriarchs; He had visibly *visited* Abraham; but He had made Himself no special dwelling-place on earth. Now, however, He comes down to *dwell* among His redeemed people; and onward from then till now He has had a dwelling on earth. After the Tabernacle came the Temple. After the Temple there came forth the Son from the bosom of the Father—"the Word became flesh, and *tabernacled* among us" (John i. 14, R.V. margin). Then, following the Incarnation, came the Church—a spiritual house, a "holy temple . . . builded together for an habitation of God through the Spirit" (Eph. ii. 21–2). This is God's present tabernacle, or dwelling-place on earth, and will be until that coming consummation of which it is written—"Behold, the tabernacle of God is with men, and He will dwell with them, and they shall be His people" (Rev. xxi. 3).

Third, observe the special *sacredness* of the Holy of Holies. When the people of Israel brought their offerings to the Tabernacle, they were allowed into the Outer Court, but were not allowed into the Holy Place, which was for the priests alone; and even the priests who ministered in the Holy Place were not allowed into the Holy of Holies. Only the High Priest was permitted into this inmost shrine, and even he only on special occasions, and after due preparation. The same applied to the Temple when, later, it took the place of the Tabernacle. That which God indwells is unspeakably sacred—a lesson which the people of God were meant to learn deeply and for all time. There cannot possibly be acceptable worship or true fellowship without a reverent recognition of the sacredness of that which is Divine. Now there were two Greek words which came to be used to denote the Temple, the one word meaning the entire precincts of the Temple buildings, while the other was used only of *the sanctuary itself*, the Holy of Holies; and it is a solemnly impressive fact that in every instance in the New Testament where the expression "temple of God" is used of Christian believers, either collectively or individually, the Greek word is that which refers to the Holy of Holies itself. Sacred privilege and responsibility, to be Christ's, and to be thus indwelt!

As the Tabernacle of old was a three-fold structure, so indeed are we by our very constitution as human beings. Corresponding to the "Outer Court" is the *body*. Corresponding to the "Holy Place" is the *soul*. Corresponding to the "Holy of Holies" is the *spirit*; and it is here in the inmost part of our being that God has taken up His dwelling, transforming us into His living temples.

There was once an old sculptor who had, among many other pieces of work in his workshop, the model of a beautiful cathedral.

Yet although it was an exquisitely finished, exact model, nobody admired it as it lay there, covered with the dust of years. Then, one day, the old attendant placed a light inside the model, and its gleams shone through the beautiful stained-glass windows, giving a new beauty to the whole thing; and all who came near stopped to admire it. The entire transformation was wrought by the shining out of the new light within. So may it be with the consecrated temples of these human personalities of ours!

> O joy of joys, O grace of grace,
> That God should condescend
> To make my heart His dwelling-place
> And be my dearest Friend!

III. THE TABERNACLE (xxv.–xl.)

DESIGNED (xxv.–xxxi.).

    Ark—Table—Candlestand (xxv.).
    Curtains—Boards—Veils (xxvi.).
    Brazen Altar—Hangings—Oil (xxvii.).
    Priests' Garments and Consecration (xxviii.–xxix.).
    Incense Altar—Laver—Anointing Oil (xxx.).
    The Workmen—The Sabbath Sign (xxxi.).

DELAYED (xxxii.–xxxiv.).

    Israel's lapse into idolatry (xxxii. 1–14).
    Disciplinary Judgment (xxxii. 15–29).
    Intercession of Moses (xxxii. 30–5).
    Israel rebuked and tested (xxxiii. 1–11).
    Moses reassured (xxxiii. 12–23).
    The further 40 days in the Mount (xxxiv.).

COMPLETED (xxxv.–xl.).

    The materials subscribed (xxxv.).
    The framework and hangings (xxxvi.).
    The Tabernacle furniture (xxxvii. and xxxviii.).
    The Priesthood garments (xxxix. 1–31).
    Work Finished: Tabernacle erected (xxxix. 32–xl. 33).
    The Tabernacle filled with Divine presence (xl. 34–8).

THE BOOK OF EXODUS (4)

Lesson Number 8

NOTE:—For this eighth study read again chapters xxv. to xxxi. and xxxv. to xl., looking up the references as they occur in our comments, so as to fix them the more clearly in mind.

DIAGRAM of the TABERNACLE
AND ITS FURNITURE

HOLY OF HOLIES

MERCY SEAT

ARK

SECOND VEIL

GOLDEN

ALTAR OF INCENSE

HOLY PLACE

GOLDEN

CANDLESTICK

TABLE

SHEW BREAD

FIRST VEIL

LAVER

OUTER COURT

BRAZEN

ALTAR

THE BOOK OF EXODUS (4)

THE FURNITURE OF THE TABERNACLE

THE FURNITURE of the Tabernacle is a really fascinating study. It consisted of seven carefully described articles, the nature of which leaves little room for us to doubt their intended symbolical and typical meaning, while their number—as in many other occurrences of the number seven—conveys the idea of completeness. Let us, in imagination, enter the sacred enclosure through the "gate" of the Outer Court, and reverently pass through the Tabernacle, pausing in turn at each of these seven objects, and noting the order in which they occur. A glance at the diagram on the opposite page will reduce this to the utmost simplicity.

First, then, on passing through the "gate" into the large Outer Court, we come to the brazen altar of sacrifice (xxvii. 1–8; xxxviii. 1–7), which is intended to teach us, at the very threshold, that the only way for sinful man to approach his holy God is through atoning sacrifice—a sacrifice which is at one and the same time a confession of man's sin on the one part, and a satisfaction to God on the other.

Moving on from the brazen altar, we next come to the laver, also of brass (xxx. 17–21; xxxviii. 8), containing the sacred water for the cleansing of those who ministered in the things of the Sanctuary; and this speaks to us of the need for spiritual renewal (hands and feet were to be washed before every act of ministering, speaking of holy conduct and walk).

Next we reach the "door" of the Sanctuary itself; and, passing through, we find ourselves in the "Holy Place." Here, on our right hand (the north side), we find the table of the shewbread (xxv. 23–30; xxxvii. 10–16), with its oblations (food) and libations (drink), speaking of sustenance for the spiritual life. On the left hand (the south side) we see the seven-branched candelabrum (xxv. 31–40; xxxvii. 17–24), speaking of spiritual illumination. Then, in front of us, and standing just before the "veil" of the "Holy of Holies," is the golden altar of incense, fragrantly symbolising acceptable supplication (xxx. 1–10; xxxvii. 25–28).

Finally, passing through the "veil" into the "Holy of Holies," we see that most sacred gold-covered acacia chest, the ark, speaking of covenant relationship between God and His people; and, above it, on the lid, the mercy seat, with the two cherubim, one at each side, facing each other and touching their outstretched wings above the mercy seat and the shekinah fire which burned just over it—the blood-sprinkled, shekinah-lit mercy seat speaking of intercession in the very presence of God, and of the very life of God imparted.

See, then, the remarkable progress and completeness of symbolical teaching in this sevenfold succession of objects—atonement, regeneration, spiritual sustenance, illumination, supplication, complete access and reconciliation through covenant relationship, and identification with the life of God, manifested and symbolically imparted in the shekinah flame.

For the sake of clarity, this, along with the *typical* meanings of these seven objects, may be set out as follows:

The Furniture	Symbolical Meaning	Typical Meaning
(1) Brazen Altar.	Atonement through sacrifice.	The Atonement of Christ.
(2) Brazen Laver.	Spiritual renewal.	Regeneration and renewal by the Holy Spirit.
(3) Table of Shewbread.	Spiritual sustenance.	Christ the Bread of Life the Holy Spirit the Water of Life.
(4) Candlestand.	Spiritual illumination.	Christ the Light of the world, and especially of His own people.
(5) Altar of Incense.	Acceptable supplication.	Prayer in the name of Jesus (see John xiv. 13, with Rev. v. 8).
(6) The Ark.	Access through Covenant relationship.	Christ as the covenant-ground of our access to God.
(7) Mercy Seat and Shekinah.	The very presence and life of God.	Christ as "Mercy Seat" (Rom. iii. 25), and (Shekinah) Holy Spirit as the imparted life of God.

A remarkable parallel has been traced between the order of this furniture in the Tabernacle and the order of the Gospel according to John. It is as though John were leading us, in exactly the same order as found in the Tabernacle, to the great spiritual *realities* which the seven articles of furniture in the Tabernacle typified. He begins by leading us to the Brazen Altar of Sacrifice; for twice over in chapter i he bids us "Behold the Lamb of God, which taketh away the sin of the world." Then, in chapter iii, he takes us to the Laver, telling us that

"Except a man be born of water and of the Spirit, he cannot enter into the kingdom of God."

Next, in chapters iv to vi, he takes us to the Table of the Shewbread, with its food and drink—recording for us the Lord's discourse to the woman concerning "the living water," of which if a man drink he shall never thirst again, and the great discourse on "the living bread," of which if a man eat he shall live for ever. Next, in chapters viii and ix, he takes us to the golden candlestand. Twice over we hear Christ saying: "I am the light of the world"; "He that followeth Me shall not walk in darkness, but shall have the light of life"; and the man born blind is given sight by the great Lightbringer.

Then, in chapters xiv to xvi there come those wonderful new lessons about praying in the name of Jesus, and we find ourselves at the golden Altar of Incense, offering prayers that became as fragrant odours by the breathing of that Name which, above all others, is dear to the heart of God.

Then, in that wonderful prayer of the Lord Jesus which is recorded in the seventeenth chapter, we are taken through the veil into the Holy of Holies and are given a glimpse of His high-priestly ministry of intercession for us in the presence of God. Nor do we see Christ there only as our High Priest, but as both the Ark and the Mercy Seat also—the covenant-ground of our access and acceptance by a new relationship, for in chapter twenty the risen One says: "I ascend unto My Father and *your* Father, and to My God and *your* God."

Finally, the reality which corresponds with the symbolic meaning of the Shekinah is disclosed. "He breathed on them, and saith unto them: *Receive ye the Holy Ghost.*" The very life of God becomes imparted to the blood-bought believer by the Holy Spirit (see John xx. 22).

How wonderful is all this correspondence of order between the long-ago Tabernacle in the wilderness and John's new pen-and-ink tabernacle of testimony! Shall we put it down to accident or Divine design? How much more wonderful still is that dear Saviour in whom we have all these seven Divine provisions, from the altar of atonement to the Pentecostal Shekinah!

THE PRIESTHOOD

We must now refer to the Priesthood, the provisions and regulations concerning which are a subject of rich interest. As we can give but the briefest treatment to this subject before passing on from Exodus to Leviticus, we must confine ourselves to one part of it, and deal with that as being representative of the whole. We shall consider the High Priest's *garments*. These are carefully described in chapter xxviii.

Turning to that chapter, we find, first, that the garments prescribed for the High Priest were to be *"for glory and beauty"* (verse 2). Arrayed with these adornments of gold and blue and purple and scarlet and fine linen and flashing gems, Israel's High Priest must indeed have looked glorious and beautiful; but who shall tell the glory and beauty of heaven's Beloved as *He* represents *us* on high?

The prescribed articles of wear for the High Priest were seven in number (see verses 4, 36, 42). They were the "breastplate," the "ephod," the "robe," the "coat," and the "linen breeches," while for the head there were the "mitre" and the "holy crown" (verses 4, 36, 42, xxix. 6).

The "breeches" were linen shorts. The "coat"—unlike our western garment of that name—was a long linen garment worn next to the body. The "robe" was a long, seamless dress worn over the "coat." It was of blue linen, and embroidered round the edge of the skirt with alternate bells of gold and pomegranates of blue and purple and scarlet. A beautifully wrought girdle secured it about the waist. The "ephod" was a short garment from the shoulders down to the waist or perhaps a little lower. The "breastplate" was a square linen container worn in front of the ephod. The "mitre" was a white linen turban; and the "holy crown" was a golden plate on the front of the mitre, inscribed with the words: "Holiness to the Lord."

Thus, these "garments" would be put on in practically the reverse order of that in which they are specified—first the "breeches," then the "coat," then, over these, the "robe," then the "ephod," then the "breastplate," and finally the "mitre" bearing the "holy crown."

Strictly speaking, the under-garments, namely, the "breeches" and the "coat," were the *ordinary* garments of the High Priest as distinct from his others, which were "for glory and beauty." Three of these latter are given special emphasis, and it is obvious that they are meant to represent great truths to us. They are the "ephod," the "breastplate," the "holy crown."

The Ephod

As already mentioned, the "ephod" (xxviii. 5–14) was a short garment from the shoulders down to the waist or perhaps a little lower. It consisted of two pieces, back and front, "joined together" at the shoulders by two "shoulder pieces" (verse 7). It was made of fine-twined linen, and embroidered with gold and blue and purple and scarlet (verse 6). It was held to the body by an artistically wrought girdle intertwining the same colours (verse 8). In line with the typical meanings everywhere present in this part of Scripture, the gold and blue and purple and scarlet and fine white linen speak, respectively, of our Lord's deity, heavenliness, royalty, sacrifice, and perfect righteousness; but most significant of all is what we are told about the two "shoulder pieces" (verses 9–12).

Two onyx stones were to be set in sockets of gold on these shoulder pieces; and in these were to be engraved the names of the twelve tribes of Israel—six on the one stone and six on the other. The reason for this is given in verse 12:

> "*Thou shalt put the two stones upon the shoulders of the ephod for stones of memorial unto the children of Israel: and Aaron shall bear their names before the Lord upon his two shoulders for a memorial.*"

Thus the names of Israel were enshrined in precious stones, set in sockets of pure gold, to be borne upon the High Priest's *shoulder*, and memorialised before the Lord.

The Breastplate

The "breastplate" (xxviii. 15–29) was a piece of finely woven linen about 17 inches long by 8½ inches wide, doubled over so as to make a kind of square bag 8½ by 8½ inches. It displayed the same colours as the "ephod," and must have been exceedingly beautiful, for in it, also, there shone twelve precious jewels, in four rows of three each—each of the twelve bearing the name of one of the tribes of Israel, and all twelve being enclosed in settings of pure gold. The breastplate was held in position by two chains of wreathen gold which hung it on to the shoulder pieces of the "ephod" (verses 22–5), and by a "lace of blue" (at the two lower corners) which fastened it to the "ephod." The reason for all this is given in verse 29:

"And Aaron shall bear the names of the children of Israel in the breastplate of judgment upon his heart, when he goeth in unto the holy place, for a memorial unto the Lord continually."

Thus, again, are the names of God's own written in jewels and set in gold, to be memorialised before Him—but this time they are upon the High Priest's *heart*.

The Holy Crown

This was a "plate of pure gold" fastened to the front of the "mitre," and bearing the inscription: "Holiness unto the Lord" (verses 36–7). The meaning of it is explained in verse 38:

"It shall be upon Aaron's forehead, that Aaron may bear the iniquity of the holy things which the children of Israel shall hallow in all their holy gifts; and it shall be always upon his forehead that they may be accepted before the Lord."

The point in this verse is that, despite the ceremonial cleansings associated with Israel's worship, both offerings and offerers, in themselves, were really unholy in the all-holy eyes of God; yet in the High Priest, who gathered up all the people into one in himself, as it were, and at the same time bespoke the atoning sacrifice which covered them all—in him, with his garments of "glory and beauty" (typifying the glorious merit and atonement of Christ), the unholiness of the people became changed into "holiness unto the Lord," and thus the people were "accepted before the Lord."

Glorious type-teaching

Now what is the meaning of all this for *us*? Why are all these details given so carefully about the "ephod" and the "breastplate" and the "holy crown"? It is because there is glorious type-teaching in it all. Here are earthly things with heavenly meanings; physical objects setting forth great spiritual realities.

Aaron the High Priest is a type of the Lord Jesus as our High Priest. First, in the "ephod," the High Priest bears Israel's tribes collectively upon his *shoulders*. Then, in the "breastplate," he bears them individually upon his *heart*. Then, as he bears them thus before God, he bears all their imperfection, and completely covers it all up in his own "glory and beauty," so that, instead, God sees "Holiness to the Lord" shining from the High Priest's brow, and the people are accepted in him. See verse 38: "It shall be always upon *HIS* forehead, that *THEY* may be accepted."

Three times in these three key verses (12, 29, 38) we have it that the High Priest shall "*bear*" his people and their interests —on his *shoulder*, on his *heart*, on his *brow*; and each time they are represented as beautiful gems and pure gold!

We see in all this a picture of Christ and His people. First, we are borne upon His great *shoulders*. The shoulder is the place of upholding power. Here, then, we see our mighty Saviour's all-sufficient power to uphold us and all our concerns, both in the presence of God and through all the experiences that come to us.

Then, we are borne upon His *heart*. The heart is the place of *love*. As each of Israel's tribes was named in those precious stones of long ago, so each blood-bought Christian is forever in the heart, in the love and tender thought of Christ as He stands before God on our behalf. Moreover, as those jewels shone from Aaron's breast, so do the people of Christ shine forth from the heart of Christ like precious gems in the presence of God.

Again, as our Lord represents us on high, "Holiness to the Lord" flashes from His *brow*. The brow is the noblest and most distinguishing feature of man. Holiness must be written here, to be seen before all else as the High Priest enters the most holy Presence. This is the first thing God beholds in *our* glorious High Priest in the heavenly sanctuary. He bears it on *HIS* forehead that *WE* may be accepted! As Aaron was to bear the "holy crown" *always* (see verse 38), so Christ bears it always for us, so that in Him *we* become *ALWAYS ACCEPTED!*

All this is taught *doctrinally* in the New Testament—especially in Ephesians and Hebrews. We are "accepted *in the Beloved*" who bears us on His heart before God. We are chosen "*in Him*" to be "holy and without blame," for He is our holiness. We are told of the Divine "*power* to us-ward who believe"—and that power is seen in Christ who bears His people on His mighty shoulder, "far above all principality and power and might, and every name that is named"! Well may our praise forever flow to God for such a Saviour!

Here we must break off, and leave all the many other wonderful typical teachings embodied in the Aaronic Priesthood to the joyous investigation of the reader.

CAN YOU ANSWER THESE?

1. What are the three principal subjects in the Book of Exodus, and what three attributes of God do they express?
2. What is the general structure of the book? What are the three parts of the Law, and what three aspects of life do they cover?
3. What four things did the outgoing from Egypt mean for Israel?
4. What are the main points of comparison and contrast between the Exodus and the Gospel?
5. Why was the Law given to Israel? Was it meant to be a *new* covenant, displacing the Abrahamic?
6. What is the relation between the so-called Mosaic covenant and the Abrahamic covenant?
7. What were the three parts of the Tabernacle, and what were their dimensions?
8. What were the articles of furniture in the Tabernacle, and their typical meanings?
9. What symbolic meaning is suggested as being latent in the dimensions of the Holy of Holies?
10. What were the High Priest's adornments, and what type-teaching do we find in them?

THE BOOK OF LEVITICUS (I)

Lesson Number 9

NOTE.—For this study read once the first seven chapters of Leviticus, and chapters xviii. to xx.

"The versatile ne'er-do-well is often castigated by the taunt, 'Jack of all trades and master of none.' In reality, however, that saying is a perversion. What the famous Benjamin Franklin actually said was that a man should be 'Jack-of-all-trades and master of *one*.' A really cultured man has been described as one who knows something about everything, and everything about something. So far as the Christian worker is concerned, and most of all the Christian minister, the specialisation-point must be the Bible. Other knowledge may be interesting, useful, important; but to be a master in Bible knowledge is *vital*."

J. S. B.

THE BOOK OF LEVITICUS (1)

A CERTAIN lady, on being asked if she had ever read the Bible right through, replied: "I have never read it right through, though I have read much of it consecutively. Three times I have started to read it through, but each time I have broken down in Leviticus. I have enjoyed Genesis and Exodus, but Leviticus has seemed such dull reading that I have become discouraged and have given up." Which did that friend the more deserve—sympathy or rebuke? To speak of Leviticus as "dull reading" misses the point of the book completely. How could we expect a book like Leviticus, which is occupied throughout with regulations, to provide exciting reading? Obviously, it is not meant just to be read, but to be *studied*. It yields little of its treasure to a mere reading; but a reasonable concentration transforms it into one of the most intriguing articles in the Scriptures.

Clearing the Ground

At the outset, let us clear away certain discouraging misunderstandings about the book. There appear to be four such. First, there are those who think it impossible for them so to master all the ritual and symbol in Leviticus as to get much spiritual profit. Second, there are those who suppose that since the Levitical prescriptions have now long passed away, with the Mosaic dispensation, they cannot sustain any living relation to the present day. Third, there are others who profess difficulty, inasmuch as certain of the Levitical commands, in their severity or seeming triviality, seem at variance with what else we know of God. Fourth, still others are discouraged because, whereas in Genesis and Exodus the main outline is easily found, there seems no such clear outline here, in this third book of Scripture.

Now, any fair study of Leviticus will quickly dispel these misgivings; for, as we shall see, it simply abounds in spiritual values; it has a living voice to our own day; its revelation of the Divine character is unique; and it is built together according to a clear plan. Its Mosaic authorship and Divine inspiration are attested by the Lord Jesus. It is referred to over forty times in the New Testament. All that follows it in the Scriptures is coloured by it; and, therefore, a clear knowledge of it contributes greatly towards comprehending the message of the Bible as a whole.

Much depends on a right approach to the book; and with a view to this we need to see its main purpose, its abiding value, its peculiar viewpoint and its structure.

Its Main Purpose

Leviticus was written to show Israel how to live as a holy nation in fellowship with God, and thus to prepare the nation for the high service of mediating the redemption of God to all the nations. Above all, then, Israel must be taught the holiness of God, and Leviticus reveals this in three ways: (1) in the *sacrificial system*, which insisted that "without the shedding of blood there is no remission," thus pressing on the most obtuse conscience the seriousness of sin; (2) in the *precepts* of the law, which insisted on the one Divinely revealed standard for character and conduct; (3) in the *penalties* attaching to violations of the law, which sternly proclaimed the inflexibility of the Divine holiness.

Involved in this revelation of Israel's holy God is the imperative insistence on Israel's *separation* from the other nations; and the laws of Leviticus are intended to ensure this separation, and to prepare the nation for the fulfilling of its high vocation. It may be added, also, that Leviticus was designed to prepare Israel for the coming Christ, by awakening a sense of need, and at the same time pointing forward, through the Tabernacle ritual, to the one all-atoning offering on Calvary.

Its Abiding Value

First, Leviticus is a revelation of the Divine character to ourselves today, as much as it was to Israel of old. God has not changed.

Second, it is a symbolic exposition of the basic principles which underlie all dealing between God and men, just as truly today as in the past; for although the Levitical priesthood and sacrifices are now done away, the spiritual realities which they pictorially declare abide for all time. Nowadays, even among professing

Christians, it is common to belittle the idea of atonement through propitiatory sacrifice: but over against this stands Leviticus, endorsed by the clear-cut witness of our Lord Himself and the inspired writers of the New Testament.

Third, Leviticus provides a body of civil law for the theocracy; and although some of the details in it are now otiose, the principles of it are such as should guide legislation today. Religion and State, Capital and Labour, land-ownership and property rights, marriage and divorce—these and other matters, which are all to the fore today, are dealt with in Leviticus. It has been truly said that "there is not one of these questions on which the legislation of Leviticus does not shed a flood of light into which our modern law-makers would do well to come and walk."

Fourth, Leviticus is a treasury of symbolic and typical teaching. Here are the greatest spiritual truths enshrined in vivid symbols. Here are the great facts of the New Covenant illustrated by great types in the Old Covenant. Supremely, it is in these ways an advance unveiling of Christ. It is a "treasury of Divinely chosen illustrations as to the way of a sinner's salvation through the priestly work of the Son of God, and as to his present and future position and dignity as a redeemed man." Moreover, in some of the figure-language of Leviticus there lie great prophecies of things which even to ourselves are still future. Dr. S. H. Kellogg says: "We must not imagine that because many of its types are long ago fulfilled, therefore all have been fulfilled. Many, according to the hints of the New Testament, await their fulfilment in a bright day that is coming. Some, for instance, of the feasts of the Lord have been fulfilled, as Passover and the feast of Pentecost. But how about the day of atonement for the sin of corporate Israel? We have seen the type of the day of atonement fulfilled in the entering into heaven of our great High Priest; but in the type He came out again to bless the people: has that been fulfilled? Has He yet proclaimed absolution of sin to guilty Israel? How, again, about the Feast of Trumpets, and that of the ingathering at full harvest? How about the Sabbatic years, and that most consummate type of all, the year of Jubilee? History records nothing which could be held a fulfilment of any of these; and thus Leviticus bids us look forward to a glorious future yet to come, when the great redemption shall at last be accomplished, and 'Holiness to Jehovah' shall, as Zechariah puts it (xiv. 20), be written even 'on the bells of the horses.'" Thus we see something of the abiding value of Leviticus!

Its Standpoint

Perhaps the first simple step toward understanding the message of Leviticus is to appreciate its standpoint. This is indicated in the first words of the first chapter—"And the Lord called unto Moses, and spake unto him *out of the tabernacle of the congregation.*"

Before this, a distant God has spoken from "the mount that burned with fire"; but now—as we see at the end of Exodus—the Tabernacle is erected "according to the pattern showed in the mount," and a God who dwells among His people in *fellowship* with them speaks "out of the Tabernacle." The people, therefore, are not addressed as sinners distanced from God, like those of other nations, but as being already brought into a new relationship, even that of *fellowship*, on the ground of a blood-sealed covenant.

In line with this, the sacrifices in Leviticus do not mean to set forth how the people may *become* redeemed (for their redemption has already been wrought through the paschal lamb of the Exodus, and is now to be forever memorialised in the Passover feast). No, the Levitical sacrifices are prescribed in such wise as to set forth *how the new relationship may be maintained.*

In their *typical* interpretation the Levitical sacrifices are a wonderful unfolding of the sacrifice of Christ in its many-sided efficacy toward those of us who have *already entered* into the new relationship of justification by faith.

This is the point at which Leviticus begins. It thus follows Genesis and Exodus with obvious sequence. In Genesis we see God's remedy for man's ruin—the Seed of the woman. In Exodus we see God's answer to man's cry—the blood of the Lamb. In Leviticus we see God's provision for man's need—a Priest, a Sacrifice, and an Altar. (It is from this that Leviticus gets its name. Israel's priests were the Levites, and the word "Leviticus" comes from the Greek *Leuitikos*, meaning, "that which pertains to the Levites.") With good reason Leviticus holds the central place among the five books of Moses, for, with its doctrine of mediation through a priest, absolution through a sacrifice, and reconciliation at the altar, it is the very heart of the Pentateuch—and of the Gospel.

As C. I. Scofield observes, "Leviticus stands in the same relation to Exodus that the Epistles do to the Gospels." In the Gospels we are *set free*, by the blood of the Lamb. In the Epistles we are *indwelt*, by the Spirit of God. In the Gospels God speaks to us *from without*. In the Epistles God speaks to us *from within*. In the Gospels we have the *ground* of fellowship with God—redemption. In the Epistles we have the *walk* of fellowship with God—sanctification. As in Leviticus, so in the Epistles, there is exhibited to us the *many-sidedness* of the work of atonement as it bears on those who are already redeemed.

This, then, is the standpoint of Leviticus, and it thus becomes of special relevance to those of us who have found redemption in Christ Jesus; for, as one has said, these Levitical sacrifices are perhaps "the most complete description" of our Saviour's atoning work anywhere given to us.

As we survey these Levitical sacrifices we gain a fuller view and a bigger conception of what happened on Calvary. The different facets of the incomparable diamond are turned successively to the eye. The matchless miracle of grace is seen in its complexity and all-sufficiency, until we break forth into singing:

> Dear dying Lamb, Thy precious blood
>   Shall never lose its power
> Till all the ransomed Church of God
>   Be saved to sin no more.
>
> E'er since by faith I saw the stream
>   Thy flowing wounds supply,
> Redeeming love has been my theme,
>   And shall be till I die.
>
> Then, in a nobler, sweeter song,
>   I'll sing Thy power to save,
> With sinless heart and raptured tongue,
>   In triumph o'er the grave.

THE STRUCTURE

And now, what about the *structure* of Leviticus? In our examination of Genesis and Exodus we have seen that to appreciate their structure is to be guided safely to their central message and permanent value. The same thing—unless we are strangely mistaken—is true of Leviticus.

Our reason for the qualifying words, "unless we are strangely mistaken," is that analyses of Leviticus, which well-known Bible teachers have issued, vary considerably. One tells us that the book is in nine divisions, another says seven, another six, another five, another two (the two parts being chapters i. to x., and xi. to xxvii.). When the doctors disagree, what shall the plain man do?

Well, in the first place, we must resolutely hold to our determination not to *make* any of the books of Scripture divide up, for this is simply to force an artificial analysis—a convenient procedure which is all too often followed by would-be Bible teachers who have an aptitude for dividing subjects under alliterative headings. We must look at each book fairly and squarely, as it lies before us. Let us try to deal in this way with Leviticus.

The Two Major Parts

What then do we find? Why, this—that whatever *sub*-divisions there may or may not be, the book is certainly in *two main parts* which are marked off in an unmistakable way, the first part covering chapters i. to xvii., the second part covering chapters xviii. to xxvii. And what is it that so clearly breaks the book up into these two parts? It is this—that throughout these first seventeen chapters we are dealing with *non*-moral regulations, whereas in the remaining ten we are dealing with regulations concerning *morals*. The first part has to do with *worship*. The second part has to do with *practice*. In the first part all relates to the *Tabernacle*. In the second part all pertains to *character and conduct*. Part one shows the *way to* God—by sacrifice. Part two shows the *walk with* God—by sanctification. The first part deals with *ceremonial* and *physical* defilement. The second part deals with *moral* and *spiritual* defilement. In the first part *purification* is provided. In the second part *punishment* is to be inflicted. The first part has to do with the people's *cleansing*. The second part has to do with the people's *clean living*.

The Central Message

Now before ever we start asking whether there are any *sub-divisions* in Leviticus, this one simple division of the book into its two major parts suggests the main idea here. We have seen, in considering the *standpoint* of Leviticus, that God here speaks "out of the tabernacle," having come down to dwell in *fellowship* with His redeemed people, and that He addresses the people as being now already brought into the new relationship of *fellowship* on the ground of the blood-sealed covenant. This idea of new relationship, of fellowship, is the key to Leviticus. In the two main parts of the book we see first (i.–xvii.) the *basis* of fellowship, in propitiatory sacrifice ; then, second (xviii.–xxvii.), the *obligations* of fellowship, in practical sanctification. In other words, part one shows us the Godward *foundation* of fellowship ; and part two shows us the manward *condition* of fellowship.

Thus Leviticus is concerned with fellowship ; and it is the supreme Old Testament illustration of that great New Testament truth expressed in 1 John i. 7—"*If we walk in the light as He is in the light, we have fellowship one with another, and the blood of Jesus Christ, His Son, cleanseth us from all sin.*" The first part of Leviticus says : "The blood cleanseth us." The second part of Leviticus says : "Yes, the blood cleanseth us, but only if we walk in the light." The message of the whole book is that through these two things together—cleansing and walking in the light—we have fellowship one with another, and truly our fellowship is "with the Father."

Let us therefore get this much clearly fixed in our minds, that Leviticus is in these two broad divisions :

1. THE GROUND OF FELLOWSHIP—SACRIFICE
(i.–xvii.).

2. THE WALK OF FELLOWSHIP—SEPARATION
(xviii.–xxvii.).

Our next step is to explore these two parts ; and here we find orderly design as beautiful as it is clear. Take the first part (i.–xvii.). The first seven chapters are exclusively occupied with the *offerings* which are to be offered. The next three chapters are all about the *priests* who were to officiate in connection with the offerings. The next six chapters are all about the physical and ceremonial cleansing of the *people*, both individually and nationally; while the final chapter in this part is given to emphasising the one *place* to which the offerings might be brought, namely, the altar within the gate of the Tabernacle. Thus we have Offerings, Priesthood, People, Altar.

Turning to the second part (xviii.–xxvii.), we find the same kind of orderly progress. In chapters xviii. to xx. we have regulations concerning the *people*. In chapters xxi. and xxii. we have regulations concerning the *priests*. In chapters xxiii. and xxiv. we have regulations concerning the *feasts*, with a closely-connected word in xxiv. about the light and the shew-bread in the Sanctuary. (The feasts were a *periodic* memorial of Israel before God: the light and the bread were a *perpetual* memorial.) Finally, in chapters xxv. to xxvii., we have regulations concerning Israel's occupancy of *Canaan*. Such is the order in part two: People, Priests, Feasts, Canaan. Here is a general analysis:—

THE BOOK OF LEVITICUS

FELLOWSHIP THROUGH SANCTIFICATION

I. THE GROUND OF FELLOWSHIP—SACRIFICE

(i.–xviii.).

THE OFFERINGS (ABSOLUTION)—i.–vii.
THE PRIESTHOOD (MEDIATION)—viii.–x.
THE PEOPLE (PURIFICATION)—xi.–xvi.
THE ALTAR (RECONCILIATION)—xvii.

II. THE WALK OF FELLOWSHIP—SEPARATION

(xviii.–xxvii.).

REGULATIONS CONCERNING THE PEOPLE—xviii.–xx.
REGULATIONS CONCERNING THE PRIESTS—xxi.–xxii.
REGULATIONS CONCERNING FEASTS, ETC.—xxiii.–xxiv.
REGULATIONS CONCERNING CANAAN—xxv.–xxvii.

THE BOOK OF LEVITICUS (2)

Lesson 10

NOTE.—For this study read chapters i. to vii. (marking off the different offerings), then chapters viii. to xvii.

"Keep the Incense burning."
On the altar fire
Let thy heart's petition,
Let thy deep desire,
Be a cloud of incense
Wreathing heaven's throne,
Till God's power within thee
Shall be fully known.

"Keep the incense burning."
Hourly let it rise,
Till from opened heavens,
Till from flame-swept skies,
Fire thy heart shall kindle
To a joyous flame,
Making thee a glory
To the Saviour's Name.

THE BOOK OF LEVITICUS (2)
PART I (i.–xvii.)

(1) The Offerings (i.-vii.)

THE FIRST seven chapters of Leviticus are occupied with the *Offerings*. Detailed study of these offerings finds in them a resistless fascination. Here we can only speak of them collectively; yet even this will be enough to indicate their richness of spiritual meaning. The section divides up as follows:

> Chapter i.—The Burnt Offering.
>   ,,   ii.—The Meal Offering.
>   ,,   iii.—The Peace Offering.
>   ,,   iv.—The Sin Offering.
>   ,,   v.—The Trespass Offering.

The remainder of the section is taken up with the "laws" conditioning these offerings (see vi. 8 to vii. 38).

Thus there were five kinds of offering prescribed; and the first thing that strikes our notice is that they are divided into three and two. The first three are "sweet savour" offerings (i. 9, 13, 17; ii. 2, 9; iii. 5, 16). The remaining two are *non*-sweet savour offerings. The first three are voluntary. The other two are compulsory. The first three comprise the first utterance of Jehovah with which the book of Leviticus opens (i. 2). The other two are introduced by the second utterance, which begins iv. 2. Let this division fix itself clearly before the eye:

> The Burnt Offering
> The Meal Offering } Sweet Savour;
> The Peace Offering   Voluntary.

> The Sin Offering } Non-Sweet Savour;
> The Trespass Offering Compulsory.

These offerings abound in spiritual significances; but their supreme value lies in their typical unfolding of the supreme sacrifice on Calvary. The sweet-savour offerings typify Christ in His own meritorious perfections. The non-sweet savour offerings typify Christ as bearing the *de*merit of the sinner. The sweet-savour offerings speak rather of what the offering of Christ means to *God*. The non-sweet savour offerings speak rather of what the offering of Christ means to *us*—and it is in connection with these that we here find the nine occurrences of the words, "It shall be forgiven" (iv. 20, 26, 31, 35; v. 10, 13, 16, 18; vi. 7).

Note the distinctive aspects of these offerings. The *Burnt*-offering typifies Christ's "offering Himself without spot to God." It foreshadows Christ on the Cross, not so much bearing sin as *accomplishing the will of God*. We are shown the perfection of Christ's *offering* of Himself, as God sees it.

The *Meal*-offering (not "meat," as in A.V.) exhibits typically the perfect manhood of Christ. The emphasis here is on the *life* which was offered. It sets forth the perfection of character which gave the offering its unspeakable value.

The *Peace*-offering speaks of restored *communion*, resulting from the perfect satisfaction rendered in Christ. God is propitiated. Man is reconciled. There is peace.

As for the non-sweet savour offerings, the *Sin*-offering typifies Christ as Sinbearer—"made sin for us" (2 Cor. v. 21), while the *Trespass*-offering speaks of sins (plural), and typifies Christ as Expiator, making restitution for the injury caused by our wrong-doing.

And now observe the *order* of these offerings. In our study of the Tabernacle we saw that the furniture of the Tabernacle is given in the reverse order of human approach. God begins with the Ark in the Holy of Holies, moving outward from Himself toward man. The same order is followed in these Levitical offerings. God begins with the *Burnt*-offering and ends with the *Trespass*-offering. He leaves off where we begin. If we take these offerings in their reverse order, therefore, they exactly correspond with the order of our spiritual apprehension of Christ.

When we first come, as awakened and believing sinners, to the Cross, the first thing we see in it (answering to our first-felt need) is forgiveness for our many *trespasses*. But scarcely have we begun to rejoice in the forgiveness of our sins before we realise that there is a further and deeper need, namely, *sin* in our nature. This further need is met by a deeper insight into the meaning of the Cross. Christ not only "died for our sins"; He bore our *sin*, as typified in the *Sin*-offering. It is then, when we realise that both sins and sin have been dealt with in the Cross, that we enter into wonderful peace with God, as set forth in the *Peace*-offering. Then, still further, we find rest and joy and complete acceptance with God in the glorious perfections of Christ as typified in the *Meal*-offering; while more and more we come into fellowship with God through the fulness of that one perfect Offering to God on our behalf which is set forth in the *Burnt*-offering. Is there not wonderful Divine design in all this?

(2) The Priests (viii.-x.)

The section about the priests is of unexcelled interest. The point of it is that if fellowship between the redeemed and their holy God is to be maintained, there must not only be a *sacrifice* (as in chapters i.–vii.), but a *priest* (as in these chapters viii.–x.). Besides absolution from guilt there must be *mediation*. Thank God, the Lord Jesus is both sacrifice and priest in one, to His believing people, so that we have access to God by "a new and living way" (Heb. x. 20)—a "new" way because it is the way of the *Cross*, which speaks of the one final sacrifice for sin; and a "living" way because it is the way of the *Resurrection*, which speaks of the one ever-living Priest on high.

The three chapters in this section run as follows:

Chapter viii.　*CONSECRATION*—the priests set apart for God;

,,　　ix.　*MINISTRATION*—the priests start their serving;

,,　　x.　*VIOLATION*—Nadab and Abihu offer "strange fire."

Take that wonderful eighth chapter in which we have the *consecration* of the priests. Is there anywhere a chapter richer in typical meanings and spiritual suggestions? Consecration means set-apart-ness. The priests are now set apart for God, and are *claimed* by Him as such in this consecration ceremony. In the first part of the chapter we have the *order* of consecration (verses 1–13.). Then we have the *basis* of consecration—the blood (verses 14–36). Observe the order of consecration:

THE HIGH PRIEST.	THE OTHER PRIESTS.
Cleansed—verse 6.	Cleansed—verse 6.
Clothed—verses 7–8.	Clothed—verse 13.
Crowned—verse 9.	Claimed—verse 30.
Claimed—verse 12.	Charged—verse 35.

The beautiful typical import in all this is too clear to need comment.

Look now at the *basis* of consecration (verses 14–30)—sacrifice. A sin-offering, a burnt-offering, and a "ram of consecration" are to be offered. Aaron and his sons are to lay their hands on the head of the sacrifice, by which *they* become identified with *it*; and then the blood of sacrifice must be sprinkled on them by which *it* becomes identified with *them*. Thus by a double identification the priests become associated with the atoning sacrifice on the ground of which they are accepted and consecrated. The right ear, the thumb of the right hand, the great toe of the right foot, must be blood-sealed (verses 23–24). "A blood-sealed *ear* was needed to hearken to the Divine communications; a blood-sealed *hand* was needed to execute the services of the Sanctuary; and a blood-sealed *foot* was needed to tread the courts of the Lord's house." The altar itself must be sprinkled (verses 15, 19, 24). The blood is the one grand foundation of all.

It will be noticed that a difference is made between the anointing of Aaron and that of his sons. Aaron is anointed *before* the slaying of the sacrifice (verse 12). His sons are anointed *after* the slaying, along with the sprinkling of the blood upon them (verse 30). True to its characteristic precision, the Scripture makes this distinction with good reason. In the type-teaching of this chapter, Aaron, the High Priest, prefigures the Lord Jesus, while his sons typically anticipate the believer-priests of the present dispensation. The sinless Lord Jesus needed no blood-sprinkling before receiving the anointing of the Holy Spirit; and in Aaron's being anointed alone, before the blood-shedding, we see a discriminating type-picture of the incarnate Son of God, Who, until He gave Himself on Calvary, stood absolutely alone. Without the blood-shedding, Aaron and his sons could not be together in the anointing. But *after* the blood-shedding, Moses anoints "Aaron . . . and his sons . . . *with him*" (verse 30). When once the blood had been shed, Aaron and his sons—typifying Christ and His priestly house—are united in the one priestly ministry: and, united as such, they all stand before God by virtue of the same sacrifice. There is now fullest identification. In the words of Hebrews ii. 11, "Both He that sanctifieth and they who are sanctified are all of one."

We can merely add a word about chapters ix. and x. In chapter ix. we see the first actual *ministration* of the priesthood; and this is set forth in such a way as to become forever afterwards a type of true priestly ministry. After offering sacrifice for the people, Aaron goes into the Holy Place as the representative of the people, and then returns with uplifted hand of benediction as the communicator of the Divine blessing to the people (verse 23). The whole of the ministry was "as the Lord commanded" (verse 10). It was therefore accepted by the Lord, and was attested by the appearing of the Divine glory (verses 23–4)—

"And Moses and Aaron went into the tabernacle of the congregation, and came out, and blessed the people: and the glory of the Lord appeared to all the people. And there came a fire out from before the Lord, and consumed upon the altar the burnt-offering and the fat: WHICH WHEN ALL THE PEOPLE SAW, THEY SHOUTED, AND FELL ON THEIR FACES."

Alas, this glorious scene at the end of chapter ix. quickly changes. In chapter x. the same fire which has gone forth and consumed the burnt-offering on the altar now leaps forth and devours two of the priests! Nadab and Abihu offer "strange fire" before the Lord, "which He commanded them not." Here is the sin of *presumption*; and it is visited with sudden and awful judgment. Over against chapter ix., with its approbation and *attestation* of the priesthood, we now see *presumption* and *rejection*! The offering of the "strange fire" by Nadab and Abihu was "will-worship." It was "of the flesh." It had no warrant in the revealed will of God. It was a vain intruding, a violating of priestly privilege, and was utterly repudiated. Israel's priests must learn at once and forever to walk by the inflexible rule of undeviating adherence to the will and word of God.

There are many Nadabs and Abihus today. Their presumption often goes long unpunished—for the present dispensation is that of *grace*; but the tenth chapter of Leviticus is a solemn warning that though judgment tarry, it will surely fall at last. God is not mocked!

(3) The People (xi.-xvi.)

If any Scripture confirmation were required for the old proverb, "cleanliness is next to godliness," Leviticus xi. to xvi. would be quite enough. These chapters tell us that God's people must be a *clean* people. They must be clean both inwardly and outwardly. There must be physical cleanliness; and there must also be ceremonial cleansing from that which defiles them morally and spiritually in the eyes of God. They are to be both sanitarily clean and sacrificially cleansed.

The purpose of the teaching in this section is to "make a difference between the unclean and the clean" (xi. 47), and to "separate the children of Israel from their uncleanness" (xv. 31). See also xvi. 30—"The priest shall make an atonement for you to cleanse you, that ye may be clean from all your sins before the Lord." Here, in this section, we have the "categorical imperative" of cleansing.

The subjects dealt with are: flesh-diet (xi.), child-birth (xii.), leprosy in bodies, garments, and dwellings (xiii.-xiv.), sex-hygiene (xv.), and national cleansing by expiatory sacrifice (xvi.). We may classify the contents of these chapters in a more easily rememberable way by saying that this section insists on—

clean foods   — xi.
clean bodies   — xii.-xiii. 46.
clean clothes — xiii. 47–59.
clean houses   — xiv. 33–57.
clean contacts — xv.
a clean nation — xvi.

We cannot here discuss the contents of these chapters. They are a separate study in themselves. They should be read carefully with the aid of a good commentary (and we would recommend, in particular, Dr. S. H. Kellogg's book on Leviticus). Chapter xvi., the great chapter about the annual Day of Atonement, we shall consider by itself later.

(4) The Altar (xvii.)

The first of the two main parts of Leviticus ends with this brief section about the Altar (xvii.). No observant reader can fail to be impressed by the solemnly emphatic language of this seventeenth chapter, concerning the one place of sacrifice. Five times, and with severe explicitness, the one Divinely ordained place is stipulated.

"What man soever there be of the house of Israel, that killeth an ox or lamb or goat in the camp, or that killeth it out of the camp, and bringeth it not unto THE DOOR OF THE TABERNACLE of the congregation, to offer an offering unto the Lord before THE TABERNACLE OF THE LORD, blood shall be imputed unto that man; he hath shed blood; and that man shall be cut off from among his people: to the end that the children of Israel may bring their sacrifices, which they offer in the open field, even that they may bring them unto the Lord, unto THE DOOR OF THE TABERNACLE of the congregation, unto the priest, and offer them for peace-offerings unto the Lord. And the priest shall sprinkle the blood upon the altar of the Lord at THE DOOR OF THE TABERNACLE of the congregation, and burn the fat for a sweet savour unto the Lord. Whatsoever man there be of the house of Israel, or of the strangers which sojourn among you, that offereth a burnt-offering or sacrifice, and bringeth it not unto THE DOOR OF THE TABERNACLE of the congregation, to offer it unto the Lord, even that man shall be cut off from among his people" (xvii. 3–9).

The meaning of this for ourselves is clear. There is one place, and only one, where God, in sovereign grace, has elected to meet with penitent sinners, and that is the Cross—of which the altar at the door of the Tabernacle was a type. None other sacrifice! None other priest! None other altar! "None other name under heaven given among men whereby we must be saved!" "There and there alone"—if we may borrow the words of another—"has God's claim upon life been duly recognised. To reject this meeting-place is to bring down judgment upon oneself—it is to trample under foot the just claims of God, and to arrogate to oneself a right to life which all have forfeited."

Fittingly accompanying this emphasis on the one place of sacrifice, the remaining verses of chapter xvii. explain the sanctity of blood, and the meaning of blood-sacrifices. In verse 11 we read: "*For the life of the flesh is in the blood, and I have given it to you upon the altar, to make an atonement for your souls; for it is the blood that maketh an atonement for the soul.*"

It is well to note, however, that even the blood has no atoning value unless it be on the altar. God says: "I have given it (the blood) to you *upon the altar*, to make an atonement for your souls." It must be the blood; and it must be the one altar.

The Scofield note on this verse says: "The meaning of all sacrifice is here explained. Every offering was an execution of the sentence of the law upon a substitute for the offender, and every such offering pointed forward to that substitutional death of Christ which alone vindicated the righteousness of God in passing over the sins of those who offered the typical sacrifices" (Rom. iii. 24, 25). And again: "The value of the 'life' is the measure of the value of the 'blood.' This gives the blood of Christ its inconceivable value. When it was shed the sinless God-man gave his life."

The shed blood is the basis of all. It is through the shed blood of Calvary's Lamb—nothing more, nothing less, nothing else— that we have our reconciliation and salvation.

Thus, in the first half of Leviticus, we have—(1) the Offerings, (2) the Priests, (3) the People, (4) the Altar.

Let us lay well to heart the great truths in these chapters!

> "The life is in the blood,"
>   And must for sin atone
> "One sacrifice" and "once for all,"
>   The blood of Christ alone.

> Oh, see the guilt of sin
>   Which needed such a price,
> And see the marvel of that Love
>   Which made the sacrifice!

THE BOOK OF LEVITICUS (3)

Lesson Number 11

NOTE.—For this study read **very** carefully chapters xviii. to xxiv.

FOCAL POINT OF LEVITICUS
(PART II: XVIII.–XXVII.)

"Here (in the words 'I am the Lord your God') we have the foundation of the entire superstructure of moral conduct which these chapters present. Israel's actings were to take their character from the fact that Jehovah was *their* God. They were called to comport themselves in a manner worthy of so high and holy a position. It was God's prerogative to set forth the special character and line of conduct becoming a people with whom He was pleased to associate His name. The moment He entered into a relationship with a people their ethics were to assume a character and tone worthy of Him. This is the true principle of holiness for the people of God in all ages. They are to be governed and characterised by the revelation which He has made of Himself. Their conduct is to be founded upon what He is, not upon what they are in themselves. The whole of Leviticus finds its focal point in the words: 'Ye shall be holy; for I, JEHOVAH YOUR GOD, am holy'" (xix. 2).

C. H. MACKINTOSH.

THE BOOK OF LEVITICUS (3)
PART II (xviii.–xxvii.)

THE SECOND part of Leviticus, as we have noted, is concerned with the *walk* of God's people—with their morals and conduct. Mere *positional* sanctification (as in part one) is not enough: there must be *practical* sanctification (which is the purpose in part two). The new chapters are introduced with this weighty charge:

"And the Lord spake unto Moses, saying: Speak unto the children of Israel, and say unto them: I am the Lord your God. After the doings of the land of Egypt wherein ye dwelt, shall ye not do; and after the doings of the land of Canaan, whither I bring you, shall ye not do; neither shall ye walk in their ordinances. Ye shall do My judgments, and keep Mine ordinances, to walk therein: I am the Lord your God. Ye shall therefore keep My statutes, and My judgments, which, if a man do, he shall live in them. I am the Lord" (xviii. 1–5).

These words—"I AM JEHOVAH YOUR GOD," express at once and forever the basic reason for God's insistence on the holiness of His people. They are to be holy because of what He Himself is. Nearly fifty times in these later chapters of Leviticus the words occur, like the reiterated keynote in a piece of music— "I AM JEHOVAH."

The four sections in this second part of Leviticus are as follows.

(1) The People (xviii.-xx.)

This section covers chapters xviii.-xx., and consists of moral regulations for the whole of the people. These three chapters, marked off, as they are, by a formal introduction (xviii. 1–5) and a formal closing (xx. 22–6), are quite clearly a distinct section. First, in chapter xviii., we have *sex prohibitions*; next, in chapter xix., *general admonitions*; then, in chapter xx., *penal sanctions* against offenders.

The prohibitions in chapter xviii. are not given as an exhaustive sex code, but are directed against those grosser violations of chastity which were shockingly prevalent among the idolatrous nations around Israel—yea, which always have been and still are prevalent amid idolatry and heathenism. The reasons for the interdicts on blood-affinities in marriage, let it be remembered, are as valid today as then. In contrast with the laxity of our own time, the prohibitions of this eighteenth chapter show us the estimate which *God* puts on chaste sex relationships. Nothing is more vital to any people than the adequate safeguarding of matrimonial and family relationships; and it has been well said that in these days when the laws covering marriage and divorce are decided by a "majority vote," regardless of the law of God, there is an urgent call for Christians to stand up for the sanctity of the marriage bond and family relationships!

Again in chapters xix. and xx., the longish lists of moral precepts and penal sanctions are not meant as exhaustive, but as covering matters outstandingly affecting Israel's well-being. We cannot go through them here. They should be carefully read with a good commentary at hand. Uprightness is demanded in all the relationships of life; and disobedience is to be punished with firmness and severity. No maudlin pity for the individual wrong-doer must be allowed to jeopardise the moral safe-guarding of the whole community. Here, too, is a lesson which many sentimental pitiers of criminals in our own day would do well to ponder.

(2) The Priests (xxi.-xxii.)

Chapters xxi. and xxii. specially concern the priests. If the people as a whole were to be sanctified unto the Lord, how much more the priests! As the Tabernacle was a three-fold structure —Outer Court, and Holy Place, and Holy of Holies, so the nation itself was arranged in a three-fold way which corresponded—the congregation, the priesthood, the High Priest. And as the three parts of the Tabernacle became successively holier, so was it to be with the nation—Israel's sanctification was to reach its culminating expression in the High Priest, who therefore wore the golden crown inscribed with the words "Holiness to the Lord."

Associated with the priesthood were the most exalted privileges. Jehovah had selected a certain tribe, and from that tribe a certain

family, and from that family a certain man; and upon this man
and his house He had conferred the exclusive privileges of drawing
nigh unto Himself as His own appointed and anointed mediaries.
The priests, therefore, must be marked by the utmost sanctity;
and it is to ensure this that these further regulations are here
communicated.

The section is in three parts: first, *prohibited practices* (xxi.
1–15), concerning the priest's social relationships; second, *prohibited persons* (xxi. 16–xxii. 16), concerning personal disqualifi-
cations from serving in or eating of the things of the Tabernacle;
third, *prohibited sacrifices* (xxii. 17–33), concerning defective
animals which must not be offered upon the Lord's altar. In
other words, these chapters tell us what the priest must not *do*,
must not *be*, must not *offer*. Above all men the priest of Jehovah
must be separated from that which defiles, lest the Sanctuary of
God be profaned. (No less than twelve times that word "profane"
occurs in these two chapters!)

How forcibly does this section of Leviticus speak to the Lord's
people today. What need there is for truer sanctity among us
who have been constituted a spiritual priesthood in Christ! How
clearly we need to grasp the difference—as illustrated in this
section—between our *standing* and our *state* as the Lord's priests!
All the sons of Aaron, whether young or old, defective or normal,
were priests to Jehovah, by virtue of their birth and life-relation-
ship with Aaron; and nothing could break that relationship: yet
those among them who were physically defective were not allowed
to officiate at the altar or to enter within the veil of the sanctuary
(xxi. 21–3); and those who were in any way defiled were not
allowed even to eat of the priests' portion (xxii. 6–7). Even so,
every true believer is a priest by virtue of life-giving union with
the Lord Jesus, and nothing can break that union where it really
exists; but all Christians do not enjoy the same intimacy of
fellowship, or exercise the same ministry within the veil! Union
is one thing: communion is another. Life is one thing: ministry
is another. Standing is one thing: state is another. Relationship
is one thing: serving within the veil is another. What deformities
and defilements debar many of us from that elevated walk and
ministry which might be ours!—yes, which "*might*" be ours;
for although there is no record of any provision for miraculously
rectifying the physical deformities which may have incapacitated

some of Aaron's sons, yet those spiritual defilements and deformities which disqualify many of ourselves from a God-glorifying, priestly ministry between the heavenly sanctuary and our fellow-men may be completely done away through the blood of the Lamb and the refining fire of the Holy Spirit.

(3) The Feasts (xxiii.)

Each new section of Leviticus seems to vie with its predecessors in interest. This catalogue of Israel's annual religious "feasts" well merits a far fuller treatment than we can spare in this short synopsis. Unfortunately, to most English readers that word "feast" is misleading, as here used, because (in the Authorised Version) the one word "feast" is used to translate two Hebrew words of different meaning from each other. There is the Hebrew word *chag* (plural *chaggim*), which rightly enough is translated by our English word "feast"; and there is the other Hebrew word, *mo'ed* (plural *mo'adim*), which means simply an appointed time or season. (The ending *im*, pronounced *eem*, is the common Hebrew plural ending—seen in such words as seraph*im* and cherub*im*, the plurals of seraph and cherub.)

For the guidance of English readers we may say that in each case where the *singular* form, "feast," occurs in this twenty-third chapter of Leviticus, the Hebrew word is *chag*; and in each case where the *plural* form, "feasts," occurs, the Hebrew word is *mo'adim* (plural of *mo'ed*).

Now the point is this—in this twenty-third chapter we have a list of *mo'adim* (= appointed seasons, or annual observances); but not all of these *mo'adim*, or appointed annual observances, were *chaggim* (actual "feasts"). As a matter of fact, only three of the *mo'adim* (annual observances) were *chaggim* ("feasts"), as we shall see: but because these three "feasts" (*chaggim*) were fixed annual observances like the others, they are here included in the fuller list of the annual set seasons (*mo'adim*).

What we have, then, in this twenty-third chapter, is a list of the "set seasons" which God appointed for Israel to observe; and it would have been better if, in our Authorised Version, they had been called by that name rather than by the word "feast," seeing that the three which *are* actually feasts are here *included* among the "set seasons," or *mo'adim*.

What then were these annual "set seasons"? They were five in number—

    1. The Feast of Passover (verses 5–14).
    2. The Feast of Pentecost (verses 15–22).
    3. The Blowing of Trumpets (verses 23–5).
    4. The Day of Atonement (verses 26–32).
    5. The Feast of Tabernacles (verses 33–44).

Of these, only three were really "feasts"; and these were (1) the feast of *Passover*—called the Feast of Unleavened Bread, in Exodus xxiii. 15; xxxiv. 18 and other places; (2) the feast of *Pentecost*—called the Feast of Weeks, and the Feast of Firstfruits, in Exodus xxxiv. 22 and other places; (3) the feast of *Tabernacles* —called the Feast of Ingathering, in Exodus xxiii. 16 and other places. The special character of these three is seen in the fact that twice in Exodus, and again in Deuteronomy, they are grouped together and emphatically enjoined as the three great annual national "feasts" of Israel, viz.—

"Three times thou shalt keep a feast unto Me in the year. Thou shalt keep the feast of unleavened bread; . . . and the feast of harvest, the firstfruits of thy labours which thou hast sown in the field; and the feast of ingathering, which is in the end of the year, when thou hast gathered in thy labours out of the field" (Exod. xxiii. 14–16).

"Three times in a year shall all thy males appear before the Lord thy God in the place which He shall choose; in the feast of unleavened bread, and in the feast of weeks and in the feast of tabernacles: and they shall not appear before the Lord empty" (Deut. xvi. 16).

All five of these *mo'adim*, or appointed seasons, however, have this in common, that they were occasions of special *sabbaths*, or rests; and they were all times of holy *convocation*, or assemblings together of the people for worship and joyous thanksgiving.

The "Scofield" Bible makes out that there are seven, instead of five, "set seasons" in this twenty-third chapter of Leviticus. This is done by dividing the Passover into three separate feasts, and calling them (1) Passover; (2) Unleavened Bread; and (3)

Firstfruits. But such a division is quite unwarranted by the text here, and is unsupported by any Scripture elsewhere. Look at verses 5 and 6, and see how obviously the Passover and the days of unleavened bread are one and the same observance—as in all other Scriptures where they are mentioned. And as for verses 9 to 14 denoting another separate feast, there is no such suggestion. What we have in these verses is simply a supplementary provision concerning future observances of the Passover when Israel has entered Canaan (verse 10). That the presenting of the first fruits of the barley harvest was included in the one Passover, or Unleavened Bread observance, is made clear from verse 11, where we are told that the sheaf was to be presented "on the morrow after the Sabbath"—that is the Sabbath during the Feast of Unleavened Bread. Moreover, to make this added provision a separate feast, and call it the Feast of Firstfruits, is to confuse it with the real Feast of Firstfruits (Pentecost) which is mentioned immediately afterwards (verses 15–22).

Others try to show that there are seven "set seasons" in this twenty-third chapter, by dividing the Passover into two feasts, and then adding, to the six thus made, the weekly Sabbath, which is mentioned in verse 3. But the weekly Sabbath is mentioned here, not to include it with these annual "set seasons," but to separate it from them; and if there were any possible doubt about that, verses 37 and 38 would surely do away with it, for we are there told that "These (five) are the feasts of the Lord . . . *beside* the sabbaths of the Lord." What is more, the seventh-day sabbath was a *weekly* observance, whereas all the "set seasons" were *annual*.

As a matter of fact, those who wish to make up the "set seasons" of Leviticus xxiii. into the symbolic number seven defeat their own purpose!—for, as we shall see, there are actually *two other* great national "set seasons" enjoined on Israel, besides these in Leviticus xxiii. These two are found in chapter xxv.; and they are the seventh-year Sabbath (or Sabbatic year), and the Jubilee year (which was to mark off each seven-times-seven of years). Thus, all told, there were seven great periodic national observances enjoined on Israel:

1. The Feast of Passover.
2. The Feast of Pentecost.

3. The Blowing of Trumpets.
4. The Day of Atonement.
5. The Feast of Tabernacles.
6. The Seventh-year Sabbath.
7. The Sabbath Year of Jubilee.

Thus, also, we see that, with the special Sabbath of the seventh month (the Blowing of Trumpets), the Sabbath system of Israel was meant to be a seven-fold revolving cycle of seventh day, seventh month, seventh year, and a seven-times-seven of years.

Associated with the *five* annual "set seasons" were Israel's special *Sabbaths*, or seasons of rest. Thus, including the weekly Sabbath, there seem to have been *ten* Sabbaths given, as follows:

1. The weekly Sabbath.
2. The first day of Unleavened Bread.
3. The seventh day of Unleavened Bread.
4. The Feast of Pentecost.
5. The first day of seventh month ("Trumpets").
6. The Day of Atonement (tenth day of seventh month).
7. The first day of Feast of Tabernacles.
8. The eighth day of Feast of Tabernacles.
9. The seventh-year Sabbath (xxv. 4).
10. The Jubilee Sabbath (xxv. 10, 11).

Besides these, the first day of each month, while not actually a Sabbath in itself, was signalised by a blowing of trumpets, and special offerings. These first days were called the "beginnings of months" (Num. x. 10; xxviii. 11, 28). They were also called the "new moons," because the Hebrew monthly calendar was lunar, and therefore the first day of the month always coincided with the "new moon" (see 2 Chron. ii. 4; Isa. lxvi. 23, etc. And for an enlightening article on the Hebrew lunar calendar see *Imperial Bible Dictionary*, article on the word "Month," by Dr. D. H. Weir). Although the Hebrew month was *lunar*, it seems equally clear that the Hebrew year was *solar*, otherwise the different months would have come at varying seasons as the years passed—the first month (corresponding roughly to our April) would sometimes have been in the spring and sometimes in the winter; whereas we know that the months were *fixed* according to the seasons, so that, for instance, the seventh month always corresponded with the harvest ingathering. The difference between the lunar year of 354 days (29½ x 12) and the solar year of 365¼ days was probably bridged every two or three years by an intercalary month.

The purpose of all these "set seasons" and monthly observances was to acknowledge that all harvest and other blessings came from God; that each new year and each new month should be dedicated to God; that the land belonged to God, and was occupied only because of His kindness; to be a memorial of Israel before God; and to be a constant reminder to Israel of their special covenant relationship with Jehovah, their God. No doubt, also, they fostered the sense of national unity. In their symbolical and typical meanings they cover the whole ground of redemption truths, and much dispensational truth also. The unifying idea running through them is the recognition of Jehovah as the Source and Sustainer of His people's life. They are called "the feasts *of the Lord*"; but alas, in New Testament times they had deteriorated into "feasts *of the Jews*" (John v. 1; vi. 4). It has been observed only too truly that "Divine institutions are speedily marred in the hands of man."

But the special interest of these "set seasons" to *ourselves*, is their typical setting forth of great New Testament truths. Let us quickly run through the five in this twenty-third of Leviticus.

The Feast of Passover (read verses 5–14).

This celebration, which began at even on the fourteenth day of the first month, was commemorative of Israel's deliverance from Egypt. It comes first because it speaks of that which comes first in redemption—the slain Lamb, and the appropriating of the shed blood as a covering from judgment.

The Passover lamb was to be slain and eaten in the evening of the fourteenth day. The slaying speaks of salvation; the feasting speaks of fellowship. Then, beginning on the fifteenth day, there were the seven days of unleavened bread. Leaven is the symbol of moral corruption, of sin; and Israel's abstention from it for seven days (a symbolic number signifying completeness) was to teach that the redeemed must separate themselves from evil, and

THE TABERNACLE

Cloud of Glory

Encampment

Veil
Boards
Holy Place
Door

Coverings
Holy of Holies

Ark
Mercy Seat
Cherubim
Shekinah Glory
Altar of Incense
Table of Shewbread
Candlestick

Gate
Court
Brasen Altar
Laver & Foot
Hangings

be a holy people. Paul applies the typical meaning of this in I Corinthians v. 7, 8.

The first and last of these seven days were to be sabbaths in which no "servile work" was to be done, but an "offering made by fire" was to be offered each day to the Lord. See the picture here—man "ceased from his own works" (Heb. iv. 10); and resting in his acceptance with God through the ascending odour of the burnt-offering.

Finally, "on the morrow after the Sabbath" (verse 11), they were to bring "a sheaf of the firstfruits" of the harvest, to be presented to the Lord. There seems to be a triple significance here. The nation Israel itself was a kind of firstfruits, or "first-born," to the Lord in His redemptive plan for the nations. Then, also, Christian believers are spoken of as "a kind of firstfruits" (Jas. i. 18). But supremely the reference is to the Lord Jesus, who, on the first day of the week (="the morrow after the Sabbath"), rose from among the dead. "Now is Christ risen from the dead, and become the firstfruits of them that are fallen asleep" (I Cor. xv. 20).

The Feast of Pentecost (read verses 15–22).

This observance was fixed for "the morrow after the seventh Sabbath," reckoning from the presenting of the Passover wave-sheaf. It fell, therefore, just "fifty days" afterwards (verse 16); hence its being named "Pentecost" in New Testament times (from *pentekoste*, the feminine of *pentekostos*, the Greek ordinal for fiftieth). The Passover barley-sheaf marked the *commencement* of the grain harvest. The Pentecost wave-loaves marked its *completion*. The Passover wave-*sheaf* was the grain as direct from God's harvest. The Pentecost wave-*loaves* were the grain as ready for man's food.

Typically, this observance speaks of that great New Testament Pentecost which took place exactly fifty days after the Lord's resurrection, namely, the coming of the Holy Spirit upon the redeemed in Christ (Acts ii.). It is "the type of God's people gathered by the Holy Spirit and presented before Him in connexion with all the preciousness of Christ."

Note the singular stipulation that the two wave-loaves must

be "baken *with* leaven" (verse 17). This is true to the design of the type here; for even in the spiritual wave-loaves of the New Testament, in that blood-bought people consecrated to God, in Christ, and fused into spiritual union by the Holy Spirit, the leaven of sin yet remains. It is comforting, therefore, to see that with the two leavened wave-loaves a *sin*-offering and *peace*-offerings were to be offered as well as the sweet-savour offerings, typifying that, despite the presence of evil in the nature, there is acceptance and communion through the Divinely provided sacrifice of Christ.

The Blowing of Trumpets.
The Day of Atonement.   (read verses 23–44).
The Feast of Tabernacles.

The Blowing of Trumpets came first in that trio of annual observances which fell in the seventh month. There are two things which it is important to note. First, they all came within a few days of each other. Second, they were separated by a wide gap from the earlier two feasts of the year. Between the feast of Pentecost and the Blowing of Trumpets on the first day of this seventh month three and a half months elapsed. Time yet to come will show how full of prophecy is this grouping of these types, with this gap between; for these observances of the seventh month look on to the time of Israel's regathering at the end of the present age.

This seventh month was pre-eminently the Sabbatic season of Israel's year. The blowing of the trumpets on the first day was Jehovah's call to Israel to regather in preparation for the two great events which followed in this seventh month, namely, the annual Day of Atonement (on the tenth day), the most august ceremony of the year, when the High Priest went into the Holy of Holies to make atonement for the whole nation (verses 26–32); and, second, the Feast of Tabernacles, the completion of the harvest ingathering, and the final religious convocation of the year (verses 33–44).

As we have seen, the full picture of the Day of Atonement is given in chapter xvi. We need not go back there except to note that the High Priest, having gone into the Holy of Holies to sprinkle the blood on and before the Mercy Seat, was to come forth again to the people, wearing his beautiful high-priestly garments. This latter part of the type has not yet been fulfilled. The Lord Jesus, Israel's true High Priest, has entered into the heavenly sanctuary, with the blood of the one perfect sacrifice, but He is yet to come forth again to His people (Heb. ix. 24–8). At that time, also, there shall be a penitent Israel; and it is significant that in this twenty-third chapter of Leviticus the emphasis is laid on that very thing. Three times are the people of Israel told that on this day they must "afflict" their souls (verses 27, 29, 32). Corresponding with this Day of Atonement, at the end of the summer and harvest season, there will come a time when the earthly Israel will say: "The harvest is past, the summer is ended, and we are not saved." Then shall they look, in believing contrition, on Him whom they pierced, and shall be saved.

It will be then, also, that the type-fulfilment of the Feast of Tabernacles (more strictly, the feast of "booths," from the Hebrew plural *succoth*) will take place, and the glory of Israel's final ingathering. This Feast of Tabernacles lasted longer than any other of the *mo'adim*, or "set seasons," of Israel's calendar; and the verses describing it show it to have been the year's supreme season of festive joy. It looked back to Israel's exodus from Egypt. "Ye shall dwell in booths seven days; all that are Israelites born shall dwell in booths: that your generations may know that I made the children of Israel to dwell in booths when I brought them out of the land of Egypt" (verses 42–3). It is of interest to note that the first pause of the Israelites on their outgoing from Egypt was at Succoth (Exod. xii. 37; xiii. 20), which name, as pointed out above, is the Hebrew plural for booths. But, in its typical significance, the Feast of Tabernacles also points us forward to that seventh millennium of history yet to be, when, in the words of Zechariah xiv., "It shall come to pass that every one that is left of all the nations which came against Jerusalem shall even go up from year to year to worship the King, Jehovah of hosts, and to keep the feast of Tabernacles. In that day shall there be upon the bells of the horses, *HOLINESS UNTO THE LORD.*"

THE BOOK OF LEVITICUS (4)

Lesson Number 12

NOTE.—For this study read Leviticus xxv. to xxvii.

" One of the most characteristic and prominent features of the Bible, considered as a whole, which runs through it from beginning to end, and which distinguishes it at once from all other books, is that it subordinates everything to the idea of GOD. It is not without reason called the Book of God; and would be so, in a very intelligible sense, even if it were wholly false, or if there were no God at all. From the first sentence to the last, He is the great theme of it, the Alpha and Omega."

HENRY ROGERS.

THE BOOK OF LEVITICUS (4)

PART II—*concluded*

(4) The Land (xxv.–xxvii.)

THE FINAL section of Leviticus consists of chapters xxv. to xxvii., and deals distinctively with Israel's occupation of Canaan. Several times already, in Exodus and Leviticus, we have come across words such as, "When ye be come into the land . . ." and this, of course, is as one would expect, since the whole of the Law given through Moses was anticipative of Israel's settling in Canaan. These last three chapters of Leviticus, however, are concerned almost exclusively with the Land, and with the terms of Israel's occupation of it. No less than thirty times in these three chapters we find reference to "the land."

Chapter xxv. enjoins the observance of the two periodic "sabbaths of *rest unto the land*," namely, the seventh year (verses 1–7), and the fiftieth (verses 8–55). These sabbaths were to be an acknowledgment of the Divine proprietorship of the land, and of Israel's tenure on the ground of covenant relationship (verse 23). They were a wise measure for the land itself, as agricultural science would now recognise. They were a graciously provided opportunity of joyous leisure for the people—for although, strictly speaking, they were times of "rest unto the *land*," yet, as a foreseen by-product, the people themselves were to enjoy the respite thus occasioned. Then, too, these land-sabbaths were to serve as a check upon covetousness. Every seventh year the Hebrew must suspend effort after gain. He must even forego his right to the spontaneous produce of his own fields, so that all alike—rich and poor, cattle and beasts—might have their fill (verses 5–6); and in the case of the Jubilee, following, as it did, the seventh of these seventh-year rests, this check covered two years running together. And if we couple with this the strict ruling that no interest was to be charged on money or goods loaned to a fellow-Hebrew (verses 35–8), and the further regulation that in the Jubilee all must go out free, we see still more clearly this restraint on greed. Furthermore, these land-sabbaths were meant to develop the people's faith in God, and to cultivate a sense of trustful dependence upon Him (verses 20–2).

It may be, however, that the foremost purpose of the regulations in this twenty-fifth chapter was to secure as far as possible "the equal distribution of wealth, by preventing excessive accumulations either of land or of capital in the hands of a few while the mass should be in poverty." We cannot here examine these most interesting regulations in detail, but we would advise that they should be carefully read with the foregoing considerations in mind.

The key to the seventh-year sabbath is the word "rest" (verse 4). It was to be a rest in three ways—(1) for the land, (2) from manual toil, (3) from debt (see Deut. xv. 1–11).

The key to the year of Jubilee is the word "liberty" (verse 10). It brought liberty in three ways—(1) to the slave, (2) to property, (3) to the ground itself (see below).

Of course, as it was with the five "set seasons" in chapter xxiii., so here, there is a typical content. Both the Sabbatic Year and the year of Jubilee were to begin on the Day of Atonement (verse 9), in which, as we have seen, Israel was to evidence special penitence for national sin ; and on that day both these Sabbath years were to begin when the High Priest made his advent to the people after having made atonement for the nation in the Holy of Holies. Both these years, being connected with the sabbatic idea, point onward to the yet final redemption and consummation.

The seventh year "sabbath of *rest*," following the six years of toil, speaks of that seventh great thousand-year period yet to be which will be brought in by the second coming of Christ, when, after the six thousand years from Adam, which are now nearing their end, the earth shall have rest under the benign rule of Israel's true King.

The Jubilee, which was to be the year *after* the seventh of these seventh-year sabbaths, and was therefore to be always in the eighth year of the sabbatic calendar, speaks of that glorious condition of things *following* the millennial reign of Christ. What our Sunday is—the *first* day of the new week, following upon and doing away with the seventh-day sabbath of the old week and the old dispensation, the day of resurrection, of the outpoured Spirit, of a new order of things, even a new creation in Christ

Jesus, so the Jubilee looks on to the new heaven and new earth yet to be (Rev. xxi.–xxii.), when, following the seventh great thousand-year day of history, during which all rule and authority shall have been brought beneath Christ's feet, and even death, the last enemy, shall have been done away, the voice of God shall be heard saying: "Behold, I make all things new!"

We have noted that the key to the Jubilee is the word "liberty." How thrillingly prophetic this Jubilee word is! As the slave was freed in the Jubilee, and returned to his forfeited inheritance, so shall it be in that consummating Jubilee of the future. Then shall we know the prophetic meaning of our Lord's word—"The meek shall inherit the earth." Then shall we know the meaning of 1 Peter i. 4–5, and Revelation xxi. 2–4. That inheritance of the earth which was forfeited through sin, this glorious Jubilee of the ages shall bring back to us. The New Jerusalem descends from heaven, and the redeemed and glorified assume the possession of the purchased inheritance.

In Genesis iii. 17–19 we are told of the curse that fell on the very ground itself because of man's sin. It is remarkable that during the sabbatic year and the year of Jubilee this curse was to be temporarily suspended, at least in appreciable measure (Lev. xxv. 20–2).

Here is liberty indeed!—for the slave, for the inheritance, for the earth itself. "The creation itself also shall be delivered from the *bondage* of corruption unto the glorious *liberty* of the children of God" (Rom. viii. 21). The sabbatic year and the year of Jubilee were to be ushered in by the blowing of the trumpet. Oh, for the time when the trumpet of God shall sound, and the universe's sabbath rest and Jubilee shall set in!

The Alternatives of the Covenant (chapter xxvi.).

We can speak but a word or two about chapter xxvi., although this is one of the most solemn and important chapters in the Bible. It sets before Israel the categoric conditions of possession and prosperity, the inexorable alternatives hinging on whether they would obey or disobey. What blessings are promised to obedience! What warnings are uttered to deter from disobedience! Truly, the higher the privilege, the deeper the responsibility!

The warnings in the second part of the chapter are an amazing epitome of Israel's later history, reaching on even to time yet to be. "So strictly true is this that we may accurately describe the history of that nation, from the days of Moses until now, as but the translation of this chapter from the language of prediction into that of history." "These facts make this chapter to be an apologetic of prime importance. It is this, because here we have evidence of foreknowledge, and therefore of the supernatural inspiration of the Holy Spirit of God in the prophecy here recorded. The facts cannot be adequately explained, either on the supposition of fortunate guessing or of accidental coincidence."

It will be noted that the final punishment is expulsion from the land, and dispersion among the nations. After the falling of the other judgments, this last one has only too patently come to pass, and the land itself, as forewarned, has lain derelict and depopulated for generations. Yet going with this warning was the Divine promise guaranteeing Israel's preservation and restoration; and the preservation of Israel is one of the uneclipsed marvels of history. Professor Christlieb says: "We point to the people of Israel as a perennial historical miracle. The continued existence of this nation up to the present day, the preservation of its national peculiarities throughout thousands of years, in spite of all dispersion and oppression, remains so unparalleled a phenomenon, that without the special providential preparation of God, and His constant interference and protection, it would be impossible for us to explain it. For where else is there a people over which such judgments have passed, and yet not ended in destruction?"

Moreover, in our days we are seeing the earlier phases of Israel's restoration in progress. The land itself, also, is being transformed in preparation for the regathering of the people; and the time seems to be rapidly nearing when these words shall be fulfilled: "And I will pour upon the house of David, and upon the inhabitants of Jerusalem, the spirit of grace and of supplications: and they shall look upon Me whom they have pierced; and they shall mourn for Him as one mourneth for his only son, and shall be in bitterness for Him as one that is in bitterness for his firstborn. . . . In that day there shall be a fountain opened to the house of David and to the inhabitants of Jerusalem for sin and for uncleanness" (Zech. xii. 10–xiii. 1). "And it shall come to pass in that day that the Lord shall set His hand again the second time to recover the remnant of His people which shall be left, from Assyria and from Egypt and from Pathros and from Cush and from Elam and from Shinar and from Hamath and from the islands of the sea: and He shall set up an ensign for the nations, and shall assemble the outcasts of Israel, and gather together the dispersed of Judah from the four corners of the earth" (Isa. xi. 11–12).

Chapter xxvii. deals with voluntary consecrations, and tithings in the land. It is a unique conclusion to Leviticus that, after all its chapters concerning *obligatory* regulations, the final chapter should concern itself with *non*-obligatory expressions of regard and love toward God. These three chapters in this final section of Leviticus are full of interest; but we cannot tarry at them here. Still, we are confident that we have said enough about these eight sections of Leviticus to indicate how full of fascination and instruction this third book of Scripture really is.

A word of caution is needed regarding the word "atonement" as it is used in Leviticus by our English version. In commonly accepted theological usage today, the word "atonement" distinctively denotes the redeeming sacrifice of Christ; but here in Leviticus it is used, somewhat misleadingly, to translate a Hebrew word which simply means *to cover*. The Levitical offerings certainly did not make atonement for sin in the theologically accepted sense of the word. They merely *covered*, or put away from judicial view, the sins of Old Testament believers, through the forbearance of God, until the one real atonement was effected on Calvary, which the Levitical sacrifices anticipated and prefigured (see Rom. iii. 25).

The central figure in Leviticus is the High Priest. The central chapter is xvi.—the annual Day of Atonement. The central theme is fellowship through sanctification. The central lesson is: "Ye shall be holy; for I the Lord your God am holy" (xix. 2). (The Hebrew word translated "holy" comes over eighty times in Leviticus.) These well deserve special study.

We may now set out a fuller analysis of Leviticus so as to see at a glance the beauty and order of its structure.

THE BOOK OF LEVITICUS

FELLOWSHIP THROUGH SANCTIFICATION

1. THE GROUND OF FELLOWSHIP—SACRIFICE
(i.–xvii.).

THE OFFERINGS (ABSOLUTION)—i.–vii.
- *The sweet-savour offerings—i.–iii.*
- *The non-sweet-savour offerings—iv.–vi. 7.*
- *The Laws of the offerings—vi. 8–vii. 38.*

THE PRIESTHOOD (MEDIATION)—viii.–x.
- *Consecration—viii.*
- *Ministration—ix.*
- *Provocation—x.*

THE PEOPLE (PURIFICATION)—xi.–xvi.
- *Clean foods—xi.*
- *Clean ways—xii.–xv.*
- *Clean nation—xvi.*

THE ALTAR (RECONCILIATION)—xvii.
- *The one place shown—verses 1–9.*
- *The one use of blood—verses 10–11.*
- *Other uses forbidden—verses 12–16.*

2. THE WALK OF FELLOWSHIP—SEPARATION
(xviii.–xxvii.).

REGULATIONS CONCERNING THE PEOPLE—xviii.–xx.
- *Sex prohibitions—xviii.*
- *General admonitions—xix.*
- *Penal sanctions—xx.*

REGULATIONS CONCERNING THE PRIESTS—xxi.–xxii.
- *Prohibited practices—xxi. 1–15.*
- *Prohibited persons—xxi. 16–xxii. 16.*
- *Prohibited offerings—xxii. 17–33.*

REGULATIONS CONCERNING FEASTS, etc.—xxiii.–xxiv.
- *The annual set seasons—xxiii.*
- *The oil and shewbread—xxiv. 1–9.*
- *The penalty of blasphemy—xxiv. 10–23.*

REGULATIONS CONCERNING CANAAN—xxv.–xxvii.
- *Sabbatic Year and Jubilee—xxv.*
- *Alternatives of the covenant.—xxvi.*
- *Consecrations and tithings—xxvii.*

SOME QUESTIONS ON LEVITICUS

1. In what three ways does Leviticus express the holiness of God?

2. What is the standpoint of the book?

3. Which are the two main parts of Leviticus, and how are they distinguished from each other?

4. What are the eight sub-divisions?

5. What is the central message of Leviticus?

6. Can you name and group the five offerings in the first seven chapters?

7. Can you explain why Aaron was anointed *before* his sons, and afterwards *with* them?

8. Can you classify the teachings concerning cleanness, in chapters xi. to xvi.?

9. Why the one altar? and why the sanctity of blood?

10. What is the basic reason for God's insistence on the holiness of His people?

11. What were the seven great periodic national observances, and what their type-meanings?

12. What is the final punishment threatened, and what the final promise given, in God's great warning to Israel?

THE BOOK OF NUMBERS (1)

Lesson Number 13

NOTE.—For this study read the whole Book of Numbers through, to get a general picture of its story.

THE BOOK OF NUMBERS

"THE GOODNESS AND SEVERITY OF GOD"		
THE OLD GENERATION (Sinai to Kadesh)	THE TRANSITION ERA (In the Wilderness)	THE NEW GENERATION (Kadesh to Moab)
I.–XIV.	XV.–XX.	XXI.–XXXVI.
THE NUMBERING (i.–iv.) THE INSTRUCTING (v.–ix.) THE JOURNEYING (x.–xiv.)	THE WANDERING	THE NEW JOURNEYING (xxi.–xxv.) THE NEW NUMBERING (xxvi.–xxvii.) THE NEW INSTRUCTING (xxviii.–xxxvi.)

THE BOOK OF NUMBERS (1)

WHO AMONG Bible readers has not fallen prey to the spell of this fourth writing from Moses' pen? Tragic record though it is, in many respects, it speaks with undying appeal to God's pilgrims in every age and clime.

How does it get its name? In an earlier study we have referred to the Septuagint Version of the Old Testament—the translation of the Old Testament Scriptures into Greek, made by seventy Alexandrian Jews in the third century B.C. It was these Septuagint translators who first gave to the Old Testament books the names under which they now appear (in their English equivalents) in our English version. Thus, although the Hebrew name for this fourth writing of Moses was *Be-midbar*, which means "in the wilderness" (from the words in the first verse of the first chapter), the Greek name given to it by the Septuagint translators was *Arithmoi* (origin of our English word "arithmetic"), which in Latin becomes *Numeri*, and in English *Numbers*—the book being so named because in it the Children of Israel are twice numbered, once at the beginning of the book, and again toward the end. The Hebrew and Greek names taken together certainly give the gist of the book—"in the wilderness" and "numbers," or "numberings."

Its Nature

Numbers resumes the narrative where Exodus left off. The last chapter of Exodus (xl. 17) tells us that "in the *first month*, in the second year, on the first day of the month, the tabernacle was reared up." Numbers i. 1 says: "And the Lord spake unto Moses in the wilderness of Sinai, in the tabernacle of the congregation, on the first day of the *second month*, in the second year after they were come out of the land of Egypt." So there is a break of just one month between the erecting of the Tabernacle, at the end of Exodus, and the command to number the people, at the beginning of Numbers—with the Leviticus instructions coming in between the two.

Numbers obviously does not intend to be a full or strictly continuous narrative. Very little, for instance, is told us about the thirty-eight years of the so-called "Wandering," while certain other happenings which must have occupied a very small space of time, comparatively, are most carefully described. In accord with the consistent practice of the Scriptures, Numbers puts the emphasis, not on mere extent of time, but on the significance of events. It covers the period of Israel's history from the second month of the second year after the Exodus (i. 1) to the tenth month of the fortieth year (see Deut. i. 3). Possibly, indeed, a few parts of Numbers overlap into Deuteronomy (xxxii. 39–42), so that we may speak of it as *the book of the forty years.*

The record is of gripping interest. First the census is taken, with the primary object of determining Israel's military strength. Then the camp is strategically distributed with a view to facilitating orderly mobility—an undertaking as vital as complex with a crowd of over two million! The services of the Levites in connection with the Tabernacle are appointed. All is made ready for the advance to Canaan's border. The march ensues, in Divinely determined stages. Jehovah Himself leads on the mighty host, by the pillar of cloud and fire. The ground is covered. Kadesh is reached. Canaan is in sight! Then comes tragic breakdown. Israel disbelieves and then rebels. Judgment falls. The forty years of the "Wandering" set in; and the many thousands who came up from Egypt, with gleam of expectation in their eyes, gradually die off, leaving a pathetic trail of carcases beneath the hard crust of the wilderness. Then, eventually, God takes up with the new generation which reassembles at Kadesh. The new numbering is negotiated. The fresh advance takes place, to the plain of Moab, on Canaan's margin; and final preparations begin, with a view to Israel's going up, at long last, to possess the land.

Its Importance

Is there any need to insist on the importance of all this? Again and again Numbers is referred to in the New Testament. Indeed, the Holy Spirit has called special attention to it in that classic statement concerning Israel's early history, 1 Corinthians x. 1–12, which please read in full—

"Moreover, brethren, I would not that ye should be ignorant, how that all our fathers were under the cloud, and all passed through the sea, and were all baptised unto Moses in the cloud and in the sea; and did all eat the same spiritual meat; and did all drink the same spiritual drink, for they drank of that spiritual rock which followed them, and that rock was Christ. But with many of them God was not well pleased; for they were over-thrown in the wilderness.

"Now these things were our examples, to the intent we should not lust after evil things as they also lusted. Neither be ye idolaters as were some of them—as it is written: The people sat down to eat and drink, and rose up to play. Neither let us commit fornication as some of them committed, and fell in one day three and twenty thousand. Neither let us tempt Christ, as some of them also tempted, and were destroyed of serpents. Neither murmur ye as some of them also murmured, and were destroyed of the destroyer.

"Now all these things happened unto them for ensamples; and they are written for our admonition upon whom the ends of the ages are come. Wherefore, let him that thinketh he standeth take heed lest he fall." (See also Rom. xv. 4; Heb. iii. 7–iv. 6.)

Note the words: "All these things happened unto them for ensamples." As we pointed out in an earlier study, the Greek word here translated as "ensamples" is *tupoi*, that is, "*types*." The things recorded in Numbers are made immortal by their having been Divinely resolved into types, for our own learning. Indeed, we think it is not too much to say with A. C. Gaebelein, that the faithless failure of Israel to enter Canaan may well fore-shadow—as it certainly illustrates—the failure of the organised Church today to possess the heavenly things in Christ. It is the presence of these typical meanings and representative lessons which gives the book its rich spiritual values for us today. He who knows Numbers well will be well admonished for the pilgrim journey to the heavenly Canaan, and will escape many a sad set-back. All who preach the Word will do well to be familiar with this book for it gives many illustrations of Gospel truth. It notably exemplifies the fact that the greatest illustrations of New Testament doctrine are found in Old Testament story.

Its Structure

The structure of Numbers is unique, and when once seen is difficult to forget. We need to remember that, unlike the Book of Leviticus, in which we are geographically stationary, Numbers is a book of *movements*; and it is these movements which mark the main divisions of the book.

But what is most vital of all is to realise that in Numbers we deal, in turn, with *two different generations of people*—first, with the generation that came up from Egypt but perished in the wilderness; and second, with the new generation that grew up in the wilderness and then entered Canaan. This at once gives the clue to the book. In the first group of chapters (i.–xiv.) we are dealing with the *old* generation. In the final group (xxi.–xxxvi.) we are dealing with the *new* generation. Coming between the two groups, and unmistakably marking them off, we have the wilderness "Wandering" (xv.–xx.)—the period of transition during which the old generation died off and the new generation grew up. This threefold grouping in Numbers is so clear that no careful reader can fail to see it.

The one query which may occur to the student's mind is: How do we *know* that chapter xx. marks the end of the "Wandering" and the taking up with the new generation? The answer to this is conclusive. That twentieth chapter records the death of Aaron. Now at what point of time did Aaron die? Chapter xxxiii. 38 tells us: "And Aaron the priest went up into Mount Hor at the commandment of the Lord, and died there, *in the fortieth year after the children of Israel were come out of the land of Egypt*, in the first day of the fifth month." If, then, Aaron's death was in the fortieth year after the Exodus, it follows that it was *thirty-eight* years after the Kadesh-barnea crisis of chapter xiv., which marked the beginning of the wilderness "Wandering," for the Kadesh-barnea crisis took place in the *second* year after Exodus. (This is clear from Numbers x. 11, which tells us that the Children of Israel started the brief journey from Sinai to Kadesh in the second month of the second year after the Exodus; and we are told in Deuteronomy i. 2 that "there are eleven days' journey from Horeb (Sinai) by the way of Mount Seir unto Kadesh-barnea," so that even allowing generously for the different halts and incidents *en route*, we may safely say that Kadesh-barnea was reached about the end of the second year.) Thus the death of Aaron marked the lapse of forty years from the Exodus, and thirty-eight years from the beginning of the "Wandering"; and we know that thirty-eight years *completed* the "Wandering," for Moses tells us so in Deuteronomy ii. 14—"The space in which we came from Kadesh-barnea until we were come over the brook Zered (see Num. xxi. 12, following on the death of Aaron) was *thirty-eight years.*" So Aaron's death *must* have marked the end of the "Wandering," which means that the twentieth chapter of Numbers marks the taking up with the new generation. Aaron's death, we may add, is the most important time-mark in the whole book of Numbers.

This point being settled, the structural features of Numbers stand out sharply. We have—

    1. The old generation (i.–xiv.).
    2. The transition era (xv.–xx.).
    3. The new generation (xxi.–xxxvi.).

Thus, also, we see that the book of Numbers is in three movements, as follows:

    1. Sinai to Kadesh-barnea (i.–xiv.).
    2. The wilderness wandering (xv.–xx.).
    3. Kadesh to Plain of Moab (xxi.–xxxvi.).

In the first of these divisions, concerning the *old* generation, we have first the numbering, or *census*; then the Canaan-ward advance, or *progress*; and then the Kadesh *crisis*.

In the final chapters, concerning the *new* generation, we have first the new *crisis* at Kadesh; then the new *progress* from Kadesh to the Plain of Moab; and then the new numbering, or *census*.

We may put it that in Numbers we have—

    Two generations (i.–xiv. and xxi.–xxxvi.);
    Two numberings (i.–iv. and xxvi.–xxvii.);
    Two journeyings (x.–xiv. and xxi.–xxvii.);
    Two instructings (v.–ix. and xxviii.–xxxvi.).

Its Central Message

Seeing these things thrown into relief suggests at once the central message of the book. This may be expressed in words which occur in the New Testament, in Romans xi. 22—

"BEHOLD THEREFORE THE GOODNESS AND SEVERITY OF GOD."

In Numbers we see the *severity* of God, in the old generation which fell in the wilderness and never entered Canaan. We see the *goodness* of God, in the new generation which was protected, preserved, and provided for, until Canaan was possessed. In the one case we see the awful inflexibility of the Divine justice. In the other case we see the unfailing faithfulness of God to His promise, His purpose, His people.

Closely running up to this central message of the book are two other lessons—two warnings to ourselves; and these also may be expressed in words from the New Testament. The first is a warning against *presumption*. Turning again to the Corinthian passage which we have just quoted in full (1 Cor. x. 1–12), we find that this warning against presumption is the lesson which Paul himself sees in the book of Numbers. After telling us that "all these things happened unto them as types" for us, he says: "*Wherefore, let him that thinketh he standeth take heed lest he fall.*"

The second warning is against *unbelief*. In Hebrews iii. 19 we read: "They could not enter in (to Canaan) because of unbelief"; and then it is added—"*Let us therefore fear* lest, a promise being left us of entering into His rest, any of you should seem to come short of it." And again: "*Take heed, brethren*, lest there be in any of you an evil heart of unbelief" (iii. 12).

Thus the New Testament itself interprets the book of Numbers for us. This fourth writing of Moses says:

1. "Behold the goodness and severity of God."
2. "Let him that thinketh he standeth take heed . . ."
3. "Take heed lest there be in you—unbelief."

Perhaps it will be helping memory through "eye gate" if we now set down our findings in a flat analysis.

(See analysis at beginning of this study: page 156.)

THE BOOK OF NUMBERS (2)

Lesson Number 14

DISTRIBUTION OF THE CAMP OF ISRAEL

North

Asher	Dan	Naphtali
Benjamin		Issachar
	Merarites	
Ephraim	Gershonites **TABERNACLE** Moses Aaron Priests	Judah
	Kohathites	
Manasseh		Zebulun
Gad	Reuben	Simeon

It is well to keep in mind that here, in this quadrangular formation of the camp of Israel, some two million people were mobilised, and that the quadrangle was about twelve miles square!

It will be noted, also, that there are now twelve tribes *besides* the tribe of Levi, which was formerly counted as one of the twelve, but which was now reckoned as a tribe apart, in connection with the Tabernacle (Num. i. 49, 50; iii. 12, 13). There still remain twelve without the tribe of Levi, because the two great families sprung from Joseph's two sons, Ephraim and Manasseh, are now and henceforth counted as two separate tribes, instead of being reckoned as the one tribe of Joseph.

THE BOOK OF NUMBERS (2)

PART I. THE OLD GENERATION (i.–xiv.)

(*Sinai to Kadesh*)

As WE have seen, Numbers is in three main parts. The first of these consists of chapters i.–xiv., and concerns the *old* generation which came up from Egypt but died during the "Wandering." This first part now breaks into three sub-sections—the numbering (i.–iv.), the instructing (v.–x. 10), the journeying (x. 11–xiv.).

The Numbering (i.–iv.)

These four chapters go in two pairs, thus—

Chapter i.—Numeration of adult males.
    ,,   ii.—Distribution of the tribes.
    ,,   iii.—Numeration of Levite males.
    ,,   iv.—Distribution of Levite duties.

First, then, in chapter i., Moses is commanded: "Take ye the sum of all the congregation of the children of Israel, after their families, by the house of their fathers, with the number of their names, every male by their polls; from twenty years old and upward, all that are able to go forth to war in Israel" (i. 2, 3). The wording here makes clear that the primary purpose of this numbering was a military one. It gives us the man-power of the newly-formed nation. The figures are of much interest.

Reuben	46,500		Manasseh	32,200
Simeon	59,300		Benjamin	35,400
Gad	45,650		Dan	62,700
Judah	74,600		Asher	41,500
Issachar	54,400		Naphtali	53,400
Zebulun	57,400			
Ephraim	40,500		TOTAL	603,550

It is on the basis of this adult male census that the sum of the whole nation is computed at between two and three million. We cannot here go into the calculations involved in the working out of this total; nor can we discuss (what has seemed a problem to some) Israel's growth from "seventy souls" (Gen. xlvi. 27) to a nation of over two millions during the sojourn in Egypt. These will be found discussed in good Bible commentaries. There is an able article by Dr. Thomas Whitelaw in the *Pulpit Commentary*.

In the census, Israel's grown sons were numbered "after their families, by the house of their fathers" (i. 2); and they were evidently to "*declare their pedigree*" (i. 18). Only true Israelites were allowed to fight Israel's battles. None of the "mixed multitude" which came from Egypt with Israel were eligible. What a lesson for us today, when all sorts of persons are allowed to serve in the organised Church who are without the Divinely required spiritual pedigree of the new birth! The first question in connection with Christian service should ever be that of spiritual pedigree. How many church workers today are far from being able to say, "The Spirit Himself beareth witness with our spirits that we are the children of God" (Rom. viii. 16)!

Next, in chapter ii., we have the distribution of the tribes and the mobilisation of the camp. The twelve tribes were each to pitch by their own standard, and were arranged in four groups of three tribes each, one group being north, another south, another east, and the other west, of the Tabernacle.

Then, in chapter iii., we have the census of the tribe of Levi, which had been exempted from the general census because God had chosen it for special service pertaining to the Tabernacle (i. 49, 50). This Levite census, unlike the other, was to include all Levite males from a *month* old (iii. 15). Along with this comes the explanation that thenceforth God would count all the Levites as peculiarly His own *instead of* the firstborn from all the other tribes (iii. 12, 13).

The Levites were in three families—Gershonites, Kohathites, Merarites; and these were located "round about the tabernacle," westward, southward, and northward respectively. As for the eastern side, where the entrance was, verse 38 says: "But those that encamp before the tabernacle toward the east . . . shall be Moses and Aaron and his sons, keeping charge of the sanctuary; and the stranger that cometh nigh shall be put to death." Here are facts of the Levite census, location, and service at a glance—

Family	Number	Location	Service
Gershonites	7,500	west of Tabernacle	external coverings
Kohathites	8,600	south of Tabernacle	internal equipment
Merarites	6,200	north of Tabernacle	structural components

A difficulty crops up as to the total of the Levite males. The above figures (from iii. 22, 28, 34) give 22,300; but verse 39 gives 22,000. For two suggested solutions see Ellicott's commentary, and Wordsworth's. It certainly seems that the level 22,000 is the right total, for verse 43 says that the number of the firstborn in *all* the tribes was 22,273, and verse 46 says that this was 273 more than the Levite males.

Finally, in chapter iv., we have a census of Levite males from thirty years old to fifty; for only these were eligible for Tabernacle duties. The total is 8,580. Mark clearly the difference between the ministry of the Levites and that of the priests. The priests had to do with the ceremonial, sacrificial, and spiritual ministries of the Tabernacle. The Levites had to do with the material of the Tabernacle itself—with its erection, transportation, preservation, and other services necessary to its maintenance, such as the driving of oxen, the tending of animals for the sacrifices, and the preparing of incense.

The twelve tribes, as we have noted, were arranged in four groups of three tribes each, one such group on each side of the Tabernacle. In these four groups the leading (and probably central) tribes were Judah, Ephraim, Reuben, Dan. Some Jewish expositors say that the device on the standard of Judah was a young lion, on that of Ephraim an ox, on that of Reuben a man, on that of Dan an eagle. If these were indeed their ensigns, we have the probable origin of the forms attributed to the four living beings in Ezekiel's vision. It may be, in fact, that these tribal ensigns were themselves taken from the symbolic forms of the cherubim in the Tabernacle.

In the Bible account of this vast camp rationalistic critics have found ample scope for scorn. Their chief objection is that such a host could not possibly have subsisted for any length of time on the scant produce of the Sinai peninsula. But recent research shows that the regions traversed by Israel were far more productive then than now. Moreover, Scripture does not say the people lived simply on natural produce. They were sustained by *super*-natural supply! The syllogisms of rationalism collapse every time because God is left out of the premises!

These first four chapters are rich with spiritual lessons. In them we have the soldier, the priest, the Levite—warrior, worshipper, worker; warfare, fellowship, service. Both warring and working are to centre in fellowship with God—in the Tabernacle at the heart of the camp. Take the first of these—warfare. Israel's grown sons were first to declare their *pedigree* ("after their families"), then rally to their tribal *standards* ("by their standards"), then all to unite in common *conquest* ("so they set forward").

The Instructing (v.-x. 10)

The first four chapters have given us the outward formation of the camp. The next five deal with the inward condition of it. The key is chapter v. 3—"That they defile not their camps, in the midst whereof I dwell." This is the foundation principle of discipline, that the Holy One Himself being in the camp, the camp must be holy. This principle applies to the Church today.

Chapter v. commands that lepers be quarantined outside the camp; that dishonest gain be confessed and recompensed; that suspected immorality be tested before God. There must be purity, honesty, and truth.

Chapter vi. gives the regulations concerning the *nazir* vow. Among the "many thousands of Israel" there were doubtless many godly souls who would feel the need not merely for the negative rulings of chapter v. but for guidance of a positive kind regarding special expressions of devotion to God. Vows of abstinence have been common among all religions. Certainly, in many cases they have been mingled with much superstition, self-will, and pride; yet in the main they have sprung from noble impulses. This Hebrew *nazir* vow was outside the compulsory requirements of the Law; and in the provision here made relating to it is the implied recognition of the free movement of the Divine Spirit in individuals. Thus, while chapter v. concerns *general separation from defilement*, chapter vi. concerns *individual separation to God*.

Chapter vii. records the free-will offering of the princes. As these leaders really represented the people as a whole, what we have here is a national recognition of the claims of the Sanctuary. Three things strike us about it—(1) the *spontaneity* of the offering; it was not commanded; (2) the *uniformity* of the gifts; each prince brought the same; (3) the *particularity* of the record; each gift is separately recorded although all the gifts were alike; for our God, who is rich beyond needing aught that man can subscribe, looks not merely at the monetary value of the total, but prizes each separate gift for what it expresses of the offerer's love to Him.

It may be asked: "*Why* was this offering brought by these princes?" The following words of Professor W. Binnie will throw light on this. "The Lord's tabernacle has been constructed, furnished, anointed, and (what is best of all) occupied by the King whose pavilion it was intended for. Yes; and the construction and furniture of this royal tent have been effected by the voluntary gifts of a willing people. The tabernacle and its furniture are completed according to the pattern shown to Moses on the mount. No necessary part is wanting. Still, there is room for some supplementary gifts. Take two examples. (1) When the tabernacle was first dedicated there would no doubt be a golden spoon for Aaron's use when he burned incense at the golden altar. One such spoon was all that was strictly necessary. But it would occasionally happen that there would be more than one call to burn incense about the same time; and it was evidently unbecoming that in the palace of the King any worshipper should have to wait till the golden spoon was available. Hence the gift of the twelve golden spoons now presented by the princes. (2) The Levites have been appointed to bear the tabernacle and its furniture. They are able to do it, but not without difficulty, especially during the sojourn in the wilderness, where it is to be emphatically a moving tent. There was room, therefore, for a present of carriages and draught oxen. There are Christian congregations to whom this chapter teaches a much-needed lesson. The roll of their membership includes men of substance, yet they suffer the sanctuary to wear an aspect of threadbare penury, and its services to be hunger-bitten. This ought not so to be."

Chapter viii. describes the consecration of the Levites. First, however, in the chapter, the following instruction is given to Aaron: "When thou lightest the lamps, the seven lamps shall give light over against the candlestick." Then, by way of explanation, it is added: "And this work of the candlestick was of beaten gold, unto the shaft thereof, unto the flowers thereof, beaten work; according unto the pattern which the Lord had showed Moses" (viii. 1–4). A. C. Gaebelein says: "The candlestick is the type of Christ as in the sanctuary. The seven lamps were to illuminate the candlestick of beaten gold, so that the gold and beautiful workmanship might be seen. The oil in the seven lamps represents the Holy Spirit. Spiritually applied, we have here the Spirit of God shedding light upon Christ. For this He is given, to glorify Christ." As it was in Israel's old-time tabernacle, and as it now is in the heavenly sanctuary, so in the assemblies of the Lord's people on earth, God would have the glorious perfections of Christ displayed before His people.

Following this, in this eighth chapter, comes the consecration of the Levites. Note the salient lessons. (i) Before they could serve they must be *cleansed* (verse 7); so must we. (ii) Their cleansing was twofold, partly wrought *upon* them and partly wrought *by* them (verse 7); even so, in our own cleansing, there is the Divine side and also the human side. (iii) The cleansing wrought *upon* them was the sprinkling of "water of purification" (lit. "water of sin"—i.e., to cleanse away sin); even so do we ourselves need that cleansing which only the blood of Christ and the renewing of the Holy Spirit can give to us. (iv) The cleansing wrought *by* them was to "shave all their flesh, and wash their clothes" (verse 7); even so, on our own part, there must be a detachment from all those habits and impurities of common life which cling to us as closely and easily as our clothes, and which seem as much a part of us as our very hair. Especially in our Christian service there must be the application of death to that which is merely natural and "of the flesh," by the bringing of the word of God to bear on heart and conscience. It has been discerningly said that "there never was a more fatal mistake than to attempt to enlist nature in the service of God." There must be the "water"—daily cleansing of our conduct in the teaching of the word; and there must be the "razor"—daily self-judgment and uncompromising disallowance of that which grows "of the flesh." (v) The acceptance of the Levites was on the ground of the *sin*-offering and the *burnt*-offering (verses 8 and 12); and even so, our own acceptance with God is solely by the atoning self-sacrifice of Christ. (vi) The Levites must be presented before, and wholly given to, the Lord (verses 13–16); even so must we too "present our bodies a living sacrifice, holy, acceptable unto God, which is our reasonable service" (Rom. xii. 1).

Chapter ix. first shows us the people keeping the Passover, and then tells us of the pillar of cloud (by day) and fire (by night) which abode over the Tabernacle when the host were to rest still, and which moved onward when they were to journey. The Passover feast speaks of *fellowship*. The pillar of cloud and fire speaks of *guidance*. Thus, after the mobilisation of the people for war (i.–ii.), the appropriation of the Levites for service (iii.–iv.), and the instruction of the camp in holiness (v.–viii.), comes the crowning lesson of fellowship and guidance (ix.–x. 10).

Here, in Numbers ix., the people's pilgrimage Passover was, in a special way, both retrospective and prospective. It was the memorial of a past deliverance, and it was the pledge of a prospective inheritance. Similarly, to the Christian pilgrim today, the Lord's table is both a memorial and a pledge. It looks back to an accomplished redemption. It points onward to a glorious consummation. It looks backward inasmuch as we thereby "*shew the Lord's death.*" It looks onward "*until He come*" (1 Cor. xi. 26). "And now abideth faith, hope, love" (1 Cor. xiii. 13). At the Lord's table *Faith* looks *back* to the *Cross*, and is *strengthened*; *Hope* looks *on* to the *Coming*, and is *brightened*; *Love* looks *up* to the *Throne*, and is *deepened*.

Note that God made provision for *all* His people to share in the Passover feast. In the camp there were "certain men who were defiled by the dead body of a man, that they could not keep the Passover on that day" (verse 6). These enquired what they should do. The mind of the Lord was that these should keep the Passover one month later (verses 7–12). This provision also covered those who should ever be "in a journey afar off."

God would have none excluded from this "feast" of redemption; nor would He have any of His blood-bought people in Christ deny themselves this fellowship with Himself on the ground of redemption and through the "Spirit of adoption whereby we cry, Abba Father" (Rom. viii. 15).

And now read again, in verses 16 to 18, about that pillar of cloud and fire covering the Tabernacle.

Here was Divine guidance, direct, continuous, unmistakable, infallible. Israel's "many thousands" were spared the confusion of being left to search out by themselves a doubtful course which might have brought them to disaster. They were to make no plans of their own. They were not to know the route for even one day ahead. When they camped they could not say how long they would be staying. When they marched they could not say how long they would be moving. To watch that guiding pillar was all they were required to do. On that guidance they were absolutely dependent; and following that guidance they were absolutely safe.

"And does God do anything less for His people living in the present age?" asks one. Nay, "Every Christian knows that he is under His care and guidance. If He guided Israel thus, how much more will He guide us who are, through grace, members of His body, one spirit with the Lord! How often we frustrate the manifestations of His power and His love by choosing our own path! We are to follow Him. It is not acting according to the letter of certain rules and regulations: it is following a living Christ." He says, "I will guide thee with Mine eye" (Ps. xxxii. 8). *Our* eye must ever be toward *His* eye. There is guidance continuous and progressive for those who truly follow. Our lifelong motto must be: "The will of God, nothing more, nothing less, nothing else, always, everywhere, and at all costs." Our Lord's *work* for us is perfect; we must *rest* in it. Our Lord's *word* to us is perfect; we must *live* by it. Our Lord's *will* for us is perfect; we must *walk* in it.

Finally, in chapter x. 1–10, Moses is commanded—"*Make thee two trumpets of silver; of a whole piece shalt thou make them; that thou mayest use them for the calling of the assembly, and for the journeying of the camps*" (x. 2). These trumpets, like the pillar of cloud and fire, were for guidance. The pillar gave guidance for the eye. The trumpets gave guidance for the ear. Four uses are assigned to these silver trumpets. They were to be, first, a rallying call to the people (verse 3); second, a signal for advance (verses 5–6); third, a clarion in time of war (verse 9); fourth, a memorial before God (verses 9–10). It was the *priests* who were to blow the trumpet; for the silver trumpet was "the trumpet of *God.*"

All these things may be related to ourselves. Does the trumpet sound a *regathering*? That trumpet is yet to sound for the re-gathering of dispersed Israel! (See Isa. xxvii. 13; Zech. ix. 14.) Besides this, when the Lord Jesus returns for His own, He shall "descend from heaven with a shout, and *with the trumpet of God*"—to gather together His redeemed to Himself (1 Thess iv. 16). "*The trumpet* shall sound, and the dead shall be raised incorruptible, and we shall be changed" (1 Cor. xv. 52). Does the trumpet speak of *war* and *conquest*? Turn to Joel ii. 1: "Blow ye the *trumpet* in Zion, and sound an alarm in My holy mountain: let all the inhabitants of the land tremble: for the day of the LORD cometh." Turn to Revelation viii. and ix. and see the angels with their trumpets sounding the Armageddon conquest of Christ. Oh for the trumpet that proclaims His coming!

The Journeying (x. 11–xiv.)

Here, then, in the first ten chapters of Numbers, we have seen the camp of Israel at Sinai, marked by every preparation and provision for advance, for conquest and possession. Get the picture of that camp well in mind. There is that mighty host, the twelve tribes lying in vast foursquare formation "far off about the tabernacle," the Levite groups encamped round about the outer court of the Tabernacle, with Moses and Aaron and the priests on the east, guarding the entrance to the sacred enclosure; while there, at the very heart, giving unity, strength, and glory to the camp, is the sanctuary, speaking of God as the centre of His chosen people, even as Christ is now the centre and life and glory of His Church.

All is now ready for advance; and "on the twentieth day of the second month, in the second year," the guiding pillar lifts from the Tabernacle (x. 11). The moment the pillar lifts, the silver trumpets sound, and the whole camp is in motion.

First come the tribes of Judah, Issachar, and Zebulun; followed by two of the Levite groups—the Gershonites, with the coverings and the curtains of the Tabernacle, and the Merarites, with the golden boards and silver sockets and other structural parts of the Tabernacle. (To help them in transporting these, the Gershonites and Merarites would use the waggons and oxen given to them in the offering of the princes—see chapter vii.) Next come the tribes of Reuben, Simeon, and Gad; with the Kohathites following, and bearing the ark, the golden altar, the golden candelabrum, and the other precious internal appointments of the Tabernacle. Next come Ephraim, Manasseh, and Benjamin; and lastly Dan, Asher, and Naphtali (x. 14–27). There have been many wonderful things in history; but has there ever been anything to eclipse the marvel of this vast national transplantation, this orderly-moving multitude of between two and three million people, with all their children, their tents, their beasts, and personal equipment?—and the ark of God leading them on? We can understand the earnestness with which Moses would pray for this great multitude the two prayers recorded at the end of chapter x.—"And it came to pass, when the ark set forward, that Moses said: Rise up, Lord, and let Thine enemies be scattered; and let them that hate Thee flee before Thee. And when it rested, he said: Return, O Lord, unto the many thousands of Israel."

Chapters x. to xiv. (the journey from Sinai to Kadesh) make sad reading. See x. 29–32. How strange to find Moses saying to Hobab, his Midianite relative, "Leave us not, I pray thee, forasmuch as thou knowest how we are to encamp in the wilderness, and thou mayest be to us instead of eyes!" How soon the temptation comes to look away from the guiding pillar of cloud and fire! Such is the weakness of the human heart. We profess to trust God, and then look to man. We find it easier to lean on a puny mortal whom we can see, than on the almighty Lord Himself whom we cannot see.

See chapter xi. 1–3. After only three days' journey the people are complaining. The ark has sought out for them a resting place. Their comfort has been provided for. Canaan is just ahead. They carry with them the pledge of victory. They should be singing songs of rejoicing. Yet they are murmuring. The fire of judgment breaks out but is mercifully stayed at the prayer of Moses. The place was thus named *Taberah*, which means a burning. Murmuring never makes the way easier. It usually brings added trouble. Those who murmur without cause are soon given cause to murmur. Murmuring against God's providences leads on, bit by bit, to open rebellion and pitiable collapse, as we see in these chapters. Let us guard against it.

See chapter xi. 4–35. The "mixed multitude" lust for the savouries of Egypt. Then the rest join them,—"Who shall give us flesh to eat?" The fire at Taberah has not chastened them! Having murmured at the way by which God led them, they murmur now at the food by which God fed them. Yet this miracle-bread from heaven (a beautiful type of Christ), and called "angels' food" in Psalm lxxviii. 25, was the perfect diet for their (intendedly brief) journeying to Canaan. Moses himself becomes discouraged (verses 10–15)—"I am not able to bear all this people alone." Seventy elders are chosen to share the burden with him; and upon these comes the Spirit of God, so that they prophesy, presumably exhorting the people to faith and obedience. Note that prophecy, which is a gift of the Spirit, has a special place in time of apostasy and failure. The craved-for flesh is miraculously provided in the form of quails; yet even as the people greedily devour the flesh, judgment falls in a plague which devours the eaters,—judgment because they greedily fall on the provision merely for the gratifying of their own fleshly lust, without repentance and without recognition of the Giver behind the gift. The plague spot became named Kibroth-hattaavah, which means "graves of lust."

See chapter xii. The murmuring has now got to Israel's highest leaders. Moses' own brother and sister contentiously question his leadership. Aaron was already High Priest. Miriam was Israel's prophetess. Jealous pride now seeks higher position still. Their reference to Moses' Gentile wife was a mere pretext. See Moses' greatness. There is no self-vindication, and no trace even of resentment (see verse 13). His gentleness makes him great. His meekness is his majesty. God vindicates him (verses 4–10). "Wherefore were ye not afraid to speak against My servant Moses?" Judgment falls on the rebels. Miriam, the obvious instigator, becomes a leper. Note, it is grave sin to speak against a true servant of God. The Christian's real safety is to leave God to vindicate him. God guards the man He calls to service. Observe Moses' forgiving spirit. He prays for Miriam, and she is healed.

This brings us to chapters xiii. and xiv., to the Kadesh crisis; and the preceding chapters have prepared us to see why the fateful failure came about. The people had been failing bit by bit before. "How often we look upon grumbling as a little sin," says one expositor; "and not until we try to check ourselves in it do we find how complete is its possession of us, and how it is ready to spring upon us at all hours of the day under the slightest provocation. The weather is bad, the tea is too sweet, the chops are half cold, the potatoes are not done, the maid is unpunctual or careless, the parcel we expected is not delivered, and we are vexed and complain. It was a secret heart-grumble that led to Eve's disobedience. Trace Israel's downward course in Numbers, from discontent to lust, despising the Lord, speaking against His servants, provoking, tempting, doubting God, rebellion, presumption, discouragement, striving with, and speaking against God, and at last gross whoredom and idolatry. Beware! To be saved from this evil thing is one step towards perfection; see Philippians ii. 14."

The details of Israel's breakdown at Kadesh are well known. The twelve spies search the land for forty days. In their report all concur that Canaan is indeed a goodly land (xiii. 27); but ten bring back the doleful advice that its conquest is impossible. The other two, Caleb and Joshua, still the people, saying, "Let us go up at once and possess it." "The Lord is with us; fear them not." The ten put the difficulty between themselves and God. The two put God between themselves and the difficulty. The ten saw with the eye of the flesh. The two saw with the eye of faith.

We know the outcome. Israel disbelieved, then rebelled, even bidding that Caleb and Joshua be stoned (xiv. 10), and suggesting the appointment of a new leader who should take them all back to Egypt (xiv. 4)! The cutting irony is that Israel was but a stone's throw from the prize. Israel disobeyed. Judgment fell. Moses' touching intercession is heard for the nation (xiv. 11–20); but the judgment of the forty years' "wandering" is imposed (xiv. 29–30). Oh, the tragedy—a whole generation must now die off in the wilderness, and forty years be spent moving about without really getting anywhere! Certainly, although human unbelief cannot finally frustrate the purposes of God, it can hold back their gracious fulfilment. But the most pronounced lesson here is surely this, that *unbelief defeats the unbeliever*!

THE BOOK OF NUMBERS (3)

Lesson Number 15

NOTE.—For this study read once or twice again chapters xv. to xx.

Ten men who failed to see God
Saw cities impregnably high;
　　Two men, "looking off" unto God,
Saw doom for those cities draw nigh.

Ten men who failed to see God
Saw giants affrightingly tall;
　　Two men, "looking off" unto God,
Saw giants as grasshoppers small.

Ten men who failed to see God,
Reported, "We're certain to fail";
　　Two men, "looking off" unto God,
Cried, "Up! for with God we prevail."

Ten men who failed to see God
Discouraged their brother men;
　　Two men perceived *God everywhere*;
Are you of the two—or the ten?

"One bold push forward, and their feet would tread on their inheritance. But, as is so often the case, courage oozed out at the decisive moment, and cowardice, disguised as prudence, called for 'further information,' that cuckoo-cry of the faint-hearted"

—ALEXANDER MACLAREN.

THE BOOK OF NUMBERS (3)

PART II. THE WILDERNESS WANDERING (xv.–xx.)

WE ARE now at the central section of Numbers—chapters xv. to xx., the chapters which cover the thirty-eight years of the so-called "Wandering." This delay-period marks the transition from the old generation to the new. It sets in immediately after the Kadesh crisis, and terminates in the year of Aaron's death (xx.), as we have already shown.

Both at the beginning and at the end of Numbers we see an Israel carefully prepared, so far as organisation is concerned, for immediate conquest and possession: but this needless, tragic delay of thirty-eight years intervenes; and Numbers thus becomes distinguishingly *the book of arrested progress*. As such it speaks to us today regarding arrested progress in the Christian Church as a whole, and in the lives of individual Christians. It took only forty hours to get Israel out of Egypt; but it took forty years to get Egypt out of Israel! Within two years the people of Israel were at Kadesh-barnea, the gate of Canaan. Thirty-eight years later, there they were again, at the very same spot. Why? Well, there was that "mixed multitude" of pseudo-Israelites who were allowed to travel with the congregation, and who were not really one at heart either with the people or with the project. That "mixed multitude" lusted, and set the others lusting too, for the flesh-pots and cheap tasties of Egypt, the fish, the cucumbers, the melons, the leeks and onions and garlic. Very soon, besides the "mixed multitude," there were mixed motives! Oh, what a curse is the "mixed multitude" in the Church of today!—and how prevalent, in consequence, are the mixed motives!—and how obvious is the arresting and thwarting of real progress! We need never wonder at God's insistence on separation. It is vital to spiritual progress and effectiveness.

The following quotation is abundantly true. "In our churches are thousands of cases of arrested development. In the case

of many the arrest, as in the case of Israel, is the direct consequence of disobedience. They heard the Divine call, they experienced the Divine deliverance, they passed from death unto life,
and they began the new life well. As young Christians they were
full of zeal, full of love: they cried in their confidence, 'All that
the Lord commanded us we will do.' They seemed ready to possess
their possessions, and to enter spiritually into all the blessed
experiences God has for those who follow Him fully. But there
was a day when the call came definitely to enter the land, definitely
to yield themselves into the hand of God for a deeper, richer
life than they had ever known. They saw the land, they confessed that it was a good land; but they saw the giants and the
walled cities; they saw the persecution, the scoffing, the isolation,
the difficult service to which full consecration would lead; and
they said, 'We could not face it; we will not go up'; and immediately an arrest was put on their progress, their religion lost
its freshness, and its power; and the truest hymn they can now
sing is that most mournful one to be found on a Christian's lips
—'What peaceful hours I once enjoyed; how sweet their memory
still! But they have left an aching void the world can never
fill.' If there be any of you whose experience this is, remember
that the cure for it is the return to Kadesh. Go back to the place
where you disobeyed God; confess your sin; take up the life
of obedience once more; and the old joy, power, and progress
will be yours again. And to those who have not put back the
purposes of God for them by wicked wilfulness, beware of the
initial sins which end in such catastrophe, the sins that lie at
the base of all backsliding—dissatisfaction and discontent. How
little Israel realised the danger of their first yielding to discontent!
Probably not one of them had any idea to what an abyss of sin
those first murmurs would lead.''

This solemn lesson of the "Wandering" should not be lost on
any reader of this Book of Numbers. Let us now briefly but
thoughtfully look again through the chapters which tell about it.

The so-called "Wandering" must be distinguished, first of all,
from the journeyings which preceded it and those which followed
it. At the Kadesh mutiny there was a collapse of organisation.
The people ceased to be pilgrims, and became nomads. We need
also to have clear views as to what the "Wandering" really was.
Most Bible readers seem to think that during those years the

whole camp of Israel moved from place to place, with the pillar of cloud and fire directing their movements, and the Levites setting up and taking down the Tabernacle at each place. Yet there is no record of any such concerted movings during this time. It would rather seem that the Tabernacle abode throughout at Kadesh, and that roving, break-away bands dispersed more or less widely into the surrounding region, recognising Kadesh as a centre, and regathering there toward the end of the long delay. We shall touch on this again at chapter xx. The earlier name of Kadesh was En-mishpat (Gen. xiv. 7). Its later name of Kadesh, which is equivalent to "the sanctuary," may possibly have been given to it because of the long stay of the Tabernacle there.

Israel was in the wilderness all this time. Kadesh itself was in the wilderness or open country, being in (or between) the wilderness of Paran (xiii. 26) and the wilderness of Zin (xx. 1; xxvii. 14; xxxiii. 36).

Further, it is well to be clear about that word "wandering." In chapter xiv. 33, where God imposes the judgment of the "wandering," the Hebrew word translated as "shall wander" is literally "shall *pasture*"—"Your children shall pasture the wilderness (or open country) forty years." Going with the judgment is an implicit assurance that the Lord will shepherd them and provide for their needs. Here is goodness as well as severity!

An Historical Suspension.

These thirty-eight years simply mark time without making history. There is an almost complete submergence of the chosen people from view. During these years the real history of Israel was actually in abeyance; for that history is the history of a theocracy, and is therefore, in the highest sense, the history of God's dealings with His own people as He leads them onward to the fulfilment of His great purposes. The thirty-eight years are a hold-up of the purposes, and therefore a gap in the history. The generation which excommunicated itself at Kadesh had henceforth no heritage in Israel. Their lives were spared at the time, but their own professed wish that they had died in the wilderness was turned back upon them (xiv. 2, 28); they must now die out, and another generation take their place before the history of the theocracy could be resumed. The Kadesh break-down and the thirty-eight years' suspension may well speak to us of that still graver breakdown at Calvary and the present long suspense-period in Israel's history, during which God is calling out for Himself a spiritual people in Christ, irrespective of nationality (see Rom. ix.–xi. with Eph. ii.–iii.).

Let us note the following facts about the so-called "Wandering." First, God did not wholly abandon the rebellious people. He continued to communicate with them through Moses (xv. 1, 17, 35, etc.); and He gave the manna and supplied water and provided raiment and shoes (Deut. viii. 2–6; xxix. 5, 6).

Second, the rite of circumcision was discontinued (Joshua v. 4–8). It seems also as though the Passover was omitted throughout. Perhaps we can understand this. The rebellious generation knew that they were never to enter Canaan, and therefore it is unlikely that they could have found much heart to celebrate the memory (now made so bitter to them) of that fruitless deliverance. Indeed it seems probable that during these years the sacrificial system as a whole fell largely into disuse.

Third, from Ezekiel xx. 10–26 and Amos v. 25, 26, we learn that during this time the Law was badly disobeyed, the Sabbaths were profaned, idolatrous practices persisted, and the people even caused their firstborn to "pass through the fire" to Moloch!

Fourth—and in the words of an Old Testament scholar— "We have no authority for supposing that the host held together during these years of wandering which had no aim but waste of time, and no end but death. The presumption is that they scattered themselves far and wide over the wilderness (itself of no great extent), just as present convenience dictated. Disease and death, and all those other incidents revived in full force which make the simultaneous march in close array of two million people an impossibility. No doubt the headquarters of the host and nation, Moses and Aaron, and the Levites generally, remained with the ark, and formed the visible and representative centre of the national life and worship."

Turning now to the chapters themselves (xv.–xx.), let us quickly pick out the main things.

Chapter xv. begins—"And the Lord spake . . . When ye be come into the land. . . ." We do not know how soon or how long after the Kadesh revolt these words were spoken, but it is striking that the first recorded word of God after Israel's turning from the land is a reference to their eventual entering it. Man's delay does not mean God's defeat. Greater than man's failure is God's faithfulness.

Verse 17 introduces another speaking of God, concerning sacrifices for sins of error, and punishment for sins of presumption. Since Israel's law is given by God, and not by any merely human authority, to disobey wilfully is to reproach Jehovah Himself, and to merit severest penalty (verses 30, 31).

Verses 32–6 give illustration of such presumption and its punishment—the "man that gathered sticks upon the Sabbath day." What may seem a trivial thing at a superficial glance was in reality a wilful scorning of God Himself.

The chapter closes with the "ribband of blue" which the Israelites were to wear. They were to make fringes (or possibly the meaning is tassels) to the borders (lit. wings) of their garments, and were to attach to the fringe or tassel a "ribband" or cord of blue. Thus did God design a mark of distinction when many other distinctions had fallen into abeyance. Blue is the heavenly colour. It was to remind them of their heavenly calling, and cause them to "remember all the commandments of the Lord, and do them" (verse 39). It was to remind them also of their separation unto God—"holy unto your God" (verse 40). It was to be in the borders of their garments, so that the reminder might be with them everywhere and all the time, and so that every time they looked selfward and earthward their thoughts might be directed heavenward. There should be that ribband of blue— that distinguishing mark of God's Spirit—about every Christian today, too.

The "Gainsaying of Korah" (Jude 11).

Chapters xvi. to xviii. really belong together. In xvi. comes the "gainsaying of Korah" which was really an attack on the Aaronic priesthood. Over fifteen thousand die in the retribution of earthquake, fire, and plague. Then, in xvii., comes the budding of Aaron's rod, the new Divine attestation of the Aaronic priesthood. Then, in xviii., we have the Divine reaffirmation of the Aaronic priesthood, spoken to Aaron himself. Thus, in these three chapters we have the Aaronic priesthood defended, attested, confirmed.

Note, in xvi., that rebel Korah was son of Kohath. The Kohathites had the choicest services among the Levites. They bore the most sacred things of the Tabernacle. Apostasy often comes from the very leaders of religion. Their censers were kept as a warning (verse 38).

Note, in xvii., that Aaron's rod, in its budding and blossoming is a beautiful miracle-type of Christ's resurrection. The founders of the non-Christian religions were dead rods, and so are the systems they originated. Christ is the rod which has budded and blossomed in resurrection life and glory; and His resurrection is the Divine attestation that He is the one true Saviour-Priest of men.

The Red Heifer (xix.).

The ordinance of the red heifer, in chapter xix., probably follows as a consequence of the Korah revolt. Besides dying at the ordinary rate, the people had been carried off in thousands by the plague. Means were required for the cleansing of the very many who became defiled by contact with the dead. The ashes of the red heifer were used for this purpose, in the way described, and probably as an emergency measure, for no such ordinance is anywhere prescribed in Leviticus.

Hebrews ix. 13–14 suggests that here we have a type of our Lord's saving death for ourselves. The red heifer was to be without blemish, even as was the character of Christ. It must be a heifer on which no yoke had come (the yoke being that which is put upon an animal to subdue its wild nature and compel subjection), even as our Lord was without any need of such a yoke, but came saying "Lo, I come to do Thy will." The heifer must be red,—and since this is the only place where the colour of a sacrificial animal is stipulated does it specially speak of our Lord's obedience even to the death of the Cross? The heifer must be slain without the camp; and so was our Lord (Heb. xiii. 12). The blood must be sprinkled seven times toward the Sanctuary, speaking of perfect atonement; and the ashes of the heifer, with water of cleansing, must be sprinkled on the defiled people, to provide cleansing. Unlike the other offerings, this one was never to be repeated. In other cases, if a man sinned, fresh blood must be spilt; but here the virtue of what had been already offered and accepted remained. Even so, the sacrifice of Christ has made provision for our complete and continuous cleansing from all the defilement of our hearts which may be contracted as we pass through "this present evil world" which, in a spiritual sense, is stamped with death everywhere. See 1 John i. 7.

End of the "Wandering" (xx.).

We are now at chapter xx., the end of which coincides with the end of the "Wandering." The first verse of this twentieth chapter is of special importance in its bearing upon the "Wandering," and it is important to understand it correctly. Rather than lengthen this present study, however, with the somewhat close reasoning involved in that connection, we deal with it in the Addenda to our studies in this Book of Numbers (at the end of the next lesson) where it can be looked up afterwards.

Meanwhile, in this twentieth chapter, we find significantly grouped together the death of Miriam, the sin of Moses, and the death of Aaron. It was because of Moses' lapse here at Meribah that he was denied leading the nation into Canaan (verse 12); yet even this, pathetic as it is, becomes overruled to teach us, typically, that the Law, which Moses represents, can never lead us into that rest of which Canaan is a type. The account of Aaron's death is touching; and, as we have already pointed out, it is this event which (by comparison with xxxiii. 38) marks the end of the "Wandering." Thus, Aaron, representative of the priesthood, could not lead Israel into the promised rest; nor could Miriam, representative of the prophets; nor could Moses, representative of the Law. This was reserved for Joshua, who in a unique way was a type of our heavenly Saviour and Captain, the Lord Jesus Christ.

The Meribah rock-smiting incident is stamped with strong type-teaching. Moses was told simply to speak to the rock; but he exasperatedly struck it twice with the rod. The rock (Christ: 1 Cor. x. 4), having been once smitten (Exod. xvii. 5), need not be smitten again. The striking of it again would imply, in type, that the one sacrifice was inadequate, thereby contradicting the finality and abiding efficacy of Calvary. However, despite Moses' action, the water gushed from the rock; for despite the misunderstandings and wrong reactions of men in relation to the Cross, the "living water" still flows "more abundantly" from the cleft Rock of Ages, to bless the souls of tens of thousands in every generation.

THE BOOK OF NUMBERS (4)

Lesson Number 16

NOTE.—For this study read again chapters xxi. to xxxvi.

" A cynical man of science long ago sneered at the Bible as ' a collection of rude imaginings of Syria,' as ' the worn-out old bottle of Judaism into which the generous new wine of science is being poured.' The cynical savant is dead, but the Bible is still alive, for it is the Book of Books. The old wines of science grow sour in their cellars, and its new vintages have their day. But the Bible shows no signs of senility. Its youth is eternal. When our men of science and their theories are forgotten, the Bible will remain what it has been for mankind for two thousand years, the one universal book of wisdom, of truth, of sublimity, and of consolation."

JAMES DOUGLAS.

THE BOOK OF NUMBERS (4)

PART III. THE NEW GENERATION (xxi.–xxxvi.)

(*Kadesh to Plains of Moab*)

THE DREARY delay is over. A new morning breaks. The old generation is no more. A new generation has arisen. Aaron is gone, and Eleazar is appointed the new high priest. Moses is soon to go, and Joshua is to be appointed the new leader. The hour has struck for a new departure. Israel is to move over to the plains of Moab, and to prepare again for entering the promised land. In this final division of Numbers we have—

> The new Journeying (xxi.–xxv.),
> The new Numbering (xxvi.–xxvii.),
> The new Instructing (xxviii.–xxxvi.).

The New Journeying (xxi.–xxv.)

The new journeying, to the plains of Moab, would take about four to five months. We gather this from the fact that the people left Mount Hor about one month after Aaron's death (xx. 29), which took place in the *fifth* month of the fortieth year (xxxiii. 38); and it was in the *eleventh* month of that same year, on their having reached the plains of Moab, that Moses commenced his great charge to Israel which constitutes the book of Deuteronomy (Deut. i. 3, 5). The journey was made much longer because Edom refused Israel the shorter way through Edomite territory (xx. 14–22; xxi. 4).

The chief halts and incidents are given in chapter xxi., which chapter opens with two significant facts. First, there is *Jehovah's new response to Israel*—"the Lord hearkened to the voice of Israel and delivered up the Canaanites" (verse 3). During the Wandering, while Israel has been out of line with the directive will of God, there has been no such response. Turn to Deuteronomy i. 44. Looking back on the beginning of the Wandering,

Moses says: "And the Amorites which dwelt in that mountain came out against you, and chased you as bees do, and destroyed you in Seir, even unto Hormah: and ye returned and wept before the Lord; *but the Lord would not hearken to your voice, nor give ear unto you.*" Now, however, with the taking up again of Israel's true history, the covenant privileges again become operative. Israel calls and Jehovah hearkens. Mark the great lesson here. When we get out of the purposive will of God for us, the real power of prayer is suspended; but if we continue in the line of that will, none can effectually stand against us. Outside that will we are misguided wanderers. Inside it we are militant pilgrims with a clear objective.

Second, here is *Israel's new victory*—"The Lord . . . delivered up the Canaanites; and they (Israel) utterly destroyed them and their cities: and he called the name of the place (lit.—the name of the place was called) Hormah" (verse 3). Hormah was the place of humiliating defeat at the *beginning* of the Wandering (see xiv. 45). Now, at the *end* of the Wandering, as Israel re-emerges into the light of the Divine purpose and favour, there is victory in the place of the old defeat. How true it is that when we turn away from the Canaan into which God would lead us we cannot stand before our *spiritual* foes! To keep in the will of God is the secret of triumphant progress.

Next, in verses 4 to 9, we have the episode connected with the lifting up of *the brazen serpent*. We shall refer to the type-teaching here later. What we would note here is Israel's discouragement (see verse 4). The people had been refused permission to go *through* the land of Edom, and were having to go *round* it. This not only made the way longer, it gave a sense of grievance which made the way seem *much* longer. Israel falls into the old sin of murmuring (verse 5), and suffers again (verse 6). This, after their recent victory! We need to be watchful in times of victory, lest we suffer depressing reactions. Note also, the brazen serpent, being in appearance like the destroying serpents which infested the camp, served both to remind the people of their wrong and at the same time to provide healing. Similarly, at Calvary we see, as nowhere else, the awfulness of our sin, and at the same time our salvation from it.

We move on now, through several stages, to *the well of singing* (verses 16–18)—"That is the well whereof the Lord spake unto

Moses: Gather the people together, and I will give them water. Then sang Israel this song:

> *'Spring up, O well; sing ye unto it;*
> *The well which the princes digged,*
> *Which the nobles of the people delved,*
> *With the ruler's staff and their staves.'"*

Thank God for song! What sighing could not do, in verse 5, singing does, in verse 17. It began to look as though Israel had forgotten how to sing. There is no record of any singing between this well of song and that which Israel had sung at the Red Sea.

Why did Israel sing at this well? Had the people at last discovered that the water from the smitten Rock was following them through all their journeyings, and that even amid the most arid stretch of desert all they had to do was to sing the song of faith, and dig through the hard crust to find the supply there, at the very point of their need? Had they now learned that besides its being unnecessary for the Rock to be *struck* more than the once, it was also unnecessary to provide *another* rock for each new need? We do not know. But have we ourselves learned not only the finality of the once-smiting on Calvary, but the continuity of supply from that once-smitten Rock ("and that rock was Christ"—1 Cor. x. 4)? Are *we* living by the continuous flow of that "living water," the Holy Spirit? Have *we* found that just beneath the hard surface of life's most arid stretches there is that crystal stream following us from the Rock, and ready to gush forth at the voice of prayer and the song of faith? Are *we* with joy drawing from the wells of salvation? Such songs and fountains transform the drabbest wilderness! In the remainder of this chapter there is nothing but victory. Had Israel sung the song of faith at Kadesh, thirty-eight years before, instead of venting the dirges of unbelief, what conquests might have taken the place of the Wandering!

And now, in chapters xxii. to xxiv., one of the strangest characters in the Bible appears on the scene—Balaam. On the problems and special features pertaining to him see our Addenda at the end of this study. These three chapters really lie athwart the narrative, as is seen by the fact that the end of chapter xxi. links right over to xxv. The great point to note here is that even the subtlest stratagems of evil against Israel are overridden now that Israel once more marches in Jehovah's will. Balaam, who tries to curse, is forced to bless.

But alas, the people themselves now turn aside and do the accursed thing. Chapter xxv.—an awful chapter—begins: "And Israel abode in Shittim, and the people began to commit whoredom with the daughters of Moab. And they called the people unto the sacrifices of their gods; and the people did eat, and bowed down to their gods: and Israel joined himself unto Baal-peor. And the anger of the Lord was kindled against Israel." From chapter xxxi. 16 we learn that Balaam, although unable to curse the sons of Israel, had evidently counselled that the women of Moab and Midian should solicit them. The sons of Israel became a foolish prey. The remainder of this twenty-fifth chapter of Numbers makes sorry reading. Twenty-four thousand die in the plague which breaks forth in judgment. What a tragedy after the recent record of victories! What a tragedy, this idolatry and obscenity in the people blessed with such high teaching and such a high calling! Of a truth, these chapters of Numbers teach us that it is not enough for us to have an outward law or ideal, however high and pure it may be. What we need is an inward change to strike down the inbred perversity of our fallen nature!

The New Numbering (xxvi.–xxvii.)

Chapters xxvi. and xxvii. give us the new military census of Israel, and certain matters consequent upon it. It is interesting to see the figures side by side with those of the earlier count.

Tribe	Old Census	New Census	Decrease	Increase
Reuben	46,500	43,730	6 per cent	
Simeon	59,300	22,200	63 ,, ,,	
Gad	45,650	40,500	11 ,, ,,	
Judah	74,600	76,500		2½ per cent
Issachar	54,400	64,300		18 ,, ,,
Zebulun	57,400	60,500		5½ ,, ,,
Ephraim	40,500	32,500	20 ,, ,,	
Manasseh	32,200	52,700		63 ,, ,,
Benjamin	35,400	45,600		29 ,, ,,
Dan	62,700	64,400		2½ ,, ,,
Asher	41,500	53,400		28 ,, ,,
Naphtali	53,400	45,400	15 ,, ,,	
	603,550	601,730		

The new numbering was evidently taken in hundreds, as the one before. The slight decrease in the new total, and the strange increases and decreases in certain of the tribes, suggest at once the genuineness of these figures. An artificial record would have avoided such difficult variations.

The new total pathetically harmonises with the whole story of Numbers. At the beginning of the forty years the number is roughly 600,000; and again at the end of the forty years the number is 600,000. They are no further forward for the whole period. There is arrested progress even numerically. The strange drop in some of the tribes may be accounted for by the plagues which fell in judgment. We gather that Simeon figured prominently in the Baal-peor sin and plague (see xxv. 14). The principle on which the land is to be apportioned is given in verses 53 to 56; and the new total of the Levites, in verses 57 to 62.

Arising in connection with this new numbering is the plea of Zelophehad's daughters respecting their family inheritance (xxvii. 1–11). It is self-explanatory and requires no comment here. Also, after the new numbering Moses receives intimation of his own impending departure (verses 12–14). Touching indeed is Moses' acknowledgment of this—

"Let the Lord, the God of the spirits of all flesh, set a man over the congregation, which may go out before them, and which may go in before them, and which may lead them out, and which may bring them in; that the congregation of the Lord be not as sheep which have no shepherd" (verses 16–17).

There is no thought of self here. It is the people and the Lord's own cause which are upon his heart. If their well-being is assured he is content. May there breathe such a spirit in our own hearts! Following Moses' prayer, he is instructed publicly to induct Joshua into office as new leader, the account of which induction closes the chapter (verses 18–23). Here, then, is newly numbered Israel's fighting strength at the change-over to Joshua's command and the going up to possess the land.

"And Moses laid his hands upon him
(Joshua), and gave him a charge, as
Jehovah had commanded" (v. 23).

The New Instructing (xxviii.–xxxvi.)

This final section of Numbers need not detain us long. Chapters xxviii. and xxix. go together. They deal with the subject of the Lord's offerings, specifying their constituents and routine, and thus amplifying the instructions already given in Leviticus xxiii. First come the daily offerings (xxviii. 3–8), then the Sabbath offerings (verses 9–10), then the new month offerings (verses 11–15), and then the offerings going with the "feasts" of the Lord (xxviii. 16–xxix. 40). For the typical aspects of these offerings and feasts look back over our study of Leviticus.

We ought just to note that the special offering for the *Sabbath* is here ordered for the first time, as also is that for the *new month*, or new moon. The *daily* offering, which was prescribed in Exodus xxix. 38–42, and which, we presume, had subsequently continued uninterruptedly, is again specified here because it was the foundation of the whole sacrificial system. Whatever else was offered was in addition to it, not in lieu of it.

Typically, all the offerings speak of Christ, and it is therefore significant that God speaks here of them as "My bread" (xxviii. 2). In Christ God has found His delight. The heart of God feeds, as it were, on Him, and is perfectly satisfied.

Chapter xxx. concerns vows—of men (verses 1, 2), of maidens (verses 3–5), of maidens betrothed (verses 6–8), of widows (verse 9), of wives (verses 10–15). On the Divine recognition of the place of vows see our note on chapter vi. The purpose of the new instructions here is to *safeguard* vows from being lightly regarded—from being either easily made or easily broken. They are to be made only to God Himself (verses 2, 3). They must not be broken (verses 2, 9, 15). In the case of maidens they must be parentally controlled (verses 3–5). In the case of the betrothed (the words of verse 6, literally translated, indicate betrothal) there must be care not to make *rash* vows (the words "uttered ought out of her lips" should rather be translated "the rash utterance of her lips"). In the case of the married woman there must be concurrence by the husband.

We may learn much from all this. There is a place for special covenanting with God, whether it be for self-denial, seasons of prayer, gifts of money, fasting, or other things; and these may provide a blessed release for the urgent love of the heart toward

God; but we should ever hold such vows or covenantings as the most inviolably sacred of all contracts. Moreover, let us say it thoughtfully, does not the old-time Hebrew vow suggest to ourselves, the redeemed at costliest price, that with utter earnestness we should vow our very selves away in life-long yieldedness to the will and service of our adorable Redeemer?

Retribution against Midian (xxxi.).

Chapter xxxi. brings the command to war on Midian. There is enough in the account to revolt the mind. The moral difficulty involved in Israel's Divinely sanctioned assault on the Canaanites here appears in its gravest form. What shall we say about it?

We suggest that the key to it is in that word "avenge." God's command is: "Avenge *the children of Israel* of the Midianites" (verse 2). Moses' transmission of the command is: "Avenge *the Lord* of Midian." If, therefore, we are dealing with honest language this war on Midian was certainly Divinely authorised and fulfilled a Divine purpose. Not that this in itself either involves or excuses the behaviour associated with the carrying out of it; but it gives the basis for a true consideration. The war on Midian was not merely a human retaliation: it was a Divine retribution. It was to "avenge *the children of Israel*" because Midian had deliberately, craftily, and gravely injured Israel, without provocation. It was to "avenge *the Lord*" because, in seducing Israel into licentious idolatries, they had knowingly (through the counsel of Balaam) been striking at Israel's holy God. Let us then be clear about this, that Midian justly merited retribution.

As to the *fact* of God's commanding Israel to destroy the Midianites, this falls in with God's command to destroy the Canaanite nations generally (Exod. xxiii. 24; Deut. vii. 1–6, etc.). There are those whose sentimental sympathies are so drawn out in commiseration for the foul-living Canaanites as to find it professedly impossible to believe that God could give such a command or sanction any such war; and on this account they reject the claim of the record to be inspired. But when we read of the utterly vile enormities of the Canaanites, in passages like Leviticus xviii. (noting specially verses 24, 27, 30), are we not driven to ask (if we are really honest) how a righteous Governor among the nations could do anything other—either in justice to these filthy-living people themselves or in consideration towards those corrupted by their influence—than effect their extermination in one way or another?

As for the *method* by which this should be effected, God has sovereign right to decide: and He commits the imperative surgery to a living nation called out to holiness and to the execution of the Divine purpose both in its necessary severity and its beneficence, so that the race as a whole might learn and heed. Now had God chosen, instead, to use pestilence, earthquake, famine, those who profess to find God's command to Israel unthinkable would make no charge of injustice; yet by these dumb agencies the lessons God wished to teach could never have been taught; and the physical suffering inflicted would have been much greater. Let us clearly and honestly face up to this, that if we believe in an overruling Providence, we must also believe that in one way or another God has provided that great wickedness in a nation shall be greatly punished; and God has the absolute right to decide the means to this end.

As for the vengeance on *Midian*, that which seems the most brutal, namely, the slaying of the women and male children (verse 17), is seen to have reason enough behind it, when we consider it in the light of all we are told. The men of Israel had spared Midian's women and children from the sword, and had brought them back prisoners. Moses' anger, coupled with words like those of Deuteronomy vii. 2, indicates that in this they had failed of full obedience. Moreover, the context suggests that the motive may have been as much sexual as benevolent. Now it was these very women who had earlier seduced the men of Israel, bringing death to twenty-four thousand (xxv. 9). What now was to be done with them? It seems an awful thing to kill a woman; yet it was the women, far more than the men, of Midian of whom there was reason to be afraid, for they would have spread physical and moral contagion through the camp. In justice to the men, and still more for the sake of Israel's own wives and mothers and maidens, it was unthinkable to let loose this host of strange women; and this appears the more forcibly when we consider the general immorality of these women, and the venereal disease certain to be rife among them. There is surely a swift recognition of this in Moses' distinction of verse 17 (and even after this, there were thirty-two thousand of the more harmless younger women left!—see verse 35).

Again, it seems a dastardly thing to slay a child; yet to suffer a whole generation of Midianites to grow up beneath the very roofs of Israel, so to speak, would have been madness; for it would have been to invite fatal national disaster. Must then these captives be driven back to their desolated hamlets to perish of hunger and disease? There was merciful perception in Moses' seemingly harsh intolerance, even though for the specific command of verse 17 he does not seem to have sought special Divine direction. Moses realised what many of his unsympathetic critics today will not allow inside the Bible but will allow outside it— that a severe evil often necessitates severe action. When mercy means compromise it is false kindness to the wrong-doer, and cruelty to the wronged.

In fairness to the men of Israel, it is well to add that throughout the account there is no trace of savagery, of torture, or of violence to the women—all of which things were the ordinary customs of war in those days.

Three remarkable things stand out about this anti-Midian action—first, the easiness of the victory; second, the largeness of the spoil (verses 25–47); third, that not one Hebrew life was lost (verse 49). Had Israel remained true to the Law of the Covenant, how quickly would the necessary dealing against the Canaanite nations have been over, and how different might have been the subsequent history of the human race!

Final Chapters (xxxii.–xxxvi.).

In chapter xxxii. we have the request of Reuben, Gad, and Manasseh, for permission to settle in the territory recently captured on the east of the Jordan. The ground of the appeal was the evident suitability of the area for their "very great multitude of cattle" (verse 1). Their request was reasonable-sounding— like most of the arguments which excuse compromise; but it was one of compromise none the less. Israel's place was inside Canaan, not just outside. Choosing by the sight of their eyes ("when they saw", verse 1), even as Lot had done, long before (Gen. xiii. 10–11), instead of in faith and according to the will of God, and being content with their portion just outside the place of promised blessing, they become types of so-called "worldly" Christians today. We see the result of their choice in 1 Chronicles v. 18–26, and 2 Kings xv. 29. They quickly bowed to the gods of the nearby peoples, and were first to go into captivity. The condition of their descendants at the time of Christ's first coming is found in Mark v. 1–17.

In chapter xxxiii. we have the summary of Israel's journeyings from Egypt to the Jordan, over which we need not tarry. Nor need we stay at chapter xxiv., except to point out that the boundaries of the land here described mark out a considerably less area for occupation than that covenanted to Abraham (Gen. xv. 18), to which fact we shall refer again later. The full inheritance reaches eastward right to the Euphrates.

The cities of refuge, in chapter xxxv., should be studied; their number (verses 6–8), their purpose (verses 9–12), their distribution (verses 13–14), their regulations (verses 15–34), and their typical lessons (along with passages elsewhere concerning them). The *final* chapter fittingly deals with the security of inheritance in the land; and it may well speak to us of the eternal security of the believer's inheritance in Christ. Thus ends this wonderful fourth book of the Pentateuch. How it invites our further and fuller study!

ADDENDA TO THE BOOK OF NUMBERS

The Hireling Prophet Balaam (xxii.–xxiv.)

Chapters xxii. to xxiv. go together. The strange wizard-prophet, Balaam, here moves before us. This section of Numbers is complete in itself. It lies athwart the Israel narrative rather than forming an ordinary continuation of it—as may easily be seen in the fact that chapter xxv. 1 continues the narrative from where the last verse of chapter xxi. left it. But this section is also strikingly marked off from the rest of Numbers by its literary form. Its form is that of a drama, in which characters and happenings of highest interest are handled with consummate art. Three problems present themselves in the person of this mongrel prophet—his knowledge of the true God, his enigmatical character, his strange prophetic gift.

How shall we account for *his knowledge of the true God* ? We believe that he is one of the many evidences of an original pure revelation of God which became perverted and obscured as time elapsed and the human race dispersed throughout the earth. Numbers xxii. 5 tells us that Balaam was of *Pethor*; and Deuteronomy xxiii. 4 tells us that Pethor was in *Mesopotamia*. Balaam himself, also, speaks of being "brought from Aram out of the mountains of the *East*" (Num. xxiii. 7). Balaam, therefore, came from the very cradle of the race; so that the natural and adequate explanation of his knowledge of the true God is that such knowledge had far from disappeared at this time from that region. The following quotation from an Old Testament scholar confirms this. "Every glimpse which is afforded us of the descendants of Nahor in their Mesopotamian home confirms the belief that they were substantially at one with the chosen family in religious feeling and religious speech. Bethuel and Laban acknowledged the same God, and called Him by the same name as Isaac and Jacob (Gen. xxiv. 50; xxxi. 49). No doubt idolatrous practices prevailed in their household (Gen. xxxi. 19; xxxv. 2; Joshua xxiv. 2), but that, however dangerous, was not fatal to the existence of the true faith amongst them, any more than is the existence of a similar cultus amongst Christians. Centuries had indeed passed away since the days of Laban; and during those centuries we may well conclude that the common people had developed the idolatrous practices of their fathers, until they wholly obscured the worship of the one true God. But the lapse of years and the change of popular belief make little difference to the secret and higher teaching of countries like the Mesopotamia of that age, which is intensely conservative both for good and evil. Men like Balaam, who probably had an hereditary claim to his position as seer, remained purely monotheistic in creed, and in their hearts called only upon the God of all the earth, the God of Abraham and of Nahor, of Melchizedec and of Job, of Laban and of Jacob. If we knew enough of the religious history of that land, it is possible that we might be able to point to a tolerably complete succession of gifted (in many cases Divinely-gifted) men, servants and worshippers of the one true God, down to the Magi who first hailed the rising of the bright and morning Star."

But what of Balaam's *character*? He is a walking paradox—a true prophet and a false prophet both in one. He is a true prophet in that he knows the true God, has a real faith in Him, has real dealings with Him, receives real communications from Him, conveys real messages from Him. Yet he is a false prophet in that he also resorts to the use of magical arts, is called a soothsayer (Joshua xiii. 22), and prostitutes his strange prophetic gift for base gain. How shall we explain such an unhallowed blend of contradictions? The writer quoted above says: "This is undeniably one of the instances (not perhaps very numerous) in which the more trained and educated intelligence of modern days has a distinct advantage over the simpler faith and intenser piety of the first ages. The conflict, or rather the compromise, in Balaam, between true religion and superstitious imposture, between an actual Divine inspiration and the practice of heathen sorceries, between devotion to God and devotion to money, was an unintelligible puzzle to men of old. To those who have grasped the character of a Louise XI, of a Luther, or of an Oliver Cromwell, or have gauged the mixture of highest and lowest in the religious movements of modern history, the wonder is not that such a one should have been, but that such a one should have been so simply and yet so skilfully depicted." Truly, Balaam is a study, drawn by an inspired hand, of a "strangely but most naturally mixed character the broad features of which are constantly being reproduced."

What now of Balaam's *prophecies*? We believe that although Balaam's other recorded speakings and doings were far from inspired, his prophecies about Israel were Divinely inspired utterances. In xxiii. 5 we read: "And the Lord put a word in Balaam's mouth, and said: Return unto Balak, and thus thou shalt speak." Again, in xxiii. 16, we read: "And the Lord met Balaam, and put a word in his mouth, and said: Go again unto Balak, and say thus." Yet again, in xxiv. 2, we read: "The Spirit of God came upon him." If we take these words in their plain meaning, we are left in no doubt.

But how could the Holy Spirit come upon such a man as this double-minded Balaam? That is the problem felt by many. Yet once we grant the *fact* of inspiration, is not the problem with Balaam more seeming than real? The Spirit of Jehovah, whom Balaam is double-mindedly invoking, comes upon this man not because he is a worthy vehicle, but despite him, crushing his secret thought to curse Israel, and sovereignly overriding the stratagems of hypocrisy, so that he who in his heart would fain curse Israel for reward is actually made the mouthpiece of marvellous benedictions. Balaam himself seems to have been driven eventually to realise the futility of any endeavouring to circumvent the will of God, for in chapter xxiv. 1 we are told that "when Balaam saw that it pleased the Lord to bless Israel, *he went not, as at other times, to seek for enchantments.*"

As for the prophecies themselves, their language is sublime and their content is profound. See chapter xxiv. 5–9 and 17–19. The following sayings are memorable, also,—chapter xxiii. 10, 19, 21, 23. To go into an interpretation of these Balaam prophecies would be a "launching out into the deep" which is beyond our present scope.

We ought just to note, however, the three New Testament references to Balaam. In 2 Peter ii. 15 we read of "the *way* of Balaam." In Jude 11 we read of "the *error* of Balaam." In Revelation ii. 14 we read of "the *doctrine* of Balaam." The *way* of Balaam is the prostitution of a spiritual gift for base gain. The *error* of Balaam is the secret idea that the will of God may be circumvented under cover of an outward respect for His word. The *doctrine* of Balaam is the counsel to ruin by seduction the people who cannot be cursed by permission (see Num. xxxi. 16).

The Brazen Serpent—a Type (xxi. 4–9)

The three main types in the Book of Numbers are, the Smitten Rock (xx. 7–11), the Brazen Serpent (xxi. 4–9), the Cities of Refuge (xxxv.). These connect up, in the New Testament, with 1 Corinthians x. 4, John iii. 14, Hebrews vi. 18. They are wonderful types. As an example, we set out here the main analogies in the Brazen Serpent. Note, in the narrative,—sin (verse 5), suffering (verse 6), supplication (verse 7), salvation (verses 8–9). This order is ever true to experience. Note further, the murmuring was twofold—about the way and the manna. Its direction was twofold—"against God and against Moses." Its punishment was twofold—pain and death. The supplication was twofold—"we have sinned" (confession), and "pray unto the Lord" (entreaty). The salvation was twofold—in the serpent, and by a look. Even so today men complain against God's way and against the living Bread He has provided in Christ. And today it is because men are not right with God that they are against Moses their fellow-man. And today sin fills the world with pain and death. And today salvation is in Christ, and by the look of faith.

Now note further—salvation by this serpent of brass was outside the Tabernacle, and apart from all ordinances, sacrifices, and priestly ministrations. So today, salvation is not by priests, confessionals, communions, or any church ceremonials. It was not Aaron the priest who had to erect the brass serpent, but Moses the layman. The Lord Jesus, according to Jewish law, was a layman, for He was neither of the family of Aaron nor of the tribe of Levi. He preached in the Temple court, but never ministered at the brazen altar. The apostles, also, were laymen. The Lord Jesus and His apostles never pointed men to the Temple or the sacrifices or the ordinances for their salvation, but to Calvary. But were not the Tabernacle and the ordinances and the priesthood of Divine origin and authority? Yes, they were, but they had not power to deal with serpent-bitten men and women. Many of the priests and Levites themselves were bitten and dying and dead, as well as other people. The point is that the Tabernacle was the appointed means of access for those who were already in covenant relationship with God, and who were healed of the serpent venom.

So, the "means of grace" today are for those who have been healed, saved, made meet for communion, through Christ the Saviour. Sinners must come to Calvary before they become true worshippers in the Sanctuary. Note the main type-aspects in the Brazen Serpent.

1. ITS APPOINTMENT

(a) It was prescribed by *God*. So the Cross of Christ is the Divinely appointed means of salvation.

(b) It was *informing*. Brass a type of judgment; the serpent, of sin. Both together show sin judged.

(c) It was the *only* Divinely appointed remedy. So the Christ of the Cross is the only way (Acts iv. 12).

(d) It was *enduring*. It was of brass. It was only destroyed long after, because superstitiously regarded.

(e) It was *conspicuous*. It was erected high in the centre of the camp. Even so is Christ uplifted.

2. ITS ALL-SUFFICIENCY

(a) It availed wherever a man was bitten. So there is provision in the Cross of Christ for all manner of sin.

(b) It availed however serious a man's condition. So the Cross saves the worst of sinners.

(c) It availed however many times a man might be bitten. So there is no limit in the Cross.

(d) It availed whoever the bitten person was,—young, old, priest, slave. So is the one Cross for all.

(e) It was infallible. There is no hint of any case in which it failed. So the Cross never fails.

3. ITS APPROPRIATION

(a) It was very *easy*. Life came simply by a look. So salvation is by the look of faith today.

(b) It may have seemed *improbable*. What connection between it and the wound? So do men speak of the Cross.

(c) It was intended as a *lesson*. They must look to a serpent, the very thing causing pain. So the Cross charges home sin even as it saves.

(d) It was *individual*. Each must look for himself. So the Cross must be individually appropriated.

(e) It brought cure *instantaneously*. No hint of any gradual or delayed cure. So it is with the Cross. It brings immediate pardon and justification.

Chapter xx. 1, and the "Wandering"

The usual idea of Israel's so-called "Wandering" in the wilderness, after the Kadesh breakdown, is that the whole camp, tabernacle and people, moved in futile procession from one place to another in the wilderness, making moves and halts, but no progress toward Canaan. The purpose of our Addendum is to show how wrong that idea is. There were not *two* comings to Kadesh-barnea—one at the beginning of the thirty-eight years of "wandering" and the other at the end. There was only the one coming. The Tabernacle and all connected therewith stayed at Kadesh-barnea throughout the thirty-eight years, while the people spread in roving bands pasturising in the open country.

The first verse of this twentieth chapter is of special importance in its bearing on the Wandering. It claims the more careful consideration because most Bible readers misunderstand it. "*Then came the children of Israel, even the whole congregation, into the desert of Zin in the first month; and the people abode in Kadesh; and Miriam died there, and was buried there.*"

These words seem to teach a second coming to Kadesh toward the end of the Wandering; and on the strength of this it is usually assumed that there were two comings to Kadesh—the first in chapter xiii., when the breakdown occurred, and the second here in chapter xx. 1, —with the thirty-eight years of the Wandering intervening.

Now we reject that assumption for certain good reasons. First, in the summary of Israel's movements given in Numbers xxxiii. only the one coming to Kadesh is recorded, with not a hint of any thirty-eight years of moving around elapsing and then another coming to Kadesh before the going to Mount Hor where Aaron died. Nay, the implication is that they stayed all the while in the vicinity of Kadesh (see xxxiii. 36–8). Similarly, in the review of the journeyings given in Deuteronomy i. and ii., there is but the one coming (see i. 19, 46; ii. 14). If there *was* a second coming it should be recorded between the last verse of Deuteronomy i. and the first verse of chapter ii., for it is quite clear that the compassing of Mount Seir (Edom) in the first verse of the second chapter corresponds with the compassing of Edom in Numbers xx. 14 and xxi. 4, at the *end* of the thirty-eight years. That the first verse of Deuteronomy ii. refers to the end of the thirty-eight years is made clear by verse 7. If, then, there was a second coming to Kadesh, it should appear between the last verse of chapter i. and the first verse of chapter ii. But there is no such hint. Surely it is no mere "argument from silence" to say that had there been such an important second coming to Kadesh, marking the death of Miriam and Aaron, and terminating the Wandering, it would certainly have found a place in both these summaries!

Second, this first verse of Numbers xx. says that Israel came to Kadesh "*in the first month.*" But which first month was this? Those who hold that this was a new and second coming to Kadesh can only connect this first month with the end of the chapter where we are told of Aaron's death. They say that the first month in verse 1 must be the first month of the year that Aaron died. Yet it surely seems strange that this "first month" should be mentioned without any connection to explain it except one which comes later,—all the more so because although Aaron's death is described in this chapter we are not told here what year or month he died,—not until away on in chapter xxxiii. 38! Surely this reference to Israel's having come to Kadesh in the first month is such as to suggest that the writer intends us to connect it with a time-mark which has gone shortly before.

That this is what he *did* intend is made clear by Bishop Ellicott's translation of the Hebrew—"Now the children of Israel *had come* . . . in the first month." The "had come" makes clear that the writer is connecting up this coming to Kadesh with that which is recorded in xiii. and xiv. when the breakdown occurred. Between that Kadesh breakdown and this twentieth chapter he has told us certain things which followed the breakdown, and now he wishes to connect back before telling us of Israel's new advance toward the plain of Moab. This is a procedure which is adopted not only in the Scriptures but in all historical writings.

This first verse of chapter xx., therefore, now becomes clear. The children of Israel had come to Kadesh (as in chapters xiii. and xiv.) in the first month of the third year after the Exodus. We know this because chapter x. 11 tells us they left Sinai in the second month of the *second* year, which gives eleven months between their leaving Sinai and their reaching Kadesh. Is it likely, then, that the journey from Sinai to Kadesh would take eleven months? It is. Deuteronomy i. 2 says: "There are eleven days' journey from Horeb (i.e. Sinai) by the way of Mount Seir unto Kadesh-barnea." Allowing for the travel difficulties arising from the hugeness of the host, with all its equipment, the necessary slowness and haltings because of babes and young children, and cattle, and belongings, beside the normally allotted rest intervals, and incidents which delayed the journeying, such as Miriam's leprosy and exclusion from the camp, when the journeying was suspended seven days,—allowing for all these things, we say, it is reasonable to suppose that the journey would take some eleven months.

That there was just this one coming to Kadesh is well supported, too, by incidental considerations. Our verse says that the people "*abode*" in Kadesh, suggesting a long stay there. The same thing is suggested by Deuteronomy i. 46. We have already shown that between this last verse of Deuteronomy i. and the first verse of chapter ii. there is no hint of a second coming to Kadesh; but now we would point out that what the last verse of chapter i. *does* say is that the people "abode in Kadesh many days." Both these verses indicate that at the one coming to Kadesh and vicinity there was a remaining there.

Again, if we say that our verse (xx. 1) indicates a *second* coming to Kadesh, at the end of the thirty-eight years, what of Miriam's age? The verse says: ". . . the people abode in Kadesh: and Miriam died there, and was buried there." Now Miriam was probably about fifteen years older than Moses (as we judge from Exod. ii. 4), which means that she was about one hundred and thirty-five, if still alive, at the end of the Wandering,—a remarkably greater age than either Moses or Aaron was allowed to reach. Yet our verse gives no hint that she was this great age, though we may reasonably have expected some such notice if she had died at that great age at the end of the Wandering. If, on the other hand, we take our verse as linking back to Israel's one coming to Kadesh, in chapter xiii., and understand that the people thereafter stayed in the Kadesh vicinity, and that Miriam's death occurred sometime *during* that period, then this note of her death, in chapter xx. 1, becomes at once quite normal. As in chapters xv.–xix., the writer is simply picking out things of special note which happened during the thirty-eight years, without concern for their exact chronological location.

Another argument in favour of the foregoing is the weakness of the objections to it. It is objected that if chapter xx. 1 links back with chapter xiii., making just the one coming to Kadesh, then all the twenty-one stopping stations given in chapter xxxiii. 16–36 must have occurred in the one short journey from Sinai to Kadesh, whereas Deuteronomy i. 2 says it was but an eleven-day journey. Going with this, it is also objected that an eleven-day journey would not take Israel eleven months. Now these objections are really confirmations. The distance would be between one hundred and fifty and two hundred miles. Divide this by twenty-one, and what could be more natural than that Israel's halts should have been at intervals of seven to ten miles, as the division indicates? As for the journey's taking eleven months, we have already pointed out the necessary slowness of so great a multitude; and when we add yet further the necessary time taken in dispensing legislation, and that the host moved or stayed simply at the guidance of the pillar, without there being the slightest suggestion that speed was in any way considered important, we see at once that the eleven months is a quite likely time for such a journey.

It is also pointed out that God's command in chapter xiv. 25 is "Tomorrow turn you, and get you into the wilderness by the way of the Red Sea." This, however, does not express a leaving of the Kadesh vicinity, but simply a turning from the danger-spot where enemies were ambushed. Read the whole verse—"Now the Amalekites and the Canaanites dwelt (lit.—are abiding, i.e. are ambushed) in the valley; tomorrow turn you (from there) and get you into the wilderness (nearby Kadesh)."

No more need be said here about this question. We are confident that further enquiry by any interested student will confirm that there was indeed but the one coming to Kadesh, and that this twentieth chapter links back thereto. This twentieth chapter, therefore, is of special importance. It not only groups the death of Miriam, the sin of Moses, and the death of Aaron; its first verse takes us back to the beginning of the Wandering, while its last verse marks the end of it.

TWELVE QUESTIONS ON NUMBERS

1. At what date and in what place does the book of Numbers commence?

2. Wherein lies its importance for ourselves? Answer by reference to the New Testament.

3. What are the structural features of the book of Numbers?

4. Which is the most important time-mark in Numbers and why?

5. How are parts 1 and 3 of the book sub-divided?

6. Why were the whole of the Levite males taken for Jehovah instead of just the firstborn?

7. What were the three families of the Levites, and what were their respective Tabernacle duties?

8. Give a diagram of the distribution of the Camp.

9. Where do we read of the silver trumpets, and what were their uses?

10. What are the main happenings recorded during the years of the Wandering?

11. Where do we read of the brazen serpent, and in what way was it typical?

12. Where do we read of Balaam, and how would you explain his knowledge of the true God?

THE BOOK OF DEUTERONOMY (1)

Lesson Number 17

NOTE.—For this first study in Deuteronomy read the first eleven chapters through twice.

" Human literature requires a lexicon and often a library of reference books to disclose its meaning. For the most part the Word of God is its own dictionary and library of reference. Within its own compass may be found either the direct or indirect definition of its own terms, making the careful student in a large measure independent of outside help, and so enabling even the poor and simple to learn its meaning, and bringing it within universal reach."

A. T. PIERSON, D.D.

THE BOOK OF DEUTERONOMY (1)

AFTER the fiery testing to which the Pentateuch has been subjected by the merciless Biblical criticism of recent years, there can remain little if any doubt that the first five books of our Bible—substantially as we now have them—are from the pen of Moses.

It is equally clear that these writings of Moses fall into the five natural divisions indicated in our Bible under the titles, Genesis, Exodus, Leviticus, Numbers, Deuteronomy. Each of the five is, in a real sense, complete in itself. Each has its distinctive subject, emphasis and message. Yet the five obviously cohere; and together they constitute one of the grand divisions of the Scriptures.

Indeed, as we have pointed out in an earlier study, the ruling messages of these five writings of Moses, when taken together, make the Pentateuch a kind of Bible in miniature. In Genesis we have *ruin* through man's sin; in Exodus *redemption* by "blood" and "power"; in Leviticus *communion* on the ground of atonement; in Numbers *direction* by the guiding will of God; in Deuteronomy *destination* through the faithfulness of God. These five books also give us a progressive revelation of God. In Genesis we see the Divine *sovereignty*, in creation and election; in Exodus the Divine *power*, in redemption and emancipation; in Leviticus the Divine *holiness*, in the insistence on separation and sanctification; in Numbers the Divine *"goodness and severity,"* in judging the old generation and preserving the new; in Deuteronomy the Divine *faithfulness*, in discipline and destination. We see, therefore, that Deuteronomy, the last of the five, which we are now to consider, is not *merely* the last in order, but the natural and beautiful *completion* of the Pentateuch.

The Hebrew name for this fifth writing of Moses was *Haddebharim*, that is, "The Words"—this name being taken from the opening verse of the book: "These be the words which Moses spake unto all Israel on this side Jordan in the wilderness. . . ." This name sufficiently marks off its special character from the more definitely historical and legislative books which have preceded it. The history and legislation of the earlier books are *reviewed* in Deuteronomy, but only as the basis for the words of admonition which are now recorded. In the truest, deepest, and profoundest sense, Deuteronomy is a book of words; for never were wiser or weightier words uttered.

Our own title, "Deuteronomy," is taken from the Greek *deuteros* (second) and *nomos* (law)—the title which the Septuagint translators gave to the book when they translated the Old Testament into Greek, somewhere about the third century B.C. In Deuteronomy we have a second giving of the Law, or, rather, a new expounding of it to the new generation of Israel who had grown up in the wilderness and were needing to have the Law repeated and expounded to them before their entering into Canaan. Deuteronomy is not the giving of a new Law, but an explication of that which was already given.

A Book of Transition

Deuteronomy is a book of *transition*. It marks a transition in a fourfold way. First, it marks the transition to a new *generation*; for with the exception of Caleb and Joshua, and Moses himself, the old generation which came up from Egypt and was numbered at Sinai, had passed away, and a new generation had grown up. Second, it marks the transition to a new *possession*. The wilderness pilgrimage was to give place to the national occupancy of Canaan. Third, it marks the transition to a new *experience*, to a new life—houses instead of tents, settled habitation instead of wandering, and, instead of the wilderness diet, the milk and honey and corn and wine of Canaan. Fourth, it marks the transition to a new *revelation* of God—the revelation of His *love*. From Genesis to Numbers the love of God is never spoken of; but here, in Deuteronomy, we have the wonderful words: "Because He *loved* thy fathers, therefore He chose their seed" (iv. 37); "The Lord did not set His *love* upon you, nor choose you because ye were more in number than any people, for ye were the fewest of all people; but because the Lord *loved* you" (vii. 7–8); "The Lord had a delight in thy fathers to *love* them" (x. 15); "The Lord thy God turned the curse into a blessing unto thee, because the Lord thy God *loved* thee" (xxiii. 5).

While speaking of the transitionary nature of Deuteronomy, it is interesting to mention that just as the Old Testament begins with five historical books—Genesis to Deuteronomy, so the New Testament begins with five historical books—Matthew to Acts; and there is a striking parallel between the Acts of the Apostles, the fifth book of the New Testament, and Deuteronomy, the fifth book of the Old. The Acts, like Deuteronomy, marks a great transition. It marks the transition from the distinctive message of the "Gospels" to that of the epistles. Like Deuteronomy, it marks the transition to a new *generation*—a *re*-generation in Christ. Like Deuteronomy, it marks the transition to a new *possession*—a *spiritual* Canaan with "all blessings in the heavenlies, in Christ." Like Deuteronomy, it marks the transition to a new *experience*—a new birth, a new life, a new dynamic, in the Holy Spirit. Like Deuteronomy, it marks the transition to a new *revelation* of God—the revelation given in the Church epistles of "the mystery which from the beginning of the world hath been hid in God," namely, the *Church*; so that now "there might be known, by the *Church*, the manifold wisdom of God" (Eph. iii. 10).

But what is equally striking is that both Deuteronomy, the fifth book of the one group, and Acts, the fifth book of the other group, are books in which God gives His people a *second chance*. What is Deuteronomy? It is *deuteros nomos*, the second giving of the Law. Before the new generation is committed to Joshua's charge, Moses, at God's command, rehearses the Law to them. What is the book of the Acts? It is the second offer of the Kingdom of Heaven to the Jews, first at the capital, to the Jews of the homeland, and then through the empire, to the Jews of the dispersion. Of this we shall say more later; but it is well to have it in mind even now.

Its Structure

The structure of Deuteronomy is simple, clear, and impressive. The first eleven chapters are all *retro*spective. The remaining chapters are all *pro*spective. In view of the transition now upon them, the people are to look backward and then forward, and to ponder both, as in the sight of God. They are to *recall*, and to *reflect*, and to *resolve*. Thus, in the first part (i.–xi.), which looks backward, we have *retrospection and reflection*; and in the second part (xii.–xxxiv.), we have *anticipation and admonition*.

Of course, in the retrospective part of the book (i.–xi.), there are passing references to the future, and in the prospective part (xii.–xxxiv.) there are references to the past; but no careful reading is required to see that in both parts such references are merely incidental to the main course of the lawgiver's dissertation. We may therefore now set forth the broad outline of Deuteronomy. It is as follows:

THE BOOK OF DEUTERONOMY

THE DIVINE FAITHFULNESS

I. LOOKING BACKWARD (i.–xi.).

REVIEW OF THE WAY SINCE SINAI (i.–iii.).
REVIEW OF THE LAW FROM SINAI (iv.–xi.).

II. LOOKING FORWARD (xii.–xxxiv.).

FINAL RULES AND WARNINGS TO ISRAEL, *before entering the earthly inheritance (xii.–xxx.).*
FINAL WORDS AND ACTIONS OF MOSES, *before entering the heavenly inheritance (xxxi.–xxxiv.).*

The Central Message

The central message of Deuteronomy, as we have already intimated, is *the Divine faithfulness.* In both parts of the book this is brought out—in God's gracious, wise, and righteous dealings with the nation in the past, and in His renewed pledges to the nation concerning the future. Despite the heart-rending perversities of Israel in the past, Jehovah has been, and ever will be, faithful to His promises, His purposes, and His people.

This is the central message of Deuteronomy: and what a source of comfort it is to us in days like our own, when things sometimes seem to have run completely out of control!

> God is still on the throne;
> And He will take care of His Own.
> His promise is true;
> He will see us right through;
> God is still on the throne.

We can never read Deuteronomy without thinking of Paul's words in I Corinthians i. 8–9. "God is *faithful*, by whom ye were called into the fellowship of His Son Jesus Christ our Lord: who shall also confirm you unto the end, that ye may be blameless in the day of our Lord Jesus Christ."

THE BASIC THINGS OF DEUTERONOMY

Deuteronomy being practically throughout a *discourse*, it is quite out of question for us here to think of going through it chapter by chapter, even in the brief way in which we have done so with Exodus, Leviticus and Numbers. Nor, however, is this needful to our present purpose; for as we stated at the outset, what we are specially concerned with in this present course of study is the getting hold of the broad outlines and principal significances of things. As for Deuteronomy, we shall best get the gist and drive of the book by picking out and clearly noting the several *basic* pronouncements in it, upon which all the other teachings are built.

(1) The Basic Fact

The basic *fact* beneath all else (and with which goes the basic command of the Law), is that which is declared in chapter vi. 4, 5—

"HEAR, O ISRAEL: THE LORD OUR GOD IS ONE LORD; AND THOU SHALT LOVE THE LORD THY GOD WITH ALL THINE HEART, AND WITH ALL THY SOUL, AND WITH ALL THY MIGHT."

Our Lord Jesus Himself has told us that this is the foundational pronouncement and "first commandment" of the Law (Mark xii. 29, 30).

It is well to be precise about the wording of this bedrock statement, since Unitarians have seized upon it as their prime argument against the orthodox doctrine that God is triune. "There now," they say, "nothing could be plainer: God is a unity, not a plurality; He is one, not three; for Deuteronomy vi. 4 says: 'Hear, O Israel: the Lord our God is *one* Lord.'"

Alas, for their argument, a closer examination of this verse shows that, far from supporting them, it actually refutes what they say it teaches; for the Hebrew original here is nothing short of a solemn declaration that Jehovah is a plurality in unity. The word translated "our God" is *elohenu,* which is the plural *elohim* (gods), with the first personal possessive plural suffix appended to it, causing it to become *elohenu,* that is, "our gods." This, then, is what the great publication to Israel says: *"Hear, O Israel: Jehovah our Gods, Jehovah is one."*

But to make the matter clearer still, the Hebrew word translated as "one" (*echad*) is a word which, strictly taken, expresses "one" in the *collective* sense. That is, it signifies, not an absolute unity, but a *compound* unity, such as is indicated in the expression "one cluster of grapes." The Hebrew word for "one" in the sense of *absolute* unity is the word *yacheed;* and this word is never used to express the unity of the Godhead. May it not also have a significance that in this solemn and basic declaration of Deuteronomy vi. 4, 5, the name Jehovah occurs just the three times? Certainly the declaration clearly conveys that God is a plurality in unity; and it possibly suggests the Divine triunity in the threefold occurrence of the name Jehovah.

This was the basic fact of Divine revelation to Israel; and this was to be the first article of Israel's religion. This is also the basic fact on which Christianity is built, even the solitariness and triunity of God. Israel's God is *our* God: there is no other. Israel's Messiah is *our* Saviour: there is no other. Christianity is Monotheistic and Christocentric.

Here, then, we have an affirmation not so much of the moneity as of the unity and simplicity of Jehovah, Israel's God, the one true God; and this affirmation of the unity of God is equally opposed to Unitarianism, Polytheism, and Pantheism. Israel's God, the alone true God, is one, indivisible, and incommunicable, the absolute and infinite One, on whom all depend, whom all must ultimately obey, and who alone is the true Object of the creature's worship. To Jehovah, therefore, Israel's undivided devotion and love are due; so that the natural accompaniment of the basic affirmation is the "first and greatest commandment"— *"Thou shalt love the Lord thy God with all thine heart, and with all thy soul, and with all thy might."* Oh that Israel had hearkened!— for then would her peace have been as a river, and her prosperity as the immovable mountains. Oh that we ourselves, God's people by a dearer covenant than that in Abraham, may truly love this glorious and gracious God with all *our* heart and mind and soul and strength!

THE BOOK OF DEUTERONOMY (2)

Lesson Number 18

"*He brought us out from thence, that He might bring us in, to give us the land which He sware unto our fathers*"—Deuteronomy vi. 23.

He brought them out!
He brought them out!
Well now may Israel sing and shout!
  Their enemies, God came to view them;
  Their enemies, God overthrew them;
  They said: "Arise, let us pursue them";
  Jehovah came; He drowned and slew them;
But Israel, He brought them out!

He brought *me* out!
He brought *me* out!
Well may my own heart sing and shout!
  From out of deepest condemnation;
  From Conscience's grim accusation;
  From inbred, Godward alienation;
  From sin, with all its implication;
Oh, praise His grace, He brought *me* out!

THE BOOK OF DEUTERONOMY (2)

(2) The Basic Truth

THE BASIC *truth* laid down in Deuteronomy is that which is expressed in chapter vi. 23—

"AND HE BROUGHT US OUT FROM THENCE, THAT HE MIGHT BRING US IN, TO GIVE US THE LAND WHICH HE SWARE UNTO OUR FATHERS."

Here is a threefold statement of truth. First, here is a *fact*—"He brought us out." Second, here is the *purpose* behind the fact—"that He might bring us in." Third, here is the *reason* behind both the fact and the purpose—"He sware unto our fathers." As for the fact—"He brought us out," we see here the *power* of God; for He brought them out with "a mighty hand." As for the purpose—"that He might bring us in," we see here the *grace* of God; for it was to bring them into a land "flowing with milk and honey." As for the reason—"He sware unto our fathers," we see here the *faithfulness* of God: He was true to His covenant.

This threefold statement is both basic and summary. It is the whole story in one sentence. What wealth of meaning did the words hold for Israel! "He brought us out from thence." No more the crack of the slave-driver's whip! No more the cruel threat of the heartless task-master! No more the blinding dust and sickening heat of the overworked brick kilns! No more the grovelling on hands and knees after straw for the tale of bricks demanded by the royal monster! No more the rigorous servitude, the iron heel, the bitter bondage, the downtrodden condition, and the shame of Egypt! It was gone! Israel was "brought out," with "not a hoof left behind"!

Yet the words assume a still greater significance when applied to Christian believers. From what an Egypt has God delivered *us*, in Christ! He has brought us out from the *condemnation* of sin; for "there is therefore now no condemnation to them which are in Christ Jesus" (Rom. viii. 1). He has delivered us from the *bondage* of sin; for "the law of the Spirit of life in Christ Jesus hath made me free from the law of sin and death" (Rom. viii. 2). And what more shall we say? He has saved us from the accusations of our awakened consciences, from Godward alienation of heart, from spiritual darkness and death, from paralysing fear of the future. In a word, God has provided for us, in Christ, a full salvation from *sin*. "He brought us out from thence."

But "He brought us out from thence *that He might bring us in*." Besides an Egypt left behind there is a Canaan on before, with its vines and fig trees, its grapes and pomegranates, its hills and streams, its olives and cedars, its milk and honey and corn and wine—a fertile, fragrant, fruitful, sun-bathed Canaan! And can we think of the earthly Canaan without thinking of the *spiritual* Canaan which is ours in Christ? In the type-teaching of Scripture, Canaan stands not so much for heaven (as many of our hymns would imply), but for an experience of holiness and spiritual fulness realisable by Christians here and now, in this present life. We think of passages and promises, like 1 Thessalonians v. 23; Galatians ii. 20; Ephesians i. 4; iii. 19; iv. 23; v. 18; John iv. 18; Colossians i. 9–11; and a score of other, similar glorious expressions of the New Testament ideal for the Christian life. The tragedy is that most of the Lord's spiritual Israel live far below their redemption rights and revealed privileges. We do not possess our possessions. We live in the wilderness when we might be enjoying the Canaan of "all spiritual blessings in heavenly places in Christ" (Eph. i. 3).

"*He sware unto our fathers*"—here we are at the heart of things. God never goes back on His word. Despite wilderness rebellings and Kadesh breakdown, God remains true to His gracious covenant. "If we believe not, yet He abideth faithful: He cannot deny Himself" (2 Tim. ii. 13). Let us gather the honey from this flower as we pass. Is the Canaan to which God calls us, in Christ, the seemingly impossible one set forth in 1 Thessalonians v. 23—"The very God of peace sanctify you wholly; and your whole spirit and soul and body be preserved blameless unto the coming of our Lord Jesus Christ"? Entire sanctification—does it seem too much to "go up at once and possess" this land? Then read the next verse—"*Faithful* is He that calleth you, who also will do it"! What we cannot attain by self-effort we may *obtain* in Christ.

(3) The Basic Requirement

The basic requirement which God makes of Israel, in Deuteronomy, is that which is found in chapter x. 12, 13:

"AND NOW, ISRAEL, WHAT DOTH THE LORD THY GOD REQUIRE OF THEE, BUT TO FEAR THE LORD THY GOD, TO WALK IN ALL HIS WAYS, AND TO LOVE HIM, AND TO SERVE THE LORD THY GOD WITH ALL THY HEART AND WITH ALL THY SOUL; TO KEEP THE COMMANDMENTS OF THE LORD, AND HIS STATUTES, WHICH I COMMAND THEE THIS DAY FOR THY GOOD."

"And now, Israel . . ." Those two little words, "and now," really gather up into a focal expression the significance of Deuteronomy. This is distinguishingly the "and now" book. The people have reviewed the faithfulness of God, in His wonderful dealings with Israel right down from the time when He entered into covenant with Abraham. They have seen how He watched over Israel during the predicted bondage in Egypt, how He brought them out with "great signs and wonders," how He constituted them an elect nation at Sinai, guarded and guided them to the borders of Canaan, suffered their many murmurings and their rebellion at Kadesh, protected, provided, preserved them through the thirty-eight years delay, bringing them again, at length, to the gateway of the promised inheritance—they have reviewed all this, *"AND NOW"* . . . what about it? What is it that is required of them as they now enter the promised Canaan? Simply this—"*to fear the Lord thy God, to walk in all His ways, and to love Him, and to serve the Lord thy God with all thy heart and with all thy soul.*"

This is the basic requirement, the obligation which comprehends all others—obedience, *loving* obedience, flowing from the grateful consciousness of covenant relationship and fellowship with this glorious and faithful God. "Obedience is the key-note of almost every chapter." It has been pointed out that the word "do" occurs over fifty times. This is the outstanding lesson of the book; and a careful examination shows that the obedience which is required has a threefold reason behind it. Jehovah it to be obeyed because of (1) what He has done for them; (2) what He is in Himself; (3) the perfection of His Law (iv. 7, 8, etc.).

This, we say, is the basic requirement found here: and is anything less required of ourselves today? Nay, because of our exalted privileges in Christ, privileges which the earthly Israel never knew, we are the more under obligation to obey, in the spirit of love and godly fear. Hear what our Lord Himself says —"He that hath My commandments, and keepeth them, he it is that loveth Me." "If a man love Me, he will keep My words" (John xiv. 21–3). May it ever be to us our supreme delight to hear His dictates, and obey!

(4) The Basic Pledge

It is important to understand that Israel entered Canaan under the conditions set forth in the Sinai covenant, the precepts, terms, and issues of which are rehearsed to the new generation of Israel in this book of Deuteronomy. The privileges and corresponding responsibilities of the Sinai covenant were such that the most solemn sanctions were attached to it and the most serious penalties were contingent upon Israel's violation of it through disobedience. We have already seen these penalties warningly set before Israel, in Leviticus xxvi., at the end of the *first* declaration of the covenant law, to the old generation, at Sinai. We now have these penalties set forth again before Israel, in Deuteronomy xxviii., at the end of the *second* declaration of the covenant law, to the new generation, at Moab. The extreme penalty threatened, both in Leviticus xxvi. and Deuteronomy xxviii., is the dispersion of Israel and the desolation of Canaan (see Lev. xxvi. 32, 33; Deut. xxviii. 63–8); and we know, alas, that Israel *did* foul the covenant, that the threatened penalties have been effected, that both the dispersion of the people and the desolation of the land have ensued. All this was pre-envisaged in the Sinai Covenant.

But the thing to grasp here is this, that the Sinai covenant is not the last word between God and Israel: it is not the end of God's dealings in covenant relationship with His chosen people. No; there is another covenant relationship between God and Israel which *stands outside* and goes *beyond* the Sinai covenant, a covenant to the force of which there is no end: that is the *Abrahamic* covenant. Nothing can destroy *this* covenant between God and Israel, which was not only sealed with blood, but confirmed with a Divine oath. No, not even can Israel's unfaithfulness nullify it! It is an unconditional and everlasting covenant to Abraham and his posterity.

Now Israel has never yet possessed Canaan under the unconditional *Abrahamic* covenant. As we have said, the nation entered Canaan under the terms of the *Sinai* covenant; and we know the result. Nor has Israel ever possessed the *whole* land as it was given to Abraham (see Gen. xv. 18), but only the portion assigned in connection with the Mosaic covenant (see Num. xxxiv. 1–12).

What we wish to stress here, however, is that the Abrahamic covenant lies *behind*, and stands *outside*, and goes *beyond* the Sinai or Mosaic covenant; and this is why, despite Israel's failure, God's covenant relationship with Israel continues. It is highly significant that in each case where the extreme penalty for violating the Sinai covenant is mentioned, namely, the dispersion of Israel and the desolation of Canaan, there is an immediate follow-up reference to the *Abrahamic* covenant, showing that even when the Sinai covenant has exhausted itself in its final penal infliction on Israel, God can (and will) still be gracious to Israel on the ground of the earlier and greater Abrahamic covenant. Take Leviticus xxvi. 33, etc.—

> "*And I will scatter you among the heathen, and will draw out a sword after you; and your land shall be desolate, and your cities waste. . . . Then . . . MY COVENANT WITH ABRAHAM WILL I REMEMBER; and I will remember the land.*"

Take Deuteronomy iv. 27–31—

> "*And the Lord shall scatter you among the nations, and ye shall be left few in number among the heathen, whither the Lord shall lead you. . . . When thou art in tribulation and all these things are come upon thee, even in the latter days, if thou turn to the Lord thy God, and shalt be obedient unto His voice (for the Lord thy God is a merciful God), He will not forsake thee, neither destroy thee, nor forget THE COVENANT OF THY FATHERS WHICH HE SWARE UNTO THEM.*"

And when we come right to the end of the Deuteronomy

reiteration of the Sinai covenant, the very last words of all are (xxx. 20)—

"That thou mayest dwell in the land which THE LORD SWARE UNTO THY FATHERS, TO ABRAHAM, TO ISAAC, AND TO JACOB, TO GIVE THEM."

Nothing can nullify the Abrahamic covenant; for Jehovah Himself accepts responsibility for the fulfilment of the whole. He undertakes for the people's part of the covenant as well as His own; for here in Deuteronomy xxx. 6, in connection with the regathering of Israel yet to be, we read: *"And the Lord thy God will circumcise thine heart, and the heart of thy seed, to love the Lord thy God with all thine heart and with all thy soul, that thou mayest live."* God Himself will do for them and in them, by His Spirit, what they themselves have pitifully failed to do under the Sinaitic covenant! It is on the ground of this Abrahamic covenant that Jeremiah looks on to the glorious time of Israel's regeneration, and sings:

"Behold, the days come, saith the Lord, that I will make a new covenant with the house of Israel, and with the house of Judah:

"Not according to the covenant that I made with their fathers in the day that I took them by the hand to bring them out of the land of Egypt; which my covenant they brake, although I was an husband unto them, saith the Lord:

"But this shall be the covenant that I will make with the house of Israel; After those days, saith the Lord, I will put my law in their inward parts, and write it in their hearts; and will be their God, and they shall be my people.

"And they shall teach no more every man his neighbour, and every man his brother, saying, Know the Lord; for they shall all know me, from the least of them unto the greatest of them, saith the Lord: for I will forgive their iniquity, and I will remember their sin no more." (Jer. xxxi. 31–4.)

It is on the basis of the Abrahamic covenant, we repeat, that such prospects are held in view; and it is in connection with this basic Abrahamic pledge that we have the crowning demonstration of the Divine faithfulness to Israel.

The so-called "Palestinian" Covenant.

We have said that Israel entered Canaan under the conditions of the *Sinai* covenant. Perhaps while we are speaking of this we ought to mention that there are certain Bible expositors who hold that in Deuteronomy xxix. and xxx. *another* covenant is set forth which is additional to the Sinai covenant, and that it was under *this* covenant that Israel entered Canaan. The Scofield Bible teaches this, and calls the supposed extra covenant the "Palestinian" covenant. We refer our student to the Scofield footnote going with chapter xxx. In our own judgment, to see in these chapters a new and different covenant is to see what is not there. Why should it be thought that we here have a further covenant, different from that at Sinai?

The argument seems to be that the *wording* of chapter xxix. indicates this. The chapter begins thus: "These are the words of the covenant which the Lord commanded Moses to make with the children of Israel *in the land of Moab, beside the covenant which He made with them at Horeb* (i.e., *Sinai*)." Then again in verse 12—"That thou shouldest *enter into* covenant with the Lord thy God, and into His oath, which the Lord thy God *maketh with thee this day.*" See also verses 9 and 14. To our own mind the objections to this are conclusive. When the covenant was made at Sinai, the covenant *sacrifices* were offered, and the people were *sprinkled* with the blood whereby the covenant was ratified; but here, in Deuteronomy xxix. and xxx., no such sacrifices or sprinkling mark off the new contract as a separate covenant. (If it be said that an altar is mentioned in chapter xxvii. 5, etc., then a mere glance at the context will show that this altar had to do with "all the words of this law" in the *Sinai* covenant: and if it be claimed that in xxix. 1, where it says, God commanded Moses to "*make*" the covenant, the Hebrew word is *lichroth*, meaning literally "to cut," and alluding to the cutting or dividing of covenant *sacrifices*, then the only possible connection is with the altar in chapter xxvii. 5, etc., which, as we have shown, has to do with the *Sinai* covenant.)

But the thing that most really reveals the artificiality of finding a separate covenant in Deuteronomy xxix. and xxx., is that even those who profess to find it cannot find anything in it but what is already included in the Sinai covenant. Scofield, in his footnote, says: "The Palestinian Covenant is in seven parts," and then lists the seven; but when we examine the seven we find that they are none other than the things contained in the *Sinai* covenant, in such passages as Leviticus xxvi.!

As for the wording in chapter xxix., which speaks of the contract here made as a covenant "*beside* the covenant which He made with them at Horeb," and speaks of the people as *then* "entering into covenant" with God, the simple answer is that God is now renewing the Sinai covenant with *the new generation* of Israel, consisting of those who were either unborn or under eighteen at the time of the Exodus. The old generation have now perished in the wilderness, through their own sin; yet the covenant with the nation, as such, holds good; and the new generation, having heard the Sinai covenant rehearsed, through the chapters of Deuteronomy, are now for themselves to "enter into" the covenant. In this sense, also (and *only* in this sense), the further contract was "*beside* the covenant which He (God) made with them (the children of Israel) at Horeb." It was a new covenant only in the sense that it was the same covenant now made with the new generation.

Moreover, God's covenant with the nation is mentioned again and again in the chapters of Deuteronomy, both before and after chapters xxix. and xxx., and the reference throughout is to the Sinai covenant. Why then try to find a different covenant inserted here, in chapters xxix. and xxx. which is never once mentioned elsewhere, either in Deuteronomy or in the rest of Scripture? It was under the *Sinai* covenant that Israel entered Canaan. Alas, the tragic story which followed we know well enough! Yet behind and beyond the Sinai covenant is the covenant with Israel through Abraham which is yet going to bear fruition in glorious consummations for God's long-scattered people.

The signs are now present in the earth that this consummation is near. After an interval of over 2,000 years Israel is once again an independent state. There is no king; and Israel will not be a *kingdom* until Christ returns; but Israel is once again an independent *state*, which fact, plus other present-day happenings, is indeed a significant sign.

THE BOOK OF DEUTERONOMY (3)

Lesson Number 19

NOTE.—For this final study in Deuteronomy read chapter xii., and then chapters xxvii. to the end.

" All our hopes for eternity, the very foundation of our faith, our nearest and dearest consolations, are taken from us, *if one line of that Sacred Book be declared unfaithful or untrustworthy.*"

—From a united protest by the Archbishops and Bishops of the Church of England, made to Bishop Colenso in 1863.

(5) Basic Differences

WE HAVE been considering the basic facts and truths enunciated through the lips of Moses in this venerable Book of Deuteronomy. We do well to ponder them most carefully, and to fix them thoroughly in our memory. Would that the people of Israel had meditated day and night in the solemn yet gracious counsels of this book! Would that they had never turned their backs upon these wise and weighty words; for then would their peace have been as a river, and their prosperity as continuing as the hills. And, as we have seen, these parting counsels of Moses speak a living message to ourselves today. It is the same God with whom we have to do today. It is *He* who has brought *us* out from Satanic bondage, that He might bring us into a wonderful inheritance in Christ. He asks no less of us today than He asked of Israel through the lips of Moses long ago, in this Book of Deuteronomy, namely, that we should love Him with all our heart and soul, and walk "in all His ways." God give us hearing ears and responsive hearts!

But now, with this Book of Deuteronomy still before us, we ought to note certain *basic differences* which it emphasises, between the old dispensation and the new, between the Old Testament and the New Testament.

Place versus Person.

One of the great differences between the Old Testament and the New is that in the one the emphasis is upon a *place*, whereas in the other all the emphasis is upon a *Person*. Under the old dispensation there was one special place of sacrifice, of worship, of the Divine presence. For instance, we read in Deuteronomy xii. 10–14:

"When ye go over Jordan, and dwell in the land which the Lord your God giveth you to inherit . . . there shall be a place which the Lord your God shall choose to cause His name to dwell there. Thither shall ye bring all that I command you, your burnt-offerings and your sacrifices, your tithes, and the heave-offerings of your hand, and all your choice vows which ye vow unto the Lord. Take heed to thyself that thou offer not thy burnt-offerings in every place that thou seest; but in the place which the Lord shall choose in one of thy tribes, there shalt thou offer thy burnt-offerings, and there shalt thou do all that I command thee."

This emphasis on a place gave focus to the religious life of the nation of Israel; it fostered the sense of national unity; it was suited to the nature of the old dispensation; and, without doubt, it took a deep hold on the thought of the people. To the old-time Hebrew, nearness to Jerusalem and to the Temple came to mean nearness to the special presence of God. The Gentiles, living in the lands beyond, were the "far off ones." It is this thought which lies behind such verses as Isaiah xlix. 1; lvii. 19; Acts ii. 39; and Ephesians ii. 17.

In the New Testament, this localisation of the Divine presence and of worship is gently but completely superseded. The emphasis is transferred from a *place* to a *Person*. It is no longer a material temple and a locality, but a spiritual Presence having the attribute of universality. This transference of emphasis may be seen in our Lord's dealing with the Samaritan woman at the well of Sychar. The woman said to Him: "Our fathers worshipped in this mountain, and ye say that in Jerusalem is the place where men ought to worship." The Lord said: "Woman, believe Me, the hour cometh when ye shall *neither in this mountain nor yet at Jerusalem* worship the Father: but the hour cometh, *and now is*, when the true worshippers shall worship the Father in spirit and in truth, for the Father seeketh such to worship Him. God is a Spirit, and they that worship Him must worship Him in spirit and in truth." Then the woman said: "I know that Messias cometh, which is called Christ: when He is come He will tell us all things." The woman herself thus looked off from place to Person; and her words evoked the wonder-inspiring reply, "I that speak unto thee am He." The Greek, literally translated, is: "*I AM who am speaking to thee.*" It is no longer God in a temple merely, but in the Person of the Lord Jesus Christ.

The same transition from place to Person is seen in Acts viii., in the account of the Ethiopian eunuch. The man had been to the right *place*—"Jerusalem." He had been for the right *purpose*—"worship." He was reading the right *book*—"the Scripture" (verses 27 and 32); but he was "returning" unsatisfied. He needed the new emphasis—on the *Person.* God sent Philip for this very purpose. "Then Philip opened his mouth, and began at the same scripture, and preached unto him *JESUS.*" The Ethiopian learned the secret of salvation and satisfaction that day, and "went on his way rejoicing."

The last utterance of our Lord before His ascension is a finally renewed emphasis on this change from place to Person: "Lo, I am with you alway, even unto the end of the age." The emphasis here upon the Person is *the strongest possible.* There are two words used in the Greek, the one emphasising the "I" the other emphasising the "am." Taken together, what do they involve? It is the God-Man speaking. "*I AM*"—with you. See here His Divine *omnipresence*—He is with us always and everywhere. See here His Divine *omnipotence*—"all power, in heaven and on earth." See here His Divine *omniscience*—seeing the end from the beginning, and speaking of the "consummation of the age." It is *He* who is with us through all the days. What a Saviour! What a glorious Presence! The omnipresent Christ is with each of His blood-bought people. He delights to be with the poorest and humblest of us; and He will never leave us or forsake us, for He is with us "to the end."

Note the striking order of the words. Literally, it is "I with you *AM*." The "with you" is sandwiched in between the "I" and the "*AM.*" Our Jehovah-Jesus is not only "with" us, He is *all round us*, to protect, preserve, provide, by His mighty, tender, personal presence! How safe are we in His blest keeping!

(6) Basic Choices

In our study of Leviticus we saw that the first giving of the Law wound up with a solemn warning of the punishments which would follow Israel's infidelity to the Covenant (see Lev. xxvi.). The same kind of ending marks the second giving of the Law in Deuteronomy. A glance back at our broad outline of Deuteronomy will remind us that the second of the two main parts (xii.–xxxiv.)

is itself in two parts. In chapters xii. to xxx. we have the main rehearsing of the Law, while in the remaining chapters (xxxi.–xxxiv.) we have, in a more personal sense, the last words and acts of Moses before his passing from the earthly scene. Now this second giving of the Law, running through chapters xii. to xxx., winds up, in chapters xxvii. to xxx., with renewed and most solemn warnings regarding the alternatives before the nation. The nation is called upon to make basic choices.

Chapter xxvii., the first of these four chapters, claims special note here, however, because it exposes in a striking way the true (and tragic) ministry of the Law. It was a ministration of condemnation and death (2 Cor. iii. 7, 9). The Law, although in itself holy, can only administer a curse upon such as Adam's fallen sons, if they are placed under it, because of the perversity of their nature. See how this is shown in Deuteronomy xxvii.

After his long and moving rehearsal of the Law and the Covenant, Moses tells Israel that when they cross Jordan and enter Canaan they are to set up "great stones" inscribed with the words of the Law (verses 2, 3, 8). These stones were to be erected on Mount Ebal (verse 4). Then Israel is to proclaim (as already commanded in xi. 29) the blessing and the curse of the Law. For this purpose six of the tribes are to station themselves on Mount Gerizim, and six on Mount Ebal. The six on Mount Gerizim are to proclaim the blessings of the Law: the six on Mount Ebal the curse.

Now two things are at once noticeable. First, on Mount Gerizim, the mount of blessing, no stones with the Law written on them are to be erected. Why? The mount could not have been the mount of blessing had the Law spoken from it; for the Law is an ethic without a dynamic, a precept without power, an outward rule without an inward renewal; and it can therefore only pronounce a curse upon such as Adam's sons, who are now, by nature, sinful.

Second, although blessings were to be proclaimed from Mount Gerizim, where are they? The chapter gives no record of any such proclamation. Twelve times the curse is solemnly uttered from Ebal (verses 15–26), yet not a word of blessing from Gerizim. How strikingly this again preaches the inability of a law system to confer blessing on such as ourselves! Well says Paul: "For as many as are of the works of the law are under the curse; for it is written: Cursed is every one that continueth not in all things which are written in the book of the law to do them."

There is a mercifully relieving feature, however, about this twenty-seventh chapter of Deuteronomy. Look again at Mount Ebal. Not only are there the great memorial stones of the Law erected on it; there is also *an altar*. See verses 5 to 7—"And there shalt thou build an altar unto the Lord thy God, an altar of stones: thou shalt not lift up any iron tool upon them. Thou shalt build the altar of the Lord thy God of whole stones; and thou shalt offer burnt-offerings thereon unto the Lord thy God: and thou shalt offer peace-offerings, and shalt eat there, and rejoice before the Lord thy God." There can be no rejoicing in the curse of the Law; but we may well rejoice at the altar which sets us free from the curse! That altar speaks of Calvary. "Christ hath redeemed us from the curse of the law, being made a curse for us" (Gal. iii. 13). As the Law testified to sin, so the sacrifices on that Mount Ebal altar testified to grace—to the provision of mercy, which lay within the Covenant, for the covering of guilt. Without this provision of grace Israel's position under the Law would obviously have been a mockery. When Israel later fouled the Covenant, she not only disobeyed the writing on Ebal's memorial pillars, she forsook the Lord's altar also, and offered to strange gods. Moreover, the approach to the Lord's own altar was often insincere or unintelligent, as the Lord Himself testifies against Israel through His prophets. Yet that altar spoke with comforting eloquence of grace to cover man's failure, if only faith and sincerity came thither. The peace-offerings and burnt-offerings speak of peace made for us with God, through Christ, and of God's perfect delight in the sacrifice of His Son, whereby we become fully accepted with Him. Oh, well may we "rejoice before the Lord our God" at that altar! The old dispensation pronounces curse, yet is made to point to the new dispensation in Christ, which administers blessing. Under the old—curse. Under the new—blessing. Thank God, the old has given place to the new!

Free from the Law, oh, happy condition!
Jesus hath bled, and there is remission!
Cursed by the Law, and bruised by the Fall,
Grace hath redeemed us, once for all!

Moses

We must not leave this parting book of the Pentateuch without taking a steady look of admiration at Moses himself. In these sunset chapters of Deuteronomy his noble character expresses itself with the richness and fulness of a maturity reached through the bearing of heavy burdens, the weathering of trying experiences, the discipline of big responsibilities, the disillusionment which comes with increasing knowledge of the human heart, and most of all by a broadening understanding of the profound majesty and patience of God. There is a ripeness, tenderness, mellowness, and a godly sagacity about Moses' deliverances in Deuteronomy which make this book—to quote G. H. C. Macgregor—"in many ways the most intensely interesting and impressive of the Pentateuch."

We cull an anonymous quotation from an article by the late Joseph W. Kemp—"Moses never appears quite so fine, noble, and practical as in Deuteronomy. His personal history comes out in great prominence, and with a solid grandeur, a calm earnestness, and affectionate persuasiveness, and unflinching fidelity to truth, a singleness of aim and unselfishness of purpose, which command the most reverent attention, bespeak the most intense sympathy, and endorse to the fullest extent the statement of Divine inspiration: 'There arose not a prophet since in Israel like unto Moses, whom the Lord knew face to face.'"

As a character-study Moses has few peers. He is one of the greatest figures in the Bible, and in all history. His life falls into three clearly marked periods of forty years each. During the first forty years he is the prince in Egypt; during the second forty the shepherd in Midian; during the final forty the leader of Israel. The time-marks indicating these three forties are Exodus ii. 11 with Acts vii. 23; Exodus vii. 7 with Acts vii. 29, 30; and Deuteronomy xxxi. 2.

Moses is an outstanding type of Christ; and the points of analogy should be traced: but what we would stress here is that quite apart from type interests Moses is a richly rewarding biographical study. Here, in Deuteronomy, is the completing of the picture; and here, in these last four chapters of Deuteronomy, we have the final words and acts of this great man, and the yielding up of his life, on Mount Nebo. The four chapters fall thus—

xxxi. The *charge* of Moses to Joshua and Levites;
xxxii. The *song* of Moses about God and Israel;
xxxiii. The *blessing* of Moses upon the tribes;
xxxiv. The *death* of Moses on Mount Nebo.

Here, then, we must leave Moses; and we cannot do so with a worthier tribute than that of the late Dr. John Kitto. "As the mind tries to rest upon the prominent points of the character which his career evinces, we find ourselves unexpectedly baffled. All the great men of sacred, as well as of profane history, possessed some prominent virtue or quality, which stood out in bolder relief than their other excellences. We think of the faith of Abraham, of the conscientiousness of Joseph, of the contrition of David, of the generosity of Jonathan, of the zeal of Elijah— but what do we regard as the dominant quality of Moses? It is not to be found. The mind is perplexed in the attempt to fix on any. It is not firmness, it is not perseverance, it is not dis- interestedness, it is not patriotism, it is not confidence in God, it is not meekness, it is not humility, it is not forgetfulness of self, that forms his distinguishing characteristic. It is not any *one* of these. It is *all* of them. His virtues, his graces, were all equal to each other; and it was their beautifully harmonious operation and development which constituted his noble and all but perfect character. This was the greatness of Moses—this was the glory of his character. It is a kind of character rare in any man—and in no man historically known has it been so completely manifested. When we reflect that Moses possessed all the learning of his age, and that he wanted none of the talents which con- stituted human greatness, we honour his humility more than his glory; and, above all, we venerate that Divine wisdom which raised up this extraordinary man, and called him forth at the moment when the world had need of him."

Moses was 120 years when he died (xxxiv. 7). He is the only man whom God himself buried. God laid His servant's body to rest in "a valley in the land of Moab," but "no man knoweth" the grave (6). The body was not left there long, however, for despite a contention of Satan (Jude 9), it was raised and glorified; and Moses reappeared in it on the Mount of Transfiguration (Luke ix. 30, 31).

CAN YOU ANSWER THESE?

1. How does Deuteronomy get its name?

2. How does Deuteronomy mark a transition?

3. What book in the New Testament parallels with Deuteronomy, and how?

4. Give the broad outline of Deuteronomy.

5. What is the basic fact and command in this book?

6. What is the basic requirement made of Israel in the book?

7. Since Israel broke the Sinai Covenant, on what basis does God continue special relationship with Israel?

8. Mention two basic differences between the old dispensation and the new.

9. What four final things of Moses do we get in the last four chapters of Deuteronomy?

10. Can you give the three verses in Deuteronomy which our Lord quoted when tempted of Satan?

THE BOOK OF JOSHUA (I)

Lesson Number 20

NOTE.—For this first study in the book of Joshua read the book right through.

"He who has once got fairly into the Scriptures can never leave them The book holds you as a magnet holds a needle, or as a flower holds a bee. If you want great thoughts, read your Bible. If you want something simple, read your Bible. If you want the deepest and highest truth that ever was, read your Bible. The book talks to us in our own mother tongue. Why should I have to ask another what my Father says? . . . The Bible to many is a dull book, as dry as an old will. But when you hear your own name read out in a will, you prick up your ears. What if there should be something in the Testament of our Lord Jesus for *you*. When I found my own name there my heart danced for joy. It was in these lines: ' God so loved the world that He gave His only begotten Son, that whosoever believeth in Him should not perish, but have everlasting life ' . . . Get your legacy at once!"

C. H. SPURGEON.

THE BOOK OF JOSHUA (1)

IN A LETTER to a certain Miss Chalmers, Scotland's Robbie Burns
wrote:

*"I have taken tooth and nail to the Bible, and am got through
the five books of Moses, and half-way in Joshua. It is really a
glorious book. I sent for my bookbinder today, and ordered
him to get me an octavo Bible in sheets, the best paper and print
in town, and bind it with all the elegance of his craft."*

In our present course of study we, too, have now got through
the books of Moses, and they have given us good reason to press
on with Burns-like zest to the book of Joshua.

Joshua is complementary to the five books of Moses, and introductory to the new historical group of twelve (Joshua to Esther).
The five books of Moses lead Israel *up to* Canaan; and Joshua
complements these by leading Israel *into* Canaan. The further
twelve books cover Israel's history inside Canaan; and Joshua
introduces these by describing the Israelite *settlement* in Canaan.
It is thus the link book between the two historical groups in the
Old Testament. It covers a period of about twenty-five years,
and describes one of the most memorable conquests in history.
"The occupation of this small strip of territory scarcely larger
than Wales, though it led to no further results in the way of
conquest, has nevertheless to a great extent moulded the moral
and religious history of the world."

Authorship

It would seem that the book of Joshua is so named because
Joshua is its focal figure, and not necessarily as implying that
Joshua himself was its author. Jewish tradition does indeed
ascribe the authorship to him, and certainly, despite the dexterous
theories of some recent scholars, there is no solid reason for
categorically rejecting it. There are evidences of other hands

than Joshua's, however, in the work as it has come to us. Possibly
these may be simply of an interpolative nature; but the probability is that while Joshua himself supplied the materials, these
were arranged and supplemented by some scribe a little later.
Or it may be that Joshua contributed the substance of the work,
while certain of the elders completed it. The really important
thing to maintain is that the editor-author was a contemporary,
or practically so, having first-hand knowledge, or authentic
documents, so that the work is really a product of the period
which it records. Such hectic higher critical arguments as that
which attributes the book to some fictitious author in Manasseh's
reign have been so effectively demolished by orthodox scholars
that there is no need to burden our minds with them here.

Structure

Joshua is a book of graphic movement, of campaign, and conquest and subjugation. We see Israel going up, winning through,
and settling in. The account is distributed in three phases, thus:

1. ENTERING THE LAND (i.–v.).
2. OVERCOMING THE LAND (vi.–xii.).
3. OCCUPYING THE LAND (xiii.–xxiv.).

Key Thought

Entering, overcoming, occupying!—if these are the three movements recorded in Joshua, then there can be no doubt as to what
is its key thought, or central message. Clearly, it is *the victory
of faith*. In this, the Book of Joshua stands in sharp contrast to
the Book of Numbers where we see the failure of unbelief—failure
to enter (xiv. 2–4), failure to overcome (xiv. 44, 45), failure to
occupy (xiv. 28–34). Spiritually interpreted, the exploits of Israel
under Joshua proclaim the great New Testament truth—"This
is the victory that overcometh the world, even our faith" (1 John
v. 4). Each of the victories in the programme of conquest was
ordered so as to exhibit that victory was due to faith in God,
not to the arm of man. To quailing unbelief, the overthrow of
giants and great cities was an *impasse*, but to the eye of faith
it was a *fait accompli*.

Typical Significance

Already, in the five books of Moses, we have found the presence of types in the Old Testament Scriptures—typical persons, events, and objects, such as Joseph, the Exodus, and the Tabernacle. Now in the case of Joshua, the whole story is one grand type. It is the Old Testament type-picture of a great spiritual reality revealed in the New Testament, as we shall shortly see. What then *is* the main typical significance of Joshua? The answer to that question depends upon the answer to the further question as to what *Canaan* typifies.

In some of our hymns, the river Jordan is taken as representing death, and the land of Canaan as representing heaven. This, however, is surely a misinterpretation of these types. If Jordan is death and Canaan heaven, then it follows that the whole of the Christian life, right till the hour of death, corresponds to the wilderness through which the Hebrews tramped—not exactly an enamouring picture—and we might feel a spark of sympathy with the argument that a death-bed conversion is preferable so as to cut the wilderness as short as possible!

Moreover, Canaan cannot very well be a type of heaven for two or three other reasons. Canaan was a place of conquest through *conflict*. There had been little fighting during the wilderness years, but as soon as Canaan was entered Israel must draw the sword. Enemies must be destroyed. Israel must fight. How then can Canaan typify the calm restfulness of the ultimate inheritance in heaven?

Moreover, it was possible for Israel to be ejected from Canaan by powerful foes; and eventually they actually *were* ejected, as we know. How then can this typify that heaven of uninterrupted felicity which is pledged to the justified in Christ?

But, to settle the question conclusively, we are expressly taught, in Hebrews iii. and iv., what the typical meaning of Canaan really is. Those two chapters should be read carefully, and they will then fix this Canaan type once for all in our intelligent understanding. They make it quite clear that Canaan pictures the believer's *present* position and possession in Christ. It was ordained to pre-figure that spiritual Sabbath-keeping into which we may enter here and now. A few verses from one of those Hebrews chapters will be enough to certify this—"For if

Joshua had given them rest He (God) would not have spoken afterward of another day (of rest). There *remaineth* therefore a rest for the people of God. For he that is entered into His rest hath himself also rested from his works as God did from His. Let us therefore *give diligence to enter* into that rest" (Heb. iv. 8–11 R.V.). The same chapter tells us that "we which have believed *do* enter into that rest" (verse 3).

The meaning of Canaan, then, as a type, is fixed, both by circumstance and New Testament explanation. Jordan does not typify death of the body and departure into the beyond, but that deeper union of our hearts with Christ in *His* death whereby we become completely separated unto Him, and introduced into "the *fulness* of the blessing of the Gospel of Christ." That New Testament phrase, "The fulness of the blessing of the Gospel of Christ," more aptly than any other sums up the type-meaning of Canaan. Certainly, as the writer of the epistle to the Hebrews says, it is the believer's "rest"; but the rest is part of the *fulness*. Canaan is that "breadth and length and depth and height" of spiritual life in which we really "possess our possessions" in Christ. The tragedy is that the majority of Christians live far below their revealed privileges and redemption rights in Christ. The Christian life is no more meant to be a wilderness than a wedding feast is meant to be a time for sackcloth and ashes. God has opened up to us in Christ a present experience of sanctification comparable to a fertile, fragrant, fruitful, sunbathed Canaan—a "land of corn and wine," a land "flowing with milk and honey."

Canaan in Christian Experience

C. H. Spurgeon says: "There is a point of grace as much above the ordinary Christian as the ordinary Christian is above the world." Speaking of those who live this higher life, he continues —"Their place is with the eagle in his eyrie high aloft. They are rejoicing Christians, holy and devout men doing service for the Master all over the world, and everywhere conquerors through Him that loved them." The experience here referred to has been called by various names—"Christian Perfection," "Entire Sanctification," "The Higher Life," "The Rest of Faith," "The Life More Abundant," "Perfect Love"; but all these are simply different names for different aspects of the one spiritual reality.

Both Scripture and the experience of many of Christ's people seem to confirm that there is a work of Divine grace in the believer, quite distinct from that which we commonly call conversion, and usually, though not necessarily, subsequent to it, in which the soul is brought into an experience of inwrought holiness and fellowship with God never known by conversion alone. "The law of the Spirit of life in Christ Jesus" makes gloriously free from "the law of sin and death" (Rom. viii. 2). There is complete renewal in the very "spirit of the mind" (Eph. iv. 23). There is effected such a love-blend of the believer's life and will with the life and will of Christ that, instead of being egocentric, the believer becomes Christocentric. Self-consciousness is sublimated in Christ-consciousness, so that the experience now is, "I live, yet not I; Christ liveth in me" (Gal. ii. 20); and "To me to live is Christ" (Phil. i. 21). The personality becomes monopolised and suffused by the Holy Spirit (Eph. v. 18). Perfect love fills the heart and casts out fear (1 John iv. 18). The soul is in Beulah Land (Isa. lxii. 4). "The winter is past and gone; the flowers appear on the earth, and the time of the singing of birds is come" (Song of Sol. ii. 11–12). There is a "walking in the light" of a cloudless "fellowship" with Heaven, while "the blood of Jesus Christ, God's Son, cleanseth from all sin" (1 John i. 7); and the believer now reads his experience in such words as these—"The sun shall be no more thy light by day, neither for brightness shall the moon give light unto thee; but the Lord shall be unto thee an everlasting light, and thy God thy glory. Thy sun shall no more go down, neither shall thy moon withdraw itself; for the Lord shall be thine everlasting light, and the days of thy mourning shall be ended" (Isa. lx. 19–20).

Characteristics of Canaan

Now this is the experience to which Canaan and the book of Joshua point in a typical way. It is therefore of the highest interest to observe what we are told about Canaan; and there are three things which are outstandingly characteristic.

First, Canaan was Israel's promised *REST*. Itineracy was to give place to settled dwelling. Instead of the inhospitable wilderness there was to be a home where they should sit down, every man "under his vine and under his fig tree." The tired hands and blistered feet were to find refreshing contrast in the responsive yields of Canaan's fertile plains and valleys. The promised rest had been wonderfully prepared for their coming. They should not need even to build the cities and houses which they would need to live in, for they were to possess "great and goodly cities which thou buildedst not, and houses full of all good things which thou filledst not, and wells digged which thou diggedst not, and vineyards and olive trees which thou plantedst not" (Deut. vi. 10–11): and here they should lie down in safety, none making them afraid (Lev. xxvi. 6).

Second, Canaan was the place of *BOUNTY*. This was the land "flowing with milk and honey," a "good land and a large" (Exod. iii. 8), a "land of corn and wine" and kissed with the dews of heaven (Deut. xxxiii. 28), a land of olives and vines, of firs and cedars, of rich fruits and harvests where an obedient people should "eat to the full," where the threshing should reach unto the vintage and the vintage unto the sowing time (Lev. xxvi. 5); a place of which God had said: "The land whither thou goest in to possess it is not as the land of Egypt from whence ye came out, where thou sowedst thy seed and wateredst it with thy foot as a garden of herbs: but the land whither ye go to possess it is a land of hills and valleys, and drinketh water of the rain of heaven: a land which the Lord thy God careth for; the eyes of the Lord thy God are always upon it, from the beginning of the year even unto the end of the year" (Deut. xi. 10–12). Yes, Canaan was the place of bounty!

Third, Canaan was the place of *TRIUMPH*. Were there enemies in Canaan? Yes: but they were a defeated foe before ever Israel struck the first blow, for God had said: "The Lord thy God shall . . . cast out many nations before thee, the Hittites, and the Girgashites, and the Amorites, and the Canaanites, and the Perizzites, and the Hivites, and the Jebusites, seven nations greater and mightier than thou" (Deut. vii. 1). Israel was to remember what Jehovah had done "unto Pharaoh and unto all Egypt" and not be afraid. Five of them should chase a hundred, and none of their enemies should be able to stand before them. God was calling Israel not merely to conflict but to an assured *victory*. Yes, to a faithful Israel Canaan was to be the place of triumph.

In all this the Spirit of God is pictorially exhibiting to us that life in the "heavenly places" (Eph. i. 3) which is our present privilege in Christ; and our conception of New Testament truth is thus vivified by Old Testament type.

Resting, abounding, triumphing!—this is our rich inheritance in Christ; and it may be ours in actual experience—

> A rest where all our soul's desire
>   Is fixed on things above;
> Where doubt and sin and fear expire,
>   Cast out by perfect love.
>
> Fair fields where peace and love abound,
>   And purest joys excel,
> And heavenly fellowship is found,
>   A lovely place to dwell.

Holiness is not something to be *attained* by self-effort; but it may be *ob*tained in Christ. Consecration and appropriation are the two hinges on which the gate to Canaan swings. If we really yield, and then plant our feet on the promises, the delectable land is ours. God will not fail us. Let us go up and possess! "Faithful is He that calleth you, who also will do it" (I Thess. v. 24).

> Sanctify me wholly,
>   Sovereign Saviour mine;
> Spirit, soul and body
>   Now make fully Thine.
> Make my motives blameless,
>   Purify my heart;
> Set me now entirely
>   For Thyself apart.
>
> Thou to this dost call me,
>   In Thy written word;
> Thou Thyself wilt do it,
>   If I trust Thee, Lord.
> Faithful is Thy calling
>   And Thy promise, too;
> Give me now to trust Thee,
>   And to prove Thee true

THE BOOK OF JOSHUA (2)

Lesson Number 21

There is a Canaan rich and blest,
　　Which all in Christ may know,
By consecrated saints possessed
　　While here on earth below.

There is a vict'ry over sin,
　　A rest from inward strife,
A richer sense of Christ within,
　　A more abundant life.

'Tis here that peace and love abound,
　　And purest joys excel,
And heavenly fellowship is found—
　　A lovely place to dwell!

Oh, this is Beulah Land indeed,
　　Where heaven itself is nigh;
Where all our emptiness and need
　　Is lost in full supply!

Lord slay all subtle love of sin,
　　Our doubt and fear remove;
Oh help us now to enter in,
　　And all Thy blessing prove!

　　　　　　　　　　　　　　J.S.B.

THE BOOK OF JOSHUA (2)

JOSHUA AND EPHESIANS

ALREADY, in our study of the Pentateuch, we have noted the correspondence between Deuteronomy and the Acts of the Apostles, and the connection between Leviticus and Hebrews. There is also a remarkable parallel between the Book of Joshua and the epistle to the Ephesians. The epistle to the Ephesians is distinctively the epistle of the "heavenly places in Christ" (i. 3). The book of Joshua, as we have pointed out, is in type that fuller Christian life in which we really "possess our possessions" in Christ, enter into heart-rest, and experience fulness of "joy and peace in believing." That Ephesian phrase, "heavenly places," or more literally, "the heavenlies," denotes the *sphere* of this higher and fuller life. It indicates a union of life and mind and will with the risen Christ, a union with Him in nature, relationships, and purposes, a union with Him in death to sin and to the flesh and to the world, a union with Him in service and suffering and desire, a union with Him in His resurrection and ascension, which lifts the believer to a level where there is a fulness of light and love and power and spiritual understanding unknown to others. This is life on the highest plane. This is the true place of the believer's present life in Christ. Seldom is it entered right away at conversion. Alas, how many believers seem never to enter it at all! Yet this indeed is God's provision; this is our inheritance in Christ Jesus; and young Christians should early be pointed to it.

Now in Joshua we see Israel entering and possessing the earthly inheritance given in Abraham. In Ephesians we see the Church entering and possessing the heavenly inheritance given in Christ.

The correspondence, however, is not merely general. There is a five-fold parallel, marked by the five occurrences of that expression, "the heavenlies," in Ephesians. The five references are Ephesians i. 3; i. 20; ii. 6; iii. 10; vi. 12. Trace the parallel briefly then between the land of Canaan in the book of Joshua, and "the heavenlies" in the epistle to the Ephesians.

1. *Each was the predestined inheritance of a chosen people.* Away back, five hundred years before Joshua led the people over Jordan, God had said to Abram: "Lift up now thine eyes, and look from the place where thou art, northward and southward and eastward and westward, for all the land which thou seest, to thee will I give it, and to thy seed for ever" (Gen. xiii. 14, 15). And when at length He brought Israel up from Egypt He said: "The Lord shall bring thee into the land . . . which He sware unto thy fathers to give thee" (Exod. xiii. 5).

Even so, turning to the first occurrence of that phrase, "the heavenlies," in Ephesians, we find that here we have the predestined inheritance of the Church, in Christ.

"Blessed be the God and Father of our Lord Jesus Christ, who hath blessed us with all spiritual blessings IN THE HEAVEN-LIES in Christ, according as He hath CHOSEN US IN HIM before the foundation of the world, that we should be holy and without blame before Him in love" (Eph. i. 3, 4).

With our eye on these two verses from Ephesians, let us note the contrastive parallel. Israel was blessed with all *material* blessings in *earthly* places in *Abraham.* The Church is "blessed with all *spiritual* blessings in *heavenly* places, in *Christ.*" Note also, that to enjoy this fulness of material blessings Israel must be *in the land.* Similarly, to enjoy the fulness of spiritual blessings in Christ we must be *"in the heavenlies."* The reason why we miss them is because we are not in the place where God bestows them.

2. *Each was opened up by a Divinely ordained leader.* In the case of Israel all was put into the hands of Joshua. It was said to him: "Unto this people shalt *thou* divide for an inheritance the land which I sware unto their fathers to give them" (Joshua i. 6); and, *"Thou* shalt cause them to inherit it" (Deut. xxxi. 7). Joshua was thus the appointed administrator of the Israelite settlement in Canaan; and we are told that at the end of the seven-years' war "Joshua took the whole land . . . and gave it for an inheritance unto Israel according to their divisions by their tribes" (Joshua xi. 23).

Even so, turning to the second occurrence of that phrase, "the heavenlies," in Ephesians, we find that the Church's inheritance is opened up by the Lord Jesus.

"That ye may know . . . what is the exceeding greatness of His power to usward who believe, according to the working of His mighty power which He wrought in Christ when He raised Him from the dead, and set Him at His own right hand IN THE HEAVENLIES . . . and gave Him to be the HEAD OVER ALL THINGS TO THE CHURCH" (Eph. i. 18–22).

Thus is Joshua a beautiful type of Christ as the trustee and representative of His people. It is the ascended Saviour who divides the goodly inheritance, and allots it to His believing people as by faith they plant their feet upon the promises.

3. *Each was a gift of grace to be received by faith.* Canaan was given to Israel in Abraham, not in Moses the man of the Law. By the Law Israel could never have become entitled to Canaan. Moses was not privileged even to lead the people in. Nor can the Law ever lead *us* into God's promised rest for our souls in Christ. Hence, Moses must die, and Joshua must take his place; and Joshua must open up the inheritance. The very first words of this book of Joshua are significantly in harmony with this— "Now after the death of Moses, the servant of the Lord, it came to pass that the Lord spake unto Joshua, the son of Nun, Moses' minister, saying: Moses my servant is dead; now *THEREFORE* arise, and go over this Jordan, thou and all this people, unto the land which I do give them, even to the children of Israel" (i. 1, 2).

So is it with the spiritual Canaan which is ours in Christ, as the third occurrence of the expression, "the heavenlies," in Ephesians, shows.

"Even when we were dead in sins (God) hath quickened us together with Christ (by GRACE are ye saved); and hath raised us up together, and made us sit together IN THE HEAVEN- LIES in Christ Jesus: that in the ages to come He might show the exceeding riches of His GRACE in His kindness toward us through Christ Jesus. For by GRACE are ye saved, through FAITH; and that not of yourselves; it is the gift of God" (Eph. ii. 5–8).

F. B. Meyer aptly says: "The law of God can never bring the soul of man into the land of Promise, not because there is any defect in it, but because of human infirmity and sin. It is the presence of this evil law in our members which makes obedience to the law of God impossible, filling us with disappointment and unrest, ceaseless striving and perpetual failure. We must therefore leave the Law, as an outward rule of life, behind us, in that lonely valley over against Bethpeor, that the Divine Joshua may lead us into the land of Promise. Not by vows or resolution or covenants of consecration signed by blood fresh-drawn from the veins; not by external rites or by ascetic abstinence from good and healthy things; not by days of fasting and nights of prayer; not even by obedience to the voice of conscience or the inner light, though attention to these is of prime importance—by none of these shall we enter the land of blessedness. They all become forms of legalism, when practised with a view to obtaining the full rest and victory of Christian experience. Valuable many of them unquestionably are, when the river is crossed and the land is entered; but they will not of themselves unlock its gates or roll back its guardian river." No; in the words of Ephesians ii. 8, it must be "by grace, through faith."

The Old Covenant rest-day was the *seventh*. The New Covenant rest-day is the *first*. Under the Old Covenant we must work the six days *up to* the rest. Under the New Covenant we work *down from* it—from a perpetual rest already possessed in Christ.

4. *Each is the sphere of a striking Divine revelation*. Israel's entering and possessing of Canaan was intended to be a revelation of the true God to the nations of that day—"That all the people of the earth might know the hand of the Lord, that it is mighty: that ye might fear the Lord your God forever" (Joshua iv. 24). "All people of the earth shall see that thou art called by the name of the Lord; and they shall be afraid of thee" (Deut. xxviii. 10). Israel's yet future regathering to Canaan will consummate that revelation. See Isaiah xi. 11, 12, Jeremiah xxiii. 5–8, and other passages in the Old Testament prophets.

Parallel with this, we find the fourth Ephesian reference to "the heavenlies" telling us that the Church is a wonderful revelation of God to the powers of the spirit-realm. Paul goes on to say, in chapter iii :—

"Unto me who am less than the least of all saints is this grace given, that I should preach among the Gentiles the unsearchable riches of Christ; and to make all men see what is the fellowship of the mystery which from the beginning of the world hath been hid in God, Who created all things by Jesus Christ: to the intent that now UNTO THE PRINCIPALITIES AND POWERS IN THE HEAVENLIES MIGHT BE KNOWN BY THE CHURCH THE MANIFOLD WISDOM OF GOD" (Eph. iii. 8–10).

The crowning revelation of the Divine wisdom and power through Israel in Canaan, as we have said, will be in the restoration yet to be. Even so the consummating display of the Divine wisdom and purpose through the Church, to the spirit-powers in "the heavenlies," will be effected by the second coming of Christ, when the completed Church will be manifested with Christ in His glory.

5. *Each is described as a scene of conflict.* In the earthly Canaan there were the giant sons of Anak, and cities "walled up to heaven." There were the Hittites and Girgashites and Amorites and Canaanites and Perizzites, and Hivites and Jebusites, who held the land with strongholds and iron chariots—seven nations "greater and mightier" than Israel. They were exceedingly *evil* nations, and they had to be dispossessed and destroyed. Therefore must Israel wield the sword against them, though not with any doubt as to the final issue, for God was with Israel; and if they would but remain true to Him none should be able to stand against them. Conflict was inevitable, but defeat was impossible, for there was an alliance invincible.

So is it with that spiritual Canaan which is ours in "the heavenlies." We turn to Ephesians again and find these words in the last occurrence of that phrase "the heavenlies"—

"We wrestle not against flesh and blood, but against principalities, against powers, against the rulers of the darkness of this world, against spiritual wickedness IN THE HEAVENLIES" (Eph. vi. 12).

Thank God, as no power could withstand Joshua and Israel, so no power in the spirit-realm can withstand the power of

Christ, for He has defeated Satan, and is now "far above all principality and power and might and dominion" (Eph. i. 21). In Him victory is ours. In Him our prayer-life may become a victorious spiritual warfare which shall be effectual to the pulling down of Satanic strongholds, the casting down of imaginations which oppose themselves to God, and the releasing of regenerating forces among men. When we are truly abiding in Him, and are "reigning in life by One, Jesus Christ" (Rom. v. 17) in "the heavenlies," all foes are beneath our feet, and we enter into the meaning of that word in Psalm ii. 4, "He that sitteth in the heavens shall laugh."

These, then, are the five points of parallel between the earthly inheritance opened up through Joshua, and the spiritual inheritance opened up to us Christian believers in Christ. Perhaps a recapitulation will help to fix them in memory.

1. Each was the predestined inheritance of a chosen people.
2. Each was opened up by a Divinely ordained leader.
3. Each was a gift of Divine grace to be received by faith.
4. Each is the sphere of a striking Divine revelation.
5. Each is described as a scene of conflict.

This parallel between Canaan, in Joshua, and "the heavenlies," in Ephesians, is as instructive as it is striking, and well merits a fuller consideration than we can give to it here. God grant that we ourselves may live in the goodly land, and "possess our possessions," to the joy of our own hearts and the glory of God!

THE BOOK OF JOSHUA (3)

Lesson Number 22

NOTE.—For this third study in the book of Joshua re-read the first twelve chapters.

They on the heights are not the souls
  Who never erred nor went astray,
Who trod unswerving to their goals
  Along a smooth, rose-bordered way.
Nay, those who stand where first comes dawn,
  Are those who stumbled—but went on.

THE BOOK OF JOSHUA (3)

THE PARTS

WE OUGHT now to glance over the three main parts of the book. Even in their broad features we shall find much to profit us. First we see Israel *entering* (i.–v.), then *overcoming* (vi.–xii.), and then *occupying* (xiii.–xxiv.).

PART I. ENTERING THE LAND (i.–v.)

The five chapters of part one run in an orderly sequence thus—

> Chapter i.—Joshua charged.
> ,,   ii.—Jericho spied.
> ,,   iii.—Jordan crossed.
> ,,   iv.—Memorials raised.
> ,,   v.—Gilgal occupied.

If we bear in mind that the key idea in Joshua is *the victory of faith*, we shall quickly see how eloquent these chapters are.

Chapter i.—Joshua charged.

The emphasis in this chapter is upon the fact that Joshua's assumption of leadership originated in a commission from God Himself. It was grounded in the word of God (see verse 9). The going up into Canaan, also, was based upon a clear Divine authorisation (verses 2–5). This is ever the beginning of things where faith is concerned—that God has spoken. True faith is therefore far removed from mere credulousness. It refuses to act on the basis of mere human reasoning : but once it is satisfied that God has spoken, it asks nothing more, for there can be no higher authority than that, and no higher reason than to obey. Here then, in chapter i., we have the *warrant* of faith, namely, the word of God. True faith always works on the principle denoted in Hebrews xiii. 5, 6—"HE hath said . . . so *we* may say."

Chapter ii.—Jericho spied.

Having received such Divine assurance of invincibility (as in i. 5–6), Joshua might easily have felt it needless to exercise cautiousness or to resort to military strategy. But this second chapter shows us that the reaction of true faith is in fact the opposite of any such carelessness. Joshua sends the two spies to Jericho; and there was good reason for his doing so, as we shall see later, for Jericho was a key city. True faith does not despise the use of means. There is a wide difference between believing and presuming. To make the promises of God an excuse for not taking reasonable precaution is to tempt God, as our Lord Jesus Himself has taught us. When the deceiver urged the Master to cast Himself from the temple tower because God had promised supernatural preservation, the Master replied: "It is written again: Thou shalt not tempt the Lord thy God." In this second chapter of Joshua we have the *prudence* of faith.

Chapter iii.—Jordan crossed.

The crossing of "this Jordan" was a major crisis of faith. The same crisis had come to the former generation of Israel some forty years earlier under somewhat different circumstances, and they had failed in their reaction to it. It was bound to repeat itself to the new generation. To be "brought out" of Egypt was one thing; but it was another thing altogether to "go over this Jordon" and thus become committed, without possibility of retreat, to the struggle against the powers of Canaan in their seemingly impregnable fastnesses, with their chariots of iron, and their large armies among which were the renowned giants. To do this was to commit themselves to a course which had been condemned by ten out of the twelve spies who had reported on the land forty years before! To the natural eye it was to hazard everything on the chance of battle, to have no retreat, and to run the risk of losing everything.

The same crisis comes in one way or another to all the redeemed —that intense crisis of the soul in which we are forced to the supreme choice whether there shall be an utter once-for-all abandon of ourselves to the will of God, so that henceforth God is absolutely first in the soul's love and life, or whether we shall take what seems to be the easier way, that is, of continuing in the Christian life, but with a reservation in our love to God. It is one thing to take Christ as Saviour from the guilt of our sin. It is another thing to make Him absolute Master of our will and life. It is one thing to be brought out from the Egypt of our unregenerate life and to join God's redeemed Israel. It is another thing altogether to bury all our self-born aims and desires in Jordan's swift-flowing flood, and to pass through to that higher life where no desires or purposes are tolerated but those of our blessed Lord Himself. It was one thing for Abram to leave Ur of the Chaldees and go out in faith at God's behest. It was another thing—a far bigger and costlier and sublimer thing—for him to climb Moriah and lift the knife to slay his beloved Isaac. Yet the crisis must be. There was no other way of decisively determining whether God was to be supreme in the life and love of the soul. There was no need for further testing after that; and God said: "By Myself have I sworn, because thou hast done this thing, and hast not withheld thy son, thine only son, that in blessing I will bless thee, and in multiplying I will multiply thy seed as the stars of the heaven and as the sand which is upon the sea shore." Abraham's Moriah and Israel's Jordan are the same crisis under different names. There is an Isaac to be sacrificed, a Jordan to be crossed, in the history of every redeemed soul. Abraham yielded his Isaac. Israel crossed the Jordan. What of you and me? This is faith's major crisis; and this is what we have in this third chapter of Joshua—the *crisis* of faith.

Chapter iv.—*Memorials raised.*

A faith that goes all the way with God leaves many a beautiful "Ebenezer" in its wake. The Jordan memorial stones were faith's witness to the power and faithfulness of God. There were two of these cairns or monumental piles—one on the west bank of the river, at Gilgal (verse 3), and the other in the river itself (verse 9), each consisting of twelve great stones representing the twelve tribes of Israel. The pile on the Canaan side of the Jordan witnessed to the *faithfulness* of God in His bringing Israel at last into the land promised to their fathers. The pile in the river itself witnessed to the *power* of God in holding back the swollen flood and cleaving a pathway across the river bed for the great host. In this fourth chapter, then, we have the *witness* of faith.

Those two memorial piles are symbolic. They witness to God's bringing His people right through the river and into the place of blessing. That preposition "through" really comprises the two ideas of "in" and "out" both in one. There must be both a going *into* and a coming *out of* to make the meaning of "*through*." Now the two memorial heaps in this fourth chapter of Joshua bear witness both to the going into and the coming out of the Jordan. Israel actually went down into that river basin; otherwise, how explain that submerged pillar of great stones amid stream? Israel actually came out on Canaan's side; hence that erection at Gilgal. Here is symbolic witness to a great truth: never does a soul go down into that *other* Jordan—the death and burial of "selfism"—to find itself deserted. As surely as there is the "*into*" there is the "*out of*." God brings the now-sanctified soul right through to the resurrection ground of "the heavenlies" in Christ.

Chapter v.—*Gilgal occupied.*

Here we see the *sealing and chastening* of faith. Strange as it might seem, the first experience in the land of blessing is one of pain, though the pain is soon over. Before ever the covenant people draw the sword against the foe, God draws the knife upon *them*. Israel has at last crossed the dividing line, and is now entering in a new way into the purposes of God. Therefore, that which has been neglected during the forty years' wandering now becomes imperative. Circumcision is re-enjoined, as the seal of the covenant between God and Israel. Israel's sons were to carry in their very persons this mark of their separatedness. Moreover, although much of the symbolic and typical meaning of things in the Israelite economy must have been unperceived by the Israelites themselves, they were left in no doubt as to the moral and spiritual significance of circumcision. Moses himself had exhorted them: "Circumcise therefore your heart, and be no more stiffnecked" (Deut. x. 16). "The Lord thy God will circumcise thine heart . . . to love the Lord thy God" (Deut. xxx. 6). Passages like Colossians ii. 11–13 make the New Testament interpretation quite clear. It is that "putting off" of "the flesh," that sharp pruning of the natural desires, which accompanies God's chastening in the soul.

Yes, Jordan must be followed by Gilgal. Even the Jordan

by itself is not enough. The Israelites must carry Gilgal's abiding
mark of their fuller separation. Even so with ourselves, that
soul-crisis of death and burial to selfism, of which Jordan is the
type, must be perpetuated by that continuous denial of "the
flesh" of which circumcision speaks. This may mean a pang at
first; but it is soon over, for God's deeper work in us when we
come through the crisis-burial of Jordan strikes a fundamental
blow at inbred sin, and so renews the desires of the heart that
the first sharp pang of "daily dying" to "the flesh" is quickly
lost in the thrill of new fellowship with God on the resurrection
ground of "entire sanctification."

Following Israel's circumcision at Gilgal comes the Passover
Feast, speaking of this new fellowship with God in the place of
blessing (verse 10). Then comes the change-over of Israel's diet
from the manna to the produce of Canaan (verse 12). Both the
manna in the wilderness and the corn of Canaan typify Christ; but
Christ will be the one or the other to us according to where we are
spiritually. He can only be to us as the rich produce of Canaan
when we have crossed the Jordan and come into the place of
complete separation to Himself.

So then, in these first five chapters we have—

Chapter   i. Joshua charged   — the *warrant* of faith.
  ,,   ii. Jericho spied   — the *prudence* of faith.
  ,,   iii. Jordan crossed   — the *crisis* of faith.
  ,,   iv. Memorials raised — the *witness* of faith.
  ,,   v. Gilgal occupied   — the *pruning* of faith.

Part II. OVERCOMING THE LAND (vi.-xii.)

In this second group of chapters we see faith's warfare and
victory. Israel is now in the place of blessing, and goes forth
"conquering and to conquer" in the might of the invisible
Captain. Vital spiritual lessons are pictured in these chapters.

Chapter   vi.—The Fall of Jericho.
  ,,   vii.—The Sin of Achan.
  ,,   viii.—The Sack of Ai.
  ,,   ix.—The Guile of Gibeon.
  ,,   x.-xii.—The Rout of the kings.

Chapter vi.—The Fall of Jericho.

This remarkable chapter sets forth in graphic type the principles by which faith works and wars and waits and wins. Faith's first rule of action is to ascertain the will and word of God. Faith's second rule of action is to obey that will and word implicitly. Faith's final rule of action is to reckon on that word, and count the thing as good as done, giving glory to God in anticipation—as the Israelites gave their mighty shout of victory before the walls of Jericho had actually fallen. Faith's principles of action, therefore, cut right across those of natural reason.

We note four things about the procedure of faith in the conquest of Jericho: (1) the seeming folly of it, (2) the inner wisdom of it, (3) the deeper meaning of it, (4) the utter triumph of it. As for the seeming folly of it, nothing could seem more useless to the natural eye than that harmless winding round and round the city walls to the blowing of rams' horns. As for the inner wisdom of it, nothing could really be wiser than to do just what God Himself had directed, however strange it might seem. As for the deeper meaning of it, nothing could be more significant than the fact that here we see God and man in *co-operation* for the pulling down of a Satanic stronghold. As for the utter triumph of it, nothing could be more marked, for with one fell blow the city was laid low, without a single Israelite casualty. Here is triumph indeed. This is the emphasis in this sixth chapter—*the triumph of faith.*

Chapter vii.—The Sin of Achan.

Alas, there is a swift lapse which, though it is soon put right, is not without cost. It is not that Israel's faith breaks down; but a secret compromise temporarily *disables* it. The men of Israel turn their backs on the foe; and thirty-six of them fall. In all the seven years' war this was the one loss. The cause of the failure is carefully exposed so that the lesson may be clearly learned. The electric wire of fellowship between God and Israel had been cut by "a trespass in the accursed thing"; and the current of power therefore ceased to flow. Israel's first inclination was to attribute blame to God instead of looking *within*. But anon the ugly deed was forced into the open; confession was made, and judgment executed upon it. Achan's smuggled loot was of little material value; but the taking of it was of deep spiritual seriousness. It was a grievous compromise with that which was forbidden. It must have been a sorrow to Jehovah to inflict the Ai reverse upon His people; yet Israel must learn by necessary pain that both for their own sake and the sake of Jehovah's holy name sin must be judged and put away. Any defeat which we sustain in the land of blessing is due entirely to some such failure within ourselves. It need never be; and our great Captain grieves over it more than we do ourselves. We must learn the lesson of this seventh chapter—that parley with sin, or permitted compromise, cuts the vital cord of communion and disables faith.

Chapter viii.—The Sack of Ai.

In this chapter we see faith re-empowered and going forth in renewed triumph. Sin confessed and judged and put away restores the cord of communion, and the Divine power begins to flow again. The invisible Captain of Jehovah's host now says to Joshua: "Fear not, neither be thou dismayed: take all the people of war with thee, and arise, go up to Ai. See, I have given into thy hand the king of Ai and his people and his city and his land." The remainder of the chapter speaks for itself. It is the picture-lesson of *faith re-empowered* after self-judgment.

Chapter ix.—The League with Gibeon.

Here behold the wiles of Satan. The Gibeonites, realising that they could not stand against such a power as that which operated through Israel, resorted to a trick of deception. A group of them, forlornly attired as wearied travellers from a distant land, came to the camp of Israel, saying: "From a very far country thy servants are come because of the name of Jehovah thy God; for we have heard the fame of Him and all that He did in Egypt . . . therefore now make ye a league with us." So clever was the disguise, so reasonable the story, so reverential the reference to Jehovah, so pitiable their plight, that Israel's compassion overflowed. Believing that these men were not of the Canaanites who were under the curse, and with whom no leagues were to be made, Israel made a covenant with Gibeon. Three days later the trickery was exposed.

Note: the most significant thing in this incident is that Israel "*asked not counsel at the mouth of the Lord*" (verse 14). We need not only the *power* of the Spirit against giants, but the *wisdom* of the Spirit against serpents! Satan is far easier to strike down as a son of Anak in warrior's armour than as a disguised Gibeonite in some pity-evoking beggar's attire. Satan's subtle wiles are more dangerous than his open assaults. He is more dangerous as "an angel of light" than as "a roaring lion." The league with these Canaanites held evil possibilities. It imperilled Israel's faith. It was not made because of any breakdown of Israel's faith at the time; but faith had been thrown off guard. Here in this ninth chapter is *faith endangered* by the failure to refer everything to God.

Chapters x.–xii.—The Rout of all Foes.

Joshua's plan of campaign here becomes clear. In first striking at Jericho and Ai, he had driven a wedge into the centre of Canaan. Now, in chapter x. he forks south, and then in chapter xi. he strikes up north. Thus we have the *central* campaign (vi.–ix.), the *southern* campaign (x.), the *northern* campaign (xi.); while chapter xii. completes the account by giving a summary of all the kings and major cities which fell before the sword of Israel. Inter-tribal quarrels between the peoples of Canaan were shelved in the presence of the one foe common to all—Israel. Those who had been each other's deadly foes now quickly made common cause against the awe-inspiring invader. Military alliances were hastily struck, and united resistance was offered. But it was all of no avail. The most formidable coalitions were no match for that supernatural power which operated through Israel. Down they went one after another—cities, kings, giants, confederacies, until it could be written:

"*So Joshua took the whole land, according to all that the Lord said unto Moses; and Joshua gave it for an inheritance unto Israel according to their divisions by their tribes.*" (xi. 23).

We group chapters x.–xii. together because whereas the overthrow of Jericho and Ai and the league with Gibeon are depicted in fuller detail, the campaigns in these further three chapters are more summarily described. And what do they show us in a spiritual sense? They shew us *faith all-victorious*. Enemies are vanquished. Israel is victor. Canaan is won. And "this is the victory that overcometh the world, even our faith."

THE BOOK OF JOSHUA (4)

Lesson Number 23

NOTE.—For this present study read again chapters xiii. to xxiv.

THE BOOK OF JOSHUA

THE VICTORY OF FAITH

I. ENTERING THE LAND (i.–v.)

i.	Joshua charged	—the warrant of faith.
ii.	Jericho spied	—the prudence of faith.
iii.	Jordan crossed	—the crisis of faith.
iv.	Memorials built	—the witness of faith.
v.	Gilgal occupied	—the pruning of faith.

II. OVERCOMING THE LAND (vi.–xii.)

vi.	Fall of Jericho	—faith triumphant.
vii.	Sin of Achan	—faith disabled.
viii.	Sack of Ai	—faith re-empowered.
ix.	Guile of Gibeon	—faith endangered.
x.–xii.	Rout of all foes	—faith all-victorious.

III. OCCUPYING THE LAND (xiii.–xxiv.)

xiii.–xix.	Division of Canaan	—faith rewarded.
xx.	Cities of Refuge	—faith protected.
xxi.	Portion of Levites	—faith preserved.
xxii.	Altar of Witness	—faith unifying.
xxiii.–xxiv.	Farewell of Joshua	—faith continuing.

THE BOOK OF JOSHUA (4)

PART III. OCCUPYING THE LAND (xiii.–xxiv.)

THIS FINAL group of chapters is rich with matters of interest, yet it can yield but a thin harvest to a casual reading; for since it deals mainly with names and places and boundary lines, it requires to be studied with map in hand. A detailed geographical tracing-out is rather beyond our present treatment of the book; but there are two or three guiding factors which we ought to note carefully.

First: it requires little imagination to see that the division of the land among the nine and a half tribes and the Levites was no simple task, but a complicated one which demanded careful direction and considerable time.

Second: the dividing of the land was by "casting lots before the Lord" (xviii. 6)—a way of doing which would commend itself because of its impartiality, while at the same time it left the sovereign Lord Himself to settle the tribes in the areas best suited to them. The same blend of impartiality and sovereignty is seen in the administration of spiritual gifts by the Holy Spirit in the Church of Christ.

"Now there are diversities of gifts, but the same Spirit. And there are differences of administration, but the same Lord. And there are diversities of workings, but it is the same God which worketh all in all. But the manifestation of the Spirit is given to every man to profit withal. For to one is given by the Spirit the word of wisdom, to another the word of knowledge by the same Spirit, to another faith by the same Spirit, to another the gifts of healing by the same Spirit, to another the working of miracles, to another prophecy, to another discerning of spirits, to another divers kinds of tongues, to another the interpretation of tongues; but all these worketh that one and the selfsame Spirit, dividing to every man severally as He will" (1 Cor. xii. 4–11).

Third: we should mark well the *principle* which governed Israel's occupation of the land, because the same principle operates in our own appropriation of the inheritance in Christ. This principle is seen if we bring together two seemingly contradictory verses. In chapter xi. 23 we read: "So Joshua *took the whole land*, according to all that the Lord said unto Moses." Yet now in chapter xiii. 1, God says: "There remaineth yet very much land *to be* possessed." These two statements in reality are not contradictory but complementary. They are two aspects of the one situation, and both are true. There was a real sense in which "the whole land" had been taken; and there was a real sense in which "very much land" yet remained to be taken. The decisive blow had been struck. The key cities had been sacked. All opposing alliances had been crushed. Any remaining foes were well within the power of Israel's individual tribes to destroy. It only remained for them now to see to it that there was a pressing home of that initial victory to the last detail.

It is the same with ourselves. The decisive blow has been struck at sin and Satan and the powers of darkness by our heavenly Captain; and thereby the entire inheritance of "all blessings in the heavenlies in Christ" is ours; but we must now apply that victory, carrying it through the whole realm of our thought and life, and pressing it home to the last detail. Especially in our prayer-life should there be a pressing forward in the power of this decisive victory. The powers of darkness can never recover from the mortal blow inflicted on them at Calvary; and even though, through the apostasy of the organised Church, they have found increasing opportunity to rally sufficiently for the waging of bitter warfare against God's spiritual Israel, they still quail before the believer who presses forward in the power of the Cross.

Yes, "the whole land" is taken, yet there remains "very much land" to be possessed. It has been aptly observed that there is a difference between the "inheritance" and the "possession." The "inheritance" is the whole land given by God, whereas the "possession" is only that part of it which is appropriated by faith. The ideal is for the possession to measure up to the full inheritance. Our *inheritance* in Christ is what He is to us potentially. Our *possession* in Christ is what He is to us actually, according to the measure of our appropriation by faith.

And now let us glance quickly at the chapters in this section. The key passage is chapter xxi. 43-5.

"*And the Lord gave unto Israel all the land which He sware to give unto their fathers; and they possessed it, and dwelt therein. And the Lord gave them rest round about, according to all that He sware unto their fathers: and there stood not a man of all their enemies before them: the Lord gave all their enemies into their hand.*

"*There failed not ought of any good thing which the Lord had spoken unto the house of Israel. All came to pass.*"

Note the three things which God gave to Israel—

"*The Lord gave unto Israel all the LAND,*"

"*The Lord gave them REST round about,*"

"*The Lord gave all their ENEMIES into their hand.*"

"All came to pass"—and thus was Jehovah's faithfulness amply exhibited. Israel at last was realising the promised inheritance, the promised rest, the promised victory.

The chapters in this final section of Joshua run thus:

Chapter xiii.–xix.—The Dividing of Canaan.
    ,,   xx.—The Cities of Refuge.
    ,,   xxi.—The Portion of Levi.
    ,,   xxii.—The Altar of Witness.
    ,,   xxiii.–iv.—The Farewell of Joshua.

Chapters xiii.–xix.—The Dividing of Canaan.

In these chapters we have the distribution of the land among the tribes. First, in chapter xiii., the settlement of Reuben, Gad, and half the tribe of Manasseh in Gilead is homologated. In chapter xiv. staunch old Caleb is planted in Hebron. In chapters xv. to xvii. we see the areas committed to Judah, Ephraim, and the remaining half of the Manasseh tribe. Then in chapters xviii. and xix. comes the setting up of the Tabernacle at Shiloh, followed by the allotments to the remaining seven tribes. Following out our spiritual interpretation of the book, we see in these chapters the *appropriation* of faith.

Chapter xx.—The Cities of Refuge.

Here we have the six "Cities of Refuge"—Kedesh, Shechem, and Hebron, on the west of the Jordan; and Bezer, Ramoth, and Golan on the east. These six were among the forty-eight cities given to the Levites (Num. xxxv. 6, 7). Their purpose is clearly explained in Numbers xxxv. and in this present chapter. They were a merciful provision to protect those who had committed certain wrongs unintendingly or by mistake. Many a man of sincere intent and godly faith might have perished but for the horns of the altars in those cities of refuge.

Thus we have here the Divine recognition of the difference between *sins* and mistakes. The holiest of men are fallible, and can make mistakes; but mistakes are not sins, and they therefore do not disqualify us for the faith-life or deprive us of our inheritance in Christ. The little girl who lovingly but ruinously put her mother's shoes in the oven to warm on a wintry night had made a mistake, but had not committed a sin! A man may have a perfect heart without having a perfect head. Sanctification can dwell with a defective memory. Let us be quick to perceive such distinctions and compatibilities.

Even when we are "in the land" we may do many things that are wrong without *realising* they are wrong. In strict justice the law of God cannot but pursue us as guilty. Yet there is provision made for this in the blood of Christ. Mistakes, inadvertences, "sins of ignorance," unintentional wrongs, are provided for in the Atonement. Christ Himself is our "City of Refuge"; and by holding to Him we are protected and covered, so that the maintaining of the faith-life in our spiritual Canaan is made possible. See in this the *protection* of faith.

Chapter xxi.—The Portion of Levi.

Here is the portion of the Levites in the land; forty-eight goodly cities with their suburbs. This distribution of the Levites through the tribes is of obvious significance. "They permeated the whole land with the hallowing influence of Shiloh. What a halo of sacred interest must have gathered round the man whose lot it was to enter into the Tabernacle of God and burn incense at the solemn hour of prayer! Then multiply this a thousandfold, and consider what a wide and wholesome effect must have been produced throughout the country, especially when Levi fulfilled the lofty possibilities of this high calling. Moreover, the teaching of the Law was a special prerogative of the Levites, who appear to have travelled through their apportioned districts. They taught

Jacob His judgments, and Israel His law; as well as put incense and whole burnt-offering on the altar. They caused the people to discern between the unclean and the clean, and in a controversy stood to judge. They acted as the messengers of the Lord of Hosts" (Deut. xxxiii. 10).

The distribution of the Levites was the Lord's provision for the preservation of Israel's faith in the land. They had entered by faith. They had overcome by faith. That faith must now be maintained in the place of blessing by the teaching of God's word. Maintained faith was the condition of maintained blessing. Faith's food is God's word. So is it always.

Chapter xxii.—The Altar of Witness.

A schismatic altar in Israel! Had not the book of the Covenant emphatically declared that there should be but the one national altar of sacrifice before the Tabernacle—at Shiloh? What then of this "great altar" erected by Reuben, Gad, and the half tribe of Manasseh hard by the Jordan? Is it to be wondered at that the other tribes, shocked and angered, gathered together against them?

But a new complexion is given to the apparent breach when the builders of the altar explain that it is meant to be not an altar of sacrifice but of *witness*—a witness to the unity of the two and a half tribes east of the Jordan with the rest of Israel.

How many there are who, like these two and a half tribes, want to feel quite sure that they have their part with God's Israel, yet are content to live just outside the land!

No doubt this altar "Ed" was well meant; but was it not *needless* if the Divine command were obeyed that three times each year all the males of Israel should appear before the Lord, in Shiloh?

Was it not also *presumptuous*? No pattern for its shape had been given of God, and no direction for its construction. Nor, apparently, had the counsel of the Lord been as much as thought of!

Now here is a noteworthy lesson concerning *the unity of faith*. Had Reuben, Gad, and the half tribe of Manasseh settled west of the Jordan with the other tribes, in the promised place of blessing, no such artificial monument of their oneness with Israel would have been required. True unity is not outward but inward. It is not achieved, nor even preserved, by external memorials. It consists in a oneness of inward and spiritual experience. The trend among the various denominations in the organised Church of today is to seek an imposing outward union by the formulation of a common creed and the inclusion of all sections in some single visible body with impressive proportions and social prestige. This is the building of a modern "altar Ed." It is the confusing of unity with mere uniformity.

The only true unity is that of a common inward life, a common spiritual experience, and a common heart-loyalty. Those who are really living "in the land," in the enjoyment of that spiritual Canaan which is in Christ, are conscious of their spiritual oneness with all the elect of God in Christ, whatever outward denominational differentiations may exist between them.

Speaking of this true unity, the late Dr. F. B. Meyer, in a fine passage, says: "Coming from all points of the compass, fired by the same hopes, suppliants at the same meeting-place, reliant upon the same blood, the common attraction establishes an organic unity like that of the tree, the multiplicity of whose parts is subsidiary to the one life-force; or like that of the body, the variety of whose members is subordinate to the one animating soul.

"The nearer we get to Christ, the more clearly we discern our unity with all who belong to Him. We learn to think less of points of divergence, and more about those of agreement. We find that the idiosyncrasies by which each believer is fitted for his specific work do not materially affect those depths of the inner life which in all saints abut on the nature of the living Saviour. As the scattered sheep browse their way up towards a common summit, they converge on each other, and there is one flock, as there is one Shepherd.

"It is the supreme vision of the Bible, granted to the most eminent saints, that though the new Jerusalem comprehends the names of the tribes of Israel and of the Apostles of the Lamb, is garnished by jewels of many hues, and has gates facing in all directions, it yet is one, 'the Bride, the Lamb's wife.' What wonder, then, that the world, and sometimes the professing Church, supposes that the Lord's prayer is not fulfilled, and that the unity has yet to be made? The unity is made; but only the spiritual with spiritual discernment can detect its symmetry.''

We cannot *make* spiritual unity. The unity of the sanctified in Christ is a spiritual reality wrought by the Holy Spirit Himself. The secret of Christian unity lies in our being west of Jordan— with the baptismal burial of that Jordan flood passed through, and the experience of the Spirit's fulness entered into. Give us back that Canaan experience of spiritual fulness which came at Pentecost, and then the overflowing consciousness of spiritual unity among Christ's own will submerge all artificial barriers. Israel's true unity lay in a common life and a common experience of God which found concentrated expression in that one altar of sacrifice at Shiloh. Even so, the true unity of the Lord's own today lies in—and is only realised *according to*—their common experience of life in Christ, finding its vital centre in the Cross and person of the Redeemer. Let this twenty-second chapter of Joshua, then, speak to us its message on the true unity of faith.

Chapters xxiii.–xxiv.—The Farewell of Joshua.

Finally, we have the parting counsels of the now aged Joshua. We must not linger over the touching scene. The faithful leader's words unveil the concern of his heart for the privileged nation. For some years now, Israel had been enjoying the rest and plenty of Canaan. What of the future? All depended on whether or not Israel would continue faithful to the covenant. Joshua's words do not conceal his apprehensiveness. Seven times he refers to the idolatrous nations still left in Canaan. He knew the snare they would be to Israel; and he therefore prescribed three safeguards.

First, there must be brave *adherence to God's word* (xxiii. 6).

Second, there must be a vigilantly continued *separation* from the Canaanite nations (xxiii. 7).

And, there must be a cleaving to the Lord with real and fervent *love* (xxiii. 8–11).

This is the gist of these closing chapters; and these are the three indispensable conditions (just as truly today as in Joshua's day) for a *continuing* in the experience of the "fulness of blessing." There must be (1) a living close to the word of God; (2) a consistent separation from all known wrong; (3) a cleaving to

God with the best love of the heart. Truly, in the words of 1 John v. 3, "His commandments are not grievous," and they who fulfil them find indeed a Canaan of spiritual blessing, of peace and joy in the Holy Spirit, of heavenly fellowship and treasure, which this world can neither give nor take away.

In these last two chapters, then, the emphasis is upon the need and the way of *continuance*. Thus, in this third part of the Book of Joshua, we have:

Chapter xiii.–xix. Partition of Canaan   — faith *rewarded*.
  ,,   xx. The Cities of Refuge   — faith *protected*.
  ,,   xxi. The Levite's Portion   — faith *preserved*.
  ,,   xxii. The Altar of Witness   — faith *unifying*.
  ,,   xxiii.–iv. Farewell of Joshua   — faith *continuing*.

And now it may be helpful to see the whole book set out in analysis, with special reference to its spiritual message which we have traced through the chapters (see page 264).

FIND OUT THE WEAK SPOTS!

1. What are the main divisions of Joshua?
2. What is the key thought of the book?
3. Is Canaan a type of Heaven? If not, why not?
4. How do Joshua and Ephesians correspond?
5. Chapter i. may be summarised as "Joshua charged." What of the other chapters?
6. What does the crossing of Jordan typify?
7. Where was Israel's first camp in Canaan?
8. What was the guile of the Gibeonites, and where is it mentioned?
9. How many cities fell to the Levites, and how many were cities of refuge?
10. What was the altar "Ed," and where is it mentioned?
11. What are the three emphases in Joshua's farewell exhortation?
12. In Chapter i. we have the *warrant* of faith. What are the characteristics of faith suggested by the other chapters?

END OF VOLUME I

EXPLORE THE BOOK

A Basic and Broadly Interpretative Course
of Bible Study from Genesis to Revelation

J. SIDLOW BAXTER

VOLUME TWO

JUDGES TO ESTHER

CONTENTS OF VOLUME TWO

THE BOOK OF JUDGES 7
Studies 24 and 25

THE BOOK OF RUTH 25
Studies 26 and 27

THE FIRST BOOK OF SAMUEL 43
Studies 28 and 29

THE SECOND BOOK OF SAMUEL 63
Studies 30 and 31

THE FIRST BOOK OF KINGS 83
Studies 32, 33, 34

THE SECOND BOOK OF KINGS 115
Studies 35 to 39

THE BOOKS OF THE CHRONICLES 163
Studies 40 and 41

THE BOOK OF EZRA 191
Studies 42, 43, 44

THE BOOK OF NEHEMIAH 225
Studies 45, 46, 47

THE BOOK OF ESTHER 257
Studies 48, 49, 50

THE BOOK OF JUDGES (1)

Lesson Number 24

NOTE.—For this study read the whole book of Judges, preferably at one sitting.

The Bible is the chart of history. It affords a panoramic view of the whole course of events from the creation and the fall of man, to the final judgment, and the inauguration of the new heaven and the new earth. It gives us, not events only, but their moral character, tracing the motives of the various actors in the drama, as well as the results of their actions. Events are shown in relation to their causes and effects, and the judgment of God as to their character is revealed. Without the Bible, history would be a spectacle of unknown rivers flowing from unknown sources to unknown seas; but under its guidance we can trace the complex currents to their springs, and see the end from the beginning.

—*Dr. H. Gratton Guinness.*

THE BOOK OF JUDGES (1)

WOULD that we might erase from the tablets of Israel's history
the many dark doings and sad happenings which make up the
bulk of this seventh book of the canon! But alas, the sin of
Israel is written "with a pen of iron and with the point of a
diamond." Though Israel wash herself "with nitre" and take
"much soap," yet is her iniquity here marked for all time and
for all to see. Says Jehovah, long afterwards, through His
prophet Jeremiah: "I brought you into a plentiful country, to
eat the fruit thereof; but when ye entered ye defiled My land,
and made My heritage an abomination" (Jer. ii. 7). As we cannot
obliterate the tragic record, let us be quick to learn from it;
for although it is such a pathetic anticlimax to the book of
Joshua, it is nevertheless one of the richest books of Scripture
in the salutary lessons and examples which it contains.

Its Name

The book of Judges obviously takes its name from its contents,
which are devoted to the period of Israel's so-called "Judges,"
and to certain of the Judges themselves. We may say that it
covers roughly the first three hundred and fifty years of Israel's
history in Canaan. This is the period of the Theocratic regime,
in which Jehovah Himself is Israel's "King Invisible."

The four-hundred-year periods of Israel's history are worthy
of note just here.

From the Birth of Abram to the Death of
    Joseph in Egypt (the family period)   about 400 years

From the Death of Joseph to the Exodus
    from Egypt (the tribal period)   .   about 400 years.

From the Exodus to Saul, the first of the
    kings (the Theocracy period).   .   about 400 years.

From Saul to Zedekiah and the Exile (the
    monarchy period) . . . about 400 years.

The period of the Judges falls in the third of these four-hundred-year periods, that is, the Theocratic. The Theocracy was a glorious experiment with superlative possibilities; and Israel's failure is therefore the more tragic.

Of the Judges as a class Dr. Joseph Angus says: "The Judges (*shophetim*) here described were not a regular succession of governors, but occasional deliverers raised up by God, to rescue Israel from oppression, and to administer justice. Without assuming the state of royal authority, they acted for the time as vicegerents of Jehovah, the invisible King. Their power seems to have been not unlike that of the *Suffetes* of Carthage and Tyre, or of the *Archons* of Athens. The government of the people may be described as a republican confederacy, the elders and princes having authority in their respective tribes."

Nature and Authorship

The records preserved for us in this book of the Judges are, of course, historically *true*; yet manifestly they do not intend to constitute a scientific *history* of the period with which they deal; for the first characteristic of a scientific history is a careful attention to chronology—a characteristic which is markedly missing from the book of Judges. The emphasis here is on the spiritual significance of selected events, not on mere chronological continuity. What we have is a collection of narratives selected because of their bearing on the main design of the book; and it is this purposeful selectivity which explains why such space is devoted to the episodes connected with Deborah, Gideon, Abimelech, and the shameful lapse of Benjamin, while long stretches are passed over in silence. It is this which explains, also, the otherwise strange non-mention of the High Priests in the body of the book, and certain other of its peculiarities. In a word, this book of Judges is not so much concerned with forging a historical chain as with driving home a vital lesson—which we will mention presently.

The authorship of this book is not known, though Jewish tradition attributes it to Samuel. "It seems scarcely open to doubt that the mass of the book consists of the original contemporary annals of the different tribes. The minute and graphic details of the narratives, Deborah's song, Jotham's fable, Jephtha's message to the king of Ammon, the exact description of the great

Parliament at Mizpeh, and many other like portions of the book, must be contemporary documents." Yet at the same time it is equally clear that these original documents were edited and compiled later. It is clear from chapter xviii. 31 and xx. 27, that the compilation took place after the Ark was removed from Shiloh. From the repeated clause: "In those days there was no king in Israel" (xvii. 6; xviii. 1; xix. 1; xxi. 25), we gather that it was made after the commencement of the reign of Saul, the first of the kings. Yet the mention of the Jebusites (i. 21), as dwelling in Jerusalem "unto this day," makes it equally plain that it was before the accession of David (who dispossessed the Jebusites from their stronghold—1 Chron. xi. 5). What could be more probable, then, than that Samuel, who links the two periods of the Judges and the Kings, should have had a large hand in the work as it has come down to us?

The reference, in chapter xviii. 30, to a "captivity of the land," has caused some to argue that the book was not compiled until the deportation of the ten tribes, hundreds of years later; but the other time-data in the book combine against this. The words obviously point to one of the earlier servitudes, in the time of the Judges, and still fresh in the memory of the people.

The original documents of the book, then, are practically contemporaneous with the events recorded; and their compilation into the present form dates somewhere in the reign of King Saul, being effected—as likely as not—by that great Israelite, Samuel; for, as Dr. Ellicott remarks, "The subordination of all the incidents of the history to the inculcation of definite lessons shows that the book, in its present form, was arranged by one person."

Its Picture of Israel

"The moral character of the Israelites, as described in this book, seems to have greatly deteriorated," writes Dr. Angus. "The generation who were contemporaries with Joshua were both courageous and faithful, and free in a great measure from the weakness and obstinacy which had dishonoured their fathers (Judges ii. 7). Their first ardour, however, had now somewhat cooled, and more than once they fell into a state of indifference which Joshua found it needful to rebuke. As each tribe received its portion, they became so engrossed in cultivating it, or so

much fonder of ease than of war, that they grew unwilling to
help the rest. Another generation arose. Living among idolaters,
the Israelites copied their example, intermarried with them, and
became contaminated with their abominations (ii. 13; iii. 6).
The old inhabitants of the land, left alone, gathered strength to
make head against the chosen race: surrounding nations and
tribes, as the Syrians, Philistines, Moabites, and Midianites, took
advantage of their degeneracy to attack them; while the licentiousness, ease, and idolatry, to which the Hebrews were giving
way, impaired their powers of defence.''

Its General Significance

The Judges whom God raised up were living object-lessons by
which God sought to preserve in Israel the understanding that
faith in Jehovah, the only true God, was the one way of victory
and well-being. But the people only responded so far as served
the selfish end of the moment—the saving of their necks from
bondage, and the grabbing of fleshly advantages. They did not
love Jehovah one whit more for His painstaking patience; nor
did they even take the lower level of serving Him from a sense
of *duty*. Speaking generally, the God of their fathers was simply
a convenient resort in time of extremity. When things were
tolerably comfortable, barefaced betrayal of Jehovah was the
order of the day. The people chafed under the disciplinary requirements of God's high calling to Israel through Abraham and
Moses. They neglected the book of the Covenant, and "turned
quickly out of the way" to indulge in the unclean and forbidden.

From time to time, out of sheer pity for His humiliated and
groaning people, God raised up these men, the Judges, whose
exploits of deliverance—despite vulgarities and crudities in the
character and behaviour of the Judges themselves—were so manifestly miraculous interventions of Jehovah, in response to faith
in Himself, that Israel was thereby forced to recognise Jehovah
again as the one true God, and was thus encouraged to return
to the first faith and the first love. Yet these gracious interventions had no durable effect; and Israel's early obstinacy
developed into incurable obduracy. So much, alas, for Israel's
first three hundred and fifty years in Canaan! It is a pathetic
anti-climax to the Book of Joshua.

Its Central Lesson

And *why* this tragic landslide? It is the answering of this question which forms the controlling purpose of this book of Judges. Its intent is to expose the cause and course of Israel's ruining downgrade in such a way as to sting the national conscience into repentant return to Jehovah: and we can well imagine how that great-souled patriot, Samuel, could compile this book with such an end in view. The plan of the book, which we mention below, leaves us in no doubt as to its central lesson. It is—

FAILURE THROUGH COMPROMISE

Every page of the book contributes to the driving home of this central truth. Of course, the exploits of the Judges teach the lesson that a return to the true faith brings renewed victory; yet in their very teaching of this they but accentuate the main, stark reality, that all the failure is due to *compromise*.

How did it all begin? Well, in the opening chapter, we are told that the nine and a half tribes which settled in Canaan did not destroy or even drive out the Canaanite nations, as God had commanded. They suffered them to remain. The other two and a half tribes—Reuben, Gad, and half the tribe of Manasseh, had already sadly compromised in choosing to settle in Gilead, on the eastern side of the Jordan. The first chapter of Judges gives us a list of eight incomplete conquests—by Judah, Benjamin, Manasseh, Ephraim, Zebulun, Asher, Naphtali, and Dan. The other two tribes, Issachar and Simeon, are not mentioned, but the presumption is that their behaviour was like that of the others. Incomplete mastery of an evil at the outset always means constant trouble from it afterwards, and often defeat by it in the end. So was it with Israel. So has it been with others. Let us beware for ourselves! It is no use taking hold of a nettle with a tender hand. It is ruinous folly to try half-measures against sin! The Divine command to Israel was austere, but necessary. Israel allowed quarter to the foe, and lived to rue it.

Next, in the second and third chapters, we find the successive steps of further compromise. Having only partially mastered the Canaanites, Israel now makes leagues with them (ii. 2)—a thing which God has prohibited. Then, having made league with them, Israel intermarries with them (iii. 6)—another thing God has prohibited. Then, having mixed blood in marriage, Israel descends to their ways, bows to their idols, forsakes Jehovah, and serves Baal and Ashtaroth (ii. 13; iii. 6). Mark well these stages—incomplete mastery, military leagues, intermarriage, idolatry and complete apostasy—followed by humiliating captivity (ii. 14, etc.). The Judges who were mercifully raised up to recall and deliver Israel, stopped the rot for the moment, but it set in again worse than before as soon as the grave silenced each Judge's voice; for in chapter ii. 18, 19, we read: "And when the Lord raised them up Judges, then the Lord was with the Judge, and delivered them out of the hand of their enemies all the days of the Judge; for it repented the Lord because of their groanings by reason of them that oppressed them and vexed them. And it came to pass when the Judge was dead that they returned and corrupted themselves *more than their fathers*, in following other gods to serve them, and to bow down unto them. They ceased not from their own doings, nor from their stubborn way."

Yes, this is the tragic story of this book of Judges—*failure through compromise*. Let the words burn into the mind, and burn out any easy-going toleration of the unholy or questionable thing. We can never enjoy God's promised rest for long if we tolerate only partially crushed sins to continue with us. If we make league with questionable things because they seem harmless, we shall soon find ourselves wedded to the desires of the flesh again, and down from the heights to which God had lifted us.

Failure through compromise! Oh that Israel had heeded the message of this book! Oh that a compromising Church today never disregard it! God's word to His people of today is still that of 2 Corinthians vi. 17, 18—

"WHEREFORE COME OUT FROM AMONG THEM, AND BE YE SEPARATE, SAITH THE LORD, AND TOUCH NOT THE UNCLEAN THING, AND I WILL RECEIVE YOU, AND WILL BE A FATHER UNTO YOU, AND YE SHALL BE MY SONS AND DAUGHTERS, SAITH THE LORD ALMIGHTY."

THE BOOK OF JUDGES (2)

Lesson Number 25

NOTE.—For this study read the whole book of Judges through again, marking in the main part of the book (chapters iii. to xvi.) the six servitudes beginning with the words, "And the children of Israel did evil in the sight of the Lord."

This, then, is the ground-plan of Judges:

THE BOOK OF JUDGES
THE BOOK OF DECLENSION

FAILURE THROUGH COMPROMISE		
EXPLANATORY PROLOGUE—i.–ii. MAIN NARRATIVE—iii.–xvi.		
Apostasy	*Servitude*	*Deliverer*
iii. 5–8	To King of Mesopotamia, 8 years.	Othniel (iii. 9–11).
iii. 12–14	To King of Moab, 18 years.	Ehud (iii. 15–30) (also Shamgar, 31).
iv. 1–3	To King of Canaan, 20 years.	Deborah (iv. 4–v. 31) (and Barak).
vi. 1–10	To Midianites, 7 years.	Gideon (vi. 11–viii. 35).
x. 6–18	To Philistines, etc., 18 years.	Jephthah (xi. 1; xii. 7).
xiii. 1	To Philistines, 40 years.	Samson (xiii. 2; xvi. 31).
ILLUSTRATIVE EPILOGUE—xvii.–xxi.		

THE BOOK OF JUDGES (2)

The Arrangement

THE orderly scheme of this book is in itself such as to argue pretty conclusively its compilation by one person rather than several. The actual records of the Judges run from chapter iii. to chapter xvi.; and it is these chapters which form the body of the book. The other chapters consist of a prologue (i.–ii.), and an epilogue (xvii.–xxi.). The prologue is by way of *explanation*. The epilogue is by way of *illustration*. The prologue explains how the unhappy conditions of the period came about. The epilogue illustrates the conditions themselves. Thus:

> Explanatory Prologue (i.–ii.).
>
> Main Body of Book (iii.–xvi.).
>
> Illustrative Epilogue (xvii.–xxi.).

As for the main body of the book (iii.–xvi.), there can be no mistaking its arrangement. Twelve Judges are successively spoken of—Othniel, Ehud, Shamgar, Deborah (with Barak), Gideon, Tola, Jair, Jephthah, Ibzan, Elon, Abdon, Samson. Of these, *six* stand out pre-eminently—because the whole story gathers round six successive apostasies and servitudes of Israel, and these six deliverers, or judges, who wrought deliverance. The six are: Othniel, Ehud, Deborah, Gideon, Jephthah, and Samson. The six major apostasies are signalised, in each case, by the words: *"And the children of Israel did evil in the sight of the Lord."* Just the six times do these words occur in the body of this book; and in each case judgment falls, and servitude ensues.

It is a striking fact that all these six servitudes of Israel are said to have been brought about *by Jehovah Himself.* First— "The anger of the Lord was hot against Israel, and *HE* sold them into the hand of Chushan-rishathaim, King of Mesopotamia" (iii. 8). Second—"The *LORD* strengthened Eglon, King of Moab, against Israel" (iii. 12). Third—"The *LORD* sold them into the hand of Jabin, King of Canaan" (iv. 2). Four—"The LORD delivered them into the hand of Midian seven years" (vi. 1). Five—"The anger of the Lord was hot against Israel, and HE sold them into the hands of the Philistines" (x. 7). Six—"The LORD delivered them into the hands of the Philistines forty years" (xiii. 1).

Israel's servitudes were not just accidents. They were punishments. This is a point for serious consideration. God may confer special privileges on certain persons and nations, but He is no respecter of persons in any sense of indulgence to favourites. Those who sin against extra privilege bear heavier responsibility and incur heavier penalty. God may give many privileges, but He never gives the privilege to *sin*. Let us beware lest a sense of privilege should beguile our own hearts into the sin of presumption.

As we read this book of Judges we may well feel amazed that such low living could go with such high calling. Yes—high calling and low living! A convention chairman once said: "It is possible to be moral without being spiritual: and it is even possible to be spiritual without being moral!" Paradoxical? Impossible? Yet have we not come across persons knowing the deeper and higher truths of the Christian life, able to converse freely in a most spiritual vein, and who, nevertheless, could stoop to behaviour that the average non-Christian would shrink from in disgust? It is only too easy for familiarity to engender callousness, and then for callousness to be hypocritically covered with an outer garment of seeming spirituality. We must watch and pray, lest we ourselves enter into this temptation.

A Strikingly Sustained Emphasis

The main narrative of Judges is remarkable for a striking four-fold emphasis which it sustains throughout. The six apostasies, servitudes, and deliverances are each set out in this quadruple order:

SINNING.

SUFFERING.

SUPPLICATION.

SALVATION.

This will be seen with ease and clearness if we set out the six episodes in parallel columns, in the actual words and the actual order of the Scripture narrative.

It is worth while for us to get the fourfold sequence vividly in our minds, for it has living applications to our own times. It may be that so far as Israel is concerned, the long period of sinning and suffering is now forever drawing to a close, and the prophesied age-end supplication and salvation drawing near.

The Six Episodes

	First iii. 7–11.	*Second* iii. 12–30.	*Third* iv. 1–v. 31.
Sin	"And the children of Israel did evil in the sight of the Lord, and forgat the Lord their God, and served Baalim and the groves . . ."	"And the children of Israel did evil again in the sight of the Lord . . ."	"And the children of Israel again did evil in the sight of the Lord when Ehud was dead . . ."
Suffering	"Therefore the anger of the Lord was hot against Israel, and He sold them into the hand of Cushan-risha-thaim, King of Mesopotamia; and the children of Israel served Cushan-rishathaim eight years . . ."	"And the Lord strengthened Eglon the King of Moab against Israel, because they had done evil in the sight of the Lord; and he gathered unto him the children of Ammon and Amalek, and went and smote Israel, and possessed the city of palm trees. So the children of Israel served Eglon the King of Moab eighteen years . . ."	"And the Lord sold them into the hand of Jabin, King of Canaan, that reigned in Hazor; the captain of whose host was Sisera, which dwelt in Harosheth of the Gentiles . . ."
Supplication	"And when the children of Israel cried unto the Lord . . ."	"But when the children of Israel cried unto the Lord . . ."	"And the children of Israel cried unto the Lord; for he had nine hundred chariots of iron; and twenty years he mightily oppressed the children of Israel . . ."
Salvation	"The Lord raised up a deliverer to the children of Israel, who delivered them, even Othniel the son of Kenaz, Caleb's younger brother," etc.	"The Lord raised them up a deliverer, Ehud the son of Gera, a Benjamite, a man left-handed," etc.	"And Deborah, a prophetess, she judged Israel at that time, . . . and she sent and called Barak, the son of Abinoam," etc.

	Fourth vi. 1–viii. 35.	*Fifth* x. 6–xii. 7.	*Sixth* xiii. 1–xvi. 31.
Sin . . .	" And the children of Israel did evil in the sight of the Lord . . ."	" And the children of Israel did evil again in the sight of the Lord, and served Baalim and Ashtaroth and the gods of Syria, and the gods of Zidon, and the gods of Moab, and the gods of the children of Ammon, and the gods of the Philistines, and forsook the Lord, and served not Him . . ."	" And the children of Israel did evil again in the sight of the Lord, . . ."
Suffering	" And the Lord delivered them into the hand of Midian seven years . . ."	" And the anger of the Lord was hot against Israel, and He sold them into the hands of the Philistines, and into the hands of the children of Ammon . . ."	" And the Lord delivered them into the hand of the Philistines forty years . . ."
Supplication	" And the children of Israel cried unto the Lord : And it came to pass when the children of Israel cried unto the Lord because of the Midianites . . ."	" And the children of Israel cried unto the Lord, saying : We have sinned against Thee, both because we have forsaken our God, and also served Baalim ; . . . Deliver us only, we pray Thee, this day . . ."	No supplication recorded, — evidently because they had said, in their last extremity : " Deliver us *only*, we pray Thee, *this* day " (see former column).
Salvation .	" And there came an angel of the Lord, and sat under an oak which was in Ophrah that pertained unto Joash the Abiezrite ; and his son Gideon threshed wheat by the winepress, to hide it from the Midianites . . . the Spirit of the Lord came upon Gideon," etc.	" Then the Spirit of the Lord came upon Jephthah, and he passed over Gilead, and Manasseh, and passed over Mizpeh of Gilead . . . thus the children of Ammon were subdued before the children of Israel," etc.	" The angel of the Lord appeared and said . . . he (Samson) shall begin to deliver Israel out of the hand of the Philistines." (Here follows the account of Samson and his exploits.)

This recurrent emphasis is meant to do its own work in the reader's mind. Let us read, mark, learn, and inwardly digest. There are things in the moral realm which are indissolubly wedded. Sin and suffering always go together. They cannot be divorced. Oh that human hearts might be persuaded of this! It is also true that supplication and salvation are similarly joined. God will be entreated by a true supplication in which there is a putting away of the evil thing; and then He will show His salvation.

GIDEON—AND HOW HE STILL SPEAKS

Some of the characters depicted in this book of Judges are worthy of careful study. We pick out Gideon for brief mention here, to show how these characters speak to us today.

Gideon, the fifth Judge of Israel, is rightly counted as one of the outstanding heroes in Israel's early history. Yet we need to realise at the outset that his heroism was not a product of his natural make-up, but the outcome of a transforming spiritual experience. It is this which gives him a living significance to ourselves today.

When first we see Gideon he cuts a pathetic figure of unbelief (vi. 11–23). He is a furtive, nervous young man secretly threshing wheat in the winepress, to hide it from the marauding Midianites. What pathetic exclamations of unbelief escape his lips when the Lord suddenly appears as a Mighty One of valour!—for undoubtedly the reading of verse 12 as "The Lord is with thee, even the Lord mighty in valour" is the correct one, and not that which makes Gideon the mighty one of valour instead of the Lord (as does our English version). Mark unconverted Gideon's reactions. He gasps—"Oh, my Lord, if Jehovah be with us, why then is all this befallen us? And where be all His miracles which our fathers told us of, saying: Did not Jehovah bring us up out of Egypt? But now Jehovah hath forsaken us . . ." A rather dismal reception this!—"Oh! . . . if . . . why? . . . where? . . . but . . ." Verse 14 continues, "And Jehovah looked upon him and said: Go in this thy might, and thou shalt save Israel from the hand of the Midianites: have not I sent thee?" These were strong and reassuring words, but Gideon can only moan, "Oh, my Lord, wherewith shall I save Israel . . .?" The Lord replies still further, "Surely I will be with thee, and thou shalt smite the Midianites as one man." Yet even this only evokes another stammering "if"—"If now I have found grace in Thy sight, then show me a sign." To be sure, in these replies of Gideon we have a fair sample of the vocabulary of unbelief. In his successive exclamations and lamentations we have the sceptical *surprise* of unbelief, then its *uncertainty* and its *questioning* and its *complaining* and its *false humility* and its *resourcelessness* and its *persistent dubiety* and its *seeking for signs*. Unconverted Gideon presents a sorry picture of the paralysis which always accompanies unbelief.

Gideon's Transformation

But now look at Gideon's transforming experience. In the first place he became *converted*. We use the word thoughtfully. By the time that the "Angel of the Lord" had completed his visit to him he had become quite convinced regarding the true God of Israel. Note verse 24, "Then Gideon built an altar there unto the Lord, and called it *Jehovah-Shalom*." There is vital significance about that altar. The altar is ever the place where God and man meet. It is the outward symbol of an inward transaction between the human soul and God. When Gideon built that altar to Jehovah he turned his back on false gods and became a worshipper of the one true God. Moreover he gave that altar a significant name—*Jehovah-Shalom*, which means, "Jehovah my peace." For the first time in his life this young Hebrew came into a sense of peace. That is always a first product of true conversion.

But Gideon went further. He became *consecrated*. He yielded his own will to the will of God. Read verses 25–7. We only need to think our way back into the circumstances a little, to appreciate what an acute challenge to Gideon's new faith and obedience this test was. The command that he should "throw down the altar of Baal" reminds us at once that Gideon lived in a time of widespread religious apostasy. Israel's religious leaders were "modernists," and had caused the people to err. To wreck Baal's altar was to run counter to the popular will, and to invite death. But Gideon did it. And how remarkable was the result! Read again verses 28–32. Gideon's father became converted too! Maybe the old man had secretly sighed for the "good old ways" and had longed for some brave champion of the old-time faith to arise and call his fellow-countrymen back to Jehovah; and now, when his son stood up for the old-time faith Joash was immediately by his side. We may apply this to ourselves. In nine cases out of ten, the reason we have so little influence for Christ among our own kith and kin is that we ourselves are not prepared to go the length of full consecration to the will of God.

Finally, Gideon became *controlled*, by which we mean that he became controlled by the Spirit of God. See verse 34, "The Spirit of the Lord came upon Gideon; and he blew a trumpet, and Abi-ezer was gathered after him." He became at once a leader and a saviour of his people. The people recognised the transforming power of God in him, and flocked to him when he sounded his clarion. The story which follows in the Scripture account tells of Gideon's marvellous victory over Midian, and his freeing of Israel from the alien yoke.

What a transformation had now taken place in Gideon! The man who had first been converted and had then become consecrated had now become controlled by the Holy Spirit. That thirty-fourth verse is noteworthy. A near translation would be: "The Spirit of Jehovah *clothed Himself* with Gideon." Gideon's personality became, so to speak, a garment in which God moved among men. What a sermon, then, is this man to us! Like Abel, "he being dead, yet speaketh." This soul-saving, life-changing, character-transforming experience through which he passed may be known by ourselves—not in its outward accidentals, of course, but in its inward essentials. *We* may become truly converted to God, truly consecrated to His will, and really controlled by the Holy Spirit. And we may be taken up and used by God as definitely as Gideon was. Converted, consecrated, Spirit-controlled!—God grant that it may be true of ourselves! We must get our eyes away from doubt-provoking circumstances, and fix them on the word of God Himself. "Faithful is He that calleth you, who also will do it" (1 Thess. v. 24).

> Doubt sees the obstacles,
>   Faith sees the way.
> Doubt sees the darksome night,
>   Faith sees the day.
> Doubt dreads to take the step,
>   Faith soars on high.
> Doubt whispers, "Who believes?"
>   Faith answers—"I."

THE BOOK OF RUTH (1)

Lesson Number 26

NOTE.—For this study read the book of Ruth right through at one sitting.

This is one of the richest rewards of truly knowing the Scriptures. No other book proves such an exhaustless mine of precious treasures to those who are content to delve deep into it. It is a field for endless study and ceaseless discovery; and the humblest believer may find hid treasure never before dug up by any other, and therefore peculiarly his own. No more unanswerable proof of the Divine origin of the Bible can be found than this capacity to reveal to every devout reader something absolutely new.

—*Arthur T. Pierson, D.D.*

THE BOOK OF RUTH (1)

PRICELESS gems have often been found in unlikely places. Many a choice flower has been found blooming in a rocky crevice. Rainbow artistries have suddenly lit up the drabbest skies. Beauty spots have charmed the traveller at surprise turns on the least-promising road. It is even so with this superbly beautiful little idyl, the book of Ruth.

It opens with the words: "Now it came to pass in the days when the judges ruled . . ."; so that its story clearly belongs to the period covered by the book of Judges—a tragic period indeed, as we have seen. Yet so touchingly beautiful is this episode, centring in Naomi and Ruth and Boaz, that it comes as a kind of redeeming contrast after our painful reading in the book of Judges. Such a lovely story we should least expect in such a setting.

The book of Judges leaves us with the all-too-well-founded conviction that the general condition was one of moral deterioration: but the book of Ruth turns a new sidelight on the scene, and shows us that amid the general degeneracy there were instances of noble love and godly chivalry and high ideal. Truly, the story is a silver star in an inky sky, a glorious rose blooming amid desert aridness, a pure gem flashing amid foul debris, a breath of fragrance amid surrounding sterility.

But it is still more. If this one instance of godly chivalry was picked out by the anonymous author, and committed to written form (maybe because of its special connection with David and the throne), may we not reasonably suppose that it represents many other such instances amid the surrounding decline, which were never recorded, and of which we know nothing? There is truth in Alexander Maclaren's word that "the blackest times were not so dismal in reality as they look in history."

This little biographical episode is given in the form of a *story*. It is a series of pastoral idyls, or pen-and-ink sketches with a rural background, showing the noble devotion of a young Moabitish widow for her widowed Hebrew mother-in-law, and the providential reward by which her self-sacrificing devotion was afterward crowned.

It is a *true* story. Its transparent simplicity bespeaks its honesty. It tells of actual happenings, and of real persons whose names figure in real genealogical records. Dr. James Morison says: "The material of the story is of such a nature that its unreality, if it had not been honest, would at once have been detected and exposed. The stuff out of which the story is woven consisted, so to speak, of very sensitive filaments. It had to do with the genealogy of the royal family. The principal personages in the story were ancestors of king David. That there was a Moabitish link in the chain of his genealogy must have been well known to the king himself, and to all his household, and to a large proportion of the people of Israel in general. It must likewise have been well known that this Moabitish link did not lie far back in the line. The existence of such a link was too great a peculiarity to be treated with indifference. We cannot doubt that the whole history of the case would be a frequent topic of narration, conversation, and comment at once within and around the royal court. The probability, therefore, is that the writer would be careful to do no violence to the facts of the case. Any alloy of fiction or romance on such a subject would have been at once resented, alike by the royal family, and by the great body of the people, the devoted admirers of the king."

Its Unique Features

This is one of the only two books in Scripture which bear the names of women. Those two are Ruth and Esther; and they stand in marked contrast. Ruth is a young Gentile woman who is brought to live among Hebrews and marries a Hebrew husband in the line of royal David. Esther is a young Hebrew woman who is brought to live among Gentiles and marries a Gentile husband on the throne of a great empire. Both Ruth and Esther were great and good women. The book of Ruth, however, is quite alone in this, that it is the only instance in the Bible in which a whole book is devoted to a woman.

The book of Ruth is a *love* story; and no doubt one of its purposes is to extol virtuous love, and to show how it can overcome all alienations and prejudices. But the remarkable thing is that it is not the story of a romantic love between a young man and a young woman; it is—as Dr. Samuel Cox says—"the story of a woman's love for a woman; and, strangely as it would sound in the ears of our modern wits, it is the story of a young wife's passionate and devoted love for her mother-in-law!"

Another striking feature about this book is its *catholicity of outlook*. The three pivotal figures in the book are Naomi, Ruth, and Boaz. All three are lovely characters; yet, somehow, without in the least detracting from the other two, Ruth excels, and with each new turn of the story the author deftly emphasises that Ruth is the heroine here, despite the fact that, unlike the other two, she is not of Israel. When we think of the jealous exclusiveness of the old-time Jews, it is remarkable to find this ungrudging portrayal of Moabitess Ruth as the focus of admiration. She is seen to excel even Israel's daughters; yet this occasions not the slightest resentment, but the admiration which it merits. That the grace and virtue of Moab's sweet-spirited daughter should have had such frank recognition speaks well for the author himself. The whole story is written in a spirit of charity and catholicity. "It is fair, and even generous, in the tone it takes toward those who were outside the Hebrew pale. It has no word of blame for Elimelech, although he left the land of his fathers to sojourn among the heathen; nor for Orpah, although she turned back from Naomi; on the contrary it records her kindness and self-devotion in at least intending to remain with her 'mother' till Naomi herself dissuaded her; while for Ruth it has no praise too high. It bases itself on the truth which Christ has made the common property of the race, that in every nation a pure and unselfish love is acceptable to God. So far from asserting the exclusive privilege of the chosen people, it rather invites other races to come and put their trust under the wings of Jehovah, by showing that as soon as they trust in Him the privilege and blessings of Israel become theirs."

Again, it is striking that this young Moabitess, Ruth, should not only have married so honourably in Israel, but have actually become the great-grandmother of David (as the closing verses show) and one of the mothers in the line from which the Messiah should eventually come. Ruth is one of the four women who are mentioned in the Messianic line. The other three—Tamar,

Rahab, and Bath-sheba, recall unworthy conduct; but virtuous Ruth redeems them.

A careful examination of the line from Adam down to the birth of Jesus shows that there were some sixty generations, and that these sixty seem to go in six tens, with the tenth man in each case being singularly representative of some great truth concerning the coming Messiah. Take the first group of ten:

Adam,	Jared,
Seth,	Enoch,
Enos,	Methuselah,
Cainan,	Lamech,
Mahalaleel,	*NOAH*.

Noah is the tenth man. As Satan had tried to cut off the Messianic hope at the very gateway of human history, by the murder of Abel, so now in Noah's day, behind the utter corruption of the race generally, he seeks to thwart it; but amid the corruption there is one man who walks with God and is clean in his generations (Gen. vi. 9); and when the whole race is destroyed there is the exception of this one man and his family; and this man is the very one in whom the Messianic line runs. All the power of Satan, and all the sin of men, cannot frustrate the purpose of the Lord God. Now take the second ten:

Shem,	Reu,
Arphaxad,	Serug,
Salah,	Nahor,
Eber,	Terah,
Peleg,	*ABRAHAM*.

Abraham is the tenth man here. Abraham is the one picked out to become the father of the chosen people from whom the Messiah should come. To him God specially reveals Himself, and gives unconditional promises which He later confirms with an oath. Now take the third ten:

Isaac,	Ram,
Jacob,	Amminadab,
Judah,	Nahshon,
Pharez,	Salma,
Hezron,	*BOAZ*.

Boaz is the tenth man here. And what of Boaz? Well, that is what our priceless little book of Ruth tells us (and may we not now be touching one of the deeper significances in the writing of the book of Ruth?). It was Boaz who took Gentile Ruth into the Davidic ancestry and the Messianic line; and as Ruth passes into that line she representatively takes all the Gentiles with her, so that now both Jews and Gentiles share common hope in the coming of Him who was to be "a Light to lighten the Gentiles, and the Glory of His people Israel." (The other "tenth" men will be mentioned later). Yes, Ruth belongs to us all, as, even more, does that wonderful Saviour who came, in the fulness of time, of that lineage in which Ruth shines like a gentle star.

> What star of Messianic truth
> More beautiful than Gentile Ruth?
> In her the Gentiles find a place
> To share the hope of Judah's race;
> Now see from royal David's line
> One hope for Jew and Gentile shine!

When it was Written

Most probably this little book was written during the reign of David—as the following considerations suggest. (1) The opening verse says: "Now it came to pass in the days when the Judges ruled. . . ." This indicates that the book was written *after* the days of the Judges, for the writer is plainly looking back on a time that had gone. (2) In chapter iv. 7, the writer speaks of a custom which prevailed in Israel "in former time"; so that the book, besides having been written after the time of the Judges, must have been written long enough after the time it writes of to allow this little custom to drop into disuse—for the fact that the writer stays to explain the custom shows that it *had* fallen into disuse. (3) The genealogy at the end of the last chapter is carried down to David, and stops there (see iv. 17–22). But *why* should it stop there if written *later* than David's time? and how could it even *mention* David if written *before* David's time? (4) The time of David's reign would be about *long enough* afterward to allow for the little custom in the earlier or mid period of the Judges to fall out of use (say 100 to 150 years), which is made clear by the fact that David, the seventh son of Jesse, was great-grandson of Boaz, and reigned, therefore, between 100 and 150 years after the happenings described in the book of Ruth; while on the other hand the time of David's reign would not be *too* long afterward to be out of keeping with the intimacy of detail shown in the book concerning persons and incidents which would have faded from memory in times *later* than that of David. (5) The Davidic reign was a literary epoch in Hebrew history. The king himself was a man of letters, and would draw literary men around him. David was also a man of deep human sympathies, and would be much interested in the recent Moabite connection with his ancestry. Moreover, he was too free from Jewish narrowness to be ashamed of his Moabitish link (especially in view of I Samuel xxii. 3–4); rather, indeed, would not David's chivalrous soul be proud of a link with such an one as Ruth? We conclude that as the book of Judges was probably written in David's time, so this choice little addition, which concerns the same period, was written then too.

And now, in anticipation of our next lesson, here is a simple outline of the book of Ruth.

THE BOOK OF RUTH

The love that suffers reigns at last

Chapter i. LOVE'S RESOLVE: (*Ruth's noble choice*).

> RUTH THE FAITHFUL DAUGHTER—cleaves to Naomi in her sorrow.

„ ii. LOVE'S RESPONSE: (*Ruth's lowly service*).

> RUTH THE MOABITESS GLEANER—responds to Naomi's pressing need.

„ iii. LOVE'S REQUEST: (*Ruth's tender appeal*).

> RUTH THE VIRTUOUS SUPPLIANT—appeals to the chivalrous kinsman.

„ iv. LOVE'S REWARD: (*Ruth's marital joys*).

> RUTH THE BELOVED WIFE AND MOTHER—joys in the blissful consummation.

THE BOOK OF RUTH (2)

Lesson Number 27

NOTE.—For this further study in the book of Ruth read the entire story again twice through, checking off the analysis which we have given at the end of the preceding study.

When the last day is ended,
 And the nights are through;
When the last sun is buried
 In its grave of blue;
When the stars are quenched as candles,
 And the seas no longer fret;
When the winds unlearn their cunning,
 And the storms forget;
When the last lip is palsied,
 And the last prayer said,
Love shall reign immortal
 While the worlds lie dead.
—Anon.

THE BOOK OF RUTH (2)

The Story

Chapter i.

SOMEWHERE in the period of the Judges a famine befell Canaan, and was felt even in such fertile districts as that around Bethlehem. Under its stress, Elimelech, a Hebrew with an inheritance in the Bethlehem locality, sought temporary refuge in the land of Moab, taking with him his wife, Naomi, and their two sons, Mahlon and Chilion. We gather that they were a godly family; and no doubt it would cost them painful cogitation before they decided to go and seek sustenance among the idolatrous Moabites. Yet they went; and without doubt they did wrong in abandoning the covenant land of Israel and their place among the elect people. Israel knew that famine was only inflicted for default (Lev. xxvi., etc.).

They reached Moab, but fared ill; for in seeking a livelihood they forfeited life itself. They sought bread but found graves. First Elimelech died; then his fatherless sons married Moabite women (another forbidden thing—Deut. vii. 3, etc.); and soon afterwards these sons themselves were laid beneath the soil of Moab, leaving their two young widows with the already widowed mother, Naomi.

Ten years have now slipped away. Naomi hears of bounty in the old home-country, and resolves to return. Her two daughters-in-law have grown to love her, and wish to go with her. They have learned of the true God in Naomi's household. The love is mutual. They set off with Naomi, but under her kindly dissuasion the one, Orpah, decides to retrace her steps to Moab. Ruth, however, has grown so to love Naomi that she is prepared to forgo everything for widowed Naomi's sake; and, in one of the purest gems of noble utterance, assures her beloved mother-in-law of her own resolve so to cleave unto her that nought but death itself should part them :—

"Intreat me not to leave thee, nor to return from following after thee: for whither thou goest I will go, and where thou lodgest I

35

*will lodge; thy people shall be my people, and thy God my God.
Where thou diest will I die, and there will I be buried. The
Lord do so to me, and more also, if ought but death part thee
and me."*

To appreciate the meaning of Ruth's self-sacrificing love here,
we need to perceive the significance in Naomi's urging the two
younger women to return to the shelter of their own parents'
homes. See verses 8 and 9—"Go, return each to her mother's
house. The Lord deal kindly with you, as ye have dealt with
the dead, and with me. The Lord grant you that ye may find
rest, each of you in the house of her husband."

Note that word "rest"—"The Lord grant you that ye may
find *REST*, each of you in the house of her husband." The
Hebrew word so translated is *menuchah*. It signifies rest, not so
much in the ordinary sense, as rather in the sense of *a safe shelter*.
This is the word by which the Hebrews used to speak of a husband's house. It was a woman's *menuchah*, or safe resort. In
the ancient Orient the position of unmarried women and young
widows was perilous. The one place where they could find safety
and respect was in the house of a husband. This alone was a
woman's safe shelter from servitude, neglect, or licence.

Now it was this fact that Naomi had in mind when she urged
the return of Orpah and Ruth to seek safety, respect, and honour,
in their parents' homes, and then in "the house of a husband."
Naomi has no more sons who can husband Orpah and Ruth, as
she sadly tells them. If they accompany her back to Israel, there
is utterly no prospect for them, nor is there even the guarantee
of safety. If they stay in Moab there is good prospect of their
finding a husband's shelter; but there is no such prospect if they
travel to Canaan, for the Hebrew sons are forbidden by the law
to marry aliens. Certainly we need feel no censure toward Orpah
in her eventually deciding to remain in Moab.

But see the glorious love of Ruth. Knowing the cost full well,
she will gladly give up all, and suffer all, for Naomi!

And so Naomi returns home—with Moabitess Ruth; and "all
the city was moved about them, and they said: Is this Naomi?"
Thus ends the first chapter, and the first scene.

Chapter ii.

With chapter ii. comes *scene 2*, and it is touchingly beautiful. Naomi is so destitute that she must allow Ruth to go even as a poverty-stricken gleaner among the roughish reapers, to fetch home at least some little for food. With beautiful self-forgetfulness Ruth goes to the fields, only too willing to make this somewhat humiliating yet honest effort after sustenance. She is providentially guided to a field of Boaz, a wealthy kinsman of Naomi. Every recorded word and act of Boaz reveal his manly piety and kindliness. He is impressed by the charm and modesty of the graceful gleaner, and, after enquiring about her, is only too glad to extend special privileges and protection to her for the full duration of the harvest, so that she may eat and drink with his reapers, and glean a goodly portion, being safeguarded the while from any improper freedom on the part of the young men. Ruth returns with the first day's welcome load to Noami, who at once perceives the hand of God in what has happened. So Ruth continues her gleaning, throughout the barley and wheat harvests, in the fields of Boaz.

Chapter iii.

Chapter iii. gives the crisis. It reads strangely to westerners, and should be carefully understood. Harvesting is ended. The daily interviews with Boaz are over. An attachment has developed between Boaz and Ruth, yet the wealthy kinsman has not taken any practical step about it. Naomi detects the sadness that creeps over Ruth's tender spirit, and contrives a plan to find out what the intention of Boaz is, so as to bring things to a head. The expedient was in full accord with old-time Hebrew custom and the teaching of the Mosaic Law. There is not the faintest touch of impurity about it. The Mosaic statute ran—"If brethren dwell together, and one of them die, and have no child, the wife of the dead shall not marry without unto a stranger; her husband's brother shall take her to him to wife, and perform the duty of an husband's brother unto her. And it shall be that the firstborn which she beareth shall succeed in the name of his brother which is dead, that his name be not put out of Israel" (Deut. xxv. 5, 6).

Now when Naomi sent Ruth to Boaz, as described in this chapter, she was really appealing to him to honour this Israelite law, and thus, at the same time, give a husband's shelter to Ruth, and honour the name of Mahlon, her deceased Hebrew husband. Boaz clearly understood this, as his noble words shew (iii. 10–13).

Notice how both Ruth and Boaz use that word "*kinsman.*" Ruth says: "Thou art a near kinsman." Boaz replies: "It is true that I am thy near kinsman: howbeit, there is a kinsman nearer than I." This word "kinsman," in the Hebrew, is *goel*; and the Hebrew law of the *goel*, or next-of-kin, is of great interest. This law is laid down in Leviticus xxv.; Numbers xxxv.; Deuteronomy xix. and xxv. There were three obligations devolving upon the *goel*:

(1) He was to redeem his brother and his brother's inheritance, according to ability, if poverty had compelled his brother to go into slavery, or to dispose of his land.

(2) He was to be the avenger of any fatal violence against his brother.

(3) He was to raise up a successor to his brother, if his brother had died without leaving a son.

The obvious purpose behind all this was the saving of Israelitish families, as such, from extinction. The *goel's* qualification was that he must be the *next* of kin, or a *near* kinsman. Each near kinsman was *one* of the "goelim"; but he who was actually the *next* of kin was distinctively *the* "goel."

Coming back, now, to this third chapter of Ruth, with this law of the *goel* in mind, we should also observe understandingly how far removed from our modern western ideas are the simple, rustic ways and surroundings in which this scene is set. As Dr. Samuel Cox truly says—"An age in which the wealthy owner of a large and fertile estate would himself winnow barley and would sleep among the heaps of winnowed corn in an open threshing floor (verse 7), is obviously an age as different from this as it is remote from it. Moreover, Ruth, in creeping softly to the resting-place of Boaz, and nestling under the corner of his long robe (verse 7), was simply making a legal claim in the approved manner of the time." When Ruth said, "spread thy skirt over thine handmaid," Boaz fully understood the appeal of widowed

Ruth for protection, as the casting of the outward garment over the bride's head was a customary ceremony at old-time eastern marriages, in token of the husbandly protection thenceforward given to the bride.

This then is what happens: Boaz wakes and finds Ruth present. For a moment he is taken aback, but, on hearing Ruth's words, sympathetically appreciates the situation. His gracious reply (verses 10–13), reveals both his own honourableness and that of Ruth. And now the two reasons are disclosed why he had not proposed wedlock to Ruth—(1) his considerable seniority in years; (2) his not being the *nearest* kinsman. It may be also that a third reason had been in the mind of Boaz, namely, that Naomi, the wife of Ruth's deceased father-in-law, really had the prior claim on him; though now, by this very act of sending Ruth, Naomi had waived her claim in Ruth's favour, The "six measures of barley" which Ruth took home next morning told Naomi that the honourable Boaz would lose no time in taking the appropriate steps.

Chapter iv.

Chapter iv. crowns the story. Boaz, without delay, contracts with the nearer kinsman, in the presence of elders and witnesses, and, according to custom, at the city gate. This anonymous kinsman admits his obligation, and is willing to buy the land which was Elimelech's, but declines when he learns that in so doing he must also take a *Moabitess* to be his wife, his objection being—"lest I mar mine own inheritance." His view would be that Mahlon and Chilion had broken the law in marrying alien women, and that the calamities which had befallen them and Naomi were due to this, and would come to himself if he married one of these widowed women. So he handed over his right to Boaz, publicly acknowledging this by the old-time custom of plucking off his shoe, and handing it to Boaz—a custom which originated in the fact that men took legal possession of landed property by planting their foot, or shoe, on the soil. The elders and witnesses in the gate then cried, "We are witnesses."

To Boaz, Ruth was far more precious than the land. She became his wife, and by him became the mother of a son who in turn became the father of Jesse, who in turn became the father

of David, Israel's greatest king. As for Naomi, her joy was brimful.
She became the babe's nurse—and never did babe have tenderer
nurse or sweeter mother; while the women of the place said to
Naomi: "Thy daughter-in-law, which loveth thee, is better to
thee than seven sons."

Thus, this story which begins with famine, death, and mourning, ends with fulness, new life, and rejoicing. Weeping has
endured for a night, but joy has come with the morning. The
sad beginning has given place to a sweet and beautiful ending.
With a voice of gentle reassurance this precious little book of
Ruth calls to us from the bygone, telling us that *the love which
"suffereth long and is kind" never fails of its reward in the end.*

Typical Aspects

A careful reading through this book of Ruth seems to show
that there is a latent typical meaning hidden in it, which develops
as the story itself develops. The very names which occur in the
story put us on the track of this; and once we get on the track
we can easily follow it right through.

The story opens at Bethlehem, the name of which means
"House of Bread" (*Beyth* = house; *lechem* = bread). The first-
mentioned figure is *Elimelech*, whose name means "My God is
King," or "My God is my King" (*Eli* = my God; *melech* = king).
This Israelite, along with his wife *Naomi*, whose name means
"pleasantness," or "favour," leaves Bethlehem in the land of
Israel, because of famine, and seeks succour in the alien land of
Moab. The names of their two sons, whom they take with them
are *Mahlon* (joy, or song) and *Chilion* (ornament, or perfectness).
Under testing they forsake the place of covenant standing, and
resort to an expedient involving compromise. In Moab, Elimelech
(my God is my King) dies; so do Mahlon (song) and Chilion (perfectness). After ten tragic years Naomi, the pathetic remnant,
returns; but instead of being Naomi (pleasantness, sweetness,
favour), she is, by her own testimony, *Mara* (bitterness).

Now if this is not a striking type-picture of Israel we are much
deceived. Israel as originally constituted in Canaan was a Theocracy. God was Israel's King. Israel was Elimelech—and could
say "My God is my King." Israel was married, as it were, to
Naomi—pleasantness, favour, and blessing; and Israel's offspring were Mahlon and Chilion—song and perfectness. But,

under testing, Israel compromised and went astray, leaving the early allegiance to Jehovah. Elimelech died. No longer could Israel say with a perfect heart before the Lord—"My God is my King." Mahlon and Chilion passed away too—the "song" of praise and the "ornament" of devout godliness died off; while eventually Naomi, the once "favoured" and "pleasant" returns, a sorry remnant, "empty" and "bitter," as in the days when the remnant returned, under Ezra and Nehemiah.

But from the point of Naomi's return, Ruth ("comeliness") takes the prominent place; and Ruth is a type of the *Church*. The type-picture is made up of three scenes—(1) Ruth in the harvest field, (2) Ruth in the threshing floor, (3) Ruth in the home of Boaz.

First we see the Ruth who gleans in the harvest field, the alien, poor and destitute; having no part or lot in Israel, or in the covenant of promise, yet seeking refuge under the wing of Jehovah, God of Israel, and begging kindness at the hand of the gracious, wealthy Boaz. The name, Boaz, means "In him is strength"; and surely Boaz, the strong, the wealthy, the noble, the gracious, is here a type of Christ, as he looks on the Gentile Ruth with generous favour and with tender love toward her.

Second, we see the Ruth who, having no hope in anyone other than Boaz, goes to the threshing floor, risking everything, believing in his kindness, staking her all on his honour and grace and his power to redeem; coming to him poor and friendless, yet loving him because he had first loved her; lying at his feet, praying the shelter of his name, asking the protection of his arm, seeking the provision which only his love could give; and finding in him more than hope had dared to expect.

Third, we see the Ruth who, having been graciously received by redeemer-Boaz, becomes united to him as his wife, shares with him his life, his home, and all his wealth and joys.

We think it does not require any very acute insight to perceive in all this a beautiful consistency of type-teaching concerning Christ and the Church. Perhaps the emphasis is slightly more on the Ruth aspect of things; yet the type parallels are quite definitely there in the case of Boaz. In acting as redeemer, Boaz must exhibit the three main and indispensable qualifications: that is, he must have the *right* to redeem; he must have the *power* to redeem; and he must have the *will* to redeem. Christ, as *our* "Goel," or Kinsman-Redeemer, has the right as our true Kinsman, and the power as the Son of God, and the gracious willingness. Nor has our heavenly Boaz merely redeemed for us the forfeited estate of Elimelech—an earthly possession; He has made us His bride, to share for ever with Him His life, His home, His wealth, and His eternal joys. In Him we boast more blessings than our father Adam lost for us!

But who is that *unnamed kinsman* who would *not* redeem (iv. 6)? I think the answer may be suggested to us if we read over again those words which occur in the book of Deuteronomy xxiii. 3: "An Ammonite or Moabite shall not enter into the congregation of the Lord; even to their tenth generation shall they not enter into the congregation of the Lord for ever." That unnamed and unwilling kinsman, in Ruth iv. 6, is the LAW. The Law, in itself, is just, but it has no smile, no place, no welcome, for alien Ruth. The unnamed kinsman would have paid the price for the *estate* of Elimelech if that had been all there was to think of (iv. 4); but as soon as he heard that Moabitess Ruth was involved he refused. And the *Law* can do nothing for *us* as sinners and spiritual aliens to God. It cannot forgive. It cannot cleanse. It cannot renew us or empower us. It can only condemn us. Thank God, the Moabite who is shut out by law is admitted by grace! And those very sinners against whom Mount Sinai thunders, "The soul that sinneth, it shall die," may hear the gracious words from Mount Calvary, "He that believeth on Me hath everlasting life, and shall not come into the judgment, but is passed from death unto life!"

> O all-embracing mercy,
> 　　Thou ever-open door,
> How could I do without thee
> 　　Now heart and eyes run o'er?
> Tho' all things seem against me,
> 　　To drive me to despair,
> I know one gate is open,
> 　　One ear will hear my prayer.

THE FIRST BOOK OF SAMUEL (1)

Lesson Number 28

NOTE.—For this study read the First Book of Samuel right through, and the first seven chapters through at least twice.

What, then, shall we think about the Bible? I will tell you very plainly what I think we ought to think. I hold that the Biblical writers, after having been prepared for their task by the providential ordering of their entire lives, received, in addition to all that, a blessed and wonderful and supernatural guidance and impulsion by the Spirit of God, so that they were preserved from the errors that appear in other books and thus the resulting book, the Bible, is in all its parts the very Word of God, completely true in what it says regarding matters of fact, and completely authoritative in its commands.

—J. Gresham Machen.

THE FIRST BOOK OF SAMUEL (1)

WE HAVE said adieu to gentle Ruth, and have turned over another page of our Bible. The "First Book of Samuel" lies before us, introducing us to one of the most venerable figures in Israel's history, and opening up a stirring new chapter in the fascinating story of God's earthly people. This "First Book of Samuel" heads what have been called the three "double books" of the Old Testament—1 and 2 Samuel, 1 and 2 Kings, 1 and 2 Chronicles. These three double books together form a complete section. They record *the rise and fall of the Israelite monarchy*.

Samuel and Kings

In the Hebrew manuscripts, 1 and 2 Samuel form but one book, as also do 1 and 2 Kings and 1 and 2 Chronicles. Their division into two books each, as we now have them, originates with the so-called Septuagint translation of the Hebrew Scriptures into Greek, said to have been made in the third century B.C. In the Septuagint, 1 and 2 Samuel and 1 and 2 Kings are called, respectively, the First, Second, Third and Fourth Books of the Kingdoms (the plural word "Kingdoms" meaning the two kingdoms, Judah and Israel). The Latin Vulgate—Jerome's famous translation of the entire Bible into Latin, in the fourth century A.D.—continues the Septuagint division of Samuel and Kings into two books each, but calls them the First, Second, Third and Fourth Books of the Kings (not Kingdoms). It is from this that there came the sub-titles to these four books in our Authorised Version. As will have been noticed, under the title: "The First Book of Samuel," it says, "*Otherwise called the First Book of the Kings.*" 2 Samuel and 1 and 2 Kings are similarly sub-titled. In the Revised Version, however, these sub-titles are dropped.

The present division into 1 and 2 Samuel has been decried by some scholars; yet undoubtedly it has much merit. *Second Samuel* is distinctively the book of David's forty years' reign; and it is well that such an epochal reign should be marked off, and given a book to itself. As for this *First* Book of Samuel, it equally clearly marks off a definite period, running from the birth of Samuel, the last of the Judges, to the death of Saul, the first of the Kings. It covers a period of about one hundred and fifteen years.

For sheer interest, 1 Samuel is unsurpassed. Not only does it recount eventful history; it is eventful history interwoven with the biographies of three colourful personalities—Samuel, Saul, David: and it is around these three that the chapters are grouped; thus—

Chapters   i. to vii. —SAMUEL.
,,   viii. to xv. —SAUL.
,,   xvi. to xxxi. —DAVID.

Of course, the three accounts overlap. Samuel lives well on into the reign of Saul, and also sees David rise to prominence; while Saul continues his reign until David is thirty years old. Yet it is none the less true that 1 Samuel is grouped as we have just indicated. In the first seven chapters Samuel is the prominent figure. In the next eight chapters all focusses on Saul, and Samuel is in the background. In the remaining chapters, although Saul is still reigning, there is no mistaking that the main attention is now on David.

Central Feature and Message

In the case of 1 Samuel there is really no need to burden ourselves with a detailed analysis. Fix it well in the mind—and the memory will easily retain it—that 1 Samuel is the book of *the transition from the theocracy to the monarchy*; and the book of the three remarkable men—Samuel, the *last* of the Judges, Saul, the *first* of the Kings, and David, the *greatest* of the kings.

If we remember this, we cannot easily forget the central *spiritual* message of the book. God had called Israel into a unique relationship with Himself; and God Himself was Israel's King invisible. Through disobedience the people had brought chastisement upon themselves from time to time, but were willing to attribute much of this, later, to the fact that they had no *human* and *visible* king, such as the surrounding nations had: and now, at length, as Samuel ages, and his sons prove perverse, the people make it the occasion to press for a human king. The fateful choice is recorded in chapter viii. which should be read carefully. It was a retrograde step, dictated merely by seeming expediency. It was the way of human wisdom, not of faith in God. It was taking the lower level. It was a refusing of God's *best*, for the *second* best—and there is much difference between the two.

The people thought it would solve their many problems, and make things wonderfully easier, if only they could have a human and visible king such as the neighbouring peoples had; but, alas, they were quickly to learn how self-deceived they were in thinking so, for new troubles were now to break upon them through the very king they had demanded: and herein lies the central message of I Samuel to us, namely: Troubles increased through choosing the seemingly easier but lower way of human wisdom, in preference to God's way—*by choosing less than God's best.*

> God has His best things for the few
> Who dare to stand the test;
> God has His second choice for those
> Who will not take His best.
>
> It is not always open ill
> That risks the promised rest;
> The better often is the foe
> That keeps us from the best.
>
> And others make the highest choice,
> But when by trials pressed,
> They shrink, they yield, they shun the cross,
> And so they lose the best.

Let us now look briefly at the three outstanding men around whom the story is woven. First of these is Samuel.

Samuel (i—vii)

As a character study Samuel has few peers; and as a factor in the early growth of his nation he is equalled only by Moses. The ministry of Samuel marks the institution of the monarchy. From now onwards we are to see Israel under the kings.

Besides this, the appearance of Samuel marks the institution of the prophetic office. There were those in Israel, even before Samuel's time, on whom the mantle of prophecy had fallen (Num. xi. 25; Judges vi. 8). Moses himself is called a prophet (Deut. xviii. 18). But there was no organised prophetic office.

Samuel founded the *schools* of the prophets, and originated the prophetic *order*. In a very real sense, therefore, he is "the first of the prophets"; and this distinction is recognised in the New Testament, as the following verses shew:

"Yea, and all the prophets from Samuel and those that follow after, as many as have spoken, have likewise foretold of these days"—(Acts iii. 24).

"And, after that, He (God) gave unto them Judges about the space of four hundred and fifty years, until Samuel the prophet"—(Acts xiii. 20).

"And what shall I more say?—for the time would fail me to tell of Gideon . . . and Samuel and the prophets"—(Heb. xi. 32).

Samuel, then, is a significant figure. He ends the period of the Judges; he heads the order of the prophets; he originates the first great educational movement in the nation; he places Israel's first king on the throne, and later anoints David, the greatest of all Israel's kings. There is a fine article about Samuel in the Pulpit Commentary, of which the following remarks are somewhat of a précis.

His Timely Appearing.

Israel's training had been remarkable. The tribes had grown up amid that mental culture in which Egypt had outstripped the world. Then, under the educated leadership of Moses, there had been the endowment of the Law, which although merely preparatory in certain civil and administrative aspects, contained a summary of the fundamental principles of morality which has never been surpassed. But great as was the impress of Moses upon Israel, we must not think that the bulk of the people had risen to the level on which he himself stood. Scarcely had Moses and his generation passed before the people reverted to barbarism; and instead of realising the grand ideal which their lawgiver had sketched for them, they sank lower and lower (as seen in Judges), until the nation seemed at the point of breaking up. The Philistines, strengthened by a constant influx of immigrants and the importation of arms from Greece, were fast reducing Israel to a subject race. Thus Judah's neglect to conquer the sea coast in the earlier days (Judges i. 18, 19), was now imperilling the nation's independence. But just when it seemed that Israel must be crushed out, Samuel came. Never did times seem more hopeless; yet Samuel arrested the nation's decay, built it up into an orderly and progressive kingdom, and planted it on the path which led it, though by an uphill and tangled route, to its high destiny as teacher of the true God to mankind.

His Educational Work.

Samuel set himself to give the nation mental culture and orderly government. These were the urgent needs. The foundation of all his reforms was the restoring of the moral and religious life of the people. One must always begin there. Moreover, Samuel was too wise to trust merely to his personal influence. Many a man who has wielded great influence in his lifetime has left nothing lasting. If Israel was to be saved it must be by institutions which would exercise continual pressure, and push the people upward to a higher level. The means he employed for this internal growth of the nation was the founding of schools. These, besides raising Israel to a higher mental level, fostered the worship of Jehovah by teaching true ideas of the Divine nature. Samuel must often have found that the chief obstacle to his work as Israel's Judge was the low mental state of the people. Nowhere in Israel were educated men to be found to bear office or administer justice. The pathetic failure of the highly gifted king Saul shews this, and proves that Samuel was right in his hesitation about creating a king. Schools were the urgent need, through which the whole mental state of Israel should be raised, and men trained for educated leadership. Up and down the land these schools were planted, where young men learned reading and writing, and gained knowledge. From these came a David, and most of David's leaders. A system of national education grew up. Other results followed, of which the whole world reaps the benefit even today. Apart from it, that series of inspired men who have given us the Scriptures would have been impossible. Isaiah and his compeers were educated men, speaking to an educated people. Both Old and New Testaments are largely the fruit of Samuel's schools.

Samuel's other great labour was the shaping of the constitutional monarchy. In this again he was ahead of his age. To a degree he was unwilling, for he saw that the time was not ripe. A limited monarchy is only possible among an educated people. Samuel's Book of the Kingdom (1 Sam. x. 25) could have little influence on a Saul who could neither read nor write: and Saul became only too like what Samuel had feared. The government which Samuel sought to establish was that of kingly power in the hands of a layman, but acting in obedience to the written law of God, and to His will as declared from time to time by the living voice of prophecy which should appeal to the king's moral sense. Not till Samuel had trained David was there a Jewish Alfred ready for the throne. Despite his private faults, David, unlike Saul, never attempted to set himself above God's law, or even to pervert it to his own use. He kept strictly within the understood limits.

We begin to see what a great figure Samuel is. He initiated the first movement toward national education, and shaped the constitutional monarchy of the nation. Samuel is indeed a great man.

THE FIRST BOOK OF SAMUEL
TRANSITION FROM THEOCRACY TO MONARCHY

SAMUEL: THE LAST OF THE JUDGES (i.–vii.).

HIS BIRTH AND HIS YOUTH (i., ii.).
HIS CALL AND HIS OFFICE (iii.).
HIS TIMES AND HIS ACTS (iv.–vii.).

Summary—vii. 15-17.

SAUL: THE FIRST OF THE KINGS (vii.–xv.).

HIS APPOINTMENT AS KING (viii.–x.).
HIS PROMISING BEGINNING (xi.–xii.).
HIS LATER FOLLY AND SIN (xii.–xv.).

Rejection—xv. 23, 28, 35.

DAVID: THE ANOINTED SUCCESSOR (xvi.–xxxi.).

HIS ANOINTING BY SAMUEL (xvi. 1–13).
HIS SERVICE BEFORE SAUL (xvi. 14–xx.).
HIS YEARS AS A FUGITIVE (xxi.–xxx.).

Death of Saul—xxxi.

THE FIRST BOOK OF SAMUEL (2)

Lesson Number 29

NOTE.—For this further study in the First Book of Samuel read again chapters eight to the end.

When for a moment, a man is off-guard, in all probability you will know more truth about him than in all his attempts either to reveal himself or to hide himself. The ever-present consciousness, habitually hidden, flashes forth. Later, he may apologise, and say he did not mean what he said. The fact is that he was surprised into saying what he was constantly thinking. In all probability Saul had never said that before, and would never say it again; but he had been thinking it for a long time—"I have played the fool." There is no escape for any man, so long as reason continues, from the naked truth about himself. He may practise the art of deceit so skilfully as not only to hide himself from his fellow-men, but in his unutterable folly to imagine that he has hidden himself from God; but he has never hidden himself from himself. In some moment of stress and strain, he says what he has been thinking all the time.

Saul had slept deeply that night, for the record tells us that "a deep sleep from the Lord was fallen" upon him. He was awakened from his slumber by the voice of David calling to him from the opposite mountain. Waking, he became keen, acute, neither dulled by food nor drugged by wine; everything was clear and sharp about him, as it so often is in the waking moment. Ere he knew it, he had said, "Behold, I have played the fool." That is the whole story of the man.

—*G. Campbell Morgan.*

THE FIRST BOOK OF SAMUEL (2)

As WE have said, this first book of Samuel is the book of *the transition from the Theocracy to the Monarchy*; and it will be well for us to remember it fixedly by this as we seek to get a broad hold on the books of the Bible. We have seen, also, that this book gathers round three men—Samuel, Saul, David. Already we have considered Samuel, the last of the Judges, and now we turn our thoughts to Saul, the first of the Kings: but we ought to note carefully beforehand how the change-over from the Judges to the Kings came about.

TRANSITION FROM JUDGES TO KINGS

The Request.

The change-over came about through the insistence of the people themselves. This we find in chapter viii., which marks the turning-point. Verses 4 and 5 say: "Then all the elders of Israel gathered themselves together and came to Samuel at Ramah, and said unto him: Behold, thou art old, and thy sons walk not in thy ways: now make us a king to judge us like all the nations." Now as Dr. Kitto says, "The demand was not the outcry of an ignorant and deluded rabble, but the grave and deliberate application of the *elders* of Israel—of those whose years or high standing in the nation gave to them the utmost weight and influence. It was not made from the mere impulse of the moment, but was the result of previous deliberation and conference; for the elders repaired to Ramah *for the purpose of* proposing the matter to the prophet; and beyond all doubt they had met together and considered the matter well before they took a step so decided."

Their approach to Samuel was marked by considerateness. They had no dissatisfaction with Samuel personally; but in view of his advanced years and the unsatisfactory behaviour of his sons they must urge that the government be put on the new basis of kingship while Samuel is yet with them, and by the sanction of Samuel's authority. Yes, they were deliberate and considerate; but they were wrong. Their eyes were away from God again. Such a request had never been born in prayer. They had held a committee meeting instead of a prayer meeting!—and now they were determined on taking a retrograde step instead of going on with God. How often is unbelief thus dressed up as the corporate wisdom of committees!

The Response.

Samuel's reaction to the request is given in verse 6: "But the thing displeased Samuel when they said: Give us a king to judge us. And Samuel prayed unto the Lord." The Divine answer is: "Hearken unto the voice of the people in all that they say unto thee; for they have not rejected thee, but they have rejected Me, that I should not reign over them. . . . Now therefore hearken unto their voice: howbeit yet protest solemnly unto them, and show them the manner of the king that shall reign over them." Samuel thereupon makes disuasive protest to them (10–18), but without avail; for verse 19 says: "Nevertheless, the people refused to obey the voice of Samuel; and said: Nay, but we will have a king over us, that we also may be like all the nations, and that our king may judge us, and go out before us to fight our battles." The request has now become a demand: and God's further word to Samuel is: "Hearken unto their voice, and make them a king" (verse 22).

Three things, therefore, we ought to note about this demand for a king. First, the outer *reason* for it was the degeneracy of Samuel's sons. Second, the inner *motive* was that the people might become like the other nations. Third, the deeper *meaning* was that Israel had now rejected the theocracy, which was the most serious thing of all; and this is emphasized in the Divine response—"They have not rejected thee, but they have rejected *ME*, that *I* should not reign over them." Alas, how many once bright Christians have been spoiled through wanting to be like the people of the world around, even as did Israel in demanding a human king! And how insidious is the temptation to lean on that which is seen and human instead of resting in the invisible God! It is a temptation to which we are all prone; but to yield to it invites a harvest of regrets.

The Result.

So then, the people claimed and exercised what in these days is called "the right of self-determination." The change-over from theocracy to monarchy was of themselves. God gave them a king and constituted a kingship. The fact would seem to be that Israel had wearied of a theocratic form of government which made their wellbeing dependent on their right conduct. Perhaps they vaguely supposed that a government under a human king would relieve them somewhat of this responsibility, inasmuch as their wellbeing would rest more with the character of the government and the qualities of the king himself.

But in giving them a king, God safeguarded the moral interests of the nation by constituting a kingship which preserved as far as possible the principles of theocratic government. The king is made directly responsible to God, and the people are no less responsible to Him through their king. Israel's king was not to be an autocratic king, but a theocratic king. The prophet and the priest, in their *official* capacity, were coördinate with, rather than subordinate to, the king, being themselves directly dependent on God; though, of course, as men and citizens they were subject to the king, like all others. As we have already said, the government was to be that of kingly power in the hands of a layman, but acting in obedience to the written law of God, and to His will as declared from time to time by the living voice of prophecy. Therefore, when we speak of the change-over from theocracy to monarchy we do not mean that all the principles of theocratic government were then waived. Theocratic responsibility still persisted through the monarchy: but absolute theocracy had ceased to be.

Observations.

We can understand the *feelings* of Israel's leaders in pressing for a human king. There were signs of trouble coming, so it would seem, from the Philistines, ever planning war, on the west, and from the Ammonites on the east (xii. 12); and it was an understandable anxiety that in Israel there was no man marked out, either by preëminent fitness or station, to be their leader in such conflicts as were likely to come. We can understand, too, the craving for outward dignity of state such as the surrounding nations had, for the Oriental mind is pervadingly regal; and maybe it was a stigma on Israel that there was no royal head of the nation. Yet in view of the theocratic privileges and high calling of Israel, this peremptory demand for a human king was gravely wrong.

The people's asking for a king had been *anticipated* in the word of God through Moses. See Deuteronomy xvii. 14–20. Maybe the elders of Israel inferred from this that it was the ultimate Divine intent to establish a monarchical government among them—and perhaps rightly so; yet even so, the least they could have done was to seek the counsel of their Divine King about this. Note further that instead of being gratefully anxious to preserve the liberties and public rights which were theirs under the theocracy, they insisted on being ruled as the surrounding peoples were ruled. In other words, they insisted on surrendering their present mild government for the overlordship of a despotic human royalty. Samuel solemnly warns them against what they were intending to bring upon themselves. See chapter viii. 11–20. Such a king would take their sons and daughters to wait on him and work for him and war for him. He would take their fields and vineyards, and the tenth of their seed and produce and flocks and other possessions; and he would do much more, so that they should cry out because of him. And without doubt, Samuel's words accurately depicted the monarchical governments which then existed round about Israel. Yet still undeterred, Israel's leaders pressed to surrender their precious immunities! The fact that the monarchy which was thereupon constituted in Israel was *not* despotic, like those around, is due, as Dr. Kitto says, to "the sagacious care and forethought of Samuel, acting under Divine direction, in securing from utter destruction at the outset, the liberties which the people so wilfully cast into the fire."

Saul : Israel's First King

Saul, the first king of Israel, is one of the most striking and tragic figures in the Old Testament. If we are at all sensitive as to the supreme values and vital issues of human life, the story of Saul will challenge us. In some ways he is very big; in others very little. In some ways he is commandingly handsome; in others definitely ugly. He began so reassuringly, but declined so disappointingly, and ended so wretchedly, that the downgrade process which ruined him becomes monumental to all who will give heed. We note the three main phases of his career—(1) his early promise, (2) his later decline, (3) his final failure.

His early promise (ix.–xii.).

Never did a young man give fairer promise or find brighter possibilities greeting his young manhood. To begin with, he was distinguished by *a striking physical superiority*. He is described as "a choice young man, and a goodly: there was not among the children of Israel a goodlier person than he; from his shoulders and upward he was higher than any of the people" (ix. 2). He had health and height and handsomeness; and while the physical is not the more important part of a man, such splendid physique as Saul had was a wonderful possession. It gave him the initial advantage of being immediately prepossessing.

Second; young Saul showed certain *highly commendable qualities of disposition*. We note his *modesty* (ix. 21; x. 22). We note his *discreetness* (x. 27). We mark his *generous spirit* (xi. 13). And there were other fine qualities too—his considerateness of his father (ix. 5), his dash and courage (xi. 6, 11), his capacity for strong love (xvi. 21), his energetic antagonism to such evils as spiritism (xxviii. 3), and his evident moral purity in social relationships.

Third, there were *special equipments* which God gave him when he became king. We read, "God gave him another heart" so that he became "another man" (x. 6, 9). Again, "the Spirit of God came upon him" so that he "prophesied" (x. 10). Such expressions cannot mean less than that Saul became inwardly renewed, and was under the special guidance of the Holy Spirit. Nor is this all: he was given a "*band* of men whose hearts God had touched" (x. 26). He also had that trusty counsellor, the inspired Samuel, at his side. To crown all this, God signalised the beginning of Saul's reign by granting a spectacular military victory which set the new king high in the confidence of the people (xi. 12).

This was the young Saul of fair promise. Extraordinarily rich in natural endowments, and specially equipped by supernatural conferments, the future seemed bright indeed. His call to the kingship was an opportunity in a million, coming to a man in a million. He was called to kingship, and he was constitutionally kingly. He was called to *theocratic* kingship, and God supernaturally equipped him for that. What scope for glorious cooperation with God! What opportunity to bless men! He betrayed none of the symptoms of vain-glory which others, less gifted than himself, have betrayed when suddenly elevated. His accession to Israel's throne was indeed a morning of fair promise.

His later decline.

Alas, Saul's early promise is a morning sky soon overcast with sullen clouds. Defection, declension, degeneration, disaster—that is the dismal downgrade which now sets in, until this giant-hero drops as a haggard suicide into ignominious death.

The first defection occurred early. See chapter xiii. It was an act of *irreverent presumption*. The Philistines were arrayed against Israel. Saul was bidden to wait for Samuel at Gilgal. When Samuel did not seem to be coming before the appointed time expired, Saul, in wilful impatience, violated the priest's prerogative, and foolishly presumed to offer up with his own hand the pre-arranged sacrifices to the Lord. We can allow for Saul's anxiety. Yet he violated that obedience to the voice of God through the prophet which was a basic condition of theocratic kingship. Samuel's rebuke was, "Saul, thou hast done foolishly: thou hast not kept the commandment of Jehovah."

The next default follows quickly. See chapter xiv. It is an act of *rash wilfulness*. Using Jonathan as his instrument, God spreads confusion among the Philistines. Israel's watchmen report what they see. Saul calls the priest, to ask God guidance, but with stupid impatience cuts short the enquiry and rushes his men off without guidance. He also rashly imposes death-sentence on any man who should eat food that day (verse 24), with the result that his men are too weak to follow up the victory (verse 30), and that his hunger-smitten men sin by eating flesh with the blood (verse 32), and that Jonathan comes under the death-sentence through ignorance, and is only rescued by the intervention of the people (verses 27, 45).

But in chapter xv. comes still graver failure. It is a blend of *disobedience and deceit*. Saul is told to destroy utterly the vile

Amalekites; but he spares the king and the best live-stock. Then
he equivocates to Samuel. He slips blame for the booty on to the
people. He even pretends the booty is for sacrifice to Jehovah.
Samuel's rebuke begins, "When thou was little in thine own
sight. . . ." Alas, humility had now given place to arrogance.
Samuel sees right through the sham to the real—"Wherefore
didst thou not obey?" "Thou hast rejected the word of Jehovah."

From this point the decline is steep. "The Spirit of the Lord
departed from Saul" (xvi. 14) and "an evil spirit" troubled him.
He gives way to a petty jealousy until it becomes a fiendish
malice—against David. Thrice he tries to kill him. Then he hunts
him for months on end, like "a partridge in the mountains." He
gives way to the basest in himself. Twice David spares Saul's
life, and twice Saul promises to leave off his blood-thirsty hunt.
He knows that in seeking to slay David he is actually fighting
against God. He admits, "I know well that thou shalt surely
be king" (xxiv. 20); yet, even after this, he resumes his dastardly
pursuit. Well does Saul say of himself, *"I have played the fool!"*
(xxvi. 21).

His final failure.

The last tragic act in the mournful drama of this man is depicted
in chapters xxviii. to xxxi. His downgrade course at length
brings him to the witch of Endor, as an embittered and desolate-
hearted fugitive from doom. This giant wreck of a man who once
enjoyed direct counsel from heaven now traffics with the under-
world. We need not dilate on the nocturnal consultation, nor
on Saul's battlefield suicide the following day. There is no need
here to pick on details. It is enough to know the stark fact, the
final plunge—witchcraft and suicide! Saul is no more. He lies
a corpse, with lovely Jonathan. How are the mighty fallen!
How is this son of the morning brought to shame! Yes, Saul—
Saul of early promise, but of later decline and final ruin, you have
"played the fool"!

And as we see this man Saul come from such heights to such
depths, do we not ask what it was which lay behind his fearful
self-frustration? It was *self-will*. Saul's two besetting sins were
presumption and disobedience to God; and behind both these was
impulsive, unsubdued *self-will*. We may trace the four progressive

stages of this ruinous self-ism in Saul: first, self-sensitiveness, then, self-assertiveness, then self-centredness, increasingly issuing in self-destructiveness.

"He being dead yet speaketh."

In sad and awesome tones the voice of Saul still speaks, and we do well to heed. First, he preaches to us that *the one vital condition for the true fulfilment of life is obedience to the will of God.* Let us mark this well—Saul was called to *theocratic* kingship; so is each one of us. Every human personality is meant to be a theocratic kingship. Saul was never meant to have a kingship of *absolute* power. It was never intended that the last word should be with *him.* He was anointed of God to be the executor of a will higher than his own. He was to be the human and visible vice-regent of Israel's Divine and invisible King, Jehovah. He could only truly rule the subjects beneath him to the extent in which he obeyed the supreme King above him. So is it with ourselves. We are not the independent proprietors of our own beings. We are God's property. He has made us kings and queens over our own personalities with their gifts and powers and possibilities; but our rule is meant to be theocratic, not an independent, self-directed monarchy. We are meant to rule for *God*, so that our lives and personalities may fulfil His will and accomplish His purpose. When we obstinately rule independently of God our true kingship breaks down; we lose the true meaning and purpose of life. In greater or lesser degree we "play the fool."

But Saul teaches this further and kindred truth, that *to let "self" get the upper hand in our life is to miss the best and court the worst.* The Philistines were not Saul's worst enemies. His worst foe was himself. Every man who lets "self" fill his vision till it blinds his inner eye to what is really true and Divine is "playing the fool." All of us who live for self in preference to the will of God are "playing the fool." The downgrade process in our life may not be as outwardly observable as it was with Saul, simply because we do not occupy as conspicuous a position, but we are just as really playing the fool, and our ultimate corruption is just as certain.

There are many other lessons, of a more incidental kind. We see that advantages are not in themselves the guarantee of success. Saul had many, yet he failed ingloriously. We dare not lean on them. We see also that wonderful opportunities do not in themselves crown men. Nor even do special spiritual equipments immunise us from the possibility of getting out of the will of God, and "playing the fool." Again, a man plays the fool when he neglects his best friends, as Saul neglected Samuel; or when he goes on enterprises for God before God sends him, as Saul did; or when he disobeys God in small matters, as Saul at first did and then went on to worse disobedience; or when he tries to cover up disobedience by a religious excuse, as Saul did, or when he allows jealousy and hate to master and enslave him, as Saul did. Oh what warnings this man utters to us! God help us each to say, and really to mean it,

> Take my will, and make it Thine;
> It shall be no longer mine.
> Take my intellect, and use
> Every power as Thou shalt choose!

THE SECOND BOOK OF SAMUEL (I)

Lesson Number 30

NOTE.—For this study read through the whole of Second Samuel and the first six chapters twice.

So pervaded are the narratives of scripture with the didactic and ethical element, that all its biographical and historical parts seem dignified by a moral purpose, teaching truth by example. The prophetic and historic are therefore so close of kin that the history seems another form of prophecy, imparting instruction at the time present and typically forecasting the time to come. The Bible becomes a picture and portrait gallery, where lessons are so taught as to impress even those dullest of comprehension. And every line and lineament is full of meaning.

—A. T. Pierson, D.D.

THE SECOND BOOK OF SAMUEL

THE BOOK OF DAVID'S REIGN

SECOND Samuel is distinctively *the book of David's reign*. It opens
with David's accession over Judah, immediately after Saul's
death, and closes just before David's death, when he is "old and
stricken in years." The book therefore covers a period of some
forty years; for that was the duration of David's reign. Chapter
v. 4 and 5, says: "David was thirty years old when he began to
reign, and he reigned forty years. In Hebron he reigned over
Judah seven years and six months; and in Jerusalem he reigned
thirty and three years over all Israel and Judah." It will be helpful, then, if we always remember Second Samuel by this—that it
is the book of David's forty years' reign.

Composite Authorship

The authorship of Second Samuel is far from certain, though
the likeliest indications still favour the older view that while
Samuel himself is responsible for the first twenty-four chapters
of the *first* of these two books which bear his name, the remaining chapters, to the end of Second Samuel, are the work of
the two prophets, Nathan and Gad. See 1 Chronicles xxix.
29–30.

As already mentioned, 1 and 2 Samuel were originally one book,
the present division being handed down from the Septuagint.
Despite those who complain that the separation of the one book
into two is "without reason or necessity," there is this definite
advantage, that it marks off the epochal reign of David, and
presents it as a subject of outstanding prominence, deserving our
special study. As David was the real founder of the monarchy,
the reorganiser of Israel's religious worship, the pre-eminent hero,
ruler, and poet of his people, and as his dynasty continued on
the throne of Judah right up to the Captivity, and as the promised
Messiah was to come of the Davidic line, it is not surprising that
so much prominence should be given to him.

The Tragic Divide

This second book of Samuel, as Matthew Henry is quick to observe, falls into two main parts. Alas, there is no mistaking it. David's great sin, recorded in chapter xi., marks the sad divide, right in the middle of the book and right in the middle of David's forty years' reign, for it falls about the end of the first twenty years. Up to this point all goes triumphantly for David; but after this there are ugly knots and tangles, grievous blows and tragic trials. In the first part, we sing David's triumphs. In the second part, we mourn David's troubles.

Mark it well that the Second Book of Samuel is cut exactly in half, with twelve chapters in each part. Chapters xi. and xii., which record David's sin and repentance, must be included in the first part, as rightly belonging there. It was through the very prosperity which had come to him by his widespread conquests that David had become exposed to the temptation of unguardedness and indulgence. At the end of that twelfth chapter there is the account of the conquest of Rabbah, the royal city of Ammon. That marks the end of any such recorded triumphs in this book. Here, then, is the outlay of the book:

THE SECOND BOOK OF SAMUEL
THE BOOK OF DAVID'S FORTY YEARS' REIGN

TRIUMPHS TURNED TO TROUBLES THROUGH SIN

I. DAVID'S TRIUMPHS (i.–xii.).

    i.–iv.—KING OVER JUDAH ONLY, AT HEBRON
       (*Civil War Period—7 years*).

    v.–xii.—KING OF ALL ISRAEL AT JERUSALEM
       (*Conquest Period—13 years*).

II. DAVID'S TROUBLES (xiii.–xxiv.).

    xiii.–xviii.—DAVID'S TROUBLES IN HIS FAMILY
       (*Amnon Sin to Absolom Revolt*).

    xix.–xxiv.—DAVID'S TROUBLES IN THE NATION
       (*Sheba Revolt to Pestilence*).

Central Spiritual Message

The central spiritual message of this book, therefore, stands out clearly, namely: *TRIUMPHS TURNED TO TROUBLES THROUGH SIN.* Or we may put it that in the two parts of the book, respectively, we have triumph through faith, and trouble through sin. Second Samuel emphasises that all sin, whether in king or commoner, whether in high or low, whether in the godly or the godless, certainly brings its bitter fruitage. Sin is the destroyer of prosperity. However full and fair the tree may look, if rot is eating its way within the trunk, the tree will surely break and fall, or else become a leafless skeleton. There is no sinning without suffering. Especially is all this true about the lust of the eye, and sexual sin, which was the point of David's breakdown. We should flee it as we would a viper. See, too, how David's sin led on to the even greater sin of murder. More often than not, one sin leads on to another of a worse kind. Let us, like Job, "make a covenant with our eyes" not to look on that which is seductive, lest, weaker than we suppose ourselves to be, we should give way to sin, and thereby heap sharp thorns into our bosom.

Key Facts to Note

There is no need for us to accompany the student chapter by chapter through this Second Book of Samuel; but we would call attention to certain key facts and events which should be carefully noted.

David at Hebron.

David reigned at Hebron for seven years and six months, over Judah only, because the other tribes would not accept him as Saul's successor. At the instigation of Abner, captain of Saul's army, Ishbosheth, a son of the deceased Saul, was proclaimed king, in opposition to David; and to Ishbosheth the tribes other than Judah gathered—a fact undoubtedly due to the pressure of the said Abner, who was a leader of much influence and renown.

Yet this repudiation of David was a grave wrong, and Israel was seriously at fault. Hereditary succession to the throne was not a principle in the constitution of the Hebrew monarchy; and even had it been so, Saul's true heir was Mephibosheth, the son of Jonathan—and Jonathan had renounced all claims for himself and his house, in favour of David.

But the guilt of Abner and Israel is the greater because in their hearts they knew well enough that David was Jehovah's appointed successor to Saul. Hear Abner's words as he quarrels with Ishbosheth—"So do God to Abner, and more also, except *as the Lord hath sworn to David*, even so I do to him; to translate the kingdom from the house of Saul, and to set up the throne of David over Israel and over Judah, from Dan even to Beersheba" (iii. 9, 10). A little later Abner says to the elders of the tribes: "Ye sought for David in times past to be king over you. Now then, do it; for *the Lord hath spoken of David*, saying: By the hand of My servant David I will save My people out of the hand of the Philistines and out of the hand of all their enemies" (iii. 17, 18). A little later still, the tribes acknowledged to David: "*The Lord said unto thee:* Thou shalt feed My people Israel and thou shalt be captain over Israel" (v. 2). Abner and Israel's leaders thus stand convicted by their own words.

Do we ask *why* Abner and Israel refused David at first? One reason may have been a jealous fear in Abner's mind that he could not hope to retain his position of supreme leadership under such a king as David, who already had his own "mighty men" of renown around him.

But there may have been another reason for Israel's refusal, namely, that the tribes had felt their faith in David shaken because of his recent sojourn among Israel's chief enemies, the Philistines, to escape Saul.

David's behaviour in the delicate situation created by Israel's refusal is commendable. He did not try to force himself to the throne by his armed power. He knew that he had been appointed of God to the throne; and his experience of God during the discipline of the preceding few years had taught him to bide God's time. Nor did God fail him. David would not act without Divine guidance (ii. 1). He was guided to Hebron. Judah welcomed him; and David reigned in Hebron, which ancient city of Abraham was Judah's capital. In the months that followed, "David waxed stronger and stronger; and the house of Saul waxed weaker and weaker" (iii. 1). The people of Israel could not but see, with self-rebuke, the contrast between the feeble character of Ishbosheth and the brilliant qualities of David, with his firm and beneficent government, the success which crowned all his projects, his victories in any clashes between Israel and Judah (ii. 12–32), and the attachment of his people to him.

Chapter v. is of outstanding importance. David is here, at last, acclaimed king of all Israel, and he transfers the seat of his government to Jerusalem. The words of Israel's leaders as they offer David the kingship are both touching and arresting. "Then came all the tribes of Israel to David, unto Hebron, and spake, saying: Behold we are thy bone and thy flesh. Also in time past, when Saul was king over us, thou wast he that leddest out and broughtest in Israel: and the Lord said to thee: Thou shalt feed My people Israel, and thou shalt be captain over Israel." Thus we see that the acknowledgment of David's right to the kingship rested on a threefold basis:

1. His human kinship—"*We are thy bone and thy flesh.*"
2. His proven merit—"*Thou leddest out and broughtest in Israel.*"
3. His Divine warrant—"*The Lord said unto thee: Thou shalt be captain over Israel.*"

Is not this a sermon in itself, speaking of *Christ's* right of kingship over *our* lives? He is our kinsman—"bone of our bone and flesh of our flesh." He is our Saviour of proven merit, who espoused our cause and fought our foe, and brought us deliverance from the guilt and tyranny of sin. And He is king by Divine warrant, the prince and Lord of His people, the One to whom is committed all administrative authority in heaven and on earth. "The government shall be upon His shoulders." Can we each say: "The government of my life *is* upon His shoulders"?

The New Centre.

Upon becoming king of a united Israel, David transferred the seat of his government to Jerusalem. Hebron, although a quite suitable capital while David's kingdom was confined to Judah, was too far south to become a metropolis for a kingdom uniting all the tribes. Jerusalem itself was about as southerly as an Israelite capital city dare be; and perhaps David's choice of it was partly dictated by a reluctance on his part to remove too far north from the tribe on which he could most surely rely, that is, the tribe of Judah, of which tribe David himself was a member.

Jerusalem at that time was called Jebus (1 Chron. xi. 4). It was a naturally strong position, which fact was also in David's mind, no doubt, when he chose to settle there. It was called Jebus after the Jebusites who still retained possession of it, or at least of that upper and fortified part of it which we know as Mount Zion. Probably in the lower part of Jebus, that is, in the *town* as distinguished from the *citadel*, Jebusites and Benjamites lived intermingled.

The Jebusites defied David to take Mount Zion. This fortress was so formidable and had so long been retained by the Jebusites, that it was regarded as impregnable. The Jebusite garrison derisively challenged David—"Except thou take away the blind and the lame, thou shalt not come in hither." It is added that they spake thus thinking: "David cannot come in hither." But David took the citadel. We are told that he said: "Whosoever getteth up to the gutter, and smiteth the Jebusites, and the lame and the blind that are hated of David's soul, he shall be chief, and captain." And to this it is added that the Jebusites therefore said: "The blind and the lame shall not come into the house." And who *were* these lame and blind who were hated of David's soul? They were not lame and blind *persons*, for David had no such hate of the lame and blind as such. He was far too generous-hearted for that. Besides, what a strange thing it would be to have had a fortress garrisoned by cripples and blind people! The blind and the lame here mentioned were the Jebusite gods. The meaning of the Jebusites in their challenge that David should not enter Zion unless he took away their gods was that David would *never* be able to take away their gods, and therefore he would never enter Zion. Probably the Jebusites brought out their gods—their idols of brass—and placed them on the fortress walls, which would explain their saying: "They shall not come into the house."

It was Joab who cleaved a way into the fortress, as 1 Chronicles xi. 6 tells us. Thenceforward Zion became "The City of David." Thus Jerusalem became the centre-city of Israel, and entered upon that historic career which has made it the most sacred and wonderful city of the world, a city, moreover, with a future even more wonderful than all its glorious and tragic past!

THE SECOND BOOK OF SAMUEL (2)

Lesson Number 31

NOTE.—For this further study in Second Samuel read chapters vii. to the end again, with special attention to chapters vii. and xi. and xii.

The reigns of David and Solomon constitute the golden period of the Jewish state. From the first, David showed the utmost anxiety that every step he took towards the possession of the kingdom should be directed by Jehovah (1 Sam. xxiii. 2, 4; 2 Sam. ii. 1.) He acted ever as "His servant"; and when established in his kingdom, his first concern was to promote the Divine honour and the religious welfare of his people (2 Sam. vi. 1–5, vii. 1, 2). As a king he sought the prosperity of the state, and as the visible representative of Jehovah he strictly conformed to the spirit of the theocracy. It was due to this character of his administration, probably, rather than to his private virtues, that he is designated as "a man after God's own heart" (1 Sam. xiii. 14; see also Acts xiii. 22), who was to "execute all His will." It is, indeed, impossible to vindicate all his acts, or to regard him as a perfect character. And yet when we look at the piety of his youth, the depth of his contrition, the strength of his faith, the fervour of his devotion, the loftiness and variety of his genius, the largeness and warmth of his heart, his eminent valour in an age of warriors, his justice and wisdom as a ruler, and his adherence to the worship and will of God, we may well regard him as a model of kingly authority and spiritual obedience.

—*Angus, Bible Handbook.*

THE SECOND BOOK OF SAMUEL (2)

The Davidic Covenant

WE MUST now turn to chapter vii., the chapter in which the Davidic covenant is made known. On no account should we fail to weigh duly the fact and the terms of this covenant; for, besides largely affecting all that follows in the Scriptures, it determinatively affects the whole history of mankind, especially that part which is yet future. It is one of the supremely great passages of the Bible, and one of the principal keys to the Divine plan of history. From the time when this covenant was announced, the Jews have always believed that the Messiah must come of David's line. They believed it in the time of our Lord, and they believe it now. That the Messiah should indeed be of David's line was later affirmed by the prophets, in such passages as Isaiah xi. 1; Jeremiah xxiii. 5; Ezekiel xxxvii. 25; and in accord with such prophecies the angel Gabriel announced to Mary, concerning Jesus: "He shall be great, and shall be called the Son of the Highest; and the Lord God shall give unto Him the throne of His father, David; and He shall reign over the house of Jacob for ever, and of His Kingdom there shall be no end."

The Davidic covenant is uttered in the following words:

> "*Also the Lord telleth thee that He will make thee an house; and when thy days be fulfilled, and thou shalt sleep with thy fathers, I will set up thy seed after thee, and I will establish his kingdom. He shall build an house for my name; and I will stablish the throne of his kingdom for ever. I will be his Father, and he shall be my Son. If he commit iniquity, I will chasten him with the rod of men, and with the stripes of the children of men; but My mercy shall not depart away from him as I took it from Saul, whom I put away before thee. And thine house and thy kingdom shall be established for ever before thee: thy throne shall be established for ever*" (2 Sam. vii. 11–16).

The first important significance of these words is that here we have *the Divine confirmation of the throne in Israel*. Hitherto, as we have seen, the throne of Israel was a man-appointed throne (see 1 Sam. viii.). It had been conceded at the clamouring of the people. Saul, the first king, was the man of the people's choice; for although he was Divinely selected and anointed and presented to the people, the choice was finally left with the people. Hitherto, also, the throne of David had rested upon the choice of the people—first of the men of Judah, and then of the other tribes. But now the throne of David is confirmed by *Divine appointment*. It now becomes statedly incorporated into God's plan for Israel, and, through Israel, for the race, from that time forth to the end of the ages.

The second important fact here is *the predicted perpetuity of the Davidic dynasty*. Three things are made sure to David—(i) a "house," or posterity; (ii) a "throne," or royal authority; (iii) a "kingdom," or sphere of rule; and then in verse 16 all three are secured to him "for ever." "Thine *house* and thy *kingdom* shall be established for ever before thee; thy *throne* shall be established *for ever*." This is emphatic language. That thrice-occurring expression, "for ever," is not just to be taken in a popular sense as meaning that Solomon's descendants should hold undisputed possession of the kingdom for many centuries. To take the expression in this popular way is ruled out by other Scriptures where we find references or allusions to this passage, notably Psalm lxxxix., which is both a confirmation and an exposition of the Davidic covenant. See verse 29: "His seed also will I make to endure for ever, and his throne *as the days of heaven*." And see verses 36 and 37: "His seed shall endure for ever, and his throne *as the sun* before Me. It shall be established for ever *as the moon*." There is no mistaking words like these. To crown the solemn emphasis, the covenant is sealed with an oath. See Psalm lxxxix. 35: "*Once have I sworn* in my holiness that I will not lie unto David." See also Acts ii. 30. This covenant, let it be most definitely understood, has to do with a literal posterity, and a literal throne, and a literal kingdom. To start "spiritualising" it into meaning a heavenly posterity and a spiritual kingdom synonymous with the Christian Church is to violate the very first drinciple of Scripture interpretation, namely, the principle that plainly spoken words should at least be accepted as meaning what they say.

The third great fact to grasp concerning this Davidic covenant

is *its Messianic implication*. The emphatic threefold repetition
of the promise to establish the kingdom of David *for ever* could
only be fulfilled in the coming Messiah; and it has always been
understood, therefore, as finding its final fulfilment in Him. In
the words spoken to David, no doubt, Solomon is first in view;
but the promise looks on through the long succession of human
kings, and on through the present long dispersion, to find its
culmination in Him who, having already been to earth as Prophet,
and having now ministered in the heavenly sanctuary as Priest,
shall yet return in glory as David's greater Son, the King of
kings and Lord of lords, of whose kingdom "there shall be no
end, upon the throne of David, to order it and to establish it
with judgment and with justice from henceforth even for ever"
(Isa. ix. 7).

It is because this Davidic Covenant finally envisages Christ
that it is *unconditional*. Certainly, inside the covenant there is a
provision made against possible sin and failure by David's
reigning sons, in the words of verse 14: "If he commit iniquity
I will chasten him with the rod of men and with the stripes of
the children of men"; but this is not a *condition* on which the
fulfilment of the covenant depends, for the next verse immediately
goes on to say: "But my mercy shall not depart away from him,
as I took it from Saul whom I put away before thee." That
clause is put into the covenant to cover Solomon and his erring
human descendants until the true and perfect King should come.
As in the Abrahamic covenant the promised "seed" was Isaac,
in the immediate sense, and Christ in the ultimate sense (Gal.
iii. 16), so, in the Davidic covenant the promised "son" is Solomon,
in the immediate sense, and Christ in the ultimate sense. Now
it is noticeable that both the Abrahamic and the Davidic covenants
are unconditional; and their being so is due to this fact that they
both find their final fulfilment in Christ, for there can be no failure
on Christ's part.

And again, this Davidic covenant marks *a fourth major development in Messianic prophecy*. The first great prophecy was made
to Adam, in Genesis iii. 15, where we are told that *the seed of the
woman* should bruise the head of the serpent. The second was
made to Abraham, in Genesis xxii. 18, "*In thy seed* shall all
the nations of the earth be blessed." The third was made through
Jacob, in Genesis xlix. 10—"The sceptre shall not depart *from*

Judah . . . until Shiloh come." The fourth is now made to David in 2 Samuel vii. See the development then. First, in the case of Adam, the promise is to the *race* in general. Then, in the case of Abraham, it is to one *nation* in the race—the nation Israel. Then, in the case of Jacob, it is to one *tribe* in that nation —the tribe of Judah. Then, in the case of David, it is to one *family* in that tribe—the family of David. Thus are we prepared for that completing word which Isaiah adds still later, namely, that the coming Seed of the woman, Son of Abraham, Lion of Judah, and Heir of David, should be *born of a virgin.*

Notice that in the covenant God says of David's son: "He shall build an house for my Name." David, being a man of *war*, could not really typify Christ as Melchisedek, who is King of Peace: this glory was reserved for Solomon. David established the kingdom over which Solomon reigned. But Christ will be both David and Solomon. As David, He will conquer all foes and set up the kingdom on earth; and, as Solomon, He will reign in everlasting peace. Even so, may He soon come!

David's Full Establishment

In chapters viii. to x. we see David's reign at its zenith. Wherever he turns he is a victorious warrior, while at home he is an upright and constructive administrator. Never before has Israel been such a power among the nations. In chapter viii. 12, 14 we find a list of the seven surrounding powers which were subdued by David—the Philistines on the west, the Syrians and Hadadezer in the north, the Ammonites and Moabites on the east, the Edomites and Amalekites in the south. The secret behind David's successive conquests is found in verse 14—"And *the Lord* preserved David whithersoever he went"; while the reason for Israel's internal consolidation is given in verse 15, namely, that "David executed judgment and *justice* unto all his people." Thus Israel becomes the central and supreme power among the peoples.

We only need to glance through these chapters to see that David was a skilful general and a virtuous ruler. Chapter viii. begins by telling us that "David smote the Philistines, and *subdued* them." Remember, David came to the throne immediately after Saul's crushing defeat by the Philistines, when almost the whole land was under their heel. His subjugating of the Philistines, therefore, is the more remarkable.

Next, we are told that "he smote Moab, and measured them with a line, casting them down to the ground: even with two lines measured he to put to death, and with one full line to keep alive." There have been many criticisms of the barbarity of David's procedure here; but actually it is meant to be the evidence of generosity. The usual procedure in those days was to slay *all* prisoners of war, often without regard either to age or sex. Here, however, is a touch of leniency. A third are to be spared, with the added clemency that of the three lines used for measuring the two-thirds to be slain and the one-third to be spared, the line to mark off the third to be spared was a "full line," which indicates that it was longer than the other two. We agree that even so the procedure was brutal; but so has war always been, and never more so than today, despite all our boasted civilisation. Is there in all past wars anything more dastardly than the modern air-bombing of innocent women and children, and the deliberate machine-gunning of drowning men and women at sea? Has there ever been any torture worse than that of the German and Russian concentration camps? Moreover, before we criticise David and the old-time Israelites overmuch, we must realise that unless they were to wage war at a great disadvantage, and with bound hands, it was unavoidable that they should wage it on the principles recognised by the peoples with whom they were brought into conflict. Let us do David the justice of at least recognising that here, in his sparing a considerable percentage of the Moabites, he was taking a forward step of humanitarianism foreign to the warfare of his time. Had he spared the whole, those foes whom he was seeking to subdue would immediately have presumed upon his leniency, and perhaps with disastrous results.

Next, we read how David smote the King of Zobah, and took from him his chariots and horsemen. The defeat which David inflicted, with infantry only, upon an army equipped with so powerful a force of chariots and cavalry (verses 3–6) indicates his military skill; and the *capture* of them shows even more clearly his clever generalship.

And so we might go on; but we must forbear. The chapters should be read through with the help of good commentaries.

They are full of interest and information. Think of the broken condition of Israel at David's accession and then remember that at his death he transmitted to Solomon a united empire extending from "the river of Egypt" to the Euphrates, and from the Red Sea to Lebanon. What an achievement this was! Besides this, the religious development of Israel received a quickening impulse from the piety of their beloved king and the influence of his sacred poetry. In the Sanctuary the services became systematically arranged, and sacred song was given prominent recognition. It has been truly said that "never was there a more earnest effort to conduct the affairs of the nation on religious principles." David's reign was truly a noble epoch in Hebrew history.

David's Great Sin

As we have said, David's great sin, recorded in chapter xi., marks a sorrowful turning-point. It is well to emphasise certain considerations which should be borne in mind whenever we think of it. Critics have seized upon it as being the evidence of the moral corruptness of one whom the Bible holds up as a hero. "There!" they exclaim—"there is your great Bible hero! What a fine specimen he is!" It has been repeatedly asked, also, how we can reconcile this shameful fall of David with the Bible statement that God Himself declared David to be "a man after Mine own heart " (1 Sam. xiii. 14; Acts xiii. 22).

Now the answer to such criticism and questioning is that in all honesty and fairness we must take into account the full facts of the case.

1. *We must view David's life as a whole.* It is not fair or honest so to emphasise this blot on David's record as to make it appear the biggest thing in his life. Critics should remember that were it not for the strict honesty of the Bible itself, this black episode could easily have been withheld from us, and we would have known nothing about it. Therefore, we must in fairness judge David by the *whole* of the Biblical account. We must see his faith and obedience toward God through many years, his general uprightness and generous-heartedness, the high-principled conduct and ardent spiritual aspirings which largely characterise him throughout his career.

2. *We must take David's repentance into account.* Never was a man more stricken and abased by self-condemnation and godly contrition than was David after this sin "Beyond all question," says Ellicott,

"Psalm li. is the expression of his penitence after the visit of Nathan" to rebuke him. Who, then, can read that Psalm of sobs without realising that David's sin was the *exception to*, and not the *expression of*, his habitual aim and desire? The sin was committed in a spasm of weakness. The repentance shows the true attitude of the man to such sin—and it is *God's* attitude.

3. *We must judge David's character in the light of his own times.* The Christian Gospel and the New Testament ethic were not at that time given to men. Judged by the moral standards of his own day, David rises head and shoulders above his fellows. Especially when we compare him with the *kings* of that age does he excel. The extravagant sensual indulgence of ancient eastern kings is notorious. Their power over the life and property of their subjects was often absolute. They appropriated women-folk at will, with little regard to crimes which lay in the way of such appropriation. Compare David with such kings, and the comparison reveals the contrast.

4. *We must see David's inner life, as revealed in the Davidic psalms.* In the books of Samuel and the Chronicles we see David's life *outwardly*. In the Davidic psalms we see his life as it was *inwardly*. Here the man's very heart is laid bare; and, as we see it thus, we can only come to one honest conclusion. Many of those who have criticised David and the Bible would be glad if their own hearts could be laid bare in such goodly terms. These psalms, so moving in their evident sincerity, furnish proof positive that David was a good man—that he was, indeed, as the Scripture says, a man after God's own heart. In warfare, a general may lose a battle and yet win a campaign. Although one or several battles may be lost, and lost badly, the result of the whole campaign may be victory. This is true of men in a *moral* sense; and, in the case of David, the full account of his life, supported by the noble testimony of his psalms, shows decisively that though there were defeats, and one outstandingly grievous fall, the final result is such as to justify the pronouncement that he was a man after God's own heart.

In our own judgment, any one of the foregoing considerations is enough to justify the Bible estimate of David; and when taken together they become conclusive. But see also the note about David at the beginning of this present study. Should critics *still* object, however, we may fall back on the fact that when David was declared to be a man after God's own heart he was then merely in his early twenties. Surely, however, no honest appraisal of David could require us to limit the words to his youth: and, as for ourselves, we will not do so. With the full facts before us, we gladly subscribe to the verdict that in David we have one of the godliest men of all the pre-Christian era. As

Augustine said, David's fall should put upon their guard all who have *not* fallen, and save from despair all those who *have* fallen.

Salient Lessons.

And now mark some of the salient lessons connected with David's sin. First, note *the honesty and faithfulness of the Scriptures* in recording such a dark incident. Had the writing of the Bible been left merely in human hands, it would have contained no such chapter. David's guilt is here exposed without the slightest effort to extenuate it, much less excuse it. There is a severe truthfulness about the way in which the Bible deals with human characters. Dr. Edersheim says: "It need scarcely be pointed out how this truthful account of the sins of Biblical heroes evinces the authenticity and credibility of the Scriptural narratives. Far different are the legendary accounts which seek to palliate the sins of Biblical personages, or even to deny their guilt. Thus the *Talmud* denies the adultery of David on the ground that every warrior had, before going to the field, to give his wife a divorce; so that Bathsheba was free."

Note, too, that *David's fall occurred when he was in prosperous ease.* All his foes were crushed. The pressure of dangers that had kept him prayerful was now removed. He had not thought it worth troubling himself to go personally with his armies to reduce the last citadel of the Ammonites, but had sent Joab at their head (see xi. 1). We little realise what we owe to those seemingly hard circumstances from which we long to get free, but which are God's means of keeping us prayerful. Prosperity and ease are always perilous; and we are never so exposed to temptation as when we are idle.

Note further that David's sin was the culmination of a process. As a rule, falls so violent as that of David do not occur without being preceded by a weakening process. David had given way to the flesh in accumulating many wives (2 Sam. v. 13), a thing expressly forbidden to Israel's kings, in Deuteronomy xvii. 17. David, by nature a man of strong passions, had indulged the flesh; and now the tragic culmination is reached. How we need to guard against the *beginnings* of sin! See James i. 14, 15.

Again, see how *David's sin led on to even worse sin.* He vainly endeavoured to hide his crime. Uriah, the wronged husband of

Bathsheba, was intoxicated so that under its influence he might become irresponsible enough for it afterwards to be said that the child born to Bathsheba was his son (II Sam. xi.) ; but this shameful trick failed through the valorous behaviour of Uriah, who, besides being one of David's "mighty men" (2. Sam. xxiii. 39), was one of David's most upright and loyal supporters. Thereupon David—who had been shocked when Joab slew Abner—made Joab his accomplice in sin, and brought about the death of Uriah! Oh, the ugly chain that one sin can forge! If we *do* fall into sin, the one safe measure is confession and restitution.

Once again, note that *David's sin resulted in years of suffering*. Incest, fratricide, rebellion, civil war, intrigue, revolt—all these are traceable to David's sin. What a sorry harvest sin brings! David's wrong was forgiven, but its consequences were not thereby obliterated: and the Divine sentence upon David, in chapter xii. 11, "Behold, I will raise up evil against thee out of thine own house," furnishes the key to David's following history, which was as troubled and adverse as his earlier reign had been happy and successful.

We must now leave the student to make independent study of the remaining chapters in 2 Samuel. In the main they are sad, but are not without touches of beauty and cheer here and there: and they are full of profitable lessons.

As we think of David's awful sin, his prostrating remorse, his heart-breaking penitence which brought him absolution from the guilt of his sin but could not obliterate its consequences, we are reminded of words written, years ago now, by that remarkable British padre of the First World War, the late Studdart Kennedy. In an article on the sin of Judas, he writes:

" Why did I do it? How could I have done it? These can be the bitterest and most tragic questions men and women ask themselves. Something done that cannot be undone, something final and irrevocable, and a man looks at it, and cannot recognise it as his own act, cannot see himself in it, and yet he knows that it is his, and must be his for ever.

> " So Judas must have looked on Christ,
> As from the Judgment hall He went
> In bonds, the blood still wet upon
> His back. Why did I do it? How

Could I have done it? I loved Him,
Yet I sold Him. How can that be?
Which am I—traitor—lover—friend
Or fiend incarnate? Am I mad?
Aye mad—stark mad—my reason rocks.
These coins are bloody—Jesus help!
I did not mean to do it. Bloody—
Wet and bloody—and they burn—hot.
Hot as hell. I cannot bear it.
I am not I. I am some damned
And dreadful thing spewed out of hell.
I am—and I must kill it—now.
I cannot live—it must go back
To hell—I must—and never see
Him—never—Jesus Mercy! Death—
I must find death.

" Remorse and repentance are human facts, peculiarly human facts. Of no other creature could that scene be true, but only of a man. It might be true of you or me. Quite ordinary people can feel like that, and do. I have seen them, sat with them, tried to comfort them. I have heard them muttering over and over again: How could I have done it? How could I have done it?

" A man cannot be really free unless he surrenders himself utterly and without reserve to the service of the highest. The real tyrants which cramp and cabin man are his own undisciplined and unorganised desires. He cannot be free except through the inner union of his passions, without that the only freedom he possesses is freedom to hang himself. However much rope you give him that is what he must use it for in the end, unless he has some great aim and purpose which gives meaning and unity to his life. If he has that aim and purpose, and his desires are organised and disciplined about it, then when he acts against that aim and purpose, when he forgets it, and follows some wayward and rebellious passion, there comes to him the sense of sin. He knows that there is something awful, something deadly, about the word or deed. It is not merely a piece of folly, a mistake, a sin against himself or his neighbour, it is a denial of the whole meaning of the world. It is a sin against his God."

THE FIRST BOOK OF KINGS (1)

Lesson Number 32

NOTE.—For this study read right through this First Book of Kings, and the first eight chapters twice.

As we have already mentioned, the two books of the Kings were originally one (see our introduction to 1 Sam.). They were first divided into two by the Septuagint translators in the third century B.C.; and this division has been followed in all subsequent versions. They open with the accession of Solomon, and close with the destruction of Jerusalem. At the beginning we see the temple built. At the end we see the temple burnt. The two books together cover a period of about four hundred years. As to their authorship, scholars are in no doubt that "the language of the two books" and their "unity of purpose" point to "a single writer." Who then was the writer? Jewish tradition says he was Jeremiah the prophet. This tradition cannot be accepted as conclusive, yet neither can it be easily refuted. Indeed there is much in its favour. Of course, Jeremiah would make use of documents already existing (1 Kings xi. 41; xiv. 29, etc.); and after him redactors would make minor contributions to the eventual completeness of the work: but substantially the work is that of one writer, and that writer was probably the aged Jeremiah. We turn now to the *first* of these two books of the Kings.—*J.S.B.*

THE FIRST BOOK OF KINGS (1)

WHAT HEIGHT of glory and depth of tragedy lie in the history which stretches before us in the books of the Kings! What deep spiritual truths and prophetic foreshadowings, also, lie in these records! The splendours of Solomon's reign and the building of the temple forepicture the glory and the worship of Christ's coming kingdom upon the earth. The ministries of Elijah and Elisha are rich with spiritual meanings and latent typical significances. It would be easy to write at great length on such fertile themes; but our purpose here is simply to give the scope and gist of these records, as the basis for further study.

The Book of the Disruption

In getting a mental hold on the books of the Bible, it is a help if we remember each book by its distinctive feature. It will help us, therefore, if we always remember this First Book of Kings as being *the book of the Disruption*, by which we mean, of course, that it is the book which records the division of the one united kingdom, over which Saul and David and Solomon reigned, into *two* kingdoms—the two kingdoms henceforth being known respectively as *Israel* and *Judah*. The kingdom of Israel, comprising ten of the tribes, becomes the *northern* kingdom, while the kingdom of Judah, comprising Judah and Benjamin, becomes the *southern* kingdom. In the northern kingdom (Israel) *Samaria* becomes the capital. In the southern kingdom (Judah) *Jerusalem* remains the capital. This, then, is the central feature of First Kings—the one kingdom is divided into two; which event is usually called the Disruption.

This First Book of Kings falls into two main parts which are almost too obvious to need pointing out. There are twenty-two chapters in the book. The first eleven are devoted to Solomon and his wonderful reign of forty years. The remaining eleven chapters cover approximately the first eighty years of the separate kingdoms of Israel and Judah. The closing verses of chapter xi. record Solomon's death, thus marking off the two equal divisions of the book. In the first eleven chapters we have the united kingdom. Then comes the disruption; and in the ensuing eleven chapters we follow the fortunes of the *two* lines of kings.

The central spiritual message of 1 Kings is unmistakable, namely, *DISCONTINUANCE THROUGH DISOBEDIENCE*. This is seen in chapter xi. 11, which marks the tragic turning point, and foretells the coming disruption, thus becoming the key to the whole story: "Wherefore the Lord said unto Solomon: Forasmuch as this is done of thee, and *thou hast not kept my covenant and my statutes, which I have commanded thee*, I will surely rend the kingdom from thee, and will give it to thy servant. Notwithstanding in thy days I will not do it for David thy father's sake; but I will rend it out of the hand of thy son. Howbeit I will not rend away all the kingdom, but will give one tribe to thy son for David my servant's sake, and for Jerusalem's sake which I have chosen" (xi. 11–13).

THE FIRST BOOK OF KINGS
The Book of the Disruption

DISCONTINUANCE THROUGH DISOBEDIENCE

I. THE GREAT FORTY YEARS' REIGN OF KING SOLOMON (i.–xi.)

SOLOMON'S ACCESSION AND EARLY ACTS (i.–iv.)
SOLOMON'S TEMPLE AND PALACE BUILT (v.–viii.)
SOLOMON'S MERIDIAN FAME AND GLORY (ix.–x.)
SOLOMON'S DECLENSION AND DECEASE (xi. 1–43)

II. THE FIRST EIGHTY YEARS OF THE TWO KINGDOMS (xii.–xxii.)

ACCESSION OF REHOBOAM: THE DISRUPTION (xii. 1–33)
JUDAH KINGS—REHOBOAM TO JEHOSHAPHAT (xiii.–xxii.)
ISRAEL KINGS—JEROBOAM TO AHAZIAH (xiii.–xxii.)
MINISTRY OF PROPHET ELIJAH TO ISRAEL (xvii.–xxii.)

King Solomon

Solomon is a figure of striking interest in three ways—historically, personally, and typically.

Viewed *historically*, his special interest lies in the fact that he represents the peak period of Israel's prosperity as a kingdom. His reign marks the most splendid and affluent period of Hebrew history. No doubt can be left in our minds, even by a superficial reading of chapters ix. and x., that Solomon's riches and Israel's abundance at that time were such as to become a marvel both then and now. "Solomon in all his glory" has become, indeed, the classic figure of royal opulence. But besides this, Solomon is of historical interest as being the *last* of the kings to reign over a united Hebrew kingdom. It was through Solomon's own disobedience that the disruption took place, as we have seen; and there never will be a king reigning over a united Hebrew kingdom again until Christ Himself returns as David's Son and Lord.

Considered *personally*, Solomon is without doubt a remarkable figure; though it is not easy to reach a true estimate of his character. His super-normal wisdom made him a wonder to all the surrounding peoples. His prayer at the dedication of the temple reveals lofty spiritual capacity. His successful governmental administration bespeaks his more than ordinary mental power. Yet somehow, as to personal godliness there is a certain lack of decisiveness about him. There is a want of moral vigour. We miss that dash of fine passion which characterised the piety of David. While, on the one hand, Solomon never indulged such impetuous and presuming disobedience as that of Saul, yet, on the other hand, he never displayed such energetic devotion to God as that of David. If he partly escapes Saul's *condemnation*, he quite fails of David's *commendation*.

But the historical and personal interest attaching to Solomon is eclipsed by his significance *typically*. Like David, he is one of the greatest Old Testament types of Christ; and, like David, he typifies Christ in His yet future reign on earth. There are those who see an interesting difference in the way that David and Solomon respectively typify the coming reign of Christ. David is the type of Christ's *millennial* reign, that is, His reign on the earth for one thousand years, as David's greater Son, over the restored and regathered house of Israel. Solomon is the type of Christ's *post*-millennial reign, which Paul calls "the dispensation of the fulness of times," when Christ shall reign in that "new Jerusalem" which cometh down "from God, out of heaven." We shall not attempt to go into that matter here (but see further our note preceding the next lesson).

The Temple (v.–viii.)

We have shown that this first book of Kings is in two parts, the first eleven chapters wholly relating to the forty years' reign of Solomon, and the remaining eleven chapters covering the first eighty years of the two kingdoms. We would now point out that each of these two periods is made memorable by an outstanding phenomenon. In the first there is the building of the wonderful temple at Jerusalem. In the second there is the remarkable ministry of the prophet Elijah to the northern kingdom. Let us here note certain matters concerning the temple.

Chapter v.

In chapter v. we have the *preparations* for the temple. Solomon applies to Hiram, king of Tyre, for cedars from Lebanon. Israel's native timber wood was the sycamore (x. 27), which, although serviceable, was coarse, and much inferior to Lebanon cedar, which was hard, and close-grained. Hiram, king of Tyre, years before this, had sent cedars to David (2 Chron. ii. 3) to build him a royal dwelling; and it was characteristic of David that he should feel compunction about living in "an house of cedar" while the ark of God still remained in a mere tent (2 Sam. vii. 2). The superiority of Lebanon cedar, coupled with the expense of bringing it from so far away, made it a kind of luxury in Israel; and those houses which were made of it were looked upon as Israel's "quality" dwellings.

The communication between Solomon and Hiram is given more fully in 2 Chronicles ii., and with additional details of much interest. Solomon "*sent*" his message to Hiram, whereas Hiram "answered *in writing*." On both sides this was the courteous thing. Solomon, who is the one making request, sends a special envoy to deliver the message orally; and to such a request Hiram must needs send a written reply, sealed with the royal seal and presumably returned by Solomon's own appointed envoy. Incidentally, also, here is an instance of communication by writing, in those long gone times.

Solomon's message to Hiram is striking in the testimony it bears to Jehovah. We have to remember that Hiram was an idolater, and that Solomon might easily have considered, therefore, that it was the more becoming to omit references to his own God, and simply mention the commercial details of his requirements. But see his glorious words in 2 Chronicles ii. 4-6—"Behold, I build an house to Jehovah my God . . . and the house which I build is great; for great is our God above all gods. But who is able to build Him an house, seeing the heaven and heaven of heavens cannot contain Him?" Here is noble testimony to the supremacy and infinity of Jehovah such as leaves no room for other supposed deities; yet the message is one of real courtesy. Still more remarkable is the reply of Hiram, who, far from being offended, acknowledged Jehovah in these words—"Blessed be Jehovah, God of Israel, *that made heaven and earth*, who hath given to David the king a wise son, endued with prudence and understanding, that might build an house for Jehovah, and an house for his kingdom" (2 Chron. ii. 12).

These were Solomon's full requirements from Hiram—"Send me now, therefore, a man cunning to work in gold and in silver and in brass and in iron, and in purple and in crimson and in blue, and that can skill to grave with the cunning men that are with me in Judah and in Jerusalem, whom David my father did provide. Send me also cedar trees, fir trees, and algum trees, out of Lebanon : for I know that thy servants can skill to cut timber in Lebanon ; and, behold, my servants shall be with thy servants" (2 Chron. ii. 7, 8). Solomon, then, required a specialist in architecture and design, skilled hewers and cutters, and large supplies in several kinds of wood. His payment was to be in terms of agricultural produce described in 2 Chronicles ii. 10.

All this agrees with what we know about Phœnicia and Israel in those times. The country of the Phœnicians, among whom Hiram reigned, ran along the coast of the Mediterranean, and the Phœnicians themselves were a nation of merchantmen, with little time for agriculture, and a limited territory which was inadequate to supple the needs of their large and populous cities. Solomon's inland kingdom, on the other hand, was rich in various fruits and cereals, and could well supply peoples outside of itself.

The later verses of chapter v. tell us that Solomon raised a levy of thirty thousand men, and employed them in shifts of ten thousand per month at Lebanon, so that each man did four months out of the twelve, with a break of two months at home between each shift—a very considerate ratio. Besides these, Solomon had seventy thousand carriers, and eighty thousand hewers in the mountains. These mere menial workers were not Israelites, but Canaanites (see 2 Chron. ii. 17, 18), and there were three thousand three hundred superiors over them. These figures make a vast total of over *one hundred and eighty-three thousand*! We begin to see the magnitude of the undertaking.

Chapter v. closes with the words: "And the king commanded, and they brought *great stones, costly stones, and hewed stones*, to lay the foundation of the house. . . ." These great foundation stones remain to this day, now known as "Haram-esh-Sheref"; and upon them there stands the Mosque of Omar. Some of these "great stones" are from seventeen to nineteen feet in length; others are over twenty-four feet in length, eight feet in width and three or four feet thick. One stone is no less than *thirty-eight feet nine inches long*! A recent report says: "This great stone is one of the most interesting stones of the world, for it is the chief corner stone of the temple's massive wall. Fixed in its abiding position three thousand years ago, it still stands sure and steadfast." There can be no doubt that these huge blocks date back to Solomon. Decipherers have recently verified that the masons' signs on them are those of the *Phœnicians*—from whom, as the Scripture tells us, Solomon asked and received such material for the temple. When we consider the size and weight of these "great stones," and reflect that they would be transported all the way to Jerusalem by means of ox-drawn low-wheeled trucks, we cannot but marvel.

Chapters vi.–viii.

In chapter vi. we have the dimensions, materials, and construction of the temple. The data here given to us, while exact and detailed concerning each part described, have not enabled scholars to agree as to the contour and external architecture of the building. The ground-plan, however, is quite clear, its measurements throughout being exactly double those of the tabernacle. It was sixty cubits long, by twenty cubits wide. The length was divided into two parts, the one being the Holy Place, which was forty cubits, the other being the Holy of Holies, which was twenty cubits. Then, in front of the building, there was a porch which was as wide as the building itself (twenty cubits), and was ten cubits in depth. This porch, therefore, brought the length of the temple up to seventy cubits (excluding the thickness of the walls). Then, around the two sides and rear of the temple, there were small rooms built against the walls, from the outside, for the use of the priests. These ran round the walls in three stories, one room above another: and so that the flooring joists of these rooms should not need to be inserted into the walls of the sacred building, the temple walls were made with ledges on which these joists, or floor beams, could rest. The width of these rooms, plus the thickness of the walls, adds ten cubits to each side of the temple, and to the rear; so that the full length is now *eighty* cubits, and the breadth *forty* cubits.

Thus we see that the temple of Solomon was not a large building. The cubit is about one foot six inches: so that a building eighty cubits long by forty cubits wide is in English measurement 120 feet by 60 feet. This means that Solomon's temple was a very small building compared with some of our own churches; and this may at first seem surprising, if not disappointing, to us. But we must remember that, in view of the purpose and object of the temple, it was never intended to be of an imposing size. Unlike our modern *churches*, which are made to accommodate congregations, the temple was *not* made for assemblies of the people. The congregation never met *within* it, but offered worship *towards* it, as being the residence of the Deity. It was a place for the Divine presence, and for the priests who ministered before it; and for no others. In this, it was like the ancient Egyptian temples, and other temples of antiquity; and viewed in this light, any surprise at its seeming smallness disappears. As Dr. Kitto says, "The importance of the temple of Solomon, which we have been led to regard as one of the wonders of the ancient world, consisted not in its size, but in the elaborate, costly, and highly decorative character of its whole interior and furniture, and also in the number, extent, grandeur, and substantial masonry of its surrounding courts, chambers, walls, and towers. Indeed, it is not too much to presume that these outer constructions, forming the massive ring in which the costly gem of the temple was set, cost as much as the sacred building itself, immense as was the quantity of gold bestowed upon it."

We cannot here speak about the exquisite ornamentation of the interior, but must simply draw attention to the outstanding fact that the whole interior was "*overlaid with pure gold*" (verse 21). This was not mere gilding, but actual gold *overlaying*, of which art there are ample specimens preserved to us from olden times. The decorative carving was first done on cedar wood; and this formed the *base* of the enchasement which appeared on the gold surface. The amount of gold expended on the interior and furniture of the temple must have been very great. It is well, however, to remember that gold, in Solomon's day, was not *money*. It was not a medium of exchange, a standard of value, as it is today. Silver was the standard of value: and it is quite probable that Solomon bought gold with silver. We should clearly understand that gold was then valued for ornamental workings, but not as money, and that, therefore, as has been truly observed, the gold which is said to have been used in Solomon's temple does not represent the monetary *cost* involved, but the actual amount of the metal used.

We cannot here speak about the two wonderful golden cherubim, each fifteen feet tall, of the two great pillars of brass, each twenty-seven feet high, in the porch at the front (which porch, be it noted, was higher than the rest of the building), of the molten sea, the lavers and candelabra and tables and vessels, and of other interesting appurtenances of the temple. These should be read up carefully with the aid of a good commentary. But there are three points we ought to mention.

First; we are told that Solomon made narrow *windows* for the temple (vi. 4); and it may be that the question arises in some mind as to how there could be such windows if there were three stories of rooms built against the exterior of the temple walls. The answer is that these three stories together were only *fifteen* cubits high (vi. 10), whereas the temple was *thirty* cubits high (vi. 2). So that, even allowing for the flooring and roofing of the three stories of rooms, there was ample space above for the windows. These windows, of course, would not be glazed, but probably filled with ornate lattice work, which was then the common way of filling such windows.

Second; the opening verse of chapter vii. says: "But Solomon was building his own house *thirteen* years." Since the temple only took *seven* years, it might seem to suggest selfishness on Solomon's part that he should take six years longer than this over the building of his own house; but we wrong Solomon if we think thus. The "But" with which chapter vii. commences should be "And" (as in the Revised Version). There is no thought of *contrast* between the last words of chapter vi. (which say that Solomon took seven years to build the temple) and the first words of chapter vii. The *palace* buildings were much larger, and the undertaking a more extensive one; nor had there been any such preparation of materials for these buildings as there had been for the temple; and probably less workmen were engaged. It speaks well for Solomon that before ever he commenced his own house he completed the house for the Lord.

Third; we should not overlook *David's* part in the temple. Although he was not permitted to be its builder, and although he knew that he must die before ever it was built, yet with characteristic generosity he set about preparing for it. He seems to have thrown himself into this with as much zest as if he himself had been going to be its builder. In 1 Chronicles xxii. 2–5 we read: "And David commanded to gather together the strangers that were in the land of Israel; and he set masons to hew wrought stones to build the house of God. And David prepared iron in abundance for the nails for the doors of the gates, and for the joinings; and brass in abundance without weight; also cedar trees in abundance; for the Zidonians and they of Tyre brought much cedar wood to David. And David said: Solomon my son is young and tender, and the house that is to be builded for the Lord must be exceeding magnifical, of fame and of glory throughout all countries: I will therefore now make preparation for it. So David prepared abundantly before his death." How characteristic of David is this generous language and behaviour! In verse 14 of the same chapter we are told that he also left for the temple "an hundred thousand talents of gold, and a thousand thousand talents of silver, and of brass and iron without weight."

Moreover, in a remarkable passage (1 Chron. xxviii. 10–19) we find that David also left for Solomon *plans* and *patterns* for the temple, which he claimed to have received from God (verses 12 and 19). And he also left for Solomon good *friends* who gave ready help. Such an one was Hiram, King of Tyre, who, we read, "was ever a lover of David" (1 Kings v. 1), and who helped Solomon for David his father's sake.

There is something noble and touching, as well as pathetic, in David's enthusiastic provision for the temple which he himself would never see. May we have a like unselfishness toward those who are to follow us! God help us to leave our children the *moral* materials for the building of their lives as living temples! May we leave our children patterns which we have received from God; and may we leave them godly friends who will be wise and willing helpers of them when we ourselves have passed beyond!

THE FIRST BOOK OF KINGS (2)

Lesson Number 33

NOTE.—For this further study in the First Book of Kings, read again chapters i.-iv. and ix.-xi.

Homer has been translated into about twenty different languages. Shakespeare has been translated into about forty different languages. Leaving out all. others, there are two books, so far as I know, that have gone out into over one hundred translations. Those are John Bunyan's *Pilgrim's Progress* and *The Imitation of Christ*, by Thomas à Kempis. The only two which have reached the three figures are those dependent upon the Bible. They are the offspring of the Bible . . . The Bible in its entirety, or parts of it, has been translated into just over *one thousand* languages of human speech.

—*G. Campbell Morgan.*

THE FIRST BOOK OF KINGS (2)

SOLOMON: HIS RISE, WISDOM, GLORY, AND FAILURE

The Accession of Solomon (i.–ii.)

SOLOMON was very young when he came to the throne. His own word is that he was "but a little child" (iii. 7). Eusebius says he was twelve. Josephus says he was fifteen. We may safely say he was not more than twenty. His early accession was precipitated by a conspiracy of Adonijah, David's eldest surviving son, who aspired to the throne. Adonijah apparently judged that he could bring off his *coup d'état* on the threefold ground of David's enfeeblement through old age, Solomon's disqualification through immaturity, and his own eminent suitability as being a favourite son of David, and a very attractive person (i. 6). He was backed up by Joab, the head of the army, and Abiathar, head of the priesthood, both of whom presumably sought their own interests—Joab to retain his leadership as under David, and Abiathar to oust his rival, Zadok.

But the stratagem proved abortive owing to the quick counter move of Nathan the prophet, who procured and then proclaimed the aged David's solemn oath that Solomon was the appointed successor. Adonijah's guilt is seen in his own confession, shortly afterward, that he had known the kingdom to be Solomon's *"from the Lord"* (ii. 15).

See chapter ii. Here is David's death-bed charge to Solomon. While the first part of it is sound and noble enough, the latter part contains certain grim touches which seem strange to a modern reader. David's word about Joab is: "Let not his hoar head go down to the grave in peace." His word about Shimei is: "His hoar head bring thou down to the grave with blood." But if these words of dying David are thought to express a revengeful spirit they are quite misunderstood. David's *personal* attitude to Joab and Shimei had been shown already. He had generously tolerated Joab through the years, and had pardoned the cursing of Shimei. His death-bed words about them are uttered from the standpoint of public duty, not of private vengeance.

See what Israel's Law enjoins—"Ye shall take no satisfaction for the life of a murderer which is guilty of death: but he shall surely be put to death. . . . *So ye shall not pollute the land wherein ye are; for blood it defileth the land: and the land cannot be cleansed of the blood that is shed therein, but by the blood of him that shed it*" (Num. xxxv. 31–3). "Thine eye shall not pity him; but thou shalt put away the guilt of innocent blood from Israel, *that it may go well with thee*" (Deut. xix. 13). Now Joab had cold-bloodedly murdered both Abner and Amasa; and he was therefore under a double guilt. It was now over thirty years since he had slain Abner, but at that very time David had evidently been thinking of the words of Israel's Divine law when he said: "I and my kingdom are guiltless before the Lord for ever from the blood of Abner the Son of Ner. Let it rest on the head of Joab, and on all his father's house" (2 Sam. iii. 28, 29). As a theocratic king, David is responsible for the maintenance of the Divine law; and it is this which lies behind his charge to Solomon. As the late Dr. J. L. Porter has said: "At the close of his life, David was roused to a sense of his neglect of this imperious duty. The kingdom was in peril. Divine vengeance was impending over it. He was then too weak to carry out the law. He was at the point of death; but, as the representative of the Divine Law-giver and Judge, he pronounced sentence upon the criminals, and charged his heir and successor to carry it out. In this there was no 'cold-blooded revenge.' There was strict, though somewhat tardy, justice."

The far sadder thing about David's charge concerning Joab is that Joab was called *so late* to pay for the blood of Abner, and that he should be punished after so long an interval *by those whom he had served so loyally and successfully*. Saddest of all was the fact that David himself had used this very man Joab as his accomplice in the murder of Uriah! It is greatly to be regretted that David should have gone down to the grave with such matters on his conscience.

In the case of Shimei there had been *treason* coupled with *blasphemy*—his cursing of "the Lord's Anointed." Solomon was not to regard him as altogether expurgated from that double crime. Shimei was a dangerous person, and not above suspicion. David had the safety of his son's kingdom at heart in his word about Shimei. Moreover, his word should be read in the light of what subsequently happened between Solomon and Shimei. In strict justice Shimei should have been put to death years beforehand; and David's clemency to him ought to have evoked a loyalty which seems to have been lacking.

The Wisdom of Solomon (iii.–iv.)

Solomon's prayer for wisdom, in preference to wealth, power, and length of days, is a beautiful passage (iii. 5–15). It reveals that the young king *already possessed* a marked degree of wisdom; for that he should *ask* wisdom above all else was above all else a *mark* of wisdom. In nothing is his early wisdom seen more clearly than that he should ask for *more* wisdom. Yet without lessening our appreciation of the noble choice here made by Solomon, it is right that we should clearly understand the *kind* of wisdom which he here besought, and with which he thereafter became supernaturally gifted; for unless we *do* understand this we shall find it puzzling to reconcile his wisdom with that later foolishness which appeared alongside of it.

Solomon's own words indicate that in asking for wisdom he did not mean *spiritual* wisdom—that insight in Divine things which comes only of regeneration and sanctification and a close fellowship with God, that wisdom of which Paul speaks in the New Testament. No; in *that* kind of wisdom Solomon falls considerably behind his father, David. The wisdom Solomon sought —and with which he became supernaturally endowed—was administrative discernment, sagacious judgment, intellectual grasp, aptitude for the acquisition of knowledge, a practical wisdom in the directing of affairs. In *this* kind of wisdom he excelled even the renowned philosophers of his day; as we read, in chapter iv. 29–34:

"*And God gave Solomon wisdom, and understanding exceeding much, and largeness of heart, even as the sand that is on the sea shore.*

"*And Solomon's wisdom excelled the wisdom of all the children of the east country, and all the wisdom of Egypt.*

"For he was wiser than all men; than Ethan the Ezrahite, and Heman, and Chalcol, and Darda, the sons of Mahol: and his fame was in all nations round about.

"And he spake three thousand proverbs: and his songs were a thousand and five.

"And he spake of trees, from the cedar tree that is in Lebanon even unto the hyssop that springeth out of the wall: he spake also of beasts, and of fowl, and of creeping things, and of fishes.

"And there came of all people to hear the wisdom of Solomon, from all kings of the earth, which had heard of his wisdom."

To the people at large, the first evidence of the young king's penetrating insight came with his decision in the case of the two young mothers who came as rival claimants to the same babe (iii. 16–28). Solomon's handling of this case is indeed striking. Any misgivings hitherto entertained on account of his immaturity were thereby removed. The people recognised a wisdom in him which was far beyond his tender years. This was indeed the wisdom of God in him. Thenceforth, Solomon held the confidence and veneration of all his people.

The Glory of Solomon (ix.–x.)

The completion of the temple and the palace mark off the first twenty years of Solomon's reign (see ix. 10). The remaining twenty are briefly dealt with in chapters ix. to xi. The two chapters ix. and x. mark the peak period. Their eloquent description needs almost no comment here. They leave us in no doubt as to the material splendour of that time. The account of Solomon's revenue and splendour (x. 14–29) is an astonishing paragraph; and when we read that Solomon made silver to be as common as stones in Jerusalem, it is well to remember that silver, not gold, was the *money* of that day!

The visit of the Queen of Sheba (x. 1–13) has an interest all its own; and Solomon's generosity to her becomes a beautiful illustration of the *heavenly* King's bounty to ourselves. In chapter x. 13 we read: "And king Solomon gave unto the queen of Sheba all her desire, whatsoever she asked, beside that which Solomon gave her of his royal bounty." The wondering-eyed Queen was fairly overcome by all the much-to-be-coveted treasures which she saw. With womanly appreciation, she simply could not resist asking for this and that and the other thing, until eventually she found herself in the quandary of seeing much more that she desired, without being able to commit the rudeness of asking still further! Solomon, however, read her heart, and gave her not only all that she *asked*, but all that she *thought*; and then, even to that, he added his "royal bounty." See, then, the three measures of Solomon's generosity which we have here—(1) All that she *ASKED*; (2) All that she *THOUGHT*; (3) Solomon's royal *BOUNTY*.

With this in mind, turn to Ephesians iii. 20—"Now unto Him that is able to do exceeding abundantly above all that we ask or think, according to the power that worketh in us." Here is the same three-fold measure of giving—(1) "all that we *ask*"; (2) "all that we *think*"; and (3) "*exceeding abundantly above*." God grant us faith to ask for big things, and to have large desires toward Him!—for giving does not impoverish Him, and withholding does not enrich Him.

It is interesting to note that in the verse above-quoted, where Solomon is said to have given the Queen of Sheba "of his royal bounty," the Hebrew reads, literally, "*according to the hand of King Solomon*." Think what that "according to" meant. Solomon was the richest king in all the earth, and his giving was such as *corresponded* with that! What lavish bounty, then, is in that "according to"! It reminds us of Philippians iv. 19—"My God shall supply all your need *according to* HIS riches in glory by Christ Jesus." May the Holy Spirit teach us the meaning of that "according to," and enrich our lives with that royal bounty which comes from Him who said, "A greater than Solomon is here."

The Failure of Solomon (xi.)

Alas, the glory of the Solomonic period was short-lived. Soon were Israel's sons to lament, "How is the gold become dim!" The fault was Solomon's alone. The following sentences, picked from chapter xi., tell the story of his failure. "But king Solomon loved many strange women." "Solomon clave unto these in love." "His wives turned away his heart after other gods." "Solomon did evil in the sight of the Lord." "The Lord was angry with Solomon." "The Lord said: I will surely rend the kingdom from thee." It was this infidelity of Solomon which precipitated the disruption into the two kingdoms. The sun of Solomon's glory set in dark clouds. Not all the gorgeous apparel of his costly wardrobe could hide the ugly blot on his character. Not only had Solomon abused marriage; he had filled his great harem with women from those nations against which Israel had repeatedly received Divine interdict—Moab, Ammon, Edom, and others, and had even built "high places" for their abominable deities. The *king's* behaviour being such, what more likely than that the *people* would quickly sink, too? Solomon had forfeited further Divine favour. The wisest of all men had become the greatest of all fools, for he had sinned against light and privilege and promise such as had been given to no other man in all the earth. The kingdom should be rent from his family, except that Judah should be retained for David's sake. Chapter xi. closes with the death of Solomon, and thus ends the first part of the book. Truly, in Solomon we see how inferior is the greatest human wisdom to true piety. If, as the psalmist says, "the fear of the Lord is the *beginning* of wisdom," then surely the highest of all wisdom is to obey the Lord in all things, and thus to walk before Him with a perfect heart.

The following quotation gives a fair criticism of Solomon: "In estimating him, we must remember his privileges and opportunities. He did not, as his father, inherit a wrecked kingdom and a demoralised army, but a kingdom established in righteousness, and an army all-victorious. Then he had the experience of the two previous kings to guide him. Peacefulness, as his name indicates, certainly characterised his reign; but how far he merited his other name, Jedidiah, 'Beloved of the Lord,' may be questioned. Abraham was the 'friend of God,' and David the man 'after God's own heart'; but Solomon did not walk in their ways. His record has its bright features, as is seen in his early humility, his wise choice of a gift, his building of the temple, and his wonderful prayer at its dedication (1 Kings iii. 7 and 9; viii. 22–53). Were these removed from the record, what would be left to the credit of his memory? He was a man of extraordinary ability, a botanist, zoologist, architect, poet, and moral philosopher; and yet a man who strangely lacked in strength of character. Moses had said that Israel's future kings should not multiply wealth, horses, or wives (Deut. xvii. 14–20), but Solomon did all three. He who was beloved of his God, not so much, one would think, for his own sake as for David's, was made to sin by 'outlandish women' (Neh. xiii. 26), after the Lord had appeared to him twice. He took to himself seven hundred wives, and from amongst those very nations against which Israel had been warned (1 Kings xi. 1, 2). This led to the introduction of false gods and false worship, for which the judgment of the Lord was pronounced against him. If any man could ever have been satisfied by getting all his heart's desire, that man was Solomon; yet he has put it on record (Eccles.) that everything under the sun is vanity and vexation of spirit. Solomon's is the self-life having its full fling, and at the end turning away sad and sick of it all."

So much, then, for king Solomon—his accession, his wisdom, his glory, and his failure. Is there anywhere a character which is more of an enigma? Is there in all history a more thought-provoking irony than this, that the wisest of all men became the greatest of fools, that the man who had wealth and fame, and pleasure above all others, should write at the end, "Vanity of vanities!—all is vanity!"? Let us read, mark, learn, and inwardly digest!

ADDENDUM ON SOLOMON'S REIGN

We have said that Solomon's reign typifies the coming reign of Christ on earth. What then were the outstanding characteristics of Solomon's reign? First, throughout his reign there was *peace* and *rest*. Not one war or internal disturbance broke the serenity of that forty years. Second, there was surpassing *wisdom* and *knowledge*, as we see in 1 Kings iv. and x. Third, there was *wealth* and *glory*—such as excelled all that had gone before. Fourth, there was *fame* and *honour*, Solomon's name being the greatest in all the countries around Israel, and Israel being honoured by all peoples. Fifth, there was *joy* and *safety*. In 1 Kings iv. 25 we read: "Judah and Israel dwelt safely, every man under his vine and under his fig tree, from Dan even to Beersheba, all the days of Solomon." See also verse 20.

Now these are certainly the predicted marks of that kingdom which Christ will yet set up among the nations. There will be *peace* and *rest*: "Nation shall not lift up sword against nation, neither shall they learn war any more." "The wolf also shall dwell with the lamb, and the leopard shall lie down with the kid; and the calf and the young lion and the fatling together; and a little child shall lead them." There will also be unprecedented *wisdom* and *knowledge*; for "the earth shall be full of the knowledge of the Lord, as the waters cover the sea."

So, also, will there be *wealth* and *glory* such as have never been known before, for "the mountain (i.e. the kingdom) of the Lord's house shall be established in the tops of the mountains (i.e. kingdoms), and shall be exalted above the hills; and all nations shall flow unto it." And there will also be such *fame* and *honour*, and such empire, as no king has ever known before; for "He (Christ) shall have dominion, also, from sea to sea, and from the river unto the ends of the earth; yea, all kings shall fall down before Him; all nations shall serve Him." And there will also be *joy* and *safety* for all the privileged subjects in that eventual kingdom; for in Micah iv. 4 we read of it that "they shall sit every man under his vine and under his fig tree; and none shall make them afraid; for the mouth of the Lord of hosts hath spoken it." There is no more engrossing study in all the Scriptures than the study of those glowing passages in the prophets, which describe the glories of this Davidic and Solomonic kingdom of Christ which is yet to be on earth. Well may our daily prayer be, "Thy kingdom come!"

—*J. S. B.*

THE FIRST BOOK OF KINGS (3)

Lesson Number 34

NOTE.—For this concluding study in the First Book of Kings read again chapters xii. to xxii.

Solomon continued the policy and shared the blessing of his father. His dominions extended from the Mediterranean to the Euphrates. and from the Red Sea and Arabia to the utmost Lebanon (1 Kings iv, 21, etc.). The tributary states were held in complete subjection, and, as they were still governed by their own princes, Solomon was literally "king of kings." The Canaanites who remained in Palestine became peaceable subjects or useful servants. His treasures were immense, composed largely of the spoils won by his father from many nations, and treasured up by him for the purpose of building a temple to Jehovah. To these Solomon added the proceeds of oppressive taxation. The largeness of his harem transgressed the bounds of even Oriental licence, though possibly dictated by worldly policy.

The wisdom of Solomon is celebrated both in Scripture and in Eastern story. Three thousand proverbs gave proof of his virtues and sagacity. A thousand and five songs placed him among the first of Hebrew poets; while his knowledge of natural history was shown by writings which were long admired.

His very greatness betrayed him. His treasures, wives, and chariots were all contrary to the spirit and precepts of the Law (Deut. xvii. 16, 17). His exactions alienated the affections of his people; and, above all, he was led astray by his wives, and built temples to Chemosh, or Baal-Peor, the obscene idol of Moab; to Moloch, the god of Ammon; and to Ashtoreth, the goddess of the Sidonians. His later days, therefor, were disturbed by "adversaries," who stirred up revolt in the tributory states; the tribe of Ephraim became a centre of disaffection; Hadad did "mischief" in Edom; Damascus declared its independence under Rezon; and Ahijah was instructed to announce to Solomon himself that, as he had broken the covenant by which he held his crown, the kingdom should be rent from him and part of it given to his servant, 1 Kings xi. 31.

—*Angus, Bible Handbook.*

THE FIRST BOOK OF KINGS (3)

THE TWO KINGDOMS

WE COME now to the second half of the book. Immediately following Solomon's death the Disruption takes place; and from this point we follow the fortunes of the *two* kingdoms and the two lines of kings. To deal separately with each of these kings is not necessary to our present scheme of study: but let us try to pick out the ruling significances of the Disruption and the subsequent course of things.

The Disruption

Israel's Tragedy.

First, the Disruption was a *tragedy*. At the close of Solomon's reign Israel had become exalted to the highest dignity in its history. Worship, religion and public instruction had become, through the provision made by David and Solomon, such as had never been known before. As the late Principal Baylee says: "The theology of the Psalms, the practical wisdom of the Proverbs, the mystical suggestiveness of the Canticles, the patriarchal teachings of Job, the archæology of Genesis, the manifestation of God in history from Joshua to 2 Samuel, gave a fulness of instruction and guidance which was calculated to make Israel the centre of light and blessedness to the whole world." The high purposes of God through Israel were developing with increasing observableness; and we can only exclaim: "Alas, what might have been if the Disruption had not struck the nation with so deadly a wound!"

Solomon's guilt.

Second, it is well to grasp clearly that the Scriptures locate the *blame* for the Disruption with Solomon. As we saw in the book of the Judges, while God may confer many privileges, He never confers the privilege to *sin*—no, not even with such an elect personage as Solomon; and therefore, much as it must have grieved the God of the Davidic covenant, the Disruption was permitted. Solomon's guilt was great. It is an awful yet true indictment of him to say that "the whole after-history of the Disruption, the gradual decline of power and influence, the corruption of morals, and at times the almost total forgetfulness of God, were only the necessary developments of those pernicious principles and practices introduced by Solomon."

Rehoboam's folly.

Third, in chapter xii. the *actual occurrence* of the Disruption is explained. In the later years of Solomon's reign the extravagant expenses of the royal court had become such as to necessitate the levying of taxes which the people were ill able to yield. Therefore, on the death of Solomon and the accession of Rehoboam, the people, under Jeroboam's leadership, sought a redress of their grievance by a diminution of this burden. Their request seems to have been a reasonable one—"Thy father made our yoke grievous: now therefore make thou the grievous service of thy father, and his heavy yoke which he put upon us, lighter; and we will serve thee" (xii. 4). The stupid behaviour and fatuous reply of Rehoboam, however, reveal his utter inability to measure such a situation (xii. 5–15), and disclose a mental inferiority which stands in painful contrast with the mental superiority of his distinguished father. His senseless threat to outdo his father's severities towards his subjects was the last straw. The ten tribes renounced any further allegiance to the house of David; and Jeroboam became their king.

Jeroboam's innovations.

Fourth, the Disruption occasioned *grave innovations* in the ten-tribed kingdom. Jeroboam was as shrewd and unscrupulous as he was energetic and forceful. He quickly perceived that although he had fortified Shechem as his capital, Jerusalem would still be regarded as the uniting centre of all the tribes unless some drastic steps were taken to negative this. The temple and the ark of the covenant, and all those things which were emblematically sacred in Israel's religion, were in Jerusalem, as also was the principal seat of learning. If the people were to continue going up to the religious festivals there the result, sooner or later, would prove fatal to the throne of the ten-tribed kingdom.

Jeroboam therefore established two new centres of worship in the ten-tribed kingdom—the one at Dan in the north, and the other at Bethel in the south, professedly on the ground that it was "too much" for the people to keep going all the way to Jerusalem (xii. 28). In each of the two new centres he installed a golden calf, and proclaimed: "Behold thy gods, O Israel, which brought thee up out of the land of Egypt." Thus was Israel led into grave sin.

It is only fair to Jeroboam to allow that in setting up the golden calves he was not meaning to introduce the worship of gods other than Jehovah; for the calves were clearly understood by the people to be symbolical figures consecrated to Jehovah. Yet Jeroboam's guilt remains great, for he evidently had the episode of *Aaron's* golden calf in mind, seeing that he used the same words as Aaron himself had used—"These be thy gods, O Israel, which brought thee up out of the land of Egypt"; and Jeroboam knew well enough the anger of God and of Moses at that sin, besides knowing that all idol-representation of Israel's God was forbidden.

Jeroboam also built "high places" for the new worship, instituted sacrifices, and ordained a feast to correspond with the Feast of Tabernacles, though he put its observance one month later than that of the feast in Judæa. Moreover, he elected a new order of priests from the lowest of the people. This he did because the true priests and Levites, much to their credit, apparently preferred to lose their livings, and resort to Jerusalem, rather than be party to Jeroboam's illicit innovations (see 2 Chron. xi. 13). It would seem, also, that the evacuating priests and Levites were joined by other faithful souls in Israel (2 Chron. xi. 16); but the ten-tribed kingdom as a whole quickly fell in with the new arrangements (1 Kings xii. 30); and thus, besides the *political* disruption which had severed Israel and Judah from each other, there now came a *religious* cleavage.

Jeroboam was a shrewd and forceful man, as we have said; but he was entirely without the spiritual insight to see that since *God* had put him on the throne, God Himself would overrule those contingencies which seemed to threaten his throne. He

went more and more deeply into sin, and dragged the people
with him. His distinguishing epitaph is "Jeroboam, the son of
Nebat, which made Israel to sin" (1 Kings xxii. 52; 2 Kings iii. 3;
x. 29, etc.). Thus, the ten-tribed kingdom had a sorry beginning;
and it rapidly went from bad to worse.

The Two Lines of Kings

Compare now the two lines of kings, up to the point where
this First Book of Kings ends. There is no need to go into a lot
of details. The broad facts tell a clear story. As we have said,
the second half of 1 Kings covers roughly the first *eighty* years
of the two kingdoms, from the Disruption. During that period
four kings reigned in Judah, and eight in Israel. Their names,
along with the number of years they reigned, and the Scripture
verdict on them, are as follows:

JUDAH		ISRAEL	
Rehoboam . . . evil	17 years	Jeroboam . . . evil	22 years
Abijam . . . evil	3	Nadab . . . evil	2
Asa . . . good	41	Baasha . . . evil	24
Jehoshaphat . . good	25	Elah . . . evil	2
Jehoram . . . (Although mentioned in chap. xxii. 50, Jehoram's reign did not begin until *after* Ahaziah's reign which is shown in the Israel column).	—	Zimri . . . evil	— (one week)
		Omri . . . evil	12
		Ahab . . . evil	22
		Ahaziah . . . evil	2
	about 86 years		about 86 years

From these figures it will be seen that, in the period covered,
Israel had twice as many kings as Judah. Eight kings in about
eighty years is not good for any nation. But what is far worse,
of the eight kings who reigned over Israel, every one was *evil*—
a tragic record. Of the four kings who reigned over Judah, the
two who reigned the longest (covering sixty-six years out of
eighty-six) were *good* kings.

The Prophet Elijah (xvii.–xxii.)

The last six chapters of 1 Kings are occupied with the ministry of the prophet Elijah in the *northern* kingdom, the kingdom of the ten tribes. This spectacular man of God rivets our attention to good purpose. He is one of the most remarkable figures in the whole story of Israel. His eminence is seen both in the religious reformation which he wrought, and in the fact that the New Testament speaks of him more often than of any other Old Testament prophet. Moreover, it was he who was chosen to appear with Moses at our Lord's transfiguration. And further, it is from this point that the ministry of the *prophets* in the two Hebrew kingdoms becomes more prominently emphasised. One of Israel's most startling and romantic characters, he suddenly appears on the scene as the crisis-prophet, with thunder on his brow and tempest in his voice. He disappears just as suddenly, swept skywards in a chariot of fire. Between his first appearing and his final disappearing lies a succession of amazing miracles. We here call attention to three things—his character, his ministry, his significance.

His Character.

The grandeur of Elijah's character is recognised by all. Even those critics who have disputed Elijah's miracles have allowed the greatness of his character. He seems to have been somewhat remarkable even *physically*. He was not a man of the city but of the open country. In fact he seems to have been a veritable bedouin, loving the haunts of the hills and the valleys, and roaming the broad, unsettled pasturages of Bashan. His rugged and austere appearance would be such as at once to attract the eye of the softer-clad townsman. When we read of Elijah's confronting Ahab, and announcing the coming drought, we must picture the shaggy-bearded, long-haired, weather-tanned sheik, or the gaunt, piercing-eyed dervish, clad with a rough sheepskin, striding into the king's presence, and lifting up a sinewy arm to heaven as he denounces the weak-willed king in tones sounding like awesome echoes from the mountains.

But Elijah is no less striking in his *moral* make-up. Three qualities are specially conspicuous—courage, faith, zeal. See his *courage.* Here is the Martin Luther of old-time Israel, who singlehanded challenged the whole priesthood of the state religion, and all the people of the realm, to the decisive test on Mount Carmel.

See also Elijah's *faith*. It was his faith which underlay his courage. What faith it required to go before Ahab and say, "There shall not be dew nor rain these years, but according to my word"! Dew and rain may be withheld through ordinary natural causes for days or even weeks or in very rare cases for some months; but for dew and rain to be suspended for years involved supernatural intervention.

Then see Elijah's *zeal*. Truly did he express his master passion when he said: "I have been very jealous for the Lord God of hosts." How much, this sun-bronzed, untutored child of the desert can teach us of jealousy for the Divine honour, of burning indignation at religious compromise, and of passionate loyalty to the word of God!

His Ministry.

Old Dr. Kitto remarks, "There were two sorts of prophets: prophets of deeds, and prophets of words. Of the latter the greatest is doubtless Isaiah. Of the former there has not been among men a greater than Elijah." This, then, is the first thing about Elijah's ministry: he was a prophet of *deeds*. So far as we know he wrote nothing; and this does not surprise us. Such devout impetuosity and tempestuousness as Elijah's seldom go with patient penmanship. Many of the most passionate and energetic reformers have been altogether ungifted as writers. They were men of action rather than diction. There is always need for such men.

But again, Elijah's ministry was one of *miracles*. At every turn miracles meet us. Because of this some recent "scholars" have summarily discarded this section of Scripture as largely mythical. Yet the narrative is so sober and circumstantial that had it not been for this miracle element in it the most destructive critic would never have questioned its veracity.

Again, Elijah's ministry was one of *reformation*. He did not originate anything. He was a protestant against the religious apostasy and resultant degradation of his nation; and he called men back to the good old ways which Israel's covenant-keeping God had marked out for them through Moses. There is need today for such outright protestation.

His Significance.

First, Elijah demonstrates the truth that *God always has a man to match the hour*. Things were dark enough when Ahab began to reign, but he soon made them a hundred times worse. It is written: "There was none like unto Ahab which did sell himself to work wickedness in the sight of the Lord, whom Jezebel his wife stirred up." Under the royal lead a grimly determined effort was made to stamp out the religion of Jehovah. Of all hours in Israel's career this was the ugliest. Yet just at zero hour God's champion arises. The same thing is seen again and again in history. When the light of evangelical truth seems on the point of being extinguished from Christendom, and Popery smothers Europe's millions beneath its evil cloak, God has his Martin Luthers and John Calvins to call back the continent to the faith once for all delivered to the saints. When politics and religion and morals become so degraded in Britain that the very vitals of the nation are jeopardised, God has His John Wycliffes and William Tyndales and Whitefields and Wesleys.

Another thing which Elijah illustrates is that *when wickedness develops into extraordinary proportions God meets it with extraordinary measures*. The Phœnician gods which Jezebel and Ahab had taught Israel to worship were largely emblems of the material elements which produce dew and rain—Baal, Ashtoreth and Ashere. Therefore the *true* God will show His superiority over all the powers of nature by suspending rain and dew for three years and six months! Over against the fake miracles of the false religion Jehovah will now intervene with *real* miracles! This is why the ministry of Elijah is one of miracles. God is meeting an extraordinary situation by extraordinary measures. And I believe that in the present days, when undoubtedly an extraordinary situation has begun to develop, we may expect God again to meet the challenge by extraordinary measures.

There are other ways in which Elijah is significant for us today; but we mention only one more. *Elijah is to come to this earth again!* Strikingly enough we are told this in the very last words of the Old Testament (Mal. iv. 5–6). There are those who scorn such an idea just as they deny a visible return of the Lord Jesus. There are those who hold that the prophecies of Isaiah and Malachi concerning the coming of Elijah were fulfilled in John the Baptist, of whom our Lord said: "Elias is come already." But while John was an interim fulfilment, he was not Elijah personally; and our Lord said (after John's death) that the real Elijah was "still to come" (Matt. xvii. 11, literal translation). If we turn on to that strange eleventh chapter of Revelation we find that one of the two "witnessess" who are to come to earth just before the crash of the present world-system and the return of Christ is Elijah (as the delineation makes clear). Truly Elijah is a significant figure. When he came on the scene long ago things quickly moved; and when he reappears in the near future still bigger things will be on the move! The Lord's own return will be at hand!

THE SECOND BOOK OF KINGS (1)

Lesson Number 35

NOTE.—For this study read right through the Second Book of Kings once or twice.

The great empires of the East, Assyria, Babylon, and Persia, will now, almost exclusively, occupy our attention (i.e. onwards from this Second Book of Kings). They all alike exercised the greatest influence upon the destinies of ancient Israel; and it is among the most welcome surprises of recent times that this long period of Israel's history should now have found such a continuous and marvellous commentary in the recovered records of those great world-kingdoms. The confirmations are so numerous and so conclusive that the critics have had to confess that here at least the Bible must be recognised as history. This has been accompanied also with the overturn of some of their earlier and most confident conclusions. For, wherever the explorer and the discoverer bring back to us the past with which the Bible deals, the critic has to retire confounded and ashamed.

—*John Urquhart.*

THE SECOND BOOK OF KINGS (1)

THIS Second Book of Kings, which opens with the translation of Elijah to heaven, and closes with the transportation of the captive Jews to Babylon, is more tragic than all which have preceded it. Nay, more than that, it is the most tragic national record ever written. The elect people, through whom the gracious purposes of God were to have been developed for the enlightenment and regeneration of the whole race, become more and more steeped in infidelity and moral degradation, until finally the measure of their wickedness is full, judgment falls, pitiless foes wreak vengeance on them, and drag them from their own land into humiliating captivity.

The Book of the Dispersion

In chapter xvii. we see the ten-tribed *northern* kingdom (Israel) going into the Assyrian captivity, from which they have never since returned; while in chapter xxv. we see Jerusalem sacked, the temple burnt, and the *southern* kingdom (Judah) going into the Babylonian captivity, from which only a remnant returned.

Although Judah did not go into captivity until over a century after the break-up of Israel, the two captivities are spoken of together as the *Dispersion*. We have seen how each of the historical books, so far, is distinguished by some controlling feature. It will repay us to fix these firmly in our memory.

1 Samuel is *the book of the Transition*—from theocracy to monarchy. 2 Samuel is *the book of David's reign*. 1 Kings is *the book of the Disruption*—of the one kingdom into two. And now, 2 Kings is always to be remembered as *the book of the Dispersion*.

We cannot read 2 Kings without thinking of Solomon's proverb —"The way of transgressors is hard." Paul's word—"The wages of sin is death," is here demonstrated on a national scale, and in clearly declared terms of poetic justice for all to see and heed. Sinning despite warning brings ruin without remedy. Inexcusable wrong brings inescapable wrath. Abused privilege incurs increased penalty. The deeper the guilt, the heavier the stroke. Correction may be resisted, but retribution cannot be evaded. "How shall we escape if we neglect . . ." God is not mocked: whatsoever a nation soweth, that shall it also reap. All these thoughts crowd in upon our minds when we read 2 Kings. As we see the battered, broken tribes of Israel dragged behind the chariots of their heathen conquerors, we surely cannot fail to see that the central message of this book is that *wilful sin brings a woeful end.*

Structure

Writers on these books of the Kings seem to find it very difficult to give a suitable analysis of their contents, because the two histories of Judah and Israel repeatedly overlap and interlock in the one narrative. But to ourselves the broad outlines are unmistakably clear. We have seen how in 1 Samuel the three parts clearly gather round Saul, Samuel, and David; and how, just as clearly, in 2 Samuel, we first have David's triumphs and then David's troubles. We have seen, also, how 1 Kings is unmistakably divided into two main parts, the first part being wholly devoted to Solomon's forty years' reign, and the second part covering the first eighty years of the two kingdoms. And now we shall find that in this Second Book of Kings the main divisions are easily discoverable and just as easily rememberable.

It will be seen that the first ten chapters are practically wholly occupied with the *northern* kingdom, Israel (the only reference to Judah being purely incidental, to mention how two of Judah's kings joined Israel in two military actions, and because of connection by marriage with the house of Ahab). In these first ten chapters the ministry of Elisha to the northern kingdom is the predominant subject.

Then, in the next group of chapters, chapters xi. to xvii., we have alternating annals of *both* kingdoms, ending, in chapter xvii., with the passing of Israel into the *Assyrian* captivity.

Finally, in chapters xviii. to xxv., we have the history of *Judah only* (since the ten-tribed northern kingdom is now dispersed in captivity); and this third group of chapters ends with the passing of Judah into the *Babylonian* captivity. For the sake of making this clear both to the outward and the inward eye, we set it out as follows:

THE SECOND BOOK OF KINGS
The Book of the Dispersion

WILFUL SIN BRINGS A WOEFUL END

I. ANNALS OF ISRAEL, THE NORTHERN KINGDOM

(i.–x.).

This part contains the ministry of Elisha, and concludes with the death of Jehu, Israel's tenth king.

II. ALTERNATING ANNALS OF BOTH KINGDOMS

(xi.–xvii.).

This part runs up to the Assyrian captivity of Israel. (Jonah, Amos and Hosea prophesied at this time in Israel.)

III. ANNALS OF JUDAH, THE SOUTHERN KINGDOM

(xviii.–xxv.).

This part ends with Judah's Babylonian captivity by which time Obadiah, Joel, Isaiah, Micah, Nahum, Habakkuk, Zephaniah, and Jeremiah had prophesied in Judah.

(For our present purpose there is no need for a more detailed analysis. It is the above three main movements which we ought to fix clearly in mind, to make the book as a whole more easily rememberable.)

Thus this second book of the Kings marks the end of both the Hebrew kingdoms, historically, though they still remain the subject of great prophecies which will be considered later on in our course of study. It is in the fulfilment of these prophecies that the final triumph of God in and through the Hebrew race will be achieved; but, viewed historically, the story of God's earthly people is one of heart-rending human failure and tragedy, as this second book of the Kings shows.

The Two Royal Lines in Completeness

Since this second book of the Kings records the dispersion and ruin of *both* the Hebrew kingdoms (the ten-tribed northern kingdom into the *Assyrian* captivity, 721 B.C., and the southern kingdom, Judah, into the *Babylonian* exile, 587 B.C.), it is well that we should scan the two lines of kings in their completeness, that is, at least, from the time when the ten tribes broke away at the "Disruption" to form their own kingdom, in 975 B.C.

It is noteworthy that nineteen kings, in all, reigned over the ten-tribed kingdom, and the kingdom lasted only some two hundred and fifty years; whereas Judah, which had twenty kings from the time of the Disruption, continued for some three hundred and ninety years from that point. Again, the nineteen kings of Israel came from no less than seven different dynasties, whereas all the twenty kings of Judah were of one and the same dynasty—the Davidic.

This leads us to make two observations.

First, although the successive kings are not dealt with in detail, but are viewed as kings rather than as men, it is noteworthy that in the case of Judah's kings *David is the standard according to which their character is estimated.* Again and again we have such words as "His heart was not perfect with the Lord his God as was the heart of David his father" (see 1 Kings xi. 4, 6, 33, 38); "Thou hast not been as My servant David" (xiv. 8); "His heart was not perfect with the Lord his God as the heart of David his father" (xv. 3); "Asa did that which was right in the eyes of the Lord, as did David his father" (xv. 11); and so on. This is a great tribute to David. Despite those personal sins which marred his life, his trust in God, his general integrity, his jealousy for the Divine honour, and his reverent recognition of responsibility as a theocratic king, were such as fully to justify his being called a man after God's own heart, and to make him a pattern to all his royal successors.

Second, it is clear that one of the ruling purposes of the Scripture history here is to show the faithfulness of God to the Davidic covenant (2 Sam. vii.), in *the preservation of the Davidic* line (see for instance 2 Kings viii. 19). Again and again the royal house of David seemed in peril of being cut off. It was threatened at the revolt of the ten tribes. Later, after the death of Ahaziah,

KINGS OF JUDAH AND ISRAEL

FROM THE DISRUPTION ONWARDS

Giving the number of years which each reigned, and showing roughly how the reigns in the two lines synchronised.

JUDAH		ISRAEL	
Rehoboam	17	Jeroboam	22
Abijam	3	Nadab	2
Asa	41	Baasha	24
		Elah	2
		Zimri	1 week
		Omri	12
Jehoshaphat	25	Ahab	22
		Ahaziah	2
		Jehoram	12
Jehoram	8	Jehu	28
Ahaziah	1		
Athaliah	6		
Joash	40	Jehoahaz	17
Amaziah	29	Jehoash	16
Azariah (Uzziah)	52	Jeroboam II	41
		Interregnum	12
		Zechariah	½
		Shallum	1 month
		Menahem	10
		Pekahiah	2
Jotham	16	Pekah	20
Ahaz	16	Hoshea	9
Hezekiah	29		
Manasseh	55		
Amon	2		
Josiah	31		
Jehoahaz	3 months		
Jehoiakim	11		
Jehoiakin	3 months		
Zedekiah	11		

when the royal city was held by a usurper, and the survival of the Davidic line through Solomon hung on the preserving of the child Joash from the usurper's sword, the woman Jehosheba saved the child and the line continued. Still later, when the as yet childless king Hezekiah was sick and apparently dying, and Jerusalem was besieged by the Assyrians, and it seemed as though the Davidic line was imperilled both by sword and sickness, God intervened, and the line continued. Still later, when the kingdom of Judah fell, on account of its sinning, the faithfulness of God continued and the line was preserved; for although God had to say of the wicked king Jeconiah, "Write this man childless," and the line of David through Solomon failed, a subsidiary line had been preserved from David through Nathan, into which line the succession now ran. And even after the Captivity in Babylon the line continues in Zerubbabel, under whose leadership the temple was rebuilt; and from him the genealogical record is preserved right down to the birth of the Lord Jesus Christ, David's Son and Lord, in whom the Davidic line is perpetuated for evermore, and by whom, at His second advent, the throne of David shall be set up on earth again in the city of Jerusalem, in fulfilment of that covenant made with David long ago.

We hear that since Israel recently became constituted and acknowledged as an independent State again in Palestine, enquiries have been set going, and certain pretensions made, with the idea of establishing a present day lineal link with the Davidic throne. Whether there be truth in this we do not know for certain; but one thing which *is* certain is that Israel will never be an independent *kingdom* again until the King himself returns, even our Lord Jesus Christ. He, and He alone, will re-establish the Davidic throne, for since His birth at Bethelehem He alone is the true Heir, according to the Scriptures of both Old and New Testaments.

> Jesus is king! Jesus is king!
> True king of Israel; David's great Son;
> Hope of the fathers; Heir to the throne;
> Lion of Judah; Lamb that was slain;
> True king of Israel, yet shall He reign.
> Jesus is king! Jesus is king!

THE SECOND BOOK OF KINGS (2)

Lesson Number 36

NOTE.—For this further study in 2 Kings, read again the first ten chapters and chapter xiii.

The newest knowledge cannot be said to be drawing us away from the Bible; on the contrary it is bringing us back to it. Our foremost scientists are feeling and finding their way through a vast undergrowth of materialistic facts towards a world horizon much more in harmony with Holy Scripture. And it has further become clear that the leaders of Science a generation ago both overestimated and overemphasized the limited knowledge of their time, and neglected to look beyond it. Because education reflects the beliefs of leading minds of the previous generation, and not those of the present, so today we are suffering from those miscalculations. But in the light of facts not then observed, or whose significance had been overlooked, scientists of the present have ceased to overestimate human knowledge; on the contrary they are emphasizing human ignorance. So-called Miracles are no longer being laughed at, they are being recognised.

—*Sir Charles Marston.*

THE SECOND BOOK OF KINGS (2)

THE PROPHET ELISHA (i.–x.)

THE PREDOMINANT subject in the first ten chapters of 2 Kings is the ministry of the prophet Elisha; and we would here call careful attention to it. The ministry of Elisha is equally remarkable as that of Elijah, and, in certain typical ways, is even more so. In our last study but one we spoke about Elijah in a threefold way—his character, his ministry, his significance. Perhaps we cannot do better than employ these three headings in connection with Elisha, laying the emphasis on the last of the three, namely, his peculiar and far-reaching significance.

His personal character.

It is always good to consider the personal character of God's outstanding servants, for by so doing we come to see the kind of persons whom God chooses and uses in signal ways. We pick out the following traits in Elisha's moral make-up as being at once noticeable.

We mark first a *spirituality of desire*. When Elijah says: "Ask what I shall do for thee," Elisha's request is, "Let a double portion of thy spirit be upon me" (ii. 9). There is no grasping after earthly advantages, though such might certainly have been chosen.

We note also *filial affection*. "Let me, I pray thee, kiss my father and mother, and then I will follow thee" (1 Kings xix. 20). There is no parallel here with the would-be disciple of Luke ix. who offered before he was called, and whom our Lord knew to be superficial. Elisha at once made a clean break from home ties; but the way he did it evinces family affection. Those who combine true family affection with their supreme love for Christ are those who usually make the sincerest and fittest servants of the Lord.

We observe further Elisha's *humility*. It would seem as though for some time his services were of a very humble sort. He is spoken of as "the son of Shaphat, which poured water on the hands of Elijah" (2 Kings iii. 11)—an allusion to the old-time Oriental custom of the servant pouring water from a ewer over his master's hands to wash them.

And again we are impressed with Elisha's *courage*. See, for instance, his first meeting with king Jehoram (iii. 13, 14). Very unlike the empty compliments of the quack diviners who fawned around Jehoram were Elisha's stinging words of denunciation. Only a brave and honest messenger of God could have spoken them.

Nor can we travel through these ten chapters with Elisha without seeing again and again his strong *faith*. Right from that first moment when he struck Jordan's waters with Elijah's mantle, believing that they would obey him as they had obeyed Elijah, we see his faith riding on from exploit to exploit. It was this faith which gave fuel to the fire of his courage. Real faith in God always makes a man fearless.

And, once more, we mark Elisha's *disinterestedness*. How rich he might have made himself by such gifts as that which was suggested by Naaman the Syrian (v. 5, etc.) and that which was sent by royal Ben-hadad (viii. 9)! But this prophet's eye is on no such rewards. He lives for one thing only—the will and the honour of Jehovah. May the Spirit of God reproduce these qualities in our own hearts and lives!

His prophetic ministry.

Elisha's ministry is an extraordinary one. Again and again the supernatural flames out through it in the most arresting ways. It is even more interspersed with miracles than was the fiery ministry of Elijah. It has been truly observed that there are no miracles in the Old Testament, except those of Moses, which can be compared in number or variety with the wonders that Elisha did. In these first ten chapters of 2 Kings there are no less than seventeen such phenomena on record. The full list, including the strange miracle at Elisha's grave, totals twenty.

How many other miracles were wrought through Elisha, without being recorded, we do not know. There may have been many. The principle of purposive selection and exclusion which is consistently observed by the Spirit-guided writers of the Scriptures, and on which we have commented in an earlier study, implies that those miracles of Elisha which have been recorded are specially noteworthy, either because of their importance at the time or because of their latent spiritual significances.

So far as we know, Elisha, like Elijah, wrote nothing; but his miracles must have created no little stir. Kings and leaders, both inside and outside Israel, were obliged to take note of him. For instance, in 2 Kings viii. 4, we read: "And the king talked with Gehazi, the servant of the man of God, saying: Tell me, I pray thee, all the great things that Elisha hath done." And all Elisha's mighty acts, let it be remembered, were unmistakable and unanswerable evidences of the reality and sovereign power of Jehovah, Israel's true God, from whom the nation had now outrageously apostatised. Elisha's ministry fell in a period which bears ominous parallels with today. The very fact that the ministries of Elijah and Elisha were so full of supernatural wonders is itself intense with meaning. God is meeting a critical situation by supernormal measures. Apostate and degenerate as the nation has become, a final bid shall be made, by special messengers and startling miraculous signs, to recall the sinning people to Jehovah and to the true faith of Israel. Even to the last, God will seek to turn His idolatry-infatuated people from their corruptions, and thus avert the culminating catastrophe of the Dispersion which must otherwise overtake them.

Alas, the louder the warning and the clearer the sign, the deafer and blinder do the unwilling people become! "The heart of this people is waxed gross." Not even the ministries of prophets like Elijah and Elisha and Jonah could turn the nation from its deadly downgrade. Doubtless there was an overridden godly remnant; but the bulk of leaders and people were wedded to their idolatries and immoral ways, and were brazen both to the appeals and the alarms of Jehovah's prophets.

Pretty much the same state of things can be seen even now developing as the present age plunges on to Armageddon. Great signs and judgments are in the earth today. All who have eyes to see *can* see if they *will*. Yet the greater are God's signs, the bolder are man's sins. The heavier the judgments, the more blindly stubborn do the nations officially become against our God and His Christ. The malady has now got beyond any gentle remedy. Accentuated apostasy and anti-Godism, going with ever-more-dangerous scientific knowledge, call for decisive Divine intervention. Judgment and destruction are again necessary; and they are even now speeding upon this present world-system. Meanwhile, however, God is gathering out His "little flock" to whom it is His "good pleasure" to "give the kingdom."

His peculiar significance.

We cannot thoughtfully linger over Elisha's ministry and miracles without sensing that there is somehow a latent typical and mystical significance clinging about him and his actions. Again and again we seem to detect that the Holy Spirit has invested him with subtle anticipations of our Lord's own ministry.

We get a hint of this in *the contrast between Elijah and Elisha.* We find the same kind of dissimilarity between Elijah and Elisha as that which is seen between John the Baptist and our Lord Jesus. This is too pronounced not to be noticed; and there is more in it than might appear at first. We know that the correspondence between Elijah and John the Baptist is more than coincidental. There is a specifically stated typological link between the two. It was announced by the angel Gabriel that John, as the Lord's forerunner, should "go before Him *in the spirit and power of Elias*" (Luke i. 17); and our Lord Himself later said of him: "*This is Elias which was for to come*" (Matt. xi 14; see also xvii. 10–12). It is not unnatural, therefore, that the question should suggest itself as to whether there may be a similar type-connection between Elisha and our Lord Jesus. And what do we find? Well, there is no actual statement anywhere to that effect, but the adumbrations are too definite to be accidental. Elijah, like John the Baptist, came "neither eating nor drinking," and was in the deserts, solitary and apart from men. Elisha, on the other hand, like our Lord Jesus, "came eating and drinking" and mingling freely among the people. There were no shaggy locks and sheepskin mantle, and there was no being fed by ravens in the lonely grot of Cherith, but a man normally shorn and clad, having a gentle and sociable presence, and a house of his own in Samaria. Instead of the fire, the storm, the sternness and judgment, there are healing acts and gentler words.

Then again, there are special features in Elisha's ministry which give it a resemblance to that of our Lord. In Elisha's recurring ministries beyond the bounds of Israel we seem to see a suggestion of Him who, besides being "the glory of His people, Israel," was to be "*a light to lighten the Gentiles.*" While again, Elisha's miracle with the twenty barley loaves, and his multiplying the widow's pot of oil, easily remind us of Him who took the five barley loaves to feed the hungry multitude in New Testament times. And yet again, the miracle of Naaman's cleansing from leprosy, at the word of Elisha, is one of the greatest Old Testament illustrations of the Gospel way of salvation. Nor can we fail to add that Elisha's weeping over the evils which he saw coming upon his nation, but which he was unable to avert (viii. 11, 12), is almost the only scene in the Old Testament which affords a parallel to our Lord's weeping over Jerusalem, as related by Luke.

We find the same parallel suggested by *the main emphasis* in Elisha's ministry. The distinctive insistence in *Elijah's* ministry, of course, like that in the preaching of John the Baptist, is the stern call to repentance, accompanied by the warning of impending judgment; but the main emphasis all through *Elisha's* ministry is that of resurrection and hope of new life, if only the people will respond. The nation has now sunk into such a state that it can scarcely be recovered except by something equal to resurrection. Therefore, through the ministry of Elisha, the people are given to see, in a succession of symbolic miracles, the power of resurrection at work, and the hope of new life which is theirs in Jehovah, if they but return to him.

Just let the mind run through some of Elisha's miracles. See how characteristic is this suggestion of life out of death. His very first miracle is the healing of the death-giving waters of Jericho, so that what had given death now gave life (ii.). Then comes the saving of the armies from death by miraculous water-supply (iii.). And in the next chapter we find the raising of the Shunamite woman's son from death to new life (iv.). This is followed by the healing of the poisoned pottage: "Death in the pot" is changed to life and wholesomeness (iv.). And in the same chapter we have the miraculous multiplication of the barley loaves. Then comes the healing of Naaman, by that symbolic baptism in Jordan, with its washing away of death, and the coming up in new life (v.). The miracle of the recovered axe-head, which next follows, speaks of the same thing in a different way. "The iron did swim"—a new life-power overcoming the downward pull of death. Finally, not to mention the intervening miracles, we have the strange miracle in which the man is brought to life at Elisha's grave, by accidental contact with the deceased prophet's bones! The emphasis on resurrection and new hope running through these miracles is surely clear to see.

But this latent typical significance which clings to Elisha reaches its most striking expression when we take Elijah and Elisha and Jonah together. These three prophets came in quick succession during the last period before the dispersion of the northern kingdom—Jonah probably lived well into the reign of Jeroboam II, after whose reign the ten-tribed kingdom only survived about another sixty years. Such "signs" were given through these three prophets as had never been given before, with the purpose of arresting the nation. Alas, the nation did not respond; but the "signs" remain, and they make these three prophets together a kind of type-trio.

It will be noticed that the idea of *resurrection* is expressed and illustrated with peculiar force through the ministry of these three. In the case of Elijah there is the raising up of the Zarephath widow's son from death to new life. Such a miracle had never been known in Israel before. Miracles had happened again and again since the days of Moses; but never had a dead person been brought back to life. The unheard-of had happened. No wonder that this man who could raise the dead could call his countrymen to Carmel! Yet that crowning miracle was repeated in the ministry of Elisha, in the raising of the Shunamite's son. Indeed it was more than repeated. An even stranger thing happened: a dead man was suddenly quickened into life again through contact with Elisha's own corpse! But, most amazing of all, there next comes *Jonah's* experience of something stranger even than death, and stranger even than being brought back to life— a resurrection not merely from bodily death, but from "the belly of Sheol"!

Now take these three prophets together. *Elisha* died and was buried—as Christ died and was buried. *Jonah*, in miraculous symbol, did more than die and become buried; he went down into Hades itself, as Christ also went into Hades. *Elijah* triumphantly smote assunder the waters of Jordan (here a type of death), passed through them, and then ascended to heaven—as Christ also overcame death, and then ascended to heaven.

But look at these three men again. *Elisha* dies and is buried, yet in his death gives life to another—as Christ, through his death, gives life to those who come into union with Him. *Jonah* goes down into "hell" itself, yet is brought up that he should not see corruption—as Christ himself was not left in Hades nor suffered to see corruption (Acts ii. 27). *Elijah*, in ascending, cast down his mantle and a "double portion of his spirit" so that his follower on earth might do "greater works" than he himself had done— as Christ also, when He ascended up on high, poured forth the Spirit so that His followers might do the "greater works" of which He had spoken.

Are all these correspondences quite fortuitous? Or were they not rather designed—strangely clear yet strangely subtle—so that godly souls, willing to be taught by God's Spirit, might be enabled to perceive Divine truths which could never be sought out by the wise and prudent of this world?

We shall speak more fully about the unique type-teachings concealed and yet so conspicuous in the story of Jonah when we come to study the little book which bears that prophet's name. Meanwhile, let us duly appreciate the significance of Elijah and Elisha and Jonah as a trio. How wonderfully, through the supernatural works and experiences of these three prophets, God prepared the minds of His earthly people for that super-miracle which was yet to be, namely, the resurrection of the Lord Jesus, Israel's Christ and the world's Saviour!

In 1 Corinthians xv. 4, Paul says that Christ "rose again the third day *according to the Scriptures.*" But to what Scriptures of the Old Testament was he referring? Perhaps he had in mind Psalm ii. 7 (which he also quoted in the same connection at Antioch in Pisidia: see Acts xiii. 33); or perhaps he was thinking of Psalm xvi. 10, 11 (which verses Peter cited as resurrection prophecies on the day of Pentecost: see Acts ii. 25–36); but we feel pretty certain that he also had in mind these three men, Elijah and Elisha and Jonah; for during those "silent" three years which Paul spent in Arabia (Gal. i. 17, 18), when the Spirit taught him "in all the Scriptures" the things concerning Christ,

Paul must have come to see in these three prophets wonderful gleamings which he had never even guessed at before! All of the more prominent features in our Lord's resurrection are fore-enacted by these three prophets, even to the three days and nights in Hades and the coming forth again on the third day: so that Paul could even say that our Lord's rising again "*the third day*" was truly "ACCORDING TO THE SCRIPTURES"!

THE SECOND BOOK OF KINGS (3)

Lesson Number 37

NOTE.—For this third study in 2 Kings read again chapters ix. to xvii. twice.

The Second Book of Kings has been much more extensively confirmed and illustrated through recent research than any other book of the Old Testament. This is due to the fact that the annals of Assyria and of Babylon, covering the same period as 2 Kings, have been so largely recovered. Light has poured in from the monuments of those two great empires, and in that light we note, with grateful astonishment, how one unexpected confirmation after another shows us the absolute fidelity and the minute accuracy of the sacred history. The lesson taught by this ought to be heeded and remembered. We have less confirmation of other parts of the Old Testament history, because we have less information regarding the countries and the times with which the Scripture narrative deals. But wherever the curtain *is lifted* we see the very things chronicled in the Bible. Could there be any fuller proof of its reliability?

—*John Urquhart.*

THE SECOND BOOK OF KINGS (3)

Evil Kings of the Northern Kingdom

As ALREADY noted (see lesson 34), up to the point at which the *First* Book of Kings closes, all the eight kings who had reigned over the northern kingdom were *"evil"* kings. What, now, of the further *eleven* who figure in this *Second* Book of Kings? The answer is as revealing as it is deplorable. It is chronicled of every one of them that "he did evil"—with the exception of Shallum, and *he* reigned only one month! Here are the references: iii. 2, 3; x. 31, 32; xiii. 2, 3, 11; xiv. 24; xv. 9, 18, 24, 28; xvii. 2. What a record! And what ruin the result!

Think of this wretched line of kings in parallel with the Davidic line of kings who reigned over Judah. We have already observed that in the annals of the kings of *Judah* the standard according to which each king is estimated is the example of *David*. It is interesting to trace this out. We see it in the case of Solomon (1 Kings xi. 6), Abijam (xv. 3), Jehoshaphat (2 Chron. xvii. 3), Amaziah (2 Kings xiv. 3), Ahaz (xvi. 2), Hezekiah (xviii. 3), Josiah (xxii. 2). Thus did David "cast his shadow" for good, even three hundred and seventy years onward, over his royal successors.

But now, returning to this unrelieved succession of "evil" men who reigned over the *ten-tribed northern kingdom*, we find an even more emphatic standard of comparison. Alas, it is no noble standard such as that which was set by David: it is the very reverse. There is no David in *this* line, to strike a norm of true godliness, or to cast any lingering lustre over the throne. The standard according to which these *Israel* kings are judged is the shameful reign of *Jeroboam*, the first king who occupied the throne of the northern kingdom after the split of the ten tribes from Judah; and the distinguishing epitaph of this brazen offender, Jeroboam, is: "*JEROBOAM, THE SON OF NEBAT, WHO MADE ISRAEL TO SIN.*" Again and again, in these records of the kings, Jeroboam is referred to by this horrible distinguishment, until the words become almost a refrain. And

135

here is a fact as striking as it is tragic: it is written of no less
than fifteen out of the eighteen kings who followed Jeroboam on
the throne of the ten-tribed kingdom that "he did evil" after
the example of this "Jeroboam, the son of Nebat, who made
Israel to sin." Here are the references: Nadab (1 Kings xv. 26),
Baasha (xv. 34), Zimri (xvi. 19), Omri (xvi. 25, 26), Ahab (xvi.
31), Ahaziah (xxii. 52), Jehoram (2 Kings iii. 2, 3), Jehu (x. 31),
Jehoahaz (xiii. 2), Jehoash (xiii. 11), Jeroboam II (xiv. 24),
Zechariah (xv. 9), Menahem (xv. 18), Pekahiah (xv. 24), Pekah
(xv. 28).

Thus did the wicked Jeroboam project *his* deadly shadow over
the throne and the throes of the ten-tribed kingdom for two
hundred and fifty years ahead, until at last, degraded and denuded
and deported, it was torn to pieces by the Assyrian dragon.

We do well to reflect, in passing, on the shadows cast by these
two men, David and Jeroboam. All of us are casting shadows
as we go through this present life. Just as our bodies cast their
shadows quite involuntarily, so are we continually and quite
involuntarily casting the shadow of our moral and spiritual
influence upon other lives. We can no more detach ourselves
from this involuntary and often unconscious influence upon others
than our bodies can rid themselves of their own shadows. What
we *can* determine is the *kind* of shadow which we cast. Our
influence, quite apart from any speech of the lips, may contribute either to the eternal salvation or the eternal damnation of
other souls. God save us from casting a shadow like that of
Jeroboam! Amid both the younger and the older everywhere
around us there are always those who, from one cause or another,
are in that sensitive poise of mind which makes them susceptible
to the shadow of some influence falling upon them from another
personality.

It is a solemn reflection that the shadow of our silent influence
may have results reaching on even into eternity. It is well to
remember, too, that our shadow often lingers here when we ourselves have passed beyond, as was the case with David and
Jeroboam. Are Voltaire and Paine and Ingersol and Huxley
dead, and other infidels who kept step to their music? Do not
their shadows still stalk the earth, gibbering their old blasphemies
in new phraseology within the walls of our schools and colleges?
And, on the other hand, are Luther and Calvin, and Wesley and

Whitefield and Moody and Spurgeon dead? Do not the Christ-filled shadows of these seraphic evangelists still fall with enduring benediction upon our national life?

Is it objected that these whom we have picked on are all outstanding men, and that the same does not apply to the inconspicuous? Well, if we are thinking *that*, we are wrong. Adolph Hitler's vile shadow, remember, includes in itself the shadows of all those other men whose names will never be published but who influenced Hitler in his earlier years, and made him what he afterwards became. We speak of Wesley and Whitefield, and the other sanctified geniuses of the Methodist revival; but remember that the heavenly shadow of that glorious epoch is really the composite influence of those thousands of obscure but consecrated men and women who are simply an anonymous multitude to the historian.

Perhaps some who read these lines are even now thanking God for the still lingering shadow of a departed saintly father or mother, or of some other departed Christian loved-one. Or perhaps some who now read these lines suffer and weep because of a darksome shadow cast over their lives by departed predecessors of a different sort. What kind of shadows are *we* going to cast today and leave tomorrow? Our lingering influence will certainly out-stay us. God keep us near to Christ! God help us to cast the shadow of a sanctified influence which will linger on to heal and bless, as Peter's shadow, long ago in Jerusalem, healed the sick ones on whom it fell!

The Dispersion of the Northern Kingdom

2 Kings xvii. records one of the most tragic anticlimaxes of history. With what prospect of high destiny had the Hebrew tribes entered Canaan under Joshua! With what wretchedness are the tribes of the northern kingdom now dragged away and dispersed! Here, in this seventeenth chapter, is the final indictment of the ten-tribed kingdom, and the deportation of its thrashed and battered people into a captivity which for ever ended their existence as a separate kingdom.

The sins for which this monster calamity was allowed to crush them are here written indelibly, as with a "pen of iron" or the "point of a diamond," so that all who come after may know the real cause of what happened, and justify the ways of God with men. Read verses 7 to 23 again. What a catalogue of outrages against Israel's covenant God! What insatiate idolatry! What stiff-necked implacability! What depth of degradation! Note specially verses 20–3. Here, right at the end of the Divine indictment, and in that last, awful, zero hour of ruin, there falls again the ugly shadow of that wicked man, the first king who sat on the throne of the ten-tribed kingdom—"Jeroboam, the son of Nebat, who made Israel to sin."

> "*The Lord rejected all the seed of Israel, and afflicted them, and delivered them into the hand of spoilers, until He had cast them out of His sight . . . For the children of Israel walked in all the sins of Jeroboam which he did: they departed not from them until the Lord removed Israel out of His sight.*"

There are certain facts of outstanding importance which we ought now to note in connection with this obliteration of the ten-tribed kingdom.

First, we see here, written in bold and terrible lines, *the operation of "poetic justice."* That is, we see Divine judgment falling upon a nation in direct correspondence to its sin, just as one line of poetry answers to another. Unfalteringly, this chapter attributes the Dispersion to the avenging hand of God Himself. If, then, this chapter is an *inspired* explanation, no philosophy of history is true which does not recognise the sovereign hand of God controlling all events and developments. There are those today who affect to scorn the idea that God thus directly visits the sins of nations back upon themselves. Well, if the Bible is the word of God, they are wrong. The God who laid this Israel kingdom low by the penal stroke of the Dispersion is still the God who rules and arbitrates above the nations. There is but the one true God. He has not abdicated. His power has not declined; and His nature is still the same. He is the Jehovah who says, "I change not." Those of us who believe and know the Bible to be the word of God have been able to grasp at least something of the meaning behind what has happened to the nations of Europe in the last few years of war and upheaval. To us, indeed, those people who say they cannot see any evidence of supernatural control in the strange anomalies of the past war and its aftermath are afflicted with a strange blindness. As truly as God overruled the revolutions of history in the days of Egypt and Assyria and Babylon and Israel, so does He now, in the history of modern Russia and Germany and America and Britain ; and as certainly as God visited the sins of nations with judgment *then*, so does He *now*.

Second, we ought to note that *the dispersion of the ten tribes occurred in two stages.* Some years before the final break-up of the kingdom, two and a half of the tribes had already been carried away captive. These were Reuben and Gad and half the tribe of Manasseh, which occupied territory on the *eastern* side of Jordan, and which therefore first fell prey to the Assyrians. Their deportation is thus narrated in 1 Chronicles v. 25, 26: "And they transgressed against the God of their fathers, and went a whoring after the gods of the people of the land, whom God destroyed before them. And the God of Israel stirred up the spirit of Pul, king of Assyria, and the spirit of Tilgath-pilneser, king of Assyria, and he carried them away, even the Reubenites and the Gadites and the half tribe of Manasseh, and brought them unto Halah and Habor and Hara and to the river of Gozan, unto this day." We learn from 2 Kings xv. 29 that the tribe of Naphtali, to the north-east, also suffered with them.

Away back in our studies in the Book of Numbers we noted that these tribes, Reuben and Gad and half the tribe of Manasseh, instead of crossing Jordan as God had directed, pleaded permission to occupy the Gilead area *east* of Jordan. The request sounded reasonable, as do most arguments which excuse compromise, but it *was* compromise none the less. Their true place was with the other tribes across the Jordan, in the covenanted place of blessing. But they chose by the sight of their eyes (Num. xxxii. 33), instead of by faith and according to the will of God, and were content with a portion just outside the place of promised blessing. They are types of so-called "worldly" Christians today. We see the after-effects of their choice. They quickly bowed to the gods of the nearby peoples ; and now *they are the first to go into captivity.* Compromise always seems an easy way out of difficulty, but it is always costly afterwards, and only too often proves fatal.

The Assyrian king who carried away these tribes is called *Tiglath-pileser* in 2 Kings xv. 29, and also *Pul*, in 1 Chronicles

v. 26. Controversy has raged around these two names. It was thought that they referred to two different persons, though the Bible seemed to use them both of one. But an ancient "Babylonian Chronicle" discovered by the late Dr. Pinches, among tablets in the British Museum, some years ago, ended the uncertainty; for it refers to Tiglath-pileser by this other name of Pull or Pulu. So the Bible is again confirmed, in yet another historical detail.

The deportation of the *other* tribes of the northern kingdom took place about thirteen years after that of the two and a half tribes, that is, *about* 721 B.C. By that time Tiglath-pileser had passed away and had been succeeded by Shalmaneser IV. See again chapter xvii. 3–6. That Samaria should withstand the practised and daring soldiery of Assyria for three years (verse 5) is remarkable. Provisions and munitions must have been accumulated in anticipation. Help, also, was daily expected from Egypt (verse 4), which, however, never came. At last the city fell. We can imagine the state of its inhabitants, and the treatment they would receive from the notoriously cruel Assyrians, who seem to have been of all oppressors the most inventive of torture-cruelties. The whole population was carried off, never to see Samaria again.

Third, this dispersal of the ten tribes *fully accords with what we know of Assyrian practice at that time.* The late Mr. John Urquhart, in his *New Biblical Guide,* says: "A marked feature of the campaigns of Tiglath-pileser III is this very carrying away captive to Assyria of the original populations of a conquered country, the planting in their stead populations which were likewise carried from a far distance, placing Assyrian officials over them, and annexing the lands in this way to Assyria. From broken men, with no common ties and with no fatherland to defend, no resistance was to be feared. The policy put an end effectually to the plottings and the alliances which had formerly sprung up in the conquered districts as soon as the Assyrian armies had withdrawn. And this policy may be said to have been Tiglath-pileser's own invention." The long-buried Assyrian inscriptions which have now been disinterred and interpreted by archaeologists show us that this policy was ruthlessly carried out. Again and again there are references to it. We have not space to quote here, except just one as an example: "I took 155,000 people and children from them. Their horses and cattle without number I carried off. Those countries to the boundaries of Assyria I added . . . like clay I trampled and the assembly of their people to Assyria I sent." Tiglath-pileser's policy was followed by those who succeeded him. It solved the problem which had hitherto baffled every conquering power, namely, how to preserve lands in cultivation by peoples who should enrich the empire without having either the spirit or the means to revolt. It would seem that Shalmaneser who besieged Samaria died the year that the city fell, and that the conquest was claimed by Sargon, his successor. Inscriptions made by Sargon have been found which actually tell of his deportation of the Israelites from Samaria (27,290 is the figure he gives), and his settling of foreigners in the land.

Fourth, *from this dispersion there has been no return.* Descendants of these exiles may have found their way back to Judaea two hundred years later, at the time when the Jewish "remnant" returned under Ezra and Nehemiah; but apart from that there has been no return, and the ten-tribed kingdom has remained non-existent. Attempts to identify these Israel tribes have been made in more recent times. The American Indians, the Armenians, and others have been suggested. The "British Israel" theory, which identifies them with the British and American peoples throughout the world, is attractive, but the more carefully we have gone into that theory, the more difficult have we found it to accept. That, however, we cannot discuss here. We confine ourselves to the historic *fact* of the dispersion of these tribes. *That* was real enough, and was a heart-rending tragedy at which one could weep even today. Among the many Assyrian writings now recovered is a deed of sale (made about fourteen years after the Israel dispersion) in which two Israelite men and one woman are sold by a Phœnician to an Egyptian for three minas of silver (about £27). This condition of perpetual slavery must have been the lot of thousands. Truly, "the way of transgressors is hard" (Prov. xiii. 15). Israel had refused to accept the ennobling service of God. She must now suffer and weep in degrading servitude to men. Oh, those words of Jesus, as He wept over Jerusalem centuries later, have a long and wide application—" I *would* "—" Ye would *not* "—" Ye *shall* not "!

THE SECOND BOOK OF KINGS (4)

Lesson Number 38

NOTE.—For this further study in 2 Kings read again from chapter xviii. to the end of the book. All these eight chapters are of great importance, leading up as they do to the culminating Divine judgment which fell on Judah by way of the Babylonian exile. They should be well read and pondered.

Those who are acquainted with critical commentaries on the Old Testament will appreciate the extent to which their contents are contradicted by this fresh evidence (i.e. of archaeology)—such, for example, as the fact that Monotheism was the original religion, and Polytheism a by-product from it. Or that the Habiru were, after all, the Hebrews and the Israelites under Joshua. Indeed, if at the present time some cynic, or candid friend, sought to make the punishment fit the crime, and proceeded to compile an Encyclopaedia of the mistakes that had been made by critics and commentators on the Old Testament, and placed beside each the real facts that have recently come to light, it would surely run into volumes.

—Sir Charles Marston.

THE SECOND BOOK OF KINGS (4)

Later Course and Downfall of Judah

THE TEN-TRIBED kingdom is no more. Its cities have been plundered, its capital laid low, its royal house swept away, its pleasant land literally scraped of Israelite inhabitants and re-peopled by a mongrel mixture imported from afar by the Assyrian overlord. And now, with the history of the ten-tribed kingdom forever closed, the last stretch of chapters in this Second Book of Kings (xviii.–xxv.) is occupied solely with the later course and downfall of *Judah*. These last eight chapters of the book, therefore, run from the fall of Samaria (721. B.C.) to the sack of Jerusalem (587. B.C.), a period of about one hundred and thirty years.

Could anything have given the sister kingdom graver cause for penitent reflection and amendment than what had now happened to the ten tribes? The long-threatened but mercifully postponed judgment had at length fallen. The warnings uttered by Jehovah's faithful prophets had materialised with tragic exactness. Israel had over-presumed upon her covenant relationship with Jehovah, and He had now utterly cast her off. The news of what had happened must have stabbed many a heart and conscience in Jerusalem with strange apprehensiveness. Yet the fact is that this terrible object-lesson in Divine vengeance had little deep or lasting effect upon Judah. Except for the reign of Hezekiah, and in a lesser way of Josiah, it is the same story of apostasy and downgrade until Jerusalem pays the agonising penalty bemoaned by Jeremiah in his "Lamentations."

So, then, we now look through these remaining eight chapters of 2 Kings. From the time of the Disruption of the ten tribes from Judah (1 Kings xii.) up to the point at which this eighteenth chapter of 2 Kings commences, twelve successors of David have occupied the throne of Judah. Eight are still to come before Jerusalem falls. These are, Hezekiah, Manasseh, Amon, Josiah, Jehoahaz, Jehoiakim, Jehoiachin, Zedekiah. Of these there are three which call for special comment. First, and by far the most commanding, is king Hezekiah.

Hezekiah

Good king Hezekiah was a really remarkable man. Soldier, statesman, architect, poet, saint—he was all these. His reign was the greatest since the days of David and Solomon. While pondering the three chapters which here tell of him (xviii.–xx) we certainly ought to read the parallel account in 2 Chronicles xxix.–xxxii. It is a noble record. Immediately upon his accession he reopened and repaired the Lord's House, he reorganised the priesthood and the Levitical services. He recalled his subjects to the worship of the true God, and led the way by his own illustrious example. Throughout the land he destroyed idols and groves and false altars. He gathered his people to a great national observance of the Passover, of which it is written, "Since the days of Solomon, the son of David, king of Israel, there was not the like in Jerusalem." He also smote Israel's enemies and extended his borders, and became "magnified in the sight of all nations" (2 Chron. xxxii. 23). Indeed, it is said of him, "He trusted in the Lord God of Israel so that after him was none like him among all the kings of Judah, nor any that were before him." Oh, what solid benefactions always result when men and kings and nations walk in the ways of the true God! Those golden hopes begin to materialise which politics, economics, legislation and education by themselves can never bring to fulfilment.

Hezekiah and the Scriptures

But Hezekiah's importance is not limited to his own reign and time. Although few may realise it, his impact is still felt in our modern world. He is really one of the *very* important men of history, and the repercussions from his labours will last to the end of the age.

It seems clear that in good degree we owe to Hezekiah *the arrangement and transmission of the Old Testament Scriptures*. Think what that has meant to the nations and to history. Note some of the evidences of Hezekiah's activities in connection with the Scriptures. We mark his zeal for the *house* of Jehovah (2 Chron. xxix. 3–19), and for the *worship* of Jehovah (verses 20–36), and his strict adherence to the Davidic pattern (verses 25, 27, 30).

Clearly, his delight was in the *word* of Jehovah. And, further, 2 Chronicles xxxi. 21 speaks of the "*work*" which he commenced "*in the Law and in the Commandments.*" Nor is this all; he formed a *guild* of men for this devout literary work. A reference to Proverbs xxv. 1 will show that these "men of Hezekiah" had a good hand in shaping the Book of Proverbs into its present form. Their work would scarcely begin and end with that one book! It has been well said that in Hezekiah's age "Israel reached its golden literary prime" with Hezekiah himself as the royal patron of piety and letters. Isaiah and Shebna and Joah were leaders among these "men of Hezekiah" (2 Kings xviii. 18, xix. 2).

There seems to be a curious confirmation of Hezekiah's work on the Scriptures in the form of a certain peculiarity which perhaps few people may know about. At the end of many books in the Old Testament, in the Hebrew originals, three capital letters occur which no transcriber has dared to omit, even though their meaning was lost. They are the three Hebrew letters corresponding to H, Z, K, the first three in the Hebrew name, Hezekiah. Nothing is more likely, says the late J. W. Thirtle, than that when "the men of Hezekiah" had completed their work of transcribing the different books, Hezekiah should have thus affixed his own sign-manual in royal confirmation. When we come to study the Book of Psalms we shall find not only that Hezekiah had much to do with the shaping of that collection, but that he himself was a composer of psalms and songs.

Now Hezekiah's reign is made unique by the fact that an extra fifteen years were added to his life (2 Kings xx.; Isa. xxxviii.). It was in those extra years that Hezekiah's literary activities reached their high point. There is more in this than at first meets the eye. Judah's days were numbered. Only five more kings were to reign before the deportations to Babylon began, and four out of the five were to prove ungodly failures. The moment had certainly come for the bringing together and editing of the inspired Scriptures, with a view to their preservation and transmission; and who should be God's man for this purpose? Who was more suitable and willing than Hezekiah? We have good cause to thank God for Hezekiah, and for those added fifteen years, and for his labours in the Scriptures which were to mean so much to posterity. Yes, Hezekiah is a great figure.

Manasseh

Talk about "studies in contrasts"! Was there ever an extremer contrast between father and son than that between Hezekiah and Manasseh? How is it that sometimes the best of fathers have the worst of sons, and the worst of fathers the best of sons? That is a nice study for the psychologists! We ourselves will not try to solve the problem, but we will try to caution ourselves by it. If men like Samuel and Hezekiah could have sons like Joel and Abiah and Manasseh, we will be careful before we allow our lips to scourge godly parents of today who have worldly-minded sons and daughters.

A short time ago we heard two Christian women harshly criticising a saintly, elderly Christian man who was known for his keenness in winning souls to the Saviour. "He would do far better to begin at home with his own unconverted son and worldly daughter," said one to the other. "His children's behaviour doesn't say much for his Christianity in the home." We were much pained by our overhearing of those caustic words, for we knew how that dear man had prayed for his children, how consistently he had lived before them, how he had pleaded with them, and how he had wept about them in our own presence only a few days earlier. Oh, what sharp-edged swords the tongues of some Christians are! How they wound the heart of Jesus every time they cut into the good name of some other Christian! We do well, changing the metaphor, to beseech the Holy Spirit to "set a watch" at the "door of our lips"! It is so easy to add cruel pangs to godly hearts which are already torn with grief over wayward sons and daughters.

And now, about this Manasseh: what a character he is! And what a grim enigma that the wickedest of all Judah's kings should be the longest-reigning one! Fifty-five years is a long stretch. In that more-than-half-a-century Manasseh wrought such things as almost defy the pen. We need not here dilate on his extremes of idolatry and spiritism, his offering of human sacrifices, his making the very streets of Jerusalem run with innocent blood (including that of the martyred prophet Isaiah), and so on. It is even said that he did wickedly "above all that the Amorites did" whom God cast out before the chosen people.

What the effect of all this would be on the nation requires little imagination to appreciate.

But there are three remarkable features which are peculiar to Manasseh, which we ought particularly to note. For these we need to turn to the parallel account in 2 Chronicles xxxiii.

First, we are told that *Manasseh was carried captive to Babylon*. Verse 11 reads: "Wherefore the Lord brought upon them the captains of the host of the king of Assyria, which took Manasseh among the thorns, and bound him with fetters, and carried him to Babylon." This verse has been a "bone of contention" to Bible critics. Had it been a Babylonian king who took Manasseh captive to Babylon all would have been normal; but that a king of *Assyria*, whose capital city was *Nineveh* away on the Tigris, should carry Manasseh captive to *Babylon*, which was three hundred miles south on the Euphrates—well, that is most decidedly a blunder! But once again the Bible proves right, and the critics themselves the blunderers. We know that the Assyrian king who reigned contemporaneously with Manasseh's father, Hezekiah, was Sennacherib, and that Sennacherib's son, who reigned during part of Manasseh's reign, was Esarhaddon (2 Kings xviii, xix; 2 Chron. xxxii.). Well, recent findings by Assyriologists have shown that of all the Assyrian kings *this Esarhaddon alone built a palace at Babylon, and lived there*!

Second, in captivity *Manasseh repented and was forgiven of God*. He thus becomes one of the most amazing instances of the pardoning love of God to extreme sinners. See verses 12 and 13. Manasseh was truly converted.

Third, *Manasseh was restored to Jerusalem*, and made amends, as far as possible, for all the evil he had done. See verses 14 to 20. Manasseh is one of the gravest warnings to all wicked-doers, for just as judgment fell on him as a direct retribution for his evil, so will it be with all others like him: yet Manasseh is also one of the most wonderful encouragements to all who are really penitent, for he shows us that, however we may have outraged God, such is the love of God that He delights in mercy to the worst.

Josiah

We skip the evil reign of Manasseh's son, Amon. After two years he was murdered by his own servants (2 Kings xxi. 19–26).

We come to the noble reign of *Josiah*. This was the one bright interval during the last hundred years of the Judah kingdom, that is, between the death of king Hezekiah in 698 B.C. and the sack of Jerusalem by the Babylonians in 587 B.C., at which time the bulk of Judah's people were carried into exile. Alas, the brightness of Josiah's reign is that of sunset. It is the final flash of a departing glory, just before the throne of David is trodden in the dust.

Josiah came to the throne about 641 B.C., when he was but eight years old. In the early years of his reign, therefore, the queen-mother, with the help of trusted advisers, would largely direct the course of government. At the age of sixteen, "while he was yet young, he began to seek after the God of David his father" (2 Chron. xxxiv. 3); and the promise of those early years was splendidly fulfilled. We shall not linger here over the noble progress of his reign. His repairing of the temple, the strange discovery of the strangely lost Pentateuch, his reading of the Law to the gathered people of his realm, his renewal of the covenant with Jehovah on behalf of the nation, his firm measures against moral evils, and his organising such a national observance of the Passover as had not been held "from the days of the Judges"—all these things are there in the record, and speak for themselves. But there are two important facts which we would pick out for special comment, as follows.

First, *Josiah's lead to his people did not really check the national downgrade.* The apparent "revival" consisted rather in outward measures taken by the king himself than in a hearty desire on the part of the people in general. There was much outward reform but no real inward return. The king's lead was deferentially respected, but there was no real heart-penitence toward the God who had been so brazenly wronged. Judah had gone too far. The moral sense of the people had now become so blurred that the popular power to respond genuinely to the king's lead was gone. Through prophet after prophet and providence after providence God had pleaded with His people, but they had repeatedly shown that they "*would* not," until now, by that deadly process which ever operates in human nature, they had reached the point where they *could* not. Apostasy and idolatry had now become ingrained in the national character. The people had lost the sense of Jehovah. The meaning of the earthly throne in Judah had been lost because they had lost the vision of the throne in the heavens. The ever-persistent stupidity of idolatry which more and more depraved the nation was the muddle-brained effort to fill the vacuum created by the lost sense of Jehovah. The moral sensitiveness of the people had now degenerated into a gross callousness. As things grew worse, great prophets were raised up; yet the mightiest and tenderest of these were left saying, "Who hath believed our report?" It is quite clear that the changes under Josiah were superficial, for the people were quite ready to sink back into idolatry and infidelity again immediately afterward. People who could imperviously spurn such messages as those of Isaiah and Jeremiah were ripe for judgment; and judgment was even now at the door. All this is only too sadly corroborated in the prophecies of Jeremiah. That great-hearted prophet commenced his ministry in the thirteenth year of Josiah, and continued until after the fall of Jerusalem (Jer. i. 1–3). The earlier chapters of Jeremiah refer to Josiah's reign. See chapter iii. 10, for the superficiality of the "revival" under Josiah. Yet it is good to detect the noble influence of Jeremiah upon the king himself, all through his reign. Perhaps Josiah would not have been what he was but for Jeremiah.

Second, *Josiah's reign occurred at one of the most fateful turning points in history.* Events of the greatest magnitude were in progress. These were—(1) The fall of the Assyrian empire after an existence of hundreds of years and after maintaining complete mastery over the other nations for about two hundred years; (2) the rise of the new Babylonian empire under Nabopolassar and his son Nebuchadnezzar, by which the most ancient mistress of the nations laid her hand once more upon the sceptre of the kingdoms; (3) the formation of the Median empire, which, a little later, as the Media-Persian empire, was to overthrow Babylon, and, through the famous "decree of Cyrus," was to bring about the rebuilding of Jerusalem and the restoration of the Jewish "Remnant," as told in the Book of Ezra; (4) the dissolution of the kingdom of Judah as an independent kingdom (the destruction of Jerusalem and the final deportation of the Jews to Babylon took place in 587 B.C., only twenty years after Josiah's death, since which time Judah has never again existed as an independent kingdom).

When later, in 536 B.C., the Babylonian empire was over-thrown by Cyrus, and the Persian empire took its place, the various regions over which Babylon had held sway thereby passed under the Persian rule ; and the hundreds of thousands of scattered Jews—both those of the ten-tribed kingdom (Israel) which had been swept off by Assyria in 721 B.C. and those of the southern kingdom (Judah) who had been carried off more recently by Babylon—thereby similarly passed under the Persian rule. The same kind of transition took place when the Persian empire gave place to the Alexandrian and then lesser empires and then the Roman empire.

Only about 50,000 of them returned to Judaea when, in 536 B.C., Cyrus gave them liberty to return. Scattered through the nations the Jews nevertheless remained a distinct people, were preserved through successive epochs of trouble, and largely increased in numbers. We find them in their millions scattered throughout the Roman world in the days of our Lord and the Apostles. James addressed his epistle to "the twelve tribes which are scattered abroad"; and Peter similarly commences his writing, "Peter. . . . to the strangers scattered throughout Pontus, Galatia, Cappadocia, Asia and Bithynia". As remarked above, however, from the time of the Babylonian Exile until our own day, Judah has never again existed as an independent kingdom. In May, 1947 Israel once again became constituted (and later acknowledged) as an independent state; but as we observed in a former study, Israel will never become an independent *kingdom* again until the King Himself returns, even our Lord Jesus Christ. He alone is the true Heir according to the Scriptures of both Old and New Testaments.

THE SECOND BOOK OF KINGS (5)

Lesson Number 39

NOTE.—For this final study in 2 Kings read carefully again chapters xviii. to the end of the book, with concentration on the last part, that is, chapters xxiii. 31 to xxv. 30.

The reformations were superficial. Immediately Hezekiah had passed away, the people returned to their old way of evil. When Hezekiah began his reformation he commenced with the temple, and before anything else could be done it took the whole company of priests and Levites sixteen days to carry rubbish therefrom, which simply means that the temple had become a lumber store. In the days when Josiah carried out his reformation, the book of the Law was found. Mark the significance of this fact that it had to be found! Moreover, its teaching so astonished Josiah that he halted in the middle of his work to enquire from the prophetess Huldah. The people had so forgotten the law of their God that, when it was found, they were absolutely unfamiliar with it.

—*G. Campbell Morgan.*

THE SECOND BOOK OF KINGS (5)

THE FALL OF JERUSALEM AND JUDAH

THE YEAR that king Josiah died, the Assyrian empire died also (608 B.C.), and with the downfall of that empire there died Judah's one earthly hope of protection against Egypt on the one hand and Babylon on the other. The Babylonian, Jehovah's avenger whose advent had been fore-announced through Isaiah over a hundred years earlier, had now appeared. The fatal stroke was to fall at last on Judah. The Babylonian exile was at hand. In the Scripture account of how this fearful retribution fell upon Jerusalem and Judah there are many incidental matters which attract our eye; but we adhere to our present purpose, and simply pick out certain facts which are of key significance.

First, we call attention to the fact that *the destruction of Jerusalem and the captivity of Judah are most emphatically ascribed to the sovereign hand of Jehovah.* Not to appreciate this is to miss nine tenths of the meaning. "Surely at the commandment of Jehovah came this upon Judah . . ." (2 Kings xxiv. 3. See also 2 Chron. xxxvi. 16, 17, 21). Because of their unique relationship with God, because they were a people chosen to embody a special revelation of God to the nations, and because God's dealings with them are permanently transmitted to the nations through the inspired Scriptures, the judgments which felled them become history's supreme object-lesson in the ways of God's government among the nations. Our statesmen of today could do nothing more profitable than to study the principles of God's disposings among the earth's peoples as revealed in the Scriptures, and as exemplified in the nation Israel. What suffering might thus be averted! But our modern statesmen are too wise to become *really* wise.

As with the judgment which fell on the ten-tribed kingdom, so with that which now falls on Judah—we see in it the operation of "poetic justice." Let those smile who will. They are welcome to their educated nonsense which would make history all a matter of blind chance. We ourselves stand with the Scripture. We believe that God orders things in history according to the behaviour of nations. He allows free rein to the human will within wide limits, so that men and nations are always fully responsible for their course; but He super-controls all other controlling powers, and works His sovereign will among earth's peoples, both to reward the good and to requite the evil. This is as true today as it was when Jerusalem fell beneath the blows of Nebuchadnezzar.

Second, it is well to note that *the deportation of Judah's people was in three stages.* The first of these fell in the third year of king Jehoiakim; and among the captives then taken from Jerusalem to Babylon was the then youthful Daniel (Dan. i. 1–4 with 2 Kings xxiv. 1, 2; and 2 Chron. xxxvi. 5–7). The second deportation occurred some eight years later, just after the death of Jehoiakim and the accession of Jehoiachin, when Nebuchadnezzar deposed Jehoiachin after a short reign of only three months, and put Zedekiah on the throne instead. Since this coincided with the beginning of Zedekiah's reign it must have been eleven years before the destruction of Jerusalem. At this second deportation Nebuchadnezzar carried off ten thousand captives comprising all the most useful and better-class Jerusalemites (2 Kings xxiv. 8–16); and among these was the priest (and later the prophet) Ezekiel—for Ezekiel himself tells us that at the destruction of Jerusalem he had already been in Babylonia for eleven years (Ezek. xl. 1).

The final deportation took place in 587 B.C. It was precipitated by a futile rebellion on the part of Zedekiah. Nebuchadnezzar now decided to break up this troublesome Jewish city and kingdom once for all. After a siege of eighteen months "a breach was made" in the city wall (2 Kings xxv. 4 R.V.). King Zedekiah and his men of war fled by night, but were overtaken. The sons of Zedekiah were slain before his eyes; then Zedekiah himself was blinded, put into brass fetters, and carried to Babylon (all of which procedure finds its parallels in the annals of eastern conquerors of that period). Jerusalem was utterly stripped of all its treasures and valuables; the temple was thoroughly dismantled and all its vessels carried away; the city walls were broken down; and then the whole city, with its desecrated temple, its desolated palaces, and its now deserted dwellings, was set on fire. All this is recorded in 2 Kings xxv. and 2 Chronicles xxxvi.

What the people suffered during and after the siege who can describe? Something of what was endured may be gathered from Lamentations and Ezekiel and Josephus. The complexions of the men grew black with famine, their skin having become shrunk and parched; the noble women searched dunghills for scraps of offal; the children died or were eaten by their parents (Lam. ii. 20; iv. 3–10); a third of the inhabitants died of this famine, and of the plague which grew out of it (Ezek. v. 12). Nearly all the remaining population were then carried off into exile, only the poorest of the land being left, to be vinedressers and husbandmen (2 Kings xxv. 11, 12).

Third, *after the Babylonians had withdrawn from Jerusalem there was a conspiracy among the Jews left in the land, which resulted in a further flight of Jews from Judæa into Egypt.* This is recorded in 2 Kings xxv. 22–6; but to understand these verses thoroughly we need to read Jeremiah xl.–xliii. (Jeremiah by his own choice stayed on with those who were left in the land). The following quotation gives the gist of what transpired.

"Nebuchadnezzar, when he carried off Zedekiah to Babylon, appointed, as governor of Judæa, a certain Gedaliah, a Jew of good position, but not of the royal family. Gedaliah made Mizpah, near Jerusalem, his residence; and here he was shortly joined by a number of Jews of importance, who had escaped from Jerusalem and hidden themselves until the Babylonians were gone. Of these the most eminent were Johanan the son of Kareah, and Ishmael, a member of the royal house of David. Gedaliah urged the refugees to be good subjects of the king of Babylon, and to settle themselves to agricultural pursuits. His advice was accepted and at first followed; but presently a warning was given to Gedaliah by Johanan that Ishmael designed his destruction; and soon afterwards, as Gedaliah took no precautions, the murder was actually carried out. Other atrocities followed; but after a time Johanan and the other leading refugees took up arms, forced Ishmael to fly to the Ammonites, and then, fearing that Nebuchadnezzar would hold them responsible for Ishmael's act, fled (against Jeremiah's remonstrances) with the great mass of the Jews that had been left in the land, from Judæa into Egypt. Here our writer leaves them (verse 26), without touching on the calamities which befell them there according to the prophetic announcements of Jeremiah (see Jeremiah xliv. 2–28)."

Thus, even those Jews whom Nebuchadnezzar left were dispersed from Judæa, and the land became utterly desolate.

Fourth, *the date on which the siege of Jerusalem began is one of utmost significance, and should be very carefully observed.* 2 Kings xxv. 1 gives the date with a noticeable preciseness: "And it came to pass in the ninth year of his (Zedekiah's) reign, in the tenth month, in the tenth day of the month, that Nebuchadnezzar, king of Babylon, came, he and all his host, against Jerusalem, and pitched against it, and they built forts against it round about." This is the first time in these historical books that an event is thus dated to the very day. Apart from anything else, therefore, the carefully-given date would catch our eye; but the fact is that this same event is referred to with a similarly impressive exactness in other parts of Scripture. At the time when Nebuchadnezzar came and invested Jerusalem, the prophet Ezekiel was far away in Babylonia where he had then been an exile for over nine years. On the day that the siege of Jerusalem began, a special message was delivered about it from God to Ezekiel. In Ezekiel xxiv. 1, 2, we read—

"IN THE NINTH YEAR, IN THE TENTH MONTH, IN THE TENTH DAY OF THE MONTH, THE WORD OF THE LORD CAME UNTO ME, SAYING: SON OF MAN, WRITE THE NAME OF THE DAY, EVEN OF THIS SELFSAME DAY. THE KING OF BABYLON HATH SET HIMSELF AGAINST (i.e. HATH BESIEGED) JERUSALEM THIS SELFSAME DAY" (see R.V.).

Is not that striking? At the very hour when the Babylonian troops were arriving to encircle the Jewish capital, the fact was revealed of God to Ezekiel those hundreds of miles away. And Ezekial was commanded to write down that date emphatically, for observation and preservation—the tenth day of the month Tebeth, 589 B.C. The day has been observed by the Jews as an annual fast ever since.

But besides this, the prophet Jeremiah marks the date with the same kind of particularity. See Jeremiah lii. 4. And *why* is such attention fixed on this day? The answer to that question is also found in Jeremiah, or, rather, is found in a comparison of Jeremiah with Haggai and Daniel. The twenty-fifth chapter of Jeremiah predicts a seventy years' period of "desolations" on

Jerusalem. We find this, later, exercising the mind of Daniel (Dan. ix. 1, 2), and mentioned again by Zechariah (Zech. i. 12). Now that seventy years' period begins from that carefully emphasised day when the Babylonian army beset Jerusalem—and this fact will help to interpret much to us a little later on in our studies.

There can be no doubt that the prophetic year in Scripture is one of 360 days (see our article on Daniel's prophecy of the "seventy weeks"). If, then, we reckon seventy years of 360 days each, from the tenth day of the month Tebeth, 589 B.C., when the siege of Jerusalem began, we come down to the twenty-fourth day of the month Chisleu, 520 B.C. Does anything special happen on that latter date? Well, turn to the little book of the prophet Haggai, chapter ii. 15–19, and see what he says to the returned exiles after their Babylonian captivity. Note the prophet's deliberate stress on the words, besides our own emphasis by the use of capitals—

"CONSIDER, *FROM THIS DAY* AND UPWARD, FROM BEFORE A STONE WAS LAID UPON A STONE IN THE TEMPLE OF THE LORD . . . CONSIDER NOW *FROM THIS DAY* AND UPWARD, FROM *THE FOUR AND TWENTIETH DAY OF THE NINTH MONTH*, EVEN FROM THE DAY THAT THE FOUNDATION OF THE LORD'S TEMPLE WAS LAID, CONSIDER IT . . . *FROM THIS DAY WILL I BLESS YOU.*"

Haggai's pronouncement marked the end of that seventy years' period. We shall refer more fully to this later. Meanwhile, let us mark well that significant emphasis on the year and month and day when Jerusalem was invested.

Fifth, let us also be clear about this, that *judgment did not fall upon the chosen people only because they had committed evils as other peoples had, but signally because they had fouled a sacred covenant.* Note a few major instances of this. (1) Israel was to keep a Sabbatic year every seventh year, and the Jubilee Sabbatic year every fiftieth, when all slaves were to be freed and all debts cancelled. See Leviticus xxv. Where is there any record of Israel's keeping these Sabbaths? See Jeremiah xxxiv. 8–22. It was because of unfaithfulness here that the seventy years of "desolations" came as a long Sabbath of judgment. See the remarkable connection between Jeremiah xxv. 11 and 2 Chronicles xxxvi. 21; and then read Leviticus xxvi. 32–5 as explaining both. (2) Israel was not to make any covenant with the surrounding nations, but to be separate (Exod. xxxiv. 12–17, etc.). Yet from the first Israel defaulted (Joshua ix. 14–16; Judges ii. 2; and many other references). And (3) Israel was to shun idolatry and the use of religious images. There is scarcely need to give references. The record is shameful. But see 2 Kings xvii. 17–23. Other examples might be given, as for instance failure in tithing, Passover observance, and so on. It was in these ways that Israel fouled the Covenant, and, in a peculiar way, merited judgment. It should be clearly grasped that all the judgments which came upon the chosen people were strictly in accord with what was threatened, under such circumstances of default, when the Covenant was first enunciated (see Lev. xxvi. 14–39).

Final Impressions

"Conquered, captive, castaway"—thus, as one has put it, ends the story of Judah as an independent kingdom. Let us now glance back over 2 Kings, and gather up our main impressions. There is always the double aspect to be kept in view—the human and the Divine. In the foreground, and in the immediate sense, is the human failure, as seen in the kings and the multitude; but in the background, and in the ultimate sense, is the Divine triumph as seen in the prophets and their messages—for let it be remembered that all the great prophets whose writings have come down to us prophesied in the period covered by 2 Kings, and it is the writings of these prophets which finally interpret to us both the present and the future tense of the Israel story.

On the human side we see, above all else, that "where there is no vision, the people perish." With departure from a simple, sincere worship of Jehovah comes a lost sense of His presence, accompanied increasingly by idolatry, ruinous alliances, inability to discern the hand of God even when it chastises, a losing of the true ideal of national life, so that moral values are belittled, and a conscience eventually so desensitised that even such messages as the inspired prophets delivered failed to arouse response. Yes, this is the message on the human side. Where the vision of God is lost there inevitably ensue, as Dr. Campbell Morgan puts

it, "degraded ideals, deadened consciences, defeated purposes."
That lesson is as true for Britain and America today as it was for
Judah and Israel long ago.

But on the Divine side there is the picture of ultimate triumph.
The greatest prophet of the era writes of Jehovah, "*HE* shall not
fail, nor be discouraged" (Isa. xlii. 4). When the throne on earth
falls to pieces the throne in the heavens rides the storm. The
chosen people may fail on earth, but the chosen purpose spans
the centuries, and the predetermined consummation is beholden
through prophets' eyes. The Babylonian exile which came as
a judgment on the Jews cured them for ever of their idolatries,
and strangely recovered to them their lost sense of Jehovah.
The Law of Jehovah became exceedingly precious to them, and
the true ideal of their nationhood began to be discerned again.
That ideal is preserved to this day. They are still the chosen
people. What a study they are! Scattered over the face of the
earth, yet strangely one; ever persecuted, yet ever preserved;
mixed in with all races, yet the most distinct people in the world;
their history is a mystery apart from the explanation given in
Scripture. Other peoples of far greater national dimensions than
they have passed away and become extinct (as, for instance, the
Assyrians and the Babylonians), yet they, the children of Abraham,
are still preserved, according to covenant-promise, and *will be*
preserved until all human failure is completely eclipsed in the
Divine triumph when David's greater Son, even the Lord Jesus,
sits on the throne in Jerusalem, and reigns in world-wide empire.

THE BOOKS OF THE CHRONICLES (1)

Lesson Number 40

NOTE.—For this study read the First Book of the Chronicles through twice.

ABOUT THOSE GENEALOGIES!

Nine chapters of genealogical tables! What waste of space! Nay, rather, what blindness to think so! No part of the Chronicles is more important. Such lines of descent were of sacred importance to all godly Jews, and rightly so, for they knew that their nation, besides being the repository of a special Divine revelation, was the possessor of wonderful Divine promises reaching on to unborn generations. The chronicler himself knew well enough that these genealogies reveal the selective process of Divine election right from Adam downwards, and that the covenant line of redemptive purpose was to culminate in the Messiah. Especially did the preservation of the trunk and main branches of Israel's family tree become vital after the Babylonian exile (when the Chronicles were written). Families had been uprooted by the thousand. Connections had been broken. Many records had been lost (see for instance Ezra ii. 59), and Judah's archives must have become largely disintegrated even where not actually destroyed. Our chronicler's lists link the *pre*-Exile with the *post*-Exile period; for (as should be clearly grasped) chapter ix. 2–34 concerns the resettlement in Judæa *after* the Exile. The break is marked by the first verse of that chapter, which should really be the last verse of the preceding chapter. The Angus *Bible Handbook* remarks: "These tables give the sacred line through which the promise was transmitted for nearly 3,500 years, a fact unexampled in the history of the human race."

—J. S. B.

THE BOOKS OF THE CHRONICLES (1)

THE SECOND Book of Kings has left us with a strange and gloomy sadness oppressing our minds. We feel like sitting down with Jeremiah, in sackcloth and ashes, and lamenting amid the ruins, "How doth the city sit solitary! How is she become a widow! How is the gold become dim! How are the precious sons of Zion esteemed as earthen pitchers!" The city is sacked. The temple is burnt. The country is laid bare. The nation is deported.

And yet we would not linger here. We would follow the thousands of Judah into the land of their exile, would sit and weep with them by the banks of the Chebar as Ezekiel did, or mingle with their captive princes in the Babylonian capital as Daniel did; and then, leaping the decades, we would return to Jerusalem and Judæa with the "Remnant," under the leadership of Ezra and Zerubbabel.

However, before we can do this, the two books of the "Chronicles" lie before us; and we may well be grateful that they do. Our Bible would certainly be the poorer without them. In one quick span, from Adam to Nehemiah, they give us the main genealogies of the Israelite nation, and the main events of the Davidic kingdom down to the time of the Babylonian exile.

Having gone carefully through the books of Samuel and the Kings we shall not need here to give more than a brief survey of 1 and 2 Chronicles. But the shortness of our treatment must not be misinterpreted as suggesting unimportance. On the contrary, not only are these "chronicles" alive on every page with sheer interest—yes, even those opening lists of genealogies!—they are of high importance to a right grasp of the Divine significance running through the story of the Israel nation. The one simple reason why we treat 1 and 2 Chronicles thus briefly is that they cover practically the same ground as 2 Samuel and the two books of the Kings.

This may sound as though they consist of repetition. So they do; but it is no "vain" repetition. It is a re-outlining of the story already told in the books of Samuel and the Kings, but from a different standpoint, with new emphases and new aspects, with significant additions and omissions, and supplying completive interpretations. In fact, it is in this repetition, with its characteristic additions and omissions, that the peculiar *viewpoint and significance* of the Chronicles are perceived; for if we read these "chronicles" side by side with the earlier accounts in Samuel and the Kings, we soon begin to notice that the additions and omissions all seem of the same sort, that is, they all seem to conform to one focal purpose. What, then, is the unifying idea running through these additions and omissions? And what is the central purpose of the Chronicles?

The Unifying Idea

First, as to *the unifying idea or emphasis,* all who have studied and written on these two books of the Chronicles are unanimous in observing the prominence given to the *temple* and matters connected with it. As representative of many others, take the following quotation from the late Dr. A. T. Pierson: "While much contained in the Books of Kings is repeated or restated in the Chronicles, much is omitted because foreign to the author's purpose. But whatever bears on the *temple,* its preservation and restoration, the purity of its worship, the regularity and orderliness of its services; whatever makes idolatrous rites or relics hateful, or lifts God to His true throne in the hearts of the people, is here emphasised."

If we have carefully read the *first* of these two books of the Chronicles, as directed at the beginning of this present study, examples of this emphasis on the temple and associated topics will quickly come to mind. For instance, beginning with chapter xi., the whole of the remaining nineteen chapters of 1 Chronicles are occupied with the reign of David. In these chapters there is no repeating the familiar tale of David's romantic adventures, or of his reign at Hebron, or of his grief over Saul and Jonathan, or of his sin against Bathsheba and Uriah, or of the revolt of Absalom (these, not to mention others, are some of the significant major *omissions*); but, on the other hand, we are given with great fulness the following matters which are *not* mentioned in Samuel and Kings—David's abundant preparation of material in advance for the temple (xxii.), his preparatory numbering and distributing of the Levites and the priests (xxiii.–xxiv.), his appointment

and arrangement of singers and players and porters (xxv.–xxvi.)
—all in anticipation of the *temple* (these, not to mention others,
are some of the significant major *additions*).

This feature persists right through the *Second* Book of the
Chronicles. The account of Solomon's reign is much shorter
here than in 1 Kings, yet no less than six out of the nine chapters
given to it in 2 Chronicles refer to the *temple*. The same significance attaches to the fact that onwards from chapter x., which
marks the disruption of the nation into the two kingdoms, the
northern ten-tribed kingdom is throughout ignored, as being
founded upon apostasy from the nation's true worship as well as
from the house of David. It is solely with Judah and Jerusalem
that the Chronicles are concerned, because it is that kingdom and
that city which hold the *temple*. And not only do all these remaining chapters (x.–xxxvi.) confine themselves to Judah, they
still further confine themselves to that viewpoint which subordinates all political and military and personal facts to the interests
of that holy religion of which the temple was the great symbol.
Thus, for instance, the reigns of Asa, Jehoshaphat, Joash, Hezekiah, and Josiah are given prominence because of the religious
reforms and temple restorations associated with them. In Kings
only *three verses* are given to Hezekiah's reforms, as against *three
chapters* in the Chronicles.

Everywhere in the Chronicles the *temple* is emphasised as the
vital centre of the nation's true life; and even where the temple
itself is not mentioned, it is obvious that the emphasis is always
upon that *religion* which the temple represented. We pick out
just one instance of this. Dr. J. H. Moulton says: "No single
incident brings out the contrast of the two versions better than
the reign of Abijah (called in the Kings Abijam). The prophetic
account (i.e. that in the Kings) of the reign is a brief notice
of the wickedness of the king, so great that only for David's
sake was the succession continued in the family. Also mention
is made of wars between Israel and Judah. The *Chronicler* relates
these wars at length, and in particular gives a fine address of
Abijah to the enemy, in which the whole spirit of the Chronicles
is concentrated"—

*"Ought ye not to know that the Lord, the God of Israel, gave the
kingdom over Israel to David for ever, even to him and to his sons*

by a covenant of salt? Yet Jeroboam the son of Nebat, the servant of Solomon the son of David, rose up, and rebelled against his lord. And there were gathered unto him vain men, sons of Belial, which strengthened themselves against Rehoboam the son of Solomon, when Rehoboam was young and tender-hearted, and could not withstand them. And now ye think to withstand the kingdom of the Lord in the hand of the sons of David; and ye be a great multitude, and there are with you the golden calves which Jeroboam made you for gods. Have ye not driven out the priests of the Lord, the sons of Aaron, and the Levites, and have made you priests after the manner of the peoples of other lands? so that whosoever cometh to consecrate himself with a young bullock and seven rams the same may be a priest of them that are no gods. But as for us, the Lord is our God, and we have not forsaken him; and we have priests ministering unto the Lord, the sons of Aaron, and the Levites in their work; and they burn unto the Lord every morning and every evening burnt offerings and sweet incense: the shewbread also set they in order upon the pure table; and the candlestick of gold with the lamps thereof to burn every evening: for we keep the charge of the Lord our God; but ye have forsaken him. And behold, God is with us at our head, and his priests with the trumpets of alarm to sound an alarm against you. O Children of Israel, fight ye not against the Lord, the God of your fathers; for ye shall not prosper" (2 Chron. xiii 5–12, R.V.).

Even the genealogies in the first nine chapters lead up to the allocation of the returned "Remnant" in Jerusalem and Judæa (after the Exile) necessary as a basis for the *temple* service, and the dues by which that service was to be supported (for it should be clearly grasped that chapter ix. 2–34 refers to the *post*-Exile resettlement. Verse 1 marks the break).

So then, without need for more illustrations, we see the unifying emphasis which runs through the Chronicles. They are not merely repetition. Nor are they merely supplemental, supplying numerous items omitted from Samuel and Kings. They relate the history of the elect people in a new way, and from a new standpoint.

The Central Purpose

But we are still left asking: "*Why* this unifying new emphasis? What is the *purpose* behind it? Here, to some degree, we must part company with the commentators. The usual reason given for the peculiar religious emphasis in the Chronicles is that the writer, or rather the compiler, was a *priest*, a priest with a very ecclesiastical outlook, to whom, quite understandably, all matters relating to organised worship and especially to the temple were of unequalled importance. For instance, Angus's *Bible Handbook* says: "It must be remembered all through that the Books of Chronicles are essentially *Levitical*. To all, therefore, that concerns the house and service of Jehovah especial prominence is given." And Moulton's *Modern Reader's Bible* says: "The whole succession of Chronicles is animated by the conscious *ecclesiastical* spirit." And Ellicott's *Commentary* says: "From the entire tone and spirit of the work it is reasonably inferred by most critics that it was the production of a Levite attached to the temple." Most others seem to take the same view.

Now the Chronicles may or may not have been compiled by a priest or Levite; but to say, as do the many, that the peculiar emphasis in the Chronicles is simply *because* the compiler was a priest or Levite, anxious to magnify his own line of things, is to miss the overruling *Divine* design in this part of Scripture, and to reduce the significance of the Chronicles to the limited outlook of an ecclesiastic who was no bigger than the office he held. If we would really appreciate the central purpose of the Chronicles, we must bear thoughtfully in mind the time and circumstances in which they were issued.

The Chronicles were compiled *after the Babylonian exile*, when the "Remnant" had returned from Babylonia to Judæa, under Ezra and Zerubbabel. This is made absolutely certain by statements and references in the Chronicles themselves, as we shall show in our next study. The Chronicles were specially written for these repatriated Jews and their descendants who were to reconstitute the Jewish national life in the homeland; and it was because of certain new circumstances which now confronted the Jewish people that the Chronicles were compiled with the unifying emphasis running through them which we have already noted, and for a special purpose which we now mention.

If we imagine ourselves back in Judæa with that "Remnant," we soon realise that there is one very great lack which forces itself upon the mind, namely, *there is no king*. That is the crucial fact to grasp, and the first key to the purpose of the Chronicles—

THE DAVIDIC THRONE IS GONE!

What that meant to all thoughtful Jews does not require much imagination to appreciate. The throne of David was unique in the earth. It was a throne founded in a Divine covenant. We have dwelt on that in a former study, and need not linger over it again here. It must have been a sore problem to thoughtful Jews, that the throne of David was no more. What we stress here, however, is that the people were returning, not to rebuild a throne, but a *temple*. Indeed, the rebuilding of the temple was the thing for which pre-eminently the Persian emperor, Cyrus, had issued the edict precipitating the return of the Jewish "Remnant" to Jerusalem and Judæa (Ezra i. 1-4). Perhaps there is here a lesson as timely as it is vital for our own days. Note it well—even before Nehemiah is sent to rebuild the *city*, Ezra and Zerubbabel are sent with the "Remnant" to rebuild the *TEMPLE*. In any national reconstruction we must begin *there*—with the temple, that is, with *GOD*! Our politicians and reconstructors of the present post-war period will not learn. They persist in the worldly-wise idea that the *city* must be built before the temple. Well, *they are wrong*.

But now, realising vividly that the throne is gone, let us see what remains. There were three things remained which meant more than all others—

1. First, there was *the teaching of the past*, a past such as no other people had ever had, with a significance attaching to it such as did not attach to the history of any other nation. The teaching of that past had reached a point of completeness in the Exile from which the "Remnant" were now just returned; that is, certain processes in the nation's past had worked themselves out completely, to their ultimate issue, and to their bitter end. In retrospect, the covenant people could now see, in grimly complete lines, just where those processes of apostasy had brought them, and it was

vital that they should now learn unforgettingly the teaching of their nation's past.

2. Second, there was *the prophetic promise for the future.* Although the Davidic throne was no more among them, the Davidic *line* was; and of this line the Messiah was to come, according to Divine promise and covenant, who should lift the Davidic throne to unprecedented splendour, and consummate Jehovah's purpose in and through Israel, by bringing in a wonderful world-rule, with its centre at Jerusalem. It was vital that they should keep this great hope ever before their eyes as they now resettled in Jerusalem and the covenant land.

3. Third, there was *the presence of Jehovah with them in the present.* That presence had been strikingly guaranteed to them in the edict of Cyrus, the Persian emperor, calling on the Jews to return to their native land and to rebuild the temple of Jehovah in Jerusalem (Ezra i. 1–4). What must have been the feelings of the Jews during the last years of their exile in Babylonia, when the fame of Cyrus the Persian began to spread?—when Babylon fell?—and when the new emperor, Cyrus, who had been actually forenamed by Isaiah two hundred years earlier, gave his edict for the rebuilding of the Temple at Jerusalem, exactly as Isaiah had foretold? (see Isa. xlv., also our article on the date of Isaiah). This, in addition to Nebuchadnezzar's proclamation of his conversion to Jehovah (Dan. iv. 1–3, 34–7), and Jeremiah's prophecies as to the exact duration of the servitude to Babylon (see Jer. xxix. 10, and the comment on it in our study of Haggai), must have shown the Jews beyond all doubt that Jehovah was with them in their return to Judæa.

These, then, were the three transcendent factors which remained—the teaching of their national past, the prophetic promise for the future, the presence of Jehovah in the present. What was now necessary? It was above all things needful that the nation should read its past and its present and its future in the true way, that is, from the Divine standpoint; *and it was with this very thing in mind—to meet this need and attain this end —that the "Chronicles" were compiled.*

Three things were naturally very important in this connection

—(1) In view of the nation's unique calling and the Davidic covenant, it was most important to retain unimpaired the nation's principal genealogies; and these are therefore carefully presented in the first nine chapters. (2) In view of the catastrophes which had occurred, it was important to recast the nation's history exclusively from a religious standpoint, at least from the beginning of the Davidic kingdom; and this we find from the tenth chapter of 1 Chronicles onwards. (3) In view of the fact that the temple represented the holy religion which had come to Israel by special Divine revelation, and the disregard of which had brought such evils on the nation, and in view of the fact that the temple was the supreme surviving link between the nation's great past and its still greater prophesied future, it was greatly important to emphasise the temple and its observances in the regard of the people; and this emphasising of the temple we find all through the Chronicles, as already noted.

The temple was now, above all things, (a) the symbol of the unity of the nation, the more so now that the earthly throne had disappeared; (b) the reminder of the nation's high calling and function; (c) the sign that Jehovah was still with His chosen people; (d) the focus of the true emphasis in the national life. It was in the light of that temple that all the past was to be read, and the present reconstructed, and the future anticipated. Hence the compiling of the Chronicles, with their sustained emphasis on the temple and the religious aspects of things. And hence the central *purpose* of the Chronicles, namely, to bring home afresh to the covenant people *where the true emphasis in Israel's national life lay*, to convince them as to *where their first duty and their only true safety lay, and thereby to challenge the elect race to a renewed consecration* as the Divinely-appointed Priest of the nations.

Perhaps we cannot do better than conclude this present study by quoting some very telling words from the pen of the late John Urquhart. "These Books of the Chronicles . . . are not mere repetitions of information supplied by pre-existing Books; nor are they made up of odds and ends left by former writers. Israel's story is told afresh with clear, distinct intention. That intention is as evident in the silence of the Books as in their speech. The story of the ten tribes is left out, and Judah alone is dealt with. In the light of the evident purpose of *Chronicles*, the reason is plain. Judah alone preserved the Divine ordinances. And for the returned Israelites was not this—name it 'ecclesiastical tone,' or whatever one may choose to call it—the one thing that the replanted people had to keep constantly before them? *Israel, unlike the other nations, has no destiny apart from God's service.* This has been proved by these more than eighteen centuries of what may be named national existence, but cannot be called national life. It will be more gloriously shown in the coming day of Israel's renewed consecration. But there is enough even now to teach the higher criticism, and also a modified rationalism, that *Chronicles* saw clearly, what is now becoming apparent as a historical phenomenon, that Israel has not existed, and cannot exist, for itself. It is the Divinely-appointed Priest of the nations. When it recognised its mission, it impressed and led the nations. When it neglected it, it sank into insignificance. When it renounced it, Israel was bereft of fatherland and of spiritual perception and power. It wanders among the nations today in its blindness, disinherited, disrobed, and yet with ineffaceable marks of its priestly destiny. The Book which proclaimed that destiny to restored Israel four-and-twenty centuries ago, not only read to them the one lesson of their past; it also read to the Israelites the story of their future. This one fact is quite enough to show the Book to be prophetic: it stamps it as Divine."

THE BOOKS OF THE CHRONICLES (2)

Lesson Number 41

NOTE.—For this further study in the Chronicles read 2 Chronicles right through twice.

As with 1 and 2 Samuel and 1 and 2 Kings, these two books of the Chronicles formed one continuous work in the Hebrew original, with the title, *Dibrê Hayyâmîm*, "Events of the Days." The division into two parts dates back to the Septuagint Version (third century B.C.), which named the two parts the first and second books of "Things Omitted." The division certainly occurs at the most suitable point, but the title, "Things Omitted," is very inadequate: it makes the Chronicles merely supplemental, and quite misses their special intent. Our own title, "The Chronicles," dates from the time of Jerome, who translated the Hebrew Scriptures into the Latin about A.D. 385–405. This famous translation is known as the "Latin Vulgate" because, from the time of Gregory I (A.D. 540–604), and with the confirmation of the Council of Trent (A.D. 1562), it was accepted as the generally authentic and current text (*vulgatis* = general, common). In some of the editions of the Latin Vulgate we find the title, *Chronicorum Liber*, that is, "Book of Chronicles," as now in our English version. Even this title is not over-commendable, for the Chronicles are really more in the nature of a retrospective and interpretative epitome than merely annals.

—*J. S. B.*

THE BOOKS OF THE CHRONICLES (2)

THUS FAR our survey of the Chronicles has been concerned with their unifying emphasis and purpose. We wish now to glance over their contents, but first there are several preliminary matters which attract attention.

Originals of Compilation

Plainly the Chronicles are a compilation from earlier documents, some of which seem to be quoted literally (see "unto this day" in 2 Chron. v. 9; viii. 8). About fourteen of these are named—

1. Book of the Kings of Israel and Judah (2 Chron. xxvii. 7).
2. A Midrash (commentary) on the above (2 Chron. xxiv. 27).
3. Words, or History, of Samuel the Seer (1 Chron. xxix. 29).
4. Words, or History, of Gad the Seer (1 Chron. xxix. 29).
5. Words, or History, of Nathan the Prophet (2 Chron. ix. 29).
6. The Prophecy of Ahijah the Shilonite (2 Chron. ix. 29).
7. The Visions of Iddo the Seer (2 Chron. ix. 29).
8. Words, or History, of Shemaiah the Prophet (2 Chron. xii. 15).
9. Work of Iddo the Prophet on genealogies (2 Chron. xii. 15).
10. A Midrash (commentary) of Iddo the Prophet (2 Chron. xiii. 22).
11. Words, or History, of Jehu, son of Hanani (2 Chron. xx. 34).
12. Acts of Uzziah, by Isaiah the Prophet (2 Chron. xxvi. 22).
13. The Vision of Isaiah the Prophet (2 Chron. xxxii. 32).
14. Words, or History, of Hozai (or the Seers) (2 Chron. xxxiii. 19).

These sources of compilation are more revealing than might seem in passing. They indicate (*a*) that the author was well-informed for his task; (*b*) that he was using well-known documents which proved the *bona-fide* nature of his work; (*c*) that many consultable writings by competent scholars had accumulated during the nation's history, which fact the more confirms to ourselves the reliability of the records that have now come down to us in our Bible; (*d*) that Israel's archives were by no means the spurious, spasmodic, almost fungus growth which some of our recent "scholars" have supposed, but a body of literature carefully composed, collected, compared, and compiled.

Note that first book in our list—"The Book of the Kings of Israel and Judah." Three times we find this title (2 Chron. xxvii. 7; xxxv. 27; xxxvi. 8). Four times we find the title partly reversed to "The Book of the Kings of Judah and Israel" (2 Chron. xvi. 11; xxv. 26; xxviii. 26; xxxii. 32). The two titles refer to the same work. This is clear, for whichever way the title occurs, the reference is to a king of *Judah*. It seems to have been a remarkable repertory of historical and biographical data (2 Chron. xxvii. 7). It is well to realise that when the chronicler refers to this "Book of the Kings" he is not meaning the earlier book in our Bible which *we* now call by that name. On the contrary, there is reason to think that both Kings and Chronicles in our Bible quote this same work. This is indicated in the fact that the books which *we* now call the Books of the Kings do not contain those matters to which the chronicler calls attention in the book which *he* knew as the Book of the Kings.

Date and Authorship

Unless we are to swallow the assumption of certain moderns, that the Chronicles are blotched all over by interpolations, we shall not be long in finding verses which settle the approximate date of their compilation. Chapters vi. 15 and ix. 1 make clear that they were put together after the carrying away to Babylon. The genealogy in iii. 16–24 shows the same. The very last words of 2 Chronicles make even the edict of Cyrus, which officially ended the Exile, a thing of the past. Most conclusive of all, unless we gratuitously label the whole of 1 Chronicles ix. a later addition, the work is brought right down to the period after the return of the "Remnant" and their partial resettlement "in the cities" and "in Jerusalem" (as is made plain by comparing this chapter with Nehemiah xi. 3–32; vii. 45; xii. 25, 26; Ezra ii. 42). And, just once again, the genealogy of Zerubbabel, in chapter iii. 17–24, brings us at least to a point very late in the life of Ezra or Nehemiah. Hebrew scholars, we may add, are agreed that the language and orthography of the Chronicles also fits this post-Exilic period. Aramaisms mark the corruption of the pure Hebrew by the Chaldean language learned by the captive Jews in Babylon.

Who the compiler was is an unsettled question. The Talmud says Ezra. We cannot here go into the discussion which clings round the matter; but we mention three points which impress us in favour of the Ezra tradition. (1) We have not yet met any weighty reason *against* it. (2) Scholars seem unanimous in tracing a single hand through the three books now called Chronicles, Ezra, and Nehemiah; and all agree it is Ezra's in at least much of the book which bears his own name. (3) No one was more fitted than Ezra; nor does our claiming him as compiler of the bulk of the work exclude completive additions by some subsequent editor.

Relation to Preceding Books

As already noted, although the Chronicles cover much the same ground as the books of Samuel and the Kings, they were written at a later date, from a different standpoint, giving a special emphasis, and having a purpose peculiar to themselves. We may now crystallise the contrastive aspects between the Chronicles and the preceding historical books, as follows. Samuel and Kings are more *biographical*; the Chronicles are more *statistical*. The former are more *personal*; the latter are more *official*. The former are more from the standpoint of the *prophet*; the latter are more from the standpoint of the *priest*. The former give the history of both the northern kingdom (Israel) and the southern kingdom (Judah) after the Disruption of the nation into the two kingdoms; whereas from the Disruption onwards the Chronicles give only the history of *Judah*. In the books of Samuel and the Kings the emphasis is upon the *throne*. In the books of the Chronicles the emphasis is upon the *temple*. In their total effect the books of Samuel and the Kings are an *indictment* of the nation, exposing its guilt; whereas the Chronicles are meant to be an *incitement* to the nation, encouraging new loyalty. The books of Samuel and the Kings are simple, faithful records of things that happened; whereas the Chronicles are a purposively selective succession of extracts all chosen to press home one focal idea. All the books of our Bible thus far, from Genesis to 2 Kings, have pursued a chronological succession of events, right from Adam's creation to Judah's captivity; but now, with the Chronicles, we come to a writing which does not carry us further forward (except in odd touches here and there which reveal its post-exilic compilation), but goes back and *reviews* the whole story in order to derive and apply a vital lesson, namely, that *the nation's response to God is the decisive factor in its history and destiny*. And this lesson, we may add, is just as true of modern Britain and America as it was of old-time Israel and Judah.

Relation to Ensuing Books

Ellicott says: "Examination of the Hebrew text of Chronicles, Ezra, and Nehemiah soon reveals that the three resemble each other very closely, not only in style and language, which is that of the latest age of Hebrew writing, but also in the general point of view, in the manner in which the original authorities are handled and the sacred Law expressly cited, and above all in the marked preference for certain topics, such as genealogical and statistical registers, descriptions of religious rites and festivals, detailed accounts of the sacerdotal classes and their various functions, notices of the music of the temple, and similar matters connected with the organisation of public worship. . . . There are other facts which combine with the above to prove that Chronicles, Ezra, and Nehemiah originally constituted a single great history." Perhaps this is confirmed by the strange termination of the Chronicles in an unfinished sentence, which the opening verses of Ezra complete; and there is actually extant part of a Greek version of these three books which shows no division between them.

Now this close affinity between Chronicles, Ezra, and Nehemiah has certain values for us. Long ago, when the Jews formed their canon of sacred writings, they put the Chronicles right at the end; and we find certain Bible teachers today who would have us think that the Chronicles ought still to come right at the end of our Old Testament, so as to show more easily the connection of their genealogies with those given by Matthew. But no, the Chronicles *must not be separated from Ezra and Nehemiah*. The right place for them is just where they come in our Bible. Surely this is *obviously* so. They belong to the *historical* books; and they are *the true link* between the pre-Exile and post-Exile periods. They look back summarisingly over the throne period, and relate it to the throneless new period. We certainly must not separate the four post-exilic books—Chronicles, Ezra, Nehemiah, and Esther; nor must we miss seeing how their distinctive subjects go together to form one progressive group, thus—

Chronicles—Retrospection.
Ezra   —Restoration.
Nehemiah—Reconstruction.
Esther   —Preservation.

Contents and Structure

And now, most interesting of all, let us try to get a quick, "all in" view of the contents of the Chronicles. Perhaps "interesting" is scarcely the best word. These Chronicles are *fascinating*, if with a little imagination we catch our author-compiler's idea, and see the purpose behind his pen taking carefully chosen form through each successive section.

Take the first section of 1 Chronicles (i.–ix.). To say that these chapters are genealogies is correct, but it is putting it in a very colourless way. They are part of our chronicler's scheme as a whole, and when seen as such they assume new meaning. What we are mainly meant to see is the family tree of a certain *people*— the people of Jehovah. The stock of Adam shoots out three great branches : the sons of Japheth, Ham, and Shem. In the electing purpose of God, the eldest is passed by, and Shem, the youngest, is chosen. So is Abram, the youngest son of Terah, selected ; so is Isaac, in preference to Ishmael ; and so is Jacob, in preference to Esau. All this is in chapter i. Next, in chapter ii., the redemptive line and selective progress descends through Jacob to Judah, then away down to Jesse, and thus to David. The chronicler here interrupts himself to preserve the genealogy of Caleb, that hero of faith who was also of Judah (ii. 18–25) ; but with chapter iii. he resumes the Davidic line—right down to the last of Judah's kings, Zedekiah. Finally, having shown the selective process from Adam down to Abraham, Isaac, Jacob, Judah, David, he reviews the genealogies of the Israel tribes in general, and their allotments in Canaan (iv.–viii.), for all share in the covenant promises. So, in these first chapters, we have, distinctively, the *PEOPLE* of Jehovah.

Now take chapters x. to xii. Here begins the reign of David, the *anointed* of Jehovah. Chapter x. (which obviously is simply transitionary) tells of Saul's death (all else about him is designedly excluded), and how thereupon God "turned the kingdom unto David." Chapters xi. and xii. tell *how* David became king, how he made Jerusalem the capital, who were his mighty men, and how all the tribes were "of one heart" to make him king. Saul had been king rather by *human* choice. David was king by *Divine* choice. Saul had possessed high *natural* qualities, yet was without true faith, and could not please God (x. 13); so his house was set aside, and the throne given to the man of *God's own choice* (x. 14). Here, then, we have the *ANOINTED* of Jehovah.

Now take chapters xiii.–xvi. Here is the first-recorded outstanding public act of king David—the bringing of the *ark* of Jehovah to Jerusalem. David sensed keenly that the secret of the nation's blessing was Jehovah's presence in the midst. Saul had never grasped this in the same way. He had let the ark of Jehovah, symbol of Immanuel ("God with us"), remain neglected (xiii. 3), which in essence was a despising of Israel's birthright, and proved Saul unworthy of the kingship. Very different is it with David, the man of faith. He plans at once to put the ark of Jehovah at the centre of His people's life. After a setback (xiii. 9–13) the ark is at length brought with due reverence to Jerusalem; and although Saul's daughter might see no glory in this act of faith, and might despise the man of God (xv. 29), God blesses this man on every side (xiv.), and David, in an inspired psalm (xvi. 7–36), can teach the people to see covenant mercy in this sacred symbol of promise. In this third section, then, see the *ARK* of Jehovah.

And next, in chapters xvii.–xxi., see the *covenant* of Jehovah. It pleased God to choose out of the race one nation—Israel, then out of that nation one tribe—Judah, then out of that tribe one family—the house of David, and to make with that house a wonderful covenant. See chapter xvii. for this covenant. Then see chapters xviii.–xx. for the immediate Divine implementing of that covenant in David's full establishment and high-point of prosperity. And although David later fell prey to a stratagem of Satan (xxi.), even this lapse was overruled to further God's plan, for it led to the fixing of the spot where the future temple was to stand (xxi. 28 with 2 Chron. iii. 1). Thus, in these chapters we have the *COVENANT* of Jehovah.

This brings us to the last group of chapters (xxii.–xxix.), which are occupied with the *temple* of Jehovah. David was not allowed to build it, but he amply prepared for it—materials (xxii.), Levites (xxiii.), priests (xxiv.), singers, porters, and other officers (xxv.–xxvii.), and a final charge in anticipation of it to Solomon and the nation (xxviii.–xxix.). Plainly, the subject here is the *TEMPLE* of Jehovah. And thus, in this first book of the Chronicles we have—

> The *PEOPLE* of the Lord (i.–ix.).
> The *ANOINTED* of the Lord (x.–xii.).
> The *ARK* of the Lord (xiii.–xvi.).
> The *COVENANT* of the Lord (xvii.–xxi.).
> The *TEMPLE* of the Lord (xxii.–xxix.).

The *subject* of these Chronicles is *the house of Jehovah*. In the larger sense that house is the whole nation Israel; in a more centralised sense it is the house of David; in the centre-most sense it is the temple. The central lesson may be expressed in the words of 1 Samuel ii. 30: "Them that honour Me, I will honour." To the man who would build God a house God says: "The *LORD* will build *thee* an house" (xvii. 10). There is no need for a minute analysis. The following will fix the framework for us.

THE FIRST BOOK OF CHRONICLES
THE HOUSE OF JEHOVAH

RESPONSE TO GOD THE DETERMINING FACTOR

1. ISRAEL'S MAIN GENEALOGIES (i.–ix.)

ADAM TO JACOB (ALSO ESAU'S LINE) (i.).
JACOB TO DAVID (ALSO CALEB LINE) (ii.).
DAVID TO ZEDEKIAH (AND POST-EXILE) (iii.).
TRIBE GENEALOGIES AND ALLOTMENTS (iv.–viii.).
Post-Exile resettlement (ix.).

2. DAVID'S REIGN AT JERUSALEM (x.–xxix.).

THE ANOINTED OF THE LORD (x.–xii.).
THE ARK OF THE LORD (xiii.–xvi.).
THE COVENANT OF THE LORD (xvii.–xxi.).
THE TEMPLE OF THE LORD (xxii.–xxix.).
Death of king David (xxix. 26–30).

And now we come to the *Second* Book of the Chronicles. For our present purpose it may be summed up very briefly. It is a tragic book, with a glorious opening and a terrible ending. The first nine chapters give us the forty years' reign of Solomon. The remaining chapters (x.–xxxvi.) give us Judah's history down to the Exile.

As for Solomon's reign, the larger part of the account is taken up with the *temple*. We need not speak here about the temple as a building: we have already done so in our study of 1 Kings. Nor need we speak again about Solomon personally, nor of the type aspects of his reign. Let us try to catch the *national* and *moral* significances of the chronicler's outline.

The Davidic covenant had provided that the seed of David should (1) inherit a firm kingdom; (2) build the temple; (3) be subject to discipline. All these three provisions begin to have fulfilment in Solomon's reign. The kingdom reaches unprecedented splendour; the glorious temple is built; and, alas, discipline has to be exercised. The promises of God concerning *ultimate* issues never have an "if" in them, because they find their final goal in *Christ* (see our note on 2 Sam. vii.); but promises concerning the intermediate processes toward those ultimate issues often *do* have an "if" in them. Thus, as someone has aptly observed, "Solomon was promised wisdom, wealth, and power, and he received them. He was promised 'length of days' *if* he persevered in his walk with God (1 Kings iii. 14). This latter gift he forfeited, and died at fifty-nine."

And what a story *after* Solomon's death—from Rehoboam and the "Disruption" to Zedekiah and the "Dispersion"! There is no need here to give each of the twenty kings separate mention. We have read the chronicler's account. We know the story. But again let us grasp the centre-point of significance. In the preceding chronicles there have risen up before us a *THRONE* founded in a Divine covenant, and a *TEMPLE* made glorious by a Divine descent into it. The throne and the temple are meant to uphold and glorify each other; but a condition of apostasy develops, and goes from bad to worse despite occasional checks, in which the throne becomes the worst *enemy* of the temple, until a point is reached where one of the two must go, and as it cannot be the temple it must be the throne. Hence the Exile and the suspension of the Davidic throne. The temple too is allowed to be burnt, for it had already been profaned far more by Jewish sinning than it now could be by Babylonish burning: and a new temple must be built in the throneless new period after the Exile.

Such is the centre-point of national significance; but let us catch the *moral and spiritual* truth of the book. Running right through the story of these kings, with its occasional reforms and ever-worsening relapses, is the solemn, vital, urgent truth that *a nation's response to God is the really determining factor in its history and destiny*. This was specially true of Israel, but it is universally true of the earth's people today. "As long as Uzziah sought the Lord, God made him to prosper" (xxvi. 5); "Jotham became mighty because he prepared his ways before the Lord his God" (xxvii. 6)—this is the stress all through 2 Chronicles. In the two books of the Chronicles taken together, we have the full historical view of the Davidic monarchy; and in it we see high calling, great blessing, ill doing, bad ending. We are meant to see, through the alternating ups and downs of the nations' history, that when king and people honoured God there was prosperity, whereas whenever they behaved unfaithfully to Him there came adversity. On page after page this truth is driven home that the nation's response to God is the really decisive factor in its history and destiny.

This truth may not seem so immediately perceptible in our modern world with its international complicatedness; but when we look at processes over a period we find it still in operation. Moral principles and spiritual convictions are the *first*-important things as regards national progress or decline, not politics and economics—as seems to be the fashionable thought in Government today. The place we give to *GOD* is that which determines our prosperity or adversity, our history and our destiny. Israel of old—kings, leaders, people—deceived themselves into thinking that they could sin with impunity, imagining that because Jehovah could not be seen He could not see: but they did not deceive God; nor can we. "God is not mocked." He rules, He chooses, He forbears; but He will not spare the persistent exploiting of privilege. The abuse of high calling by low living always brings ruinous ending. Oh, that nations, leaders, peoples, might realise that today!

The following outline will help to fix the main points in mind.

THE SECOND BOOK OF CHRONICLES
THE TEMPLE VERSUS THE THRONE

RESPONSE TO GOD THE DETERMINING FACTOR

1. SOLOMON'S FORTY YEARS' REIGN (i.–ix.).

SOLOMON'S EARLY ESTABLISHMENT (i.).
SOLOMON REARS THE TEMPLE (ii.–vii.).
SOLOMON IN ALL HIS GLORY (viii.–ix.).
Death of Solomon (ix. 29–31).

2. JUDAH'S HISTORY TO THE EXILE (x.–xxxvi.).

THE "DISRUPTION" OF THE KINGDOM (x.).
THE TWENTY KINGS OF JUDAH (xi.–xxxvi.).
DEPORTATION TO BABYLON (xxxvi. 15–21).
Edict of Cyrus (xxxvi. 22, 23).

Concluding Reflections

In our brief survey of the Chronicles we have had to leave many interesting points untouched. Perhaps a few hints or suggestions may be acceptable as we close.

These Chronicles are an endless mine for preachers. Every part is full of spiritual suggestion. As just one instance, in 2 Chronicles, take the four deliverances wrought for Judah— (1) under Abijah against Jeroboam; (2) under Asa against the Ethiopians; (3) under Jehoshaphat against the Moabites; (4) under Hezekiah against the Assyrians; and note how in every case the victory is attributed to God's fighting for Judah (see xiii., xiv., xx., xxxii.). Or go through the chapters noting the two persistent perils to the temple and the true worship—(1) neglected, or (2) corrupted. Or again, the reforms under Hezekiah are a grand study, showing the first steps to be taken, both negatively and positively, in *any* national reconstruction.

Again, as Dr. J. H. Moulton says, "There can be few better exercises in the study of historic literature than to compare these two divisions of Bible history (Chronicles *versus* Samuel and Kings), in their treatment of the same incident." We give overleaf a list of the parallel passages.

PARALLEL PASSAGES

A comparison with the books of Samuel, Kings and certain chapters in Isaiah is necessary in the study of Chronicles. To assist in this, we give a complete list of the parallel passages with which Chronicles should be studied.

1 Sam. xxvii.	.	.	.	1 Chron. xii. 1–7
xxix. 1–3	.	.	.	xii. 19–22
xxxi.	.	.	.	x.
2 Sam. v. 1–5	.	.	.	xi. 1–3
v. 6–10	.	.	.	xi. 4–9
v. 11–16	.	.	.	xiv. 1–7
v. 17–25	.	.	.	xiv. 8–17
vi. 1–11	.	.	.	xiii.
vi. 12–23	.	.	.	xv. and xvi.
vii.	.	.	.	xvii.
viii.	.	.	.	xviii.
x.	.	.	.	xix.
xi. 1–27	.	.	.	xx. 1
xii. 29–31	.	.	.	xx. 1–3
xxiii. 8–39	.	.	.	xi. 10–47
xxiv. 1–9	.	.	.	xxi. 1–6
xxiv. 1–9	.	.	.	xxvii. 23, 24
xxiv. 10–17	.	.	.	xxi. 7–17
xxiv. 18–24	.	.	.	xxi. 18–xxii. 1
1 Kings ii. 1	.	.	.	xxiii. 1
ii. 1–4	.	.	.	xxviii. 20, 21
ii. 10–12	.	.	.	xxix. 23–30
ii. 46	.	.	.	2 Chron. i. 1
iii. 4–15	.	.	.	i. 2–13
v.	.	.	.	ii.
vi.	.	.	.	iii. 1–14 ; iv. 9
vii. 15–21	.	.	.	iii. 15–17
vii. 23–6	.	.	.	iv. 2–5
vii. 38–46	.	.	.	iv. 6, 10, 17
vii. 47–50	.	.	.	iv. 18–22
vii. 51	.	.	.	v. 1
viii.	.	.	.	v. 2 ; vii. 10
ix. 1–9	.	.	.	vii. 11–22
ix. 10–28	.	.	.	viii.
x. 1–13	.	.	.	ix. 1–12
x. 14–25	.	.	.	ix. 13–24
x. 26–9	.	.	.	ix. 25–8 ; i. 14–17
ix. 41–3	.	.	.	ix. 29–31
xii. 1–19	.	.	.	x.
xii. 21–4	.	.	.	xi. 1–4
xii. 25	.	.	.	xi. 5–12
xii. 26–31	.	.	.	xi. 13–17
xiv. 22–4	.	.	.	xii. 1
xiv. 25–8	.	.	.	xii. 2–12
xiv. 21, 29–31	.	.	.	xii. 13–16
xv. 1	.	.	.	xiii. 1, 2
xv. 6	.	.	.	xiii. 2–31
xv. 7, 8	.	.	.	xiii. 22 ; xiv. 1
xv. 11, 12	.	.	.	xiv. 1–5
xv. 13–15	.	.	.	xv. 16–18
xv. 16–22	.	.	.	xvi. 1–6
xv. 23, 24	.	.	.	xvi. 11–14
xxii. 1–40, 44	.	.	.	xviii.
xxii. 41–3	.	.	.	xvii. 1 ; xx. 31–3
xxii. 45	.	.	.	xx. 34
xxii. 47–9	.	.	.	xx. 35–7
xxii. 50	.	.	.	xxi. 1

PARALLEL PASSAGES (*continued*)

2 Kings	2 Chron.
i. 1 ; iii. 4, 5	2 Chron. xx. 1–3
viii. 16–19	xxi. 2–7
viii. 20–2	xxi. 8–15
viii. 23, 24	xxi. 18–20
viii. 25–7	xxii. 1–4
viii. 28, 29 ; ix. 1–28.	xxii. 5–7, 9
x. 11–14	xxii. 8
xi. 1–3	xxii. 10–12
xi. 4–20	xxiii.
xi. 21 ; xii. 1–3	xxiv. 1–3
xii. 6–16	xxiv. 4–14
xii. 17, 18	xxiv. 23, 24
xii. 19–21.	xxiv. 25–7
xiv. 1–6	xxv. 1–4
xiv. 7	xxv. 11–16
xiv. 8–14	xxv. 17–24
xiv. 17–20	xxv. 25–8
xiv. 21, 22 ; xv. 1–4	xxvi. 1–15
xv. 6, 7, 27, 28	xxvi. 22, 23
xv. 32–5	xxvii. 1–8
xv. 38	xxvii. 9
xxvi. 1, 2.	xxviii. 1, 2
xvi. 3, 4, 6	xxviii. 3–8
xvi. 7	xxviii. 16–19
xv. 29	xxviii. 20
xvi. 8–18.	xxviii. 21–5
xvi. 19, 20	xxviii. 26, 27
xviii. 1–3	xxix. 1, 2
xviii. 13	Isa. xxxvi. 1
xviii. 14–16	2 Chron. xxxii. 2–8
xx. 1–11	{ 2 Chron. xxxii. 24 ; Isa. xxxviii.
xx. 12–19.	Isa. xxxix. 1–8
xviii. 17–37	{ 2 Chron. xxxii. 9–19 ; Isa. xxxvi. 2–22
xix. 1–5	{ 2 Chron. xxxii. 20 ; Isa. xxxvii. 1–4
xix. 6, 7	Isa. xxxvii. 6, 7
xix. 8–19.	{ 2 Chron. xxxii. 17 ; Isa. xxxvii. 8–20
xix. 20–37	{ 2 Chron. xxxii. 21 ; Isa. xxxvii. 21–38
xx. 20, 21	2 Chron. xxxii. 32, 33
xxi. 1–16	xxxi. 1–9
xxi. 17, 18	xxxiii. 18–20
xxi. 19–26	xxxiii. 21–5
xxii. 1, 2 .	xxxiv. 1–7
xxii. 3–20	xxxiv. 8–28
xxiii. 1–3	xxxiv. 29–32
xxiii. 21–3	xxxv. 1–19
xxxiii. 24–6	xxxiv. 33
xxiii. 28–30	xxxv. 20–7
xxiii. 30–3	xxxvi. 1–3
xxiii. 34–7	xxxvi. 4, 5
xxiv. 8, 9	xxxvi. 9
xxiv. 15–17	xxxvi. 10
xxiv. 18, 19	xxxvi. 11, 12
xxiv. 20	xxxvi. 13–16
xxv. 8–21	xxxvi. 18–21

The above list of parallel passages we have taken the liberty of reproducing from the *Annotated Bible*, by the late A. C. Gaebelein, which work we are happy to recommend.

It is good to know that recent archaeological discovery has wonderfully confirmed the Chronicles. See the late John Urquhart's *New Biblical Guide*, volumes 6 and 8, and other books on Bible archaeology.

Most of all, may that central message of the Chronicles grip our minds, namely, *that response to God is the really decisive factor*. It is true both nationally and individually. It was true of old: it is true today. The first *duty* and the only true *safety* of the *throne* lies in its relation toward the *temple*. Our national leaders of today might well ponder that fact. When God is honoured, government is good and the nation prospers. But when God is *dis*honoured, the cleverest statesmanship cannot avert eventual disaster. The call to our nation today, as clearly as in the Edict of Cyrus quoted at the end of 2 Chronicles, is to "*go up*" and *REBUILD THE TEMPLE*.

THE BOOK OF EZRA (1)
Lesson Number 42

NOTE.—For this study read through the Book of Ezra twice. Make a note of problematical points or references. Some of these, at least, will be found dealt with in the two ensuing studies. For a note on the Jewish "months" see appendix to our next study in Ezra.

It is maintained by many that the Book of Ezra is the work of several different hands, and that such unity as it possesses has been given to it by a compiler. The compiler is by some believed to have been Ezra, by others an unknown Jew contemporary with him. This latter theory rests upon the fact of the curious transitions from the third to the first person, and back, which occur in the later chapters (vii. 28; x. 1). . . . In the earlier portion of the Book it is supposed that different styles may be traced. . . . The simple view that Ezra, who is admitted to have written at least one section, really composed the whole, using for the most part his own words, but in places inserting documents, is to the full as tenable as any other hypothesis. The general harmony of the whole Book, and the *real* uniformity of its style, are in favour of this view. The objection from the changes of person is of no great importance, changes of this kind often occurring in works admitted to be the production of a single writer, as in Thucydides and in Daniel. Moreover, tradition ascribes the whole Book to Ezra; and if Ezra wrote Chronicles, which is the view of many critics, then the connection of the Book with Chronicles will be an additional argument in favour of Ezra's authorship.

—*Rev. George Rawlinson, M.A., in "Pulpit Commentary."*

Note: The above quotation refers to "curious transitions" (plural) from third to first person and back, as though they occurred several times. The actual fact is that there is one complete section in which the change to first person is sustained throughout, without alternation (vii. 27—ix. 15). We mention this because it seems yet further to strengthen the likelihood that Ezra was the author-compiler, rather than that "unknown few contemporary with him."

—*J.S.B.*

THE BOOK OF EZRA (1)

THE THREE little books which now lie before us—Ezra, Nehemiah, Esther—complete the seventeen historical books which form the earlier part of the Old Testament. These three belong together as the three books which record God's dealings with the Jews *after* their going into captivity. Ezra and Nehemiah deal with the "Remnant" which returned to Jerusalem and Judæa, while the book of Esther has to do with those who stayed on in the land of their captivity. While we are reading these three sketches at the end of the seventeen *historical* books, we ought to read the three prophets at the end of the seventeen *prophetical* books, namely, Haggai, Zechariah and Malachi, for these were the three prophets whom God raised up among His people in the post-Exile period.

The Return of the Remnant

The subject with which this Book of Ezra deals is one of the most important in Jewish history, namely, *the return of the Remnant*. This event took place about the year 536 B.C., that is, at the end of the seventy years' servitude to Babylon. Both the Exile and the return were predicted before ever the Exile began (see Jer. xxv. 11–12, and xxix. 10, 11); and the Book of Ezra recognises this in its opening words—"Now in the first year of Cyrus, King of Persia, *that the word of the Lord by the mouth of Jeremiah might be fulfilled*, the Lord stirred up the spirit of Cyrus, King of Persia, that he made a proclamation throughout all his kingdom, and put it also in writing, saying:

"JEHOVAH, GOD OF HEAVEN, HATH GIVEN ME ALL THE KINGDOMS OF THE EARTH; AND HE HATH CHARGED ME TO BUILD HIM AN HOUSE AT JERUSALEM WHICH IS IN JUDAH. WHO IS THERE AMONG YOU OF ALL HIS PEOPLE?—HIS GOD BE WITH HIM, AND LET HIM GO UP TO JERUSALEM WHICH IS IN JUDAH, AND BUILD THE HOUSE OF JEHOVAH, GOD OF ISRAEL (HE IS THE GOD) WHICH IS IN JERUSALEM."

At the outset, then, let us clearly note these two facts—first, that the return was foretold in prophecy; and second, that it was actually set on foot by the decree of Cyrus.

The Size of the Remnant

As to the *size* of the returning Remnant, in the second chapter of Ezra thirty-three family groups are enumerated, making a total of 24,144. Then follow four groups of priests totalling 4,289. Then come groups of Levites and others to the number of 1,385. These three totals added together give the combined total of 29,818. This total, however, seems to be the aggregate of the *males only*; for in verses 64–5 we read: "The whole congregation together was forty and two thousand, three hundred and three score; beside their servants and their maids, of whom there were seven thousand, three hundred, thirty and seven." Thus, the final total of males, females, and servants is 49,697; and we may therefore put the size of the Remnant at the round figure of 50,000.

Such a number, out of the national total, was very small. It was, indeed, merely a "*remnant*." During the years of captivity in Babylonia many of the older generation had died off, and the new generation of Jews who had grown up amid their foreign environment would not feel just that smarting sense of strangeness, humiliation, and resentment which their parents had felt. Understandably, therefore, though not excusably, the pull of their fatherland was not so strong upon these latter as it had been upon their exiled parents. Historic changes, also, had taken place during those years of Jewish exile. The power of Babylon had crumpled and perished before the resistless spread of the Persian empire (which accounts for the fact that it was a Persian king, Cyrus the Great, who issued the edict which precipitated the return of the Jewish remnant to Jerusalem); and the Jews seem to have fared none too badly under the Persian rule. Thus when the providential opportunity came for repatriation, the bulk of the nation, to their shame, preferred their tolerable and perhaps even lucrative life under Persian rule, to which they had now become quite accommodated.

A Further Return

So, then, there was this return of fifty thousand, in response to the decree of Cyrus, in 536 B.C.—which return was under the leadership of Zerubbabel (see ii. 2), who was a lineal descendant of the kings of Judah. But about *eighty years later*, in the year 456 B.C., there was a further return, though of a very much smaller number, under the leadership of Ezra, the priest and scribe. It was occasioned by a decree of Artaxerxes, the then reigning Persian king; and the twelve groups of those who comprised the expedition along with the Nethinims (viii. 20) totalled about 2,000, though this is said to be the number of males only (viii. 3., etc.). With this further expedition under Ezra in mind, we may say that the repatriating of the Remnant was in two stages. It was *commenced* under Zerubbabel, in the first year of Cyrus (536 B.C.), and was *completed* eighty years later, under Ezra, in the seventh year of Artaxerxes (456 B.C.).

The further return under Ezra is described in chapters vii. and viii., and marks off this book of Ezra into its two main parts: Part I—The Return under Zerubbabel (i.–vi.); Part II—The Return under Ezra (vii.–x.).

The " Book " of Ezra

As we pointed out in our study of the Chronicles, there is reason to believe that 1 and 2 Chronicles, Ezra, and Nehemiah were originally one undivided work. The Jewish and early Christian view is that Ezra was the author-compiler of that original. Perhaps we may profitably mention here again three points in favour of the Ezra tradition: (1) we have not yet encountered any weighty reason *against* it; (2) scholars agree that a single hand may be traced through Chronicles, Ezra, and Nehemiah, and that it is certainly Ezra's in part of the book which bears his own name; (3) it is difficult to find an alternative. Who was more fitted or more likely? And as for that over-refined critical expertness which professes to discern *several* different "styles" in the original, it is surely answer enough that Ezra's being the author-compiler of the work in bulk does not rigidly exclude God-guided completive touches here and there by some competent hand a little later, nor does it exclude that the autobiographical parts in the Book of Nehemiah were written by Nehemiah himself.

As to the *date* of the book, obviously, it must have been written after the latest event which it records, and that is the reformation under Ezra, the year after his arrival at Jerusalem, 456 B.C. Probably it was written a few years after that event.

Perhaps the central *spiritual* significance of the book may be best expressed in the words of Lamentations iii. 32—"*Though He cause grief, yet will He have compassion.*" God had certainly brought grief upon His elect people, for judgment had become necessary, and the grief was richly deserved: but now the span of exile was over; God had not forgotten to be gracious, and there was a compassionate restoration made possible. Oh, that most wonderful truth—that the God of Israel, and of the universe, is a *compassionate* God! Let us never forget it, especially in times when men's sins bring vast calamities upon the world.

The *structure* of the book is simple and interesting. As already mentioned, it is in two clearly divided parts. In chapters i. to vi. we have the return under Zerubbabel, and what ensued; then in chapters vii. to x. we have the further return under Ezra, and what ensued. It should be most definitely understood that between these two parts (i.e. between the end of chapter vi. and the beginning of chapter vii.) there intervenes *a gap of sixty years*. The return under Zerubbabel was in the first year of Cyrus (i. 1) which was 536 B.C. The return under Ezra was in the seventh year of Artaxerxes (vii. 1, 8) which was in 456 B.C., that is, *eighty* years later. The first six chapters of the book cover the first *twenty* years (approximately) after the return under Zerubbabel, which leaves about *sixty* years between the end of chapter vi. and the opening of chapter vii. During the earlier part of this sixty years' gap the critical events narrated in the Book of *Esther* took place.

There is a noticeable parallelism between the two main parts of this Book of Ezra. In preference to an ordinary paragraph-by-paragraph analysis, we ought to get into our minds a picture of the book in this parallel form. Part 1 begins with the decree of Cyrus; part 2 begins with the decree of Artaxerxes. In part 1 the central figure is Zerubbabel; in part 2 the central figure is Ezra. In both parts we are given a careful list of the persons who returned, and of the sacred vessels. In part 1 there is the ministry of the prophets, Haggai and Zechariah; in part 2 there is the ministry of the priest-scribe, Ezra. At the end of part 1 the main outcome is the temple rebuilt; at the end of part 2 the main outcome is the people re-separated.

THE BOOK OF EZRA
THE BOOK OF RESTORATION

> *"Though He cause grief, yet will He have compassion."*

THE RETURN UNDER ZERUBBABEL (i.–vi.)	THE RETURN UNDER EZRA (vii.–x.)
The decree of Cyrus (i. 1–4)	The decree of Artaxerxes (vii. 1, 11–26)
The leader, Zerubbabel (i. 8 ; ii. 2)	The leader, Ezra the scribe (vii. 1–10)
Names and number of Remnant (ii. 3–65)	Names and number of company (viii. 1–20)
Sacred vessels and gifts (i. 6–11 ; ii. 68–70)	Sacred vessels and gifts (vii. 15–22 ; viii. 24–35)
The coming to Jerusalem (iii. 1)	The coming to Jerusalem (viii. 32)
Prophet ministry: Haggai, Zechariah (v. 1–vi. 14)	Intercessory ministry of Ezra (ix. 1–15)
Main outcome — Temple re-built (vi. 15–22)	Main outcome — People re-separated (x. 1–44)

The Two Leaders

If this book of Scripture were named according to its subject rather than after its author, it would be called "The Book of the Remnant," or "The Book of the Restoration," or "The Book of the Repatriation," rather than "Ezra." Or, if it were named after its leading parts or personalities, it would be "The Book of Zerubbabel and Ezra," rather than of Ezra alone. This is worth mentioning, lest from repeated reference to the book as "The Book of Ezra" we fall into thinking of Ezra himself as the principal actor in the story. Ezra certainly is the leader of the expedition and re-separation in chapters vii. to x., but the real leader of the Remnant, eighty years before Ezra's expedition, and the chief administrator of affairs among the Remnant after the resettlement in Judæa, was Zerubbabel. The contemporary prophet, Haggai, uniformly addresses him as "Zerubbabel, governor of Judah." Since he must have been well into adult years when he led the Remnant back to Judæa, we presume that he must have been dead a considerable time when Ezra came to Jerusalem, eighty years after the Remnant. The last historical reference to Zerubbabel is in chapter v. 2. Both these leaders are very important figures in the story of Israel.

Zerubbabel.

In this Book of Ezra, Zerubbabel is also called by two other names—"Sheshbazzar" (i. 8, 11; v. 14–16), and "The Tirshatha" (ii. 63). The former is his Babylonian or Chaldee name; the latter is a Persian title meaning governor. His personal name, "Zerubbabel," means *"descended of Babylon,"* which indicates that he was actually a child of the Exile, born in Babylonia, or probably in the city of Babylon itself. This also suggests that in the case of Zerubbabel personally, the coming to Jerusalem with the 50,000 Remnant was not a "return" but *his first coming.* There is nothing to suggest that he had ever seen Jerusalem or Judæa before.

He is called, "Zerubbabel, the *son of Shealtiel"* (elsewhere called Salathiel). His full lineage is given in 1 Chronicles iii. That he was indeed one of the generation born in captivity is definitely shown in 1 Chronicles iii. 17–19 (see R.V. for verse 17). His lineage makes his leadership of the Remnant the more noteworthy. He was directly in the royal line of David, being the great-grandson of king Jeconiah (who began to reign at the age of eighteen but was carried captive to Babylon three months later: see 2 Kings xxiv. 8–16). So important does the chronicler deem Zerubbabel's lineage that, after connecting it right back with David, he carries it down several generations *after* Zerubbabel—in fact to the latest point of time anywhere in Chronicles, Ezra or Nehemiah. When we turn on to the New Testament we at once find Matthew completing the links, until, of David and Zerubbabel's line, according to the flesh, *CHRIST* is born.

Of Zerubbabel's personal character we know nothing except by inference from scantiest data. His religious zeal is implied, of course, in his very leadership of the Remnant. We note his care to conform the restored worship to the word of God (Ezra iii. 2–5, 11), and his response to the two prophets (v. 1, 2; Hag.

i. 12). But the threefold glory which immortalises him is that he (1) captained the Remnant back to Judæa, (2) laid the foundation of the new temple, (3) completed the erection of the new temple (compare iii. 8 and vi. 15 with Zech. iv. 9).

Ezra.

Jewish tradition, via the Talmud, has made Ezra one of the most celebrated personages in all the history of his people. Five great works are attributed to him: (1) The founding of the so-called "Great Synagogue," or synod of learned Jewish scholars —concerning which see the note sub-joined to our next study; (2) the settlement of the sacred "canon," or recognised list of authoritative Hebrew Scriptures, and its threefold arrangement into the Law, the Prophets, and the Writings; (3) the change-over from the writing of the Hebrew Scriptures in the old Hebrew script to the new, with its square Assyrian characters; (4) the compilation of the Chronicles, along with the book which now bears his own name, and the Book of Nehemiah; (5) the institution of local synagogues.

If these five big accomplishments provenly and directly originated with Ezra, then he certainly is of a stature to be eyed with some wonder; but *did* they all originate with him? Scholarly investigators into these Jewish traditions have pronounced them largely legendary. This much, however, is quite factual, that these far-reaching developments took shape in or near the period of Ezra's moral and literary leadership, and that he had no small part in them. Thus, it is not without reason that he should be regarded as something of an epochal figure.

But let us glance at Ezra *personally*. He was one of the captives in Babylonia, where, also, almost certainly, he was born. He was a lineal descendant of Israel's first high priest, Aaron; and all the links in the chain of descent are given in chapter vii. 1–5. So he was a *priest*. Also, he was a "*scribe*"—a "ready scribe in the Law of Moses" (vii. 6), which really means that he was an *expert instructor* in the Scriptures. Apart from this, Ezra would never have become the leader that he was. He shows us how God can use a man who studies to a proficient grasp on the written word of God. He shows us what a noble and vital qualification for highest leadership it is to have a full and careful knowledge of the Scriptures. In his personal *character*, also, Ezra is a fine example. See his *godly purpose* (vii. 10) ; his *godly thankfulness* for success (verses 27, 28) ; his prayerful *dependence on God* (viii. 21–3) ; his acute *grief* at the sin of the people (ix. 3, 4) ; his *deep humility* before God (verses 5–15) ; his prompt, brave *action against that which was wrong* (x.). These aspects of Ezra's character richly repay reflection, and may well send us to our knees with the prayer that the same qualities may be reproduced in ourselves, through the sanctifying ministry of the Holy Spirit.

THE BOOK OF EZRA (2)

Lesson Number 43

NOTE.—For this further study read the Book of Ezra through again, at one sitting.

One of the most brilliant French scientists of our time—Dr. Alexis Carrel, of the Rockefeller Institute of New York—has lately . . . affirmed that the negative attitude towards miracles *can no longer be sustained* in the face of the facts observed by Science during the last fifty years. And this authority in medical research goes on to accept miracles of healing through prayer, including even organic diseases, such as cancer. The evidences for unusual happenings in human life have always existed, but they are only now at last being recognised, recorded, and vouched for by Science. Since this is being done, it follows that the well informed and unprejudiced cannot henceforth reject the Bible narrative because it records the occurrence of unusual happenings some thousands of years ago. A section of our clergy who call themselves Modernists might make themselves familiar with this advance in knowledge if they desire to retain their title; otherwise they have clearly become " Ancient Modernists ".

—*Sir Charles Marston.*

THE BOOK OF EZRA (2)

THIS BOOK of Ezra contains remarkable spiritual lessons, some of which we wish to mention; but before we come to these, we ought perhaps to touch on several points in the narrative which may not be quite clear to the minds of some readers. The story of the book becomes all the more interesting when these obscure bits here and there are cleared up, and when certain sidelights are brought to bear upon it.

Explanatory Notes and Sidelights

Duration of the Exile.

The Jewish exile in Babylonia is often spoken of as the *seventy years'* exile, on the basis of Jeremiah xxix. 10 and 2 Chronicles xxxvi. 21. But it will occur to any thoughtful reader that if the Exile lasted seventy years, practically none of those who went into it as adults could have been alive, let alone physically able, to join the returning "Remnant" at the end of it. Yet chapter iii. 12 says: "But many of the priests and Levites and chief of the fathers, who were ancient men, that had seen the first house (Solomon's Temple), when the foundation of this (the new) house was laid before their eyes, wept with a loud voice." Are we then to think that these "many" were all men of ninety and over? No, for the Exile lasted fifty-one years only, not seventy. It began in 587 B.C., and ended with the decree of Cyrus, 536 B.C. In Jeremiah xxix. 10, the words "at Babylon" should be "*for* Babylon" (as in R.V.). God did not say His people would be *at* Babylon seventy years, but that there would be a seventy years' rule *for* Babylon (which came true exactly: see our note re this in the study on Haggai). These older men who came back to Jerusalem with the "Remnant" need not have been more than the three-score-years-and-ten. Even so, they were brave and zealous to caravan those seven hundred miles from Babylon to Jerusalem, a journey which meant five months of daily travel.

Assyria, Babylon, Media-Persia.

That part of Israel's history which is recorded in the latter part of the Kings and the Chronicles, and in Ezra, Nehemiah, and Esther, has for its successive background three world-empires— Assyria, Babylon, and Media-Persia. With the Book of Ezra before us we have reached a point in our Bible study where we ought to have at least a skeleton sketch of this background in our minds. This is the more so because in this little book of Ezra no less than seven different kings are mentioned, representing all three world-empires, and the story means so much more when these references are intelligently distinguished. For instance, we must not think that the emperor Darius here is the king Darius of the book of Daniel; nor must we think that the Artaxerxes of chapter iv. is the Artaxerxes of chapter vii. So, then, a few words about Assyria, Babylon, and Media-Persia will be useful.

First comes the *ASSYRIAN EMPIRE*. The story of the kingdom of Assyria begins a long, long way back, and runs in three periods, the first being from about 1430 to 1000 B.C., and the second from about 880 to 745 B.C., in both of which there was a period of rise to power followed by long decline. It is the *third* period which has so much to do with *Israel*, in which Assyria became world-mistress. This period began in 745 B.C., with the able and cruel usurper-general, Pul, who took the reigning name of Tiglath-Pileser III, and it continued till Nineveh was finally destroyed, about 612–608 B.C., when Babylon took the lead. Here are the Assyrian emperors and their connections with Scripture history:

Tiglath-Pileser III (745–27). 2 Kings xv. 19, 29; xvi. 7, 10; 2 Chron. v. 26.

Shalmaneser IV (727–22). 2 Kings xvii. 3; xviii. 9.

Sargon (722–05). 2 Kings xviii. 11; Isa. xx; x. 12, 28–34 (R.V.).

Sennacherib (705–681). 2 Kings xviii.–xix.; 2 Chron. xxxii.; Isa. xxxvi.–xxxvii.

Esar-haddon (681–68). 2 Kings xix. 37; 2 Chron. xxxiii. 11; Ezra iv. 2.

Assur-bani-pal (668–26). Ezra iv. 10 ("Asnapper")?

With the death of Assur-bani-pal this greatest period of

Assyria fell into decline. In 625 B.C. Babylon regained independence under Nabopolassar (Nebuchadnezzar's father) who reigned at Babylon till 606 B.C. Also the kingdom of the Medes regained independence. Later the Medes and Babylonians made alliance and overthrew Nineveh about 608 B.C., which ended the Assyrian empire for ever (see further on this in our study of Nahum).

Now comes the *BABYLONIAN EMPIRE*. On the fall of Nineveh, the even more ancient city of Babylon laid her hands once more to the sceptre of the nations. Her new lead began in 606 B.C. with the young and brilliant Nebuchadnezzar; yet it only lasted until 536 B.C., thus exactly fulfilling Jeremiah xxix. 10. During the latter fifty years of this time the Jews were captives in Babylonia. Had the undermentioned kings who followed Nebuchadnezzar been as imposing as their names, perhaps the empire might have had better fortunes!

Nebuchadnezzar (606–562).
Evil-Merodach, or Amil-Marduk (562–559). 2 Kings xxv. 27.
Nergal-sharezer, or Neriglissar (559–55). Jer. xxxix. 3. 13.
Labashi-Marduk, or Laborisoarchod (555, 9 months)
Nabonidus, or Nabunahid (*whose viceroy was the "Belshazzar" of Daniel v.*) (553–36).

And now the *MEDIA-PERSIAN EMPIRE* succeeds Babylon. We have already mentioned how the kingdom of the Medes regained independence and made alliance with Babylon to overthrow Assyria. That alliance ended with the end of Nebuchadnezzar's reign. Two or three years later the Medes and the Persians became one empire, under Cyrus the Persian. The Medes and the Persians were akin to each other, and followed the same customs and religion. An insurrection dethroned the last *Median* king, in 559 B.C., and the taking of the throne thereupon by Cyrus transferred the supremacy to the Persians. Cyrus had a wonderful career of conquest. To quote the words of another—"In but twelve years, with his handful of Persians, he destroyed for ever three great empires—Media, Lydia, and Babylonia, conquered all Asia, and secured to his race for two centuries the dominion of the world." This is the Cyrus with whose edict for the restoration of the Jews to Judæa the Book of Ezra opens.

After conquering Babylon, Cyrus made a certain Gobryas viceroy there. This Gobryas is seemingly the "Darius" of the

Book of Daniel. Also, Cyrus reversed the policy of transportation which the Assyrians and Babylonians had practised since the time of Tiglath-Pileser, and permitted subject peoples to return to their own countries, and to restore their own religions and institutions. His idea was to attach them to his government by gratitude instead of fear. It was in keeping with this that the Jewish state was resuscitated in Judæa, though, of course, it still remained vassal to Persia.

The Persian empire lasted from 536 B.C. (first year of Cyrus) until 330 B.C., when it was overthrown by Alexander the Great, and gave place to the *Greek* empire. Here follow its kings, except for two or three minor usurpers in its later years. The names in brackets are the *personal* names or stigmas of these kings, as apart from their *throne* titles.

Cyrus the Great (536–29). Ezra i., etc.; Isa. xlv.
Cambyses (529–21). Ahasuerus of Ezra iv. 6.
Gaumata (pseudo-Smerdis) (7 mths). Artaxerxes of Ezra iv. 7.
Darius I (Hystaspis) (521–486). Re-allowed Temple: Ezra v., vi.
Xerxes I (485–64). Ahasuerus of Esther.
Artaxerxes I (Longimanus) (465–24). Ezra vii. 1; Neh. ii. 1; v. 14.
Xerxes II (424–24).
Darius II (Nothus) (424–04). Neh. xii. 22?
Artaxerxes II (Mnemon) (404–359).
Artaxerxes III (Ochus) (359–38).
Darius III (Codomanus) (336–30). Neh. xii. 22?

The Decree of Cyrus.

One cannot read such books as Ezra, Nehemiah, Esther, without being struck by the wonderful way in which God over-rules during times of trouble and crisis. Let us not miss the point that in Ezra i. 1 the "proclamation" of Cyrus which occasioned the return of the Remnant is directly attributed to Divine constraint—"The LORD stirred up the spirit of Cyrus, king of Persia, that he made a proclamation. . . ." Men and nations are free agents, and God permits them, within wide limits, to work out their own history, yet never so as to elude His own super-control. There are Divine intervenings, sometimes visible but more often invisible, which, without violating the free-will of man, ensure the fulfilment of the ultimate Divine purposes. In these later days of this present age it is well to keep this truth firmly in mind, that human freedom does not rule out Divine control. It has a steadying effect when evil and exciting developments seem to run on unchecked. High above God's *permissive* will is His *directive* will which can never know defeat.

The *wording* of Cyrus's proclamation is certainly remarkable: "Jehovah, the God of heaven, hath given me all the kingdoms of the earth; and He hath charged me to build Him an house at Jerusalem which is in Judah." How came this Persian emperor to have such knowledge of, and reverence for, and guidance from the God of Israel? Note particularly his later words in the proclamation: "Jehovah, God of Israel, He is *the* God." Modernist critics have felt that their only escape from the problem of the surprising wording here is to depreciate it as "a Judaizing paraphrase of the original." Once again they would insinuate that the Bible writers resort to distortions and misrepresentations. But the problem of these critics then becomes: If this edict of Cyrus was *not* as it is worded in the Scripture transcription of it, then *why* did Cyrus issue this proclamation of his favour to the Jews at all? There certainly was no *political* reason for it, for the Jews, unlike the Babylonians and certain other peoples conquered by Cyrus, were quite powerless either to help or to harm the new dominion.

The fact is that in some way or other *Cyrus had come under the influence of Jewish religious teaching*. The Jewish historian, Josephus, tells us how. He tells us that after Cyrus's conquest of Babylon, the new emperor was shown the remarkable prophecy of Isaiah xliv. 24—xlv. 6, written two hundred years earlier, in which Cyrus is actually named in advance as the destined restorer of the Jews and rebuilder of the temple. Josephus tells us that Cyrus, having seen the Isaiah prediction, was at once seized with "an earnest desire and ambition to fulfil what was so written." And there is much more which Josephus tells us about Cyrus and his edict, not all of which, perhaps, we need accept. But there can be absolutely no doubt about the *fact* of the edict or that the Bible transcription of it is literally *exact*; and this implies, of course, that Cyrus (as Josephus actually states) had come to recognise Jehovah as the supreme God. To say the least, it is understandable that the Isaiah prophecy would stir up a keen appetite in the mind of Cyrus to know more of Israel's inspired Scriptures.

How wonderful then, indeed, is the Divine overruling! Even that black calamity, the Babylonian exile of the Jews, is overruled to the conversion of Nebuchadnezzar, the Babylonian emperor, and of Cyrus, the Persian emperor; moreover it cured the covenant people of their idolatry once for all, and, by spreading the knowledge of the one true God throughout the nations of the ancient world, prepared for the coming of the Gospel of our Lord and Saviour, Jesus Christ.

What about those "ten tribes"?

If we read this Book of Ezra carefully we find ourselves again running counter to that fanciful theory according to which the so-called "lost ten tribes" are Britain and America. This is not a place where we can discuss the British Israel case separately; but there are certain features in the Book of Ezra which directly bear upon it, and which ought to be noted. The British Israel position is that the Jews are one tribe only (Judah), and that the other tribes are the British and American peoples. It is claimed that only the tribe of Judah returned to Palestine under the decree of Cyrus, and that the other tribes (ten apart from the Levite tribe) became "lost." The whole theory bristles with difficulties, but just to take one aspect alone, let us see what the Book of Ezra says about the composition of the Remnant.

First, in chapter i. 3, the edict of Cyrus is to *all* Israel. Let it be remembered that Assyria (which took the ten-tribe kingdom into captivity) had later become absorbed in the Babylonian empire, which in turn had now become part of Cyrus's dominion: so *all* the tribes were now in his domain. Understandably, the chiefs of Judah and Benjamin responded, seeing that it was to Jerusalem and Judah that the Remnant was to return; but with these were "*all* whose spirit God had stirred" (verse 5, R.V.).

Now see chapter ii. 2. In this verse we are given the leaders of the Remnant. Compare it with Nehemiah vii. 7. There were twelve leaders. Is anything more reasonable than to understand that these twelve were heads of the twelve tribes? If not, why twelve?

Next go to chapter ii. 70. Not only was Jerusalem reoccupied, but so were the other Judæan cities (see ii. 1); and so we now read that "*all* Israel" dwelt "in their cities." Can this mean less than that the return was participated in by all the tribes?

Pass on to chapter vi. 17. Is it without significance that at the dedication of the new temple the number of the he-goats offered for a sin-offering was twelve, and was for "all Israel"? And is it without significance that again in viii. 35 there are twelve bullocks and twelve he-goats offered for "all Israel"?

And in chapter viii. 29, what can be meant by "the princes of the fathers' houses of Israel" if the whole of the tribes were not represented? Nothing can be clearer than that the Return was participated in by all the tribes, even though, understandably, Judah and Benjamin took the lead. It was not, as the British Israel advocates say, simply a return of Judah-ites.

Moreover, these indications that the Remnant was composed from all the twelve tribes are strengthened by two important facts outside the Book of Ezra. The first of these is that before ever the ten tribes were carried away there had been large infiltrations from them into Judah (2 Chron. xi. 13–17; xv. 9; xxxiv. 6–9). The second is the fact that the names "Jew" and "Israelite" became synonymous during the Exile. Who can doubt this when the Book of Esther speaks of the "Jews" as scattered right through the one hundred and twenty-seven Persian provinces from India to Ethiopia (Esther i. 1; iii. 8, 12, 14)? The Book of Esther makes no distinguishment between Jew and Israelite; nor does our Lord Jesus, nor do the writers of the New Testament. Remember, it was only a small part, even in the case of the Judah tribe, who returned to Judæa. We have practically as much reason, therefore, to speak of the major part of Judah as "lost" as we have of the other tribes. When the apostle James, five and a half centuries later, writes to "the twelve tribes which are scattered abroad" (Jas. i. 1), he writes to a scattered people who were *all* known as "Jews"; and, similarly, those people who are known to us *today* as the Jews are the posterity of *all* the Israel tribes, not just of Judah.

Chapter iv. 4–24.

This passage presents a problem which it is well just to note. Through artful misrepresentation, adversaries cause a suspension in the rebuilding of the Temple. Verse 5 says they "hired counsellors" against the Jews, "to frustrate their purpose all the days of Cyrus, *even unto the reign of Darius*." This Darius came next-but-two after Cyrus. Glance back at our list of Persian kings. The frustration lasted from the second year of Cyrus (iii. 8) to the second year of Darius (iv. 24), about fourteen years.

The problem begins at verse 6: "And in the reign of *Ahasuerus*, in the beginning of his reign, wrote they unto him an accusation against the inhabitants of Judah and Jerusalem." Then verse 7 says: "And in the days of *Artaxerxes* wrote Bishlam," etc. It is these two names, Ahasuerus and Artaxerxes which make the problem. See our list of Persian kings again. The two thus named did not reign until *after* Darius in whose second year the rebuilding suspension was ended; and, therefore, if these are the two who are really meant in Ezra iv. 6, 7, then verses 6 to 23 are a long *parenthesis* telling of what happened thirty years later, and then again what happened another twenty years or more after that.

Not a few have adopted this parenthesis idea; but in our own view it is wrong and needless. It has really nothing in its favour but the sequence of the royal names, which in this case is of very doubtful weight, for Persian kings often had more than one name. Moreover, such a parenthesis here seems a quite foreign and pointless interruption. But what is clearly fatal to the idea is the nexus of verses 23 and 24. That last verse of the chapter says: "*Then* ceased the work of the house of God which is at Jerusalem. So it ceased unto the second year of the reign of Darius king of Persia." That "*then*" surely connects with what immediately precedes. We need have no headache, therefore, about the poser of those two royal names in verses 6 and 7. They are the Cambyses and Gautama who reigned between Cyrus and Darius, or else *both* names refer to Cambyses alone.

Who were the "Nethinims"?

Seventeen times in Ezra and Nehemiah we read of the *Nethinims*. They are mentioned only once elsewhere (1 Chron. ix. 2, which also refers to the post-Exile resettlement). Strictly, the "s" is not needed at the end of the word, for the ending "im" is itself the Hebrew plural. Who, then, were these Nethinim? The Hebrew word means "the given ones." Ezra viii. 20 calls them "the Nethinim whom David appointed for the service of the Levites." That seems a sufficient clue. In both Ezra and Nehemiah they are closely connected with another order—"the servants of Solomon," who seem to have been descendants of the Canaanites Solomon used in building his Temple (2 Chron. ii. 17), and whose duties were possibly even humbler than those of the Nethinim. Maybe the Nethinim were originally captive foreigners who had been given from time to time by the kings for the more menial work of the temple. Certainly, the personal names of some of them seem to indicate a non-Israelite diversity of origin. Only about the time of the Return does the name "Nethinim" seem to have definitely crystallised upon this class of helpers—presumably because their services then became so much the more needed. Nehemiah xi. 21 points to their having been organised into a sort of guild under their own leader. They are not mentioned in Scripture again. Probably, with other groups, they became gradually incorporated into the general body of Levites.

ADDENDA

THE "GREAT SYNAGOGUE"

According to Rabbinic tradition, a great council was convened some time after the return of the Jewish Remnant from Babylon, to reorganise the religious life of the people. Smith's smaller *Bible Dictionary* gives the following summary. "It consisted of 120 members, and these were known as the men of the Great Synagogue, the successors of the prophets, themselves, in their turn, succeeded by scribes prominent, individually, as teachers. Ezra was recognised as president. Their aim was to restore again the *crown*, or *glory* of Israel. To this end they collected all the sacred writings of former ages and their own, and so completed the canon of the O.T. They instituted the feast of Purim. They organised the ritual of the synagogue, and gave their sanction to the *Shemôneh Esrêh*, the eighteen solemn benedictions in it. Much of this is evidently uncertain. The absence of any historical mention of such a body, not only in the O.T. and the Apocrypha, but in Josephus, Philo, and the *Seder Olam*, so that the earliest record of it is found in the *Pirke Aboth*, circ. the second century after Christ, has led some critics to reject the whole statement as a Rabbinic invention."

It is true that many recent scholars have rejected this tradition; yet, as the late Dr. James Orr says, "It is difficult to believe that declarations so circumstantial and definite have no foundation at all in actual history." The excessive scepticism of certain modern schools in such matters is an intellectual *fashion*, rather than a product of scholarly cautiousness.

JEWISH MONTHS IN EZRA, NEHEMIAH AND ESTHER

In Ezra, Nehemiah, Esther, Jewish "months" are referred to thirty-five times. We ought to familiarise ourselves with the Jewish calendar. There were really *two* Jewish "years"—sacred and civil. Originally the new year began in the autumn (Exod. xxiii. 16), but from the Exodus the seventh month (Nisan) was made the first month (Exod. xii. 2). Josephus says: "Moses appointed that Nisan should be the first month of their festivals because he brought them out of Egypt in that month; so that this month began the year as to all solemnities they observed to the honour of God; although he preserved the original order of the months as to selling and buying and other ordinary affairs." Mostly in Scripture the months are those of the sacred year. The pre-exilic names of most of them have not come down to us; but they seem to have been based on the seasons, *Abib* meaning grain in the ear, and *Ziv* the beauty of spring flowers. The twelve months were lunar; and therefore every three years or so a thirteenth, intercalary month was added to readjust the year with the sun.

Month	*Sacred*	*Civil*	*English*
Abib or Nisan	1st.	7th.	Mar.–Apr.
Ziv or Ivar	2nd.	8th.	Apr.–May
Sivan	3rd.	9th.	May–June
Tammuz	4th.	10th.	June–July
Ab	5th.	11th.	July–Aug.
Elul	6th.	12th.	Aug.–Sept.
Ethanim or Tisri	7th.	1st.	Sept.–Oct.
Bul or Marchesvan	8th.	2nd.	Oct.–Nov.
Chisleu	9th.	3rd.	Nov.–Dec.
Tebeth	10th.	4th.	Dec.–Jan.
Shebat	11th.	5th.	Jan.–Feb.
Adar	12th.	6th.	Feb.–Mar.

THE BOOK OF EZRA (3)

Lesson Number 44

NOTE.—For this study read the book again, noting the course things took in chapters ii.–vi.

When people say that the doctrine of plenary or full inspiration of the Bible fails to do justice to the individuality of the Biblical writers, they simply show that they do not know what they are talking about, Yes, what a wonderful variety there is in the Bible. There is the rough simplicity of Mark, the unconscious yet splendid eloquence of Paul, the conscious literary art of the author of the Epistle to the Hebrews, the matchless beauty of the Old Testament narratives, the high poetry of the Prophets and the Psalms. How much we should lose, to be sure, if the Bible were written all in one style! We believers in the full inspiration of the Bible do not merely admit that. We *insist* upon it. The doctrine of plenary inspiration does not hold that all parts of the Bible are alike; it does not hold that they are all equally beautiful or even equally valuable; but it only holds that all parts of the Bible are equally true, and that each part has its place.

—*J. Gresham Machen.*

THE BOOK OF EZRA (3)

WE DID not intend our Ezra studies to run into a third instalment. It is an important tract of Scripture, however, marking a major turning-point, and well merits this further consideration. In this final study we review it exclusively from a spiritual point of view. It is replete with spiritual lessons of ever-fresh relevance; but we here limit ourselves to that *main* spiritual lesson which develops as the story of the book itself develops.

MAIN SPIRITUAL APPLICATIONS

The subject of the book, as we have seen, is the repatriation of the Jews, under the edict of Cyrus. It is the book of the *Restoration*. What we ought not to miss is that this historical restoration of the Jews strikingly exemplifies the laws and factors which operate in all true *spiritual* restoration.

First of all, the very *fact* of the Jewish restoration is spiritually eloquent. It speaks deep comfort concerning the restoration of Christian believers who become "bewitched" by this "present evil world," or ensnared by Satan's "devices," and fall into "backsliding." God had permitted great grief to engulf the covenant people, even to the extreme expedient of disintegrating the twelve tribes in the lands of heathen captors. Their being the covenant people did not immunise them from the penalty of sinning. Nay, their privilege increased their responsibility. Their apostasy and presumption were answered by unsparing chastisement. Yet even under the lash they were still Jehovah's people. The covenant still stood, and God did not go back on it. He had cast them out, but He did not cast them off; and He now made a way of return and restoration for all who would avail themselves of it.

And as this was true of Israel nationally, so it is true of God's people in Christ individually. We may wander from the place of blessing. We may lose our first love and grow spiritually cold. We may backslide into worldliness and become lured away by its deceptive glamour. God may allow heavy chastisement to reduce us to sore straits. He may allow evil powers to lead us captive in some degree. The grieved Spirit of God may withdraw all consciousness of His presence from us. Yet if we are truly the Lord's by a genuine conversion, if we are truly born of the Spirit and sprinkled with the covenant blood of Calvary, then God will never utterly cast us off or allow us finally to "fall from grace." However sadly we may have backslidden there is a way of return and restoration. God has made that truth plain in His Word; and the restoration of the Jews illustrates it. Indeed, in the case of the Jews, God not only opened up the way of return, but it was He who also "stirred" the hearts of those among His people who responded (i. 5). And even so does the Holy Spirit still minister in the hearts and consciences of backslidden believers. The very desire to return is His work within us, and an evidence of our election. Oh, the patience and tender grace of God toward us for Christ's sake! May we never ungratefully presume on it!

But to proceed; in the first half of this Book of Ezra (i.–vi.) there are *six steps* particularised in connection with the restoration of the Jews, and these six steps or stages correspond with the main factors in *spiritual* restoration.

1. *Back to the Land.*

The first step in Israel's restoration was *the return to the land* (i. 3). To the nation Israel, Canaan was in a special sense the place of blessing. It was their covenant inheritance, and their full enjoyment of the blessings of the Abrahamic covenant were associated with their occupation of it. Jehovah might preserve them distinct even amid dispersion, but there could be no fulfilment of the covenant promises and purposes while they were outside the land. So the first step in restoration was a return to the *place* of blessing.

And it is the same in the restoration of the *soul*. Is there, perchance, some reader of these lines who has lost the first joy, the early vision, the once-bright flame, through backsliding into the world? And is there a longing for restoration? Then let this be clearly grasped: the way of restoration is open, and the Lord waits to be gracious, but we must first get back to the *place* where He can bless us. That is, we must turn our backs on the Babylon of this world which has held us captive, we must forsake that which has occasioned our declension, and get back to the old ground of acceptance and blessing, namely, *God's promise in the Gospel.* What Canaan was, with all its material provisions, to the Israelite, the Gospel is, with all its spiritual provisions, to the Christian. The first thing for any distressed backslider is to get back to the clear word of God in the Gospel, and to stand *there.* That is the ground on which alone God deals with us in restoring grace. We must get back there, and take up the old position of repentance toward God, and faith toward our Lord Jesus, and obedience toward the written Word. We must get back there on the old basis, that salvation is by grace alone on God's part, and faith alone on our own part. Then, when we are *there*, we may possess the promise, and begin to rejoice in restoration.

But *which* promise? Well, take that very well-known promise in I John i. 9. We cannot here start expounding it; but a few minutes' reflection on it will show to any sorrowing backslider what a wonderful provision it is. Often have we seen restored backsliders weeping tears of joyous relief when once they have had faith to count on it. Until we get our mind fixed on some such word of God there is no relief; but when we firmly focus our mind on some precious promise of the Word, the Holy Spirit gets His opportunity to witness within us, on that basis, to the reality of our restoration.

2. *The Altar Rebuilt.*

The second thing with the Jewish Remnant was *the rebuilding of the altar* (iii. 1–6). It was built just where the former one had been. Doubtless, the altar here, as in many other places, typically anticipates the great altar of Calvary, as we ourselves, with our fuller light, can now see. But what did it mean to those returned Jews? Symbolically, that altar, with its various offerings, and especially with its freewill offerings, spoke of *consecration to God*; for the offerer symbolically offered up *himself* with his offering.

And that is precisely what we ourselves must do, if we would be restored from our backslidings. We must rebuild in our hearts the altar of dedication to Christ. There must be a complete yielding of our lives to Him. You will notice that with the re-erection of the altar in Jerusalem, the old-time worship was re-established, that is, the old *fellowship* was restored. So is it with ourselves when the altar is re-erected and we are yielded again to our true Lord.

3. *The new Temple commenced.*

Those returned Jews were under a commission, not only from Cyrus, but from God himself, to build up, on the old site, a new temple to Him (i. 2, 3). After the altar had been rebuilt and the true worship restored, work on the new Temple was commenced. This speaks of *service* and *witness*. It was indeed their special purpose and service to raise up this new house of witness to Jehovah among the surrounding nations—"an house of prayer for all people" (Isa. lvi. 7).

Even so are *we* to erect a *spiritual* house of praise and witness to the Lord, in our own lives, in each local Christian church, in each community, and throughout all nations. Yes, there must be a restored service and witness to Christ in our lives; and in truth there *will* be, if we are back on the ground of Gospel promise, with the altar of consecration rebuilt, and the old fellowship restored.

4. *"Adversaries" encountered.*

Sometimes those of the Lord's people who have been restored from backsliding are so overjoyed at their sense of renewed acceptance and communion with God, that they tend to imagine, as many new converts do, that they have now reached a place where their difficulties are all at an end. But they soon find otherwise—as did the Jewish Remnant long ago when they started the rebuilding of the Temple. In all human history there has never been a true work for God without there being opposition from the devil. The opposition usually begins in a subtle way; then, if subtlety fails, it develops into open hindrance, and employs all sorts of crooked counter-measures.

That is just what happened in long-ago Palestine. There were "adversaries" (iv. 1), and they sought to hinder the rebuilding of the temple in three ways: (1) by trying to deceive the Jews into an unreal union—"Let us build with you"; (2) by open hindrance—"they weakened the hands of the people of Judah"; (3) by misrepresentation—"they hired counsellors against them." The first of these was the most dangerous; but it did not succeed. Yet here is one of those seeming enigmas which occur in work for God, namely, that although the Remnant stood firm, the "adversaries" were allowed to gain a victory for some time. They got the work suspended, and then the Remnant grew disheartened. We must be prepared for "adversaries," for strange and disappointing setbacks, even when we are faithfully working for God. Our motto throughout must be, "No compromise"; and we must also forearm our minds against disappointments, for somehow, under the present system of things on earth, testings are a necessary element in spiritual progress.

5. Prophets raised up.

New voices are now heard among the Remnant, exhorting and encouraging them with a special word from God. The prophets Haggai and Zechariah appear. Their words are like a strong breath from the hills. Zerubbabel and his helpers feel that God is among them again of a truth, and they resume the building with renewed resolution.

This carries a step still further the remarkable parallel between the story of the Remnant and the spiritual experience of Christian believers today. Let it be keenly realised that the Hebrew prophets were men under the constraint of a most definite supernatural inspiration (see our opening study on the prophets). They were the living voice of God to the covenant people, and it is noticeable how God raised up such men in times of accentuated need. The Old Testament prophets, like the New Testament apostles, are now passed from us, not only as individuals but as an *order* which we no longer need. We now have the completed canon of the Divinely inspired Scriptures by which we are "throughly furnished" for all exigencies of Christian life and service. These Scriptures are the living and vitalising word of God to us, and they have a prophetic ministry to our hearts akin to that of Haggai and Zechariah in those bygone days. In all our work for God, and especially in time of opposition, discouragement, or apparent failure, we need to live close to the written Word. That is one of the vital secrets of perseverance and final achievement. God help us to learn it!

6. *The work completed.*

If a work is truly of God it cannot know final defeat. This is one of the inspirations of Christian service, and it finds illustration in the completed work of the long-ago temple rebuilders. On the third day of the month Adar, in the sixth year of Darius, "*this house was finished*" (verse 15). The dedication was an event of great joy (verses 16, 22). Thereupon the Feast of the Passover and of Unleavened Bread was held, which, as we saw in our Leviticus studies, speaks typically of salvation and fellowship. So then, despite opposition, in the end there is completion, victory, joy, fellowship. Faith and work triumph in the name of the Lord.

Yes, this is the sure outcome of work that is truly of God and done for Him in the obedience of faith. We need have no doubt. This sixth point in the parallel between those old-time temple rebuilders and the experience of the Lord's people today is true to fact. And thus we see in this six-fold development in the first half of the Book of Ezra a striking historical object-lesson depicting the laws and factors which operate, as we have said, in all true spiritual restoration and Christian service. Note the points of parallel once again—

1. Return to the land (i. and ii.)—back to right basis.
2. Altar re-erected (iii. 1–6)—dedication renewed.
3. New Temple begun (iii. 8–13)—service and witness.
4. "Adversaries" obstruct (iv.)—faith under testing.
5. Prophets exhort (v. 1–vi. 14)—need of God's word.
6. Temple finished (vi. 15–22)—faith wins through.

PART 2; EZRA (VII–X)

We have already spoken about the character of Ezra, and need not cover the second half of the book again which tells of him and his expedition. But here too we find rich spiritual values which we ought just to jot down in skeleton form even though we cannot give space to a fuller study of them. The four chapters which tell of Ezra and his mission mark a fourfold progress. In these chapters Ezra is a model of service and leadership.

1. EZRA'S PREPARATION FOR THE TASK (vii.).

True preparation: "Ezra had prepared his heart" (1) to "seek"; (2) to "do"; (3) to "teach."

2. EZRA'S PROSECUTION OF THE TASK (viii.).

True dependence on God. See verses 21-3. "To seek a right way." Also note Ezra's care of detail.

3. EZRA'S CONSTERNATION AT COMPROMISE (ix.).

See verses 2, 4, etc. "The holy seed have mingled." True resort: "I spread out my hands to the Lord."

4. EZRA'S RESTORATION OF SEPARATION (x.).

The true course of action—put the wrong right. See verses 6, 7, 10, "Make confession," "Separate."

THE GODWARD ASPECT

Up to this point we have been occupied with the *manward* aspect of the spiritual teachings in this Book of Ezra; but now let us gather up into a few paragraphs its main *Godward* significance. This is profound, yet full of rich comfort.

We go back to the first verse of the book—"Now in the first year of Cyrus, king of Persia, *that the word of Jehovah by the mouth of Jeremiah might be fulfilled . . .*" So the restoration of the Jews was in fulfilment of prophecy made seventy years earlier. This connects back to Jeremiah xxv. and xxix., from which take the following excerpts:

"And this whole land shall be a desolation and an astonishment; and these nations shall serve the king of Babylon seventy years. And it shall come to pass, when seventy years are accomplished, that I will punish the king of Babylon and that nation, saith Jehovah, for their iniquity, and the land of the Chaldeans, and will make it perpetual desolations" (xxv. 11–12).

*"After seventy years be accomplished for Babylon, I will visit
you and perform my good word toward you in causing you to
return to this place. For I know the thoughts that I think toward
you, saith Jehovah, thoughts of peace, and not of evil, to give
you hope . . . and I will bring you again unto the place whence
I caused you to be carried away captive"* (xxix. 10–14, R.V.).

These prophecies were uttered before Jerusalem fell, and
Jeremiah had a bad time of it for saying that the king of Babylon
would be successful. But just as the restoration of the Jews by
Cyrus must be read in the light of these prophecies, these
prophecies themselves must be read in the light of another great
pronouncement, in Jeremiah xviii. 1–6, concerning the *sovereignty*
of Jehovah.

*"The word which came to Jeremiah from the Lord, saying: Arise
and go down to the potter's house, and there I will cause thee
to hear My words. Then I went down to the potter's house, and
behold, he wrought a work on the wheels. And the vessel that he
made of clay was marred in the hand of the potter: so he made
it again another vessel, as seemed good to the potter to make it.
Then the word of Jehovah came to me, saying: O house of Israel,
cannot I do with you as this potter? Behold, as the clay is in the
potter's hand, so are ye in Mine hand, O house of Israel."*

Get the tremendous facts here. God is the potter. Israel is
the clay. History is the wheel. "The vessel was marred"—that
is the Israel story right from the Exodus to the Exile. "He made
it again another vessel"—that is the story in Ezra and Nehemiah.
The time had come when God was shaping a new vessel, though
out of the same clay.

"He made it again"—oh, lay hold of that! It is wonderful
—wonderful because it tells us that which is the ultimate thing
in the Divine sovereignty. The final fact is not that the vessel
was "marred," but that it was "made again." *That* is the ultimate
word in the Divine sovereignty. How it contrasts with the *human*
idea and practice of sovereignty! Man's idea and exercise of
sovereignty is that if you have had your chance, and have failed,
sovereignty treads you down and rejects you. The last word in
God's sovereignty is "He made it again."

What comfort there is in this—"He made it again"! Reflect, it is true about us as *individuals*. I am that marred vessel. I have failed to reach even my own ideal, let alone God's ideal for me. I have allowed this life of mine, which might have been a vessel of beauty, to become distorted, ugly, full of failure, "marred." The word of the Divine sovereignty is, "I will begin again." Does someone say, "Oh, it's too late now: I'm sixty. I cannot live my life again"? Well, if we were simply made for three score years and ten, that might be so; but "the grave is not our goal." There is a destiny of ages before us. The vital thing is to be willingly in God's hand. The dishonoured clay may be cleansed in the fountain of Calvary. The obstinate hardness may become pliableness through the renewing influence of the Pentecostal Spirit. If we are unreservedly in the master Potter's hand, he can make each of us a "vessel unto honour."

"He made it again"; this is also the final thing about *Israel*. Beginning with Abraham, God made a new vessel of the chosen *family*; but that vessel had to be broken in Egypt. Beginning again at Sinai, God made of the same clay another new vessel, the chosen *nation*; but that vessel had to be broken in the Assyrian and Babylonian exile. Beginning again at the Restoration under Zerubbabel and Ezra, God made of the same clay yet another new vessel, the returned *Remnant*; but that vessel had to be destroyed by the dispersal under the Romans in A.D. 70. The vessel is still broken: but the ultimate fact is that God will yet "make it again," and will fashion it into such a vessel of beauty and perfection as will occasion astonishment to men and glory to God. The Jew, who today is a vexation to all peoples, is to become the loveliest character on earth. The nation which today is crushed and broken beyond all others shall display the Divine ideal of nation-hood in unsullied moral integrity and material prosperity.

THE BOOK OF NEHEMIAH (1)

Lesson Number 45

NOTE.—For this study read through the Book of Nehemiah twice.

The Babylonian Exile sounded the death-knell of the Hebrew language. The educated classes were deported to Babylon or fled to Egypt, and those who remained were not slow to adopt the language used by their conquerors. The old Hebrew became a literary and sacred tongue, the language of everyday life being probably Aramaic. Whatever may be the exact meaning of Nehemiah viii. 8, it proves that the people of that time had extreme difficulty in understanding classical Hebrew when it was read to them. Yet for the purpose of religion, the old language continued to be employed for several centuries.

—*T. H. Weir, in "International Standard Bible Encyclopaedia."*

THE BOOK OF NEHEMIAH (1)

NEHEMIAH is a gem of a book in the spiritual lessons which it teaches us. It tells how, under the new leadership of Nehemiah, the walls of Jerusalem were rebuilt by the returned Remnant, and how the people themselves were reinstructed in the Law which God had given to their nation, long before, through Moses. This rebuilding of the city wall is like a graphic object-lesson illustrating those truths which lie at the heart of all true service for God; and he who will give heed to the lessons here vividly pictured will be a wise and successful builder in spiritual things.

Although in this course of study we are more or less self-restricted to the leading ideas and significances of each book of Scripture, and do not wish to cumber ourselves with technical or scholastic questions, we are almost bound to take certain of these into consideration here and there. We shall find this more so when we come to books like Job, Isaiah, Daniel, and Jonah. Meanwhile, with each book we ought to know something, at least, about authorship, date, and background.

Who Wrote It?

As for this Book of Nehemiah, our remarks concerning author-ship and date need only be few, for certain facts are patent even at a first reading. First, there can be no doubt that Nehemiah himself is the writer of the parts which are in the first person. These are chapters i. to vii., and xii. 27 to xiii. 31 where the book ends. Second, the intervening stretch (viii. 1–xii. 26) was probably incorporated by Nehemiah himself with his own record, even if, as scholars seem agreed, its style suggests a different author. Some suggest Ezra for this part. Third, the genealogical list of the returned Remnant, which closes chapter vii., is evidently derived from an official list drawn up earlier; while the list in chapter xii. was probably commenced by Nehemiah himself, and added to at a later date (for the name, Jadua, in verses 11 and 22 takes us down to the time of Alexander the Great). We may say, then, that Nehemiah is *certainly* the actual *composer* of much of the book, and probably the *compiler* of the whole (allowing for supplementary touches as in xii. 11, 12, 23).

When was it Written?

The *date* at which Nehemiah completed the work would be about 430 B.C., that is, following upon his return to Jerusalem after his temporary recall to Babylon (xiii. 6, 7). The royal edict authorising Nehemiah's *first* coming to Jerusalem was "in the month Nisan, in the twentieth year of Artaxerxes" (ii. 1). The late Sir Robert Anderson, in his book, *The Coming Prince*, has shown, with the corroboration of the British Astronomer Royal, that this date was the 14th March, 445 B.C. Nehemiah's *second* coming to Jerusalem after his brief visit to Babylon was "in the two and thirtieth year of Artaxerxes" (xiii. 6), and was therefore twelve or thirteen years later, which brings us to 432 B.C. Then, allowing for the activities recorded in the closing paragraphs of the book, we find ourselves definitely at the conclusion that the book could not have been completed *before* 432 B.C., and was probably written *soon after* that date, for the events are still poignantly fresh in the writer's mind (xiii. 22, 29).

What is the Background?

As we have seen, Nehemiah came to Jerusalem in 445 B.C. The restored Jewish "Remnant" had then been back in Judæa over ninety years. Zerubbabel and his contemporaries were now passed away, and another generation filled their place. What had happened during those ninety years? The new temple had been built, much inferior to the original, of course; but although the actual building had taken only four years five months and ten days (Hag. i. 15 with Ezra vi. 15), the Remnant had been back twenty-one years when it was completed! Some sixty years after this, Ezra had come from Babylon to Jerusalem with his company of between two and three thousand (Ezra vii. gives 2,000, but this is males only). Moral and spiritual conditions in Judæa then were far from satisfactory. Princes, rulers, priests, Levites and people alike had largely intermarried with the surrounding idolatrous peoples, and although not themselves worshipping idols were thus conniving at idolatry and allowing its infiltration, to the jeopardising of the rising generation. Unchecked, such a fusion of the Remnant with the outnumbering Gentiles then in Palestine would have meant complete absorption and obliteration of them as a distinct people, and we can well understand Ezra's consternation at discovering it (Ezra ix. 3–15). Maybe the laxity came about during the interval of governmental debility between the death of Zerubbabel and the advent of Ezra. The default, however, had been drastically corrected by Ezra, whose timely measure was accompanied by widespread penitence (Ezra x.).

And now, when Nehemiah came to Jerusalem, another twelve years after Ezra, circumstances were far from consoling. The walls and gates of Jerusalem were still in ruins, a discouragement to eye and heart; and the people were in much "reproach" (Neh. i. 3). There was dearth (v. 3). Some of the poorer were mortgaged to their own better-off fellow-Jews (verse 5). There had been laxity about Sabbath observance and other obligations, as the covenant in chapter x. indicates. Such is the background of the book.

Subject and Structure

Nehemiah's special objective was the rebuilding of *the city walls*. We have seen how the Book of *Ezra* is in two main parts. In the first part, under the leadership of Zerubbabel, we are concerned with the rebuilding of the *temple*. In the second part, under the leadership of Ezra, we are concerned with the restoring of the *worship*. Similarly, this Book of Nehemiah, which is a natural sequel to the Book of Ezra, is in two main parts. In the first part we are occupied with the reconstructing of the *walls* (i.–vi.). In the second part we are occupied with the reinstructing of the *people* (vii.–xiii.). Thus, in Ezra and Nehemiah we have the restoring of the temple, the worship, the walls, the people. We have seen that Ezra is distinctively the book of the *restoration*. Nehemiah is distinctively the book of *RECONSTRUCTION*. When we come to the epic of Esther, we shall find that Esther is distinguishingly the book of preservation. Thus in this trio of books at the end of the seventeen historical books of the Old Testament, we have—

EZRA	RESTORATION
NEHEMIAH	RECONSTRUCTION
ESTHER	PRESERVATION

THE BOOK OF NEHEMIAH

THE BOOK OF RECONSTRUCTION

THE RECONSTRUCTING OF THE WALL (i.–vi.)

NEHEMIAH'S INTERCESSION (i. 1–11).
NEHEMIAH'S EXPEDITION (ii. 1–16).
NEHEMIAH'S EXHORTATION (ii. 17–20).
THE REBUILDING ATTEMPTED (iii. 1–32).
THE REBUILDING OBSTRUCTED (iv.–vi. 14).
THE REBUILDING COMPLETED (vi. 15–19).

THE REINSTRUCTING OF THE PEOPLE (vii.–xiii.)

RE-REGISTRATION OF THE REMNANT (vii.).
RE-INCULCATION OF THE LAW (viii.).
RE-CONSECRATION OF THE PEOPLE (ix.–x.).
RE-POPULATION OF THE CITY (xi.).
RE-DEDICATION OF THE WALLS (xii.).
RE-EXTIRPATION OF ABUSES (xiii.).

This undetailed skeleton will amply serve our purpose here. It gives the scope and shape of the contents at a glance. The book, however, lends itself to further analysis, and some of the sub-sections are pointedly instructive when analysed and given a spiritual application, as we shall show.

Spiritual Message

As we watch this strong, earnest, godly hero, Nehemiah, resolutely leading the rebuilding in the first part of the book, then resolutely resisting compromise and laxity and intrigue in the second part of the book, we find the spiritual message of it all coming home to us with great force. Let us heed its voice to us. There is no winning without working and warring. There is no opportunity without opposition. There is no "open door" set before us without there being many "adversaries" to obstruct our entering it (1 Cor. xvi. 9). Whenever the saints say, "Let us arise and build," the enemy says, "Let us arise and oppose."

There is no triumph without trouble. There is no victory without vigilance. There is a cross in the way to every crown that is worth wearing.

Lessons and analogies are everywhere in this book. There are the walls of a city of God to be built in every individual human heart. There are the walls of a city of God to be built among the nations of the earth. Nehemiah exemplifies the vital principles which are involved in all such building, if it is to be successful building in the true sense. And we must add that Nehemiah himself is a really first-rank character-study. He stands out conspicuously as a man of *prayer*, a man of *faith*, a man of *courage*, a man of *action*. Look up the verses and incidents which indicate these qualities. They are an inspiration to read and reflect on. The late Rev. Samuel Chadwick, beloved by all sound Methodists, once used the following words, or words very like them, in a prayer at a service which he was conducting in Manchester: "O Lord, make us intensely spiritual, but keep us perfectly natural and thoroughly practical." As we recall that prayer we cannot but think how Nehemiah illustrates those three expressions—intensely spiritual, perfectly natural, thoroughly practical. Both Nehemiah and Samuel Chadwick eminently fulfilled the terms of that prayer, and both were singularly owned of God as spiritual builders and soldiers. May God raise up a numerous succession to them among the needy churches of our day!

THE MAN AND THE STORY

In this Book of Nehemiah, the man and the story are inseparably wedded to each other. How different a story the rebuilding of Jerusalem might have been if that huge burden and *hazard* had fallen to a man of different calibre from Nehemiah! If ever a crisis-hour was matched by a man, it was so in that city-rebuilding episode.

Yet it is not only the man who makes the story. It is almost equally true that the story makes the man. The perils and problems of the undertaking bring out all that is finest in the man. How often that happens! How much we owe to the difficulties and setbacks, the obstructions and oppositions, which have been permitted to try us! The things which we have thought were breaking us were in reality *making* us—as we now see in retrospect.

So then, let us follow this man from the beginning of his story to the time when the walls of Jerusalem were rebuilt. In the little book which bears his name we see Nehemiah in three capacities—(1) the cupbearer; (2) the wall-builder; (3) the governor.

Nehemiah the Cupbearer (i. 1–ii. 10)

Nehemiah was "the son of Hachaliah" (i. 1), and apparently of the tribe of Judah (ii. 3). Evidently he was reared in exile, and in early manhood became attached to the Persian court, where he rose to the lucrative position of royal cupbearer before Artaxerxes Longimanus and queen Damaspia, in the royal residence at Shushan. *I was the king's cupbearer,*" he says of himself (i. 11). To us western and modern readers, that may sound a rather unimportant position, not unlike that of a butler among our aristocracy; but we are wrong in so thinking. To quote Dr. Angus, it was "an office which was one of the most honourable and confidential at the court"; and to quote Dr. W. M. Taylor, it was an office "referred to by ancient writers as one of great influence." We know the great influence which Pharaoh's butler had on behalf of Joseph; and we see what high rank the foul-tongued "Rab-shakeh" (or chief cupbearer) had in the empire of Assyria (2 Kings xviii.).

One day, while Nehemiah was in attendance at the royal court, his brother, Hanani, and a group of Jews, brought him such a pitiful report concerning the condition of Jerusalem and the restored Jewish community in Judæa that he was quite overcome with grief. He learned that his countrymen away in the homeland were in dire straits because, among other things, the city walls were still in ruins, and the gates remained just as they had been burned and broken by the Babylonians a hundred and forty years earlier. Walls and gates mean nothing to cities nowadays, but long ago, in the east, they meant almost everything. Those torn-down walls and gates left the inhabitants always open to attack and plunder by vicious neighbours; and it is quite probable that Hanani's report to Nehemiah was made the more poignant by the fact that the citizens of Jerusalem had at that very time been suffering in this way from the deceitful and treacherous peoples who surrounded them.

Nehemiah, stricken with grief, thereupon gave himself to fasting and mourning and prayer (i. 2–11). During this process the

conviction ripened in him that he himself should undertake the huge
task of the rebuilding; but he was not his own master; and however difficult it might be to get *into* the Persian palace, when one
did secure a position there it was even more difficult to get *out*.
Nehemiah's grief and fasting, however, had so altered his appearance in four months that Artaxerxes asked what was wrong.
The emperor's words seem to indicate that he had become really
attached to his servant. None the less, as Dr. Kitto remarks,
Nehemiah had reason enough to be *"very sore afraid"* (ii. 2),
for it was considered a capital offence to appear sad in the royal
presence (see also Esther iv. 2). Nehemiah answers with humble
courtesy, not daring even now to make any request, but earnestly
praying God to overrule; and the upshot is that Nehemiah is
most generously commissioned to undertake the project which
lies on his heart. Thus closes the first scene—Nehemiah the cupbearer.

Note: *real godliness is not incompatible with earthly success.*
Indeed it often happens that godliness is a first factor in pro-
moting and furthering such success. One gets sick of hearing that
to be a real Christian is impossible in the business world of today,
and that to apply godly principles in modern commercial tran-
sactions is to invite bankruptcy. We could give many examples
to the contrary. Certainly there is a price to pay, and there may
be losses to incur; but observation convinces us that true Christian
character and principle, allied to normal business ability, definitely
contribute to success. If Nehemiah could keep his conscience
unseared amid the cabals of that Persian court, so may we ourselves blend uprightness with success in modern business. Such
present-day Nehemiahs are the salt of the commercial world.
Better lose our job than sell our conscience! But in nine cases out
of ten, keeping a good conscience will help us toward material
as well as spiritual success, and will keep us steady when success
actually comes.

THE BOOK OF NEHEMIAH (2)

Lesson Number 46

NOTE.—For this study read through chapters ii. to vi. again, marking those verses which reveal the special virtues or traits of Nehemiah's character.

Further Note.—For the benefit of any reader who may be interested in a fuller exposition and application of the spiritual lessons contained in Nehemiah's rebuilding of Jerusalem, we would add that the contents of the following study will be found, in considerably expanded form, in the last chapter of the author's book, *Mark These Men.*

—*J. S. B.*

It is not the arithmetic of our prayers, how many they are; nor the rhetoric of our prayers, how eloquent they are; nor the geometry of our prayers, how long they be; nor the music of our prayers, how sweet our voice may be; nor the logic of our prayers, how argumentative they may be; nor the method of our prayers, how orderly they may be—which God cares for. Fervency of spirit is that which availeth much.

—*William Law.*

THE BOOK OF NEHEMIAH (2)

THE MAN AND THE STORY—*continued*

Nehemiah the Wall-builder (ii. 11–vi. 19)

ARMED with royal authority, thrilled with a sense of Jehovah's overruling graciousness, and yet solemnised by keen appreciation of the hazards involved in his undertaking, Nehemiah sets off for Jerusalem, accompanied by an escort of Persian soldiers, and completes the journey in about three months. On his way he has to pass through the provinces of certain Persian satraps and governors. To those "beyond the river" (i.e., the Euphrates) he carries letters (ii. 7, 8) which he duly delivers (verse 9). Among such governors was a certain Sanballat, who, according to Josephus, was "satrap of Samaria." Also there was a certain "Tobiah the servant," who was either another petty governor or, more probably, a kind of secretary to Sanballat. These two, we are told, were greatly annoyed "that there was come a man to seek the welfare of the children of Israel" (verse 10). With these two, Nehemiah is now about to have much trouble.

Nehemiah safely reaches Jerusalem, and, after an interval of three days, makes a secret survey of the ruins by night, so as to escape observation by hostile spies from Samaria. Nor does he divulge his mission even to the leaders at Jerusalem until he has made plans to ensure that the whole work shall be started and finished within a few weeks (ii. 12–18).

His plan, so it turns out (for the account clearly implies it), was to *sectionise* the rebuilding among different work-parties, all acting simultaneously, and each responsible for its own section of the wall (iii.). The plan so succeeded that in spite of opposition the wall was completely rebuilt in just over seven weeks (vi. 15), after which solid folding-doors were placed at the gateways (vii. 1), guards were appointed, and regulations imposed concerning the closing of the gates at nightfall and their reopening in the morning (vii. 3). Thus Nehemiah's main objective was achieved —all within six months of his mandate from Artaxerxes!

See here also *the blending of practical organising with intense spiritual-mindedness.* The task is sectionised and systematically prosecuted. Nehemiah set each of the forty-two different work-groups to work on that part of the walls which was nearest to where its members themselves lived (iii. 10, 23, 29, 30). This gave them a special interest in the work. Our first obligation for Christ is always our own neighbourhood.

We find this blending of the practical with the spiritual all the way through the story of Nehemiah. In chapter iv. 9, for instance, we read: "We made our *prayer* unto God, and set a *watch* against them (the adversaries) day and night." Nehemiah never let presumption displace precaution. Organised Christianity is *over*-organised today, and we complicate our own progress by too elaborate machinery. Yet the real trouble is not so much the machinery itself as that the vital driving-force behind it all has largely failed. Organising has crowded out agonising. There is too much working before men and too little waiting before God. There is more and more motion, but less and less unction. It is the Nehemiahs whom God uses—the men and women who *blend* the practical and the spiritual.

Again and again, as we watch Nehemiah, we are reminded of Cromwell's famous words, "Trust in God, and keep your powder dry." Speaking generally of today, there is a brilliant but frustrating over-emphasis on the human, the energetic, in religious service. More than ever before we wrestle with social problems in committees and conferences, but less than ever do we wrestle on our knees against evil spirit-powers which lie behind the social evils of our day. Nearly everybody in committee has a fine programme, but few indeed seem to have a real spiritual burden. The practical has overridden the spiritual; and when that happens, the practical becomes utterly *un*practical.

But perhaps the most telling lessons of all in this story of Nehemiah occur in connection with the *obstructions and setbacks* which Nehemiah had to overcome in those months of rebuilding. There were three forms of opposition from *without*—scorn (iv. 1–6), force (iv. 7–23), craft (vi. 1–19). And there were three forms of hindrance from *within*—debris (iv. 10), fear (iv. 11–14), greed (v. 1–13). Each is a lesson, a study in itself, strikingly corresponding with what we are up against today in a spiritual sense.

OPPOSITION FROM WITHOUT

Scorn (iv. 1–6).

Take the opposition which Nehemiah encountered from outside. First it took the form of *scorn*. See chapter iv. 1–3.

Never was there more derisive sarcasm than in Sanballat's question—"What do these feeble Jews?" And that is exactly the first reaction of the worldly-wise today towards the spiritually-minded minority scattered through the churches. "What do these feeble folk?" they ask contemptuously. What are a few little prayer meetings compared with a European Pact or a revolutionary change-over to a Socialist Government or a United Conference of Nations? What is this paltry idea about converting people one by one compared with scientific, legislative, educational, economic and sociological programmes which can affect millions at a sweep?

Well, how did Nehemiah meet the scorn of Sanballat and Tobiah? Verses 4, 5 and 6 in that same fourth chapter tell us. He just kept on praying and kept on building. "Hear, O our God," he says; "for we are despised." And after his prayer he adds, "So built we the wall . . . for the people had a mind to work." That is the way to meet scorn—not by counter-scorn! The scorn of Sanballat and Tobiah soon began to look stupid as the walls of Jerusalem rose higher and higher. Always our best answer to the world's scorn is to keep on praying to God for Pentecostal blessing, and keep on striving to win souls for Christ. God always honours such earnest prayer and effort. It is always a big victory for the devil if he can laugh us out of some worthy work for Christ, and I fear he manages this far too often. We do well to learn a lesson from Nehemiah!

Force (vi. 7–23).

But look again at this opposition which Nehemiah encountered from outside. When taunts and sneers failed it took a more menacing form. Scorn gave place to *force*. Taunts became threats, and sneers became plots. Such enemies as Sanballat and Tobiah were not the sort to be content with venting their spleen in idle mockery. Their keenest shafts of sarcasm were lost on a devout soul like Nehemiah. So scorn now gives place to force. Read again in that fourth chapter, from verse 7 onwards.

Things certainly looked pretty serious. The opposition had now developed into a formidable alliance—Sanballat, Tobiah, Arabians, Ammonites, Ashdodites! It is remarkable (or is it?) how again and again mutual enemies will become mutual friends to make common cause against the people of God. Pilate and Herod patched up their quarrel and became "friends" in their joint condemnation and abuse of Jesus (Luke xxiii. 12). Romanism and paganism have joined hands before today against the true Protestant faith. Communist Russia and Nazi Germany once shook hands in common purpose against Christianity!

We must not be surprised even today if the Lord's enemies resort to force. And if this happens what are we to do? Well, what did Nehemiah and his company do? They did as before— kept on praying and kept on working; only now they had to join *watching* with praying, and *warring* with working. See verses 9 and 17.

"We made our prayer unto God, and set a watch against them,
    day and night" (verse 9).
"Every one with one of his hands wrought in the work, and with
    the other hand held a weapon" (verse 17).

Was not prayer alone enough, then? Why this setting of a watch and this arming with weapons if they trusted the Lord? It was because Nehemiah was not the fanatic to blunder into the delusion that faith is presumption.

Praying, watching, working, warring! How all this speaks to us today! We are not suggesting for a moment that when physical force is used against Christians they should resort to physical weapons, as Nehemiah was obliged to do; but there is a spiritual application. There is a proper place for resisting and attacking and exposing error, deception, falsehood, and sin, on the part of those who oppose the truth as it is in Christ Jesus. Nor must we shrink from such warring, whatever the risk or cost.

Craft (vi. 1–19).

But there was yet another kind of opposition from exterior foes which Nehemiah had to encounter. When scorn and force had failed, Sanballat and Tobiah and their confederates resorted to *craft*. This took four turns. First they tried *pretence* (vi. 1–4). "Come, let us meet together in one of the villages in the plain of Ono." This was an enticement to a pretendedly friendly conference on neutral ground, presumably with the suggestion that an alliance should now be made between Nehemiah and themselves. But Nehemiah saw through their hypocrisy (verse 2), and each time they repeated their request he repeated his reply—"I am doing a great work; I cannot come down" (verse 3). This is ever the one safe answer to such pretence—uncompromising separation.

Next they tried *bluff* (verses 5–9). They said that a charge was being lodged with the emperor against Nehemiah and the Jews, to the effect that they were planning rebellion, and that Nehemiah's only answer to this was to "take counsel with themselves." Nehemiah's reply is frank denial, renewed prayer, and a continued separation.

Next, and worst of all, they managed to intrigue some of Nehemiah's own kinsmen, and thus employed *treachery* against him (verses 10–14). Even some of the prophets were bribed. Nehemiah, however, refused to do the cowardly or shady thing even on the advice of a prophet. The perfidy of these Judases among his own followers was a cutting sorrow to Nehemiah, but he overcame by his courageous honesty and by prayer (verses 11, 14).

It seems an awful thing to say, yet it is true, that there are betrayers like Shemaiah and Noadiah (verses 10–14) in most Christian congregations today—men and women who have professed conversion to Christ, who share in the fellowship and labours of the saints, who nevertheless seem to find a cruel pleasure in the fall of a Christian leader. To his face they are friendly, fussy, saintly, but behind his back they are mischief-makers. They profess loyalty and concern, yet if he slips or falls they love to gossip it among the brethren or talk it round the town. Oh, what heart-pangs such disloyal brethren give to Christian ministers, pastors, superintendents, and leaders! They are Tobiahs, Quislings, Satan's fifth-columnists. All that the Christian leader can do in his dealings with them is just to keep on building for God through "evil report and good report" (2 Cor. vi. 8), courageously refusing all shady expedients, and continually casting himself on God by prayer.

But Nehemiah's enemies did not cease their crafty activities even when this special bit of treachery had failed. They sought continually to unnerve and discourage Nehemiah through *cliques of compromised brethren* (verses 17–19). The artful Tobiah had become son-in-law to a leader in Israel with a large following. Then his son had taken a Jewish girl to wife; so that Tobiah was now both a son-in-law and an uncle to Israelite people; and there had grown up a clique in Jerusalem who let social and family ties with Tobiah override moral and spiritual duty. Oh, how compromise complicates things!

It must have been a sore problem to Nehemiah, to find that many of the leading men in Judah were hobnobbing by post with Tobiah, and that many, indeed, were "sworn unto him" because both he and his son had married into Israel.

And does not the same sort of thing curse Christian congregations today? How often it ties the hands and paralyses the lips and breaks the hearts of earnest Gospel ministers! Many a man in the ministry gives way, bit by bit, for reasonable comfort's sake; but he ceases to be a real Nehemiah. It is not easy to maintain the Nehemiah position; yet in the end it is the only one which wears the crown of Divine approbation and true success.

HINDRANCES FROM WITHIN

We have seen something of the opposition which came to Nehemiah from outside Jerusalem, but now look at the hindrances which he encountered from the *inside*. They were threefold—debris (iv. 10), fear (iv. 11–14), greed (v. 1–13).

Debris (iv. 10).

First, there was the problem of *debris*. "And Judah said: The strength of the bearers of burdens is decayed, and there is much rubbish, so that we are not able to build the wall." We can easily understand such discouragement. At the very beginning of the rebuilding Sanballat had sarcastically referred to the huge "heaps of the rubbish." It must have seemed a heart-breaking as well as a back-breaking job to get without all this before each part of the wall could be reconstructed; and now there had needed to be a reduction of workmen, owing to the appointing of a guard against attack from outside (verse 9), so that the remaining labourers removing the rubbish seemed near to exhaustion.

This has a pathetic counterpart in much Christian work today. There is many a devout servant of the Lord who cannot get on with the wall God has given him to build, because of the hindrance through "much rubbish." Oh, the "rubbish" in many of our churches today! I recently received a letter from a minister in the south of England asking advice whether to leave or stay on at a certain church. It is impossible, he says, to make any spiritual headway because of "much rubbish." The preceding ministers were Modernists. They have deposited all sorts of doubts and disbeliefs in the people's minds about the Bible, so that now his own references to the Scriptures are largely discredited and his messages thwarted.

But that is not the only sort of "rubbish." In a letter from another minister in England I read: "The people here have no ear for any spiritual challenge. They resent it. For years the place has been run on whist drives, social evenings including dancing, and so on." Yes, there is much rubbish!

Fear (iv. 11–14).

But there was another discouragement from within, namely, *fear*. Jews from outlying districts brought repeated warning that a surprise attack was being planned by Nehemiah's enemies (verses 11, 12). This spread fear among the workers. Nothing is more paralysing than fear; and how it often paralyses evangelical work today! It arises mainly from looking at circumstances and consequences instead of looking to God. Nehemiah's men were scared by the numerical superiority of Sanballat's forces. There is a parallel today. Never did the foes of evangelical Christianity seem bigger and deadlier than now. In Soviet Russia and Hitlerite Germany we have seen the State itself solidly against it—with Siberian exile or Nazi concentration camps as the penalty for faithfulness to Christ. Is it surprising that fear should have blanched many a cheek and stifled many a testimony?

It is instructive to see how Nehemiah turned the tables on this fear which had beset his men. First, they were to *look to*

God instead of at circumstances. "Remember the Lord, great and terrible!" cries Nehemiah (verse 14).

Second, they were to *reflect* on the issues. "Fight for your brethren, your sons and your daughters, your wives and your houses" (verse 14). Everything was at stake! No mercy could be expected from their spiteful foe.

Third, they were to be *armed in readiness* (verses 16–23). Henceforth they were to hold a tool in one hand and a weapon in the other. What wisdom there was in this union of sword and trowel! Even the nuisance diversion of anti-invasion preparation must not stop the building of the wall, for in the long run that rebuilt wall would itself be the supreme defence. Even battling must not exclude building!

How these three things come home to ourselves today! We must *"remember the Lord."* There is no antidote to fear like a vivid God-consciousness.

Second, we must *keep the issues in mind.* If the distinctive doctrines of the evangelical faith are really true concerning the Bible and the person of Christ and the shed blood of Calvary and the message of the Gospel, then the distinctive doctrines of the Modernists and the Romanists are wrong. And the issues are measurelessly graver than were those in the Nehemiah episode. Souls are at stake! Eternal destinies hang in the balance!

And third, we must not forget our need of being *armed to fight.* Our weapons are: (1) the Bible, which is "the sword of the Spirit"; (2) prayer, which can avail to thwart error just as much as to save souls; (3) the continually-renewed infilling of the Holy Spirit.

Greed (v. 1–13).

Alas, there was a third hindrance from within, a plague of *greed.* This came nearer to wrecking Nehemiah's project than all the stratagems of Sanballat and Tobiah, for it threatened internecine strife among Nehemiah's own men. The circumstances were most disturbing. Many of the people, in order to raise money with which to buy corn (verse 3) or to pay tribute (verse 4), had been obliged to mortgage land holdings, and in some cases even to pledge their sons and daughters; and the richer

Jews, instead of sinking private interests in the critical public need, had selfishly exploited it until a point was reached where there was an outcry.

If Satan cannot ruin a work for Christ today by "much rubbish" or by "fear" of one sort or another, he will try to do so through self-seeking and other wrong motives between Christian and Christian. He will seize on every possible circumstance to provoke this; and his heart-rending success is known in earth and heaven! How disheartened Nehemiah must have been! And how disheartened many a godly minister is today when he finds that even among his keenest and ablest workers there are wrong motives and feelings which thwart blessing and frustrate revival despite all the praying and working.

See now how Nehemiah dealt with this trouble. First, he challenged the offenders by prompt, even drastic action (verse 7). Second, he appealed to them by his own example (verses 8–11). Third, the offending party admitted their blame and made restitution (verses 12, 13). Oh, what a good thing is promptness, frankness, boldness, in such matters! Nehemiah is a robust example to all leaders in Christian work.

The trouble in Nehemiah's day was put right because the offenders, being frankly charged with wrong, admitted their blameworthiness, and repented, and put the wrong right. No wonder that "all the congregation said, Amen, and praised the Lord" (verse 13)! Would that ills and grudges and animosities among Christian groups today might be as fearlessly and faithfully dealt with. It would bring spiritual revival much nearer.

Thus the setback through greed, like the other troubles, was overcome, and the building of the wall went on. Look back, once more, over the difficulties which brave Nehemiah encountered and surmounted—from *without* scorn (iv. 1–6), force (iv. 7–23), craft (vi. 1–19); from *within*, debris (iv. 10), fear (iv. 11–14), greed (v. 1–13). In each case the difficulty becomes more acute and deadly, but in each case the victory becomes more telling, until, stone by stone, and day by day, despite all opposition from without and all hindrance from within, *the wall is completed!*

These, then, are some of the lessons which come home to us from Nehemiah's rebuilding of that city wall. May we read, mark, learn, and act accordingly! The days in which we live have an intensity and complexity such as eclipses that of all former times. The need is vast. The issues are tremendous. The time is short. The wall must be built, even "in troublous times." God help us to keep at it, warring and working, watching and waiting, battling and building! Let us mark this man, Nehemiah, the man who rebuilt Jerusalem, and keep him in mind as we work for God today under difficult conditions. He will be an inspiration to us. God is building with us; and at last we too shall certainly see the walls of God's "New Jerusalem" completely built up on the earth, and "the nations shall walk in the light of it."

> We are builders of a city
> In the minds and lives of men,
> And we work with love and pity,
> Using voice and deed and pen;
> It shall certainly be finished,
> Tho' as yet we know not when,
> This fair city of true worship
> To the one true God again.
>
> And this city, we must build it
> In the nation's social life,
> For if but the many willed it,
> It would end our social strife.
> And this city we are building
> Must encompass every land,
> Tho' it has no outward gilding,
> Yet the wise ones understand.
>
> Though Sanballats and Tobiahs
> In their thousands may oppose,
> God has still His Nehemiahs
> Who at last repulse all foes;
> Oft resisted, ne'er defeated,
> With our trowels on we plod,
> Till that city is completed
> By the reigning Christ of God!

THE BOOK OF NEHEMIAH (3)

Lesson Number 47

NOTE.—For this final study in Nehemiah read chapters vii. to xiii. again, picking out those verses which reveal the special virtues of Nehemiah's character.

The Theory of Evolution has dominated the critical mind in complete disregard of historical facts. Whatever may be said for the evolution of the material universe, there is little that can be said for the evolution of Man, as a dogma. Thus history teaches us that while civilization is progressive it is also retrogressive. When its moral and spiritual factors decline, civilization destroys itself. But the evolution conception, being based upon the idea of steady consistent progress, from barbarism to the present day, underestimated the knowledge and culture of Old Testament times, and postulated something far too primitive. Thus, for example, the Israelites should have been illiterate; but it will now be seen (i.e. in the evidence of recent archaeological findings) that they possessed facilities for literary expression, from the days of Moses onwards, that were actually superior to those of their contemporaries.

Sir Charles Marston.

THE BOOK OF NEHEMIAH (3)

Nehemiah the Governor (vii.—xiii.)

FINALLY, in our rapid review of this man and his story, we see Nehemiah as the *governor*, that is, as governor of the rebuilt Jerusalem and the province of Judæa, under the Persians. We see him in this capacity in the second half of the book, chapters vii. to xiii.

Many a man who is a genius in ruling a crisis is a failure in the follow-up process. Not so Nehemiah, as these chapters show. There is much here to catch the eye and hold the mind, but our comments must be limited simply to pointing out the main lines and lessons.

There is a downrightness and forthrightness about Nehemiah which strikes us throughout the story, and which now comes out most of all in these later chapters telling of his governorship. Whether we approve or not his *method* of handling this or that irregularity, his *motive* is always clear as noon and sound as a bell. There is not a fleck of camouflage anywhere in his character or conduct. Mark his four outstanding qualities here—

1. Clear-seeing.
2. Plain-speaking.
3. Firm-dealing.
4. God-honouring.

And now let us just glance through the chapters.

Security precautions (vii. 1–3).

First, in chapter vii. 1–3, we see Nehemiah making the necessary regulations for the security of what had now become a first-class fortress. His assigning the guarding of the gates to Levites (verse 1) may seem strange, but we need to remember that just then the priests formed nearly half the scanty population (compare xi. with 1 Chron. ix. 10–19). Then he appoints two

municipal officers to have general charge over all such matters
—his own brother, Hanani, and a certain Hananiah who was
already "commandant of the fort" or temple tower (verse 2,
see R.V.).

Population problem (vii. 4–73 with xi.).

Next Nehemiah tackles the problem of the too scant population
(verse 4), and decides on a census as a first step (verse 5). In this
connection he looks up the genealogy of "them which came up
at the first" (i.e. ninety years earlier with Zerubbabel); and the
rest of this seventh chapter reproduces that register (which we
have seen before, in Ezra ii.).

The lack of population is rectified by the casting of lots, to
bring one in every ten from the Judæan population *outside*
Jerusalem to live *inside* the now rebuilt capital (see xi., which
connects back to this seventh chapter).

Note in verse 5, that the keeping of these careful birth-registers
in Israel was *according to the mind of God*. It was important to
determine who were the true seed of Israel, especially so as
Israel looked for the coming of One who should give an imperishable glory to her genealogies, even David's greater Son who
should spring from this very line of Zerubbabel and finally "turn
again the captivity" of Judah; the supreme Zerubbabel, who
should consummatingly restore the temple; the supreme Ezra,
who should write the Law in the very hearts of the chosen people;
the supreme Nehemiah, who should build up the walls of Zion
for ever (Isa. liv. 11, 12; Zech. vi. 12, 13; Jer. xxxi. 33; Ps. xlviii.
12, 13; Isa. lx.).

"Back to the Bible" movement (viii.–x.).

Chapter viii. should really begin with the last clause of chapter
vii., thus: "And when the seventh month came (i.e. the specially
sacred month), the children of Israel were in their cities; and all
the people gathered themselves together as one man into the
street that was before the water gate; and they spake unto Ezra
the scribe to bring the book of the law of Moses, which the Lord
had commanded to Israel."

Then follows the remarkable account in chapters viii., ix., and x., of what we should call today a great "back to the Bible" movement. There was held a most remarkable religious convention. The people themselves ask for the Scriptures to be expounded to them (viii. 1). Ezra and his helpers explain afresh the Law. The observance of the Feast of Tabernacles is revived. A great day of humiliation is observed in which the people confess their sad failures and acknowledge the wonderful mercy of their long-suffering God (ix.). Then they enter into a self-imposed covenant, with deep moral purpose to order their ways in future according to the revealed will of God in the Scriptures (x.).

The new census (xi.).

Chapter xi. gives the main results of the new census taken by Nehemiah. Verses 3 to 19 tell us of the dwellers at Jerusalem. Verses 20 to 36 tell us of the "residue" in the other Judæan cities. Note in verse 2 that "the people blessed all the men that willingly offered themselves to dwell at Jerusalem." These were the men, one in every ten, on whom the "lot" fell that they should come and dwell in the capital. The words indicate that they accepted the fall of the "lot" gladly, and patriotically submitted, even though apparently no compensation was made to them. It is not surprising that the people applauded them, for the transfer would mean, in many cases, the quitting of possessions, exchange of riches for poverty, leaving a comfortable house for one half in ruins, giving up the life of a small, landed proprietor for that of an artisan or hired labourer. (We may mention, incidentally, that forced enlargements of capital by transfers of this kind were not uncommon in the ancient world, where the strength of states was considered to depend greatly on the size and predominance of the capital.) The city census in this eleventh chapter is that of the now *augmented* population.

The dedication of the walls (xii. 27–47).

So far the chapters have been quite straightforward reading, and detailed comment has scarcely been needed; but an explanatory word is certainly called for when we come to the passage narrating the dedication of the walls. To the unwary reader it

would seem as though this passage (xii. 27–47) follows immediately and without any interruption upon what goes before,
whereas the fact is that there is *a break of some twelve years*
between the end of chapter xi. and this dedication of the walls.

There are three circumstances which indicate this. First, if
the *dedication* of the walls had taken place immediately after the
rebuilding it is unlikely that the narrator would have separated
the two events by five and a half chapters. Second, between the
end of chapter xi. and xii. 27 there is inserted (presumably by
another hand than Nehemiah's) a descent of the *high priests*
right from Jeshua (ninety years *before* Nehemiah) down to
Jaddua (about ninety years *after* Nehemiah), so that there is
definitely a break here in the narrative.

But third, Nehemiah himself gives us certain time-marks which
conclusively settle it. In chapter xiii. 6 he says that when Eliashib
the priest treacherously gave Tobiah an apartment in the Temple
courts, he himself (Nehemiah) was "*not* at Jerusalem," but away
on recall to the Persian emperor. Now Eliashib's treachery
during Nehemiah's absence is introduced by the words, "And
before this . . ." (xiii. 4), which means that it was before the
incident recorded in verses 1–3, in which the people rediscovered
what the Law of Moses had said about the Ammonite and the
Moabite (Tobiah was an Ammonite, remember: see ii. 10). But
then *this* incident itself begins with the words, "*On that day* . . ."
(xiii. 1), which means that it coincided with the restoration of the
temple services, described just before it (xii. 44–7); and we know
from chapter xii. 44 that this *coincided with the dedication of the
walls*. This means that Nehemiah's absence and Eliashib's treachery *preceded* the three incidents which are related before them,
including the dedication of the wall; and as Nehemiah's brief
absence occurred twelve years after his first coming to Jerusalem
as wall-builder (compare ii. 1 with xiii. 6), it means that *the
dedication of the wall was about twelve years after the completion
of the rebuilding.*

What struggles Nehemiah had known before he saw those walls
rebuilt! And what struggles he afterwards had before he gained the
reward of seeing a spiritually revived people gratefully dedicating
those walls to God! Truly, there is no triumph without travail.
The only service which really tells is that which really costs. There
seems to be a cross in the way to every crown worth wearing!

The dedication of the walls was performed with all due pomp and circumstance, with full religious ceremony and solemnity; and the people seem to have entered into it with zest and reverence. The ceremony took a three-fold course: first there were two processions of singers who chanted praises to God; second, the reading of the Law; and thirdly the separation of the mixed multitude from the true Israel. It must have been a heart-gladdening day indeed for Nehemiah and Ezra. As the dedication (xii. 27–47) really *followed* in point of time, the happenings recorded in chapter xiii., it is really the climax of the book. It is a lovely climax too: "That day they offered great sacrifices, and rejoiced; *so that the joy of Jerusalem was heard even afar off*" (xii. 43).

Last glimpses of Nehemiah (xiii.).

Glance again at chapter xiii. See how quickly evil compromises had devoloped during Nehemiah's short absence from Jerusalem; and see how firmly he attacked these on his return. (By the way, there is further corroboration that this thirteenth chapter really precedes chapter xii. in point of time, inasmuch as the treacherous high priest Eliashib, who here consorts with Tobiah, is never once mentioned in chapter xii., in the account of the dedication of the walls. Understandably he was in disfavour.)

In this thirteenth chapter we see Nehemiah's zeal for God enduring strong to the end. He returns to Jerusalem, and immediately fights the new outbreak of evils. He will not tolerate for one minute longer the intrusion of Tobiah's "household stuff" where the sacred vessels belong (verses 4–9). He will not tolerate self-indulgence at the expense of the service of God (verses 10–14). He will not tolerate dishonour to the Sabbath day, business being put before religion (verses 15–22). He will not tolerate the breaking down of Israel's separatedness through intermarriage (verses 23–8).

There are touches of grim humour in some of the drastic measures taken by this man of flashing eye and godly indignation. He never lets time slip away while he ponders whether a course of action is "usual" or dignified. He has the firm hand and confident stride of one whose purpose and conscience are absolutely honest before God. Such men never hesitate in dealing with sin.

Promptness and firmness are more than diplomacy! We cannot resist a smile as we see Nehemiah actually throwing Tobiah's household furniture out-of-doors (verse 8), or "smiting" and "plucking off the hair" of those Jews who had married wives outside of Israel (verse 25), or, "chasing" the young Jew who had become son-in-law to Sanballat (verse 28). Yet all this must have cost Nehemiah much. Indeed his ejaculatory prayers, three of which occur in these paragraphs, show us plainly enough how keenly he felt all these things in his own spirit.

Summary of Nehemiah as governor.

See how really great this man was. Cast the eye back over these chapters, and gather out the various reforms effected by him. They make an impressive aggregate.

1. Augmentation of population of Jerusalem (xi. 1).
2. Redemption of Jews sold into slavery among heathen (v. 8).
3. Abolition of borrowing on mortgage and of money-raising by selling children (v.).
4. Strict Sabbath observance restored, also the Sabbatical year (x. 31; xiii. 15–22).
5. Annual levy of one-third shekel instituted toward temple services and fabric (x. 32).
6. System of wood-supply introduced for temple sacrifices (x. 34).
7. Profanations of temple rectified and interdicted (xiii. 4–9).
8. Re-enforcement of tithe payment (x. 37; xiii. 10–13).
9. Divorce of all foreign wives and re-effecting of national separation (xiii. 1–3; 23–8).
10. Various others such as regulations regarding city gates, etc. (xiii. 19–22).

Oh, Nehemiah is a grand example to us all, but especially to all public Christian workers and leaders. His clear-seeing and plain-speaking and brave-dealing, and his God-honouring motive throughout, are both a challenge and an inspiration. For we cannot forget that all his efforts to effect the various reforms just mentioned were resisted by an influential group among the priests and nobles who were bent on secularism, were addicted to inter-marriage with the surrounding Gentile peoples, and in fact were quite willing for fusion with those other peoples. Any ordinary man might have quailed at opposing the will of such a strong party, upheld as it was by the high priest himself, and supported by neighbouring princes. Yet Nehemiah resolutely set himself to "contend with the rulers" (xiii. 11) and "the nobles" (verse 17) on these urgent and sensitive issues; and he adorns with an abiding lustre the great truth that one consecrated man and God are more than a match for all the powers and subterfuges of evil.

There are many lessons running through this Book of Nehemiah, which we cannot stay to point out here; but we would call special attention to *Nehemiah's ejaculatory prayers*. There are eight of them (ii. 4; iv. 4, 5; iv. 9; v. 19; vi. 14; xiii. 14; xiii. 22; xiii. 29). Undoubtedly, in this habit of ejaculatory prayer we have a principal key to the fine temper and sanctified drive and God-glorifying exploits of one of Israel's greatest figures. Nehemiah's ejaculatory prayers presuppose three things—first that God is *sovereign* every minute; second that God is *present* in every place; third that God *really hears and answers each sudden call.*

Oh, it is a great thing to cultivate the habit of ejaculatory prayer to this wonderful "God of heaven" (ii. 4) whose will is sovereign over emperors and kingdoms, whose presence is ever with us in every place, and who hears instantaneously every SOS of the soul, every whisper of adoration, every sigh for holiness, every cry for help, every appeal for strength, every prayer for guidance, every secret utterance of the heart! Every day we ought to be in touch with Him again and again by this wonderful "communication-cord" of ejaculatory prayer. It will keep us calm and steady. It will keep us patient and cheerful. It will keep our minds on a high level. It will enrich and sanctify us. It will bring a thousand streams of blessing into our lives from the hills of God.

Just a parting word. We have shown that this Book of Nehemiah is in two parts—

> The rebuilding of the wall (i.–vi.).
> The reforming of the people (vii.–xiii.).

There is a climax to each part. The climax in part one is the *completion* of the wall—"So the wall was finished." The climax in part two is the *dedication* of the wall—at which "the joy of Jerusalem was heard even afar off." The signs of our times are that the return of Nehemiah's heavenly Antitype is rapidly nearing. Then will be the climax of all climaxes. The walls of Zion shall be built up for ever, and "the joy of Jerusalem" shall again be "heard even afar off"!

THE BOOK OF ESTHER (1)

Lesson Number 48

NOTE.—For this study read the whole Book of Esther through twice or three times.

There is no situation in human life or experience for which a message of God cannot be found through the Book. I do not care whether it be a personal, social, national, or international situation. And about the future, this Book has no hesitation. There is much it does not reveal, but the reality of it is insisted upon from beginning to end. The great fundamental things that we need to know in this preparatory life are all here in this Book.

—*G. Campbell Morgan.*

THE BOOK OF ESTHER (1)

THE THREE little books of Ezra, Nehemiah and Esther record God's dealings with the Jews after their going through the predicted seventy years of their servitude to Babylon: but while Ezra and Nehemiah deal with the remnant of the people which returned to Judæa, the book of Esther is concerned with those—the far greater number—who stayed on in the land of their captivity.

Esther is a *crisis* book. It is a drama—not of fiction, however, but of genuine fact. It is set on the stage of real history, and gathers round actual personages. Five figures move before us—Ahasuerus, the Persian monarch; Vashti, the deposed queen; Haman, the Jew-hater; Mordecai, the Jewish leader; and Esther, the Jewish girl who became queen. In the background are the royal palace, the Persian capital, and the several millions of Jews scattered throughout the emperor's domains.

Esther is the *crucial* figure in the drama inasmuch as everything turns upon her elevation to the throne and her influence as queen. The book, therefore, is fittingly called after the name of Esther. It describes events which took place at Susa, the principal Persian capital, and covers a period of some twelve years.

A Drama of Providence

The *purpose* of the book is to demonstrate the providential care of God over His people. It is vital to see this, for herein lies the living significance and permanent value of the book. The great thing here is the fact of *providential preservation*—"providential" as distinct from what we call the "miraculous." We are meant to see providential *overruling* as distinct from supernatural *intervening*.

That word "providence" comes from the Latin *provideo*, which means that I see a thing beforehand (*pro* = before; *video* = I see); so that the root meaning of providence is foresight. Inasmuch, however, as foresight always occasions *activity* in relation to that which is foreseen, providence comes to have the acquired meaning

of *activity arising from foresight.* Strictly speaking, there is only
One who has foresight, and He alone, therefore, is able to act
on the basis of foreknowledge. Providence, then, in its one absolute
sense, is the Divine foreknowledge and the Divine activity which
arises therefrom; and such providence implies that God wields
absolute power over all the works of His hands.

Providence Demonstrated

It is this which we see demonstrated in the Book of Esther.
The crisis about which the book is written is providentially anticipated and then providentially overruled just at the crucial
moment. No miraculous intervention is resorted to. All the
happenings recorded are the outworking of circumstances in their
natural sequence. Yet while there is no miracle recorded, the
whole thing, in its ultimate meaning, is a mighty miracle—the
mighty miracle whereby a sovereign Deity so manipulates all
non-miraculous events as to bring about a predetermined outcome; and this miracle is all the more miraculous just because
it achieves the predetermined outcome without the *need* for using
miracles! Truly, this mysterious reality which we call providence, this sovereign manipulation of all the ordinary, non-miraculous doings which make up the ordinary ongoing of human
affairs, so as to bring about, by natural processes, those results
which are Divinely predetermined, is the mightiest of all miracles;
and it is this, we repeat, which is strikingly demonstrated in this
Book of Esther.

The non-mention of God

It is this which explains why the name of God does not occur
in the Book of Esther. This non-mention of God in the story
has been a problem to many. Martin Luther, in one of his
occasional lapses of self-restraint, went so far as to say that he
wished the book did not exist! Others have contested its right
to a place in the canon. Yet surely to find a problem in this
non-mention of God is to miss that which above all else we are
intended to see! We say it reverently, yet none the less unhesitatingly, that if God had been specifically mentioned in the story,
or, still more, if the story had specifically *explained*, in so many
words, that it was God who was bringing about all those happenings which are recorded, the dramatic force and moral impact of
the story would have been reduced; for, above all, we are meant

to see, in the natural outworking of events, how, without violating
human free will, and without interrupting the ordinary ongoing
of human affairs, a hidden Power unsuspectedly but infallibly
controls all things. There may have been other reasons why the
anonymous author omitted any direct reference to God, as, for
instance, that the book was intended for Persians as well as Jews;
and there may also be, as some have suggested, the deeper reason
that inasmuch as the Jews were away from their own land,
following the rupture in their special relationship with God, the
name of Jehovah is avoided as being in keeping with this broken
relationship: but we believe one main reason to be that which
we have given, namely, the emphasising of God's invisible activity
in providence.

As a matter of fact the name of God *does* occur in this Book
of Esther, in a most remarkable way. The name "Jehovah" is
secretly hidden four times in an acrostic form, and the name
Ehyeh ("I am that I am") once. In several ancient manuscripts
the acrostic consonants which represent the name are written
larger, to make them stand out, as though we might write it in
English thus—*JeHoVaH*. There are no other acrostics in the
book, so that the intentionalness of these five is clear. The five
places where the acrostics occur are i. 20; v. 4; v. 13; vii. 7;
vii. 5.

In the four acrostics which form the name of Jehovah, the four
words forming the J H V H are in each case consecutive. Each
of the four is spoken by a different person. In the first two cases
the acrostic is formed by the *initial* letters of the words. In the
other two it is formed by the *final* letters of the words. In the
first and third acrostics, the letters spell the name *backwards* and
the speakers are *Gentiles*. In the second and fourth, the letters
spell the name *forwards* and the speakers are *Hebrews*. There are
other points of interest, also, which we need not stay to mention here. The point we now make is that the name of Jehovah
is actually here, in the Book of Esther, in this secret form—as
though the anonymous author would anticipate any who might
stumble at his non-mention of God in the story. The writer says
to us, in effect: "Lest you should think that God is left out of
consideration, see the recognition of Him in these five acrostics,
which, being themselves secretly hidden in the writing, are symbolic of God's secret working throughout the story." Yes, God

is in this Book of Esther, not in so many syllables, but in events; not in miraculous interventions, but as guiding the wheels of providence; not in open communication, but as the unseen Power overruling all.

Who was Ahasuerus?

Who was this king Ahasuerus? We ought to ask this before we go further. Can we regard him as a real historical figure? In the opening verse of the book he is said to have reigned over an empire of a hundred and twenty-seven provinces stretching from India to Ethiopia. Until quite recent times his identity has remained puzzlingly obscure; but now, thanks to diggers and decipherers, the mystery is cleared up, and Ahasuerus is definitely identified. He is known to us in history outside the Bible as Xerxes, which is the Greek form of his Persian name. This Xerxes reigned over the Persian empire from 485 to 465 B.C.

The laurel for the first identifying of Ahasuerus as Xerxes goes to Georg Friedrich Grotefend, who, when he was a young student at the University of Göttingen, set himself patiently to decipher the curious, wedge-shaped Persian characters which had been found on inscriptions among the ruins of the ancient Persian city of Persepolis. The name of the son of Darius was deciphered as *Khshayarsha*, which, when translated into Greek, is *Xerxes*, and which, when translated into Hebrew, is, practically letter for letter, *Akhashverosh*, that is, in English, *Ahasuerus*. As soon as the name was read in Persian, the identity of Ahasuerus was settled; and later findings have corroborated Grotefend.

What then of Xerxes? This is the king who ordered a bridge to be built over the Hellespont, and who, on learning that the bridge had been destroyed by a tempest, just after its completion, was so blindly enraged that he commanded three hundred strokes of the scourge to be inflicted on the sea, and a pair of fetters to be thrown into it at the Hellespont, and then had the unhappy builders of the bridge beheaded. This is the king who, on being offered a sum equivalent to five and a half millions sterling by Pythius, the Lydian, towards the expenses of a military expedition, was so enraptured at such loyalty that he returned the money, accompanied by a handsome present; and then, on being requested by this same Pythius, shortly afterwards, to spare him just one of his sons—the eldest—from the expedition, as the sole support of his declining years, furiously ordered the son to be cut into two pieces, and the army to march between them. This is the king who dishonoured the remains of the heroic Spartan, Leonidas. This is the king who drowned the humiliation of his inglorious defeat in such a plunge of sensuality that he publicly offered a prize for the invention of some new indulgence. This is the king who cut a canal through the Isthmus of Athos for his fleet—a prodigious undertaking. This is the king whose vast resources, and gigantic notions and imperious temper made the name of Persia to awe the ancient world. Herodotus tells us that among the myriads gathered for the expedition against Greece, Ahasuerus was the fairest in personal beauty and stately bearing. But morally he was a mixture of passionate extremes. He is just the despot to dethrone queen Vashti for refusing to expose herself before his tipsy guests. He is just the one to consign a people like the Jews to be massacred, and then to swing over to the opposite extreme of sanctioning Jewish vengeance on thousands of his other subjects.

Two Main Movements

Look now at the story itself. In our English Version it is given in ten short chapters. As we read through these chapters we cannot fail to see that in the first five chapters everything is leading up to the crisis-point in the drama. Events move quickly toward the threatened disaster, until, at the end of chapter v., the very gallows are prepared for Mordecai, and it seems as though nothing can avert the impending tragedy. Then, with chapter vi., there comes a sudden turn in the story. The crisis has been providentially anticipated, and is now overruled. The tables are turned. God's people are both saved and avenged. Threatened tragedy gives place to triumph and blessing. The black clouds break apart; the sun bursts through; the earth is green again; and there is a song of prosperity.

We note, then, that this drama of providential preservation is in two main movements. In chapters i. to v. we have *crisis anticipated*, while in chapters vi. to x. we have *crisis overruled*. Thus we see, in this historic episode, that union of Divine *pre*-vision and *pro*vision which constitutes providence. We see, also, that this Book of Esther fills a unique and necessary place in the canon of the inspired Scriptures, as being distinctively *the book of providential preservation*. We see, still further, the central

spiritual message of the book, namely, that amid the shadows
God stands, keeping watch upon His own. He sees and knows
and cares for His own. He may be out of their sight: but *they*
are never out of *His* sight. "He that keepeth Israel shall neither
slumber nor sleep." He may be invisible, but He is infallible.
He may seem strangely silent, but He remains actively sovereign.
He may be unsuspected; yet omnisciently, omnipresently, omni-
potently, He guides and guards. Evil may be temporarily permitted, but ultimately it is frustrated. Behind a frowning providence God hides a smiling face. We may now set all this out in
the following analysis.

THE BOOK OF ESTHER
THE BOOK OF PROVIDENTIAL PRESERVATION

GOD IN THE SHADOWS WATCHES HIS OWN	
CRISIS ANTICIPATED (i.–v.)	CRISIS OVERRULED (vi.–x.)
QUEEN VASHTI DEPOSED (i.)	MORDECAI IS HONOURED (vi.)
ESTHER BECOMES QUEEN (ii.)	HAMAN IS EXECUTED (vii.)
HAMAN PLOTS MASSACRE (iii.)	THE JEWS ARE AVENGED (viii.)
MORDECAI PLEADS HELP (iv.)	PURIM IS INSTITUTED (ix.)
ESTHER CONTRIVES AID (v.)	MORDECAI MADE PREMIER (x.)

Whatever else we may see in chapters i. to v., we miss their
supreme significance if we fail to see in them a most remarkable
providential predisposing of all contributory factors in anticipation of a foreseen crisis. The feast of Ahasuerus to his lords
and satraps, his inebriate jollity and indecent request, Vashti's
valorous refusal and her dethronement—these things seemed far
from having any connection whatever with the as-yet-undreamed-
of peril to the Jews which was to head up through the anti-
Jewish hatred of Haman, who at this time had not even risen
to public eminence. Yet these things were being so overruled
as to subserve the unsuspected Divine preparation for that which
was to come later. Indeed, the crisis had been anticipated years
before ever Ahasuerus's feast-making took place, in the bestow-
ment of an extraordinary feminine beauty upon Mordecai's

cousin ; and now, as a result of the vacancy created by Vashti's deposal, the matchless Esther is elected to be queen, so that she is in the place of influence when the critical moment comes, to avert the seemingly inescapable disaster, and to turn the tables on Israel's wicked enemies.

Oh, this wonderful fore-planning of providence! It is here brought vividly out to view so that through our seeing it thus clearly demonstrated in this one notable episode we may believe in the fact of its operation through *all* the vicissitudes of our life, and through all the history of the human race, and especially in those trying times when rampant evil seems to have snatched the reins of government from higher control.

THE BOOK OF ESTHER (2)

Lesson Number 49

NOTE.—For this further study in the Book of Esther read again chapters vi to x.

Higher criticism is not an evil thing in itself. It is the discussion of dates and authorship. Of course, when the method adopted is that of rationalism and naturalism, it becomes destructive and pernicious. When Jesus attributed the 110th Psalm to David, He was in the realm of higher criticism. It is perfectly proper to discuss dates and authors, but one may spend one's whole life trying to find out how many men wrote Isaiah, who was the author of the Pentateuch, or who wrote the letter to the Hebrews, without ever studying the Bible.

—*G. Campbell Morgan.*

THE BOOK OF ESTHER (2)

NOTES ON THE STORY

LONG-CONTINUING royal banquets on an enormous scale like that which is described in this first chapter of Esther were not uncommon among the Persians. References in ancient Greek authors leave us in no doubt about this. Royal state seems to have reached its highest splendours in the great Persian empire; and sumptuous banquets were a prominent feature in the life of the Persian court. Such a lavish feast and display as here described would be much to the taste of the vainglorious and ostentatious Ahasuerus.

The occasion of this huge festal gathering is now known, almost with certainty, to have been the summoning together of all the chief men of the kingdom, and especially of the satraps, or "princes of the provinces," to deliberate upon the contemplated expedition against Greece.

The king's order that Vashti (Vashti means "beautiful woman") should come and immodestly display herself before a vast company of half-intoxicated revellers was not only a gross breach of Persian etiquette, but a cruel outrage which would have disgraced for life the one whom, above all other, the king should have protected. Vashti's refusal was courageous and fully justified: though we can well understand that such a public rebuff to one who was an absolute monarch, and vainglorious in the extreme, must have been as humiliating and exasperating as it was richly deserved.

Without doubt, it would have a suddenly sobering effect upon the emperor and the high lords of the realm. Nor is it surprising that when the king's high council of wise men came to consider the matter, they concluded that Vashti must forfeit her royal diadem.

About four years slip away (compare i. 3, 4, with ii. 12 and 16) between the end of chapter i. and Esther's being elected queen —which is the principal happening recorded in the second chapter. During this time Ahasuerus has undertaken his expedition against Greece, and has returned ingloriously frustrated. Maybe he is

269

the more disposed through this to turn his mind from uneasy war thoughts to the pleasures of the seraglio.

Esther, the Jewish orphan girl, daughter of the deceased Abihail, and cousin of Mordecai, is now selected to become queen. Verses 7, 9, 15, leave us in no doubt that Esther must have been a most beautiful young woman. Verses 9 and 15 also suggest a winsome nature. The process by which choice was made was in full accord with Persian and Oriental custom. Esther's Hebrew name was Hadassah, which means *myrtle*, while the Persian name Esther, which was given to her, means a *star*. Jewish, tradition says that Mordecai tried to hide Esther so that she should not be taken by the royal agents. Mordecai also instructed her not to make her Jewish parentage known (ii. 10), presumably lest it should occasion prejudice or intrigue against her. That such prejudice could have been aroused by her Jewish parentage is shown by chapter iii. 4.

Mordecai himself was evidently employed in the service of the royal court, for in chapter ii. 5, where he is first mentioned, we are told that he was resident in "Shushan the Palace" (not just in the city, which was quite separate from the palace, as archæologists have now clearly shown). No one who was not connected with the royal service would have been permitted to reside within those jealously guarded precincts. In chapter ii. 19, 21 we see him fulfilling a regular duty at "the king's gate," and in chapter iii. 2 we see him counted among "the king's servants" which served at the gate. In chapter vi. 10 we see that the king himself knew him as "Mordecai the Jew, that sitteth at the king's gate." Had not Mordecai been there on royal service, the palace guards would have summarily dispatched him on his refusing to obey the decree regarding Haman.

Haman

Another five years have passed by the time we reach the middle of the third chapter (see verse 7). A new character, Haman, appears on the scene. This man, Haman, has so risen in the king's favour as to have become grand vizier of the realm. The king has even commanded that every knee shall bow to him. But while others bow the knee there is one who refuses, even "Mordecai the Jew." Unlike the Persians, who, according to Plutarch, regarded their king as the very image of God, Mordecai will not yield to any man the reverence which belongs alone to the one true God in whom he believes, any more than Daniel would pay Divine homage to king Darius. Haman's fury at this results in the decree for the slaughtering of all the Jews in the Persian empire, on the thirteenth day of the twelfth month.

From the fact that Haman is actually designated "*The enemy of the Jews*" (viii. 1; ix. 10, 24), and from his words to the king about the Jews as a *race*, and from the fact that it was when he had learned Mordecai's Jewish nationality that he decided to make his revenge the occasion for a general anti-Jewish massacre, we infer that Haman was a hater of the Jews before ever Mordecai's refusal of homage had stung his pride.

The light and careless way in which Ahasuerus handed away to Haman the lives of tens of thousands of his industrious and useful subjects is deservedly branded as "perhaps the most shocking example of oriental despotism on record." It ranks with the recent callous announcement of Nazi Hitler, that he was prepared to sacrifice the lives of a million Germans to invade England. Conscience and common sense alike protest the wrongness of such wide power being in the hands of any one man. A really sound and good man will refuse to bear such a responsibility singly. A bad man can only abuse it. Democracy may be beset with many complex difficulties, but it is immeasurably preferable to despotism or dictatorship. Such was the fatuous conceit of Ahasuerus that besides heartlessly handing over an unknown number of men, women and children to cold-blooded murder, he actually made a present to Haman of the ten thousand talents of silver which Haman had offered to pay into the royal treasury, to compensate the emperor financially for the destruction of the Jews (iii. 11)! Even when Haman's real motives were later exposed by Esther, and the king's anger burned against his guilty favourite, the anger was not because Haman had been deceiving him into the committing of a savage crime, but because the crime concerned the people *to which the queen belonged*! (vii. 5).

The awful decree for the annihilation of the Jews was duly promulgated (iii. 12–15). Chapter iv. records the grief and mourning of Mordecai and the Jews, Mordecai's appeal to Esther, by Hatach, one of the king's chamberlains, and Esther's courageous decision to risk her life in an appeal to the king. The risk arose from the awing Persian law that whoever entered unbidden into the king's inner court paid the death penalty (iv. 11). At the time, Esther had not been called in for a whole month (iv. 11), which possibly indicated a cooled regard towards her; so that the risk which she would run in intruding was a very real one. But she resolved to take the risk, saying: "If I perish, I perish" (iv. 16).

At this point in the story the implicit recognition of God is unmistakable. Mordecai's urgent words: "Who knoweth whether thou art come to the kingdom for such a time as this?" are really the key to the whole episode, and reveal his sudden perception of the providential anticipation underlying Esther's strange exaltation to the throne. Moreover, his words, "If thou altogether holdest thy peace at this time, then shall there enlargement and deliverance arise to the Jews from another place," reveal his unshakable faith in Jehovah, and in the indestructibility of His people. Esther's appeal to Mordecai for a three days' fast for her among the Jews is really a plea for prayer, and a casting of herself on the mercy of God in the matter; for, in the Old Testament, fasting is a symbolic form of prayer.

On the third day Esther enters the inner court, and stands opposite the gate of the king's throne-room so as to attract his notice. The king is sitting on his throne at the time, looking down the pillared vista and through the open door, where he beholds, with some surprise, the graceful figure of his young and beautiful wife. His immediately extended sceptre assures Esther that any breach of etiquette is excused. Then the king, realising that only some grave concern could have brought Esther thus, generously reassures her with the words: "What wilt thou, queen Esther? It shall be even given thee to the half of the kingdom." Esther asks that the king and Haman should come to a banquet for them later that day.

By such a banquet as she knew the king loved, she would make the more sure of his favour, and at the same time ensure the presence of Haman himself when she exposed his wicked plot. Haman would thus be tongue-tied. He would not be able to deny the truth of the accusation, nor would he dare to contradict the queen in the very presence of the king, nor would he get any opportunity of misrepresenting the matter to the king in the queen's absence. When the feast took place, however, Esther apparently did not think the most advantageous moment had come, but she promised to make her request certainly known at a further banquet on the following day.

There was a higher Mind than Esther's at work in this postponement, however. During that day the gloating Haman caused the gallows to be prepared for Mordecai; and during that night the sleepless king determined that the same Mordecai should be exalted before all the people! The crucial moment had been prepared for Esther to speak.

The Turning Point

With the opening of the sixth chapter comes the sudden new turn of events. The crisis which has been providentially anticipated is now amazingly overruled. With consummate skill, He that sitteth in the heavens turns the tables on the wicked, and delivers His own people. A few master strokes, and the whole situation is revolutionised. The dramatic irony of the new developments which now rapidly succeed each other leaves us exclaiming, "Truth is stranger than fiction!"

The king cannot sleep. The night drags. He calls for the chronicles to be read to him. He hears how a plot against his own life was foiled through the timely action of Mordecai, and is surprised to find that Mordecai has not been rewarded. He resolves that Mordecai shall be rewarded without delay. The night is now wearing into early morning. He asks who is in the court, and learns that Haman is there (for Haman had come for the earliest possible interview with the king, to obtain sanction for the hanging of Mordecai). The king asks Haman: "What shall be done unto the man whom the king delighteth to honour?" Haman, headily presuming that he himself is the man in the king's mind, and that he is the prospective candidate for still further preferments, swells with self-congratulation, and then makes the following glamorous proposal: "Let the royal apparel be brought which the king useth to wear, and the horse that the king rideth upon, and the crown royal which is set upon his head; and let this apparel and horse be delivered to the hand of one of the king's most noble princes, that they may array the man withal whom the king delighteth to honour, and bring him on horseback through the street of the city, and proclaim before him: Thus shall it be done to the man whom the king delighteth to honour!" Haman's proposal lays bear his unbounded conceit, his sickly thirst for the praise of men, and his paltry idea of greatness. His pulse throbs the more quickly as he imagines himself being thus publicly borne aloft amid the adulations of his fellows. Then he hears the king say: "Make haste, and take the apparel and the horse, as thou hast said, and do even so—*to Mordecai the Jew*"! What!—do this to Mordecai the Jew! Are Haman's ears mocking him? No; it is real enough: the king has spoken, and must be obeyed! The subtle gleam pales from Haman's eyes. The swollen bubble of his pride suddenly bursts. A sickening pall turns his heart cold. For a few age-long seconds he stands, dumbfounded, before his royal master; then he slowly withdraws, with leaden footsteps, to exalt Mordecai in the very way which he, Haman himself, had so stupidly proposed. "He that sitteth in the heavens shall laugh. The Lord shall have them in derision." The utter irony of it! Haman, through his own stupid conceit, has tripped himself into publicly exalting and parading the very man for whose death-warrant he had come to apply, and for whom he had already presumed to prepare the gallows!

Haman's Doom

Chapter vii. tells of Esther's second banquet to the king and Haman. It is a much changed Haman who now sits uneasily at the royal board. His mind is the more disturbed because his "wise men" and his wife Zeresh have said to him: "If Mordecai be of the seed of the Jews, before whom thou hast begun to fall, thou shalt not prevail against him, but shalt surely fall before him" (vi. 13). Yet Haman little guesses how suddenly he is now to be precipitated to his miserable end. In the king's sleepless night, and the exaltation of Mordecai, and the chagrin of Haman, and the now obvious good will of the king, Esther recognises the control of a higher Power, and knows that the moment to speak has come. The king again asks what her special request is, and is amazed to learn that it is a plea *for her life to be spared*—"O king, if it please the king, let my life be given me at my petition, and my people at my request: for we are sold, I and my people, to be destroyed, to be slain, and to perish." The astonished Ahasuerus looks on the lovely face and form of his wife, who is now deeply wrought with emotion, and exclaims: "Who is he, and where is he, that durst presume in his heart to do so?"— to which Esther replies: "The adversary and enemy is this wicked

Haman." Then, in a flash the king sees through Haman's hypocrisy. Rising from the banquet, the king strides agitatedly into the palace garden. Haman, in a frenzy of cowardly terror, oversteps the bounds of etiquette, and falls upon Esther's couch, pleading with her to spare his life. The king re-enters to find him thus; and, either in reality or in sarcastic pretence, misconstruing Haman's action as implying immoral motive, speaks words which immediately cause the attendants to remove Haman, with his face covered—the covering of the face being a Persian custom to indicate that a person was no longer fit to see the light. Without delay, Haman is sent to his doom. Before another sunrise sheds its light over Shushan, the corpse of Haman dangles fifty cubits aloft, on the very gallows which he himself had caused to be made for Mordecai.

Lest it should be thought incredible that the gallows would be so high ("fifty cubits"—about seventy-five feet), we would mention that the Hebrew word translated as "gallows" means a tree. The tree which Haman had selected was in the grounds of his own house (vii. 9); and it was here that, with awful irony, he was made to swing before the horrified gaze of his own family!

THE BOOK OF ESTHER (3)

Lesson Number 50

NOTE.—For this final study in this Book of Esther read again right through the whole book, asking: "Do the figures and incidents in this story suggest or seem to parallel with spiritual or prophetic truths elsewhere enunciated in Scripture?"

I was never out of my Bible.—*John Bunyan.*

I am a man of one Book.—*John Wesley.*

That Bible on the table is a book to you. It is far more than a book to me. It speaks to me; it is as it were a person.

—*Napoleon Bonaparte.*

If we abide by the principles taught in the Bible, our country will go on prospering; but if we and our posterity neglect its instructions and authority, no man can tell how sudden a catastrophe may overwhelm us and bury all our glory in profound obscurity.

—*Daniel Webster.*

THE BOOK OF ESTHER (3)

LATENT TYPE-TEACHING

THIS Book of Esther, besides being of high interest historically, seems to contain latent *type-teachings* which ought not to escape our notice.

The Persian Jews

First of all, and without doubt, *the Persion Jews as a whole* are here used as a type of *the worldly among the Lord's people*.

We have already referred to the non-mention of God in the story. The more we ponder it, the more remarkable does this resolute non-reference to God or to anything religious become; and the more definitely do we see it to have been *intentional* on the part of the writer, for some special reason.

Can we really believe that in a crisis which threatened death to every Jew in the Persian empire there was no agonised calling upon the God of their fathers? Can we believe, too, that after the amazing deliverance which came to them there was absolutely no voice of thanksgiving to God?

No; never could there have been more heart-wrung prayer. Never could there have been more fervent praise. Why then is there absolutely no word of this? Is it due to the author's spiritual blindness or to an unpardonable forgetfulness? If so, how shall we account for the fact that such a stupid, blameworthy book should have been given a revered place in the Hebrew canon? If, on the other hand, the non-mention of God was *not* due to spiritual blindness or godless forgetfulness, there is only one possible inference—*the silence was intentional*.

Why, then, this intentional silence? I think we are not left in doubt. More than fifty years before this Esther episode, the Persian emperor, Cyrus, had made the proclamation which permitted and exhorted all Jews to return to Judæa, as reported in the Book of Ezra (i. 2–4).

Now Ezra is careful to say that this proclamation of Cyrus was in fulfilment of Jeremiah's prophecy which had been made before ever the captivity of the Jews had begun. The seventy years of captivity had been forefixed (Jer. xxix. 10, etc. See also xxv. 11, 12). Moreover, the prophet Isaiah had actually spoken of Cyrus by name, as the coming restorer of Jerusalem, before ever Cyrus was born (Isa. xliv. 28, etc.).

Here, then, was the voice of Jehovah to His people throughout the Persian empire. Here was the Divine recall of the Jews to Jerusalem and Judæa. There could be no mistaking it. It bore a supernatural seal. First the release had been predicted; and now it had been effected. Not a Jew ought to have remained in Persia. The people, without exception, should have flocked to Zion with thanksgiving. Yet the unhappy truth is that only a remnant returned. The rest were content to stay on in Persia. Of course they were ready to applaud those who were returning, and to say how splendid it was of them to undertake the re-building of Judah's ruined cities and Jehovah's temple; but they themselves did not find it convenient at the time to break away from their Persian connections. In truth, they were selfishly indisposed to leave the plenty of Persia for the leanness of desolated Judæa, even though that was the place of covenant blessing. They believed in Jehovah, and acknowledged Him as the one true God; but their hearts were set on the things of this world.

Undoubtedly these Jews are types of the worldly among the Lord's people today. They are the figures of those who profess faith in Christ but who love the world and the flesh too well to make renunciation for Christ's sake. They want to be numbered with the redeemed of the Lord; but they also want to enjoy the pleasures of the world for a season.

And what of these worldly believers, these modern correspon-dents of the old-time Jews who stayed on in Persia? Well, just this—God will not allow His name to be bound up with them any more than He allowed His name to be associated with the Jews who stayed on in Persia. God watched over those Persia-loving Jews, and remained faithful to them even though they had slighted Him. In their trouble they cried to Him, and He delivered them; but He would not allow His name to be bound up with them. His deliverance of them, in the Esther episode, was so recorded that the striking circumstances unmistakably demonstrated His providential care over them; *yet His name must not be once mentioned in the account.*

Let the absence of God's name from the Book of Esther burn this truth into our minds: God will not associate His name with the worldly among His professing people today, any more than He would associate it with those old-time Jews in Persia. Through the centuries, God is developing His purpose for the earth's salvation; and, in the end, those who have "come out" from the Babylon of this world, to "be separate" unto Him, will shine as stars in the eternal kingdom: but those who have said "Lord, Lord," without renouncing the world, will not be known in that day. Their record will not shine on high. They may be saved, as by fire, but they will never hear the King of kings say to them: "Come, ye blessed of my Father; inherit the kingdom." Our Lord's promise to the overcomer is: "I will give him a white stone, and in the stone a new name written, which no man knoweth saving him that receiveth it"; but there will be no such "secret of the Lord" for the worldly disciple. The final description of the glorified saints says that the very name of God shall be "written on their foreheads"; but God's name will never be imprinted on those who have loved self and the world in preference to sanctification. It is possible to be saved from Gehenna, the final doom of the lost (as the Jews in Esther's day were saved from massacre) and yet to miss that "eternal weight of glory" which God has prepared for them that love Him with all their heart.

But we may go further. These Persian Jews of Esther's time were also types in a dispensational and prophetic sense. They typically portrayed the history of *the Jewish race as a whole*, right on to the end of the present dispensation, in which fact we see a still more meaningful reason why the name of God is omitted from the book of Esther. This cannot be better expressed than in the following quotation. "These Persian Jews are the types of their fellow-countrymen who were afterwards to reject God's salvation in Christ, and who, scattered among the nations, were again and again to be threatened with destruction. God's name and theirs have not been bound together for nineteen hundred years. God has been working marvellously in these centuries; but those rebellious Jews and He have not been found together. God's temple has been reared, and it is being reared now; but the work is done by other hands than theirs. God's battles have been fought and won; but *their* names have not been inscribed in the glorious story." Yet, on the other hand, "He has watched over His rebellious people, and He watches over them still. Haman may plot their destruction; but he plots against his own life and the lives of all that are dear to him. Let every foe of that apparently God-forsaken people take heed to it: God will avenge the wrong done to His people even though they have despised their heritage." Their unbelief cannot make God forget His word: "I will bless them that bless thee, and curse him that curseth thee" (Gen. xii. 3). Never have the Jews suffered more than they have recently suffered in Nazi Germany and Rumania and other European countries. Germany already curses the day she followed Hitler in his anti-Jewish atrocities; and Hitler himself, like Haman of old, has perished forever on gallows of his own making.

Haman

The wicked *Haman* prefigures "the man of sin" who is predicted to appear, toward the end of the present age, as the last and worst enemy of God's people on earth. Haman is a type of the "man of sin" in six ways.

First, mark his *name*. In chapter vii. 6 Esther brands him as "Haman the wicked"; and it is a singular fact that the numerical value of the Hebrew letters which make up his title is 666, the number of Antichrist (Rev. xiii. 18).

Second, see Haman's *power*. With meteoric rise he outranks all his fellows. The opening verses of chapter iii. tell us that his place was set up above all the princes of the realm, and a royal decree was issued that every knee should bow to him. Thus does he foreshadow the fearsome "beast" of Revelation xiii., which receives its power and eminence from the dragon, and the "little horn" of Daniel vii. 8, which has "the eyes of a man and a mouth speaking great things."

Third, observe Haman's *pride*. Hear him boast his glory and riches to Zeresh, and to his friends (v. 11). See his conceited exasperation when Mordecai withholds obeisance (v. 13). Hear him planning to ride the king's own horse, clad in the royal apparel, wearing the crown royal, and being borne ostentatiously aloft amid the adulations of the people (vi. 7–9). Thus does Haman forepicture that coming "man of sin" who, as Paul says, "opposeth, and exalteth himself above all that is called God" (2 Thess. ii. 4).

Fourth, mark Haman's *hate*. Four times over he is designated as "the enemy of the Jews" (iii. 10; viii. 1; ix. 10, 24). Five times, also, he is called an "Agagite" (iii. 1, 10; viii. 3, 5; ix. 24). Modern discovery has shown that Agag was a territory adjacent to Media; but symbolically interpreted this word "Agagite" connects Haman with the Agagites mentioned earlier in the Scriptures. Agag was king of the Amalekites (1 Sam. xv. 8), who were descended from Esau (Gen. xxxvi. 12). Amalek is always Israel's enemy (Exod. xvii. 16; Deut. xxv. 17–19). But there was to come a Star out of Jacob and a Sceptre out of Israel which should bring destruction to Amalek (Num. xxiv. 17–20); even as the New Testament says that Christ shall yet smite the Antichrist (2 Thess. ii. 8). The coming "man of sin" will be the latter-day Haman. He will be history's supreme Jew-hater.

Fifth, note Haman's *plot*. He makes Mordecai's conscientious resistance the occasion for a contemplated annihilation of the whole Jewish race. With specious guile he works toward this through his political power, so that the Jews are plunged into great sorrow and suffering (chapters iii. and iv.). So yet will the coming Antichrist, the evil "prince" of Daniel ix., plunge the Jews into the "great tribulation" by a political betrayal (Dan. ix. 26, 27).

Sixth, see Haman's *doom*. While he is in power he is terrible; but he lasts only a few years (compare ii. 16 with iii. 7); and his end is as sudden as it is ironic. One day he vaunts himself: the next day he hangs by his own rope. Moreover, all his progeny perish with him; for in chapter ix. 7–14, we find that Haman had ten sons who were hanged along with him.

Just as suddenly and ironically will the coming Antichrist perish. Weymouth's translation of 2 Thessalonians ii. 8 is: "The lawless one will be revealed, whom the Lord Jesus will slay with the breath of His mouth, and overwhelm by the splendour of His coming." Thus suddenly will the "man of sin" meet his doom. He who has overcome men by supernatural wonders will himself be overcome by a bigger wonder still! Moreover, as Haman had ten sons who perished with him, so the final form of Gentile government, at the end of the present age, is to be that of "ten kings" who reign for "one hour" through whom Antichrist works, and who perish along with him (Dan. vii.; Rev. xvii.). Haman, then, is a grimly significant figure!

Esther

We have left ourselves little space to trace out the type meaning of Esther and Mordecai. Esther may be taken as a type of the Church.

First, she is so *in her Jewish antecedents*. She was the daughter of Jewish parents; but her parents were dead. Even so, the Church, considered historically, emerged from Jewish antecedents. The Saviour Himself was a Jew. The Scriptures which prepared the way for the Christian Church were Jewish. The first Christian community was Jewish. Yet, in its very emergence from Judaism, the Church carried with it the sign that its Jewish antecedents were now passed away. The Law was done away in Christ. The Mosaic economy was now dead. As Esther's parents were passed away, so were those Jewish antecedents from which the Church had emerged.

Second, Esther is a type of the Church *in her womanly beauty*. God had given her a beauty which surpassed that of all others. Even so has God given a surpassing beauty to the Church of Christ—even the very beauty of Christ Himself. We become "the righteousness of God in Him." We are "accepted in the Beloved." We are yet to be presented as Christ's bride, "a glorious Church, not having spot or wrinkle, or any such thing" (Eph. v. 27).

Third, Esther typifies the Church *in her exaltation*. She becomes married to one whose title was "King of kings"—and although Ahasuerus, in his personal character, is far from typifying Christ, yet, in his being a "king of kings," he may fitly speak to us of the Church's royal Bridegroom who, indeed, is "*The* King of kings, and Lord of lords."

Fourth, Esther typifies the Church *in her intercession*, Esther went in to the king "on the third day," which speaks symbolically of resurrection, and of interceding in resurrection power. It was against the "law" for Esther thus to go in before the king. The law excluded her; yet she was accepted on the ground of pure grace; for the king beheld her wearing the royal apparel which he himself had given her (v. 1). Even so, we ourselves are excluded by the Law; but we are fully accepted on the ground of free grace when we appear in the royal robes which Christ Himself has given us. It was through Esther's intercession that deliverance came to the Jews. Will it not be through the intercession of the Church's believer-priests that deliverance comes to the Jews in their *final* tribulation? Are not the "golden vials full of incense" said to be "the prayers of the saints"? (Rev. v. 8).

Mordecai

As for *Mordecai*, he may fitly represent to us the faithful Jewish remnant which will be preserved through the great tribulation, to enter the millennial kingdom. We see this in four ways.

First, *in his refusal to bow to Haman*. When the king's servants asked Mordecai: "Why transgressest thou the king's commandment?" he "told them he was a Jew" (iii. 4); so that his refusal was clearly because of his Jewish faith. He would not yield to man that which is due to God alone; even as the faithful Jewish remnant in the final tribulation will not bow to the beast nor receive his mark upon them.

Second, Mordecai typified the Jews of the tribulation period *in his bitter mourning and fasting and weeping*, which becomes shared by thousands of other Jews, and which forepictures that preparation of penitence which will finally lead the Jews to "look upon Him whom they pierced," and own Him as their King.

Third, he typifies the Jewish remnant *in his marvellous deliverance*. As he was delivered so will his brethren of the future be. The seventh chapter of Revelation shows us the sealing of the Jewish remnant before "the wrath of God" is poured upon the earth. They are sealed and saved.

Fourth, Mordecai typifies these *in his wonderful exaltation*. The closing chapter of Esther shows him exalted above all his fellows, made the grand vizier of Persia, and next to the king and queen! Even so, through the faithful remnant will the Jews and Jerusalem take the supreme place among the nations in the coming kingdom of David's greater Son.

This brings us to the end of the seventeen historical books of the Old Testament, and to the end of volume 2 in our course of study.

EXPLORE THE BOOK

A Basic and Broadly Interpretative Course
of Bible Study from Genesis to Revelation

J. SIDLOW BAXTER

VOLUME THREE
POETICAL BOOKS (JOB TO SONG OF SOLOMON)
ISAIAH, JEREMIAH, LAMENTATIONS

CONTENTS OF VOLUME THREE

	Page
THE POETICAL GROUP	7
Preliminary	
THE BOOK OF JOB	23
Studies 52 to 56	
THE BOOK OF PSALMS	81
Studies 57 to 61	
THE BOOK OF PROVERBS	129
Study 62	
THE BOOK OF ECCLESIASTES	141
Studies 63 to 65	
THE SONG OF SOLOMON	169
Studies 66 to 68	
THE BOOKS OF THE PROPHETS	197
Study 69	
PROPHECY AND THE PROPHETS	205
Study 70	
THE BOOK OF ISAIAH	215
Studies 71 to 74	
THE BOOK OF JEREMIAH	257
Studies 75 and 76	
LAMENTATIONS OF JEREMIAH	277
Study 77	

THE POETICAL BOOKS

THE BOOK OF JOB
THE BOOK OF PSALMS
THE PROVERBS
ECCLESIASTES
SONG OF SOLOMON

Lesson Number 51

Parallelism, where one clause answers to another, pertains to the genius of Hebrew poetry, the rhythm and rhyme of thought taking the place of those of words, one member of the parallelism corresponding to another in sentiment, and sometimes in terms. To discover and develop this correspondence or juxtaposition often gives the clue to exposition. In some cases one member of a complex parallelism is left unexpressed and wanting; but, being implied, must be supplied to make the whole complete; and this is one form of the enigmas, or "dark sayings of the wise," to be solved by study.

—Arthur T. Pierson, D.D.

THE POETICAL BOOKS

A Glance Backward

THE SEVENTEEN *historical* books which comprise the first part
of the Old Testament now lie behind us. A much smaller and
very different group of books lies before us, consisting of the five
poetical books—Job, Psalms, Proverbs, Ecclesiastes, and the Song
of Solomon. In these we shall find ample vistas of interest opening
up to us: but before we press forward we ought perhaps to glance
backward over the trodden way. We have come through some
magnificent scenery, though there have been ugly breaks, and
unforgettable scenes of desolation. Over sunlit hilltops, and
through gloomy valleys, and by many windings of the way, we
have passed, at length, through the eventful story of God's
dealings with Israel up to the time of expulsion from Canaan.
The writings of the Hebrew prophets, when we come to them,
will be found to turn new light on Israel's past and future; but
the actual historical records, in the first seventeen books of
Scripture, we have now thoughtfully examined; and there are
certain dominant features which we ought to retain securely in
our memory.

The seventeen historical books, as we have seen, are divided
into five and twelve. In the first five (Genesis to Deuteronomy)
we have seen Israel's *preparation* for Canaan. In the remaining
twelve (Joshua to Esther) we have seen Israel's *occupation* of
Canaan, ending with the nation's failure and exile. The twelve
may be further divided into nine and three. In the first nine
(Joshua to 2 Chronicles) the whole nation is in Canaan. In the
remaining three (Ezra, Nehemiah, Esther), only a very small
remnant is in the land. Let us firmly fix it in mind, then, that
in these three groups of *five* and *nine* and *three*, we have—

PREPARATION — (Genesis to Deuteronomy)
OCCUPATION — (Joshua to 2 Chronicles)
DISPOSSESSION — (Ezra to Esther).

9

We have seen also, how each of the books, thus far, may be represented by some particular word which expresses its distinctive feature. We may be wise, at this point, to look back over these and make sure that we have learned them. For instance, we saw that the central significance of 2 Samuel, the book of David's forty years' reign, is really expressed in the word *confirmation*. By this we mean that following upon the transition from Theocracy to monarchy, which we have in the *First* Book of Samuel, and following the rejection of the throne of Saul, God now accepts and *confirms* the throne in Israel, in the great covenant with David. In the case of the other books the distinguishing words speak for themselves—

Genesis	— Destitution.
Exodus	— Deliverance.
Leviticus	— Dedication.
Numbers	— Direction.
Deuteronomy	— Destination.

Joshua	— Possession.
Judges, Ruth	— Declension.
1 Samuel	— Transition.
2 Samuel	— Confirmation.
1 Kings	— Disruption.
2 Kings	— Dispersion.
1 & 2 Chronicles	— Retrospection.
Ezra	— Restoration.
Nehemiah	— Reconstruction.
Esther	— Preservation.

The Poetical Books

We turn, then, to the "Poetical Books"; but before we examine them separately, we ought to note certain characteristics which belong to them collectively.

The seventeen books which lie behind us are *historical*. These five poetical books are *experiential*. The seventeen historical books are concerned with a *nation*, as such. These five poetical books are concerned with *individuals*, as such. The seventeen have to do with *the Hebrew race*. These five have to do with *the human heart*.

These five so-called "poetical books" are *not the only poetry* in the Old Testament Scriptures. There are stretches of unexcellable poetry in the writings of the prophets, which we shall come to later. This, however, does not affect the fact that these five— Job, Psalms, Proverbs, Ecclesiastes, and the Song of Solomon— are distinctively the poetical *group*.

We ought clearly to understand, also, that the term "poetical" refers only to their *form*. It must not be thought to imply that they are simply the product of human imagination. There is glorious poetry here; but there is nothing of the merely fanciful or unreal. These books portray real human experience, and grapple with profound problems, and express big realities. Especially do they concern themselves with the experiences of the *godly*, in the varying vicissitudes of this changeful life which is ours under the sun. Moreover, experiences which are here dealt with were permitted to come to men in order that they might be as guides for the godly ever afterward. These experiences are here recorded and interpreted for us by the Spirit of inspiration through "holy men of old" who spoke and wrote "as they were moved" by Him. Thus, in these poetical books we have a most precious treasury of spiritual truth.

Spiritual Progress

There is another thing which we ought to note before we pass on to consider these poetical books separately, and that is *the spiritual progress* which they collectively express; for, after all, what we are most concerned about is to grasp their spiritual meaning. As we have said before, we believe that God overruled in the arranging of the *order* in which the books of our Bible now appear, as much as He overruled in their original inspiration. The beauty of a perfect spiritual progress is seen in these five poetical books; and we cannot alter their present arrangement without spoiling this.

In the Book of Job we see *the death of the self-life*. Through the fires of affliction and a new vision of God, Job is brought to the end of himself. He sees himself as God sees him. The self-life, with its self-goodness and self-reason and self-religion and self-everything, is laid bare and laid low. The man who at first is said to have been the best man on earth (i. 8), is found at last on his face before God, exclaiming, "I abhor myself in dust and ashes!" (xlii. 6).

Next, in the Psalms we see *the new life in God*, expressing itself in praise and prayer, in adoration and supplication and intercession, in faith and hope and love, in fear and joy and song and sigh, and in every frame that godly hearts know.

Then come the books of Proverbs and Ecclesiastes. In Proverbs we are in God's school, learning a heavenly but practical wisdom for life on earth; while in Ecclesiastes we are taught not to set our affection on anything under the sun, but to let our treasure be on high. Finally, the Song of Songs completes the progress by symbolically expressing the sweet intimacy of communion with Christ in all the fulness of His love. In these five books, then, we have the death of the old life in self, the flame of the new life in God, the practical disciplining of the soul in the school of God, the weaning of the heart from worldly desires, and the rapture of communion with the heavenly Bridegroom. Is not this a beautiful spiritual progress?

It is well to learn, too, that this beautiful progress in the order of the poetical books is the necessary order in true Christian experience. That which the Song of Solomon represents *can never* be experienced until that which is represented in the Book of Job has been experienced. Death is peaceful enough; but *dying* is hard. The self-life never dies without a struggle; but the "nevertheless afterward" makes rich compensation!

Or, to put it in another way, in the words of one who simply calls himself anonymously "A Bondservant of Christ": "The first step in the spiritual life is to abhor equally one's badness and one's goodness; the second step is to live by the faith of the Son of God, that is, to live in the energy of the faith by which the Messiah lived; the third step is the subjection of the will to Christ, the Wisdom of God; the fourth step is deliverance from the spirit of this present world; and the climax is the joy unspeakable of union and companionship with Christ."

Leading Ideas

We have seen how, in the seventeen historical books which we have now studied, the distinctive feature of each book is so clear that it may be expressed in a single word. Similarly with each of these five poetical books, the ruling idea may be concentrated into a single phrase.

The Book of Job	— Blessing through Suffering.
The Psalms	— Praise through Prayer.
The Proverbs	— Prudence through Precept.
Ecclesiastes	— Verity through Vanity.
Song of Solomon	— Bliss through Union.

HEBREW POETRY

We ought to say a word here about the *nature* of Hebrew poetry, as it is different from our own in certain marked ways. Much of our modern poetry is couched in *rhyme* or parallelism of sound. Besides this, there is *rhythm*, or parallelism of time. In rhyme we get the pleasure of *phonetic* agreement. In rhythm we get the pleasure of *metric* agreement. There are many who would say that rhyme is not necessary to poetry. Some of our greatest English poetry is written in so-called "blank verse," or rhythm without rhyme. Certainly, rhyme and rhythm do not in themselves constitute real poetry, which, at heart, consists in the quadruple genius of insight, imagination, analogy, and expression; yet they are bound up with it in a subtle intimacy; and although *rhyme* is considered to be quite unnecessary by many, felicity of *rhythm* seems to be one of the generally accepted canons by which English poetry is judged.

Now in Hebrew poetry there is neither the sound parallelism of rhyme nor the time parallelism of rhythm, but there is parallelism of *ideas*. This parallelism of ideas is in three kinds—completive, contrastive, and constructive.

By *COMPLETIVE* parallels we mean those in which the second member of the parallel concurs with the first, and develops it to an intended further point. Take the following as examples:

The righteous shall flourish like the palm tree;
He shall grow like a cedar in Lebanon.

(Ps. xcii. 12.)

God is our refuge and strength,
A very present help in trouble.

(Ps. xlvi. 1.)

The law of the Lord is perfect,
    restoring the soul;
The testimony of the Lord is sure,
    making wise the simple.

(Ps. xix. 7.)

Thou hast turned for me my mourning into dancing;
Thou hast loosed my sackcloth and girded me with
    gladness.

(Ps. xxx. 11.)

It will be seen at once that in each of these couplets the sense of the second member is in close affinity with that of the first. Yet this close affinity is not actual identity. The similarity is not synonymity. Other than being mere empty repetition, the second member colours, enriches, develops, completes the first. Take the following example of *triple* parallelism, from the first verse of the first of the psalms—

O, the happiness of the man
Who walketh not in the counsel of the ungodly;
And standeth not in the way of sinners;
And sitteth not in the seat of the scornful.

The opening exclamation here belongs to each line of the succeeding triplet. In each of the three lines which make up the triplet there are three *word*-members which correspond with each other and mark a completive progress, thus—

walketh	*counsel*	*ungodly*
standeth	*way*	*sinners*
sitteth	*seat*	*scornful.*

The development here is almost too obvious to need comment. The *walking*, in line one, which speaks of no more than being on friendly terms, gives place to *standing*, in line two, which implies a closer intimacy, while this in turn gives place to *sitting*, in line three, which speaks of a permanent connection. Again, in the first line the word "counsel" simply betokens general advice, whereas the word "way," in the second line, indicates a chosen course of conduct, and the word "seat," in the third line, implies a set condition of mind. Yet again, in line one, the word "ungodly" describes the *negatively* wicked, while in the next line the word "sinners" describes the *positively* wicked, and in the last line the word "scornful" describes the *contemptuously* wicked.

Take now a few examples of *CONTRASTIVE* parallels. The Book of Proverbs abounds in these.

Trust in the Lord with all thine heart;
And lean not upon thine own understanding.

(Prov. iii. 5.)

Faithful are the wounds of a friend;
But the kisses of an enemy are deceitful.

(Prov. xxvii. 6.)

Weeping may endure in the evening;
But singing cometh in the morning.

(Ps. xxx. 5.)

The house of the wicked shall be overthrown;
But the tent of the upright shall flourish.

(Prov. xiv. 11.)

Many sorrows shall be to the wicked ;
But he that trusteth in Jehovah, mercy shall encompass him.

(Ps. xxxii. 10.)

It will be seen at once that in each of the above parallels the second member is set in contrast with the first. In some cases these parallels are not strictly *antithetic*—as, for instance, in the first of the above examples, where the second line is really simply the *negative* of the first—but the second member is always *contrastive* in its terms. It will be seen also that in some of these contrastive parallels there is progress of thought, even as in the *completive* parallels. Take, for instance, the fourth of the above examples. In the first line we have the word "house," telling us that the *strongest* structure of the wicked shall perish ; whereas in the second line we have the word "tent," telling us that the *lightest* structure of the upright shall endure. There is a careful choosing of words in each parallel. Note the following four-line stanza in which we have not merely a contrastive parallel between

two single lines, as in the above examples, but between two
completive parallels.

> *Yet a little while, and the wicked shall not be;*
> *Thou shalt look for his place and it shall not be found;*
> *But the meek shall possess the land,*
> *And delight themselves in abundant prosperity.*
>
> (Ps. xxxvii. 10, 11.)

Again, in the following example we have a *succession* of contrastive parallels.

> *Behold, My servants shall eat;*
> *But ye shall be famished.*
> *Behold, My servants shall drink;*
> *But ye shall be thirsty.*
> *Behold, My servants shall rejoice;*
> *But ye shall be confounded.*   (Isa. lxv. 13.)

Take now the following examples of *CONSTRUCTIVE* parallelism, in which successive parallels are built up together into
structural form until they unitedly express one complete idea.

> *The eye that mocketh at his father,*
> *And despiseth to obey his mother;*
> *The ravens of the valley shall pick it out,*
> *And the young vultures shall eat it.*   (Prov. xxx. 17.)

In these four lines the one subject is the "eye"; and it takes
both pairs of lines (for the four lines are in two pairs—two completive parallels) to express the one complete idea about it.

Turn to Psalm xxi. for another example. Here the four-line
stanza is again made up of two completive parallels which are
built together to express the one complete idea.

> *In Thy strength, O Jehovah, the king shall rejoice;*
> *And in Thy salvation how greatly shall he exult!*
> *The desire of his heart Thou hast granted him;*
> *And the request of his lips Thou hast not denied.*
>
> (Ps. xxi. 1, 2.)

The beautiful development in the above lines will be immediately apparent. The word "strength," in the first line, is developed into "salvation" in the second; and the word "rejoice," in the first line, gives place to "exult" in the second. The "desire of the heart," in the third line, becomes the "request of the lips" in the fourth; and the clause "Thou hast granted," in the third line, is turned to "Thou hast not denied" in the fourth line (the last expression being a heightened form of emphasis, in Hebrew usage, just as the words, "The Lord will not hold him guiltless," are really an emphatic way of saying that the Lord *will most certainly* hold the person guilty).

And now take a further example of this constructive parallelism, in which two *contrastive* couplets are built together.

> *These trust in chariots, and these in horses;*
> *But we boast the name of Jehovah our God.*
> *They are bowed down, yea are fallen:*
> *But we are arisen and stand upright.*
>
> (Ps. xx. 7, 8.)

Turning away from the Poetical Books just for a moment, take the following example of constructive parallelism from a well-known passage in the prophet Isaiah.

> *Seek ye Jehovah while He may be found;*
> *Call ye upon Him while He is near:*
> *Let the wicked forsake his way,*
> *And the unrighteous man his thoughts;*
> *And return to Jehovah, for He will have mercy;*
> *And to our God, for He will abundantly pardon.*
>
> (Isa. lv. 6, 7.)

Here are three completive parallels going together to constitute a united whole. Note the progress in each of the completive parallels, and the progress running through the whole structure. In the first line men are simply exhorted to "seek," and are simply told that Jehovah may be "found." In the second line men are exhorted to "call," and are correspondingly assured that Jehovah is actually "near." In the third line it is the "*wicked*" man (the *positive* committer of wrong) who is exhorted to forsake his "*way*" (or habitual behaviour). In the fourth line it is the "*unrighteous*" man (the *negative* omitter of right) who is exhorted to forsake the very "*thought*" of wrong. In the fifth line men are exhorted to return to "Jehovah," and are promised "mercy." In the sixth line men are the more encouraged to return because Jehovah is "*our* God," and will "*abundantly* forgive." Surely this is a beauty of progress which cannot but appeal to our minds.

Of course, under this heading of *constructive* parallels, we ought to mention that there are several varieties of such structures. For instance, there is *introverted* parallelism. A striking example of this kind of structure is provided in Psalm cxxxv. 15–18.

> *The idols of the heathen are silver and gold,*
> *The work of men's hands.*
> *They have mouths but they speak not;*
> *They have eyes but they see not;*
> *They have ears but they hear not;*
> *Neither is there any breath in their mouths;*
> *They who make them are like unto them;*
> *So are all they who put their trust in them.*

It will be seen here that the first line corresponds with the last; for in the first line we read of "the idols of the heathen," and in the last line we have simply another name for the heathen, namely, "they who put their trust in them (idols)." Then, it will be seen that the line next to the first corresponds with the line next to the last; for both speak about the *making* of the idols (in the one case the making, and in the other case the makers). Further, it will be noted that the line next but one to the first corresponds with the line next but one to the last; for the one says that the idols have no speech in their mouths, and the other says that they have no breath in their mouths. Finally, the two middle lines agree; for in the one line the idols are said to have eyes without any faculty of vision, and in the other line the idols are said to have ears without any faculty of hearing.

Take a simpler case of this introverted parallelism, from Hosea xiii. 14 :—

I will ransom them from the power of the grave;
From death I will redeem them;
O death, I will be thy plague;
I will be thy destruction, O grave.

Here the first and last lines go together, and the two inner lines go with each other. Take just one more instance, from Psalm li. 1.

Have mercy upon me, O God,
According to Thy loving-kindness;
According to the multitude of Thy tender mercies
Blot out my transgression.

Perhaps we ought to say that these three kinds of parallelism —completive, contrastive, and constructive—have usually been called "synonymous," "antithetic," and "synthetic." These names, in our own judgment, are open to objection. Those parallels which are called "synonymous" are rarely if ever really synonymous, inasmuch as the second member of the parallel almost invariably amplifies or diversifies the first; while in some of those which are called "antithetic" the second member is not really in opposition to the first in idea, although contrastive in its *terms*. So we prefer to call the three main kinds of Hebrew poetic parallelism by the more accurate terms—"completive," "contrastive," "constructive": and these three should be carefully remembered.

To understand this Hebrew parallelism is not only poetically interesting; it is important in the *interpretation* of Scripture. The corresponding members in each parallel throw light upon each other. Obscure words are often explained thereby, inasmuch as the same idea usually lies at the foundation of both members of the parallel. Sometimes the one member expresses the idea figuratively, while the other expresses it literally. Sometimes the one member expresses the idea positively, while the other expresses it negatively. Sometimes the one member expresses the idea in what to us seems obscure phraseology, while the other expresses it in words which are too clear to admit any possible doubt. For instance, when we read: "The Lord is in His holy temple," we may find ourselves asking: "*Which* temple—earthly or heavenly?"

But when we interpret the statement in its poetic parallel we see that it is the heavenly temple which is meant.

> *The Lord is in His holy temple;*
> *The Lord, His throne is in heaven.*
>
> (Ps. xi. 4.)

It happens that in this instance we know on *historical* grounds that the reference is to God's heavenly abode; for it is practically certain that the earthly temple at Jerusalem was not built when these words were written. None the less, however, this instance illustrates what we are saying about the interpretative value of parallelism.

Take a more difficult case—that of Psalm x. 4, which reads: "The wicked, through the pride of his countenance, will not seek *after God*: God *is* not in all his thoughts." The italicised words in our Authorised Version, "*after God*," and "*is*," do not come in the original. They have been inserted to make the statement read coherently in English; and then the verse has had to be made to end with the words: "God is not in all his thoughts." Now the verse, in the original, runs thus: "The wicked, in the height of his scorn—will not requite—no God—all his thoughts." There is really nothing about "not seeking after God," as in our Authorised Version. Does not this text yield up its true sense when it is interpreted by its parallels?—

> *The wicked in his haughty scorn—*
> *"He will not requite,"*
> *"There is no God"—*
> *These are all his thoughts.*

Thus paralleled we see the outward scorn and the inward thoughts of the wicked. We see, also, how the wicked man's denial of Divine judgment, in the words "He will not requite," leads on by an easy step to his final delusion that "There is no God."

We must speak just one further word about this Hebrew poetry of parallel ideas. Its peculiar genius makes it wonderfully suitable for *translation into any language*. Nothing is harder than to translate other kinds of poetry from one language into another;

but this Hebrew poetry can be reproduced in any language without any necessary diminution of its beauty or force. When we try to translate rhyme or rhythm from one language into another we are up against almost insuperable obstacles. If, for instance, I want to translate two rhymed lines of eight syllables each from English into Greek, the one line ending with the word "God," and the other line ending with the word "trod," I find that the Greek word for God is *Theos*, which is a word of two syllables, unlike our English word "God"; and the Greek word for "trod" is *periēpatēsen*, a word of no less than six syllables, instead of one, and thus hopelessly different from our English word "trod"; so that at once, with these two words, my rhyme and my rhythm are both alike ruined.

There are no such difficulties in the translating of Hebrew poetic parallel. The five-fold group of the poetical writings which we now come to in our study of the Holy Scriptures were meant to be a book of prayer and praise and precept for all men, the Book of the Psalms in particular being, as it were, a Prayer Book for all generations; and in gracious wisdom, therefore, the Spirit of inspiration so ordered it that the kind of poetry which should clothe these prayers and praises should be a *universal* poetry. We may well thank God for this wise *pre*vision and rich *pro*vision; and, further, we may discern in it yet one more indication of the Divine inspiration of the Scriptures.

What do you think of the following?—

Even a *tree* hath hope.
If it be hewn down it will sprout anew,
The young shoot thereof will not fail;
Though in the earth its root waxed old,
Or in the ground its stock should die,
Yet at the scent of water it will spring,
And shoot forth boughs like a new plant.
But a *man* dies and is cut off.
Yea, when men die, they are gone;
Ebbs away the water from the sea;
And the stream decays and dries;
So when men lie down they rise not;
Till the skies vanish they never wake,
Nor are they roused from their sleep.

Behold of wrong I cry, but am not heard,
I cry for help, but there is no judgment.
He hath stripped me of my glory,
And taken my crown from my head.
He hath broken me down on every side,
And uprooted my hope like a tree.
He hath also kindled his wrath against me,
And counted me among His adversaries.
His troops advance on me together,
And cast up their way against me,
And encamp round about my tent.
He hath put my brethren far from me.
Even my confidants are estranged from me.
My kinsfolk, too, have failed,
My familiar friends have forgotten me.
I call my servant, but he gives no answer,
I have to entreat him with my mouth.
Even young children despise me;
If I arise, they talk against me.

.   .   .   .   .

Have pity, have pity on me, O my friends,
For the hand of God hath touched me!

.   .   .   .   .

Oh, that my words were written!
That they were inscribed in a book!
That with an iron stylus and lead
They were graven in the rock for ever!
For I know it: my REDEEMER liveth,
And at last on earth shall stand up;
And though my skin may be destroyed,
Yet in my flesh shall I see God,
Whom I shall see FOR MYSELF,
And *my* eyes shall see (not just another's)
My reins (longings) burn within me (i.e. for the day)

.   .   .   .   .

Is not that alluring poetry? It is from the Book of Job, the first
of the poetical books, which we shall now inspect in the ensuing
group of studies.

THE BOOK OF JOB (1)

Lesson Number 52

NOTE.—For this study read the whole Book of Job through once, marking Job's protestations of innocence and his expressions of perplexity concerning God.

"We cannot understand the meaning of many trials; God does not explain them. To explain a trial would be to destroy its object, which is that of calling forth simple faith and implicit obedience. If we knew why the Lord sent us this or that trial, it would thereby cease to be a trial either of faith or of patience."

—Alfred Edersheim, D.D.

THE BOOK OF JOB (1)

ALTHOUGH the Book of Genesis comes first in our Bible, it may not have been the first to be written. There are grounds for believing that the Book of Job is of an even earlier date. In fact, this Book of Job may be the oldest book in the world.

Yet despite the changing scenery of the forty centuries which have elapsed since the author of this old-world epic laid down his pen, can we find anywhere a more poignantly up-to-date treatise on the pathos of human experience?

Moreover, besides thus blending antiquity with enduring reality, the Book of Job is characterised by a transcendent literary excellence. Dr. Richard G. Moulton, an acknowledged literary authority, declares it to be his belief that if a jury of persons well instructed in literature were empanelled to pronounce as to which is the greatest poem in the world's great literatures, the large majority would give their verdict for the Book of Job. It is a literary masterpiece.

Subject and Method

The subject here is that ever-present problem—*the mystery of suffering*, but specially as concerns the godly. We have already referred to the elasticity of Hebrew poetry, and its freedom from any hard-and-fast metrical uniformity. This is particularly advantageous in the treatment of such a variable subject as suffering. To quote Dr. Moulton: "The philosophical discussion (of suffering) is also a dramatic debate; with rise and fall of passion, varieties of personal interest, quick changes in the movement of thought; while a background of nature, ever present, makes a climax in a whirlwind which ushers us into the supernatural. Interest of rhetoric is added for emphasis: the argument is swayed out of its course by sustained outbursts of verbal workmanship such as are wont to rouse assemblies of men to strong feeling."

The different aspects of this grave and sensitive subject are introduced by the different speakers as the dialogue proceeds;

while representative mental attitudes toward it are successively exhibited in Job's three friends—Eliphaz the Temanite, Bildad the Shuhite and Zophar the Naamathite, with the addition of Elihu the Buzite, a younger man, who speaks later, when Job and his three fellow-patriarchs have apparently exhausted their discussion in an agreement to differ. The poem then winds up in a Divine intervention expressed in language of the utmost majesty and impressiveness.

It is a pity that in our Authorised Version this mighty poem is not reproduced in its poetic form. The Revised Version, however, restores the parallelism for the English reader, and is a real help in our reading the poetical books of Scripture. In this Book of Job, the poem commences at chapter iii. Chapters i. and ii. are not poetry, but an *historical prologue* to the poem. The poem ends at chapter xlii. 6, with Job's words—

> I had heard of Thee by the hearing of the ear;
> But now mine eye seeth Thee:
> Wherefore I abhor myself
> And repent in dust and ashes.

The final eleven verses of the book are not poetry, but an *historical epilogue* to the poem. Thus, this book of Job may be fitly called "A Dramatic Poem framed in an Epic Story."

Object and Message

In a general sense the design of this book is "to justify the ways of God to man," by correcting certain misconceptions which arise from men's imperfect knowledge: but the *special* object is to show that there is a benevolent Divine purpose running through the sufferings of the godly, and that life's bitterest enigmas are reconcilable with this benevolent Divine purpose, did we but know all the facts. Could Job but have seen into the counsels of heaven just before his trial came, as *we* are permitted to glimpse into them, in the prologue to the poem; and could Job but have foreknown the outcome of his ordeal, as *God* foreknew it, and as *we* now see it in the epilogue to the poem, how differently would he have reacted to it all!

But then that is just the point which gives the whole book its meaning for us—Job did *not* know; and, simple as this point may seem, it is through failure to appreciate its significance that most readers miss the message of the book. Get the picture. Between the prologue, which shows how Job's trial *originated* in the counsels of heaven, and the epilogue, which shows how Job's trial *eventuated* in enrichment and blessing, we have a group of patriarchal wiseacres theorising and dogmatising from incomplete premises and deficient data. They knew nothing about the counsels of heaven which had preceded Job's trial; and they knew nothing about the coming epilogue of compensation. They were philosophising in the dark. It is in this that the book has its message to us. We are meant to see that there *was* an explanation, even though Job and his friends did not know it, so that when baffling affliction comes to ourselves we may believe that the same holds good in our own case—that there is, indeed, a purpose for it in the counsels of heaven, and a foreknown out-come of blessing.

Job not meant to know

The fact is, Job was *not meant* to know the explanation of his trial; and on this simple fact everything hangs. If Job *had* known, there would have been no place for faith; and the man could never have come forth as gold purified in the fire. We are meant to understand that there are some things which God cannot reveal to us at present, inasmuch as the very revealing of them would thwart His purposes for our good. The Scriptures are as wise in their *reservations* as they are in their *revelations*. Enough is revealed to make faith intelligent. Enough is reserved to give faith scope for development.

In this, we repeat, lies the message of the book—that there *was* an explanation, but that Job did not know it and *was not meant* to know it. Because of failure to appreciate this adequately the book has been said to present a problem without a solution. Certainly, if we misjudge the subject of the book to be the problem of suffering *as a whole*, then the book *does* present a problem without a solution: but when we see that the subject is really *one aspect only* of that problem—namely: why do the *godly* suffer?—then the book is far from being a problem without a solution. The solution is found in the explanation of the *prologue* and the consummation of the *epilogue*. This solution, we admit, is not the *final* solution even of this one aspect of suffering. It is an *interim* solution, in which the godly heart may find rest until the full and final solution is given in a day yet to be. The purpose of the book is to show that the final solution is as yet withheld, and that an interim solution is provided, namely, that suffering fulfils a Divine purpose and exercises a gracious ministry in the godly. *Behind* all the suffering of the godly is a high purpose of God, and *beyond* it all is an "afterwards" of glorious enrichment. Such suffering, as we learn from this Book of Job, is not judicial, but remedial; not punitive, but corrective; not retributive, but disciplinary; not a penalty, but a ministry. This is the interim solution. The final solution will be given in that promised day when, instead of seeing through a glass darkly, we shall see "face to face" and shall "know even as we *are* known."

BLESSING THROUGH SUFFERING

The central message of Job, then, may be expressed as: "*BLESSING THROUGH SUFFERING*." Through bitter calamity comes blessed discovery. "Self" is slain and God is known through trial. The book is a grand illustration of Paul's words: "All things work together for good to them that love God, to them who are called according to His purpose" (Rom. viii. 28), and of that other word, in Hebrews xii. 11: "No chastening for the present seemeth to be joyous, but grievous; nevertheless afterward it yieldeth the peaceable fruit of righteousness unto them which are exercised thereby." As the late Dr. J. L. Porter says: "All things—the sorest trials, the bitterest persecutions, the private sorrows that sometimes wring the very heart, and seem calculated to surpass patience, and to quench hope—all these, under the guidance of a God infinite in wisdom and in power, co-operate for the real, because the eternal, welfare of God's people. This is the grand lesson taught by the Book of Job." As William Cowper's well-known couplet puts it—

> *Behind a frowning providence*
> *God hides a smiling face.*

We may now set all this out in the following outline:

THE BOOK OF JOB
BLESSING THROUGH SUFFERING.

PROLOGUE (i.–ii.)	DIALOGUE (iii.–xlii. 6)	EPILOGUE (xlii. 7–17)
	JOB: OPENING LAMENTATION (iii)	
JOB—*his piety in prosperity* (i. 1–5)	FIRST TRIAD Eliphaz v Job iv.–vii. Bildad v Job viii.–x. Zophar v Job xi.–xiv.	JOB—*his proven integrity.* (xlii. 7)
SATAN—*his lie and malignity* (i. 6–19)	SECOND TRIAD Eliphaz v Job xv.–xvii. Bildad v Job xviii.–xix. Zophar v Job xx.–xxi.	FRIENDS—*their rebuked perversity* (xlii. 8)
JOB—*his piety in adversity* (i. 20–2)		JOB—*his ended captivity* (xlii. 10)
SATAN—*his further malignity* (ii. 1–8)	THIRD TRIAD Eliphaz v Job xxii.–xxiv. Bildad v Job xxv.–xxxi. Elihu speaks xxxii.–xxxvii.	FAMILY—*their restored society* (xlii. 11)
JOB—*his piety in extremity* (ii. 9–13)	*GOD: CLOSING INTERVENTION* (xxxviii-xli)	JOB—*his final prosperity* (xlii. 12–17)

Fact or Fiction?

It has been argued by some that the Book of Job is not a narrative of historical fact, and that Job himself was not a real person. Others have held the book to be *partly* historical and partly otherwise, that is, a fiction elaborated around a *nucleus* of facts, like the historical plays of Shakespeare or the historical romances of Sir Walter Scott. Job himself, according to this latter theory, was probably enough a real person, though the Job whom we see in the story is a fictional development of the real person who bore that name. The objections to the historical nature of the book, however, are far from convincing.

Supposed numerical artificiality

One such objection is the supposed *numerical artificiality* of Job's possessions—his 7,000 sheep and 3,000 camels and 1,000 oxen and 500 she-asses, and his having exactly double these figures after his trial. Yet surely these round numbers are not only credible, but just such as might be expected in the describing of a very wealthy man's possessions, and just such as, in fact, commonly occur in the enumeration of herds, flocks, tribes, towns and armies. Job's possessions were such that he was "the greatest of all the men of the east"; and, therefore, in the giving of the totals of his livestock, it would have been trivial for the writer to give an odd ten or fifty, or even an odd hundred in figures running into thousands. The round figures which are given are obviously intended to be taken as approximate, and, as such, are quite compatible with actual fact.

The recurrence of the numbers 7 and 3—in the 7 sons and 3 daughters, the 7,000 sheep and 3,000 camels, and the 3 "friends" who sat with Job for 7 days and nights, have been said to suggest symbolic significance rather than actual fact. Yet all must admit that each of these figures, considered by itself, is such as seems *likely* to be true; and even if these figures *did* contain some symbolic significance, that would not render them historically untrue any more than Jacob's twelve sons become unhistorical because of the Scriptural prominence and symbolic significance of the number twelve.

Satan's Interviews with the Lord

Another objection to the historicity of the book has been found in its description of *Satan's interviews with the Lord*. Could such really have taken place as here described? Well, obviously, since any real knowledge which men possess of the invisible realm can only come by supernatural revelation, it follows that the dealing between God and Satan as here described must either have been Divinely revealed or was a pure invention on the part of the writer. If it was the latter, what shall we say of all the other places in the Scriptures where similar disclosures are recorded? Are these, too, fictitious? However, we shall consider this point more fully when we speak of the prologue to the poem, in our next study.

Poetry and Profundity

Yet another objection to the historicity of the book has been found in its very *poetry and profundity*. It is urged that a dialogue clothed in such grand poetry, and marked by such elaborate structure, could not have been carried on in the spontaneous way here indicated. It has been replied to this that nothing is more remarkable among the Shemitic nations of western Asia than the prevalence of poetic imagination and expression, going with an equally remarkable faculty for pouring forth well-reasoned addresses more or less extemporaneously.

Surely, however, the true reply is that the speeches in the dialogue were probably *not* extemporaneous. There are indications that the interview between Job and his friends continued for a considerable period. They sat in solemn silence for a whole week to begin with (ii. 13), which certainly suggests the opposite of haste! Then, although the speeches are long and contain invectives and reproaches which would almost certainly have occasioned interruptions in any extemporaneous discussion, each speaker is heard without interruption to the end; and the same is true of each reply. Surely, if there was a seven days' pause for consideration *before* the speeches, there would be pauses for reflection *between* the speeches! Moreover, it does not in the least imperil the doctrine of the inspiration of the Scriptures to say that perhaps we largely owe the grand *poetry* of the book to the anonymous *author*, who himself may have been inspired to clothe these weighty addresses in their present rich, poetic garb.

The witness of Scripture

But the historicity of the Book of Job is decisively settled by the testimony of other Scriptures. In Ezekiel xiv. 14, God Himself is represented as saying: "Though these three men, Noah, Daniel, and Job, were in it (Jerusalem), they should deliver but their own souls by their righteousness, saith the Lord God." We have the same in verses 16, 18, and 20. Now Noah and Daniel were certainly historical figures; and is it thinkable that in such words God would use the example of two men who were real and a third who was a mere fiction? Would God speak about a mere feigned person as "delivering his own soul"? Let those answer in the affirmative who will; but to our own judgment these solemn words leave no doubt about the historicity of Job.

Then again, in the Epistle of James, chapter v. 11, the apostle writes: "Ye have heard of the patience of Job, and have seen the end of the Lord, that the Lord is very pitiful and of tender mercy." Now if James was not a writer inspired by the Holy

Spirit he may have been deceived: but if he was writing under the inspiration of the Holy Spirit, as we believe he was, then his reference to Job means that Job was indeed a real person; for if Job were merely a fictitious character it is unthinkable that the Holy Spirit would have lifted him up as an *example* to us. If the person held up as an example be unreal, then there is no real example! Such a model is useless to us; for men are not incited to patient endurance by the patient endurance of somebody who never existed! Moreover, to hold up such an one *as* an example, would surely be unworthy of God. We do well to take it as settled, then, that Job was a real person, and that the Book of Job is really historical.

THE BOOK OF JOB (2)

Lesson Number 53

NOTE.—For this second study in Job read the first two chapters twice, also chapter xlii. 7–17.

Then let us cheerfu' acquiesce;
Nor make our scanty pleasures less,
   By pining at our state;
And, even should misfortunes come,
I here wha sit hae met wi' some,
   An's thankfu' for them yet.
They gie the wit of age to youth;
   They let us ken oursel',
They make us see the naked truth,
   The real guid and ill.
Though losses and crosses be lessons right severe,
There's wit there, ye'll get there, ye'll find nae other where.
         —Robert Burns in " Epistle to Davie."

THE BOOK OF JOB (2)

THE PROLOGUE

THERE is an alternating movement in the prologue to the Book of Job, thus—

JOB—*his piety in prosperity* (i. 1-5).

SATAN—*his lie and malignity* (i. 6-19).

JOB—*his piety in adversity* (i. 20-2).

SATAN—*his further malignity* (ii. 1-8).

JOB—*his piety in extremity* (ii. 9-13).

We shall speak of the character and behaviour of Job a little later, in the light of the conclusion to the poem; but we must pause here to consider the references to Satan.

Satan and God

The interviewing between Satan and God, which we find described in this prologue to the Book of Job, is certainly, on the face of it, one of the strangest bits in the Bible. To some minds it has seemed to give ground for what is perhaps the strongest of the several arguments against the historicity of the Book of Job. Could such interviews really have taken place as here described? The answer to this question is certainly vital, for the truth and value of the whole book depend upon it, as a little reflection will show.

Obviously, as we remarked in our last lesson, since any real knowledge which men possess of the invisible realm can only come by supernatural revelation, it follows that the dealing between God and Satan as here described must either have been Divinely revealed, or else was a pure invention on the part of the writer. There is no middle choice; therefore the reliability of the whole book either stands or falls by it.

If it was by Divine revelation, then the **dealing** between God and Satan actually occurred, even though, of course, the description of it is *anthropopathic*, that is, pictured to us in terms of human action and speech so as to make it understandable to the human mind.

If, on the other hand, it was a pure invention by the author, the whole book is really reduced to meaninglessness; for Job's trial—which is the subject of the whole book—is said to have *originated* in this dealing between God and Satan; so that if this dealing in the invisible realm never took place, but was a mere invention, then *why* Job suffered is absolutely unknown, for it did *not* so originate; it loses any special significance to us; the Divine intervention at the *end* of the book becomes equally fictitious; and the whole book becomes a matter of mere human imagination.

There is no middle choice, we repeat. The book stands or falls on whether this dealing between God and Satan *was* or was *not* a Divine revealing of what actually took place. The vital question, then, is: *Was* it a Divine revelation of what really happened? —and the answer to that question, in the light of other Scriptures, is surely "*Yes.*"

Is not God again and again represented to us, with similar anthropomorphism, as seated on a throne, surrounded by cherubim and seraphim, ministered to by the angel hosts, and conducting His government through their instrumentality? Is not Satan represented as having access to God, as the "accuser of the brethren," in Revelation xii. 10? And do we not see Satan standing in the Lord's presence to accuse Joshua, in Zechariah iii. 1, 2? And are there not still other passages which show us that Satan has indeed a permitted, though limited, power of sifting or testing the Lord's people? See Luke xxii. 31, 32, and 1 Corinthians v. 5, and 1 Timothy i. 20, and 2 Timothy ii. 26.

Perhaps, however, the most striking corroboration of the Satan passages in Job is found in our Lord's word to Simon Peter, in Luke xxii. 31, the more accurate translation of which is: "Simon, Simon, behold, *Satan hath obtained you, by asking that he might sift you as wheat.*" Note, too, our Lord's further word— "But *I have prayed for thee* that thy faith may not utterly fail." Both verbs—Satan's having obtained, and Christ's having prayed,

—are in the Greek tense which indicates an act already past, as though Christ himself had taken part in some such transaction as those described in Job and Zechariah, and had prevailed against the Accuser and Tempter.

With all these instances before us, need we doubt the reality of the Satan passages in Job i. and ii.? To do so calls other Scriptures equally into question, and even the words of the Lord Jesus himself. We believe that these interviews actually took place between God and Satan, that the fact and purport of them was Divinely revealed, that they are anthropopathically described to us, and that they supply us with the primary explanation of Job's trial. But besides this, these interviews are so described as to furnish us with certain most precious and enlightening facts; and some of these we will now consider.

Arresting Implications

Accepting, then, that these colloquies in heaven took place as recorded in the prologue, we note certain arresting truths concerning Satan.

We see that *Satan is accountable to God.* Does it seem strange that Satan should have access to God as here recorded? To see it in that light is to miss the real implication. Are we not to infer from this passage that angel intelligences must gather periodically to the great white throne to give account? These "sons of God" come to "present themselves" before Jehovah; not to participate in the governmental deliberations of the Divine Mind, but to render account, as servants of the Crown, concerning their respective ministrations. Satan also must give account. The point here is not that Satan has the privilege of access, but that he is compelled to come. He, no less than other creatures, is subject to the Divine authority, however unwillingly. His appearing before the throne is neither a privilege from God nor a presumption of his own, but a compelling ruling of the Most High which the arch-rebel dare not and cannot evade. To be brought thus and exposed before the white fire of that awful throne, what intense torture to that naked, malignant spirit!

Second, we see here that *even the dark mind of Satan is an open book to God.* It might sound at first as though God's words,

"Hast thou considered my servant Job . . .?" were a provocation or incitement to Satan. No; God knew what was already there in that evil-designing mind, just as he knew all Satan's goings to and fro before ever he asked, "Whence comest thou?" The questions are asked, not because God does not know, but to compel confession on the part of Satan. More literally translated, God's question is: "Hast thou set thine heart on (or against) my servant Job because there is none like him. . . .?" Satan's reply immediately revealed that he *had*, and that he believed his lack of success was because God had hedged Job in too protectedly. It is good to reflect that God knows all that is in Satan's mind, at all times, against any of the saints.

Third, we see from this passage that *Satan is behind the evils that curse the earth.* In reply to the question, "Whence comest thou?" he says: "From going to and fro in the earth. . . ." It seems clear that Satan has a special activity towards this earth. Genesis attributes the origin of sin in humanity to him, and the Scriptures make it progressively plainer that he is largely behind the evils that afflict our race. Satan's words: "going to and fro" and "walking up and down" indicate his restless and unintermittent activity. His sinister genius is ever erupting malevolent stratagems. He knows nothing of the joyous peace which inheres in loyal and beneficent service. The ban of Cain is upon him, that of vagabond restlessness. This perpetual motion of unrest is ever the mark of the evil, banished from God. See Isaiah lvii. 20, 21; Matthew xii. 43. But besides restlessness, there is perpetual purpose of evil in Satan's peregrinations. He is "the god of this age" who blinds the minds of the unbelieving. We never get very far in dealing with social problems or in preaching or in praying until we realise that behind the world's evils is the energising and organising mind of a personal devil.

Fourth, we see from Satan's words and doings in this prologue that *the evil one is neither omnipresent nor omniscient.* Many of the Lord's people seem to have a vague sort of idea that Satan is everywhere; but he is nothing of the kind. He may move with almost lightning-like rapidity, maybe, but none the less he is a created and therefore *local* being. He is only in one place at a time. At the risk of its sounding rather crudely put, we mean that if the personal Satan himself is this moment engaged in one particular part of this world, say Africa, he is not in any other part, say Australia or America. Many Christians seem to think that Satan himself is somehow always hovering about them in a shadowy sort of way; but they are wrong. While there may be many invisible spirit-agencies operating in alliance with Satan upon human beings, he himself is a restricted, localised being. With characteristic insight, John Bunyan, in his *Pilgrim's Progress*, has recognised this; for although Pilgrim encounters all manner of enemies on the road to the celestial city, he only encounters the dread Apollyon himself once. Nor must we think that Satan is *omniscient*—as many seem hazily to imagine. God can see into all our minds; but Satan cannot; he is not God. Here is comfort for the saints! Satan could not see clearly into Job's mind. He thought he knew what was there, but he was mistaken, and was defeated. Satan can indeed take possession of a human mind, as he did of Judas's, and as he does with many a spiritist medium, either directly or through some other evil spirit, and either intermittently or continually; but that is because there has been permission granted from the human side, in response to deceptive temptation. He cannot read my mind, much less force access, unless I let him. If this were not so, the dignity of human personality would not exist. Let us never forget it—Satan is neither everywhere nor all-knowing. We *dare not* underrate him; but it is also bad strategy to *overrate* him.

Fifth, we note, in this prologue to the Book of Job, that *Satan can do nothing without the Divine permission*. His machinations are under the perpetual surveillance of the Almighty. He is as free and restless as the restless, raging waters of the swelling seas—and at the same time just as bound. "Hitherto shalt thou come, but no further: and here shall thy proud waves be stayed" (Job xxxviii. 11). It is because Satan can do nothing without such permission that God is able again and again to overrule his doings to the ultimate good of those whom he would ruin.

Sixth, let us also be quick to learn from this prologue that *in every such permission there is a definite limitation*. The first limitation is: "Only upon himself put not forth thine hand" (i. 12). Then, when Job has sublimely survived the test, there is a further permission, but also a further limitation: "Behold, he is in thine hand; but touch not his life" (ii. 6). Here again is comfort for the saints. Satan has absolutely no power against a saint beyond what God allows, any more than Pilate had against

Christ (John xix. 11). If God set a limit to Satan's power in the trying of Job, then he will do likewise in the case of others, especially those who are less able to withstand the adversary's assaults. See 1 Corinthians x. 13 for the classic New Testament pronouncement on this.

Finally, let us learn afresh from this prologue that *God's eyes are ever on his own people, and especially so in times of trial.* God's question to Satan was: "Hast thou set thine heart against my servant Job . . .?" The very question indicates that God also had Job in his thought. Note how God particularises Job by name, dilates on Job's godly character, commends his piety, and evinces special regard for him by calling him "My servant." So is it with *all* God's Jobs. Lowell's words come to mind—

> Careless seems the great Avenger,
>   History's pages but record
> One death grapple in the darkness,
>   'Twixt old systems and the Word;
> Truth for ever on the scaffold,
>   Wrong for ever on the throne;
> Yet that scaffold sways the future,
>   And behind the dim unknown
> Standeth God within the shadows,
>   Keeping watch upon his own.

An Alternative Theory

Perhaps we ought to mention here that there is an alternative theory concerning the "sons of God" who come to "present themselves before Jehovah" in Job i. 6 and ii. 1. There are those who hold that these were not angels, but the *godly men* of that time. We need to remember the high antiquity of this Book of Job. Its language, tone, style, the manners, customs, institutions and the general mode of life described in it, all indicate that it belongs to Patriarchal times, possibly long enough before the Exodus. In those times God revealed Himself in visible form to men far more than was the case later; and it is argued that the coming of these "sons of God" before Jehovah was the gathering of godly patriarchs to the place of Divine manifestation, for the purpose of worship. For instance, Mr. George Rapkin, in his book on Genesis, says—

"We have, in the Book of Job, the statement in chapters i. 6 and ii. 1, 'The Sons of God came to present themselves before the Lord.' The expression here for 'sons of God' is the same as in the Hebrew of Genesis vi. 2, namely, *beni ha Elohim*. It has been concluded by scholars that Moses was the author of the Book of Job, and that he (Job) lived in the Patriarchal period, probably before the Flood. Here, again, is the expression, 'the presence of the Lord.' Now can it be assumed that the angels are not always in His presence? But these *beni ha Elohim* were not always there, and came at certain seasons for this purpose.

"The story of Job opens by telling of a devout father, who, when he knew his children were feasting, offered sacrifice for them, lest they should have blasphemed God. Then came the day of appearing before God, and of Satan being granted the permission to harass the father.

"The 'sons of God' were the godly men of the time who came for worship in the presence of the Lord. They came before the Lord just as David later urged the congregation to do, when urging thanksgiving. Coming before the Lord and entering His presence is not so striking when we find the Bible speaking of men and congregations doing this. Nimrod is said to have been a 'mighty hunter before the Lord,' but we do not stretch our fanciful imagination to the extent of saying he must have been an angel. Now Job and his sons, with other righteous men, were the sons of God who presented themselves before the Lord for the act of worship and sacrifice, the father then acting as the head, or priest, of the family worship and sacrifice."

Mr. Rapkin is by no means alone in holding this view. It is surprising how much may be said for it. As we have remarked, the Book of Job is perhaps the oldest in the Bible, going back to earliest times when there seem to have been visible and set manifestations of the Divine presence among men, in connection with worship. These sons of God in Job came before such a "presence of Jehovah," and it was from the same "presence" that Satan went forth. It is just the same expression as in Genesis iv. 16, where we read that "Cain went out from the presence of

Jehovah"; and just the same as with Jonah who fled from "the presence of Jehovah" (Jonah i. 3, 10).

Now no one would say that either Cain or Jonah were going out from some audience with God *in heaven*! They were both, quite definitely, on earth; and they passed out from some visible presence of God on earth (which incidentally gives the lie to those who stupidly make out that Jonah thought he could escape from the *general* presence of God. Jonah's own words in verse 9 should have shown them otherwise). Similarly, so it is claimed, the "sons of God" in Job were not angels coming before God *in heaven*, but godly men coming before Him *on earth*.

It is also urged that these "sons of God" in Job came into the presence of Jehovah *voluntarily*, inasmuch as it says that they came to "*present* themselves" before Him. And it is still further pointed out that they are said to have come before "*Jehovah*," the name "Jehovah" being especially a name of God toward *man*. And there are other arguments as well.

After careful thought we ourselves incline to the other and more usual view of the prologue. But the crucial fact, whichever view we take, is that there was *a definite interview between Satan and God concerning Job*, in which, all unsuspected by Job and his fellows, lay the origin and the explanation of his fiery trial.

THE BOOK OF JOB (3)

Lesson Number 54

NOTE.—For this study read chapters iii. to xxxi. (in the Revised Version preferably, or in some modern translation where the poetic parallelism is shown).

But before reading those chapters again read the study herewith, then read the chapters, checking off in them what we have said in our summaries of the speeches by Eliphaz, Bildad and Zophar.

Be still, my soul; the Lord is on Thy side.
Bear patiently the cross of grief or shame.
Leave to thy God to order and provide;
In every change He faithful will remain.
Be still, my soul; thy best, thy heavenly Friend
Through thorny ways leads to a joyful end.

Be still, my soul; thy God doth undertake
To guide the future as He hath the past.
Thy hope, thy confidence, let nothing shake;
All now mysterious shall be bright at last.
Be still, my soul; the waves and winds still know
His voice who ruled them while He dwelt below.

—*Katherine von Schlegel.*

THE BOOK OF JOB (3)

THE DIALOGUE

WE COME now to the main body of the book, that is, to the poetic dialogue or debate. It moves before us with something of dramatic form, in successive rounds or triads. There are six speakers—Job, the three friends, a younger man named Elihu, and God.

The centre-problem is: Why does Job suffer? This necessarily involves the question of human suffering as a whole. Job's three friends seek to interpret Job's case in particular by their conception of providence in general. The results are far from satisfactory. Then, at the point of pathetic deadlock, Elihu suddenly speaks up and elaborately submits at least one important proposition which has hitherto been quite overlooked. Deep darkness, however, still remains. Finally, the voice of God Himself breaks in from a tornado, bringing the discussion to a majestic yet unexpected climax.

Now if we are to appreciate the living message of this old dramatic dialogue, there are two main things we must do. First, we must catch the main significance of the discussion itself. Second, we must watch the remarkable process going on in Job the sufferer. What, then, is the main significance of the discussion? We shall most quickly get at this by referring, not to Job's own speeches, but to the other speakers and their respective viewpoints.

Take first Job's three friends, Eliphaz the Temanite, Bildad the Shuhite, and Zophar the Naamathite. They speak to the debate, one after another, in the order in which we have here named them, presumably because this is the order of seniority (though all three were definitely old men: see xxxii. 6). They come from far to console Job (ii. 11–13); but, as the dialogue develops, their condoling turns to condemning, and Job's suffering is thereby aggravated to a point of almost unendurable poignancy. What, then, is the philosophy and argument of these men?

Eliphaz

To begin with, let us glance quickly again through the three speeches of Eliphaz, the eldest and wisest. An observant reader will soon notice the peculiarity which distinguishes Eliphaz from Bildad and Zophar, namely, that he rests his philosophy of life on a two-fold basis—(*a*) on general observation, and (*b*) on a supposed special spiritual illumination. As to the first of these, see the recurrence of "I have seen" in chapters iv. 8; v. 3, 27; xv. 17. As to the second, see his reference to a secret vision, in chapter iv. 12–16, and his reference to a special wisdom handed down from his Temanite predecessors, in chapter xv. 18, 19, R.V. So we may say, in a word, that Eliphaz bases his argument on *EXPERIENCE*.

His three speeches may be easily summarised. The first occupies chapters iv. and v. It is in four parts. In the opening verses he commends Job's former piety (iv. 3–7). Then, in the main body of his speech, he declares what he has learned by observation (iv. 8–v. 7), namely, that suffering is always the direct outcome of sin, and is God's judgment on it. Next he avows what his own pious reaction would be if he himself were in such a trouble as Job's (v. 8–16). Finally, he applies all this to Job in a poetically arresting appeal which begins, "Behold, happy is the man whom God correcteth" (v. 17–27).

His second speech occupies chapter xv. Its tone is much severer. It is much shorter than the first. In point of argument it marks no advance on the first speech. It is in two parts. Verses 2–16 are a venerable rebuke. Verses 17–35 are an even more insistent declaration than in the first speech of what he has "seen" and learned.

His third speech fills chapter xxii. Again there is no advance in argument. It is the old theory, with its necessary corollary that Job must have sinned. It is in three parts. In verses 1–9 he outrightly condemns Job, especially so in verses 5–9, where he flatly contradicts his own commendation of Job in the first speech. Next, in verses 10–20, he draws his hard and fast conclusion about Job, beginning with that unmistakable "Therefore . . ." Job is in reality a hypocrite (see verse 13). Finally, in verses 21–30, there comes Eliphaz's parting appeal, beginning with, "Acquaint now thyself with Him and be at peace."

So much for the disquisitions of Eliphaz. This man and his views may be summed up in the following fourfold way:

1. He rests his philosophy of life peculiarly on his own observation and experience (iv. 8, 12; v. 3, 27).
2. He is committed to a fixed theory, with a much too narrow and rigid view of Providence (v. 3–7, 12–16; xv. 20–35).
3. This rigid and inadequate theory finds focal expression in chapter iv. 7, at the beginning of his first speech: "Remember, I pray thee, who ever perished being innocent? Or where were the upright cut off?"
4. This theory, as applied to Job, finds focus in chapter v. 17: "Behold, happy is the man whom God correcteth: therefore despise not thou the chastening of the Almighty." *Job suffers because he has sinned.*

Bildad

Take now the speeches of Bildad. They occur in chapters viii., xviii., and xxv. respectively. They do not have the same air of courtesy as those of Eliphaz. Bildad is the forthright declaimer rather than the reflective reasoner. His opening speech is noticeably severer than that of Eliphaz, though this may be because Job had already uttered his first reply to Eliphaz before Bildad spoke.

Unlike Eliphaz, who rests his philosophy of life on his own observation and experience, Bildad rests on *tradition*. See chapter viii. 8–10. See also chapter xviii., where practically his whole speech (verses 5–20) seems to be but a succession of traditional maxims or proverbs drawn from "the wisdom of the *Beni Kedem*" (or sons of the east: 1 Kings iv. 30). So, then, in Bildad we have the voice of *TRADITION*.

His three speeches are easily epitomised. The first is an appeal; the second is a rebuke; the third is an evasion. They occur in chapters viii., xviii., and xxv.

The first comes in chapter viii. It is an appeal, and is in three parts. Verses 2–7 are an appeal to *appearances*, that is, to the sudden deaths of Job's children as indicating Divine judgment on them for sin (verse 4), and to Job's further trouble as therefore indicating that Job himself cannot be "pure and upright" (verses 5, 6). Note the three "ifs" in verses 4, 5, 6, which mark Bildad's reasoning from these appearances. Next, verses 8–19, the main body of the speech, are an appeal to *tradition*; and finally, verses 20–2 are really an appeal to Job's own intelligence, the force of which is: "God will not cast away a perfect man" (verse 20), and therefore "He will yet fill *thy* mouth with laughter" (verse 21), if *thou* art such a man.

Bildad's second speech comes in chapter xviii. In point of argument it marks no advance on the first. It is simply reaffirmation in fiercer form. In fact it contains no actual *reasoning* at all, but rather consists of proverb-quoting. It is a rebuke, and is in two parts. Verses 1–4 are a rebuke in the form of indignant personal questions. Verses 5–21 are a rebuke in the form of traditional moral maxims. Note the determined "Yea" and "Surely" at the beginning and the ending of the second part (verses 5 and 21).

Bildad's third speech comes in chapter xxv., which has only six verses. It is simply a few sententious couplets, and is really an evasion. It completely shirks Job's preceding challenge (xxiv.) as to the fact that it is the wicked and not the righteous who are often the more prosperous. It simply touches on two well-worn topics again—the all-holy majesty of God (verses 2, 3), and the sinfulness of man (verses 4–6). Its closing words—"The stars are not pure in His sight, how much less man?"—are merely an evasive truism as applied to Job; for Job had never claimed to be without sin, but only that his sins had not been such as to account for his trouble.

These, then, are the contributions of Bildad. We may sum up this man and his views thus:

1. His outlook on life is moulded and limited peculiarly by tradition (viii. 8; xviii. 5–20).

2. Like Eliphaz, he is committed to a far too rigid view of Providence (viii. 11–19; xviii. 5, etc.).

3. This circumscribed theory finds focal expression in chapter viii. 20: "God will not cast away a perfect man; neither will He uphold evil-doers."

4. This theory as applied to Job finds focus in chapter viii. 6: "If thou wert pure and upright, surely now God would awake for thee." *Job is a hypocrite.*

Zophar

And now, what about Zophar? Unless, as some scholars think, chapters xxvii. (from verse 7) and xxviii. should be attributed to him, he speaks only twice to the debate, for in the third round his place is taken by Elihu. The two speeches occur in chapters xi. and xx. Zophar is less courteous and more drastic than either Eliphaz or Bildad. This may be due in part to the fact that by the time he entered the argument Job had already answered both the other two, contradicting their philosophy, and upholding his own innocence with increasing tenacity. Zophar's opening words denote that he already feels aggravated (xi. 2, 3).

Zophar, like the other two, has his distinguishing feature. Eliphaz, as we have seen, bases his view on observation and experience. Bildad rests on tradition. But Zophar is content with mere *ASSUMPTION*. There is at least reasoned deduction in Eliphaz, and intelligent orthodoxy in Bildad, but this man Zophar assumes and pronounces with a finality which would make even Job's daring to differ a sin. He is the pure dogmatist. From beginning to end of his speeches there is not a semblance of *reasoning*. There is not a semblance of Eliphaz's "I have seen," or of Bildad's "Enquire, I pray thee, of the former age." Zophar's word is a dogmatic "Know thou." It occurs in both his speeches, and in both cases right at the beginning of his main proposition. See chapters xi. 6 and xx. 4 (the latter reads as a question in our English versions, but the Hebrew is simply, "Know thou").

Zophar's first speech (xi.) is in three parts. Verses 1–6 are *a condemnation of Job*—for verbosity (verse 2), presumption verses 3, 4), sinfulness (verses 5, 6).   Next, verses 7–12 are *a vindication of God*—as above human understanding (verses 7–9), above human interference (verse 10), above human deception and evasion (verses 11, 12). Finally, verses 13–20 are *an admonition to repentance*—the alternatives being repentance and restoration (verses 13–19), or impenitence and death (verse 20).

Zophar's second speech comes in chapter xx. It is throughout a vehement though covert denunciation of Job as a deservedly punished evil-doer and hypocrite. It falls into three parts. Verses 1–3 give the *introduction*, i.e. Zophar is provoked. Then verses 4–28 give the *proposition*, i.e. the prosperity of the wicked is shortlived. Finally, verse 29 gives the *application*, which is meant to be taken by Job himself, i.e. that Job is suffering the portion of "*a wicked man.*"

We may sum up Zophar and his views thus:

1. He is a religious dogmatist (xi. 6; xx. 4).
2. Like Eliphaz and Bildad, he is mentally cramped by a much too rigid view of Providence (xi. 13–20; xx. 5, etc.).
3. His narrow dogmatism finds focal expression in chapter xx. 5: "The triumphing of the wicked is short. . . . "
4. This theory, applied to Job, finds concentration in chapter xi. 6: "Know therefore that God exacteth of thee less than thine iniquity deserveth."

The Three Compared and Contrasted

Compare and contrast these three men. Take first the points of difference. Eliphaz rests his view of things on *observation*; Bildad rests on *tradition*; Zophar rests on *assumption*. Eliphaz is the religious *moralist*. Bildad is the religious *legalist*. Zophar is the religious *dogmatist*. Eliphaz is the *apologist*. Bildad is the *lecturer*. Zophar is the *bigot*; he is full of convictions, but they are assumptions, not reasoned conclusions. In a rough sort of way, we have in Eliphaz the voice of philosophy; in Bildad the voice of history; and in Zophar the voice of orthodoxy; but none is able to give satisfying answer to a problem like Job's. These three men may be represented largely, perhaps, by the three words, "IF," "MUST," "IS." Eliphaz takes the hypothetical attitude that *if* Job were not sinful, this trouble would not have come. Bildad takes the inferential attitude that Job *must* be sinful seeing that the trouble has indeed come. Zophar begins with the assumption that Job *is* a sinful man and deserves his affliction.

Take now the points of similarity. (1) All these three men are committed to what is substantially the same fixed theory of life, namely, that calamity is always the direct outcome of sin, and that the Divine favour or disfavour is indicated by a man's material prosperity or adversity. (2) They all therefore have a far too narrow and rigid view of Providence; yet they are so sure that their view is right that they look on resistance to it as resistance to God: see chapter xi. 5, for instance. (3) They all want to prove that goodness and wickedness are always rewarded and punished *in this present life*: they are all silent concerning human destiny and Divine retribution in a life beyond this present one. Their philosophy and doctrine have no horizon beyond this earth. (4) From the standpoint of argument they are all absolutely static. Although there is marked advance in the thinking of Job himself, there is no advance at all on the part of these three "friends," except in the *expression* of their views. (5) They all fail to give any real or convincing answer to Job, as is recognised by those who witness the debate: see chapter xxxii. 3, 5, 11, 12. (6) They all condemn Job; for on their philosophy, they must either justify Job at God's expense or justify God at Job's; and, understandably, they choose the latter (xxxii. 3).

Job Versus the Trio

So far as mere argument is concerned, Job undoubtedly has the better of it. Admittedly, he gives way here and there to passionate and reckless utterances which he afterwards regrets and confesses to have been rash; but these were simply wrung from him in moments of terrible intensity when, in addition to his already extreme mental and physical suffering, he was goaded to exasperation by the stubborn unfairness and lack of real sympathy on the part of the three professed sympathisers.

Job is suffering far too keenly to aim at any mere victory of argument. He would gladly lose the argument if thereby he could get at the truth. Yet his very suffering gives a realism to his arguing and questioning which is lacking from the speeches of Eliphaz, Bildad, and Zophar, and which these men cannot withstand.

Glance back over the three rounds or cycles of the dialogue. In the first round the three friends are one in the contention that God always prospers the upright and punishes the perverse. Job's reply is that his own experience proves their argument defective, for he himself is upright and yet is afflicted.

In the second round Eliphaz insists that it is *only* the wicked who suffer. Bildad insists that the wicked *always* suffer. Zophar insists that any seeming prosperity of the wicked is *shortlived*. Job replies to each. Observation shows that it is *not* only the wicked who suffer: the righteous suffer as well. Nor do the wicked *always* suffer; many seem to escape. Nor is the prosperity of the wicked always shortlived; for it often continues until death and extends to the children who are left.

In the third round Eliphaz merely restates the old theory, though with more vehemence. Bildad re-endorses it, but only in a few evasive platitudes. Job's answer is a protracted and solemnly passionate protestation of innocence. Zophar is silent.

Thus the discussion exhausts itself in a sheer deadlock; and there is an arresting significance in this very fact. It has been discerningly observed that this historic debate in the Book of Job is "the first recorded struggle of a new experience with an established orthodox belief." It is "the first fierce collision" of a new fact of experience with the accepted creed which "will not stretch to cover it." The orthodox formula of the trio on the one hand, and Job's experience on the other, were simply irreconcilable. Job knew that although he was a sinner, as all men are sinners, he had been conscientiously upright according to the light given to him, and that he was utterly sincere in his protestation to the three friends; and he therefore felt (as others of us have felt in other connections perhaps) that no creed can be true or adequate if it contradicts that which is deepest and truest and most native in our human constitution. The verdict of God Himself later comes down on Job's side. Thus the book brings home to us the fact that experience is an essential factor in the interpreting of revealed truth.

So much, then, for the interchanges between Job and the trio. The argument is broken off inconclusively and disappointingly. But there are two other voices which now speak to the debate and bring it to a majestic finale. These we shall consider in our next two studies.

THE BOOK OF JOB (4)
Lesson Number 55

NOTE.—For this study read the speech of Elihu in chapters xxxii. to xxxvii. Then read our interpretation of it herewith, and go through the speech again, checking off what we have said in this study.

Not oft mid busy servings
   Life's deepest truths are learned;
Not oft mid noisy strivings
   The Spirit's voice discerned.
Not in life's crowded places,
   Where jostling cares intrude,
But, in life's lonely spaces,
   God speaks in solitude.

The solitude of illness—
   The loneness, ling'ring drear,
'Tis oft predestined stillness,
   The voice of Heav'n to hear.
Old age—sad isolation
   When friends of yore are gone,
Oft brings most revelation
   Of the abiding One.

Affliction's deprivation—
   Blind eyes, deaf ears, spent powers,
Ah, painful separation
   To lonely, trying hours!
The loneness when heart breaketh,
   And none on earth can ease;
Ah, most of all God speaketh
   In solitudes like these.

The prophet's lone vocation,
   Some heavenly call pursued,
The far-flung mission station—
   These bring their solitude.
Thrice-blessed heart-break places,
   Where lone and drear we plod!
For in life's loneliest spaces
   We most discover—*GOD*.

           —*J. S. B.*

THE BOOK OF JOB (4)

A New Voice—Elihu

THE LAST verse of chapter xxxi. marks a major break—"The words of Job are ended." Chapter xxxii. introduces a harangue by a new speaker, Elihu. He is a much younger man than the others (verse 6). He has evidently heard all the debate, and has held his tongue until now in deference to seniority (verses 4, 6, 7). Now, however, as he hears Job still stubbornly justifying himself while the trio increasingly condemn him without being able to answer him, he cannot stand by any longer silently biting his lip. He must now speak (verses 2, 3, 5); and he breaks forth in a spirit of "Elihu to the rescue." Albeit, the rescue is not so easy as Elihu has presupposed, though he certainly contributes a valuable corrective to the discussion. There is one aspect of the problem which has been overlooked, and it is to this that our new speaker calls attention.

Elihu's discourse, which fills no less than six chapters, has been criticised as verbose and as the speech of a conceited young man, disrespectful in its tone and adding nothing to the argument. A more careful reading refutes this unkindly misjudgment. It is the most courteous speech of the debate, and undoubtedly surpasses all the preceding speeches in spiritual grasp. It moves on a higher level than the speeches of Eliphaz, Bildad and Zophar. What is most of all important, however, in relation to the problem under discussion, is that it introduces three new factors. First, there is a new *approach*. Second, there is a new *answer*. Third, there is a new *appeal*.

A New Approach.

Elihu accepts Job's position that any true wisdom in man comes only by inspiration from God, but he has become convinced that such wisdom is not given only to the aged (xxxii. 9). There is "a spirit in man" capable of receiving inspiration (verse 8), and Elihu believes that he himself is now receiving such inspiration (xxxiii. 4; xxxvi. 2–4). But more than this, Elihu believes that he is so inspired as to fulfil Job's longing for a daysman between God and himself, to whom he could set out his case. In pathetic desperation Job had lamented the lack of such a daysman (ix. 33), and his own inability to gain an interview with God (xxiii. 3–7); and, in fact, his last words before Elihu breaks in are—

"Oh that I had one to hear me! (Lo, here is my signature; let the Almighty answer me), and that I had the indictment which mine adversary hath written! Surely I would carry it upon my shoulder; I would bind it unto me as a crown. I would declare unto Him the number of my steps; as a prince would I go near unto Him" (xxxi. 35–7).

Elihu believes himself to be so inspired as to be the answer to this longing of Job. Note his remarkable words in chapter xxxiii. 6—

"Behold, I am according to thy wish in God's stead. I also am formed of clay."

Thus Elihu claims a special inspiration from God, yet can take Job's part also as being of the same clay. This is a quite different approach from that of Eliphaz, Bildad and Zophar with their hard and fast philosophy and their treatment of Job's problem as detached onlookers. *They* had wished to be *judges*; whereas *Elihu* would be a *brother*. He would seek to sit with Job in the fellowship of human sympathy, yet at the same time speak the real truth from *God's* side. Such is the new approach.

A New Answer.

Elihu's answer reaches its full statement in chapters xxxvi. and xxxvii.; but glance first at what leads up to that, in chapters xxxiii. to xxxv.

God is greater than man, and therefore man has no right or authority to require an explanation of Him (xxxiii. 12, 13). There must of necessity be some things which God does that are incomprehensible to man. Yet God *does* speak to men if they will listen (verses 14-16), with a view to restraining and rescuing them from evil (verses 17, 18). Moreover, God not only speaks, He *chastises* (verses 19-22), and this, if only there were one to interpret it, is always with a view to healing and restoring men (verses 23-8). This covers the very experiences through which Job was passing. What he has lacked is an interpreter; and it seems clear that Elihu considers himself the required interpreter (verses 29-33). Job's suffering is *educational*. God is dealing with him to some higher issue. This is in chapter xxxiii.; and obviously it touches a higher level than the other speeches.

It is followed, in chapter xxxiv., by the argument that God's government, besides being sovereign and gracious (as in xxxiii.) must necessarily be absolutely righteous and impartial (verses 10-19). It is also perfect in its discernment (verse 23), which makes quite superfluous Job's demands for an audience with God, in which to state his case (verse 23). God knows all the facts absolutely. Special trial is unnecessary. It is just because of this that some of God's doings seem mysterious (verses 24-6). Yet they are always with good moral purpose (verses 27-30).

And so Elihu moves to the final development of his answer to Job, in chapters xxxvi. and xxxvii. And what *is* it which makes his answer new and distinctive? It is this: He sees a different and superior *purpose* in suffering from that which Eliphaz and Bildad and Zophar have seen. It is a much higher and more spiritual purpose. The other speakers have all been bound hand and foot by the theory that suffering is necessarily the punishment of past sinning. Elihu sees beyond that, to a truer and wider meaning. Suffering is not exclusively punitive; it is also *corrective*. It is not only penal; it is *moral*. It does not only come to requite a man; it comes to *restore* a man. It does not always come just to chastise; it often comes to *chasten*. It is not only the judge's rod; it is the shepherd's goad.

See how this new interpretation of Elihu runs through his discourse, reaching its full expression in chapters xxxvi. and xxxvii. See how through suffering man is restrained and refined and restored.

RESTRAINED.
"He (God) openeth the ears of men,
And sealeth their instruction,

That He may *withdraw man from his (evil) purpose*
And hide pride from man.
He keepeth back his soul from the pit,
And his life from perishing by the sword."

(xxxiii. 16–18.)

CHASTENED.

"He is also *chastened* with pain upon his bed,
And with continual strife in his bones,
So that his life abhorreth bread,
And his soul dainty meat."

(xxxiii. 19–20.)

RESTORED.

"If but there be with him . . . an interpreter,
To show unto a man what is right for him,
Then He is gracious unto him, and saith,
Deliver him from going down to the pit,
I have found a ransom.
His flesh shall be fresher than a child's;
He returneth to the days of his youth;
He prayeth unto God, and He is favourable,
So that he seeth His (God's) face with joy,
For He restoreth to man his righteousness.
He singeth before men and saith,
I have sinned and perverted the right,
And it profited me not.
He hath saved my soul from going to the pit,
And my life shall behold the light."

(xxxiii. 23–8.)

Ere he ends this first part of his speech, and pauses to give Job chance to interpose any comment (verses 31–3), Elihu rounds off this threefold view of suffering with the summary reiteration—

"Lo, all these things doth God work,
Twice, yea thrice, with a man,
To bring back his soul from the pit,
That he may be enlightened with the light
of the living."

Next, in chapter xxxiv., Elihu goes on to argue that in thus afflicting men, God ever acts with absolute righteousness, impartiality and discernment.

"Far be it from God to do wickedness,
    And from the Almighty to commit iniquity . . .
Shall One that hateth right govern?
And wilt thou (Job) condemn Him (God) that
        is just and mighty?
Is it fit to say to a king, Thou art vile?
Or to nobles, Ye are wicked?
How much less to Him that respecteth not the
        persons of princes,
Nor regardeth the rich more than the poor?
For they all are the work of God's hands."

                              (verses 10, 17–19.)

"For His eyes are on the ways of a man,
And He beholdeth all his goings.
There is no darkness nor shadow of death
Where workers of iniquity may hide (from Him);
For He needeth not further to consider a man,
That he (i.e., a man) should go before God in
        judgment (i.e. as Job wished to do)."

                              (verses 21–3.)

Elihu then makes the case that on this principle affliction comes even to the mighty men of the earth, and that it only continues to the point of complete destruction where there is refusal toward God.

"He breaketh in pieces mighty men, in ways
        past finding out,
And setteth others in their stead."

                              (verse 24.)

"Because they turned from following Him,
And *would not heed* any of His ways."

                              (verse 27.)

Had there been repentance on the part of any of these persons, the outcome would have been different; but all of those who had perished had refused to learn by affliction.

> "For hath any (of them) said unto God,
> I have borne chastisement, I offend no more;
> That which I see not, teach Thou me,
> And if I have done iniquity I will do it no
> more?" (verses 31, 32.)

Then Elihu turns to Job and asks him if, in view of all this, he considers himself better qualified than God to decide such recompense.

> "Should God's recompence be according to *thy*
> mind,
> Seeing thou refusest them (God's judgments)?
> For thou must choose, and not I;
> Therefore say what *thou* knowest (i.e. better
> than God)." (verse 33.)

This is a hint to Job to submit to God's dealings as chastening with a good purpose, rather than to be all the while rebelling against them as unrighteous punishments. God is trying to teach Job something, and the suffering is being prolonged by Job's resentful unsubmissiveness.

In chapter xxxv. Elihu continues his answer by submitting that Job's appeals and protestations to God are not acknowledged because they are not in a right spirit. Many others suffer on for the same reason. Read verses 9 to 12, culminating with,

> "There they cry, but He doth not answer,
> Because of the pride of (those) evil-doers."

As for Job himself, how can *he* expect answer or explanation from God when he insists that God cannot even be found or approached and that He treats Job as an enemy?

> "Surely God will not hear vanity,
> Neither will the Almighty regard it;
> How much less (thee, Job) when thou sayest
> Thou seest Him not?" (xxxv. 13, 14.)

In chapters xxxvi. and xxxvii. Elihu brings his theory to its final expression. Once again he emphasises that affliction, other than being always judicial, is often remedial.

> "Behold, God is mighty and despiseth not any;
> He is mighty in strength of understanding.
> He preserveth not the life of the wicked,
> But giveth to the afflicted their right.
> He withdraweth not His eyes from the upright,
> But (exalts them) with kings on the throne;
> He setteth them for ever and they are exalted.
> If they (others of them) be bound in fetters
> And be taken in the cords of affliction,
> He (thus) showeth them their . . . transgressions,
> That they have behaved themselves proudly.
> He (thus) openeth their ear to instruction,
> And commandeth that they return from iniquity.
> If they hearken and serve Him
> They spend their days in prosperity,
> And their years in pleasantness.
> But if they hearken not they shall perish . . .
> And they shall die without knowledge."

(xxxvi. 5–12.)

This is stated again later, and is directly applied to the case of Job—

> "He saveth the afflicted *by* his affliction
> And openeth their ear in adversity.
> Yea, He would have led *thee* out of distress
> Into a broad place where is no straitness."

(verses 15, 16.)

But, as Elihu now complains, Job, instead of learning by affliction, has "fulfilled the judgment of the wicked" (i.e. has displayed the same attitude toward God as the wicked). That is why Divine judgment *still* afflicts him (verse 17). And Elihu warns Job that his affliction may even lead to death if there is no change of mind—

> "Because there is wrath, beware,
> Lest He *take thee away* with His stroke;
> Then a great ransom cannot deliver thee.
> Will thy riches suffice (then) . . .
> Or all the forces of thy strength? . . .
> Take heed! Regard not iniquity,
> For this thou hast chosen (i.e. to murmur)
> rather than (submission to) affliction."
>
> (verses 18–21.)

Lastly, at verse 26 and running right through chapter xxxvii., Elihu brings his harangue to a dramatic and poetic climax by referring to a gathering storm which he graphically describes and uses to illustrate his thesis, namely, that affliction is educative as well as retributive, disciplinary as well as destructive.

> "Yea, He ladeth the thick cloud with moisture,
> He spreadeth out the cloud of His lightning,
> And it is turned about by His guidance,
> That they may do what He commandeth them
> Upon the face of the habitable world,
> Whether it be for *correction* or for (the sake of)
> the earth."
>
> (xxxvii. 11–13.)

A New Appeal.

So much, then, for Elihu's new answer. We have given rather more space to it than we at first intended; but perhaps we ought not to begrudge that, for it is important to see clearly the special point of it (which many readers seem strangely to miss), and any further reducing of our key-quotations would have been prejudicial to the clearness of our presentation of it.

Mark now the new *appeal* which goes with Elihu's new approach and new answer. The appeal of Eliphaz, Bildad and Zophar (if "appeal" it could be called) finally amounted to, "Own up, and cease being a hypocrite." The appeal of Elihu has nothing of that in it. It is an appeal for a new attitude in Job toward his affliction. Eliphaz, Bildad and Zophar had kept harping on some supposed wicked behaviour *in the past*. Elihu is concerned with a wrong attitude *in the present*. He does not discuss whether Job has committed grievous sin in the past. He accepts Job's protestation of innocence, and his point is that although Job's protestation of innocence may be genuine enough, his present attitude and spirit are wrong. Job's suffering may not be for past sin at all. His suffering is more probably a chastening with some ultimately good purpose; but Job is thwarting his own good by his impossible attitude.

So, then, in line with his philosophy of affliction as being corrective and educative rather than judicial and punitive, Elihu's appeal is for a teachable *humility* on Job's part. This is where Job has mainly failed. As with others who have not been heard by God because their motive was wrong (xxxv. 12), so even Job's requestings and protestings, earnest though they have been, have sprung from a wrong motive, namely, pride—a pride which has been self-righteously occupied with the vindicating of Job himself even to the point of impugning *God's* righteousness. God will not hear such "vanity" (xxxv. 13). Job needs to realise his own impotence and ignorance (xxxvii. 14–24). This is certainly discerning.

But Elihu's appeal is also for submissive *patience*. All God's judgments proceed from His absolute understanding (xxxiv. 21–3), and are both right (verses 10–12) and resistless (verses 13–20, 29). Therefore it is wisdom in a man to submit and have patience to learn. As he says in chapter xxxv. 15, "The cause is before Him; therefore *wait thou for Him*" (see R.V. margin). This also is discerning.

Yet again, Elihu's appeal is for Job to have *faith in God Himself* rather than in some demanded explanation. The true wisdom is to have faith in God Himself despite the lack of all explanation, seeing that God is all-knowing and all-righteous (xxxvi. 5, etc.). His closing word is, "Touching the Almighty, we cannot find Him out; He is excellent in power; and in judgment and plenteous justice He will not afflict. *Let men therefore fear Him*" (xxxvii. 23, 24). This also is discerning.

What then?

What then of Elihu's speech in total and in fine? What we have said will have substantiated that it moves on a higher level than the preceding speeches. There is ampler spiritual grasp and truer spiritual insight. Admittedly, here and there Elihu is somewhat *incorrect*, as when he says that God is unaffected either by man's sin or uprightness (xxxv. 6, 7). The complete Scripture revelation shows that God's heart of love is indeed affected. Here and there, also, Elihu is *inadequate*, as when he says that a true response to affliction always brings restoration to prosperity (xxxiii. 23–30). But there are also *strikingly true* things, as when he charges Job, not with suffering because of sinning (as the other three speakers had said), but with sinning because of his suffering! (xxxiii. 8–11; xxxiv. 36, 37; xxxv. 15, 16).

Elihu's philosophy of suffering certainly does not cover all the ground; and, of course, so far as Job's sufferings in particular were concerned Elihu was just as ignorant of their real cause (i.e. the slander of Satan and the challenge of Jehovah) as the other speakers in the dialogue. Yet his view of suffering is undoubtedly nearer the truth than anything submitted by Eliphaz, Bildad or Zophar; and especially is he bordering on tremendous truth when, at the end of his speech, he advocates that faith in God Himself is better even than an explanation. It is at this point, significantly enough, as we shall soon see, that Jehovah Himself breaks in by a whirlwind voice from the storm which has been gathering over the land toward the end of Elihu's speech.

Yes, Elihu's was a great theme. In fact it was *too* great for him. He was not equal to it. A more-than-human voice needed to speak now; and it *did* speak. In our next and final study on the Book of Job we shall hear the last and greatest Speaker of all.

THE BOOK OF JOB (5)

Lesson Number 56

NOTE.—For this final study in the Book of Job read chapters xxxviii. to xlii. Appreciate the magnificent sweep and poetry even if the purport is not so clear at first. Ask and try to answer the question: What is the purpose of this speech of Jehovah?

Then read the ensuing study, and go through the speech again, checking off our comments upon it. This will prove really rewarding.

He never fails the soul that trusts in Him;
Tho' disappointments come and hope burns dim,
    He never fails.
Tho' trials surge like stormy seas around,
Tho' testings fierce like ambushed foes abound,
Yet this my soul, with millions more has found,
    He never fails; He *never* fails.

He never fails the soul that trusts in Him;
Tho' angry skies with thunder-clouds grow grim,
    He never fails.
Tho' icy blasts life's fairest flow'rs lay low,
Tho' earthly springs of joy all cease to flow,
Yet still 'tis true, with millions more I know,
    He never fails; He *never* fails.

He never fails the soul that trusts in Him;
Tho' sorrow's cup should overflow the brim,
    He never fails.
Tho' oft the pilgrim way seems rough and long,
I yet shall stand amid yon white-robed throng,
And there I'll sing, with millions more, this song—
    He never fails; He *never* fails.

                      —*J. S. B.*

THE BOOK OF JOB (5)

THE VOICE FROM THE WHIRLWIND

SUDDENLY, in chapters xxxviii. to xli., the profound but pathetic dialogue is brought to a climax by the interposition of God Himself, speaking out of a whirlwind. "Then the *LORD* answered Job out of the whirlwind, and said . . ." The storm had spread itself across the skies while Elihu was speaking, and eventually had silenced him. The five men are now struck dumb with awe as that voice "like the sound of many waters" breaks upon them from the whirling air.

Now obviously if there is one point more than another in this ancient poem-drama of Job where everything depends on whether it is genuinely historical or only fictional, it is at this terrific crisis-point. Either it really *is* God Himself who speaks, or it is only God impersonatedly and pretendedly. If the former, then it is alive with vital significances. If merely the latter, then all we have to do is to admire the imaginative genius of the human composer, or else feel anger at his irreverence in thus "pretending" God.

That is why it was so important, in our first study on the Book of Job, to settle whether it is really and fully true, or only at best a fictional elaboration around some mere nucleus of fact. We need not go over the *pros* and *cons* again here. We have submitted that the only view of the book which does justice to the data is that which accepts it as a record of what genuinely happened, given to us in superb poetical rendering. This means that in these climax chapters, xxxviii. to xlii., it is indeed the Eternal One who speaks with that awesome voice out of the tornado.

And what is it that the Voice Divine says? Well, when we read these chapters through the first time, all the while expecting to come upon some mighty paragraph which gives Job at last and once for all the Divine solution of his problem, we are unconcealably disappointed. There is not even the slightest move to explain Job's suffering or to dissolve the problem of providence

67

provoked by it! (Incidentally, we may observe that this, in conjunction with other factors, is a pretty sure corroboration that it really *is* God who here speaks. Had it been no more than the voice of God as pretended by a clever human composer, it is practically certain that *some* climactic explanation would have been attempted, according with chapters i. and ii., so that the debate should not be left argumentatively unresolved, as it now is.)

Another thing which strikes us disappointingly is that this Divine interposition is not even an argument. It is rather a series of interrogations. The language, the poetry, the rich imagery, the universal sweep of ideas and illustrations—all these certainly eclipse everything that has preceded, and probably they are unsurpassed in all literature, ancient or modern: but there is neither explanation nor argument! Why? Well, we shall see.

We have given short but careful analyses of the speeches by Eliphaz, Bildad and Zophar, and have tried to show, by selected quotations, the new aspect represented in the ample dissertation of Elihu; but there is scarcely need for an analysis of this over-awing climax-speech from the whirlwind in order to find its drift and purpose. Not that it is *without* orderly progress. A careful rereading will show that its subject and course are as follows—

(Here see outline on page 73.)

One senses an intended touch of kindly ludicrousness here and there in the way that the contrast between Jehovah and Job is brought out, as for instance in chapter xxxviii. 19–21:

"Where is the way to the dwelling of light?
   And as for darkness where is the place thereof? . . .
   Doubtless thou knowest, for thou wast then born,
   And the number of thy days is great!"

In fact this latter couplet serves to indicate the intended irony underlying the whole address. Job, of course, is as old as the Almighty, or at least coeval with creation, or else he could not presume, as he *has* done, to arraign the moral government of the Creator. But the irony is benevolent throughout, not sarcastic. The Divine purpose is to humble Job, but not to mock him or even humiliate him (and there is a wide difference between being humbled and being humiliated!). There is a sublime majesty and dignity going with a conversational condescension all through the speech.

One cannot but be arrested, also, by the references in this speech to living creatures of peculiar features or habits. The ostrich is cited, not just on account of its gorgeous wings, however, but rather because of certain innate stupidities; and we are told that these very stupidities are "because God hath deprived her of wisdom" in certain ways. The lion, the wild ass, the crocodile —why are such fierce and untamable and fearsome creatures referred to? Job would need no explaining on that point. The distinctive features and peculiarities of the various creatures are determined and conferred by the wisdom and power of God. Some of these differentia are not attractive to us human beings nor are they what *we* should have chosen if we had been in charge of things. They are the more significant for that very reason, because they show us that nature is not ordered according to *our* thought, and yet the whole description shows that it is ordered well and for a grand, total result of life far beyond anything which *we* could have imagined.

Job would both sense the underlying irony of the speech and see the general purpose of it, just as we ourselves do. By simply exposing Job's profound ignorance of God's *natural* government it shows his utter incapacity to pass judgment on that which is far more incomprehensible and mysterious, God's *moral* government.

Yes, Job would grasp this; yet even so we are still left asking what is the special significance of this whirlwind address so far as the *sufferings* of Job were concerned. As we have said, it is superlative poetry, magnificent description, profound comprehension; yet it is not an explanation of Job's affliction, nor an answer to his questioning, nor a solution to the problem of suffering, nor does it contain even a promise that Job's affliction would end in renewed prosperity. What then *is* its significance in relation to this man's adversity? An unreflective reading of it may easily *miss* its significance and cause disappointment.

Well, the first significance of it is that Job was *not meant* to know the explanation of his sufferings. Had Job been told the real explanation, i.e. the slander of Satan and the challenge of Jehovah, he certainly would have opened his eyes wide with astonishment, yet at the same time the whole purpose of his trial would have been nullified thereby. Had he been told this strange origin of his calamities (as described in the prologue) and assured of the rewarding outcome of his ordeal (as described in the epilogue), then obviously his whole reaction would have been affected. His fortitude would have been artificial. There would have been no real test of character. Nor would there have been any place for the genuine exercise and education of faith. On this simple fact everything hangs in our understanding of the book. By means of the prologue we ourselves are *shown* the explanation of Job's sufferings before ever they began, so that when the explanation is *withheld* from Job we may appreciate at once that an explanation *could* have been given, easily enough, if God had so willed. As we now read the record of this august speech from the whirlwind, with its wonderful exhibition of the transcendence, immanence and providence of God, yet its absence of explanation concerning Job's problem, we are meant to learn the lesson that there are *some* things about human suffering which God cannot possibly explain to us without destroying the very purpose which they are designed to fulfil. *That* is the first significance of this speech from the whirlwind.

And its second significance is its indication of the Divine *concern* in Job's affairs. Although that aerial voice from the cyclone did not vouchsafe an explanation, it evinced that God had been watching, hearing, caring. Job would immediately realise this with a sudden, new vividness. What tumult of emotion and rush of regret that he had allowed Eliphaz and Bildad and Zophar to aggravate him into saying rash things about the unconcern of God! Under the power of that dread voice he now knew in a flash, and without any telling, how wrong they had been. Yet deeper than all else, the speaking of that hitherto silent Heaven meant to Job that God felt concern and sympathy! Job and his grief meant enough to God to cause Him to speak! Doubtless this is one of the main reasons why, in the overruling purpose of God, this story of Job was preserved—that men might know through it the fact of this Divine concern and sympathy, particularly so until the crowning demonstration of it should be given in the cross of our Lord Jesus Christ.

But there is a third and even deeper significance in this speech from the storm-cloud, and once again it arises from the strange-seeming absence of any explanation to Job. The Divine purpose is to bring Job to the point where he rests in *God Himself*, apart from explanations. If only Job can be brought there, where he trusts God as being absolutely righteous and benevolent over against *all* unexplained adversities, then Satan's slanderous libel (in the prologue) is proved false, and the devil is defeated. Job *does* get there, as chapter xlii. shows ; and *we* are meant to get there too. Baffling enigmas abound in the life of even the godliest Christians. In the final analysis faith is to trust God Himself over against all seeming contradictions, and in the absence of all present explanations. This is not mere *blind* faith. We have the completed Scripture revelation, throwing much light on the mystery of human sin and suffering—of its origin, of Satanic activity behind it, of its being Divinely overruled, and of its eventual abolition. Most wonderful of all, God has shown us, in Christ, how He Himself suffers *with* us. Faith, therefore, has much to encourage it. Yet even so, there are the still-clinging curtains of what are to us impenetrable mysteries. There are things which God cannot divulge to us at present. Over against the much that is revealed is the much that is as yet unrevealed. The victory of faith is to rest with full confidence in God Himself.

And we must mention one further significance in that speech from the whirlwind. Clearly, the Divine purpose is to bring Job to *the end of himself*—to the end of his own self-righteousness, self-vindication, self-wisdom, self-everything, so that he may find his all in God. This is indicated by an interesting fact. The speech from the whirlwind is divided into two parts by an interlude half-way through, in which God directly addresses Job, and Job replies. See chapter xl. 1–5.

> "Moreover the Lord answered Job, and said,
> Can he who cavils contend with the Almighty?
> He that argueth with God let him answer it.
> Then Job answered the Lord, and said,
> Behold, I am of small account : what shall I answer Thee?
> I lay mine hand upon my mouth.
> Once have I spoken, and I will not answer ;
> Yea twice, but I will proceed no further."

Job is learning his lesson, but he has not yet learned it fully enough. Had he done so, the speech from the whirlwind would have terminated at this point. There is a spiritual breaking-down process going on in Job. Going with the outward speech from the whirlwind is the inward illumination of God's Holy Spirit. Job is coming to see God in a new way; and he is coming to see himself in a new way too. He sees himself of "small account" against the mighty background of the universe and the Divine infinity, and he says, "What shall *I* answer *THEE*?" "I lay mine hand on my mouth." Yes, Job is learning his lesson. He is bowed in confession. Yet his contrition is not full enough; so the speech from the whirlwind continues; and it continues until Job breaks in, with an uttermost convictedness and convincedness, at the opening of chapter xlii.

Unfortunately, the first six verses of chapter xlii., which are the crisis-climax of the whole book, are generally misunderstood because they are all attributed to Job instead of being distributed between Job and God. The chapter begins, "Then Job answered the Lord, and said . . ." This easily enough gives the impression that all the verses up to verse 6 are the words of Job, whereas they should be read as follows—

JOB
  "I know that Thou canst do all things,
   And that no purpose of Thine can be restrained."

VOICE FROM WHIRLWIND
  "Who is this that hideth counsel without knowledge?"

JOB
  "Therefore have I uttered that which I understood not,
   Things too wonderful for me, which I knew not.
   Hear, I beseech Thee, and I will speak."

VOICE FROM WHIRLWIND
  "I will demand of thee, and declare thou unto Me."

JOB
  "I had heard of Thee by the hearing of the ear,
   But now mine eye seeth Thee.
   Wherefore I abhor myself (or loathe my words),
   And repent in dust and ashes."

These, then, are the main significances of the speech from the whirlwind: Job was *not meant* to know the explanation of his sufferings; but God was concerned and *sympathetic*; the Divine purpose was that Job should rest in *God Himself*, apart from explanations; also that Job should come to the end of his *self-ism* and find his all in God. When these significances are perceived, the august and prolonged interruption from the whirlwind assumes wonderful meaning, not only for Job, but for ourselves as well.

JEHOVAH VERSUS JOB

A CHALLENGE BASED ON CONTRAST

The infinite creative and controlling power of Jehovah versus the littleness, ignorance and impotence of Job.

1. IN RELATION TO THE EARTH (xxxviii. 1–18).

Its creation	verses 4–7.
The oceans	,, 8–11.
The morning	,, 12–15.
Hid sources	,, 16–18.

2. IN RELATION TO THE HEAVENS (xxxviii. 19–38).

Light and dark	verses 19–21.
The elements	,, 22–30.
Stars and Zodiac	,, 31–2.
Laws of nature	,, 33–8.

3. IN RELATION TO LIVING BEINGS (xxxviii. 39–xxxix.).

Beast and bird of prey	verses 39–41.
Beasts preyed upon	,, 1–12.
Bird and beast of beauty	,, 13–25.
Two fiercest vultures	,, 26–30.

4. IN RELATION TO SPECIAL CASES (xl.–xlii. 6).

Proud wicked-doers	verses 6–14.
Behemoth (hippopotamus)	,, 15–24.
Leviathan (crocodile)	chapter xli.
Job himself (in reply)	chapter xlii. 1–6.

Job himself as a study.

In these reflections on the Book of Job, we have not considered Job himself as a separate character-study. We have been more concerned to set forth the meaning and message of the *book* as such. But before we conclude this final study on Job we ought to get at least a silhouette of the man himself. In this epic story and poem we see a man of exemplary integrity progressively stripped of all those dearest possessions and most sacred confidences with which men clothe their souls, until he stands as a consciously naked soul before his Maker.

First he loses all his *wealth*. All in a few hours, by a few swift, fell strokes, he passes from plenty to poverty. Then he loses all his *children*. By one awful, complex blow, he is bereaved of all his seven sons and three daughters. Next he loses his *health*. He becomes so repulsive outwardly that his closest kin will not come near him, and so tortured by inward discomfort that his existence is a continual burden. Next he loses the fellowship of his *wife*. Frenzied by the terrible spectacle of her husband, she exclaims, "Curse God and die!" The cord of co-believing snaps between wife and husband; and thus a terrible loneliness is added to Job's other losses. Next he loses the sympathy of his three sagest friends. Sympathy turns to censure; and instead of consoling they unite in condemning, until poor Job cries out, "Have pity upon me, O ye my friends!"

But besides all these more external losses there is a terrible stripping process going on inside the man's very soul and spirit. His extreme adversity strips away even his sense of *self-worth*. Earlier he has been able to say, "Naked came I forth . . . and naked shall I return," and in that statement he has recognised the worth of his own personality as being more than all his possessions. But later he longs supremely to be blotted out. Next he loses the sense of God's bona fide relationship to him. No longer can he say, "The Lord gave; the Lord hath taken away: blessed be the name of the Lord." In those words there was a perception of graciousness blended with the Divine sovereignty. But later he can only ask in bitterness of soul, "Why hast Thou set me as a target for Thee?" Lastly he seems to lose even the conviction of the goodness of the *Divine government*. Earlier he has been able to say, "Shall we receive good at the hand of the

Lord, and not evil?" But that earlier recognition of sovereign good breaks down as the debate moves on, and Job is desolate indeed.

All these things with which men mentally and spiritually clothe themselves are now gone; and we stand watching the naked spirit of this man. There are but two final realities left. *God* is left. *Self* is left. But both are problems. God is a problem because Job can neither understand Him nor find Him. Self is a problem because Job cannot escape himself. God and himself are final certainties; but there is no place of meeting.

What then? Job *must* find God. It has been truly observed that Job's speeches, in their deepest utterances, are not so much an answer to Eliphaz, Bildad and Zophar as the wail of a desolate soul to a God who could not be found, from a self which could not be escaped, and an anguish which could not be explained. For these heart-wrung cries and questions see chapters ix. 2, 3, 32, 33; xiv. 7–10, 14, 15; xvi. 18–21; xix. 23–7; xxiii. 3, 4; xxxi. 35–7.

And this stripped and naked soul *finds* God! Although a sinner in the sense that all men are, he is no hypocrite such as his "miserable comforters" have alleged. He is a sincere soul in an agony of desire really to know God, and God cannot deny him. God speaks from the storm. The voice does not argue. It simply makes vivid the majesty and sublimity of the Divine government. The result is an overpowering sense of the infinite wisdom, power, holiness and goodness of God. In a way which only those can understand who have experienced sudden Divine enlightenment at conversion or in some never-to-be-forgotten spiritual crisis, Job sees and understands God as he never had before, and he cries out,

> "I had heard of Thee by the hearing of the ear,
> But now mine eye seeth Thee!"

And with this new discovery of God, there comes to him, as is invariably the case, a new knowledge of his own heart; so that he now says,

> "Wherefore I abhor myself (or, my words),
> And repent in dust and ashes."

Thank God, the voice from heaven which spoke to Job has now found a better vehicle of expression than that long-ago whirlwind. "God, who at sundry times and in divers manners spake in time past unto the fathers by prophets, hath in these last days spoken unto us in His SON." Let all who "suffer according to the will of God" (I Pet. iv. 19) bathe their weary hearts in the revealing and comforting consolations of the New Testament. Not everything is revealed to us yet by a long way; but enough is now revealed to make faith intelligent despite persisting dark problems. What is still unrevealed is reserved in order to give faith scope for development. If Job could say it, then certainly *we* can, with far fuller reason—"Though He slay me, yet will I trust Him" (xiii. 15).

Epilogue and Final Reflections

We need not add much concerning the brief epilogue (xlii. 7–17). The poetry ends with verse 6, and the epilogue is in prose. It reads quite simply, and there are no points needing explanation to the general reader. But there *are* certain points of spiritual significance which ought not to be missed.

The first significance, of course, is that there *is* an epilogue. It is a "happy ever after" ending, too, such as is quite out of fashion with modern fiction writers; but it is a sequel of real fact, and no mere fairy-tale. Job is vindicated and rewarded. And because this is a real account of God's dealings with a man, its meaning is profound. Job, remember, is a Divinely intended object-lesson through which we are meant to apprehend certain great truths pertaining to the trials of the godly. In the Job of the epilogue we see that for the godly sufferer there is a "nevertheless afterward" of compensation and reward. It may not come in this present life-time, as Job's did; but come it surely will. In Job's case it *had* to come in this life-time in order to fill out the object-lesson for us; but human life has a larger context than the present three-score years and ten; and we must read this epilogue in the light of that "better land" beyond earth's sunsets, or with those precious promises before us which tell of our Lord's second coming and millennial kingdom.

The next thing that catches the eye is the Divine rebuke of *Job's three "comforters."* God's wrath is kindled against them (verse 7). Why? Because they have more nearly wrecked Job's soul than even the devil himself. When Satan had done his worst, it could still be written, "In all this did not Job sin with his lips" (ii. 10); but as the three "friends" prosecuted their pious misrepresentations of both God and Job, the poor sufferer was simply driven into sinning with his lips. Mark well: Satan has no more dangerous tools than those who, under the guise of piety, and in the name of religious orthodoxy, offer false comfort or give untrue impressions of God. Far better be silent in the presence of suffering than say what is wrong.

Implication concerning Inspiration

And further, we note here the implication concerning *the inspiration of the Scriptures*. In this epilogue God says to Eliphaz, Bildad and Zophar, "Ye have not spoken of Me the thing that is right." This can only mean that the speeches of those three men were not Divinely inspired. There are some impossible people who say, "Oh, if the Bible is verbally inspired as you teach, then one ought to be able to open the Bible anywhere and say of any verse on any page, 'This is the word of God, and must be obeyed.'" Such an attitude is utterly stupid. Words of wicked men like Ahab, and even of Satan, are recorded in Scripture, and all that inspiration involves in such cases is the accuracy of what is reported. Even so, in the Book of Job, we obviously cannot take any or every statement made by Eliphaz, Bildad or Zophar and say, "That is Divinely inspired." The *record* of their speeches is inspired, but not what they say. Of course, there is much that is elevated and true enough in their speeches, but it is only men who are speaking; and some of their statements are definitely wrong, as God Himself now says in the epilogue. What we ought to grasp clearly is that this is no argument whatever against the verbal inspiration of the Bible; for although the speeches of the five men in this Book of Job may not be inspired, the whole book is an inspired record of real doings and sayings, with a Divine purpose in view. In this true and vital sense the epic story and poem is an inspired book, and has a Divine message for us.

We pass by other points of interest, to mention the New Testament comment on this Book of Job. In James v. 11 we read, "Ye have heard of the patience of Job, and have seen the end of the Lord, how that the Lord is full of pity and merciful." That is the ultimate fact about this Book of Job—"the end (or point aimed at) of the LORD." We are only meant to see Job that we may see beyond him to *God*, to the God who is sovereign throughout the universe, Satan included, and whose sovereignty is one of gracious purpose toward man. And we are meant to see that although there are some things which God cannot make plain to us yet, the gracious purpose of God toward us interpenetrates and persists through the most painful mysteries of our earthly experience.

Look again at Job: see how for the godly sufferer "Paradise Lost" becomes "Paradise Regained." See the three main features of the epilogue—transformation, vindication, restoration. First, there is the *transformation* of Job as regards his own character, for he comes forth as "gold tried in the fire." Second, there is the *vindication* of Job before his friends, for God calls him "My servant" and makes him a priest to them (verse 8). Third, there is the *restoration* to Job of all his former prosperity, and indeed far more, for "the Lord gave Job twice as much as he had before" (verse 10). Yes, the "end of the Lord" is very gracious. Let every godly sufferer "rest in the Lord, and wait patiently for Him."

Is Job a latent Parable?

Such, then, is the Book of Job. Take just one further, parting glance back over the whole book—prologue, dialogue, epilogue. The whole is an inspired record of what actually happened. Yet can it be that *behind* the literal facts and direct significances there is a mystic parable of the human *race* as such? The Job of that prologue and the Satan of malicious design, do they speak of Eden and what man was at first? The suffering Job of the potsherd and the ashes, does he speak to us of humanity as it is at present? The purified and reinstated Job of the epilogue, does he speak of the humanity that is yet to be? This, at any rate, is true: there are latent meanings in the written word of God which are deeper and more wonderful than the wisest of men have yet discovered.

SOME TEST QUESTIONS ON JOB

1. What order of spiritual progress do the Poetical Books collectively express? And could you state in a single phrase the ruling idea in the Book of Job?

2. What are the three kinds of parallelism in Hebrew poetry? And which parts of the Book of Job are respectively poetry and prose?

3. What are the main objections to the historicity of the Book of Job, and what are the answers to those objections?

4. Give two Scripture references which seem to settle conclusively that the book is genuinely historical.

5. Summarise the object and message of the book in a few lines.

6. If the interviews between God and Satan are fiction and not fact, why is the book reduced to meaninglessness?

7. What are the main points of contrast between Eliphaz, Bildad, and Zophar?

8. What are the points of similarity between Eliphaz, Bildad, and Zophar?

9. Describe briefly the new approach and the new answer and the new appeal of Elihu.

10. What are the four main divisions in the speech of Jehovah? The first is: In relation to the earth (xxxviii. 1–18).

11. What is the main significance of the speech from the whirlwind?

12. What bearing does the Lord's rebuke of Eliphaz and Bildad and Zophar have on the inspiration of the Bible?

THE BOOK OF PSALMS (1)

Lesson Number 57

NOTE.—For this study read psalms i. to xli., noting how many are ascribed to David. Read them in the Revised Version, and appreciate the thought-parallels of their poetic form. Read each psalm through at least twice.

I wonder at the hardihood with which such persons undertake to talk about God. In a treatise addressed to infidels they begin with a chapter proving the existence of God from the works of Nature . . . this only gives their readers grounds for thinking that the proofs of our religion are very weak. . . . It is a remarkable fact that no canonical writer has ever used Nature to prove God.

—*Pascal.* "*Pensées,*" IV, 242, 243.

THE BOOK OF PSALMS (1)

WHAT words can adequately introduce this Book of Psalms to us? Who shall say how much it has meant to godly hearts down the years? Here is poetry which more than vies with that of Milton and Shakespeare, yet it is the poetry of downright reality; and, as "the body is more than the raiment," so here, the reality is greater than the poetry which expresses it. Here, too, is strong theology—not, however, any merely theoretic theology, but the practical theology of vivid human experience; and, as "the life is more than meat," so is concrete experience more than abstract doctrine. It is this, fundamentally, which has made the Book of Psalms such a treasure to the godly.

"Hymns to the gods of Greece have been preserved," says C. J. Ellicott, "but how vast is their difference from the Psalms! Let the reader compare one of those translated by Shelley, with any song out of the Psalter. Pretty compliments and well-turned flatteries intended to propitiate he will find, set, indeed, in melodious verse that celebrates the birth of gods and demi-gods; but no wrestling in prayer with tearful eyes and downcast head, and the full assurance of faith, such as has made the Psalms for all time the expression of the devotional feelings of men."

This Book of Psalms is a limpid lake which reflects every mood of man's changeful sky. It is a river of consolation which, though swollen with many tears, never fails to gladden the fainting. It is a garden of flowers which never lose their fragrance, though some of the roses have sharp thorns. It is a stringed instrument which registers every note of praise and prayer, of triumph and trouble, of gladness and sadness, of hope and fear, and unites them all in the full multi-chord of human experience.

John Calvin said: "This book I am wont to style an anatomy of all parts of the soul; for no one will discover in himself a single feeling whereof the image is not reflected in this mirror. Nay, all griefs, sorrows, fears, doubts, hopes, cares, anxieties— in short, all those tumultuous agitations wherewith the minds of men are wont to be tossed—the Holy Ghost hath here represented to the life."

Spiritual Value

We may say, then, that the first great value of this Book of Psalms is that it provides for our emotions and feelings the same kind of guidance as the other Scriptures provide for our faith and actions. Ambrose of Milan said: "Although all Scripture breatheth the grace of God, yet sweet beyond all others is the Book of Psalms. History instructs, the Law teaches, Prophecy announces, rebukes, chastens, Morality persuades; but in the Book of Psalms we have the fruit of all these, and a kind of medicine for the salvation of men."

Ever since they were written, the Psalms have played a large part in the life of God's people. The old-time Hebrews used them in the temple worship; and the Jews of today still use them in the synagogue. The Christians of New Testament times sang them (as we see from Col. iii. 16, and Jas. v. 13); and all denominations of Christendom use them today.

But above all, they have ever been precious to the *individual*. In this Book of Psalms the tempted and tested gain fortitude from pilgrims of yesterday, whose feet have bled along the same thorny pathway. Here the suffering and sorrowing find a fellowship of sympathy which takes the bitterness out of their tears. Here the persecuted and the forsaken find reassurance in their time of need. Here the weeping penitent finds that which suits the broken and the contrite heart. Yea, here the Christian believer discerns the figure of His Lord, moving among the psalms of David as truly as among the seven golden candlestands of the Apocalypse. To all the godly these Psalms are an unmatched treasury of devotion, of comfort, of sympathy, and of gladdening reassurance. They are the sighings and singings of "men of like passions" with ourselves; yet the very breath of heaven is in them.

With the sixty-six books of the Bible before us, must we not reverently acknowledge that the Holy Spirit has vouchsafed to us no more precious bequeathment than this "Book of Psalms"?

The word "psalm" comes to us from the Greek word *psalmos* (plural, *psalmoi*), which meant "a poem to be sung to a stringed instrument." It was in the third century B.C., in the Septuagint translation of the Hebrew scriptures into Greek, that this word *Psalmoi* was first used as the general title for this collection of Hebrew poems; and from there, per the Latin Vulgate, the name reappears in our English version.

This name is certainly appropriate, for many of these poems are undoubtedly *odes*, or poems written to be set to music, as is shown by the fact that fifty-five of them are addressed to "the chief musician," that is, to the choir-leader, or precentor, of the Hebrew religious worship. Many of them are *lyrics*, or poems expressing the individual emotions of the poet, and intended for accompaniment by the lyre or harp or "stringed instruments," as we see in those which have the word *Neginoth* attached to them. It is because of this that the Book of Psalms is known almost equally as well as the Psalter, from the Greek word *psalter*, that is, a harp or stringed instrument.

The usual Hebrew name for the book is *Tehillim*, which means "Praises." Another Hebrew title is *Tephiloth*, that is, "Prayers" —a title taken from such verses as psalm lxxii. 20, where we read: "The prayers of David the son of Jesse are ended." Neither of these titles, however, is strictly descriptive of all these poems, though taken both together they well express their spiritual nature, which our own title, "Psalms," fails to do. Still, seeing that both the praises and the prayers were poems to be set to song, we come back to the title "Psalms." Moreover, besides being equally applicable to all these poems, this title, "Psalms," is endorsed by New Testament usage (Luke xx. 42; Acts i. 20; xiii. 33).

Collection and Formation

The Book of Psalms is obviously a *collection*. The superscriptions in the Hebrew text ascribe seventy-three of them to David; twelve to Asaph, who was one of the heads of David's choir at Jerusalem (see 1 Chron. vi. 39; xv. 17, 19; xvi. 5; see also 2 Chron. xxix. 30); eleven to the sons of Korah, or rather twelve, since it is pretty clear that the superscription to psalm xlii. covers xliii. as well; one to Heman the Ezrahite; one to Ethan the Ezrahite; and one to Moses. This makes a total of exactly one hundred. The other fifty are left anonymous.

Either by a single editor or by several, these poems, written by different persons at different times, were brought together into one volume; and probably the formation of the collection was gradual. It is likely that a first collection of the Davidic psalms was made soon after David's death, that the Korahite group were added a little later, and the Asaph group still later, with a number of further, anonymous psalms; while probably Ezra the scribe had much to do with the bringing of them into their present arrangement.

They are in five groups, the end of each group being marked by a doxology, or special ascription of praise to God. These doxologies are not integral to the psalms at the end of which they occur, but are simply appended to mark off the group divisions.

The five groups are—(1) i.–xli.; (2) xlii.–lxxii.; (3) lxxiii.–lxxxix.; (4) xc.–cvi.; (5) cvii.–cl.

The first two groups are mainly Davidic; the third mainly Asaphian; the fourth mainly anonymous, or "orphan" psalms, as the Rabbis call those which lack inscriptions; and the fifth partly Davidic and partly anonymous.

It seems likely that the first group was collected by Solomon, the second group by the Korahite Levites, the third by Hezekiah, the fourth and fifth by Ezra and Nehemiah. Thus, the formation and completion of our "Book of Psalms" took over five hundred years.

A Poetic Pentateuch

The fivefold division of the Book of Psalms makes it a kind of poetic *Pentateuch*. From the time of Ezra downwards, and coinciding with the first appearing of synagogues among the now-scattered Jews, there arose a system of commenting upon and explaining the meaning of the Hebrew scriptures. This doubtless arose from the necessity of expounding the Hebrew Law to congregations of Jews in which many did not, or might not, understand the language in which it was read. At first the commentaries were merely oral and extempore; but later they became crystallised into definite form, and still later were made permanent in writing. When they assumed this definite and written shape they became known as the *Midrashim* (plural of *midrash*, which means "investigation" or "interpretation"). Now the Midrash, or Jewish comment, on the first verse of the first psalm speaks of the fivefold division of the Psalms in these words: "Moses gave to the Israelites the five books of the Law, and as a counterpart to these, David gave them the Psalms, which consist of five books." In modern times, also, the Hebrew scholar Delitzsch, has said: "The Psalter is also a Pentateuch, the echo of the Mosaic Pentateuch, from the heart of Israel. It is the fivefold book of the congregation to Jehovah, as the Law is the fivefold book of Jehovah to the congregation."

There are those who have seen an even closer correspondence between the Book of Psalms and the Pentateuch, the five groups of the psalms corresponding in order, by affinity of subject, with Genesis, Exodus, Leviticus, Numbers, and Deuteronomy. The first group, corresponding with Genesis, has much to say about *man*. The second group, corresponding with Exodus, has much to say about *deliverance*. The third group, corresponding with Leviticus, has its emphasis in the Asaph psalms, upon the *sanctuary*. The fourth group, corresponding with Numbers, and beginning with Psalm xc., the prayer of Moses, stresses the time when unrest and wandering will cease in the coming worldwide kingdom when the nations shall bow to God's King. The fifth group, corresponding with Deuteronomy, has much of thanksgiving for the Divine faithfulness, and lays much emphasis upon the word of the Lord, as, for instance, in the longest of all the psalms, which has for its theme the written word of the Lord. We suggest to the student that here, at least, is a very interesting field for exploration.

Spiritual Message

The central spiritual message of this Book of Psalms may be said to be *PRAISE THROUGH PRAYER*. Again and again, in individual psalms, we see how sighing is turned into singing through praying; while if we take the book as a whole, we see this idea moving forward ever more definitely until the whole book is wound up in the five "Hallelujah" psalms with which it closes, each of which begins and ends with the exclamation, *"Praise ye the Lord!"*

It may help the eye if we now put down our findings thus far compactly, as follows:—

THE BOOK OF PSALMS

The Book of Devotion

PRAISE THROUGH PRAYER		
First Group (i.–xli.)	Mainly Davidic	Suggests Genesis
Second Group (xlii.–lxxii.)	Mainly Davidic	,, Exodus
Third Group (lxxiii.–lxxxix.)	Mainly Asaphian	,, Leviticus
Fourth Group (xc.–cvi.)	Mainly Anonymous	,, Numbers
Fifth Group (cvii.–cl.)	Partly Davidic and partly anonymous	,, Deuteronomy

In our next lessons we shall consider together the inscriptions which go with the psalms, the different groups of psalms, and certain of the psalms in particular as being representative of the whole. Meanwhile, let us get this general outlay of the collection well in mind, thanking God for such a matchless treasury, and praying that the Holy Spirit may give us eyes to see wonderful things therein.

There are two opposite extremes which we should ever avoid in our study of the Bible. We should guard, on the one hand, against being *fanciful*, and seeing what is not there. We should guard, on the other hand, against being *mechanical*, and missing what is actually there in latent or hidden form. Some minds have an imaginative spiritualising faculty which tends to bring a magical streak into the Bible. Others are so suspicious of anything beyond the literal wording that the Scriptures can no more reveal their latent treasures than our Lord would say a single word to the inquisitive but gross-hearted king Herod. It is the precious function of the Holy Spirit to anoint our inward eyes that we may clearly see what is *really there* for us in the Word of God.

THE BOOK OF PSALMS (2)

Lesson Number 58

NOTE.—For this study read psalms xlii. to lxxii., noting again that they are mainly Davidic. Read them in the Revised Version. Note specially the doxology at the end of psalm lxxii. indicating the end of the second main group of psalms. Read each psalm twice.

The Word of God, notwithstanding its Divine origin and authorship, is also a human product, and to be studied as literature. It pleased God to use a book as the medium of His Self-Revelation, and human minds, tongues and pens as instruments of conception and expression. All this must qualify and modify the result, and makes needful to fix, as far as may be, the reasonable limits within which to subject such joint product of God's authorship and man's agency to reverent criticism as a form of literature.

—*Arthur T. Pierson, D.D.*

THE BOOK OF PSALMS (2)

PSALM INSCRIPTIONS

WHO, IN reading the psalms, has not been interested, and probably puzzled, by the inscriptions which are affixed to some of them? When were these inscriptions affixed? and what do the strange-sounding Hebrew words mean which occur in some of them? The matter of these inscriptions is a somewhat complex, yet singularly interesting one; and we ought to say a little about it here, because if we would appreciate to the full the force and beauty in some of the psalms, we need to appreciate the inscriptions which go with them.

First of all, let us reduce the seemingly complex part of the subject to simplicity. Of the one hundred and fifty psalms which make up the book, only *thirty-four* are without any title whatever. These are psalms i., ii., x., xxxiii., xliii., lxxi., xci., xciii., xciv., xcv., xcvi., xcvii., xcix., civ., cv., cvi., cvii., cxi., cxii., cxiii., cxiv., cxv., cxvi., cxvii., cxviii., cxix., cxxxv., cxxxvi., cxxxvii., cxlvi., cxlvii., cxlviii., cxlix., cl.

Next, there are *fifty-two* psalms with only meagre titles such as "A Psalm of David," "A Psalm of Asaph," "A Prayer of David," "A Psalm for Solomon," "A Psalm for the Sons of Korah." These are psalms xi., xiii., xiv., xv., xvii., xix., xx., xxi., xxiii., xxiv., xxv., xxvi., xxvii., xxviii., xxix., xxxi., xxxv., xxxvi., xxxvii., xl., xli., xlvii., xlviii., xlix., l., lxiv., lxv., lxvi., lxviii., lxxii., lxxiii., lxxix., lxxxii., lxxxiii., lxxxv., lxxxvi., lxxxvii., xc., xcviii., c., ci., ciii., cviii., cix., cx., cxxxviii., cxxxix., cxl., cxli., cxliii., cxliv., cxlv.

Next, there are *fourteen* psalms with inscriptions explaining their *historical connection*, such as "A Psalm of David when he fled from Absalom, his Son." These are psalms iii., vii., xviii., xxx., xxxiv., li., lii., liv., lvi., lvii., lix., lx., lxiii., cxlii.

Next, there are *thirty-nine* psalms which have what we can only call, at the moment, *special-word* inscriptions, such as, "A Song upon Alamoth," or "To the chief muscian, on *Neginoth* upon *Sheminith*." These are psalms iv., v., vi., vii., viii., ix., xii., xvi., xxii., xxxii., xxxix., xlii., xliv., xlv., xlvi., lii., liii., liv., lv., lvi., lvii., lviii., lix., lx., lxi., lxii., lxvii., lxix., lxxiv., lxxv., lxxvi., lxxvii., lxxviii., lxxx., lxxxi., lxxxiv., lxxxviii., lxxxix., cxlii. (But see our footnote on page 97.)

Next, there are *four* psalms which express *purpose*, such as "A Psalm or Song for the Sabbath day." These are psalms xxxviii., lxx., xcii., cii.

Next, there are *fifteen* psalms following consecutively upon each other, each bearing the title, "*A Song of Degrees*." These are psalms cxx. to cxxxiv.

This, then, is how the one hundred and fifty psalms are made up—

Psalms without inscriptions	34
Psalms with simple inscriptions	52
Psalms with historical inscriptions . . .	14
Psalms with inscriptions denoting purpose . .	4
Psalms entitled "Songs of Degrees" . . .	15
Psalms with special-word inscriptions—39 (less 8 of these which also bear *historical* inscriptions and are included with the 14 such given above) . . .	31
	150

When were the Inscriptions Affixed?

The *antiquity* of the inscriptions attached to the psalms is undoubted. They were in existence when the Septuagint translation was made in the third century B.C., and must have been so for a good while *before* that, since the meaning of those which we have called "special-word" inscriptions had already by that time gradually become lost, as is evidenced by the fact that the Septuagint translators did not attempt to translate these words, but simply let them stand untranslated in the inscriptions. Their antiquity is thus thrown back easily to the fifth century B.C., that is, to the time of Ezra, who, it is generally agreed, made a recension, or revisal, of the Scriptures as existing in his day, and therefore had much to do with bringing the Book of Psalms into its present form. Are we then going to say that *Ezra* affixed all or most of these psalm-inscriptions? I think not; especially in view of the fact that Hebrew lyrical compositions from earliest times have come down to us with inscriptions attached to them. What is more likely than that the psalm-inscriptions came down to Ezra along with the psalms themselves? Indeed, a detailed study of them reveals every likelihood of their having been a part of the primitive sacred text. That they were so is certainly our own belief.

A Puzzle—

This brings us to a matter of intriguing interest, namely, the *significance* of these inscriptions. It is an admitted fact that the key to them has been lost for over two thousand two hundred years. Bishop Jebb, who issued a monumental work on the Psalms, in 1846, regretted that "so great are the difficulties attending this enquiry, that in many instances little more than conjectures can be offered." The late Dr. E. W. Bullinger said: "No subject of Biblical study has appeared to be more incapable of solution." That great Hebraist, Franz Delitzsch, said of these so-called psalm "titles": "The Septuagint found them already in existence, and did not understand them. . . . The key to their comprehension must have been lost very early." Many other such quotations could be given. Some scholars, as, for instance, the late Bishop Perowne, resort to arguing that the titles are of no necessary authority, and are merely the expression of conjecture or tradition.

—and a Solution

But it may now be said with confidence that *the long-lost key has been discovered!*—and it so simply unlocks the psalm-inscriptions that one marvels at its having lain so long overlooked. When we go back to the ancient Hebrew manuscripts we find that there are no breaks or spaces separating the psalms from each other such as there are in our modern Bible. The only mark of division between them is the number in the margin. The inscriptions, therefore, which have always been more or less gratuitously assumed to be the titles of the psalms *following* them, might just as truly be footnotes to the psalms *preceding* them. Yet, strangely enough, the former has been so taken for granted that the latter has remained apparently unsuspected until quite recently. It was at the beginning of the present century that the late Dr. James W. Thirtle, LL.D., found what is undoubtedly, in our own judgment, the key to the psalm-inscriptions, by asking whether, instead of being *super*-scriptions to the psalms which follow them, they might be *sub*-scriptions, either wholly or in part, to the psalms which precede them. Is there, anywhere outside the Book of Psalms, a psalm standing by itself from which we can learn what was the Hebrew practice in this connection? There is; and it is in the third chapter of the prophet Habakkuk. In that composition of Habakkuk we find—

1. The *Super*scription—"A Prayer of Habakkuk the prophet, upon *Shigionoth*" (verse 1).

2. The "Prayer," or Psalm, itself—from verses 2 to 19.

3. The *Sub*scription—"To the Chief Musician upon *Neginoth*."

We find the same three-fold arrangement in Isaiah xxxviii. 9–20, in king Hezekiah's Psalm of Praise and Thanksgiving for his recovery from sickness, as follows—

1. The *Superscription*—"The writing of Hezekiah, king of Judah, when he had been sick and was recovered of his sickness" (verse 9).

2. The "*Song*," or Psalm, itself—from verse 10 down to verse 20.

3. The *Sub*-scription—"Therefore we will sing my songs to the stringed instruments, all the days of our life, in the house of Jehovah."

These two instances give the key to the inscriptions found in the Book of Psalms. As an outcome of the Babylonian Exile, detailed knowledge of the original temple worship became obscured; and by the middle or end of the third century B.C., when the Septuagint Translation of the Hebrew Scriptures was made into Greek, it had become quite lost. Since there was no space-break between the psalms, there was nothing to tell the Septuagint translators whether the inscriptions *between* some of them belonged to what went before or what came after; and, because *some* of them were almost certainly titles to what followed, the Septuagint translators erroneously assumed that *all* of them were, with the result that all these inscriptions have been handed down, ever since, as psalm "titles," and now appear as such in our English Bible.

It is because of this that many readers of the psalms have noticed that some of these so-called "titles" have little or nothing to do with the psalms over which they stand; while some of our commentators venture the remark that certain of these titles actually seem more appropriate to the psalms which precede them than to those at the head of which they appear!

Inscriptions which need dividing

With the two instances of Habakkuk and Hezekiah before us, then, we shall find that in the case of those psalms which have titles, in our English version, many of these titles must be divided. The first part of the title must be treated as the *sub*-scription of the psalm which goes before; and the remaining words, such as, "A Psalm of David," will remain as the *super*-scription of the psalm which follows—just as the words, "A Prayer of Habakkuk," head the composition in Habakkuk iii.

As an example take psalms iv., v., and vi. In each case the first words of the title are not *really* a part of the title at all, but a sub-script to the psalm which goes before; and the simple title to each of these three psalms is: "A Psalm of David."

Now as soon as we get this key in our hands, the special words used in some of these sub-scripts light up with new significance.

Shoshannim and Gittith

Take the two words, *Shoshannim* and *Gittith*. The former means "lilies," and belongs at the end of psalms xliv. and lxviii. (not at the beginning of psalms xlv. and lxix., as in our English version). The latter means "wine-presses," and belongs at the end of psalms vii., lxxx., and lxxxiii. (not at the beginning of viii., lxxxi., and lxxxiv., as now in our Bible). The "lilies" speak of Springtime; and the "wine-presses" speak of Autumn; for the universal symbol of Spring is *flowers*, and that of the Autumn is *fruit*. Now the *first* of the annual sacred "feasts" in the Jewish calendar was the feast of the *Passover* which came in the *Spring*; while the last of these feasts was the feast of *Tabernacles*, which came in the Autumn ; and these psalms which bear the *Shoshannim* and *Gittith* sub-scripts are meant to be associated respectively with these two feasts. The Passover feast commemorated *redemption* and *deliverance*. The feast of Tabernacles commemorated the Divine *preservation* of Israel, when, after the deliverance from Egypt, God "made the children of Israel to dwell *safely* (the Hebrew form of the verb is emphatic) in booths" (Lev. xxiii. 43). Read these *Shoshannim* and *Gittith* psalms again now in the light of this, and see their relevance.

Muth-labben

But again, take the expression *Muth-labben*. In our English version it comes as the caption to psalm ix., thus—"To the Chief Musician upon *Muth-labben*. A Psalm of David," but we must divide this inscription so that the words, "To the Chief Musician upon *Muth-labben*," are sub-joined to psalm viii., leaving the simple title, "A Psalm of David," at the head of psalm ix.

What, then, does *Muth-labben* mean? All concur that *muth* means "death," and that *ben* is the Hebrew for "son"; so that the natural meaning of the compound term is, "Death of (or for) the son." But it is pointed out that *ben* may probably be *beyn*, written without the long vowel, the omission of the vowel sign being frequent in Hebrew; and in this case the expression *muth-labbeyn* would mean, "death to the one coming between." In fact, this is how the inscription reads in the ancient Jewish Targum—"To praise, relating to the death of the man who went out between the camps." Does that suggest anything? Why, of course, it suggests Goliath; for in 1 Samuel xvii., 4, 23, Goliath is actually called the "*man between the two hosts*," though we do not see this in our English version because the Hebrew term is translated as "a champion." Read psalm viii. again now in the light of this sub-script, and see in it the celebration of David's great victory over Goliath.

But for a fuller and most fascinating treatment of these psalm-inscriptions see Dr. James W. Thirtle's *The Titles of the Psalms*, and Dr. E. W. Bullinger's *The Chief Musician*. Having drawn attention to what we believe is the true key, we must here content ourselves by giving the following meanings of the special Hebrew words which are found in the different inscriptions.

Words	Meanings	Where
Aiieleth-Shahar	The hind of the morning (*meaning the day dawn*).	end of Ps. xxi.
Alamot	The singing maidens, or the maidens' choir.	end of Ps. xlv.
Al-Tashchith	Destroy not.	end of Pss. lvi., lvii., lviii., lxxiv.
Gittith	Winepresses.	end of Pss. vii., lxxx., lxxxiii.
Jeduthun (see footnote)	" Praise-giver "; name of one of the three Directors of Temple worship (1 Chron. xvi. 41, 42 ; xxv. 1–6; 2 Chron. v. 12).	end of Pss. xxxviii., lxi., lxxvi.
Jonath-Elem-Rechokim	The dove of the distant woods. (*Note : David is the dove, in flight from Absalom.*)	end of Ps. lv.
Mahalath (*should be M'choloth*)	The great Dancing.	end of Ps. lii.
Mahalath-Leannoth	Dancings with shoutings.	end of Ps. lxxxvii.
Maschi	Instruction, understanding.	Pss. xxxii., xlii., xliv., xlv., lii., liii., liv., lv., lxxiv., lxxviii., lxxxviii., xxxix., cxlii.
Michtam	Engraven (indicating emphasis and permanence).	Pss. xvi., lvi., lvii., lviii., lix., lx.
Muth-labben	Death of the Champion.	end of Ps. viii.
Neginoth	(*pl. of Neginah*) Stringed instruments.	end of Pss. iii., v., liii., liv., lx., lxvi., lxxv.
Nehiloth (*should be Nahaloth*)	Inheritances.	end of Ps. iv.
Sheminith	Probably the eighth group or division (*in the procession bringing back the Ark. See* 1 Chron. xxiv. 1, 5 ; xxvi. 1, 12).	end of Pss. v., xi.
Shiggaion	A crying aloud (*either of grief or joy*).	Ps. vii., title.
Shoshannim	Lilies.	end of Pss. xliv., lxviii.
Shoshannim-Eduth	(*also Shushan-Eduth*) Lilies of testimony.	end of Pss. lix., lxxix.

Note: As *Jeduthun* refers to a person, a Levite chief singer, perhaps our analysis on pages 91 and 92 should have placed the psalms addressed to him with the "meagre-titles" group rather than with those having "special-word" inscriptions.

THE BOOK OF PSALMS (3)
Lesson Number 59

NOTE.—For this study read psalms lxxiii. to lxxxix., and psalms cxx. to cxxiv., the latter group being the "Songs of Degrees." Use the Revised Version.

In the Old Testament we have an interpretation of human need; and the New Testament is a revelation of the Divine supply. In the Old we have unveilings of the human heart. In the New we have the unveiling of the heart of God, and the way in which He has answered humanity's need in Christ.

—*G. Campbell Morgan.*

THE BOOK OF PSALMS (3)

GROUPS OF PSALMS

WE CANNOT read thoughtfully through the Book of Psalms without observing that certain of the psalms fall into distinctive classes or *groups*. Although the psalms comprising any one of these groups may be irregularly separated from each other, they clearly belong together by similarity of subject-matter, or by some other distinguishing characteristic.

The Songs of Degrees

First we take that group of fifteen psalms known as the "Songs of Degrees." Unlike the other groups which we shall mention, these "Songs of Degrees" *do* run consecutively. They are psalms cxx. to cxxxiv. Each one of these psalms is entitled, "A Song of Degrees."

To what does this title refer? An old Jewish notion was that these fifteen psalms were so called because they were sung, each in order, on the fifteen steps of the Temple; but the difficulty is to prove that there ever *were* fifteen steps to the Temple!

Luther took the title as meaning "A Song in the higher choir," while Calvin thought it meant that these psalms were sung in a higher key. Bishop Jebb's idea was that these psalms were so called because they were sung in connection with the "going up" of the Ark to Mount Zion. Other outstanding scholars, taking the Hebrew word as meaning *ascents* rather than "degrees," have supposed that a gradation, or series of ascents, in the poetic parallelism of these psalms is indicated, in which each line of a parallel carries the meaning of its predecessor a degree further or an ascent higher; but the difficulty about this supposed explanation is that not all these fifteen psalms possess this feature, while *other* psalms, besides these fifteen, *do* have this feature! Others again have suggested that these fifteen psalms were associated with Israel's going up to the three annual feasts at Jerusalem; but as one scholar points out, the majority of these psalms have, as it seems, "nothing at all" to do with pilgrimages! Yet again, the modern school makes all these psalms post-exilic, and says that they were songs of the exiles returning from the Babylonian captivity! Others spiritualise the psalms, and interpret them as referring to the Church; but the psalms themselves speak only of Israel, Judah, Jerusalem and Zion!

So there we are! Suggestions are plentiful; but does any one of those which we have mentioned commend itself as being the true explanation?

What, then, of these fifteen "Songs of Degrees"? Is there a really satisfactory solution? There is. Nor need we go outside the Bible, to Tradition or to the Fathers or to human ingenuity. The explanation, as Drs. Thirtle and Bullinger have shown, is inside the Bible itself.

The first thing to note is that the title, "A Song of Degrees," has the definite article, in the Hebrew, before that word "Degrees," and should therefore read: "A Song of *THE* Degrees." This at once suggests that certain well-known "degrees" are alluded to. Are there, then, any such mentioned in the Bible? There are: and they are the *only* "degrees" of which the Bible tells us. These were the degrees on the great sun-dial of King Ahaz, at Jerusalem. Like other such royal sun-dials of long-ago, the sun-dial of Ahaz would be an elaborate and conspicuous edifice, with its scores of steps mounting up like a long, straight stairway, to a considerable height, and on which, step by step, or degree by degree, the shadow would be registered from the gnomon.

Are we told anything special about this sun-dial of Ahaz? We are: something *very* special. It was on this sun-dial, in the reign of Hezekiah, the son of Ahaz, that the shadow went back ten "degrees" or "steps," as a sign that fifteen years were to be added to Hezekiah's life! This supernatural happening is recorded in 2 Kings xx. 8–11 (which, please look up), where the word "degrees" is certainly given emphasis by repetition.

Is there any likelihood, then, that the "Songs of the Degrees" relate to Hezekiah and the degrees on the sun-dial of Ahaz? There is. To begin with, we know that Hezekiah was the godliest of Judah's kings (2 Kings xviii. 5, 6) and that he was just the man, considered from a spiritual point of view, to write such pieces as the "Songs of the Degrees." Secondly, we know that Hezekiah was very interested in psalms and spiritual songs. It was he who restored the Temple worship (2 Chron. xxix.), taking great care that all was done "according to the commandment of David" (verse 25), and "with the instruments ordained by David" (verse 27), and "with the words of David" (verse 30).

It is generally agreed by scholars that Hezekiah had a large part in shaping the Book of Psalms into its present form; and we know that the same is also true of the Book of Proverbs (Prov. xxv. 1). But, thirdly, Hezekiah was himself a psalm-writer; for in Isaiah xxxviii., beginning at verse 9, we find one of the psalms which he wrote. What is still more striking is the reference, in that chapter, to a set of "songs" composed by Hezekiah. What "songs" could these be? It seems almost certain, from their connection, that they were the "Songs of Degrees" which now appear in our Book of Psalms; for in verse 9 we are told that the psalm there recorded was a "writing of Hezekiah, king of Judah, *when he had been sick, and was recovered of his sickness*" (the sickness in connection with which the shadow went back ten degrees: see verse 8); and at the end of that psalm Hezekiah says: "The Lord was ready to save me. Therefore we will sing *my songs* to the stringed instruments all the days of our life in the house of the Lord" (verse 20).

Is still further evidence required? Then let us note that the number of the "Songs of the Degrees" is *fifteen*; and the number of the years which were added to Hezekiah's life is also *fifteen*. The shadow went back *ten* degrees on the sun-dial; and *ten* of the "Songs of the Degrees" are left anonymous, while the remaining five are *not* left so, four being attributed to David, and one to Solomon. Reasons are not lacking why Hezekiah should leave the ten by himself without name. A proper sense of humility would be enough, apart from anything else; and it may be that since the "songs" were known quite well to be Hezekiah's, the putting of his name with them was deemed to be quite unnecessary. It went without saying that they were his. He himself spoke of them as "*MY* Songs"—as though, even then, they were already well-known.

That they were carefully *arranged* into their present order is clear. There are five groups of three psalms each. In each group two are by Hezekiah, and one by David or Solomon. In each trio the first psalm is one of *trouble*; the second, one of *trust*; and third, one of *triumph*.

But, added to all that we have said, the completing evidence that these fifteen "Songs of the Degrees" did indeed relate to Hezekiah and the degrees on the sun-dial, is the correspondence between their contents and the historical account, in Kings and Chronicles, of Hezekiah's illness and the siege of Jerusalem at that time by the Assyrian king. This, however, is a study all in itself; and we must leave the interested student to consult Bullinger's book, *The Chief Musician*, or, better still, to trace out the correspondence independently.

The Messianic Psalms

Running through the Book of Psalms there is a remarkable prophetic element; and many of the psalms can never be worthily appreciated apart from a recognition of this. The New Testament warrants our speaking so, for not only is the Book of Psalms quoted more frequently in the New Testament than any other book of the Old Testament, but most of the quotations from it are on prophetic lines.

The most noteworthy feature about this prophetic content of the psalms is found in what are known as the *Messianic* psalms —psalms, that is, which, besides having a real reference to the time in which they were written, have their ultimate explanation and fulfilment in Christ.

Three themes are covered by the prophetic psalms—(1) the humiliation and exaltation of the Messiah; (2) the sorrows and eventual deliverance of Israel; (3) the future blessing of all the nations through Israel's reigning Messiah.

The principal Messianic psalms are: ii., viii., xvi., xxii., xxiii., xxiv., xl., xli., xlv., lxviii., lxix., lxxii., lxxxvii., lxxxix., cii., cx., cxviii. In these and others we have Christ's birth, betrayal, agony, death, resurrection, ascension, coming again in glory, and world-wide reign, all pictured with inspired vividness. It has been observed that there are more prophetic statements on this theme of themes in the psalms "than in the Book of Isaiah or in any of the other prophetic books."

Here, in these psalms, we find some of our Lord's prayers

pre-written, and some of the very expressions by which He vented His sufferings, not to mention other adumbrations of His humiliation which are found over and over again. Quite apart from anything else, these Messianic psalms, when read in the light of the New Testament, constitute an unanswerable testimony to the Divine inspiration of the Scriptures.

Take psalm xxii. for instance. Could there be a more amazing fore-enactment of our Lord's death on the Cross than we find described in this psalm? It opens with the very words which our Lord used in the fourth of His seven utterances from the Cross—"My God, My God, why hast Thou forsaken Me?" Through the human writer of this psalm the pre-incarnate Christ Himself actually speaks as though He were already on that never-to-be-forgotten Cross. He speaks of Himself, in the first person, as "despised" and "scorned" and taunted by the words, "He trusted on the Lord that He would deliver Him: let Him deliver Him, seeing He delighted in Him"—and these are some of the very words used at Calvary by the Jewish leaders, who certainly did not obligingly express themselves thus in order to effect the artificial fulfilment of a prophecy which was written against themselves! Perhaps most astounding of all, the psalm goes on to say: "The assembly of the wicked have enclosed Me: they pierced My hands and My feet. I may tell all My bones: they (the wicked) look and stare upon Me. They part My garments among them, and cast lots upon My vesture." When we remember that these words were written hundreds of years before our Lord's incarnation, and that death by crucifixion was then a thing unknown (being introduced later by the Romans), we cannot but wonder at the psalmist's language here, about the piercing of the hands and feet. He is a strangely blind reader of the psalms who can only see here the human David describing some unheard-of experience in his own life; for David was never reduced to the crucifixion-extremity portrayed in this psalm; and besides this, as we well know, the parting of the garments, and the gambling away of the vesture, were literally fulfilled while our Saviour was hanging on the Cross!

Take psalm lxxii. Its title is simply "A Psalm for (or concerning) Solomon"; but we cannot read it discerningly without exclaiming: "A greater than Solomon is here!" It paints in rich colours the glories of Messiah's kingdom. In an earlier study we have seen how God's covenant with David concerning his "son" was to have a primary fulfilment in Solomon, and its ultimate fulfilment in Christ (see on 2 Sam. vii.). Agreeing with this, we find that in this seventy-second psalm the blessings of Solomon's reign are sublimated into a prophetic picture of the coming kingdom under Christ. Note the four great facts about it:

1. Its character—"righteousness" (verses 2-7).
2. Its extent—"to the ends of the earth" (verses 8-11).
3. Its prosperity—"abundance" (verse 16. See R.V.).
4. Its duration—"as long as the sun" (verse 17).

These Messianic psalms are a rich study in their varied witness to Christ. They witness to His *person*, as the Son of God (ii. 7; xlv. 6, 7; cii. 25-7); as the Son of man (viii. 4-6, etc.); and as the Son of David (lxxxix. 3, 4, 27, 29). They witness to His *offices*, as Prophet (xxii. 22, 25; xl. 9, 10); as Priest (cx. 4); as King (ii., xxiv., etc.). It is to be noted that such references as psalms xlv. 6, 7, and cii. 25-7 carry the implication of our Lord's essential deity, especially so in the light of Hebrews i. 8-14. In the Messianic psalms, then, we have a treasure of pure gold.

Other Psalm-groups

We ought just to note two or three other groups of psalms. There are the *Hallelujah* psalms, of which there are ten, and they are psalms cvi., cxi., cxii., cxiii., cxxxv., and cxlvi. to cl. The special characteristic of these is that each of them begins with the expression "Hallelu-Jah" (given in our English Version as "Praise ye the Lord"); and all but two of them (cxi. and cxii.) also *end* with "Hallelu-Jah." This expression of praise occupied a place as a choral refrain in Hebrew worship corresponding with the *Gloria Patria* of Christian worship.

Then there are the *Penitential* psalms. These are seven in number—psalms vi., xxxii., xxxviii., xxxix., li., cii., cxliii.— though, of course, there are lesser penitential passages in other psalms besides these.

Then there are pairs and trios and smaller groups which go together by reason of their *complementariness to each other*. Take psalms xxii., xxiii., and xxiv. These make a trinity in unity.

Psalm xxii. is the psalm of the *suffering Saviour*. Psalm xxiii. is the psalm of the *living Shepherd*. Psalm xxiv. is the psalm of the *exalted Sovereign*. In these three psalms we have the Cross, the Crook, and the Crown! Further: these three psalms strikingly correspond with the three outstanding New Testament references to our Lord's "shepherd" work. In John x. He is the *"good"* Shepherd who gives His life for the sheep—*as in Psalm xxii.* In Hebrews xiii. 20, 21, He is the *"great"* Shepherd, who, being brought again from the dead, perfects that which concerns His flock—*as in psalm xxiii.* In I Peter v. 4, He is the *"chief"* Shepherd, who is to reappear in glory, bringing crowns of reward— *and going with psalm xxiv.* Thus, in psalms xxii., xxiii., and xxiv. we have the "good," the "great" and the "chief" Shepherd —a sublimely beautiful, triune forepicturing of the Lord Jesus as the true Shepherd of His people.

Take psalms xlvi., xlvii., and xlviii. These are not usually included with the Messianic psalms, yet knowing the latent prophetic import of the Psalter it is easy to see in these three psalms a striking triple foreview of the Messianic reign which is yet to be. In psalm xlvi. we have the *coming* of the kingdom— through great tribulation. In psalm xlvii. we have the *range* of the kingdom—even "all the earth." In psalm xlviii. we have the *centre* of the kingdom—even Zion, the "city of our God." Look up these three psalms, and see whether these things be so or not.

Or take psalms xc. and xci. The former is attributed to Moses, and the latter is presumed to be from the same hand. These two great poems make a wonderful exposition of Moses' parting words, in Deuteronomy xxxiii. 27—"The eternal God is thy refuge, and underneath are the everlasting arms." In psalm xc. we have the "eternal God"; and in psalm xci. we have the "everlasting arms." Further examples might be given, but the above will suffice to show what highways and byways of pleasant and instructive discovery lie everywhere around us in this peerless Book of the Psalms.

We recall the advice of an old preacher to a young friend just starting in the ministry. "My young brother, if you would have your spiritual life rich, and your preaching powerful, learn well the psalms of David and the epistles of Paul."

THE BOOK OF PSALMS (4)

Lesson Number 60

NOTE.—Read now psalms xc. to cxix. Mark the doxology at the end of psalm cvi., indicating the break between the fourth and fifth main groups of the psalms.

Love can forbear, and Love can forgive . . . but Love can never be reconciled to an unlovely object. . . . He can never therefore be reconciled to your sin, because sin itself is incapable of being altered; but He may be reconciled to your person, because that may be restored.

—Traherne, "Centuries of Meditation," II, 30.

THE BOOK OF PSALMS (4)

The Imprecatory Psalms

HERE and there in the Psalter, like jagged thorns in a chain of roses, there occur certain psalms which express vehement anger and imprecation against enemies and evil-doers. These are known as the "Imprecatory Psalms." There are also occasional shorter passages of a similar nature elsewhere in the psalms. These imprecatory psalms and passages have been a sore perplexity to many a reader. The imprecatory psalms are xxxv., lviii., lix. lxix., lxxxiii., cix., cxxxvii. The lesser passages are: v. 10; vi. 10; xxviii. 4; xxxi. 17, 18; xl. 14, 15; xli. 10; lv. 9 and 15; lxx. 2, 3; lxxi. 13; lxxix. 6 and 12; cxxix. 5–8; cxl. 9, 10; cxli. 10; cxlix. 7–9. To some minds, these imprecatory psalms and passages are perhaps a more difficult obstacle than any other in the way of a settled confidence in the Divine inspiration of the Scriptures. What then shall we say about them?

First of all, we shall not hesitate to say that, for our own part, we have never found these psalms and passages to be the difficulty which they are supposed to be. We may be thought hard or superficial or both, by a certain type of mind, for saying this so unhesitatingly: but we are not in the least perturbed by that; for, having thoughtfully pondered the circumstances, we are persuaded that it is the objection itself which is superficial, being mainly the expression of sentiment rather than of sound logic and careful reasoning. Let us briefly analyse the objection, and seek an answer.

There seem to be four elements in the objection. These imprecatory psalms are said to be (1) contrary to the higher feelings of human nature, such as the common sentiments of compassion within us; (2) against the dictates of even natural religion, which shows us that God sends His rain upon both the just and the unjust, and does good to the worst of men; (3) utterly contrary to the teaching and spirit of the New Testament, which teaches love to enemies and forgiveness of injuries; (4) inconsistent with the psalmists' own profession of ardent trust in God.

Certain supposed explanations of these psalms have been put forward which, in our own judgment, would have been better left unsaid. For instance, it has been argued that many of the passages which, in our English version, express imprecatory desire are in the future tense in the Hebrew, and should therefore be translated simply as declaring what will happen, and not what the psalmist *wishes* or prays might happen. But this argument offers no solution of those other passages where the verb is in the imperative, such as psalm lv. 9—"Destroy, O Lord, and divide their tongues." Nor does it cancel out such statements as "Happy shall he be who taketh and dasheth thy little ones against the stones!" Quite apart from other weaknesses, therefore, *this* argument is obviously inadequate.

Again, it has been argued that these imprecatory sentiments are peculiar to the old dispensation. This argument, however, while it attempts to limit the difficulty, certainly does not remove it; for what is essentially bad at one period must be so always. Moreover, under the old dispensation, God emphatically inculcated kindness, not only to widows and orphans, but to the stranger, and the Egyptian, and the slave who was of foreign birth. Moreover, the attitude found in the imprecatory psalms is also found in the New Testament; as, for instance, in Paul's words: "Alexander the coppersmith did me much evil. The Lord reward him according to his works!" (2 Tim. iv. 14). See, also, for a most solemn execration, Galations i. 8, 9.

Yet again, it has been argued that the imprecations in the psalms only call down *temporal* calamities, and not such as affect the soul in the beyond. We are relieved to find that this certainly seems to be so; yet the *principle* remains the same whether the anathemas relate to the present life only or to the hereafter. If the *attitude* expressed in the imprecatory psalms is wrong, then it is wrong whatever the imprecations themselves may be: and that is the real difficulty.

Can we, then, justify these imprecatory psalms and passages without resorting to artificial "explanations"? I think we can. There are certain facts concerning them which seem to have been either overlooked or insufficiently emphasised, and which we ought to note at the outset.

First: it seems to be a fairly well-established principle of Scripture interpretation that the first mention of any given subject provides the key to all that is afterwards said about it. Many instances of this could be given did space permit. Now as it is with other classes of texts in the Scriptures, so here, the first of these imprecatory verses gives the key to all those that follow. It is psalm v. 10, where David says: "Destroy Thou them, O God; let them fall by their own counsels. Cast them out in the multitude of their transgressions; for they have rebelled against Thee." The imprecation here is against rebellious transgressors; and it is against them solely *because* they are such, as we see from the last clause—"for (or because) they have rebelled against Thee." In other words, the imprecation is against ungodly wicked-doers *as such*. David's words here are those of a man who sees sin in its real nature as rebellion against God. They are the words of a man who has identified himself with God against sin, and who hates sin because God hates it. It is the attitude crystallised in psalm cxxxix.—"Do not I hate them, O Lord, that hate Thee? and am not I grieved with those that rise up against Thee? I hate them with perfect hatred: I count them mine enemies."

This, we repeat, is the attitude in the first of the imprecatory verses; and it is important to grasp this, for it at once clears the psalmist's *motive*. It is not, like many other human imprecations, the evil wish of a bad man against a good man whose goodness condemns him. Nor is it the evil wish of an ambitious man against some other, either bad or good, who stands in his way. It has nothing to do with jealousy or spite or ambition. The imprecation is not against these men simply as men, *but as evil-doers*. Now a careful examination of all the imprecatory passages shows that two thirds of them are specifically against evil-doers as such; and even in the remainder the same motive seems to be there by implication. While we are far from saying that this fact alone clears up these imprecatory passages, we stress its initial importance as at any rate clearing their *motive*.

Another fact which should be noted is, that out of the twenty-one instances of imprecation which we have cited, sixteen are from David, who, be it remembered, was a *theocratic* king. Unlike Saul, David ever had a keen sense of theocratic responsibility. This reveals itself in the fact that, despite personal delinquencies, he never set himself above the Law or tried to pervert it to his own use. As a theocratic king, he knew that he was anointed by *God*, that he ruled *for* God, and that he was directly *responsible* to God. In an earlier study (on 1 Kings ii.) we have seen how, on his very death-bed, David, conscious of this theocratic responsibility, charged Solomon to inflict punishment on certain wrong-doers whom he himself had neglected to punish earlier: and this death-bed charge to Solomon parallels with the imprecatory verses in the Davidic psalms. In these verses, David is speaking out of the consciousness of his theocratic kingship. Those who were fighting him, betraying him, contriving his downfall, were assaulting *God*; for he, David, was *Jehovah's anointed*! There are many indications of this in the Davidic psalms; but to pick out two or three such from the imprecatory psalms themselves, we would point to psalms lix. 11 and lxix. 6 and xl. 9, 10. While again we are far from saying that this fact alone clears up these imprecatory passages, we stress its importance as making clear their *standpoint*, which is not merely personal but theocratic. These Davidic imprecations are uttered from the standpoint of public justice and not of private vengeance.

As for the five imprecatory passages which are *not* Davidic, these are in each case *national* and not personal. They are psalms lxxxiii.; cxxxvii.; lxxix. 6 and 12; cxxix. 5–8, cxlix. 7–9.

Yet another fact which should be carefully noted about these imprecatory passages is one which concerns the *spirit* in which they were written. It is asked: "Why did not the psalmist show a spirit of kindness to those who were maltreating him?" The answer is that he had *already done so*, and it had been abused. Here and there in the imprecatory psalms we come across such words as, "They rewarded me evil for good"; "I restored that which I took not away"; "They have rewarded me evil for good, and hatred for my love" (xxxv. 12; lxix. 4; cix. 5).

There are many people who seem incapable of distinguishing between *forgiving* and *condoning*. It is Christian and beautiful to forgive acts of wrong against oneself; but when forgiveness is taken advantage of, and wrong-doing impenitently persisted in, continued forgiving degenerates into the *condoning* of that which calls for condemnation. We should distinguish between forgiving a wrong *act* and condoning a wrong *attitude*. Some years ago I witnessed the reunion of a husband and wife, after a separation of eighteen years due to the husband's immorality. It was beautiful to see the wife's forgiveness of the husband's wrongs. A little later, however, it was found that the evil-minded fellow was still hypocritically continuing in his immoral ways while simultaneously professing ardent love for the woman whose life he had already so cruelly blighted. What was the Christian thing for that wife to do? To condone such vile sin? Is any passage in the imprecatory psalms too strong for such behaviour? This distinction between forgiving and condoning ought to be borne in mind in the reading of the imprecatory psalms. While once again this does not clear up the whole difficulty of these imprecatory psalms, it is important as justifying their *spirit*.

Surely, then, it is true to say that at least there are reasonable grounds on which we may sympathetically appreciate the *motive*, and the *standpoint*, and the *spirit* of the so-called "imprecatory" psalms. This prepares us for what, in our own judgment, is decisive in their favour.

Having in mind their motive, standpoint, and spirit, we honestly believe that they are fundamentally in accord with the truest and highest instincts of human nature, and with the teachings of Christianity.

There are certain crimes which by their very extremeness call forth the intense indignation of all right-thinking men and women. The dastardly outrages committed by such monsters as Ahab, Herod, Xerxes I, Antiochus Epiphanes, Nero, the Fouquier Tinvilles and the Carriers of the French Revolution—can any normal-minded man or woman read of such outrages without experiencing reactions of vehement condemnation and imprecation? The revolting circumstances and diabolical cruelty of Hitler's recent persecution of the Jews; the gloating savagery of the Nazis in systematically dive-bombing and machine-gunning the helpless and unoffending women and children of Belgium and France; their sickening brutality in purposely mangling the bodies of terror-stricken refugees beneath the iron rollers of their tanks; their fiendishly destructive spite against cities like Belgrade; their inhuman hardness in gunning life-boats, and hospital ships, and even wrecked seamen struggling for very life in the water; their organised lying and treachery and murderous trickery—can we think of these diabolical atrocities without experiencing, not only revulsion, but an instinctive upflaming of intense indignation and imprecation? Is it to be wondered at that when the Nazis utterly scorned all humanitarian considerations and persisted in their calculated cruelty to defenceless civilians, the people of Britain were gradually exasperated to cry out that the cities of Germany should be given a dosing of the same sort of suffering (thus echoing the very sentiment of Psalm cxxxvii.)? Such misdeeds as those which I have mentioned, whether long past or recent, shock the innate moral sense of human nature in a way which no lapse of time diminishes. Common conscience demands reparation. We feel that if such deeds were to go unpunished the moral constitution of the very universe would be violated; and we are relieved when we hear that retribution has been inflicted.

Such a reaction, we affirm, is native to our very nature; and nothing so clearly shows it to be so than to analyse it. A first constituent in it is an intuitive *anger* against the wrong—not merely the sort of mental disapproval which comes after reflection and reasoning, but a spontaneous upsurge of protestation which is as instinctive as it is instantaneous. A second ingredient is that of *sympathy*—immediate sympathy with the victim or victims of such cruelties. By our very nature we side at once with the injured party. And again there is a perturbing consciousness of *desire*—a desire springing from that sense of justice which is inherent in our moral constitution, that righteous retribution shall square things out. This is no mere cry for revenge, for the ill-deed may not have been against ourselves. Nor is it a shortlived emotion, for reflection only serves to confirm it. Even if we ourselves are the doers of the wrong we experience this; for while on the one hand we may seek to avoid the pain of the penalty, we long, on the other hand, for the mental relief which comes of knowing that the penalty has been borne.

Argue as we will, this imprecatory reaction against outstanding wrongs springs from what has been called "an original principle of our nature." The same feelings, at least in kind, are aroused whether the perpetrator is someone who lives today or someone who lived centuries ago, whether he lives in our own locality or away at the antipodes; and this at once proves that the imprecatory reaction does not spring merely from any personal malice toward the wrong-doer.

How this bears on the imprecatory psalms will be obvious. That which is an irrepressible instinct of our moral nature we cannot pronounce to be wrong without impugning the God who made us. And if such imprecation against blatant atrocities or vile outrages springs from our native instincts and feelings, may there not be circumstances in which it is right to *express* it by lip or pen? We know of at least one thoughtful man whose qualms about the imprecatory psalms have been forever cured by his own native reaction to the atrocities committed by the Nazis, for he found himself venting his sheer indignation in terms equally forcible as those in the imprecatory psalms! He now knows, by the teaching of his own moral constitution, whether it is right or not to feel and to express imprecation against such wrong-doers! Let anyone without prejudice examine the circumstances which called forth, or are thought to have called forth, the sterner imprecations found in the psalms, and there will be found nothing in them which contravenes either the truest instincts of human nature or the teachings of Christianity.

But there is something else to be added which puts these imprecatory psalms in an altogether new light. Careful examination shows that there is a supernatural *predictive* element in them. This prophetic seal settles it that they are Divinely inspired. The late Dean Farrar, who, with remarkable literary brilliance, popularised many rash ideas about the Scriptures, contemptuously sneered, "Can the casuistry be anything but gross which would palm off such passages as the very utterance of God?" But though canons to the right of us and deans to the left of us volley and thunder their doubts, it still remains that the seal of prophecy is the seal of *God*. Read carefully the following words of the late Bishop William Alexander:

"It may be plausible to deny, not without bitter indignation, the Messianic application of the 110th psalm, or the subjectively Messianic character of the 69th or 109th psalm, on the ground that imprecation can never issue from those gentle lips; that images of war and carnage have nothing in common with the Messiah of the New Testament. Yet, after all, who uttered the sentence, 'Those Mine enemies who would not that I should reign over them, bring hither and slay before Me'? Who is to say, 'Depart from Me, ye cursed,' 'Depart from Me, all ye workers of iniquity,' in the words of the 69th psalm?

"No passage in the Psalms has given more offence than that which comes at the close of the tender 'Super flumina' (By the rivers of Babylon):

" 'O daughter of Babylon! who art to be destroyed,
　Happy he who shall reward thee as thou hast rewarded us;
　Happy he who will take and dash thy babes against the
　　rock.'

"But for the attentive student, the doom of Babylon hangs in the air of prophecy. We close the Psalter for a time, and after many days, as we draw near to the end of the whole volume of revelation, we are startled by a new echo of the words in the old 137th psalm, 'Babylon the great is fallen, is fallen. *Reward her even as she rewarded you;* and double unto her double according to her works.' "

Yes, after all these centuries there is still a remaining prophetic significance in the words, relating to something even yet to happen. But even if we hark back to the long-ago fall of the actual ancient Babylon, we find that there was a startling fulfilment of the strangely prophetic import of the psalmist's words; for, as things eventuated, such were the terrible doings at the overthrow of Babylon, that he would have been a kind friend, truly enough, who had dashed the little ones against the rock and thus saved them from a fate even worse! Bishop Alexander aptly adds: "Unless it is wrong and incredible that God should punish terribly, it is not wrong or incredible that His Son should give warning of it in the most vivid and impressive way." Let it never be forgotten, then, that there is this prophetic strain latently present in the so-called imprecatory psalms; and let it never be forgotten that whatever men may think or say, the prophetic seal on Scripture is the seal of God Himself.

To sum up: The imprecatory psalms are sound in their *motive,* in their *standpoint,* in their *spirit.* They express a constitutional moral sense of human nature, and not an individual desire for revenge. The supernatural predictive element in them seals them as genuinely inspired. There are also passages in the New Testament which fully correspond. We therefore deduce that objections to these psalms arise from the sentimental susceptibilities of human nature rather than from logical reasoning. But when sentiment disagrees with sound logic, sentiment is wrong and must be firmly restrained.

THE BOOK OF PSALMS (5)

Lesson Number 61

NOTE.—Before this final study in the Psalms read psalms cxx. to cl. Use the Revised Version. Read each psalm twice. Study carefully psalm cxxxix. along with our notes on it in this study.

Compared with this, how poor religion's pride,
   In all the pomp of method, and of art,
When men display to congregations wide
   Devotion's every grace, except the heart!
The Power, incensed, the pageant will desert,
   The pompous strain, the sacerdotal stole:
But, haply, in some cottage far apart,
   May hear, well pleased, the language of the soul;
And in His book of life the inmates poor enrol.
        —*Robert Burns, "The Cotter's Saturday Night."*

THE BOOK OF PSALMS (5)

Individual Psalms

BEFORE we leave this Book of Psalms we ought just to glance at a few of the psalms separately. Not only do many readers fail to appreciate the glorious poetry of the psalms, as we have lamented in an earlier lesson, but they also read them too casually to perceive the structural beauty which many of them possess.

Psalm cxxxix.

Turn to psalm cxxxix. Here is a poem the literary excellence of which is only equalled by the majesty and sublimity of its spiritual message. Far from being a mere string of loosely connected verses, it is a methodically constructed composition. This may be traced quite easily even in our Authorised Version, although it does not set out the psalm in its poetic form. The twenty-four verses of the psalm run in four strophes of six verses each. In the first six verses we have the Divine *omniscience*. In the second six we have the Divine *omnipresence*. In the third six we have the Divine *omnipotence*. In the final six we have the psalmist's reaction to these lofty considerations, ending with an earnest prayer; for his contemplation of the Divine attributes brings him to his knees in adoration and fervent entreaty.

Take the first six verses on the Divine *omniscience*. The first verse reads: "O Lord, Thou hast searched me and known. . . ." There is some kind of ellipsis here in the original. Instead of filling it with the pronoun "me," as in our English versions, perhaps we ought to read it: "O Lord, Thou hast searched me and known my heart." This makes a true parallel between the opening sentence of the psalm and its closing prayer—"Search *me*, O God, and know *my heart*." It is not indispensable to read the first verse thus in order to see the development in these first six verses, but it brings out even more clearly their sequence and completeness, speaking, as they do, of heart, thoughts, actions, and words. These verses, then, tell us that the omniscient God knows—

MY HEART—"O Lord, Thou hast searched me and known my heart" (verse 1).

MY THOUGHTS—"Thou understandest my thought afar off" (verse 2).

MY ACTIONS—"Thou . . . art acquainted with all my ways" (verse 3).

MY WORDS—"Not a word in my tongue, but Thou knowest it altogether" (verse 4).

This covers the whole moral man, the whole of our inner and outer life. The Divine omniscience is here viewed, not as a mere theological or philosophical abstraction, but as an arresting reality bearing upon our whole individual life and being. It is not surprising that in verses 5 and 6 the inspired poet, subdued to reverent wonder, should add: "Thou hast beset me behind and before, and laid Thine hand upon me. Such knowledge is too wonderful for me: it is high, I cannot attain unto it."

And now read the *second* strophe, covering the second group of six verses. Here we have the Divine *omnipresence*; and it is expressed in five extremes. First there is the extreme of *height*: "If I ascend up into heaven, Thou art there" (verse 8). Next there is the extreme of *depth*: "If I make my bed in Sheol, behold, Thou art there!" (verse 8). Note David's exclamation of surprise, his "behold!" that God is in the depth of Sheol as well as in the height of heaven. Next come the two extremes of *east* and *west*: "If I take the wings of the morning"—a poetic reference to the sunrise, and therefore to the east; "or dwell in the uttermost parts of the sea"—a reference to the Mediterranean Sea, and therefore to the west; "even there shall Thy hand lead me, and Thy right hand shall hold me" (verses 9, 10). Finally comes the extreme of *darkness*: "If I say, Surely the darkness shall cover me; even the night shall be light about me" (verse 11). Note the emphasis here—"If I say *surely* the darkness shall cover me." Dense darkness is considered the surest of all coverings. Wherever a man may hide in the daylight, he can be seen if any should chance that way; but the darkness is such a screen as no mortal eye can see through. Height, depth, east, west, light, darkness—God is present in them all.

And now read the *third* strophe, covering the third group of six verses. Here we have the Divine *omnipotence* (verses 13–18). Here the royal poet speaks with delicate skill concerning the mystery of human birth and life, beholding in man the crown of creative achievement, and at the same time the evidence of the Divine omnipotence. We must leave these verses to the student's private reading. They express with striking vividness the marvel of the human constitution. The complexity, delicacy, intricacy, and exquisite mechanism of the human system are such as inspire the psalmist with a sense of awe, in which he would have ourselves also join. As we ponder the power, the thought, the love, the care, which God exercises toward man, toward men as individuals, toward each of ourselves, do we not find ourselves joining with David in the words by which he closes this third strophe?—"How precious also are Thy thoughts unto me, O God! How great is the sum of them! If I should count them, they are more in number than the sand. When I awake I am still with Thee."

And now read the *final* six verses of the psalm. David has reflected on the Divine attributes of omniscience, omnipresence, and omnipotence; he has recognised the *spirituality* of God (verse 7), the *love* of God (verse 17), and now he reflects on the *holiness* of God (verse 19), which, translated more literally, reads: "Oh, if thou wouldst smite the wicked, O God! (Ye men of violence depart from me!) for they rebel against Thee with wicked deeds, and lift up against Thee vainly." Such a view of God as David has had means a clean break with sin. Hence his strong words here against sin in others and his intense concern about sin in himself: and hence the prayer with which the psalm closes. David's contemplation of God has brought him to his knees in prayer. So should it be with each of ourselves. However, what we are particularly concerned with just here is the structural beauty of this grand psalm; and perhaps we have said sufficient to exhibit at least something of this.

Psalm xxiii.

Turn now to another favourite psalm, the twenty-third. The opening words, "I shall not want" are the key to the whole. The Prayer Book version brings out the full force—"The Lord is my shepherd, therefore can I *lack nothing*." Unlock the verses of this psalm with this key, and how beautifully do they open up to us! "He maketh me to lie down in green pastures"—so I shall not lack *provision*. "He leadeth me beside the still waters" —so I shall not lack *peace*. "He restoreth my soul"—so I shall not lack *restoration* if I faint or fail. "He leadeth me in the paths of righteousness"—I shall not lack *guidance*. "Yea, though I walk through the valley of the shadow of death, I will fear no evil"—I shall not lack *courage* in the dark hour. "Thy rod and thy staff, they comfort me"—so I shall not lack true *comfort*. "Thou preparest a table before me in the presence of mine enemies"—I shall not lack *protection, preservation, and honour*. "Thou anointest my head with oil"—I shall never lack *joy*, of which the oil is a symbol. "My cup runneth over"—I shall never lack fulness of *blessing*. "Surely goodness and mercy shall follow me all the days of my life"—I shall not lack the Divine *favour* as long as I live on earth. "And I will dwell in the house of the Lord for ever"—I shall not lack a *heavenly home* when my earthly journeyings are done.

This twenty-third psalm begins, "The Lord is my shepherd." The little copula, "is," does not come in the Hebrew. That is why it is put in italics in our Authorised Version. The Hebrew simply says: "Jehovah my shepherd." Should not the words be read as an exclamation of joyous discovery?—"Jehovah—my Shepherd!" This exclamation, in the Hebrew, is *Jehovah-raah*, and this is very significant. In the Old Testament we find seven instances of compound Jehovistic titles. They are as follows:

Jehovah-jireh—"The Lord will provide" (Gen. xxii. 13–14).
Jehovah-rapha—"The Lord that healeth" (Exod. xv. 26).
Jehovah-shalom—"The Lord our peace" (Judges vi. 24).
Jehovah-tsidkenu—"The Lord our righteousness" (Jer. xxiii. 6).
Jehovah-shammah—"The Lord ever-present" (Ezek. xlviii. 35).
Jehovah-nissi—"The Lord our banner" (Exod. xvii. 8–15).
Jehovah-raah—"The Lord my shepherd" (Ps. xxiii. 1).

It is an impressive fact that all these seven wonderful Divine provisions which are indicated in these seven compound Jehovistic names are gathered up in this twenty-third psalm.

Jehovah-jireh (The Lord will provide)—"I shall lack nothing";
Jehovah-rapha (The Lord that healeth)—"He restoreth my soul";

Jehovah-shalom (The Lord our peace)—"He leadeth me beside the still waters";

Jehovah-tsidkenu (The Lord our righteousness)—"He leadeth me in the paths of righteousness";

Jehovah-shammah (The Lord ever-present)—"I will fear no evil, for Thou art with me";

Jehovah-nissi (The Lord our banner)—"Thou preparest a table before me in the presence of mine enemies";

Jehovah-raah (The Lord my shepherd)—"The Lord is my Shepherd."

Other Examples

To close with, here are a few further examples, given more briefly.

Take psalm xlv. This psalm is a Royal Marriage Hymn. Its title is: "A Song of Loves"; and, as we shall see later, it is the Scripture key which unlocks to us the mystic meaning of the Song of Solomon. The first chapter of the Hebrews epistle tells us, also, that this psalm has reference to the Lord Jesus Christ. The psalm has three parts to it—(1) a brief exordium or preface—verse 1; (2) an Address to the royal bridegroom—verses 2 to 9; (3) an Address to the royal bride—verses 10 to 17. In the address to the royal bridegroom we have four sub-divisions—(a) in verse 2, the beauty of his person; (b) in verses 3 to 5, the valour of his conquests; (c) in verse 6, the stability of his kingdom; (d) in verses 7 to 9, the gladness of his marriage. Similarly, in the address to the royal bride we find four sub-divisions—(a) in verses 10 and 11, an appeal for complete devotion; (b) in verse 12, a promise of high honour; (c) in verses 13 to 15, a eulogy of the bride's charms; (d) in verses 16 and 17, a pledge of unceasing Divine favour.

Take psalm xc.—the "Prayer of Moses, the man of God." It is in three clear parts—(1) the Divine sovereignty and human history—see verses 1–6; (2) the Divine severity and human iniquity—see verses 7–11; (3) the human appeal for compassion and favour—see verses 12–17.

Or again, take psalm xix. Dr. Moulton's title for this psalm is: "The Heavens above; the Law within." It is the psalm of

Science and Religion. Here the two are shown to be fundamentally one. In masterly paragraphs this brief but majestic psalm handles this much-controverted subject, and with an understanding and clear vision unsurpassed by any modern scholarship. The first fourteen lines are devoted to the revelation of God in *the works of Nature*. The next fourteen lines are devoted to the revelation of God in *the words of Scripture*. Then, after these equally balanced parts, the psalm closes with the prayer: "Let the words of my mouth, and the meditation of my heart, be acceptable in thy sight, O Lord, my Rock and my Redeemer." In part 1 the psalmist's name for God is *El*, "the Mighty One." In part 2 he changes to the name *Jehovah*, which is distinctively the redemption name of Deity (indicated in our English version by the word LORD, in capitals). This name Jehovah is used seven times in the latter part of the psalm, but the name El not once. The psalmist chooses with intelligence and care. The name of God in the realm of Science is El, or Elohim. The name of God in the realm of religion is Jehovah. The God of Science and the God of Religion are not two different deities, but one and the same God—the only true God, who is both the God of creation and the God of redemption.

Yet again, take psalm iii., and see how its three "Selahs" divide it up into (1) Trouble, (2) Trust, and (3) Triumph. Or turn to psalm xxxviii., and see how its twenty-two verses are exactly halved between (1) the plague within, and (2) the foes without.

Then there is that wonderful psalm cxix., which is in twenty-two sections—one section for each of the twenty-two letters of the Hebrew alphabet, in order; each section consisting of sixteen lines, with the sixteen lines going in eight parallel pairs or couplets, and each of the eight couplets of the section beginning with the same letter of the alphabet. Or see psalm cxi., which, after the opening "Hallelujah," has twenty-two lines, each line beginning with a letter of the Hebrew alphabet, so that the twenty-two initial letters of the lines run consecutively right through the alphabet. (There are eight of these Alphabetic or Acrostic psalms —ix., xxv., xxxiv., xxxvii., cxi., cxii., cxix., cxlv.)

The most familiar psalms may often surprise us with new beauties. To go back yet once more to psalm xxiii., it has been suggested that there is a beautiful triple message in it, inasmuch as we have three metaphorical figures in it—

(1) The Shepherd and the sheep (verses 1, 2).
(2) The Guide and the traveller (verses 3, 4).
(3) The Host and the guest (verses 5, 6).

Look the precious old psalm up again, and see whether the above analysis will stand the test of a careful study.

Look up psalms xlii. and xliii., and see whether you think these two ought to go together as one. Certainly the one title seems to cover them both. Their subject-matter, also, seems akin. But what is most suggestive is the recurring of the refrain—

> *Why art thou cast down, O my soul?*
> *And why art thou disquieted within me?*
> *Hope thou in God;*
> *For I shall yet praise Him,*
> *Who is the health of my countenance,*
> *And my God.*

It will be seen that this refrain comes in the *middle* of psalm xlii., and again at the *end*; and yet *again* at the end of psalm xliii.

These two psalms prescribe a lovely cure for depression. See the psalmist's diagnosis—"cast down" and "disquieted." Then see him expose the causes and symptoms: interrupted communion with God (1, 2); misunderstanding by others (3); unhelpful brooding over the past (4). Then see him indicate the treatment to effect recovery: the determination to remember God (6); new confidence in His sympathy, faithfulness, presence (7, 8); and a resolve to pray the matter through (8, 9). The prayer itself is psalm xliii. Thus fear gives place to hope, and sighing to singing.

There we must stop. We commend this exhaustless treasury of the psalms once again to the prayerful exploration of every Christian. The joy and enrichment which these precious poems of human experience and Divine inspiration have brought to the people of God down through the ages can never be measured or expressed. To God be the praise and thanksgiving!

DO YOU KNOW THE ANSWERS?

1. What is the origin and meaning of the title, "Psalms"?

2. What, in a sentence, is the general spiritual value or purpose of the Book of Psalms?

3. What are the so-called "orphan" psalms, and how many are there?

4. Of the hundred psalms which have their authors' names, how many did David write, and who wrote the others?

5. Can you give six of the special Hebrew inscription-words and their meanings?

6. Give reasons why some of the psalm-inscriptions should be taken as *sub*-scriptions to the psalms which precede them rather than as superscriptions to those which follow.

7. Which are the five main groupings of the psalms?

8. Which are the "Songs of the Degrees," and what reasons are there for thinking they were compiled by Hezekiah in relation to the sun-dial of king Ahaz?

9. Can you cite ten of the Messianic psalms?

10. In what way do psalms xxii., xxiii., and xxiv. make a trio?

11. Can you give four considerations in justification of the so-called "imprecatory" psalms?

12. Can you show by a general analysis that psalm cxxxix. is a methodical composition?

THE BOOK OF PROVERBS

Lesson Number 62

NOTE.—For this study read the whole Book of Proverbs through, but not too many chapters at once. With successions of maxims such as (mainly) we have here, overloading is the enemy of remembering. Read the book according to the following grouping: First read twice through chapters i. to ix., which are all on the extolling of "Wisdom." Then read twice through chapters x. to xxiv., which consist of 375 proverbs (x.–xxii. 16), and 16 epigrams (xxii. 17–xxiv.) on various matters. Then read twice through chapters xxv. to xxxi., which consist of proverb-clusters, the Sayings of Agur (xxx.), the Oracle of Lemuel's Mother (xxxi. 1–9), and the Acrostic on the Virtuous Woman (xxxi. 10–31).

A proverb is a wise saying in which a few words are chosen instead of many, with a design to condense wisdom into a brief form both to aid memory and stimulate study. Hence proverbs are not only "wise sayings," but "dark sayings"—parables, in which wisdom is disguised in a figurative or enigmatic form like a deep well, from which instruction is to be drawn, or a rich mine, from which it is to be dug. Only profound meditation will reveal what is hidden in these moral and spiritual maxims.

—*Arthur T. Pierson, D.D.*

THE BOOK OF PROVERBS

OUR BIBLE is both a book and a library. It is a book inasmuch as it is a diversity in *unity*, all its sixty-six parts combining to make one progressive whole. It is a library in the sense that it is a unity in diversity, with its different groups of books given up to the principal different branches of knowledge. Not only do we have history and politics and poetry and prophecy and devotional literature; we also have here that distinctive order or learning and teaching which goes by the name of *philosophy*. This we find in Job and Proverbs and Ecclesiastes.

This library must not be measured merely by number of words, but by its depth of truth, by its breadth and fulness, by its superiority and finality. The Bible may seem very small against the imposing shelves of many a large library; yet with this one volume in our hand we may stand within the largest library on earth and truthfully say that all the tens of thousands of books therein collected cannot teach us more about the fundamental realities of the universe and of human life than we learn in these Scriptures. To struggle through hundreds of the profoundest and most erudite of other books, whether ancient or modern, and yet remain ignorant of *this* book, is infinite deprivation; whereas to know no other volume but this is to be made wise unto salvation, and to be furnished with a knowledge of fundamental realities which comes to us stamped with Divine certainty.

Prudence Through Precept

So, with growing appreciation of the varied treasure which we possess in our Bible "library," we now turn on from the devotional passion of the Psalms to the practical wisdom of the Proverbs.

As a preliminary, we note right away that the Proverbs are meant to be to our *practical* life what the Psalms are to our devotional life. This is their general significance. Here are pointed precepts for practical prudence. Here are laws from heaven for life on earth. Here are counsels from above for conduct here below. Here are the words of the wise on the ways of the world. Here is homely wit for the daily walk; but it is human wit shot through with Divine wisdom; and he who is well versed in it will be soundly guided and safely guarded. We may put it that the general message of this Book of Proverbs is *Prudence through Precept*.

Genius of the Proverb

The English word "proverb" means a brief saying in the stead of many words (*pro* = for; *verba* = words). In popular usage it signifies any pithy, sententious saying or terse maxim. The Hebrew word, however, which we translate as "proverbs" (*mishle*) has a much wider meaning, and is used of many discourses, sentences, and expressions which would not be classed as proverbs in English today. This accounts for the fact that not all the writings in the "Book of Proverbs" are proverbs in the usual English sense. The larger part of them, however, *are* true proverbs, and are proverbs of the highest order, too.

The genius of the proverb lies in its shrewd concentration of a truth or of some sagacious counsel in a terse and striking way, so that it catches on, and becomes easier to remember than to forget. A proverb does not argue: it assumes. Its purpose is not to explain a matter, but to give pointed expression to it. An aphorism or proverb has several ways of catching on to the mind and the memory. It may do so by elegance of diction, by the beauty of a rhetorical figure, by its oracle-like brevity, or by its smart focusing of a poignant truth. It is not surprising, therefore, that the use of the proverb has figured largely in every nation, more so in the past than in the present era of widespread systematic education, and most of all among Oriental peoples, to whose mental cast the proverb seems peculiarly adapted.

Who Wrote the Proverbs?

There can be little doubt that the bulk of the Proverbs are from Solomon. The book opens with the words, "The proverbs of Solomon, the son of David, king of Israel." Likewise, chapter x. begins, "The proverbs of Solomon." Yet again, chapter xxv. begins, "These are also the proverbs of Solomon, which the men of Hezekiah, king of Judah, copied out." The book itself, therefore, testifies to Solomonic authorship. In I Kings iv. 32 we are told that among his diverse writings Solomon "spake three thousand proverbs." What then is more likely, in view of this and the claim of the book itself, than that this Book of Proverbs is in the main from Solomon, and was arranged substantially in its present form during the reign of Hezekiah, at which time, also, the Thirteen Sayings of Agur (xxx.) and the Oracle of Lemuel's Mother (xxxi.) were appended? Arguments for the composite authorship of the book are based on unconvincing assumptions; though the work of different hands here and there may admittedly be perceived as contributing to the arrangement of the work in its present completed form.

Analysis

The Book of Proverbs is in three main divisions. These are indicated by the three places, already referred to, where the book ascribes the authorship to Solomon. These are chapters i. 1; x. 1; and xxv. 1. The first nine chapters are a little book in themselves, all devoted to one theme, namely, the extolling of Wisdom. In these chapters we do not find "proverbs," in our common English sense of the word, but *sonnets*, by which we mean a short poem devoted to one particular theme and moulded into some special form. (According to strict definition, a sonnet, in English, consists of fourteen lines, after the Italian pattern; and still more strictly, the fourteen lines originally consisted of an octave and a sextet expressing two phases of the same thought. The essential distinction of the sonnet, however, does not really lie in the mere number of its lines, but in the moulding of thought to a special form. In these first nine chapters of Proverbs there are fifteen sonnets and two monologues.)

Then, in chapters x. to xxiv. we have a long run of proverbs proper—three hundred and seventy-five aphorisms in couplets, followed by sixteen epigrams and sayings which commence at chapter xxii. 17.

Finally, beginning at chapter xxv., we have seven epigrams and proverb-clusters, fifty-five couplets, thirteen sayings of Agur, and the oracle of Lemuel's mother, ending with the acrostic on the Virtuous Woman.

In our Authorised Version there is nothing to indicate to the ordinary reader where the different sonnets and epigrams begin or end; nor is it very much better in the Revised Version, although the paragraph marks are certainly a help. We shall do well to call a literary specialist to our aid, and let him pick out for us the fifteen sonnets in Book 1, and the various epigrams in Books 2 and 3. In the following analysis, therefore, while the three main headings are our own, we have followed Dr. R. G. Moulton's *Modern Reader's Bible* in the details given under these headings. It will be good for us to go carefully through this analysis, marking off the different sonnets and epigrams in our study Bibles for future reference. (*See next page.*)

Although in this present scheme of studies we devote only one chapter to the Book of Proverbs, let not this be thought to indicate that we deem it comparatively unimportant. The briefness of our treatment is due simply and solely to the nature of the book. To deal with it more fully would involve more or less our dealing separately with its hundreds of sententious sayings and sagacious aphorisms, an undertaking which obviously would require a book all to itself. What we are here seeking to do is to exhibit the genius of the proverbs as a species, the main groupings of them in this *book* of proverbs, and the rich value of the complex collection which is here preserved for us. After that, the only thorough way to study and know the book is to read it again and again, slowly and reflectively, and not too much at a time, letting its pithy contrasts and parallels rivet themselves in the mind. They who know the book well in that way will have "wit and wisdom" for every situation.

Structural Method

First, learn to appreciate the main features of proverb *structure*. Most common is the *contrastive* proverb, which catches the mind and emphasises a truth by the compact presentation of some striking contrast. Proverbs of this type may be known at once by the almost invariable "but" which starts the second line or member of the proverb; as in—

A merry heart doeth good like a medicine;
But a broken spirit drieth the bones.

THE BOOK OF PROVERBS

THE BOOK OF PRACTICAL WISDOM

PRUDENCE THROUGH PRECEPT

BOOK 1. SONNETS EXTOLLING WISDOM (i.–ix.).

15 SONNETS. Introduction (i. 1–9); Enticements of Sinners (i. 10–19); Wisdom the Deliverer (ii. 1–22); The Reward of Piety (iii. 1–10); Wisdom the Supreme Prize (iii. 11–20); Wisdom and Security (iii. 21–6); Wisdom and Perversity (iii. 27–35); Tradition of Wisdom (iv. 1–9); The Two Paths (iv. 10–19); Wisdom and Health (iv. 20–7); The Strange Woman (v. 1–23); Suretyship (vi. 1–5); The Sluggard (vi. 6–11); The Discord Sower (vi. 12–19); Adultery (vi. 20–35); House of Wisdom versus that of Folly (a sonnet quartette: ix.).

2 MONOLOGUES. Wisdom's Warning (i. 20–33); Wisdom and the Strange Woman (vii.–viii.).

BOOK 2. MAXIMS ENJOINING PRUDENCE (x.–xxiv.).

375 PROVERBS or aphorisms in the form of contrastive or completive or comparative couplets (x. 1–xxii. 16).

16 EPIGRAMS. Introduction (xxii. 17–21); Mixed Epigrams (xxii. 22–29); Awe before Appetite (xxiii. 1–3); Fleetingness of Riches (xxiii. 4–5); Evil Hospitality (xxiii. 6–8); Mixed Epigrams (xxiii. 9–18); Gluttony (xxiii. 19–21); Three Sayings (xxiii. 22–5); Whoredom (xxiii. 26–8); Wine and Woe (xxiii. 29–35); Mixed Epigrams (xxiv. 1–10); Duty of Rescue (xxiv. 11–12); Wisdom and Honey (xxiv. 13–14); Four Epigrams (xxiv. 15–22); Respect of Persons (xxiv. 23–5); Three Sayings (xxiv. 26–9); The Field of the Slothful (xxiv. 30–4).

BOOK 3. MORE MAXIMS ON PRUDENCE (xxv.–xxxi.).

7 EPIGRAMS and Proverb-clusters. The King (xxv. 1–7); Various (xxv. 8–xxvi. 2); On Fools (xxvi. 3–12); The Sluggard (xxvi. 13–16); Social Pests (xxvi. 17–26); Various (xxvi. 27–xxvii. 22); Good Husbandry (xxvii. 23–7).

55 PROVERBS or aphorisms in the form of contrastive or completive or comparative couplets (xxviii.–xxix.).

THE THIRTEEN SAYINGS OF AGUR (xxx.).

THE ORACLE OF LEMUEL'S MOTHER (xxxi. 1–9).

AN ACROSTIC ON THE VIRTUOUS WOMAN (xxxi. 10–31).

It has been said that antithesis, or contrast, is the very life-blood of the proverb.

Then there are many proverbs of the *completive* type, in which the second line or member of the proverb agrees with the first, and adds to it, or carries the thought of it to some further point. These may usually be known by the "and" which leads the second line or member of the proverb; as in—

> Commit thy works unto the Lord;
> And thy thoughts shall be established.

Then again, there are those proverbs which are *comparative* in their structure. Some of these are very striking in their figures of comparison; and not infrequently they may be at once known by the "than" which leads the second line or member; as in—

> Better is a little with righteousness,
> Than great revenues without right.

Imagery and Analogy

One should not miss the sheer poetic pleasure of the rich and clever and varied imagery of the proverbs. Many of the analogies are apt and "knowing" to a degree. Who can miss the grim humour of the proverb which likens a "fair woman without discretion" to a "jewel of gold in a swine's snout"? Or what masculine nature can help feeling a twinge of knowing sympathy with that other proverb which likens the tongue of a nagging woman to "a continual dropping in a very rainy day"? Was there ever a more delightful simile than—"As cold water to a thirsty soul, so is good news from a far country"? Who can forget such analogies and pictures as we find on page after page of the proverbs?—the sluggard who is like vinegar to the teeth and smoke to the eyes of his employer; the offended brother who is harder to win than a strong city; the coming of poverty like "an armed man" upon the slothful; the likening of wise reproof to an earring of gold on an obedient ear; of boastfulness to wind and clouds without rain; of conscience to a lamp of God in man; the picture of riches flying away on wings like those of an eagle; the contrasting of the faithful wounds given by a friend with the profuse kisses of an enemy; not to mention many more such instances. Quite apart from the moral and spiritual value of the proverbs, the wit and imagery which we find in them are a tonic to the mind, unless we are without a single streak of humour and poetry in our make-up.

Proverb Cameos

Running through the practical philosophy of the proverbs is a keen aliveness to the perpetual struggle which goes on between good and evil for the upper hand in men's lives. It is because of this that the proverbs retain a vivid up-to-dateness even though much of their language relates to a simple state of society far removed from our modern western world. Some of the cameo pictures of social types which abound in the proverbs might have been carved out for us this morning. They stand out; they live on; they are as characteristic as any of Dickens' characters, and as typical as any of the figures in Bunyan's *Pilgrim's Progress*, even though presented in far fewer words. The following quotation picks a few of them out for us: "There is the prating fool, winking with his eye; the practical joker, as dangerous as a madman casting firebrands about; the talebearer, and the man who 'harps upon a matter,' separating chief friends; the whisperer whose words are like dainty morsels going down into the inner-most parts of the belly; the backbiting tongue, drawing gloomy looks all around as surely as the north wind brings rain; the false boaster, compared to wind and clouds without rain; the haste to be rich; the liberal man that scattereth and yet increaseth, while others are withholding only to come to want; the specu-lator holding back his corn amid the curses of the people; the man of wandering life, like a restless bird; the unsocial man that separateth himself, foregoing wisdom for the sake of his own private desire; the cheerfulness that is a continual feast"—and so on. What pages of immortal interest there are in these proverbs!

How to Read

Our *"NOTE"* at the beginning of this present study says, "Read the whole Book of Proverbs through, *but not too many chapters at once.*" The intelligence of that advice will be at once apparent. These chapters of proverbs are not meant to be read in the way one reads narrative chapters (as in the historical books), or full cycles of debate (as in the Job dialogue), or complete poems (as in the Book of the Psalms), or progressive argument (as in Ecclesiastes). They are meant to be read lingeringly, ponderingly, memorisingly. Not, however, that the memorising of them is to be a forced work, like the memorising of rules in the learning of a language. Proverbs are meant so to aid the memory as to be difficult to forget. It is wonderful how these Scripture proverbs light up with significant wisdom, and how unforgettably they engrave themselves in the mind when they are read musingly and fairly often. Take chapter iii. 5—

> Trust in Jehovah with all thine heart;
> And lean not on thine own understanding.

How reasonable it seems to "lean on our own understanding"! Is not man's intellect his distinguishing superiority? Was it not implanted by God, to be a lamp of guidance? Is there not then something strange-sounding in this proverbial counsel? Maybe at a glance there is; but when we reflect on it as set off against "Trust in Jehovah . . ." it opens up with sage spiritual meaning. That intellectual faculty which crowns man as being "in the image of God" was never meant to make men *independent* of God, but to make possible co-operative *fellowship* with God. Now that Adam's posterity is a fallen race, man's highest faculty can be his deepest snare, the more so as there is an active deceiver "going to and fro in the earth". And so we might go on, as this little proverb goes on opening up big reflections to us.

We are reluctant to leave the book without displaying the facets of at least one captivating jewel from this manifold casket. Take the last chapter, with its acrostic on the "virtuous woman." Never was a worthier ode sung in praise of wifely virtue. It consists of twenty-two couplets, corresponding with its twenty-two verses in our own translation (more clearly shown in R.V.). Each of the twenty-two couplets begins with a letter of the Hebrew alphabet, so that the twenty-two run right through the alphabet in proper order. The special features may be set out like the manuscript notes of an address.

MRS. "FAR-ABOVE-RUBIES"

Proverbs xxxi. 10–31

She is a Good Woman

She works diligently	"She worketh willingly with her hands" (vv. 13, 15, 19)
She contrives prudently	"She considereth . . . and (then) buyeth" (v. 16). Also vv. 22 and 24
She behaves uprightly	"Strength and honour are her clothing" (v. 25)

She is a Good Wife

She seeks husband's good	"She will do him good all the days of her life" (v. 12)
She keeps his confidence	"The heart of her husband doth safely trust in her" (v. 11)
She aids his prosperity	"Her husband is known . . . among the elders of the land" (vv. 23, 24)

She is a Good Mother

She clothes family wisely	"All her household are clothed with scarlet" (v. 21)
She feeds household well	"She riseth and giveth meat to her household" (v. 15). Also v. 27
She shops sensibly	"She bringeth her food from far" (rather than get inferior near by) (vv. 14 and 18)

She is a Good Neighbour

She helps the poor	"She stretcheth out her hand to the poor" (v. 20)
She uplifts the needy	"She reacheth forth her hands to the needy" (v. 20)
She speaks graciously	"In her tongue is the law of kindness" (v. 26)

Her value—"Her price is far above rubies."
Her praise—"Her children arise and call her blessed."
Her pre-eminence—"But thou excellest them all."
Her secret—"A woman that feareth the Lord."

Perhaps we ought just to add that the New Testament enables us to fill in the complete picture of this acrostic heroine of the Proverbs. Mrs. "Far-above-rubies" lives at "Godly House," the Way of Holiness, Blessing-town. The house is built on the Rock of Ages, over which the Way of Holiness runs, leading to the Celestial City. The house overlooks the boundless sea of "the riches of grace"; and as it is built foursquare on the Rock, the "Sun of Righteousness" is always shining in through one or more of the windows, which are "Pray without ceasing," "Rejoice evermore," "In everything give thanks," and "Quench not the Spirit." The house is built with the "exceeding great and precious promises" of the Scriptures, "Jesus Christ Himself being the chief corner stone." The rooms are lighted with "the light of the knowledge of the glory of God in the face of Jesus Christ." The house is well furnished with "every good and perfect gift from above." The servants of the house are "Goodness and Mercy"; and they are such faithful servants that they follow Mrs. "Far-above-rubies" all the days of her life. The wholesome diet of the house is the Bread of Life and the Water of Life, and the grapes of Eshcol, and the milk and honey and corn and wine of Canaan; and truly their mouths are "satisfied with good things"! In the garden of the house there grows "the fruit of the Spirit"—"love, joy, peace, longsuffering, gentleness, goodness, faith, meekness, temperance"; and the fragrant aroma which is exhaled from these fruits and flowers of the garden pervades the whole atmosphere of the place. Yes, this is where Mrs. "Far-above-rubies" lives.

THE BOOK OF ECCLESIASTES (1)
Lesson Number 63

NOTE.—For this study read the whole twelve chapters of Ecclesiastes at one sitting, so as to follow the several arguments through. Then read them a second time, noting the writer's interim conclusions at the end of chapters ii., v., and viii., and his final conclusion at the end of chapter xii.

Ecclesiastes is an inspired confession of failure and pessimism, when God is excluded, when man lives under the sun, and forgets the larger part, which is always over the sun, the eternal and abiding things. If you want to know what a man of great privilege, and of great learning and great wisdom can come to, read this record of a man who has put God out of count in his actual life.

—*G. Campbell Morgan, D.D*

THE BOOK OF ECCLESIASTES (1)

THE BOOK of Ecclesiastes is a *sermon*. There is the announcement of a theme, a brief introduction, a developing of the theme, and a practical application in conclusion. The theme is: What is the chief good? The standpoint is that of natural reason. We are meant to see where the quest for the chief good leads us when conducted simply on the ground of natural experience, observation, and induction. In the opening verse (and six times later) the author styles himself *Koheleth*, which is translated as "The Preacher" (though perhaps the Hebrew term rather conveys the idea of "Master of Assemblies," or "Teacher"). Our title, "Ecclesiastes," comes from *Ecclesiastes*, the Latin form of the Greek word for a preacher.

Who Was the Preacher?

Who was this preacher-author of Ecclesiastes? Dispite all that has been said to the contrary, we resolutely hold that he was Solomon. We have read the arguments which have been put forward for a post-Exile authorship, and we are not impressed by them. An able summary of these has been given by the late Charles A. Fox in his book on Ecclesiastes. There is a certain plausibility about them; yet an evident superficiality. The first argument is based on certain philological niceties. Words and forms occur in Ecclesiastes, it is said, which are found only in post-exilic writings. But these Aramaic words are proved by other scholars to have been in common use among the nations around Israel long before then; and we know that the widely-read Solomon would have all the available literature of that age at his command, not to mention his familiarity with foreigners through marriage and diplomacy.

The argument that "the whole social state" described in Ecclesiastes does not agree with that of Solomon's time, is similarly unimpressive. The references given are chapters iv. 1, 3, 5, 6; vii. 26, 28; viii. 3, 4, 5, 8; ix. 9, 11, 14, 15; x. 4, 6, 7, 16, 18, 19, 20. We have examined these; and there is not one thing mentioned in them which might not have been frequently seen *in* or appropriately said *to* the society of Solomon's time, either in Israel or among the surrounding peoples.

Another, and surely puerile argument is that whereas Solomon gives his name to Proverbs and the Song of Songs, he does not give it to Ecclesiastes; and that the writer only says "I *was* King over Israel in Jerusalem," implying that at the time of writing he was king no more—as though, if a man of today were telling us of something that happened a few years ago, and said: "I was a married man at the time," it would imply that he could be no longer married at the time of speaking! To ourselves it is childishly obvious that Solomon used the past tense simply because he was describing an experiment which he had made in the past, but after he had come to the throne. How *else* could he have expressed himself?

And, as for the argument that Solomon's *personal history* precludes him from the authorship, why surely the very opposite is the truth! His super-normal wisdom, going with his love of fleshly pleasures, his wealth, and his opportunities to make just such an experiment as he describes in Ecclesiastes, his literary gifts, and what we know of his later years, all mark out Solomon as the author.

See what the book itself says about its authorship in chapters i. 1, 12, 16; ii. 9; xii. 9. Let anyone read this clear testimony of the author himself, with unbiased mind, and surely the conclusion will be that it is King Solomon who is here speaking to us, and not some unidentified rabbi of six centuries later, writing in a feigned name and indulging a "dramatic *impersonation*" of Solomon!

What is the Sermon?

The preacher's text is: "Vanity of vanities; all is vanity"; and the question which he propounds is: "What profit hath man of all his labour which he taketh under the sun?" This question suggests at the outset that the sermon is to be the expounding of a *quest*; and such it proves to be, when we read through it. Ecclesiastes is *the quest of the natural man for the chief good*. It is not easy, in our English translation, to pick out the true links and breaks in the thesis; and at first, indeed, it may seem impossible to systematise it into logical periods: but after a little patient reading and re-reading we begin to see that there are orderly movements in a planned progress.

In the first two chapters the "preacher" tells us how he sought the chief good by *PERSONAL EXPERIMENT*. First of all he sought it by *wisdom* (i. 12–18); but he found that this striving after the true good *by*, or *in*, natural wisdom was "vexation of spirit" (literally, a striving after wind), for there was always something which eluded him (i. 15); and with increased knowledge came increased sorrow (i. 18). So next he turned to conduct his quest in *pleasure* or folly (ii. 1–11); but here again he found that both physical and aesthetic gratifications alike were "vanity," or emptiness to his *soul*. Whereupon, he found that wisdom excels folly even "as light excelleth darkness" (ii. 13), but that life itself is vanity inasmuch as the same event, even death, overtakes both the wise man and the fool—a point on which he enlarges (ii. 15–23). His conclusion is: "There is nothing better for a man than that he should eat and drink, and that he should make his soul enjoy good in his labour" (ii. 24); and he perceives that "this is from the hand of God."

Next, in chapters iii., iv., and v., Koheleth pursues his quest by *GENERAL OBSERVATION* of the world and of human affairs. Here, on the one hand, he finds himself up against what seems to be an impenetrable mystery of *Divine providence*, namely, an apparently immutable forefixedness of all happenings which is as inexorable as it is inscrutable (iii.), and from which it is easy to recoil into a kind of religious fatalism. On the other hand he finds *human* society disfigured by injustices, inequalities, enigmas, and superficialities (iv.), from which he can only turn away saying: "Surely this also is vanity and a striving after the wind." As the preacher ponders the resistless round of the Divine providence, on the one hand, and the ironies of human possession and ambition and position, on the other hand, he can only counsel us (read chapter v.) to maintain a prudential observance of religion in view of the one (verses 1–7) and not to set our hearts on the other (verses 10–12). He then comes to the same conclusion as he had come to when seeking the chief good in wisdom and pleasure— "Behold, that which I have said holds good, that it is well for a man to eat and to drink, and to enjoy the good of all his labours wherein he laboureth under the sun, through the brief day of his life which God hath given him; for this is his portion" (verse 18).

Next, in chapters vi., vii. and viii., Koheleth renews his quest in the realm of *PRACTICAL MORALITY*. The secret he is after must surely lie in "the golden mean," in finding the true centre of conduct, in achieving the even balance between things, the proper poise in behaviour, the correct middle-course of *expediency*. In chapter vi. he points out that though a man have riches, wealth, and honour, he cannot enjoy it unless God permits him to do so (verse 2); and, moreover, all the labour of man for his mouth cannot satisfy his *soul* (not "appetite," as in the Authorised Version). Therefore, "Who knoweth *what* is good for a man in this life?" (verse 12). Surely the answer is to be found in an expedient course of behaviour. So, beginning with the aphorism, "A good name is better than precious ointment" (vii. 1), the preacher presses along this further route of inquiry. But, alas, *is* the true good to be found here?— for he has seen righteous men perish in their righteousness, and wicked men live long in their wickedness (vii. 15); the best of men are still sinners (vii. 20); the best of men are spoken against (vii. 21, 22); and there are not a few other equally discouraging anomalies (see chapter viii.). More and more the preacher is being driven to see the necessity for God (vii. 13, 14, 18; viii. 12, 13, 17); yet once again he concludes, as before, that "a man hath no better thing under the sun, than to eat and to drink, and to be merry; and that this should accompany him in his labour all the days of his life, which God giveth him under the sun" (viii. 15).

Finally, in chapters ix. to xii., we have the quest *REVIEWED AND CONCLUDED*. Looking back over the way he has come, the preacher now says: "For all this I laid to my heart, even to explore all this, *that the righteous and the wise, and their works, are in the hand of God*" (ix. 1). With these words he commences a review, after which he submits his final conclusion. First, he faces us once more with the fact that "All things come alike to all" (ix. 2). Then, in view of this, he reaffirms that the true good is not to be found in *pleasure*, or the absorptions of this present life (ix. 3–12); nor in human *wisdom* (ix. 13–18), though wisdom is admittedly superior to folly; nor in expedient *behaviour* (x. 1–xi. 8), because of the many anomalies which exist (x. 5–7), and because of the inevitable end (xi. 8).

What, then? Why, this—the highest good at present open to man is a wise, temperate, grateful use and enjoyment of the present life (xi. 9, 10), combined with a steadfast faith in God and in the life to come (xii. 1–7). This is what the preacher says:

"*Rejoice, O young man, in thy youth; and let thy heart cheer thee in the days of thy youth, and walk in the ways of thine heart, and in the sight of thine eyes: but know thou, that for all these things God will bring thee into judgment. Therefore remove sorrow from thy heart, and put away evil from thy flesh; for youth and prime of life are vanity.*

"*Remember also Thy Creator in the days of thy youth, or ever the evil days come, and the years draw nigh when thou shalt say: I have no pleasure in them . . . and the dust return to the earth, as it was, and the spirit to God who gave it.*"

In the above quotation, the words, "But know thou, that for all these things God will bring thee into judgment," have been gravely misunderstood. They have been taken in an ironic sense, as though the preacher, immediately after encouraging the young man to get the best out of life, mocks him with the threat of retribution for so living. That is not the true sense of the words at all. We get the sense more truly by changing the "but" into "and"—"*and* know thou that for all these things . . ." The fact of a righteous judgment hereafter is mentioned not as a scare but as a comfort, because it is then and there that the ironies and enigmas which make this present life vanity, even to the righteous and the wise, will be answered by a final explanation, restitution, and compensation. It is an anticipation of Paul's word in Romans viii. 20, that although the creation has been made "subject to vanity," it has been thus subjected "in *hope*." Admittedly, the thought of that final judgment is meant *also* to be a deterrent to folly and sin; but the main thought here is that of *hope* in it; and that is why the preacher, having mentioned it, immediately adds, "Therefore, remove sorrow from thy heart, and put away evil from thy flesh." It is important, also, to realise that the advice to "eat and drink and enjoy," in Ecclesiastes, has nothing of Epicureanism or godless, fleshly indulgence in it. It is simply a periphrasis for living in a legitimate comfort and prosperity (see Jer. xxii. 15), due to Jehovah's bountifulness.

So, then, this present life of man beneath the sun, when considered by itself, or when lived for as an end in itself, is vanity;

and the preacher therefore, in his final paragraph, comes right
back to where he was when he began—"Vanity of vanities, saith
the preacher; all is vanity" (xii. 8). It is the thought of that final
judgment, and that life beyond, which gives the grand significance
to life; and the preacher therefore winds up to his solemn, weighty,
wise, and inspired conclusion—

"Let us hear the conclusion of the whole matter: fear
God, and keep His Commandments; for this is the
whole duty of Man. for God shall bring every work
into judgment, with every secret thing, whether it
be good or evil" (xii. 13, 14).

ECCLESIASTES: The Quest for the Chief Good

INTRODUCTION I. 1–11

1. THE QUEST BY PERSONAL EXPERIMENT (i.–ii.).

The search in Wisdom (i. 12–18).
The search in Pleasure (ii. 1–11).
Comparison of the two (ii. 12–23).
Ad interim conclusion (ii. 24–6).

2. THE QUEST BY GENERAL OBSERVATION (iii.–v.).

Forefixedness of the natural order (iii.).
Ills and enigmas of human society (iv.).
Advice in view of the foregoing (v. 1–17).
Second ad interim conclusion (v. 18–20).

3. THE QUEST BY PRACTICAL MORALITY (vi.–viii.).

Material things cannot satisfy the soul (vi.).
So expedient morality advocated (vii. 1–viii. 8).
But there are strange anomalies (viii. 9–14).
Third ad interim conclusion (viii. 15–17).

4. THE QUEST REVIEWED AND CONCLUDED (ix.–xii.).

The big evil remains—one event to all (ix. 1–6).
Mirth, wisdom, morals, all fare same (ix. 7–xi. 8).
True good—a wise enjoyment of present (xi. 9., 10).
Going with faith in God and life beyond (xii. 1–7).
FINAL CONCLUSION, xii. 13–14.

THE BOOK OF ECCLESIASTES (2)

Lesson Number 64

NOTE.—For this further study in Ecclesiastes read the book through once more, carefully checking off the analysis given in our first study.

No investigation of Scripture, in its various parts and separate texts, however important, must impair the sense of the supreme value of its united witness. There is not a form of evil doctrine or practice that may not claim apparent sanction and support from isolated passages; but nothing erroneous or vicious can ever find countenance from the Word of God when the whole united testimony of Scripture is weighed against it. Partial examination will result in partial views of truth which are necessarily imperfect; only careful comparison will show the complete mind of God.

—*Arthur T. Pierson, D.D.*

THE BOOK OF ECCLESIASTES (2)

THIS BOOK of Ecclesiastes has been a much misunderstood book. Pessimists have found material in it to bolster up their doleful hypotheses. Sceptics have claimed support from it for their contention of non-survival after death. Others have quoted it as confirming the theory of soul-sleep between the death of the body and the yet future resurrection. Besides these, many sound and sincere believers have felt it to be an unspiritually-minded composition, contradictory to the principles of the New Testament, and awkward to harmonise with belief in the full inspiration of the Bible. It is the more needful, therefore, that we should clearly grasp its real message, and understand its peculiarities.

Misapprehensions such as those just mentioned come about through a wrong way of reading. People read the chapters simply as a string of verses in which each verse is a more or less independent pronouncement, instead of carefully perceiving that the verses and paragraphs and chapters and sections are the component parts of a cumulative treatise. Ecclesiastes is not the only part of Scripture which is wronged by this kind of reading; but it suffers the more by it because when the links in the chain of reasoning are thus wrenched apart they lend themselves to an easy misunderstanding. Those interpretations of this or that or the other verse, which contradict the design and drift and declaration of the book as a whole, are wrong.

Pessimism?

Is the Ecclesiastes view of life *pessimistic*? The answer to this question must obviously be found in the message of the book as a whole, and not in a few passages here and there. Admittedly, there is a persistent ground-tone of sadness in the discourse, because the larger part of it has to do with some of the most sombre realities in human life: but the facing up to these is not pessimism. Rather is it a brave honesty.

Follow the process of the preacher's reasoning right through. He steadily faces up to all the dark enigmas; and although at first he sees only tantalising ironies and wearying repetitions, as he steadily gazes he perceives that through the fixed operations of nature and the permitted distortions of human society there moves an all-embracing Divine control (iii. 17; ix. 1) making toward a future restitution (xii. 14). After each recoil from things "under the sun," God is recognised, as a careful reading of the book will show (ii. 24–6; iii. 10–14; v. 19; viii. 17; ix. 1), until at last the author sees through present "vanity" to the final *verity*. He sees that since God has "set eternity" in men's hearts (iii. 11, R.V.), men can never be really satisfied by the things of this present life "under the sun" (v. 10–12; vi. 7). Indeed, he perceives that God has actually allowed the enigmas of the present order to remain so that men might be exercised thereby, and caused to think on higher things (ii. 25; iii. 10; vii. 14).

It is thus that the writer gradually reaches his final conclusion, and lands us at the very antipodes of pessimism, namely, that if we honour and obey God we may enjoy the good things of this life with a thoroughly easy conscience, and look forward, also, to a time when the other things—the ills and wrongs—shall be put right (iii. 17; viii. 5–12; xi. 9; xii. 14).

This, we repeat, is the very opposite of pessimism, with its melancholy idea that life is but a deepening shadow, an ill unrelieved by hope, a problem without a solution. Here, in Ecclesiastes, the wise philosopher has discovered that although the Creator has subjected this present life to "vanity," He has subjected it thus in *hope*. There is a warm light shining through the mystery. There is much to comfort and gladden us in the present: and beyond the question mark which overhangs much of the present is the exclamation mark of a final Divine solution.

Scepticism?

The Book of Ecclesiastes has been charged with *scepticism*. One unfriendly scholar goes so far as to call it "The Canticle of Scepticism"; but it is the scholar himself who is the sceptic, and not Koheleth. There is a certain class of scholars who only see what they *want* to see; and these would not be persuaded even though Koheleth himself were to come back from the grave to assure them. Apart from these, the mistaken idea that scepticism taints Ecclesiastes arises from that superficial way of reading which we have already mentioned, in which verses are regarded in isolation from their context and the conclusion of the book as a whole.

Koheleth is supposed to be sceptical concerning *the present running of things*, in such passages as chapters i. 8, 12–18; iii. 9; viii. 16, 17. A closer examination of these references, however, and a relating of them to the whole argument, shows otherwise. Underlying all Koheleth's animadversions is an unwavering confidence in the justice and wisdom of a governing Providence, as we have seen; and such belief is the opposite of scepticism. Koheleth does not doubt the ultimate, though the mysteries of the present have caused him grave reflection: and even on these mysteries of the present he does not *theorise*, either sceptically or otherwise, his purpose being concerned with the practical, as distinguished from the metaphysical or theological. Further, although poignantly impressed by the ignorance and limitedness of man, he does not deny to men the power of reaching any certitude or mastering any verity, for he is no agnostic. When he declares the "vanity" of human wisdom and knowledge, he means that since human reason has such strict limits, and is utterly incapable of penetrating the present mysteries of Providence, perfect intellectual satisfaction is impossible by that means. The wise thing is a hearty acquiescence, with trust in God; and this certainly is not scepticism.

Again, Ecclesiastes is said to be sceptical about *life after death*. We are referred to chapter iii. 19–21 (which look up). But this passage, other than denying survival, actually implies it when taken carefully with the context. Verses 19 and 20 tell us that physically men suffer the same end as the lower animals, and "all go unto one place," namely, the earth. If we were limited to these verses we might well infer that the writer did not believe in the continuance of life beyond the grave; but it will be noticed that verse 19 is linked on to what goes before, by the conjunctive "for." If, then, we look back to verse 17, we find that it was just *because* men and beasts seemed to perish alike that the writer found refuge in the thought of a life beyond. Verse 17 reads: "God shall judge the righteous and the wicked, for there is a time THERE (i.e.—with God, in the beyond) for every purpose and every work." Look now at verse 21 (in R.V.). If by the "spirit" here is meant the *ego* of man, life after death is at once implied, in contrast with the spirit of the beast, which perishes in the earth. If less than this is meant, there is still *no denial* of life after death.

So is it with chapter ix. 3–6 (which please look up). These verses must be read in connection with verse 10, where we are told of a *Sheol* to which humans go beyond the present life. When the author says in this tenth verse, "There is no work nor device nor knowledge nor wisdom in *Sheol* whither thou goest," he means merely that there these things come to an end *in the sense in which they are known and pursued on earth.* He by no means necessarily implies a cessation of consciousness; for his words must be interpreted in the light of the final pronouncement (xii. 7) to which he is now hastening, namely, that at death the body returns to the earth, and *the spirit returns to God*—which surely teaches, in view of the predicted Judgment in the beyond (xii. 14), a survival of the individual soul as such, and not any mere vague absorption. Admittedly, in Ecclesiastes, the life beyond is only touched on in its negative aspect, for fuller revelation on the subject is as yet awaited; but the *fact* of a life beyond is clearly believed in; so that to allege scepticism here is wrong.

Inspiration?

As we have remarked, there are those who seem to find this Book of Ecclesiastes awkward to harmonise with belief in the full inspiration of the Bible. This is due, once again, to the reading of it without due appreciation of the fact that the whole book is one sustained argument, with various incidental inferences, three *ad interim* conclusions (which mark off, respectively, the first three of the four main parts of the argument), and a final conclusion. There are indeed verses and paragraphs which, taken by themselves, seem contradictory to the teachings of the New Testament; but these become quite harmonious if we pay heed to three things—(1) their place in the progress of the argument, (2) the standpoint of the argument as a whole, (3) the nature of inspiration.

First, then, the tentative conclusions which Koheleth records in the course of his dissertation should all be read carefully *in connection with their setting, and especially in the light of the final conclusion.* For instance, take that troublesome passage about men and beasts apparently dying alike, in chapter iii. 19–22. We may perhaps ask: "Since the writer of Ecclesiastes is so definite, in his final conclusion, that the human spirit lives on after the death of the body, and returns upwards to God, why does he not say so here in chapter iii.?" The answer is that the stage of the argument required this as-yet unsatisfying statement. We are meant to follow the processes of the man's mind in his great quest, if the final conclusion is to mean to us what is intended. That this is so is surely indicated also by the fact that he twice prefaces these verses with "I said in mine heart"—to show that he refers to what he thought at an earlier time.

Second, we must keep in mind *the standpoint of the treatise as a whole.* This is the book of man "under the sun." It is written from the standpoint of human reason. Under the guidance of the Holy Spirit the writer is led to adopt this standpoint so that we may be shown where a proper exercise of human reason and intuition will lead us, if we will honestly follow. Despite the limitations of human reason, and despite the dark enigmas which scourge the present order of things, human reason, if it be really honest with all the data, will show us the vanity of living merely for earthly things, and will conduct us to a reverent faith in God, a keeping of His commandments, and belief in a judgment beyond. Certainly, the final conclusion of the writer is true and great, though, of course, there is nothing of our precious New Testament Gospel in it; but inasmuch as the purpose of inspiration here is to teach us lessons by exhibiting the *process* of human reasoning toward that final conclusion, we must not assume that all the incidental inferences and sayings of the reasoner are recorded as independent pronouncements of inspiration.

This brings us to our third point. We need to be clear as to *the nature of inspiration.* Not long ago, a minister of very modern ideas said to me: "If the whole Bible is inspired, as you say, then you ought to be able to open it at any page, and take any verse you hit on as an inspired precept to be obeyed." Did anybody ever hear such unreasonable stupidity? Even the old rationalists like Tom Paine and Bob Ingersol did not so unjustly injure the Bible. Considerable parts of the Bible are *history*, without doctrine or precept. In such parts, inspiration fulfils its purpose by simply guaranteeing the veracity of the narrative. Besides this, again and again in the Scriptures, the utterances of various persons are reported simply as such, including those of theorisers like Zophar, of wicked men like Ahab, and even of the devil himself—and which were certainly never intended to be taken as Divinely inspired. All that inspiration involves in such cases is the veracity of the report. Similarly, in the case of Ecclesiastes, we are given to see the processes of thought by which an enquiring soul arrived at a great and true conclusion; but this does not necessarily mean that all the incidental inferences and minor conclusions are inspired.

Besides this, let it be remembered that revelation is *progressive*; and it is this which explains the absence of more positive teaching in Ecclesiastes concerning the after-life. As to the *fact* of a life beyond, and of a righteous judgment there, Ecclesiastes rings true and clear; but as to the nature, course, and details of that life, nothing is said. Had our author been tapping Egyptian or other heathen mythological sources, he need have been at no loss for colourful details of Sheol and its denizens; but he is held by a sacred reticence. No rein is given to imagination. He speaks only as he is moved. At this stage of Divine revelation, life beyond is disclosed only in its negative aspect, as the place where earthly works and devices and knowledge and wisdom come to an end (ix. 10). To elucidate the *positive* aspects of the life beyond, further revelation was needed; and, thank God, further revelation has been given, disclosing the continuance of conscious life between death of the body and its resurrection (Isa. xiv. 9–11; Matt. xxii. 32; Mark ix. 43–8; Luke xvi. 19–31; John xi. 26; 2 Cor. v. 6–8; Phil. i. 21–3; Rev. vi. 9–11), along with many other precious and vital unveilings in many other passages.

When rightly understood, there is nothing in Ecclesiastes which *contradicts* later revelation regarding the after-life or any other matter. When it is read today by ourselves, its place in the progress of Scripture revelation should be carefully borne in mind.

Purpose and Message

In view of what we have just said, some practical-minded student may perhaps ask: "If fuller revelation comes later, why go back to Ecclesiastes?" The answer to that question lies in *the central purpose and message* of the book. Above all else Ecclesiastes would teach us the emptiness of everything apart from God. That word "vanity" which recurs throughout the book does not mean merely foolish pride, but the emptiness, in its final result, of all life lived for this world alone. This book would wean us from love of the world. It says to us all, "Love not the world, neither the things that are in the world: for all that is in the world, the lust of the flesh, and the lust of the eyes, and the pride of life, is not of the Father, but is of the world. And the world passeth away, and the lust thereof: but he that doeth the will of God abideth for ever" (1 John ii. 15–17). It says to us: "Lay not up for yourselves treasures upon earth, where moth and rust doth corrupt, and where thieves break through and steal: but lay up for yourselves treasures in heaven, where neither moth nor rust doth corrupt, and where thieves do not break through nor steal: for where your treasure is, there will your heart be also" (Matt. vi. 19–21). Yes, Ecclesiastes says to every Christian: "Set your affection on things above; not on things on the earth" (Col. iii. 2).

Make no mistake, we need Ecclesiastes in our Bible. Do not listen to those who think they know better, and would exclude it as being of inferior moral quality. Do not be misled even by those very spiritual friends who aver that the sentiments of Koheleth are unspiritual. It is a Divine kindness which includes Ecclesiastes within the compass of Holy Writ. One of the saddest ironies is the proud folly by which successive generations of human beings commit the same sins, repeat the same big blunders, fall prey to the same ensnaring stupidities, and suffer the same agonising disillusionments, as those who have lived and died before them; all because they will not take to heart such a testimony as that of Koheleth. We are reminded of a rather grim little poem entitled, "Sympathetic Lines of a Father to a Daughter in Bed with Mumps", from which we cull the following wistfully philosophical rhymes—

> Thus generations come and go,
> From youth to age they wiser grow;
> Yet as they pass they all relate
> They learn their lessons just too late.
> Our junior wisecracks dodge the truth
> That dense old parents once were youth,
> That present youth must older grow,
> Oft haunted by, "I told you so",
> And all their youthful bombast rue
> When *they* as parents suffer too!

When they as parents suffer too,
As with strange certainty they do,
They marvel at the self-sure ways
The *next* relay of youth displays.
They hear the same old arguments
Arrayed in fresh accoutrements—
The times are different, so are we,
Just let us have *our* way, and see.
For artful Nature oft repays
Her rebels in ironic ways.

Thus generations, as they go,
Perpetuate the tale of woe.
They will not learn from yesterday,
But choose to learn the harder way—
Experience shall be teacher, please;
And well he teaches—but what fees!
What fees he charges those he schools
Before he makes wise men of fools!
How oft his scholars have confessed,
"Ah yes, poor Dad and Mum knew best"!

Each generation soon is past,
So sure at first, so sad at last.
As ranks of youth successive rise,
Each thinks, "We are supremely wise".
They each a lot more knowledge know,
And yet a bit less wisdom show.
O sanguine youth, God's word revere—
Honour your parents while they're here;
And you will find in later days
What handsome dividends it pays!

THE BOOK OF ECCLESIASTES (3)

Lesson Number 65

NOTE.—For this final study in Ecclesiastes read again the first two chapters and the last two, contrasting the regrets in the first two with the advice in the last two.

> Truth shall retire,
> Bestruck with slanderous darts, and works of faith
> Rarely be found; so shall the world go on,
> To good malignant, to bad men benign,
> Under her own weight groaning, till the day
> Appear of respiration to the just,
> And vengeance to the wicked, at return
> Of Him, . . . thy Saviour and thy Lord;
> Last in the clouds of Heaven to be revealed
> In glory of the Father.
> —*Milton, "Paradise Lost,"* xii. 535.

THE BOOK OF ECCLESIASTES (3)

THERE are other weighty considerations pertaining to this Book of Ecclesiastes which we ought at least briefly to reflect upon, before we turn to the Song of Songs. They will help us to appreciate more truly its rich spiritual values.

A Challenge to Faith

There is certainly a challenge to *faith*. Koheleth argues his way through disillusionments and doubts to a point where he rises into the clear shining of a reasoned faith in the Divine justice and wisdom and goodness. If he, with his much more imperfect knowledge than ours, rose above the depressing disappointments of human experience and found composure in a faith which conquered mistrust, how much more should we Christian believers, who stand in the full rays of Gospel revelation! Never for a moment should we give way to misgivings concerning the dealings of Providence. With the Divine love-pledges of the Bethlehem manger and the Cross of Calvary and the empty tomb of that first Easter morning before us, how can we longer doubt the goodness of God's fundamental purpose in the universe and for the human race? Strange and hurting inequalities and enigmas and tragedies there certainly are in plenty everywhere around us; yet even the sum-total of these cannot outweigh the profound and reassuring significance of the Incarnation, the Crucifixion, and the Resurrection of God's Son, our Saviour. As one of the old Puritans used to say, we should "never let what we do *not* know destroy our faith in what we *do* know." However many things there are which are still mysterious to us, they do not destroy the reality and meaning of those things which actually *are*, and which we *know*. Over against all the sufferings and problems and mysteries of man's earthly lot is the fact of CHRIST. He is a real fact; and He is the Divine guarantee of a coming daybreak which will bring a full and final answer. With unswerving trust, let us "commit the keeping of our souls to Him in well doing, as unto a faithful Creator" (1 Pet. iv. 19).

Sensible Resignation

But Koheleth would teach us also to have the attitude of sensible *resignation*. It is no use fretting and fighting and fuming against the established order of nature. It is simply dashing our silly heads against the rocks of stubborn facts which all our hot tempers can never alter. If we will consider thoughtfully, there are enough indications to show us that a Divine super-control operates everywhere. We get glimpses of an unmistakable logic about things. Strange, half-deciphered unities appear, running through the history of the past and the happenings of the present, which in contemplative moments suddenly become luminous to the mind, giving coherence to everything. We see with an unmistakable convincingness that there is a Divine harmony behind earth's discords, and a settled goal beyond the disturbing disorders of the present. The controlling presence of a good Divine purpose in the universe becomes the one, obvious key which fits all the chambers of the lock. A hundred coincidences all suddenly fit together and show us that there is a unifying benevolent purpose underlying and overruling all that is providentially permitted. It is to this that Koheleth approximates. First he sees that life is full of "vanities" which *mock* men. Then he sees that these "vanities" are *meant* to mock men. Then he sees that these "vanities" are not just meant to mock men cruelly, but with a *benign purpose,* namely, to lead men to seek their true happiness in God Himself. He sees that these things are "from the hand of God." (ii. 24). And he sees that these things are allowed because God "hath set eternity" in men's hearts (iii. 11), and seeks to lead them to a true view of life in relation to material things. All this is indeed discerning, and is a true voice of wisdom to us.

It is well to pick out and ponder the ten "vanities" which Koheleth sees as occasioning the ironies and frustrations of human life, and which make so much of human life "vexation or a striving after wind". What agonising disillusionments men and women would spare themselves if only they would pause and ponder these ten "vanities" of Koheleth!

The Ten " Vanities "

ii. 15–16.	The "vanity" of human wisdom,	*Wise and foolish alike have one end, death.*
ii. 19–21.	The "vanity" of human labour,	*Worker no better than shirker in the end.*
ii. 26.	The "vanity" of human purpose,	*Altho' man proposes it is God who disposes.*
iv. 4.	The "vanity" of human rivalry,	*Much success brings envy more than joy.*
iv. 7.	The "vanity" of human avarice,	*" Much" feeds lust for "more," yet oft eludes.*
iv. 16.	The "vanity" of human fame,	*Is brief, uncertain, and soon forgotten.*
v. 10.	The "vanity" of human insatiety,	*Money does not satisfy. Increase only feeds others.*
vi. 9.	The "vanity" of human coveting,	*Often gain cannot be enjoyed, despite desire.*
vii. 6.	The "vanity" of human frivolity,	*It only camouflages the inevitable sad end.*
viii. 10, 14.	The "vanity" of human awards,	*Bad often honoured. Good and bad get wrong deserts.*

Yet again, this Book of Ecclesiastes should teach us the need of further Divine *revelation*. This is one of the things it is undoubtedly *meant* to show us. The mental struggles of this man, Koheleth, are a lesson for all time, and point to the need for supernatural light to be given from heaven. Natural religion and man-made faiths are not enough. Human reason can take us so far and no farther. Even the Mosaic Law, with its Ten Commandments and its high social ethics, cannot give us that which we most need to know and possess. This Book of Ecclesiastes cries out for Him who said: "He that hath seen Me hath seen the Father," and, "I am come that they might have life, and that they might have it more abundantly."

Authorship Significances

Always in our reading of Ecclesiastes we should keep in mind that *Solomon* is the author. It gives such added force to many of the sentiments which are expressed. Is the book the product

of a late repentance? Many think so. Is Solomon seeking to atone
for past follies, and to warn others from his own bitter experience?
Perhaps so. When he speaks about an "old and foolish king"
and a "poor and wise youth" who follows him by usurping the
throne (iv. 13–16), is he speaking, with prophetic prescience, of
himself, soon now to pass away, and of the scheming usurper,
Jeroboam, who thereupon sets himself up as king over ten of
the Israel tribes? When he speaks so bitterly of woman, in
chapter vii. 26–9, and says that the seductress is "more bitter
than death," and that he has not found one true woman "in a
thousand," is he recalling his countless wives and concubines?
Oh, that the gifted Solomon who began so wisely should have had
to write such a book as this! What intensity it gives to his doctrine of the "vanity" or emptiness of everything, apart from God!
We can never read it without being reminded of the poet Byron's
words, written shortly before his premature death, after a life
lived wholly for the world and its pleasures—

My days are in the yellow leaf,
    The flowers and fruits of love are gone;
The worm, the canker, and the grief
    Are mine alone!

The fire that on my bosom preys
    Is lone as some volcanic isle;
No torch is kindled at its blaze—
    A funeral pile.

The hope, the fear, the jealous care,
    The exalted portion of the pain
And power of love I cannot share,
    But wear the chain.

The Cause and Cure of Pessimism

This Book of Ecclesiastes suggests a sermon on *the cause and
cure of pessimism*. We have shown that in its final conclusion
the book is *not* pessimistic; but it may be freely granted that many
of the sentiments expressed in the argumentative processes of
the book *are*. They are the sombre surveyings of eyes which

selfish sinning has filmed and dulled; yet although these eyes cannot see very far, they are seeing more truly and steadily than when they were bright and young and inflamed with wine. *Whence*, then, the lines of pessimism in Koheleth's review?

There are three causes. First, he views life *selfishly rather than socially*. He has lived to get, instead of to give; and he has found what all such persons find, namely, that the more one lives for self, the less do earthly things satisfy. When one lives just to "get," the more one gets the less one really has. It is a true paradox that the more one gives the more one gets. And those who do most for others do most for themselves. Koheleth had been a great social mixer, but only outwardly. Inwardly he had been an isolationist. He had been wrapped up in his own selfishness, viewing all others simply in relation to his own self-gratification. To live so, whatever our social status may be, sooner or later brings an ironic sense of having had no real joys at all, and makes the late Lord Beaconsfield's famous words seem all too true—"Youth is a mistake, manhood a struggle, and old age a regret."

But second, Koheleth views life as *apart from God rather than as controlled by Him*. God is scarcely mentioned, and even then only distantly. All seems in the hands of men (iv. 1–3). One of the main reasons for the pessimism about human life and history which is so prevalent in our own times is that God is pushed more and more away from it by our twentieth-century industrialisation and urbanisation, and by popular science with its evolutionary jargon about the "origin of species" and the "survival of the fittest" and the "reign of natural law" and the "impossibility of miracles" and the *a priori* rejection of everything "supernatural." When the universe becomes, as W. T. Stead put it, "the empty eye-socket of a dead deity," it is never long before pessimism rules human philosophy.

And third, Koheleth views human life as *bounded by the grave rather than as having destiny beyond*. Man dies as the beast, he says; and this is his greatest problem of all. "For that which befalleth the sons of men befalleth beasts; even one thing befalleth them. As the one dieth, so dieth the other; yea, they have all one breath; and man hath no pre-eminence above the beasts: for all is vanity. All go unto one place; all are of the dust, and all turn to dust again" (iii. 19, 20). What then is the use of life's struggle? It may be said, indeed it *is* being said by some today, that we must take an unselfish view, and be willing to play our little part and then pass out, finding satisfaction in the thought that humanity is gradually progressing to a perfect age. That might sound better if we could only be *sure* that such a perfect humanity was really evolving. But we are *not* sure. And besides, scientists tell us that at the present rate of evolution, by the time that the prospective perfect race has emerged, the conditions on this planet will not allow human beings to live here at all! The sun is gradually losing its heat. Or it is gradually getting too hot in relation to the earth. Taking the long view, we must inevitably perish either by extreme cold or by extreme heat! Perhaps it is not so surprising that one or two scientists have recently averred that the best thing for our earth is that some stray planet should collide with it and finish it *that* way!

But coming back to Koheleth's gloomy observation that men and beasts die alike; some perhaps would say, "Why should the thought of death worry men? Why not live simply in the present and enjoy it?" The answer is that although the beasts can and *do* live simply in the present, man simply *cannot* do so, the reason being that God has "set eternity" in the human heart (iii. 11). There is that in man's constitution which simply cannot be satisfied merely with the present and the material, however much another part of him may be mesmerised by the things of time and sense. Man simply cannot live merely in and for the present. He has a capacity for things intellectual and spiritual, and a consciousness that projects itself into the future. Yet over against this is the stark fact which was so perturbing to Koheleth, that men and beasts seem to die alike.

What then? Well, *Koheleth was wrong.* No man can have a true view of life who looks at it selfishly rather than socially, and apart from God, and as bounded by the grave. And when all the available data are considered, no man *needs* to view it as Koheleth did. Nor did Koheleth himself so view it at the time when he wrote his treatise; for it must be remembered that he was describing how he had thought *earlier* (as his use of the past tense all through the book indicates).

Koheleth's final conclusion is right. It is *fully* right, as far as it goes; but it is far from adequate. That is, it is far from adequate as a motive and power to inspire human conduct. We can learn very much from what he has told us; but as we have said, we need to turn on through the pages of holy writ and see how much more its developing revelation from God has to say to us. We must turn on to the pages of the prophets and find there whole continents of further truth and wonderful new horizons spreading out before us. And most of all, we must turn on to the New Testament, to the crown of Divine revelation, even the incarnate Son of God Himself.

Oh, what a different view of life we get when we see it through the eyes of the Lord Jesus! With Him there is no viewing of life selfishly rather than socially. None was ever so social-minded as the Son of Man. There was pure "otherism" and absolutely no egoism. He "went about doing good." He was the best of all mixers. He was at home in every circle, for wherever He was, He was there to forget Himself in the good of others. And with Him there was no viewing of human life as apart from God. He saw the Father's hand everywhere. Everything was significant of good purpose and of faithful Divine supervision. And with Him there was no viewing of life as bounded by the grave. The very opposite! It is there, beyond the mortal present, that the vast issues of our life are. There is no "vanity of vanities" with Jesus! He comes to declare *the reality of realities*, that there is a Divine meaning and purpose running all through our human life. Even the Cross, if it be the Father's will, is the pathway to a throne. There is benevolent purpose everywhere in the universe. We may trust God. We may know His love and presence in our lives. Life is not a mockery. God is *LOVE*. Behind every frowning providence there is a smiling face. God is not only Creator, King, and Judge: He is the *FATHER*!

But we must add one word more, lest even now we give a wrong impression about this Book of Ecclesiastes. True enough, so far as life after death and certain other big matters are concerned, we need to pass on from its pages to the further and fuller unfoldings of Scripture revelation: yet this fact does not detract from its importance. Strange as the remark may seem to some, we do not hesitate to say that if there is one book more than another in the Old Testament which we would like to send for special consideration to millions of our fellow-countrymen today, it is Ecclesiastes. And though it may sound still stranger, if there is one Old Testament book more than another which many *Christians* of today need to read and pray over, it is Ecclesiastes.

Would that the people of our time had learned the central lesson of this little suite of essays from the quill of disillusioned Solomon, namely, that a life lived for self and the world, and without God, is "vanity," and that nothing "under the sun" can ever really satisfy the human heart! Would that many who call themselves Christians had learned that same truth: "Set your affection . . . not on things on the earth"! Certainly, it is only when we have really learned the *"vanity of vanities"* in Ecclesiastes that we can appreciate the mystic message of the *"Song of Songs"* in the book which follows.

Meanwhile, perhaps we cannot more fittingly end these reflections on Ecclesiastes than by quoting some lines from Scotland's Robbie Burns.

> It's no in titles nor in rank:
> It's no in wealth like Lon'on bank,
>   To purchase peace and rest;
> It's no in making muckle mair;
> It's no in books; it's no in lear;
>   To make us truly blest;
> If happiness hae not her seat
>   And centre in the breast,
> We may be wise, or rich, or great,
>   But never can be blest;
> Nae treasures, nor pleasures, could make us happy lang:
> The heart aye's the part aye that makes us right or wrang.
>   —ROBERT BURNS, *in "Epistle to Davie."*

THE SONG OF SOLOMON (1)

Lesson Number 66

NOTE.—For this study in the Song of Solomon read the whole book
through twice, in the Revised Version.

O happy love!—where love like this is found!
    O heart-felt raptures! bliss beyond compare!
I've pacèd much this weary, mortal round,
    And sage experience bids me this declare—
"If Heaven a draught of heavenly pleasure spare,
    One cordial in this melancholy vale,
'Tis when a youthful, loving, modest pair,
    In either's arms breathe out the tender tale,
Beneath the milk-white thorn that scents the evening gale."
                —ROBERT BURNS, *in "The Cotter's Saturday Night."*

THE SONG OF SOLOMON (1)

"THE SONG of songs, which is Solomon's"—such are the introductory words to this exquisite composition. Fitly is it called the Song of Songs, for it is on the theme of themes—*love*. Its literary excellence is such as to make it well worthy of the gifted king to whom it is attributed. It bears clear marks of having come down to us from the Solomonic period; and there seems to be no weighty reason why we should not accept it as being actually from the pen of the royal author whose name it bears.

Interpretation

But the question of first concern is the *interpretation* of this love-poem. It has been truly said that "Nowhere in Scripture does the unspiritual mind tread upon ground so mysterious and incomprehensible as in this book, while the saintliest men and women of the ages have found it a source of pure and exquisite delight." What, then, shall we say about it? Is it just a poem of human love and nothing more, or has it a spiritual meaning and a Divine message for us? If the latter, then what *is* the spiritual meaning and Divine message? "There is no book of Scripture on which more commentaries have been written and more diversities of opinion expressed than this short poem of eight chapters"—so says a learned expositor. We shall be wise, therefore, to avoid adding unprofitably to an already liberally discussed subject. Fortunately, in the process of the long-continued discussion certain broad facts have gradually emerged with increasing clearness, all converging toward the same result; so that we are now in a position to sum up and draw fairly mature conclusions.

Three theories of interpretation have been advanced—the naturalistic, the allegorical, and the typical.

Naturalistic Theory.

The *naturalistic* theory would have it that the book is simply a collection of erotic songs, or idylls of love, put together on the ground of literary merit, and without any allegorical or typical meaning, though possibly intended to describe ideal human love. This theory leaves the inclusion of the book in the sacred canon an inexplicable anomaly. When we remember how the Hebrews venerated their sacred Scriptures, and how careful they were that only inspired writings should be included in the canon, we cannot believe that the Song of Songs should have been given its decided place in the Scriptures simply on the ground of literary merit. Not one of the books is there simply as a piece of literature. Each has its place because of its religious character or its special connection with the peculiar national position of the Hebrew people. The very canonicity of the poem, therefore, argues its spiritual significance.

Allegorical Theory.

At the other extreme is the *allegorical* theory, which ignores as of no concern whether the poem has any historical foundation in a real love-suit between Solomon and Shulamith, and treats the whole as a purely figurative and mystical fiction. To read some of the absurd and fanciful expositions associated with this theory, such as that the hair of the bride represents the mass of the nations converted to Christianity, is too much for a God-given sense of humour, and brings the whole theory into disrepute.

Typical Interpretation.

Coming between the naturalistic and allegorical theories is the *typical* interpretation, which recognises the distinctive elements in each of the other two without going to the extreme of either. The writing has an historical basis; but in harmony with the rest of Scripture, it also has a religious purpose and a spiritual content. An ideal human love is represented, to lead the soul into the thought of fellowship with God. Fundamentally, the facts are historical; but they are lifted up into the region of poetry for a religious purpose; the facts are idealised and given, by the Spirit of inspiration, a spiritual meaning.

We need not be deterred from a chastened perception of typical significances in Scripture because of the foolish extremes to which fanciful allegorisers have gone. Again and again, in the Scriptures, metaphors based upon the marriage relationship are used of Israel's relationship with God, and of the Church's relationship with Christ, and of the individual soul's communion with God. The use of the marriage metaphor is noticeably prominent in Paul and John; and we may well ask if they would thus have used the metaphor had not the Old Testament Scriptures already familiarised the people of God with it. A true interpretation of the poem, therefore, will recognise in it a duality in unity; for while it is primarily the expression of "pure marital love as ordained of God in creation, and the vindication of that love as against both asceticism and lust," the deeper and larger meaning has reference to the heavenly Lover and His bride, the Church.

The Scriptural Key

Has the Holy Spirit, who inspired the Scriptures, provided anywhere a key which really fits the lock and opens up to us the mystic doors of this love-poem in such a way as to assure us that we are rightly interpreting it? I think we may reverently say that He has. Accepting it as a principle of Biblical exegesis that scripture is to be explained by scripture, we believe that the key to the Song of Solomon is psalm xlv.

We get a prefatory hint of this in the *title* of this psalm, which is: "A Song of Loves" (the earlier part of the title as it appears in our English version belongs to the preceding psalm, as we explained in a former lesson on the Titles of the Psalms).

When we look at this "Song of Loves" we find that it is a song of *royal* love. In fact it is a royal *marriage* hymn; and it refers to *Solomon*. But while the primary reference is to Solomon, the ultimate reference is to Christ, as is conclusively settled by Hebrews i. 7, 8. Thus, as Solomon is a type of Christ in his wisdom and riches and fame, so here, in this forty-fifth psalm, he is a type in this marriage union. This at once does away with the supposed difficulty that in the Song of Songs such an one as Solomon cannot fittingly be thought of as a type of the heavenly Bridegroom. Moreover, on the very face of it, this forty-fifth psalm is just such as goes with the Song of Solomon. It might almost have been written to be read with it, as a kind of complement or epilogue, setting the crown on the happy issue of the love-suit.

After the brief preface in verse 1, the psalm divides into two equal parts—(1) an address to the royal bridegroom, in verses 2 to 9; (2) an address to the royal bride, in verses 10 to 17. In each of these two parts we find four sub-divisions. In the address to the royal bridegroom we have—(a) in verse 2, the beauty of his person; (b) in verses 3 to 5, the valour of his conquests; (c) in verse 6, the stability of his kingdom; (d) in verses 7 to 9, the gladness of his marriage. Similarly in the address to the royal bride, we have—(a) in verses 10 and 11, an appeal for complete devotion; (b) in verse 12, a promise of high honour; (c) in verses 13 to 15, a eulogy of the bride's charms; (d) in verses 16 and 17, a pledge of unceasing Divine favour.

A comparison of this psalm with the Song of Solomon will show us certain striking correspondences such as that between the newly married queen's evident longing towards her now distant Lebanon home, and the exhortation to her, in verse 10 of the psalm: "Forget also thine own people, and thy father's house." But without going further into this here, we shall accept it, in the light of psalm xlv., that the love-suit in the Song of Songs is between Solomon and Shulamith, and that this exquisite love-suit is a most sacred type of the spiritual union between Christ and His Church.

Moreover, there is truth in the observation that "What so many of God's people (right down the course of the years) have recognised (in the Song of Solomon) must be substantially the mind of the Spirit."

There is a theory, though it has never been widely held, that the love-suit in Solomon's Song is between some anonymous shepherd and Shulamith, and that Solomon is a type of the World, against whose allurements the bride eventually proves true to her shepherd-lover. This view is carefully set out by E. W. Bullinger in his *Companion Bible*, and we have carefully examined it; but it is so obviously artificial, and so distorts the poem, that it stands at once discredited, and gives the greater reason for believing that the love-suit here, as in psalm xlv., is between the royal Solomon and this maid of the mountains.

Thus, if the Song of Solomon spoke to Israel, it speaks in an even more profound and beautiful way to the spiritually-quickened members of the true Church, concerning their relationship with the heavenly Bridegroom—of which relationship Paul was speaking when he wrote to the Ephesians: "Husbands love your wives, even as Christ also loved the Church, and gave Himself for it, that He might sanctify and cleanse it with the washing of water by the word, that He might present it to Himself a glorious Church, not having spot or wrinkle or any such thing, but that it should be holy and without blemish" (Eph. v. 25–7).

That the love of the Divine Bridegroom should "follow the analogies of the marriage relation," in this Song of Solomon, "seems evil only to minds so ascetic that marital desire itself seems to them unholy." The book has been a source of exquisite delight to the saintliest men and women of the ages.

We see here, then, in hallowed type, the Lord Jesus and His mystic bride, the Church; and, therefore, by a warrantable appropriation, each Christian believer may claim a true individual application.

Central Message

It is this mystic presence of Christ and the Church in the Song of Songs which gives it its deepest wonder and inmost meaning. It is this which has made it unutterably precious to the inner circle of the Lord's lovers; and it is from this that there comes to us its central *message*, namely: Such is the union between Christ and His redeemed people, when realised in its deepest and tenderest meanings, that it can only be expressed to us under the figure of an ideal marriage union. This is true whether we think of this union as between Christ and His people collectively, as the *Church*, or between Christ and His people individually, as the redeemed and sanctified *members* of that Church.

Various figures are used in Scripture to express the various aspects of this wondrous union. Christ is the Head and we are the body; for it is a *living* union. Christ is the Foundation and we are the building; for it is a *lasting* union. Christ is the Vine and we are the branches; for it is a *fruitful* union. Christ is the Firstborn and we are His brethren; for it is a union of *joint-heirship*. But the sublimest and tenderest meaning of this union can only be expressed—and even then imperfectly—by that most sacred of all human relationships, marriage. Christ is the Bridegroom and we are the bride; for in the truest sense our union with Him is a *loving* union. This is the wonderful meaning which lies at the heart of Solomon's Song: and thus the Song of Solomon is the sheer opposite of Ecclesiastes; for in Ecclesiastes this present vain world is found too small ever to fill and satisfy the human heart, whereas in Solomon's Song the heart is filled and satisfied by Christ.

The Climax

What, then, is the *climax* of this ideal espousal? It is the joy of mutual possession, as expressed in chapter ii. 16—"*My Beloved is mine, and I am His.*" This, also, is the quintessence of that holy joy which the Christian saint finds in His spiritual union with the adorable Son of God. It is the assurance of possessing and being possessed. Each one of us, as the Lord's redeemed, may unhesitatingly take these words on our lips as applying to ourselves—"My Beloved is mine, and I am His."

In my little book, *His Part and Ours*, I have spoken of the cords which bind our Beloved to us and us to Him. On the one hand, *He* is bound to *us* by (1) the unbreakable cord of His own *promise*, (2) the unseverable cord of an eternal *covenant*, (3) the golden cord of the Divine *love*, (4) the proven cord of our own *experience*. On the other hand, *we* are bound to *Him* by (1) the old cord of *creation*, (2) the red cord of *redemption*, (3) the strong cord of *election*, (4) the new cord of our own *choice*. Seven out of these eight precious bands are those which our Lord Himself has tied; and even the eighth is really the work of His Holy Spirit within our hearts. These love-cords will last for evermore: blessed be His dear Name!

To some it may seem that the language of Solomon's Song is too intimate or extravagant to express the communion of the saints with the heavenly Bridegroom; yet it is a fact that the most ardent lovers of the Lord have here found a relief of expression such as could be found nowhere else. There is a rapture of communion with Christ which no ordinary phraseology can utter. Take the following words of Samuel Rutherford—

"*Every day we see some new beauty in Christ, His love hath neither brim nor bottom. If there were ten thousand thousand millions of worlds, and as many heavens full of men and angels, Christ would not be pinched to supply all our wants, and to fill us all. This soul of ours hath love and cannot but love some*

*fair one; and oh, what a fair One, what an only One, what an
excellent, lovely, ravishing One is Jesus! All men speak well
of Christ who have been at Him. Men and angels who know Him
will say more than I now do; and think more of Him than even
they can say. Oh for arms to embrace Him!"*

Or take these further words, from that lovable old character,
John Fawcett, the author of the hymn, "Blest be the tie that
binds our hearts in Christian love"—

*"O blessed Jesus, Thy love is wonderful. The experimental sense
of it sweetens all the bitterness of life, and disarms death of its
terrors. When I am favoured with the light of Thy countenance
and the sense of Thy love, my soul is filled and satisfied. Thou
art to me the full ocean of never-failing delights and satisfaction.
Through all the ages of a blissful eternity I humbly hope to
proclaim the wonders of redeeming love, and tell to listening
angels what that love has done for my soul."*

Or turn to the hymnbook. See, again and again, in its
pages, the same eager, affectionate language. Take the following
well-known verses from hymns by Charles Wesley, Antoinette
Bourignon, F. W. Faber, and C. E. Mudie, respectively:—

> O Love Divine, how sweet Thou art!
> When shall I find my willing heart
>   All taken up by Thee?
> I thirst, I faint, I die to prove
> The fulness of redeeming love,
>   The love of Christ to me.

.   .   .   .   .

> Thee I can love, and Thee alone,
> With pure delight and inward bliss;
> To know Thou makest me Thine own,
> Oh, what a happiness is this!

> Nothing on earth do I desire
> But thy pure love within my breast;
> This, only this, will I require,
> And freely give up all the rest.

.   .   .   .

O Jesus, Jesus, dearest Lord,
  Thy sacred name I say
For very love within my heart
  A thousand times a day.

I love Thee so, I know not how
  My raptures to control;
Thy love is like a burning fire
  Within my very soul.

Oh, light in darkness! joy in grief!
  Oh, wealth beyond all worth!
Jesus, my love, to have Thee mine
  Is heaven begun on earth.

.   .   .   .   .

I lift my heart to Thee,
    Saviour Divine;
For Thou art all to me,
    And I am Thine.
Is there a closer bond
    On earth than this,
That my Beloved's mine,
    And I am His?

Truly, there is a rapture of communion with Christ which no ordinary phraseology can utter. There is an inner circle of our Lord's disciples in which the love of God is so "shed abroad" that those who experience it must say with Bernard of Clairvaux, "The love of Jesus, what it is, none but His loved ones know". And should not the response of our own hearts be that which is expressed in a further verse of Mr. Mudie's hymn?—

To Thee, Thou bleeding Lamb,
    I all things owe;
All that I have and am,
    And all I know.
All that I have is now
    No longer mine;
And I am not my own,
    Lord, I am Thine.

THE SONG OF SOLOMON (2)

Lesson Number 67

NOTE.—For this study read right through the book again, marking a separating break at the end of each of the following verses: II. 7; III. 5; v. 1; vi. 3; vii. 10; viii. 4.

"We see in burning-glasses, where the beams of the sun meet in one, how forcible they are, because there is a union of the beams in a little point. Let it be our labour that all the beams of our love may meet in Christ, that He may be our Beloved. As all streams meet in the great ocean, so let all our loves meet in Christ. We cannot bestow our love and our affections better than upon Christ. It is a happiness that we have such affections as joy, delight, and love, planted in us by God; and what a happiness is it that we should have such an excellent Object to fill those affections, yea, to transcend, and more than satisfy them!"

—Richard Sibbes.

THE SONG OF SOLOMON (2)

Its Literary Form

THE SONG of Solomon, as we have said, is a poem. It will be well, however, if we now amplify that definition, and say that it is really *several* short poems combined into one. This does not detract either from its literary appeal or its spiritual meaning, for these several poemettes, or idyl fragments, obviously belong together as different aspects of the same love-suit.

According to Dr. Richard G. Moulton's *Modern Reader's Bible*, the Song of Solomon is "*A Suite of Seven Idyls.*" These, the titles of which we have reworded somewhat, are as follows:

Idyl 1. *The Royal Wedding Lived Over Again* (i. 1–ii. 7).
  „   2. *The Bride's Courtship Reminiscences* (ii. 8–iii. 5).
  „   3. *The Occasion of the Betrothal Recalled* (iii. 6–v. 1).
  „   4. *The Bride's Troubled Dream Related* (v. 2–vi. 3).
  „   5. *The King's Meditation on His Bride* (vi. 4–vii. 10).
  „   6. *The Bride Longs to See Her Old Home* (vii. 11–viii. 4).
  „   7. *The Renewal of Love at Lebanon* (viii. 5–viii. 14).

Perhaps that word, "idyl," calls for comment. It comes from the Greek *eidullion*, which means "a little picture." Historically, its use in connection with poetry comes down from the great Sicilian poet, Theocritus (third century B.C.). The idyls of Theocritus were pictures of the ordinary, open-air shepherd life of the people of Sicily: and from that time until the present, literary usage has reserved the word "idyl" for that which is pastoral or homely as in contrast with that which is epic, heroic or dramatic. An idyl, then, is a short pictorial poem on some pastoral or homely subject; a short descriptive or narrative poem, especially one which gives to familiar or everyday scenes a tinge of romance.

To say that the Song of Solomon is a cluster of idyls may seem quite unimportant at first. What does it matter whichever particular form of poetry it is in? Actually, however, it is of very *real* concern to classify the technical form of this work; for upon this depends the very *interpretation* of the story which the poem intends to convey. A moment's reflection will make this clear. If we take the poem as *dramatic*, rather than idyllic, then the Song of Solomon is a *consecutive story*: that which comes in chapter ii. is later in point of time than that which comes in chapter i.; that which comes in chapter iii. is later in point of time than that which comes in chapter ii., and so on. Drama presents a story; and therefore dramatic action can never go back. If, then, we take the Song of Solomon as dramatic, our interpretation will be correspondingly affected.

On the other hand, if we see in the Song of Solomon a cluster of lyric idyls, then our interpretation will not be restricted by any necessary adherence to sequence; for these lyric idyls may, with perfect propriety, pick on different parts of the story, passing from the later to the earlier, without restriction as to the order of time.

Hear Dr. Moulton again: "Those who hold that Solomon's Song is a drama find the plot of that drama to consist in a struggle between king Solomon and a humble shepherd wooer for the love of the fair Shulamite woman, Solomon in the end giving way, and the heroine and her humble wooer becoming united. To me this result seems to be wrung out of the words of the poem with a good deal of straining. On the other hand, if we allow the work the wider range of lyric idyls, there needs no straining of interpretation to arrive at a story which is certainly not less interesting than the other. For by this interpretation we are able to identify the humble lover with Solomon himself. The story becomes this: King Solomon, with a courtly retinue visiting the royal vineyards upon Mount Lebanon, comes by surprise upon the fair Shulamite. She flies from them. Solomon visits her in the disguise of a shepherd, and so wins her love. He then comes in all his royal state, and calls her to leave Lebanon and become his queen. They are in the act of being wedded in the royal palace when the poem opens."

It is wonderful how this Song of Solomon lights up with added beauties when it is set out in this seven-fold idyllic form, with each separate idyl arranged to full poetic effect. It is quite impossible for us to give all seven thus set out here; but with much gratitude to Dr. Moulton, whose great work we whole-heartedly recommend, we will take the liberty of here reproducing (abridged) his presentation of Idyls one, five and seven.

IDYL I (i. 1–ii. 7)

THE WEDDING DAY

Outside the Palace. The Bridal Procession approaches: the Royal Bridegroom leading the Bride, followed by an Attendant Chorus of Daughters of Jerusalem.

THE BRIDE

Let him kiss me with the kisses of his mouth:
  For thy love is better than wine (etc.).

A pause is made at the threshold of the Palace.

THE BRIDE (*to the Bridegroom*)

Draw me—

ATTENDANT CHORUS

We will run after thee.

The Bridegroom lifts the Bride across the threshold.

THE BRIDE

The king hath brought me into his chambers.

ATTENDANT CHORUS

We will be glad and rejoice in thee,
We will make mention of thy love more than of wine.

THE BRIDE

In uprightness do they love thee.

Inside the Palace. The Bride addresses her Attendant Chorus.

THE BRIDE

I am black, but comely, O ye daughters of Jerusalem,
  As the tents of Kedar (etc.).

The Bride and Bridegroom whisper reminiscences of their courtship: how she sought to penetrate his disguise and he answered mysteriously.

THE BRIDE (verse 7).
THE BRIDEGROOM (verse 8).

The Procession from the Banqueting House to the Bridal Chamber.

THE BRIDEGROOM (verses 9–11).
THE BRIDE (verses 12–14).
THE BRIDEGROOM (verse 15).

THE BRIDE (i. 16–ii. 1).
THE BRIDEGROOM (ii. 2).
THE BRIDE (ii. 3–6).
REFRAIN (ii. 7).

I adjure you, O daughters of Jerusalem,
    By the roes, and by the hinds of the field,
That ye stir not up, nor awaken love,
    Until it please.

IDYL V (vi. 4–vii. 10)

THE KING'S MEDITATION ON HIS BRIDE

THE KING MUSES ON HER BEAUTY

Thou are beautiful, my love, as Tirzah,
Comely as Jerusalem,
    Terrible as an army with banners.
Turn away thine eyes from me,
    For they have overcome me.
Thy hair is as a flock of goats
    That lie along the side of Gilead.
              (etc. to end of vi. 9)

THE MUSING BECOMES (IN DRAMATIC FORM) A REMINISCENCE OF THE FIRST MEETING

(a) Surprise of the Court

"Who is she that looketh forth as the morning,
"Fair as the moon, pure as the sun,
    "Terrible as an army with banners?"

(b) Surprise of the Shulamite

"I went down into the garden of nuts,
    "To see the green plants of the valley . . .
"Or ever I was aware, my soul set me
    "Among the chariots of my princely people".

(c) Cry of the Royal Court

"Return, return, O Shulamite;
    "Return, return, that we may look on thee".

(d) Confusion of the Shulamite

"Why will ye look upon the Shulamite
"As upon the dance of Mahanaim?"

THE KING RESUMES HIS MUSING ON THE BRIDE'S BEAUTY

How beautiful are thy feet in sandals,
    O prince's daughter!
The joints of thy thighs are like jewels,
The work of a cunning workman. . . .

(and so, to verse 9)

IDYL VII (viii. 5–14)

THE RENEWAL OF LOVE IN THE VINEYARD OF LEBANON

Arrival of Royal Pair (unattended) at place where they first met.

Who is this that cometh up from the wilderness,
    Leaning upon her beloved?

KING SOLOMON

Under the apple tree I awakened thee:
There thy mother was in travail with thee,
There was she in travail that brought thee forth.

THE BRIDE

Set me as a seal upon thine heart,
    As a seal upon thine arm:
For love is strong as death;
    Jealousy is cruel as the grave;
The flashes thereof are flashes of fire,
    A very flame of the LORD.
Many waters cannot quench love,
    Neither can the floods drown it:
If a man would give all the substance of
    his house for love,
It would utterly be contemned.

*The Bride recalls riddling speeches of her Brothers when she was a
child: she understands them now.*

"We have a little sister" (etc.)

(*Here read verses 8, 9 and 10.*)

The Bride renews her vows to her husband: Solomon shall be the landlord of her heart as he is the landlord of her home.

THE BRIDE

Solomon had a vineyard at Baal-hamon ;
   He let out the vineyard unto keepers ;
   Everyone for the fruit thereof was to bring a thousand
     pieces of silver.

My vineyard, which is mine, is before me :
   Thou, O Solomon, shalt have the thousand,
   And those that keep the fruit thereof two hundred.

The Escort heard approaching to conduct them back from Lebanon: there is just time for a final embrace.

KING SOLOMON

Thou that dwellest in the gardens,
   The companions hearken for thy voice :
   Cause me to hear it.

THE BRIDE

Make haste, my beloved,
   And be thou like to a roe or to a young hart
   Upon the mountains of spices.

To see these idyls presented in this way enhances their interest, and clarifies their sense. It adds to their literary charm, and at the same time helps our perception of their spiritual meaning ; for let us most of all remember that the Lord Jesus and His bride, the Church, are mystically present everywhere in this sevenfold poem ; and anything which helps us in our understanding of this is important.

In our next and final study in the Song of Solomon, we shall summarise the seven idyls, each in turn, and then give certain instances of spiritual lessons which are to be found in them. Meanwhile, we cannot do better than to close this present study by once again recommending the reader to get Dr. Richard G. Moulton's *Modern Reader's Bible*—if and when circumstances allow.

THE SONG OF SOLOMON (3)

Lesson Number 68

NOTE.—For this study read again the seven idyls which constitute the full poem, but read them separately, along with the brief comments which we have made on them.

No angel's tongue above
Could e'er express His love;
Nor harp of sweetest sound
Like his dear voice be found.
No lustrous seraph there
Could e'er with Him compare—
The fairest of the fair
   is Jesus.

Sweet wonder, all Divine,
That He should now be mine!
The rapture, who shall tell,
Where He has cast His spell?
Perfection's crown is He,
The sum of bliss to me,
My endless heaven to be
   is Jesus.
      —J. S. B.

THE SONG OF SOLOMON (3)

The Seven Parts

HAVING now noted the composite and idyllic form of this exquisite composition, and having seen two of the seven idyls set out so as to show the underlying incidents to which the poetry refers, let us sum up the seven idyls in turn. Modern and western readers should guard against mentally picturing the wooing and wedding here as being according to occidental form and custom.

Idyl 1 (i. 1–ii. 7).

Here, in vivid touches, is the royal marriage. The bridal procession reaches the palace. The royal bridegroom, according to customary ceremony, lifts the bride over the threshold (i. 4), whereupon the attendant "daughters of Jerusalem" break into chorus—"We will be glad, and rejoice in thee. We will make mention of thy love more than of wine" (i. 4). Inside the palace, the bride, whose marriage raises her from rustic obscurity to the throne of the land, gracefully excuses her country complexion to her more artificial, city-bred wedding-maidens (i. 5, 6); though, of course, that for which she modestly apologises is, in Solomon's eyes, part of her superlative charm. The two lovers now exchange whispered reminiscences of their courtship (i. 7, 8), after which comes the procession from the banqueting house to the bridal chamber. Here the bride and bridegroom are heard exchanging affectionate appreciations of each other (i. 9–ii. 6), until the poet's refrain (ii. 7) draws the curtain on that final picture of the happy day—

> I adjure you, O daughters of Jerusalem,
> By the roes, and by the hinds of the field,
> That ye stir not up, nor awaken love,
> Until it please.

189

Idyl 2 (ii. 8–iii. 5).

In this second idyl, the bride indulges in reminiscences of the courtship days. She re-lives that unforgettable day in the fair springtime, when her princely lover first came to her mountain home, and when their love had its beginning (ii. 8–14). As she thinks upon her new-found lover's ardent words at that time, she also recalls how the harsh voices of her brothers had interrupted with the cry that the foxes had got into the vineyard (ii. 15). After this there follow the reminiscences of a happy dream in which she found her lost lover (iii. 1–4); and then the second idyl closes with the same refrain as that which closed the first (iii. 5).

Idyl 3 (iii. 6–v. 1).

In this superb song the day of the betrothal is re-lived. Already king Solomon, in shepherd disguise, has wooed and won the fair heroine; but now he comes in state (iii. 6–11). Having arrived, he pours out his love to the Shulamite (iv. 1–5). The maiden's momentary interruption of modest embarrassment before such ardent praises is given in verse 6; and after this comes the actual proposal of marriage (iv. 7–15). Solomon invites her to leave Lebanon (verse 8), for she has ravished his heart (verse 9). Her rustic fragrance is better to him than all manner of "spices"— the more artificial perfumery of the city maidens (iv. 10). Yet while she is away amid her country surroundings she is like "a garden shut up" and inaccessible (verse 12). So, under this metaphor of a garden shut up—a delicate symbol of maidenhood —marriage is proposed; and, under the same metaphor the beautiful Shulamite accepts, in the words of verse 16—

> Let my beloved come into his garden,
> And eat his pleasant fruits.

Solomon's joyous response is (in v. 1): "I am come into my garden, my sister, my bride." This idyl then closes with a final touch from the poet (in v. 1)—

> Eat, O friends;
> Drink, yea, drink abundantly of love.

Idyl 4 (v. 2–vi. 3).

Idyl 4 relates a troubled dream of the bride. She dreams that her beloved comes to her in the night, seeking admission. She hesitates. There is a little delay while she quickly attends to her personal appearance, and dips her hands in the myrrh (v. 3). In that pause, her beloved withdraws himself; and when she opens the door he is gone (v. 6). She wanders forth in the night, seeking her lost lover (v. 7). The watchmen find her. They smite and wound and insult her (v. 7). In her troubled dreaming she now fancies herself accosting the chorus of bridesmaids, to whom she pours out her grief (v. 8). To them she gives a description of her beloved which is surely a masterpiece of language, unexcelled for choiceness (v. 10–16). Her rapturous eulogy of his charms has the effect of lifting her dream out of its troubled darkness and bringing it to a happy issue. She finds where her beloved has gone (vi. 2), and is relieved to awake with a song upon her lips (vi. 3).

Idyl 5 (vi. 4–vii. 10).

This is a meditation of the king upon his bride. It is both passionate and rapturous. In the first part (vi. 4–9), the king muses on her beauty. The language is richly expressive. At verse 10 the meditation seems to become a reminiscence, and may well refer to the first meeting of Solomon and Shulamith. We seem to hear, in verse 10, the words of surprise and praise from the royal party when they unexpectedly came upon the maiden.

> Who is she that looketh forth as the morning,
> Fair as the moon, pure as the sun,
> Terrible as an army with banners?

The next six lines may well express the feelings of the maiden, sensitive under the admiring gaze of the royal party (verses 11, 12).

The next couplet (verse 13) may well fit the royal party as the maiden flees from them—

> Return, return, O Shulamite;
> Return, return, that we may look upon thee.

And the next couplet gives the response, either spoken or unspoken, of the maiden—

> Why will ye look upon the Shulamite,
> As upon the dance at Mahanaim?

The king's meditation is then resumed (at vii. 1) and runs on to the closing refrain (vii. 10).

Idyl 6 (vii. 11–viii. 4).

There is but one voice in this, the shortest of these lyrics. It is that of the bride. Amid the palace splendours she yearns to see the country home on Mount Lebanon again. In these choice stanzas she makes tender appeal that she and her husband should visit it, and there renew their love (vii. 11–viii. 3). This idyl then closes with a snatch from an earlier refrain (viii. 4).

Idyl 7 (viii. 5–14).

Here is the renewal of love in the Lebanon vineyard. In the opening couplet the royal pair reach the spot where they had first met: "Who is this that cometh up from the wilderness, leaning on her beloved?" Solomon speaks (verse 5); then his bride (verses 6, 7). The bride now recalls remarks of her brothers which had puzzled her in younger years, and which she now understands (verses 8–10). And now she renews her love-vow to Solomon under the figure of a vineyard and its landlord. The voices of the escort are now heard. There is but time for a last word of love; and the poem ends.

Spiritual Lessons

When once the mystic presence of Christ and the Church is seen in this Song of Solomon, it simply abounds with precious spiritual applications. The little space which here remains to us allows merely a fractional illustration of this.

Turn to the beginning of Idyl 4 (v. 2). Here we have the bride's reminiscence of a love-dream. Her beloved comes to her, gently appealing for admission: "Open to me, my sister, my love, my dove, my undefiled; for my head is filled with dew, and my locks with the drops of the night." The spouse allows self-considerations to delay her response: "I have put off my coat; how shall I put it on? I have washed my feet; how shall I defile them?" When she eventually opens the door, her dear one has gone away; and with anguished heart she must now seek him through the night, must weep for him, and suffer at the hands of the city watchmen, before she finds him again. Oh, how often has that very thing happened in our own experience! Self-interests have delayed our response to Christ when He has come in some special way to enrich the heart: and when we have afterwards sought the blessing, our Beloved has withdrawn Himself, night has surrounded us, fears have beset us, and we have waded through pools of tears before we have found Him. Well have we understood at such times the truth of those lines from the hymn book—

> Our midnight is Thy smile withdrawn;
> Our noontide is Thy gracious dawn.

Oh that we may be quick to the voice of our heavenly Bridegroom!—that we may make eager response to Him!—that we may not forfeit His choicest secrets and blessings! The Scofield Bible note on the bride's delay is well worth prayerful reflection: "The bride is satisfied with her washed feet while the Bridegroom, His 'head filled with dew,' and His 'locks with the drops of the night,' is toiling for others. The state of the bride is not one of sin, but of neglect of service. She is preoccupied with the graces and perfections which she has in Christ through the Spirit (1 Cor. xii. 4–11; Gal. v. 22, 23). It is mysticism, unbalanced by the activities of the Christian warfare. Her feet are washed, her hands drop with sweet-smelling myrrh; but He has gone on, and now she must seek Him."

But now let us turn up just one other such instance in the Song of Solomon. We will limit ourselves to one verse only. It is chapter ii. 14. Here the royal lover addresses Shulammith thus: "O my dove, in the clefts of the rock, in the secret of the stairs; let me see thy countenance, let me hear thy voice; for sweet is thy voice; and thy countenance is comely." Read these same words now as coming from the lips of Christ to His own; and observe the beautiful progress of thought in them.

First, we have the bride's *character*, as it is in the estimation of the bridegroom. He calls her "My dove," a metaphor which means to express gentleness, tenderness, comeliness, and purity (see v. 2 and vi. 9). Although, in themselves, Christ's people are deeply unworthy and are defiled by sin, yet, in Him, they are made beautiful. Covered by His perfect righteousness, they are "accepted in the Beloved." Sanctified by the love of God, which is shed within them by the Holy Spirit, they are made "blameless and harmless."

Next, note the bride's *safety*. The dove is "in the clefts of the rock." The rock-doves, as the reader may know, actually do live in the clefts of the rock, safe from the storms, which, whatever else they may destroy, cannot shake the immovable rock. Interpreted in the light of other Scriptures, the "rock" in this fourteenth verse of chapter ii. is Christ Himself. He is the "Rock of Ages," cleft for us; and we are hidden in Him, hidden, as it were, in the riven side of Christ who died to make us His own.

See, further, the bride's position of *privilege*. She is said to be "in the secret of the stairs" (omit the italicised word "places," in the Authorised Version). This "secret of the stairs" speaks of access and ascent. Not only is our true life "hid with Christ in God" (Col. iii. 3), and not only are we personally safe in the clefts of the Rock, but we have the secret of ascent and the privilege of access (Eph. ii. 18; Heb. x. 19–22).

Just once again, see the bride's *belovedness* to her royal lover. He says: "Let me see thy countenance, let me hear thy voice; for sweet is thy voice, and thy countenance is comely." The spiritually-minded Christian reads these words, and hears them falling, not merely from the lips of Solomon to the maid of Lebanon, but from the lips of the Son of God to those whom He has bought with His own precious blood; for it is written that "Christ loved the Church, and gave Himself for it . . . that He might present it to Himself a glorious Church . . . holy and without blemish" (Eph. v. 25–7).

This Song of Solomon abounds with similarly tender correspondences between the royal love-suit of long ago and the far more wonderful union of Christ and the Church. Again and again, as we read it prayerfully and adoringly, we find ourselves softly singing Charles Wesley's lines—

> O Love divine, how sweet Thou art!
> When shall I find my willing heart
> All taken up by Thee?
> I thirst, I faint, I die to prove
> The fulness of redeeming love—
> The love of Christ to me.

CAN YOU MANAGE THESE?

1. What is the genius of the proverb, and what the general purpose of the *Book* of Proverbs?

2. What is the threefold division of the Book of Proverbs?

3. Can you give three proverbs exemplifying, respectively, contrastive, completive, and comparative structure?

4. Indicate the four main parts or movements in the quest or argument of Ecclesiastes.

5. Inasmuch as Ecclesiastes consists of argumentative processes not every word can be picked on as being in itself an inspired precept: but how then does that fact bear on the inspiration of the Bible?

6. In what way is the Book of Ecclesiastes a challenge to faith?

7. What are the ten "vanities" mentioned in the Book of Ecclesiastes?

8. What were the three sources of Koheleth's pessimism?

9. What are the three theories of interpretation regarding the Song of Solomon?

10. Which psalm seems to be the Scripture key to the typical meaning of the Song of Solomon?

11. What would you say is the central message of the Song of Solomon?

12. Which are the seven idyls of which the complete suite is composed?

13. Why is it important to decide whether the form of the Song of Solomon is dramatic or idyllic?

14. Answer the objection that Solomon cannot be a type of Christ in the Song of Songs because of his personal unsuitability.

15. Give one specimen of the spiritual applications (to Christ and His people) which may be made from the Song of Solomon.

THE BOOKS OF THE PROPHETS
Lesson Number 69

By whatever process it has come to be, teachers and disciples far and wide now regard the Old Testament from an angle totally different (I use the words deliberately) from that taken by our Lord Jesus Christ, alike before and after His resurrection from the dead. To Him, tempted, teaching, suffering, dying, risen, *"it is written"* was a formula of infinite import. The principle this expressed lay at the heart of His teaching. It is not too much to say that it belonged to the pulse, to the vital breath, of His message to others, and, what is mysteriously yet more, to His certainty about Himself.

—Sir Robert Anderson

THE BOOKS OF THE PROPHETS

INTRODUCTORY

IN OUR progressive study of the Bible, we have now reached the final group of writings in the Old Testament. Twenty-two books now lie behind us. A further seventeen stretch before us, namely, the seventeen books of the Prophets. These we shall find to be an arresting concentration of inspired doctrine and prediction.

A Backward Look

It is well that just here we should look back for a moment over the ground which we have already traversed. We did this at the beginning of the Poetical Books, but we ought to do the same again here. The first group of writings in the Old Testament, as we have seen, is comprised of seventeen *historical* books. These are the books running from Genesis to Esther. This group of seventeen sub-groups itself into five and twelve. The first five, Genesis to Deuteronomy, clearly belong together. They are all from the pen of Moses, and they all have to do with Israel's *preparation* for Canaan. The remaining twelve, Joshua to Esther, equally clearly belong together. They are from different pens, but they all have to do with Israel's *occupation* of Canaan. Thus, at the beginning of the Old Testament, we have a group of *seventeen* books which are all *historical*, and which are divided into two sub-groups of five and twelve.

The twelve may be further divided into nine and three, for in the first nine, which are pre-exilic (Joshua to II Chronicles) the Davidic kingdom is still in the land, whereas in the remaining three (Ezra, Nehemiah, Esther) only the post-exilic "Remnant" is back in the land.

And now, as we come to the third and final group of books in the Old Testament, we find a further group of *seventeen* which are *prophetical*. What is more, we find that these, like the foregoing seventeen historical books, are divided into five and twelve, i.e. the five writings of the "Major" Prophets, and the twelve so-called

"Minor" Prophets. And the twelve may be still further divided into nine and three, for in the first nine, which are pre-exilic (Hosea to Zephaniah) the Davidic kingdom is still in the land, whereas in the remaining three (Haggai, Zechariah, Malachi) only the post-exilic "Remnant" is back in the land.

As we have pointed out before, the division of the seventeen prophetical books into "Major" and "Minor" is no artificial distinction. In the former we find all the basic ethical features of Old Testament prophecy and of Messianic prediction. In Isaiah the coming Messiah is seen both as the suffering Saviour and as the ultimate Sovereign who reigns in world empire. In Jeremiah, where we also have Jehovah's full case against Israel, He is the righteous "Branch" of David, and the ultimate restorer of the judged and dispersed people. In Ezekiel, looking beyond intermediate judgments, we see Him as the perfect Shepherd-King in whose glorious reign the ideal temple of the future is to be erected. In Daniel, who gives us the most particularised programme of times and events in their successive order, we see the Messiah "cut off" without throne or kingdom, yet standing up at last as universal Emperor on the ruins of the crashed Gentile world-system.

The twelve writings grouped as the "Minor Prophets", though they amplify various aspects, do not determine the main shape of Messianic prophecy. They conform to the general frame already formed for us in Isaiah, Jeremiah, Ezekiel and Daniel.

Coming *between* the seventeen historical books and the seventeen prophetical books, we have the five-fold group of the "poetical" books, which are neither historical nor prophetical, but *experiential*. Thus, the thirty-nine books of the Old Testament are grouped as follows:

HISTORICAL	EXPERIENTIAL	PROPHETICAL
SEVENTEEN 5 + 9 + 3	FIVE	SEVENTEEN 5 + 9 + 3

It is well, also, at this point, to let our eye travel back over the distinctive features of the books which we have studied. We have found, up to this point, that the distinctive feature of each book in the Old Testament is so pronounced that we may denote it by a single word or phrase.

Genesis	— *Destitution* (through the sin of man).
Exodus	— *Deliverance* (through the power of God).
Leviticus	— *Dedication* (accepted through atonement).
Numbers	— *Direction* (by the Divine guidance).
Deuteronomy	— *Destination* (by the Divine faithfulness).

Joshua	— *Possession* (Israel occupies the land).
Judges, Ruth	— *Declension* (Israel betrays her trust).
1 Samuel	— *Transition* (Theocracy now a Monarchy).
2 Samuel	— *Confirmation* (Davidic throne confirmed).
1 Kings	— *Disruption* (break-away of ten tribes).
2 Kings	— *Dispersion* (both kingdoms into exile).
Chronicles	— *Recapitulation* (Adam down to the Exile).
Ezra	— *Restoration* (Remnant returns to Judæa).
Nehemiah	— *Reconstruction* (Jerusalem wall rebuilt).
Esther	— *Preservation* (of the *non*-returned Jews).

Book of Job	— *Blessing through Suffering* (self-life dies).
The Psalms	— *Praise through Prayer* (the new life in God).
The Proverbs	— *Prudence through Precept* (in Wisdom's school).
Ecclesiastes	— *Verity through Vanity* (world cannot satisfy).
Song of Songs	— *Bliss through Union* (Christ fully satisfies).

We cannot stress too strongly the practical usefulness of getting such a synopsis as that given above firmly fixed in the mind and memory. The interest, not to say the intelligibility, of the books of Scripture which still lie before us depends in considerable degree upon our grasp of that which now lies behind us. To learn and retain the above summary is to have an advantageous background. The main movements of the Scripture story are kept vivid to the mind. The gist of the message is given fixity. In fact, unless we have well learned the foregoing, large tracts in the writings of the Prophets, to which we now come, will be almost like words without meaning; for, whatever else may be true of the Prophets, this is true, that primarily they were men who spoke to their own times, and whose messages are coloured by the history of the chosen people, Israel. So much, then, for the way by which we have already travelled.

And now, before we look at each of these prophetical books by itself, let us anticipate the whole seventeen as a *group*. In our English version they do not appear in their chronological order; but it is most important that we should see and learn them in their chronological order, because our understanding of them is in no small degree bound up with rightly relating them to the day and the circumstances in which they were spoken and written. Here, then, they are, in their chronological order (according to Ussher's dating), with the Assyrian captivity of the ten-tribed northern kingdom, and the Babylonian captivity of Judah, the southern kingdom, shown in relation to them.

CHRONOLOGICAL GROUPING OF OLD TESTAMENT PROPHETS

Prophets of northern king-dom (Israel).	Jonah	B.C. 862	(down to perhaps 830).
	Amos	787	
	Hosea	785–725	
Prophets of southern king-dom (Judah).	Obadiah	887	
	Joel	800	
	Isaiah	760–698	—Here Israel, northern kingdom, goes into
	Micah	750–710	Assyrian captivity (721 B.C.).
	Nahum	713	
	Habakkuk	626	
	Zephaniah	630	
	Jeremiah	629–588	
	Lamentations		—Here Judah, southern kingdom, goes into Babylonian captivity (587 B.C.).
Prophets during and after Exile.	Ezekiel	595–574	
	Daniel	607–534	
	Haggai	520	—Here the " Remnant " returns to Jerusalem
	Zechariah	520–518	and Judæa (from 536 B.C.).
	Malachi	397	

From these dates, given in relation to the Assyrian and Babylonian captivities, we see that the Prophets were a succession of messengers raised up for a special period—a period of declension and apostasy. It has been truly said that they were primarily "revivalists and patriots" who spoke on behalf of God to the heart and conscience of the nation: but their deeper significance is that they were specially raised up and inspired of God to transmit a message of warning and entreaty ere the stroke of Divine judgment laid the two Hebrew kingdoms low beneath the heel of their heathen captors.

It will be noted, too, that Jeremiah's tear-drenched elegy, the "Lamentations," marks Judah's actual plunge into the night of the Babylonian exile. (We have read the arguments which some modern scholars have put forward for the much later date and the composite authorship of the "Lamentations," and are convinced that they are wrong.)

Once more, it should always be borne in mind that the last three of the seventeen *prophetical* books (Haggai, Zechariah, Malachi) should be read with the last three of the seventeen *historical* books (Ezra, Nehemiah, Esther), for in both cases the three books are *post*-exilic. Haggai and Zechariah and Malachi, that is, are the prophets of the returned "Remnant."

And now, for the sake of even greater clearness, we ought perhaps to set out the line of prophets in relation to the kings during whose reigns they conducted their ministries. In the following lists the prophets whose names are given in italics are the non-writing prophets, or prophets of whose writings nothing has come down to us. The numbers in brackets give the years that the different kings reigned.

Also, in the following catalogue the reason why the kings of Judah are spaced out a little in several places is to show, as nearly as possible, the kings of the two lines, respectively, who reigned at the same time as each other, or whose reigns overlapped.

THE PROPHETS IN RELATION TO THE KINGS

Saul	(40)	*Samuel, Nathan,*
David	(40)	*Gad, and Ahijah.*
Solomon	(40)	

JUDAH			ISRAEL		
Rehoboam	(17)	*Shemaiah*	Jeroboam	(22)	*Ahijah* (1 Kings
Abijam	(3)	(2 Chron. xii.)	Nadab	(2)	xi., xiv.)
Asa	(41)	*Azariah*	Baasha	(24)	
		(2 Chron. xv.)	Ela	(2)	*Jehu* (1 Kings
		Hanani	Zimri	(one week)	xvi. 2 Chron. xix.)
Jehoshaphat	(25)	(1 Chron. xvi.)	Omri	(12)	
Jehoram	(8)		Ahab	(22)	*Elijah, and*
Ahaziah	(1)	OBADIAH ?	Ahaziah	(2)	*Micaiah*
Athaliah	(6)		Jehoram	(12)	(1 Kings. xiv. 22).
Joash	(40)	JOEL ?	Jehu	(28)	
			Jehoahaz	(17)	*Elisha.*
Amaziah	(29)		Joash	(16)	JONAH
Azariah	(52)		Jeroboam 2	(41)	and AMOS.
(Uzziah)			(interregnum)	(12)	
Jotham	(16)		Zechariah	(½ year)	
		ISAIAH	Shallum	(1 month)	
		and	Menahem	(10)	HOSEA.
		MICAH.	Pekahiah	(2)	
Ahaz	(16)		Pekah	(20)	
Hezekiah	(29)		Hoshea	(9)	
Manasseh	(55)	NAHUM.			
Amon	(2)	ZEPHANIAH,			
Josiah	(31)	HABAKKUK,			
Jehoahaz (3 mths.)		*Huldah.*			
Jehoiakim	(11)	JEREMIAH.			
Jehoiachin (3 mths.)					
Zedekiah	(11)				

NOTE—

(1) We must be careful not to think that the above-named prophets were the *only* prophets of Judah and Israel. The truth is very much otherwise. Ever since Samuel's days there had been an organised prophetic order with prophet schools up and down the land. This accounts for the fact that besides the above-named prophets, unnamed prophets are again and again referred to (see 1 Kings xiii. 1, 11, 18; xviii. 4; xx. 13, 22, 35; xxii. 6, etc.).

(2) It should be borne in mind that although the above prophets whose names are given in italics are classed as non-writing prophets, they are only so classed because no writings of theirs have come down to us. It seems *probable* that many of them *did* write, because it is *certain* that a number of them did, whose writings, nevertheless, have not been preserved to us. See, for instance, references to the writings of Nathan (2 Chron. ix. 29), of Gad (1 Chron. xxix. 29), of Ahijah (2 Chron. ix. 29), of Jehu (2 Chron. xx. 34), of Shemaiah (2 Chron. xii. 15), of Oded (2 Chron. xv. 8), of Iddo (2 Chron. xiii. 22).

PROPHECY AND THE PROPHETS

Lesson Number 70

THE PROPHETIC ELEMENT IN SCRIPTURE

This is one of seven elements which together constitute the whole body of the Word of God, namely: History, Biography, Prophecy, Ethics, Devotion, Messianic Revelation and Spiritual guidance. This prophetic element pervades all the rest. It is the *eye* of Scripture, with supernatural vision—backsight, insight and foresight, or power to see into the past, present and future. It is, therefore, the miracle of utterance, as other miracles are wonders of power, and evinces omniscience, as they do omnipotence, thus reflecting the image of the glory of God.

—Arthur T. Pierson, D.D.

PROPHECY AND THE PROPHETS

BEFORE delving into these writings of the Hebrew prophets, we ought to have a clear understanding as to the nature of prophecy and the significance of the prophetic order in Israel.

Prophecy Not Merely Prediction

To begin with, prophecy is not merely *prediction*. The common idea today is that prophecy is wholly a matter of foretelling the future, but that idea is erroneous. It is founded on a wrong etymology; for the *pro* in "prophet" is not that which means *beforehand*, as in the word "provide," but that which means *in place of*, as in the word "pronoun." The remainder of the word "prophet" is from the Greek *phemi*, which means *to speak*. So, then, a prophet is one who speaks in place of another. Thus, when Moses quailed at the thought of being sent to Israel in Egypt, on account of his supposed inability as a speaker, God said to him: "See, I have made thee a god unto Pharaoh; and Aaron thy brother shall be thy *prophet*" (Exod. vii. 1). Aaron was to be his brother's prophet in that he was to speak in his name, and *in place of him*.

It is well to realise, then, that while all prediction is prophecy, not all prophecy is prediction. Prophecy may concern the past or the present as well as the future. In the former case it is an inspired *forth*-telling; in the latter, it is an inspired *fore*-telling. Prophecy in the *non*-predictive sense is a declaring of truth, on any given subject, received by direct inspiration from God. Prophecy in the *predictive* sense is a declaring of the future such as is impossible to the unaided wisdom of man, and which can only come by direct inspiration from God.

Prophecy a Product of Inspiration

We would stress the fact that prophecy, in the Scripture sense, is the product and expression of a direct and special *inspiration* from God. The Hebrew word for a prophet is *nabhi*, which derives from a word meaning to boil up or boil forth, like some hot spring or fountain, thus suggesting a pouring forth of words from fervent animation or Divine inspiration. The very name "prophet," therefore, indicates the supernormal constraint under which the prophets wrote and spoke. Their constant refrain is "Thus saith the LORD." Unlike the teachers of the Gentiles, these Hebrew prophets came before the people, not to present "moral discourses, metaphysical treatises, or philosophical reasonings," as an old writer puts it, but "to make known the will of One above them, and to express higher thoughts and purposes than their own." They spoke "not as from man to men, but as those entrusted with direct authority from God to speak in His name to sinful men."

This, of course, prompts the question: What was the *nature* of the inspiration under which the prophets wrote and spoke? In the words of 2 Peter i. 21, these "holy men of God" were "moved by the Holy Ghost"; and the Greek word which is here translated as "moved," means to be borne along, or even driven along. Thus, Weymouth translates it as "impelled," and Moffatt as "carried along." The same word is used in Acts xxvii. 15, 17, to describe how the ship on which Paul was a passenger was "driven along" by the tempestuous wind, Euroclydon. It is a strong word, therefore; and it certainly teaches that the inspiration of the prophets was a most definite supernatural work wrought in them, by which they spoke *direct from God*. The *Twentieth Century New Testament*, in fact, uses those very words, "direct from God," to give the sense of this verb, thus: "No prophetic teaching ever came in the old days at the mere wish of man; but men, moved by the Holy Spirit, spoke direct from God." That which the Holy Spirit wrought in the prophets was an inspiration in all respects fully adequate to the end in view, namely, the transmission, without error, of truth Divinely revealed to them.

What Inspiration Implies

The prophets were far from being infallible in themselves, nor did they live in a state of *perpetual* inspiration which gave infallibility to *all* their words and actions. This is strikingly illustrated in the case of the prophet Nathan, who at first commended David's purpose to build a temple to the Lord, but was afterwards sent back with a Divine message to David *not* to build it. In his earlier commendation of David's project, Nathan had gone so far as to say: "Go, do all that is in thine heart, for the Lord is with thee"; notwithstanding, he had been expressing merely his own human judgment in the matter, and had to be corrected of God. Moreover, it is noteworthy that when God sent Nathan back to David, the prophet was instructed to begin with: "Thus saith the LORD." It was a clear case of "Thus saith Nathan," at first, versus "Thus saith the LORD" afterward (see 2 Sam. vii.).

Yet in all their transmissions of special or direct communications from God, the inspiration of the prophets by the Holy Spirit was such as to render them infallible as vehicles of the Divine message. It was this being "moved," impelled, borne along, inspired, by the Divine Spirit which both constrained and authorised them to speak in the name of Deity, and to say: "Thus saith the LORD." When they *thus* spoke, they were *infallible*. This was the result secured by the supernatural work of inspiration. The *fact* that this inerrancy was secured in these human vehicles of the Divine message is far more important than curious speculations as to the *ways* by which the Holy Spirit wrought it. It is the reality of it, and not merely the psychology of it, which is the vital thing. As the late Dr. Kitto observes, "How far this object was secured by direct suggestion, by negative control, or by an elevating influence upon their natural powers, is a question of little practical importance to those holding the only essential doctrine—that the inspiration was in all respects such as rendered those who received it incapable of error. Any inspiration beyond this could not be needed; any less than this would be worthless."

Inspiration and the Prophet Himself

It may be asked: What was the condition of *the prophet himself* while under the influence of inspiration? Did he retain normal possession of his natural faculties, so as to be master of himself as at ordinary times? Or were his natural powers rendered inoperative for the time being, either by a supernatural ecstasy or by a state of abnormal passivity? Perhaps we cannot better answer this than by quoting from an article by C. Von Orelli.

"This inspiration is not such that it suppresses the human consciousness of the recipient, so that he would receive the word of God in the state of sleep or trance. But rather the recipient is in possession of his full consciousness, and is able afterward to give a clear account of what happened. Nor is the individuality of the prophet eliminated by this Divine inspiration. The individual peculiarity of the prophet is a prime factor in the form in which the revelation *comes* to him. In the one prophet we find a preponderance of visions; another prophet has no visions. But the visions of the future which the prophet sees are given in the forms and the colour which have been furnished by his own consciousness. All the more, the form in which the prophet *gives expression* to his word of God is determined by his personal talents and gifts as also by his experiences."

The early Christian apologists, living amid paganism, were well warranted in pointing to the contrast between the frenzied hysteria of pagan pseudo-inspiration and the dignity, self-possession, and active intelligence of the Hebrew prophets.

THE PROPHETS AS A CLASS

In a former study we have seen that the origin of the prophetic order in Israel dates back to Samuel. Of course, there were those in Israel, even before Samuel's time, on whom the mantle of prophecy had fallen (Num. xi. 25; Judges vi. 8). Moses himself is called a prophet (Deut. xviii. 18). But before Samuel there was no organised prophetic *office* in Israel. It was Samuel who originated the "schools" of the prophets, and thus, also, the prophetic *order*. In this sense he is "the first of the prophets"— a distinction which the New Testament clearly recognises, in Acts iii. 24; xiii. 20; and Hebrews xi. 32. From Samuel's time the "schools of the prophets" were planted up and down the land (2 Kings ii. 3, 5); and it was from these that there came, in due course, such men as Isaiah and his compeers, who, as their writings show, were men of education.

It is in connection with Samuel that we first find mention of any such colony of prophets; and this was at Ramah (1 Sam. xix. 20). Thereafter, in other places, bands of youths seem to have gathered around experienced and accredited prophets, forming small colonies around them, learning from them, and seeking to imbibe their spirit.

But besides this, it is clear that the Holy Spirit Himself frequently operated in supernatural ways through these "schools of the prophets," and among these "sons of the prophets." They were centres of religious life, where "communion with God was sought by prayer and meditation, and where the recollection of the great deeds of God in the past seemed to prepare for the reception of new revelations" from Him. These schools, moreover, were centres of theocratic ideas and ideals from which consecrated young men went out to exert considerable influence in the nation, and to hold up the torch of Divine truth amid the dark days of apostasy. It seems likely, too, that sacred music and poetry were cultivated at these schools, and that sacred traditions were here treasured and transmitted both orally and in writing. It was in these colonies of devout young students that the Holy Spirit found a unique opportunity to express the mind of God to the nation through prepared vessels. It was in this way that there grew up in Israel a recognised prophetic *order*.

The Prophets in Relation to Priests and Levites

Thus, we have now marked, in the course of Israel's national history, the rise of five distinct orders—Priests, Levites, Judges, Kings, Prophets. This will immediately prompt the question to some minds: What was the relationship of the prophetic order to the priests and Levites? In the law of Moses we find the priesthood and the Levitical order clearly instituted; but there is no such institution of a prophetic office, though there certainly is a promise that from time to time God would send prophets when they were needed (Deut. xviii. 18, 19). What, then, of the relationship between the new order of the prophets and the long-established order of priests and Levites? The following answer is worth carefully remembering.

"The office of the prophet was extraordinary rather than ordinary. As His ordinary servants and teachers, God appointed the priests and Levites. They taught what the Law, as it stood, enjoined; and they performed the sacred rites which it demanded. But when, under this more formal teaching, the nation slumbered; when they came to rest on the mere letter of the Law; when they misapprehended its real character; or when they turned away from it—then appeared the prophet, to rouse, to excite, to warn the people, and to call them back to the real purport of their own institutions."

Yet although they were *extra*ordinary ministers of God, the prophets did not stand apart from the Law, or in any way act independently of it. They were neither to add to it nor to "diminish ought from it," any more than were the people themselves. We find, therefore, that "prophecy always takes its *ground* in the Law, to which it refers, from which it derives its sanction, and with which it is fully impressed and saturated. There is no chapter in the prophets in which there are not several references to the Law. The care of the prophets was to explain it, bring it home to the hearts of the people, and to preserve it vital in its *spirit*. It was, indeed, also their duty to point to future advancement, and to announce the dawn of better light, when the ever-living spirit of the Law should break through its hitherto imperfect forms, and make for itself another, more complete: but, for their own times, they thought not of altering any of the laws in question, even as to their form, and much less as to their spirit. For all change, for all essential development, they directed the view of their countrymen forward to the time of the Messiah, who Himself came not to destroy the Law, but to fulfil it, superseding its ritual symbols only by accomplishing all they were designed to shadow forth."

But we would emphasise that the *vital* distinction between the ordinary teachers of Israel and these *extra*ordinary teachers, the prophets, lay in the fact of which we have already spoken, namely, that the prophets were the subjects of a special Divine inspiration.

Finally, it is worth noting that, as 1 Samuel ix. 9 tells us, in earlier times prophets in Israel were called "seers." It says: "He that is now called a prophet was beforetime called a seer." The older name, "seer," however, although used far less than the name "prophet," persists right on to the time of the captivities (2 Chron. xxxiii. 18; xxxv. 15), and is used as synonymous with "prophet" (2 Sam. xxiv. 11; 2 Chron. xvi. 7, 10). This older name "seer" is noteworthy as indicating that which lay behind the inspired utterance of the prophet. He was a "seer"—a man supernaturally enabled to "see" things which lay beyond ordinary human knowledge. It is wise to note, however, that although a prophet is said to have "seen" some given matter, it does not mean necessarily that he must have seen it in the form of an optical vision, with his natural eyes. The prophet could "see" *words*, with his *inner* eyes (see Isa. ii. 1—"The *word* which Isaiah *saw*"). Similarly, when we are told that God *spoke* to the prophet, we are not necessarily to understand that there must have been a voice which could be heard by the physical ear. The vital thing in each case is that the prophet must have been able to distinguish sharply the Divine communication from his own personal consciousness. Only thus could there be either the authority or the compulsion to speak as the mouthpiece of God.

We need not speculate concerning the *modes* by which the Holy Spirit communicated special truth to these men—whether by dream, vision, voice, sign, or by a direct inward impact upon the mind. Mystery about such revelation and inspiration there assuredly is; but this in no wise discounts the proven facts which proclaim the *reality* of it.

TWELVE "SPIES" TO SEARCH THE LAND

Can they bring a good report?

1. What are the seven main book-groupings of the Old Testament?

2. Can you express in a single word or phrase the distinctive feature of each Old Testament book from Genesis to the Song of Solomon?

3. The books of the Prophets in our Old Testament are not in their chronological order. Could you give them in their chronological order—first, those to the northern kingdom (Israel), then those to the southern kingdom (Judah), then those during and after the Exile?

4. With which three *historical* books of the Old Testament should Haggai, Zechariah and Malachi be read?

5. Could you cite indications that some of the prophets whose names have come down to us, but without any writings from them, *did* write?

6. What is the etymological meaning of our word, "prophet"? What is the Hebrew word for a prophet? And what is prophecy in the non-predictive sense?

7. Illustrate from Nathan that although the Old Testament writings of the prophets are Divinely inspired, the prophets themselves were far from being infallible or perpetually inspired.

8. From what point of history do the prophets as a school or class begin? The first-mentioned *colony* of prophets—where was it, and with whom specially connected?

9. What, briefly, would you say was the relation of the prophets to the priests and Levites?

10. What, briefly, would you say was the mental condition of the prophet himself while under the influence of inspiration?

11. What was the older name for a prophet in Israel, and what does it signify?

12. At what date did the ten-tribed kingdom go into captivity, and to which nation? And at what date did Judah go into captivity, and to which nation?

THE BOOK OF THE PROPHET
ISAIAH (1)

Lesson Number 71

NOTE.—For this study read the whole Book of Isaiah through, marking any reference which Isaiah makes to himself and to his times. Note also that the four chapters xxxvi. to xxxix. are an historical interlude between the two main parts of the book.

According to the old tradition, the prophet *Isaiah* was sawn asunder. Of the truth of the tradition we cannot be sure, but we know that one of the earliest feats of the Higher Criticism was to perform the like operation upon his prophecy. So much is the theory of a divided prophecy gaining ground, that no one must make any pretension to scholarship if he hesitates to accept the double authorship of Isaiah. From chapter xl. to the close was written, we are told with tiresome iteration, not by Isaiah, but by a prophet of the Exile— the *Great Unknown*. By the way, it is remarkable how many *unknown* great men flourished among the Jews, and remained unknown to their posterity, until, in these enterprising days, the Higher Critics arose and discovered them, brought them into light *with the exception of their names*. How wondrously modest, how self-effacing, these writers had been! and how strangely unmindful of their best men had the people been! True, we know they did not always receive the God-sent messengers; they killed the prophets, and stoned them that were sent unto them. But *killing* a man is a different thing from *ignoring* a man. You cannot well put a man to death without recognising the fact that he had existence.

—*Archibald McCaig, LL.D.*

THE BOOK OF ISAIAH (1)

WHAT Beethoven is in the realm of music, what Shakespeare is in the realm of literature, what Spurgeon was among the Victorian preachers, that is Isaiah among the prophets. As a writer he transcends all his prophet compeers; and it is fitting that the matchless contribution from his pen should stand as leader to the seventeen prophetical books. All who have any sense of literary appreciation must be impressed by the combined excellences of Isaiah's style—its grandeur and dignity, its energy and liveliness, its profusion of imagery, its vividness of description, its forceful play on words, its dramatic and rhetorical touches, and last, but not least, its wonderful variety. If we were here making a literary study of Isaiah, we might find fascinating occupation in classifying the abundant examples of these literary excellences; but as our purpose is with spiritual meaning rather than literary merit we must not digress into this tempting "By-path Meadow"!

The *social status* of Isaiah seems to have been high. He had familiar interviews with kings Ahaz and Hezekiah (vii., xxxvii., etc.). He was historiographer at the Judæan court in Jotham's reign, and wrote accounts of the reigns of Uzziah and Hezekiah (2 Chron. xxvi. 22; xxxii. 32). His "book" bears throughout the stamp of a well-educated man. Nothing is known of his father, Amoz. Isaiah himself was a married man (vii. 3) and had two sons *Shear-jashub* ("A-remnant-shall-return"), and *Maher-shalal-hash-baz* ("Haste-ye-haste-ye-to-the-spoil"). His wife also possessed the gift of prophecy (viii. 3).

The *period* of Isaiah's ministry lay "in the days of Uzziah, Jotham, Ahaz, and Hezekiah, kings of Judah (i. 1). Therefore, even if he only commenced his prophetic career near the end of Uzziah's reign he continued for some sixty years. Allow say five years under Uzziah; add the sixteen years each of Jotham and Ahaz; then the first fourteen years of Hezekiah (when Isaiah announced the further fifteen years of life to Hezekiah; 2 Kings xviii. 2; xx. 6). This gives fifty-one years; and Isaiah evidently lived on after this. Jewish tradition says that he lived into the reign of Manasseh, under whom he suffered a horrible martyrdom for resisting that wicked king's doings, being placed in the hollowed trunk of a tree, and then "sawn asunder." It is thought that Hebrews xi. 37 alludes to this.

The *character* of Isaiah claims note. See his *boldness*, whether to king or people. He never stoops to curry favour. See his ardent *patriotism*. He is the enemy of all that is against the best interests of his nation. Yet equally there is a *tenderness*, and a *sympathy* which reaches out to other nations, uncramped by any narrow race-egoism. There is also a stormy *indignation* expressing itself in sarcasm and satire; but this is offset by a deep *reverence* and *spirituality*. The usual title for God is "The Holy One"; and there is a vivid sense of the majesty of God. Outward forms of religion are nothing without inward reality. Read through the book again, underscoring where these qualities speak. Boldness, patriotism, tenderness, broad sympathy, stormy indignation at hypocrisy, with deep spirituality and a profound sense of the Divine majesty—oh, these are grand qualities, and just such as need restoring to the preaching of our day!

The Times of Isaiah

When Isaiah came to the fore in Judah, the ten-tribed northern kingdom (Israel) was nearing its destruction by Assyria, after its apostate career of some two hundred years, under no less than nineteen kings, of eight different families. Against the fierce menace of the Assyrian emperor, Tiglath-Pileser II, effort was made among the nations of Palestine and Syria to form a confederacy under the leadership of Damascus, capital of Syria (Syria must not be confused with *Assyria*, the far greater power, of which the capital was Nineveh). Ahaz, king of Judah, would not join this confederacy. So Syria and Israel invaded Judah, to coerce Ahaz, and dealt heavy blows (2 Kings xvi.; 2 Chron. xxviii.). Ahaz then humbly craved the aid of the great Assyrian, who marched forth a great army which overthrew Syria and Israel; but Judah thereby became vassal to Assyria.

A little later, Tiglath-Pileser's successor, Shalmaneser IV, determined on the final destruction of Israel. After a three years' siege Samaria fell (2 Kings xvii. 4–6). Israel was "carried away into Assyria," and the ten-tribes were distributed through "the cities of the Medes." Isaiah would then be between fifty and sixty years old.

Judah remained vassal to Assyria till the reign of Hezekiah who rebelled (2 Kings xviii.). This move would be supported by Isaiah who ever advocated reliance on Jehovah, and freedom from foreign alliances. There were other voices, however, to which Hezekiah listened. These urged alliance with Egypt, the one power equal to Assyria (Isa. xxx. 2–4). When the Assyrian monarch (now Sennacherib) came to lay low the rebellious Jews Egypt failed to send aid, Judæa was overrun, and Hezekiah was forced to buy off the Assyrian with much gold and silver, and become vassal again (2 Kings xviii. 13–16). But Judah's intrigues with Egypt continued; and Sennacherib soon came back. While his main force cut off Egypt from Judah he sent a smaller force to threaten and if possible seize Jerusalem (Isa. xxxvi.; xxxvii.). At last Hezekiah fell back on Isaiah's advice. The result we well know. A mighty disaster befell the Assyrian army, from which Sennacherib never recovered. Judah was freed from threat of invasion, and enjoyed a good spell of peace.

Such were Isaiah's times. If this brief memorandum is kept in mind, passages which seem obscure will become vividly intelligible.

The "Book" of Isaiah

Until a hundred years ago Isaiah's authorship of the book which bears his name was unquestioned. Then a theory stole in among rationalistically inclined Bible scholars, that chapters xl.–lxvi. were from a different writer, at the end of the Babylonian captivity, some two hundred years after Isaiah. But this theory of dual authorship did not long appease the dissective mania of more modern critics. Ewald discovered seven authors in the book. Yet even seven soon became inadequate for some of the dissectors. Thanks to the ingenious insight of the modern school, the theory of composite authorship has been elaborated into a perfect complexus. Professor Cheyne wrote: "It is becoming more and more certain that the present form of the prophetic Scriptures is due to a literary class (the so-called Sopherim, 'scribes' or 'Scripturists') whose principal function was collecting *and supplementing* the scattered records of prophetic revelation. *They wrote, they recast, they edited. . . .*" In the *Cambridge*

Bible for Schools and Colleges Professor Skinner wrote: "The book which bears the name of Isaiah is in reality a collection of prophetic oracles, showing manifest traces of composite authorship, and having a complicated literary history behind it. Not much less than two thirds of its bulk consists of anonymous prophecies . . . to this class belongs first of all the whole of the latter part of the book . . . but even when we confine our attention to chapters i.–xxxix. we still find abundant evidence of great diversity of authorship." So there we are!—our "Book of Isaiah" is a sheer patchwork from a combination of anonymous authors whose number no one knows!

But is this *really* so? The plurality of authorship has been argued on three grounds—(1) differences of vocabulary; (2) differences of ideas and forms of expression; (3) differences in historical references. All agree that the book is in two main parts (i.–xxxix. versus xl.–lxvi.), and that these two have a different "feel" from each other. Yet the difference is no greater than that between other writings from one author. As is now well proven, several writings from one author often differ strikingly in all three ways mentioned above, simply according to difference of subject. If Isaiah's modern critics applied their methods to the writings of present-day authors they would be a laughing-stock. Fortunately for them, Isaiah is not here to reprove them; but their superficiality has been exposed by other modern scholars who have checked their so-called "findings."

Plural Authorship Argued from Vocabulary

In the earlier phases of the controversy stress was laid on difference of *vocabulary*. Dr. Driver supported his "two Isaiahs" theory by words which he said occurred *only* in the second part of the book; but the late John Urquhart so exposed his mistakes as to reduce his argument to contempt. The word *bachar*, "to choose," was one such word, but it was replied that it came four times in the first part: so Dr. Driver then explained that it was only in the sense of God's choosing Israel that it only came in the second part. Even then he overlooked that it occurs in that very sense in chapter xiv. 1.

Tehillah—"praise," and *halal*—"to praise," were said to come only in the second part; yet *halal* comes in chapter xxxviii. 18, translated as "celebrate"! Even in part two it only comes twice! *Tehillah* comes nine times in part two, and it is clear why, namely, that it accords with the writer's new subject. This same word, simply for the same reason, comes more often in the Book of Psalms than in all the other books of the Old Testament together. Dr. Driver wanted to show that these words were *late* words which only a writer long after Isaiah would use; but, as we have shown, *halal* comes in the first part of the book, which he allows came from the real Isaiah; and as for *tehillah*, it comes no less than six times in the first group of the psalms (i.–xli.), which group, as all critics agree, contains probably the oldest psalms in the Psalter! *Tehillah* also occurs away back even in Deuteronomy (x. 21; xxvi. 19), in places which only extreme acrobatics of criticism can make post-exilic!

We can only glance at one more specimen, so we pick from the end of Dr. Driver's list. He says that *pa-er*, which, in its reflexive form means "to deck oneself" or "to glory," comes in chapters xliv. 23; xlix. 3; lv. 5; lx. 7, 9, 13 21; lxi. 3, and that, its use is "especially of Jehovah either glorifying Israel or glorifying Himself in Israel." He admits that it comes once in Isaiah proper (i.–xxxix.), in chapter x. 15, but only in its use of "the axe" as "*boasting itself*" against its user. This is hair-splitting if you like! But there is more than this. Once again Dr. Driver was careless. The word comes in chapter iii. 20, used exactly as in the second part of the book! Compare chapter iii. with lxi. 3. The latter verse speaks of "beauty for ashes"; and the word "beauty" here is a form of *pa-er*, meaning, literally, a headdress, or garland. In chapter iii. 20 it is used in exactly the same sense, only it is translated as "bonnets."

We say no more. Dr. Driver was singled out because he was considered a brilliant champion of this linguistic argument. Such tissue-paper expedients have so crumpled up that another eminent critic, Professor Cheyne, has had to say: "My own opinion is that the peculiar expressions of the latter prophecies are, on the whole, not such as to necessitate a different linguistic stage from the historical Isaiah; and that, consequently, the decision of the critical question will mainly depend on other than purely linguistic questions."

But we may now turn round on the critics, and say that if Isaiah *was* the author of the whole book, there will be linguistic evidences of it. Such evidences there are in abundance. The late Professor T. R. Birks of Cambridge found them so numerous that he limited himself just to words beginning with *aleph*, the first letter of the Hebrew alphabet. We have not room to detail these here. He cites forty of them, all arguing the falsity of any supposed duality or plurality of authorship based on vocabulary. Even by the grudging admission of the critics themselves, the facts point the other way; and all who know how jealous our modern scholars are not to concede a point to the more conservative school will realise that such admission really means that on linguistic grounds the evidence is in favour of *one author for the whole book.*

On this question of vocabulary and style I cannot do better than append the following quotation from a pamphlet by the late Dr. T. W. Fawthrop, which he sent to me for this purpose, shortly before his passing.

"We all agree that there are the differences, but these do not necessarily demand another authorship. Isaiah is versatile, and doubtless had several styles. His long experience would give him fluency of expression, and these later prophecies belong to his quiet years of retirement, at the close of his political career. Now if Isaiah, after writing his account of Sennacherib's invasion, had retired from active life, and spent about twenty years in restful meditation, and then reappeared in literary life with his mind filled with Messianic prophecy, and a deeper spirituality, is it not highly probable that this later thought would be presented in different style and language? Compare the sermons of a busy preacher, in a populous working-class district, with those preached in life's later retirement of quiet thought, balanced conclusions, and deeper spirituality.

"Consider again the different style of authors. Would anyone have thought that *The Pickwick Papers* and *The Tale of Two Cities* were both from the pen of Charles Dickens; or *The Lord of the Isles* and *Kenilworth* by Sir Walter Scott? But all the differences in the Book of Isaiah are consistent with his authorship. The author sorrows in his retirement over an erring nation, and our all-beneficent Heavenly Father grants him visions of restoration. The first part of the book ends in Exile, causing gloom to the faithful expecting redemption, so the second part tells of the Restoration and the triumphs of Messiah's kingdom, to remove the shadows. There is a unity running through both parts. Disappointing history merges into prophetic promise. There is a resemblance to our three historical Gospels, and the Master's conversations in St. John's Gospel. The mellowness of the second part shows it belongs to the prophet's later years.

"When the Book of Isaiah was compiled, what induced the scholars to add part II to part I? Although the closing verses of the Book of Amos refer to the doom of Edom (Amos ix. 12), and the twenty-one verses of the Book of Obadiah continue about Edom, the scholars have not added them to the Book of Amos. Why? It is because they knew them to be by another prophet. Why add part II to Isaiah? Because they knew the second part was also his; they knew no second Isaiah. All antiquity, and all Hebrew (Jewish) scholars, know but one Isaiah.

"The two parts of Isaiah have likenesses as well as differences. When the destructive critics have parted the supposed authors at the end of chapter xxxix, their theories require portions of part I to be transferred to part II, and of part II to part I. For if Isaiah's prophecies end with the Exile, then all relating to the Fall of Babylon, and later than the Exile, found in part I, must be transferred to part II. There is much to transfer.

"But are these critics, by their rules, able to detect the different authors? We cannot do it today. Tate and Brady together wrote the hymn, 'As pants the hart for cooling streams,' who is going to tell us how much is by Tate, and how much by Brady? Sir W. Robertson Nicoll tells of Robert Louis Stevenson collaborating with Lloyd Osborne in a certain novel. Professor Neil, of Cambridge, was confident that he could detect the parts which each had written. When his decisions were taken to the one who had arranged the novel, Neil was wrong in nearly every decision. But if the critics fail in modern literature, what of 2,650 years ago? We shall have need of better proof before we swear allegiance to Isaiah II."

Plural Authorship Argued from Ideas

But plural authorship is also said to be indicated by *differences of ideas and forms of expression*. Kuenen says: "There are diversities of language and style which compel us to distinguish the author of chapters xl.–lxvi. from Isaiah himself. The Deutero-

Isaiah uses a certain number of words foreign to Isaiah, or rather which are employed by him in a different sense. Thus Jehovah, for the Deutero-Isaiah, is He who *formed* Israel (xliii. 1, etc.). He is the *creator* (xliii. 1, 15); the *saviour* (xlv. 15, etc.); the *redeemer* (xli. 14, etc.); the *comforter* (li. 12) of Israel; He *has mercy* on His people (xlix. 10). In the authentic prophecies of Isaiah, Jehovah bears none of these names, any more than one finds the expressions *as nothing* (xl. 17, etc.); *all flesh* (xlix. 26, etc.); and a multitude of others."

Will it seem too strange to believe?—each of these words *is* used in the first thirty-nine chapters, with just the same *idea* as in the later chapters! We have not space to show this in each case. Take simply the *first*, as evidence of our honesty about the others. The Hebrew word here for "formed" is *yatsar*. Turn now, in the first part of the book, to chapter xxvii. 11, where the same word and idea occur—"*He that formed them will show them no favour.*" Is it surprising that we should distrust the dicta of such men?

There is really no need to give further instances. The critics themselves have been obliged to make the almost humorous plea that the "Deutero-Isaiah" (or Isaiahs) *copied the style* of the real Isaiah! Cheyne says: "The 'Great Unnamed,' if a different writer from Isaiah, often imitated his style and knew his prophecies by heart"! L. Seinecke says: "No other prophet has so maintained the spirit of Isaiah as the author of chapters xl.-lxvi. With no other do we find his *characteristic manner of speaking* so well reproduced"! Orelli says that the author of the second part, if not Isaiah, has "assumed his form." Other examples might be given; but is there need? This badly battered argument of the critics has been floored and "counted out" by those who backed it!

No one has ever denied that certain words and phrases *do* occur more often in chapters xl.-lxvi. than in chapters i.-xxxix., but the obvious explanation lies in change of subject. The first part is mainly upbraidings for sin, and warnings of coming judgment. In the second part the judgment is seen as having fallen, and Israel is felled to the ground. The message is now one of comfort and hope and healing. How could there *not* be noticeable differences in the thoughts expressed and the words used? Not one of these differences is incompatible with the older view of *one author for the whole book*. As a matter of fact, the Hebrew in the second part of the book is irreconcilable with a late exilic date. An author born and bred in Babylonia would have given us a writing as clearly marked by Aramaisms as those of Daniel and Ezekiel, whereas the language of Isaiah xl.–lxvi. is among the purest Hebrew in the Old Testament.

The supposed difference of ideas in the two parts of the book is sometimes put in another way. It is said that the theology in the second part is more advanced. In reply to this we quote Dr. Fawthrop again.

"All students note this advanced theology, but the destructive critics can only account for it on the lines of evolutionary and chronological progress. We maintain that the days of Isaiah were much more likely to attain to this excellence, than the decadent days of the Exile. As Dr. Orr points out, it is unlikely that a prophet of the rank of the writer of the second part of Isaiah would arise in the days of Ezra, or Nehemiah. But if these later chapters were the product of Isaiah's retirement from public life, then the marked advance in spirituality can be accounted for by his study, meditation, prayer and growth in grace. The lapse of twenty years would bring new visions of God, and deeper understanding of His Word. How different is the forceful, buoyant style of the young preacher, from the thoughtful maturity of life's latest years! Did not St. John, a son of thunder (Boanerges), ripen into the disciple of love?

"As to the magnificence of the picture, in Isaiah liii., of the suffering Servant of Jehovah dying for humanity, it is the climax of prophecy. The prophet minutely foretells the sufferings of Jesus, who lived seven hundred years later. The Jews admit this, although they adopt various subterfuges to avoid the acceptance of Him as Messiah. But the Ethiopian eunuch was assured by Philip the Evangelist, that Isaiah referred to Jesus Christ (Acts viii. 32–5). How could the name of the prophet of such mighty utterance have been permitted to vanish away? Well might Ewald describe him as "The Great Unknown." How can we think of him as some nameless wanderer, whom, for the lack of a better name, we call the second Isaiah! Better far is it to visualise Isaiah meditating on his own sufferings, his appeals spurned, and himself despised, his martyrdom drawing near; then he is given for his support the greater visions of the sufferings of the Man of Sorrows, the highest and holiest prophecy of redemption, and the dawn of the Messianic kingdom of the Christ who is to be."

Author's Note

Parts of these studies in the *authorship* of the Book of Isaiah were written in the nineteen-thirties. Some of the names of Higher Critical scholars mentioned in them have quickly receded and already begin to seem "yesterdayish"; but it is to be remembered that their conclusions and positions are still the intellectual "fashion" in many theological seminaries, so that the arguments here submitted against them are still as needed as ever.

I think it is true to say that "Modernism" as a *school* has been well and truly answered, and that as a *phase* it is passing, if not now past; but that as a *spirit* and *attitude* it lingers still and seems like doing so for some time. The so-called "Neo-Orthodoxy" associated with Barth and Brunner, and to a considerable degree including leaders like Tillich, Niebuhr, Kraemer and Edwin Lewis, has sounded the death-knell on the older form of Modernism; yet that older form of it, which will always be associated in our minds with the so-styled "Higher Criticism," has left a miserable residuum of doubt concerning the literal veracity of the Bible, and a stolid disinclination to accept the definitely supernatural in Scripture. We cannot but have this in mind through all our ensuing studies in the Old Testament prophets. My own reading convinces me that the leaders of the "Neo-Orthodoxy" *assume*, generally speaking, the results of the more radical "Higher Criticism." The Higher Critics argued. The Neo-Orthodox assume. The former attacked the historical facts of the Christian faith; the latter now by-pass them as not vitally necessary to Christian faith. There is a brilliantly presented new emphasis, but the inner attitude of mind toward the Bible and the historical facts of Christianity and the miraculous is practically the same as that of the older Modernism.

THE BOOK OF ISAIAH (2)

Lesson Number 72

The Old Testament literature falls into two main periods: that composed before and during the Babylonian Exile, and that which falls after the Exile. But even between these two periods the differences of language are comparatively slight, so that it is often difficult or impossible to say on linguistic grounds alone whether a particular chapter is pre- or post-exilic, and scholars of the first rank often hold the most contrary opinions on these points.

—*Thomas Hunter Weir*

THE BOOK OF ISAIAH (2)

Plural Authorship Argued from Historical References

THE COMPOSITE authorship of our "Book of Isaiah" has been argued most of all on the ground of its *divergent historical references*. The big contention is that the standpoint of the writer, or writers, in chapters xl.–lxvi. is that of an exile, or exiles, in Babylonia, writing after Jerusalem and the temple had for years lain in ruins. This brings us to one of the most serious defaults in the "modern" school of higher criticism. The purpose underlying much of the arguing for the composite authorship of the book is the eliminating of the supernatural from it. Not a few of the moderns evidently disbelieve in supernatural prediction, and, therefore, to them, it is not allowable that Isaiah should speak of an event long before its occurrence. Thus, when they come to any passage which is predictive they immediately assign it to an origin late enough to nullify this supernatural element. We do not assert this without qualification of *all* those critics who have questioned the unity of the book; there are shades and grades; but it is true of *many*; and it is because of this that in still more recent days not only has there been argued a different authorship for the second part of the book (xl.–lxvi.) from that of the first part, but even the first part has been represented as a veritable mosaic from a variety of anonymous writers. Let us not wrap it up—this is the motive, and the arguments about differences of style and ideas are merely props to supply a seemingly scholarly support.

Do we seem to be unkindly misrepresenting the scholars in question? Then let us hear what some of their own representatives say. Knobel says: "Isaiah, at the Assyrian epoch, was not able to announce the deliverance from the captivity, by Cyrus, seeing that in his time that captivity had no existence." Vatke says: "At the time of Isaiah the kingdom of the Chaldeans had as yet no existence; it began to exist only in 625 B.C., how then would the prophet have been able to represent it as near to its decline?" Noldeke says: "A prophecy in which Cyrus is called by his name is not naturally the work of Isaiah, who could not know in advance either the exile of the people to Babylon, or the deliverance from that exile by Cyrus." Some of our British and American critics have adopted a more apologetic attitude, perhaps, yet they really take the same position. Professor Skinner, for instance, says of Isaiah xiii. and xiv. that they cannot be from Isaiah himself because they refer to what is future, and then adds: "On the principle that the prophet always addresses himself primarily to the circumstances of his own time, we must assign these chapters to the closing years of the Babylonian captivity."

Hostility to the Supernatural.

We know now where we are! It is this *hostility to supernatural prediction* which underlies the more rabid higher criticism. The one answer is to exhibit the plentiful and unanswerable evidence of fulfilled prediction throughout the Scriptures. This has been done again and again by able students, and it is neither needful nor possible to cover all that ground again here: it would require a volume to itself! One only needs to read a work like *Keith on Prophecy*, not to mention more recent works on the same line, to know how full and final the argument is. Moreover, among the moderns themselves, the more thorough and straightforward are obliged to recognise that not even the late-dating of chapters xl.–lxvi. can quite expunge supernatural prediction. Thus, Professor G. A. Smith agrees that chapter liii. "as a prophecy of Jesus Christ is surely as great a marvel if you date it from the Exile as if you date it from the age of Isaiah."

So, then, with the more outright critics, the position is, that since supernatural prediction is *a priori* out of the question, those passages which refer to events and circumstances later than Isaiah's own time must be by a later author. In order to bolster up this position they try to make out that the whole scenery of chapters xl. to lxvi. is Exilic and not Isaian.

Now to those of us who believe in the Divine inspiration of the Scriptures, the miracle of prediction presents no difficulty whatever: but what of the *scenery* of chapters xl. to lxvi.? That is something that should be settled. Does it favour a Babylonian origin or a Judæan and Isaian?

Geographical and Historical Background

Now without a doubt, the first thing that strikes the mind of a careful reader is that the local background is *the same in both parts of the book*; the next thing is that this common background is *Palestinian and not Babylonian*. We here give references indicating that this is so in *both* parts of the book; for, in more recent days, as we have already mentioned, many passages in the *first* part of the book (i.–xxxix.) have been assigned to the late, exilic date, as well as chapters xl.–lxvi.

Perhaps we scarcely need point out the many references to *Lebanon*, with its mighty cedars (ii. 13; x. 34; xiv. 8; xxix. 17; xxxiii. 9; xxxv. 2; xxxvii. 24; xl. 16; lx. 13). Let the *trees* to which the book refers bear their testimony—"cedars," "oaks," "firs," "pines," "box trees," "sycamores," "cypresses," "shittah trees," "olives," "vines," "myrtles" (i. 8, 30; ii. 13; iii. 14; v. 1–10; vi. 13; vii. 23; ix. 10; xiv. 8; xvi. 8–10; xvii. 6; xxiv. 7, 13; xxvii. 2; xxxii. 12; xxxiv. 4; xxxvi. 16, 17; xxxvii. 24, 30; xli. 19; xliv. 14; lv. 13; lx. 13; lxi. 5; lxv. 21). All of these trees are Palestinian, or at any rate Syrian. And with this put the fact that there is not one single mention of the palm tree, which was the chief tree of Babylonia. Note, too, that in the above references, each of these trees is mentioned in the *second* part of the book, except for the sycamore and olive. Bashan, Sharon and Carmel are mentioned (ii. 13; xxxiii. 9; xxxv. 2; xxxvii. 24; lxv. 10). The water spoken of is that of "fountains," "streams," "pools" or reservoirs and "springs" (xxx. 25; xxxiii. 21; xxxiv. 9; xxxv. 6, 7; xli. 18; xlii. 15; xlix. 10; lvii. 6; lviii. 11)—all common to Palestine; whereas the great river Euphrates, the glory of Babylon, is only mentioned anonymously in one passage, and that passage is one which, so far as I know, all critics agree to be a genuine prophecy of *Isaiah himself* (vii. 20; viii. 7). But read again—of "rocks" and "ragged rocks" and "clefts in the rocks" and "holes in the rocks" (ii. 10, 19, 21; vii. 19; xxxiii. 16; xlii. 22; lvii. 5)—utterly out of keeping with Babylon! Mountains, forests, woods, wild beasts of the forests—the mention of these, too, but adds to the Palestinian scenery which is everywhere in evidence (ii. 14; ix. 18; x. 18, 34; xiii. 4; xl. 12; xlii. 11; liv. 10; lv. 12, 13; lvi. 9; lix. 11, etc.).

Is it surprising that some of the critics themselves have had to admit the force of all this against the so-called "Babylonian standpoint" of chapters xl.–lxvi.? Cheyne says: "Some passages of Isaiah II are in various degrees really favourable to the theory of a Palestinian origin. Thus in chapter lvii. 6, the reference to torrent-beds is altogether inapplicable to the alluvial plains of Babylonia; and equally so is that to subterranian 'holes' in chapter xlii. 22; and though no doubt Babylonia was more wooded in ancient times than it is at present, it is certain that the trees mentioned in chapter xli. 19 were not for the most part natives of that country, while the date-palm, the commonest of all the Babylonian trees, is not once referred to."

But if the scenery is thus Palestinian, what of the *historical* allusions? Well, how shall we reconcile such a passage as chapter lvii. with the supposed Babylonian standpoint of chapters xl.–lxvi.? Take verses 4 to 7—

"Are ye not children of transgression, a seed of falsehood, enflaming yourselves with idols under every green tree, slaying the children in the valleys under the cliffs of the rocks? Among the smooth stones of the stream (or torrent) is thy portion; they, they are thy lot; even to them hast thou poured a drink-offering. . . . Upon a high and lofty mountain hast thou set thy bed: even thither wentest thou up to offer sacrifice."

"Rocks," "valleys," "high mountains," stony-bedded "torrents" —where were these to be found on the flat stretches of Babylonia? And what of verse 9?—

"And thou wentest to the king with ointment, and didst increase thy perfumes, and didst send thy messengers far off, and didst debase thyself even unto hell."

This is no picture of the Jews in exile. Judah here is still a *kingdom*—an anxious little kingdom sending ambassadors to seek alliances with foreign powers, and debasing herself thereby. Does it not at once suggest the times of Ahaz and Hezekiah, the very time when Isaiah himself lived? So strong is the indication of Palestinian origin in such passages that one by one these chapters have been slowly conceded to the older view of pre-exilic authorship. Here, again, a closer study shows that the real facts are in favour of *one author for the whole book.*

Positive Arguments for Isaian Authorship

Finally, we sum up very briefly the evidences for Isaiah's authorship of the whole book. These may be grouped as external and internal. As for the *external* evidences, we put first the witness of the *Septuagint*. This standard version of the Hebrew Scriptures into Greek, remember, was made in the third century B.C., yet as early as that it ascribes the whole book to Isaiah. We cannot think this was merely an uncritical convenience, for the same version is careful not to ascribe all the psalms to David, though it would have been a similar convenience to give his name to the whole book, as being its main author.

Next, we take the apochryphal book of *Ecclesiasticus*, written by Jesus, the son of Sirach, which also dates back to the third century B.C. He distinctly ascribes chapters xl.–lxvi. to Isaiah; and his witness is weighty, for he is declared to have been a man of "great diligence and wisdom" and of "great learning." He certainly speaks for all the learned Jews of his time.

Next we hear *Josephus*, the famous Jewish historian of the first century A.D. His testimony is striking. He reports this decree of Cyrus: "Thus saith Cyrus the king: Since God Almighty hath appointed me to be king of the habitable earth, I believe that He is that God whom the nation of the Israelites worship; for, indeed, He foretold my name by the prophets, and that I should build Him a house at Jerusalem, in the country of Judæa." Josephus adds: "This was well known to Cyrus by his reading the book which Isaiah left behind him of his prophecies." It may be said that we should not give too much credence to Josephus here; but his word certainly fits with the decree of Cyrus which is given both at the end of 2 Chronicles and in the first verses of Ezra, wherein Cyrus says: "Jehovah, God of heaven . . . hath charged me to build Him an house at Jerusalem which is in Judah." But how did Cyrus know that Jehovah had "*charged*" him? Say that Isaiah wrote the prophecies which bear his name, and the answer is clear.

Most of all, there is the witness of *the New Testament*. Quite apart from references to other parts of Isaiah, there are nine places where the New Testament refers to the *second* part (xl.–lxvi.) and attributes the authorship to him. Critics have tried to nullify the force of these by suggesting that Isaiah's name is only mentioned by way of reference, without the point of strict authorship being in mind at all. Deny the unique inspiration of the New Testament, and you are at liberty to claim this—though you must also explain, as one has put it, "how this uninspired New Testament stands peerless amid all the literature of the Christian ages." But if the New Testament be indeed the inspired word of God its witness on this point is final.

Both parts of Isaiah are quoted by St. John (xii. 38–40), and accredited to the one Isaiah; from part II, "That the saying of Isaiah the prophet might be fulfilled which he spake, 'Lord, who hath believed our report?'" (Isa. liii. 1); from part I, "Therefore they could not believe because that Isaiah said again, 'He hath blinded their eyes,'" (Isa. vi. 9). Notice, "Isaiah said again," not another, either first or second Isaiah, but the same. Then Jesus *puts the two sayings together*, exclaiming, "These things said Isaiah, when *he* saw His glory," not, when *they* saw (John xii. 41).

But now we return to certain *internal* proofs that Isaiah wrote the whole book. Here, first, we mention *similarity of quality and genius throughout the book*. Not only is the genius which expresses itself in the disputed chapters equal to that in the undisputed, but it is genius of exactly the same kind. This has had to be acknowledged even by those who have doubted Isaiah's authorship of the latter part. How could they but acknowledge it with chapters xl., xliii., li., lii., liii., lxiii., and other such sublime passages before them?

Second, there is *similarity of language and constructions*. To demonstrate this would require an expert, elaborate treatise which we are not able to furnish; but it will be enough to array some of the specialists who vouch for it—Delitzsch, Professors T. R. Birks and Stanley Leathes, Dr. William Kay, of *The Speaker's Commentary*, Dean Payne Smith, Dr. S. Davidson, in his *Introduction to the Old Testament*, and T. K. Cheyne, whose verdict against the linguistic argument for a plural authorship has been already noted.

Next, we mention *similarity of ideas*. It would take pages to exhibit this with adequacy. We can but give a few leading examples. The dominant thought of the Divine holiness, with the favourite title for God as "The Holy One of Israel" (twelve times in the first part, thirteen in the second, and only five times in the rest of the Old Testament); the thought of the Divine *power*, of God as "the Mighty One of Israel"; the entering of the high and holy One into covenant with Israel; their having rebelled and broken the covenant; their being cast off yet not wholly forsaken; the "remnant," the "return," the calling of the Gentiles, the coming King and His reign of righteousness—these are all recurrent in both parts of the book.

There is also a clear *similarity of images*. We think of "light" and "darkness," of "blindness" and "deafness," of humanity as "the flower that fadeth," of the "rod" and the "stem," or "sprout," as applied to the Messiah; the "stakes" and "cords" of the tent as used of Jerusalem; the "wolf" and the "lamb" dwelling together in the future kingdom, and there being no "hurting or destroying" in all God's "holy mountain"—these, not to mention others, are all found in both parts of the book.

There are also correspondences between the two parts by way of *repetition*. Noteworthy instances of this are picked out in the *Pulpit Commentary*. In chapter xi. 7 we read: "The lion shall eat straw like the ox." We have the same in chapter lxv. 25. These are other references—chapters i. 13 with lxvi. 3; i. 29 with lxvi. 17; xi. 9 with lxv. 25; xiv. 24 with xlvi. 10; xvi. 11 with lxiii. 15; xxiv. 19, 20 with li. 6; xxiv. 23 with lx. 19; xxv. 8 with lxv. 19; xxvi. 1 with lx. 18; xxvii. 1 with li. 9.

But there is one other point which we must mention. To our mind it absolutely settles the matter. *There are quotations from the second part of Isaiah by other Old Testament prophets who wrote before the Exile*, and these, of course, prove that the second part of Isaiah must *already* have been written! All agree that the first two chapters of Zephaniah were written years before the Exile: yet Zephaniah ii. 15 is a quotation from the words of Isaiah xlvii. 8–11. The prophet Nahum was only a few years later than Isaiah himself; yet in Nahum i. 15 we find an appropriation of Isaiah lii. 7. The prophet Jeremiah was later, yet he was pre-exilic; and can we mistake the derivation of his phraseology in chapter xxxi. 35 from Isaiah li. 15? It is futile to suggest that instead of these three prophets having quoted from Isaiah, the anonymous "second" Isaiah (or Isaiahs) quoted from *them*; for the words are unmistakably Isaiah's *style*, and in each case they occur in *obvious sequence* and as *natural parts* in the progress of the passages in Isaiah where they occur, whereas in the other three prophets the connection is less intimate and spontaneous. With this topstone of evidence, the case for Isaiah's authorship is, to our own judgment, complete. We believe that the book is one, and that it was written by the Isaiah who prophesied "in the days of Uzziah, Jotham, Ahaz, and Hezekiah, kings of Judah."

THE BOOK OF ISAIAH (3)

Lesson Number 73

NOTE.—For this third instalment on Isaiah read the first thirty-five chapters afresh, marking the main breaks in subject which by now will be making themselves clear.

Human philosophy starts with a question. The Bible starts with an assumption: "In the beginning *God*". The deduction from that assumption is that all wisdom is in God; that in the last analysis there is no such thing as a riddle of the universe. When philosophy has wrought its way round the circle, it will arrive where these men start—GOD.

—*G. Campbell Morgan, D.D.*

THE BOOK OF ISAIAH (3)

WE ARE now ready to explore this Book of Isaiah. Its main arrangement cannot easily be forgotten. As there are sixty-six books in the Bible, so there are sixty-six chapters in this Book of Isaiah as it appears in our English version; and as the sixty-six books of the Bible are divided into the thirty-nine of the Old Testament and the twenty-seven of the New, so the sixty-six chapters of Isaiah are divided into thirty-nine and twenty-seven. Moreover, as the thirty-nine books of the Old Testament are mainly occupied with the Law, and the judgment which comes on those who disobey it, so the first thirty-nine chapters of Isaiah are mainly occupied with the thought of judgment on the covenant people because of their disobedience to the Law; and as the twenty-seven books of the New Testament are mainly occupied with the message of Divine grace, and the salvation which it brings, so the last twenty-seven chapters of Isaiah are a message of Divine grace and comfort, and of coming salvation. Thus, the Book of Isaiah is a kind of Bible all in itself.

So much for the main arrangement; but is there any methodical *sub*dividing of the two main parts? To be quite frank, it may be that some of us, on reading this book for the first time or two, thought it almost impossible to resolve its many chapters into orderly and progressive groups. Yet method and progress there certainly are. It is quite fascinating to see how the book opens to a patient and observant eye. Let us pick our way through it, and note down what we find.

We start at the opening words of chapter i. The august introduction here makes it clear that this is the *true* beginning (not chapter vi., as some have suggested)—

"HEAR, O HEAVENS, AND GIVE EAR, O EARTH,"
"FOR JEHOVAH HATH SPOKEN"

This chapter is the initial indictment; and we note that it is addressed to *Judah and Jerusalem* (verses 1, 8, 21, 26, 27).

Chapters ii.–vi.

Next, we note that chapters ii. to v. are obviously linked together; *first*, by the fact that, whereas the opening words of
chapter ii. indicate a new vision, the opening words of the other
chapters indicate continuity; *second*, because all these chapters
are about the same subject, namely, the "day of Jehovah"
(ii. 11, 12, 17, 20; iii. 7, 18; iv. 1, 2; v. 30); *third*, because they all
directly concern *Judah and Jerusalem* (ii. 1, 3, 6; iii. 1, 8, 16;
iv. 3–5; v. 3). We also note that this section closes with six
"WOES" (v. 8, 11, 18, 20, 21, 22).

Chapter vi. clearly stands apart as to its subject. It is a striking
flash of autobiography. The prophet's new vision here is not of
his nation, but of God Himself; and it is meant to prepare him
for larger prophetic ministry. There is a new *vision* (verses 1–5),
a new *unction* (verses 6, 7), and a new *commission* (verses 9, 10).
But the big thing here is that Isaiah saw Jehovah as *KING*. The
high point is the awed exclamation: *"Mine eyes have seen the
King—Jehovah of Hosts!"* If we may anticipate the coming
chapters just for a moment, we are going to see that from this
point Isaiah's prophetic range wonderfully widens out; but
it was first needful that he should see Jehovah as King of all
nations, so as to sense vividly and be able to declare forcefully
that behind and above and beyond all the convulsions of which
he was to prophesy was the sovereign grip and purpose of the
universal Emperor, Jehovah. The *immediate* reference of this
sixth chapter, however, is again to *Judah and Jerusalem* (verses
5, 9–13); so that at any rate we may now mark off the first six
chapters of Isaiah as going together, in that they all *directly
concern Judah*, and in that their main subject is the "*day of
Jehovah.*"

Chapters vii.–xii.

We pass on to chapter vii. and those which follow. Here we
find six chapters which refer mainly to *Israel* (the northern, ten-
tribed kingdom, of which Samaria was the capital). See how
chapter vii. begins—"It came to pass . . . that Rezin the king
of Syria, and Pekah the son of Remaliah, king of *Israel*, went up
toward Jerusalem to war against it. . . ." See also verse 2,
where the name "Ephraim" is an alternative for Israel. Now

glance through the whole chapter again: it is all about Israel. To any reader who may be using the "Scofield Bible" we can only say that the inserted heading at verse 17 is surely wrong which says that the subsequent verses predict an invasion of *Judah*. Context and circumstances alike are so plain that it seems strange for such a mis-heading to occur. Syria and *Israel* are the invaders (verses 1, 2). It is *Israel* that is to be "broken that it be not a people" (verse 8). King Ahaz of Judah, who is besieged by Syria and Israel, is told that the land (Syria and *Israel*) before the two kings of which he is afraid, shall be forsaken (verse 16, see R.V.). The whole message is one of comfort to the besieged Ahaz (verses 3–16); but what strange comfort to be suddenly told, without any reason for the transition, that a far more deadly trouble was coming to Judah than anything just said of Israel!

No, at verse 17 it is the king of *Israel* who is now addressed directly. The wording makes this clear: "The Lord shall bring upon thee and upon thy people, and upon thy father's house, days that have not come, from the day that *Ephraim departed from Judah*: even the king of *Assyria*." In other words, there were days coming on Israel such as had not been since the ten-tribes set up as a separate kingdom; and the trouble was coming from *Assyria*. Now we well know that it was *Israel* which was destroyed by Assyria, not Judah; for although Assyria was also allowed to trouble Judah, Jehovah intervened, Assyria sustained a crippling reverse, and Judah was spared.

Chapter viii., which continues the same subject, makes it even clearer that it is Israel which is here spoken of. See verse 4: "The spoil of *Samaria* shall be taken away before the king of Assyria." See also verse 6, where the people who "rejoice in Rezin and Remaliah's son" certainly are not Judah! See also verse 7; and note verse 8 which clearly says that Assyria would, indeed, also "overflow" into Judah, exactly as Micah i. 9 says (see our comment on that verse), and thus distinguishing Judah from the words just uttered about Israel. The remainder of chapter viii. speaks of the "confederacy" which Syria and Israel wished to force on Judah (see our introductory remarks on the Times of Isaiah); but Israel comes to the fore again towards the end, and in chapter ix.

The connection between chapters viii. and ix. makes the main reference to Israel clearer still. It is a pity that the translation here in our Authorised Version is so confusing. Read it in the Revised Version. The last line of chapter viii. should really be the first of chapter ix., and instead of reading, "they shall be driven to darkness" (note the italicised words, showing that the translators felt difficulty here) it should read: "Yet the thick darkness shall be driven away." Thus, the last verse of chapter viii. and the first verse of chapter ix. should read—

And they shall look upward,
And they shall look earthward,
And behold distress and darkness,
Even the gloom of anguish.
Yet the darkness shall be driven away,
And there shall be gloom no more
    to her that was in anguish.
As in former time He brought to contempt
The land of Zebulon and the land of Naphtali,
So in the latter time He hath made it glorious,
The tract by the sea, the region beyond Jordan,
    Galilee of the nations. . . .

Observe, above, the mention of "Zebulon" and "Naphtali" and "Galilee," showing again that the reference is to *Israel*, not Judah. The reference to Israel is addedly clarified in the verses which follow (see verses 8, 9, 10, 12, 14, 21).

Chapter x. continues the same prophecy. Among other things, this is shown by the solemn refrain, "For all this His anger is not turned away, but His hand is stretched out still" (ix. 12, 17, 21; x. 4). In verses 5 to 34 the prophet breaks away to address *Assyria*, the power which was to destroy *Israel* and also afflict Judah (verses 11, 12). In the end Assyria herself should be destroyed. This leads to chapters xi. and xii. which describe the coming reign of the Messiah, in which the "outcasts of Israel" and the "dispersed of Judah" should be reunited (xi. 12).

We must pause here, at the end of chapter xii., for a mere glance at the opening words of chapter xiii. tells us that we there break away to a different subject. Looking back over chapters vii. to xii. we see that, just as chapters i.–vi. were mainly concerned with *Judah*, ending (in vi.) with a wonderful vision of Jehovah as the reigning King in heaven, so chapters vii.–xii. are mainly concerned with *Israel*, ending with a glorious vision of Jehovah as the reigning King on earth, in the Messianic kingdom which is yet to be. Nor must we omit to add that in chapters vii. to xii., just as in chapters i. to vi., we find recurrent references to the "day of Jehovah" (vii. 18, 20, 21, 23; x. 20, 27; xi. 10, 11; xii. 1, 4). Thus we may now say that the first six chapters concern the "day of Jehovah" mainly in relation to *Judah*, and the next six chapters the "day of Jehovah" mainly in relation to *Israel*.

Chapters xiii.–xxiii.

The remaining chapters in this first part of Isaiah group themselves with little difficulty. Chapters xiii. to xxiii. clearly belong together, for they are a succession of "*burdens*," all but one (that of the "Valley of Vision") being on the surrounding *Gentile* nations, as follows—

xiii.–xiv. 27	The burden of	Babylon.
xiv. 28–32	,,	Philistia.
xv.–xvi.	,,	Moab.
xvii.–xviii.	,,	Damascus.
xix.–xx.	,,	Egypt.
xxi. 1–10	,,	Desert of sea.
xxi. 11, 12	,,	Dumah (Edom).
xxi. 13–17	,,	Arabia.
xxii.	,,	Valley of Vision.
xxiii.	,,	Tyre.

Note also in these chapters the "day of Jehovah" (xiii. 6, 9, 13; xiv. 3; xvii. 4, 7, 9; xix. 16, 18, 19, 21, 23, 24; xx. 6, xxii, 12, 20, 25; xxiii. 15).

Chapters xxiv.–xxvii.

And now, in chapters xxiv. to xxvii. we have the "day of Jehovah" in relation to *the whole world*. That the language here does in reality embrace the whole earth is agreed by all expositors. Mark specially chapters xxiv. 1, 4, 5, 16, 19, 20, 21; xxv. 6, 7, **xxvi**, 21; xxvii. 1. See *now* how Isaiah's grasp is immensifying, and how necessary was that overawing vision in chapter vi.!— first of all the message was to *Judah*, then to *Israel*, then to all the surrounding *Gentile* nations, and now it is to *the whole world*!

There is no mistaking the subject in these four chapters: once again it is the "day of Jehovah" (xxiv. 21; xxv. 9; xxvi. 1; xxvii. 1, 2, 12, 13).

Chapters xxviii.–xxxiii.

The next six chapters (xxviii. to xxxiii.) group themselves off equally sharply. They consist of six "*woes.*" These all specially concern Jerusalem, which is ever the centre of all God's earth-dealings. Even though the first "woe" (xxviii.) turns its opening words on the "drunkards of Ephraim," these are but used as a warning to Judah. The words, "They also," in verse 7 (compare verse 14) swing the "woe" round on Judah. And although the last of these "woes" speaks anonymously of Assyria, as the "spoiler," yet the message is clearly to Jerusalem. Thus, the six "woes" of chapter v. on Jerusalem are now paralleled by these further six. The city of highest privilege is the city of heaviest responsibility! These are the six "woes"—

xxviii.	Drunkards of Ephraim and Judah.
xxix. 1	Hypocrites (verse 13) of Ariel.
xxix. 15	Evil schemers of Jerusalem.
xxx.	The revolters against Jehovah.
xxxi.	The Unholy Alliance-makers.
xxxiii.	The Assyrian Spoiler.

Notice the phrase, "the day of Jehovah" several times again in these "woe" chapters (xxviii. 5; xxix. 18; xxx. 23; xxxi. 7).

Chapters xxxiv.–xxxv.

Finally, in chapters xxxiv. and xxxv., we have the climactic prophetic outburst in this first part of Isaiah. They depict Jehovah's *world-vengeance* and *Zion's restoration.* Note chapter xxxiv. 8— "It is the day of Jehovah's vengeance, and the year of recompenses for the controversy of Zion." Although in this thirty-fourth chapter the fury is unleashed against Edom, in particular, yet it is perfectly clear that Edom is here used typically. See how the chapter begins—"Come near, ye *nations*, to hear; and hearken, ye people: let the *earth* hear, and all that is therein; the *world*, and all things that come forth of it. For the indignation of Jehovah is upon *all nations.* . . ." Isaiah here not only embraces all nations of the earth, he reaches right on to the end of history. Then, after this awful picture of vengeance, with its dark and lurid hues, he brings us to the tranquil, triumphant, and delectable picture of the final kingdom, in chapter xxxv. It is the picture of final grace and glory after sin and judgment. In chapter xxxiv we are in the "great tribulation" at the end of the present age. In chapter xxxv we are in the Millennium!

How remarkable, then, is the expanding development in this first part of Isaiah! Glance back quickly through these thirty-five chapters again. In the first six we are limited to Judah. But after the transforming vision of Jehovah as King of all nations and ages, in chapter vi, the prophecies reach out more and more, until they have comprehended all nations and all history! If in the first six chapters we are confined to Judah, in the next six we reach out to the ten-tribed kingdom of Israel. Then, in the next group (xiii to xxiii) all the main kingdoms of Isaiah's day are girdled. Then, in the next four chapters (xxiv to xxvii) the whole world is revolving before the eye of prophecy. Next, in chapters xxviii to xxxiii, it is Jerusalem which becomes the focus-point as being the centre of all Jehovah's dealings and controversy with our race. While finally, in chapter xxxiv, we are plunged into the "great tribulation" at the end of the present age, and then brought through to the lovely climax of the Millennium, in chapter xxxv! Is not that a wonderful expansion, development, progress, design? And does it not argue *one* human author behind the whole of it, even as it also indicates the one *Divine* Author behind the human?

An historical addendum.

At the end of the prophecies in this first part of Isaiah, there is an historical addendum of four chapters (xxxvi.–xxxix.). We cannot discuss the contents of these here, but we do want *this* fact to be grasped, that these four historical chapters are an evidently designed *transition* from the first part of the book to the second. The first two of these chapters are about the invasion of Judah by *Assyria* (after which time Assyria declines to her doom). The remaining two are about Hezekiah's illness, recovery, and contact with *Babylon*—which new world-power now begins to fill the scene. Thus these four chapters are a clearly intended transition from chapters i.–xxxv., in which *Assyria* is the dominant world-power, to chapters xl.–lxvi., in which *Babylon* is the dominant world-power.

So, then, we may now set out our findings in the first part of Isaiah as follows—

> i.–vi. The Day of Jehovah, and Judah.
> vii.–xii. The Day of Jehovah, and Israel.
> xiii.–xxiii. The ten burdens on the Nations.
> xxiv.–xxvii. The "Day," and the whole world.
> xxviii.–xxxiii. The six "woes" upon Jerusalem.
> xxxiv.–xxxv. The final wrath : Zion restored.
> xxxvi.–xxxix. Historical transition to part II.

THE BOOK OF ISAIAH (4)

Lesson Number 74

NOTE.—For this final study in Isaiah read chapters xl. to lxvi. again, marking carefully all references to Jehovah's "Servant" and those also which seem to refer to Him even though He is not actually referred to as the "Servant."

Men talk of the Divine history of the human race, but there is no such history. The Old Testament is the Divine history of *the family of Abraham.* The call of Abraham was chronologically the central point between the creation of Adam and the Cross of Christ, and yet the story of all the ages from Adam to Abraham is dismissed in eleven chapters. And if, during the history of Israel, the light of revelation rested for a time upon heathen nations, it was because the favoured nation was temporarily in captivity. But God took up the Hebrew race that they might be a centre and channel of blessing to the world. It was owing to their pride that they came to regard themselves as the only objects of Divine benevolence.

—Sir Robert Anderson

THE BOOK OF ISAIAH (4)

THE FIRST thirty-nine chapters of Isaiah have opened up encouragingly. What of the remaining twenty-seven? Do we find similarly clear arrangement in these? We do. In fact there is something more than arrangement merely: there is a most significant grouping. These chapters (xl.–lxvi.) which make up the second part of the book, by their very grouping proclaim a truth of utter importance and preciousness.

These twenty-seven chapters are a poem. They are a *Messianic* poem. Their ever-recurrent subject is the coming Christ, the redemption of Israel, and the ultimate consummation. The chapters are not detachable from each other: they go together to form the greatest Messianic poem in the Bible.

The twenty-seven chapters are arranged in three groups of nine chapters each, the end of each group being marked off by the same solemn refrain. Thus, at the end of the first nine (xlviii. 22) we read: "There is no peace, saith Jehovah, unto the wicked." Then, at the end of the second nine (lvii. 21) we read: "There is no peace, saith my God, to the wicked." Finally, at the end of the third nine (lxvi. 24) we have this again, but in amplified form: "Their worm shall not die, neither shall their fire be quenched; and they shall be an abhorring unto all flesh."

Whoever made the present arrangement into chapters, there can be little doubt that this tripartition of these twenty-seven chapters was definitely intended. But there is something deeper than merely human intention. There is Divine design. By common consent the greatest of all Old Testament passages concerning the atonement of Christ is Isaiah liii.; and is it not luminously significant that this immortal "Lamb" chapter is the middle chapter of the middle nine? At the very centre of this tremendous Messianic poem God has put the *LAMB*. He is the crux, the focus, the centre, the heart. Let us keep the Lamb where God has put Him—in the centre! Christ as the *Lamb* of God must be central in our faith and hope and love, in our preaching and teaching and witness-bearing, in our thought and prayer and Bible-study, even as God has made Him the centre of prophecy and history and redemption.

But we owe a closer look at these three nine-fold groups before we pass on. Each group has its own unmistakable emphasis. In the first group it is the *supremacy* of Jehovah. In the second group it is the *"Servant"* of Jehovah. In the third group it is the *challenge* of Jehovah.

Take the first group (xl.–xlviii.), where the stress is on the *supremacy* of Jehovah. There is clear progress of thought. In the first two chapters of this group (xl., xli.) Jehovah is seen as supreme in His *attributes* of omnipotence, omniscience, and omnipresence. Note, for instance, great passages like chapters xl. 12–28; xli. 4, etc., and 21–9. Next, in chapters xlii.–xlv., we have the supremacy of Jehovah in *redemption*. See chapters xlii. 5–9, 13–16; xliii. 1, 3, 10, 11, 12, 25; xlv. 5–8, 15–17, 20–2. Finally, in chapters xlvi.–xlviii., we see the supremacy of Jehovah in *judgment*. These three chapters are about judgment on Babylon and its gods, Bel, Nebo, etc. But note the further marked reference to the supremacy of Jehovah, in chapters xlvi. 5, 9, 10; xlvii. 4; xlviii. 12–14, 20–2.

And now take the second group (xlix.–lvii.), where the stress is on the *"Servant"* of Jehovah. The "Servant" has been mentioned before, in the earlier group, but is now brought into fuller prominence. In chapters xlix.–l. the reference, without a doubt, is primarily to the elect nation, Israel; though even here there is a latent, ultimate reference to Christ. But from chapter lii. 13 to the end of chapter liii. there is a breaking through into clear, full, glorious reference to the personal Messiah-Redeemer who was to come. Springing from this, in chapters liv. and lv. we have the restoration of the nation Israel, and the reigning of the Christ (lv. 4, etc.) as Davidic leader and commander. This group then closes, in chapters lvi., lvii., with an urgent appeal and a renewal of promise.

Finally, in the third group (lviii.–lxvi.) we have the *challenge* of Jehovah. There is a threefold presentation. First, there is the challenge in view of *present default* (lviii., lix.). Then there is the challenge in view of the simply *epochal prospects* rising up before Israel (lx.–lxv.). Chapter lxvi. winds up the wonderful poem with a closing challenge of final promise and warning.

Perhaps we ought now to set out in flat analysis both parts of this book of Isaiah. The central message is that *Jehovah is supreme Ruler and only Saviour*. In part one the key chapter is the sixth, where we have the prophet's vision of Jehovah as King. In part two the key chapter is the fifty-third, where we see the Lamb, first suffering and then triumphing.

THE BOOK OF ISAIAH

Jehovah, Supreme Ruler and only Saviour

ORACLES OF RETRIBUTION AND RESTITUTION

(i.–xxxix.)

i.–vi. The Day of Jehovah, and JUDAH.
vii.–xii. The Day of Jehovah, and ISRAEL.
xiii.–xxiii. The ten burdens on the NATIONS.
xxiv.–xxvii. The "Day" and the whole WORLD.
xxviii.–xxxiii. The six "woes" upon JERUSALEM.
xxxiv.–xxxv. The final wrath: ZION RESTORED.
xxxvi.–xxxix. Historical addendum to part one.

ORACLES OF REDEMPTION AND CONSUMMATION

(xl.–lxvi.)

GROUP 1. THE SUPREMACY OF JEHOVAH (xl.–xlviii.).
Jehovah supreme in attributes (xl.–xli.).
Jehovah supreme in redemption (xlii.–xlv.).
Jehovah supreme in punishment (xlvi.–xlviii.).

GROUP 2. THE "SERVANT" OF JEHOVAH (xlix.–lvii.).
Firstly Israel: finally Christ (xlix.–liii.).
Israel restored: Christ reigns (liv.–lv.).
Thus, present urge and promise (lvi.–lvii.).

GROUP 3. THE CHALLENGE OF JEHOVAH (lviii.–lxvi.).
In view of present wrong-doing (lviii.–lix.).
In view of future great events (lx.–lxv.).
Final challenge, promise, warning (lxvi.).

There is a noteworthy parallel between the two parts of Isaiah and chapters iv. and v. of the Book of Revelation. The whole movement in the first five chapters of Revelation is to put the Lamb on the throne. In chapter iv. we have an august unveiling of the THRONE. In chapter v. we see the LAMB in the throne. So is it with the two parts of Isaiah. In the first thirty-nine chapters we see the THRONE, with Jehovah as supreme Ruler. In the remaining twenty-seven chapters we see the LAMB in the throne, expressing the truth that Jehovah is the only Saviour.

The " Servant " of Jehovah

Isaiah's doctrine of Jehovah's *"Servant"* is arresting; but certain passages in it will have perplexed some of us. The difficulty is to decide whether this figure of the "Servant" refers to Christ or to the nation Israel. The following remarks may be helpful.

Biblical scholarship now fully appreciates that the prophetic writings usually have their *first* meaning, at least, in connection with the times when they originated. Here and there, undoubtedly, are predictions which directly overleap the centuries; but usually the prophet's message has a clear first reference to his own time. Thus, in the miracle of inspiration, it often occurs that a passage may have both a present and a future reference, the one patent, the other latent. The phraseology is more than can be fairly limited to the immediate historical occasion: it assumes an amplitude which anticipates far greater issues of which the immediate historical occasion is but a foreshadowing.

It is not surprising, therefore, that in the "Servant" prophecies there should seem an alternation of reference between Israel and Christ; for the corporate Israel itself was a standing *type* of Christ—Israel, that is, abstracted from its grievous failures, and viewed in the light of its Divine mission. That the prophet sometimes means the *nation* when he speaks of the "Servant" is made clear in such places as chapter xlix. 3. But there are four special places where the prophet so strongly *individualises* the "Servant" that no candid reader can take them merely as poetic personifications of the nation. These are chapters xlii. 1–7; xlix. 5, 6; l. 4–10; lii. 13–liii. 12.

The prophet's own thought-process would seem to be as follows His conception of the *nation* as "Servant" of Jehovah would inhere in the very fact of Israel's unique election in Jehovah's redemptive purpose for the human race. But as the nation's unfaithfulness and pre-revealed dispersion more and more pressed on his consciousness there would come the inescapable necessity of abstracting the idea of the true Israel from the actual; and thus, in the second stage of his thought, the "Servant" is no longer the actual, but the *ideal* Israel, represented by the godly "remnant" *within* the nation. Yet even here his mind does not find final rest. Peering ahead, as it were, and failing to glimpse even this ideal Israel collectively achieving the Divinely-intended high destiny, his mind is led on, both by human longing and Divine guiding, not only to idealise, but to *individualise* the true Israel, to draw its portrait in the features of a Person, a "Servant" of Jehovah who should be the perfect flower, the final embodiment, and the personal Head of the elect nation. Hence the seeming ambiguity in certain passages, and the clear transition from the nation to the Person in the "Servant" passages taken as a whole. In this connection it is helpful to look up the New Testament appropriations of the "Servant" passages as referring definitely to Christ.

The Fifty-third Chapter

It is generally agreed that the last three verses of the preceding chapter really belong to this fifty-third chapter. It is the most extraordinary of all the "Servant" passages—and the most precious. This is one of the places where the inspired prophet so strongly individualises the "Servant" that no unprejudiced student can see merely a poetic personification of the nation. Even here we need not deny to the critics that there may have been a primary and more superficial reference to the exiled nation; but the truer, deeper, fuller, and final reference to Christ is so emphatic that none but the wilfully blind can fail to see it.

It has been truly said that "the prolonged description of chapter liii. suits only one figure in all human history—the Man of Calvary." The following twelve points absolutely confirm this, for in their totality they cannot possibly be applied to any other. (1) He comes in utter lowliness—"a root out of a dry ground", etc. (2) He is "despised and rejected of men," etc. (3) He suffered for the sins and in the place of others—"He was wounded for our transgressions," etc. (4) It was God Himself who caused the suffering to be vicarious—"The Lord hath laid on Him the iniquity of us all." (5) There was an absolute resignation under the vicarious suffering—"He was afflicted, yet He opened not His mouth," etc. (6) He died as a felon—"He was taken from prison and from judgment." (7) He was cut off prematurely— "He was cut off out of the land of the living," etc. (8) Yet He was personally guiltless—"He had done no violence, neither was any deceit in His mouth." (9) And He was to live on after His sufferings—"He shall see His seed; He shall prolong His days." (10) Jehovah's pleasure was then to prosper in His hand—"The pleasure of Jehovah shall prosper in His hand." (11) He was to enter into mighty triumph after His suffering—"He shall divide the spoil with the strong", etc. (12) By all this, and by "justifying many" through His death and living again, He was to "see of the travail of His soul, and be satisfied."

As trait after trait is contributed, can we possibly write any other name under this amazing portrait than *JESUS OF NAZARETH*? And can we fail to marvel at the miracle of inspiration in this prophetic anticipation of the Man of Sorrows, when we reflect that it was written probably seven hundred years B.C.?

But look at this wonder-chapter again. Right at the heart of it we read: *"He is brought as a lamb to the slaughter"*; and on each side of this central declaration there is a seven-fold setting forth of *vicarious* suffering. In the verses that go before, it is from the *human* standpoint. In the verses which follow, it is from the *Divine* standpoint. Go through the verses, and pick these out, beginning at verse 4—"*He* hath borne *our* griefs." No wonder this chapter means so much to those of us who have fixed our hope for ever on Calvary!

Other Great Chapters

Our space is almost done; but we would whet the appetite of each reader for the study of the many other great chapters in Isaiah. How they open up to the mind which prayerfully concentrates on them! If we may pick out just one instance, take another of the "Servant" chapters—chapter xlii. This, with the two chapters which follow it, is really a great sermon which Isaiah preached on the sovereign grace of Jehovah in redemption. See how the chapter opens up. In verses 1 to 4 we have the Servant *described*. In verses 5 to 9 we have the Servant *addressed*. In verses 10 to 20 we have a declaration of what Jehovah will *do* through His Servant. And in verses 21 to the end we have Isaiah's own *appeal* to his countrymen. When verse 21 says: "Jehovah is well pleased for *His* righteousness' sake," the "His" refers to the Servant, of course. It was *Christ* who should "magnify the law, and make it glorious." Going back to the opening verses, also, note the connection between verses 3 and 4. Verse 3 says: "A *glimmering* wick shall He not quench." Verse 4 uses the same word, and says: "*HE* (Christ) shall not glimmer till He has established righteousness in the earth."

Translation Snags

We are so keen that these great chapters of Isaiah shall be appreciated to the full that we return, in closing, to urge the use of a modern translation along with the Authorised Version. Certainly there are translation snags in the Authorised Version which wreck the sense of some grand passages. Take, for instance, chapter ix. 5–7. Verse 5 reads: "For every battle of the warrior is with confused noise, and garments rolled in blood; but this shall be with burning and fuel of fire." Read thus it conveys little or no sense, and certainly it has no intelligible connection with what follows—"For unto us a Child is born," etc. But read it now as it should be, and see what a magnificent prediction we have. "All the armour of the armed men in the onslaught, and the garments rolled in blood, shall be for burning, shall be fuel for the fire; for (and this is *why* all the implements of war shall at last become fuel for the fire) unto us a Child is born, unto us a Son is given; and the government shall be upon His shoulder; and His name shall be called Wonderful Counsellor, Mighty God, Everlasting Father, Prince of Peace. Of the increase of His government and of peace there shall be no end, upon the throne of David and upon his kingdom, to establish it and to uphold it with judgment and with righteousness, from henceforth for ever. The zeal of Jehovah of hosts shall perform this."

Here we must leave Isaiah; and we do so with the longing prayer that soon the above words may leap into their Millennial fulfilment. "Even so, come, Lord Jesus!"

ARE THESE QUESTIONS ON ISAIAH ENJOYABLE
· OR TROUBLESOME TO YOU?

1. During which reigns did Isaiah prophesy? Name the Judæan kings, and then say how this bears on the *duration* of Isaiah's ministry.

2. How do we know that Isaiah's social status was high, that he was well-educated, that he was married and a father?

3. What big event happened to the northern kingdom (Israel) when Isaiah was between fifty and sixty years old?

4. What are the three grounds on which the Book of Isaiah is nowadays claimed to be a composite production of two or several or even many different contributors?

5. Could you show just briefly, giving an example or two, that the above-mentioned "three grounds" of the higher critical argument for plural authorship may be refuted?

6. What would you say, in a sentence or two, is the main purpose of the rationalist Higher Critics in arguing for a plural authorship of the book?

7. Could you mention any references which show that the geography of the second part of Isaiah (chapters xl. to lxvi.) is Palestinian and not Babylonian?

8. Could you name four witnesses, outside the Book of Isaiah, which testify that the whole is from the pen of the one Isaiah? (The first of the four is a famous translation, third century B.C.)

9. Could you give three lines of indication *inside* the Book of Isaiah which also confirm that both parts are from the one author?

10. In what way do the prophets Zephaniah and Nahum coincidentally yet conclusively prove that the one Isaiah is the author of the whole work?

11. Give in broad outline the structure of the Book of Isaiah, showing how the prophecies in part one are developingly expansive, and showing how in part two there is a threefold grouping?

12. Could you give nine points in Isaiah liii. which together show that it can be fully applicable to only one Person in all history, namely, our Lord Jesus Christ?

THE BOOK OF THE PROPHET JEREMIAH (1)

Lesson Number 75

NOTE.—For this study read the whole Book of Jeremiah right through. Do not try to read it quickly through at one sitting. Read it grouped as follows:

First, chapters i. to xx., noting that all the prophecies therein are undated.

Second, chapters xxi. to xxxix., noting that these are more or less particular and dated.

Third, chapter xl. to the end of the book, making a break at the end of chapter xliv., before the prophecies on the Gentile nations begin.

While God's government of the world has undergone several changes, which we, following the example of Paul, term dispensations, still these dispensations, vary as they may in laws and conditions, are ever constant to one main object. They all combine to prove that in no conceivable circumstances is man able to preserve or recover his integrity, and to save himself from corruption; that his sole hope lies in a direct interposition of the Eternal, and so wondrous infusion of the Holy Spirit that an entire change is wrought in his nature.

—*Pember, "The Great Prophecies of the Centuries"*

THE BOOK OF JEREMIAH (1)

JEREMIAH is one of the bravest, tenderest, and most pathetic figures in history; and his book of prophecies is one which everybody should read. Indeed, there is good reason why we should read the prophecies of Jeremiah with much thoughtfulness just now, for there is no little correspondence between the fateful days of this noble prophet and our own.

We have already remarked that these books of the prophets should be read in close connection with the times and circumstances in which they were written. This is especially so in the case of Jeremiah. The man and his message and his times are inseparably bound together, and must be interpreted together. In an earlier study we spoke of the Second Book of the Kings as "the most tragic national record ever written"; and the most tragic part of that tragic record is the final part, which covers the period in which Jeremiah lived. It was some eighty or a hundred years after Isaiah's death that Jeremiah exercised his ministry, a ministry which continued for well over forty years, during the reigns of Judah's last five kings (i. 1–3). One has but to name these kings—Josiah, Jehoahaz, Jehoiakim, Jehoiachin, Zedekiah—to realise the darkness of those days. The late Dr. Moorehead's words are apt and true: "It was Jeremiah's lot to prophesy at a time when all things in Judah were rushing down to the final and mournful catastrophe; when political excitement was at its height; when the worst passions swayed the various parties; and the most fatal counsels prevailed; . . . to see his own people, whom he loved with the tenderness of a woman, plunge over the precipice into the wide, weltering ruin." Jeremiah was the prophet of Judah's midnight hour.

Jeremiah Himself

The man himself is a rich subject for study. He blends in his character, to a degree of striking fineness, feminine tenderness with masculine strength, nervous sensitiveness with transparent simplicity, so that his nature reveals its reactions to outside

259

goings-on as sharply as the limpid waters of Alpine lakes reflect every mood of the changeable skies above them. I know of no man who reveals a truer heart-likeness to Jesus Himself than does Jeremiah, in his suffering sympathy both with God and men, in his unretaliating forbearance, his yearning concern for his fellows, his guileless motive, his humility, his willingness for self-sacrifice, and his utter faithfulness, even to the point of unsparing severity in denunciation. All disappointed, disappreciated, disregarded, misunderstood, misrepresented, and persecuted Christian workers today, sticking on at their work, but with a leaden weight at the heart and a choke of grief in the throat, should turn aside again and again to commune with the heroic great-heart of these pages. Indeed, we cannot properly study this Book of Jeremiah without studying Jeremiah himself; for the man is as much the book as the prophecies which he uttered.

No man ever shrank from publicity as did Jeremiah; yet singularly enough, it is this man who, of all the prophets, gives us the fullest revelation of his own character. This is because the man and his message are in such passionate oneness under such tragic circumstances. Jeremiah's nature was such that he simply could not be merely a *transmitter*, able to detach his own feelings from that which he was commissioned to declare. With an intensity of love and sympathy, he himself lived and felt and suffered in his message. His own heart-strings vibrated to every major and every minor chord. The man and his message were one.

We believe that there was Divine design in this. Jeremiah was a man raised up specially for such a time as that in which he lived. Indeed, we are told this with significant emphasis in chapter i. 5—"Before I formed thee . . . I knew thee; and before thou camest forth . . . I sanctified thee, and I ordained thee a prophet unto the nations." Thus, Jeremiah was specially fitted for his sad but noble task. The Holy Spirit would have us look at this *man*, as well as hear his words.

And what is it that impresses us first about Jeremiah as we read through these chapters? It is *his suffering sympathy*. His sorest inward trial was the tearing of his heart between two rival sympathies—on the one hand, a sympathy with God such as few men have entered into, and on the other hand a grieving, yearning, loving sympathy with his fellow-countrymen, which made him suffer with them. In all their afflictions he himself was afflicted. Somehow, in his relation to God, Jeremiah was a prophet, and something more; and similarly, in his ardent identification of himself with his people he was a patriot, and something more. He entered both into the life of his people and into that of Jehovah. He did not merely speak *for* God; he felt *with* Him: and he did not merely speak to the people; he felt with *them*. In the earlier chapters it seems as if, at times, these two sympathies offset each other to a point of fine balance. We seem to sense that the prophet's sympathy is at first so poignantly with his people that he could almost side against the threatened chastisements of God as too severe (see iv. 10, 19, 20; x. 23–5; xiv. 7–13, 19–22). But gradually we note a change. As Jeremiah himself spends his noble love and pleadings in vain upon this obdurate people, as he suffers their derisive mockery, discovers their thankless plots against his own life, and undergoes the ignominious punishments which they inflict on him, he is gradually forced to identify his own judgment with God's. Indeed, he is actually driven by their cruel treachery to cry out that God shall punish them—not at all out of a spirit of revenge, but from a sense of outraged justice and kindness (see xi. 19, 20; xviii. 18–23; xx. 10–12; xxxii. 16–23; xlii. 20–2). Jeremiah's own suffering through this struggle of dual sympathy within his heart is seen in passages such as chapters iv. 19; viii. 21; ix. 1; xv. 10, 18; xx. 14–18; xxiii. 9, etc.

But further, we cannot fail to be impressed by Jeremiah's *patient perseverance*. Only pure love and goodness persevere as graciously as this man did, through such a protracted and forlorn ministry. Most of the other prophets do seem to have produced a measure of reform. Although Isaiah asked, "Who hath believed our report?" how plainly is his influence seen in Hezekiah's reign! But through forty years Jeremiah never once saw any grateful response. He stood alone, as God's spokesman, unheeded, humiliated, yet bravely persistent. Love alone keeps a man thus persevering in face of such discouragements. "Love suffereth long, and is kind . . . beareth all things, believeth all things, hopeth all things, endureth all things." And remember that the persevering love of *God* is struggling to express itself through this lonely, lovely man; for he has become so sympathetically one with God and with his message that he himself, as it were, *becomes* the message. Every prediction of coming judgment is soaked in tears: every pleading is punctuated with sobs. Jeremiah becomes an object-lesson for all time, of the persevering love of God. Dr. G. Campbell Morgan truly says: "In the story of Jeremiah's shrinking and pain and tears we have a picture of a man in such perfect fellowship with God that through him God was able to reveal His own suffering in the presence of sin."

We can mention only one other characteristic, namely, *his utter faithfulness.* His sensitive nature shrank from certain aspects of the tragic ministry which was committed to him. He pours out his heart in touching appeal against having to pronounce such fearful retributions. His own heart feels the pain of the judgments which are coming on his kinsmen. He suffers with them. He feels he cannot drag his leaden steps to declare these woes of God upon them. Yet through all the years he faithfully declares the whole counsel of God to his unrepenting generation. Yes, "Jeremiah, the son of Hilkiah, of the priests that were in Anathoth, in the land of Benjamin" (i. 1), is a noble figure and a rewarding study. Never did he lose that native simplicity of heart with which he first responded to the Lord—"Ah, Lord God, behold I cannot speak; for I am a child" (i. 6); and he persevered with heroic faithfulness right to the bitter end.

Jeremiah's Prophecies

It is quite clear that the chapters and messages in this Book of Jeremiah are not arranged in chronological order. Chapters xxxv. and xxxvi., for instance, are earlier in point of time than chapter xxi.; and so on. For the most part it would seem as though little attention was paid to chronological order in the compilation of our prophet's writings. Is there, then, arrangement according to *subject*? It scarcely seems so. Writers on this book seem to be agreed that it cannot be reduced to any logical analysis. Of course, we can pick out the different chapters which belong to the reigns of the different kings, and make our own classification in that way, grouping those chapters which belong to the reign of Josiah, and those which belong to the reign of Jehoiakim, and so on. But what of the book as it now stands? Is there any sign of orderly purpose in its actual present arrangement? I think there is; and it is an orderly arrangement which is quite easy to remember.

To begin with; this much is clear, that chapters i. to xxxix. are all *before the fall of Jerusalem.* First, then, let us look at these thirty-nine chapters. Is there any indication of order in these? There is. Take them just as they stand. In chapter i. we have the prophet's call and commission, which is introductory to the whole book. Then, next, we note that all the chapters from ii. to xx. are a series of prophecies which are *general and undated.* The only time-mark in all these chapters is a very general one in chapter iii. 6—"In the days of Josiah," which simply indicates that at any rate the first six chapters were Jeremiah's earliest prophesyings. It is probable, indeed, that the first *twelve* chapters fall in Josiah's reign, and that all of these first *twenty* chapters fall in the earlier years of Jeremiah's ministry. This section ends with an account of the reaction and result at the close of this first phase of Jeremiah's ministry—opposition and persecution. See chapter xx. Also note that the "Pashur" of chapter xx. 1 is not the same as "Pashur, the son of Melchiah" in chapter xxi. 1.

Next, we observe that all the prophecies in chapters xxi. to xxxix. are *particular and dated.* They are clearly stated to have occurred in connection with this or that or the other historical event, or at such and such a time (see the opening words of the chapters). Lest it should be thought that chapters xxii. and xxiii. are an exception to this, we point out that both these chapters continue the prophecy commenced in chapter xxi. Look this up carefully to verify it. Note that chapter xxii. (which obviously continues chapter xxi.) speaks of all the last four of Judah's kings—Jehoahaz (Shallum) in verse 11; Jehoiakim in verse 18; Jehoiachin (Coniah) in verse 24; and Zedekiah (to whom the whole prophecy is addressed); see chapter xxi. 3 with chapter xxii. 1. These evil kings were the false "shepherds" who led the people astray: and it is with this in mind that chapter xxiii. begins: "Woe be unto the shepherds that destroy and scatter the sheep of My pasture! saith Jehovah." Now note in chapter xxiii. false pastors (verses 1, 2), false prophets (verse 9), false priests (verse 11).

Perhaps we ought just to add that, similarly, chapters xxx. and xxxi. continue chapter xxix. In chapter xxix. Jeremiah addresses the first batch of *captives* who had been deported from Judah to Babylon (some years before the final siege and fall of Jerusalem). Then, in chapter xxx. he is instructed to commit the foregoing to written form for preservation. That the captives and the captivity are still in mind is clear from the link between chapter xxix. 31 ("Send to all them of the *captivity* . . .") and chapter xxx. 3 ("I will bring again the *captivity* . . ." etc.).

So, then, the first thirty-nine chapters cleave into two clear groups: chapters i. to xx., prophecies *general and undated*; chapters xxi. to xxxix., prophecies *particular and dated*.

As for the remaining chapters, the arrangement is simple and clear. In chapters xl. to xliv. we have Jeremiah's ministry to the Jews *after the fall of* Jerusalem, first in Judæa (xl.–xlii.), then in Egypt (xliii.–xliv.).

Chapters xlv. to li. are plainly a group all by themselves, being Jeremiah's collected prophecies on the surrounding *Gentile nations* —nine of them (on chapter xlv. see next lesson). And, finally, chapter lii. is an historical appendix and conclusion to the whole book, in which we see the last of Judah's kings dragged from his throne, blinded, humiliated, and carried captive, the city sacked, the temple burned, and Jeremiah's word fulfilled to the last degree.

The *central thought* of the book may be expressed by bringing together the two recurrent expressions, "I will punish" and "I will restore." While there is present failure through the sin of man, there shall be final triumph through the love of God. There is *wrath to the full*, but there is *love to the end*. Jeremiah's message is crystallised in chapter xxvi. 12, 13—"The Lord sent me to prophesy against this house and against this city all the words that ye have heard. Therefore now amend your ways and your doings, and obey the voice of the Lord your God; and the Lord will repent Him of the evil that He hath pronounced against you." This was a clear and gracious eleventh-hour offer, but it was not responded to.

The key to the whole book is found in chapters xxx. and xxxi., especially in chapter xxx. 15–18: "Because thy sins are become immense I have done these things unto thee. . . . Yet all they that devour thee shall be devoured. . . . For I will restore health unto thee, and I will heal thee of thy wounds, saith the Lord."

THE BOOK OF JEREMIAH

INTRODUCTION—Jeremiah commissioned (i).

PROPHECIES, GENERAL AND UNDATED (ii.–xx.).

First message, ii. 1–iii. 5; second message, iii. 6–vi. 30; third message (at Temple gate), vii. 1–x. 25; fourth message (the broken covenant), xi. 1–xii. 17; fifth message (sign of linen girdle), xiii. 1–27; sixth message (on the drought), xiv. 1–xv. 21; seventh message (sign of the unmarried prophet), xvi. 1–xvii. 18); eighth message (at city gates), xvii. 19–27; ninth message (the potter's vessel), xviii. 1–23; tenth message (the earthen vessel), xix.; result, xx.

PROPHECIES, PARTICULAR AND DATED (xxi.–xxxix.).

First (to Zedekiah), xxi.–xxiii.; second (after first deportation), xxiv.; third (fourth year of Jehoiakim: The coming Babylonian captivity), xxv.; third (early reign of Jehoiakim), xxvi.; fourth (early reign of Jehoiakim), xxvii.–xxviii.; fifth (to captives of first deportation), xxix.–xxxi.; sixth (tenth year Zedekiah), xxxii.–xxxiii.; seventh (during Babylonian siege), xxxiv.; eighth (days of Jehoiakim), xxxv.; ninth (fourth year Jehoiakim), xxxvi.; tenth (siege), xxxvii.; result xxxviii.–xxxix.

PROPHECIES AFTER FALL OF JERUSALEM (xl.–xliv.).

Babylonian kindly treatment of Jeremiah (xl. 1–6); ill-doings in land of Judæa (xl. 7–xli. 18); Jeremiah's message to remnant in the land (xlii. 1–22); Jeremiah carried down to Egypt (xliii. 1–7); first prophetic message in Egypt (xliii. 8–13); second prophetic message to Jewish refugees in Egypt (xliv. 1–30); result—further rejection of the message by Jewish refugees.

PROPHECIES UPON GENTILE NATIONS (xlv.–li.).

Preceded by a prefatory note to Baruch the faithful scribe who wrote them (xlv.); first (against Egypt), xlvi. 1–28; second (against the Philistines) xlvii. 1–7; third (against Moab), xlviii. 1–47; fourth (against the Ammonites), xlix. 1–6; fifth (against Edom), xlix. 7–22; sixth (against Damascus), xlix. 23–7; seventh (against Kedar and Hazor), xlix. 28–33; eighth (against Elam), xlix. 34–9; ninth (against Babylon and Chaldea), l. 1–li. 64.

CONCLUSION—Jerusalem overthrown (lii.).

THE BOOK OF JEREMIAH (2)

Lesson Number 76

NOTE.—For this second study in Jeremiah read the whole book through again, marking off its main divisions as given in our preceding lesson; and making careful note of the following:

(1) All references to Jeremiah himself, in which there are many precious spiritual teachings;

(2) All those passages which tell of the coming Messiah and of Israel's final restoration;

(3) Chapter xxv., which gives us the starting-point of Jeremiah's prophetic ministry, and other pivotal facts, as we shall also show in the ensuing study.

The Bible shows that all righteousness is rooted in religion. If we destroy man's relationship to God, and his consciousness of Him, we destroy the possibility of man's right relationship with his fellow-man. That is what the world has lost sight of so largely. Perhaps it may come back through blood and misery and tears in these appalling days.

—*G. Campbell Morgan, D.D.*

THE BOOK OF JEREMIAH (2)

THIS Book of Jeremiah "grows" on us the more we read it. Having seen its general lay-out, we really must tarry, even though briefly, to appreciate some of its main features.

Basic and Vital Lessons

Basic and vital lessons lie before us on these pages. To begin with, here is the solemn truth, vehemently emphasised and tragically illustrated, that *all national deterioration and disaster is due fundamentally to the disregarding and disobeying of God.* Read again Jeremiah's opening impeachment of the Jewish nation, in chapter ii., noting specially verses 8, 19, and 35.

"The priests said not, Where is Jehovah? And they that handle the Law knew Me not. The rulers also transgressed against Me; and the prophets prophesied by Baal, and walked after things that do not profit."

"Thine own wickedness shall correct thee, and thy backslidings shall reprove thee. Know therefore and see that it is an evil thing and bitter that thou hast forsaken Jehovah thy God, and that My fear is not in thee, saith the Lord, Jehovah of hosts."

"Yet thou sayest: I am innocent; surely His anger is turned away from me. Behold I will enter into judgment with thee."

In the first of these verses we see the spiritual breakdown among the *leaders* of the nation. In the second we see the inevitable entailment of such breakdown, namely, wickedness and bitterness. In the third we see the blindness which this process begets: sin gradually ceases to be recognised as such, and innocence is professed even amid wrongdoing and defilement.

When once the national downgrade has set in, it is not easy to check the momentum. The wrong which is indulged in by those in authority soon becomes the fashion among the people at large. We only need to turn on to Jeremiah's second message for an illustration of this. See chapter v. 31—"The prophets prophesy falsely, and the priests bear rule by their means; *and My people love to have it so."*

Moreover, the nation and people that dishonour God by *denying* Him usually degenerate into *defying* Him. How clearly this is demonstrated in the later chapters of Jeremiah! The king himself burns God's message in the fire (xxxvi. 27); the princes put Jeremiah into a dungeon (xxxviii. 4); and as for the nation as a whole there is a defiant deafness to all appeal (xxxvii. 2). This downgrade process has one inevitable end. Corrupt leadership inoculates the whole nation with moral poison; and inward, moral failure issues in outward, national ruin.

You cannot rightly explain the history of any nation if you leave God out of the picture. Judah's politicians were busy explaining that the kingdom's troubles were due to a geographical dilemma—Egypt to the south, and Assyria to the east; but Jeremiah's message was that the nation's calamities were judgments of God for her iniquities. The miserable policy of Judah's leaders was to try and play off Egypt and Assyria against each other, or, when this seemed too precarious, to make an alliance with one of them as a safeguard against the other. Jeremiah denounced such wretched expedients (ii. 18, 19, 36; xxxvii. 7), and declared that the country's lamentable condition was due to the people's apostasy from the true God.

Sin is still in the world, and God is still God; and therefore history repeats itself. Our politicians are still floundering about among second causes. The fundamental cause of all our troubles is that God is forgotten. We discuss policy instead of putting away sin. It is the same today as it was in Jeremiah's time. When will nations learn that national decay and ruin are, at root, due to failure towards God? Jeremiah's message may well be heeded by our leaders today.

But we must add a word more. This Book of Jeremiah reveals to us *the process of the Divine judgment in national life.* Speaking of Jeremiah's days, Dr. G. C. Morgan says: "We read the history merely and say: What an unfortunate succession of kings; how singularly these people failed to produce statesmen who were able to cope with the political situation! This lonely figure, observing the race to ruin, said: The failure of your kings and the failure of your policy prove that the hand of God is upon you in judgment. It is He who breaks down the power of your king. It is He who will bring to nought your intrigue with Egypt, and hand your city over to the Assyrian who is already at your gates." Yes, and we know that Jeremiah was right. The judgment of the Almighty on the nation was operating through these things which, to sin-warped little human minds were simply (as men call them) "*misfortunes.*" When sin has quenched the vision of God, it also renders the mind incapable of seeing the operations of Divine judgment in the things which are permitted to happen.

So it was then. So it is today. Events moved on and vindicated Jeremiah. So do events move on and vindicate God's Jeremiahs among men today. The great lessons of this Book of Jeremiah speak to all peoples in all ages. Where sin has destroyed the vision of God, men think that the calamities which are permitted to come upon them are indications that God has abandoned interest in them; but where the vision of God is clear, as it was with Jeremiah, the things which are permitted to happen are seen in their true significance; and these very calamities are seen to be the evidences that *God has not abandoned His throne!*

There is another lesson in this book, too, which stands out prominently, and which should be very comforting to all sincere Christian workers today. *God does not reckon the worth of service for Himself merely in terms of success.* Nor must we, on our part, judge the blessing of God upon us merely by the degree of success that comes to us. Judged by that standard, where is Jeremiah? We must learn to be faithful even where we cannot be successful —as Jeremiah was, so conspicuously. This lesson has special relevance to the Lord's witnesses today. We are almost—if not quite—at that point in the history of Christendom which corresponds to the time of Jeremiah in the history of Judah— the eleventh hour, the hour leading to the midnight zero of the final apostasy under "the Man of Sin," and the final outbreak of the Divine judgment at Armageddon. This being so, or very probably so, we may find that people in general are less and less inclined to hear our message, and are more inclined to resist and persecute us. Let us then recognise the hour in which we witness for God; and let us take great comfort and encouragement from Jeremiah, who, through nearly half a century of discouragement, bravely kept on.

Messianic and Restoration Passages

Jeremiah's mission was to a people who had shut their eyes and ears until they had become blind and deaf. Their sins were "bound" upon them. Judicial blindness and deafness had become an accomplished fact. They *would not* hear in their prosperity (xxii. 21). They *cannot* hear now in their adversity (vi. 10). In one sense they were past praying for; and three times it is said, "Pray not for this people" (vii. 16; xi. 14; xiv. 11). God's awful word, in chapter xv. 1, is: "Though Moses and Samuel stood before Me, yet My mind could not be toward this people: cast them out of My sight, and let them go forth." The point is that the sentence of judgment was now irrevocable. As at Kadesh-barnea of old (Num. xiv.), so was it now again, in Jeremiah's time—that generation was doomed. Because of this, Jeremiah's message was largely one of coming judgment.

But the sad ministry of this prophet carries a golden promise at its heart. The Everlasting Love, though veiled by these gathering and passing thunder-clouds, shines through, again and again, in simply dazzling promises. No passages, even among the rapturous rhapsodies of Isaiah, surpass some of the glorious promises of restoration and consummation which are found in these pages of Jeremiah. Like almost-blinding sunbursts from a cloud-draped heaven they recur through the book.   See the following passages again: chapters xxiii. 3–8; xxx. 1–10, 17–22; xxxi. 1–14, 31–40; xxxii. 37–44; xxxiii. 14–26; iii. 16–18; xii. 14–15; xvi. 14, 15.

Right at the heart of this book, then, there is a *GOSPEL*—good news of *great days yet to come!* "For, lo, the days come that I will bring again the captivity of My people. . . . I will cause them to return to the land, and they shall possess it . . . and I will raise up unto them David, their King" (xxx.). This is a scene of millennial blessedness. The *people* are to be regathered. The *land* is to be repossessed. The *Messiah-King* is to reign; and the glory of His reign shall *never end*!

It is as plain as can be that these Messianic and millennial predictions are not merely florid poetical exaggerations of events which are now past; and it is equally clear that if they are to be taken at their face value they have not yet had their fulfilment. They look on to the second advent of the Lord Jesus Christ, and His coming reign on earth in a world-wide empire centred at Jerusalem. These great "restoration" passages should be studied collaterally, and memorised, and enjoyed by all the Lord's people.

Also, it is in connection with these "restoration" promises that we first come across *the manifesto of a wonderful "NEW COVENANT"* which God was going to make with Judah and Israel. Read onward from chapter xxxi. 31—one of the most remarkable paragraphs in Old Testament prophecy. Jeremiah saw that if there was to be any hope of salvation for his people, it could not be by a return merely to the old system on the basis of the covenant made through Moses: and he learned that there was to be this wonderful "new" covenant. It was to be a covenant of grace, not law. Instead of being an outward command demanding obedience, it should be an inward renewal providing holy desire and motive. It should be deep-grounded in forgiveness, and would produce a complete change in Israel. The new covenant was to centre in a perfect Ruler who was to come—the Son of David.

The promised One has now indeed appeared. The "new covenant" has been sealed with His own redeeming blood. But the application of all the wonderful provisions in it for the covenant people awaits the time when they shall "look on Him whom they pierced," and acclaim Him their Messiah-Saviour-King. Jeremiah was not given to see this present, intervening age of the Church; but he clearly saw the kingdom glories beyond it. At the moment when "out of the throne proceeded lightnings and thunderings," announcing Judah's doom, he saw "a rainbow round about the throne" (Rev. iv.)—the rainbow of a new promise, a new covenant, every line rich with hope and beauty!

The Babylon Doom-song

The final prophecy of the book is on the doom of Babylon It runs through one hundred and ten verses, and is the longest single prophecy in the book. It is an arresting article, and has been fulfilled to the letter. Such prophecy and fulfilment, of course, is proof absolute of inspiration; and it is not surprising, therefore, that this Babylon doom-song has attracted the subtle attentions of our modernist scholars, who would fain post-date it so as to eliminate the presence of supernatural prediction. Their effort is to argue that Jeremiah could not have been the writer because (as they put it) its "standpoint" is later than his day, by which they mean (in Dr. Driver's words) that "the destruction of the Temple is presupposed, the Jews are in exile, suffering for their sins," and so on.

But there are three facts which completely smash this "higher critical" contention. *First:* even the critics themselves have to admit that no prophecy in the whole book bears more clearly the literary characteristics of Jeremiah. Graf, for instance, says: "The style presents all the characters of the special style of that prophet." *Second:* no prophecy in the whole book is more significantly authenticated than this one. It begins with: "The word that the Lord spake against Babylon . . . *by Jeremiah* the prophet"; and it ends with: "Thus far are the words *of Jeremiah*." Thus it is clasped by a double guarantee. And then, to complete a "threefold cord" of evidence, it is carefully dated—the fourth year of Zedekiah (see li. 59–63), that is, seven years before the fall of Jerusalem. *Third:* there are parts of this prophecy which look far beyond the end of the captivity in Babylonia. See chapter l. 14–16, where the destruction of the walls and foundations of Babylon is foretold. This demolition, not to mention other items in the prediction, did not occur at the conquest of Babylon by Cyrus at the end of the predicted captivity; it happened over five hundred years after that! But would the critics now argue that because the "standpoint" here "*presupposes*" this destruction of Babylon's walls, the prophecy was not written until five hundred years after the Exile, when our own Christian era had begun? Presumably, that is what the " standpoint " theory would require!

This "standpoint" theory of the critics is nonsense. Are there not great predictions in this book, and in the other scriptures, which overleap the centuries right on to the Millennium? And are we therefore to infer that because their "standpoint" is in the Millennium, the *writer* is also millennial—and therefore not yet born? Nay, as one writer has said, the "standpoint" of all true prophecy is "the standpoint of *omniscience*"—of God Himself. In other words, Jeremiah's Babylon prophecy, like all other true prophecy, was *the inspired word of God.*

A Pivotal Chapter

Chapter xxv. should be carefully re-inspected. First, it marks for us precisely the starting-point of Jeremiah's prophetic ministry (verse 3). Second, it definitely predicts the seventy years' servitude to Babylon, a full twenty years in advance (verse 11, with date in verse 1). Third, it clearly shows that chapters xlvi. to li.—Jeremiah's batch of prophecies on the Gentile nations— were already in "book" form (verses 13, 17–26), here in "the fourth year of Jehoiakim," twenty years before the Exile, even though they are now placed right at the *end* of the "Book of Jeremiah" as it has come down to us.

Chapter xxv. also explains, incidentally, why that tiny *forty-fifth* chapter, addressed to Baruch, comes where it does. Writers on Jeremiah seem to have taken it for granted that *this* little chapter, at least, is quite out of its proper place. Certainly it cannot be an addendum to what precedes it, in chapters xliii. and xliv., for in those two chapters we are with the aged Jeremiah in Egypt, some time after the fall of Jerusalem, whereas this forty-fifth chapter is dated away back "in the fourth year of Jehoiakim." But is this forty-fifth chapter connected with the prophecies on the Gentile nations, which come *after* it? It is; and surely the connection is disclosed in chapter xxv. The prophecy in chapter xxv., which, as we have just seen, mentions the "*book*" of Jeremiah's prophecies on the Gentile peoples as being already written, is dated, "*the fourth year of Jehoiakim.*" Probably this "book" of prophecies on the Gentiles was written actually in that year. Who was the scribe? *Baruch* was Jeremiah's scribe, or writer (xxxvi. 4, 17; xliii. 6, etc.). It would be he who wrote out this "book" of prophecies on the Gentile nations. See now how chapter xlv. begins: "The word that Jeremiah the prophet spake unto Baruch, the son of Neriah, *when he had written these words in a book*, at the mouth of Jeremiah, in *the fourth year of Jehoiakim.*" Is not the connection too clear to doubt? When it says he wrote "*these* words" it means those that *follow*, in the prophecies on the Gentile kingdoms; for verse 4 speaks of judgment coming on "the whole earth" (not just "this whole land" as in A.V.), and verse 5 speaks of evil coming on "all flesh"— referring, surely, to the world-prophecies which follow. After all, then, chapter xlv. is in its right place—as a prefatory note to chapters xlvi.–li.

Typical Significance of Jeremiah

We close with a final word about Jeremiah himself. It would almost seem as though a kind of *typical* significance clings to this meek, brave, faithful, suffering prophet of tears, in the experiences which came to him, and in the emotions which were wrought within him. See chapters ix. 1; xi. 19; xiii. 17; xv. 16–21; xx. 10; xxvi. 11–15; xxxvii. 15, 16; xxxviii. 6; Lamentations iii. 1–14. Certainly, no figure that moves before us anywhere in the Bible comes nearer to expressing the sorrowing, patient, gracious love of Christ over those He suffers to save than does Jeremiah. Most of us, I fear, cannot ever read the story of this man without inward self-rebuke that we ourselves fall so short of this generous-hearted, meek-spirited heroism. If Jeremiah is not actually a type of Christ, he is certainly an advance reflection of Him.

Dr. G. Campbell Morgan truly says: "We have read this prophecy very carelessly if we have simply seen in it the sorrows of a man, '*Oh that my head were waters, and mine eyes a fountain of tears, that I might weep day and night for the slain of the daughter of my people!*' Can we find anything to match that? We have already done so. We have travelled through the centuries until we have stood upon the slopes of Olivet with a Man more lonely than Jeremiah, and have seen Him looking at Jerusalem, and have heard Him pronounce its doom, weeping as He did so. That is the fulfilment of the prophecy of Jeremiah. . . . The interpretation of Jeremiah's suffering is to be found in the suffering of Jesus; and the interpretation of the suffering of Jesus is to be found *in the suffering of God.*"

Mark well then, this remarkable man, Jeremiah; and as the mind lingers appraisingly upon him let the heart's prayer be—

> *Teach me, O Lord, to serve as Thou deservest,*
> *To give, and not to count the cost;*
> *To fight and not to heed the wounds;*
> *To toil, and not to seek for rest;*
> *To labour and not to ask any reward,*
> *Save only of knowing that I do Thy will.*

THE LAMENTATIONS OF JEREMIAH

Lesson Number 77

NOTE.—For this study read the whole of this poem-dirge, "Lamentations," through twice, noting that each chapter has 22 verses in it, except the middle chapter, which has exactly three times that number. Try to pick out carefully when it is Jehovah speaking, when Jerusalem, and when Jeremiah.

Behold therefore the goodness and the severity of God . . .

Romans xi. 22.

Desperate tides of the whole world's anguish
Forced through the channel of a single heart.

Frederick Myers in "St. Paul."

There is a budding morrow in midnight.

Keats.

Poets learn in sorrow what they teach in song.

Anon.

THE LAMENTATIONS OF JEREMIAH

"O JERUSALEM, Jerusalem, thou that killest the prophets, and stonest them which are sent unto thee, how often would I have gathered thy children together, even as a hen gathereth her chickens under her wings, and ye would not! Behold, your house is left unto you desolate!" Such was the tear-drenched plaint of the Man of Sorrows over the impenitent city which was soon to crucify its Messiah-King: but six hundred years before then, those words were anticipated and adumbrated, in more elaborate form, by the brave but broken-hearted prophet, Jeremiah, in his five-fold poem, the "Lamentations."

Authorship

That this little scroll which we call the "Lamentations" is indeed the work of Jeremiah we do not for one moment doubt, even though no author's name is attached to it in the Hebrew original. We have just read the learned T. K. Cheyne's argument against Jeremiah's authorship of it; but the very weakness of his case confirms our own adherence to the older view. Dr. Cheyne himself is obliged to say of chapter iii. that "if we take the poem literally, it points to Jeremiah more distinctly than to any other known individual"; and he cannot escape the admission that even the other chapters are characterised by "expressions and ideas familiar to us in Jeremiah." His case, like that of the other modern critics who have shared his view, rests on unconvincing minutiæ in the text, and on the fact that the fifth lament is not in the acrostic form (which we will mention presently) of the other four. The way our modern school of literary Biblical critics have often professed to discover variant authorship in variant forms of expression is, in our own judgment, unworthy of serious scholarship. That much of it is disguised guess-work is shown by the way in which the results of the different literary critics clash with each other.

Right through these five elegies or lamentations we descry the hand and the heart of Jeremiah: nor is there any tenable alternative to Jeremiah's authorship. Jewish tradition, as far back as we can go, ascribes the authorship to him. The historian Josephus confirms it. The Massoretic editors of the Hebrew Scriptures undoubtedly believed it. Later Jewish and Christian scholarship endorsed it. *We* therefore accept it. That the writing of the book was contemporaneous with the sufferings which it describes is transparently evident; and that being so, then as C. J. Ellicott says, "There is absolutely no other writer living at the time to whom it can be ascribed with the slightest shadow of probability." Into the many parallel traits between the Lamentations and the Book of Jeremiah we cannot go here. Ellicott's Commentary has a fine little paragraph which can be looked up in this connection, and which, to our own judgment, is conclusive as to the fact that this weeping prophet of the "Lamentations" is none other than Jeremiah.

Characteristics

This pathetic little five-fold poem, the Lamentations, has been called "an elegy written in a graveyard." It is a memorial dirge written on the destruction and humiliation of Jerusalem by the Babylonians in 587 B.C. It is a cloudburst of grief, a river of tears, a sea of sobs. In the Jewish grouping of the Old Testament Scriptures it is one of the five *Megilloth*, or "Rolls." The five are the Song of Songs, Ruth, Lamentations, Ecclesiastes, Esther; and they were called the "Rolls" because each of them was written on a roll for reading at Jewish festivals—the Song of Songs at the Passover, Ruth at the Feast of Weeks or Pentecost, Ecclesiastes at the Feast of Tabernacles, Esther at the Feast of Purim, and Lamentations at the anniversary of the destruction of Jerusalem.

But further, this five-fold poem is built up in an *acrostic* form. Even the reader of our English version has a slight clue to this in the fact that all the chapters except the middle one have the same number of verses, that is, twenty-two, while the middle chapter has exactly three times the number of each of the others, that is, sixty-six. This is because there are twenty-two letters in the Hebrew alphabet; and the verses of these five elegies (each elegy being represented by one complete chapter in our English version) run successively through the alphabet, each verse beginning, in order, with one of the twenty-two letters of the Hebrew alphabet. The reason why the third elegy (iii.) has sixty-six verses instead of twenty-two is that it runs in *triplets* of verses, each of the *first three* verses beginning with the first letter of the alphabet, each of the *next three* verses beginning with the second letter of the alphabet, each of the *next three* verses beginning with the third letter of the alphabet, and so on, thus taking sixty-six verses to run through the full twenty-two letters. The acrostic lettering is not continued in the fifth and shortest of these elegies, but the number of the verses is still twenty-two. We will give examples of this acrostic arrangement after we have briefly examined the structure of these five elegies as a whole.

Structure and Analysis

The structure of this quintuple poem is remarkable. These five elegies are not unconnected digits: they belong together, and make one complete poetic quintuplet. When this is clearly seen it gives a final indication that all five are from the one author.

The two *outer* poemettes—the first and the fifth, correspond. The two *inner* ones—the second and the fourth, correspond. The *middle* one—the third, which is the most elaborate in conception and the most finished in execution, is three times the size of the others, and stands at the centre like a great throne draped with mourning.

Take the first of the five (i.). The subject here is *Jerusalem's plight*. The little piece is in two parts. Notice that verses 1 to 11 are all in the *third* person—"she," "her," "the city," "Jerusalem," "Judah." This is because in these verses it is the prophet himself who is speaking *about* the city. At verse 12 there is a change. All the verses from 12 to 22 are in the *first* person—"my," "me," "I." This is because in these verses the *city* is represented as speaking *of itself*. This first chapter, then, is the elegy of "Jerusalem's Plight." In verses 1 to 11 *the prophet describes it*. Then, in verses 12 to 22, *the city bemoans it*.

Look now at the second lament (ii.). The subject here is *Jehovah's anger*. All the way through, the emphasis is on the fact that Jerusalem's humiliation has been brought about by Jehovah Himself. The expressions, "The Lord hath" and "He hath," occur no less than thirty times, not to mention verbs like "He burned," "He slew," "He poured out," all emphasising this fact that Jerusalem's discomfiture was *the Lord's* doing. This second lament, like the first, is in two parts. In verses 1 to 12 Jehovah's anger is *described*. Then, at verse 13, there is a change from the third person to the second, and the anger-smitten city itself is *exhorted*.

Pass on now to the third and central elegy (iii.). Here, at the heart of this five-fold memorial, we have *the prophet's own sorrow*. So sensitively is his own spirit identified with his people, so afflicted is he in all their afflictions, that in some verses it could be either the prophet himself, or the personified nation speaking; the words are so true of both. The background throughout, however, is that of Jeremiah's own personal suffering. This third dirge, like the former two, is in two parts. In verses 1 to 39 we have *affliction* (verses 1–21), *but with hope* (verses 22–39). In the remaining verses, 40 to 66, we have a resultant *prayer-appeal* to God—national (verses 40–51) and personal (verses 52–66). As already mentioned, the verses or stanzas of this third elegy run in triads. The first three verses all begin with the first letter of the Hebrew alphabet. The next three verses all begin with the second letter of the alphabet; and so on. Thus, in the first part of this third elegy (verses 1–39) we cover the first thirteen letters of the alphabet, and in the second part (40–66) the other nine.

This brings us to the *fourth* poemette. Here we are back to twenty-two verses. The subject, as in the second poemette, is *Jehovah's anger*, but with this difference, that whereas in the second acrostic the Lord's anger is *described*, in this fourth one it is explained, or *defended*. It is because of Jerusalem's sin. Verse 6, which is the centre verse of the first part of the chapter, says: "For the iniquity (not 'punishment' as in A.V.) of the daughter of My people is greater than the sin of Sodom." Verse 13 further explains that the vengeance is "For the sins of her prophets, and the iniquities of her priests, that have shed the blood of the just in the midst of her," etc. This fourth acrostic, like the others, is in two parts. In verses 1 to 11 we have *a series of contrasts* between the Zion that was and the Zion that now is. In verses 12 to 22 we have the thoughts and actions of the *onlooking Gentile nations* about it.

And now, glance at the last of these five laments. Although having twenty-two verses, and thus corresponding with the Hebrew alphabet, like its predecessors, it is not an acrostic. Also, although it has twenty-two verses, it is shorter than the others with twenty-two, which is because its verses are short couplets, and not long-lined triplets such as mainly make up the other laments. It is throughout a *prayer*, and the speaker is *Jerusalem*. In the first eighteen verses the plea springs from Jerusalem's pitiful plight. In the remaining four verses the appeal is to Jehovah's abiding sovereignty and faithfulness. So then—

THE BOOK OF THE LAMENTATIONS

Lament 1 *Jerusalem's Plight*	Lament 2 *Jehovah's Anger*	Lament 3 *Jeremiah's Grief*	Lament 4 *Jehovah's Anger*	Lament 5 *Jerusalem's Prayer*
THE PROPHET BEWAILS IT (1–11).	THE ANGER DESCRIBED (1–12).	AFFLICTION, YET HOPE (1–39).	CONTRASTS— AND WHY (1–11).	PLEA : ZION IS STRICKEN (1–18).
THE CITY BEMOANS IT (12–22).	THE CITY EXHORTED (13–22).	PLEA : NATIONAL, PERSONAL (40–66).	ONLOOKERS— KINGS, EDOM (12–22).	PLEA : JEHOVAH CAN RESTORE

Hebrew Elegiac Poetry

Although, as we pointed out in an earlier study, the parallelism in Hebrew poetry is one of ideas rather than of rhyme or rhythm, there does seem indication that rhythm was used to some extent. A certain peculiar metre seems to have been reserved for poems of mournful reflection such as we have in the "Lamentations." The first feature of this is the unusual length of the line, to give a slow, solemn movement. A second feature is the breaking of the lengthy line into two unequal parts, the first part being about the same length as one normal line in any average Hebrew lyric, and the second part much shorter, almost like another line abbreviated, and "seeming to suggest," as Professor W. F. Adeney puts it, "that the weary thought is waking up and hurrying to its conclusion." Often the effect of this is impaired in translation; yet in our English version it often comes through with unmistakable force. Take just a couple of examples:

Her princes are become like harts—that find no pasture,
And they are gone without strength—before the pursuer (i. 6).

Jehovah's mercies! We are not consumed—for His mercies fail
not;
They are new every morning—great is Thy faithfulness (iii. 22).

Examples of this funereal metre are scattered through the poetry of the Old Testament. Some are to be found in the Psalms. An early specimen among the prophets is given by Amos, who, after announcing that he is to utter a *lamentation* over Israel, puts it into the elegiac couplet—

The Virgin daughter of Israel is fallen—she shall no more rise;
She is cast down upon her land—there is none to raise her up.

A remarkable instance is Isaiah's sudden transition to elegiac form in chapter xiv. 4, for his ironic lament over Babylon and Lucifer—

How hath the oppressor ceased—the golden city ceased!
Jehovah hath broken the staff of the wicked—the sceptre of the
rulers, etc.

Simply now, as specimens of the rest, we set out the first three verses of the first and of the third of Jeremiah's "Lamentations."

A *How doth the city sit solitary—that was full of people!*
   How is she become as a widow—that was great among nations!
   Princess among the provinces—how is she become tributary!

B *She weepeth sore in the night—and her tears are on her cheeks;*
   There is no comforter for her—out of all her lovers;
   All her friends dealt treacherously by her—are become her
   enemies.

C *Judah is removed because of affliction—and through much*
   servitude;
   She dwelleth among the heathen—she findeth not rest;
   All her persecutors have overtaken her—amid (her) straits.

A   *I am the man that hath seen affliction—by the rod of His wrath.*

A   *He hath led me and caused me to walk in darkness—and not in light.*

A   *Surely against me He turneth His hand again and again—all the day.*

B   *My flesh and my skin hath He made old—He hath broken my bones.*

B   *He hath builded against me—and set round me gall and travail.*

B   *He hath made me to dwell in dark places—as the dead of old.*

C   *He hath hedged me about, I go not out—He hath made my chain heavy.*

C   *Yea, when I cry and call for help—He shutteth out my prayer.*

C   *He hath hedged my way with hewn stone—hath made my paths crooked.*

It may seem strange to us modern westerners that such passionate sentiments as we have in these "Lamentations" should be put into the artificial form of alphabetic acrostics. It may seem to give a touch of unreality. A little reflection, however, will convince us otherwise. These elegies were probably meant for liturgical use rather than for merely private reading; and the acrostic arrangement is an expedient to aid the memory. There is another value, too, in the acrostic scheme: it indicates self-possession amid deep emotion on the part of the writer: what he writes is the product of reflection and deliberation. Moreover, such is the genius of these "Lamentations" that, although they are within this acrostic framework, the underlying thought remains uncramped, unforced, and spontaneous. Pain, pathos, genius, inspiration and beauty, are all here, in these "Lamentations" of Jeremiah.

Our space is done, and we have scarcely touched on the spiritual significances of this little book. One very tender truth here is that *God suffers with those whom He chastises.* This is immortally objectified in Jeremiah, who had become so sympathetically one with God, and at the same time with his countrymen, that he suffered a double agony in his own heart. No truth is more affecting than that God still loves and suffers with those whom He is obliged in righteousness to smite.

The heart of the poem, both literally and spiritually, is the middle passage of the middle chapter. Five times that word "hope" occurs. Affliction does its humbling work (verse 20). The sufferer grasps its meaning, and cries out, "*I have HOPE*" (verse 21). The new hope is in God alone, as the context shows. This is emphasised again as the poem closes—"THOU, O LORD, REMAINEST" (v. 19). The final prayer of the poem will yet be fulfilled—"*Renew our days as of old*" (v. 21); and Zion will be supreme among the nations; for although God's covenant people may suffer the fiercest fires of affliction and persecution, yet, like the burning bush of Horeb, they are not consumed! They can sing, through the years, the words of Lamentations iii. 22, "*It is of Jehovah's mercies that we are not consumed!*" Nor shall they be consumed, but shall be preserved until David's greater Son shall take the throne and reign gloriously in Jerusalem. Then will their troubles be over for ever.

We must add a final word. If we are earnest disciples of our Lord, we cannot study this little fivefold poem, the "Lamentations", as something merely objective, historical, and far removed from ourselves. It certainly does concern what is now distant; yet in a spiritual sense it is poignantly up-to-date. God is the same today as ever in His dealings with nations and individuals. High calling, flaunted by low living, inevitably issues in deep suffering. Election is never indulgent favouritism, whether in relation to Israel or to the members of the true Church today. Since the Divine Sinbearer bore all the sin of all believers, God never *punishes* His born-again children when they sin. The legal aspect was comprehensively dealt with at Calvary. The relationship is now that of Father and child, rather than that of Judge and culprit. Yet the sins of Christian believers bring grievous *chastisings* and *chastenings* upon them; and we may well heed Paul's appeal in Ephesians iv. 1, "*Walk worthy of the vocation wherewith ye are called*".

TRY TO ANSWER THESE QUESTIONS ON JEREMIAH AND LAMENTATIONS

1. Name the kings through whose reigns Jeremiah prophesied, and say what was the catastrophe to which the kingdom of Judah was heading.

2. Mention three outstanding and most exemplary characteristics of Jeremiah personally which reveal themselves through his ministry.

3. Which passage would you say gives the key to the whole book, or focalises its message?

4. Which are the four main parts into which the Book of Jeremiah falls? Simply give the headings to these groups of chapters.

5. Can you cite four great Messianic prophecies in the Book of Jeremiah?

6. Which is the longest single chapter in the book, and where does it occur?

7. Mention three facts which prove that the prophecy on Babylon is a genuine prophecy of Jeremiah, and not a writing of later date.

8. Why is chapter xxv. of special, pivotal importance?

9. In what way can Jeremiah himself be said to be a kind of typical figure?

10. What catastrophic event does the elegy, "Lamentations," bemoan?

11. Show broadly the subject-arrangement of the five "laments" which make up the full poem.

12. What acrostic features are found in "Lamentations"?

EXPLORE THE BOOK

*A Basic and Broadly Interpretative Course
of Bible Study from Genesis to Revelation*

J. SIDLOW BAXTER

VOLUME FOUR
EZEKIEL TO MALACHI

CONTENTS OF VOLUME FOUR

	PAGE
THE BOOK OF EZEKIEL	7
Studies 78 to 81	
THE BOOK OF DANIEL	47
Studies 82 to 85	
HOSEA, JOEL, AMOS	87
Studies 86 to 90	
OBADIAH, JONAH, MICAH	135
Studies 91 to 96	
NAHUM, HABAKKUK, ZEPHANIAH	195
Studies 97 to 99	
HAGGAI, ZECHARIAH, MALACHI	225
Studies 100 to 103	

THE BOOK OF THE PROPHET
EZEKIEL (1)
Lesson Number 78

NOTE.—For this study read the whole Book of Ezekiel through once, but not attempting to read it hurriedly at one sitting. Read it with the chapters grouped as follows:

First, chapters i. to iii., pondering the opening vision and the call of the prophet;

Second, chapters iv. to xxiv., noting that they all refer to Jerusalem;

Third, chapters xxv. to xxxix., noting that they mainly refer to the future and the destinies of various Gentile peoples;

Fourth, chapters xl. to xlviii., which are quite apart, and are wholly occupied with the vision of the final temple and city.

The sum of it (God's sovereignty) lies in this proposition, namely, that the great God, blessed for ever, hath an absolute power and right of dominion over His creatures, to dispose and determine of them as seemeth Him good.

—*Elisha Coles, "A Practical Discourse of God's Sovereignty"*

THE BOOK OF EZEKIEL (1)

IN OUR course of studies we have noted that twelve of the prophetical books are pre-exilic, and five post-exilic. The five post-exilic are, Ezekiel, Daniel, Haggai, Zechariah, Malachi. All the others belong to the period *preceding* the fall of Jerusalem and the Babylonian exile of the Jews, except, of course, that Jeremiah, the last of the pre-exilic prophets, actually lived to witness that tragic event, and wrote his "Lamentations" as a sad memorial to it.

With the prophet Ezekiel we make a new departure. His book, like that of Daniel which follows it, was written in the period after the Babylonian exile of the Jews had set in. Both Ezekiel and Daniel, however, were carried captive to Babylon some years before the final siege and sack of Jerusalem in 587 B.C. —for there were two earlier and smaller deportations of Jewish captives to Babylon, as we see from 2 Kings xxiv. 8–16; Jeremiah xxiv. 1, and Daniel i. 1–4. These were the first-fruits of that harvest for captivity which the Babylonians eventually reaped even to the gleanings.

Ezekiel Himself

Ezekiel, like Jeremiah, was a priest as well as a prophet (i. 3). He was one of ten thousand captives taken to Babylon by Nebuchadnezzar at the time when Zedekiah, Judah's last king, commenced his miserable reign of eleven years at Jerusalem. This deportation is reported in 2 Kings xxiv. 11–18. Since it coincided with the accession of Zedekiah it must have been eleven years before the final overthrow of Jerusalem; for it was in the eleventh year of Zedekiah's reign that the overthrow occurred. We know that Ezekiel must have been among that ten thousand, because he himself tells us, in chapter xl. 1, that "the fourteenth year after the city was smitten" was the twenty-fifth of his own captivity in Babylon—which shows that he had been in Babylon for eleven years before the fall of Jerusalem.

Perhaps, instead of saying that Ezekiel and his fellow-captives were in Babylon, we ought to use the wider term and say that they were in Babylonia, lest it should be imagined that they were actually in the *city* of Babylon. Ezekiel tells us exactly where he was located in his exile, and just when he commenced his prophesying there. His exilic home was at Tel-abib (iii. 15) on the banks of the river Chebar (i. 1). The name, Tel-abib, means "hill of corn ears," and perhaps indicates the fertility of the district. The river Chebar is said to be now known as the *Kabour*. It flowed into the Euphrates north of Babylon city, and was also called *Nar-kabari*, that is, the great canal. Of the Jewish exiles Dr. Joseph Angus says: "These captives were distributed into different settlements throughout Babylonia, forming small communities with a certain organisation and freedom to worship, each in their 'little sanctuary.'" One such colony had been planted at Tel-abib on the Chebar, consisting, as some think, of better-class Jews. Among these the most notable figure was the priest-prophet Ezekiel, whom they evidently respected, but whose words they resisted for the most part, clinging to the false hope of an early return to the land of their fathers.

The Ministry of Ezekiel

Ezekiel tells us that he commenced his prophesying in the fifth year after Jehoiachin's deposition, which, of course, was also the fifth year after Zedekiah's accession (i. 2). This was also the fifth year of Ezekiel's captivity in Babylonia; and it is important to note here that wherever Ezekiel gives the date of his visions or prophecies (which he does thirteen times) he reckons from that outstanding, tragic year of his life when his exile started in Babylonia. He himself makes this clear in chapters xxxiii. 21 and xl. 1. The *latest* date which Ezekiel gives us for any of his prophesyings is chapter xxix. 17—"And it came to pass in the seven and twentieth year . . ." which gives a stretch of twenty-two years from the opening vision in chapter i. If our reading of chapter i. 1 is right, Ezekiel was thirty years of age when he commenced his prophetic ministry to the exiles; which means that he was carried to Babylon when he was twenty-five.

Since Ezekiel began his prophesying in the fifth year after his arrival in Babylon (i. 2), he was exercising his ministry to the exiles for six years before Jerusalem fell. That is why, in the first twenty-four chapters, there is so much about coming judgment on Jerusalem (for none of the first twenty-four chapters is dated later than the ninth year, whereas it was in the *eleventh* year that Jerusalem fell).

Ezekiel's ministry among the exiles was a very difficult one. A brief consideration of the circumstances will show why. Ominous blows had lately fallen on Jerusalem. Two deportations of Jews to Babylon had already deprived it of the flower of its nobility. Yet instead of reading in these things Jehovah's ultimatum to them to mend their ways or else perish, the idol-mad, vice-intoxicated populace had steeped themselves the more deeply in superstition and immorality. This we saw in our study of Jeremiah.

After the deportation of the ten thousand in which Ezekiel was included, God gave to Jeremiah the sign-message of the good and the evil figs (Jer. xxiv.), the good figs representing those who had been carried away from Jerusalem, and the bad figs, which were *very* bad, those who remained. Yet so senselessly had the people of Jerusalem misconstrued the meaning of that deportation as to flatter themselves that while their now exiled kinsmen were probably being justly enough punished for their sins, they themselves, the spared remainder in the city, were heaven's favourites, to whom the land was given for a possession (see Ezek. xi. 15 and xxxiii. 24).

Other than dreading an imminent expulsion from the land, they persuaded themselves that the Babylonian armies would not return, and that Jehovah's city was inviolate. Undoubtedly this popular delusion was considerably due to the false prophets who dealt their deadly dope in the name of Jehovah (Jer. xxvii. 9; xxviii. 1–11, etc.). It was in vain that Jeremiah told them that their city's fate was sealed (Jer. xxi. 7; xxiv. 8; xxxii. 3–5; xxxiv. 2, 3).

The same mood apparently asserted itself with equal obstinacy among the exiled Jews in Babylonia, among whom Ezekiel laboured. While there would doubtless be some kindred spirits to Ezekiel, who recognised Jehovah's judgments in the calamities that were occurring, and mourned over Zion with contrite hearts (see psalm cxxxvii.), yet the majority clung to their idolatries and wrong ways (xiv. 4, etc.; xxxiii. 32; see also ii. 4; iii. 7–9). These exiles, also, were permeated by the delusive idea that their captivity would soon be ended, and that Jehovah could never allow Jerusalem, His chosen city, to be ruined. There were false prophets among them, as there were at far-away Jerusalem, who were all the while inculcating this (xiii. 16, 19). It was to counter the influence of these deceivers that Jeremiah wrote his letter to the Jewish exiles in Babylonia (Jer. xxix.), exhorting them to settle down quietly there and seek the good of that land. Note how Jeremiah hits out at the false prophets among the exiles. Read his letter again. Maybe the exiles would have accepted Jeremiah's counsel the more readily but for the persistence of these impostor-prophets, one of whom, Shemaiah the Nehelamite, actually sent a reply to Jeremiah's counsels, suggesting that the priest Zephaniah should imprison Jeremiah as a madman (Jer. xxix. 24–8).

It is certainly clear that there was need for such a prophet as Ezekiel among the exiles, and it is equally clear that his task was a very difficult one. His first task was to disabuse them of their false hope, which required much courage. He was also to interpret to his exiled people the stern logic of their past history. But the rainbow is seen again in the cloud; for Ezekiel, like Jeremiah, had a glorious picture to paint of the after-days, and a consummating vision in which he saw a reunited people, a re-erected temple, and a reorganised worship, and a regenerated Israel.

Probably after the fall of Jerusalem there would be a readier ear to Ezekiel's message. The only other points which we need mention here about him are that he was a married man (xxiv. 16–18), that he evidently had his own house at Tel-abib (iii. 24; viii. 1), that his wife's death, in the ninth or tenth year of their captivity, came as a grievous blow to him (xxiv. 16, 17), and that according to Jewish tradition he was eventually slain by a fellow-exile whose idolatries he had rebuked.

The opening vision and commission of Ezekiel (i–iii) have special relevance for Christian workers. Note the end of the vision, "I saw", "I fell", "I heard". That is ever how prophets are made. But immediately he is "on his face", the Spirit sets him "on his feet" (ii. 2). Let us read, mark, learn!

The " Book " of Ezekiel

Although this Book of Ezekiel is a large one, it presents no obstacles to a clear general analysis. It follows a clear order. Let us glance through it, and note its main features.

First, it is perfectly clear that the opening three chapters belong together. In them we have *the initial vision and Divine commission of the prophet*. Next, it will be seen that all the chapters from iv. to xxiv. are concerned with *God's judgments upon Jerusalem and the covenant people*; and all the dates which Ezekiel affixes to these chapters fall before the overthrow of Jerusalem (i. 2; viii. 1; xx. 1; xxiv. 1). Next, it will be seen that chapters xxv. to xxxix. are all occupied with *the future destinies of the nations*—first of the Gentile nations (xxv.–xxxii.) and then of Israel (xxxiii.–xxxix.). Finally, in chapters xl. to xlviii., we have a wonderful vision symbolically portraying the ideal temple and worship of the ultimate future.

We do not have to look deeply to find the *key idea* and the *focal message* of Ezekiel. They confront us on almost every page. With slight variations, that expression, "They shall know that I am Jehovah," occurs no less than seventy times. It is used twenty-nine times in connection with Jehovah's punishment of Jerusalem; twenty-four times in connection with Jehovah's governmental judgments on the Gentile nations; and seventeen times in connection with the coming restoration and final blessing of the elect nation. To see this is to see the heart of the book unveiled. The elect people, and all other peoples, are to know by indubitable demonstration that Jehovah is the one true God, the sovereign Ruler of nations and history; and they are to know it by three revelations of His sovereign power—first, by the punishment of Jerusalem and the captivity of the chosen people, which came true exactly as foretold; second, by the judgments prophesied on the Gentile nations of Ezekiel's day, which also have come true exactly as foretold; and third, by the preservation and ultimate restoration of the covenant people, which had a partial fulfilment in the return of the "Remnant" under Ezra and Nehemiah, and which is still being fulfilled in the marvellous preservation of Israel, and which is even now hastening to its millennial consummation. This, then, is Ezekiel—"*THEY SHALL KNOW THAT I AM JEHOVAH.*"

Let us mark well these three main movements in this book of Ezekiel—

1. THE PRESENT JUDGMENTS ON JERUSALEM
(iv.–xxiv).

2. THE FUTURE DESTINIES OF THE NATIONS
(xxv.–xxxix).

3. THE FINAL TEMPLE, PEOPLE, AND CITY
(xl.–xlviii).

And now let us pick out the *sub*divisions. Take the first movement (iv. to xxiv.). Here it will be seen that chapters iv. to vii. consist of similes and messages of the imminent doom.

It is equally obvious that a new section starts with chapter viii., for chapters viii. to xi. describe a *vision*—a carefully dated vision—of the Temple and Jerusalem defiled by the idolatries and sins of the Jewish people, its special point and climax being that the glory of Jehovah now leaves the Temple and the city (x. 18; xi. 23).

Then, from chapter xii. to xxiv. we have a further stretch of similes and prophecies of the judgments which were even now beginning. Note that chapter xxiv., which ends this first of the three main movements in Ezekiel, and which brings us exactly half way through the book, coincides with the very day on which Nebuchadnezzar's armies commenced the fateful siege of the Jewish capital. See 2 Kings xxv. 1 with Ezekiel xxiv. 1, 2. On the very day that Jerusalem was invested, God revealed the fact of it to Ezekiel, away in Babylonia. In this twenty-fourth chapter, also, Ezekiel's wife dies, the "desire of his eyes," and she is to be unmourned, as a tragic type of Jerusalem. Thus ends the first movement of the book.

Chapters xxv–xxxix

Take now the second movement (xxv.—xxxix.). Here we have Jehovah's purposes with the nations. Here national destinies are written in advance. First we have the coming judgments on Gentile powers—Ammon, Moab, Edom, Philistia (xxv.); Tyrus and Zidon (xxvi.–xxviii.); Egypt (xxix.–xxxii.). But at chapter xxxiii. there is a break. Ezekiel turns again to his own nation: "Again the word of the Lord came unto me, saying: Son of man, speak to *the children of thy people.* . . ." From here to the end of chapter xxxix. we are dealing with the future destiny of Israel. Jerusalem has now fallen. In this very chapter, "one that has escaped out of Jerusalem" comes to Ezekiel with the word, "The city is smitten!" (see verse 21, which connects back with xxiv. 26). The word of Jeremiah and Ezekiel has come true! The false prophets are now exposed! There will now be a different mood and outlook among the Jewish exiles! In consonance with this, Ezekiel is now *recommissioned*, in this thirty-third chapter, as Jehovah's watchman to Israel (verse 7). Note the special word to those who, in the light of what had happened, would turn from their wickedness (verse 11, etc.). Then, in chapter xxxiv., there begins the message that after judgment there was to be a glorious destiny for Israel.

Chapter xxxv., the judgment on Mount Seir, may seem, at a glance, to cut across this high theme; but in reality it is certainly meant to fit in here by way of sharp contrast. Mount Seir is the metonymic name for *Edom*, the twin nation to Israel (see our study on Obadiah). The Edomites had descended from Esau, Jacob's twin-brother, yet they had been from the very start Israel's bitterest foe, with a strange, fierce, implacable, spiteful, gloating hatred. One of the preludes to Israel's final blessing should be the final putting out of wicked Edom. We find a similar singling out of Edom in Lamentations iv. 22. Chapters xxxvi. and xxxvii. are a wonderful anticipation of the national reunion and spiritual renewal of God's earthly people. The culminating age-end assault of Gog and Magog is foredoomed in chapters xxxviii. and xxxix., and the thirty-ninth chapter ends with *all nations recognising Jehovah as the true God, through His marvellous doings with Israel.* Thus ends the second movement of the book.

The last nine chapters

As for the third main part of the book; it is clear that this vision of the ideal temple, worship, land, and city, which covers no less than the last nine chapters of the book, stands by itself. It is carefully dated—the fourteenth year after the fall of Jerusalem (xl. 1), and its subdivisions scarcely need pointing out. We may now, therefore, set out our findings thus—

THE BOOK OF EZEKIEL

"They shall know that I am Jehovah"

OPENING VISION AND CALL OF EZEKIEL (i.–iii.).

1. THE PRESENT JUDGMENTS ON JERUSALEM
(iv.–xxiv.).

SIMILES AND PROPHECIES OF IMMINENT DOOM (iv.–vii.).
VISION OF TEMPLE AND CITY: GLORY DEPARTS (viii.–xi.).
FURTHER TYPES AND MESSAGES OF JUDGMENT (xii.–xxiv.).

2. THE FUTURE DESTINIES OF THE NATIONS
(xxv.–xxxix.).

PROSPECTIVE JUDGMENTS ON GENTILE POWERS
(xxv.–xxxii.).
AFTER PRESENT JUDGMENTS ISRAEL RESTORED
(xxxiii.–xxxvii.).
GOG AND MAGOG DESTROYED: ISRAEL EXALTED
(xxxviii.–xxxix.).

3. THE FINAL TEMPLE, WORSHIP, AND CITY
(xl.–xlviii.).

THE RE-ERECTED TEMPLE, AND NEW GLORY
(xl. 1–xliii. 12).
THE RENEWED WORSHIP, AND HOLY RIVER
(xliii. 13–xlvii. 12).
THE REDIVIDED LAND, AND CITY OF GOD
(xlvii. 13–xlviii. 35).

The Book of Ezekiel lends itself to a much more detailed analysis, of course, than the one here submitted; but this is all that is needed for our present purpose. It is good to fix well in mind the main, threefold structure, with the key idea and focal message—"They shall know that I am Jehovah".

THE BOOK OF EZEKIEL (2)

Lesson Number 79

NOTE.—For this study read Ezekiel, chapters i. to iii., especially lingering over the vision in chapter i. Read also chapters iv. to xxiv. again.

That there is such a power (i.e. the Divine sovereignty), and that this power belongs to God, no other reason needs be assigned but that "He is God, and there is none beside Him". There can be no more, because (1) There can be but one Infinite; for such a being fills heaven and earth; and so no place or room for another. (2) There can be but one Omnipotent; for He that is such hath all others under His feet; besides, where one can do all, more would be impertinent. (3) There can be but one Supreme; supreme power may reside in many (as in mixed monarchies and commonwealths), but as lawmakers and supreme they are but one. (4) There can be but one First Cause, from which all beings else derive their original; and that is this blessed One we are speaking of: "Of whom and for whom are all things" (1 Cor. viii. 6). And if He be the Author of all, He needs must have a sovereign right and power to determine all, both as to their being, order, efficacy, and end.

Elisha Coles, "A Discourse of God's Sovereignty."

THE BOOK OF EZEKIEL (2)

THE OPENING VISION

EZEKIEL'S opening vision is one of the most remarkable in the Bible; and so needful is it for us to grasp its meaning that we devote the whole of this present study to it. It is described mainly in chapter i. Its contents are threefold. So also is its purpose. As to its threefold contents, there is a background, and there is a centre-group, and there is a super-climax. If we understand these rightly we shall know the threefold purpose.

The Background.

First, then, see the background in this vision. The prophet sees a "whirlwind" and a "great cloud" and a "fire infolding itself," coming "out of the north" (verse 4). That expression, "a fire infolding itself," is literally "a fire *catching itself.*" The flames flashed round and round the whirling cloud with such lightning swiftness that each seemed to catch hold of the flash before it. The picture is that of some terrific, whirling thunder-cloud, enclosed in a lurid surround of flashing fire. But the prophet also tells us that "out of the *midst*" of this whirling globe of cloud and fire there was "as the colour of amber." The Hebrew word here translated "amber" is peculiar to Ezekiel, and is now recognised as meaning some kind of luminous metal. The prophet's meaning is that there was a brilliant centre-glow to this fire-swathed storm-cloud. From this the living figures of the vision presently emerged; but first let us get the meaning of this background.

What is the significance of this tempest and storm-cloud and fire? There can be only one answer: these are the symbols of *judgment.* This is corroborated by the fact that they came "out of the north," for it was from Babylon, via the north, that judgment was coming on Jerusalem (see Jer. i. 14, 15; iv. 6; vi. 1). This is further corroborated by the fact that at the end of the vision a "hand" gave Ezekiel a "roll of a book" which was found to contain "lamentations and mourning and woe" (iii. 9, 10). The approach from "the north" does not lose its force through Ezekiel's being in Babylonia, not Jerusalem, at the time; for in an inward sense he was transported far enough from Babylonia; and we are plainly told that afterward "the Spirit" lifted him "away," *back* to the exiles in Babylonia (iii. 14). The standpoint, as in Ezekiel's other visions, is Jerusalem; and the purpose behind the symbols is to reveal the approach of judgment.

The Centre-group.

Out from the fiery heart of this whirling storm-cloud Ezekiel sees "four living creatures" (verse 5), each with four faces and four wings and four hands (verses 6, 8). It should be realised that these four are actual living beings. They are the "cherubim" —Ezekiel himself calls them so in chapter x. That is, they are the living beings who appear in Genesis, guarding the gate of Eden, and who reappear in the Apocalypse as the mysterious guardians of the ineffable throne in heaven (Rev. iv., etc). Yet it must be just as clearly realised that the *presentation* of them here is merely symbolic. Spirit-beings do not actually have "faces" or "wings" or "hands." Symbols are used to express as nearly as possible to our human minds the nature and functions of these wonderful heavenly beings. Ezekiel himself is careful to say that it was only the "likeness" of these four living ones which he saw (verse 5). So very careful is he on this point that he uses the word "likeness" fifteen times. What then do the "likenesses" of these four living ones convey to us?

First, each had four faces—the face of a lion, of an ox, of a man, of an eagle. The fourfold meaning here is obvious—strength, service, intelligence, heavenliness. Here, in symbol, is strength at its greatest, service at its meekest, intelligence at its fullest, and spirituality the most soaring.

These beings also had four wings and four hands each—a wing and a hand on each of their four sides, these together symbolising fulness of capacity for service (verses 6, 8).

Next, "they went every one straight forward: whither the Spirit was to go, they went; and they turned not when they went" (verse 12). Here is symbolised their undeviating prosecution of the Divine will.

Next, their appearance was "like burning coals of fire, like lightnings" (verse 13)—a symbolic expression of their utter holiness. And again, they "ran and returned as the appearance of a flash of lightning" (verse 14), which expresses their utter swiftness of action.

Thus, in these cherubim, we have strength, service, intelligence, spirituality, at their highest; fulness of capacity for service; undeviating prosecution of the Divine will; absolute holiness; and uttermost swiftness of action.

But now, at verse 15, a strange new marvel presents itself. Four awesome wheels appear "by" (that is, *beside*) these four living beings. That these wheels were four in number is stated in verse 16. One wheel was beside each of the four living beings, as we see in verse 16 (also in x. 9). The size and sweep of these wheels was vast. They reached down to the earth (verse 15), yet they reached up to heaven. Verse 18 says: "As for their rings (rims) they were so high that they were dreadful." Mark well, then, that these four wheels connect these heavenly beings with the earth.

Perhaps the most curious thing about these immense wheels is that each wheel was two in one. Verse 16 says that their appearance was "as it were a wheel in the middle of a wheel." Many readers misunderstand the meaning here. They picture a large wheel with a smaller one in the middle of it, revolving in the same direction. This is not Ezekiel's meaning. What he means is made clear by a striking little word which he speaks both of the wheels and the living creatures. He says: "They turned not when they went; they went every one straight forward" (verses 9, 12, 17). Now how was it that the four living beings turned not when they went? It was because, having four faces, they each faced north, south, east, west, simultaneously, and therefore needed not to turn in any direction. Nor did they need to turn when they flew, for each had four wings, one on each of their four sides, so that they simply needed to use the appropriate pair of wings for any of the four directions, without any necessity to turn. And, similarly, the *wheels* needed not to turn, for they were two wheels in one, the one being through the other, that is, *crosswise* to each other, the one revolving north-south and the other east-west, so that there was no need to turn for any direction. Such a wheel, of course, would be impossible actually to construct; but we are here seeing *symbol*.

These wheels, which thus whirled with lightning-like rapidity in every direction, without need of turning, had their vast rims "full of eyes" (verse 18). These countless eyes looked simultaneously in every direction from the crosswise rims. They saw everything. Nothing could be hid from them. This, undoubtedly, is the symbol of *omniscience*.

Finally, these awesome wheels were filled with the life of the living beings themselves. "The spirit of the living creatures was in the wheels" (verse 20). Because of this these wheels expressed with absolute exactitude the will and movement of the four living beings (verse 21).

Try now to catch the full picture of these cherubim with their wheels, and the meaning will be unmistakable. Ezekiel, remember, had just seen the symbols of a coming judgment. The Babylonians were soon to overrun Judæa and carry the nation into exile. In these cherubim and their wheels Ezekiel was meant to learn that the judgments which were about to happen on earth were but the expression of what was happening in the invisible realm. The events which take place on this earth should never be viewed apart from that invisible realm. Fundamentally there is a spiritual and Divine meaning in all that is permitted. Ezekiel was meant to learn this particularly in connection with the overthrow of Jerusalem. We ourselves should learn it afresh in connection with the big developments of our own era. The purpose, then, in this centre-group of Ezekiel's vision is to show that *behind the events which take place on earth are the operations of supernatural powers in heaven.*

See how significantly the *wheels* show this. They rest down on earth, yet they reach up to heaven. They run to and fro down here, yet they move by a power from above, for "the spirit of the living creatures was in the wheels"! Those vast, awesome wheels are *the wheels of the Divine government*, the wheels of so-called "Providence," with an especial reference here, to the exercise of providential *judgment*. Those wheels of the Divine government run with resistless, lightning-like swiftness in all directions over all the earth. They never need to turn, for they face every way, and they are everywhere, and they are full of eyes which look north, south, east, west, simultaneously, and see everything, everywhere, every minute.

And now, just as the wheels connect the events of earth with the powers of heaven, see how the four living creatures *above* the wheels connect up with God Himself. These four living creatures above the wheels express most strikingly, in symbolic form, *the life of God*. As we have seen, the four faces of each expressed the fourfold idea of strength, service, intelligence, and spirituality at their highest, with the added suggestion of inaccessibility and mystery, in the symbol of the eagle. Now each of these four living ones could only have each of his four faces looking one way (verses 10, 12); but when they appeared to Ezekiel in square formation, they were evidently so placed, each at one corner of the square, that the face of a man looked every way, the face of a lion every way, the face of an ox every way, and the face of an eagle every way. Thus, not only did the myriad eyes of the four double wheels look in every direction, but the sixteen faces of the living beings, in four fours, also looked in every direction; and as the four awesome wheels expressed the omniscience, omnipotence, and omnipresence of God, so the faces of the living beings expressed the moral and intellectual nature of God—for we must remember that as the spirit of the living creatures was in the wheels, so the Spirit of Jehovah Himself was in the living creatures (verse 12). Thus, then, these wheels connect the events of earth with the cherubim in heaven; and the cherubim in turn connect them with God.

Both Ezekiel and John make it clear that these four living ones somehow live nearest of all God's creatures to the throne of God Himself, and most nearly express His life. It is not surprising, therefore, that when the very Son of God became incarnate there should be seen a correspondence between Him and these four symbol-clad figures of Ezekiel's vision. It is seen in the distinctive emphasis of the four Gospel writers. In Matthew it is the lion; in Mark, the ox; in Luke, the man; in John, the eagle.

The Super-climax.

This brings us to the super-climax of Ezekiel's vision. It is in truth a "super" climax, for Ezekiel now sees above the cherubim a superstructure of almost blinding glory. He suddenly hears a voice from the firmament over the heads of the cherubim (verse 25), and on looking up he sees "the likeness of a throne, as the appearance of a sapphire stone." On the throne is a fire-enveloped Figure having "the likeness as the appearance of a man." Mark again Ezekiel's cautious language. It is "the *likeness* as the *appearance* of a man" upon "the *likeness* of a throne." It is not the Divine Being Himself whom Ezekiel sees, but certain appearances to make vivid to him the character and attributes of Him whom "no man hath seen nor can see."

As the *general* form of the cherubim, apart from divergent peculiarities, was that "of a man" (verse 5), so here, again, the general impression is that of "the appearance of a man" (the same basis being retained, presumably, because of there being no higher symbol of intelligence that would be understandable to the human mind) ; but that which is added here (unlike the description of the cherubim) is vague, being incapable of description. The Figure is wreathed in fire. There is a centre-glow as of luminous or molten metal ("amber"), and a "brightness round about." The symbols are expressive of awful holiness and unapproachable glory. Ezekiel at once recognises in it "the appearance of the likeness of the glory of Jehovah," and falls in prostrate adoration.

The *purpose* in this super-climax is as clear as that in the other parts of the vision. If the cherubim and their wheels express the fact that behind the events of earth are the operations of heaven, this super-climax of the throne expresses the fact that *both behind all events on earth and above all supernatural powers in heaven is the sovereign throne and will and purpose of the infinite Jehovah Himself.*

Ezekiel hears and sees, and falls on his face. But even that is not all. He has caught sight of something, after everything else, which he can never forget. He has seen a *rainbow* round about that throne (verse 28), which crowns all the awful glory with a gentle beauty. It is the token of a Divine covenant. It is the symbol of the Divine faithfulness. It is the pledge of a final clear shining after the dark thunder-clouds of judgment have passed away. It says that amid wrath to the full there will be love to the end. Even the awful holiness and ineffable glory of that supreme throne are over-arched by grace! Thank God, that rainbow is always there! Man's sighs shall yet become songs; and where sin has abounded, grace shall ultimately triumph in a redeemed human society which is "holiness unto the Lord."

The Threefold Purpose.

So, then, in this opening vision there is a threefold purpose. First, in the background of storm and cloud and fire the purpose is to show the approach of judgment. Second, in the centre-group of cherubim and wheels the purpose is to show that behind the events of earth are the operations of heaven. Third, in the super-climax of the throne and rainbow the purpose is to show that supreme over all is Jehovah Himself, that His sovereign will overrules all, that in wrath He remembers mercy, and that in the end judgment issues in the triumph of grace and righteousness.

When the tragedy of Jerusalem's ruin came, Ezekiel was not to let his faith go to pieces, thinking that Jehovah, after all, had proved unable to preserve His own chosen city, that the reins had been snatched from His grasp, and that the gods of the heathen were mighty. He was to know that before ever the judgment fell it was foreknown and actually predetermined, that behind it was the operation of supernatural power, and that beyond it there would be an outcome of final blessing.

What this vision meant to Ezekiel, and how clearly he grasped its threefold purpose, is seen all through his prophecies. We cannot but be struck by the fact that this man who was in even more hopeless circumstances than Jeremiah, inasmuch as he was actually in exile, was full of hope and jubilant conviction as to the eventual restoration of Israel. Though he never dissolved in tears as did Jeremiah, yet his vision of the ultimate triumph of Jehovah's purpose through His people was even clearer. In fact he saw right through to the glory of that final temple which is yet to be built, and the wonder of that city of God which shall one day be named, "Jehovah-Shammah"—"The Lord is there."

We, too, need to catch that vision in days like these. Science has put staggering new powers and weapons into man's hands. Wickedness finds much bigger and far more terrifying forms of expression than ever before. Things move on such a vast scale, and with such frightening contingencies, and at the beck of such organised anti-God forces, that the international situation easily becomes profoundly disturbing. The reins of providence seem to hang loosely. Evil forces in large areas of the earth seem to have it pretty much their own way. It is easy for our eyes to become so held by the startling evolution of human history today that we lose our vision of that glory-flashing throne high over all, and our sense of the Divine sovereignty.

Yes, we need to see that throne again today. We need to see it with clarified inward eyes. And we need to see again, above that throne, the overarching rainbow which speaks of the Divine faithfulness. The presence of that lovely rainbow there gives to the four symbolic seraphim a significance which we have not hitherto mentioned, but which we ought to note here. Each of those seraphs had the face of a lion, and the face of an ox, and the face of a man, and the face of an eagle. It has been aptly observed that the lion represents all the untamed beasts. The ox represents the tamed and serviceable animals. The man represents the human race. The eagle represents the birds of the heavens. The rainbow at once reminds us of God's covenant with Noah, and through Noah with all the human race and the lower animals who occupy the earth along with man. Ezekiel's vision shows that covenant as still sealing and crowning the Divine government of the earth. God remembers His covenant with man and with all the creatures, even when His judgments must fall upon the earth and strange things must be permitted. Thank God that rainbow is still there, as the present age careers onward through its closing decades to its culminating convulsions! We need not lose heart. We need not lose faith. That rainbow still arches the throne of omnipotent sovereignty; and even the night of the "great tribulation" shall be but a black-robed herald of the glorious Millennium which is on its way!

THE BOOK OF EZEKIEL (3)

Lesson Number 80

NOTE.—For this study read again chapters xl. to xlviii., twice over.

The apostate angels, or wicked spirits, though the testimony we have from these is not from love or good will, yet is as great an evidence of God's sovereignty as any other, in that, being enemies to God, proud and imperious, they are yet overawed and compelled to submit. And hence it was that the devil dared not answer again when the fatal sentence was pronounced upon him for seducing our first parents.

Elisha Coles, "A Discourse of God's Sovereignty"

THE BOOK OF EZEKIEL (3)

THE TRIO OF VISIONS

EZEKIEL has been called "the Patmos-seer of the Old Testament." As to the exiled John on the island of Patmos, so to the exiled Ezekiel by the river Chebar, extraordinary *visions* were given. The first of these, which we have already examined, is described mainly in chapter i. A second and much longer one is described in chapters viii. to xi. A third, which is much longer still, is described in chapters xl. to xlviii. To get the point of these three main visions is to comprehend the total message of the book.

The First Vision (i.–iii.).

We devoted our preceding lesson to this first vision. We went into its symbolism, and therefore need not do so again in the second vision; for the same symbolic presentation of cherubim and glory reappears, with only minor divergences. We have seen the central purpose of the first vision. In general it was to show that behind all events of earth are the operations of supernatural powers, and that above all is the will of God Himself. More particularly, it was to show Ezekiel that behind the judgment coming on *Jerusalem* was the sovereign activity of Jehovah.

The Second Vision (viii.–xi.).

This second vision came "in the sixth year" (viii. 1), that is, five years before the overthrow of Jerusalem. In it Ezekiel was transported to Jerusalem (viii. 3). The vision moves in four stages. First, in chapter viii. we see Judah's profanation of the temple. Second, in chapter ix. we see Jehovah's judgment on the people. Third, in chapter x., the "glory" of Jehovah leaves the temple. Fourth, in chapter xi., the "glory" also leaves the city.

In chapter viii. Ezekiel is shown the profanation of the temple. At the north gate of the inner court he sees an "image of jealousy which provoketh to jealousy" (verse 3). This was an idol set up in the very precincts of Jehovah's house. Yet Israel's God had said: "Thou shalt not make unto thee any graven image . . . for I, Jehovah, am a jealous God" (Exod. xx. 4; and see Deut. xxxii. 16, 21). Mark the contrast here: immediately after pointing out the "image of jealousy," Ezekiel exclaims, "And behold, the glory of the God of Israel was there!" (verse 4). Oh, the provocation—a false god reared *there*! Judah's guilt was measured by the contrast between this ugly idol and that heavenly shekinah.

But Ezekiel is now shown an *inferno* of idolatries. He is let into the secret chamber of a clandestine theriomorphic cult, in which seventy Jewish elders offer incense to beast-gods (verses 7–12). Next, at the north gate of the outer court he is shown "women weeping for Tammuz" (verses 13–15), the "Adonis" of Greek mythology. The annual feast of Tammuz consisted of a weeping by the women, for his death, followed by a rejoicing over his return, and was accompanied by phallic abominations. Next, Ezekiel is shown twenty-five men standing between the altar of sacrifice and the door-porch of the holy place; but instead of worshipping toward the holy place of Jehovah, they have turned their backs on it, and face eastward, worshipping the sun (verse 16). These twenty-five men, being in the court of the priests, are presumably the high priest and the heads of the twenty-four courses.

Thus, in these different parts of the temple, Ezekiel sees the general image-worship of the *people*, the secret animal-worship of the *elders*, the sex-corruption of the *women*, and the shameless apostasy of the *priesthood*. All classes are involved in the debasing infidelity. Corruption in religion always brings general moral breakdown; so we are not surprised to read in verse 17, "They have filled the land with violence."

Chapter ix. now follows with a symbolic picture of *judgment* on the wicked populace. Seven men are dispatched, one to spare the godly minority, six to slay the rest. This slaying, note, is the command of Jehovah Himself (verses 5–7). Then comes chapter x., with its significant ceremony of the departure of the Divine presence from the *temple*. In verse 4 the "glory" moves from the cherub over the ark in the Holy of Holies, to the threshold of the house. In verses 18 and 19 it leaves the temple altogether. Finally, in chapter xi. the "glory" departs from the *city* also. The doom of the now God-forsaken city is sealed.

The main import of all this is unmistakable. If the *first* vision means to show that the power behind the coming judgment is that of God Himself, the purpose of this second vision is to show that the *reason* for the coming judgment is the guilt of Judah. The first vision says that the judgment is from *God*. The second vision says that the judgment is for *sin*. The first vision explains the *fact* of the judgment. The second vision explains the *cause* of it.

The Third Vision (xl.–xlviii.).

We turn to Ezekiel's third vision. Here he sees a temple and city of the future in which the glory of God shall abide for ever. In some senses it is the most remarkable passage of the book; but the interpretation of it is a matter of dispute. Let us see if we can briefly resolve our own views about it.

First, Ezekiel's description here is not that of the *former* temple, which Solomon built, and which was now destroyed. Equally clearly, it is not the *later* temple, erected by the "Remnant," after the Exile. Nor does the still later temple which Herod built at Jerusalem fulfil the requirements. All will agree thus far. So, then, as there has been no Jewish temple at Jerusalem since the destruction of Herod's in A.D. 70, and as Ezekiel's description certainly cannot be "spiritualised" into meaning the present Christian Church, his temple and city must be *still future*.

Yet, even so, the question remains: Is Ezekiel's description to be taken *literally* or only *symbolically*? We reject off-hand the theory of certain moderns, that this new temple and worship and city were simply a product of Ezekiel's own mind, devised as a pattern for the reorganising of Israel after the Exile; for Ezekiel's own word is that what he describes was shown him by supernatural agency (xl. 1, 2). Are we, then, to interpret literally or symbolically?

Well, first, we believe it to be a sound principle of exegesis in general that unless there is some serious objection to the literal interpretation of a passage, this should be given first preference. Are there, then, serious objections to our taking Ezekiel's description literally? There are. Certain of its main features are such that a literal fulfilment of them is surely unthinkable.

Take the size of the *temple* and of the *sacred area* going with
it. The "outer court" of the temple is 500 reeds long by 500
wide (xlii. 15–20; xlv. 2); and as the reed is about ten feet, this
court is one mile long by one mile wide, which means that this
temple covers a space as large as the whole city enclosed by the
walls of old Jerusalem. Certainly, *this* temple could not possibly
be contained on Mount Zion, inside Jerusalem. But when we
pass from the temple to the sacred area, or "oblation" of land,
going with it, we find this to be 25,000 reeds long by 25,000 wide
(xlviii. 20), that is, forty-seven miles north to south, and the
same east to west, covering an area between six and seven times
that of modern London! Of this an area forty-seven miles by
nearly nineteen is reserved for the priesthood alone (xlv. 3, 4;
xlviii. 10), and an area the same size for the Levites (xlv. 5;
xlviii. 13). There is also a third area, in which, although small
compared with the whole "oblation," is a "city" with a circuit
of 20,000 reeds, or nearly thirty-eight miles (xlv. 6; xlviii. 15–19),
whereas Josephus reckoned the circuit of Jerusalem in his day
at only *four* miles! Now is it thinkable that there is to be a
literal counterpart to this temple which itself is as large as the
whole of Jerusalem, and in a sacred area of over two thousand
two hundred square miles?

Moreover, this sacred area is *physically impossible*—unless
the river Jordan be moved further east! The boundaries of
the land are the Mediterranean on the west and the Jordan
on the east (xlvii. 18); and this great square of forty-seven
miles by forty-seven cannot be put between the two, for the
distance between them in places is scarcely forty miles. Even
if we bend the great square to the slope of the coast we cannot
get it in—the less so because on each side of the square, in
Ezekiel's vision, is an *additional* area called "the portion for
the prince" (xlv. 7; xlviii. 21, 22). Admittedly, God could
move the Jordan; but is it thinkable that we are meant to infer
this?

There is the further difficulty that although this great area is
forty-seven miles by forty-seven, it *does not include the site of
Jerusalem*; so that this "city" which Ezekiel sees is not Jerusalem. If, then, we are to take this vision literally, what of all
those other prophecies which speak of Jerusalem as the glorified
centre of the coming new order?

Ezekiel's vision also places the new temple 500 reeds (some nine and a half miles) *away north from the "city,"* in fact, fourteen and a quarter miles from the *centre* of it. Now the connection between the temple and Jerusalem is so deeply laid, both in the Scriptures and in the thought of the Jews, that to interpret literally a vision which separates them without giving the slightest reason seems again unthinkable. As C. J. Ellicott says, "A temple in any other locality than Mount Moriah would hardly be the temple of Jewish hope." Hard as we find it to picture Ezekiel's mile-square temple spread over the variety of hill and valley which the country presents, we find it even harder to think of the new city as miles away from Jerusalem, and the new temple still another fourteen miles north, and, in fact, well on the way to Samaria.

Another problem in the way of a literal interpretation is found in the waters which Ezekiel saw flowing from beneath the eastern threshold of the temple (xlvii. 1–12). To quote C. J. Ellicott again, "These waters run to the 'east country' and go down 'to the sea,' which can only be the Dead Sea: but such a course would be physically impossible without changes in the surface of the earth, since the temple of the vision is on the west of the watershed of the country. They had, moreover, the effect of 'healing' the waters of the sea, an effect which could not be produced naturally without providing an outlet from the sea: no supply of fresh water could remove the saltness while this water was all disposed of by evaporation; and Ezekiel (in xlvii. 11) excludes the idea of an outlet. But above all, the character of the waters themselves is impossible without a perpetual miracle. Setting aside the difficulty of a spring of this magnitude upon the top of 'a very high mountain' (xl. 2) in this locality, at the distance of 1,000 cubits from their source the waters have greatly increased in volume; and so with each successive 1,000 cubits, until at the end of 4,000 cubits (about a mile and a half) they have become a river no longer fordable, or, in other words, comparable to the Jordan. Such an increase, without accessory streams, is clearly not natural. But, beyond this, the description of the waters themselves clearly marks them as ideal. They are life-giving and healing; trees of perennial foliage and fruit grow upon their banks, the leaves being for 'medicine,' and the fruit, although for food, never wasting."

Even if we admit the physical possibility of all these things, there is another kind of difficulty, which in some ways is still greater. In this temple of Ezekiel's vision the system of *animal sacrifices* is re-instituted (xliii. 13–27, etc.). Is it thinkable that after the one perfect sacrifice of Christ there should be, in the yet future temple, a reversion to these? Does not such an idea insult the New Testament? Did not that perfect sacrifice do away for ever with the merely typical and temporary system of the Old Testament? Those who would literally interpret Ezekiel's vision are certainly taxed here. One writer suggests that these sacrifices will be reinstated in a *commemorative* capacity, just as the Lord's Supper is now observed in a commemorative capacity; but he forgets that even the Lord's Supper is only a temporary commemoration until the Lord Himself returns. And can we think that when the simple, beautiful commemoration with the bread and wine has ceased, the animal sacrifices of the Mosaic economy will be set going again as a commemoration of Calvary? Is *that* the kind of commemoration God wants in the consummation? Can we really think that when the glorified Lord is Himself visibly reigning on earth such a system of artificial commemoration could be needed or perpetuated? Surely not!

But if the passage is *not* to be interpreted literally, what then? Well, as a principle of sound exegesis, it should be borne in mind that we are here dealing, not with direct prophecy, but with *vision*. This very fact should put us on our guard. Our reading of this vision must be guided by the two earlier visions. In the vision of the cherubim we saw that although the cherubim are actual beings, the presentation of them was highly symbolic. In other words, what we have is *central, literal fact surrounded and expressed by symbolism*. Again and again we find this in Scripture. Even so, with this final vision of Ezekiel's, there is a core of real fact, surrounded and expressed by symbols. The millennial temple and city will be concrete realities. The symbols used of them in this vision are meant to express figuratively their principal features.

The main meanings of the striking symbols are clear. The vastness of the dimensions in the vision indicate the *transcendent greatness* of the final temple and city. The various cube measurements symbolise their *Divine perfection*. In the description of the sacrificial ritual we see the *absolute purity* of the final worship.

The marvellous waters gushing from the sanctuary foretell *fulness of life*, and *worldwide blessing*. The returning of the Divine "glory," never to depart again (xliii. 1–7), tells of *sin forever removed* and of *righteousness finally triumphant*; while the putting of Jehovah's throne "in the midst for ever" (xliii. 7) expresses the *ever-enduring glory* of the consummation.

These, then, are the main ideas symbolised concerning the temple and worship and city of the coming age—transcendent greatness, Divine perfection, absolute purity, fulness of life, worldwide blessing, sin forever removed, righteousness finally triumphant, and Jehovah Himself in the midst, reigning in neverending glory.

The Three Visions Together

And now, finally, see the three visions together. All three were necessary to give Ezekiel the full view of things. The central idea of the first vision is that of God *overruling*. The central idea of the second vision is that of God *intervening*. The central idea of the third vision is that of God *consummating*. In the first God overrules in sovereign *government*. In the second God intervenes in righteous *judgment*. In the third God consummates in gracious *restoration*. In the first we see glory *transcending*. In the second we see glory *departing*. In the third we see glory *returning*. In the first vision Ezekiel must see the throne of Jehovah high over the wheels of government. In the second he must see the activity of Jehovah behind the stroke of judgment. In the third he must see the victory of Jehovah in the ultimate realisation of the ideal. In other words, Ezekiel was to see, in these three visions, the purpose of Jehovah *above* all, and *behind* all, and *beyond* all.

This triple truth Ezekiel grasped and understood. He lived and wrought in the light and power of it. We, too, need to live and work in the light and power of this vision, or we shall faint at the discouragements of the times. Servant of Jesus, stand with Ezekiel again: get the sound of the wings and the chariot wheels in your ears again: see again the man with the inkhorn sealing the godly remnant: and look on to the temple and city which are yet to be. This is the triune vision which turns fear to hope, and sighs to songs. May it be ever before our eyes!

Jehovah hath spoken it, and it shall surely come to pass.

THE BOOK OF EZEKIEL (4)

Lesson Number 81

NOTE.—For this final study in Ezekiel read again chapters xxv. to xxxix. Note specially the passages on Gog and Magog, and on Israel's coming restoration.

Thy Spirit animates eternal years,
Pervades and broods above,
Changes, sustains, dissolves, creates and rears.
Though earth and man were gone,
And suns and universes ceased to be,
And Thou wert left alone,
Every existence would exist in Thee.

Emily Brontë.

THE BOOK OF EZEKIEL (4)

EVERY page of Ezekiel gleams with attraction for the keen student of the Bible. From the opening vision of the Divine glory to the final vision of the future temple there is not a dull paragraph. Three *modes* of prophetic activity are conspicuously before us— visions, sign-sermons, and direct predictions. We have given two full lessons to Ezekiel's visions, because of their bearing on the message of the book as a whole; but if we are to keep within the intended limits of these present studies, our consideration of Ezekiel's sign-sermons and direct predictions must be severely brief.

Ezekiel's Sign-sermons

I wonder if we have appreciated the force of these. As Jehovah's witness among a "most rebellious" people, Ezekiel was directed to perform various symbolical or typical *actions* before them, at different times, all portraying, in one aspect or another, the impending judgment on Judah. Certain of these involved him in keen personal discomfort, and would be as irksome to him as they now seem strange to ourselves: but there is a peculiar significance in them which few, perhaps, have noticed.

This significance will become clearer if we look back to our analysis of the book. The first of the three main movements covers chapters iv. to xxiv., and is wholly occupied with the overhanging doom of Jerusalem. Now in these chapters there are no less than ten of these sign-actions, whereas in all the remaining chapters (xxv.–xlviii.) there is only one (xxxvii. 16). Why is this? The answer is found in three paragraphs which tell us that Ezekiel was to be in a certain sense *dumb* until the fall of Jerusalem. First, in chapter iii. 26, 27, right at the beginning of Ezekiel's ministry, God says to him: "I will make thy tongue cleave to the roof of thy mouth, and thou shalt be dumb." Next, in chapter xxiv. 27, four and a half years later, God says to him: "In that day (when Jerusalem falls) shall thy mouth be opened

. . . thou shalt be no more dumb." Third, in chapter xxxiii.
21, 22, we read: "One that had escaped out of Jerusalem came
unto me saying: The city is smitten . . . and my mouth was
opened, and I was no more dumb."

Does this seem a bit mystifying? It is not so in reality. The
point of it is just this, that to a people whose ears were largely
closed God was largely dumb. God had filled Ezekiel's heart
with a great and wonderful message which, although it included
the alarm of approaching judgment, looked on to the days beyond,
and lustred them with gracious promises of Divine forgiveness
and restoration; but his obdurate fellow-exiles were so wedded
to their evil ways as to be utterly unfit to hear such a message.
They remained in this state until Jerusalem had actually been
laid low. Then they saw that the word of prophets like Jeremiah
and Ezekiel was truly the word of Jehovah. Yet even before
Jerusalem fell, witness for Jehovah *must* be borne to them,
"whether they will hear or whether they will forbear" (ii. 5, 7,
etc.), even though it was restricted to a declaration of retribution
against their sin. It was in this sense that Ezekiel was a "watchman" to the house of Israel (iii. 17). God will not have even the
most "stiffhearted" and "rebellious" laid low by final judgment
without a witness and a warning being uttered to them right up
to the midnight knell.

So deaf, however, to the spoken word of God, had these old-
time Jews become, through their disobedience, that even the
warning of judgment must be conveyed to them in the form of
these *sign-actions*, with the purpose of at least arousing curiosity
and causing enquiry; and also with the further purpose, possibly,
of lessening somewhat the guilt which would more and more have
accrued from their repeatedly hearing and rejecting a forthright
declaration from God. That these sign-actions *did* cause enquiry we know from verses such as xii. 9 and xxiv. 19.

But beyond a doubt there was also this yet further purpose in
these sign-sermons: God was thereby indicating His withdrawment from any further reasoning or pleading with them. Such
was their obduracy that a point had now been reached where
God would not speak to them directly any more (xiv. 3). Since
they had treated the declared word of God as cheap, God would
now be dumb (though He would still faithfully warn them),
and they should now be left to puzzle out His intentions from

strange sign-actions. Thus, by his sign-sermons, Ezekiel is a last tragic witness for God, to "a crooked and perverse generation."

Taking a last glance at the three texts which speak of Ezekiel's dumbness, we note that from the first of them (iii. 26) to the second (xxiv. 27) his dumbness was only *partial*; for in chapter iii. 27 God adds, "But when I speak with thee I will open thy mouth, and thou shalt say . . ." But from the second text (xxiv. 27) to the third (xxxiii. 21, 22) the dumbness is *total*; for in the intervening chapters (xxv. to xxxii.) Ezekiel has not one word for his own people, but addresses the Gentile nations only (for according to Ezekiel's own time-marks, these prophecies on the Gentiles come in the period before the fall of Jerusalem, except for the added section of the prophecy against Egypt: see xxix. 17). Ezekiel's *last* sign-sermon to his own people, before his total dumbness for about a year and a half, was the culminating, tragic sign of his own wife's death (xxiv. 15–27).

We may learn much from these sign-sermons. We must be prepared to witness in any way God chooses, and even among those who disdain our message. We must be willing to yield up our dearest possession for the sake of bringing saving truth home to the hearts of men, even as Ezekiel was submissively prepared to part with his wife, who was "the desire of his eyes." Note that Ezekiel was instructed not to express his heart-break in any of the conventional modes of mourning, nor even in tears and crying (xxiv. 16, 17). He was to have his personal sorrow swallowed up in the bigger bereavement, namely, the ruin of Jerusalem and of his nation. So we, also, must bravely sink personal sorrows and grievances in the larger, desperate calamity of the perishing multitudes all around us, who are heading to a Christless eternity. Moreover, as Ezekiel spoke by sign-actions, and as he himself became a sign (xxiv. 24), so there must be the sign of Christ over every part of our life—over our home life and business life and social life, and over our reactions to all the experiences of life. God help us to be Ezekiels to our day and generation!

As for going into Ezekiel's sign-actions one by one here, that is quite beyond our present scope. Some of them are extremely interesting. Those who would appreciate their details and their aptness will do well to linger over them with some good modern verse-by-verse commentary. So far as this present study is concerned, we must reluctantly leave them.

Ezekiel's Direct Predictions

Here, again, we open the gate on a wide and wonderful field. Some of the most remarkable predictions in the Old Testament, both concerning Israel and the Gentile nations, are found in Ezekiel. We can only pick out two or three brief references here to illustrate this.

Take the prophecy on *Tyre* (xxvi.–xxviii.). Tyre was the greatest maritime commercial centre of the ancient world, and one of the most impregnable fortresses. Her continuity seemed secure above that of all other places. But one little strip of Ezekiel's doom-song about her runs—"Thus saith the Lord God: Behold, I will bring upon Tyrus Nebuchadnezzar, king of Babylon . . . he shall break down thy towers . . . he shall enter into thy gates . . . thy strong garrisons shall go down to the ground . . ." (xxvi. 7–11) ; and all this came true, even though it took a siege of no less than thirteen years before Nebuchadnezzar overcame the mighty city.

This, however, by no means exhausted Ezekiel's prophecy. It was but one incident in it, meant to be a sign and guarantee that the remainder would surely come true. In verse 4 God says : "I will also scrape her dust from her, and make her like the top of a rock." This is repeated in verse 14. Also, according to verse 5, Tyre, despite her world-embracing commerce and her proud affluence, was to become merely "a place for the spreading of nets in the midst of the sea." This, too, is repeated in verse 14, with the fateful addition, "Thou shalt be built no more."

Nearly two hundred and fifty years slipped away, and still there seemed no sign of these words being fulfilled. After their experience with Nebuchadnezzar, the Tyrians had resolved never to expose themselves to a like defeat again. The bulk of their treasure they removed to the island half a mile from the mainland. Thus they had a liquid bulwark round them which was far more to them than the stoutest walls of man's building. With this, and her great fleet, the new Tyre was secure above all places. But, after two and a half centuries, the hour struck, and Ezekiel's

words came true to the letter. Alexander the Great turned on
Tyre. He looked across that half mile of water, and actually
determined to lay a solid causeway through it. He pulled down
the walls, towers, palaces, and other buildings of the older Tyre
on the mainland, and laid them through the water, thus fulfilling Ezekiel's strange words—"They shall lay thy stones and
thy timber and thy dust in the midst of the water" (xxvi. 12).
Such was the need of material for this huge effort and amazing
assault that the debris and the very dust seem to have been
"scraped" away for use, till the site was indeed "like the top of
a rock." Thus was Tyre scraped bare; and it has never been
rebuilt to this day. It has been a place "for the spreading of nets"
by fisher-folk, and still is.

Take now the equally arresting utterance against *Egypt*,
that land of ancient might and marvel and mystery (xxix.–xxxii.).
The doom here meted out in advance must have seemed so unlikely at the time of the prophecy that no unaided human mind
could possibly have foreseen it. In chapter xxix., verses 8 to 12,
we find the prediction of a forty years' desolation. This is followed,
in verses 13 to 15, by these words:

*"Yet thus saith the Lord God: At the end of forty years will I
gather the Egyptians from the people whither they were scattered.
And I will bring again the captivity of Egypt, and will cause
them to return into the land of their habitation; and they shall
be there a base kingdom. It shall be the basest of the kingdoms;
neither shall it exalt itself any more above the nations: for I
will diminish them, that they shall no more rule over the
nations."*

It will be seen that at verse 17 a *further* short prophecy is
appended, which Ezekiel wrote some seventeen years later (compare verses 1 and 17). This later addition tells of an apparently
impending attack on Egypt by Nebuchadnezzar, after his successful siege of Tyre (verses 17–20). Now since this addendum of
Ezekiel is dated "the seven and twentieth year," we are at the
sixteenth year after the fall of Jerusalem; that is, we are at
571 or 570 B.C. and it was in 570 B.C. that Pharaoh-Hophra of
Egypt came to his end. There seems doubt as to the exact
circumstances of his death, but it is clear that it was at the hands
of enemies—as was predicted, also, by Jeremiah (see Jer. xliv. 30),

who seems to connect it with Nebuchadnezzar. The historian
Josephus actually tells us that Nebuchadnezzar invaded Egypt
and "slew the king that then reigned"; though his date does not
seem to correspond with Ezekiel's. It may be that further light
is still to come on this, and also as to whether Nebuchadnezzar's
invasion brought on the forty years' desolation. But as to the
larger prophecy regarding Egypt's subsequent history down to
the present—and of which the more immediate prophecy about
Nebuchadnezzar was evidently meant to be a dread guarantee—
there can be no doubt, but only marvelling.

Although other great peoples like the Assyrians and the
Babylonians were to become extinct, the Egyptians were to
continue—and they continue to this day. They were also to
continue as a *kingdom*—and they are still a kingdom. Yet they
were to be the *basest* of kingdoms—and this they surely continue
to be. Their Khedive is dependent on outsiders. Their kingdom
is under mandate. Their taxes are levied and controlled by
foreigners. They are just a kingdom, and no more. The fulfilment of the word through Ezekiel lives on for all the world
to see.

But how stirring are Ezekiel's predictions concerning his own
people, *Israel*! Who can read, without emotion, such passages
as chapters xxxv. 11–16, 22–31; xxxvi. 8–12, 22–38; xxxvii.
1–28; xxxix. 21–9? How apt and gripping is that vision of the
valley and the dry bones, in chapter xxxvii.! Ezekiel's people
had known both reverses and revivings in the past; but now that
all twelve tribes were scattered in exile, and the temple was no
more, and Jerusalem was laid in ruins, it would seem a mocking
of the people's misery to preach a returning of prosperity. Ezekiel's vision of the dry bones and their miraculous reanimation
takes full cognizance of Israel's extremity, but reveals Jehovah
as the God of the impossible.

We need to remember, of course, that this is *vision*, not direct
prophecy. We must watch against unwarranted literalism in
interpreting this symbol of resurrection from the dead. Nobody
would dream of saying that the two "sticks," in verses 16 to 19,
were literally Judah and Israel. They are symbols. Even so,
in this vision of the dry bones we must not take the bones as
meaning literally the bones of Israel's dead. We must carefully
keep to the interpretation which God Himself gives. Verse 11

says: "These bones are the whole house of Israel: behold they say, Our bones are dried, and our hope is lost." Thus, the bones represent the exiled people, not the actually dead. The vision is a symbolic picture of *national restoration*, not of individual resurrection. The physical resurrection of individuals is taught elsewhere in Scripture. The point we make here is simply that this is not what is symbolised in Ezekiel's vision. The wonderful prospect here is the re-emerging of all Israel's tribes from the graves of their captivity, in *national* resuscitation. Verse 14 says they are to be placed in their own land again—which again shows that it is the scattered exiles, and not the actually deceased, who are thought of here; for the bulk of Israel's actual dead were buried *in the land*, and would not need to be regathered to it, if a resurrection of bodies were here thought of! Verse 19 speaks of *reunion* as well as renewal. The two kingdoms shall be one again, as symbolised by the two sticks which became one. Verse 24 foretells the reign of the coming Messiah-King David over the restored kingdom. Verse 26 predicts a "covenant of peace" which shall continue perpetually, and tells of Jehovah's sanctuary being set up in the midst again, nevermore to depart! It is a marvellous prophecy. It yet awaits fulfilment; but as the predictions concerning Tyre and Egypt and other nations have come true, and as other predictions concerning the nation Israel have already come true, so surely will these glowing passages concerning Israel's ultimate destiny.

Here we must leave Ezekiel. His message will live on with us. Jerusalem has failed, and lies weeping in the dust; but Jerusalem's God drives on through the ages to the predestined consummation. He will not rest until the *new* Jerusalem becomes the queen city of a new order, inscribed with *JEHOVAH-SHAMMAH*—"The Lord is there." The ravages of sin are still round us; but we have heard the chariot-wheels of God: we have seen a rainbow round about the throne: we have caught the vision of a temple and city which are yet to be. He has opened our eyes to His magnificent purpose, and we "rejoice in hope of the glory of God"!

> Oh, blessed hope! with this elate,
> Let not our hearts be desolate;
> But, strong in faith, in patience wait
>   Until *HE* come!

A TEST PAPER ON EZEKIEL

1. When was Ezekiel carried to Babylonia? How old was he then? And how long was it before the overthrow of Jerusalem?

2. What is the event from which Ezekiel reckons all his datings?

3. Mention a factor which made Ezekiel's earlier ministry among the exiles more difficult.

4. What are the three main movements or chapter-groupings of the book?

5. Could you briefly interpret the opening vision (i.) and give its main purpose?

6. What was the substance of Ezekiel's second vision (viii.–xi.), i.e. of the corrupt temple and city?

7. Give reasons for thinking that parts of the great temple-vision (xl.–xlviii.) cannot be *literally* fulfilled.

8. Give the main symbolic meanings in the temple vision.

9. Give three significant reasons why "sign" actions were used instead of direct speech, in chapters iii.–xxiv.

10. Mention some of the nations concerning which Ezekiel prophesies in chapters xxv.–xxxii. And show briefly how some particular one of them had a remarkable fulfilment.

THE BOOK OF DANIEL (1)

Lesson Number 82

NOTE.—For this study read the Book of Daniel through once, preferably at one sitting. Note the remarkable presence of the supernatural throughout, and pay special attention to chapter xi.

Owing to the unhappy fact that Modernist Biblical criticism has made the Book of Daniel one of its chief points of attack against the older view of the Bible as a directly and supernaturally inspired revelation of God, we have felt obliged, in the first three of these Daniel studies, to give most of the space to reconsidering the *pros* and (supposed) *cons*, for and against the genuineness and supernaturalness of the book. This, however, proves to be of much profit, for it brings different points and passages into prominence which definitely help us in our understanding and appreciation of the book.

J.S.B.

THE BOOK OF DANIEL (1)

FOR SHEER interest this Book of Daniel surely stands first among the writings of the prophets. It is full of supernatural marvel, both in the events which it records and in the visions which it describes. But its interest is eclipsed by its importance; for it preserves to us not only unique links in the chain of history, but also vital keys to the interpretation of prophecy. Alas, scholars of some modern schools, for these very reasons, have made it such a focus of criticism that before we can settle to a constructive study of it we are almost obliged to reassure ourselves as to its genuineness.

THE CONTENTIONS OF THE CRITICS

To our sceptical critics the book is merely one of the *pseudepigrapha*, or Jewish writings of the first and second centuries B.C., issued under a spurious name. It was written about 164 B.C., to hearten loyal Jews amid their trials in the time of the Maccabees. This means that it was written three and a half centuries after the time which it pretends. Its miracles are imaginations. Its predictions are simply history pretended to be foretold three hundred and fifty years earlier.

Now the critics may eulogise the noble intentions and literary merits and high ethics of the book, but their verbal drapery does not deceive us. The blunt truth is that either this book was written when it purports to have been written, and is therefore inspired of God, or else, if it was not written until the date assigned to it by the critics, it is a forgery. Which of the two is it?

The Prominence of the Supernatural

The first contention against its genuineness is *the prominence of the supernatural* in it. The more thorough-going modernist critics believe neither in miracle nor prophecy. The following words of Noldeke are sufficiently representative: "The Book of Daniel is not authentic . . . the majority of the facts recorded

49

in the book belong to the category of fable, and could not have happened." Now when supposed Bible-scholars take this outright rationalistic position, that miracles just could not have happened, reasonable argument is scarcely possible. Who are *they* to decide what the Almighty could not or would not do? The whole subject of miracles is brought up, not just those in Daniel; and obviously we cannot re-argue that, every time we come across some new instance of the supernatural. If miracles just could not have happened, we may as well throw our Bible away: its pages are lies; the four Gospels are wrong; the foundations of Christianity are false. Thank God, we know better! The miracles of Scripture rest on a secure basis; and none is surer than that which seals all the rest, namely, the resurrection of Christ. To those whose minds are not warped by modernist scholastic infidelity, the miracles in Daniel will be no barrier to credibility, providing the book is proved sound in other respects.

As a matter of fact, however, there is *a special reason* why the supernatural is so prominent in Daniel. Israel was now in captivity. Jerusalem was ruined. Even the temple—that last hope —was gone. Jehovah, after all, had proved unequal to the gods of the Babylonians! Bel-Merodach had conquered Jehovah! That is what the Babylonians exultantly supposed. That is what the Jews were tempted to believe. There seemed no possibility now of national restoration. What though Jeremiah had given it as Jehovah's word that there should be a return after seventy years? Had not Jehovah's promises to David and Solomon now proved false?

Now the miracles in this Book of Daniel were a *sign from God*, both to Israel and the Gentiles. When the earthly sovereignty was transferred from Israel to Nebuchadnezzar, God raised up this notable man, Daniel, to represent Him at the Babylonian courts, so that through his lips, and by these supernatural attestations, He might teach Nebuchadnezzar, and impress upon the Gentile world-empires, through Nebuchadnezzar their head, the delegated nature of their authority, and their accountability to the one true God, even the God of Israel. Thus, when the testimony to Jehovah ceased at Jerusalem, God raised up this supernatural witness to Himself at the heart of the Gentile world-empire. The chosen people were to know that Jehovah's eye was watching, and His hand still guiding the course of things on earth, that He was as near to His people in exile as He had been to them in their own land, and just as able to deliver them from Babylon as when, of old, He had brought their fathers out of Egypt. The prominence of the supernatural, then, in Daniel, is at once understandable. In fact it is such as might be expected at such a critical juncture.

The *actuality* of these extraordinary miracles is witnessed to by their impact upon the Jews. During the exile a profound transformation took place in the religious conceptions of the Hebrew people, one of the most astounding in the history of any nation. The Jews went into that exile helpless addicts to idolatry. Their idolatrous proclivities had cursed them for nearly five hundred years, and had at last become such a demoralising infatuation as to cause their expulsion from Canaan. Yet they emerged from that brief interval of the Exile what they have remained to this day—the most rigidly monotheistic people in the world. Our modern critics have striven in vain to account for this. It certainly cannot be attributed to Babylonian influence, for Babylon was a hotbed of idolatry. Nor can it be attributed to the Persians, for Cyrus and his successors were all idolaters. How then did it happen?

Well, if we admit the authenticity of Daniel the explanation is clear; for this greatest revolution in Israel's history took place *in the very interval covered by this Book of Daniel.* We know from the contemporary prophet, Ezekiel, that Daniel, even in his earlier years at Babylon, had become famed. How could it be otherwise with such miracles as those recorded in chapters ii. and iii.? And certainly Nebuchadnezzar's proclamation to the whole empire (iv.), in acknowledgment of Israel's God, must have had a simply indescribable effect on the Jews. How they would ponder Daniel's supernaturally attested prediction of the world-empires which were to follow Babylon! How they would now turn again to Jeremiah's prophecy concerning the duration of their exile, and to that earlier prophecy of Isaiah's in which the very name of their coming deliverer was foretold (Isa. xlv.)! With what eagerness would they now look for the fulfilment of these! And what would be their feelings when the fame of Cyrus the Persian began to spread?—when Babylon fell?—when the new emperor, Cyrus, who had been actually forenamed by Isaiah two hundred years earlier, gave his edict for the rebuilding of the temple at Jerusalem, exactly as foretold? How could it be otherwise than that Jewish doubt should now be utterly silenced, and adoration of the one true God cure them for ever of their idolatry?

The " Greek " words in Daniel

A more concentrated attack, however, has been made against this book, in connection with the alleged *"Greek" words in it*. These words have been singled out as proof irrefragable of late authorship. Do they not show that by the time the book was written not only had Alexander subdued the East (about 330 B.C.), but that a considerable time must have elapsed even after that for these Greek terms thus to have embedded themselves in Hebrew speech? Could there be any proof more conclusive that the book was not written until about 160 B.C.?

But once again the "assured results" of our modern "higher critics" were doomed to humiliation. As these words were subjected to the keen scrutiny of other scholars, the results were such that, when Dr. Driver wrote more recently on Daniel, the list had dwindled to three words, these being the names of three musical instruments, with even one of these admitted not to be conclusive by itself! The other two are *pesanterin* and *sumphonyah*, which are supposed to be derived from the Greek *psalterion* and *symphonia*. Dr. Driver says it is "incredible" that these two can have "reached Babylon about 550 B.C." (which is about the time that the Book of Daniel purports to have been written).

The excavations of ancient Greek cities in Egypt now tell a very different tale! The late John Urquhart says: "The old contention that Greece carried nothing to Babylonia before the time of Alexander the Great is now too absurd for serious discussion . . . we discover the trace of a very busy commercial intercourse between Greece and Babylonia about a century before the time when Daniel was written . . . a brisk trade was then carried on in musical instruments." The seven-stringed harp invented by the Greek poet and musician, Terpander, in 650 B.C., is now found to have been in use in Babylonia less than twenty-five years after that date! We need say no more. It is now clear that Greek musical instruments, known by their Greek names, were at Babylon long enough before Daniel.

The Prophecy in Chapter Eleven

But a very different sort of attack has been made on the book, in connection with *the prophecy in chapter xi*. In this chapter critics have found what they claim is an irrefutable evidence of late authorship, in that part which refers (as all are agreed) to Antiochus Epiphanes (verses 21–45). Dr. Driver puts the case thus: "While down to the period of Antiochus' persecution the *actual* facts are described with surprising distinctness, after this point *the distinctness ceases*: the closing events of Antiochus' own life are, to all appearance, not described as they actually occurred." The transition to indistinctness here referred to comes at the end of verse 39. At that point, according to Professor Charles, we make "a transition from history to prophecy"! Now up to verse 39 we certainly do find fuller detail than in the few remaining verses of the chapter, and it may be true that our information concerning Antiochus' later years does not so clearly tally with verses 40 to 45; but to assert on this ground that verses 1 to 39 are "nothing more than past history put into the garb of prophecy," that verses 40 to 45 are simply "speculation on the part of the author as to what he thought likely to happen in the immediate future," and that this "seeming" prophecy, therefore, must have been written at that point of time (verse 40) where it "begins to fail of accomplishment"—this is surely Biblical criticism gone mad! May not the less detail in verses 40 to 45 be simply because there was less to give, since Antiochus was now nearing his end? May it not be that if we had more data about his later years we might get more light on these verses? Such questions immediately spring to mind: though fortunately, quite apart from them, there is a clear reply to the critics.

Chapter xi. does not stand alone. Chapters x. to xii. are all one vision and prophecy: and according to x. 14 the special purpose is to disclose what should happen to *Daniel's own nation* in the latter days. That is why Antiochus Epiphanes is given prominence. He was by no means one of the greatest of the old-time kings, but he figures in prophetic light because of his doings in connection with the covenant people and their land. It is this which determines what is put in and what is left out, both up to verse 39 and after it.

But let us agree that there *is* this comparative indistinctness from verse 40. There is a deep significance in this to which the critics are blind. In each case where Antiochus Epiphanes is featured in this Book of Daniel he is the prototype of "the man of sin" (2 Thess. ii. 3–10) who is even yet future (see viii. 9–14, 23–5). With this in mind, look again at verse 40. It distinctly tells us that from this point we overleap the centuries, to "the time of the end"; and we know that this means the "end time" which is *yet to be*, because the first three verses of chapter xii., which uninterruptedly continue the closing verses of chapter xi., make this plain beyond all doubt. So, then, this sinister figure of Antiochus, which here moves before us, casts a shadow which reaches right on to the final crisis of the present age. And if some of the traits do not seem to fit merely to the Antiochus of past history, it is because of this latent and further meaning in the words.

Moreover, to see in the alleged break at verse 40, as do the critics, the evidence of a spurious author whose pretended prophecies simply retell the past in prophetic garb, down to the reign of Antiochus Epiphanes, is to do violence unpardonable to the rest of the book. Nothing in the book is plainer than that the four metals in Nebuchadnezzar's dream-image represent Babylon, Media-Persia, Greece, and Rome (see our final Daniel study); but by making the forecasts reach down only to Antiochus, the critics must force the four metals into meaning four kingdoms which terminated then; and this cuts out Rome, which had not then risen to world power.

The Opening Verse

Perhaps, also, we ought to note, in passing, an objection based on the opening verse of the book, which says that Nebuchadnezzar besieged Jerusalem "in the *third* year" of Jehoiakim. This statement is said to be a blunder, and contrary to the other Scriptures, inasmuch as not only is there no reference elsewhere to any such siege then, but Jeremiah, in a prophecy dated the *fourth* year of Jehoiakim (xxv.), speaks as though the Babylonians had not even then come against Jerusalem.

Once again the answer is clear. Jeremiah xxv. 1 says that the *fourth* year of Jehoiakim's reign was the *first* year of Nebuchadnezzar's, which means that the *third* year of Jehoiakim's reign was the year *before* Nebuchadnezzar became king of Babylon. Now the Babylonian historian, Berosus, records that in this very year young Nebuchadnezzar led a military sweep against the west, including Palestine. He says: "When Nabolassar, father of Nabuchodonoser (Nebuchadnezzar), heard that the governor whom he had set over Egypt and over the parts of Celesyria and Phœnicia had revolted from him, he was not able to bear it any longer; but committing certain parts of his army to his son, Nabuchodonoser, who was then but young, he sent him against the rebel. Nabuchodonoser joined battle with him, and conquered him, and reduced the country under his dominion again. Now it so fell out, that his father, Nabolassar, fell into a distemper at this time, and died in the city of Babylon, after he had reigned twenty-nine years. But as he (Nebuchadnezzar) understood, in a little time, that his father Nabolassar was dead, he set the affairs of Egypt and the other countries in order, and committed *the captives he had taken from the Jews* and Phœnicians and Syrians, and of the nations belonging to Egypt, to some of his friends . . . while he went in haste . . . *over the desert* to Babylon."

Perhaps the critics will explain how Nebuchadnezzar had those Jewish captives if he had not invaded Judæa, and how he reached Egypt if not via Palestine! They have argued that all this took place in Jehoiakim's *fourth* year, so as to fit it with Jeremiah xlvi. 2, which says that Nebuchadnezzar smote the Egyptians in *that* year, at Carchemish. The late Dr. Driver argued that it was after this *Carchemish* victory that Nebuchadnezzar hastened back to Babylon "over the desert." But he forgot that Nebuchadnezzar could not have returned to Babylon *over the desert* from Carchemish on the Euphrates! And as for the supposed silence of other Scriptures, the critics have strangely overlooked 2 Kings xxiv. 1, where we find a coming of Nebuchadnezzar to Jerusalem which *must* have been in the early years of Jehoiakim! So there we are! This first verse of the book is correct enough. The attacks on this Book of Daniel have resulted, not in confounding it, but in *confirming* it. Once again we are reminded of Paul's words in 2 Corinthians xiii. 8, "We can do nothing *against* the truth, but *for* the truth."

THE BOOK OF DANIEL (2)

Lesson Number 83

NOTE.—For this study read again the Book of Daniel through once, this time noting carefully all time-marks and geographical references which might bear on the genuineness of the book.

The Higher Criticism starts with the assumption that everything in Scripture needs to be confirmed by external evidence.

True criticism seeks to elucidate the truth: the higher criticism aims at establishing prejudged results.

The critic is a specialist; and specialists, though often necessary witnesses, are proverbially bad judges.

Sir Robert Anderson.

THE BOOK OF DANIEL (2)

THE Modernist case against this Book of Daniel has been a badly built vessel beating itself to pieces on the rocks of stubborn fact. We can leave the floating wreckage to tell its own ironic tale. To those who would follow out more fully the reply to the critics we recommend a reading of the late Sir Robert Anderson's devastating little book, *Daniel in the Critic's Den*. In this present study let us consider certain *positive* evidences for the genuineness of the book.

THE TESTIMONY OF THE REAL FACTS

First we cite the witness of *the prophet Ezekiel*. The genuineness and usually accepted date of the Book of Ezekiel have never been seriously questioned. In fact, De Wette's opinion, that Ezekiel wrote everything with his own hand, has been largely endorsed by scholars; and the latest date fixed on is the twenty-fifth year of the Captivity. All agree, therefore, that the whole of Ezekiel was written in Babylonia, and was contemporary with Nebuchadnezzar.

Now Ezekiel mentions Daniel three times. See chapters xiv. 14, 20; xxviii. 3. The two references in chapter xiv. were penned about the sixth or seventh year of Ezekiel's captivity (see viii. 1 and xx. 1, between which xiv. falls). At that time Daniel had been in Babylon about fifteen years, for he was carried there eight years before Ezekiel (compare Ezek. i. 2 with Dan. i. 1). So even if Daniel was only eighteen when carried captive, he must now have been about thirty-three. The probability is that he was more. Ezekiel's other mention of Daniel (xxviii. 3) was written about the *eleventh* year of Ezekiel's captivity (see xxvi. 1), at which time Daniel would be thirty-eight or more.

Here, then, in Ezekiel, we have contemporaneous testimony to a Daniel who, even at that time, was widely known, and was looked upon as such an outstanding saint and sage that he could

be coupled with Noah and Job. The words bear clear witness
to Daniel's historicity, integrity, wisdom, and fame; and they
were written just when Daniel had been at Babylon long enough
to become thus famous. Such evidence as this will be almost
enough by itself to convince any open mind. What then do our
critics say? Unbelievable as it may seem, rather than accept it
they try to explain it as referring to some other famous Daniel
who flourished at an earlier time; yet with comic incongruity
they have to admit that this other Daniel, despite his fame, has
never been heard of outside these supposed references in Ezekiel!
Truly, Ezekiel's mention of Daniel, besides giving witness to the
true Daniel, forces the critics to expose their own casuistry.

First Book of Maccabees

It is a matter of general consent that among the books of the
Apocrypha the First Book of the Maccabees has an excellence,
veracity, and value above the rest. It was written about 110
B.C., and it bears clear witness to the Book of Daniel. In chapter
ii. 51–61, the dying Mattathias recalls godly heroes of Israel's
past history, exhorting his sons to similar loyalty. After mentioning seven such, he says,

"Ananias, Azarias, and Misael, by believing, were saved out of
the flame.
Daniel, for his innocency, was delivered from the mouth of
lions."

Who, with unbiased mind, can read this narrative, the integrity of which is generally conceded, without seeing that this
mention of Shadrach, Meshach, Abed-nego, and Daniel, along
with the other great worthies and incidents in Israel's history,
indicates that the contents of our Book of Daniel were at that
time known and accepted all over Jewry as being *equally true
history* as that of the other accepted Jewish Scriptures?

To this witness from First Maccabees we would add that the
earliest of the so-called "pseudepigraphs," the Book of Enoch,
the nucleus of which dates back to about 200 B.C. or even earlier,
gives evidences of the influence of the Book of Daniel; which
fact means, of course, that the Book of Daniel must have been

in existence long enough *before* then, and, therefore, *far* earlier than the date assigned by our "new theology" experts. In fact, as J. E. H. Thomson says in the *International Standard Bible Encyclopaedia*, *all* the apocalyptic writings of this period take Daniel as their model, thus proving, not only its prior existence, but its great influence and generally accepted authority even then.

Inclusion in the Canon

But now, an even more decisive witness to the genuineness of the book is *its inclusion in the Old Testament canon.* According to strong Jewish tradition, the canon of the Old Testament was largely settled by the men of the "Great Synagogue" which was called together in Nehemiah's time and continued periodically for over a hundred years, until it gave place to the Sanhedrim. The critics have cast opprobrium on this, however, so we will not press it. This is certain, however, that the canon of the Old Testament was settled before the time of the Maccabees.

Turning again to the Apocrypha, we find that Jesus Ben-Sira, in his introduction to the Book of Ecclesiasticus, speaks of "the Law, the Prophets, and the other books of our fathers," and again to "the Law itself, and the Prophets, and the rest of the books." This is precisely the threefold arrangement of the Old Testament to which our Lord Himself refers in Luke xxiv. 44: "All things must be fulfilled which were written in the law of Moses, and in the Prophets, and in the Psalms, concerning Me." He calls the third part the "Psalms" simply because that book stood first in it, and sometimes gave its name to it. All must admit that "the other books" which Ben-Sira puts with the Law and the Prophets must mean that third part of the Old Testament, the part which became commonly known as "The Writings." His words surely cannot imply much less than *a recognised set* of Scriptures in *his* day.

At what date, then, did Ben-Sira write? He says it was soon after his entering Egypt, "in the eight and thirtieth year . . . when Euergates was king." That, say the scholars, was about 132 B.C. Now this Book of Ecclesiasticus is not the Hebrew original, but only Ben-Sira's Greek translation of it. The original work, as he tells us, was from the pen of *his grandfather*; and this, it is computed, must have been written not later than

200 B.C., and possibly was written as early as 240 B.C. What Ben-Sira tells us, then, is that the Hebrew Scriptures were *already* arranged into their threefold form *even in his grandfather's day*; which means that as far back as about 250 B.C., at least, there was this threefold division; and this certainly implies a recognised set of sacred books even at that time. Unhesitatingly, therefore, we may say with the always cautious Joseph Angus that "in the 250 years from Ezra to (the grandfather) Ben-Sirach (444–200 B.C.) a canon of sacred books was formed, practically identical with that of the Hebrew Scriptures." The one question that remains—and it is absolutely decisive—is: *Did this canon, or recognised set of sacred Jewish books, include the Book of Daniel?* If it did, then the loud argument against the book is laid low at a single blow.

Well, there is evidence that the book *was* included. To begin with, there are *three quotations* from it in this Book of Ecclesiasticus, which fact alone, to an impartial mind, will show that Daniel was one of the "other books" referred to in Ben-Sira's prologue. But, if the critics reject these quotations there is further evidence.

A remarkable testimony concerning the Jewish canon comes down to us from the pen of Josephus, the Jewish priest-historian, who, in such a matter, could make no mistake. It was written about A.D. 90. Note specially the parts we italicise.

"For we (Jews) have not an innumerable multitude of books among us, disagreeing with and contradicting one another (as the Greeks have), but only *twenty-two books*, which contain the records of all the past times; which are justly *believed to be Divine*; and of them, five belong to Moses, which contain his laws and the traditions of the origin of mankind till his death. This interval of time was little short of three thousand years; but as to the time from the death of Moses till the reign of Artaxerxes king of Persia, who reigned after Xerxes, *the prophets* who were after Moses wrote down what was done in their times, in thirteen books. The remaining four books contain hymns to God and precepts for the conduct of human life. It is true, our history hath been written *since* Artaxerxes (i.e. since the time of Nehemiah) very particularly, but *hath not been esteemed of the like authority with the former* by our forefathers, because there *hath not been an exact succession of prophets since that time*: and how firmly we have given credit to *those* books of our own nation (i.e. those up to Nehemiah's time) is evident by what we do; for *during so many ages as have already passed*, no one has been so bold as either to add anything to them, to take anything from them, or to make any change in them; but it becomes natural to all Jews, immediately from their very birth, to esteem those books to contain Divine doctrines, and to persist in them, and, if occasion be, willingly to die for them."

So, then, those books which eventually constituted the Jewish canon were admitted only after long recognition as Divinely inspired. No book was admitted which was not believed to have been in existence in the time of Nehemiah; for the Sanhedrim held that inspiration ceased with the prophets, and that no "prophet" (i.e. no Divinely inspired teacher) had come since the time of Nehemiah. During "*so many ages*" as had "*already passed*" when Josephus wrote, since those twenty-two books had come to form the canon, nothing had been added and nothing deleted. That means, of course, that if the Book of Daniel was in that canon at all, then like the other books in the canon, it had been in for these "so many ages." That it actually *was* in is certain. In A.D. 32 we find our Lord Jesus Himself referring to the Book of Daniel in just the same deferential way that He refers to the other books of the Old Testament canon, as being just as truly inspired, and just as commonly accepted, as the other canonical Scriptures by those who heard Him (Matt. xxiv.). And the Book of Daniel was just as certainly in the twenty-two books of Josephus, in A.D. 90. And yet again it appears in the carefully ascertained list of the Jewish canonical books as left by Melito, bishop of Sardis, about another ninety years after Josephus.

And, remember, such was the zealous concern of the Jews to allow only the truly time-tested and inspired books into the canon, that, not only did they resolutely exclude books of great repute like Ecclesiasticus and First Maccabees, but they even challenged canonical books like Proverbs and Ecclesiastes and even Ezekiel: yet, as the late Dr. Edersheim says, "*The right of the Book of Daniel to canonicity was never called in question in the Ancient Synagogue.*"

Surely this evidence alone is conclusive. The Modernist fabrication, that the Book of Daniel is a spurious historical romance of as late as 164 B.C., covertly relating to the reign of Antiochus Epiphanes in the form of a prophecy pretendedly originating centuries earlier, and then somehow smuggled into the canon in the post-Maccabean years—this, we say, is preposterous.

Especially is this seen to be so when we reflect on the calibre of the Jewish leaders at that time. As Sir Robert Anderson has said, "The Sanhedrim of the second century B.C. was composed of men of the type of John Hyrcanus; men famed for their piety and learning; men who were heirs of all the proud traditions of the Jewish faith, and themselves the sons of successors of the heroes of the noble Maccabean revolt. And yet we are asked to believe that these men, with their extremely strict views of inspiration and their intense reverence for their sacred writings —that these men, the most scrupulous and conservative Church body that the world has ever known—used their authority to smuggle into the sacred canon a book which, *ex hypothesi*, was a forgery, a literary fraud, a religious novel of recent date. Such a figment is worthy of its pagan author, but it is wholly unworthy of Christian men in the position of English ecclesiastics and university professors."

Some of the critics may disown saying that the book was "smuggled" into the canon. They prefer to put it rather more mildly and say that the Jews were *deceived* by it. But this is equally unthinkable. The competence of the Jewish scholars to judge as to the genuineness of the book was as clear and sure as that of our modern hyper-critics is dubious. Sir Robert Anderson does not hesitate to say that if the critics are right, then these men of old, who were the Divinely appointed custodians of the Hebrew Scriptures (Rom. iii. 2), were either fools or knaves. If they were deceived by a literary forgery of their own time they were the former, he says. If they shared in a plot to get the fraud into the canon, they were the latter. "If the book was not genuine it was a forgery palmed off upon the Sanhedrim. And like all forgeries of that kind, the MS. must have been 'discovered' by its author. But the 'finding' of such a book at such a period of the national history would have been an event of unparalleled interest and importance. Where then is the record of it?"

The critics have also argued that although the book was received into the canon it was "relegated to the *Kethuvim*, side by side with such a book as Esther." We have already mentioned that the Hebrew Scriptures were in three parts—the Law (*Torah*), the Prophets (*Neveeim*), and the Writings (*Kethuvim*). The suggestion is that the *Kethuvim* were considered inferior to the rest of the Scriptures. Now that is absurd, even though the Jews naturally had a most special regard for the Law. We only need to recall that books like the Psalms and the Chronicles and Ezra are found among the *Kethuvim*: and as for Esther, which is there, that book has been given special honour in Jewish esteem from early times. Moreover, it is obviously natural that those who later arranged the Hebrew Scriptures should think of putting the Book of Daniel just before Ezra and Nehemiah, for it belongs to that point of Israel's history. However, we need not bother to argue this any more, for Charles Boutflower, in his scholarly work on the Book of Daniel, has gathered unanswerable evidence to show that originally the book stood, not among the "Writings," as it later came to do, but *among the Prophets*! Josephus (A.D. 90) clearly has Daniel there. So has Melito, bishop of Sardis (A.D. 180), in his carefully ascertained list of the books in the Jewish canon.

So there we are: the evidence simply cannot be gainsaid that the Book of Daniel was in the Old Testament from the very time that the canon was completed—long enough before the time of Antiochus Epiphanes! The book, therefore, is unquestionably genuine, and an inspired part of the word of Divine truth. The Modernist theory is a broken pitcher that can hold no water!

THE BOOK OF DANIEL (3)

Lesson Number 84

NOTE.—For this study read the Book of Daniel once through again, this time noting the clear division of it into two clear parts, the historical and the prophetical. Note specially chapter iv., in which the key truth of the book is three times expressed, and chapter vii. in its references to the coming kingdom of the Son of Man.

After busying myself with the Old Testament in its original text for over forty-eight years, I can bear witness with fullest truth that whatever cleaves to the Old Testament of imperfection, yea, perhaps, of offence, in a word, of "the form of a servant", has from year to year for me ever the more shrivelled up into nothingness, with an ever deepening penetration into the overmastering phenomenon of prophecy.

Kautzsch.

THE BOOK OF DANIEL (3)

WE BELIEVE that the evidence already adduced will have been enough to convince any candid thinker that our Book of Daniel is genuine enough; but there are other proofs also, which, although they can be set forth much more briefly than the foregoing, are, if possible, even more decisive.

Fulfilled Prediction

There is the witness of *fulfilled prediction*. Nothing more strongly proves the inspiration of the Bible than fulfilled prediction. Justin Martyr said, long ago, "To declare that a thing shall come to be, long before it is in being, and then to bring about the accomplishment of that very thing according to the same declaration, this or nothing is the work of God." To that we must all agree. Such fulfilled prediction is proof absolute of Divine inspiration. Therefore, if any one of the Daniel predictions can be shown to have had unmistakable fulfilment such as none but God could have foreknown or predetermined, then the inspiration and genuineness of the book are put absolutely beyond question.

Such proof—clear and incontestible—can certainly be given. We refer to chapter ix., to the prophecy of the "seventy weeks." Daniel is there informed that from the "commandment to restore and to build Jerusalem" down to the time when the Messiah should be "cut off" would be sixty-nine weeks, or sevens; that is, four hundred and eighty-three years. Obviously, then, this long period reaches right on to the A.D. era, to the year when our Lord Jesus, the Messiah, was "cut off," at Calvary. And it can be shown that this prophecy came true, not merely to the year, but to the very day, in A.D. 32 (see our next study).

What can our pseudepigraph theorists say about *this*?—for according to *their* theory the book was not written till about 164 B.C., to hearten loyal Jews in the evil days of Antiochus Epiphanes; its pretended predictions were penned *after* the events supposedly foretold; and, of course, they look *no further* than the reign of this Antiochus. The late Dean Farrar, who put the Modernist case over in popular form to the British public, could only wriggle from the quandary with such remarks as, "To such purely mundane and secondary matters as close reckoning of dates, the Jewish writers show themselves manifestly indifferent." What a view of Bible inspiration! And what shameful misrepresentation of the real facts! No writers of old were more punctilious about exact datings and chronologies than those of the Bible.

But the critics have also tried to make the starting-point of the four hundred and eighty-three years the *destruction* of Jerusalem, so as to squeeze all but some sixty years (which apparently is neither here nor there to them) into the space between the destruction of Jerusalem and the death of Antiochus Epiphanes. Yet could anything be a more pitiful case of "handling the word of God deceitfully"?—for in clearest language the starting-point is the "commandment to *restore* and to *build* Jerusalem." We say no more about the wrigglings of these men. This one true prophecy, which was fulfilled with unmistakable clearness in the death of our Lord, is enough in itself to verify the Book of Daniel to all who are willing to accept honest evidence.

The Witness of our Lord Himself

The books of the Bible stand or fall together. They are so truly a plurality in unity that the validity of the whole is bound up with the veracity of each. If "one member suffer, all the members suffer with it." Again and again we have seen that it is impossible to disparage any one part without involving some other. This is emphatically true in connection with this Book of Daniel. So closely has it entered into the warp and woof of the New Testament that, in the words of famous Isaac Newton, "To reject Daniel's prophecies would be to undermine the Christian religion." Paul's doctrine of the coming Antichrist obviously reflects Daniel vii. and xi. Still more are the visions of John in the Apocalypse bound up with those of Daniel.

But, most vital of all, the authority of Christ Himself is bound up with this Book of Daniel; for He has chosen to put the seal of a special recognition upon it. His self-given and oft-repeated title, "the Son of Man," as all agree, was taken from the pages of Daniel. As plainly as can be, when He speaks of "Daniel" He means a real person, not the mere *nom de plume* of a comparatively recent fiction. He speaks, mark, of "Daniel *the prophet,*" meaning one through whom Divine revelation was transmitted. Three times in His Olivet discourse (Matt. xxiv.) He quotes from Daniel. In verse 15 He refers to Daniel viii. 13; ix. 27; xi. 31; xii. 11, and gives His disciples the sign therefrom, when to leave Jerusalem. In verse 21 He describes the coming great tribulation on the basis of Daniel xii. 1. Then, in verse 30, He describes His own second advent in the words of Daniel vii. 13. Most august and solemn of all, in that terrific moment when the High Priest exclaimed, "I adjure thee, by the living God, that thou tell us whether thou be the Christ, the Son of God," our Lord replied: "Thou hast said: moreover I say unto you, Hereafter shall ye see the Son of Man sitting on the right hand of power, and coming in the clouds of heaven"—words again taken from Daniel (vii. 13, 14).

But this passage, Daniel vii. 13, 14, really forms the groundwork of *all* our Lord's pronouncements concerning His second coming (see Matt. x. 23; xvi. 27, 28; xix. 28; xxiv. 30; xxv. 31). And in addition to this, as Charles Boutflower comments, "Our Lord's description of the resurrection, in John v. 28, 29, runs on the lines of Daniel xii. 2; while the next verse, Daniel xii. 3, is paraphrased by Him in Matthew xiii. 43, when describing the future glory in store for the righteous: 'Then shall the righteous shine forth as the sun in the kingdom of their Father.'"

Nor is the witness of Christ to Daniel found only in the Gospels. We simply have not space here to discuss the interweaving of Daniel's visions with those of John; yet we cannot but point out that the very title of the Apocalypse—"The revelation of *JESUS CHRIST*, which God gave unto *HIM*, to show unto His servants"—means that all the way through this wonderful book the ascended Christ is again setting His seal on the Book of Daniel!

Now this unmistakable witness of Christ to Daniel makes the issue clear. It is either Christ or the critics. It is either the "higher critics" or the *highest* Critic. To those of us who worship Him as God the Son, His word will be final. To hear it suggested that He played up to popular ignorance on such matters outs us to the core as being unspeakably dishonouring to Him. As with the Pentateuch and Jonah and Isaiah, so here again, with

Daniel, the word of Christ is the touchstone. On His authority we accept the book as being indeed the inspired word of God.

And Now—Daniel Himself

And now, with absolute confidence in this vital book, we pass on to a brief examination of its contents and message. First, however, we ought just to collect the main data concerning Daniel himself.

Our information concerning this heroic saint and seer is derivable almost wholly from the book which bears his name. In the opening verses of the first chapter we learn that he was one of a small band of Jewish captives carried off from Jerusalem by the young Babylonian conqueror, Nebuchadnezzar, in the third year of Jehoiakim's reign over Judah (2 Kings xxiii. 36, etc.). That would be about eight years before Ezekiel was similarly carried captive, and about nineteen years before the destruction of Jerusalem.

At the time of his deportation to Babylon, Daniel was still a youth. This is inferable, first, from verses 3 and 4, in which Nebuchadnezzar charges the master of his eunuchs to bring "certain of the children of Israel, and of the king's seed, and of the princes; children in whom was no blemish, but well-favoured, and skilful in all wisdom, and cunning in knowledge, and understanding science, and such as had ability in them to stand in the king's palace, and whom they might teach the learning and the tongue of the Chaldeans." C. J. Ellicott comments: "If the Babylonian customs were similar to the Persian, it is probable that the course of education would commence at an early age. So elaborate a system of science as the Babylonian, whether theological, astronomical, or magical, would naturally require an early training." We may reasonably suppose, therefore, that these Hebrew "children" who were to adorn the proud conqueror's courts were still youths.

Besides this, Daniel's youthfulness at the time of his expatriation seems implied by the length of time he lived in Babylon. See chapters i. 21; vi. 28 and x. 1. The last of these three verses tells us that Daniel was still there in "the third year of Cyrus, king of Persia." Now if, as we have seen, Daniel was carried to Babylon nineteen years before the fall of Jerusalem, he begins there in 606 B.C.; and since the third year of Cyrus was 534 B.C., Daniel must have lived there for no less than seventy-two years. How much longer he lived we do not know; but it is plain that when he was taken to Babylon he must have been quite young, and when he died he must have been a great age.

The remarkable fact will also be seen from this that Daniel lived *right through the period of the seventy years' servitude.* He outlived the thirty-four years' reign of Nebuchadnezzar, and saw his son, Evil-merodach (=Amel-Marduk, "servant of Merodach") come to the throne for his brief reign of two years, to be followed by Neriglissar (=Nergal-shar-utsur, "Nergal protect the king"), Nebuchadnezzar's son-in-law, who reigned for about four years. Neriglissar's son, Labashi-Marduk, then reigned, for four months only, and was succeeded by a usurper, Nabonidus. Daniel witnessed all this, and then saw the sudden downfall of the Babylonian dominion. Nabonidus puts Belshazzar, his son, in command at the city of Babylon. Belshazzar makes his great feast, and the handwriting appears on the wall. That night Belshazzar is slain. Babylon is taken by the Persians, under Cyrus. The Babylonian empire is no more. The empire of Media-Persia takes its place. Cyrus makes his great proclamation for the return of the Jews to Jerusalem. Daniel is still in Babylon when the "Remnant" leaves for Jerusalem, led by Zerubbabel. Our last glimpse of him is in his old age, in "the third year of Cyrus." Thus Daniel links the pre-Exile and post-Exile periods together.

Going back again to the first chapter of the book, we gather that Daniel, besides being youthful at that time, was of goodly physique and handsome appearance (verse 4). It seems probable, too, that he was of royal descent (verse 3). But the thing which strikes us most of all, right from his youth to his old age, is his moral courage, or shall we call it his *unwavering godliness?* How can we but admire Daniel the youthful, refusing to defile himself with "the king's meat" and the "wine"? And how can we but admire Daniel the aged, going into the lions' den rather than forgo his life-long practice of daily prayer?—for he was then three score years and ten! Oh, this beloved Daniel is a grand character! He is one of the few men about whom God says only good. Thrice he is called "greatly beloved" (ix. 23; x. 11, 19). What John, the beloved disciple, was among the apostles in the New Testament, that was Daniel among the prophets of the Old Testament. They had a like close place to the Divine heart. To both were great visions given. They were admitted, we may say, into the very arcana of the Deity. A deep and prayerful study of this man's peerless moral character will enrich any of us. He is an outstanding figure even as regards intellectual capacity and executive ability. We think of him as holding high administrative office with both the Babylonians and the Persians (ii. 48; vi. 1–3). Yet through all, his faith remains simple, his heart humble, his character unblemished, and his godliness supreme.

Naturally, we cannot but connect Daniel's early faith and godly resolve with the influence of the good king Josiah and the great prophet Jeremiah. It was in the third year of Jehoiakim, or just afterward, that he was carried to Babylon (i. 1). King Josiah had then been dead scarcely four years. If, then, Daniel was about eighteen to twenty when taken to Babylon, he must have been about fourteen to sixteen when Josiah died. Josiah's was a long reign of thirty-one years. Daniel was born about the middle of it, and, being of princely descent, grew up in closest connection with it. Now it was in Josiah's reign that the temple was repaired, and the worship reformed, and the Book of the Law re-discovered, and the great national Passover kept. The godly king gave a grand, royal lead which could have saved the nation if the people had really responded. Also, it was in the thirteenth year of Josiah that Jeremiah commenced his powerful public witness (Jer. xxv. 3), which was still continuing at Jerusalem when young Daniel was carried away. The influence of these two men was never lost on the future prime minister of Babylon. More than sixty years later we find Daniel pondering the words of Jeremiah concerning the seventy years' servitude (ix. 2). A godly example and influence are never without power over *someone*. There is almost always some young Daniel watching and listening. Here is a ministry which we can all exercise. We need not be kings or prophets. What a power can be wielded by the godly example of a father, a mother, a brother, a sister, a friend, a teacher, a business associate! Let us take *heed*—and, if we have become discouraged, let us also take *heart*. Nor must we miss that great truth which is both the centre and the crown of Daniel's personal history, namely, that *God honours those who honour Him* (1 Sam. ii. 30).

The " Book " of Daniel

There is really no need to set out an analysis of the *Book* of Daniel: the arrangement of it is so clear. Its twelve chapters fall into two equal parts, the first six chapters being *historical*, and the remaining six *prophetical*. The key thought and central purpose of the book are expressed in chapter iv.—three times over for emphasis (verses 17, 25, 32)—"THAT THE LIVING MAY KNOW THAT THE MOST HIGH RULETH IN THE KING-DOM OF MEN, AND GIVETH IT TO WHOMSOEVER HE WILL." It is significant that this key utterance is made to come to us through the lips of the humbled Nebuchadnezzar, who was the golden "head" and first world-ruler of "the times of the Gentiles." It is noteworthy, too, that this central purpose in Daniel parallels with that in Ezekiel, the *other* book of the captivity. Ezekiel's stress is: "THEY (ISRAEL) SHALL KNOW THAT I AM JEHOVAH." Daniel's is: "THAT THE LIVING (ALL NATIONS) MAY KNOW THAT THE MOST HIGH RULETH."

A striking feature of this Book of Daniel is that it is written *in two languages*. From chapter ii. 4 to the end of chapter vii. the language is Aramaic. Elsewhere it is Hebrew. Is there some special significance in this? We think there is. There is a correspondence unmistakable between Nebuchadnezzar's dream-image in chapter ii. and the first of Daniel's visions, in chapter vii. They both give in general outline the whole course of "the times of the Gentiles"; whereas the later visions foretell the future specially in relation to the covenant people. Accordingly, chapters ii. to vii. are in Aramaic, which was, at the time, the Gentile language of commerce and diplomacy over the whole known world. We may see, therefore, in this passing from the language of the Jew to the common language of the Gentiles, a significant symbol of what was actually then happening in history, by the sovereign act of God.

But there is even more in it than this. It is one more proof that the book was really written when it says it was. *Before* the time of Daniel the Jews did not understand *Aramaic* (see 2 Kings xviii. 26). *After* the time of Daniel they ceased to understand *Hebrew* (see Neh. viii. 8). But *in* the time of Daniel *they knew both languages*. If the book was written by a pretender, nearly four hundred years later, wanting to console his fellow-country-men, why did he lock half of it up in a language which they could no longer read? Or, if he wanted to lock it up in the Hebrew, to invest it with a sacred and ancient value, why did he go and put those middle chapters in the common tongue of his own day? Here is a pretty little puzzle for the late-daters to solve! Mean-while, we ourselves are grateful to see in the phenomenon a further seal upon the book from the hand of God.

THE BOOK OF DANIEL (4)

Lesson Number 85

NOTE.—For this study read twice through chapters vii. to xii.

The reign of Nebuchadnezzar was chronicled by Berosus, "the Manetho of Chaldæa." His writings have mostly perished, but, as in the case of the Egyptian historian, Josephus, in his treatise *Against Apion*, has preserved a fragment which at least illustrates Nebuchadnezzar's boast, recorded in Daniel iv. 30, "Is not this great Babylon which I have built?" This is also the burden of the "East India House" inscription of the king, discovered among the ruins of Babylon in 1803.

The list of public works which the king had undertaken for the improvement of Babylon is amazing. They comprised more than twenty temples, with strengthened fortifications, the excavation of canals, vast embankments by the river, and the celebrated hanging gardens. Another inscription on two barrel cylinders in the British Museum gives a very similar account of the architectural works by which this great monarch enriched his metropolis and kingdom. All through Babylonia the discovery of bricks enstamped with Nebuchadnezzar's name attests his enterprise as well as his opulence and taste. . . . In the Book of Daniel the sequel of Nebuchadnezzar's boast was his attack of madness and his seclusion from public affairs. Neither Berosus nor any of the hitherto-discovered inscriptions refers directly to this fact, which need excite no surprise, as references to what was inglorious and humiliating were out of the line of such monumental records.

Angus's "Bible Handbook".

THE BOOK OF DANIEL (4)

THERE is gripping interest in the first six chapters of Daniel—the historical half of the book. Point by point they have been assailed by our modern critics; and more than equally have they been vindicated by sounder scholars. We wish we could give them fuller treatment than our present scheme allows; but in this, our final instalment on the book, we must turn to its *prophecies*.

The prophecies of Daniel are a vital key to Scripture prophecy as a whole; hence the importance of understanding them. In the Book of Daniel itself there are two prophecies which are basal to the others—that in connection with Nebuchadnezzar's dream-image in chapter ii., and that of the "seventy weeks" in chapter ix. The one is basal to prophecy concerning the *Gentile* nations, the other to prophecy concerning *Israel*.

Nebuchadnezzar's Dream-image

Never did a more epochal dream come to a man. Moreover, it was just as necessary that Nebuchadnezzar should *forget* it as that he should dream it. Had the king himself been able to relate the dream there might have been competing interpretations; but that it should become a sheer blank and then be recalled by the inspired Daniel was proof beyond question that both the dream and its interpretation were from the Most High.

What then of the interpretation? With Daniel's words before us and the record of history behind us, we surely see that the head of gold is *Babylon*, the breast and arms of silver *Media-Persia*, the lower trunk of brass *Greece*, the legs of iron *Rome*. We might have assumed that this would be at once accepted had not the Modernist school forced other meanings on the image; but as these alternative interpretations have been advanced, we refer to them here for the sake of verifying the true interpretation.

To their own humiliation, as we have seen, the critics have striven to make the Book of Daniel a mere *pseudepigraph* of about 164 B.C., in which the supposed predictions are simply history retold down to that time. As Rome had not then risen to world-empire the four metals of Nebuchadnezzar's dream-image must somehow be made to mean four great kingdoms *before* Rome (as also Daniel's *other* prophecies must be similarly limited). But if Rome be excluded, how can the four metals be accounted for? Four expedients have been resorted to. *First*, the head of gold has been restricted to Nebuchadnezzar alone, with the later history of Babylon as the breast and arms of silver. Thus the abdomen of brass becomes Media-Persia, and the iron legs Greece. *Second*, the Media-Persian empire has been divided, so that the silver becomes the Medes and the brass the Persians, with the iron again Greece. *Third*, with the golden head as Babylon, and the silver chest and arms as Media-Persia, the brass trunk, instead of representing the Greek empire as a whole, has been restricted to Alexander the Great, with the legs of iron representing his successors. *Fourth* (despite Daniel's word to Nebuchadnezzar, "Thou art this head of gold"), the head of gold has been made to mean the Assyrian empire which preceded that of Babylon, so that the silver chest and arms now become Babylon, the brass trunk becomes Media-Persia, and the iron legs Greece.

Now it will be seen that three out of these four expedients agree that *Babylon* must not be divided into two; three agree that *Media-Persia* must not be divided into two; and three agree that *Greece* must not be divided into two. Thus, by the consensus of the critics themselves, the image begins with Nebuchadnezzar; Babylon is one metal, Media-Persia is one metal, Greece is one metal. What then about the fourth metal? The critics themselves have forced us to the conclusion that *it can only be Rome*. Moreover, the conflicting contentions and concessions of the critics tell us that they themselves are not satisfied with any one of their four expedients. Each one is open to grave objection, such as, for instance, the artificiality of representing the Medes and Persians as the second *and* third empires—as the silver *and* the brass. The Medes certainly never held what could be described as a world rule; and they were never masters of Judæa. But without needing to disprove these four makeshifts in turn, we believe it can be shown from other parts of Daniel that the four metals do indeed signify Babylon, Media-Persia, Greece, and Rome.

In chapter viii. the two empires, Media-Persia and Greece, are each mentioned *by name*, and in such a way as absolutely forbids our making either of them into more than one of the metals. Daniel is shown "a ram which had two horns, but one was higher than the other, and the higher came up last" (verse 3). The heavenly interpreter says: "The ram which thou sawest that had the two horns, they are the kings of Media and Persia" (verse 20). So *the one figure*, the ram, represents Medes and Persians as one kingdom, while yet the twofold character of that kingdom is preserved in the two horns, the smaller being the Medes, the later and higher one the Persians, who, later, under Cyrus and his successors, assumed the supremacy. The correspondence here with the silver breast and arms of the image will be seen at once, the two horns and the two arms in each case denoting the dual nature of Media-Persia, while yet the unity of that empire is preserved in the one ram and the one metal.

Equally clearly are we told the identity of the "he-goat" which destroys Media-Persia (verses 5–7). "The rough goat is the king of Grecia; and the great horn that is between his eyes is the first king" (verse 21). In the vision, however, "the great horn" (Alexander the Great) was broken, and for it came up four notable ones toward the four winds of heaven" (verse 8). This also is explained: "That (the great horn) being broken, four kingdoms shall stand up out of the nation, but not with his power" (verse 22). Here, then, while the later divisions of the Greek empire are clearly anticipated, Alexander and his successors are represented as forming *one empire*, under this figure of the he-goat. Definitely, then, if Media-Persia is the silver breast and arms of the image, Greece must be the lower trunk of brass.

We can still further verify this. In chapter vii. the four kingdoms represented by the four metals are seen again, as four beasts of prey. Special attention is focused on the *fourth* beast. The correspondence between it and the fourth metal of the image cannot be missed—"strong exceedingly, and it had great *iron* teeth," etc. (verse 7). This fearsome beast has ten horns (the horn is the symbol of ruling-power), and among these a new horn arises which uproots three of the others, and has a "mouth speaking great things." Daniel says: "I beheld, and the same ·horn made war with the saints, and prevailed against them, *until* the Ancient of Days came, and judgment was given unto the saints of the Most High, and the time came that the saints possessed the kingdom" (verses 21, 22). The fourth kingdom, therefore, in its parts—the legs, the iron-clay feet, and the ten toes—is to continue "*until*" the coming of the Messiah's world-wide kingdom. This, certainly, can only be Rome.

Thus, if the iron represents Rome, the brass *must* represent Greece, which is figured in chapter viii. as *one* empire; and then the silver *must* be Media-Persia, which also is figured as one empire; and thus the golden head *must* be Babylon, in accord with Daniel's word to Nebuchadnezzar, "Thou art this head of gold."

And now, having learned from the word of God itself the meaning of the four metals, and knowing how wonderfully history has unfolded their prophetic significance, we survey that image with awe. We see in it the whole course of history delineated beforehand, from Daniel's day, two thousand five hundred years ago, to the end of the present age. If that is not evidence of Divine inspiration, nothing is.

Now there are two big facts revealed through that dream-image which relate momentously to ourselves in this twentieth century. First, the end of the present age is not to come by gradual betterment until some high point of excellence is reached, but *by a crisis, a crash, a sudden catastrophe*; for in the days represented by the ten toes a "Stone cut out without hands" (Christ in His Messianic kingdom, as shown in chapter vii.) smites the image and crushes it to powder (ii. 34, 35, 43–5). As William Newall has said, "All modern dreams of Millennium before Christ comes are heresies begotten of vain human self-confidence or of Satanic delusion direct." The world will be saying "Peace and safety" when "sudden destruction" smites the whole present system of things.

Second, *the end of the present age is now near*. The two legs representing Rome are true to historical fact; for, as is well known, the Roman empire split into two great halves—the eastern and western empires. *The division took place in* A.D. 395. Thus, from the accession of Nebuchadnezzar (606 B.C.) to the dividing of the Roman empire into the legs of iron (A.D. 395) is just one thousand years in popular chronology. We will risk no date-fixings! Yet we need not hesitate to say that in the light of this interpreted dream-image we must be today somewhere in the end-period

represented by the feet and the toes. Present-day developments corroborate this. Count the thrones which have given
place to republics in recent years. See the portentous movements of "labour" today. The iron and the clay now go together
as in the feet of that image. With such portents before our eyes,
we who are Christ's may well "look up," knowing that "our
redemption draweth nigh." And, seeing we know such things,
"what manner of persons ought we to be in all holy conversation
and godliness"!

The " Seventy Weeks "

In Daniel ix. we find one of the most notable predictions in the
Bible. In verses 24–7 Daniel is told that "seventy weeks (or
sevens) are determined" on his people. From the going forth of
the "commandment to restore and to build Jerusalem" to the
time when the Messiah should be "cut off" would be "seven
weeks, and threescore and two weeks," or sixty-nine weeks in
all; that is 483 years. The seventieth week is treated as distinct.
In it an evil ruler violates covenant with the Jews, and desecrates
Jerusalem.

To understand this prediction we must ascertain when the
"command to restore Jerusalem" was issued, so as to know the
starting-point of the 483 years. We must also know whether the
years are solar or lunar or lunisolar. Three decrees affecting
Jerusalem are mentioned in Ezra—that of Cyrus in 536 B.C., that
of Darius Hystaspis about 519 B.C., and that of Artaxerxes
Longimanus about 458 B.C. (i. 1; vi. 3; vii. 11). None of these can
be the decree foretold to Daniel, for all three relate only to the
temple and worship. The one edict in history for the rebuilding
of the city itself is that which was issued by Artaxerxes at the
appeal of Nehemiah—"That thou wouldst send me unto Judah,
unto the city of my fathers' sepulchres, *THAT I MAY BUILD
IT*" (Neh. ii. 5). Nehemiah himself gives the date—"the month
Nisan, in the twentieth year of Artaxerxes (ii. 1). This, then, is
the starting-point: Nisan, 445 B.C. Nisan is the first month of the
Jewish year. The first of Nisan is New Year's Day. As Nehemiah
names no other day, the prophetic period must be reckoned,
according to common Jewish custom, from the New Year's Day.
Now as the Jewish year was regulated by the Paschal moon,
the date of any Nisan can be definitely calculated in relation to

our own Julian dating. In his book, *The Coming Prince*, Sir Robert Anderson has shown, with the corroboration of the Astronomer Royal, that Nehemiah's date was the 14th March, 445 B.C.

And now, what kind of *years* are we to reckon? We are not left in doubt. The interrelation of Daniel's visions and those of John is patent to all; and a comparison of the two will settle it that the prophetic year is a lunisolar year of 360 days. Both Daniel and John speak of "a time, and times, and half a time" (that is three and a half "times"); and both make it clear that three and a half "times" are three and a half *years* (Compare Dan. vii. 25; ix. 27; Rev. xii. 14; xiii. 5). But John goes further and splits up the three and a half years into *days* (compare Rev. xi. 2, 3; xii. 6, 14), showing us that the three and a half years equal 1,260 days. This settles it that the prophetic year is one of 360 days.

So then, from the edict to rebuild Jerusalem, down to the cutting off of the Messiah, was to be 483 years of 360 days each. Was the prophecy fulfilled? It was. Once only did our Lord offer Himself publicly and officially as Israel's Messiah. It was on that first, memorable "Palm Sunday." Sir Robert Anderson rightly emphasises the significance of this. "No student of the Gospels can fail to see that the Lord's last visit to Jerusalem was not only in fact but in intention the crisis of His ministry. From the time that the accredited leaders of the nation had rejected His Messianic claims, He had avoided all public recognition of those claims. But now His testimony had been fully given, and the purpose of His entry into the capital was to proclaim openly His Messiahship, and to receive His doom. Even His apostles themselves had again and again been charged that they should not make Him known; but now He accepted the acclamations of 'the whole multitude' of the disciples. And when the Pharisees protested He silenced them with the indignant rebuke, 'I tell you that if these should hold their peace, the stones would immediately cry out.' These words can only mean that the Divinely appointed time had arrived for the public announcement of His Messiahship, and that the Divine purpose could not be thwarted." It was on this day that our Lord looked on Jerusalem and exclaimed: "If *thou* also hadst known, even *ON THIS DAY*, the things that belong to thy peace . . .!" (see R.V.). And we are expressly told that this day was the fulfilment of Zechariah ix. 9 (Matt. xxi. 4, 5). Such concentrated emphasis on this day surely cannot be mistaken. This was the predicted day of His public offer to the nation; and which directly occasioned His being "cut off." Here, then, we find the *terminus* of the 483 years, emphasised too clearly to be misunderstood.

See now how *exactly* Daniel ix. was fulfilled. No date of history is made clearer than the commencement of our Lord's public ministry. Luke tells us that it was "the fifteenth year of Tiberius Cæsar" (iii. 1). Now the reign of Tiberius began 19th August, A.D. 14, so that the *fifteenth* year of his reign, when our Lord commenced His public ministry, was A.D. 29; and the first Passover of our Lord's ministry was in the month Nisan of that year. Three Passovers after this, in A.D. 32, our Lord was crucified. We give a final quotation from Sir Robert Anderson: "According to Jewish custom, our Lord went up to Jerusalem on the 8th Nisan (John xi. 55; xii. 1; and Josephus, *Wars*, book vi. chapter 5, paragraph 3), which, as we know, fell that year upon a Friday. And having spent the Sabbath at Bethany, He entered the Holy City the following day, as recorded in the Gospels. The Julian date of that 10th Nisan was Sunday the 6th April, A.D. 32." What then was the length of time between the decree to rebuild Jerusalem and this climactic public advent of Christ—between the 14th March, 445 B.C. and the 6th April, A.D. 32? Sir Robert tells us that it was EXACTLY 173,880 DAYS, THAT IS, 483 PROPHETIC YEARS OF 360 DAYS! Again, if this is not evidence of Divine inspiration, then nothing is.

What about that *seventieth* week? It is yet to be. Between the Messiah's being "cut off" and that seventieth week, the whole of the present "Church" age intervenes. As we have said before, the Church of the present dispensation is nowhere the subject of direct prediction in the Old Testament. It was the "secret" kept "hidden" during preceding ages (Eph. iii.). Again and again in the Old Testament we find both advents of Christ foretold in the same verse or passage, but with no light given as to the intervening of the present age between them (see Gen. xlix. 10; Isa. liii. 11, 12; Mic. v. 3; Isa. lxi. 1, 2, with Luke iv. 17–19; Zech. ix. 9, 10; Mal. iii. 1; 1 Pet. i. 10, 11).

We cannot here go further into Daniel's prophecies; but we hope that our brief study of these two basal passages may serve as a useful beginning to some for further investigation. Meanwhile, with that seventieth week in view, we await the trumpet-blast from heaven, the voice of the archangel, the descent of the Lord, the opening of the graves, the resurrection of the saints, the possessing of the kingdom, and the glory that shall follow.

QUESTIONS ON THE BOOK OF DANIEL

1. What have the rationalistic critics said concerning the date and authorship of this book, and why?

2. Give a special reason for the large presence of the supernatural in the book, and say what impact the miraculous happenings had on the Jews.

3. What coincidental and yet very weighty witness does Ezekiel bear to the contemporary historicity of Daniel?

4. Can you mention three other witnesses to the genuineness of Daniel and his book? (One of these is a book of the Apochrypha.)

5. How do our Lord and the New Testament witness to the genuineness of Daniel and his prophecy?

6. When was Daniel carried to Babylon, and how do we know that he lived there at least seventy-two years?

7. What are the two main chapter-groups of the Book of Daniel?

8. What was Nebuchadnezzar's dream-image? What do you think its several parts represent, and why?

9. How does that image seem to show that the end of the present age must be near?

10. Could you show by certain dates and facts how the prophecy of the Seventy Weeks, up to the "cutting off of the Messiah," was fulfilled exactly?

THE PROPHET HOSEA (1)

Lesson Number 86

NOTE.—For this study read the Book of Hosea right through once or twice. For reasons mentioned later, the book should be read in a modern translation, or at least in the Revised Version, especially from chapter iv. onwards.

The original Scriptures were written in Hebrew, with some parts in Chaldee, and others in a peculiar dialect of Greek. Attempts were naturally made to make these originals available by translations into other vernacular tongues. But translation is necessarily imperfect. Languages are not uniform in vocabulary or significance, and exact equivalents are not always to be found. Hence arise difficulties of rendering which perplex the most learned linguist, and all that is practicable is to choose the best available words to reproduce the original. No inspiration can be claimed for such human reproductions, yet they are practically safe guides.

A. T. Pierson, D.D.

THE BOOK OF HOSEA (1)

HOSEA is the prophet of Israel's zero hour. The nation had sunk to a point of such corruption that a major stroke of Divine judgment could no longer be staved off. What the weeping Jeremiah was to Judah, the southern kingdom, nearly a century and a half later, that was the sob-choked Hosea to Israel, the northern kingdom. Poignantly, though unprevailingly, he expostulated with his obdurate countrymen during those tragic decades which culminated in the utterly deserved yet none-the-less heart-rending catastrophe of the Assyrian invasion. Nay, more, just as Jeremiah saw his fellow-countrymen of the south actually plunged into the thick night of the Babylonian captivity, and broken-heartedly memorialised it in his "Lamentations," so, probably, did Hosea actually see the ten tribes of his beloved Israel dragged away from the land which they had shamefully defiled, into that exile and dispersal among the nations from which, even yet, they have not been regathered. Perhaps, indeed, he became a refugee in Judæa, bringing his prophetic writings with him, from which this "Book of Hosea" has come down to us.

Background

It is especially true with Hosea that if we would clearly understand the man and his message we must see him against the background of his times. The opening verse of the book says: "The word of the Lord that came to Hosea, the son of Beëri, in the days of Uzziah, Jotham, Ahaz, and Hezekiah, kings of Judah, and in the days of Jeroboam, the son of Joash, king of Israel." Note the mention of *Hezekiah* here. That Hosea was still prophesying in the days when Hezekiah reigned in *Judah* settles it that our prophet lived on through the fifty years or so in Israel between the death of Jeroboam II and the Assyrian invasion; for that invasion took place while Hezekiah reigned in Judah (Isa. xxxvi.). It also indicates that the *beginning* of Hosea's prophesying must have been *near the end* of Jeroboam's reign.

Now this period, from Jeroboam II on to the captivity, was the awful "last lap" of iniquity in Israel's downward drive. We cannot read these pages of Hosea without seeing that things have become shockingly worse in his days even than they were in the days of his prophet-predecessor, Amos. With the death of Jeroboam II, and the murder of his son, the dynasty of Jehu expires (see 2 Kings x. 30, with xv. 8–12.) Jeroboam is the last king who reigns in Israel with any semblance of Divine appointment. The kings who follow seize the throne by murdering its occupant at the time. Shallum slays Zechariah after only half a year's reign; Manahem slays Shallum after a reign of only one month; Pekah kills Pekahiah, the son of Menahem; while Hoshea, the last of them, in turn slays Pekah.

It is an awful period. Loyalty to the throne is all but extinct; conspiracies are rife; there are outbreaks of anarchy; conditions are deplorable (iv. 1, 2; vii. 1, 7; viii. 4; ix. 15, etc.). Around the degraded and tottery throne the nation tosses in disorder. As the late George Adam Smith has said: "It is not only, as in Amos, the sins of the luxurious, of them that are at ease in Zion, which are exposed; but also literal bloodshed, highway robbery with murder, abetted by the priests. Amos looked out on foreign nations across a quiet Israel; his views of the world are wide and clear; but in the Book of Hosea the dust is up, and into what is happening beyond the frontier we get only glimpses. There is enough, however, to make visible another great change since the days of Jeroboam. Israel's self-reliance is gone. She is as fluttered as a startled bird; *They call to Egypt; they go to Assyria*' (vii. 11). But everything is hopeless; kings cannot save; for Ephraim is seized by the pangs of a fatal crisis." (In Hosea, "Ephraim" is used as representing the whole of the ten-tribed nation, Israel.)

Things were even worse morally and spiritually than they were politically. Ever since the days of the *first* Jeroboam, when the ten tribes had disrupted from the house of David to form a separate kingdom, the worship of the golden calf at Bethel had been a snare to Israel. Although the Bethel calf (like that at Dan, in the north) was supposed at first to represent Jehovah, yet more and more the idol itself became the object of worship. This became an open door to other forms of idolatry; and the alliances which Israel's kings made with foreign powers brought in the immoral idolatries of Syria and Phoenicia. Thus the way was paved for the course, cruel nature-worship associated with the names of Baal and Ashtaroth, with all the attendant abominations of child-sacrifices and revolting licentiousness.

Pick out some of the evils which Hosea laments or denounces —swearing and falsehood (iv. 1, 2); murder and bloodshed (iv. 2; v. 2; vi. 8); robber-gangs, and murder-gangs of priests (vi. 9; vii. 1); wide-prevailing adultery (iv. 2, 11; vii. 4); perversion, false-dealing, and oppression (x. 4; xii. 7); idolatry (iv. 12, 13; viii. 5; x. 1, 5; xiii. 2); drunkenness (iv. 11; vii. 5); utter heedlessness of God (iv. 4, 10; viii. 14). Such was the sorry state to which Israel had sunk! Things were all too disturbing even in the days of Amos; but since then there had been a veritable landslide of wickedness. The people were steeped in evil— idolatry, drunkenness, debauchery, perjury, violence, banditry, adultery. In fact, adultery was consecrated as a part of the religious rites connected with the idolatrous calf-worship (iv. 14). It was to these people, and at this time, that the sensitive-hearted Hosea lifted up his voice in the name of Jehovah!

Characteristics

One thing quickly becomes clear as we read this Book of Hosea; the first three chapters belong together, in distinction from all those that follow. They are *narrative*, whereas all the remainder are addresses. But besides this, these first three chapters are *symbolical* narrative. The prophet's wife, Gomer, and the three children, Jezreel, Lo-ruhamah, and Lo-ammi, and the tragedy of the prophet's married life, of which these chapters speak, are all symbolical of the relationship between Jehovah and Israel. The narrative is continuous. The style is fluent and easy.

But with chapters iv. to xiv. it is very different. There is neither narrative nor symbol; nor apparently are these chapters amenable to logical analysis. The modern scholar already quoted tells us that here we have "a stream of addresses and reflections, appeals, upbraidings, sarcasms, recollections of earlier history, denunciations and promises, which, with little logical connection and almost no pauses or periods, start impulsively from each other, and for a large part are expressed in elliptic and ejaculatory phrases. . . . The language is impulsive and abrupt beyond all comparison. There is little rhythm in it, and almost no argument. Few metaphors are elaborated. Even the brief parallelism of Hebrew poetry seems too long for the quick spasms of the writer's heart."

Such seems to be the mind of Bible scholars in general about chapters iv. to xiv., so that usually this Book of Hosea is simply regarded, without further analysis, as having but the one division —that between the three symbolic chapters at the beginning, where we have the faithless wife and her faithful husband, and the remaining eleven chapters, where we have the faithless Israel and her faithful God. Yet although this is the usual view, and despite the passionate brokenness of Hosea's style here, I think we shall see shortly that if we have an observant eye to the prophet's phraseology, there is undoubtedly clear division and significant development in chapters iv. to xiv.

Symbolic Prologue

If we are going to be really captured by the pathos, the passion and the startling meaning of Hosea's message, we must first see the significance of the first three chapters, in which we have the symbolic story of Hosea's unfaithful wife and her children. The fact is, these three chapters should not be taken as a "division" in Hosea's treatise, but rather as a *prologue* to it. That is surely why they are put at the beginning, and not in the middle or at the end! The treatise proper begins at chapter iv. 1, with the words—

"HEAR THE WORD OF JEHOVAH, YE CHILDREN OF ISRAEL; FOR JEHOVAH HATH A CONTROVERSY WITH THE INHABITANTS OF THE LAND."

The symbolic narrative of Hosea's marriage tragedy, in the first three chapters, is forefixed because all that follows in "the Lord's controversy" is meant to be interpreted in the light of it.

What, then, is the special relevance of this prologue? It is this: *The prophet, through the heartbreak of his own marriage tragedy, had come to see Israel's sin against God in its deepest and most awful significance.* Hosea had loved, with a pure, deep, tender, sensitive love. He had honourably taken to himself the woman of his choice, and entered into what he anticipated would be a union of life-long happiness. After the birth of the first child, however, painful suspicions were aroused in his mind as to Gomer's loyalty; and these were confirmed later by the discovery of adultery. The first child Jezreel is definitely said to have been born to Hosea (i. 3), but the others are not. The second child he does not own. He names the little girl *Lo-ruhamah*, which means Unloved, or she-that-never-knew-a-father's-love. The third child he disowns outright, calling it *Lo-ammi*, which means Not-my-people, or No-kin-of-mine.

We can imagine the conflict of emotion in Hosea's heart, the sense of shame in his desecrated home. He had forgiven his beloved but weak and disloyal Gomer once . . . twice. . . . He had pleaded and warned. But things had at length reached the point where separation was necessary. After this, so it would appear, Gomer had sold herself for money, and later drifted into slavery, from which, however, she was redeemed by the still compassionate Hosea (iii. 2), though there could be no thought of reunion without a process of discipline and chastening (iii. 3).

This story is told consecutively, and at each point the symbolism is explained and applied. Gomer is the nation, Israel. The children are the people of that nation. Hosea's sorrow, patience, compassion, and his final act of redeeming, chastening, and restoring Gomer are, in adumbration, the sorrow, patience, compassion, and love of God toward sinning Israel. The whole tragic story of Israel is here, in these first three chapters, yea, and the ultimate triumph of that day yet to be, when God shall say: "I will betroth thee unto Me in righteousness, and in judgment, and in lovingkindness, and in mercies" (ii. 19); "I will say to them which were not My people: Thou art My people; and they shall say: Thou art my God" (ii. 23).

It will be quite clear to any careful reader that the first verse of chapter ii. should really end chapter i. It will be equally clear that chapter ii. is the *application* of chapter i.; also that chapter iii. looks right on to the end of the present age, for its last words are: "Afterward shall the children of Israel return, and seek the Lord their God, and David their king; and shall fear the Lord and His goodness *in the latter days*" (iii. 5). Yes, the whole story of Israel, past, present, and future, is here, in this symbolic prologue.

But the deepest and most awesome thing of all in these chapters is that through his own cruelly desecrated relationship with Gomer, Hosea came to understand the true meaning of Israel's sin: it was *spiritual adultery*, and even *harlotry*! The sin of adultery has been defined as that of "seeking satisfaction in unlawful relations." That is what Israel had done. Harlotry is even worse. It is the sin of "prostituting high possessions for the sake of hire and gain." That, too, is what Israel had done. As Hosea tells them, God had taken them to Himself in a special relationship, had loved them, carried them in His arms, taught them to walk, been Husband and home to them; and they had gone after other gods!—and had prostituted their high privileges to the lascivious indulgence of idolatry!

Such sin, then, is spiritual adultery! To see it in this light is to see it in its ugliest enormity, and at the same time to realise with a cutting keenness *the suffering which it causes to the heart of God.*

Now this is the thought which underlies all the remaining chapters in Hosea; and chapters iv. to xiv. should be read with this all-the-while in mind. The sin of a people with such high privilege and sacred relationship as Israel is the most heinous sin thinkable. Deeper down and worse than merely fleshly sins is that of *wilful infidelity to love*—even to that love which is "passing the love of women"!

Outraged but Persevering Love

Hosea is the prophet of *outraged but persevering love.* Here is the love that "suffers long and is kind." Here is the love that never lets us go, and never gives us up. Here is the love that many waters cannot quench—wounded, outraged, grieved, disappointed love, which, although it flames and flashes with white-hot indignation at sin, sobs out, "How shall I give thee up, Ephraim? How shall I deliver thee, Israel?"

We have already referred to the brokenness of Hosea's style in chapters iv. to xiv. May we not detect in this brokenness of style a sensitive vibrance with the brokenness of the times, and an expression, too, of the brokenness of Hosea's own spirit over the sin and coming calamity of his people?

The difference between Amos and Hosea is strongly marked.

Perhaps we may be permitted to give one further quotation from George Adam Smith concerning this. "There could be no greater contrast (than Hosea) to that fixture of conscience which renders the Book of Amos so simple in argument, so firm in style. Amos is the prophet of law: he sees the Divine processes work themselves out, irrespective of the moods and intrigues of the people, with which, after all, he was little familiar. So each of his paragraphs moves steadily forward to a climax, and every climax is doom—the captivity of the people to Assyria. You can divide the book by these things; it has its periods, strophes and refrains. It marches like the hosts of the Lord of hosts. But Hosea had no such unhampered vision of great laws. He was too familiar with the rapid changes of his fickle people; and his affection for them was too anxious. His style has all the restlessness and irritableness of hunger about it—the hunger of love." Yes, Hosea is the prophet of the hungering, persevering love of God to men; and the prophet himself has entered into the great, suffering, yearning love of God through his own lonely grief over wayward Gomer.

This is an aspect of the Divine love upon which, perhaps, we do not dwell often enough. We think of God as angry, threatening, hostile, towards wicked-doers; and we are right in so thinking, for such must God necessarily be, as the moral Governor and Judge of the human race. Not only is it true that God *does not* and *will not* "clear the guilty"; He *cannot* if He is to remain consistent with His own holy nature. Yet there is another aspect. It is that which is represented in Hosea, and which reappears in the guise of father-to-son compassion in the parable of the prodigal son. God sustains four principal relationships to mankind— (1) Creator, (2) King, (3) Judge, (4) Father. Which of these four is it which supplies the fundamental motive and purpose in the bringing of the human race into being? Did God create merely to possess? Did God create merely to reign? Did God create merely to judge? No, the three relationships of Creator, King, Judge, do not supply the basic motive. It is the fatherhood which is ultimate. God created us for *fellowship* with Himself. This means that human sin hurts the great, loving heart of God. In its deeper aspect, sin does not merely break God's law, it breaks His heart. Calvary says so. Whether it be under Hosea's metaphor of the grieved and wounded husband, or our Lord's picture of the sorrowing and compassionate father, the truth is there: *human sin hurts God!* "Lost souls" are a loss to the heart of God!

And we must add a further word—a warning against the veneration of supposedly sacred objects. All the trouble in that ten-tribed kingdom of long ago originated in the worship of the two golden calves which king Jeroboam installed at Dan and Bethel. By the time Hosea lived, those calves and the illicit cult which grew up around them had brought the nation to such a moral condition that Divine judgment could be staved off little longer. Those calf-worshippers of Hosea's day were in the same category as the Romanist image-venerators of our own day. They claimed that in worshipping the golden calves they were worshipping Jehovah in symbolic form; but in reality it was the idols and the idol system which held their worship. This opened up the way for full idolatry, causing sins of outrageous flagrance, and thus provoking the severest judgments of God. "Little children, keep yourselves from idols" (1. John v. 21).

Organised Protestant Christianity today is marked by a decline in the teaching of evangelical doctrine, and a resurgence of ritualism. The breakdown in Biblical indoctrination is an outcome of that theological liberalism commonly styled "Modernism". The reversion to ritual is a clerical effort to fill the gap created by this breakdown, but it is a deceptive and futile substitute. It is the attempt to conceal inward death by outward show. It is like putting an elaborately dressed-up corpse in the place of a living organism. Those golden calves are back again! God save us from them! It is by doctrine—by the teaching of Bible truth as the very word of God, that men learn and live and nations prosper.

THE BOOK OF HOSEA (2)
Lesson Number 87

NOTE.—For this study read right through the book again, and chapters iv. to the end twice. The need for a more modern and clarifying translation will have now become clear in the reading of these chapters.

If we look at a sundial we may understand the use and import of the figures; yet can we not attain a knowledge of the time unless the sun shine upon it. So it is with the Word of God; we may understand the general meaning of the words, yet can we not receive its spiritual instruction unless we have the unction of the Holy One, whereby we may know all things.

Charles Simeon.

HOSEA

THE PROPHET OF PERSEVERING LOVE

PROLOGUE (i.–iii.)—The whole story in symbol.

ISRAEL'S SIN INTOLERABLE: GOD IS HOLY (iv.–vii.).

THE FIVEFOLD INDICTMENT (iv., v.).
ISRAEL'S UNREAL "RETURN" (vi.).
HEALING MADE IMPOSSIBLE (vii.).

ISRAEL SHALL BE PUNISHED: GOD IS JUST (viii.–x.).

THE TRUMPET OF JUDGMENT (viii. 1).
These chapters throughout are expressions of wrath to come.

ISRAEL SHALL BE RESTORED: GOD IS LOVE (xi.–xiv.).

DIVINE YEARNING (xi. 1, 4, 8, etc.).
YET ISRAEL MUST SUFFER (xii., etc.).
THE FINAL VICTORY OF LOVE (xiv.).

THE BOOK OF HOSEA (2)

WE COME now to the body of the book, chapters iv. to xiv. Here we must express sympathy with those who may have found these chapters discouragingly difficult to get hold of as they appear in the Authorised Version. Admittedly, the abruptness of Hosea's style in these chapters makes translation less easy; but the Authorised Version—much as we dislike to say an unkind word about our grand old "A.V."—so confuses the verb-tenses in some places and obscures the sequence in others that it is awkward, even with careful reading, to pick out the train of thought and the true breaks in it. The Revised Version makes improvements; but these chapters should be read in a thoroughly modern translation; for despite the emotional brokenness of the writing here, the progressive periods and logical breaks are present, as we shall soon find, and can be seen as the outline of hills can be seen through vapoury summer showers—until, in the last chapter, the rains and vapours clear away, and the landscape is bathed in clear shining.

What is more, when we really see the threefold progress in these chapters we are struck by the completeness and beauty of the message which together they express to mankind for all time.

Let us now pick our way through these chapters. The first thing which will be clear to us is that chapters iv. and v. obviously belong together as one progressive address of indictment. It will be good to set these two chapters out here, in part, so as to see more clearly the order and progress in the prophet's address.

JEHOVAH'S ADDRESS OF INDICTMENT

(a) To the whole nation

Chapters iv. and v.

Hear the word of Jehovah, ye children of Israel; for Jehovah hath a controversy with the inhabitants of the land, because there is no truth nor real love nor knowledge of God in the land.

2. *Swearing and falsehood and murder and thieving and adultery!—they break out, and blood strikes upon blood.*

3. *Therefore doth the land wither, and every dweller therein languisheth, even to the beast of the field and the fowl of the heaven; yea, even the fish of the sea are swept up.*

(b) To the Priesthood

4. *Yet let no man contend, let no man reprove, for thy people are contenders against Me, O priest.*

5. *Thou hast stumbled today, and the prophet shall stumble with thee tonight, and I will destroy thy mother (i.e. the nation).*

6. *My people are destroyed for lack of knowledge. Because thou hast rejected knowledge (O priest), I reject thee from being priest to Me; and as thou hast forgotten the Law of thy God, I also will forget thy children,* etc.

(c) An " aside " to Judah

15. *Though thou, Israel, play the harlot, let not Judah bring guilt on herself. And come not to Gilgal, and go not to Beth-Aven, nor swear, As Jehovah liveth!*

16. *Israel has gone wild like a wild heifer. How now can Jehovah feed them like a lamb in a broad meadow?*

17. *Ephraim is wedded to idols: leave him alone (O Judah!)*

18. *Their carouse over, they continue with harlotry: her rulers are fallen in love with shame!*

19. *A wind hath wrapt them up in her skirts, and they shall be put to shame by their sacrifices.*

(d) To Priests, People, and Princes

Chapter v. 1. *Hear ye this, O priests, and hearken, ye house of Israel, and give ear, O house of the king; for on you is this sentence!—for ye have become a snare at Mizpeh, and a net spread out upon Tabor;*

2. *And the revolters are gone deep in corruption; but I shall be the scourge of them all.*

3. *I know Ephraim, and Israel is not hid from Me; for now, O Ephraim, thou hast played the harlot, and Israel is defiled.*

4. *Their doings will not let them return to their God,* etc.

(e) Judgment certain on Israel

8. *Blow the trumpet in Gibeah, the clarion in Ramah; shout the slogan, Beth-Aven—"After thee, Benjamin!"*

9. *Ephraim shall become a desolation in the day of rebuke! Among the tribes of Israel I have made known what is certain!* etc.

14. *For I will be unto Ephraim as a lion, and as a young lion to the house of Judah. I, even I, will rend and go away; I will carry off, and there shall be none to deliver.*

15. *I will go and return to My place, till they feel their guilt and seek My face. In their trouble they will soon seek Me!*

Thus we see, in chapters iv. and v., an address marked by clear order and progress as well as deep emotion. But besides this, we shall now find that chapters vi. and vii. continue and develop this address, so that chapters iv., v., vi., and vii. all belong together. This will become clear if we watch the recurrent words and ideas. To begin with, in chapter v., the Lord twice speaks of withdrawing Himself from Israel:

"They shall go with their flocks and with their herds to seek Jehovah, but they shall not find Him: He hath withdrawn Himself from them" (v. 6).

"I will go and return to My place till they acknowledge their guilt and seek My face. In their affliction they will soon seek Me" (v. 15).

Chapters v. and vi. should be linked by the word "saying," thus: "In their affliction they will soon seek Me, saying: Come, and let us return unto the Lord. . . ." But the profession of returning to the Lord is superficial, as the Lord's immediate rejoinder shows—"O Ephraim, what can I make of thee? O Judah, what can I make of thee? for your goodness (or professed love) is like a morning cloud, and as the dew which soon passes away" (vi. 4). This thought of *returning* (hypocritically) recurs, connecting chapters vi. and vii.

"Come and let us return unto the Lord, for He hath torn, and He will heal us" (vi. 1).

"Yet for all this they have not returned unto the Lord their God" (vii. 10).

"They return, but not to Him that is on high" (vii. 16).

But now look at an even clearer link-word to show the connection of chapters iv. and v. with chapter vi. It is that word "knowledge"—

"The Lord hath a controversy with the inhabitants of the land, because there is no . . . knowledge of God in the land" (iv. 1).

"My people are destroyed for lack of knowledge. Because thou hast rejected knowledge I will also reject thee" (iv. 6).

"Come, and let us return unto the Lord . . . and let us know, let us follow on to know the Lord" (vi. 1–3).

"I desire mercy and not sacrifice, and the knowledge of God more than burnt offerings" (vi. 6).

Just a further word. The second half of the last verse in chapter vi. reads: "When I returned the captivity of My people." The chapter break here is cruel; for these words obviously go with the opening words of chapter vii. Also, instead of the past tense, "returned," we should read, "When I would return"; so that chapter vii. now begins—

"When I would return the captivity of My people, when I would heal Israel, then the iniquity of Ephraim reveals itself, and the wickedness of Samaria."

This thought, that God would fain have healed and delivered Israel, comes again in the thirteenth verse of this seventh chapter —*"Though I would have redeemed them they spoke lies against Me."*

Now these different words, which are like links and keys to these four chapters, do not thus recur in the later chapters; but they certainly bind chapters iv., v., vi., and vii. together, and at the same time interpret them for us. The progressive argument is as follows.

The knowledge of God was destroyed in the land (iv. 1, 6); and this was the tap-root of all manner of evils (iv., v.). Because of Israel's impenitent persistence in these evils Jehovah purposes to exact retribution and to withdraw Himself from them (v. 6, 15). Whereupon Israel superficially "returns" to "know" Jehovah, taking it presumptuously for granted that "after a couple of days" there will be a reviving (vi. 1–3). But their professed return is merely ritualistic, and Jehovah protests, "I desire real love, and not sacrifice, and the knowledge of God more than burnt offerings" (vi. 6). Jehovah, however, still longs to spare and restore Israel, but when He would do so the determined wickedness of the nation prevents Him. The upshot of these chapters is that *Israel's sin has reached the point where it is intolerable.*

Chapters viii. to x.

The remaining chapters of Hosea can be dealt with simply and briefly. If, in the chapters just reviewed (iv.–vii.), we have the exposure of Israel's awful *sin*, it is equally clear that in the next three chapters (viii.–x.) we have the utterance of the awful *judgment* which is swiftly coming upon it. Chapter viii. begins, "*Set the trumpet to thy mouth!*"—that is, sound the alarm of impending calamity. Thereafter, every verse, or every other verse, in these three chapters is a vehement expression of wrath to come. Run the eye quickly again through these chapters, and see that this is so.

"The eagle is down upon the house of Jehovah!" (viii. 1). "Israel shall cry . . . but the enemy shall pursue him" (verses 2, 3). "Thy calf, O Samaria, He hath cast off. . . . Mine anger is kindled" (verse 5). "The calf of Samaria shall be broken in pieces. . . . They have sown the wind, and they shall reap the whirlwind" (verses 6, 7). "The bud shall yield no meal: if so be it yield, strangers shall swallow it up" (verse 7). "Israel is swallowed up. Now shall they be among the Gentiles as a vessel wherein is no pleasure" (verse 8). "Now will He—Jehovah— remember their iniquity, and visit their sins" (verse 13). "I will send a fire upon his cities, and it shall devour the palaces thereof" (verse 14). So is it all the way through these chapters. The verses are like one unbroken scourge of curses. The centre verses of the three chapters focus the whole of their contents— "The days of visitation are come; the days of recompense are come; Israel shall know it. . . . He (Jehovah) will remember their iniquity; He will visit their sins" (ix. 7-9). Thus, our second finding in chapters iv. to xiv. is that chapters viii. to x. are occupied with *judgment on Israel's sin.*

Chapters xi. to xiv.

Finally, in chapters xi. to xiv., we find a noticeably different emphasis or tone from the preceding chapters. Dr. R. G. Moulton calls these chapters "The Yearning of God." The yearning is that of *love.* See the opening words—"When Israel was a child, then I *loved* him . . ." See verse 4—"I drew them with cords of a man, with the bands of *love* . . ." See verses 8, 9, 10, 11 —"How shall I give thee up, Ephraim? How shall I deliver thee, Israel? . . . Mine heart is turned within Me, My repentings are kindled together . . ." See also xii. 6, 9, 10; xiii. 14; xiv. 6. Note also in these chapters the recurrence of *plaintive retrospect* (xi. 1-4, 8, 9; xii. 3-6; xiii. 4-6). And note that although the inevitability of judgment is reiterated, as in xi. 5, 6; xiii. 3, 7, 8, 13, yet the note is now that of sorrowing regret that it must be so, as is shown in each case by the verses immediately following the above references.

But most of all here is the final triumph of love, culminating in the last chapter. It is a grand and beautiful climax. Judgment is finished. Sin is forsaken. Backsliding is healed. Love reigns. See verse 8, which is really the closing verse, for verse 9 is a brief epilogue. Ephraim says: "What have I to do any more with idols?" Jehovah responds: "I have answered and will regard him." Ephraim again says: "I am like a green fir tree"; and Jehovah again responds: "From Me is thy fruit found."

Thus we have a striking, triple message in these chapters of Hosea, as is shown in the simple analysis which we have prefixed to this present study (see page 98).

THE PROPHET JOEL (1)

Lesson Number 88

NOTE.—For this study read the prophecy of Joel through twice.

The Bible is indeed a deep book, when depth is required, that is by a deep people; but it is not intended particularly for profound persons. And, therefore the first, and generally the main and leading idea of the Bible is on its surface, written in the plainest possible Greek, Hebrew, or English, needing . . . nothing but what we all might give—attention.

John Ruskin, " Modern Painters."

THE BOOK OF JOEL (1)

BOTH in style and subject this Book of Joel is arresting. For vividness of description and picturesqueness of diction Joel is scarcely equalled. His pen-pictures of the plague-stricken land, the invading locust-army, and the final gathering of all nations to the valley of judgment, are miniature masterpieces of graphic vigour.

Joel, whose name means "Jehovah is God," calls himself "the son of Pethuel" (i. 1). Beyond this we are told nothing about him. His book makes it tolerably certain, however, that he exercised his prophetic ministry in or near Jerusalem. It is the inhabitants of that city whom he addresses (ii. 23). It is Jerusalem which he sees in danger (ii., 9). It is in Zion that the "alarm" is to be sounded (ii. 1, 15). It is in Mount Zion and in Jerusalem that deliverance shall be in the after-days (ii. 32). It is the captivity of Judah and Jerusalem which is then to be ended (iii. 1); and it is Judah and Jerusalem which shall "dwell for ever" (iii. 20). The ten-tribed northern kingdom is not once mentioned.

Early or Late?

As for the *date* when Joel wrote this message, scholars are far from unanimous. He has usually been regarded as one of the earliest, if not actually the very first, of the writing prophets: but certain moderns contend, paradoxically enough, that he was probably the very latest of them. We have inspected the arguments on both sides; and it has not taken us too long to conclude that the earlier view is the true one. It is not needful to our present study to discuss this fully here, though we may mention that one strong indication of the earlier date assigned to the book is that the only enemies of Judah mentioned in it are the Phoenicians, Philistines, Edomites, and Egyptians. Now while these were vexatious enough enemies, what were they compared with the awful Assyrian and Babylonian world-powers which rose later, and crushed the Palestinian nations, leading both Israel and Judah into captivity? Surely it is almost incredible that if Joel prophesied *after* the onsets of these mighty powers he should leave them unmentioned, the more so if, as is asserted, he wrote after the Babylonian exile itself had occurred!

Notwithstanding this, Sir George Adam Smith's book on the Minor Prophets categorically asserts that the *post*-exilic date of Joel is "proved" by chapter iii. 2, which says that the heathen have scattered Israel among the nations and parted their land. But Sir George should have been more careful to take this text in its context. It is the Phoenicians and the Philistines who are here in mind (see verse 4), and it is *these* who are said to have plundered the land and sold the Israelites to other peoples and removed them far from their own land (see verses 5 to 7)—long enough before the Exile! And if corroboration be required for this, one only need turn to Amos (whom Sir George admits to be pre-exilic) chapter i. 6, 9, to find the same predatory assaults of the Philistines and the same Phoenician traffic in Israelite captives referred to. And if an actual historical instance of this carrying away of Judah's sons from their own land be asked, we have it in 2 Chronicles xxi. 17, where we are told that the Philistines broke in and carried away all the king's sons except one—the youngest. Needless to add, perhaps, these would not be the only persons carried off in that particular raid.

But even if Joel iii. 2 *did* refer to the Exile, as Sir George has asserted, it would not prove that Joel wrote *after* that event, for this verse comes (as Sir George himself admits) in the *predictive* part of Joel's little treatise; and therefore there is no reason at all why Joel should not have written of the Exile before ever it happened, just as other prophets speak of events long in advance. As a matter of fact, in Joel iii. 2 and its context we have an instance of something that is found again and again in the prophetic writings, namely, the prophecy is so worded that while there is a primary reference to an historical happening with which the prophet's contemporaries were familiar, there is a further and larger fulfilment envisaged away in futurity. Some of the other "modern" arguments for a *post*-exilic Joel are more like those of young schoolboys than degreed scholars. We shall here ignore them, and are confirmed in the older view that Joel prophesied in the latter half of the ninth century B.C.

Contents and Analysis

Let us now go through the book and analyse it, and thus seek to know its central message.

First, we must re-read chapter i. Here we have a moving description of the desolation in the land, resulting from successive locust ravages (verse 4). The thing to settle here is: Are we to understand that the desolation which Joel here describes was actually present when he wrote, or (as frequently happens in the prophetic writings) was he using the present tense for the sake of vividness to picture something that was yet coming? My own first impression was that he was using the graphic present to depict, as though it were already there, a calamity yet to break on the nation, just as Isaiah, hundreds of years before our Lord's incarnation, used the present tense concerning Him, in the words, "Unto us a Child is born; unto us a Son is given." My impression seemed confirmed by verse 15, where Joel slips into a momentary use of the future tense—"Alas—for the day! for the day of Jehovah is *at hand*, and as a destruction from the Almighty *shall it come*." Most writers on Joel, however, take it that the desolation described by him in chapter i. was actually present; and I think we must take that view ourselves after careful reading. The question seems settled, in fact, by chapter ii. 25, where the Lord says: "And I will restore to you the years that the locust *hath eaten*, the cankerworm and the caterpillar and the palmer-worm, My great army which I *sent* among you." This verse makes it absolutely clear that the land was already stricken by the locust scourge. So, then, as our first item in the analysis of this book, we write down that chapter i. describes a desolation already present, with (in verse 15) an alarm of some still further and greater calamity impending.

Chapter ii.

If we now read on through chapter ii., we shall find that the first eleven verses in it are a most gripping and awesome picture of this still further and greater trouble which was about to break on the nation. This is too clear to need comment. The chapter begins: "Blow ye the trumpet in Zion; and sound an alarm in My holy mountain!" An alarm is not sounded for what is already past, but to warn of that which is imminent. Thus, the verse continues: "Let all the inhabitants of the land tremble; for the day of Jehovah *cometh*, for it is *nigh at hand*." Then follows the description of the strange, dread army which was to overrun the land. It is enough to strike fear into any heart. This visitation, whatever its nature, was to be so grave and extraordinary that it could be described by no less an expression than "the day of Jehovah"—an expression which comes not only in verse 1, but again in verse 11, where we read, "The day of Jehovah is great and very terrible; and who can abide it?"

At verse 12 there is a break too clear to miss. It is marked, in our Authorised Version, by the word "Therefore"; and from this twelfth verse down to verse 17 there is an imploring *appeal* to the nation to repent before the dread stroke falls. The appeal begins: "Therefore also now, saith Jehovah, turn ye unto Me with all your heart. . . ." Instead of the word "therefore," the Revised Version has, "Yet even now"; and this is preferable, for it emphasises that this is an *eleventh-hour* appeal. In the mercy of God there is always this eleventh-hour chance before a major stroke of judgment falls. We see this illustrated in the history of both Israel and Judah. It happens again and again in the lives of individuals. Modern European history exemplifies it, too, if we have eyes to discern the hand of God in things.

And now, at verse 18, there comes a further break. There is a gracious *promise*—a promise of salvation if the eleventh-hour appeal is heeded. This promise runs from this eighteenth verse to verse 27. Most writers on Joel suppose that the appeal was heeded, and that therefore these verses (18–27) describe what actually happened. That, however, is a gratuitous "reading between the lines" what is not there, all because verse 18 is in the past tense—"Then did Jehovah become jealous for His land, and took pity upon His people." But none of the verses which follow verse 18 is in the past tense; and this eighteenth verse is put in the past simply as a way of vivid emphasis as the prophet introduces the gracious promise, or because, for encouragement's sake, he momentarily visualises the Divine response, if the people repent, as though it had already happened. Again and again we have the past tense used in this way in the prophetic writings. The fifty-third chapter of Isaiah, for instance, gives its wonderful picture of the suffering Saviour practically wholly in the past tense.

An Annex (ii. 28–iii. 21).

Finally, from chapter ii. 28 to iii. 21, where Joel's little book ends, we have a section which plainly stands by itself, for it is all *predictive* of what will happen in the after-days; and this is the only part of Joel's writing which is predictive of the days beyond the prophet's own time. The apostle Peter, in his discourse on the day of Pentecost, definitely relates Joel ii. 28, and what follows it, to "the last days" (Acts ii. 15–21). At this point, therefore, we are reassuringly guided in our analysis and interpretation of Joel by a clear New Testament pronouncement. So, then, from Joel ii. 28 to the end of the book we have a predictive *annex* concerning the after-days. And thus we may now set out our analysis as follows.

THE BOOK OF JOEL

"The Day of Jehovah cometh!"

AN ALARM—INVASION BY PLAGUE! (i. 1–ii. 11).

> The present desolation (i. 1–20).
> The yet further threat (ii. 1–11).

AN APPEAL—ELEVENTH-HOUR HOPE! (ii. 12–27).

> Appeal: "Turn ye to Me" (ii. 12–17).
> Promise: "I will restore" (ii. 18–27).

AN ANNEX—ON THE AFTER-DAYS (ii. 28–iii. 21).

> Epochs of the end-time (ii. 28–iii. 16).
> Ultimate glory of Zion (iii. 17–iii. 21).

But there is one point in our analysis which may seem to require further verification. Our first heading is "Invasion by Plague"; yet are we *sure* that the invading host in chapter ii. is a locust plague, and not an army of *men*? This is important. Three answers have been given.

First, there are those who expound this passage as *apocalyptic*, that is, as referring wholly to the dread "day of the Lord" at the end of the present age. This explanation of the passage is called "apocalyptic," of course, from the Greek word, *apocalupsis*, which means an unveiling or revelation (and which is the title of the last book in our Bible because that book is an unveiling of the future). An example of the apocalyptic interpretation of this Joel passage is found in the Scofield Bible, which heads it: "THE DAY OF THE LORD: THE INVADING HOST FROM THE NORTH PREPARATORY TO ARMAGEDDON." The footnote adds: "In Joel ii. the literal locusts are left behind, and the future day of Jehovah fills the scene." "The whole picture is of the end-time of this present age."

But we cannot accept this theory; for besides other exegetical difficulties there is one fact outstandingly which decides against it. Can we really believe that the prophet, although purporting to address and arouse his own generation, was not really addressing them at all, but a future generation nearly three millenniums away? Such an artificiality as that would be unworthy of the inspired Word. Surely, as clearly as language could make it, Joel here addresses his own contemporaries, and sounds an alarm of some calamity which was imminent then and there. He certainly *intends* them to think this. If we read the passage with a really open mind we cannot escape this. Whatever *latent* significances may lie in his words, their genuine first sense has to do with Joel's own time; and we do not serve the best interests of our Bible when, with zeal for seeing prophetic meanings, we exalt the apocalyptic at the expense of the historical integrity of Scripture.

But there is also the *allegorical* explanation. According to this, Joel was describing a coming crisis simply under the *figure* of a locust plague. There had recently been actual locust ravages in the land (as chapter i. shows); and now the prophet imagines an even worse locust plague, and uses it as a figure of the fateful coming crisis which he calls "the day of Jehovah." In line with this, it is argued that while the description has its *ground* in a locust plague, the language is too ominous to be limited by it. These locusts of chapter ii. are really the "*nations*" of chapter iii. Certain features in the description, it is said, imply a *human* army. The invaders are said to be "a great *people* and a strong" (verse 2). They assault cities and terrify the people (verses 6, 7). They are to be destroyed in a way which is inapplicable to locusts (verse 20). The priests are urged to pray that the "*nations*" may not "rule over" Israel (verse 17). The scourge is from the *north* (verse 20), whereas locusts usually swarm Palestine from the south. All these things, it is argued, indicate something more than a locust plague. As to which event is here "allegorised," opinions vary. The later invasions by the Assyrians, Babylonians, Persians, and Romans, of course, have been hit on; and there are those who would also include a final apocalyptic reference to Armageddon.

But the allegorical theory will not do. The idea that the description exceeds that of a locust plague breaks down on fuller knowledge, as we shall see. So does the idea that certain details are not applicable to locusts; for they invade towns just as Joel says, while Joel's further word about their stealing into houses "like a thief" certainly fits locusts more than a military assault! Moreover, Joel's account of the damage inflicted on the land is agricultural rather than military (verse 3), and there is not even a hint of that which goes with a *military* invasion—massacre and plunder. But the allegorical theory is finally disproved by verses 4 to 7 where Joel says the invaders are *like* horsemen, and sound *like* chariots, and scale the wall *like* men of war. It has been aptly observed that Joel would never have compared a *real* army with itself.

Yet even more than this, both the apocalyptic and allegorical theories are surely proved wrong by a comparison of verses 11 and 25; for in the one the invaders are called *Jehovah's* army, and in the other Jehovah Himself says: "I will restore unto you the years that *the locust* hath eaten, the cankerworm and the caterpillar and the palmerworm, *My great army* which I sent among you." Could language make it plainer, that the threatened *further* calamity, in chapter ii. 1-11, was to be of the same kind—though in even severer degree—as that which had already taken place (as described in chapter i.)?

No; Joel's locusts were neither "apocalyptic" nor "allegorical." In our next lesson we shall see that he meant locusts quite literally, and that the visitation was to be such that he could even call it by that awesome name, "The day of Jehovah." Meanwhile, let us get our analysis well fixed in our minds:—(1) An *alarm*, invasion by plague! (2) An *appeal*, eleventh-hour hope! (3) **An** *annex*, on the after-days.

THE BOOK OF JOEL (2)

Lesson Number 89

NOTE.—For this study read the prophecy of Joel through again twice.

I always do, and always will exhort you that at home you accustom yourselves to a daily reading of the Scriptures.

St. Chrysostom.

We have done almost everything that is possible with the Hebrew and Greek writings. . . . There is just one thing left to do with the Bible; simply to read it.

Professor Richard Moulton.

THE BOOK OF JOEL (2)

Invasion by Locusts!

"Blow ye the trumpet!" "Sound an alarm!" "The day of Jehovah cometh!" "It is nigh at hand!" If these words have honest meaning, then they mean that some extraordinary crisis was imminent at the very time when the prophet wrote. *Following* these words there is the description of a terrifying, desolating, resistless invasion-host which was to come up over all the land (ii. 2–11); and, as already pointed out, a comparison of verse 11 with verse 25 shows conclusively that this threatened disaster was an invasion by *locusts*.

Those who hold that the prophet's language here is too awesome to be used of an actual plague of locusts have fallen back either on the *apocalyptic* explanation, which refers the passage exclusively to the end of the present age, or on the *allegorical* explanation, which says that the passage describes those *human* enemies of the covenant people which were later to invade their land. But, as we saw in our last study, neither of these explanations will bear careful examination.

We shall now furnish some external proofs of the fact that the true interpretation is, indeed, that which takes the passage *literally*, as referring to real locusts. Read the passage carefully, once again, noting the seeming peculiarities, from that unusual expression in verse 2, about "the morning spread upon the mountains," down to verses 10 and 11, where we read even of the earth quaking and the heavens trembling. Then read the following accounts from competent witnesses. It will be found that Joel's description is literally true, and that little, if anything, need be taken as hyperbole or poetic licence.

The following quotation is from Van-Lennep's work, *Bible Lands*.

"The young locusts rapidly attain the size of the common grasshopper, and proceed in one and the same direction, first crawling, and at a later period leaping, as they go, devouring every green thing that lies in their path. They advance more slowly than a devouring fire, but the ravages they commit are scarcely inferior or less to be dreaded. Fields of standing wheat and barley, vineyards, mulberry orchards, and groves of olive, fig, and other trees are in a few hours deprived of every green blade and leaf, the very bark being often destroyed. The ground over which their devastating hordes have passed at once assumes an appearance of sterility and dearth. Well did the Romans call them 'the burners of the land,' which is the literal meaning of our word 'locust.' On they move, covering the ground so completely as to hide it from sight, and in such numbers that it often takes three or four days for the mighty host to pass by. When seen at a distance, this swarm of advancing locusts resembles a cloud of dust or sand, reaching a few feet above the ground, as the myriads of insects leap forward. The only thing that momentarily arrests their progress is a sudden change of weather; for the cold benumbs them while it lasts. They also keep quiet at night, swarming like bees on the bushes and hedges until the morning sun warms them and revives them and enables them to proceed on their devastating march. They 'have no king' nor leader, yet they falter not, but press on in serried ranks, urged in the same direction by an irresistible impulse, and turn neither to the right hand nor to the left for any sort of obstacle. When a wall or a house lies in their way, they climb straight up, going over the roof to the other side, and blindly rush in at the open doors and windows. When they come to water, be it a mere puddle or a river, a lake or the open sea, they never attempt to go round it, but unhesitatingly leap in and are drowned, and their dead bodies, floating on the surface, form a bridge for their companions to pass over. The scourge thus often comes to an end, but it as often happens that the decomposition of millions of insects produces pestilence and death. History records a remarkable instance which occurred in the year 125 before the Christian era. The insects were driven by the wind into the sea in such vast numbers that their bodies, being driven back by the tide upon the land, caused a stench which produced a fearful plague whereby eighty thousand persons perished in Libya, Cyrene, and Egypt. The locust, however, soon acquires its wings, and proceeds on its way by flight, whenever a strong breeze favours its progress. Our attention has often been attracted by the sudden darkening of the sun in a summer sky, accompanied by the peculiar noise which a swarm of locusts always makes moving through the air; and, glancing upward, we have seen them passing like a cloud at a height of two or three hundred feet."

We call particular attention to the above mention of the fire-like effects of the locusts; of the noise made by their wings; of the darkening of the sun; and of their destruction at the sea shore exactly as Joel describes (ii. 20). But if a locust *"swarm"* is so awful, what must a locust *"plague"* be! It is little wonder that when Moses announced a coming plague of locusts Pharaoh's counsellors exclaimed in desperation, "Knowest thou not yet that Egypt is destroyed?"

Mr. James Bryce, in his *Impressions of South Africa*, writes: "It is a strange sight, beautiful if you can forget the destruction it brings with it. The whole air, to twelve or eighteen feet above the ground, is filled with the insects, reddish brown in body, with bright, gauzy wings. When the sun's rays catch them it is like the sea sparkling with light. When you see them against a cloud they are like the dense flakes of a driving snow-storm. You feel as if you had never before realised immensity in number. Vast crowds of men gathered at a festival, countless tree-tops rising along the slope of a forest ridge, the chimneys of London houses from the top of St. Paul's—all are as nothing to the myriads of insects that blot out the sun above and cover the ground beneath and fill the air whichever way one looks. The breeze carries them swiftly past, but they come on in fresh clouds, a host of which there is no end, each of them a harmless creature which you can catch and crush in your hand, but appalling in their power of collective devastation."

Or, to quote, in an abbreviated form, from W. M. Thomson's classic work, *The Land and the Book*: "Their number was astounding; the whole face of the mountain was black with them. On they came like a living deluge. We dug trenches, and kindled fires, and beat and burned to death 'heaps upon heaps'; but the effort was utterly useless. Wave after wave *rolled up* the mountain side, and poured over rocks, walls, ditches and hedges —those behind covering up and bridging over the masses already killed. It was perfectly appalling to watch this animated river as it flowed *up* the road, and ascended the hill above my house. For four days they continued to pass on toward the east . . .

millions upon millions. In their march they devour every green thing, and with wonderful expedition. The noise made in marching and foraging was like that of a heavy shower on a distant forest. Nothing in their habits is more striking than the pertinacity with which they all pursue the same line of march, like a disciplined army."

In the *Journal of Sacred Literature*, October 1865, a writer recorded: "Our garden finished, they continued toward the town, devastating one garden after another. Whatever one is doing one hears their noise from without, like the noise of armed hosts, or the running of many waters. When in an erect position their appearance at a little distance is like that of a well-armed horseman." Another writer says: "To strength incredible for so small a creature, they add saw-like teeth, admirably calculated to eat up all the herbs in the land." Another says: "After eating up the corn, they fell upon the vines, the pulse, the willows, and even the hemp, notwithstanding its great bitterness." And another says: "For eighty or ninety miles they devoured every green herb and every blade of grass." And another says: "The gardens outside Jaffa are now completely stripped, even the bark of the young trees having been devoured, and look like a birch-tree forest in winter." And still another: "The fields finished, they invade towns and houses, in search of stores. Victual of all kinds, hay, straw, and even linen and woollen clothes and leather bottles, they consume or tear in pieces. They flood through the open, unglazed windows and lattices; nothing can keep them out." W. M. Thomson tells us that when the millions upon millions of locust eggs hatch, the very dust seems to waken to life, and the earth itself seems to tremble with them; and later, when the vast new breed have acquired wings, the very heavens seem tremulous with them. And as for Joel's likening of the locusts to "dawn scattered on the mountains," G. A. Smith says: "No one who has seen a cloud of locusts can question the realism even of this picture; the heavy gloom of the immeasurable mass of them, shot by gleams of light where a few of the sun's imprisoned beams have broken through or across the storm of lustrous wings. This is like dawn beaten down upon the hilltops, and crushed by rolling masses of cloud, in conspiracy to prolong the night."

We need add no more. The foregoing evidence settles two things conclusively: the *awfulness* of a really bad locust plague; and the *literalness* of Joel's description. There can remain no doubt that the invasion which Joel announced as imminent was an invasion by locusts; nor can we doubt that it was this to which he referred, in the first place, when he said: "The day of Jehovah is at hand." The connection in the context is too clear to mistake.

" The Day of Jehovah "

Five times in this effusion from the pen of Joel we find the phrase, "The day of Jehovah" (i. 15; ii. 1, 11, 31; iii. 14). In fact we may say that Joel is distinctively *the prophet of "the day of Jehovah."* What is more, his use of the expression furnishes us with a guide as to its use in Scripture prophecy generally.

Let us note, then, that Joel uses this appellation in three ways. First, in chapters i. 15; ii. 1 and 11, he uses it of *the threatened locust plague*, as the context shows, and especially a comparison of ii. 11 with ii. 25, as already mentioned. Second, in chapter ii. 31, he uses it of a "great and terrible" day which is even yet to come, at *the end of the present age*; for, as the New Testament comment on this passage shows (Acts ii. 14–21), the context here refers to "the last days." Thirdly, in chapter iii. 14, he uses it of a day of Divine judgment which was even then "near" upon *the Palestinian nations* which had afflicted Israel; for the context addresses these (iii. 4–8); and their being gathered to "the valley of Jehoshaphat" (iii. 2, 12, 14) was for a "day of Jehovah" which, as plainly stated in verse 14, was *"near"* even when Joel wrote. Yet in this case the language is such that we cannot *restrict* it to this event of long ago. The description is couched in terms which evidently intend the event to adumbrate that final "day of Jehovah" which is yet to be; so that this *third* way in which Joel uses the expression *combines* both the historical and the prophetical, both the local and the racial, both the near and the far, both the now past and the yet future—a remarkable feature which we find again and again in the prophetical writings of Scripture.

This phrase, then, "The day of Jehovah," is used in three ways —first in a *local* sense; second in a *final* sense; and third in a *double* sense. Examples of each of these are found in the following references: Isaiah ii. 12; xiii. 6, 9; xiv. 3; Jeremiah xxx. 7, 8; xlvi. 10; Lamentations ii. 16; Ezekiel vii. 19; xiii. 5; xxx. 3, 9;

Amos v. 18, 20; Obadiah 15; Zephaniah i. 7, etc.; Zechariah xiv.; Malachi iv. 5.

Therefore the phrase must not *always* be interpreted of the end of the present age. Sometimes it must *not* be. Sometimes it *must* be. Sometimes it *may* be. If we take a purely local reference and give it an apocalyptic interpretation we get confusion. We see this in the Scofield Bible note to Joel ii. 11. It says that although the invading army in verses 1 to 10 is the host against the Lord at Armageddon, yet the army in verse 11 is a different one; it is now the *Lord's* army (because it says, "The Lord shall utter His voice before *His* army"). Now this idea is flatly contradicted by verse 25 which plainly says that the Lord's army was the *locust* army, the effects of which are lamented in chapter i., and an imminent further invasion of which is described in chapter ii. 1—11; so that *all* these first eleven verses of chapter ii. refer to the Lord's army, and not just verse 11 as the Scofield note says! There is much that is excellent in the Scofield notes; and while we express occasional criticism we do not lack appreciation; but the many Bible readers who unquestioningly accept the Scofield word on a passage should at least pay the respect of exercising a little kindly suspicion here and there. Certainly we cannot make the above Joel passage apocalyptic without doing violence to it.

But we must add that even where this expression, "The day of Jehovah," does not look right on to the end of our own age it is reserved to denote only the most extraordinary visitations of Divine judgment. Here in Joel, for instance, where it is used of the threatened locust-plague, the plague is such that "*there hath not been ever the like, neither shall be any more after it, even to the years of many generations*" (ii. 2). Knowing what we now do about the awfulness of locust plagues, we can appreciate what blackness of horror such an announcement would mean. Many observers have confessed that the earthquake and the locust-plague, above all other physical disasters, produce a helpless, awesome, ominous sense of the supernatural. How indescribably awful, then, this super-plague of Joel ii. was to be may be easily inferred.

What "the day of Jehovah" at the end of the present age will be passes the power of imagination to anticipate. We only need to look up the references to it in both Testaments to realise that all the events of past history will be dwarfed by this magnitudinous culmination. It will suddenly burst into occurrence with the return of the Lord Jesus Christ in supernatural splendour. This will precipitate Armageddon, when the "Beast" and the "False Prophet" and the anti-Christ "kings of the earth with their armies" shall be utterly overwhelmed, the present world-system smashed, Satan flung into the bottomless abyss, and all powers of evil crushed to the dust. And this will inaugurate the world-wide empire of Christ, with a restored Israel in Palestine, and all the peoples of the earth forming the one kingdom of "our God and His Christ." This "day of Jehovah" will be heralded by cosmic disturbances and other preternatural signs; it will continue for a thousand years; it will end with a Divinely permitted final insurrection of evil inspired by Satan; then the final abolition of evil from the earth, the general judgment of the human race at the Great White Throne, and a cataclysm of fire, followed by a "new heaven and a new earth."

Seeing then that we look for such things, "what manner of persons ought we to be in all holy conversation and godliness!"

Addendum on Joel ii. 28 etc.

It is usually held that the inauguration of the Christian church dates back to Pentecost. Acts ii. 16, however, explains Pentecost as, "This is that which was spoken by the prophet Joel . . ." And the Joel passage (ii. 28—iii. 21) refers, not to the church, but to the even yet future "great and terrible day of Jehovah", the final regathering of Israel, and the Messianic kingdom. But if that Joel prophecy is even yet unfulfilled, how could Peter say at Pentecost, "This is *that*"? The answer is as follows.

In fulfilment of promise, our Lord proclaimed the kingdom to the Jews, and offered Himself as Messiah. (How certain anti-dispensationalists can deny this is passing strange.) The Jews, who had doted on the material aspects of the promised kingdom, to the neglect of its spiritual requirements, rejected and even crucified Christ—which, however, was foreknown and overruled of God to effect a world-wide Gospel of individual salvation.

On the Cross, our Lord prayed, "Father, forgive them, for they know not what they do". In answer, the Jews were given a further opportunity in the period covered by the Acts, when the new offer was accompanied by the additional message (and proofs) of the resurrection and ascension of the Lord Jesus, and the outpouring of the Holy Spirit. The Pentecostal miracles were God-given *signs* that the kingdom was verily drawing near again in offer. Hence Peter's "This is *that*. . ." But Israel again rejected; and as the further rejection crystallised, the Pentecostal signs were withdrawn, as also was the kingdom. The Joel passage now awaits the second coming of Christ, when the church age ends, and the kingdom age begins.

TEN QUESTIONS ON HOSEA AND JOEL

1. Was Hosea a prophet to the northern or the southern kingdom? And why may we call him the prophet of zero hour?

2. Can you mention some of the evils which existed in Israel, and which Hosea denounced?

3. What was the name of Hosea's wife, and what were the names of his three children?

4. What are the three main chapter-groups in Hosea?

5. In what way is the narrative in the first three chapters of Hosea symbolical?

6. Give reasons for the early date of the book of the prophet Joel.

7. Give a brief outline of the Book of Joel.

8. Why cannot we accept the apocalyptic and allegorical interpretations of Joel, chapter ii.?

9. Give reasons for believing that the invading host predicted in chapter ii. was to be an actual locust plague.

10. What are the three ways Joel uses the expression, "The day of the LORD"? And what great passage is quoted from Joel by Peter at Pentecost?

THE PROPHET AMOS

Lesson Number 90

NOTE.—For this study read the prophecy of Amos through at least twice.

Note on Amos v. 26, 27.

These verses read in the Authorised Version:

"But ye have borne the tabernacle of your Moloch and Chiun your images, the star of your god, which ye made to yourselves. Therefore will I cause you to go into captivity beyond Damascus, saith the Lord, whose name is the God of hosts".

The word rendered as "tabernacle" in verse 26 is the Hebrew *Succoth*, and research has now shown that it is the name of a heathen god, not just the Hebrew word for a tent or tabernacle. The more correct rendering is, "Succoth your king".

Schrader translates the verse: "Thus shall ye then take Succoth your king and Kēwān your star-god, your images which ye have made for yourselves, and I will carry you off into captivity. . . ."

It was the forewarning of expulsion to a people who had forsaken Jehovah and made idols their gods.

J.S.B.

THE BOOK OF AMOS

Amos, the herdsman-prophet, is a singular figure among the Old Testament prophets. His writing, too, is distinguished by a peculiar forcefulness and rural freshness. Although we are devoting less space to Amos than to some of the other prophets, this must not suggest a lesser estimate of him. Far from it! We give extra space and attention to a book like that of Jonah simply because of the aggravated problems and prevalent misunderstandings associated with it. This book of Amos ranks high among the writings of the prophets. Let us glance at the man himself, and then briefly examine his prophecies.

THE MAN

In chapter i. 1, the prophet speaks of himself as "Amos, who was among the herdmen of Tekoa." So he was a rustic from away down south, from the wild country west of the Dead Sea, the wide stretch of open land known as "The Wilderness of Judæa." The sparse ruins of the little Judæan town, Tekoa, are identifiable even today, some six miles south of Bethlehem. Mile after mile the open country stretches away to the east of Tekoa and Bethlehem till it reaches the Dead Sea, fifteen miles or so away.

It was here, in this so-called "Wilderness of Judæa," that David kept his sheep, and where he afterward roamed a refugee from the court of Saul. It was here, nearly three centuries later, that Amos went forth with the herdsmen of his day; and it was here that he heard the call of God to become a prophet to the northern kingdom, Israel. In chapter vii. 14, 15, he says: "I was no prophet, neither was I a prophet's son; but I was an herdman and a cultivator (not just a 'gatherer,' as in the Authorised Version) of Sycamore fruit (that is, the Sycamore-*fig* tree): and the Lord took me as I followed the flock, and the Lord said unto me: Go, prophesy unto My people Israel."

When Amos says he was not a prophet nor the son of a prophet, he means this merely in the technical or professional sense. He had not been trained in any of the "schools of the prophets," and therefore was not, in the usual sense, a member of the recognised prophetic order. He was what we would call today a "layman." He is a great encouragement to thousands of Christians today who have had no academic or theological training. God is sovereign in His choice of servants. He is not tied to any bishop's hands. He is not bound to any set of officials. He is not restricted in His workings to any recognised ministerial order. "The wind bloweth where it listeth"!

Mark the definiteness with which Amos speaks of his Divine call—"The Lord took me"; "The Lord said unto me: Go, prophesy." What confidence does the consciousness of such a call give a man, especially in face of opposition or discouragement such as Amos had to meet! What straightforward speaking it always puts in a man's mouth! What a sense of authority (along with humility) it gives him!—"*The Lord* said unto me: Go, prophesy unto My people Israel. *Now, therefore*, hear the word of the Lord." It is that ring of "now, therefore" which is absent from many of our preachers today; and therein lies their weakness. It is the conviction of a Divine call deep in the soul which makes any man or woman a telling witness for God.

Amos, although a native of Judæa, was called to prophesy in the northern kingdom, Israel. Try to imagine the impression that his appearance and preaching would make at the capital, or at Bethel. Alexander Maclaren says: "If one fancies a godly Scottish Highlander sent to the West End of London, or a Bible-reading New England farmer's man sent to New York's 'Upper Ten,' one will have some notion of this prophet, the impression made, and the task laid upon him." We know that Amos went to Bethel, the main centre of Israel's golden-calf worship (vii. 13), and there, like a solitary Luther, he denounced the prelate and the priests and the state idolatry, under the very shadow of "the king's chapel."

Amos himself tells us the *time* when he prophesied. It was "in the days of Uzziah, king of Judah, and in the days of Jeroboam, the son of Joash, king of Israel" (i. 1). The *style* of Amos may not be marked by sublimity, but there is a clearness and regularity, an elegance and colour and freshness about it, which give

it a literary charm all its own. His vocabulary, his figures of
speech, his illustrations, are all redolent of the country life from
which he came. There was an unconventional bluntness about
him which must have been pretty disconcerting to the college-
trained professional prophets of the Bethel calf-worship, with
their polished ambiguities and evasions. They would certainly
feel a cold shiver down their spines to hear Amos address the
upper-class ladies of Samaria as "cows"!—"Hear this word, *ye
cows* of Bashan that are in the mountain of Samaria, which
oppress the poor, which crush the needy, which say to their
masters: Bring, and let us drink" (iv. 1).

No doubt Amos created a stir when he appeared on the scene;
and probably he was hailed with appreciation at first, for he
began by announcing coming judgments on the surrounding
nations. But when he suddenly wheeled round with scathing
threat of coming judgment on Israel, the visage of his hearers
changed. A public man in *our* land today may fling invectives at
other nations to his heart's content; but let him really charge
his own countrymen to their face with the rottenness and crooked-
ness of their ways, and his popularity is doomed; nor need he
be astonished if he finds the leaders of the national religion among
his enemies. Bethel was Israel's Canterbury: the head priest of
Bethel was Israel's primate: and we find the primate of Israel
denouncing Amos as a conspirator, to the king himself (vii. 10, 11),
and afterwards telling Amos to flee the country (vii. 10–13).

Whether Amos later returned to Judæa or not we do not know
for certain, though the traditional site of his tomb at Tekoa
suggests that he probably did. Of this, however, we may be
assured, that this dauntless messenger of God did not return
until he knew that his witness was fully given—not until God's
word was true of him, as it later was of Ezekiel, "They shall
know that there hath been a prophet among them." Amos is the
kind of prophet-preacher needed in many places today. As we
think of him again, Charles Wesley's lines come to mind—

> Shall I, to soothe the unholy throng,
> Soften Thy truth or smooth my tongue,
> To gain earth's gilded toys, or flee
> The cross endured, my Lord, by Thee?

THE BOOK

We have noted that the language of Amos is marked by clearness and regularity. We shall now see that the subject-matter of his little treatise is arranged with a corresponding orderliness.

Chapters i. and ii.

First, in chapters i. and ii. we find eight prophetic "*burdens*," or messages burdened with the news of coming retribution. These eight burdens concern eight Palestinian nations—Syria, which is addressed through Damascus its capital (i. 3–5); Philistia, which is represented by its fortress-city of Gaza (i. 6–8); Phoenicia, which is represented by its great seaport, Tyre (i. 9, 10); Edom (i. 11, 12); Ammon (i. 13–15); Moab (ii. 1–3); Judah (ii. 4, 5); Israel (ii. 6–16).

There are several points to notice about these eight burdens. First, each is prefaced by the formula, "For three transgressions and for four . . ." The phrase is not to be taken arithmetically, to mean a literal three and then four, but idiomatically, as meaning that the measure was full, and more than full; the sin of these peoples had overreached itself; or, to put it in an allowable bit of modern slang, they had "gone one too many," and "tipped the scale." The first time they had done the evil, God had rebuked. The second time, He had threatened. The third time, He had menaced with uplifted hand. Now, at the fourth time, He smites! Let the nations know that though God may bear long with the wicked, they can sin once too often! God is not mocked: there cannot be cumulative sin without a culminative stroke of retribution. The prophets believed in "poetic justice"—a retribution corresponding to the guilt, as truly as one line of poetry parallels another. The operation of such poetic justice may be seen all through history—and it operates today, as events and issues in World War II impressively demonstrated to all observant eyes.

Second, in each of these burdens the symbol of judgment is *fire* (i. 4, 7, 10, 12, 14; ii. 2, 5)—the most destructive of all the elements. Extreme guilt brings extreme doom.

Third, in each case (except Judah and Israel) the sins to be punished are *cruelties against other peoples*. See the recurrence

of "Because they . . ." God hates inhumanity. Yet never
in all history have nations shown such coldly calculated inhumanity to other nations as have certain nations of today.
And is God blind to this? And will He not punish?

Chapters iii. to vi.

Next, in chapters iii. to vi., we have three short *sermons*, or
perhaps we ought to call them sermon "breviates," as they are
doubtless written precís of the prophet's much lengthier *utterances*. These three addresses are easily picked out. They each
begin with "Hear this word . . ." (iii. 1; iv. 1; v. 1). The
first of them runs through chapter iii. The second runs through
chapter iv. The third runs through chapters v. and vi.

Each of them is divided by an emphatic "*therefore*," so that
in each we have, in the first part, judgment *deserved*, and in the
remainder, judgment *decreed*. In the first of these addresses
(iii.) the "therefore" is at verse 11. In the second address (iv.)
the "therefore" is at verse 12. In the third address (v., vi.) the
"therefore" is in the fifth chapter, at verse 16. (In this fifth
chapter there are two "therefores" which come before this, in
verses 11 and 13, but they are merely incidental, whereas see
the emphasis at this sixteenth verse: "Therefore, Jehovah, the
God of Hosts, the Lord, saith thus . . .") It will be observed
that these three addresses grow in intensity, and that the third
is made longer than the others by two culminating "woes"
which are appended to it (see v. 18 and vi. 1).

The first of these addresses declares the fact of Israel's guilt
in the *present*. The second stresses Israel's sin in the *past* (see
verses 6 to 11, which recount Jehovah's repeated but unavailing
chastenings of Israel, and note the five-times occurring mournful
refrain, "Yet have ye not returned unto Me, saith Jehovah"—
verses 6, 8, 9, 10, 11). The third address stresses the punishment
of Israel's sin in the *future* (see v. 1–3 and v. 16 to vi. 14). Note
the vehemence and intensity at the end (vi. 8–14). Yet notice,
also, in this third address, the eleventh hour warning in the
thrice-uttered appeal of Jehovah: "Seek ye Me, and ye shall
live," etc. (v. 4, 6, 14).

Note further about these three addresses that in the first we
see the *principle* underlying Divine judgment—"You only have

I known of all the families of the earth; *therefore will I punish you* for all your iniquities" (iii. 2). This is the key verse of this book. Amos is the prophet of *judgment for abused privilege*. Judgment is always determined according to privilege. Increased privilege is increased responsibility. Israel had been supremely favoured, and therefore was supremely responsible. Here is a solemn lesson for all of us to learn.

In the second address we see the *forbearance* behind Divine judgment. Before the stroke of a final major judgment is allowed to fall on the nation, there comes a succession of minor judgments, to warn (iv. 6–11). It is when these are ignored and the Divine patience is outraged that the culminative judgment falls (iv. 12).

In the third address we see the uncompromising *severity* of Divine judgment on the impenitent, where sin has been obdurately persisted in (v. 2, 3; vi. 8–14).

Chapters vii. to ix.

Finally, in chapters vii. to ix. we have five *visions*. In chapter vii. 1–3 there is the vision of the *grasshoppers*, or locusts, eating up the product of the soil. But in answer to the prophet's entreaty to "forgive," the plague is *averted*.

Next, in verses 4 to 6, we have the vision of the devouring *fire*. This is definitely the symbol of judgment; yet in response to the prophet's entreaty to "cease," the fire is stayed: so that here we have judgment *restrained*.

Next, in verses 7 to 9, there is the vision of the plumbline (fitting symbol of judgment according to a righteous, Divine standard). Here God says: "I will not again pass by them"; and there is no intercession of Amos. Here, then, is *judgment determined*.

Following this there is the parenthetical episode of Amaziah's rebuke to Amos (vii. 10–17), making it clear that the nation, at least officially, was certainly set against the appeals of Jehovah. Then, in chapter viii., we find the vision of the basket of *summer fruit*. The fruit, that is, was dead ripe; and once fruit has reached that point, especially in hot lands, it is on the point of quickly perishing. Here, then, we see judgment *imminent*.

Lastly, in chapter ix., in one of the most awing visions of the Bible, we are shown Jehovah Himself "standing upon the altar" —that is, upon the false altar at Bethel. No symbol is here used, as in the visions of the grasshoppers, the fire, the plumbline, and the summer fruit. It is the Lord Himself; and He says: "Smite the lintel of the door, that the posts may shake, and cut them in the head, all of them. . . ." Here is judgment *executed*.

Thus, in these five visions we have, successively, judgment averted, restrained, determined, imminent, executed; and thus we see that there is an increasing intensity in the five visions, as there is in the three sermons. Yet even amid the execution of the culminative judgment, not one grain of the pure wheat was to be allowed to perish (see ix. 9)! Even "in wrath" God "remembers mercy"!

Such then is the Book of Amos. We are sorry that we cannot expand our treatment of it; but if the foregoing is firmly grasped we may feel some satisfaction. For the sake of clarity and easy remembrance we will set out our findings in a flat analysis.

THE BOOK OF AMOS

JUDGMENT FOR ABUSED PRIVILEGE

---

1. EIGHT "BURDENS" (i.–ii.).

DAMASCUS (i. 3); GAZA (6); TYRE (9); EDOM (11); AMMON (13); MOAB (ii. 1); JUDAH (4); ISRAEL (6). Note: "For three transgressions and for four."

2. THREE SERMONS (iii.–vi.).

JUDGMENT DESERVED (iii. 1–10); DECREED (iii. 11–15). JUDGMENT DESERVED (iv. 1–11); DECREED (iv. 12–13). JUDGMENT DESERVED (v. 1–15); DECREED (v. 16–vi.).

3. FIVE "VISIONS (vii.–ix.).

GRASSHOPPERS (vii. 1); FIRE (vii. 4); PLUMBLINE (vii. 7); SUMMER FRUIT (viii.); GOD OVER THE ALTAR (ix.). Note the final promise to Israel (ix. 11–15).

THE BOOK OF OBADIAH
Lesson Number 91

NOTE.—For this study read through the prophecy of Obadiah several times at one sitting, noting the divisive "But" at verse 17, which divides the little prophecy into its two parts, the one concerning Edom, the other concerning Israel.

Whatever has to do with God is, of necessity and in the nature of things, supernatural and superhuman, extraordinary and unique. It belongs on a level of its own, standing alone and apart, by itself, unapproachable, defying alike competition and comparison. We should therefore expect both sublimity and originality, elevation and isolation, much that transcends all the limits of human thought, involving more or less the element of the inscrutable: and the presence of such characteristics instead of an obstacle to faith is rather an argument for it.

A. T. Pierson, D.D.

THE PROPHET OBADIAH

THIS remarkable fragment from the pen of Obadiah is the shortest and perhaps the earliest of the writings which have come down to us from these Hebrew prophets. It has one subject only, namely, *judgment* on Edom, though this is offset in the closing verses by a contrastive reference to the final salvation of Israel.

Of Obadiah himself nothing is known. Not even his father's name is given in the title of the book. The name, "Obadiah," was common enough among the Hebrews, and means a worshipper, or servant, of Jehovah; but our prophet cannot be identified with any of the persons so named in Scripture. The contents of his prophecy, however, indicate that he belonged to Judah, the southern kingdom. We need not here discuss the *pros* and *cons* as to the *date* of this writing, for in the case of Obadiah the question of date is not vital from an interpretative point of view.

" Concerning Edom "

The prophet begins: "Thus saith the Lord God *concerning Edom.*" First, then, we must jog our memory as to the *identity* of the Edomites. The name "Edom" means *red*. It is the name which was given to Jacob's brother, Esau, because he sold his birthright for Jacob's red pottage. See Genesis xxv. 30: "Esau said to Jacob: Feed me, I pray thee, with that same red pottage, for I am faint. Therefore was his name called Edom." The Edomites were Esau's descendants, and their country was Mount Seir. Genesis xxxvi. 8, 9, says: "Esau dwelt in Mount Seir: Esau is Edom . . . the father of the Edomites in Mount Seir."

This "Mount Seir" was not just one mountain, but a mountainous *region* extending from the south of the Dead Sea to the Gulf of Akabah, and it was named "Seir" after Seir the Horite. In Genesis xiv. 6 and xxxvi. 20 we read: "The Horites in their Mount Seir. . . . These are the sons of Seir the Horite ("Horite" means, a rock-dweller), who inhabited the land." So, then, the Horites, or rock-dwellers, were the earlier inhabitants of Mount

Seir, and the land was called after the early Horite chief, Seir. The Edomites, or Esauites, later displaced the Horites and settled in Mount Seir. This we read in Deuteronomy ii. 12: "The Horims (Horites) dwelt in Seir beforetime; but the children of Esau succeeded them, when they had destroyed them, and dwelt in their stead."

It is a coincidence that the name "Seir" means hairy, rough, rugged. Whether the Horite cheif, Seir, was so named because he was a hairy, rough, rugged man is not said, though it may possibly be suggested that he was such a man by the fact that he and his fellow tribesmen were rock-dwellers. This, however, is certainly true, that the name of this man after whom Mount Seir was called was a most appropriate name for the *territory* where he and his people lived, with its straggling bushes and tufts, its ragged crags, and serrated ridges. It is an added coincidence that Esau himself is said to have been a hairy man (Gen. xxvii. 11), and that he was called Esau for that very reason (Gen. xxv. 25)—for the name "Esau" means rough, or hairy. It may have been because of this, and because of his love for the field and the hunt and the wild life of the open, that Esau was first drawn to Mount Seir and its Horites, or rock-dwellers. At any rate, this was the identity and background of the Edomite people who are addressed by the prophet Obadiah. Their Father was Esau. Their country was Seir.

The area occupied by the Edomites, although mountainous and craggy, had no lack of fertile valleys and fruitful soil. The ancient capital was Bozrah, a few miles south of the Dead Sea; but in Obadiah's days the capital was the famous Sela, or Petra, the rock city, which, because of its peculiar position, its difficult access, its rock-hewn dwellings, and its precipitous natural defences, was considered impregnable, and had fostered a spirit of fierce independence and security in the Edomites, which defied attack and scorned all attempts to subjugate them.

Edomite Anti-Jacobism

Now the Edomite people were like both their father and their country. Their nature was marked by a hard earthiness. They were profane, proud, fierce, cruel; and these tempers found concentrated vent in a strangely persistent, implacable, bitter, gloating spite against Israel, the nation which had descended from the twin-brother of their own national father, Esau. This violent nastiness had expressed itself again and again in the history of the two peoples. A never-forgotten instance of it was away back in the days of Israel's wilderness wanderings, when, with vicious threat, Edom had flung refusal to the courteous appeal of Moses that Israel might be allowed to pass through the Edomite country (Num. xx. 14–22).

In the times of our prophet, Obadiah, this undying Edomite anti-Jacobism had flamed out more wickedly than ever, in unprovoked treachery. See verses 10 to 14. In the day of Jerusalem's disaster, instead of befriending or at least sympathising, the people of Edom had indulged the passive cruelty of looking on with gloating satisfaction (verses 11, 12), and had egged on the plunderers. It was this Edomite venom that the Judæan captives in Babylon recalled, in the words of psalm cxxxvii. 7—"Remember, O Lord, the children of Edom in the day of Jerusalem, who said: Rase it, rase it, even to the foundation thereof."

But passive callousness had given place to active alliance with Jerusalem's destroyers. The Edomites had "entered the gate"; they had robbed and despoiled Jacob; they had barred the escape of the refugees, and had delivered up the remnant to the spoilers (verses 13, 14). We shall see shortly the arresting significance of all this; but for the moment we simply note the fact of it.

Sentence on Edom

It was for this long-accumulating guilt that Divine retribution was now determined against Edom, as stated in this writing of Obadiah. If in verses 10 to 16 we have seen the *reason* for this coming requital, in the earlier verses (1 to 9) we see the *certainty* of it. Note specially verses 3 and 4—"The pride of thine heart hath deceived thee, thou that dwellest in the clefts of the rock, whose habitation is high; that saith in his heart: Who shall bring me down to the ground? Though thou exalt thyself as the eagle, and though thou set thy nest among the stars, thence will I bring thee down, saith the Lord."

Writers on Obadiah seem usually to hit on the last verse (21) as the key here. That verse reads: "And saviours shall come up on mount Zion to judge the mount of Esau; and the kingdom shall be the Lord's." But while this is the *final* thought, it is not the *key* truth here. The key verse is 15—"*As thou hast done, it shall be done unto thee.*" Whoever be the prophet, and whatever be his prophecy, the ultimate prospect before the eye of all true prophecy is that "the kingdom shall be the Lord's"; but here, in this particular prophecy about Edom, we are meant to learn emphatically that there is a principle of "poetic justice" operative in the Divine government of the earth's peoples. This is the distinctive contribution of this Edom prophecy. Obadiah, let us remember it well, is *the prophet of poetic justice.*

Poetic Justice!

See how this key truth is amplified by the context. Edom had indulged in treachery against Judah (verses 11, 12); therefore Edom should perish through the treachery of confederates (verse 7). Edom had seized the chance to rob Judah (verse 13); therefore Edom should be robbed even till his hidden things, or treasures, were searched out (verses 5, 6). Edom had lifted the sword and shown violence against Judah (verse 10); therefore Edom should perish by slaughter (verse 9). Edom had sought the utter destruction of Judah (verses 12-14); therefore Edom should be utterly destroyed (verses 10, 18). Edom had even sought to hand over and dispossess the remnant of the invaded Jerusalem (verse 14); therefore, in the end, the remnant of Jacob should possess the land of Edom (verse 19). Yes, poetic justice!—the penalty corresponding to the iniquity as one line of poetry corresponds to another! And have we not had eyes to see the operation of poetic justice in our own day in the anti-Axis war? Never was there a war with such strange anomalies. To mention only one —was it altogether without significance that Britain was forced off the European mainland, first in the north, at Dunkirk, and then in the south, from Greece, and made to stand aside for the time, while Germany and Russia, the two nations which, officially and more blatantly than all others, had blasphemed God, slaughtered each other, despite their recently-signed pact of friendship? Were not the shocking brutalities of both these nations to the Jews paid back to them in identical terms? Yes, if we believe the Hebrew prophets, and Obadiah in particular, then we believe in poetic justice!

It should be noted that Obadiah predicts even the *extinction* of Edom. "Thou shalt be cut off for ever" (verse 10), "There shall not be any remaining of the house of Esau" (verse 18). At the time when the prophet wrote, Edom might have seemed far more likely to survive than Judah; yet history has strikingly endorsed the prophecy. Edom has perished, Judah persists.

Although there is no explicit record, it would seem that the Edomites, despite their rocky bulwarks, fell beneath the yoke of Babylon some five years after they had helped that same nation to raze Jerusalem. A comparison of Jeremiah xxvii. 3–6 and Malachi i. 3, 4, with the writing of Josephus on the Babylonian campaign makes this practically certain. Thereupon, the Nabathæans, an Arabian tribe, occupied Edom's capital, Petra. Possibly they were sent there by Nebuchadnezzar. Later, in 312 B.C., Antigonus, one of the generals of Alexander the Great, crushed these people and despoiled Petra. Still later, in the second century B.C., the Edomites themselves, who had now settled in southern Palestine, sustained crushing defeats from Judas Maccabæus (1 Macc. v. 3, 65). Josephus tells us that still later Alexander Jannæus completed their ruin. The small Edomite remnant were almost entirely put to the sword in the massacre at the siege of Jerusalem. The survivors took refuge among desert tribes, in which they became absorbed; and Origen, in the third century A.D., spoke of them as a people whose name and language had altogether perished. Thus, the sentence on Edom was executed, and Obadiah's prophecy fulfilled.

The contents of Obadiah's prophecy may be set out very simply, as follows.

THE BOOK OF OBADIAH
THE PROPHET OF POETIC JUSTICE

---

1. THE DESTRUCTION OF EDOM (verse 1–16).

> THE CERTAINTY OF IT, verses 1–9.
> THE REASON FOR IT, verses 10–16.

2. THE SALVATION OF ISRAEL (verses 17–21).

> THE PROMISE OF IT, verses 17–18.
> THE FULNESS OF IT, verses 19–21.

Latent Type-teaching

But finally, we shall miss the inmost meaning of this little book if we fail to discern its latent *typical* sense. It is here that its living message and permanent values lie. Esau-Edom is a type of the "natural man," of the Adam-nature, the "flesh," the old "self-life" in us.

There is a strangely fascinating, symbolic interest about the successive *pairs of sons* away back in Genesis—Cain and Abel, Ishmael and Isaac, Esau and Jacob. In these pairs, Abel, Isaac, Jacob are the spiritual men, and they represent different aspects of the new life which is ours through union with Christ. On the other hand, Cain, Ishmael, Esau are the "natural" men, who are "of the earth, earthy," and they represent different aspects of the self-life, or the "flesh." Cain is the natural heart in its antipathy to *redemption*. He is all for a religion of culture. He would offer the fruits of the ground—of that which is under the curse through sin. He has no eye for the bleeding lamb, and will not admit the need for atonement. He tills the ground, builds cities, and finds his portion in the life that now is. As for the next of these men—Ishmael, in him we see the self-life in its antagonism to that which is of *faith*, as Paul tells us in Galatians iv. 29 (which please look up in its context). And next, in Esau, we see the self-life in its disappreciation of that which is *spiritual*. He is the man "who for one morsel of meat sold his birthright" (Heb. xii. 16). From these three pairs of sons let us learn that the "flesh" persists with us—a sad reminder of the rock from which we were hewn and the pit from which we were digged; and let us see its hostility to redemption, to the life of faith, and to the things of the Spirit.

But Esau is of special interest, for in him we see the "flesh," the Adam-nature, *in its fairest form*. In certain respects he is attractive and lovable. He is a decided advance on Cain and Ishmael. From Genesis xxv. 25 we learn that two characteristics distinguished him from his birth; he was "ruddy," and he was "hairy," which two things speak of beauty and strength. He was a bonnie babe and a comely youth, marked by physical grace and power. Yes, there is no doubt that in Esau the "flesh" is attractive. But wait; see how soon the beauty corrupts. Esau the "ruddy" becomes Edom, "the red one"; and his hue, like that of the red horse and the red dragon and the scarlet beast in Revelation vi., xii. and xvii., betokens the fierce life within. The hair which at first bespeaks strength soon comes to indicate animal coarseness. Esau the strong becomes Edom the wild, the hunter, the slayer. After all, in the Hebrew, the word "Edom" is actually a form of the word "Adam." Edom is Adam, and Esau is the "flesh" again—outwardly fair but inwardly fierce. When he really expresses himself, see the value he puts on spiritual things; for a dish of lentils he scorns his birthright, even though he knows that the birthright from his grandfather Abraham downwards carries the Divine promises of great spiritual and future blessing. This is the "flesh" in every age. For a momentary gratification it will despise the hope of a heavenly glory, and esteem an earthly morsel in the present far more than a Divine promise for the future.

It is an illuminating study to trace out the recurring references to Edom in the Scriptures. We cannot do this here; but throughout, Edom is the "flesh"; and in our prophet Obadiah we see the ultimate expression of this. Look again through these verses of Obadiah, and let Edom picture the "flesh" or Adam-nature. See first its pride—"The pride of thine heart" (verse 3); then see how strong its hold is—"Thou that dwellest in the clefts of the rock" (verse 3); then see its defiance—"Who shall bring me down?" (verse 3); then see its ambition—"though thou set thy nest among the stars" (verse 4); then see its hatred of the spiritual—"thy violence against thy brother Jacob" (verse 10); then see its real cruelty (verses 11–14). But, on the other side, see its self-deceivedness (verse 3); its detestableness to God (verse 2); its eventual defeat by the sons of faith (verses 17–21); and its final destruction by God (verses 10, 18).

Truly, in the light of New Testament teaching such as we have in Romans vi. 6–14, and Galatians v. 17–25, all this is full of vivid meaning! Nor must we fail to note that Edom is a type of all nations hostile to God, and foreshows the coming action of God against the present Gentile world-system. Nor must we fail to note yet again the truth that no weapon against God's covenant people prospers, and that nations pay dearly, in due course, for their anti-Israel policies. Thus, although the Book of Obadiah is the shortest of the prophetic writings, it is certainly *multum in parvo*, much in little.

TWELVE QUESTIONS ON AMOS AND OBADIAH

1. What little town did Amos come from? Where was it? And in what verse does he tell us that he was from there?

2. What does Amos say of himself in regard to the prophetic office and his own occupation?

3. Where and when did Amos prophesy? And what was his style of speaking?

4. What noticeably repeated preface to his prophecies does Amos use in the opening chapters, and what is the significance of that expression?

5. Give a general outline of the book of the prophet Amos.

6. What is the subject of the prophecy of Obadiah?

7. What does the word "Edom" mean? Whose descendants were the Edomites?

8. Where was the region named "Mount Seir," and how did it get its name?

9. What act of hostility to Israel did the Edomites show in the days of Moses? And what does Obadiah say about their spite in his own day?

10. What is the key verse in the little prophecy of Obadiah? What is the distinctive truth of the book?

11. What is the two-fold division of the prophecy of Obadiah?

12. What latent type-teaching does it contain for us concerning Edom?

THE PROPHET JONAH (1)

Lesson Number 92

NOTE.—For this study read the story of Jonah through twice at least.

The religious revolt of the sixteenth century rescued the Bible from the Priest. God grant that the twentieth century may bring a revolt which shall rescue it from the Professor and the pundit.

Sir Robert Anderson.

All knowledge begins and ends with wonder; but the first wonder is the child of ignorance, and the second is the parent of adoration.

Coleridge.

THE BOOK OF JONAH (1)

Fact or Fiction?

THE BOOK of Jonah—is it history, allegory, or romance? Was Jonah a real person? Was he really housed in the great fish as the book declares? Did he really preach Nineveh to a repentance which averted Divine judgment? Or is the book merely fictional? The answer to these questions is of much deeper consequence than many persons realise; for if the book is really a narrative of actual fact it brings to us one of the most striking revelations of God, and one of the most priceless messages of Divine comfort ever given; whereas, if it be merely fictional, it contains no authentic significance at all. Moreover, this question as to whether it is really historical or not involves both the integrity of the Scriptures as a whole, and the word of the Lord Jesus Himself, as we shall see. The true answer to the question, so we ourselves believe, is clear and convincing to any candid mind.

Modernist theologians, true to their Sadducean lineage, would discredit the book because it relates that which is miraculous; but their own supposedly scholarly "explainings" so ludicrously contradict each other that we turn back to the Scripture again, preferring even the miraculous to the ridiculous!

Meanwhile, on the one hand, this Book of Jonah, more than any other book of Scripture, has been the butt of the scoffer, while, on the other hand, those who accept it, and have taken the trouble to discover the tender message which lies at the heart of it, will appreciate Charles Reade's description of it as "the most beautiful story ever written in so small a compass," and the words of another, who speaks of it as a "highwater mark of the Old Testament revelation."

First, then, without wasting time on the merely negative theories of the critics, let us examine the positive evidences for the historicity of Jonah and his book.

Is Jonah Himself Historical?

That Jonah himself was a real person there can surely be no doubt. The opening verse of the book calls him "Jonah the son of Amittai," and says: "Now the word of the Lord came unto Jonah," thus indicating that he was a prophet. Do we read anywhere else of such a person? We do. Turn to 2 Kings xiv. 25. "He (king Jeroboam II of Israel) restored the coast of Israel from the entering of Hamath unto the sea of the plain, according to the word of the Lord God of Israel, which He spake by the hand of His servant Jonah, the son of Amittai, the prophet, which was of Gath-hepher." Now this king Jeroboam was a real enough person. He was, in fact, the greatest and longest-reigning of all the kings who reigned over the northern kingdom. In a moral and religious sense there was little to choose between him and his evil predecessors on the throne, but in military prowess he remarkably excelled. His recaptured and newly annexed territories reached up as far as Hamath, over two hundred miles north of Samaria, so that his domain became almost as extensive as David's had been!—and all this is plainly said to have been in fulfilment of a prophecy by "Jonah, the son of Amittai, the prophet which was of Gath-hepher." Surely, then, if this Jeroboam, who *fulfilled* Jonah's prophecy, was a real enough person, so was this Jonah himself who *uttered* it!—and if confirmation is required outside the pages of the Bible, it may be worth noting that Gath-hepher is now identified with a village name El Meshed some miles north of Nazareth, in Zebulon, where, according to a firm tradition dating back to Jerome's time, the tomb of Jonah is pointed out even to this day.

No, we cannot doubt that this prophet Jonah who is mentioned in 2 Kings was a real person; nor can we doubt that this prophet Jonah in 2 Kings is identical with the Jonah of the book which bears that name; for in both cases Jonah is the son of Amittai, and neither of these two names, "Jonah" and "Amittai," do we find anywhere else in the Old Testament. Incidentally the reference in 2 Kings fixes the *time* of Jonah's ministry. It was during the later years of Joash, and (presumably) the earlier years of Jeroboam II. He would probably be one of the leaders among the "schools of the prophets" when Elisha was nearing the end of his remarkable ministry.

Is the Narrative Historical?

Jonah himself was a real enough person; but can we believe what the book says *about* him? Is the *narrative* historical? In reply, we call attention to the following points.

First, *there is nothing in the book to suggest otherwise*—except, of course, to our modern critics, to whom *any* narrative which records the supernatural is *ipso facto* incredible.

An unprejudiced reading will satisfy any reader that the narrative is at least *meant* to be taken as a record of actual fact. The rationalistic schools of theologians would have us believe on supposedly philological grounds, that the book is a fiction written about three hundred years later than Jonah's time; but they stupidly contradict each other; for while some of them are thus arguing a very *late* date for the book, others tell us that such crude notions as that of Jonah's fleeing "from the presence of the Lord" belong to the time of Israel's undeveloped *earlier* ideas of God! We had better leave the critics to settle their own disagreements! The fact is, that in all probability the historicity of the book would never have been called in question but for the large presence of the supernatural in it. Apart from the admitted presence of striking miracles, there is nothing whatever to suggest that the book is not meant to be read as a narrative of true fact.

Second, *tradition strongly attests its historicity*. Its early and unquestioned place in the Hebrew Scriptures at once argues the original belief of the Hebrews in its historicity. The apocryphal Book of Tobit, written probably in the fourth century B.C., includes these death-bed words of Tobit to his son, Tobias: "Go into Media, my child; for I surely believe all the things which Jonah the prophet spake of Nineveh, that it shall be overthrown." Philo, the Jewish philosopher of the first century A.D. and Josephus, the historian, both hold its historicity; and, in fact, this has been the unbroken Jewish belief from earliest times.

Moreover, until recent days, the Christian Church has emphatically endorsed this Jewish belief. In the Catacombs of Rome, those subterranean cemeteries of the early Christians, no Biblical representation is found more often than that of Jonah, whose deliverance from the deep had now become a Christian symbol of faith in the coming resurrection of the saints. Jerome, Irenæus, Augustine, Chrysostom, and others of the Christian Fathers, all indicate their belief in the historicity of the book. So, in later days, do Calvin, Luther, and the other great Bible-men of the Reformation. It is only in recent days that certain schools of rationalistic "higher critics" have endeavoured to fling the mantle of doubt over it; and the outstanding feature of even these men is the way they contradict each other.

Third, *the word of Christ Himself conclusively confirms it.* In Matthew xii. 39, 40, He says: "An evil and adulterous generation seeketh after a sign; and there shall no sign be given to it but the sign of the prophet Jonas; for as Jonas was three days and three nights in the whale's belly, so shall the Son of Man be three days and three nights in the heart of the earth." Surely, to a straight-thinking Christian mind this testimony of our Lord Himself will settle the matter; yet the critics, to save their own faces, will even call our Lord's own words into question. Some of them try to show that these words are an *interpolation*; but unfortunately for them the manuscript evidence is quite sound; and still more unfortunately for them, Luke also records the same words!

Others, forced to disown the interpolation theory, try to argue that our Lord was simply citing the Jonah story just as a preacher today might use a well-known incident from Bunyan's *Pilgrim's Progress*, or from one of Shakespeare's plays, without implying for a moment its actual historicity. But, alas for the critics, this idea is broken to bits by our Lord's further words about Jonah, in that twelfth chapter of Matthew. He says: "The men of Nineveh shall rise in the judgment with this generation, and shall condemn it; because they repented at the preaching of Jonas; and, behold, a greater than Jonas is here." Will anyone dare to maintain that the Son of God was here teaching (as one has well put it) that "imaginary persons who at the imaginary preaching of an imaginary prophet repented in imagination, shall rise up in that day and condemn the *actual* impenitence of those, his *actual* hearers, that the fictitious characters of a parable shall be arraigned at the same bar with the living men of that generation?" To maintain this is monstrous! Nor dare we allow the dishonouring theory that our Lord "accommodated" his teaching to the ignorance of his hearers. Our Lord was "The Truth," and He spoke the truth. An honest reader of the New Testament must surely see that the Lord Jesus was the most *un*accommodating preacher who ever preached!

What then? Why, this: Our Lord really spoke the words about Jonah as recorded by Matthew and Luke; and in those words He clearly and conclusively confirmed the historicity of the *Book* of Jonah.

As for such objections as that we cannot believe the narrative because there is no reference in secular history to Nineveh's repentance; or that the book must have been written long after Jonah's time because it uses the past tense in chapter iii. 3— "Now Nineveh *was* . . ."; or that there are certain Aramaic words used by the writer, which indicate its late date; we can only say that to ourselves they appear to be the despairing petty subterfuges of critics who, when their other criticisms have been soundly trounced, are bent on destroying faith in the book by any means whatever; and in any case, these objections have been easily and fully disposed of again and again. We may settle it in our minds, both from the convincingness of the evidence *for* it, and from the utter poverty of the supposed arguments *against* it, that this Book of Jonah is, indeed, a narrative of true happenings.

But What of the " Whale "?

Someone, however, even yet, is sure to trot out the hackneyed old question: *What about the whale?* So we must needs add a patient little word about this, although the question has been answered time and time again. This matter of the "whale" has been aggravated into an altogether disproportionate prominence by the contention which our modern critics have created around it. Were it not for that, we would not trouble to add this extra word here; for there is no fundamental difficulty about it to those who believe in God and in the inspiration of the Scriptures. The truth is, that this *physical* miracle of the "whale" is not nearly so wonderful as the *moral* miracle of Nineveh's repentance, or as the *spiritual* miracle of the Divine Self-revelation at the end of the book. This much is certainly true, that just as often as critics have held up this "whale" incident to ridicule, able writers have turned the ridicule of the critics back upon their own heads.

The three questions are: *Could* it happen? *Would* it happen? *Did* it happen?

As to whether it *could* happen, the obvious answer, for all who believe in God, is that *of course* it could!—for if God created *all* the fish in the seas, He could very easily create one specially for the purpose of preserving Jonah. As a matter of fact, however, we are under no necessity to believe that God actually *created* a whale to receive Jonah; for the narrative simply says that God "*prepared*" a great fish; and the Hebrew word which is here translated as "prepared" has no thought of direct creation. What is more, the narrative does not say that the fish was a whale, but only that it was "a great fish"; and although the word "whale" *is* used in Matthew xii. to describe this "great fish," we need to remember that our New Testament is translated from the Greek; and the Greek word which is translated as "whale" would be better translated as "sea-monster" (as in the margin of the Revised Version). It *may* or may *not* have been a whale.

Now our modern critics have urged that no kind of fish ever heard of could perform such a feat as the swallowing and containing of a grown man; but alas for them, they have thereby exposed their own ignorance of the submarine world, as the following cullings will show.

In the *Daily Mail* of December 14th, 1928, Mr. G. H. Henn, a resident of Birmingham, gave the following testimony.

"My own experience was in Birmingham about twenty-five years ago, when the carcase of a whale was displayed for a week on vacant land in Navigation Street, outside New Street station.

"I was one of twelve men, who went into its mouth, passed through its throat, and moved about in what was equivalent to a fair-sized room. Its throat was large enough to serve as a door. Obviously it would be quite easy for a whale of this kind to swallow a man."

Or again, in the late Sir Francis Fox's book, *Sixty-three Years of Engineering*, the manager of a whaling station informs us that the sperm whale swallows lumps of food eight feet in diameter, and that in one of these whales they actually found "the skeleton of a shark *sixteen feet in length*"!

Mr. Frank Bullen, in his book, *The Cruise of the Cachalot*, furnishes the information that the cachalot, or sperm whale, always ejects the contents of its stomach when dying. Parts of one such ejection he himself witnessed, consisting of huge masses, some of which were estimated as about "eight feet by six feet into six feet," the total being equal to the bodies of "six stout men compressed into one!"

Most striking of all, perhaps, is an incident related by Sir Francis Fox, which, he assures us, "was carefully investigated by two scientists, one of whom was M. de Parville, the scientific editor of the *Journal des Debats* of Paris, well-known as "a man of sound judgment, and a careful writer." The incident is as follows:

"In February 1891, the whale-ship *Star of the East* was in the vicinity of the Falkland Islands, and the look-out sighted a large sperm whale three miles away. Two boats were lowered, and in a short time one of the harpooners was enabled to spear the fish. The second boat attacked the whale, but was upset by a lash of its tail, and the men thrown into the sea, one being drowned, and another, James Bartley, having disappeared, could not be found. The whale was killed, and in a few hours the great body was lying by the ship's side, and the crew busy with the axes and spades removing the blubber. They worked all day and part of the night. Next day they attached some tackle to the stomach, which was hoisted on deck. The sailors were startled by spasmodic signs of life, and inside was found the missing sailor, doubled up and unconscious. He was laid on the deck and treated to a bath of sea-water which soon revived him; but his mind was not clear, and he was placed in the captain's quarters, where he remained two weeks a raving lunatic. He was kindly and carefully treated by the captain, and by the officers of the ship, and gradually gained possession of his senses. At the end of the third week he had entirely recovered from the shock, and resumed his duties.

"During his sojourn in the whale's stomach Bartley's skin, where exposed to the action of the gastric juice, underwent a striking change. His face, neck, and hands were bleached to a deadly whiteness, and took on the appearance of parchment. Bartley affirms that he would probably have lived inside his house of flesh until he starved, for he lost his senses through fright and not from lack of air."

Bartley is also said to have explained that after being hurled into the sea the waters foamed about him, evidently from the lashings of the whale's tail. Then he was drawn along into darkness and found himself in a great place where the heat was intense. In the dark he felt around for an exit and found only slimy walls around him. Then the awful truth rushed into his mind, and he became unconscious till the sea-water bath revived him on the ship's deck.

And where now are the critics who have declared the swallowing of Jonah to be an impossible feat?

As to whether this providential miracle *would* happen, when we come to consider the contents of the narrative in a later lesson we shall see that it is thoroughly congruous. As for the fact that it actually *did* happen, we have the confirmatory word of the infallible Christ Himself; and, so far as we ourselves are concerned, *that settles it.*

Yes, "that settles it," and the very saying so reminds me of an incident which my dear mother related to me in connection with the famous evangelist, D. L. Moody. Years ago, when my mother was a young deaconess in the Manchester City Mission, Moody and Sankey, who were big names by that time, came for their memorable Manchester campaign. Along with other deaconesses, my mother was there to hear and to help. At first she was not greatly impressed, and Moody's American nasal twang was an annoyance; but he "grew" on his hearers as the meetings progressed, and a wonderful work of conversion attended the preaching. There was a big-hearted love always pouring itself through the messages, and yet at the same time there was an air of unhesitating finality which might have caused resentment toward a preacher of different personality. But the thing which ever afterwards stood out in my mother's memory was his conclusion to a sermon on John iii. 7, "Ye must be born again". Whether Moody felt he was wasting words or somehow not making headway with his hearers I do not know, but he suddenly and abruptly ended by exclaiming, "Men and women of Manchester, ye *must* be born again. Jesus said it. *That settles it*".

That is where every *true* believer on the Lord Jesus Christ is. What *He* says settles it. It settles it regarding Jonah, and the whole of the Old Testament, and every other subject on which He made pronouncement. Our Christ is no mere *kenosis* Christ of modern criticism, but the Christ of whom, when He actually incarnate, John wrote, "We beheld His glory. . . . *FULL* of grace and *TRUTH*".

THE BOOK OF JONAH (2)

Lesson Number 93

NOTE.—For this second consideration of Jonah, read the whole of the short story again, asking: Do the chapter breaks really represent the different movements in the story?

Since writing the foregoing instalment on Jonah we have come across the following news-item in the Madras *Mail* of November 28th, 1946:

"Bombay, November 26.—A twelve-foot tiger shark, weighing 700 lbs., was dragged ashore last evening at the Sassoon Docks. When the shark was cut open a skeleton and a man's clothes were found.

"It is thought that the victim may have been one of those lost at sea during the recent cyclone.

"The shark was caught by fishermen thirty miles from Bombay."

THE BOOK OF JONAH (2)

HAVING satisfied ourselves that this Book of Jonah is a genuine bit of history, we are now ready to learn its priceless significance.

The little story is in four parts, which correspond with the four chapters into which it is divided in our English version, except that the last verse in chapter i. should be the first verse of chapter ii. (as, in fact, it *is* in the Hebrew). Jonah is the central figure, until the closing verses, where the prominence is transferred to the Lord Himself, and the supreme message of the book is uttered. The four movements of the story are—

> Chapter i. JONAH AND THE STORM.
>   ii. JONAH AND THE FISH.
>   iii. JONAH AND THE CITY.
>   iv. JONAH AND THE LORD.

In these four movements we have Jonah's disobedience, preservation, proclamation, and correction. In chapter i. he is *fleeing from* God. In chapter ii. he is *praying to* God. In chapter iii. he is *speaking for* God. In chapter iv. he is *learning of* God. If we get at the real point in each of these chapters, we shall find that the final message of the book is one of captivating tenderness. First, then, we turn to chapter i.; but here, right away, we are faced with a question the answering of which will determine our appreciation of the whole story; and we must devote careful thought to it, the more so because there has been much misunderstanding in connection with it.

Why did Jonah Flee?

The crucial question is: *Why did Jonah flee?* Our answer to that question will decide for us whether Jonah was a petty-spirited bigot or one of the most heroic patriots Israel ever produced. Our answer, also, will either enhance or reduce for us the force of the book as a whole.

The common idea is that Jonah was a narrow-minded Jew, unwilling to carry a merciful warning to a Gentile people. For instance, even a writer of such keen insight as the late Dr. A. T. Pierson says: "His national prejudice construed God's election of Israel as a rejection of all others. His religious intolerance was mixed with no mercy for the heathen. His legal spirit inclined more to vengeance than to grace. His disloyal temper made him wilful and wayward." The late Dr. Kitto, whose writings we have gratefully quoted a number of times in this Bible Course, goes so far as to say: "One cannot love this Jonah or think well of him. We seem unable to recognise in him those signs of grace which we expect to see adorning the commissioned servants of God. It may be recollected that we do not know all Jonah's character, but only some parts of it, excited under rare and extraordinary influences. Yet it must be confessed that there is such a pervading homogeneity in *all* the traits which appear in his history, as to suggest that we see in them his real and natural character—a character, no doubt, solidly good, and open to conviction, but habitually irascible and morose, and apt, under exciting circumstances, to view things in their worst and most gloomy aspects."

In face of such words we can only protest that poor Jonah is surely the most misunderstood personality in the Bible. If such was indeed the spirit and temper of this man, then, far from his merely needing to be corrected on this or that or the other point, he was unfit for the prophetic office and for spiritual leadership. On occasions, God can and does use strange vessels; but that God should sustain, through years of inspired prophetic ministry, such a man as Jonah is here said to have been is surely hard to believe.

Now this, the common idea about Jonah, is mainly due to our misunderstanding the motive for his flight, in chapter i. The usually suggested reasons for it are three—(1) cowardly *fear* of going to Nineveh, (2) bigoted *prejudice* against the Gentiles; (3) selfish *jealousy* for his own prestige. But these three supposed reasons may be seen to be untenable simply by reading through chapter i. It certainly was not *fear* that deterred this prophet-successor of the brave Elijah and Elisha; for on board ship he shows utter fearlessness of death, himself urging the sailors to cast him overboard! Nor was it anti-Gentile *prejudice*, however keen his national spirit may have been; for he displays immediate compassion toward the idol-worshipping Gentile sailors, even to the point of being willing to die for their safety's sake! Nor was it selfish *jealousy* lest, by prophesying a destruction of Nineveh which should afterward be averted, he should injure the professional reputation which he had gained in Jeroboam's court as the predicter of Israel's expansion; for surely it is hard to believe that the prophet who was willing to sacrifice not only his reputation but his life itself for the distressed mariners, would peevishly set his own prestige against all the thousands of lives in great Nineveh!

What, then, is the *real* reason why Jonah fled, rather than deliver his message to Nineveh? The answer is found in Jonah's own words, in chapter iv. 2, coupled with certain information which we know Jonah possessed about Assyria, of which Nineveh was the capital. In chapter iv. 2, Jonah says to God: "Therefore I fled to Tarshish, because I knew that Thou art a gracious God, and merciful, slow to anger, and of great kindness, and repentest Thee of the evil." Nothing could be franker than that! —*Jonah did not want God to spare Nineveh.* Moreover, Jonah had shown himself prepared to forfeit his prophetic office, prepared to flee into exile, prepared even to resign life itself, rather than that Nineveh should be spared! Now such deliberate self-abandon, followed by such frankness to the One who, as Jonah well realised, could read his inmost motive, surely will persuade us that Jonah must have had some far greater reason than any thought of personal safety, or prejudice, or prestige, for wishing to leave Nineveh to its doom: and, as a matter of fact, we know that Jonah *did* have such a reason—a reason which transforms his motive from apparent pettiness to something touchingly heroic.

There were two awesome facts about Assyria which gave Jonah a vehement dread lest the threatened judgment on its wicked capital, Nineveh, should be averted, through the compassion of God. First, *Assyria was the rising world-power destined to destroy Israel*; and Jonah knew this. Second, the notorious brutality of the Assyrians was such as to make the surrounding peoples shudder with a sickly terror of ever falling prey to them. Without a doubt, the Assyrians were the German Nazis of those days. The inscriptions on Assyrian monuments which have been interpreted for us by our archaeologists reveal how they revelled in hideous cruelty on those whom they vanquished.

Speaking of this grim testimony from Assyrian inscriptions, the late John Urquhart says: "No considerations of pity were permitted to stand in the way of Assyrian policy. It could not afford to garrison its conquests, and it practised a plan which largely dispensed with the necessity for leaving garrisons behind the Assyrian armies. There was unsparing slaughter to begin with. The kings seem to gloat in their inscriptions over the spectacle presented by the field of battle. They describe how it was covered with the corpses of the vanquished. This carnage was followed up by fiendish inflictions upon individual cities. The leading men, as at Lachish when Sennacherib had conquered that city, were led forth, seized by the executioners, and subjected to various punishments, all of them filled to the brim with horror. Some of the victims were held down while one of the band of torturers, who are portrayed upon the monuments gloating fiendishly over their fearful work, inserts his hand into the victim's mouth, grips his tongue and wrenches it out by the roots. In another spot pegs are driven into the ground. To these, another victim's wrists are fixed with cords. His ankles are similarly made fast, and the man is stretched out, unable to move a muscle. The executioner then applies himself to his task; and, beginning at the accustomed spot, the sharp knife makes its incision, the skin is raised inch by inch till the man is flayed alive. These skins are then stretched out upon the city walls, or otherwise disposed of so as to terrify the people and leave behind long-enduring impressions of Assyrian vengeance. For others, long sharp poles are prepared. The sufferer, taken like all the rest from the leading men of the city, is laid down; the sharpened end of the pole is driven in through the lower part of the chest; the pole is then raised, bearing the writhing victim aloft; it is planted in the hole dug for it, and the man is left to die."

The late Professor Sayce says: "The barbarities which followed the capture of a town would be almost incredible, were they not a subject of boast in the inscriptions which record them. Assurnatsir-pal's cruelties were especially revolting. Pyramids of human heads marked the path of the conqueror; boys and girls were burnt alive or reserved for a worse fate; men were impaled, flayed alive, blinded, or deprived of their hands and feet, of their ears and noses, while the women and children were carried into slavery, the captured city plundered and reduced to ashes, and the trees in its neighbourhood cut down." Nor is this all about the horrible Assyrian mania for blood and vengeance; but we forbear.

Every man in Israel knew these things. Jonah most certainly did, for he came of a border town, and may even have witnessed Assyrian savageries in frontier raids. Let Nahum express the mind of the Hebrew prophets about Nineveh, the representative city of Assyria. "Woe to the bloody city! It is all full of lies and robbery; the prey departeth not . . . there is a multitude of slain, and a great number of carcases, and there is none end of their corpses; they stumble upon their corpses, because of the multitude of the whoredoms of the well-favoured harlot, the mistress of witchcrafts, that selleth nations through her whoredoms, and families through her witchcrafts." "The lion (Nineveh, as representing Assyria) did tear in pieces enough for his whelps, and strangled for his lioness, and filled his holes with prey, and his dens with ravin." "All that hear the bruit of thee (i.e. the news of Nineveh's destruction) shall clap their hands over thee; for upon whom hath not thy wickedness passed continually?" (Nahum iii. 1–4; ii. 12; iii. 19). Not a spark of pity mingles with Nahum's delight at the destruction of Nineveh and the foul butchery of Assyria. *He* felt just as *Jonah* did about it!

Now besides knowing full well the blood-curdling savagery of the Assyrians, Jonah knew that Assyria was the nation which was predicted to destroy his own beloved land and people. For some years before the ministry of Jonah, Assyria had been rising as the dominant world-power, and had already been laying her hands on the nations of the Mediterranean coast. The Hebrew prophets were made aware of what was to happen consequent upon Assyria's rise to the mastery. Twenty or thirty or more years before the event, Isaiah foretold how Assyria would despoil Israel (vii. 17, etc.); and Hosea, hard on the heels of Jonah, foretells the same (ix. 3; x. 6, 7; xi. 5); and Amos, whose ministry possibly overlapped the last bit of Jonah's, tells of the judgment God was soon sending, not only on Israel, but on the nearby nations too, and adds, "The Lord God will do nothing but He revealeth His secret unto His servants, the prophets"

(iii. 7). Yes, Jonah knew the bitter role that Assyria was intended to play; and when the almost unbelievable Divine announcement came to him, that Nineveh was to be destroyed within forty days, his heart must have leapt with a sudden sense of relief. Gladder news had never come to him!—for we must not forget that besides being a prophet he was a man, and a man of Israel, and an ardent patriot, who loved his native land, and yearned as a shepherd over his beloved but wayward countrymen. What would he not have done or given for their salvation? With what emotion he would cogitate on the Divine command—"Arise; go to Nineveh, that great city, and cry against it; for their wickedness is come up before Me"! So Nineveh's cup was full! The great Judge had passed sentence; and if Nineveh perished, then—oh, the gladness of the thought—Israel was saved! There was but one thing Jonah feared—Jehovah was a merciful God; and if Nineveh cried to Him, even at the eleventh hour, Assyria might be spared, and then Israel would perish. Oh that he might be quite sure that Nineveh would not be spared! But how could that be? Well, there was one way—he could leave Nineveh without the warning! Thus she would be left to reap the deserved harvest of her wickedness.

Jonah must now make the most costly choice of his life. He must choose between suffering the Divine vengeance upon himself for awful disobedience, and thus save Israel; or else he must go to Nineveh, and possibly cause the salvation of Nineveh, which would result in Israel's ruin. His mental agony resolves itself into the determination to flee rather than risk delivering the message. He would sacrifice himself that Israel might be saved; for if it came to a choice as to which should not be spared, Nineveh or Israel?—then let it be wicked Nineveh!

Let those who would pillory Jonah as the peevish bigot think of all this. Let them imagine themselves in Jonah's position. Nay, more than that, let us put Jonah where he really belongs —with Moses, who prayed: "If Thou wilt forgive their sin—; and if not, blot me, I pray Thee, out of Thy book"; and with Paul, who said: "I could wish that myself were accursed from Christ for my brethren, my kinsmen according to the flesh." Yes, that is where Jonah really belongs. God knew the motive of His servant; and surely that is why He preserved and restored him; and surely that is why Jonah could express himself with such intense frankness to God afterwards. Let us admire Jonah's self-abnegation and sympathise with his motive, even though we must still condemn his disobedience to God. His spirit was that of the famous words, "Who dies if England lives? Who lives if England dies?" It has been truly said that "with a patriotism no less deep, and a flaming consciousness of all that the preservation of the elect nation meant for the fulfilment of the Divine promises made to the fathers, Jonah in his heart, in the crisis of his renunciation, might have said: Who dies if Israel lives? Who lives if Israel dies? What matter if I perish?" Truly Jonah had the spirit of the martyrs.

Let it be clearly understood, too, that when Jonah "rose up to flee unto Tarshish *from the presence of the Lord*," he certainly did not think he could go where God was not! No; his going out from "the presence of the Lord" was his renunciation of his prophetic standing before Jehovah, as we shall see later.

Jonah knew well enough the omnipresence of God. He knew that he could not escape Him: but he was willing to suffer the inescapable vengeance of Heaven if only Israel might be saved. Yes—if only Israel might be saved—*that* was why Jonah fled! Let us never again stigmatise Jonah as merely an obstinate bigot, or a coward, anxious only about the safety of his own skin. He stands out with a unique emphasis as Israel's prophet-*patriot*; and his motive is touchingly heroic even though, at the Nineveh crisis-point, it misguides him into regrettable disobedience to his Divine commission.

I seem to have noticed more than once or twice that those of the type who criticise Jonah for his supposed narrowness or meanness have exhibited the same spirit, though without suspecting its presence in themselves. I recall an upright Christian man who quite seriously warned us that the too speedy evangelisation and education of the negroes would hasten a major crisis between blacks and whites, and that therefore it should be slowed down! I remember another who argued that similar enlightenment was prejudicial to the retention of India in the British empire! And yet another comes to mind, who said he could never bring himself to help displaced and parentless German children because of the atrocities committed by their nation in the Second World War!

One can understand the human proneness to such feelings under aggravating circumstances, and it is rather grimly pathetic how Jonah's highest-minded critics can be far worse Jonahs themselves without suspecting themselves of it; but such attitudes simply must not be tolerated, either in ourselves or in others. No such passionate pettiness must ever be allowed to come between us and God's gracious will toward others to whom He sends us with the message of His redeeming love in Christ.

That big-hearted evangelist, D. L. Moody, has pictured the scene on that mountain slope when the risen Lord Jesus commissioned His first disciples to go into all the world and preach the Gospel to every creature. Moody pictures Peter's wide-eyed wonder as he asks Jesus if they must go to those who drove the nails through His hands. Again Peter asks if they must go to the man who drove the spear into the Master's side; and Jesus says, "Yes, tell him there's a nearer way to My heart than that". And those early disciples entered into the compassions of their Master. His Spirit came upon them and broke down all their little human boundary-walls.

What Jonah needed, and what we all need, if we are to be the Lord's true servants and messengers, is so to get our minds and feelings in the great, wide flow of the Divine compassions for sinning, suffering, struggling, sorrowing men and women that all lesser considerations are submerged. God's Jonahs must go even to Nineveh.

THE BOOK OF JONAH (3)

Lesson Number 94

NOTE.—For this further instalment on Jonah, read the story through yet again, noting carefully the wording of Jonah's prayer, and the comments on Nineveh.

The Book of Jonah . . . which, in any case, is earlier than the close of the prophetic Canon, contains a prayer of Jonah (chapter ii. 2–10), admittedly based on passages from different parts of the Psalter. This implies some collection of these psalms.

James Orr, D.D.

God moves in a mysterious way
  His wonders to perform ;
He plants His footsteps in the sea,
  And rides upon the storm.
William Cowper.

THE BOOK OF JONAH (3)

IN THIS, our third instalment on the Book of Jonah, we shall glance through the first three chapters, reserving our fourth and final lesson for the last chapter and the closing message of the book.

Jonah and the Storm

In chapter i. we see Jonah amid the storm at sea. The storm came *because* of him—because of his fleeing "from the presence of Jehovah." Three times in the first ten verses we have it that Jonah's flight was "from the presence of Jehovah." These words were never meant to suggest that Jonah thought he could sail to a place where God was not! Obviously not, for Jonah himself says to the sailors: "I am an Hebrew, and I fear Jehovah, the God of heaven, which hath made the sea and the dry land." Long before Jonah's day, David had written: "If I ascend up into heaven Thou art there: if I make my bed in Sheol, behold Thou art there. If I take the wings of the morning (the uttermost east), or dwell in the uttermost parts of the sea (the uttermost west—where Jonah was now going), even there shall Thy hand lead me, and Thy right hand shall hold me." Indeed, the twenty-four verses of that sublime one-hundred-and-thirty-ninth psalm, running in four strophes of six verses each, are devoted successively to the omniscience, omnipresence, and omnipotence of Israel's God, and then the psalmist's awe-inspired reaction to these infinite Divine attributes. This psalm, of course, not to mention other and similar writings from inspired pens in Israel, was in Jonah's possession. The language of his prayer from the interior of the great fish shows how familiar he was with the writings of his nation. And, in fact, from the very days of Israel's constitution as a nation, under Moses, the Hebrew people had believed in the omnipresence of Jehovah, as the God of gods. No, Jonah certainly was not imagining the possibility of out-sailing the reach of God!

These words, "from the presence of Jehovah," must be interpreted in the light of Elijah's and Elisha's words, "As Jehovah liveth, *before whom I stand,"* and such words as those to the priests, in 2 Chronicles xxix. 11, "Jehovah hath chosen you *to stand before Him."* When Jonah "rose up to flee unto Tarshish, from the presence of the Lord," he was voluntarily forfeiting his prophetic office and his prophetic standing before Jehovah. That is undoubtedly the significance of the words, and should be clearly understood.

Jonah *knew* that the storm had come because of himself. He explained so to the sailors (i. 12). But even before this the sailors themselves seem to have sensed that there was something uncanny about it, for they resorted to the casting of lots, to find for whose sake it had come (i. 7). Jonah's being found asleep tells its own story of sheer fatigue after nights of sleepless cogitation followed by his fugitive haste for the ship.

Note verses 9 and 10. Jonah had *already* told the sailors that he fled "from the presence of Jehovah"; but now, when they realise the greatness of Jehovah from Jonah's own words, they are filled with consternation at having one of His prophets—a disobedient one—on board with them. Understanding fully, now, Jonah's identity, they try their very utmost to spare him (as we see in verses 12 and 13), but without avail; and at last—try to imagine the scene—they reluctantly swing him, unresisting, from the deck of the plunging vessel into the foaming fury beneath: and lo, the storm at once dies away into dead calm! We are not surprised to read, in verse 16, that these amazed men "feared Jehovah exceedingly, and offered a sacrifice unto Jehovah, and made vows."

One wonders what the next move of these sailors was after their scaring experience. They certainly could not have proceeded with their intended voyage, for all their cargo had been jettisoned (i. 5), and probably their boat was damaged (i. 4). Presumably they would return to Joppa, to report on the happening, and to make new preparations. And what a strange report it was which they carried back! One wonders if they had actually seen the fish appear, and Jonah pass into its great wide mouth. Nor can one help wondering how soon and how far the story got round—possibly even as far as Nineveh, before ever Jonah himself got there!

Jonah and the Fish

We are now at chapter ii. Let us clearly grasp the fact that the swallowing of Jonah by the "sea-monster" was not an act of punishment but of preservation. That, perhaps more than anything else, confirms the belief that Jonah's *motive* in fleeing was, as we have said, the high motive of Israel's salvation.

Note the following points about Jonah's prayer from inside the great fish. It is not a cry for deliverance. Jonah knew that he was already being delivered. His prayer is really a psalm of praise, a "Te Deum," a "doxology." I know of a man who once sang the "Doxology" with his head in his empty flour barrel, as an expression of faith that God would send a further supply of flour! But the novelty of singing a doxology with your head —and all the rest of you—inside a great fish, in mid-ocean, is absolutely without rival!

There is not one word of petition in Jonah's prayer. It consists of thanksgiving (verses 2–6), contrition (verses 7, 8), and rededication (verse 9). Inside that fish Jonah realised in a new way the wonderful love and care of his God. He learned, as never before, that underneath and round about him were the "everlasting arms" of Jehovah. It was there, too, that he came to understand with vividness the folly and futility of disobedience to God; for he said: "They that observe lying vanities forsake their own mercy" (rebuking himself, in these words, for his own self-willed subterfuge). Still more, it was there, in that fish, that Jonah re-covenanted with God, saying, "I will pay that which I have vowed"; while his final word is, "Salvation is of Jehovah." Thereupon, the fish discharged its unusual cargo, safe and sound at an unnamed port of call.

Jonah and the City

Most remarkable of all, perhaps, is chapter iii., which recounts Nineveh's repentance. How great this moral miracle was may be judged from the size of the city. Three times God speaks of Nineveh as "that *great* city." In this third chapter, also, we have it that "Nineveh was an *exceeding* great city of three days' journey." Then, in the last verse of the last chapter, we find it referred to as having had in it "more than six score thousand persons that cannot discern between their right hand and their left hand, and also much cattle."

Now consider how great this city was. The late Professor C. F. Keil, in his *Archaeology of the Old Testament*, says: "The conclusion to which recent discoveries lead is that the name of Nineveh was used in two senses: first, for one particular city; and secondly, for a complex of four large primeval cities (including Nineveh proper), the circumvallation of which is still traceable . . . the mounds of which cover the land." The names of these four component cities which made up the vast Nineveh quadrangle are Nimrud, Koyunjik, Khorsabad, and Keramles. To go the round of these would be to cover a distance of sixty miles, which, according to the old reckoning of twenty miles to a day, would be a "three days' journey."

This quadrangular picture of ancient Nineveh is borne out by Diodorus Siculus, the famous Sicilian historian and contemporary of Julius Cæsar. He asserts that it was a quadrangle one hundred and fifty stadia in length, ninety in breadth, and four hundred and eighty in circumference; so that it was a parallelogram, with its longer sides making thirty-six miles, and its shorter sides twenty-four miles, the circumference being about sixty miles. The walls were one hundred feet high, and so broad that three chariots could be driven abreast on them. They were fortified with fifteen hundred towers, each of these being two hundred feet in height. Based on a trigonometrical survey of the locality, the full area of the Assyrian metropolis has been computed as three hundred and fifty square miles, which is some twenty miles more than that of London today!

Of course, it must be understood that Greater Nineveh included great gardens, orchards, and even pastures and corn-fields. This need not surprise us. The great walled towns of Babylonia seem to have enclosed large spaces for cultivation and pasture, so that in case of long siege they were largely self-contained. It is this fact which explains the mention of "much cattle" in Nineveh (iv. 11). Modernist critics have smiled with superior toleration at such a mistaken slip as that reference to the "much cattle"; but today the *really* modern scholar, with the evidence of archaeology before him, may smile at the presumptuous ignorance of the critics!

On the basis of the Scripture reference to the great number of young infants in Nineveh, namely, the "six score thousand persons that cannot discern between their right hand and their left hand" (iv. 11), and the size of the place, and fuller knowledge of these great old-time cities, the population of Nineveh is estimated at about one million, probably more, and certainly "not less than six hundred thousand." Thus, it will be seen that Nineveh was indeed "an exceeding great city."

Can we believe, then, that the whole of this vast and populous metropolis repented, with an immediate and genuine repentance, at the preaching of this lone prophet from Israel? Once again the critics have found occasion to smile; but once again the likelihoods are against them. We *can* believe it; and that for several reasons.

We must always be careful not to read into the Scriptures what is not there: yet undoubtedly there is room, again and again, for a legitimate "reading between the lines," inasmuch as the Scriptures often compress very much into very small compass. For instance, in this very chapter, we are simply told that Jonah's words to Nineveh were, "Yet forty days and Nineveh shall be overthrown"; yet obviously he did not merely repeat and repeat and repeat this without variation or addition without a single word of explanation or amplification. Who had given him this message? What was his authority? Who was he? Was he a prophet in all sanity and reality? Or was he some unbalanced fanatic? And if there really was a message from the God of gods, what must Nineveh do to appease Him? Quite plainly, Jonah would tell them how Jehovah's message had come to him, and *why* Nineveh was to be overthrown. Maybe he would also tell them of his own disobedient flight, of his miraculous preservation, and of his further commission to warn Nineveh. It surely takes little imagination to visualise the at-first curious, then serious, then perturbed Ninevites besieging Jonah with questions, and at least getting earnest replies to some of them. Less than this there surely could not have been, unless we rob the story of all naturalness. Yet this is not stated in so many words.

Now the most significant clue to the reason why Jonah's appearance and proclamation at Nineveh created such an immediate stir is found in the New Testament, in our Lord's words

—"This is an evil generation: they seek a *sign*; and there shall no *sign* be given unto it, but the *sign* of the prophet Jonas. For as Jonas was a *sign* unto the Ninevites, so shall the Son of Man be to this generation" (Luke xi. 29, 30). We have emphasised that word "sign." Jonah was a *sign* unto the old-time Ninevites, by his miraculous experience in the great fish: but the question at once presents itself: How could Jonah have been a sign to them if the Ninevites *did not know* of Jonah's experience? And if they had been given no evidence for it besides Jonah's own word, would they have given it credence?

Now let us do just a little "reading between the lines." Our thoughts turn back to chapter i., to the sailors. When Jonah booked his passage on that boat, certain questions would be asked of him. We have noted already (i. 10) that before ever the storm broke, Jonah had told them "that he fled from the presence of Jehovah": but would he, or *could* he have given this most unusual explanation without telling them at least *why* he was thus fleeing? At the time, Jehovah was only a "god" by hearsay to these Gentile sailors; and what Jonah may have said to them about the message for Nineveh may have meant nothing to them: but when that uncanny storm swept about them and they learned the omnipresent greatness of Jehovah, and when Jonah's disappearance in the water brought that equally uncanny calm, what would their thoughts be! Their cargo had been thrown overboard (i. 5). Their boat was badly knocked about (i. 4). What could they do but make back for port? And what a tale they had to tell! Along that seaboard no little Assyrian commerce was done. One of the most amazing revelations which recent archaeological discovery has brought us is that of the travel and traffic which were carried on over wide distances in the days of which we are now speaking. What intense interest would the Jonah occurrence have to those who went to and from Nineveh!

But what of the feelings of all, when the supposedly drowned Jonah himself reappeared, and recounted his none-such experience, and announced his purpose of now going to Nineveh! How could it be otherwise than that this phenomenal story should reach Nineveh before ever Jonah got there?

And so, without resorting to any such explanation as that Jonah's experience in the "whale" had perhaps left a bleached appearance about him (!), we can well imagine what a startling and solemn "sign" he would be to the astonished Ninevites.

Strangely enough, too, it appears that Jonah's mission to Nineveh coincided with a period when fear of some impending calamity lurked there in many hearts. Although Assyria was rising to become the proud and cruel mistress of the nations, there was one period when she suffered reverses and temporary decline, and when it seemed that still greater calamity might be coming. Babylon at this time, as Professor Rawlinson has pointed out, refused further submission. Israel, and Judah, and Syria all ceased to pay tribute. Jeroboam, King of Israel, as we have seen, reclaimed and annexed much territory. Other revolts shook Assyria's hold, and contracted her boundaries. It began to look as though Assyria's hour was coming. Jonah's sudden cry came just at the most telling moment. It was like a spark on dried wood, or a thrusting in of the sickle when the harvest was dead ripe. The hearts of Nineveh's thousands were bowed as the heart of one man.

Nor is there any difficulty in believing that the king and the nobles led Nineveh's mourning for sin, and that a general fast was proclaimed by royal edict; for, as Professor Sayce says, "It is just such a fast as was ordained by Esarhaddon II when the northern foe was gathering against the Assyrian empire, and prayers were raised to the sun-god to 'remove the sin' of the king and his people." Nor is there any difficulty in believing that the animals were included in the edict; for other cases of this occurred, as the Greek historian, Herodotus, has shown us.

No, there is no real reason why we should not believe that Nineveh's repentance took place just as the Book of Jonah declares. It is just such as *could* have taken place; and that it actually *did* take place is settled by the words of Christ Himself —"The men of Nineveh repented at the preaching of Jonas." We have seen that there is no getting over our Lord's words about Jonah and Nineveh: and they who will not bow to the clear word of Christ should not dare to call themselves Christians.

> How can I call Him Lord, and yet forsooth
> Diverge from Him who said "I am the Truth",
> And offer Him that strangest disrespect
> Of much preferring my own intellect?

THE BOOK OF JONAH (4)
Lesson Number 95

NOTE.—For this final study of Jonah read the whole story through once again, but with special concentration on the last chapter.

Should a voyager chance to be on the point of shipwreck on some unknown coast, he will most devoutly pray that the lesson of the missionary may have reached thus far. . . .

Charles Darwin.

I will not believe that it is given to man to have thoughts higher and nobler than the real truth of things.

Sir Oliver Lodge.

For the love of God is broader
   Than the measures of man's mind;
And the heart of the Eternal
   Is most wonderfully kind.

F. W. Faber.

THE BOOK OF JONAH (4)

WE HAVE seen that this little book of Jonah is in four movements —chapter i., Jonah and the *storm*; chapter ii., Jonah and the *fish*; chapter iii., Jonah and the *city*; chapter iv., Jonah and the *Lord*. In this, our final consideration of the book, we are at chapter iv. We shall briefly reflect on this chapter, and then make two or three parting observations on Jonah himself, before passing on to the next of Israel's prophets.

Jonah and the Lord

Chapter iv. gives us the supreme message of the book. This can be expressed in few words, but it is one of affecting tenderness. The chapter is a dialogue between Jonah and the Lord.

Jonah cuts a sorry figure; but if we would rightly appraise his attitude we must realise afresh the intense identity of interests which existed between him and his nation. So passionate was his religious patriotism that all self-interests were sunk in his deep concern for Israel. The earlier chapters have already made this clear to us. We have protested that Jonah's motive in fleeing, rather than deliver the warning to Nineveh, was not anti-Gentile prejudice, but the high motive of concernedness for Israel's salvation; and we would re-emphasise that. Yet we are keenly alive to this, also, that while Jonah's mind may not have been warped by actual prejudice, his very consciousness of the Divine privileges conferred upon Israel may have occasioned a looking upon other peoples as somewhat inferior. Such a grave error needed to be corrected; and in this fourth chapter we see with what condescending patience the correction is given.

Note verses 1, 2, and 3. Jonah is not only "displeased" and "angry," but his dismay at Israel's dark future, now that Nineveh is to be spared, so overcomes him that he prays for his life to be taken away. The Lord tenderly reproves him with the question, "Doest thou well to be angry?" (verse 4). Thereupon Jonah, thinking that possibly there was still a gleam of hope, "went out of the city, and sat on the east side of the city, and there made him a booth, and sat under it in the shadow, *till he might see what would become of the city*" (verse 5). Here the Lord patiently and tenderly reasoned with His overwrought servant, by three "prepared" things—a gourd, a worm, a wind.

First, God "prepared a *gourd*, and made it to come up over Jonah, that it might be a shadow over his head, to deliver him from his grief." It has been truly observed that "the tenderness in the heart of God is manifested not only in His compassion for repenting sinners, but also in His patience with repining saints." The Hebrew word which is here translated as "a gourd" has been thought by some to refer to the castor-oil plant, which, because of its broad, palmatic leaves, would provide just such a comforting screen as Jonah would appreciate. Dr. W. M. Thompson, however, in *The Land and the Book* raises forceful objection to this. "Orientals never dream of training a castor-oil plant over a booth, or planting it for a shade," he says; "and they would have but small respect for anyone who did. It is in no way adapted for that purpose, while thousands of arbours are covered with various creepers of the general gourd family." So much, then, for that; but whichever plant of the gourd family it may have been, its growth was miraculously accelerated, for it "came up in a night" (verse 10), and was thus "prepared" by the time the hot sun mounted the sky again. It would form a welcome draping around Jonah's booth of tree branches, and we are not surprised to read that "Jonah was exceeding glad of the gourd."

But with the next sunrise God also "prepared" a *worm*, which "smote the gourd that it withered" (verse 7). Either this was a single gourd-worm which punctured the main stem of the plant, and thus caused the whole of it to wither, or else, collectively, it was a *swarm* of such worms or caterpillars which, in short time, stripped the plant of all its leaves—a common enough happening in many an Oriental locality, where a warm, moist night will product a host of such caterpillars. Thus Jonah was now left exposed to the sun again.

Still further, however, God "prepared" a *sultry east wind*. It is a pity that our Authorised Version here gives it as a "vehement" east wind. The Revised Version rightly changes it to "sultry." Perhaps even the word "wind" here tends to convey a wrong impression to us who live latitudes away from the tropics. A "wind," to us, on a hot day, would be a welcome refresher: but the wind which our text refers to was what might be described as a kind of hot breath almost suffocating the land. Dr. Thompson has told us of one such dust-laden *sirocco*, or hot wind, which he experienced when travelling from Lydd to Jerusalem. "There is no living thing abroad to make a noise. The birds hide in the thickest shades; the fowls pant under the walls with open mouth and drooping wings; the flocks and herds take shelter in caves and under great rocks; the labourers retire from the fields, and close the windows and doors of their houses; and travellers hasten, as I did, to take shelter in the first cool place they can find." The languor, enervation, and weariness which such a *sirocco* can cause is easy to imagine. Poor Jonah, dispirited at the thought of Israel's dark future now that Nineveh is to be spared, inadequately screened from the glare of the merciless sun, and reduced to utter lassitude by the sweltering heat, sinks down and yearns that he might die (verse 8).

He is roused by a voice, however. It is God speaking. "Doest thou well to be angry for the gourd?" Jonah's reply is: "I do well to be angry, even unto death" (verse 9). This occasions the wonderful Divine utterance with which the book closes.

"Then said Jehovah: Thou hast had pity on the gourd, for the which thou hast not laboured, neither madest it grow; which came up in a night, and perished in a night. And should not I spare Nineveh, that great city, wherein are more than six score thousand persons that cannot discern between their right hand and their left hand, and also much cattle?"

This is the revelation of the heart of God to which the whole book has been moving, and for which, indeed, it was written. Therefore, as soon as this point has been reached, the book closes. We are not told what Jonah said or did further, for Jonah was not intended to be last in our minds at the close of the book. We are left in the presence of God, face to face with this moving revelation of the Divine compassion. To some the book seems to end with a strange abruptness and incompleteness. This is because they have not perceived the one real purpose of it. They have not sensed the genius and motive of the Scripture writings. Nothing is told us for the mere sake of the telling. All has a moral and a Divine aim. The Book of Jonah was never written merely to tell us the story of Jonah as an end in itself. A thousand times, No! We are told the story of this man and Nineveh because of what it reveals to us of *God*. That is the vital reason why it was written. Once that purpose has been served, the writer is content to lay down the pen. He has no mind to add more, for the mere sake of interesting us. He is under the guidance of the inspiring Spirit; and the Spirit guides him where to stop as clearly as He guides him what to write.

Ponder, then, this revelation of God, in the closing three verses of this book. It is perhaps the tenderest anticipation of John iii. 16, and the parable of the prodigal son, and the world-embracing message of the Gospel, to be found anywhere in the Old Testament. God's tender patience with the resentful prophet, and His tender concern for the Ninevites, despite their wickedness, together give us a unique expression of the Divine compassion. See here the compassion of God toward penitent wicked-doers, and toward innocent little children, and even toward the dumb animals! Truly, "His tender mercies are over all His works," as the psalmist says. He is as slow to punish as He is quick to pardon where there is penitence.

Jonah needed to learn that God's special favour toward Israel did not mean a lessened love for other peoples. He must learn that the Divine election is not arbitrary, but for the fulfilling of high purpose. Israel had not been chosen simply for Israel's own sake, but to fulfil a Divine purpose, the end of which was the blessing of *all* peoples. The election of the one nation did not mean the rejection of others! God loves *all* His human creatures "without respect of persons"—yea, even the wicked sinners of Nineveh, much as He hates their sin itself! It was by revelations such as this to Jonah that the Hebrew people came to learn that their omnipresent Jehovah had an omnipresent care and concern and compassion toward *all* men and women, boys and girls, and even the lower animals. Yes, even the oft-misrepresented Jonah helped to prepare the way for Jesus to say: "God so loved the world, that He gave His only-begotten Son, that whosoever believeth in Him should not perish, but have everlasting life."

There is one point of tender significance which seems to have been overlooked in the parallel between Jonah's pity for the gourd and God's pity for Nineveh. Jonah's pity for the gourd was not only because a thing of beauty and fragrance had been ruined, but because the loss of the plant meant much *to himself*. Even so, God's pity toward the Ninevites is not wholly because of their intrinsic preciousness as human souls, but because they mean much *to His own heart*. How the comparison must have set Jonah thinking! And how precious to ourselves is this thought that each one of us means much to the heart of the Eternal! And how it pulls at our heart-strings to know that each man and woman and boy and girl, of whatever race or clime or colour, means something very tender in the mind of God! Surely this is the deepest inspiration of all overseas missionary activity!— and this revelation was given to the first foreign missionary ever sent out from Israel! This revelation of God at the end of the book of Jonah is such that even a modern critic like Dr. Arthur Peake is obliged to say: "That out of the stony heart of Judaism such a book should come, is nothing less than a marvel of Divine grace"; while another recent critic, Cornill, says: "One of the deepest and grandest things ever written. I should like to exclaim to anyone who approaches it: Put thy shoes from off thy feet, for the place whereon thou standest is holy ground." Yes, as we come to this final word in the Book of Jonah, we may well tread reverently and adore; for here the heart of God is revealed with special tenderness.

Jonah as a Type

We must not close this lengthened treatment of the Book of Jonah without noting that, in addition to the spiritual and historical values of this book, Jonah himself has significance as a *type*. This is markedly so in three ways.

First, Jonah typically foreshadows *the history of his own nation, Israel*. If we watch the movements of this man discerningly, we shall see the whole nation of Israel moving with him, just as a man's shadow on a wall behind him moves with him. As is often the case, the shadow is much bigger than the man himself. We see here the *national* Jonah, the Hebrew nation. As Jonah moves, so Israel's history moves before us. See here the people of Israel

—disobedient to the heavenly commission, as Jonah was; out of their own land, as Jonah was; finding precarious refuge with the Gentiles, as Jonah did; everywhere a trouble to the Gentiles, as Jonah was on that ship; yet witnessing to the true God, among the Gentiles, as Jonah did to those sailors; cast out by the Gentiles, as Jonah was cast out by the troubled seamen; yet miraculously preserved amid their calamities, as Jonah was miraculously preserved in the deep; calling on Jehovah, at last, in penitence and rededication, as Jonah did from inside the great fish; finding salvation and deliverance in Jehovah-Jesus, as Jonah found salvation in a new way in the deep, concluding his prayer with the words, "Salvation is of Jehovah"; and in the end becoming missionaries to the Gentile nations (see Zech. viii. 13, 20, 23), as Jonah, in the end, became God's missionary to Gentile Nineveh.

Second, Jonah typically anticipates *the death and burial and resurrection of Christ.* Chapter i. tells us that Jonah was inside the great fish "three days and three nights." Why was he thus retained for this duration? So long as the fish had served the purpose of preventing drowning, might not the prophet have been discharged from the fish without further delay? Our Lord Jesus has given us to know why Jonah was in the fish for that duration. He says, "As Jonah was three days and three nights in the sea-monster, so shall the Son of Man be three days and three nights in the heart of the earth." There is a strange impressiveness about this fact that, hundreds of years before our Lord's incarnation, Jonah's entombment in the great fish should be sovereignly overruled to become a type in this way. As we have said before, the latent typology of the Old Testament is one of the most impressive credentials of its Divine inspiration.

There are those who hold that Jonah actually died inside the fish, and that he was literally brought to life again, so as to make him a type absolute of our Lord's resurrection. To press this, however, is not really necessary to Jonah's typifying our Lord's death and resurrection. Indeed, to our own mind, he fulfilled the type more truly by remaining conscious in the fish; for the interior of that fish is likened, in Jonah's prayer, to *Sheol* (the Hades of the New Testament), into which our Lord went between the death and resurrection of His body, and where He "preached unto the spirits in prison" (1 Pet. iii. 19).

In an earlier study we have shown that the three notable prophets who came in quick succession during the last period before the destruction of the ten-tribed kingdom, namely, Elijah, Elisha, Jonah, are a kind of *type-trio*. Elisha dies and is buried, but in his death gives life to another—as our Lord by His death gives life to others. Jonah, in symbol, not only dies, but goes down into Sheol, and then comes up that he should not see corruption—as also did our Lord. Elijah ascends to heaven and casts down his mantle—as our Lord ascended and sent down the Pentecostal Spirit to us.

Third, Jonah is a type of *Christ Himself, as God's "sign" Messenger*. Our Lord Jesus said: "As Jonas was a sign unto the Ninevites, so shall also the Son of Man be to this generation." What did His words mean? We give a grandly worded reply to that question from the pen of the late Rev. John Urquhart. "Look back over those well-nigh nineteen centuries," he says, "and you will read the answer. When Jonah, having become a curse for his people, came back, as it were, from the dead, whither did he carry the word of the Lord? To Israel? No; to the Gentile city of Nineveh. And there he beheld what he had in vain longed and prayed to see among his own people—the turning of a whole city to God—the leaders leading for once in the right direction, and the entire people following and seeking God with purpose of heart. When Christ came back from the grave, and the word of the Lord was once more to be proclaimed, whither was it carried? It was borne to the Gentiles. And how fared it with the message there? The Word of Life, which Israel had rejected, these received. Age after age the Jew has been confronted with that sign. Out of the grave of the Crucified has come this power that has tamed the barbarian, changed the savage, cleansed and raised the hopelessly debased, brought back the outcast races into the brotherhood of man, and given to all who have received the message, the nobleness, the spiritual insight, the compassions, and the purity of the children of God. He who said that the Jew should have that sign read the future. He gave a promise, and, rising from the grave, He has kept it. He has proved His claim to be the Son of God and the world's Saviour. He has attested the Book of Jonah; He has attested the entire Scripture; and for us that attestation is final."

AND NOW, TRY THESE . . .

1. What reference in the Old Testament *historical* books proves that Jonah was a real figure of history?

2. How does this reference to Jonah in the historical books guide us as to the *time* of Jonah's ministry?

3. How do our Lord's words about Jonah unmistakably confirm that Jonah and what is related of him were really historical?

4. What are the four movements in which the story of Jonah is arranged?

5. What, briefly, was the real reason why Jonah fled rather than go to Nineveh?

6. What is the number of Nineveh's little children given in chapter iv. 11, and what is the full population of the city inferred from this?

7. Why was it that Jonah was such a convincing preacher to the people of Nineveh?

8. What were the three "prepared" things by which God reasoned with Jonah, in chapter iv.?

9. What is the great lesson, or revelation of God, to which the story moves and with which it ends?

10. In what ways is Jonah a *typical* figure?

THE PROPHET MICAH

Lesson Number 96

NOTE.—For this study read right through the prophecy of Micah at least twice. Then read it through again in a modern translation or the Revised Version.

As in any organism, no member or part, however minute, can be fully understood aside from its relation to the whole; so, in scripture, every paragraph and sentence is part of its totality, and must be studied in relation to all the rest. The text will be illumined by the context, or scripture immediately preceding and following. Every occurrence and utterance should be studied in its surroundings. How, why, when a word was spoken or an act done, helps to explain it, is its local colouring. Hidden relationships must be traced like underground roots and subterranean channels.

A. T. Pierson, D.D.

THE BOOK OF MICAH

IT IS good to know that in the Judæan capital, long ago, the great prophet Isaiah had such a trusty comrade and such a doughty fellow-champion of truth as "Micah the Morasthite." With the first few strokes of his pen Micah tells us that he prophesied "in the days of Jotham, Ahaz, and Hezekiah, kings of Judah"; which means that he and Isaiah wrought contemporaneously (compare Isa. i. 1). Isaiah, however, who was the elder of the two, not only continued with Micah through these three reigns, but commenced his ministry even earlier, in the reign of Uzziah; so that he had already been championing the cause of Jehovah for some years when the prophetic mantle fell on Micah. Although Isaiah was a man of the schools and Micah a man of the fields, these two giants of faith would no doubt have their heart-to-heart consultations on the stirring doings of those eventful days; and we are not surprised, therefore, that in their writings certain sentiments, expressions, and historical references are common to them both. Probably Isaiah's ministry was more to the upper classes, and Micah's more to the lower—with which by descent his sympathies were the more closely connected.

The Hebrew name translated "Micah" means "Who is like Jehovah?" We detect a little play on this when Micah winds up his message with the question, "Who is a God like unto Thee?" (vii. 18). Our prophet calls himself a "Morasthite," which means that he was of Moresheth, a little place in Judæa, near Gath on the Philistine border (called Moresheth-gath in i. 14, that is, "Territory of Gath"). He records no events of his life; so the little we may know of him must be deduced from this short synopsis of his preachings which has come down to us as "The Book of Micah." This much is clear: he was a prophet of Judah, with Jerusalem as the centre-point of his prophetic ministry and message (though he often also includes Samaria).

Moderns have doubted the superscription that Micah prophesied "in the days of Jotham, Ahaz, and Hezekiah"; but, as we have repeatedly seen, one part of Scripture cannot be impugned without the involving of some other. This is another instance; for in Jeremiah xxvi. 18 we have an incidental yet decisive corroboration of Micah's superscription, along with a noteworthy tribute to his remarkable influence as a preacher. Furthermore, all the historical allusions in Micah correspond with those times, as comparison with 2 Kings and 2 Chronicles shows; but into this we need not enter here.

The Book and its Message

Perhaps to the ordinary reader this book may not open up too intelligibly at first. This is partly due to obscurities in translation. Yet even to the reader who is limited to the Authorised Version it opens up rewardingly after a little further patience. No one can read these seven chapters carefully without noting (even while bits here and there remain obscure) that chapters i. to iii. are an announcing of *imminent judgment* because of sin; that chapters iv. and v. mark a gladsome contrast to this by fixing our eye on the *ultimate blessing* of the covenant people; and that the remaining two chapters consist of exhortations to *repentance* in view of the message delivered. Some Bible teachers have it that the little work consists of three addresses, each opened by the word "Hear" (i. 2; iii. 1; vi. 1). This is simply division according to literary form rather than subject-matter. If we would get the message of the book as a whole we must analyse according to subject-matter; and when we do this we find, as just shown, a triple message, the logical sequence of which is clear:

1. IMMINENT JUDGMENT DECLARED (i.–iii.).
2. ULTIMATE BLESSING PROMISED (iv.–v.).
3. PRESENT REPENTANCE PLEADED (vi.–vii.).

The obscure verses in Micah should be read in a modern translation. It is one of the most rewarding books when clearly understood. The central thought is: *PRESENT JUDGMENT BUT FUTURE BLESSING.* The present judgment is because of Israel's unfaithfulness to the Covenant. The future blessing is because of Jehovah's *unchanging faithfulness* to it. In the case of Micah we scarcely need give a fuller analysis, though the book lends itself to this. With our limited space let us rather glance through the three main parts to clear up verses which may still seem obscure.

Chapters i. to iii.

The "it" and the "he" in chapter i. 9 may have seemed awkward. The "wound" in this verse is the stroke of retribution (as the Septuagint renders). There had been earlier chastisements, but this coming one was to be "incurable," that is, there would not be recovery from it. Jehovah's rod to inflict the stroke was Assyria: and after the Assyrians had laid low the northern kingdom (Israel) they also invaded the southern kingdom (Judah), even to Jerusalem itself (see 2 Kings xviii. 9–xix. 37), so that this ninth verse truly says in advance of the event: "It (the stroke) is come unto Judah; it (not 'he') is come unto the gate of *my* people, even to Jerusalem."

The unfamiliar names in verses 10 to 16 are names of *places* in the locality where Micah was reared—places dotted among the broad, fertile glens of the Shephelah, or range of low hills which lay between Judah and the Philistine plain, stretching away west of Judah to the Mediterranean. Micah foresees these places bearing the brunt of invasion, which will come from the south-east because the Assyrians will first strike at Egypt (on which Judah foolishly relied) and then march on Judah through Micah's own home-locality. There is an intriguing play on these place-names. David's words, "Tell it not in Gath" (in his elegy over Saul: 2 Sam. i. 20) had become a proverbial saying; and Micah here says (i. 10) in effect, "Tell it not in Tell-town." The words "Weep ye not at all" (verse 10) are really "Weep ye not at Weep-town" (*Acco*). Again in verse 10, "Aphrah" is dust; so Micah says, "Roll thyself in dust at the House of Dust." In verse 11 "Saphir" is beauty; so Micah says, "Pass away inhabitress of Beauty-place, in nakedness and shame." Again in verse 11, "Zaanan" is March-town; so Micah says, "The inhabitress of March-town marches not forth." Again, "Beth-ezel" (verse 11) is the "House-of-the-side," that is, "Neighbourtown"; and Micah says that the mourning of Neighbour-town shall be such as to take away any neighbourly "standing" or support. "Maroth" (verse 12) means bitter, evil; and Micah says, "Evil hath come down from Jehovah." In verse 13 "Lachish" means Horse-town; and Micah says, "Bind the chariot to the swift beast, O inhabitant of Horse-town." In verse 14 "Achzib" means a deceit, a lie; and Micah says, "The houses of Lie-town shall be a lie to the kings of Israel." In verse 15 the word "heir" should be "possessor" or "conqueror"—meaning the Assyrian.

In chapter ii., verses 6 and 7 may have been perplexing. Some would simplify them by changing the word "prophesy" here to "prate" or "sputter"—as referring to false prophets, because Micah's word here is not the common one for prophesying. But the same word is used elsewhere of *true* prophesying (in Ezek. xx. 46, for instance, where the Lord certainly did not mean Ezekiel either to prate or sputter!). Micah ii. 6, 7 must be seen as part of the contrast between the false prophets and the true (see last clause of verse 7 with verse 11, in which latter "the spirit" should be "wind". Note iii. 7, 8). Now read chapter ii. 6, 7 thus:

"Prophesy not"—so they (the false prophets) prophesy— "Let none prophesy such things" (as Micah did). "Their insults (lit. 'shames') are endless!" (Now comes Micah's reply)—"Shall this be said (not 'named'), O House of Jacob? Is the Spirit of Jehovah to be restrained? Are such things His doings? Do not my words do good to him that walketh uprightly?"

Chapters iv. and v.

As we have said, these two chapters picture the ultimate blessing of the covenant people. In chapter iv. we have the future *kingdom*, in chapter v. the future *king*. To Micah and other Hebrew prophets it was given by the Spirit of inspiration to foresee a golden day-break of restoration beyond the grim nightfall of retribution. They were not given to see all the intervening historical processes; they did not discern the long period between the Messiah's *first* coming, as the suffering Servant to bear the curse of the Law, and His *second* coming, as King of kings, to administer the blessings of the Abrahamic and Davidic covenants; but they *did* see the eventual consummation. In 1 Peter i. 11 we learn that they actually studied their own writings to ascertain "what manner of time the Spirit of Christ which was in them did signify when He testified beforehand the sufferings of Christ, and the glory that should follow." The present age of grace and of the Church was a secret of God not divulged until apostolic times (see Eph. iii.).

There is something rather thrilling, all the same, in the fact that these Hebrew preachers of twenty-five centuries ago should be telling us even today of things which are still to happen. An unbiased consideration of such predictions as we have in Micah iv. and v. will convince any honest mind that there has not yet been a fulfilment which satisfies all their intent. They await the Millennial era for their full realisation. They will burst into consummating occurrence at the reappearing of Israel's great Deliverer, the now-rejected Christ. If only they were heeded, these Hebrew prophets have grand wisdom and mighty comfort for the harassed nations of today. They were brave men; they would not conceal the awful retribution and dispersal which were coming to their people; yet they were men of glad heart, for they had glimpsed the shining height beyond the fearsome valley; they had caught the song beyond the storm; they had seen the flashing sunrise of a new age beyond the thunder-clouds of judgment and the frowning enigmas of the present.

And now, in this fourth chapter, note the opening phrase, "In the last days." It clearly lifts the passage from any application merely to the prophet's own time, and points to the far future. Also note verse 2. The nations other than Israel are to be in the Messianic kingdom and are to walk in the ways of Jehovah. This largely clears the apparent difficulty of verse 5, which seems to contradict verse 2. It should read: "*All the peoples now walk in the name of their god, but* shall *walk in the name of Jehovah our God for ever.*"

See, too, the sharp contrast Micah makes between the restoration promised for the *last* days, and the judgment imminent in *his own*. In verses 1 to 8 he speaks of "in the last days" and "in that day" (verse 6); but see verse 9—"*NOW* dost thou cry . . ."; and verse 10—"*NOW* shalt thou go . . . to Babylon"; and verse 11—"*NOW* also many nations are gathered against thee"; and chapter v. 1—"*NOW* . . . he hath laid siege against us"; and see chapter v. 3 where we are told that the time of God's giving up the nation to humiliation is "*UNTIL*" the coming of Christ.

This brings us to Micah's remarkable prediction of the place of Christ's birth (v. 2). Micah and Isaiah give the two clearest predictions concerning our Lord's incarnation. Isaiah foretells His birth of the *Virgin*. Micah tells the *place* of His birth so plainly that when the Magi long after enquired of Herod where the King of the Jews should be born, the scribes answered without hesitation: "In Bethlehem of Judæa; for thus it is written by the prophet" (Matt. ii. 5). Note that between the first half of Micah v. 3 and the second, the present age, with its further scattering of the Jews, intervenes—which Micah was not given to foresee. The rest of this fifth chapter looks on to the kingdom-age yet to be. Note Israel's double aspect in verses 7 and 8—fresh as the dew, strong as the lion! Mark the regeneration of Israel in verses 10 to 14. And in verse 15 see the coming wrath on the earth's impenitent peoples. This verse should read: "I will execute vengeance in anger and fury upon the nations which do not hearken."

Chapters vi. and vii.

The last two chapters of Micah are in the form of a *colloquy*; and when read as such they light up with new interest. All we can do here is to point out where the different speakers come in. First, in chapter vi. 1, 2, the *mountains* are exhorted to listen, like stately referees, to Jehovah's "controversy." Then, in verses 3 to 5, *Jehovah* pleads. In verses 6 and 7 *Micah* speaks, representing those in the nation who would fitly respond. In verse 8 the overhearing mountains break in—"He hath showed thee, O man, what is good; and what doth Jehovah require of thee but to do justly, and to love mercy, and to walk humbly with thy God?" Next, in verses 9 to 16, *Jehovah* speaks to "the man of wisdom," wheresoever he is, in the city, exposing the nation's sin, and showing why the nation suffered. Then, in chapter vii. 1 to 6, the unhappy *nation* is impersonated as confessing its baneful state. In verses 7 to 10 the "man of wisdom" speaks again. In verses 11 to 13 it is Jehovah. In verse 14 the "man of wisdom." In verse 15 Jehovah. Finally, from verse 16 to the end it is the "man of wisdom." These two chapters, reflect, are Jehovah's pleading for *repentance*. They are the "application" of the great sermon preached in the foregoing chapters. Moreover, they maintain through-out a high-water mark of literary excellence.

Great Truths

Some of the mightiest truths in the Old Testament are expressed in Micah. As our prophet relates the sovereignty of Jehovah to human life and history he recognises and emphasises resultant realities of immense importance.

Note first *the profound significance of the Divine dealings with the Hebrew nation.* Micah addresses a small people in a strip of land merely about the size of Wales, yet in chapters i. 2 and vi. 1, 2, he commands the whole earth, the mountains, the hills, to attend (in Scripture usage mountains and hills frequently symbolise kingdoms). This is no mere rhetoric. Micah realised that the covenant people were brought into their unique relation-ship with Jehovah so that through them the sovereignty of the true God, in its governmental administration among the nations, might be objectified to all peoples and for all time. Had Israel remained faithful she would have displayed the munificence of the Divine government. Alas, Israel exhibits a tragically different yet vastly significant aspect of the Divine government; and well may the nations of today heed it!

Note, too, the solemn yet glorious significance of the contrast which Micah strikes by *the unmasking of false rulership versus the unveiling of true rulership in Christ.* God delegates authority to human rulers. Micah recognises this fact in the Divine economy, and addresses the princes, priests, and prophets as the ordained representatives of the Divine administration. Their responsibility is commensurately great. See Micah's scathing indictment of false rulership in chapter iii. versus the arresting description of the *true "RULER,"* in chapter v., who was yet to come. Christ is God's ideal of rulership. Micah traces the perversion and adversity of the people to the misrule of those over them; and all who abuse such authority incur equal penalty. Let the rulers of today take heed!

Finally, we revert to Micah's *august declaration as to the true essence of religion.* A great scholar has said of Micah vi. 1-8: "These few verses in which Micah sets forth the true essence of religion may raise a well-founded title to be counted as the most important in the prophetic literature." Underline that eighth verse. Note that God "*REQUIRES*," for He is *God*. And God also *REVEALS*, for "He hath *showed* thee, O man, what is good . . ." (a reference to the Law of Moses: see Deut. x. 12). Yet even this is not enough. If we would know the full chord in the music we must turn on to the New Testament, and learn there that God *REDEEMS*. He "requires" because He is *God*. He "reveals" because He is *good*. He "redeems" because He is *love*. The Christ of God has been already to redeem. He will come again to restore. Meanwhile let us view all our life in the light of the Divine purposes and the future reappearance of the great "RULER" whose goings forth have been "from of old, even from everlasting."

THE PROPHET NAHUM
Lesson Number 97

NOTE.—For this study read right through the short prophecy of
Nahum three times, and then again in a modern translation
or the Revised Version.

Also, turn back again to our third study in Jonah and
re-read what is said there about the great city of Nineveh.

For all things exist only as seen by Thee, only as known by Thee.
All things exist
Only in Thy light, and Thy glory is declared even in that which
denies Thee; the darkness declares the glory of light.
Those who deny Thee could not deny, if Thou didst not exist; and
their denial is not complete, for if it were so, they would not exist.
They affirm Thee in living; all things affirm Thee in living.

T. S. Eliot.

THE BOOK OF NAHUM

As WE make our way through the writings of these Hebrew prophets, one thing must impress us ever more forcibly; these inspired men profoundly realised the sovereignty of God, especially in its governmental super-control of nations and history. This is vividly re-emphasised in Nahum's vehement oracle on the doom of Nineveh.

Of this prophet who tolls the knell over Nineveh practically nothing is known. He comes to us simply as "Nahum the Elko-shite"; that is, he was of Elkosh, a place which cannot now be located with certainty. It is surmised that he was of Galilee. His name is thought to have been preserved in the Galilæan city of Capernaum, the name of which (Kaphar-Nahum) means Village-of-Nahum. The present-day village of *El-Kauzeh*, which lies in the area long ago occupied by the tribe of Naphtali, is supposed by some to be the modern continuer of Elkosh. Nahum's reference to Carmel, Lebanon, and Bashan, also, is said to indicate special interest in the northern part of the Holy Land. If Nahum was indeed a man of Galilee, then it may be that when the Assyrian monarch, Esarhaddon, repeopled the northern province with a mongrel population, after the deportation of the ten tribes of Israel (2 Kings xvii. 5, 6), Nahum, with others of his disconsolate fellow-countrymen who had been left, evacuated to Judah. All this, however, lies in the realm of conjecture. This much is certain: Nahum *addresses Judah* (i. 13, 15); and the impression left on the reader's mind is that he also wrote *from* Judah.

The *date* of Nahum's writing seems settled by his reference, in chapter iii. 8, to the overthrow of No-Amon (not "populous" No, as in Authorised Version). No-Amon was the famous Egyptian city of Thebes, where the god, Amon, was worshipped; and it is now known, from discoveries in the Assyrian monuments, that the Assyrian monarch, Assurbanipal, overthrew that city in 665 or 664 B.C. Nahum wrote soon after that; and thus he follows Isaiah, in the reign of Judah's wickedest king, Manasseh.

Jehovah and Nineveh

Nahum's oracle is given to one subject alone—*the doom of Nineveh*, capital of Assyria, and (when Nahum wrote) the world's greatest city. It is noteworthy that *two* of the books among the so-called Minor Prophets are devoted wholly to Nineveh. Over a century before Nahum, Jonah had lifted up his voice for Jehovah in the great thoroughfares of Nineveh; and the Ninevites had learned through him that "Jehovah is slow to anger" (Jonah, iv. 2). Jonah would certainly preach this to the Ninevites, and it would strike a sharp contrast between Jehovah and the fierce-tempered deities of the Assyrians. To this strangely welcome compassion of Jehovah, uttered through His unique ambassador, the Ninevites had responded; but soon afterward they had presumed upon it, going to greater lengths of wickedness than ever before. They must now learn, therefore, through Nahum, that "Jehovah is a jealous God" (i. 2), jealous, that is, of His rights over His creatures. They must now learn that wrath restrained (as in Jonah's time) is wrath *reserved*, if there is wilful return to wickedness (i. 2). Nahum, so to speak, takes up where Jonah left off. Like Jonah, he says, "Jehovah is slow to anger" (i. 3), but he adds the other side of the truth—"and great in power, *and will not at all acquit the wicked.*"

These words in chapter i. 3 are, in fact, the *key* to this doom-song of Nahum, and they utter its message for all time—"*Jehovah will not acquit.*" The fact that *two* of the Minor Prophets are devoted to Nineveh emphasises its significance. This mighty metropolis of a bygone empire was meant to objectify for all peoples and for all time the governmental method of God with the Gentile nations. Let nations and peoples take heed! Let all who would presume upon the Divine patience and silence beware! Though God will forgive sin repented of, He will not condone sin persisted in. "God is not mocked," and there is no escaping Him; for, as Nahum goes on to say, "Jehovah hath His way in the whirlwind and in the storm, and the clouds are the dust of His feet . . ." (i. 3–6). Since the lesson of the past is lost on the Assyrians, Jehovah will now have His way with them even in the whirlwind and the storm. The righteous principles of His administration among the earth's peoples are unchanging. Compassion can never be exercised at the expense of righteousness. There must be a settling of accounts. Nineveh was the proudest and fiercest, as well as the vilest of cities. The surrounding peoples cringed at her feet. She swelled with pride in the imagination of her seeming invulnerability. But now, besides rebuking Nineveh's pride, oppression, idolatry, and defiance of the sovereign Jehovah, Nahum publishes the irreversible decree that she shall be forever destroyed. With Nineveh before our eyes, we may well say with Paul, "Behold, therefore, the goodness and severity of God"—His goodness through Jonah, and his severity through Nahum.

Let the peoples of today take a long, steady, thoughtful look at old-time Nineveh. She is one of God's special object-lessons to all rulers and nations. It is the same God who super-rules the world today. He is not one whit less severe than He was in Old Testament times, and He is not one whit more compassionate. He is just as uncompromising toward sin, just as compassionate toward the penitent, the same from age to age. The idea that the Gospel of Christ somehow tones down the severity in the Divine character is wrong. Certainly, the Gospel is the supreme *expression* of the Divine graciousness; but it does not in the slightest degree modify the inflexible principles of righteousness by which God governs nations. God has always been gracious. God has always been intolerant of wickedness. He is the same today. Unless we are strangely unseeing, the Anti-Nazi war demonstrated again how surely the hand of God still controls, to bring guilty nations to book. Let the modern leaders of Europe mark God's dealings with old-time Nineveh!

There is no need to give a detailed analysis of Nahum's prophecy if we get hold of its main movements. Practically throughout it is poetic in form, and it is poetry unsurpassed for power of description. It opens with a description of the attributes and operations of God, and runs in three strophes, answering to the three chapters in our English version. Chapter i. asserts the *certainty* of Nineveh's overthrow. Chapter ii. depicts the *siege and capture* of the city. Chapter iii. tells of the *wickedness* which provoked the retribution, ending with the words, "Upon whom hath not thy wickedness passed continually?" Thus—

Chapter i.—NINEVEH'S DOOM DECLARED.
    ,, ii.—NINEVEH'S DOOM DESCRIBED.
    ,, iii.—NINEVEH'S DOOM DESERVED.

Use a modern translation along with the Authorised Version. This will make the three movements clearer. For instance, in chapter i. 12, the words, "Though they be quiet" will become "Though they be very strong," which gives the true sense, namely, that though the Assyrians were very strong and very many, they should be cut down. Again, in chapter ii. 2, instead of "For the Lord hath turned away the excellency of Jacob," we shall read that the Lord "bringeth again" or "restoreth" the excellency of Jacob, which makes the verse at once intelligible and in keeping with the context. Verses 3 and 4 in chapter ii. describe the *attackers* of Nineveh. Verse 5 describes the enfeebled *defenders*. The words, "He shall recount his worthies" refer to Nineveh's king.

Nineveh's Vastness and Vileness

Beyond all doubt, Nineveh is one of the most remarkable cities in history. Recent discovery has shown that it was really a complex of four cities in one, making a vast quadrangle no less than sixty miles round. The walls were one hundred feet high, and so broad that three chariots could be driven abreast on them. These walls were fortified with fifteen hundred towers, each two hundred feet high. Based on a trigonometric survey, the full area has been computed as three hundred and fifty square miles— the area of modern London! Of course, greater Nineveh included spacious gardens, orchards, pastures, and grain fields. This need not surprise us. Babylonia's great walled towns enclosed large spaces for pasturage and produce so that in case of siege they were self-provided for. The reference, in Jonah iv. 11, to "much cattle" in Nineveh is therefore easily understandable. The mention, in that same verse, of "six score thousand persons that cannot discern between their right hand and their left hand," means that there were some hundred and twenty thousand infants there alone. From this it has been estimated that Nineveh's population in Jonah's time was about one million. It would be even more in Nahum's time.

But Nineveh's vastness was eclipsed by its *vileness*. The brutality of the Assyrians toward the victims of their conquests was such as to make the flesh creep. The surrounding peoples shuddered with a sickly horror at the thought of ever being prey to them. Their mania for blood and savagery was gruesome and foul (look back over our second lesson on Jonah). And Nahum now drags out to view the violence, murder, witchcraft, whoredom, and vile corruption *inside* the harlot city (iii. 1–7). The word of God to her is: "I will make thy grave, *for thou art vile*" (i. 14).

Nahum's Prophecy Fulfilled

The decisive test of prediction is fulfilment. One of the unanswerable arguments for the superhuman origin of the Bible is its amplitude of fulfilled prediction. Nahum's oracle on Nineveh is an impressive instance. His reference to "the gates of the rivers" being opened, and the palace "dissolved," in chapter ii. 6, is striking in view of what actually happened. Read the following abbreviated extract from an article on Nahum in the *Pulpit Commentary*.

"This prophecy, so precise and assured, was the result of no human prevision. When Nahum prophesied, Assyria was at the height of its prosperity. No enemy in its neighbourhood was left unsubdued; the distant Egypt had submitted to its arms; Phoenicia and Cyprus owned its sway; Judah paid annual tribute; commercial enterprise had drawn unto it the riches of all nations. No one at this epoch could have foreseen the speedy end of this prosperity. In fifty years the end came. On the death of Assurbanipal, matters began to assume a dangerous attitude. Egypt rose against its former conqueror; Babylon revolted; the Medes, now a powerful monarchy, prepared to attack Nineveh. The successor of Assurbanipal himself marched against the latter, sending Nabopolassar to recover Babylon. The Medes were defeated, and for a time driven back. Nabopolassar also was successful, and received as a reward for his services the title of King of Babylon. Here he managed affairs so skilfully, and strengthened himself so effectually, that after fifteen years he found himself able to throw off the Assyrian yoke. Nabopolassar made alliance with all the enemies of Assyria, and became the ruling spirit of a strong confederacy which comprised Medes and Persians, Egyptians, Armenians, and other nations, all animated with the fierce desire of revenging themselves on Assyria. About 612 B.C. the allied forces attacked Nineveh, but were repulsed with loss. Victory for some time hovered over the Assyrians; but the enemy, reinforced from Bactria, proved irresistible. The

Ninevites, fearing for their final safety, attempted to escape from the city. They were overtaken, and again shut up within their walls. Here they defended themselves for more than two years, when a circumstance against which no remedy availed laid them at the mercy of the besiegers. An unusually heavy flood of the Tigris carried away a large section of the huge rampart that surrounded the city. Through the gap thus formed the enemy forced their way within the walls and captured the place. The town was sacked, and a great number of the inhabitants were massacred. Thus fell Nineveh, 608 B.C., according to the prophecy of Nahum." So completely was Nineveh destroyed, we may add, that in the second century A.D. even the site of it had become uncertain. See, also, Ezekiel xxxii. 22, 23.

Parting Reflections

The name of the prophet Nahum means *Comfort*; and let us frankly agree that in Nahum's dirge there is very real comfort for the godly. It is the comfort of knowing that in the righteous government of God, the outrages of impenitent evil-doers against their fellow-humans are Divinely requited. The desire for revenge is not Christian; but the appeal that God Himself shall avenge outraged justice, and vindicate the right against impenitent evil-doers, is fully in accord with Christian principles. Note the fact that Nahum scarcely mentions his own nation. The reason for this is clear. He does not exult in Nineveh's downfall merely for Judah's sake, or for his own. Nineveh had sold whole peoples by her whoredoms and witchcrafts. Nahum voices the outraged conscience of mankind. Other than merely indulging revenge, he identifies himself with the government of God in its guarantee that such wrongs shall not go without redress.

Yes, there is comfort here. As we think of the outrages which are committed with apparent impunity against the godly, as we see how the wicked often flourish and gloatingly grind down the innocent, we find relief in Nahum's assurance that "Jehovah will not acquit." There is comfort for the godly in the very anger of God. Nineveh proclaims to us the final vindication of right against wrong; and therein is comfort. That, indeed, is what the elect cry for, day and night (Luke xviii. 7, 8; Rev. vi. 10, 11); and the Almighty has pledged Himself to avenge, in a day which is yet to be (Rom. xii. 19, etc.).

Again, Nineveh figures to us "this present evil world," in its outward display, its seeming security, its superficial response to God's message, its false religion, its inward corruption, its cruelty to the souls of men, and its eventual overthrow by Divine judgment. But there is another significant correspondence. In chapter i. 11, Nahum says to Nineveh: "There is one come out of thee that imagineth evil against Jehovah, a wicked counsellor (lit., a counsellor of Belial)." Possibly Nahum here harks back to Rab-shakeh, who, a few years earlier, had come from Assyria to terrify Jerusalem (2 Kings xviii.; xix.; Isa. xxxvi.). Rab-shakeh certainly was a "counsellor of Belial," a "man of sin" with a foul mouth speaking insolent things, and exalting the Assyrian sovereign above all gods, even above Jehovah Himself. He certainly adumbrated, if he did not actually typify, the "man of sin" who is to appear toward the end of the present age. Again and again, in the course of history, the world-spirit, the spirit of anti-Christ, has expressed itself with blatant concentration through some outstanding evil personality. A braggart instance was Hitler; and so again is Stalin. But there is yet to appear the Rab-shakeh whose number is 666, through whom the forces of evil will vent their culminating defiance of the true God and His Christ. It will then be as it was with Rab-shakeh and the suddenly death-smitten Assyrian host (Isa. xxxvii. 36); for it is written, in 2 Thessalonians ii. 8, "Then shall the lawless one be revealed, whom the Lord shall consume with the breath of His mouth, and shall destroy with the brightness of His coming." Yes, Nineveh is fallen, is fallen! Jehovah will not acquit! His government is righteous. He is the stronghold of the godly. Christ is His supreme pledge. Lo, He comes, and every eye shall see Him! Wrongs shall be righted. The valleys shall be exalted, and the mountains brought low. The dark shall be made light, and the crooked straight; and the kingdoms of this world shall yet become the kingdom of our God and His Christ.

We cannot emphasize too strongly that this doom-song on Nineveh is no mere human cry for revenge. If it had been, it would not have been worthy of a place in the canon of Scripture, and certainly would never have been included. Nahum does not even view Nineveh's coming destruction with patriotic gratification from the standpoint of his own nation and countrymen. The predicted requital is viewed solely from the requirements of Divine justice.

God Himself has implanted in our human nature a constitutional sense of right, of justice, of fair-play, of demand that the wicked, wanton, cruel hurter of souls does not finally "get away with it", even though he may not have hurt ourselves personally. We do not want any mere human revenge; but there is a sense of moral necessity in us which cries out that God Himself shall *avenge* such wrong. And when we read such a message as that of Nahum on such a monster of vileness and cruelty as old-time Nineveh, our innate sense of justice "amens" the Divine sentence. Read again our study on the Imprecatory Psalms; for this doom-oracle of Nahum casts further light on those psalms, as well as belonging to the same category.

That this prophecy of Nahum actually *is* a product of Divine inspiration, and not just a vehement thirst for human revenge, is made sure, of course, by the fact that it was fulfilled to the very letter. And in these days when monstrosities of wickedness terrorise the earth, on a scale never known before, when Christian and godly and innocent people in many lands suffer coldly calculated or brutally inflicted cruelties for the sake of upright principles, it is a thoroughly Christian attitude to pray for and to take refuge in the soon-coming final vengeance of God on the wicked, and His vindication of the upright.

THE PROPHET HABAKKUK

Lesson Number 98

NOTE.—For this study read right through the short prophecy of Habakkuk three times at one sitting, and then in a modern translation.

The heart is commonly reached, not through the reason, but through the imagination, by means of direct impressions, by the testimony of facts and events, by history, by description. Persons influence us, voices melt us, looks subdue us, deeds inflame us. Many a man will live and die upon a dogma; no man will be a martyr for a conclusion.

J. H. Newman.

Speak to Him then, for He hears,
    And spirit with spirit can meet;
Closer is He than breathing,
    And nearer than hands or feet.

Tennyson.

THE BOOK OF HABAKKUK

HUMAN personality is an endless study. No two minds react in exactly the same way. Each individual is unique. We are impressed by this again as we go through the writings of these Hebrew prophets. All of them are conscious of Divine inspiration, and give good evidence of it; yet their inspiration does not swamp their individuality, but leaves ample play for it. Each has his own distinguishing characteristics. Each makes his own distinctive contribution. Each stamps his own individuality on what he writes.

This, in particular, is true of the prophet Habakkuk. Unlike the other peophets, he does not address either his own countrymen or a foreign people: his speech is to God alone. Again, unlike the other prophets, he is not concerned so much with delivering a message as with solving a *problem*—a problem which vexed his own sensitive soul relating to Jehovah's government of the nations. The first part of this prophecy (i. and ii.) is a *colloquy* between Habakkuk and Jehovah. The remainder (iii.) is an exquisitely beautiful ode describing a majestic *theophany*, or visible coming of God to the earth. Both in the colloquy which it relates and in the theophany which it describes, this Book of Habakkuk is unique.

The focus of Habakkuk's problem and prophecy is *Babylon*. Of the enemies which afflicted the covenant people long ago, three were outstanding—the Edomites, the Assyrians, and the Chaldeans, or Babylonians. It was given to three of the Hebrew prophets specially to pronounce the doom of these three powers. The prophecy of Obadiah sealed the fate of Edom. The prophecy of Nahum tolled the knell over Assyria. The prophecy of Habakkuk dug the grave of Babylon.

This, of course, bears on the question of the *time* when Habakkuk wrote. Of Habakkuk himself we know no more than we do of Nahum, though conjectures are not lacking: but the time he wrote does not seem too difficult to settle within fairly clear limits. We are plainly told that it was when the Chaldeans were rising to power (i. 5–11). Now it was not until Nineveh had been destroyed that Babylon rose above the nations as the new dominating world-power, which fact at once suggests that Habakkuk wrote either a little while *before*, or, more probably, soon *after* the fall of Nineveh, in 608 B.C. The latter is supported by Habakkuk's omission of any reference to Nineveh, which suggests that all menace from Nineveh had now passed.

Years before Habakkuk, the prophet Isaiah had forewarned king Hezekiah that his treasures should be carried to Babylon, and his sons become eunuchs in the palace there (Isa. xxxix. 6, 7); but at that time it was Assyria which Judah feared; and it was only after the fall of Assyria, in Habakkuk's time, that the menace from Babylon became suddenly imminent. King Josiah of Judah was slain in battle just before Nineveh fell. When the Egyptians came up to join with the other allies against Nineveh, Josiah, who was vassal to Nineveh, went out to resist the Egyptians, but was killed at Megiddo (2 Kings xxiii. 28–30). Josiah's son Jehoahaz, reigned only three months, and was then carried captive to Egypt by Pharaoh-Necho of Egypt, who put Judah under tribute to Egypt, and made Josiah's *other* son, Eliakim, king of Judah, changing his name to *Jehoiakim* (2 Kings xxiii. 31–7). We conclude, therefore, that it was probably in Jehoiakim's reign that Habakkuk wrote, somewhere about 600 B.C., and we are confirmed in this by 2 Kings xxiv., which gives the reign of this Jehoiakim as the time when the Babylonians began their harassing of Judah which eventually culminated in Judah's seventy years' Babylonian servitude.

Thus Habakkuk, contemporary of Jeremiah, was a prophet of fateful days in Judah. The dark storm-clouds were massing over Jerusalem. Josiah, Judah's last good king, had been followed by Jehoiakim, the wicked king who burned Jeremiah's "roll" (Jer. xxxvi.). The last two or three decades had set in for Judah when Habakkuk took up his pen to write; and it was perhaps to Habakkuk that God first revealed *how near* the end was.

This prophecy of Habakkuk puts into words a struggle and triumph of faith which took place in the soul of the prophet himself. It begins with a sob, and ends with a song; and it is in the process from the one to the other that the little book discloses the heart of its meaning to us. There can be no mistaking the author's own *arrangement* of what he writes. There are three parts, corresponding to the three chapters of the book in our English version (except that perhaps the first verse of chapter ii. should go at the end of chapter i.). The first part (i.) begins: "The *burden* which Habakkuk the prophet did see." The second part (ii.) begins: "The Lord answered me and said, Write the *vision*, and make it plain upon tables, that he may run that readeth it ; for the *vision* is yet for an appointed time. . . ." The third part (iii.) begins: "A *prayer* of Habakkuk the prophet, upon Shigionoth " (i.e. set to a triumphal strain). So then, in these three parts we have—

Chapter i.—A "BURDEN."

„   ii.—A "VISION."

„   iii.—A "PRAYER."

A glance through the book again will show that these three titles truly represent the contents of the three parts. But let us now inspect the "burden" and the "vision" and the "prayer" a little more closely, to get a true understanding of them.

Chapter i.—A "Burden."

The prophet here is in an agony of perplexity. He is beset by a double enigma of the Divine providence, or, at any rate, what *seems* to be so. He sighs—

"O Lord, how long shall I cry, and Thou wilt not hear? I cry out unto Thee of violence, and Thou wilt not save! Why dost Thou show me iniquity, and look upon perverseness?" (*read verses 2 to 4*).

Habakkuk's problem was the silence, inactivity, and apparent unconcern of God. Violence abounded ; lawlessness was rife ; blatant evils defied all protest from God's prophets ; and God seemed to be doing nothing. But Habakkuk's problem on this score was cleared up by a special word from God—

"Behold ye among the nations, and regard, and wonder marvellously; for I work a work in your days which ye will not believe though it be told you. For, lo, I raise up the Chaldeans, that bitter and hasty nation; which march through the breadth of the earth, to possess dwelling-places that are not theirs" (*read verses 5 to 11*).

This, however, to the distraught Habakkuk, only solved the one problem by raising a still bigger one. Certainly the crushing requital coming to Judah was deserved; but why should God punish Judah by means of a people far more wicked and ruthless than the Jews themselves? The thought of this was a painful shock to Habakkuk. It seemed hard to reconcile with his belief in the righteousness of Jehovah's government over the nations of the earth. It was the same kind of problem which some of ourselves felt when Hitler wrought such havoc in Europe, struck France, bleeding, to the ground, and even seemed likely to wreak his evil will on Britain. We could understand that Britain, with other peoples, was being punished for her godless ways; but why should it be by the Nazis, the most brutal, immoral, and anti-Christian horde on earth?

Habakkuk's plaintive further appeal to God is given in verses 12 to 17, which should be read again in the Revised Version. What can Habakkuk do about it? After all, God is sovereign. It is no use beating one's head against a wall. Will God be gracious and give His servant some understanding of this matter? Habakkuk resolves to await God's word. He says: "I will stand upon my watch, and set me upon the tower, and will look forth to see what He will speak with me" (ii. 1).

Chapter ii.—A "Vision."

In this chapter we have the wonderful "vision" which God gave to Habakkuk; and here faith finds a solution, though not a solution in the *logical* sense, but a *spiritual* solution which is thoroughly intelligible to faith. The chapter should be read again with special regard to two great pledges which God gives, in verses 4 and 14. Verse 4 says: "Behold his soul (the Babylonian's) is puffed up; it is not upright in him; *but the just shall live by his faith.*" Verse 14 says: "*For the earth shall be filled with the knowledge of the glory of the Lord.*" If, then, in chapter i. we have a double problem, in chapter ii. we have a double pledge.

What is the meaning of these two assurances? Take the first of them—"*The just shall live by his faith.*" The words might almost seem to occur in a merely incidental way; yet in reality they are so significant that they are quoted no less than three times in the New Testament as a decisive factor in evangelical argument (see Rom. i 17; Gal. iii. 11; Heb. x. 38). It should be understood at once that the words look beyond the body to the *soul*. This is indicated by the earlier half of the sentence, in which God says of the proud Chaldean, "Behold, his *soul* is puffed up; it is not upright in him." That word "soul" betokens the deeper sense in which we are to read the remaining words of the sentence, namely, "the just shall live by his faith." The words look beyond the outward to the *inward*, beyond the merely physical to the *spiritual*, beyond the present to the *future*, beyond the intermediate and episodal to the *ultimate* and *eternal*. It is as though God said to Habakkuk: "Yes, your estimate of the Chaldean is quite right; his soul is all wrong; but though I use him to chastise My people, he himself shall be brought to woe in the end; and although in the present painful process the righteous suffer with (and by) the wicked, yet the righteous shall never perish in the end like the wicked, but shall live because of his faith, as will yet be seen, for the earth shall yet be filled with the knowledge of the glory of the Lord." The fact is that this word to Habakkuk is one of those prolific words of the Old Testament which must be read in the light of New Testament revelation if we are to grasp the full meaning. Those who by faith in the God of the Lord Jesus are justified, or made righteous, in Christ, *do* "live" by their faith, in the sense that they *receive* new spiritual life here and now, and *shall* live forever with Christ beyond the short years of mortality on earth.

As for the second pledge—"*For the earth shall (yet) be filled with the knowledge of the glory of the Lord*", that also must be read anew in New Testament light. Not yet have the words had fulfilment. They await the return of Christ. They look on to the Millennium. *Then* the meek shall inherit the earth, and the controversy of history be resolved in the final vindication of the right and true. God's word to Habakkuk is: "Though it tarry, *wait* for it; because it will surely come" (ii. 3). God has given supreme pledge in Christ that He is indeed working out great and gracious purposes for mankind. Habakkuk himself grasped something of this, and said, "Jehovah is in His holy temple; *let all the earth keep silence before Him*" (ii. 20).

Chapter iii.—A "Prayer."

This "prayer" of Habakkuk is really a sublime rhapsody of faith. It begins, however, with an appeal to God, to grant a gracious revival "in the midst of the years," before ever His ultimate purpose for history has worked out to its final fulfilment (iii. 2). Then, from verse 3 to verse 15 there is a glorying in Jehovah's mighty doings of the past, His coming forth for the emancipation of Israel, His marvels from the time of the Exodus onwards. There can be no doubt that Habakkuk here refers to these things; yet significantly enough he puts his verbs in the *future* tense, so that from the imagery of the Exodus and the journeying to Canaan there is a solemn picturing of a far greater coming of God to judgment which is yet to be. Thus, verse 3 should really read: "God *shall come* from Teman, and the Holy One from Mount Paran"; similarly the future tense in most of the verses. "Teman" and "Paran," we may just add, are the land of Edom, and the land between Edom and Egypt.

Finally, in verses 16 to 19, we have a postlude, in which faith soars on wings above all doubts and fears. It does the heart good to read such exulting words of assurance in days like these. Although the prophet had "trembled" at the coming judgment upon his own people (verse 16), he now speaks of himself as "I who shall *rest* in the day of tribulation." That is the more literal translation. Though he should be brought to utmost destitution, as in verse 17, yet, says he, "I will rejoice in Jehovah; I will joy in the God of my salvation" (verse 18). The literal is, "I will jump for joy in the Lord; I will spin round for delight in God." Here is the hilarity of faith!—joy at its best with circumstances at their worst! What a victory! May it be ours!

Such, then, is the Book of Habakkuk—in chapter i. a *"burden"*; in chapter ii. a *"vision"*; in chapter iii. a *"prayer."* In chapter i. we have a twofold *problem*; in chapter ii. a twofold *promise*; in chapter iii. a twofold *product*—praise for the past and confidence for the future. In chapter i. we have faith *sighing*; in chapter ii. faith *seeing*; in chapter iii. faith *singing*. Perhaps we cannot do better than set it out thus—

Ch. i. A "BURDEN": FAITH GRAPPLING WITH PROBLEM.

,, ii. A "VISION": FAITH GRASPING THE SOLUTION.

,, iii. A "PRAYER": FAITH GLORYING IN ASSURANCE.

The key verse to Habakkuk is chapter ii. 4—"The just shall live by his faith"; and around this truth precious lessons for faith are written. The living message of the little book is clear. Faith has still its problems. If Habakkuk's days seemed draped with dark enigmas, even more do our own. But this book tells us not to judge merely by the appearances of the hour. God has given us great promises, and is working out great purposes. He cannot tell us the whole in so many words; but He has revealed enough to make faith intelligent, and to give it scope for development.

There is also truth of high value for us in the *process* by which Habakkuk passed from his sob of doubt to his song of trust. First, he told his honest doubt to *God*, and not to any mere human "brains trust." If we would only do that instead of sighing abroad our doubts on *human* ears, what unrest we would escape! But second, Habakkuk resolved to *wait* on God. He said: "I will get to my watchtower. I will wait to see what it all means." Nor did God mock him. Nor does God ever mock such a man. We do not know how long Habakkuk waited; but we *do* know God answered him. Oh, if we would only give God time, so that He might prepare our minds for what He has to say! People say that God does not speak to men today as He did long ago. The truer statement is that men do not listen today as they did of old. To the man who waits, God does not remain silent. Thus, thirdly, Habakkuk broke through to joyous certitude and song. He had seen a vision. All was changed. When he had looked at circumstances he was in despair. When he waited and heard God speak he began to sing.

Finally, let us keep Habakkuk's golden hope before us, that the earth shall yet be filled with the glory of the Lord. The age is far spent. The final epoch hastens to us. The vision has tarried; but now it speeds to its full realisation. Christ is coming soon; the big events of our time are the solemn heralds of His return. God help us to wait with the patience of a true hope, to watch with the eye of a true faith, to work with the zeal of a true love— until He come!

> Oh, the golden dawn may be at hand
> Which dries the mourner's tears!
> War and woe shall be abolished and unknown!
> Men shall batter swords to plowshares,
> And to pruning hooks their spears,
> When the Lord returns in glory for His own!

THE PROPHET ZEPHANIAH

Lesson Number 99

NOTE.—For this study read the little Book of Zephaniah right through at least twice, and then in a modern translation.

One of the most characteristic and prominent features of the Bible, considered as a whole,—that which runs through it from beginning to end, and which distinguishes it at once from all other books, is that it subordinates everything to the idea of GOD. It is not without reason called the Book of God; and *would* be so, in a very intelligible sense, even if there were no God at all. From the first sentence to the last, HE is the great theme of it, the Alpha and Omega. Infinitely various as are its contents, this is the keynote which runs through the whole.

Henry Rogers.

THE BOOK OF ZEPHANIAH

IN INTRODUCING himself to us, Zephaniah gives his pedigree more fully than any other of the prophets. He is "Zephaniah, the son of Cushi, the son of Gedaliah, the son of Amariah, the son of Hizkiah" (i. 1). The reason for this lies in the last of these names, "Hizkiah," which should really be "Hezekiah" (as in the Revised Version). There does not seem to be any weighty reason for doubting that this Hezekiah was the godly *king* Hezekiah; and we can understand how a prophet like Zephaniah would be grateful to show his near descent from a king like Hezekiah. So then, Zephaniah is by distinction the prophet of royal descent. He is a prince of the house of David, and the great-great-grandson of king Hezekiah.

Zephaniah also tells us *when* he prophesied. It was "in the days of Josiah, the son of Amon, king of Judah" (i. 1). This carries with it the information that he was a contemporary of the prophet Jeremiah (see Jer. i. 2); though, of course, Jeremiah would outlive him. We can well appreciate that king Josiah, in his noble religious reforms, would have the ardent backing of his prophet-cousin; and, without reading too much between the lines, it may be that much of the urge toward these reforms came from Zephaniah, who would have the intimate influence of a relative in the royal house.

There is something pathetic, however, about the religious reform in the days of King Josiah. Outwardly it was impressive perhaps, but inwardly it was far from what was needed. It was an outward reformation sponsored by the king, rather than a real spiritual revival among the people themselves. Read again 2 Kings xxii.–xxiii. and 2 Chronicles xxxiv.–xxxv., noting particularly the words of prophetess Huldah to Josiah, in 2 Kings xxii. 15–20. In effect, the prophetess said: "Yes, king Josiah, do all that is in your mind; it is good: but the heart of this people is become gross; there will not be a real heart-turning to God such as would avert judgment." Certainly Josiah's clean-up of Judah's religious abuses, and his reorganising of religion on the older lines, gave a grand royal lead; but even a king cannot "organise" a real revival; and the movement in Josiah's time was reformation as distinct from regeneration. It did not get down to the undercurrents of the nation's life. This is made clear by Jeremiah iii. 6, 10. The stream of iniquity flowed on unstemmed. Judgment was unavoidable, though the storm was not unleashed until good king Josiah's reign was over.

We are not greatly surprised, therefore, that our prophet Zephaniah does not make mention of these outward reforms. His perceiving eye left him in no doubt as to the real state of the nation's life. He exposes the transgressions and pollutions of his days, and with a stern vehemence warns his people that the "Day of Jehovah" hastes toward them, with its tornado of Divine wrath. The two prophets Joel and Zephaniah are in an emphatic way the prophets of judgment against Judah; yet both of them, having delivered their message of judgment, foretell a glorious aftermath. The final passage from Zephaniah's pen is one of the most beautiful in the Scriptures. It looks on to that promised age which is yet to be, when Israel's Messiah, the Church's Divine Husband, shall hold empire over all the earth.

Zephaniah's Threefold Message

Let us now look through the book, to find its main movements, and to get at its central message. If we read carefully we soon see that what Zephaniah has to say falls into three parts, though these three parts, unfortunately, do not coincide with the three chapters into which the book is arranged in our English version.

Part one runs from chapter i. 1 (or, strictly, from i. 2) to chapter ii. 3. A glance through these verses will show us at once that everything here refers to the judgment that is coming on *Judah* (see specially i. 4, 7, 8, 11, 12; ii. 1; and note that "Maktesh" in i. 11 was a depression, or small valley, in Jerusalem where the bazaars were). In all this run of verses there is no mention of the outside nations. The one theme is the sin and coming judgment of *Judah*. Note the one grimly significant *"because"* in chapter i. 17. Why is all the terrible calamity which is described in the foregoing verses coming on Judah? Verse 17 gives the simple, fundamental, awful answer—"Because they have sinned against Jehovah." And note, also, that this part of the book ends with an appeal for repentance, and an encouraging word to the little company of upright ones among the degraded populace (ii. 1–3).

Part two runs from chapter ii. 4 to chapter iii. 8. There can be no mistaking it—in this part the prophet looks away from Jerusalem and Judah to *the surrounding nations.* First he turns west, to Philistia and the Philistines (ii. 4–7). Then he turns east, to Moab and Ammon (ii. 8–11). Then he turns south, to Ethiopia (ii. 12). Then he turns north, to Nineveh and Assyria (ii. 13–15). Note that this part concludes with a sudden turning round on Jerusalem again, the point being that if God so smites the surrounding nations with judgment, how certainly will he smite the people of Judah who have had privileges above all others! That this is the point of this wind-up to part two is clear from the last three verses in it—"I have cut off the nations; their towers are desolate; I made their streets waste, that none passeth by; their cities are destroyed, so that there is no man, that there is none inhabitant. I said, Surely (in view of all this) thou (Jerusalem) wilt fear Me, thou wilt receive instruction . . . but they rose early and corrupted all their doings. . . . Therefore . . . I rise to the prey" (iii. 6–8).

Part three runs from chapter iii. 9 down to verse 20, which is the last verse of the chapter and of the book. Here the prophet is not just looking *within*, at Jerusalem and Judah, nor looking *around*, at the other nations; he is looking *beyond*, to a time of healing and blessing which shall come to Israel and to all peoples alike, after the days of judgment have served their purpose. The passage begins: "For then will I turn to the *peoples* (not singular, as in the Authorised Version, but plural, as in the Revised) a pure language, that they may *all* call upon the name of Jehovah, to serve Him with one consent." In this the vision of Zephaniah is like that of other prophets. The coming Messianic kingdom is to embrace all the nations. Yet the covenant people are to be the centre of that kingdom; and therefore Zephaniah concludes by picturing the exalted blessings of Israel in that golden age. There is to be a regathering of the dispersed (verse 10). There is to be a changed temper and behaviour in the people (verses 11–13). There is to be complete banishment of evil, and an exulting joyousness (verses 14, 15). God Himself is going to find utter pleasure in the Holy City and her people; it shall be said to Zion: "Jehovah, thy God, is in the midst of thee, the Mighty One who will save; He will rejoice over thee with joy; He will rest in His love; He will joy over thee with singing" (verses 16, 17). All afflictions are to be forever over, and Israel is to be made "a praise among all the peoples of the earth" (verse 20). It is a delectable picture indeed, and sets our longing hearts praying the more fervently: "Even so, come, Lord Jesus" (Rev. xxii. 20).

For memory's sake let us now set all this out in flat analysis. There is really no need for any more elaborate analysis than that which here follows.

THE BOOK OF ZEPHANIAH

Through Judgment to Blessing

LOOK WITHIN!—WRATH COMING ON JUDAH (i. 1–ii. 3).

THE PURPOSE OF JEHOVAH TO JUDGE (1–6).
THE "DAY" OF JEHOVAH "AT HAND" (7–18).
And so—plea to Jerusalem (ii. 1–3).

LOOK AROUND!—WRATH ON ALL NATIONS (ii. 4–iii. 8).

WEST, EAST—PHILISTIA, MOAB, AMMON (4–11).
SOUTH, NORTH—ETHIOPIA AND ASSYRIA (12–15)
And so—"Woe" to Jerusalem (iii. 1–8).

LOOK BEYOND!—AFTER WRATH, HEALING (iii. 9–20).

CONVERSION OF GENTILE PEOPLES (9).
RESTORING OF COVENANT PEOPLE (10–15).
And so—the new Jerusalem (verses 16–20).

The key thought in Zephaniah is not expressed so much in any one verse as in the *contrast* between the very first verse and the very last. After the super-scription, the first word is, "*I will utterly consume.*" This is the fierce fire of judgment. But the last word of the book is, "*I will make you a name and a praise.*" This is the final fulness of blessing.

God has a glorious end and purpose in view; but even that golden goal must not be gained at the expense of absolute justice and righteousness in the present; and therefore present sin must be equated by present judgment. Yet, even so, the ultimate purpose shall be realised; for the sovereign Jehovah so over-rules, that, however grievously His people sin, and however grievously He must punish, the present process of judgment shall eventually issue in the final blessing. This is what we have in Zephaniah. There must be the smiting with retribution before there can be the smiling of restoration. Thus we may say that the key thought of Zephaniah is, *"THROUGH JUDGMENT TO BLESSING."* Closely allied with this is the thought that "Jehovah is in the midst." He is in the midst of Jerusalem to *judge* (iii. 5); and He is in the midst of Jerusalem to *save* (iii. 15, 17). Well may we sing—

" And though His arm is strong to smite,
'Tis also strong to save."

Big Meanings

This prophecy of Zephaniah is loaded with big meanings for us today. Here was a man who had the mind of God on the national and international situation when few others, if any, had taken the measure of it or sensed the gravity of it; and he declared it even though it was severely unpopular. This is ever the mark of the true prophet. This man saw beneath the sudden new burst of religious activity, and judged it for what it was really worth. He looked out also on that larger crowd of the populace, the irreligious lot, who simply nodded an artificial respect for the new stir of Jehovah-worship because the king was chief patron, but who said among themselves that these religious ideas were now played out, that "Jehovah will not do good, neither will He do evil" (i. 12), or, in other words, that Jehovah just didn't bother and didn't matter—Zephaniah looked out on these and saw the tragic farce of their unconcern: he had heard the sickening thud and rumble of a coming judgment which would crush the nation to pieces: he knew that soon there would be upon them the biggest calamity since Israel had become a nation. Zephaniah was the man who knew; and he cried to his countrymen, "The Day of Jehovah is at hand!" (i. 7). This is his great theme, especially in the first part of his prophecy (i. 1–ii. 3).

If we mistake not, there is a correspondence between Zephaniah's day and our own. We are far from claiming to be prophets in the sense that Zephaniah and his compeers were; yet in another sense we shall not shrink from holding that we are truly the Lord's spokesmen. If we do not have the special kind of inspiration by which God spoke through the Hebrew prophets, that is not now needed, since "the volume of the Book" is now completed for our guidance; but we *do* claim to have the illumination of the Holy Spirit, and we *do* claim to be honestly interpreting the word of Scripture, in declaring our conviction that the time is once more here when we must lift up our cry that "The Day of the Lord is at hand!" Zephaniah's fervid depicting of "The Day of Jehovah"—the awful judgment which was determined on his own generation, is really an adumbration of that all-eclipsing "Day of the Lord" which is to be at the end of the present age; and unless we are strangely deceived, the words of the Book, together with the signs of the times, point to its near approach. The religious and social conditions are morally similar to those of Zephaniah's days. Despite the new bursts of religious activity, in movements such as the Anglo-Catholic and other ritualistic groups, and the strong passion for conferences on denominational reunion, the spiritual condition of the churches and the people is worse than at any time since just before the Methodist revival. Modernism has done its deadly work through its "fifth-columnists" in the pulpits and schools of our land; and the gulf between organised religion and the masses grows steadily wider. We fix no dates. We give no limit of years. We simply keep to the clear words of the Book and the big indications of our time. We are surely in that period now which is to move up quickly to the august, awful day of Christ's return.

That day will be joy superlative for Christ's own, the blood-bought, Spirit-born members of the true Church; but it is well that we should cry aloud the *terror* of that day to many others. This is the aspect of it which grips and excites Zephaniah. Mark his phrases as he struggles to impress his lethargic fellow-countrymen with the dread of it: "That day is a day of wrath, a day of trouble and distress, a day of wasteness and desolation, a day of darkness and gloominess, a day of clouds and thick darkness, a day of the trumpet and alarm against the fenced cities and against the high towers" (i. 15, 16). The "day of Jehovah" which came upon Judah long ago was all that Zephaniah had foretold; and if that day, then, was meant to adumbrate the supreme "day" which is yet to be, in which all God's earth-judgments will have their awful culmination, then that coming day is one that should cause all who refuse the Gospel of Christ, and all who live impenitently in sin, to tremble with fear. In recent days we have seen the horrors which men can inflict on their fellow-men by the weapons of modern warfare; but what are these compared with the terrors of the Almighty upon the wicked? What will it be when the seven trumpets of the Apocalypse are sounded, and the seven vials of the Divine wrath are poured out, and the blazing fury of Armageddon breaks loose! Well may we cry to the careless, unawakened sinners around us, "Flee from the wrath to come! Flee from the wrath to come!" The popular attitude today is exactly that of Zephaniah's time —"The Lord will not do good, neither will He do evil," that is, God doesn't act in human affairs: He neither blesses nor punishes: the world is governed by "natural laws," and God doesn't inter-fere with these laws to give supposed answers to prayers. God's existence is remotely admitted; but His interest and activity in human affairs is denied. That "day" which is soon coming will heap burning coals on the tongues of those who thus dis-honour God.

Finally, let us learn the threefold truth that God permits, but punishes, and in the end perfects. Men are free agents. God allows enough freedom to the human will for any man to know at any time that he is thinking and speaking and choosing and acting of his own volition. Thus God *permits* sin—and suffering. If God were to intervene every time the innocent are made to suffer by the wicked there would be no history at all. But God *punishes* the wicked—usually by overruling natural processes, and not by miracles. Thus, he allows Israel to be punished through the agency of wicked nations; but in turn He punishes these nations for their own wrongs. In this process the innocent often suffer; but God has pledged a final restitution; and He has pointed us to a time when the present darkness shall give way before a sorrowless daybreak, and the present travail shall be forgotten in the tender triumph of love and virtue. The faith of many has been shaken by the recently permitted cruelties of war. Why should such suffering be allowed? God has overruled the natural processes of human sin to bring judgment on wicked nations, and the innocent again have suffered with the wicked; but the age is far spent, and the longed-for dawn is about to bring in that better time. Smiting will give place to smiling. The peoples shall serve the Lord "with one consent." God will *perfect* His purpose, and fulfil all His promises. Christ shall reign. The curse shall be gone. God will rejoice over His redeemed sons and daughters. He will rest in His love. He will "joy over them with singing."

THREE QUESTIONS EACH ON
MICAH, NAHUM, HABAKKUK, AND ZEPHANIAH

1. In what reigns did Micah prophesy? And what was the name of his great prophet contemporary?

2. How were Micah and his ministry different from Isaiah and his ministry?

3. What is the threefold arrangement of the Book of Micah, and what the central thought?

4. What is the subject of Nahum's prophecy? What is the key verse? What contrastive offset to the Book of Jonah do we see in it?

5. What is the threefold division of the prophecy of Nahum?

6. Could you show, briefly, how Nahum's prophecy was strikingly fulfilled?

7. Which city is the focus of Habakkuk's prophecy? How does his referring to that city help fix the date of his prophesying?

8. What is the threefold division of Habakkuk's prophecy? What, briefly, was his problem?

9. What great text in Habakkuk is quoted three times in the New Testament? And how did Habakkuk pass from his sob of doubt to faith?

10. Of which king was Zephaniah the great-great-grandson? And in which king's reign did he prophesy?

11. To which kingdom (Judah or Israel?) did Zephaniah prophesy? And who was his famous prophet contemporary?

12. Can you give the key thought of Zephaniah's prophecy, and a brief outline of the little book?

THE PROPHET HAGGAI

Lesson Number 100

NOTE.—For this study read Haggai's short prophecy through three times, and then in a modern rendering.

These are Thy glorious works, Parent of good,
Almighty! Thine this universal frame,
Thus wondrous fair: Thyself how wondrous then.
Unspeakable! Who sitteth above these heavens
To us invisible, or dimly seen
In these Thy lowest works; yet these declare
Thy goodness beyond thought, and power Divine . . .
On Earth join, all ye creatures to extol
Him first, Him last, Him midst, and without end.

John Milton.

THE BOOK OF HAGGAI

THIS "Book of Haggai" is really a momentous little fragment. Although it covers a period merely of about four months, it puts on record one of the crucial turning-points of the Divine dealings with Jerusalem and the covenant people. It has to do with the Jewish "Remnant" who returned to Jerusalem and Judæa after the Babylonian exile, and should be read along with the Book of Ezra.

It was in 520 B.C. that this otherwise unknown prophet Haggai stood forth and voiced his message to the leaders of the returned Jews. Sixteen years before this, the Persian emperor, Cyrus, had issued his historic decree for the rebuilding of Jehovah's temple at Jerusalem; and the "Remnant," numbering some fifty thousand, had returned to Judæa, under the leadership of Zerubbabel, to implement the royal proclamation (Ezra i. and ii.). Two years later the foundation of the temple had been laid, amid mingled praises and tears (Ezra iii. 8–13), and the prospects for the rebuilding had seemed bright.

But now, in 520 B.C., circumstances were gloomily otherwise. Adversaries, from the mongrel race of the Samaritans, had "hired counsellors" to misrepresent the cause of the Jews all through the reign of Cyrus; and at the accession of his successor, Artaxerxes, they had managed to bring about a complete suspension of the project (Ezra iv.). Fourteen years had now dragged by; the temple remained unbuilt, and the foundations were silted with debris and overgrown with weeds.

The repatriated Jews seem to have accepted the situation with an almost fatalistic resignation. This was the result, so it would appear, at least in part, of a wrong reaction to prophecy. Jeremiah had predicted a seventy years' period of "desolations" on Jerusalem (Jer. xxv.). We find this later exercising the mind of Daniel (Dan. ix. 1, 2), and mentioned again by Zechariah (Zech. i. 12). The Jews of the returned "Remnant" seem to have mistakenly inferred (despite God's sign to them by the edict of Cyrus) that even the *temple* could not be rebuilt until the period of the "desolations" on the city had run its course. It is this which the prophet has in mind in his very first words—"This people say, *The time is not come, the time that Jehovah's house should be built*" (i. 2). They were paralysed by a wrong attitude to prophecy. We shall touch on this again later.

Now the pivotal significance of Haggai lies in the fact that this very year in which he uttered his fourfold prophecy, 520 B.C., was *the year which ended the period of the "desolations" and introduced a new period of Divine blessing.* Whether the Jewish leaders, or even Haggai himself, understood this clearly is another matter; but in actual fact it was so, as is made very plain in the word of God. Through the lips of the inspired Haggai, the Spirit of God has marked and emphasised the point of transition, to the very month, and even to the very day. Turn to chapter ii. 15–19, and note the deliberate stress on the words—

"*Consider from this day and upward, from before a stone was laid upon a stone in the temple of the Lord . . . consider now from this day and upward, from the four and twentieth day of the ninth month, even from the day that the foundation of the Lord's temple was laid, consider it . . . from this day will I bless you.*"

Could language be more definite? But even so, how do we *know* that this underscored date ended the period of the desolations? The answer is most interesting. Turn back to Ezekiel xxiv. 1, 2. Here we find another date made equally conspicuous by a similarly significant emphasis—

"*Again, in the ninth year, in the tenth month, in the tenth day of the month, the word of the Lord came unto me, saying: Son of man, write the name of the day, even of this selfsame day. The king of Babylon hath set himself against (i.e. hath besieged) Jerusalem this selfsame day*" (see R.V.).

This tenth day of the tenth month in the ninth year of Ezekiel's captivity in Babylonia, is also clearly given in 2 Kings xxv. 1, as the day when the siege began. This is the first time in the historical books that an event is dated to the very day. The same exact date is also given in Jeremiah lii. 4. At the very hour when the Babylonian army was in the act of surrounding the Jewish capital, the fact of it was revealed of God to the prophet Ezekiel, hundreds of miles away in Babylonia, where, at this time, he had already been in exile since Nebuchadnezzar's earlier deportation of Jewish captives, recorded in 2 Kings xxiv. 11–16. This day, then, which marked the investing of Jerusalem, Ezekiel is told to write down emphatically for observation and preservation—the tenth day of the month Tebeth, 589 B.C. This day has been observed as an annual fast by the Jews ever since. It was this day, the tenth of Tebeth, 590 B.C., which marked the *beginning* of the seventy years' period of the "desolations." The momentous fact to grasp is that from this date down to the date emphasised by Haggai, namely, the twenty-fourth day of the month Chisleu, 520 B.C., was a stretch of 25,200 days, that is, exactly *seventy years of 360 days each.*

That the prophetic year in Scripture is one of 360 days is abundantly shown (see our preceding article, on Daniel's prophecy of the "seventy weeks"). Thus, as we have said, Haggai puts on record for us a *transition-point* in the Divine dealings with Jerusalem.

There are *two* seventy years' periods predicted by the prophet Jeremiah which should not be confused. The one is the seventy years' *servitude* to Babylon ; the other is the period of the "*desolations.*" The servitude to Babylon began with Jehoiakim's submission to Nebuchadnezzar, in 606 B.C., and ended with the proclamation of Cyrus, in 536 B.C., freeing the Jews to return to their own land. This seventy years' servitude is spoken of in Jeremiah xxix. 10, where, unfortunately, our Authorised Version misleads the reader by putting "*at* Babylon" instead of "*for* Babylon." In the Revised Version the verse reads: "Thus saith the Lord: After seventy years be accomplished *for* Babylon, I will visit you, and perform My good word toward you, in causing you to return to this place." Jeremiah nowhere predicts that the Jews would be *at* Babylon for seventy years; but he *does* say that God had appointed a seventy years' period *for* Babylon, as ruler over the nations, during which period Jerusalem and Judæa, with the other Palestinian peoples, should be in *servitude* to Babylon.

But *besides* this seventy years of servitude, Jeremiah foretells an epoch of actual *"desolations"* which would come upon Jerusalem and Judæa as a consequence of further impenitence (Jer. xxv. 9–11); and both Daniel and Zechariah understand this as being for seventy years (Dan. ix. 1, 2; Zech. i. 12). This, we repeat, was the period which ended with the prophecy of Haggai on the 24th Chisleu, 520 B.C. The last deep shadow of that night slinks away. A new sun has risen. Here is a word of new hope, heralding good things to come. This is Jehovah's announcement—*"FROM THIS DAY WILL I BLESS YOU."* Let us get this significant turning-point clearly in mind, for it is the crux of Haggai's message.

Perhaps it scarcely needs pointing out that this little scroll from the hand of Haggai is in four parts. Four times within four months in that notable "second year of Darius," 520 B.C., the "word of Jehovah" came through the lips of this prophet. Each of the four communications is carefully dated, and each has its own clear focus-point; so that we may set the whole down thus—

THE BOOK OF HAGGAI

"From this Day I will Bless You."

FIRST MESSAGE—TO AROUSE (i. 1–15).

Date—Sixth month, first day.
Crux—"Build the House" (verse 8).

SECOND MESSAGE—TO SUPPORT (ii. 1–9).

Date—Seventh month, 21st day.
Crux—"I am with you" (verse 4).

THIRD MESSAGE—TO CONFIRM (ii. 10–19).

Date—Ninth month, twenty-fourth day.
Crux—"From *this* day will I bless you."

FOURTH MESSAGE—TO ASSURE (ii. 20–3).

Date—Ninth month, twenty-fourth day.
Crux—"In *that* day I will make thee . . .".

The Four-fold Message

Let us now briefly consider this four-fold message of Haggai. In his *first* address (i.) his purpose is to reprove the people for their neglect, and to arouse them to immediate action. They were presuming on prophecy, and saying, "The time is not come, the time that the Lord's house should be built." Whatever semblance of reason there may have been in this at first, there is no doubt that it had degenerated into a mere excuse for negligence of religious duty and for the pursuance of selfish interests. "Consider your ways!" cries the prophet. "Is it 'time' for you (you who say the 'time' is not come)—is it 'time' for *you* to dwell in *your* ceiled houses (expensive and embellished houses), while *this* House (of Jehovah) lies waste?" (verse 4).

This reproof through the lips of Haggai has a relevance to our own day. There are those among us today who presume on prophecy, and say, "The time is not come." They mislead or excuse themselves into inactivity on this plea, when they ought to be spending themselves in the effort to win our present generation for Christ. There is a right attitude and there is a wrong attitude to prophecy. We need ever to remember that although inspired prediction is infallible, our own interpretation of it is *not* infallible. The mistake of the returned Jewish exiles is a case in point. We should learn from it. Instead of proving a tonic to them, prophecy had become a narcotic. They had given way to a feeling that there was a hopeless inevitability in things. Present effort was of no use; they must just wait until the clock of prophecy struck the predestined hour. The result was indifference; and the cause of God suffered. The people were getting used to being without a temple; and this would have proved fatal.

We need to be ever on our guard against this attitude. This was the attitude of gruff old Dr. Ryland of Northampton when he overrode young William Carey with the rejoinder, "Young man, sit down. When God pleases to convert the heathen, He'll do it without your aid or mine." This is the attitude of those today who say, "There's no use hoping for any great revival of Christianity today. The Word of God does not foretell any such great revival toward the end of the present age. Things are just to go from bad to worse until Christ returns." What a paralysing idea this is! It is enough, apart from anything else, to cut the nerve of prayer and effort. Yet what stupid presuming this is! What of the glorious revivals which have swept through our land in the past? Can we put our finger on chapter and verse in the Bible where any one of them is foretold? Where is there any chapter or verse which says that there *cannot* or *will not* be another great ingathering of souls before Christ returns? "Consider your ways," says Haggai. "Go up . . . and build the House." We must not let any such presuming on prophecy paralyse endeavour for Christ.

Some time ago a number of evangelical ministers met in conference, to discuss the possibility of a co-ordinated nation-wide evangelistic effort. Their hearts were heavy because of the deplorable moral and spiritual condition of the country. There were several sessions, at each of which one of the brethren gave an address on some aspect of the subject. There was a marked unanimity of outlook, until the final session, when the introductory speaker pressed the view that all such human organising was really to little purpose unless *God's* predestined time had come to take action, and that when God *did* take action He usually did it independently of human organising. This occasioned a good deal of warm discussion; but eventually the conference voiced its united conviction that *while regeneration and revival are the sovereign act of God, evangelism is the constant obligation of the Church*. It is well always to remember that. The fallacy of the last speaker at that conference was that he was making antitheses of two things which are not antithetic. The Divine sovereignty and human endeavour are not mutually exclusive; they are meant to be co-operative. It is not a case of "either . . . or. . . ." It is not a case of *either* "waiting on God" *or* "working for revival"; it must be the two together—"waiting" *and* "working." It is not a choice between agonising in prayer or organising an effort. Agonising and organising are to go together. We must never allow the truth of the Divine sovereignty or the fact of Scripture prophecy to dull our perception of human responsibility. This great fact, perhaps more than any other, is brought home to us today by this prophecy of Haggai.

Haggai's *second* message is a striking one. Its purpose was to encourage. Some of the older Jews who remembered the former temple were downcast at the contrast between it and that which was now being built. Haggai therefore heartens them by a declaring of three great facts. First, Jehovah's covenant with Israel still stands, and Jehovah's faithfulness thereto continues (verse 5); second, the Spirit of God still remains among them (verse 5); third, God's promise is that there shall yet be a great shaking, that One shall come who is the Desire of all nations, and that "the glory of this latter House shall be greater than of the former" (verses 6–9). These are the three great things, also, which must ever inspire *ourselves*—the covenant, the Spirit's presence, the promised return of the King. A shaking—an advent—a glory-filled temple; this is the landscape of promise. See Hebrews xii. 26, 27 for a striking comment on this part of Haggai.

We have already mentioned the significance of Haggai's *third* message, on the twenty-fourth day of the month Chisleu. The people had expected a return of material prosperity from the very first day that they had responded to Haggai and recommenced work on the temple, three months earlier (i. 15); but Haggai now points out that they certainly must not view their renewed work on the temple as giving them a pious merit which, so to speak, put God under obligation to them. Nay, it was far otherwise. If a person ceremonially unclean touched some article, that article also became defiled (ii. 11–14), and so, in reality, was it with themselves. Other than having special merit, they were defiled; and it was grace on God's part to accept them. Yet now, none the less, God *would* give them a special sign of His favour, for *from this day* onwards He would bless them (verses 15–19).

The *fourth* message is to Zerubbabel himself, the leader of the returned Jews; and yet, quite evidently, it looks far beyond him to the ultimate consummation of the Davidic line in the coming reign of Christ. It should be clearly grasped that Zerubbabel is here addressed as the *representative* of the Davidic line. Once more God speaks of the great shaking which is to come, but adds that "in THAT DAY" Zerubbabel shall be "*as a signet*" (the sign of authority). It is peculiarly noteworthy that this figure of the signet should be used here of Zerubbabel, for it was used of his grandfather, king Jeconiah, in a tragic way, to express God's rejection of him—"As I live, saith the Lord, though Coniah (Jeconiah) the son of Jehoiakim King of Judah were the signet upon my right hand, yet would I pluck thee thence" (Jer. xxii.

24). In the last great victory of the Divine purpose, Christ, the greater Son and wonderful Antitype of David and Zerubbabel, will be Jehovah's signet whereby He shall impress and imprint upon all nations His own majesty, His own will and ways, His own perfect ideal, and His own very image.

THE PROPHET ZECHARIAH (1)

Lesson Number 101

NOTE.—For this study read the whole Book of Zechariah through at one sitting. Then read the first eight chapters again twice, using the Revised Version.

Hebrew prophecy will be acknowledged by most to be a perfectly unique phenomenon in the history of religions. Whatever the etymology of the name (*Nabi*) the prophet himself stands clearly out as one who is conscious of receiving a message directly from Jehovah, which he is commissioned to impart to men. . . . It was certainly an error of the older apologetic to place the essence of prophecy, as was often done, in prediction. The prophet was in the first instance a man speaking to his own time. . . . It must be put to the account of modern criticism that it has done much to foster this better way of regarding prophecy, and has in consequence greatly vivified the study of the prophetic writings, and promoted a better understanding of their meaning. On the other hand, the modern view, in its desire to assimilate prophecy as much as possible to the utterances of natural human genius, does palpable violence to Scriptural teaching in denying, or making light of, this element of prediction.

James Orr, D.D.

THE BOOK OF ZECHARIAH (I)

AFTER the short, forthright message of Haggai, this Book of Zechariah may seem discouragingly complicated; yet it is not so in reality, as we shall see. To an observant reader it quickly sorts itself out; and it is full of good things. Zechariah was contemporary with Haggai (Ezra v. I). The prophecies of the two men relate primarily to the same point of history, which, as we have seen in our study of Haggai, was a *turning-point* in the Divine dealings with Jerusalem and the covenant nation. If we have really grasped the crucial significance of that emphatic key-word in Haggai—"*From this day will I bless you*" (ii. 15-19), we shall not be long in getting to the crux of Zechariah's message; for these prophecies of Zechariah take up from this same point, supplementing, developing, and amplifying the message of Haggai. So really is this true, in fact, that the little scroll of Haggai might almost be an *introduction* to this larger work from the pen of Zechariah.

Zechariah both priest and prophet.

With Zechariah, then, as with Haggai, we begin in the year 520 B.C., in "the second year of Darius" of the Medo-Persian empire (i. I), and we are among the fifty thousand or more of the Jewish "Remnant" who have returned (sixteen years earlier) from their Babylonian exile, to repeople and rebuild Judæa and Jerusalem. These two men, Haggai and Zechariah, have been raised up of God, and inspired to animate the flagging zeal of the Jewish leaders and people. Zechariah was both a priest and a prophet. He was "the son of Berechiah, the son of Iddo" (i. I). This Iddo was one of the priests who returned from Babylon with Zerubbabel and Jeshua (Neh. xii. 4). This means that Zechariah was of the family of Aaron. We are told that he exercised his sacerdotal office in the days of Joiakim, the son of Jeshua (Neh. xii. 12, 16).

There was a special suitability that the ministry of both prophet and priest should be united in the one person at that juncture.

Only too often in earlier years had prophets been obliged to stand in sharp antagonism to the priests. When the priest was a mere formalist, and callous to the inner meaning of the holy rites which he administered, the prophet had needed to recall the minds of his countrymen to the vital truths enshrined in the outward ritual. Zechariah united in himself all the sacerdotal traditions of the Aaronic priesthood with the zeal and authority of the prophet. Nothing could have been more timely than that the one voice should have this double appeal. Nothing was more fitted to hearten the people amid discouraging setbacks, and at the same time to arouse them from their apathetic dilatoriness in the rebuilding of the Lord's House.

It is worthy of note that from this time the priesthood takes the lead in the nation. As to government, the history of the covenant people falls into three main periods. First, from Moses to Samuel we have Israel under the *Judges*. Second, from Saul to Zedekiah we have Israel under the *Kings*. Third, from Jeshua and the repatriation of the "Remnant," down to the destruction of Jerusalem in A.D. 70, we have Israel under the *Priests*.

About Chapters ix. to xiv.

Perhaps before we come to examine and analyse this Book of Zechariah we ought just to notice that chapters ix. to xiv. have been called in question by some of our more recent Bible critics. It has been argued, with more confidence than reason, that these chapters are not from the hand of Zechariah, but from a writer (or writers) who lived, according to some, as early as 770 B.C., or, according to others, as late as 330 B.C. One scholar sees a difference of authorship in the fact that while the style of the first eight chapters is prosaic, feeble, poor, that of the remaining six is *poetic, weighty, glowing*; but another scholar bases his contention on "the *lifeless* language" of these later chapters! We cannot resist the observation that there surely must be something strangely faulty with a system of Biblical criticism which from the same data, leads to such contradictory extremes, both as to date and style.

We need not stay here, however, to discuss the attack on these chapters. The critics have been answered, and the integrity of the book demonstrated, again and again, by scholars of a sounder calibre. An able treatment of the question, in small compass, is easily accessible in C. J. Ellicott's *Commentary*, also in the introduction to the Book of Zechariah in the *Pulpit Commentary*. In earlier studies in this series we have examined the Modernist attacks on the Books of Jonah, Isaiah, and Daniel, and have shown how fallacious are the arguments against those scriptures. The attempt against these later chapters of Zechariah falls into the same category and reveals a similar result, namely, that the scholarly "blitz" spends itself, only to prove more clearly than before the thorough genuineness of the precious old Book.

Contents and Analysis

If we pick our way carefully through this Book of Zechariah two or three times, we soon find its arrangement becoming clear to us. We are sure to see, first of all, that there is a major break between chapters viii. and ix., which divides the book into two main parts. There can scarcely be any mistaking this, for the characteristics of the two parts are markedly different from each other. The first eight chapters are mainly *vision*-prophecies; the remaining six chapters are wholly *direct* prophecies. The first eight chapters were written during the rebuilding of the temple; the remaining six chapters were written considerably *after* the temple was rebuilt. The first eight chapters have a *particular and immediate* reference to the Jewish "Remnant" now back in the land; the remaining six chapters have a *general and far-reaching* reference to Israel as a whole, to the ultimate future, and to the Gentile nations. The contents of the first eight chapters are carefully dated (i. 1; i. 7; vii. 1); the contents of the remaining six chapters are *nowhere* dated.

The Two Parts.

In the first part (i.–viii.) we have *seven visions* (i.–vi.) with a follow-up message of application to "all the people of the land" (vii. 5; viii. 9, 11, 12). There are those who make the number of the visions eight, by making the symbol of the "ephah" in chapter v. a separate vision in itself; but a careful reading of that chapter, we think, will show that it is to be understood as essentially one vision in three dissolving views—the scroll, the ephah, the women. Verse 6 shows the connection of the ephah with what goes before. Certainly there are not *ten* visions in these chapters, as the Scofield Bible makes out by artificially splitting the vision of the four horns and carpenters into two (i. 18–21), and the vision of Joshua likewise (iii.), as well as that of the scroll and the ephah (v.). Check these seven visions off carefully, and see how aptly Zechariah's *spoken* message in chapters vii. and viii. follows them up.

The *second* part of the book (ix.–xiv.) consists of one continuous, unfolding prophecy which looks beyond the prophet's own time to the conquests of Alexander the Great, and the sway of the Greek empire, and the heroic struggles of the Maccabees, and the coming of Israel's Shepherd-King, the Messiah. It trumpets the King's first advent, then, in veiled, mystic phraseology, tells of His rejection, and then sweeps on to His second advent, over-leaping the present age and depicting the final travail and triumph of Zion, when the bells on the horses and the pots in the kitchens shall be "holiness unto the Lord." It is not the easiest of passages for the average reader of our Authorised Version to get hold of, but this is due in part to translation difficulties. When once we appreciate its three main movements, and clear up translation obscurities here and there, we quickly grasp that it is one of the most amazing prophecies ever written. It runs in three movements. First, in chapters ix. and x., we have the coming Shepherd-King, and Zion's consequent blessing. Second, in chapter xi., we have the offending of the Shepherd-King, and its tragic results. Third, in chapters xii. to xiv., we have Zion's final travail and triumph, and Jehovah's ultimate victory.

What is the *key-word* to this prophecy of Zechariah? In ous study of Haggai we saw that the key-word there was, "From thir day will I bless you" (ii. 19). Jehovah had turned to Jerusalem again in blessing, after the seventy years of the "desolations." Following this up, the key-word here in Zechariah is, "I am (become) jealous for Zion (again); I am returned unto Jerusalem with mercies" (i. 14–16; viii. 1–3, R.V.). This thought, that Jehovah has now become jealous again for Jerusalem, runs right through the book, as we shall see presently, when we glance through the chapters in turn. But let us, at this point, set down our findings in flat analysis:—

THE BOOK OF ZECHARIAH

"I AM JEALOUS FOR ZION"

EARLY PROPHECIES: TEMPLE BEING REBUILT
(i.–viii.).

A sevenfold vision: the four horses (i. 8–17), the four horns and smiths (verses 18–21), the measuring line (ii.), the reclothing of Joshua (iii.), the golden candlestand (iv.), the roll, ephah, and women (v.), the four chariots (vi.).
A fourfold message: vii. 1–7, 8–14; viii. 1–17, 18–23.

LATER PROPHECIES: AFTER TEMPLE REBUILT
(ix.–xiv.).

The coming Shepherd-King, and Zion's consequent blessing
(ix.–x.).
The offending of the Shepherd-King, and its tragic results
(xi.).
The final travail and triumph of Zion: Jehovah's victory
(xii.–xiv.).

The Seven Symbolic Visions

The seven visions described in the first part of the book are really seven in one, for they all came, so it would seem, in the one night, that of "the four and twentieth day of the eleventh month (Sebat), in the second year of Darius" (i. 7). This was exactly five months after the rebuilding of the temple was resumed (Hag. i. 15). What were these symbolic vision-scenes meant to convey to Zechariah and the Jews? I think we need not be left guessing for long as to their central significance. Let us run through them and try to pick out the essential point in each.

Take the first of them, that of *the four horses and their riders* (i. 8–17). Zechariah sees an angel patrol drawn up among the myrtles in the vale. Our Authorised Version gives the impression that behind the first rider, the man on the red horse, there were a goodly number of horses; but the Revised Version rightly corrects this, showing that there were but four in all. These heavenly "scouts" (verse 10) report to the Angel of Jehovah the result of their survey of world conditions; the nations are "at ease" (compare verses 11 and 15). Zechariah is intended to grasp that although the surrounding nations are at careless ease while Jehovah's "remnant" suffer hardships, and although there may seem little sign that judgment is about to fall on these wicked nations, according to Jehovah's word through Haggai (Hag. ii. 22), yet in the invisible realm, God is watching, and the heavenly powers are already preparing for the stroke of retribution. That such is the meaning is put beyond question by what now follows in the vision. The Angel of Jehovah asks, "O Jehovah of hosts, how long wilt Thou not have mercy on Jerusalem and on the cities of Judah, against which Thou hast had indignation these threescore and ten years?" The answer is, "Thus saith Jehovah of hosts: I am jealous for Jerusalem and for Zion with a great jealousy. And I am very sore displeased with the nations that are at ease, for I was but for a little (while) displeased (with Jerusalem and Judah) and they (the nations) helped forward the affliction (lit. 'they helped for evil'). Therefore, thus saith Jehovah: *I am returned to Jerusalem with mercies: My house shall be built in it, saith Jehovah of hosts, and a line (a measuring-line for its rebuilding) shall be stretched forth upon Jerusalem.*" Clearly, then, the essential point in this first vision-picture is that Jehovah has now become jealous again for Jerusalem, and is about to punish the nations for their abuse of His covenant people.

The second and third visions re-express this very same fact under different symbols. In the *second* vision (i. 18–21) Zechariah sees "four horns" and then "four carpenters" which come to "fray" them. The four horns are the nations which have "scattered Judah, Israel, and Jerusalem," and the four carpenters are Jehovah's agencies of judgment against these nations. In the *third* vision (ii. 1–13) Zechariah sees "a young man" with a "measuring line" going to "measure Jerusalem." But a heavenly messenger runs to this young man, saying, "Jerusalem shall be inhabited as *towns without walls*, for the multitude of men and cattle therein" (that is, it would exceed all the wall measurements which this young man was intending taking, so great would be its prosperity). Jehovah Himself should be Jerusalem's wall, as the fifth verse continues—"For *I*, saith Jehovah, will be unto her a wall of fire round about, and will be the glory in the midst of her." Here again, then, in the second and third visions, we have the judgment of the nations, and the return of Jehovah's favour toward Jerusalem (see especially verses 6–13). Once again Jehovah has become "jealous for Zion."

Next, in the *fourth* vision-scene (iii. 1–10), Zechariah is shown "Joshua the high priest (of the returned remnant) standing before the Angel of Jehovah, and Satan standing at his right hand to resist him." There is no need to go into the minor details: the main purport of this symbolic reclothing of Joshua is too clear to miss. During the period of the "desolations" Jerusalem has been rebuked and chastised, and her priests and people have suffered Jehovah's indignation. But now there is a change. It is shown in this reclothing of Joshua, who is here the representative of the covenant people. Instead of rebuke against Joshua, it is now Satan who is rebuked, and Joshua, as representative of the returned Remnant, is "a brand plucked out of the fire." Joshua's filthy garments are removed (verse 4), the symbolic meaning of which we are plainly told is *the removing of iniquity* from him (as representing his people). Joshua is then clothed with "*rich* apparel"; and a "diadem" is set on his head (see verse 5, R.V.); and a new commission and promise for the future are given him. If this is not a symbolic expression of the same fact which has been expressed through the earlier visions, then it means nothing. Quite clearly the meaning again here is Jehovah's return of favour to His people and city. Once again Jehovah has become "jealous for Zion."

The *fifth* vision, that of the golden candlestick and two olive trees (iv. 1–14), is a special encouragement to Zerubbabel, the *civil* leader of the Remnant (verses 6–10), as the preceding vision was to Joshua, the *religious* leader. The mountain should become a plain before him, and he should certainly complete the rebuilding of the temple. Verse 10 is the crux (see R.V., as A.V. obscures the sense). It should read: "Who hath despised the day of small things (the poor-looking beginnings of the rebuilding)? For these seven eyes of Jehovah (the seven lamps of the candlestick) which run through all the earth *shall behold with joy the plummet in the hand of Zerubbabel.*" Once again, therefore, the meaning is that of Jehovah's new pleasure and favour toward Zion. See also verse 12, which should read: "What be these two olive branches which through the two golden spouts (or tubes) pour out from themselves the golden oil?" (the oil dropped of itself from the fruit-bearing branches into two "spouts" or channels which conveyed it to the central reservoir). The answer is, "These are the two sons of oil which stand by the Lord of the whole earth" —Joshua and Zerubbabel (though there may be latent further meanings), as representing the covenant people, and through whom the Spirit of Jehovah was now flowing again to bless. Once again Jehovah has become "jealous for Zion."

In the *sixth* vision (v. 1–11) Zechariah sees a huge scroll, twenty cubits long and ten cubits wide (thirty feet by fifteen), passing through the air, and is told that this is "the curse" which "goeth forth" against wickedness in the land. When God sets up His House in the land (as in the preceding vision) His word goes forth (as in this new vision) to judge and sentence all that is not in harmony with that House. There cannot be a restoration of Jehovah's blessing without the expulsion of that which is evil. That large, floating scroll, open for all to read, explained why, up to that juncture, there had been such adversity among the Remnant: it was Jehovah's curse upon the evil which was still permitted. But now, Zechariah is shown what is to be done with the evil. He sees an "ephah" (the largest of the dry measures in use among the Jews, equal to six or seven gallons), in some large container, and is told that this represents the wicked of the land. Verse 7 should be read in the Revised Version. A leaden disc is lifted from the mouth of the ephah, and there, inside, is a woman. The interpreting angel says to Zechariah, "This is wickedness." Then he casts the woman down into the ephah, and the leaden weight on the mouth of it. Suddenly, now, two other women, each with the wings of a stork (an unclean bird) appear, with the wind in their wings, and bear away the evil ephah to Babylon. Whatever latent meanings may lie in the peculiar details of this sixth vision, its salient point is plain enough. Let the false-swearing and thieving which were execrated on the flying scroll (verse 3) go where they properly belong, even to Babylon, the seat of anti-Godism right from the days of Nimrod (Gen. x. 10). If the "ephah" was the old-time Jewish symbol for *trade*, then the woman in the ephah would represent Babylonian corruption which was leavening commerce among the returned Remnant. The proper home for such corruption is not Jerusalem, the city of Jehovah, but Satan's rival city, Babylon.

The very fact of Jehovah's new jealousy on behalf of Zion means a renewed intolerance of that which is unholy.

Finally, in the *seventh* vision (vi. 1–8), and the symbolic *crowning of Joshua*, which follows it (verses 9–15), we see again Jehovah's coming judgment on the Gentile nations, and His return of favour toward Jerusalem. There can be little doubt that the four war-chariots of this vision represent swift-coming Divine judgment. The four angel drivers are "the four spirits of the heavens which go forth from standing before the Lord of all the earth" (verse 5) —thus corresponding with the "four angels" of Revelation vii., as Jehovah's agents of *judgment*. Special judgment is meted to "the north country" from where the great Gentile invaders had come (verses 6, 8). But in marked contrast with this, there comes to Zechariah—apparently at dawn—the instruction to enact a remarkable *coronation ceremony* (verses 9–15). He was to receive silver and gold from certain Jewish visitors who were present from Babylon, and to make a composite diadem wherewith to crown Joshua, the new high priest at Jerusalem. Then he was to say: "Behold the man whose name is the BRANCH, and he shall grow up out of his place, and he shall build the temple of Jehovah. . . ." There is a type-reference to Christ, of course, here. But the *immediate* meaning of it, none the less, and once again, is that Jehovah, besides sending forth his chariot-judgments on the surrounding Gentile powers, has "returned with mercies" and gracious promises to the remnant of His people.

These, then, are Zechariah's seven visions; and we think it will now be clear that the key thought or unifying idea running through them is that which is uttered in connection with the first of them—"*I am jealous (again) for Jerusalem and for Zion with a great jealousy*; and I am very sore displeased with the nations that are at ease; for I was but a little while displeased, and they helped for evil. Therefore, thus saith Jehovah: *I am returned to Jerusalem with mercies*" (i. 14–16). If final corroboration is required for this we need only read on through the remaining two chapters of this first part of the book (vii. and viii.). See chapter viii. 1–3 and 9–15 (R.V.).

Of course, we must not pass from these chapters without recognising that here and there they look beyond the immediate and local, to an ultimate fulfilment at the second coming of Christ. See ii. 10–13; iii. 8–10; vi. 12–14. The *reason* why the full realisation of such passages is even yet future is that when the Messiah-King came and offered Himself to His people, they rejected and crucified Him, thus suspending the promised age of blessing. We shall touch on this again, however, in our next lesson, when we examine Zechariah's great prophecy in chapters ix. to xiv.

THE BOOK OF ZECHARIAH (2)

Lesson Number 102

NOTE.—For this study read again chapters ix. to xiv. It is really important to master them. Read them carefully in the Revised Version or some modern translation; and read them through at least twice at one sitting.

"In the volume of the Book, it is written of Me" (Ps. xl. 8). The Holy Scriptures and the Person of the Lord Jesus Christ are so inseparably bound together, that whatever impairs the integrity and authority of the one correspondingly affects the other. The written Word is the Living Word enfolded: the Living Word is the Written Word unfolded. Christ is the Cornerstone of all faith, but that Cornerstone is laid in Scripture as a bed-rock, and to disturb the Scripture authority unsettles the foundation of the believer's faith and of the church itself.

Arthur T. Pierson.

THE BOOK OF ZECHARIAH (2)

WE ARE now at chapters ix. to xiv. As we have said, they constitute one of the most remarkable prophecies ever penned. The whole passage, however, may seem rather complicated at first, but if we pick out its three main movements, and then clear up obscurities of translation here and there in our English version, it opens up grandly to us. Its meanings are lit up by other Old Testament predictions which we have now studied, and even more so by what transpired during the first advent of the Lord Jesus, Israel's Messiah. It is really important to master the meaning of this great Messianic prophecy; and, therefore, we here submit a considerable part of it in a translation and presentation which will help to simplify it, with brief explanations in brackets where we think needful, and comments between some of the paragraphs.

PART I

THE COMING SHEPHERD-KING, AND ZION'S CONSEQUENT BLESSING (ix.–x.)

The burden of a word of Jehovah is against the land of Hadrach, and Damascus is its goal (for Jehovah hath an eye on mankind and on, all the tribes of Israel); also (it is) against Hamath which bordereth thereon [*note: these were cities of Syria*]; also (against) Tyre and Sidon, though very wise (as they think), and Tyre doth build a bulwark to herself, and heapeth up silver as dust, and gold as the dirt of the streets: behold, the Lord will dispossess her, and strike her power in the sea, and she shall be consumed with fire [*note: these were cities of Phoenicia*]. Ashkelon shall see it, and fear; Gaza also, and shall be sore pained, Ekron also, for her confidence shall shrivel up: and the king shall perish from Gaza; and Ashkelon shall lie deserted; and a bastard people shall dwell in Ashdod; and I will cut off the pride of the Philistines [*note: these were cities of Philistia*]. And I will take away his (the Philistine's) blood out of his mouth, and his abominations from between his teeth [*a reference to Philistine idolatrous sacrifices*]; and even he shall be a remnant for our God, and become like a clan in Judah, and Ekron as the Jebusite [*the Jebusites, it will be remembered, were allowed to dwell with the children of Judah in Jerusalem as equals, and not as a conquered race: see Joshua xv. 63*]. And I will encamp about

249

Mine house as a garrison (saith Jehovah), that none pass through or return: and no oppressor shall pass through against them ever again: for now do I watch it with Mine eyes.

So much for verses 1 to 8. But now, at verse 9, in contrast with this prelude of predicted judgments on the Gentile nations, Zechariah breaks out in rhapsody over the coming King and the coming blessing of Zion.

> Rejoice greatly, O daughter of Zion;
>   Shout aloud, O daughter of Jerusalem:
> Behold thy King cometh unto thee,
>   Vindicated and victorious;
> Lowly, and riding upon an ass,
>   Even upon a colt the foal of an ass.

And I will cut off the chariot from (against) Ephraim, and the horse from (against) Jerusalem, and the battlebow shall be cut off: and He (the coming King) shall speak peace to the nations; and His rule shall be from sea to sea, and from the river even to the ends of the earth.

As for thee (Zion) also, because of the blood of the covenant with thee [*Jehovah's covenant with the nation*] I have set free thy prisoners from the pit (Babylon) wherein is no water [*here Zechariah returns for a moment to the more immediate circumstances*]. Return to the stronghold (that is, to Zion) ye prisoners of (such a) hope [*this is an appeal to the Jews who had chosen to stay on in Babylon after the term of the exile was over, instead of returning to Judæa with the Remnant*]; even today do I proclaim that I will render double unto thee [*that is, a double recompence of blessing to Zion for all her chastisements*]. For I have drawn Judah for My bow, and filled it with Ephraim; and I will stir up thy sons, O Zion, against thy sons, O Greece, and will make thee as the sword of a mighty one [*note: this striking reference to Greece looks beyond the prophet's own time, to the coming conquests of Alexander the Great, and the sway of the Greek empire, and to the later heroic victories of the Maccabees: though the verses which now follow look on, also, to a mightier victory which is yet to be, and which was suspended through Jewish unbelief when Christ came and offered Himself as their promised Messiah-King, nineteen hundred years ago*].

Then shall Jehovah appear over them,
    And his shaft shall go forth like lightning;
And the Lord Jehovah shall blow the trumpet,
    And shall go with whirlwinds of the south.

Jehovah of hosts shall cover them,
    And they shall devour and trample (their enemies like) spent sling-
        stones;

Yea, they shall drink and make noise as by wine;
And shall be filled as a bowl, like the corners of the altar.

And Jehovah their God shall save them in that day as the flock of His
   people;
For they shall be as the stones of a crown glittering on His land.
For how great their goodliness and their beauty!
Corn shall make the young men flourish, and new wine the maidens.

It will have been noticed, perhaps, that in the foregoing passage (chapter ix.) the central idea is that which we found in the first part of the book, namely, that Jehovah is now about to punish the nations, and that now again He has become "jealous for Zion." We shall find this yet again in chapter x. which now follows. But before we read the tenth chapter we ought to realise that the period of the Maccabees, which we have found predicted in chapter ix., and which led up to the first coming of Zion's King (ix. 9), *could* have led right on to the final struggle and victory of Zion which is now depicted in this tenth chapter, had it not been for the unbelief and sin of the Jews. As a result of what happened when Zion's King first came and offered Himself, nineteen hundred years ago, the final struggle and victory now depicted in chapter x. are postponed, and the present age intervenes (as it does between verses 9 and 10 in chapter ix). Zechariah, like the other Old Testament prophets, is not enlightened as to the present long interval of the "Church" age (Eph. iii.). It may be asked: Why did not God reveal this in advance since He foreknew that it would come to pass? The answer is twofold. First, if God had plainly revealed this beforehand, then the Lord Jesus could never have come and made a real, *bona fide* offer of Himself as Messiah; and God could never have tested the Jews in relation to Him. Second, God *has* been pleased to foreshow the rejection and crucifixion of Christ again and again in Old Testament prophecy, so that we ourselves, in this present age, both Jew and Gentile, may know that He had anticipated and graciously overruled the unbelief and sin of the Jews when Christ first came to them. And now (in part) we give chapter x., which simply carries on from the end of chapter ix.

Ask ye of Jehovah rain in the time of the latter rain. Jehovah shall make lightnings, and shall give them rain in showers, to every man herbage in the field. For the teraphim have spoken emptiness, and the diviners have seen falsehood, and the dreamers speak vanity, they comfort in vain: therefore they (the covenant people) have wandered like a flock; they are afflicted because there is no (true) shepherd. My wrath burns against the (false) shepherds [*that is, the surrounding kings, as we shall see again later: see also Isaiah xliv., where king Cyrus is called a shepherd*], and I will punish the he-goats; for Jehovah of hosts hath visited His flock, the house of Judah [*note that Judah is here called Jehovah's "flock": it will guide us later*], and shall make them as His goodly horse in battle. From him shall come forth the cornerstone, from him the stay, from him the battle-bow; from him shall go every exactor together . . . [*now at verse 9*] And though I sow them among the peoples they shall remember Me in far countries, and bring up their children, and return. I will bring them home from the land of Egypt, and gather them from Assyria, and I will bring them into the land of Gilead and Lebanon, and place shall not be found for them. And He (Jehovah) shall pass through the sea of affliction and smite the sea of waves, and all the depths of the Nile shall dry up, and the pride of Assyria shall be brought down, and the sceptre of Egypt swept away. And I will make them mighty in Jehovah; and in His name shall they walk up and down, saith Jehovah.

PART II

THE OFFENDING OF THE SHEPHERD-KING, AND ITS TRAGIC RESULTS (xi.)

This part begins, like the former, with an outburst of calamities on the surrounding powers—"Lebanon" and "Bashan" and "the pride of Jordan" denoting areas north and north-east and east, just beyond the bounds of the area which was now occupied by the Jews. Then Zechariah tells us how Jehovah instructed him to "feed the *flock of slaughter*" (Judah, as seen above), and how he did so (emblematically), and what eventuated.

> Open thy doors, O Lebanon,
> That the fire may devour thy cedars!
> Howl, O fir tree, for the cedar is fallen,
> For the goodly ones are destroyed!
> Howl, ye oaks of Bashan,
> For the mighty forest is come down!
> Hark to the howling of the shepherds,
> For their glory is destroyed!
> Hark to the roaring of the young lions,
> For the pride of Jordan is blasted!

Thus said Jehovah, my God: Shepherd the flock of slaughter (the covenant people) whose buyers slaughter them without any sense of guilt, and whose sellers say, Blessed be Jehovah, I am become rich, and whose shepherds have no pity on them: for neither will I have pity any more on the inhabitants of the earth, saith Jehovah. For behold, I am going to hand over mankind, each into the hand of his neighbour and into the hand of his king: and they shall smite the earth, but I will not give deliverance from their hand.

So I shepherded the flock of slaughter—even you, most afflicted flock. And I took unto me two staves; the one I called Grace, and the other I called Union; and so I shepherded the flock. And I cut off the three (false) shepherds in one month. But my soul was grieved with *them* (Jehovah's own flock), and they on their part abhorred *me*. Then I said: I will not shepherd you: that which dieth, let it die; and that which perisheth, let it perish; and those which survive, let them consume each other's flesh. And I took my staff, Grace, and cut it asunder, to make void my covenant which I had made with all the peoples [*i.e. the purpose or covenant of judgment above-mentioned, whereby Jehovah's flock were to be succoured, and their afflictors requited*]. So it was broken in that day; and they of the afflicted flock who watched me knew that it was Jehovah's word. And I said to them: If it be good in your sight, give me my hire; and if not, forbear. So they weighed out for my hire thirty pieces of silver [*the price merely of a foreign slave: Exodus xxi. 32*]. And Jehovah said to me: Throw it to the potter [*so contemptible is the price that it is flung to the meanest of craftsmen*]. O the magnificence of the price that I was apprised at of them! [*said ironically*]. So I took the thirty pieces of silver, and cast them to the potter, in the house of Jehovah. Then I cut asunder my second staff, Union, so as to break the brotherhood between Judah and Israel.

Thus the true Shepherd is despised and rejected, with tragic consequences. The remaining few verses of this chapter, which we need not re-translate here, tell of a *faithless* shepherd who should exploit the flock. The big fact to grasp in the foregoing passage is that the transaction of the thirty pieces of silver, in the light of Matthew xxvii. 9, 10, clearly has reference to *Christ*. As a result of His humiliation the Jews have been under false shepherds ever since; and the falsest of all shepherds is yet to exploit them as the present age draws to its close. No wonder our Lord wept over Jerusalem, on the very day when He fulfilled Zechariah ix. 9, "If thou hadst known in this day, even thou, the things which belong unto thy peace! But now they are hid from thine eyes" (Luke xix. 42).

PART III

THE FINAL TRAVAIL AND TRIUMPH OF ZION: JEHOVAH'S VICTORY (xii.–xiv.)

In this third part of Zechariah's great Messianic prophecy, we need only to translate snatches here and there by way of guidance. The language makes it clear that this passage passes over the present "Church" interval, right on to that culminating epoch at the end of the present age, when, after all the tragic delay caused through the rejection of the true Shepherd-King, Jehovah shall again take up and complete His grand purposes with and for and through Israel.

The burden of a word of Jehovah on *Israel* [*note, then, that this passage specially concerns Jehovah's own people*]. Thus saith Jehovah, who stretched out the heavens, and founded the earth, and formed the spirit of man within him; Behold I will make Jerusalem a cup of reeling to all the peoples round about; and even over Judah, too, shall it (the cup of reeling) be, in the siege against Jerusalem. And it shall come to pass in that day that I will make Jerusalem a burdensome stone to all the peoples; all who burden themselves with it shall be sore wounded; and all the nations of the earth shall be gathered together against it [*such language, of course, transcends any past fulfilment, and looks on to the end-time, to the gigantic world-drama yet to be, of which Jerusalem will be the storm-centre, and which will precipitate the second advent and world-empire of Christ: pass now to verse 10*].

And I will pour upon the house of David and upon the inhabitants of Jerusalem the spirit of grace and of supplication; and they shall look unto ME whom they have pierced [*we know from John xix. 37 that this refers to Christ*], and they shall lament for HIM as one lamenteth for an only son, and grieve bitterly for Him as with grief for a firstborn [*note the " ME " and the "HIM." However much this may have perplexed the first readers of this prophecy, we ourselves now know how truly both pronouns apply. Jehovah Himself was "pierced" when Jesus Christ was crucified: see Rev. i. 7*]. In that day there shall be a great mourning in Jerusalem. . . . [*pass now to xiii. 1*].

In that day a fountain shall be opened to the house of David and to the inhabitants of Jerusalem, for sin and for uncleanness. And it shall be in that day, saith Jehovah of Hosts, that I will cut off the names of the idols from the land, and they shall no more be remembered. And also I will expel the (false) prophets and the unclean spirit from the land. And it shall be that if any man prophesy (falsely) again, his father and mother who begat him shall say to him: Thou shalt not live, for thou speakest falsehood in the name of Jehovah: and his father and mother which begat him shall thrust him through when he (thus) prophesieth [*so great the zeal for Jehovah's honour!*]. And it shall be in that day that the (false) prophets shall be ashamed, each of his vision when he prophesieth; nor shall they wear a hairy garment to deceive; but he shall say: I am no prophet, I am a tiller of the ground, for the ground is my occupation from my youth. Even so [*super-tragedy that the true Prophet-Priest-King Himself should be treated actually in the same way as these false prophets!*], it shall be said to HIM [*the "Him" looking back to xii. 10—"they shall mourn for HIM"*]: What are these wounds in *Thine* hands? And He shall reply: Those with which I was wounded in the house of My friends. (Yes!) Awake, O sword, even against My Shepherd, and the Man that is My Fellow, saith Jehovah of Hosts. Smite the Shepherd, and the flock shall be scattered [*our Lord Jesus refers this prophecy to Himself at His first coming: see Matthew xxvi. 31. The time when it will be asked: What are these wounds in Thine hands? is His* second *coming: see Revelation i. 7*]; but I will turn mine hand toward the little ones (a remnant), and it shall be, saith Jehovah, that although two parts throughout the land shall be cut off, and die, a third shall be left therein; and I will bring the third part (the remnant) through the fire, and refine them as silver is refined, and try them as gold is tried. They shall call upon My name, and I will hear them: I will say: This is my people; and they shall say: Jehovah, my God! [*that remnant still exists, and that promise will yet be fulfilled*].

Chapter xiv. now continues. The following verses are enough to show that it looks right on to the end of the present age.

Behold a day of Jehovah cometh when thy spoil (O Zion) shall be divided in thy midst. For I will gather all nations to besiege Jerusalem. . . . (now verse 3). Then shall Jehovah go forth and fight against those nations, as when He fought in the day of battle. And His feet shall stand in that day on the Mount of Olives which is over against Jerusalem on the east: and the Mount of Olives shall split into halves, from east to west, by a huge ravine; and half the mountain shall slide to the north, and half to the south. . . . And Jehovah, my God, shall come, and all the holy ones with Thee (the change into the second person here denotes the prophet's own joyous anticipation) . . . (now verse 9) And Jehovah shall be King over all the earth in that day. . . . (now verse 11). And there shall be no more curse; but Jerusalem shall dwell safely. . . . (now verse 20). In that day there shall be "Holy to Jehovah" even on the bells of the horses, and the very pots in the house of Jehovah shall be as the (sacred) bowls before the altar. Yea, every pot in Jerusalem and in Judah shall be holy to Jehovah of Hosts; and all who sacrifice shall come and take of them and cook therein. And in that day there shall be no more any trafficker in the house of Jehovah.

Such, then, is the Book of Zechariah. It is like some unique masterpiece of music, with simpler movements in the first part, followed by a final, riotous rhapsody, with crashing chords and lightning runs and sudden alternations between major and minor, and a triumphant finale. Yet both in the *earlier* movements (i.–viii.) and in the *later* (ix.–xiv.) we hear the same recurrent key-note all the way through—Jehovah is "jealous for Zion." The *Pulpit Commentary* remarks on chapter ix. 13, *"Nothing but inspiration* could have enabled Zechariah and Daniel to foresee the rise of the Macedonian dynasty, and the struggle between the Jews and the Syro-Grecian power in Maccabean times, which is here announced." What then shall we say about those passages in Zechariah which look right on to the Messiah's first and second comings—to His public entry into Jerusalem in lowly dignity, riding on an ass; to His being "wounded" in the house of His own kinsmen; to the "smiting of the Shepherd and the scattering of the flock;" to the preservation of the "remnant" even as at this very day; to the "mourning" for Him, which is yet to be, when the Jews "look on Him whom they pierced"; to the last super-conflict and the final kingdom-glories? Yes, what shall we say to all this? Is it not a marvel of inspiration? Oh for that final triumph which Zechariah has predicted! *"Even so, come, Lord Jesus!"*

THE PROPHET MALACHI
Lesson Number 103

NOTE.—For this study read Malachi's short prophecy through at least twice at one sitting, and then in a modern translation of it.

In the New Testament, every book of the Old Testament is quoted from, except Ruth, Ezra, Nehemiah, Esther, Ecclesiastes, Canticles, and Lamentations. Or to take that mathematically, in another way: In the New Testament there are 260 chapters; 209 have references to the Old Testament, leaving only fifty-one chapters with no reference. Thus the Old and the New Testament are interwoven with the weave of constant reference, allusion, and quotation; and no single reference in the New contradicts the Old, or undermines its authority. They all accept its full authority and its Divine nature.

G. Campbell Morgan, D.D.

THE BOOK OF MALACHI

MALACHI calling!—the last call of the Old Testament before the voice of prophecy dies into a silence of four hundred years. One great phase of Divine revelation is now to close. The last spokesman utters his soul, and retires behind the misty curtains of the past. A peculiar solemnity clings about him. What does this last speaker say? What is the final message? What is the parting word?

We need spend no time here replying to those moderns who would tell us that Malachi was not a real person. They cannot produce a shred of positive evidence; and they have been ably answered elsewhere. Some of them give us the impression that they love to differ from the older views just for the sake of differing. They strain at gnats and swallow camels. Their arguments here, as in not a few other connections, are as weighty as feathers. For short but good synopses of the question we refer to the introductory articles on Malachi in Ellicott's *Commentary* and the *Pulpit Commentary*, which, although not the latest-written, remain thoroughly sound today.

Our first step toward appreciating the message of Malachi is to see him amid his own times. He does not date his prophecy, but there are pointers to the approximate time of it. All agree that it is post-exilic, and later than the other two post-exilic prophets, Haggai and Zechariah. The likelihood is that it was written *a little later than the days of Nehemiah*. It is well to fix in mind the main dates and events relating to the Jewish Remnant, from the time of the return, down to the ministry of Malachi. They are as follows:

B.C. 536. At the decree of Cyrus, the 50,000 return to Judæa, under Zerubbabel (Ezra i. and ii.).

534. The foundations of the new temple are laid (Ezra iii.) —but the rebuilding is held back.

520. Ministry of prophets Haggai and Zechariah. Temple rebuilding resumed (Ezra v.; Hag. i. 15).

516. Restoration Temple completed (Ezra vi. 15), just twenty years after return of the 50,000.

457. Return of the further 1,800 (plus wives, daughters and servants) under Ezra (Ezra vii.).

445. Nehemiah comes to Jerusalem by royal edict, as Governor, to rebuild *the city* (Neh. ii.).

430. (approx.) Nehemiah returns to Jerusalem after absence on visit to Artaxerxes (Neh. xiii. 6, 7). Malachi prophesies sometime after this.

When did Malachi write?

Now the likelihood, we say, is that this little Book of Malachi belongs to the period following the days of Nehemiah. We think this because it does not easily fit any earlier juncture. To begin with, it does not fit the early days of *Ezra* in Judæa. The offerings and sacrifices and other observances of the temple service have become perverted and profaned when Malachi prophesies (i. 7, 8, 12; ii. 8), but despite the other evils which *Ezra* had to encounter, we nowhere find his having had to reform such abuses in connection with the new temple service. Moreover, in Ezra's days all the necessaries for the temple services were provided from the royal revenues (Ezra vi. 9, 10; vii. 17–20), so that Malachi's rebukes of the people for their niggardliness toward the temple (i. 13; iii. 8–10) would scarcely apply. Still more, Malachi's opening words about the desolate state of the land of Edom (i. 3–5) would have been of little comfort to the Jewish Remnant if at the same time their own Jerusalem was still "lying waste, and the gates thereof consumed with fire." No, the city has been rebuilt when Malachi prophesies; and this brings us on to the days of Nehemiah.

Did Malachi prophesy, then, in the days of *Nehemiah*? Well, he certainly did not prophesy during Nehemiah's *first twelve years* as Governor of Jerusalem, when such grand restorations were effected (Neh. vii.–xii.). Did he prophesy, then, during the brief *interval* that Nehemiah was away at the Persian court (Neh. xiii. 2)? Scarcely, for there is a settled attitude and behaviour, and a state of callousness and defiant hostility, indicated in the time of Malachi which were not the product merely of a sudden collapse all within a couple of years, but a growth through a longer period (i. 6, 7, 10, 13; ii. 8, 9, 17; iii. 7). Certainly, Nehemiah found, on his return, that certain abuses had already reappeared (xiii.), but it is just as clear that they did not represent the whole nation, as was the case when Malachi prophesied (iii. 9). Again, if the extreme of corruption denounced by Malachi all developed in the short absence of Nehemiah, then it says very little for Malachi's effectiveness if he prophesied *then*!

Did Malachi prophesy, then, during Nehemiah's *second* term at Jerusalem? Hardly, for it is difficult to think that such a condition of things as Malachi exposes would develop while Nehemiah was still in control, and while Ezra possibly still lived. Also, there is a reference to "the Governor" in Malachi i. 8 which surely seems inexplicable if Nehemiah was Governor at the time. Would Malachi have referred thus namelessly to such an one as Nehemiah? It is possible, of course, but is it likely? Moreover, this verse speaks of "offerings" for the Governor; but Nehemiah expressly tells us that *he* made it his practice to maintain himself *apart from such Governors' dues* (Neh. v. 14, 15); and it is not likely that he changed later!

We conclude, therefore, that Malachi prophesied *after* the days of Nehemiah—and long enough after for the settled, corrupt condition of things to have developed which he deplores and denounces. The Book of Ezra *does* refer to the two prophets, Haggai and Zechariah, who prophesied during the period covered by that book: but the Book of Nehemiah nowhere suggests the presence of Malachi; and in this, again, we see a further, slight corroboration of our conclusion that Malachi came on the scene somewhat later. Nehemiah, it will be realised, may have lived for a considerable time beyond the last event recorded in the book which bears his name; and so long as he lived he would exert a strong influence for moral and religious purity: but the conditions described by Malachi suggest a deterioration which had come about *after that influence was withdrawn.* Not only had the earlier zeal of people and priests cooled down; it had given place to a complex of slovenly formalism (iii. 14) and even deceitful evasion (i. 14). Our last glimpse of Nehemiah in Jerusalem is at about 430 B.C., but he probably continued there for some years after that; so we put the ministry of Malachi somewhere between 420 and 397 B.C.

Daniel's First " Seven Weeks "—and Malachi

This brings us to a most noteworthy consideration. It has to do with Daniel's prophecy of the "seventy weeks" (Dan. ix). Daniel was told that from the date of the decree to rebuild Jerusalem, to the cutting off of the Messiah, was to be "seven weeks, and threescore and two weeks." The date of the decree, most definitely, was 445 B.C. (see our earlier study on Daniel). Why should the sixty-nine weeks from then to the cutting off of the Messiah be divided into "seven weeks, and threescore and two weeks"? Clearly the Scripture has some important boundary-point in view at the end of that first "seven weeks," or forty-nine years; and it is hard to resist the conclusion that this boundary-point was *the ceasing of prophecy with Malachi*. This would make Malachi's ministry *end* at 397 B.C., a date which, in fact, well suits the circumstances. Thus Malachi bounds the forty-nine years, or "seven weeks" of the predicted "troublous times" (Dan. ix. 25). In a special way God now waits to be gracious. In the light of this, how significant is that great, final promise of Jehovah through Malachi—"BRING YE ALL THE TITHES INTO THE STOREHOUSE, THAT THERE MAY BE MEAT IN MINE HOUSE; AND PROVE ME NOW HEREWITH, SAITH JEHOVAH OF HOSTS, IF I WILL NOT OPEN YOU THE WINDOWS OF HEAVEN, AND POUR YOU OUT A BLESSING, THAT THERE SHALL NOT BE ROOM ENOUGH TO RECEIVE IT" (iii. 10)!

The Meaning and Message of the Book

And now, what is the special purpose, the central message, the key thought, of the book? We need not make any close analysis to find this. If we mentally place ourselves in the ring of Malachi's first audience, and read through the book at speaking pace, letting it speak to us as though it were the living voice of the prophet himself ringing in our ears, we simply cannot miss seeing that from beginning to end this little book is AN APPEAL—a powerful, passionate, pleading appeal—an appeal to *repent* of sin and to *return* to God—an appeal accompanied by rich *promise* if the people respond, and by stern *warning* if they refuse. Read the little book through again, and get into the eager, urgent flow of the prophet's thoughts and words, and see if this is not so— "If I be a Father, where is mine honour? and if I be a Master, where is my fear?" (i. 6); "I pray you, beseech God that He will be gracious unto us" (i. 9); "Have we not all one Father? hath not one God created us? Why then do we deal treacherously every man against his brother, by profaning the covenant of our fathers?" (ii. 10); "Even from the days of your fathers ye are gone away from Mine ordinances, and have not kept them. RETURN UNTO ME, AND I WILL RETURN UNTO YOU, SAITH JEHOVAH OF HOSTS" (iii. 7); "BRING YE ALL THE TITHES INTO THE STORE- HOUSE . . . AND PROVE ME NOW HEREWITH, SAITH JEHOVAH OF HOSTS" (iii. 10); "REMEMBER (GIVE HEED AGAIN TO) THE LAW OF MOSES . . . WHICH I COMMANDED" (iv. 4).

Now we need not try to analyse this little book into five or six or seven parts which burden the mind to remember. The simple fact to note is that this APPEAL of Malachi quite natur- ally falls into *TWO PARTS*. In chapters i. and ii. the appeal is made in view of *the present sin of the nation*. In chapters iii. and iv. it is in view of *the coming "Day of Jehovah."*

Glance again, now, through chapters i. and ii. After the few verses by way of introduction (verses 1–5) it is the *priests* who are first addressed (see i. 6; ii. 1, 7). It will be noticed that *Jehovah Himself* addresses these priests directly, and that all the way through, to chapter ii. 9, the verses are in the first person. Then, at chapter ii. 10, there is a change. It is the *prophet* now, who speaks *on behalf of* Jehovah. It is no longer the priests who are addressed, but *the people generally*. The prophet puts him- self among them, and asks: "Have we not all one Father? Hath not one God created us? . . ." And from this point all the verses are in the *third* person. So much, then, for chapters i. and ii.

Now glance through chapters iii. and iv. A new note is struck. The prophet views the present *in the light of the great "Day of Jehovah" which is to come*. It will be noted that beginning with the first verse of chapter iii. it is Jehovah Himself who speaks directly again, using the first person, "I," "Me," "My," right to the end of the book. First, in verses 1 to 6, we are told that *the coming One* who was the nation's hope of future blessing was coming to *judge* (not merely, as was being presumed, to bless the nation indiscriminately!); and arising from this there is *renewed appeal* to the people to "return" and to "bring all the tithes" and to "prove" Jehovah's present offer of blessing (verses 7–12).

Then, from verse 13 to the end of the book, there is a further addition about this coming "Day of Jehovah"—not only will it judge the guilty (as just said); it will *vindicate the godly minority* (iii. 13–iv. 3); and arising from this is the closing appeal of the book, to "give heed" again to "the Law of Moses" (iv. 4–6). This final section of the book which runs from chapter iii. 13 is not brought out clearly enough in our English version. There is a contrast between two classes—between the larger number who *resisted* Jehovah and "spake together" (verse 13), and the minority who "*feared*" Jehovah, and "spake often one to another" (verse 16). There are *only two tenses* in the Hebrew language, and the *context* must decide which tense they are given in our *English* translation. Verses 13–16 should read—

"Your words are stout against Me, saith Jehovah; yet ye say, What do we speak in our conversation together against Thee? Ye say, It is a vain thing to serve God. . . .
But those also who fear Jehovah speak one to another, and Jehovah doth attend and hear. And a book of remembrance is being written before Him, of them that fear Jehovah, and that esteem His name. And they shall be to Me a peculiar treasure, saith Jehovah of Hosts, in the day that I am preparing. . . ."

This Book of Malachi should be read in the Revised Version. Young's *Literal Translation*, also, is a great help here, as in many other places. A careful reading in either of these will bring out clearly the arrangement of the book as shown in this study.

" Behold, He shall come . . . but "

The key thought of Malachi is found in chapter iii. 1, 2— "*Behold, He shall come, saith Jehovah of Hosts; but who may abide the day of His coming?*" In our study of Haggai we saw that the Jewish Remnant had become indifferent to the rebuilding of the temple through a wrong attitude to prophecy. On the strength of Jeremiah's prediction that seventy years of "desolations" were determined on Jerusalem, the leaders and people were saying, "The time is not come, the time that Jehovah's House should be built" (Hag. i. 2). Thus they excused themselves into blameworthy indolence—and were rightly rebuked for it. A hundred years later, in Malachi's time, there is *a wrong attitude to Divine PROMISE.* The earlier prophets had foretold of the coming One who should bring final deliverance and age-long blessing to the covenant nation; Ezekiel and Daniel had continued the strain; the post-Exile prophets, Haggai and Zechariah, had carried it still further; the time was now surely drawing nearer, and the promised One would come to exalt the nation in untold dignity and prosperity. All would then be well, so the leaders and priests and people told themselves, and the present did not very much matter. Thus they sank into a nonchalant formalism, and even into unblushing hypocrisy in their dealings both with God and with each other. Malachi now shows them that the Divine promise is a two-edged sword. Not only will the coming "Day" slay the enemies *outside* the nation, but also the wicked *inside* the nation. The "Messenger of the Covenant" in whose promised coming they were "delighting" (iii. 1) should surely come, as promised; *but* (let them mark it well, this very big "but")—who should "abide the day of His coming"? for He would come as a "refiner's fire" and would be a "swift witness" against all the evildoers (verse 5). Yes, there is a "but" in the promise. "Behold, He shall come . . . *but.*" That is the centre-thought in Malachi. Let us now set out our findings in a simple, flat analysis.

THE BOOK OF MALACHI

"Behold, He shall come . . . but"

APPEAL (A)—IN VIEW OF THE PRESENT SIN (i.–ii.).

Jehovah the speaker: the priests are appealed to
(i. 6–ii. 9).
Malachi the speaker: the people are appealed to
(ii. 10–17).

APPEAL (B)—IN VIEW OF THE COMING "DAY" (iii.–iv.).

The day will judge the guilty (iii. 1–6)
therefore appeal (verses 7–12).
The day will bless the godly (iii. 13–iv. 3)
therefore appeal (iv. 4–6).

Closing Observations

This last fragment of Old Testament Scripture is richly full of vital truths and living applications to our own days. In these closing paragraphs we can merely mention a few of them.

First, we note that the Old Testament leaves us with *a final promise of the coming of Christ*. Thus the very first promise and the very last, in the Old Testament, are concerning *HIM*. But what a wealth of development lies between Genesis iii. 15 and Malachi iv. 6! The united voice of the Old Testament Scriptures is, "Behold He comes!" We note, also, that the coming of Christ which is described in Malachi is that which even to ourselves is yet future. Our Lord's first coming as the suffering Servant is most certainly a fact of *history*: and His second coming as King and Judge is just as certainly a fact of *prophecy*. The present interval between the first coming and the second was not revealed to Malachi, nor to any other of the Old Testament prophets. This we have noted again and again. And yet, none the less the *two aspects* of His coming—as suffering Servant and as universal Sovereign—are unmistakably present to the eye of Old Testament prophecy. There is a real sense in which John the Baptist was Malachi's Elijah-forerunner (Mal. iv. 5 with Matt. xvii. 12, 13); yet it is equally clear that, as a result of our Lord's rejection there is to be a more dramatic, *final* fulfilment of Malachi's Elijah prediction (Matt. xvii. 11, "shall"; and Rev. xi.).

We must make a sharp distinction always between Divine foreknowledge and Divine fore-ordination. God foreknew the Jewish rejection of Christ; but He did not fore-*ordain* it. God never predestinates to *sin*! In His government of this world God does not allow His larger purposes for the human race to rest upon the uncertain behaviour of the human will; yet He does leave enough scope for the free action of the human will to make men conscious at all times that they are acting of themselves, and by their own intelligent choice. Thus He permitted even the crucifixion of Christ. But He foreknew it, and fore-provided against it, so that *the crucifixion of Israel's Messiah became the coronation of the world's Saviour*, and from the ugly debris of Jewish failure there emerged God's further purpose, that is, the *CHURCH*, and the proclaiming of a *WORLD-EMBRACING GOSPEL* of personal salvation throughout the present age. God could not reveal all this, however, to the Old Testament prophets; for, had He done so, Christ could never have come and made a *bona fide* offer of Himself as Israel's Messiah. We have touched on this before; but it is so important to grasp it clearly that we think it wise to speak of it again.

Then again, with this little scroll of Malachi before us, we should ever guard against *a wrong attitude to Divine promise*. We have seen how this wrong attitude cursed Malachi's generation. It is also in evidence today. There are those whose attitude to the hope of Christ's return begets complacent indifference. "Thou wicked and slothful servant!"—will those awful words ever fall on some of *us* who have been believers in the Lord's second coming? Oh, may the dear prospect of His coming ever be an incentive to holiness, and an urge to the winning of other souls to Him!

Again, if we have read Malachi observantly, we cannot have missed seeing that the two besetting evils of his day were *formalism* and *scepticism*. In these we see the beginnings of the Pharisaism (formalism) and the Sadduceeism (scepticism) which later reached their harvest-whiteness in our Lord's days. How these two things curse us today! And how they cause men to argue back against God! Seven times the priests and people of Malachi's time are faced with the vital issues of real heart-religion; and seven times they answer back with that word, "wherein?" "Wherein hast Thou loved us?" (i. 2). "Wherein have we despised Thy name?" (i. 6). "Wherein have we polluted Thee?" (i. 7). "Wherein have we wearied Him?" (ii. 17). "Wherein shall we return?" (iii. 7). "Wherein have we robbed Thee?" (iii. 8). "Wherein have we spoken against Thee?" (iii. 13). The formalist does not like to have his formalism *disturbed*. The sceptic does not like to have his scepticism *disproved*. Both will evade the real issues of heart-religion by self-justifying counter-argument. Verily, "they have their day"! But "the day cometh that shall burn as an oven" (Mal. iv. 1); and, as D. L. Moody put it, "A cloak of false profession will make an awful blaze when God burns up the stubble!"

And finally, in Malachi we see how precious to God are the godly minority in times of declension. A "book of remembrance" is kept; and they, God's remnant, are to be Jehovah's "peculiar treasure" in the "day" which He is "preparing." Thus, as the

Old Testament closes, we see the godly remnant speaking softly to one another of a great hope—"He is coming!" Then, for four hundred years they disappear from sight, until they reappear from obscurity in New Testament times, in the aged Simeon and Anna, who are found in Jerusalem, "waiting for the Consolation of Israel" (Luke ii. 25). And so it is today. They who fear and love Jehovah-Jesus speak one to another amid the closing decades of the present age, comforting one another with the words, "He is coming!" And God's book of remembrance is being kept. Yes, He is surely coming—for "Unto you that fear My name," saith Jehovah, "shall the Sun of Righteousness arise, with healing in His wings!" And our prayer is, "Even so, come, Lord Jesus."

Yes, comforting, thrilling prospect, He is coming, coming a *second* time. The inviolable guarantee of this is the historical fact of His *first* coming, as vicarious Saviour, which fulfilled scores and scores of greater and lesser Old Testament predictions, with Divine precision. That first batch of fulfilments, two thousand years ago, constitutes the mightiest conceivable guarantee that *all the other* predictions and promises concerning His reign on earth in world-wide empire will similarly be fulfilled. Yes, He is coming! *HE* is coming—the Church's Bridegroom, Israel's Messiah, and God-Man Emperor of all nations!

> Jesus, my Lord, Thou art coming!
>   Thy Spirit assures me within.
> Coming, dear Lord, Thou art coming,
>   To banish the empire of sin.
> Jesus, Thy people are yearning;
>   The world cries unknowing for Thee.
> Oh, for Thy promised returning,
>   Thy face and Thy glory to see!

"EVEN SO, COME, LORD JESUS!"

FOUR QUESTIONS EACH, ON HAGGAI, ZECHARIAH, AND MALACHI

1. What picture does Haggai give of the moral condition of the returned "Remnant"?
2. What is the crucial turning-point which Haggai puts on record? What is the date of it?
3. What are the two seventy-year periods prophesied by Jeremiah which should not be confused?
4. What, as to their crux or gist, were the four messages of which the Book of Haggai consists?
5. When did Zechariah prophesy—which year, and in which Medo-Persian king's reign? How long had the "Remnant" then been returned?
6. The Book of Zechariah falls into two parts: which are they?
7. What, in simple statement, were the seven parts of Zechariah's sevenfold vision in the first six chapters? And what the meaning of the first?
8. What are the three main parts of the great Messianic prophecy in Zechariah, chapters ix. to xiv.? (Simply give the headings to the three main parts.)
9. What reasons could you give for saying that Malachi prophesied some little time after the days of Nehemiah?
10. Could you mention any possible connection between the date of Malachi and the first seven weeks of Daniel's famous prophecy of the Seventy Weeks?
11. Give a brief outline of the Book of Malachi, and say what is its key verse or idea.
12. How do both Haggai and Malachi warn us against a wrong attitude to prophecy?

EXPLORE THE BOOK

*A Basic and Broadly Interpretative Course
of Bible Study from Genesis to Revelation*

J. SIDLOW BAXTER

VOLUME FIVE

INTER-TESTAMENT AND THE GOSPELS

FOREWORD TO NEW TESTAMENT SECTION

In issuing the New Testament section of this Bible course we are encouraged by generous appreciations of its earlier parts, and would make three remarks on these further instalments.

(1) In this work we are not trying to satisfy the whims of some who always want the "latest" in theology. Nowadays "theology" is in danger of becoming mere religious speculation, away from its proper moorings in a supernaturally inspired Bible. These studies assume that the Bible is both an *inspired* and a *completed* revelation, with the corollary that this present age is not one of continuing *revelation* but of Spirit-guided human *apprehension*.

(2) Not in the least do these studies pretend to be either a "commentary" or a symposium of theological papers. They are an exploratory opening-up of the Bible to show how inviting and rewarding are its pages, and to provide briefly but amply a general preparation for more particularised study of its various parts.

(3) Do we devote too many pages to the inter-Testament centuries? Possibly; yet in pursuance of the above-mentioned purpose we are convinced that an adequate knowledge of the eventful interval, and of the notable Jewish institutions which developed from it, is more valuable in the study of the New Testament than many realise. A close acquaintance with that "great divide" often causes passages in the Gospels, Acts and Epistles to "live" with new relevance—as in the Sermon on the Mount, where our Lord's recurrent "Ye have heard that it was said . . . But I say unto you" strikes a cleavage, not with the Old Testament (as many mistakenly suppose) but between His own words and those merely of the *"Oral* Law" which had developed during the inter-Testament period.

J.S.B.

CONTENTS OF VOLUME FIVE

	Page
INTER-TESTAMENT PERIOD	9
Studies 104, 105, 106, 107	
NEW TESTAMENT AND OLD	87
Study 108	
NEW TESTAMENT AS A WHOLE	99
Study 109	
FOUR GOSPELS COLLECTIVELY	115
Study 110	
GOSPEL ACCORDING TO MATTHEW	135
Studies 111, 112, 113, 114	
GOSPEL ACCORDING TO MARK	187
Studies 115, 116, 117	
GOSPEL ACCORDING TO LUKE	227
Studies 118, 119, 120	
GOSPEL ACCORDING TO JOHN	269
Studies 121, 122, 123	

INTRODUCTORY

THE INTER-TESTAMENT PERIOD

I. THE POLITICAL ASPECT

Lesson Number 104

NOTE.—(1) The ensuing synopses of the inter-Testament interval are meant for learners. The need is not to say anything new about it, but so to arrange and present it as makes it easiest to remember. For those who wish to scan the period more fully we recommend Professor John Skinner's primer, *Historical Connection Between the Old and New Testaments*.

(2) In His great mercy God has made the soul-saving truths of His written Word independent of our either knowing or not knowing the course of history outside it, so that the ignorant equally with the informed may become saved. But if we would also acquire a fuller and ever-more-profitable understanding of His Word, then a knowledge of such history outside it as bears upon it is most important to us, and we should be at pains to learn it. That is why we have given such considerable space to the inter-Testament period in the ensuing studies. We advise that these synopses of that period be read carefully and repeatedly, as a really worthwhile preparation for the study of the New Testament Scriptures themselves.

BETWEEN MALACHI AND MATTHEW

WE WOULD not say that a knowledge of the period between the Old and New Testaments is *vital* to one's understanding of the four Gospels, but it is very desirable, and indeed quite necessary, if we would fully appreciate many of the scenes and incidents on which Matthew lifts the curtain. It gives a background against which we see with sharpened clearness the connections and relevances of the sayings and doings which occupy the earlier pages of our New Testament.

Yet it is surprising how little is known of this period by the generality of Bible readers. We have often wished that the standard editions of our Authorised and Revised Versions of the Bible gave a brief synopsis, to light up for the average reader this long and divisive inter-Testament hiatus. We think it will be useful to give a brief delineation of the period here as a prelude to our study of the four Gospels.

THE PERIOD IN GENERAL

The period between Malachi and Matthew covers some four hundred years, if we accept the usual date assigned to Malachi. Modern historical criticism has given a later date to Malachi, bringing Joel and parts of Isaiah down to the same period, placing Zechariah about 250 B.C. and Daniel even within two hundred years of our Lord's birth; but such post-datings are based solely on subjective grounds and are really nothing more than theoretical conjecture. We may with confidence accept the Old Testament canon as closing with Malachi at about 397 B.C.

This four-hundred-year interval has been called "the dark period" of Israel's history in pre-Christian times, because throughout it there was neither prophet nor inspired writer. With Malachi the waning sun of prophecy sets, and the wail of Psalm lxxiv. 9 seems to find a sad fulfilment in the ensuing four centuries: "We see not our signs; there is no more any prophet; neither is there among us any that knoweth how long."

Our sources of information concerning the period are Books XI, XII and XIII of Josephus, two books of the Apocrypha, 1 and 2 Maccabees, plus references here and there in Greek and Latin historians: Polybius, Tacitus, Livy and Appian. Gentile historians refer only sparsely to Jewish concerns of those days, probably because of dislike for the covenant people, and an inability to appreciate the spiritual aspects of the conflicts which repeatedly broke out between the Jews and the idolatrous peoples around them.

The condition of the Jews as a nation and race at the beginning of this four-hundred-year period should be clearly borne in mind. Two hundred years earlier Jerusalem had been overthrown and the Jewish people carried into the Babylonian exile (587 B.C.). Fifty years after that, while the Jews were still in captivity, the Babylonian empire itself had been overthrown and succeeded by that of Media-Persia, second of the world-empires predicted in Daniel; and Cyrus, the Persian emperor, had issued his famous decree (536 B.C.) occasioning the return of the Jewish "Remnant" to Jerusalem and Judæa, under Zerubbabel, some fifty thousand in all. Twenty-one years later, after many setbacks, the building of the new temple had been completed in 515 B.C. Then another fifty-seven years later, in 458 B.C., Ezra the scribe had joined the repatriated "Remnant" at Jerusalem with a much smaller contingent of two thousand with their families, and had restored the Law and the ritual. Still another twelve years later, in 446 B.C., Nehemiah had come to Jerusalem to rebuild the walls and function as governor. So there was now again a Jewish state in Judæa, though of course under Persian overlordship.

But the returned "Remnant" was *only* a remnant. The bulk of the nation preferred to stay on in Babylonia and Assyria (now under Persian rule), where they were prospering, and where, from the commencement of the Media-Persian rule, they were treated more as colonists than as captives.

Such, then, is the picture of the Jewish people at the beginning of the four-hundred-year period between Malachi and Matthew: the Jewish Remnant back in Judæa about one hundred and forty years; a small, dependent Jewish state there, Jerusalem and the temple rebuilt, the Law and the ritual restored; but with the mass of the people remaining dispersed throughout the Media-Persian empire.

Naturally it is upon the *Remnant*, the repatriated and reconstituted Jewish community in Judæa, that our interest specially fixes, for it is in them that the continuity of Jewish history, nationally and politically, is preserved between the Old and New Testaments, i.e. it is they who are the Jewish *nation*, in distinction from the Jews as a scattered and disintegrated race.

If we are rightly to appreciate this Jewish community as it re-emerges in the pages of the New Testament, we need to trace its course in two ways: first, as to *external* developments (the political aspect); and, second, as to *internal* developments (the religious aspect).

External Developments

Viewed externally and politically, the varying course of the little Jewish nation in Palestine simply reflects the history of the different world-empires and other great powers which successively secured the mastery of Palestine, with the exception of one short juncture, namely, the Maccabean revolt, when for a short spell there was independent government again. We may say that Jewish history during those four centuries between the Testaments runs in six periods: the Persian, the Greek, the Egyptian, the Syrian, the Maccabean and the Roman.

The Persian Period (536–333 B.C.)

The Persian rule over Palestine, which commenced with the decree of Cyrus in 536 B.C. for the return of the Jewish Remnant, continued until 333 B.C., when Palestine fell under the power of Alexander the Great and his Græco-Macedonian empire (the third of the Gentile world-empires foretold by Daniel). This means that at the end of Malachi the Jews were still under Persian rule, and remained so for about the first sixty years of the inter-Testament era.

The latter part of the Persian period seems to have been more or less uneventful. Information concerning it is scant. Palestine was part of the Syrian satrapy, and Persian rule seems to have been tolerant. The sacerdotal form of Jewish government was respected, and the high priest given an increasing degree of civil power in addition to his religious offices, though of course he was responsible to the Persian governor of Syria.

It would seem that the only notable disturbance during this time was an anti-Jewish reprisal which the Jewish leaders themselves provoked through intrigue and assassination in their evil rivalries for the coveted office of high priest—for the civil power invested in the sacred office had already made it an object of political ambition. In the very temple Jonathan, the grandson of Eliashib, murdered his own brother Joshua, who was a favourite with the Persian governor. The Persians wreaked vengeance upon Jerusalem, defiled the temple, imposed a severe fine, partly laid waste the city, and persecuted the Jews for some time afterwards.

Perhaps one other point should be noted about this Persian period. It has to do with Samaria, the province adjoining that of Judæa, and part of the Syrian satrapy. In 2 Kings xvii. 24–41, we are told how, away back in 721 B.C., after destroying the ten-tribed kingdom of Israel and dispersing the Israelites through "the cities of the Medes," the Assyrian emperor repeopled the cities of Israel with a mongrel people who became known as the Samaritans, the territory being known as Samaria, the name of its chief city, formerly the Israelite capital. Later, it was from this area and people that Nehemiah encountered spiteful opposition when he came from the Persian emperor, in 446 B.C., to rebuild the walls of Jerusalem. And now, long years later, in the opening stages of the inter-Testament centuries, and toward the end of the Persian rule, it would appear that the rival *worship* of Samaria (John iv. 19–22) became established, by the founding of the Samaritan temple. That event dates the total separation of Jew and Samaritan. Henceforth Samaria survives as an insulated community within a narrow area. The rival worship was part of a more general rivalry, keen and resentful, which persisted right on until New Testament times.

The Greek Period (333–323 B.C.)

Alexander the Great is such a meteoric phenomenon in history that one cannot but wonder what his total impact on the world would have been had he not suddenly died at the premature age of thirty-two. Catapulted into leadership through the assassination of his father when he, Alexander, was but a youth of twenty, he completely transformed the face of the world, politically, in little more than a decade. He is the "notable horn" in the "he-goat" vision of Daniel (see Daniel viii. 1–7).

In his Syrian campaign he marched southward on Jerusalem. Josephus tells how the high priest Jaddua, in his priestly garments, and heading a procession of white-robed priests, issued forth to invoke the conqueror's clemency. Alexander, who is said to have recognised in Jaddua the fulfilment of a dream, not only spared Jerusalem and offered sacrifice to Jehovah but also had the prophecies of Daniel read to him concerning the overthrow of the Persian empire by a king of Grecia; and thereafter he treated the Jews with marked preferment, according them full rights of citizenship with the Greeks in his new city, Alexandria, and in other cities. This, in its turn, created decidedly pro-Greek sympathies among the Jews, and, along with Alexander's spreading of the Greek language and civilisation, had its far-reaching repercussions in the Hellenistic spirit which developed among the Jews and greatly affected their mental outlook afterward.

The Egyptian Period (323–204 B.C.)

This is the longest of the six epochs in the inter-Testament era. The untimely death of Alexander precipitated an interval of confusion which resolved itself into a fourfold break-up of his empire under four generals: Ptolemy, Lysimachus, Cassander and Selenus. These are the four "notable ones" which take the place of the "great horn," as predicted in Daniel viii. 21, 22.

After severe fighting, in which Judæa, along with the other part of Syria, became again both "the prize and the victim" of the strife for empire between East and West, Judæa now fell to Ptolemy, along with Egypt. This was Ptolemy Soter, the first of the Ptolemaic dynasty, i.e. the line of *Greek* kings over Egypt. (For a list of the Ptolemies see end of this study.)

Ptolemy wrested the Syrian provinces from a rival general, Laomedan. The Jews refused to break their oath to Laomedan, but Ptolemy captured Jerusalem on a Sabbath, which the Jews scrupled to break even in self-defence. From one hundred thousand captives Ptolemy drafted thirty thousand to garrison his most important cities, particularly in Libya and Cyrene, which he had newly annexed. This he did because of the fidelity which the Jews had showed to their allegiance with Laomedan.

For a time Ptolemy Soter dealt heavily on the Jews, but afterwards became just as friendly. His successor, Ptolemy Philadelphus, continued this favourable attitude, and his reign is made notable not only by his founding the renowned Alexandrian library but by the fact that the famous Septuagint translation of the Old Testament Scriptures was then made from the Hebrew into the Greek language, which had now become the language of the civilised world. It is thought that the Pentateuch was translated about 285 B.C., and the remainder of the Scriptures in later stages. The Jews were now so numerous in Egypt and North Africa that such a translation had become a necessity. It came into general use well before the birth of our Lord, and made the Scriptures known to many of the Gentiles.

During the humane and sometimes kindly treatment of the first three Ptolemies the Jews in Judæa grew in numbers and wealth, developing their commerce, which the fall of Tyre had increased; but during the later part of the Egyptian period they had anything but an enviable time. Palestine was increasingly becoming a battle-ground between Egypt and the now very powerful Seleucidae (i.e. the line of *Syrian* kings from Seleucus I). Lying there, between Syria and Egypt, Palestine was once again "between the hammer and the anvil." Antiochus the Great of Syria claimed that the Syrian province had originally been assigned to Seleucus at the break-up of Alexander's empire. In a big battle at Raphia, near Gaza, Antiochus was defeated by Ptolemy Philopater (the fourth Ptolemy), which settled it that Palestine remained an Egyptian province to the end of Philopater's reign. Philopater, however, at this time alienated the Jews by his rash intention of entering the Holy of Holies. He was resisted by the high priest, Simon II, whereupon Philopater, returning to Alexandria, persecuted the Jews, and even started measures to extirpate them throughout his dominions (3 Maccabees ii). From the reign of Ptolemy Philopater the power of Egypt quickly waned. The star of empire was finally sinking for Egypt, and a civilisation lasting from early post-deluvian history was soon to be crushed under the iron heel of Rome.

When Ptolemy Philopater died, his successor, Ptolemy Epiphanes, was only five years old. Antiochus the Great seized his opportunity and in 204 B.C. invaded Egypt. Judæa, with other territories, soon after became annexed to Syria and passed under the rule of the Seleucidae. (For a list of the Syrian Seleucidae see end of this study.)

The Syrian Period (204–165 B.C.)

There are two points of special note about this period. First, it was at this time that Palestine became sectionised into the five provinces which we find there in New Testament times, namely: Judæa, Samaria, Galilee, Peræa, Trachonitis. (Sometimes the first three of these are collectively called Judæa.) Second, this Syrian period was the most tragic part of the inter-Testament era for the Jews of the homeland.

Antiochus the Great was harsh towards the Jews. So was his successor, Seleucus Philopater. Yet the Jews in Judæa were still permitted to live under their own laws, administered by the high priest and his council as the nominal rulers. But with the accession of Antiochus Epiphanes (175–164 B.C.) a "reign of terror" befell Jewry.

By this time there had developed in Judæa a Greek-minded or Hellenising party, advocating un-Jewish innovations. They were for relaxing orthodox observance of Judaism with the national exclusiveness which it entailed, in favour of Greek liberty of thought and manners and forms of religion. The wranglings between Nationalists and Hellenists for the control of affairs caused much bitter contention and even murders.

After several earlier interferences with the temple and priesthood, Antiochus Epiphanes now used this Jewish factiousness as a provocation to vent his spleen on them to the full. He wreaked a terrible havoc in 170 B.C. Jerusalem was plundered, the wall torn down, the temple coarsely desecrated, and the population subjected to monstrous cruelties. Thousands were massacred. The women and children were sold into slavery. The temple sacrifices were abolished. The Holy of Holies was rifled and its costly furniture carried away. Jewish religion was banned. Circumcision was prohibited on pain of death. A foreign governor was appointed, a traitor made high priest, and paganism forcibly imposed on the people. A commissioner was appointed to pollute both the temple at Jerusalem and that at Samaria, and to rededicate them, respectively, to Jupiter Olympius and Jupiter Xenius.

All copies of the Law which could be found were either burned or defaced with idolatrous pictures, and the owners executed. The first book of Maccabees says that many Jews apostatised, and that some even joined in the persecution. In 168 B.C. Antiochus caused a sow to be offered on the altar of sacrifice, and then, on the very altar, had a statue erected to Jupiter Olympius. In this awful decade Palestine Jewry was indeed in the valley of the shadow of death.

The Maccabean Period (165–63 B.C.)

Like the sudden flashing of brilliant stars through a break-up of the clouds on a dark night, the Maccabean episode now breaks on us. It is one of the most heroic passages in all history. To appreciate it as it deserves one needs not only to know the facts but to get into the spirit of them.

The revolt and resistance movement was provoked by the sheer excesses of Antiochus. It was started by an aged priest, Mattathias, and developed by his son Judas, known subsequently as Judas *Maccabeus*, from the Hebrew word for hammer. Against a background of terrible darkness, and in defiance of overwhelming odds, the godly faith of Mattathias and his sons blazed out with glorious brightness and called forth the willing self-sacrifice of a godly multitude. The devotion of hundreds of thousands led them to martyrdom. Hardly in the Old Testament or in the Christian era can we find a nobler outflaming of holy jealousy for the honour of God.

The spark which ignited the desperate indignation into a blaze was a courageous and drastic retaliation by the angered old priest. Antiochus's commissioners, in their circuit of the land to obliterate Judaism and replace it by the king's state-religion, visited Modlin, the town of Mattathias. He, a prominent figure, refused compliance, slew Antiochus's commissioner, along with a disloyal Jew, and destroyed the idolatrous altar. He and his five sons then took refuge in the mountains of the wilderness, and many of the faithful with their families gathered to them. Philip the Phrygian pursued them and slew about a thousand of them with their wives and children, burning them alive in the caves where they were sheltering. This he was easily able to do because they scrupled even to defend themselves on the Sabbath. Mattathias thereupon persuaded the survivors that self-defence under such circumstances was right even on the Sabbath.

Mattathias and his band grew into an army. They attacked town after town, striking down the traitorous Jews, overthrowing the idol altars, and restoring the true religion. About a year later Mattathias died, having deponed his son Simon as chief counsellor and his son Judas as military commander.

Judas now developed a powerful guerilla warfare, the land being well suited to such tactics. His army grew bigger. Two invading armies he defeated in pitched battle, and slew both commanders, namely, Appollonius and Seron. A third and much larger expedition of some fifty thousand sent direct from Antiochus under the joint command of his generals Ptolemy Macron, Nicanor, and Gorgias, ended in a debacle. Whereupon a great army of sixty-five thousand picked footmen and horsemen invaded Judæa under the chief of all Antiochus's generals, Lysias. The result was the same. Judas's ten thousand men fought with such terrifying desperateness and seemingly superhuman strength that the Syrians were scared, and Lysias retired, realising that nothing but a major campaign would meet the situation.

Judas now assumed the offensive. Jerusalem was captured, the temple refurnished, and on 25th December, the anniversary of its profanation three years earlier, the orthodox sacrifices were re-instituted (which date the Jews still observe as the Feast of the Dedication: see John x. 22). Judas also captured the chief posts up and down the land. Antiochus, it would seem, now contemplated a huge revenge, but a heavy reverse at Elymais in Persia, in addition to the successive defeats in Judæa, seem to have brought upon him a superstitious dread which developed into a fatal sickness. He is said to have died in a state of raving madness.

What might have seemed like a God-given signal of final deliverance, however, proved to be the very opposite. The deadliest crisis of all now came. Antiochus's son was very young. Lysias was the self-appointed Syrian regent. And he now invaded Judæa with an army of one hundred and twenty thousand. Judas and his army were defeated at Bethsura and retired to Jerusalem. There was a long siege. The Maccabees valiantly resisted, but provisions failed. Many of the besieged deserted through sheer hunger. Judas's numbers grew less and less, until capitulation seemed inevitable and the cause lost.

But just when zero-point seemed reached, Lysias suddenly heard of a rival regent at the Syrian capital and induced the young son of Antiochus, with the Syrian princes, to make peace with

Judæa on friendly terms, promising them the restoration of all their religious liberties. Thus the Maccabean revolt, just as it seemed on the point of being crushed, was crowned with success!

Further troubles arose later, however, from a new successor on the Syrian throne, Demetrius I. After anti-Maccabean interferences at Jerusalem, he at length sent an army under Nicanor to kill Judas. Judas defeated it and slew Nicanor. About this time Judas sought an alliance with Rome, which had now become one of the most commanding powers on earth; but before any fruits of such an alliance could be reaped he was slain in battle against a further Syrian army, courageously resisting a multitude with a mere handful of men.

We cannot here narrate the further ups and downs of Judæan Jewry during the ensuing decades, the swayings to and fro between orthodox Maccabeans and the heterodox Hellenising party, continually complicated, as they were, by unintelligent interference from foreign powers. The following comments, however, will indicate the course which things took.

Under Jonathan, the younger brother of Judas Maccabeus, the orthodox party gained the ascendency. He proved an able warrior, gaining signal victories; and through sheer force of circumstances outside Judæa the Syrian and other rulers were obliged to pay him respect. Jonathan, also, became high priest, thus uniting the civil and priestly authority in one person, and thus commencing the "Asmonean" or "Hasmonean" line of high priests (so called from Hashmon, great-grandfather of the Maccabee brothers). Later, however, he was tricked and murdered by a foreign power (143 B.C.), and his brother Simon assumed leadership.

Simon, also, led well. Having captured all other Syrian strongholds in Judæa, he actually forced the Syrian garrison in the *citadel* at Jerusalem to surrender. Thus Judæa was freed of all alien troops; and from that time (about 142 B.C.) was once again under independent Jewish government. Except for one short lapse, this continued until Judæa became a Roman province, in 63 B.C.

Simon, besides ejecting the Syrian garrison from the citadel in Jerusalem, actually levelled down the "mountain" on which it had stood. The people worked night and day for three years, until it was reduced to the ordinary ground-level of the city, so that it might never mean such mischief to them again, and that the temple might now be the highest of all the buildings. Simon was greatly beloved; but after eight years in office he and two of his sons were treacherously murdered by a son-in-law who coveted the high-priesthood.

Simon's remaining son, the able John Hyrcanus, now became high priest. After an initial reverse and a short interval of acknowledged servitude to Syria, he remarkably extended the power of Judæa. In fact, since the break-away of the ten tribes after Solomon's reign no Jewish king had held so spacious an area. He is indeed a notable figure. With him the Asmonean dynasty (135–63 B.C.) is usually reckoned as beginning; though perhaps more truly it commenced with Simon his father, in 140 B.C., when a great assembly at Jerusalem made the dual office of prince and high priest hereditary in the Asmonean family.

John Hyrcanus had a prosperous reign of twenty-nine years, and died in 106 B.C. After him, alas, the record of Jewish independence is far from honourable. The later rulers of the Asmonean line did not have the earlier Maccabean qualities. Bitter partisan controversies became aggravated into recurrent internecine strife and a civil war which was only terminated by later Roman intervention.

When the said John Hyrcanus was dead, his son, Aristobulus, made the leadership into a *kingship* for himself, imprisoning and starving his mother to death in the process, incarcerating three of his four brothers, and negotiating the murder of the other. But this Aristobulus lived only about a year after these evil deeds.

He was followed by Alexander, who, in the internecine bloodshed which stained his reign, slew fifty thousand of his own countrymen. His widowed queen managed to hold the crown for some nine years after his decease, but on her own demise there was bitter contention between her two sons—another Aristobulus and another Hyrcanus.

The Herod family now appears on the scene. Antipater, father of the Herod who reigned at the time of our Lord's birth, managed to secure, by his adroit machinations, the support of the Roman general Pompey for the brother named Hyrcanus. The other brother, Aristobulus, defied Rome. The result was a siege of Jerusalem. After a siege of three months Pompey took the city.

At that time, with callous disregard, he strode into the Holy of
Holies—an action which at once estranged all loyal Jewish hearts
toward the Romans. That was in 63 B.C.

The Roman Period (63 B.C. onwards)

Pompey's subjugation of Jerusalem ended the interval of
Judæa's regained independence. Judæa now became a province
of the Roman empire. The high priest was completely deprived
of any royal status, and retained priestly function only. This
high priest, John Hyrcanus, marks the end of the Asmonean and
Maccabean line of high priests. The governing power was exercised by Antipater the Idumean, who was appointed procurator
of Judæa by Julius Cæsar in 47 B.C.

Antipater appointed Herod (his own son by marriage with
Cypros, an Arabian woman) as governor of Galilee, when Herod
was only fifteen years of age (according to Josephus).

During the war between Pompey and Cæsar the concerns of
Judæa were submerged for the time being in bigger issues. But
after the murder of Cæsar, Herod fled from the disorder which
that event had provoked in Palestine, and appealed to the trium-
virate at Rome, where his manœuvres eventually captured for
him the fond ambition of his heart, even the crown of Judæa. He
was appointed king of the Jews about 40 B.C.

On returning to Judæa he sought to ingratiate himself with the
Jews by his marriage with Mariamne, the beautiful granddaughter
of the Asmonean, John Hyrcanus, and by making her brother
Aristobulus high priest. He also greatly increased the splendour
of Jerusalem, building the elaborate temple which was the centre
of Jewish worship in the time of our Lord.

But he was as cruel and sinister as he was able and ambitious.
He seems to have had an almost Satanic determination to obliterate the Asmonean family; and in pursuance of this he stained
his hands with awful murders. He slew all three of his wife's
brothers—Antigonus, Aristobulus and Hyrcanus. Later he murdered even his wife Mariamne, though she seems to have been the
only one he was ever capable of loving. Again, later, he murdered
his mother-in-law Alexandra. And still later he murdered his own
sons by Mariamne—Aristobulus and Alexander. This is that
"Herod the Great" who was king when our Lord was born.

Such, then, in brief, is the contour of Jewish history in Palestine, viewed externally and politically, during the four centuries between Malachi and Matthew. It is good to fix in memory the six periods which we have outlined. We proceed now to review the period from a religious and spiritual standpoint.

FOR YOUR REFERENCE

in connection with the foregoing review of the period
between Malachi and Matthew

THE PTOLEMIES

(i.e. the dynasty of Greek kings who ruled Egypt during the last phase of Egypt as an empire)

THE SELUCIDAE

(i.e. the dynasty of kings originated by Seleucus Nicator, the founder of the Syrian Monarchy)

THE PTOLEMIES		THE SELUCIDAE	
Ptolemy Soter	323–285	Seleucus Nicator	312–280
Ptolemy Philadelphus	285–247	Antiochus Soter	280–261
		Antiochus Theos	261–246
Ptolemy Euergetes	247–222	Seleucus Callinicus	246–226
		Seleucus Ceraunus	226–223
Ptolemy Philopater	222–205	Antiochus the Great	223–187
Ptolemy Epiphanes	205–181	Seleucus Philopater	187–175
		Antiochus Epiphanes	175–163
Ptolemy Philometer	181–146	Antiochus Eupater	163–162
		Demetrius Soter	162–150
Ptolemy Physcon	146–117	Alexander Balas	150–146
		Demetrius Nicator	146–144
Ptolemy Soter II	117–107	Antiochus Theos	144–142
		Usurper, Tryphon	142–137
Ptolemy Alexander I	107–90	Antiochus Sidetes	137–128
Ptolemy Soter II (further		Demetrius II (again)	128–125
reign)	89–81	Seleucus V	125–124
		Antiochus Grypus	124–96
Ptolemy Alexander II	19 days	Seleucus Epiphanes	95–93

Ptolemy Dionysus	80–51	Soon after this the Syrians, worn out with the civil broils of the Selucidae, handed the kingdom to Tigranes, king of Armenia, in 83 B.C. It became part of the Roman empire in 69 B.C.
Ptolemies XII and XIII with Queen Cleopatra	51–43	
Egypt succumbed to Roman subjection in 30 B.C.		

Such, then, in brief, is the course of Jewish history in Palestine, viewed externally and politically, during the four centuries between Malachi and Matthew. It is good to fix in memory the six periods which we have outlined. We proceed now to review the period from a religious and spiritual standpoint.

FOR YOUR REFERENCE

in connection with the foregoing review of the period between Malachi and Matthew

THE PTOLEMIES		THE SELEUCIDAE	
(a Greek dynasty of kings who ruled Egypt during the last phase of Egypt as an empire)		(the dynasty of kings originated by Seleucus Nicator, the founder of the Syrian Monarchy)	
Ptolemy Soter	323–285	Seleucus Nicator	312–280
Ptolemy Philadelphus	285–247	Antiochus Soter	280–261
		Antiochus Theos	261–246
Ptolemy Euergetes	247–222	Seleucus Callinicus	246–226
		Seleucus Ceraunus	226–223
Ptolemy Philopater	222–205	Antiochus the Great	223–187
Ptolemy Epiphanes	205–181	Seleucus Philopater	187–175
		Antiochus Epiphanes	175–163
Ptolemy Philometer	181–146	Antiochus Eupater	164–162
		Demetrius Soter I	162–150
Ptolemy Physcon	146–117	Alexander Bala	150–146
		Demetrius Nicator	146–144
Ptolemy Soter II	117–107	Antiochus Theos	144–142
		Tryphon	142–137
Ptolemy Alexander I	107–90	Antiochus Sidetes	139–128
Ptolemy Soter (restored reign)		Demetrius II (restored)	128–125
		Seleucus V	125
Ptolemy Alexander II	108–95	Antiochus Grypus	125–95
		Seleucus Epiphanes	95–93
Ptolemy Dionysos	80–51	Soon after this the Syrian monarchy fell, with the dual throne of the Seleucidae. Tigranes, king of Armenia, in 83 B.C. became part of the Roman empire in 64 B.C.	
Ptolemies XII and XIII with Queen Cleopatra	51–43		

Egypt succumbed to Roman subjection in 30 B.C.

THE INTER-TESTAMENT PERIOD

II. The Religious Aspect

Lesson Number 105

It is of the greatest importance to remember . . . that only a minority of the Jews, consisting in all of about 60,000, originally returned from Babylon, first under Zerubbabel and afterwards under Ezra. Nor was this inferiority confined to numbers. The wealthiest and most influential of the Jews remained behind. According to Josephus, with whom Philo substantially agrees, vast numbers, estimated at millions, inhabited the Trans-Euphratic provinces. To judge even by the number of those slain in popular risings (50,000 in Seleucia alone), these figures do not seem greatly exaggerated. A later tradition had it, that so dense was the Jewish population in the Persian Empire, that Cyrus forbade the further return of the exiles, lest the country should be depopulated. So large and compact a body soon became a political power. Kindly treated under the Persian monarchy, they were, after the fall of that empire, favoured by the successors of Alexander. When in turn the Macedono-Syrian rule gave place to the Parthian empire, the Jews formed, from their national opposition to Rome, an important element in the East. Such was their influence that, so late as the year A.D. 40, the Roman legate shrank from provoking their hostility. At the same time it must not be thought that, even in these favoured regions, they were wholly without persecution. Here also history records more than one tale of bloody strife on the part of those among whom they dwelt.

—A. Edersheim, D.D.

BETWEEN MALACHI AND MATTHEW (2)

WE CANNOT read far into the pages of our New Testament without sensing that great changes have come over Jewry since the last writer of the Old Testament laid down his pen. It is not simply that Palestine has changed hands half a dozen times, as foreign powers have successively wrested it from each other, and that these changes have chiselled their marks deeply on the nation. Jewry itself has changed. There are new sects or parties—Pharisees, Sadducees, Herodians. There are new institutions—Synagogue, Scribes, Sanhedrin.

In fact Jewry has now developed into a kind of national "ism," i.e. *Judaism*. A remarkable condition of things has evolved in which the whole nation is practically identifiable with this cultus, this Judaism which has grown up round the Old Testament Scriptures. Jewry (the people) and Judaism (the religion) are now practically co-extensive, and each implies the other.

All these changes—the rise of these new sects and institutions, and the evolution of Judaism—have come about during those four hundred years between the Old Testament and the New. This in itself shows what importance attaches to the inter-Testament interval. So, then, having already reviewed those four centuries as to the exterior course of Jewish history, let us now briefly trace the major internal and religious developments.

Internal Developments

To begin with, if we are to understand in general the spirit and trend of the Jewish community during that stretch of centuries we must appreciate the profound impact made upon the nation by the *Babylonian exile*. Let the mind travel away back for a moment to the Books of the Kings. After the death of King Solomon there was a disruption in the Hebrew commonwealth which was never repaired. Ten of the tribes broke away from the house of David and set up a kingdom of their own, so that henceforth there were two kingdoms instead of the one. There was the ten-tribed northern kingdom, with Samaria as its capital; and there was the southern kingdom of Judah, with Jerusalem as its capital. After an inglorious career of two and a half centuries, the ten-tribed kingdom was swept away by the Assyrians, the tribes were dispersed in foreign territories, and the Assyrian emperor re-peopled their land with a heterogeneous mixture of captives drafted there from other regions. That dispersion was in 721 B.C., and the substitute people who were afterward deposited in the former Israelite territory became known as the Samaritans.

The southern kingdom Judah continued another century and a half, then succumbed to Babylon, the new world-power which had now supplanted the Assyrian empire. In 587 B.C. Judæa was overrun, Jerusalem was reduced to ruins, and the bulk of the people were carried away to Babylonia. That Babylonian exile is often spoken of as the *seventy-years* exile, but actually it was not that length. It certainly is true that for exactly seventy years (from 606, when Daniel and other Judæan princes were carried away, to 536, when the Babylonian empire fell) God used Babylon to scourge His covenant people; but the exile itself was only *fifty* years in duration. It had such a profound impact upon the Jewish people that we need to see just how decisive it was if we are to understand Jewish religious developments during the inter-Testament period.

Inveterate Idolatry Cured

When one reflects on the unique privileges and covenant relationship and high calling of the chosen people, the exile was a superlative catastrophe. Yet it was Divinely overruled to bring about such a transformation in the religious conceptions of the Hebrew people as can only be described as one of the most astounding revolutions in the history of any nation. The Jews went into that exile with what seemed a hopelessly incurable infatuation for idolatry; they emerged from it what they have remained to this day, the most monotheistic people in the world, the custodians and promulgators of belief in the one true God, Jehovah.

Look back over their history. Scarcely are they out of Egypt before they are worshipping the golden calf. Scarcely are they settled in Canaan before they are in the groves of Baalim, and prostrating themselves before Ashtaroth of the Phœnicians. In the peak period of the monarchy Solomon himself leads the nation in the worship of Milcom, the abomination of the Ammonites, and of Chemosh, the abomination of the Moabites, and of Molech and others equally abominable. After the break-away of the ten tribes we find Jeroboam setting up his golden calves in Dan and Bethel; and that was but the beginning of one long and shocking record of idolatry, aggravated by such reigns as that of Ahab and his heathen wife Jezebel, until the incurably apostate kingdom was dissolved in the Assyrian dispersal. As for the southern kingdom, i.e. Judah, despite the reigns of several godly kings, the evil of idolatry went from bad to worse, until, in the reigns of Manasseh, Jehoiachin and Zedekiah, things came to an intolerable pass. Jeremiah, the prophet of Judah's zero hour, cries, "According to the number of thy cities are thy gods, O Judah."

Yet here is this extraordinary fact, that after the Babylonian exile the Jewish people are totally and for ever converted from idolatry into convinced worshippers of the one true God.

How shall we account for it? What was it, in that short interval of fifty years, which so decisively achieved what all previous chastisements and prophetic exhortations and royal reformations and divine warnings had failed to effect? It certainly was not the Babylonian environment, for Babylon was the hotbed of idolatry. Its gods and altars and shrines were well nigh as old as civilisation and were venerated far and wide. Babylon might well have increased the idolatry of the Jews, but it certainly could not have cured it.

Yet there must be *some* explanation of Israel's swift and final renunciation of idolatry; for no people can undergo such a basal and enduring transformation of ideas without there being some overpowering compulsion. What, then, was it which so fully and finally converted the whole of this people?

The Supernatural Factors

The answer is that it was *the miracle of prophecy being fulfilled before their very eyes*. Away back in the writings of their own prophets, Isaiah and Jeremiah, the very happenings that were now upon them had been clearly foretold. The destruction of Jerusalem, the exile of Judæa's sons and daughters in Babylon, the subsequent sudden overthrowing of Babylon itself, the brilliant conquests of Cyrus the Persian who overthrew Babylon, the ensuing edict of Cyrus for the restoring of the temple at Jerusalem—these were all foretold two hundred years in advance, along with Jeremiah's more recent and even more specific prophecies concerning the seventy-year period assigned of God to Babylon for the scourging of Judah, and the shorter interval of actual exile in Babylonia (see Isa. xliii. 14, xliv. 28, xlv. 1–7, xlvi. 1–11, xlvii. 1–11, xlviii, 3–7; Jer. xxv. 8–14, l., li.).

Little did the Jews think, as they were dragged into Babylonia, that within fifty years the mighty, opulent and seemingly unassailable capital of Nebuchadnezzar's wide-spreading empire would be overthrown for ever, that Cyrus the Persian would be the conqueror, and that almost immediately he would give the Jews the opportunity to return to Judæa in possession of a royal edict for the rebuilding of the temple. Yet it all happened; and the exiled Jews, with wondering eyes, saw it all happening exactly as foretold by JEHOVAH through His Hebrew prophets! There was absolutely no gainsaying it all. It was evidence conclusive. The historian Josephus as good as tells us that the emperor Cyrus was himself converted through the marvel of it.

And, in addition to this, God had put a *wonderful witness to Himself in the very court at Babylon.* After the emperor himself, the most renowned figure of the era was the man DANIEL. Through him, this far-famed Jew, this man of uncompromising loyalty to Jehovah, such miracles of Divine wisdom and power had been wrought as had outclassed all that the arts and magic of Babylon could do. Daniel was indeed a wonderful monument to the reality and supremacy of Jehovah. Every Jew in Babylon must have marvelled and pondered. And how the Jews must have marvelled at the gracious promises which God had attached to some of Isaiah's predictions about the Babylonian exile—promises of blessing and restoration if the exiled people would renounce their idolatry and become the true servants of Jehovah!

Thus, at length, the Hebrew people were startled into the realisation that the gods of the heathen were lying vanities, and that Jehovah was the one true God, the Creator of all things, the sovereign Ruler of the universe, whose will alone is sovereign over the armies of heaven and among the inhabitants of the earth. Once and for all they were cured of their idolatry; and they became for ever afterwards the confirmed worshippers of their covenant God Jehovah.

Rise and Growth of Judaism

And now, recognising in that profound, national reconversion the most determining of all factors in subsequent Jewish history, let us travel in thought with the fifty thousand who returned from Babylonia to Judæa in response to the edict of the Emperor Cyrus.

Those fifty thousand are known as the "Remnant." They were *only* a remnant: the bulk of the nation remained in Babylonia. Doubtless there would be large numbers to whom the uprooting from Babylonia and the traversing of those hundreds of miles back to Judæa would be very difficult, if not impossible. Some would find it so for family reasons, others for reasons of age or ill-health. Some would feel unequal to the struggle of resettling in ruined cities and villages, and reclaiming the weed-entangled ground, uncultivated now for half a century. Others would intend to return, but later. And apparently many others, even though their convincement against idolatry was genuine and permanent, did not equally feel it a point of conscience to return to the land itself.

Of this we may be quite sure, those fifty thousand who returned were the devoutest of the devout. They knew what they believed, and why they believed it. They knew why they were returning. They realised, at least in part, the difficulties awaiting them; and they well knew what they intended to do in Judæa.

Back in Judæa: so what?

So then we return to Judæa with the Remnant. What do they find? Try to get into their minds. Besides those things which strike the eye—the silted ruins and tangled undergrowth and heart-sickening reminders of earlier tragedies, there are certain *absences* which strike the *mind*. There is no *king* and no throne; the royal line of David is gone. There is no *temple*; and even though a new one may be built on the old foundations, it can never take the place of its incomparable predecessor. And no longer is there any *national independence*, for, although the fifty thousand have returned with the purpose of re-establishing a Jewish state in Judæa, they are only there on sufferance as a subject province in a restricted area covering merely a small part of the former kingdom of Judah.

No throne, no temple, no independence! What is left? Why have these Jews returned to such ruins and wastes and hardships? Why have they returned with such devout eagerness? It is because there is still one thing left which has recently become the most precious and vital possession in all the world to them and their fellow nationals: it is the treasure of their sacred SCRIPTURES. These have now proved themselves beyond doubt to be the inspired word of the one true God, Jehovah; and they are the articles of Jehovah's covenant with the people Israel. In the Law of Moses, the Pentateuch, these Jews now read with new eyes the basis of their commonwealth and vocation; and also, with strange new emotions, they see therein the threatened penalties for disobedience which have now been fulfilled with terrible exactness in the disbanding of the kingdom and the exiling of the tribes.

But besides this, these Jews now see in their Scriptures, especially in the prophets, the wonderful succession of predictions concerning the coming of a Messiah who should permanently regather and exalt the chosen people, and under whose glorious reign all the promised blessings of the Abrahamic covenant should burst into fulfilment. All the other predictions have come true, as these Jews have themselves lived to witness, and so will all these further promises which tell of this coming Messiah. Thus do these fifty thousand returned exiles rightly reason within themselves; and they return to their homeland, therefore, animated by new zeal for the Law and with new hope for the future.

Law from Past: Hope for Future

Now these two things—this new zeal for the Law and this Messianic hope—lie at the very root of "Judaism," the system of Jewish religion which originated just after the Exile and developed during the inter-Testament period. The Jewish state, as restored under the Remnant leaders Zerubbabel and Jeshua, belongs to a different order of things from the earlier kingdoms of Judah and Israel. More often than otherwise, in those pre-exile kingdoms, the higher truths of Israel's religion had been maintained only by the prophets and a small minority, while the vast majority played fast and loose with various idolatries, and apparently recognised little essential difference between Jehovah and other gods. But *now* there is an utter aversion to idolatry, and the people as a whole recognise the immeasurable superiority of Israel's religion to every form of paganism. There is now an impelling new desire to grasp the imperishable truths of the revelation which has been committed to them as the covenant nation, and a passion that the nation shall fulfil its vocation as the guardian of that peerless deposit of Divine truth which will ultimately mean salvation to the ends of the earth. These fifty thousand purpose to fashion the new Jewish state as the holy people of Jehovah, separated from all others by the most scrupulous observance of His Law.

To translate this lofty concept into actual operation, however, in the forming and running of a new social organism, proved to be beset with difficulties. One of these, of course, was the unhalting process by which people die and others grow up in their place. Many of the fifty thousand who returned were aged or elderly (Ezra iii. 12). Their return to the land only preceded their demise by a few years. The children who grew up could not perhaps feel quite the same vividness of emotion about the repatriation, and there was much to discourage even the stoutest heart among them. Thus, not only was there opposition from external enemies, but also apathy and compromise among the people themselves. Still, the root ideas of Judaism had really taken hold, and there was no compromise in the matter of idolatry. What the people needed was a new and systematic teaching of the Law; and when Ezra the scribe came, eighty years *after* the return of the fifty thousand, the people responded; there were decided improvements, and the first objective seemed to become possible of realisation again.

As Professor John Skinner says: "Under Ezra's auspices, a great reformation was carried through. The principle of separation from the heathen was revived and relentlessly enforced by the dissolution of all mixed marriages (Ezra ix., x.). In a great assembly of the people the book of the Law was adopted as the written constitution of the state and the authoritative rule of individual life (Neh. viii.–x.). Ezra's efforts were vigorously seconded and continued by Nehemiah, who had set himself, in the first instance, to render Jerusalem safe from attack by rebuilding the walls. By the joint labours of these two men Judaism was at last placed on a secure foundation. The Law now became at once the standard of holiness and the symbol of nationality; and in spite of disintegrating tendencies still at work, it gained such a hold on the affections of the Jewish people that all danger of their being absorbed by the surrounding nations was at an end."

Synagogue, Scribes, Oral Law

Thenceforth the local *synagogue*, in which the Scriptures were read and expounded, and the order of the *scribes*, who were the specialists in translating and explaining those Scriptures, assumed an ever-increasing importance.

Alas, from that time, also, there began to form that elaborate system of interpretations, amplifications and additional regulations of which the Judaism of our Lord's time was the result. We know what that finished product was, and how utterly lacking in vital spirituality our Lord found it to be.

Judaism originated while the living voice of prophecy was still speaking through the post-exile prophets, Haggai, Zechariah and Malachi, but its distinguishing characteristics were developed during the succeeding centuries between Malachi and Matthew when that voice had become silent. Haggai, Zechariah and Malachi all reiterate the high ethics of the pre-exile prophets— their stern rebuke of mere formalism, and their glowing prophecies of the ultimate restoration of Israel, in national and religious supremacy, under the coming Messiah. Judaism began with the passion and purpose to keep alive that exalted ideal amid outward persecutions and inward divisions, but pedagogues and synagogues gradually brought in such slavery to the mere letter of Scripture that the living spirit of true religion could scarce survive. More and more the trend became one of legalistic literalism and religious externalism. There accumulated around the Scriptures, and especially around the Law of Moses, that mass of comment, interpretation and supplementation which became known as the *Oral Law*, and which was handed down with such traditional sanctity that by the time our Lord was on earth obedience had become transferred from the Law to the traditional interpretation.

Mishna and Talmud

This MISHNA, or Oral Law, with its *Halachoth* (legal exegesis or determinations) and its *Haggadoth* (moral, practical, and often fanciful expansions), after being handed down orally for generations, was gradually committed to writing in its various parts and forms, until finally, about the end of the second century A.D., it was all compiled by Rabbi Jehuda into the TALMUD, which is in two main parts: (1) the *Mishna*, or Oral Law, and (2) the *Gemara*, or commentaries upon the *Mishna*; and the Talmud remains the revered and largely authoritative encyclopædia of Jewry to this day.

In our Lord's time the Oral Law was *still* mainly oral. We can appreciate what a formidable obstacle He found it. To contradict it, as He did (Matt. xv. 1–9, xxiii. 16–18, 23), was to go against the whole weight of scholarly opinion, devout conviction, and public sentiment. Moreover, we can well understand that when, in the Sermon on the Mount, our Lord six times (see Matt. v.) used the formula "Ye have heard that it was *said* . . . but *I* say unto you . . ." He was not putting His "I say unto you" over against the Old Testament Scriptures (as some modern critics have tried to make out) but against maxims of this *oral* or traditional law. His customary way of referring to the Scriptures themselves was, "It is written."

So much, then, for "Judaism." We need not forget that there were *good* elements preserved in it. In its earlier stages it certainly restored the Scriptures to their proper place in the popular mind; and its two most characteristic institutions—the synagogue and the scribe—were meant to perpetuate this. It certainly did maintain the regular and systematic public reading of the Scriptures. It fostered devout regard for the Sabbath, and it kept aflame the Messianic hope, though not in the earlier and truer spirit. Its evil lay in that which it *superimposed* upon the Scriptures. In the end it resulted in such a hard and ceremonial religiosity, generally speaking, that when our Lord came the most formidable obstruction to His gracious mission was the dead-weight of religious externalism, formalism, and self-effort righteousness by which Judaism had well nigh obliterated the spiritual truths of God's Word.

The Synagogue

There is not a word about synagogues in the Old Testament, not even in the latest-written chapters; but as soon as we read on into the four Gospels we find them everywhere, a synagogue to practically every occupied locality of the land; and when we read on into the Acts of the Apostles we find them similarly estab-

lished everywhere among the many Jewish communities throughout the Roman empire.

That is a remarkable fact, and it may well be noted by the
Christian believer, for it was from the synagogue and not from
the temple that the early Christian Church, as organised by the
apostles, took its constitution and main forms of worship. Our
Lord Himself evidently visualised His Church on earth as assuming the synagogal form when He promised that He would be in
the midst wherever two or three were gathered in His name and
when He gave authority to such groups to exercise discipline
(Matt. xviii. 17–20). Furthermore, the titles given by the New
Testament epistles to Christian church office-bearers, i.e. "Elders"
(*presbuteroi*), "Bishops" (*episkopoi*), "Deacons" (*diakonoi*), are
all carried over from the synagogue, while never once is the title
"Priest" (*hierus*) appropriated from the Jewish temple.

The synagogue has been called "the most characteristic and
lastingly influential of all Jewish institutions." When, why, and
how did it originate? The facts seem to be as follows.

Non-existent before Exile

First, the synagogue did not exist *before* the Exile. Jewish
rabbins, in their zeal to enhance the venerableness of Israelite
institutions, have elastically exaggerated the antiquity of the
synagogue, tracing it as far back as Abraham. But the uncontra-
dictable fact is that the synagogue, in the proper sense of the
word, as a regularly constituted religious assembly with a definite
object and fixed officials, never existed, nor did anything like it,
before the Exile.

It may be said that the word "synagogues" occurs in psalm
lxxiv. 8; but that is purely a matter of translation. The Hebrew
word (*mo'adah*) so translated occurs two hundred times in the
Old Testament, and this is the only place where it is translated
as "synagogue." That fact will speak for itself. The word
properly refers to the *solemn feasts* or *set seasons* in Israel's
religious calendar, and then, by extension, to the places where
these were observed. It has nothing to do with the synagogue
idea. Psalm lxxiv. was written soon after the Babylonians had
desolated the land, and therefore synchronises with the Lamentations of Jeremiah. In Lamentations we have the same word used

in chapter ii. 6, 7, 22, and one only needs to look at the "solemn feasts" or "solemn appointments" mentioned there to see that there is no possible connection with the synagogue. Moreover, the same word reappears with the Remnant after the return from Babylon, in Ezra iii. 5 and Nehemiah x. 33, where it is again translated as "set feasts," and where obviously any idea of the synagogue is utterly foreign.

In 2 Chronicles xvii. 7–9 we are told that King Jehoshaphat had to send certain princes and Levites and priests, carrying the book of the Law with them, to teach the people, up and down the land; and in chapter xxxiv. 14–21 we are told of the amazement and alarm awakened in the mind of King Josiah when the book of the Law was rediscovered in his days (only forty years before the Exile), so that the synagogue certainly could not have existed before the Exile.

Soon in being after Exile.

Yet it is equally certain that the synagogue was in being *soon after* the Exile. In Acts xv. 21 we find the Apostle James saying? "For Moses *of old time* hath in every city them that preach him, being read *in the synagogues* every Sabbath day." So the synagogues must then have been several hundred years old. And correspondingly with this, in Nehemiah viii. (ninety years after the return of the Remnant) something very nearly approaching the synagogal worship in its fully developed state meets us. There is the elevated pulpit of wood, the reading of the Law by Ezra and others, the explanation of the Law by the scribes, the praying and praising in the name of the congregation, with the responses of the people, all being after the usual pattern of the synagogue worship. And, significantly enough, it is the people themselves who "spake unto Ezra the scribe, to bring the book of the Law of Moses which the Lord had commanded to Israel." The narratives concerning Ezra certainly seem to imply a background in which the practice of organised, periodic meetings had become familiar (Ezra viii. 15; Neh. viii. 1, 2, ix. 1).

The conclusion seems clear, therefore, that the synagogue originated *during* the Exile, synchronising with the remarkable conversion of the Jewish people from idolatry and their awakening to an intense new interest in their sacred Scriptures. With that upsurge of religious revival there came a heart-cry to know more of those wonderful Scriptures. Devout souls, impelled by common longing and impulse, now began to meet regularly and more systematically for the purpose of learning the contents of those inspired Rolls. There was no longer a Jewish temple, and they were in a foreign land, but their captivity in Babylon was not of the sort which proscribed meetings together for religious purposes. The urgent new demand and the opportunity went hand in hand. The demand was the greater because all but the older Jews were now losing their knowledge of the Hebrew language, and were speaking in the language of Babylonia. Thus, regular gatherings would begin to take shape, for the reading and interpreting of the Scriptures.

That is how the synagogue *came into being*, and it explains at once why synagogues were so widely spread among the Jews of the dispersion as well as in the new Jewish state which the Remnant set up in Judæa. Undoubtedly during the five hundred years from the end of the Exile to the time of our Lord the synagogue would undergo many modifications, but its basic ideas and forms remained the same.

Basic Idea, Method, Features

The basic idea of the synagogue was *instruction in the Scriptures*, not worship, even though an elaborate liturgical service developed later, with public prayers read by appointed persons, and responses made by the congregation. Also, since the public reading of the Law had now to be by translation into the Aramaic tongue which the people had learned in Babylonia (see Neh. viii. 8, where such translation is implied), the transition from translation to *exposition* and even to *discourses* was easy, though no doubt it took place gradually.

That such synagogue discourses were common *in our Lord's time* is seen in such references as Matthew iv. 23, ix. 35; Luke iv. 15, 44; Acts xiii. 5, 15, xiv. 1, xvii. 10, xviii. 19. These verses also show us that the right to utter instruction was not confined to those who were the regularly trained and appointed teachers. The leader of the congregation might invite *any* suitable person whom he saw present to address the people; and anyone could *offer* to do so. Thus we find that our Lord, though not trained in any of the schools, could everywhere preach and teach in the synagogues. Similarly, we find in Acts xiii. 15: "And after the reading of the law and the prophets the rulers of the synagogue sent unto them [i.e. Paul and Barnabas, who were strangers], saying: Ye men and brethren, if ye have any word of exhortation for the people, say on."

As to its *constitution*, the most important feature of the synagogue was that it was *congregational*, not priestly. Priests were always honoured when present, but they had no special synagogue privileges, their functions being regarded as belonging specially to the temple, where their right to perform those functions was hereditary. In the synagogue the office-bearers were *not* hereditary; they were constituted by congregational vote or consent. There was a "ruler" or president, and a council of elders who also were called "rulers" (Mark v. 22; Acts xiii. 15). There was a "legate," whose duty it was to recite the prayers. There were "deacons," who looked after the alms. There was the *chazzan*, who called out the names of the appointed readers and stood by the readers to see that the lessons of the day were read accurately, pronounced properly, etc. It was he, also, who took care of the Scripture rolls, blew the trumpet which announced the approach of the Sabbath, saw to the lighting of the lamps, superintended the synagogue furniture, and applied the scourge when punishment was afflicted. (He is referred to as "minister" in Luke iv. 20.)

As to *discipline*, the jurisdiction of the synagogue became very extensive, which was inevitable in a constitution where the ecclesiastical and the civil law were one, as in post-exile Jewry.

The synagogue became and has remained the most characteristic and influential of all Jewish institutions. It has been truly said: "It was the great means of religious instruction, the great centre of religious thought. However trifling may have been the tone of its teaching at times in the hands of the recognised instructors of Israel, it was in it, at least, and in it alone, that the Law was publicly read, that explanations of it were given, free discourses delivered, and the minds of the people stirred. The great institution of preaching—one entirely unknown to heathenism—took its rise in the synagogue; and that zeal for the Law, by which Israel was so strikingly marked from the period of the return from Babylon to the coming of Christ, was cherished and increased by its arrangements more than any other agency."

THE INTER-TESTAMENT PERIOD

III. Scribes, Pharisees, and Sadducees

Lesson Number 106

The history of Israel and all their prospects were intertwined with their religion; so that it may be said that without their religion they had no history, and without their history no religion. Thus history, patriotism, religion, and hope alike pointed to Jerusalem and the temple as the centre of Israel's unity.

—*A. Edersheim.*

BETWEEN MALACHI AND MATTHEW (3)

(1) THE SCRIBES

WHO AND what were the "scribes," those none-too-attractive figures who appear so frequently in the Gospel narratives? That they were an influential class is evident; and we ought to know something about them as we travel through our New Testament.

We read of scribes away back in Old Testament times, but *they* must be distinguished from that further order of scribes which developed during the inter-Testament period and had acquired such important status in our Lord's time.

The scribes who meet us in the Gospel narratives were a class of professional experts in the interpretation and application of the Law and the other Old Testament Scriptures. If we give them their Hebrew name, they were the *sopherim* (*im* is the Hebrew plural), from the Hebrew verb *saphar,* which means to write, to set in order, to count. In the Greek of the New Testament their usual title is the plural, *grammateis*, uniformly translated as "scribes." Less frequently they are called "lawyers" (*nomikoi*), as in Luke vii. 30.

Origin as a Class

As to their *origin* as a class, much the same may be said of them as about the synagogue. Whatever may have been the functions and characteristics of Israelite scribes in Old Testament times, and whatever may have been the guild of transcribers fostered by King Hezekiah about a century before the Babylonian exile, there can be no doubt that from the time of that Babylonian exile there developed a new line of scribes who were not just penmen, recorders, transcribers, secretaries, but a new *body* of men who became the guardians, the expounders, the doctors of the Law and of the other Scriptures, to the whole nation, and whose power as a class increased the more as time went on. They were not just scribes in the older sense, but *"the* scribes," as a specially distinguished order in the nation.

The transition was due to five factors: (1) the mid-exile conversion of the Jewish people from idolatry to a passionate new faith in their own religion and Scriptures; (2) the need which the exiled people now felt for special teachers, owing to separation from their own land and capital and temple; (3) the change-over from Hebrew, as a spoken language, to Aramaic, necessitating a new kind of specialist in the study and exposition of the sacred Scriptures; (4) the rise and spread of the synagogue during and after the Babylonian exile; (5) the cessation of the living voice of prophecy, with Malachi, and the accentuated interest which that occasioned in the *written* word of inspiration, i.e. the Scriptures.

It is not difficult to see how, when once this new order of scribes came in, it rapidly gained great power. The very nature of the new Judaism made this almost inevitable, for as it has been truly observed, "The aim and tendency of Judaism was to make every Jew personally responsible for the keeping of the whole Law"; and therefore "a definite rule" had somehow to be extracted from the Law to cover practically every activity of daily life. This endeavour to make the Law such a detailed code created a complex and sometimes acute problem. In some way or another the Law had to be made to speak even on circumstances to which it did not specifically apply; and when one requirement seemed to be contradicted by another, some hidden harmony or other suitable explanation must be shown. As Dr. John Skinner adds: "How to be faithful to God's covenant under such conditions came to be a serious theoretical difficulty, and it could only be overcome by the continuous labours of a body of trained experts, who made the study of the Law the great business of their lives." What this came to mean in a society where the civil and religious law were one can easily be imagined.

We may say that the new order of scribes originated with the great and saintly Ezra, though Ezra must not be associated with the elaborate deteriorations which developed later. It was in 458 B.C., some eighty years after the Jewish Remnant had left Babylon to resettle in Judæa, that Ezra followed, with his smaller contingent of two thousand some hundred persons. He is described with an emphasising distinctness as "a ready scribe in the Law of Moses," and "a scribe of the words of the commandments of the Lord, and of His statutes to Israel" (Ezra vii. 6, 11). Even in the decree of Artaxerxes he is named "the scribe of the Law of the

God of heaven" (Ezra vii. 21). It is quite clear that with Ezra the office of scribe reaches a new dignity. In Nehemiah viii. 1–8 we see Ezra elevated in a pulpit, reading and expounding and applying the Law, and, along with Levite assistants, "causing the people to understand the Law" (now that Hebrew was no longer their spoken language). Thenceforward there gradually developed that class of specialists who employed themselves in the Hebrew Scriptures and sought to administer them as a directory for all practice, even down to details. No doubt at first they rendered a valuable service; for so long as the living voice of prophecy continued, before which all Israel bowed, their subordination preserved their usefulness.

Subsequent Misdirection

As the late Dr. William Milligan says: "It is after the inspiration of the prophetic period was over, and when the canon was complete, that we must look for the degenerating of their spirit and for the increase of their power. Amidst the multiplied foreign influences which, from this period onward to the beginning of the Christian era, were ever threatening the existence of all that was most distinctive of the chosen people, the Law needed to be preserved with the most jealous care. It had at the same time to be studied, and its precepts applied to the ever-changing circumstances of the national condition and life. This application of it, however, was made not by unfolding the spirit of the Law, but by positive prescriptions—prescriptions indeed which only professed to explain it, but which, doing this in a concise, sententious, authoritative manner, and leaving nothing to the judgment of the hearers, could not fail to invest the rules thus given with an authority hardly less great than that of the inspired writings themselves. . . . Hence, accordingly, it was almost impossible to avoid what seem to have become the two leading principles of the scribes: first, the multiplying of oral traditions; and secondly, the introduction of such a system of interpretation and exposition of Scripture as utterly destroyed its meaning, and, under pretence of honouring it, in reality overthrew it."

In course of time this ever-multiplying body of handed-down oral tradition became regarded as being even above the Law itself. "Step by step the scribes were led to conclusions at which, we may believe, the earlier representatives of the order would have

started back with horror. Decisions on fresh questions were
accumulated into a complex system of casuistry. The new precepts, still transmitted orally, more precisely fitting into the circumstances of men's lives than the old, came practically to take
their place. The right relation between moral and ceremonial
laws was not only forgotten but absolutely inverted." The study
of the Scriptures themselves degenerated into an absorption with
mere minutiae, a concentration on supposedly hidden meanings
even in syllables and letters, fuddling engrossment with the
mere "letter" of the Word, until idolatry of the letter destroyed
the very reverence in which it had originated, and true spiritual
instruction became all but extinct. It is not surprising that the
people were arrested by the contrast between the forthright teaching of Jesus and that of the scribes (Matt. vii. 28, 29); nor is it
surprising that our Lord condemned this hyper-veneration for the
"tradition of the elders" (Mark vii. 7, 8), or that the scribes,
eager to retain their hold, determinedly opposed our Lord and
His teaching.

Some Necessary Distinctions

The scribes must be carefully distinguished from the *priests*.
To ourselves, perhaps, it may seem rather strange that the occupation of expounding and administering the Scriptures did not
from the first become identified with the priesthood in Israel; but
it is not so strange in reality. The function of the priest related
entirely to the official ceremonies and duties of the temple worship.
Of course, a man might be a priest and yet devote his free time
to a study of the Law and the other Scriptures, thus becoming
both a priest and a scribe (as the great Ezra himself was: see
Ezra vii. 1–11), and no doubt many priests did this; but the two
activities were always recognised as quite distinct. Several times
in the Gospels we find the scribes and the priests coupled together,
which indicated their consciousness of close connection in the one
religious system. Notwithstanding this, however, their functions
were separate. Most of the earlier scribes were laymen who,
through concentrated study, had acquired proficiency in the
Scriptures and Oral Law according to the required standards;
though later, in many cases, there was a course of study at the
school of some rabbi in Jerusalem.

The scribes must also be distinguished from the *Pharisees*. Again and again in the Gospel narratives they are mentioned in conjunction with the Pharisees (Matt. v. 20, xii. 38, xv. 1, xxiii. 2; Mark ii. 16; Luke v. 21, 30, etc.), but although this reveals closeness of affinity it does not imply oneness of identity. The Pharisees were an ecclesiastical *party*, held together by their peculiar aims and views, whereas the scribes were a body of experts in a scholastic sense. Certainly a man might be both a Pharisee and a scribe; and the fact is, that practically all the scribes *were* Pharisees in outlook and association, hence their being so often mentioned *along with* the Pharisees; yet the two fraternities were different from each other. The scribes were not a kind of *section* of the Pharisaic party: they acted an independent part and are mentioned separately in a number of places (Matt. vii. 29, xvii. 10; Mark ix. 11, 14, 16, etc.). A man might conceivably be all three—a priest, a Pharisee and a scribe—yet those three connections covered quite distinct areas of his life: the first related to daily occupation, the second to religious conviction, the third to special vocation. Similarly a man might be a priest, a scribe and a Sadducee, though there is no clear evidence that any of the scribes *was* a Sadducee, which circumstance was due presumably to the rationalistic attitude of the Sadducean party.

We cannot here name and describe the several parts which made up the so-called Oral Law and which eventually (in the second century A.D.) became fixed in written form. We shall refer to that in an addendum on the Jewish Talmud.

That there was much corruption behind the outward sanctity of the scribal profession is all too true, and our Lord severely denounced it (Matt. xxiii. 13–28). Yet it should not be supposed that *all* the scribes were of that sort. Names of such men as Nicodemus and Gamaliel and the renowned Hillel prove otherwise. To an anonymous scribe our Lord once said, "Thou art not far from the kingdom of heaven." It has been truly said, however, that in the main "they constituted a caste marked not only by the worst type but by the very quintessence of Pharisaism; and the general tendency of their spirit and instructions was, as appears by all records of it in the Talmud, the very antipodes of the Gospel of Christ. Hence the severity of the Saviour's reproofs, and the righteousness of the woes which He denounced against them."

(2) THE PHARISEES

However much we may dislike the obtruding characteristics of the Pharisees as we see them in the Gospel narratives, we cannot but sense that collectively they were an influential and extraordinary sect. Our Lord said such things *of* them and *to* them, and their bitter opposition to Him had such deadly consequences that we ought to know who and what they were.

Their origin as a movement may be compared to a river which flows underground for some distance before coming to the surface and flowing visibly onwards. The typical spirit and attitudes of Phariseeism were present in post-exile Jewry long enough before the fraternity took its historical form under the name "Pharisees."

Causal Factors: (1) Separatism Based on the Law

For the protogenesis of the Pharisee movement we must go right back again to the beginning of the inter-Testament period. When the Remnant returned to Judæa after the Exile, their aim was to reconstruct the repatriated Jewish community as a nation *separated* from all others to Jehovah by the most scrupulous observance of His law. The incarnation of this idea in and through the new social organisation was much more problematical in practice than in theory, and there were many setbacks; but the ideal was ever there, especially among the more devout.

As we have said, when Ezra and his addendum "remnant" of some two thousand came to Jerusalem eighty years after the main body had settled there he headed up an already needed reformation in which the first ideal of separation became supreme again. By common consent all mixed marriages were dissolved, and other irregularities corrected. In a mass meeting, and by signed covenant, the book of the Law was acclaimed as the binding standard for both state and individual. Separation to Jehovah was the controlling ideal.

Causal Factors: (2) Mounting Influence of High Priest

From that time (approx. 458–445 B.C.) during the comparatively uneventful period of Persian overlordship (536–333 B.C.) the importance and prestige of the high-priesthood steadily mounted. That is not surprising. Holding as he did, by inherited right, the supreme sacred office in a state which had no king but God, he was bound to wield a unique influence from the outset. Both the sacred and the civil authority became more and more merged in the one figure, until, instead of installing separate *civil* governors, the Persian government left the Jewish high priest solely responsible for the whole civil administration and the tribute levy to Persia.

There came other developments, too, which are not so surprising, human nature being what it is. The high-priesthood gradually became the coveted office of ambitious ecclesiastics who thought far more of its political advantages than of its spiritual responsibilities. Nor is it very surprising that this led, later on, to unscrupulousness, criminality, and degradation of the office, which harmfully affected the course of the national history. Nor is it surprising that over against this there should be provoked into existence *a movement all the more sharply advocating strict adherence to the God-given national Law and the original ideals of Judaism.*

Causal Factors: (3) Rise of Two Opposing Bodies

The first signs of two main opposing groups inside the nation are found fairly early in the inter-Testament period. Dr. Skinner says: "From a very early period there were two ruling classes in Judæa, each aspiring to supreme influence on its own lines— the priests on the ground of their official position, and the scribes on the ground of the authority of the Law.

"It is a remarkable fact that of all circles of Jewish society the upper ranks of the priesthood were the least influenced by the theocratic spirit, the most susceptible to foreign influences, and the readiest in times of temptation to abandon the fundamental principles of their religion. . . . The scribes, on the contrary, were the zealous champions of the integrity of the Law, and the upholders of all that was distinctive in Judaism. They were the life and soul of the popular resistance to paganism, which carried the nation safely through the dangers of the Greek period, in spite of the apostasy of the chief priests."

It was through the scribes during the Persian period (536–333 B.C.) that "the great principles of holiness through separation became deeply rooted in the mind of the community, and the Jewish character gradually acquired the austere exclusiveness and devotion to the externals of religion which ever afterwards excited the antipathy of the heathen world."

There was no healing the rift between the priestly clique and the scribes. It went on and on, until it eventually crystallised itself into "Sadducees" versus "Pharisees."

Historical Features: (1) First Mention by Name

So, then, keeping in mind this picture of these two opposing attitudes, groups, tendencies, inside the little Jewish state, travel on in thought beyond the later Persian period, through the Greek period (333–323 B.C.), through the Egyptian period when Palestine was in the empire of the Ptolemies (323–204 B.C.), on through the Syrian period (204–165 B.C.) and into the Maccabean period (165–63 B.C.).

Following the heroic struggles of the Maccabees (165–135 B.C.) and due to the decay of the Syrian power, the Jewish state gained one short period of independence (after four and a half centuries of subjection to other powers). This ran from 135 B.C. down to 63 B.C., the date of the Roman conquest. John Hyrcanus became high priest; and although he never assumed the title of king, he really reigned as such, commencing what is known as the Asmonean dynasty. ("Asmonean" was the inherited family name of Mattathias, father of Judas Maccabeus and his brothers, and grandfather of John Hyrcanus.)

This John Hyrcanus recaptured most of the territory which had been Israel's long before. No Jewish king had held so large an area since the break-away of the ten tribes after the death of King Solomon. It is in the days of John Hyrcanus, also, that the *Pharisees*, named as such, first appear on the scene as an historical movement.

As we have said, the Pharisees represent and continue that section of the Jewish leaders and people with whom loyalty to the Law and religion of Jehovah, and separation to the first ideals of Judaism, were everything; only it must be presumed that by this time a considerable mass of *oral* law had accumulated, with multiplied external religious observances. More immediately, the Pharisees were the spiritual successors of the *Chasidim*, i.e. the "Pious Ones," who, thirty or forty years earlier, had banded themselves together in a secret league to preserve the Jewish faith when the maddened Antiochus Epiphanes was trying to stamp it out by fearful atrocities. So strictly and literally did those *Chasidim* live "according to the Law" that many allowed themselves to be murdered rather than lift a hand in self-defence on the Sabbath day. When Judas Maccabeus commenced his liberation struggle large numbers of the *Chasidim* rallied round him.

So much, then, for the antecedents and historical emergence of the Pharisees. The name *Pharisees* means "Separatists"; and it is not unlikely that they were first so labelled by enemies because of their pious but proud and often petty exclusiveness. They would fain have held aloof from earthly politics, but religious issues were continually at stake, which turned them into fiery partisans. Separation was the all-dominating feature and the vital virtue in the Pharisee's concept of religion, and going with this was a fanatical adherence to the letter of the Law.

Historical Features: (2) Inevitable Tendencies

It was inevitable that the Pharisees should have much in common with the scribes, those specialists in the *Written* Law, and in the ever-enlarging *Oral* Law. Indeed, as we have mentioned earlier, most of those who were scribes by vocation would be Pharisees in conviction. To scribes and Pharisees alike separation and sanctity by strict fulfilling of both written and oral law was the supreme aim.

On the other hand, an unhappy proclivity of the Pharisees was a sanctimonious snobbery toward the common people, who had not the slightest chance, and knew it, of fulfilling the complex requirements of the scribal code.

A further snare was their easy liability to *hypocrisy*. First they solemnly laboured to perform all the scribal enjoinments; then, failing in this, they rested in mere *outward* compliance; then they excused outward correctness *only*; then they masqueraded in an outward profession of piety while covertly sinning; until finally, becoming used to this, they tolerated it, and even practised it, thus becoming the worst of hypocrites.

The mass of the people gave up trying altogether and were resigned to being hapless sinners. Yet they still admired the Pharisees as representing something which somehow ought to be, even though the Pharisees despised them. This was the situation as it seems to have developed in the time when our Lord was on earth.

Historical Features: (3) Other Notable Aspects

Yet, even so, we cannot with fairness leave the picture just there. Undoubtedly in the Pharisee movement there were many sincere and aspiring souls, however misguided they may have been. Moreover, it was such as they who kept the Messianic hope aflame and influential in inter-Testament Israel, and preached the hope of bodily resurrection for the faithful when the Messiah should bring in His kingdom.

In his *Antiquities of the Jews* (Book XVII) Josephus tells us that the Pharisees in Herod's time numbered some six thousand. Perhaps they were never a large body numerically, but their influence was out of all proportion to their number. They had, in fact, such a hold on the popular mind that no governing power could afford to disregard them.

Several times during the inter-Testament period we find that in struggles for the ruling power the Pharisees were the determining factor. In the reign of Alexander Jannæus (a son of John Hyrcanus) it was the Pharisees who led the people in a civil war against king and Sadducees, compelling the king to flee. It was they who headed another insurrection in the reign of Aristobulus II (a grandson of Hyrcanus). It was the eighty years of independence under the Asmonean (Maccabean) dynasty, *plus* the teaching of the Pharisees, which made the Jews so troublesome a little later, when Judæa became part of the Roman empire.

We need only read the four Gospels to see what sway they had in our Lord's days on earth—and what influence they had in bringing about His crucifixion.

THE SADDUCEES

Our giving less space to the Sadducees is not because they were proportionately less noteworthy, but simply because, in connection with the Pharisees, we have already discussed the factors which originated the two divergent groups and need not cover that ground again.

The two movements were embryonic in the early disaffection

between priest and scribe. They could not develop in post-exile Jewry while inspired prophets continued and represented the theocracy in its noblest form; but in the inter-Testament period, when the living voice of prophecy had died, the opposing tendencies increased until eventually, just after the Maccabean revolt, they emerged *by name* as "Pharisees" and "Sadducees."

It seems settled that the name "Sadducees" comes from "Zadokites"; but whether "Zadokites" is from "the sons of Zadok," who held the high-priesthood right from Zadok in David's reign (2 Sam. viii. 17, etc.) down to Maccabean times, or from a certain Zadok who lived about 250 B.C., or from a Hebrew word meaning "righteous," has not been so easy to determine. Most likely it derives from that long-continuing priestly house of Zadok. As late as the mid-exile period Ezekiel names "the sons of Zadok" representatively for the whole priesthood (xl. 46, xliii. 19, xliv. 15, xlviii. 11). What could be more probable, then, when the high-priesthood passed to the *Asmonean* house after the Maccabee victory, than that the Jewish priestly group, anxious to retain the prestige and advantage of such venerated tradition for their aims and policy, should now stress in a new way that although they loyally supported the Asmonean priesthood they were still, in reality, the *Zadokites*?

That a cleavage should have early developed between priest and scribe in the inter-Testament era certainly does seem strange after the way Ezra combined the two in himself (Ezra vii. 6, 12). There was no *constitutional* cause. It just *grew* from early tendencies. As we have said, to the scribes the theocratic idea and the Messianic hope were everything; whereas the priests seem to have tended toward absorption with the official and earthly aspects of the high-priesthood, as it increasingly united in itself both the spiritual and political headship of the nation.

Later, when the empire of Alexander spread the Greek language and culture throughout the civilised world, and a struggle began in Jewry between Judaism and Hellenism, it was the priestly line who gave way to compromises, while the influence of the scribes was the very nerve of the resistance movement which eventually veered the nation away from those seductive siren voices and ruinous rocks.

Long after Alexander and his empire had gone, the Greek

"culture" continued to spread among the nations. The cities all round Judæa had fallen a willing prey. Danger was unavoidable as the Jews came into contact with the colourful refinements, liberty of thought, and voluptuous pleasures of those Greek-living communities. It was always the aristocratic group associated with the priests who showed proclivities toward slackening Judaism in favour of Greek liberties: and this was the group later known as the Sadducees.

A vivid little snapshot of their distinctive features is given by Professor Skinner in the following paragraph: "The Sadducees seem to have been in the first instance neither a religious sect nor a political party, but a *social clique*. Numerically they were a much smaller body than the Pharisees, and belonged for the most part to the wealthy and influential priestly families who formed the aristocracy of the Jewish nation. The leaders of the party were the elders with seats in the council, the military officers, the statesmen, and officials who took part in the management of public affairs. With the mass of the people they never had much influence; like true aristocrats, they did not greatly care for it. Their one ambition was to make themselves indispensable to the reigning prince, that they might conduct the government of the country according to their own views. The Sadducees held, like some more modern politicians, that the law of God had no application to politics. If Israel was to be made great and prosperous it must be by well-filled treasuries, strong armies, skilful diplomacy, and all the resources of human statecraft. . . . To expect a Divine deliverance merely by making the people holy, they accounted as sheer and dangerous fatalism."

Yet it should be understood that in their own way they were as jealous for Judaism as the Pharisees. It was their *idea* of it which was radically different. They totally rejected the Oral Law accumulated by the scribes, and professed to stand by the Written Law alone; though it must be regretted that their doing so was from a sceptical rather than a spiritual turn of mind. We glean from Matthew xxii. 23 and Acts xxiii. 8 how sceptical was their attitude even to the Written Law, for we are told that they denied bodily resurrection, and did not believe either in angels or spirits. As a body they seem to have been just as astute about the worldly aspects of religion and politics as the Pharisees were indifferent to them, and just as indifferent to the Messianic hope as the Pharisees were taken up with it. The two groups *provoked each other* into existence and mutual opposition. Wherever the characteristics of the one appeared they excited the hostile reactions of the other. The very fanaticism of the Pharisees provoked the scepticism of the Sadducees. The other-worldliness of the one group irritated the worldly-mindedness of the other. And so the feud continued. The Pharisees tried to influence the nation from the people *upwards*. The Sadducees tried to influence the nation from the ruling power *downwards*. In the Gospels and Acts we see how influentially the Sadducees figured in the Sanhedrin. During our Lord's public ministry the high priests were Annas and his son-in-law Caiaphas, both Sadducees. Acts v. 17 speaks of "the high priest and all they that were with him, *which is the sect of the Sadducees.*" We can well understand how intolerable to such a group were the teachings and character and Messianic claims of our Lord Jesus. Their hatred is measured by their readiness to consort even with the detested Pharisees in order to kill Him. It was they, in fact, who were directly responsible for His crucifixion (compare Luke iii. 2; John xi. 49, xviii. 13, 14, 24, xix. 15; Mark xv. 11).

Yet, even so, we must be careful not to imply that *all* the priests were necessarily "Sadducean." It was a devout priest and his sons who led the Maccabean revolt. It was to a righteous priest that the angel Gabriel announced the coming gift of a son who should be the Lord's forerunner. A generation later, after the ascended Christ had poured out the Holy Spirit on His waiting disciples, we find that, despite the bitter hostility of the *chief* priests, "a great company of the *priests* became obedient to the faith" (Acts vi. 7).

THE INTER-TESTAMENT PERIOD

IV. Essenes, Herodians, Zealots, and the Judæa of Our Lord's Day

Lesson Number 107

JOSEPHUS ON THE ZEALOTS

But of the fourth sect of Jewish philosophy (i.e. the Zealots), Judas the Galilean was the author. These men agree in all other things with the Pharisaic notions; but they have an inviolable attachment to liberty, and say that God is to be their only Ruler and Lord. They also do not value dying any kinds of death, nor indeed do they heed the deaths of their relations and friends, nor can any such fear make them call any man Lord; and since this immoveable resolution of theirs is well known to a great many, I shall speak no further about that matter; nor am I afraid that any thing I have said of them should be disbelieved, but rather fear that what I have said is beneath the resolution they show when they undergo pain; and it was in Gessius Florus's time that the nation began to grow mad with this distemper, who was our procurator, and who occasioned the Jews to go wild with it by the abuse of his authority, and to make them revolt from the Romans.

BETWEEN MALACHI AND MATTHEW (4)

THE ESSENES

ALTHOUGH our New Testament does not mention the peculiar Jewish sect known as the *Essenes*, we should spare it a glance, as contributing a further significant feature to the later inter-Testament period. It is remarkable how in each age the same three types reappear—the "orthodox," the "heterodox" and the "peculiars." The Pharisees were all for the *letter* of the Law. The Sadducees broke from all but the broad *sense* of it. The Essenes would fain live in the *spirit* of it; and to do this they withdrew from ordinary human society to haunts of their own in rural solitudes, where they practised a monastic kind of life and a mystical kind of Judaism.

It is strange, also, how in each age different groups can be so blind to their own self-contradictoriness. The Essenes were ultra-Judaistic. Moses was their paramount authority. Yet, as with most mystics, their ethereal contemplativeness rarefied into something else the plain meanings of the authority they profoundly venerated.

They dissociated themselves from the temple sacrifices, having supposedly purer lustrations of their own which stressed the spiritual meaning. They could not mix with the vulgar crowd of temple-frequenters, who, they held, defiled its precincts. It was more in accord with the *spirit* of the Mosaic prescriptions to stay apart and render sacrifice in the holier sanctuary of their own dwelling. Yet they showed their reverence for the temple by sending regular incense-offerings. Their passion was a holy mind, a spiritual religion, and self-humbling separation to God, by means of monastic withdrawment, ascetic discipline, and barest simplicity of living.

They were a community apart. They "lived by themselves in houses of their own, working in the field or at useful crafts, but shunning trade as tending to covetousness." Each meal was prepared by their own priests and partaken of as a sacrifice to God.

One dish alone was set before each of them. They were, on principle, opposed to war. They disallowed the use of oaths. The stricter part of them even abjured marriage—an asceticism utterly alien to Mosaic teaching. Members were only admitted after protracted probation, and were most solemnly bound to keep the rules and secrets of the order; to exercise devout piety toward God and uprightness toward man; to hate the wicked and help the righteous; to speak only the truth, and to injure no one.

Yet their monastic spirituality was overlaid by a slavish externalism! They kept the Sabbath so rigidly to the letter of the Law that they could neither kindle a fire nor allow food to be prepared. They counted it defilement ever to eat food cooked by any but their own fraternity, and would even have preferred death to it. They superstitiously refrained from spitting, especially on the right side. If they were ever touched by an uncircumcised person they must at once undergo corporeal ablutions.

Contradictory mixture though they were, they exhibited godly virtues which lifted them much above the generality (see Josephus's tribute, postfixed to this study). The motive was good; but the method was mistaken. Their exclusivism, asceticism and mysticism were disguised escapism. Their ultra-Judaism became almost un-Jewish. Their *mystical* liberty with the Written Word did not bring them *spiritual* liberty, but left them still slaves to form. After all, they did not penetrate the shell to the true spirit of the Law. It cannot be done *their* way. Our Lord Jesus showed the true way; and He was no recluse. The Essenes were understandably held in high repute for their piety, as also for their religious insight; and it is said that their predictions of the future were regarded as almost infallible. But they were wrongly out of touch with men. Hence they made no real impact on their times, nor do they receive mention in the New Testament. Yet they are significant as showing yet further the hungerings and reactings of the Jewish people during those inter-Testament centuries.

THE HERODIANS

In Matthew xxii. 16, Mark iii. 6 and xii. 13 we find yet another Jewish ring cited, namely, the *Herodians*. Who, then, were *they*? No explicit information has been handed down as to their original banding together, but their very name, of course, advertises their distinguishing role and *raison d'être*. Whatever the religious preferences or aversions of its members may have been, the group as such was in no sense a religious cult or union. It was political; and the leading aim of its adherents was to further the cause of the Herod government. Whether they were directly subsidised from the Herod household or throne is conjectural, but obviously the ready seal of royal approval would be theirs, and each of the wily but uneasy Herods would have his agents co-operating with them.

We can well imagine that many would consider it sound policy to strengthen the hold of the Herod house on Jewish leaders and public. After the torturous insecurity and gory rivalries and almost suicidal expedients which had cursed Jewish rule since Maccabean days, what could be wiser than to back the Herodian throne, enjoying as it did the favour of Rome, and thus giving Judæa the protection of that mighty empire? Many would see in the Herods the one Jewish hope of separate national continuance; the one alternative to direct heathen rule. Others, too, would be inclined to favour a blend of the ancient faith and Roman culture such as the first Herod and his successors had sought to effect as the highest consummation of Jewish hopes.

On the other hand, there must have been many who detested the very name. The Herod family were not Jews but Idumeans. Had not the first Herod murdered all but two of the Sanhedrin? Had he not compromised the Jewish faith which ostensibly he had earlier embraced? Had he not built at Paneas a white marble temple to the worship of Augustus? Outside Judæa, was he not the undisguised patron of heathenism? Had he not built a Roman theatre in Jerusalem, with a huge amphitheatre outside the walls, and instituted gladiatorial shows? And although he had built the magnificent new Jewish temple in Jerusalem, had he not blazoned a golden Roman eagle over the main entrance to the outer court? Were not the Herod family stained with the blood of the most shocking crimes? Did they not, after all, represent the power of the hated Roman conqueror? We can imagine how the Pharisees, for instance, must have hated the Herodians! The two parties were bitterly intolerant of each other, which makes the consorting of the Pharisees with the Herodians against our Lord all the more astonishing.

THE ZEALOTS

In Matthew x. 4 and Mark iii. 18 a certain "Simon the Canaanite" figures among the twelve apostles. In Luke vi. 15 and Acts i. 13 he is "Simon Zelotes." The word "Canaanite" should be "Cananæan" (see R.V.), as it refers to a movement, not to the Canaanite race. "Zelotes" means "the Zealot." Both these appellations—"Cananæan" and "Zealot"—name the same movement, the former in Aramaic, the latter in Greek. Who and what, then, were the Zealots? They were in a drastic way the Jewish *nationalist* party. It was they, indeed, who eventually brought on the mad clash with Rome which resulted in utter ruin and the sack of Jerusalem by the Roman general Titus in A.D. 70.

For their beginnings as a movement we must hark back to somewhere about 63 B.C., when the Maccabean independence-period ended and Judæa passed under the Roman yoke. There was wide difference between the turbulent Jewish community which then became vassal to Rome and the Remnant who had been submissive under Persian rule at the beginning of the inter-Testament period! Not only were they now much larger in number; they were markedly different in temper. Those seventy years of self-government, interpenetrated by Pharisee influence, had done something to the spirit of the nation which made them perhaps the most aggravating community which the Romans had to manage.

Whereas the Judæan Jews at the beginning of the inter-Testament were resigned to a waiting submissively until their Messiah should come and deliver a people faithfully keeping the sacred Law, there was now an impetuous contention that miraculous intervention would only come to a people prepared to fight for Israel's deliverance from foreign domination. There was the same Pharisee-fanaticism for the letter of the Law, but with a fiery new nationalistic turn which outmoded the pious aloofness of the earlier Phariseeism.

Furthermore, twenty-six years after Rome had become Judæa's master, the scheming, hated foreigner, Herod, had waded through blood and savagery to seize the throne of Judæa, with backing from Rome but against bitter resistance by the Jews. It was his accession, so it would seem, which inflamed the Zealot reactionaries into an organised movement or party; and Dr. Edersheim does not hesitate to say that "a deeper and more independent view of the history of the times (i.e. from then onwards) would perhaps lead us to regard the whole country as ranged either with or against that party."

The more violent activities of the movement seem to have been at first in the Galilee area. In A.D. 6, when Quirinus, the Roman Legate of Syria, ordered a taxation census in Palestine, Judas the Galilean, with Sadok, a Pharisee, headed a revolt against the Roman domination, calling upon his countrymen as the people of God to resist human despotism. He was for restoring completely the theocratic polity. A large band flocked to his ensign, but were easily dispersed by Quirinus, and Judas himself was slain (Acts v. 37). Yet, as the late Dr. W. A. Lindsay says: "From this time forward to the destruction of Jerusalem and the scattering of the Jewish race the outer history of the Jews is chiefly a record of the struggle of those who were zealous for the Law against the encroachments of Roman power and Hellenic culture."

The sons of Judas carried on the cause, two of whom, Jacob and Simon, were crucified by Tiberius Alexander, a later procurator. A third son, who gave out that he was the Messiah, was slain by a mob.

But the opposition of the Zealots to Rome by force of arms, alas, gradually degenerated into a pretext for violence even against their own countrymen. During the last few decades before the destruction of Jerusalem, in A.D. 70, they had become lawless brigand-bands and were a terror to the land. It is not improbable that Barabbas and his confederates were Zealots, also the two robbers who were crucified with our Lord. Note that the name Barabbas is Aramaic; that both he and *a band of conspirators* were in prison as having committed murder in an *"insurrection"* (Mark xv. 7). The two malefactors who were crucified with our Lord were violent robbers, not just "thieves." The word "thieves" in Matthew xxvii. 44 is rightly changed to "robbers" in the Revised Version. Maybe the *penitent* robber, like others, had thought at the outset that the "kingdom of God" could be brought by force. Watching Jesus on the Cross he suddenly saw differently.

JEWRY IN OUR LORD'S TIME

And now, to follow up our inter-Testament sketch, let us try to sense the resultant political and religious atmosphere during the time when our Lord Jesus lived in Palestine.

The Roman World

The civilised world of that day was co-extensive with the Roman empire. One common subjection bound all nations to the one throne. One common military control kept order everywhere with iron hand. One common language, i.e. Greek, linked larger towns and educated men in a world-wide interchange of thought never known before. One common culture, the Græco-Roman, prevailed more or less through all lands. The famous Roman roads facilitated land communications and became great highways of trade. The Mediterranean shipping routes connected a world of peoples all kept at peace with each other. Commerce flourished by land and sea. So, despite many facinorous officials, a rough justice was maintained on a world level such as had not been before. Loyalty to Rome gained corresponding leniency. Local religions and customs were respected; and provinces were allowed a large degree of self-government in their own domestic affairs. Palestine was part of one such Roman province (that of Syria) at the beginning of our Christian era.

Palestine

At that time Palestine was in five sub-areas—Judæa, Samaria, Galilee, Peræa, Trachonitis. The first Herod (inanely misnamed "Herod the Great" instead of Herod the Gory!) had reigned over all five; but at his death (about the time our Lord was born) the kingdom had been partitioned to three of his sons, as directed in his will. To his eldest son, Archelaus (Matt. ii. 22), he bequeathed Judæa and Samaria. To his son Herod Antipas he left Galilee and Peræa. To another son, Philip, he left Trachonitis. Ten years later Rome had deprived Archelaus of Judæa and Samaria because of misrule, and had appointed instead a procurator known as "Governor of Judæa." During our Lord's public ministry the fifth of these procurators was in charge, namely, Pontius Pilate. He was responsible to the Roman Legate over Syria, who exercised supervisory control of all Palestine, and who in turn was accountable to the emperor. The procurator's ordinary residence was not at Jerusalem but at Cæsarea, which to the Romans was of greater political importance. At such times as the feast of the Passover, however, when Jerusalem was crowded, and Jewish nationalist feeling might excite thoughts of revolt, the procurator took up temporary residence in the capital —which explains Pilate's presence there when the fracas occurred which occasioned our Lord's crucifixion.

At that time, also, Herod Antipas ruled as Tetrarch over Galilee and Peræa. He was the son of Herod the Great and Malthace, a Samaritan woman. Half Idumean and half Samaritan, there was not a drop of Jewish blood in his veins; and "Galilee of the Gentiles" seemed a fitting domain for such a prince. The Gospels indicate him to have been a superstitious, immoral and cruel man. He, too, was at Jerusalem when the clamour for our Lord's crucifixion broke out. Pilate, therefore, on learning that Jesus was of Galilee, sent Him round to that Herod: but Herod threw back the responsibility on Pilate.

Judæan Jewry

As for Judæa religiously at that time, Pharisees, Sadducees, Herodians were all pressing their own views in their own way. There was great activity in the schools of the *Pharisees*. Some of the most famous among scribes had adorned the days of Herod the Great. Indeed, the great Hillel and Shammai, most famous of all Jewish scribes since Ezra, and founders, respectively, of the rival Babylonian and Palestinian schools of rabbinical hermeneutics, were both at their zenith when Jesus was born. The Pharisees had much influence with the people; and Herod therefore treated them with a careful forbearance.

The power of the *Sadducees* had been greatly weakened by Herod's murdering forty-five of their leaders early in his reign. Herod had also abolished the hereditary high-priesthood—another blow to the Sadducees. Notwithstanding, the Sadducees remained influential in top circles. The hereditary priestly families were still the native aristocracy of the land. In their higher ranks they were still motivated by political rather than spiritual aims. If Herod had not shown such early savagery toward them for their support of the Asmonean high-priesthood, they would have been far more predisposed to Herod's reign and Hellenising innovations than the Pharisees; but they now shared the Pharisee hatred of the Herod regime. They still had a powerful hold on the high-priesthood and the Sanhedrin. Both at the end of the Gospels and in the early chapters of the Acts the high priest and chief priests are Sadducees, with much influence in the Sanhedrin (see Acts iv. 6, v. 17, etc.).

The Herodians, Nazi-like, moved among the people, their tactics more cautious since Herod's son was replaced by a procurator in Judæa. They shared the resentment of Pharisees and Sadducees toward that official, but not their Jewish hatred of Rome. They had no scruples against using spy-ring tactics, and always had a double-faced card to play. To the Herods they were the determined devotees of that house. To the Roman "Governor" they were equally the loyal upholders of Roman domination, from which the authority of the Herods was derived.

They had only cynical scorn for the Messianic hope of Jewish pietists, but were all alert at the big excitement as to whether Jesus was this expected King of the Jews, with supposed claims on the throne of Judæa. Their hostility was immediate. He was dangerous, and should be handed over for the Governor to silence (Luke xx. 20).

They were evidently known as having an organised spying personnel. Hence Mark iii. 6: "The Pharisees went forth and straightway *took counsel with the Herodians,* how they might destroy Him." Their surreptitious manœuvres against our Lord are exposed in Luke xx. 20 (which Matthew xxii. 16 fastens on them): "They *watched* Him, and sent forth *spies,* which should feign themselves righteous men, that they might take hold of His words, and so *deliver Him unto the power and authority of the governor.*"

An Evil Triangle

Yes, Pharisees, Sadducees and Herodians were all there in Judæa at that time. Each group hated the others with venomous and vituperative spite. Yet in that strange frenzy of hatred which pure goodness involuntarily provokes against itself in minds that are set on selfish wrong, all three groups became one in their murderous opposition to the guileless God-Man who was "meek and lowly in heart."

Jerusalem at that Time

Perhaps we cannot more suitably leave this snapshot of Palestine Jewry in our Lord's time than by glimpsing at Jerusalem itself, in the following paragraph from Dr. Alfred Edersheim.

"There were two worlds side by side in Jerusalem. On the one hand was Grecianism with its theatre and amphitheatre ; foreigners filling the court, and crowding the city ; foreign tendencies and ways, from the foreign king downwards. On the other hand was the old Jewish world, becoming now set and ossified in the schools of Hillel and Shammai, and overshadowed by temple and synagogue. And each was pursuing its course by the side of the other. . . . If Greek was the language of the court and camp, and indeed must have been understood and spoken by most in the land, the language of the *people,* spoken also by Christ and His apostles, was a dialect of the ancient Hebrew, the Western or Palestinian Aramæan. . . . Indeed it was a peculiar mixture of two worlds in Jerusalem, not only of the Grecians and the Jewish, but of piety and frivolity also."

But there is one very important aspect of that old-time Jewry which we must not on any account overlook. It is not only courts and schools and leaders and parties which compose a nation, but those thousands and thousands of individuals who are only known anonymously and collectively as "the common people." The historian's pages necessarily leave them unnamed and unsung. Yet they are just as human, and just as personally precious to God, as the figures of far-flung fame. It is they who, in their vast total and procreative continuity, constitute the living body of the nation and race. It is they who are the real subject of history. The conspicuous few are only so because of their impact upon *them.* Even so, away back in Judæa, about the time when B.C. gave place to A.D., it was ordinary men and women, boys and girls, who made up the ever-moving life of the community. They each had their own little-big world of interests and concerns, pleasures and burdens, joys and sorrows. They grew, they aged ; they worked, they played ; they laughed and wept ; they sang and sighed ; they hoped and feared ; they lived and died.

What of *them,* in that old-time Jewry? Alexander Maclaren has a haunting little word that "the blackest times were not so dismal in reality as they look in history." Was there ever a blacker time in Israel's pre-exile history than that of the Judges? It was black with religious apostasy and civil confusion; and the tragic book ends with the final sigh, "In those days there was no king in Israel; every man did that which was right in his own eyes." Yet on the very heels of that last sentence in the Book of Judges comes the priceless little Book of Ruth, opening with the words, "Now it came to pass *in the days when the judges ruled,*"—reminding us at once that even in those ugliest of days there were loveliest characters, godliest believers, and most chivalrous hearts. And so it was in Judæa as Jewry emerged from those tortuous and torturous inter-Testament centuries into Gospel times.

There was pure love, godly uprightness, prayerful aspiration; and many were wistfully waiting for "the Sun of Righteousness" to arise "with healing in His wings." "Then they that feared the Lord spake often one to another; and the Lord hearkened and heard." "In the carpenter of Nazareth and his virgin wife; in the parents of John the Baptist, in the shepherds who kept their flocks in the fields of Bethlehem, in the little group of saints who gathered round the infant Saviour in the temple, we recognise the humble representatives of the purest type of Jewish piety. Men and women like these had lived and died in Israel during all those centuries. Far removed from the pomp of earthly courts and the strife of factions and the heated atmosphere of political and religious fanaticism, they had waited for the consolation of Israel. And now at last to such as these the long expected Messiah had been revealed. In the hour of Israel's deepest degradation, when Herod's kingdom seemed to mock the aspirations of all faithful Israelites with its counterfeit semblance of Messianic glory, their eyes beheld the Lord's Anointed, the true King of the kingdom of God, the Ruler 'whose goings forth were from of old, from everlasting.' "

THOSE JEWISH SECTS—AND TODAY

It is remarkable how those long-ago Jewish sects resurrect themselves and don fresh garb in each new age. Make no mistake: they live again today; they wear up-to-date apparel, and are busy in modern Christendom.

Away back in that old-time Jewry the Essenes and the Zealots kept far from our Lord's pathway. He was too social for the Essenes, and too gentle for the Zealots. The Essenes stayed away in their monastic solitudes, and the Zealots in their hilly lurking-places. Our Lord took no message to the former, and asked no help of the latter.

But the Pharisees and the Sadducees and the Herodians were "on the spot" and in active opposition to Him all the time. Oh, stark tragedy!—in their blind conceit they were withstanding that which they professedly existed to further. Observe them carefully, for they are highly significant types. The Pharisees were the old-time *ritualists*. The Sadducees were the old-time *rationalists*. The Herodians were the old-time *secularists*.

The mark of the Pharisee—the ritualist—is that he is always *adding to*. He is not content with the written Word of God, and with the plain truth of the Gospel, and with the faith once for all delivered to the saints. He must start adding his own ideas and ordinances, until religion and salvation are a highly complicated matter. This is just what the Pharisees did, until, with the weight of their accumulated religious ceremonies and observances, they made religion a burden too heavy for men to bear.

On the other hand, the mark of the Sadducee—the rationalist —is that he is always *taking from*. He cannot accept the written Word of God in its entirety, nor the truth of the Gospel as it stands; nor can he accept, without drastic deletions, the faith once for all delivered to the saints. Everything must be tried at the bar of human reason. This, that, and the other thing must be cut out to make faith reasonable and tenable. This was precisely the attitude of the Sadducee. He could not, or rather *would* not, believe either in angels or demons, either in the resurrection of the dead or in any other miracle.

As for the Herodian—the secularist—he cared neither for adding to nor taking from. Like the careless Gallio, he "cared for none of these things." The written Word of God, the message of the Gospel, the faith once for all delivered to the saints, were far from his first concern. His prime consideration was *the life that now is*. What does it matter that a heathen Herod reigns on a throne made crimson with crime so long as material interests are furthered? While the ritualist Pharisee was busy *adding to*, and the rationalist Sadducee was sceptically *taking from*, the secularist Herodian was heedlessly *passing by*.

Ritualist, Rationalist, Secularist

We have these three groups with us today. The Pharisee—the ritualist—is the modern "high" churchman, the Anglo-Catholic, the Roman Catholic. He is not content with the written Word of God, the plain truth of the Gospel with its good news of salvation by grace alone on God's part, and by faith alone on our part; nor is he content to stand by the faith once for all delivered to the saints. No, he must start *adding to* these his vestments, candles, images, sacraments, confessionals, penances, ceremonies, and all the other deceiving draperies of his hyper-religiosity.

On the other hand, the Sadducee—the rationalist—is the modern religious sceptic, the modernist, the "broad" churchman—and he is so broad that sometimes you cannot tell where his theology begins or ends. He is far happier telling you what he *cannot* or rather *will not* believe than declaring what he *does* believe. True to his Sadducean lineage, he is always *taking from*. He cannot accept the written Word of God in its entirety, nor the truth of the Gospel as it stands; nor can he accept, without drastic deletions, the faith once for all delivered to the saints. This, that, and the other thing must be cut out. He cannot believe Moses, Isaiah, Daniel. Much of Scripture history and doctrine is mythical and crude. Even Christ Himself is not infallible. The miraculous and supernatural must be eliminated until the only miracle left is the miraculous infallibility of modern scholarship!

As for the Herodian, he is the modern secularist. Just as his *quondam* prototype would have "Hellenised" and "Herodised" Judæan society (all in the name of modern progress, of course!), so does the twentieth-century antitype want to quash what he thinks are effete religious quakes and qualms and quibbles. With bland-faced, so-called "progressiveness" he would trample underfoot the sacredness of the Christian Sabbath, and bloat the day with secular amusements, under charitable slogans such as "Brighter Sundays for the People."

The Three Great Enemies

These three—the Pharisee, the Sadducee, the Herodian, alias the modern ritualist, rationalist, secularist—are the three great enemies of true, evangelical Christianity today. With the ritualist the battle-centre is the Lord's Table—is it a *table* or an *altar*?

With the rationalist the battle-centre is the Bible—is it *God's* Word or only *man's*? With the secularist the battle-centre is the Sabbath—is it a *holy* day or only a *holiday*?

Perhaps the sorriest feature of all in the behaviour of those long-ago Pharisees and Sadducees and Herodians was that, although they hated and strove against *each other,* they all united in common cause against *HIM.* Is there anything more astonishing than to read, even early in our Lord's ministry: "The Pharisees went forth, and straightway took counsel *with the Herodians* against Him, how they might destroy Him" (Mark iii. 6)? How intense the hate which made them so lower themselves! And is it not surprising to read a bit later on: "Then the Pharisees *with the Sadducees* came tempting Him" (Matt. xvi. 1)? And was there not a grim strangeness in the way that all three groups closed in *together* upon Him at the end (Matt. xxii. 15, 16, 23) in a final, *concerted effort* to undo Him?

We would not sound harsh, yet we must plainly state our view that ritualists, modernists and secularists of today reject the Christ of the Gospels as really and as mistakenly as the Pharisees and Sadducees and Herodians. The Christ of the Gospels is not acceptable—*not just as He really is*—to the high churchman, or to the broad churchman, or to the no-churchman. They can seem, respectively, "so spiritual," "so intellectual," "so charitable"; but touch the sensitive nerve, and at once they betray their deep-down aversion to the real Christ and the real Gospel. The ritualist will not have Christ and the Gospel in their *simplicity*. The modernist will not have them in their Divine *infallibility*. The secularist cannot bear them with their "crude" emphasis on salvation *through the blood*.

These three groups feelingly differ from each other; yet they will make common cause against *evangelical* Christianity—which asks only that Christ Himself and the written Word of God shall be the sole court of appeal! How often in recent days has the ritualistic Church of Rome joined hands with godless secular authorities to suppress Protestant evangelicals whose only offence has been that they were preaching Christ and the Gospel in strict accord with Scripture! In the now-evolving œcumenicity represented by the World Council of Churches, Modernist Sadducees will sponsor Socialist or even Communist ideas, will hob-nob with the venerable-looking Pharisees of the Greek Orthodox Church, and invite the elaborate dignitaries of Papal Rome; yet they are *angered* by those who insist on keeping strictly to the Christ of the Gospels, and to the Scriptures as the inspired and solely authoritative Word of God. We forbear to add more; but if some who belong to the above-mentioned groups should happen to read these lines, and be stirred to anger, we advise, "Examine yourselves, whether ye be in the faith" (2 Cor. xiii. 5); "Search the Scriptures, whether these things are so" (Acts xvii. 11).

Spiritual Relevances

In other ways, too, those defunct Jewish sects have a continuing voice to us. There is a *"golden mean"* of truth, which, when adhered to, begets in men a sane, sound godliness; but when men and movements deviate from it they become in corresponding degree ill-balanced and liable to unsound extremes. We see this objectified in the Pharisees, the Sadducees, the Essenes, the Zealots and the Herodians. Think back on them again. The Pharisees were passionately punctilious about the very letter of the Law, and they became *hyper*-spirituals. The Sadducees forked away contrariwise, refusing the Word except with limited meanings; and they became *infra*-spirituals. The Essenes read far more "between the lines" than in the lines themselves, convinced that by peculiar insight they had broken through to the inmost reality of it all; and they became *ultra*-spirituals. The Zealots impatiently broke away at another angle, arguing that true loyalty to the Word is not shown by preoccupation either with its outer letter or its inner meaning, but by physical activity, even fighting if need be; and they eventually became *un*-spirituals. The Herodians slanted away, insinuating that the most practical thing was to blend the Hebrew Scriptures with the Greek philosophers; Judaism with Hellenism; religion with pleasure; and they became *anti*-spirituals.

Hyper, infra, ultra, un, anti—they are all with us today! We need not start identifying them. They all display their own differentials. We should guard against the *tendencies* which developed into those Judæan movements. We should guard against them in ourselves individually and among our churches. The "golden mean" of which we spoke is to have a firm belief in the Bible as the inspired Word of God, and in the Lord Jesus Christ as the perfect Saviour-Examplar; and then to keep simple-heartedly close to the common-sense meanings of Holy Writ. If we do so, it will guide us in the way of truth and guard our feet from by-ways of error. In us and through us it will answer that prayer of Sam Chadwick's which comes to mind again: "Lord, make us intensely *spiritual*, but keep us thoroughly *practical* and perfectly *natural*."

EXCURSUS ON THE SANHEDRIN

There is one further Jewish institution which we ought to notice as bearing upon our reading of the four Gospels: that is, the Sanhedrin, which in New Testament times was the supreme civil and religious tribunal of the Jewish nation. With that representative body must lie for ever the real responsibility for the crucifying of Israel's Messiah, the incarnate Son of God. Pontius Pilate was merely the "rubber stamp" of imperial Rome implementing the ghastly injustice. More-over, in order to expedite the crime, the Sanhedrin violated its own code of honour.

The Sanhedrin is referred to in all the following verses, though an unapprised reader might not suspect so, for the Greek word *sunedrion* is translated as "council": Matthew xxvi. 59; Mark xiv. 55, xv. 1; Luke xxii. 66; John xi. 47; also Acts iv. 15, v. 21, 27, 34, 41, vi. 12, 15, xxii. 30, xxiii. 1, 6, 15, 20, 28, xxiv. 20.

It was a remarkable institution, as even our brief notes on it will show. Besides the central, Metropolitan Sanhedrin, there were smaller, local sanhedria or "councils" (Matt. v. 22). Indeed there were two such in the capital itself, at the entrance to the temple mount and the temple hall respectively, which dealt with lesser issues than those handled by the "Great Sanhedrin." But our main concern in these notes is with the "Great Sanhedrin," the supreme judicial and adminis-trative council of the Jewish people.

Origin

Jewish tradition, with its facile ingenuity for antiquating Judaistic innovations, finds the institution of the Sanhedrin away back in Moses' appointment of the seventy elders as magistrates (Num. xi). Later, so it goes, at the beginning of the monarchy period, King Saul was president of it and Jonathan vice-president. It persisted through the Babylonian exile, and was afterward reorganised by Ezra among the returned Remnant in Judæa.

But the Sanhedrin of the Gospels and Acts has no such ancient origin, though undoubtedly it is by that time some centuries old. Neither the historical nor the prophetical books of the Old Testament mention any such convention as could be identified with the Sanhedrin.

Nor is there any commensurate body indicated in the early post-exile years. As the four inter-Testament centuries began, there *may* have been, even under the Persian rule, some court coacting with the high priest in his administrative responsibilities, but there is no *evidence* of it.

The name *Sunedrion,* by which the institution has come down, suggests an origin after the Greek impact of 333 B.C. Moreover, a supreme council such as the Sanhedrin could only have come into being during a time when considerable self-government was allowed the Jews, which again points to the sub-Greek period, when the first three Ptolemies (323–222 B.C.) all favoured such increase of self-government. Furthermore, if, as Jewish tradition says, the "Great Synagogue" ceased about 300 B.C., with Simon the Just, the hand-over from it to some such synod as developed into the Sanhedrin would fit the juncture we have mentioned. And as a completive historical datum, we know that such a synod or senate *was* functioning and evidently well-known by 202 B.C., for a decree of Antiochus the Great then refers to it as the *Gerousia*—a name indicating governing elders, which reappears in Acts v. 21, translated "senate."

It was from this *Gerousia*, which presumably originated early in the third century B.C. and succeeded the "Great Synagogue," that the Sanhedrin evolved. About the end of the inter-Testament period we find it powerful enough to arraign young Herod (later Herod the Great) for excesses as governor of Galilee—though it lost its nerve when Herod appeared in royal purple and with armed guards. We may say that the Sanhedrin of the Gospels and Acts was an institution of up to three hundred years old, though of course it gathered up in itself traditions and connections reaching much further back than its own historical origin.

It would seem that the Sanhedrin was temporarily dissolved during the Maccabean revolt, owing to stress of circumstances, but restored after the victorious conclusion of that struggle.

Constitution

Most of the interesting data under this and the following sections are extracted from various parts of the Mishna and Gemara.

The Sanhedrin consisted of seventy-one members, made up, so it would seem, of: (1) the high priest; (2) twenty-four "chief priests" who represented all twenty-four orders of the whole priesthood: see 1 Chronicles xxiv. 4, 6; (3) twenty-four "elders," who represented the laity, often called "elders of the people," as in Matthew xxi. 23, xxvi. 3; Acts iv. 8—and reminding us of Revelation iv. 4; (4) twenty-two "scribes," who were the expert interpreters of the Law in matters both religious and civil.

When the word *Sanhedrin* is used, as in Mark xiv. 55, it denotes this fourfold assembly; and vice versa, where "chief priests and elders and scribes" are all mentioned together, as in Matthew xvi. 21, etc., it is a periphrasis for the Sanhedrin. An alternative name for the elders is "rulers." In some places we find just "chief priests and rulers" (Luke xxiii. 13) or simply "rulers" (Acts iii. 17) used as a synecdoche for the whole Sanhedrin.

There was a president, who was public figurehead of the Sanhedrin; a vice-president ("father of the house of judgment"), who supervised deliberations in the sessions; and a *chakam*, or skilled referee, who pre-examined pending matters and then laid them before the house. The Sanhedrin elected its own president, vice-president, and *chakam*. Only the king was ineligible for the presidency, because it was forbidden by law to contradict him.

Operation

At the time of our Lord's birth the Sanhedrin held its sessions in the "Hall of Squares" on the south side of the temple, but about the time of His crucifixion it removed to the "Hall of Purchase" on the east side of the temple mount. There were daily sittings, between morning and evening sacrifice, excepting sabbaths and festivals. The president occupied a raised seat, vice-president at his right hand, referee at his left, while the members sat on low cushions, Oriental fashion, in a half-moon, so that all could see each and each see all. Before them sat three rows of disciples—future judges—also two notaries, one on the right hand, the other on the left. Twenty-three members were a quorum, which allowed two-thirds to be free at any given time for their own business concerns; but no member must leave if thereby he would deplete the quorum.

Membership

Most illuminating is the following quotation from the late Dr. C. D. Ginsburg on the qualifications for membership: "The applicant had to be morally and physically blameless. He had to be middle-aged, tall, good-looking, wealthy, learned both in the Divine Law and diverse branches of profane science such as medicine, mathematics, astronomy, magic, idolatry, etc., in order that he might be able to judge in these matters. He was required to know several languages, so that the Sanhedrin might not be dependent on an interpreter in case any foreigner or foreign question came before them. Very old persons, proselytes, eunuchs and Nethinim were ineligible because of their idiosyncrasies, nor could such candidates be elected as had no children, because they could not sympathise with domestic affairs, nor those who could not prove that they were the legitimate offspring of a priest, Levite, or Israelite, who played dice, lent money on usury, flew pigeons to entice others, or dealt in produce of the Sabbatical year. In addition to all these qualifications, a candidate for the Great Sanhedrin was required, first of all, to have been a judge in his native town, to have been transferred from there to the small Sanhedrin which sat at the entrance of the temple hall before he could be received as member of the seventy-one."

Jurisdiction

The jurisdiction of the Sanhedrin was acknowledged both by the Jews of the homeland and those of the *diaspora*, though of course those in other lands had to observe the civil laws of the communities where they lived. Its *religious* jurisdiction was binding on Jews everywhere. Comprehensively, its grand function was the specialised interpretation and application of both Written and Oral Law, and thereby to adjudicate in matters of dispute as the exemplary head court of the land. How important this was in a state which was regarded as a theocracy can be easily appreciated.

The main functions of the Sanhedrin have been particularised somewhat as follows: (1) Surveillance over the lineal and legal purity of the priesthood, including careful pedigree registers. (2) Adjudication in cases of alleged immorality among wives or daughters of priests. (3) Superintendence over the religious life of the nation, with special watchfulness against any lapse into idol-worship. (4) Apprehension and trial of false prophets or dangerous heretics. (5) Watchfulness that neither king nor high priest should act contrary to the Divine Law. (6) Decision whether any war contemplated by the king should be waged or not, and the giving of permission. (7) Determination whether boundaries of the holy city or temple should at any time be enlarged, as only the Sanhedrin could pronounce ground consecrated. (8) Appointment of smaller local sanhedria. (9) Regulation of Jewish calendar and harmonising of solar years with lunar by intercalary days.

Administration

As to the usual mode and tenor of administration, we must take the liberty of quoting Dr. Ginsburg again: "They always manifested an anxiety to clear the arraigned rather than secure his condemnation, especially in matters of life and death. Their axiom was that 'the Sanhedrin is to save, not to destroy life.' Hence no man could be tried and condemned in his absence; and when the accused was brought before the tribunal the president of the Sanhedrin at the very outset of the trial solemnly admonished the witnesses, pointing out to them the preciousness of human life, and earnestly beseeching them carefully and calmly to reflect whether they had not overlooked some circumstances which might favour the innocence of the accused. Even the attendants were allowed to take part in the discussion if a mild sentence could thereby be procured; whilst those members of the Sanhedrin who during the debate once expressed themselves in favour of acquitting the accused, could not any more give their votes for his condemnation at the end of the trial. The taking of votes always began from the junior member, and gradually went on to the senior, in order that the lowest members might not be influenced by the opinion of the highest. In capital offences it required a majority of at least two to condemn the accused, and when the trial was before a quorum of twenty-three, thirteen members had to declare for the guilt. In trials of capital offences, the verdict of acquittal could be given on the same day, but that of *guilty* had to be reserved for the following day; for which reason such trials could not commence on the day preceding the Sabbath or a festival. No criminal trial could be carried through in the night. The judges who condemned a criminal to death had to fast all day. The condemned was not executed the same day on which the sentence was passed; but the votes *pro* and *con* having been taken by the two notaries, the members of the Sanhedrin assembled together on the following day to examine the discussion and see whether there was any contradiction on the part of the judges. If on the way to execution the criminal remembered that he had something fresh to adduce in his favour, he was led back to the tribunal, and the validity of his statement was examined. Clemency and humanity, however, were manifested toward him even when his criminality was beyond the shadow of a doubt and when the law had to take its final course. Before his execution a stupefying beverage was administered to the condemned by pious women to deprive him of consciousness and lessen the pain. The property of the accused was not confiscated, but passed over to his heirs."

The Sanhedrin and Christ

All this, of course, connects up with the circumstances of our Lord's life and death as recorded in the Gospels. The rule that no man could be tried in absence recalls at once Nicodemus's "point of order" in John vii. 51: "Doth our law condemn any man before it hear him?" Our Lord's being taken by night before the ex-high priest Annas (John xviii. 13), the make-believe nocturnal trial before Caiaphas in the high priest's palace (19–27), the sentence and execution without an intervening day, not to mention other features, were utterly against the Sanhedrin code of fair play.

If we ask why this sinister eagerness to "push through" with the prosecution and conviction, Dr. Ginsburg tells us that the one exception to all the forementioned legal leniencies was "one who gave himself out as the Messiah, or who led the people astray from the doctrines of their fathers. Such an one had to endure all the rigours of the law without any mitigation. He could even be tried and condemned the same day or in the night." Dr. Ginsburg, however, quotes as his authority for this the Talmudic *Tosefta Sanhedrin x.*; but the Toseftas, as we have mentioned in our article on the Talmud, were additions dating after the official Mishna was completed in the second century A.D., and it is obviously doubtful whether any such special waiving of regulations was invented until after those Jewish leaders had so shamefully violated the code of their own Sanhedrin in the unconstitutional condemnation of our Lord Jesus.

And on any showing it was illegal for the Sanhedrin to meet in the high priest's palace (John xviii. 15) instead of its own council hall, and still more so for the high priest to usurp the presidency for the occasion!

Perhaps it mitigates these dark doings somewhat to say that this was an *abnormal* summons of the assembly and not a statutory meeting —certainly it is difficult to think that men like Gamaliel and Nicodemus and Joseph of Arimathea were present; yet *many* of the members must have been there, as indicated by Matthew xxvi. 59 (even if with some of the best manuscripts we omit "elders"). Is there a more tragic verse anywhere in the history of Israel: "Now the chief priests and elders and *all the Sanhedrin* sought *false witness* against Jesus, *to put Him to death*"!

Shortly before that time the power of inflicting capital punishment had been taken away from the Jewish rulers (their later stoning of Stephen was illegal); so they had to get sanction from Pilate for the crucifixion. But why should they have clamoured for *such* a death? From time immemorial the Jewish modes of inflicting judicial death were stoning, burning, beheading and strangling.

After the destruction of Jerusalem in A.D. 70 Jerusalem ceased to be the administrative centre of the Jewish religion; and the Sanhedrin, after several removals, eventually located itself at Tiberias. Its power gradually declined, until it died out about A.D. 425.

Our Lord presumably had in mind the president and seventy senators of the Sanhedrin when He chose His seventy representatives and co-workers, as recorded in Luke x., just as He had the twelve tribes of Israel in mind when He appointed the twelve apostles. His choice of those seventy was prophetic perhaps, among other significances, that the authority of that old-time Jewish court *was indeed* now passing away in favour of a new "seventy" under His own presidency.

EXCURSUS ON THE JEWISH TALMUD

We came across a student not long ago who, in reply to the question, "What is the Pentateuch?" answered, "The period between Easter and Whitsuntide." Another student answered a question on the Talmud by saying, "The Talmud was a famous Jewish rabbi of long ago"! Perhaps they are two rather extreme instances of inventive genius gone astray; yet they certainly warn us not to take too much for granted when dealing with "freshers." It may be that some who are now traversing these studies are far from clear as to what the Talmud really is and how it came into being. So the following synopsis may be useful.

The Talmud is that large collection of writings which retrospectively embody and largely determine the religious and civil laws of the

Jewish people; those precepts, rules, interpretations and institutions by which (in addition to the Old Testament) they are professedly guided. It is a fulsome miscellany of tractates and breviates on matters of religion, philosophy, medicine, jurisprudence, history, and the various aspects of practical morality. No decision would be counted valid if against the agreed meaning of the Talmud: though present-day Jewish "liberals," while regarding it as a venerable work of antiquity, say that it has no final authority for faith and life.

It is in two parts: (1) the *Mishna*, i.e. the Oral Law; (2) the *Gemara*, i.e. commentaries on the Oral Law.

The Mishna

The *Mishna,* or Oral Law (often called the Second Law) is that copious aggregation of rules and regulations which by scribal methods of interpretation were accumulatingly deduced from the *Written* Law of Moses, mainly during the inter-Testament period.

Traditional origin

Jewish tradition reaches back much further, and claims that the Oral Law was actually given *along with the Written Law* to complete and explain it. This is what the scribes and Pharisees of our Lord's time believed. Along with all the precepts, regulations and ceremonials in the Pentateuch God had given to Moses explanations relating to their proper application and supplementation, to be transmitted by word of mouth. Such is the common belief to this day among traditionally orthodox Jews.

The classic passage on this, in the Mishna itself, reads thus: "Moses received the (oral) law from Sinai, and delivered it to Joshua, and Joshua to the elders, and the elders to the prophets, and the prophets to the men of the Great Synagogue." (Note: the "Great Synagogue" is a traditional college or assembly of one hundred and twenty men soon after the days of Ezra, to which the Jews assign an important share in the formation of the Old Testament and the handing on of the Oral Law.) From the men of the "Great Synagogue" the *Mishna* or Oral Law was then transmitted (supposedly) to the scribes or rabbis who followed, who in turn faithfully passed it on from generation to generation.

We ourselves, of course, do not believe in any such fantasy as that God gave to Moses, along with the written Law, this "oral" law. Nor can we accept the story of the "Great Synagogue" in its Jewish traditional form; though we readily agree that Ezra and his co-scholars had much to do with the shaping of the Old Testament canon, and that Nehemiah probably convened some such assembly which may have been followed by annual reassemblings. As Dr. Edersheim says, "Ezra left his work uncompleted. On Nehemiah's second arrival in Palestine, he found matters again in a state of utmost confusion. He must have felt the need of establishing some permanent authority to watch over religious affairs. This we take to have been 'the Great Assembly', or as it is commonly called, 'the Great Synagogue.' It is impossible with certainty to determine either who composed this assembly or of how many members it consisted. Probably it comprised the chief priests, elders, and 'judges'—the latter two classes including the scribes, if indeed that order was already separately organised. Probably, also, the term, 'Great Assembly' refers rather to a succession of men than to one synod—the ingenuity of later times filling the historical canvas, where left blank, with fictitious notices."

As for the Jewish *tradition* that God gave Moses the Oral Law along with the Written Law, and that it was thence passed orally down, that tradition had its birth and growth, like the Mishna itself, during the inter-Testament period, in the fertile minds of scribes anxious to invest the oral law with sanctity and authority.

Real Origin of the Mishna

How, then, in reality, did the *Mishna*, or Oral Law, develop? And how did it come to be in the Talmud? It originated in what are known as the Midrashim. And what were they? They were commentings on the Law and other Old Testament Scriptures which began to be made from about the time when the Remnant returned to Judæa after the Babylonian exile. When the writings of Moses and the pre-exile prophets became unintelligible to the mass of the people, who now spoke Aramaic, public expositions of the Scripture became necessary in a new way, and were delivered on a much larger pattern by the "lawyers" or "scribes." Often, perhaps, the public teacher would limit himself to paraphrasing the Scriptures in the Aramaic vernacular; but the understandable tendency was to expand into exegesis and application. As time went on, paraphrasing became needed from Hebrew into *other* languages besides Aramaic, for the Jews were more and more spread among the different peoples of the world; and this led to translations or versions in Chaldee, Syrian, Greek (such versions being known as *targums*). Also the early commentings on the Scriptures developed into more definite though still oral commentaries, i.e. the *Midrashim*.

The Halachoth

These *Midrashim*, or commentaries, almost inevitably divided themselves into two main categories, namely the *Halachoth and the Hagadoth* (*oth* is a Hebrew plural).

The *Halachoth* were the binding rules or precepts which were deduced or developed from the Written Law to cover all those details of human conduct which the Written Law itself did not mention. When one remembers that the returned Jews had adopted the Law of Moses as both the written constitution of the state and the authoritative rule of individual life, and that there were simply endless new civil and personal problems inevitably arising, one can well appreciate how it gave rise to the continuous labours of a large body of trained men who made the study of the Law the great business of their lives. One can easily see, also, how those legal rules or precepts, those guaranteed extendings of the Written Law to cover particular circumstances, gradually came to acquire an importance equal to, or even greater than, that of the Written Law itself. They are known collectively as the *Halachic Exegesis*, or "Deductions from the Law," or as the *"traditional* law" in distinction from the *"Written* Law" of Moses. As time went on and the *Halachoth* grew, they covered "every possible and impossible case, entered into every detail of private, family, and public life; and with iron logic, unbending rigour, and most minute analysis, pursued and dominated man, turn wither he might, laying on him a yoke which was truly unbearable."

The Hagadoth

But besides the *Halachoth*, there were the *Hagadoth*. The former were legal prescriptions, doctrinal, binding, fixed, stable; whereas the latter were free interpretations, homiletical, discoursive, exhortative, practical, and accompanied by illustration, comment, anecdote, clever or learned sayings, etc. The *Halachoth* were confined to the Pentateuch, whereas the *Hagadoth* ranged over the whole Scriptures. They contain "beautiful maxims and ethical sayings of illustrious men; attractive mystical expositions about angels and demons, paradise and hell; Messiah and the prince of darkness; poetical allegories; symbolic interpretations of all the feasts and fasts; charming parables; witty epithalamiums; touching funeral orations; amazing legends; biographical and characteristic sketches of Biblical persons and national heroes; popular narratives and historical notices of men, women, and events of bygone days; philosophical disquisitions; satirical assaults on the heathen and their rites; able defences of Judaism, etc. etc." Is it to be wondered at, that such a sacred and national lore became far more interesting to the people at large than the dry musts and must nots pertaining to the legal enactments contained in the *Halachoth*? Indeed, although both the *Halachoth* and the *Hagadoth* had developed from the early *Midrashim*, or commentings, the word Midrashim later became commonly used of the *Hagadoth* only.

Eventual Compilation in Talmud

For centuries the *Halachoth* were transmitted *orally* and were therefore also called *Shematha*, which means that which was heard or received, i.e. by those in the chain of tradition. To write them down was frowned on as a religious offence. The only touches of writing, for centuries, were those by a few learned rabbis who here and there wrote out certain of these laws, or indicated them by signs or hints in their Pentateuch scrolls, solely to aid memory: and those documents are called *Secret Scrolls*. It was between 200 B.C. and A.D. 200 that the compiling and redacting and rubricating of this now-accumulated mass of juridico-political and religious *halachoth* took shape. By and by, the circumstances of the times indicated the need for fixedness and order, and more or less complete collections of the *Halachoth* were made. The learned Hillel (75 B.C.–A.D. 14) made a first attempt, classifying the *Halachoth* under six *sedarim* or orders (which still remain). A much fuller collection is attributed to Rabbi Akiba (about A.D. 135). The compilation of *Halachoth* and *Hagadoth* together, in finalised form, as the authoritative *Mishna*, and as now in the Talmud, was accomplished by Rabbi Jehuda, who died about the end of the second century A.D. "The language of the Mishna is that of later Hebrew, purely written on the whole, though with a few grammatical Aramaisms, and interspersed with Greek, Latin and Aramaic words which had become naturalised."

Divisions of the Mishna

The Mishna, as now in the Talmud, is in six *Sedarin* or orders, the titles of which indicate their main subject: (1) *Sedar Zeraim* —agriculture; (2) *Sedar Moed*—the festivals; (3) *Sedar Nashim* —women; (4) *Sedar Nezikin*—civil and criminal law; (5) *Sedar Kodashim*—sacred things; (6) *Sedar Taharoth*—purifications.

These six orders or books are divided into tractates. There are 11 tractates in the first, 12 in the second, 7 in the third, 10 in the fourth, 11 in the fifth, 12 in the sixth—making a total of 63 tractates. These tractates are subdivided into *perakim* (chapters)—525 in all; and again into 4,187 *mishnas* (verses)—for the word *mishna* is used of any such verse of the whole Mishna, just as we ourselves use the word "Scripture" to mean the whole Bible, yet speak of any particular verse as such-and-such a scripture.

The Boraitas and Toseftas

But not even did this official *Mishna* manage to incorporate all the Midrashim, or traditional precepts and interpretations. Many others existed, which are preserved in part in the *Sifra*, or Commentary on Leviticus; the *Sifri* on Numbers and Deuteronomy; the *Mechilta* on Exodus; and the second *Sifri* on Numbers.

Still further, there are the *Toseftas*, or "Additions," dating from soon after the official Mishna was completed. There are *Toseftas*, or "Additions," to fifty-two out of the sixty-three Mishna tractates.

Substance and Influence of the Mishna

For such a diverse and complex compilation, the Mishna is thus systematised with great skill; but in substance it treats men like children. Its precepts, with their "musts" and "must nots," formalising the minutest particulars of ritual observances, kept men for ever at the mere letters of the alphabet in matters religious, spiritual and moral. It prevented the development of real *theology* and plastered men's minds with pedagogic "do's" and "don'ts." As Dr. Edersheim says: "The *Halachah* indicated with the most minute and painful punctiliousness every legal ordinance binding on the conduct. But it left the inner man, the spring of actions, untouched alike as regarded faith and morals. What he was to believe and what to feel was chiefly matter of the Haggadah. A man might hold or propound almost any views so long as he adhered in teaching and practice to the traditional ordinances. . . . Thus, Rabbinism had no system of theology; only what ideas, conjectures, or fancies the Haggadah yielded concerning God, angels, demons, man, his future destiny and present position, and Israel, with its past history and coming glory. What a terrible mass of conflicting statements and debasing superstitions, legendary colouring of Biblical narratives and scenes, incongruous, and degrading to them; the Almighty Himself and His angels taking part in the conversations of rabbis, and the discussions of academies; nay, forming a kind of heavenly Sanhedrin, which occasionally require the aid of an earthly rabbi. The miraculous merges into the ridiculous and even the revolting. Miraculous cures, miraculous supplies, miraculous help, all for the glory of great rabbis, who by a look or word can kill and restore to life. At their bidding the eyes of a rival fall out, and are again inserted. Nay, such was the veneration due to rabbis, that R. Joshua used to kiss the stone on which R. Elieser sat and lectured, saying: 'This stone is like Mount Sinai, and he who sat on it like the Ark.'"

Read all this, and then bear in mind that the Mishna represents the traditions which were current among the scribes and the Pharisees when our Lord was on earth. Its influence was a dead weight against the new message of the kingdom of heaven which our Lord had come to proclaim.

The Gemara

So far we have dealt only with the first part of the Talmud, i.e. the *Mishna*; but there is a second part, the *Gemara*, for the *Mishna* is only a smaller area of Jewish traditionalism. As we have said, the Mishna reached standardised completion at the hands of Rabbi Jehuda toward the end of the second century A.D. Thenceforward, because of obscurity in many of its enjoinments, the *Mishna* itself became the subject of elucidation and comment. Just as the Mishna purports to expound and expand the Written Law, so now in turn must the Mishna be expounded and supplemented! That is what developed during the period of the Amoraim, or public expositors of the Oral Law from about A.D. 200 to 500. During those three centuries commentaries ranging over the whole *Mishna* came into being.

Formation of the Gemara

These commentaries, containing the "discussions, illustrations, explanations and additions" which the Mishna provoked "in its application or in the academies of the Rabbis," were eventually brought together and arranged in order: and it is these commentaries collectively which form the *Gemara*. The word *gemara* means "that which is learned," and is therefore practically synonymous with the word *"talmud."* It is well to note that; for although the entire work popularly known as the Jewish Talmud comprises both the *Mishna* and the Gemara, as often as not when the Jews themselves speak of the Talmud they mean the *Gemara* only, in distinction from the *Mishna*.

Two Gemaras

But there is yet a further feature to mention. There are *two* of these *Gemaras* or Talmuds. There is the Jerusalem *Gemara*, and there is the Babylonian. They are so named because the one came from the Palestinian academies and the other from the Babylonian. It should be borne in mind that ever since the return of the Remnant to Judæa after the exile in Babylonia the Jews of the homeland were a minority. The much larger part of their race continued as the "Dispersion." By the time Josephus wrote (A.D. 37–98) there was "no nation in the world which had not among them part of the Jewish people." But it was between the Euphrates and the Tigris, in the area formerly known as *Babylonia,* that the largest and wealthiest and least-Hellenised Jewish communities remained (see note prefixed to study number 107). It was from there that the greatest teachers had come to restore and expound the Law in Judæa—the great Ezra, just before the inter-Testament period, and the renowned Hillel just at the end of it. After the overthrow of Jerusalem in A.D. 70 political stress shifted the real centre of rabbinical Judaism to Babylonia.

The *Jerusalem* Talmud is the earlier but much smaller of the two, and it gives the discussions of the Palestine *Amoraim* (expositors) from about A.D. 200 to 400. The *Babylonian* Talmud is some four times larger, and covers more than thirty-six of the sixty-three tractates of the *Mishna*. It is nearly eleven times longer than the Mishna itself, and fills close on six thousand large pages. It was completed somewhere about A.D. 500. Both *Gemaras* began to be known by that name from about the ninth century onwards. The Jews consider the Babylonian Talmud the higher authority of the two. The succinctness of the Jerusalem Talmud, however, compared with the diffuseness of the Babylonian, saves it from many fables, fictions and absurdities.

Character and Style

Neither of these *Gemaras* is complete. Both have the same *Mishna,* but differ considerably in the *Gemara*. In both of them the Mishna is commented upon *seriatim,* tenet by tenet. Dr. Edersheim says: "Of the character of these discussions it would be impossible to convey an adequate idea. If we bear in mind the many sparkling, beautiful, and occasionally almost sublime passages in the Talmud, but specially that its forms of thought and expression so often recall those of the New Testament, only prejudice and hatred could indulge in indiscriminate vituperation. On the other hand, it seems unaccountable how any one who has read a Talmudic tractate, or even part of one, could compare the Talmud with the New Testament, or find in the one the origin of the other."

Offsetting Dr. Edersheim, however, the learned Bishop Lightfoot, speaking of the Babylonian *Gemara,* says: "The almost unconquerable difficulty of the style, the frightful roughness of the language, and the amazing emptiness and sophistry of the matters handled, do torture, vex, and tire him that reads them (the Talmudic authors). They do everywhere abound with trifles in that manner as though they had no mind to be read; with obscurities and difficulties, as though they had no mind to be understood; so that the reader hath need of patience all along to enable him to bear both trifling in sense and roughness in expression."

With that well-deserved Anglican grumble, perhaps we ought now to leave the Talmud, lest others start grumbling, too!

JOSEPHUS ON THE ESSENES

"The doctrine of the Essenes is this: That all things are best ascribed to God. They teach the immortality of souls, and esteem that the rewards of righteousness are to be earnestly striven for; and when they send what they have dedicated to God into the temple, they do not offer sacrifices, because they have more pure lustrations of their own; on which account they are excluded from the common court of the temple, but offer their sacrifices themselves; yet is their course of life better than that of other men; and they entirely addict themselves to husbandry. It also deserves our admiration, how much they exceed all other men that addict themselves to virtue, and this in righteousness: and indeed to such a degree, that as it hath never appeared among any other men, neither Greeks nor barbarians, no, not for a little time, so hath it endured a long while among them. This is demonstrated by that institution of theirs, which will not suffer any thing to hinder them from having all things in common; so that a rich man enjoys no more of his own wealth than he who hath nothing at all. There are about four thousand men that live in this way, and neither marry wives, nor are desirous to keep servants; as thinking the latter tempts men to be unjust, and the former gives the handle to domestic quarrels; but as they live by themselves, they minister one to another. They also appoint certain stewards to receive the incomes of their revenues, and of the fruits of the ground; such as are good men and priests, who are to get their corn and their food ready for them."

SOME QUESTIONS ON THE INTER-TESTAMENT PERIOD

1. Can you name and date the six successive periods of Judæa's history during the inter-Testament period?
2. When and how did the rival worship of Samaria begin?
3. Why and how did Alexander the Great show favour to the Jews? What repercussions did it have among the Jews?
4. Who were the Ptolemies? Who was the second, and which two happenings made his reign notable?
5. The Maccabean revolt: why and how and by whom was it started? By whom was it continued?
6. What was the Asmonean dynasty? How did it begin? Who is usually reckoned first in it? How did it end?
7. Whom did the Romans first appoint as procurator of Judæa? Can you also name his even more notable son? Of what race was the family?
8. Herod's will divided his kingdom among three of his sons. Who were they, and what were their respective domains?
9. How, or why, did the Babylonian exile cure the Jews of idolatry?
10. What, in a sentence or two, was Judaism? How did it come into being and develop? What is the Oral Law?
11. When did the synagogue begin to appear, and what do you think gave rise to it?
12. What was the basic purpose of the synagogue? Who was the *chazzan*?
13. Who were the scribes? How did they originate as a class? Wherein did they err?
14. Who were the Pharisees? When do they first appear as a sect so named?
15. What were the originating causes and leading features of the Pharisee sect?
16. Who were the Sadducees? Can you explain the likely origin of the name? What, briefly, was their outlook or viewpoint?
17. Who and what were the Essenes?
18. Who and what were the Herodians?
19. Who and what were the Zealots?
20. How do the Pharisees, Sadducees, Herodians reflect on our times?

THE NEW TESTAMENT AND THE OLD

Lesson Number 108

In the Old Testament we have an interpretation of human need; and the New Testament is a revelation of Divine supply. In the Old we have unveilings of the human heart. In the New we have the unveiling of the heart of God, and the way in which He has answered humanity's need in Christ.

G. Campbell Morgan.

THE NEW TESTAMENT AND THE OLD

WHEN POWERFUL ideas grip men's minds they affect the whole mental outlook, sometimes revolutionarily. Perhaps there is far more of grim seriousness than of artistic humour in a recently published pamphlet which tells us that having come through the Ice Age, and the Stone Age, and the Bronze Age, and the Iron Age, and the Industrial Age, we are now entering the *Ideological* Age!

It is true that today, on an immenser scale than ever before, ideas are the deciding factor. From ideas come ideologies. Hitler, with his overmastering idea of world-rule by *one race*, created the Nazi ideology—with what vast and ghastly outcome! Marx, with his volcanic idea of world-rule by *one class*, progenerated the Communist ideology—with what ultimate global concussions yet remains to be seen. We are pointedly reminded that in modern warfare "nations are out-*thought* before they are out-*fought*." The Russian Vishinsky has said: "We shall conquer the world, not with atomic bombs, but with our ideas, brains and doctrines."

Those of us who know the prophetic word of Scripture are comfortingly assured that just as the Hitlers and Marxes and Lenins and Trotskies and Stalins all *die*, so there will never be *any* complete global monopoly again until the risen Christ Himself returns to set up *His* universal kingdom. But those anti-Christian leaders and ideologies are none the less loudly eloquent in the way they exemplify the power of *ideas*. Let modern history show us how momentous it is for men and nations to have *right* ideas!

But looking off from these outer and larger considerations to our own minds individually, how unspeakably important is it that we ourselves should be enlightened and inspired, dominated and energised, by the truest and purest and highest ideas! All our life is either enriched or impoverished, ennobled or vulgarised, dignified or degraded, blessed or cursed, by the ideas which govern our minds.

It is with such reflections that we now come to our exploration of the New Testament. Of all books on earth, it is the most wonderful in its matter and meaning and message. Its pages are immortalised by the loftiest of all ideas and ideals. And not only are those ideas and ideals ethically incomparable; they are "alive" with an inexhaustible vitality. There is a glorious moral and spiritual explosiveness in them which makes new *men,* and shakes whole *nations,* and wakes new *eras,* and will even yet issue in a new *world.*

And *why* is this? It is because those ideas, unlike the ideologies of Nazism and Communism, are grounded in indestructible historical *facts.* That is, they are not *solely* ideas, the products of philosophical evolution, the creations of mere human reasoning —they are "ideas *plus.*" They are not merely *theories,* like those of Nazism and Communism—they are *truths* arising from imperishable historical certainties.

Already the ideas and ideals of so-called Communism have badly deteriorated. "Communism" is now a misnomer for what should be dubbed "Russianism" or "Sovietism." But the redeeming and transforming truths of the New Testament have an inextinguishable Divine fire flaming through them. Though necessarily static in their historical fixity, they are endlessly vital and mobile, with ever-developing, ever-surprising new relevancies to changing times and passing centuries; always abreast of the times; always ahead of latest discoveries; always revealing new breadths of meaning; always speaking with new voice to new generations of human pilgrims.

> *This wisdom grows not obsolete,*
> *Tho' ancient, never "old";*
> *A school, a learning, all-complete,*
> *Man's inborn higher quest to meet;*
> *Each new-born age its leaves repeat*
> *New guidance to unfold.*

> *Here truths beyond the wisest sage*
> *Shine out as clear as morn,*
> *While many a deep predictive page*
> *Enfolds millennia unperceived,*
> *Which finite reason ne'er conceived,*
> *And ages yet unborn.*

The greatest need of our troubled twentieth century is a return to the New Testament. It can do more for us than all the economic or political theorists and theories. It goes right to the heart of the human problem—for the heart of the human problem is the problem of the human heart. It makes new men, and through new men a new society. It did this in the *first* century A.D. It can do it in the *twentieth*. Superficially, the twentieth century is very different from the first, but fundamentally it is very much the same. There is the same heart-need, the same heart-cry; and there is still the same unchanging, all-sufficient answer given by the New Testament. That answer is JESUS CHRIST.

The New Testament first of all sets before us *facts*—the most wonderful facts in all history. Then it exhibits the tremendous *ideas* or meanings embodied in the facts. From these come the great *truths* which save men, and the high *ideals* of Christian humanhood. It is good to get this fourfold logical sequence of New Testament revelation well in mind: (1) Facts, (2) Ideas, (3) Truths, (4) Ideals.

THE DOMINANT IDEA—FULFILMENT!

But we must give a new turn to our remarks about "ideas" and the New Testament. We have sometimes heard the advice given that in coming to the New Testament we should try to have *no* preconceived ideas, but just let it speak to our completely open minds as though it had been put into our hands for the first time. Perhaps there is value in that advice, particularly when given to sceptics or unbelievers, most of whom seem scared simply to give the book a fair chance; but so far as others are concerned the advice needs tempering.

We who are going through these studies already prize the precious pages of the New Testament, and long to apprehend their meanings still more enrichingly. We certainly want to discard all *wrong* ideas, and to read with "completely open minds." Yet an "open" mind is not necessarily a *blank* mind. We may miss much if we come to our New Testament without certain *right* ideas.

Here we mention one only, which, if it be borne in mind from the outset, gives complexion and glow and thrill from beginning to end. It is this: Dominating all the writings of the New Testament the characteristic concept is that of FULFILMENT.

Matthew, right at the beginning, sets the key, and for emphasis strikes the key-note twelve times over with his "That it might be *FULFILLED*" (i. 22, ii. 15, 17, 23, iv. 14, viii. 17, xii. 17, xiii. 35, xxi. 4, xxvi. 56, xxvii. 9, 35). Right away, in his first-recorded public discourse of our Lord, he reports as the very crux of it, "I came . . . to *FULFIL*." But Matthew is not alone in this emphasis. What was the very first word spoken by our Lord as He commenced His public ministry? According to Matthew it was this: "Thus it becometh us to FULFIL" (iii. 15). According to Mark it was: "The time is FULFILLED, the kingdom of God is at hand" (i. 15). According to Luke it was "This day is this scripture FULFILLED in your ears" (iv. 21). John, as is usual, contrastively counterpoints the three synoptists, and instead of giving us our Lord's own first declaration gives us the reaction of those who first "received" Him—"We have FOUND!" (i. 41). "We have FOUND!" (i. 45). And thereafter, seven times over, he reiterates Matthew's key-note: "That it might be *fulfilled*" (xii. 38, xiii. 18, xv. 25, xvii. 12, xix. 24, 28, 36).

So is it, in varying form and phrase, all through the Acts and the Epistles. The New Testament is the fulfilment of the Old; or, to be more precise, the CHRIST of the New Testament is the fulfilment. He is the fulfilment of all that prophets saw, and psalmists sang, and godly hearts hoped for.

The New Testament is the ANSWER to the Old. Without it the Old is like a river which loses itself in the sands. It is revelation without destination; something pre-visualised but never post-realised; promise without fulfilment; preparation without consummation. If the New Testament is *not* the answer to the Old, then the Old has *never* had an answer, and never *can* have an answer. But the New Testament IS the answer. It is THE answer. It is the TRUE, CLEAR, GLORIOUS FULFILMENT.

Let us see how this is so.

The Unfinished Symphony

Try to imagine yourself reading or studying the Old Testament for the first time. Let us suppose that you have a Jewish friend who says to you, "Our Hebrew Scriptures are wonderful; you should read them." You reply, "I presume you mean the Bible."

He rejoins, "No, no, the Bible is the Old and New Testaments. We Jews believe only in the Old. *That* is our Scripture. Don't bother about what these Christians call the New Testament. Read the *Old* Testament; and don't just read it once, it is too wonderful."

So you read the Old Testament a first time, and, of course, the first section which you traverse is the *Torah* or Law—the "Pentateuch." The thing which probably strikes you most is the prevalence of animal sacrifice. It begins away back in Genesis iv. It occurs again in chapters ix. and xii. and xxii. It presents itself more clearly in Exodus, until in Leviticus there is an entire organisation of sacrifices, offerings, rites, ceremonies. Everywhere the impression clings that these sacrifices and ceremonies somehow point to realities outside of themselves, yet this is nowhere clearly explained. However, you read on through the remaining books, hoping to find an explanation. You travel through the historical books (Joshua to Esther), and the philosophy books (Job to Song of Solomon), and the prophetical books (Isaiah to Malachi); but although the sacrifices and ceremonies of the Law are referred to again and again, you come to the end of the Old Testament without the light that you need; and you have a disappointing sense that the Old Testament is a book of *UNEXPLAINED CEREMONIES*.

Still, you have decided that the Old Testament is just about the most wonderful book you ever read, and that the Jews are a remarkable race. Is it really so, that the Jews are God's "chosen people," with high purpose and destiny? Then you must read about it all again. So you start again at Genesis. You see the obliteration of the antediluvian civilisation, also God's covenant with Noah that the race should never be flood-destroyed again. Next you encounter the far-reaching covenant with Abraham in Genesis xii., xv., xvii., xxii., renewed later to Isaac and Jacob. Later you see the twelve tribes freed from Egyptian bondage by Jehovah's outstretched arm, welded into a nation at Sinai, given a Law and ordinances, and constituted a *theocracy*. You watch the covenant people invade and occupy Canaan: the future is florid with possibilities. But alas, the Book of Judges follows with its sordid declensions and servitudes. The First Book of Samuel recounts the change-over from theocracy to monarchy. 1 Kings brings disruption of the one kingdom into two. 2 Kings ends with both kingdoms swept into exile. 1 and 2 Chronicles review the tragic story. In Ezra, Nehemiah, Esther, a Remnant returns to Judæa; but it is *only* a remnant. The walls of Jerusalem are rebuilt, but the Davidic throne is no more. In Judæa the Jews are a minor dependency; outside they are scattered to the four winds. You read on through the philosophy books, but there is nothing further about them there; nor is there in the prophets, except in the last little trio, Haggai, Zechariah, Malachi, where things are far from well with the returned Remnant. Thus you finish your second reading of the Old Testament with a sad sigh that it is a book of *UNACHIEVED PURPOSES*.

One thing, however, now stands out with captivating power, and it is this: in its *spiritual* aspects the Old Testament is surely unmatched, and you can well understand the pride of the Jews in it. You really must read it yet again, for here, surely, the true God is revealed, as also the way to find Him! You start at Genesis again. Surely this is the most credible and sublime account of origins ever penned! You re-peruse Exodus, Leviticus, Numbers, Deuteronomy. Surely this is the most wonderful Law ever given! But your *special* interest is now focused on those *philosophical* books in the fivefold poetic group, Job to Solomon's Song, for it is those which deal with the aching problems of the individual human heart. In them you will surely find solution! But do you? Nay, for although there are indeed illuminating, penetrating, practical, reassuring counsels and lessons and promises, somehow there are no clear or final solutions to the dire problems of sin and pain and death and the beyond. You are still left groaning with Job, "Oh that I knew where I might find HIM!" In the ensuing writings of the Prophets you find loftiest ethics and most startling predictions, but they do not solve your spiritual quest; and you end your third reading of the Old Testament equally aware that it is a book of *UNAPPEASED LONGINGS*.

Yet even now you cannot finally forsake its pages, for in reading it you have yourself become an earnest seeker after reality, and, besides, you have found in it a certain astonishing phenomenon such as is found in no other religion or philosophy under the sun. This unique feature has impressed you more each time you have gone through the book. It is the marvel of Old Testament *prophecy*, especially prophecy in the sense of *prediction*.

There can be no surviving doubt as to genuineness. Boldly drawn, time-spanning, markedly detailed foretellings on Egypt, Assyria, Babylon, and other mighty powers were hazarded and then fulfilled with such accuracy that any candid investigator must consent, "This is the seal of the living God upon these Scriptures." Moreover, the fulfilling of those prophecies guarantees the similar consummation of the many others which reach on into a more distant futurity. The main body of the Old Testament prophecy speaks as no other known literature about the *future*, and garnishes it with the most compensating ultimate restitution. It all focuses in the idea that *SOMEONE IS COMING* who will be God's answer to the cry of the ages. Away back in Genesis iii. 15 the "Seed of the woman" is to "bruise the head" of the serpent. The promise of this "Seed" is renewed to Abraham, Isaac, Jacob, in chapters xii., xvii., xxii., xxvi., xlix. There are traces of it in all the succeeding Old Testament scrolls, until, in Isaiah and his compeers, the stream of Messianic prophecy reaches floodfulness. Yet when you reach Malachi again, although empires have perished, and centuries have filed into antiquity, and the seers lie in their graves, the promised One has not come. "Behold, He shall come!" exclaims Malachi, as he, too, the last of the prophets, recedes behind the misty curtain of the past; but he must leave off there; and you close the Old Testament realising that it is a book of *UNFULFILLED PROPHECIES*.

Yes, the Old Testament, in its four successive compartments, i.e. the organisational, the historical, the philosophical, the prophetical, is a book of (1) UNEXPLAINED CEREMONIES, (2) UNACHIEVED PURPOSES, (3) UNAPPEASED LONGINGS, (4) UNFULFILLED PROPHECIES.

The Completed Masterpiece

But now let us suppose that, having thus read the Old Testament, you meet a Christian friend who persuades you to read the *New* Testament. What do you find? You read it once, twice, thrice, and all the time you are discovering a book of corresponding fulfilments. The very first chapter of Matthew sings out the soon-familiar refrain, "That it might be fulfilled . . ." The Jesus who is to "save His people from their sins" is lineally certificated right back to royal David and patriarch Abraham, through whom God's two great "covenants of promise" were made with

Israel. His birth of the virgin immediately unlocks the secret of Isaiah vii. 14: "Now all this was done that it might be fulfilled which was spoken by the Lord through the prophet, Behold the virgin shall be with child, and shall bring forth a son, and they shall call his name Emmanuel, which being interpreted is, God with us."

Thereafter you read about the Jesus of the New Testament, whose birth, life, death, resurrection and ascension are historically *recorded* in the Gospels, spiritually *interpreted* in the Acts and Epistles, and prospectively *consummated* in the Apocalypse.

In His vicarious death and atoning self-sacrifice, His resurrection and ascension, His present high-priestly ministry in heaven, and His promised return, you see the *unexplained ceremonies* of the Law suddenly flame into new meaning. They all point to *HIM* —as for instance the five different kinds of offerings in Leviticus, the tabernacle ordinances, the annual entering of the high priest into the Holy of Holies with covenant blood-sprinkling, and his later re-emerging in his glorious garments to bless his people.

As you read of the Saviour's birth, and hear the announcing angel say, "He shall be great, and shall be called the Son of the Highest: and the Lord God shall give unto Him the throne of His father David . . ." you realise that the *unfulfilled histories* of the Old Testament are being taken up again, and are finding fulfilment in *HIM*.

As you read His teachings about the love and fatherhood of God; as you hear Him say, "Come unto Me, all ye that labour and are heavy laden, and I will give you rest"; as you see Him, not only ascending to heaven but shedding forth the Holy Spirit and thereby coming to indwell the hearts of His redeemed people —you see the *unappeased longings* of the Old Testament philosophy books finding lovely fulfilment.

And as for the *unfulfilled prophecies* of the Old Testament Christology, from the time of His miraculous birth at Bethlehem right on to the climax of His miraculous ascension from Olivet, He is fulfilling those predictions of the older dispensation. He *claims* to be their fulfilment—as when He says in the synagogue: "This day is this scripture fulfilled in your ears." He *proves* to be their fulfilment, in His sinless life and miracle-attested ministry, and most movingly in His Calvary death; for of whom could such passages as Isaiah liii. be written if not of Him to whom John the Baptist pointed as He exclaimed: "Behold, the Lamb of God, which beareth away the sin of the world"?

Yes, the Jesus of the New Testament is the fulfilment of Old Testament ceremony, history, philosophy, prophecy. In the Old Testament He is *coming*. In the Gospels He has *come* in visible humanity. In the Epistles He has come *in* by the invisible Holy Spirit. In the Apocalypse He comes *back* in the glory of world empire. The fulfilments at His *first* coming prove Old Testament prophecy to be Divine; and they equally guarantee that the still-unfulfilled remainder, in both Old and New Testaments, will just as certainly burst into occurrence when the predestined hour strikes.

> *Praise we the God of light*
> *Whose revelation pure*
> *Ends superstition's deadly night*
> *By truth Divine and sure;*
> *Whose Self-revealing grace,*
> *Through patriarchs begun,*
> *Now shines in fulness from the face*
> *Of His incarnate Son.*

THE NEW TESTAMENT AS A WHOLE

Lesson Number 109

It must first be remembered that the New Testament was not given and received as one volume, but that it *grew together* by recognition and use. As the several books gradually coalesced into unity, it might be expected that there would be many varieties of arrangement, but that they would on the whole tend to assume their relative places, according to the law of internal fitness, rather than on any other principle which might exercise a transient influence, as for instance that of the relative dignity of the names of their authors, or that of their chronological production or recognition. In fact, this tendency shows itself at once, in the earliest period to which our enquiries are carried back by extant manuscripts, by ancient catalogues of the sacred books, and by the habitual arrangement of the oldest versions. . . . The order in which we now read the books of the New Testament is that which, on the whole, they have tended to assume ; and the general internal arrangement, by which the entire collection forms for us a consecutive course of teaching, has been sufficiently recognised by the instinct and fixed by the habit of the Church.

—T. D. Bernard.

THE NEW TESTAMENT AS A WHOLE

THE NEW TESTAMENT is the most vital book in the world. Its supreme *subject* is the Lord Jesus Christ. Its supreme *object* is the salvation of human beings. Its supreme *project* is the ultimate reign of the Lord Jesus in boundless and endless empire.

Christ is *the* subject of its pages. Is He not also the subject of the Old Testament? Yes, but not in the same way or with the same exclusiveness. He who figures in the Old as the Christ of *prophecy* now emerges in the New as the Christ of *history*. He who is the super-*hope* of the Old is the super-*fact* of the New. Expectancy in the Old has become *experience* in the New. *Pre*-vision has become *pro*vision. That which was latent has now become patent. The long-predicted is the now-presented.

This is concentratedly true of the four Gospels, which we are now to study. As Job exclaimed, when he made his new discovery of God: "I had heard of Thee by the hearing of the ear, but now mine eye seeth Thee!" so may *we* say, as we reverently encounter the Christ of the four Gospels. In the earlier Scriptures we have heard of Him "by the hearing of the ear," but now "our eye seeth Him." Before this, we have seen Him "through a glass darkly," whereas now it is "face to face."

For this reason the four Gospels are the very *crux* of the Bible. They are the historical focus of Old Testament prophecy, and the factual basis of New Testament theology. They are not the *terminus* of Old Testament prophecy, much of which runs on into times even yet future; but they are the main-line *junction,* on which all Old Testament branch-lines converge. All lines now become one main line in the historical JESUS OF NAZARETH. We "change" here from that which is distinctively Jewish to that which is distinctively Christian; from the old covenant and dispensation to the new covenant and dispensation; from Moses to Christ; from law to grace.

Before we travel through the four Gospels successively, we ought to review them collectively: (*a*) in their structural relation to the New Testament as a whole; (*b*) in their interrelation to each other as a quartette. In this present study let us consider:

The New Testament as a Whole

Away back at the outset of this Bible course we pointed to the structure of the New Testament as exhibiting Divine design. It will be well worth while just here to repeat and amplify what we then said. Structurally the New Testament is built together in the form of a literary *archway*. When one pauses to reflect on it there is no kind of edifice which so accurately expresses the spiritual function and significance of the New Testament as an archway. What *are* these twenty-seven documents, these collected memoirs and letters which comprise the New Testament, but a literary archway leading to something beyond themselves? Are they not, in their total union, God's wonderfully constructed archway into saving truth, into the true knowledge of Himself, into eternal blessedness?

We know, of course, that many profess the Christian faith whose views of inspiration are such as to make it seem incredible to them that there should be superhuman system and progress determining even the arrangement of the books in our New Testament. To them, the present lay-out of its contents is purely accidental, or at most simply one of several ways in which human hands have collected them. We shall refer to this again later, and would simply remark here that to our own judgment it has always seemed a reasonable inference, if not a necessary corollary, that since God has expressed Himself in such a written revelation by means of supernatural *inspiration*, and guarded it through centuries by providential *preservation*, He should shape and control its finalised *integration*. To our own mind, the absence of predetermined design from such Divine oracles seems as unthinkable as the *presence* of it apparently seems to others! It has been truly said that "God never leaves loose ends"!

The Gospels and the Acts

As we turn over the earlier pages of the New Testament we find ourselves traversing five writings which are entirely narrative, namely, Matthew, Mark, Luke, John, and the Acts of the Apostles. These form a group by themselves, inasmuch as they are the only *historical* books of the New Testament, and are foundational to all that follows.

The Christian Church Epistles

The abrupt ending of the Acts brings us to a series of letters. The first *nine* of these unmistakably group themselves together. All nine are from the pen of the same human author, the apostle Paul. They are letters of teaching and instruction in Christian truth and practice; i.e. they are mainly *doctrinal*. They are all addressed to Christian assemblies, or "churches," and are rightly called the "Christian Church Epistles"; i.e. Romans, 1 and 2 Corinthians, Galatians, Ephesians, Philippians, Colossians, 1 and 2 Thessalonians.

The Pastoral Epistles

After the "Christian Church Epistles" we still continue with Pauline writings, but his remaining letters are not addressed to churches. They are to individuals; and there are *four* of them. The first two are written to Timothy, one of Paul's sons in the faith, who was now a pastor over a Christian congregation. The third is sent to Titus, of whom the same may be said as of Timothy. The fourth is to Philemon, a Christian leader at Colosse, who also led a "church" which met in his own "house." These, especially the first three, are known as the "Pastoral Epistles."

The Hebrew Christian Epistles

There are still nine other writings left in the New Testament: Hebrews, James, 1 and 2 Peter, 1, 2 and 3 John, Jude, Revelation. They, also, are *letters* of varying length. Even the last and longest of them, although commonly known as "The Revelation," is in reality a letter or epistle. It is an epistle of our Lord Jesus Himself (even though transmitted per the apostle John), as its opening words indicate: "The revelation *of Jesus Christ*, which God gave unto Him, to show unto His servants things which must shortly come to pass: and He [i.e. our Lord Jesus] *sent and signified it* by His angel unto His servant John; who bare record of the word of God and of *the testimony of Jesus Christ*. . . ."

One does not have to look over-intently into these nine to see that they are not just a miscellaneous addendum to the "Christian Church" and "Pastoral" epistles. They cohere homogeneously into a complete, final group. They are not addressed to Christian churches, however, as the earlier nine are. The first of them, i.e.

Hebrews, is obviously addressed to *the Hebrew nation* as such. The next of them begins: "James, a servant of God and of the Lord Jesus Christ, *to the twelve tribes scattered abroad*," by which the writer obviously means the Hebrew people. Next comes Peter, beginning with: "Peter, an apostle of Jesus Christ, *to the strangers scattered throughout Pontus, Galatia, Cappadocia, Asia, and Bithynia*," by which, again, the Jews of the "Dispersion" are denoted. Next comes John's first epistle, bearing no opening direction at all. His short second and third letters, however, are both addressed to Jewish individuals. Their inter-Jewish standpoint reveals itself in such remarks as that in 3 John 7, where the apostle refers to certain servants of the Lord as having gone forth "taking nothing of the *Gentiles*." John would never have thus referred to the Gentiles had he been writing *to* Gentiles.

Unmistakably, these last nine epistles of the New Testament are different from the nine "Christian Church Epistles." Not only are they not addressed to local Christian churches, there is nothing in them about *the* Church, i.e. the Church *mystical*—the mystical body and bride and temple of God's dear Son, except in an anonymous and visionary form at the end of the Apocalypse. All of that teaching on the Church mystical, which is so precious to the Lord's own, is in the "Christian Church Epistles." These *later* nine are rightly called "The *Hebrew* Christian Epistles." Make no mistake, they are "*Christian*," and some of the most magnificent Christian doctrines are treated in them. Yet they are distinctively Hebrew in their primary adaptation and application. Their standpoint, approach and atmosphere certainly make them the "*Hebrew* Christian Epistles."

An Archway of Written Truth

Is it not easily perceivable, then, that the twenty-seven oracles of our New Testament, in their several groups, form themselves, so to speak, into an *archway* structure of written revelation? First the four Gospels and the Acts lay down a solid five-fold slab, or five basal steps, of historic fact beneath our feet. Then rising up on the right hand and on the left, like two beautifully elaborated side-pillars of a handsome arch, are the two nine-fold groups of epistles—the "Christian Church Epistles," and the "Hebrew Christian Epistles," both being bridged above by the four "Pastoral Epistles," the whole thus framing itself into the likeness of an archway, and reaching its high vertex in the transcendent epitome of Gospel truth: "Great is the mystery of godliness: God was manifest in the flesh, justified in the Spirit, seen of angels, preached unto the Gentiles, believed on in the world, received up into glory" (1 Tim. iii. 16).

London's famous "Marble Archway," the "Arc de Triomphe" of Paris, the ancient Arch of Titus in Rome—what are they compared with this literary archway of Divine revelation into soul-saving truth and eternal blessedness?

Inter-correspondences

This archway structure of the New Testament opens up a fascinating subject which could absorb many pages. The contrastive and completive interrelationships between the four Gospels we shall consider in our next study; as also we shall later point out the latent methodicity and mutual correspondences in the two ninefold pillars of epistles. But even here it is well to note again a few of the more obvious comparative and contrastive parallels between those two sets of epistles.

Both groups open with a great doctrinal treatise—in the one case Paul's Epistle to the Romans; in the other, the Epistle to the Hebrews. Both groups end with an unveiling of our Lord's return and of "things to come"—in the one case the pair of epistles to the Thessalonians; in the other, the Apocalypse, or Book of Revelation.

At the beginning of the one group the Epistle to the Romans shows us that salvation through our Lord Jesus Christ is the *only* way. At the beginning of the other nine the Epistle to the Hebrews shows us that salvation through our Lord Jesus Christ is the *better* way—there is a "better" *Deliverer*, even Jesus; and a "better" *sacrifice*, i.e. Calvary; and a "better" *principle*, i.e. faith. At the end of the first group the Thessalonian letters show us the second coming of Christ especially in relation to the *Church*. At the end of the other nine the Book of the Revelation shows us the second coming of Christ in relation to *Israel* and the *nations*.

We shall add to this later; but what we have said here will already have indicated that the New Testament is far from being a string of writings succeeding each other with little or no reference to order. There are designed divisions and groupings, a supernaturally supervised over-all pattern, and a significant archway-structure.

Design Plus Development

But lest our figure of the archway should suggest something merely static, we must add that there is an orderly *unfolding movement* observable in the New Testament, which blends itself with the set group-arrangement of the twenty-seven parts. It has been aptly called "progress of doctrine." Besides design there is *development*. Besides pattern there is *progress*.

This "progress of doctrine" in the New Testament cannot long remain doubtful to a diligent and discerning reader. It is the more noticeable because, in contrast, the writings do *not* adhere to any formal progress according to the *calendar*.

The four Gospels show us right away that succession simply according to date, while it is never misleadingly violated, is always subordinated to a higher pattern and purpose. In the ancient manuscripts and versions, as well as in catalogues of the New Testament books, the four Gospels almost always occur in the familiar order—Matthew, Mark, Luke, John; but neither in that nor any other order are they the four parts of one consecutive narrative. Although Mark follows Matthew, he does not take on where Matthew leaves off; he turns back again to begin at the ministry of John the Baptist. Luke follows Mark, but starts even further back than Matthew, telling us not only of our Lord's nativity but about the parents of the forerunner.

To take Matthew, in particular, we soon find that he is more concerned to present our Lord's sayings and doings in purposive *groupings* rather than by progressive *datings*, the first grouping of sayings being the Sermon on the Mount, in chapters v. vi. and vii.; and the first groupings of doings being the miracles in chapters viii. and ix. The miracle which Matthew first *reports* is not the one which our Lord first *performed*; whereas John, who comes *last* of the "holy quaternion," starts with the *first* of the miracles, i.e. at Cana of Galilee.

So it is with the epistles. Their order is not determined by date of composition. Almost uniformly the nine "Christian Church Epistles" have come down to us in their present order; yet 1 and 2 Thessalonians, which were written first, stand last; while Romans, which was written almost last, stands first. The nine "Hebrew Christian Epistles" show similar disregard for any strict order according to date.

Yet, the more plainly off-setting this non-adherence to strict sequence of chronological *fact*, there is consistent sequence of revelational *truth*. In its main divisions the New Testament exhibits a "progress of doctrine" which, it would seem, is permanently fashioned for our instruction. The several examples of this which we shall here adduce must be taken as representative of many.

Order of the Gospels

This "progress of doctrine" shows itself in the four Gospels. Before we can say one word about it, however, we shall be parried by the objection: "Is not the present order of the four Gospels purely accidental? How then can there be any such predesigned or over-all 'progress'? Is it not just imaginary?" The late T. D. Bernard answered that objection once for all: "When this particular arrangement of books, which may be, and often have been, otherwise arranged, is treated as involving a course of progressive teaching, it may seem that an unwarrantable stress is laid on an accidental order which some may regard as little more than a habit of the printer and the binder . . . [but] if the familiar order *does* exhibit a sequence of thought and a sustained advance of doctrine, then the several documents are in their right places according to the *highest kind of relation* which they can bear to each other." The fact is, that if these four Gospels had been submitted to any of us, with the request that we should study them so as to arrange them in their most advantageous and progressive order, we should have been obliged to put them in the very same succession as that which they have assumed in our New Testament.

Their familiar order has an internal fitness and is evidently *meant* by a higher than human control. How could Matthew be anywhere but first, or John anywhere but last? Who can help noticing that the four are divided into three and one (as has *always* been recognised)—the first three preparing us for the completive interpretation of the fourth? The first three familiarise us with the *visible* aspects of the wonderful manifestation, and educate us for the crowning presentation in John, where the *inward* mystery and majesty of it is interpreted to us.

Matthew necessarily leads, for his speciality is the linking up of the Gospel with the Hebrew Scriptures, thus introducing the New Testament as the fulfilment of the Old. "That it might be fulfilled which was spoken," is his distinguishing refrain; and he plainly adapts his narrative to the Jews, of whom, as to the flesh, Christ came.

Just as plainly Mark fits next, and Luke next again. Lest Matthew's account should seem to suggest that the Gospel is a development merely *in* and not *from* the Jewish faith (some would fain have so contracted it), Mark and Luke follow with their memoirs in which, to quote apt words, our Lord is "disengaged from those close connections with Jewish life and thought which the first Gospel is studious to exhibit."

According to more than tradition, Mark was coadjutor of Peter, as Luke was of Paul. Early Christian Fathers name Mark as Peter's *amanuensis*, or even as translator-continuator of an original "Gospel" written by Peter himself in Aramaic.

The connection of Mark with Peter, and Luke with Paul, is indelibly evident in their two memoirs. It was Peter who first "opened the door of faith unto the Gentiles" (Acts x., with xv. 7); yet Peter remained the "apostle of the circumcision" (Gal. ii. 8, 9), whereas Paul broke right out as the "apostle of the Gentiles" (Rom. xi. 13, etc.). Correspondingly, Mark's Gospel moves away from the studied Jewish adaptation of Matthew. There is no genealogy of our Lord's Davidic and Abrahamic descent. Only twice (as against twelve times in Matthew) do we find "that it might be fulfilled." Our Lord is seen not so much fulfilling the past as commanding the present. He is the wonder-Worker with power over both visible and invisible realms. This is the Gospel of *action*, and its first-intended approach seems to be to the Roman rather than the Hebrew. It was perfectly adapted to such Roman converts as those in Acts x., and may well be summarised in Peter's words to them: "God anointed Jesus of Nazareth with the Holy Spirit and with power, who went about doing good, and healing all those who were oppressed of the devil."

Yet although Mark moves away from the more exclusive Hebrew features of Matthew and sketches a wonder-working

Jesus with arresting meaning for the Gentile, it is Luke who, in the widest sense, presents Him as "the Son of *Man*." In Luke the door swings wide open. Here is broadest human sympathy, catholicity of outlook, and a Saviour so presented as to engage the Gentile mind at large. The very preface prepares us for this. The other evangelists, according to Hebrew form, begin without a dedication, whereas Luke not only prefaces a dedication in Greek fashion and classic style but dedicates his Gospel to a Gentile convert. Thereafter, in a way which we cannot detail here but which is so featured that any careful reader sees it, the narrative brings out, as none of the others does, the common humanity of the perfect Man with all the human family and without regard to national distinctions or the older demarcation between Jew and Gentile.

Progress Parallels

This outward "progress" from Matthew through Mark to Luke corresponds with the racial affinity of the three writers. Matthew, also called "Levi, the son of Alphaeus," was a Jew, and a near kinsman of our Lord. Mark, or "John Marcus" (Acts xii. 12), was half Jew and half Gentile, hence, presumably, his name John (Hebrew) and surname Marcus (Greek). Luke, or Lucas, was a Gentile, as his Greek name, Greek style of writing and Paul's references to him seem to make certain, though of course it is quite probable that his parents had become proselytes to Judaism.

Again, this outward "progress" of the Gospel, from Jewish Matthew, through Jew-Gentile Mark, to Gentile Luke, parallels with the three stages of expansion in the Acts of the Apostles. First the Gospel is preached within the confines of Jewry (Acts i.–vii.). Then it spreads through Samaria, reaches to the Ethiopian chancellor, and breaks with Pentecostal effusion on the Gentile (Roman) household of Cornelius (viii.–xii.). Finally, through the missionary travels of Paul, it is propagated freely and fully to the whole Gentile world (xiii.–xxviii.).

The Fourth Gospel

But if, in our three synoptic Gospels, the presentation of the historical Christ shows these progressive stages, from its originating Jewish aspect to its most catholic Gentile adaptation, the

fourth Gospel is its perfective and protective climax. That which
has been rightly *inferred* from the reports of the three is now
plainly *declared* in the review by the fourth: the historical Jesus
is the eternal Son. He who is Israel's Messiah is Himself Jehovah.
He who is the world's Saviour is the world's Maker. He not only
teaches truth: He *is* the truth. He imparts life because He *is* the
life.

John wrote his Gospel when the earlier three writers had passed
beyond. He was providentially kept alive to a great age for a
purpose which proved only too necessary. Soon enough after the
completed data of the historical manifestation had been fixed and
preserved by Matthew, Mark and Luke there emerged those subtleties of controversy in which a speculative theosophy began tampering with the person of Christ. It was *the* moment—long
enough after the historical facts were circulated, yet soon enough
to answer at the outset all such deviations from the true doctrine
of Christ—for an authoritative endorsement and interpretation
of the three synoptists. It required the voice of a still-living *eye-
witness* who could say, "That which we have seen with our eyes,
and our hands have handled"; but the eye-witness needed to be
also an *apostle*, who, besides thus supplying the certification of
the senses, could endorse and interpret the facts with authoritative permanence for the Church. The aged John was both eye-
witness and apostle. So, as we have said, the fourth Gospel is
both "perfective" and "protective."

There are many other features of such "progress" in the four
Gospels, but we must leave them for the time being. It should
be noted, however, that these stages of progress in the Gospels,
as well as others to be mentioned later, are constituted only by
difference of degree. It is a marvel how they remain essentially
alike even while they aspectively differ. It may be truly said:
"There is nothing expanded in one book which has not been
asserted in another. Take whatever may seem to you the distinguishing idea of any one of them, and you find a strong expression
of it in all the others. The Judaism of St. Matthew reaches out to
the calling of the Gentiles; and the catholic spirit of Luke falls
back upon its Jewish origin. St. John, in exhibiting the Divine
nature of Christ, exhibits only what the others have everywhere
implied and frequently affirmed." They are an unmatched literary
phenomenon of exquisitely balanced *di*vergence and *con*vergence.

The Book of the Acts

We can give little more than a passing glance at the continuance of this progress in the Acts and the Epistles.

The *geographical* progress in the Acts has been noted already. It follows the course pre-delineated by our Lord Himself in chapter i. 8: "Ye shall receive power after that the Holy Spirit is come upon you; and ye shall be witnesses unto Me, both in Jerusalem and in all *Judæa*, and in *Samaria*, and unto the *uttermost part of* earth."

As for *doctrinal* progress in the Acts, was there ever a more wonderful unfolding of events and truths going hand-in-hand? We start with the renewed offer of the "kingdom" to the *Jews*, and end with "churches" planted throughout the lands of the *Gentiles*; and from beginning to end, under the control of the now-invisible Lord, the evolution of outward *events* is made to register the corresponding evolution of evangelical *doctrine*. The Lord who was visible in the Gospels is now invisible, but at every necessary point there is an unmistakably supernatural intervention, so that the guiding of the history might be seen as the sealing of the doctrine.

The Acts must immediately *follow* the four Gospels, for we need to see the now-completed external facts of our Lord's life, death, resurrection and ascension in their *first* meaning for the *Jews*. Equally must the Acts *precede* the Christian Church Epistles, for we are thereby prepared to see the Christ-facts in their *fuller* meaning for the *Church*.

Yes, as the story opens, Jesus crucified, risen, ascended, is Israel's *Messiah*; but more and more as the story unfolds He is the world's *Saviour*. Yes, all over the earlier pages we find *"To the Jew first"*; but more and more legibly, as the later pages are turned, we find *"and also to the Gentile."* Yes, wonderful are the outward miracle-signs which fill the earlier pages, then later decrease; but far more wonderful are the inward soul-saving truths which go on expanding all the way through.

The Messianic kingdom has now been twice offered and twice rejected. In the Gospels it was offered through the lips of Christ Himself, but Israel rejected it and nailed Him to the Cross. Now, in the Acts, it is offered again by the crucified, risen, ascended

Jesus, through Spirit-fired, miracle-attested messengers; and Israel rejects it again. First the Jews of the homeland finalise *their* rejection in the martyring of Stephen. Later, the Jews of the Dispersion, gathered in their representative thousands at Jerusalem, signalise *their* rejection in the attempted lynching of Paul (Acts xxii.).

Yet although Israel, civically and representatively, has now twice rejected Jesus and the offered kingdom, there are *groups* of men and women, both Jews and Gentiles, in Judæa and Samaria and throughout the Roman world, who *have* believed on Him and who *do* own Him as King. What of *them*? Why, they now become the very crux of the story. As Israel's refusal crystallises into hard-set fixity, there gradually emerges the realisation that the very failure of Israel is being sovereignly overruled in the formation of the CHURCH, of which those many scattered groups of believers are the first units!

But if the "kingdom," in its visible, Messianic aspects, is being withdrawn, what is this "Church," this *ecclesia*, which is now developing on earth and bringing to light a hidden purpose of God? That is the point where the book of the Acts leaves us and where we are ready for the Christian Church Epistles.

The Epistles

Sorry as we are, in connection with the Gospels and the Acts, that our reference to "progress of doctrine" must be so skimpy in one short section like this, we are the more so as we now advert briefly to the Epistles. We are comforted, however, inasmuch as we shall have opportunity to refer to such progress in the two main groups of epistles when we reach our study of them in this series. We shall attempt no more here than to point out a few *general* lines of designed development.

There are three words which concentrate for us the meaning of the Christian life, at least on its human side. They are "faith" and "hope" and "love." As 1 Corinthians xiii. 13 puts it: "And now abideth faith, hope, love, these three: but the greatest of these is love." In the spacious vestibule of a beautiful European cathedral the floor consists of three massive slabs on which three Latin words are inscribed in large letters. On the first slab is the Latin *CREDO*; on the second, *SPEIRO*; on the third, *AMO*.

First comes *credo*, "I believe." Next comes *speiro*, "I hope." Then comes *amo*, "I love." Now the three principal writers of our New Testament epistles are Paul, Peter and John, and they come in that order. They all speak about faith and hope and love, yet each of them has an emphasis. First comes Paul, who is distinctively the apostle of *faith*. Next comes Peter, the apostle of *hope*. Last comes John, the apostle of *love*. If you change their *positional* order, you foil the true *spiritual* order. Their present arrangement is designed to indicate the true order of spiritual progress.

Take the nine Christian Church Epistles. The first four emphasise the *Cross*; the next three the *Church*; the last two the Lord's *second coming*. Is not that true progress?

Take the nine Hebrew Christian Epistles and their characteristic emphases. The first two stress *"faith"* and *"works."* The next two emphasise *"hope"* and *"growth."* The next four (John and Jude) *"love"* and then *"contending."* Finally, the Apocalypse speaks of *"overcoming"* and *"inheriting."* What notable system of progress is *there*! Look it through leisurely and see how the spiritual balance is preserved at each forward step of the progress.

From beginning to end of the New Testament there is a sustained movement of progress until the thorn-crowned Christ of the Cross is the glory-crowned King of the new Jerusalem.

Now, of course, the fact of this "progress" implies the *unity* of the whole. Mere succession is of many, but progress is of one—which here indicates one controlling Mind. But this progress also implies a Divine *plan* predesigned so as to achieve the progress. And again it implies that the *same* Mind is speaking to us *from first to last*; for while there may be advance in human *apprehension*, there cannot be progress of Divine *revelation* unless it is Christ Himself speaking just as really in the Acts and Epistles as in the Gospels.

How important, also, is it for preachers and expositors to recognise this fact of revelational progress in the New Testament! It is well said that the sufficient foundations of Christian doctrine lie less in single texts than in "the combination and convergence" of the Scriptures in their progressive totality.

How wonderful, too, is the blending of the human with the Divine all through the New Testament! In this inspired "original" of Christian fact and truth, what is it that is being recorded—the

Divine *revelation* of truth, or the human *apprehension* of it? In the Acts and the Epistles revealed truth is presented to us not only as a communication from God but also as an apprehension by man. The two are so united that the former repeatedly expresses itself through the latter, thus clothing the Divine act in human story and fashioning these Divine oracles into the most human book ever written.

> *Praise we the God of Love,*
> *Whose wondrous thoughts to men*
> *Have been transmitted from above*
> *Through inspiration's pen;*
> *Whose Spirit moved and wrought*
> *Through holy men of old,*
> *And thus to all the ages brought*
> *The Book of worth untold.*

THE FOUR GOSPELS COLLECTIVELY

Lesson Number 110

About "Harmonies" of the Gospels

Beneath their divergent details the Gospel narratives exhibit a unity which has occasioned many attempts to combine all four into one. It has been argued that thus to combine them would preserve us all the matter, yet provide one shorter memoir, and present it in strict order. All such attempts, however, while they are valuable in further demonstrating the consistency of the four accounts, necessarily fail to produce the perfect *"one."* The fact is, we are neither furnished nor intended to make the four into one *that* way. Such a literary unit would destroy those very features and emphases which the Holy Spirit, by His use of four writers, purposes shall arrest our minds and comfort our hearts. Matthew, Mark, Luke and John were inspired *impressionists*. Their accounts are pen-pictures, not annals or even diaries. Exact chronological sequence is not their aim. So a chronological "harmony" or unification into one strictly consecutive story is scarcely feasible. We pass on the following paragraph by the late Rev. E. A. Thompson, from a little book now long out of print:

"A harmony of the Gospels in strict chronological order is impracticable. We cannot possibly work it out, at least with anything like scientific certainty; for this plain and obvious reason, that with the exception of the beginning and the end of their narratives, which, as connected with a biography, almost necessarily correspond, the evangelists do not write chronologically: each of them has his own distinct plan and system of arrangement; and this is so independent of chronological order that if we attempt to put them together in such an order we find ourselves at once entangled in inextricable difficulties, and expose ourselves to the caustic rebuke of a sagacious citizen respecting an old minister of the High Church of Edinburgh, who was engaged for many years in constructing a Harmony of the kind: 'He *is* a minister, *that*, who spends his time and strength in trying to make four men agree that never quarrelled.'"

THE FOUR GOSPELS COLLECTIVELY

LET US now fix our attention on the four Gospels. Never were a more wonderful set of memoirs penned; and this is most of all true when we examine them *collectively*. It is not just that one inserts what the other omits, or vice versa: each contributes a unique aspect, yet all blend in such a fourfold unity of presentation as only Divine superintendence could have effected. That this is no exaggerated statement we shall presently see.

Why Four Instead of One ?

To begin with, we find ourselves asking: Why is it that there are *four* Gospels, especially when the first three seem to cover much the same ground? Would not just one have been better?

Well, as we are dealing with Divinely inspired writings, the ultimate answer, of course, is that there are four because God willed it so: but we may reverently add that there are clear *reasons* why God willed it so.

We need not *invent* reasons, such as, for instance, that it needed "more minds than one" to set forth "the most wonderful life ever spent on earth"; for if the Holy Spirit had so determined He could just as effectively have concentrated through *one* what He has distributed through *four*. Genesis ii. 10 tells us that "a river went out of Eden to water the garden; and from thence it was parted into four heads." The water in all four head-streams was that of the one feeder-river, divided to fulfil a geographical purpose. So does the great feeder-river of Divine inspiration spread itself through the four Gospels to fulfil a *spiritual* purpose.

Preliminary Inferences

Even before we come to *inner* indications why there are four Gospels instead of one we need not hesitate to infer that a first reason is one which springs from Divine considerateness for our human weakness, namely, to enhance the sheer *interest* of the Gospel data. Just as, in the later part of the New Testament, Christian doctrine is taught by a sheaf of endlessly intriguing *letters*, or "epistles," rather than by formal dissertation (Christianity is the only religion which teaches by letters), so here the historical *basis-facts* of the Christian faith are presented by means of four pen-sketches in which, while there is all-controlling Divine guidance, there is no swamping of human personality or idiosyncrasy (how different is Matthew from Luke, and Mark from John!), so that the four memoirs become at once humanly interesting to all who read with reasonable desire to know, and endlessly engaging with ever-fresh surprises for those who study them deeply or compare them carefully.

Besides this, it seems equally inferable that there are four, rather than only one, so as to give us a more *heart-satisfying* picture of the historical Christ. Some time ago I was visiting a friend whose wife had recently died. On a cabinet in his sitting-room there was a satin-wood, gold-embroidered, quadrifolding photograph-holder, standing concavely to the room and containing four coloured pictures of his lost loved-one. He explained that those four gave him just the characteristic expressions which were dearest to him. No one photograph was enough—all four were needed. Sometimes this one, and sometimes that one, spoke most to him, but each in its own way brought a flood of affecting memories to his mind. And would not any of us prefer several life-like aspects of those whom we best love rather than have them forever restricted to one?

Why then try to make the four into one, as some have tried to do with the four Gospels? (See our addendum on so-called "Harmonies of the Gospels".) Would any of us ever dream of cutting up four different photographs of the same loved-one, and trying to unify the scissored bits into one new picture so as to construct what we might call the basic likeness? What futile inanity that would be! Even so, the four Gospels have each an individuality which was never meant to be obliterated. Read the life of Socrates as written by Xenophon the soldier. Then read the same ancient philosopher as depicted by the contemplative Plato. In the one you will see Socrates as the practical moralist. In the other you will see him as the speculative thinker. Two more widely differing biographies of the same person it would be hard to find. Yet they are both faithful to Socrates. Either, without the other, would be misleadingly onesided, yet by their very contrasts the two together preserve the true identity of their hero.

It may sound strange, but the "harmony" of the four Gospels is best appreciated not by destroying but by preserving their diversities. It is their unity of subject *plus* their diversity of treatment which makes them so interesting to the mind, and so satisfying to the heart, in their portraiture of the historical "Jesus of Nazareth."

Difference yet Concurrence

But now let us trace some of the *inner evidences* of Divine design in our four Gospels. Their mutually complementary character has often been pointed out. The famous exegete, Bengel, aptly compares them to a vocal quartette in which the voices, although they may sometimes sing apart, unite the four parts to produce a complete, concordant whole.

That there are surface "differences" between the four accounts need not be denied, even though some of these at a first glance might even seem like disagreements. They serve a good purpose, for they are the indications of independent authorship and of genuineness. Nowhere are these differences incompatible with historical accuracy. They are variations but not contradictions. They appear simply because different aspects or points of view are being emphasised. Indeed, upon careful examination they are seen to be none other than the hall-marks of supernatural design.

Had four *un*inspired men written separate and *independent* accounts we should almost certainly have been faced with real contradictions and inadvertent inaccuracies, even allowing for the thorough sincerity of the writers ; while again, if four uninspired accounts had been written *in collusion* meticulous care would have been taken to eliminate all such variations as we have in our four Gospels, and there would have resulted a "faultily faultless," artificial agreement which would have created suspicion regarding the reliability of the writers and the reality of the great Figure being portrayed. Have we not reason to thank God that these things were not left to the unguided mind and will of man?

The truth is that with perfect naturalness Matthew, Mark, Luke and John have given us four unique presentations of the Lord Jesus, each having its own distinctive emphasis, each being from a point of view peculiar to itself, each being in a real sense complete in itself, yet all four going completively together to make the full portrayal of the God-Man which the Spirit of inspiration purposes to set before us.

A Significant Parallel

Most of us, perhaps, are familiar with the parallel which has often been noted between the four Gospels and the four "living creatures" in the opening vision of the prophet Ezekiel. The four "living creatures," or cherubim, are thus described in Ezekiel i. 10: "As for the likeness of their faces, they four had the face of a man, and the face of a lion, on the right side; and they four had the face of an ox on the left side; they four also had the face of an eagle." The lion symbolises supreme strength, kingship; the man, highest intelligence; the ox, lowly service; the eagle, heavenliness, mystery, Divinity.

In Matthew we see the Messiah-King (the lion).
In Mark we see Jehovah's Servant (the ox).
In Luke we see the Son of Man (the man).
In John we see the Son of God (the eagle).

It needs all four aspects to give the full truth. As Sovereign He comes to reign and rule. As Servant He comes to serve and suffer. As Son of Man He comes to share and sympathise. As Son of God He comes to reveal and redeem. Wonderful fourfold blending—*sovereignty and humility; humanity and deity!*

But it may be asked *why* there should be this correspondence between the four Gospels and those four seraphic beings of Ezekiel's vision. It is interesting, no doubt, but is it *only* a matter of interesting coincidence? Or is there some significance in it? The answer is that there is a most profound significance in it which all of us should perceive. Mind you, we are not suggesting (as some have imaginatively advocated) that those four "living creatures" were a *type* of the four Gospels! We should warily distinguish between types and mere illustrations. A type is a Divinely adapted prefigurement of some truth to be revealed afterward. An illustration has no such type-intention in it, but is simply an illuminating of one thing by another with which it happens to have useful correspondences. When we use those four "living creatures" of Ezekiel's vision (seen again by John in

Revelation iv. 6–8) as paralleling with Matthew, Mark, Luke and John we are simply using a time-honoured similitude. The *Pulpit Commentary* scarcely puts it too strongly when it says: "The patristic interpretation which finds in the four living creatures the *symbols* of the four evangelists . . . must be considered as the play of a devout imagination, but not as unfolding the meaning of either Ezekiel or St. John."

Indeed, the comparison is not so much between the four seraphim and the four evangelists as between the four faces of *each* seraph; for each one of them had the four faces, i.e. of the lion, the ox, the man, the eagle. Well, even though the striking similarity between those four faces and the four Gospel records is used *only* as an illustration, it still remains true that there is a simply profound significance in it, and it is as follows.

Those four seraphs in Ezekiel's vision are, of all created beings, the nearest to the throne of God (see again our exposition of that vision, in study number 79) and we are meant to understand that *they therefore express most accurately the likeness of the Divine nature*.

Those four faces which each seraph possessed, and all the other symbolic characteristics, are meant to express to us the Divine being and attributes. The outstanding and most arresting thing is the revelation of the *moral nature* of God given by the four faces. There is that which corresponds with the lion—which is at once understandable. But there is also that which corresponds with the ox—at which fact we may well marvel, for the ox is the symbol of lowly service. There is that which corresponds with the man, i.e. highest intelligence, reason, emotion, volition, knowledge, love, sympathy, understanding. And there is that which corresponds with the eagle, greatest of all creatures in the natural heavens, solitary, transcendent, mysterious.

Now it was inevitable that when the very Son of God became incarnate the same four qualities or features should reappear; for how could it be otherwise than that HE should exhibit the moral nature of the Godhead more clearly than even those sinless, glorious seraphs, the highest of all created beings, could ever express it? Our Lord Jesus Christ actually *is* the Divine nature become incarnate. "The Word became flesh, and dwelt among us." Therefore this quadruple revelation represented by the lion, the ox, the man, and the eagle re-expresses itself in Matthew, Mark, Luke and John. But the re-expression of it in suchwise that *each* of the four evangelists unmistakably (though perhaps unsuspectingly) sets off *one* of the four aspects, so that the four aspects and the four memoirs correspond respectively, is one of those artistries of Divine design in the Scriptures which we cannot but admire.

In thus touching upon this lion-ox-man-eagle formation of the four Gospels we find it difficult to restrain an eager pen from enlarging upon it and going into details in a way which would carry our present article far beyond the limits imposed upon it by this course of studies; and we can only hope to write more fully on it elsewhere. But we wish, at any rate, to convince those to whom these things may be rather new that in the most plentiful and conclusive way the inner traits and proofs of this fourfold pattern inhere throughout the Gospel narratives. And they are purposive, not just decorative. They mean us to see a wonderful Christ who blends and expresses what the four seraphic beings of Ezekiel's vision symbolically represented.

There is no doubt about it that it is the "lion" in Matthew, the "ox" in Mark, the "man" in Luke, the "eagle" in John. We say this the more deliberately because there are those who have tried to arrange the correspondences otherwise. Nor need we be surprised that different parallels should have been attempted, for as it was with those flashing seraphs and awesome wheels of Ezekiel's vision—"they four had one likeness" and "two wings of every one were joined one to another"—so it is with the four Gospels: amid their marked diversity they all portray "one likeness," the same wonderful Person, and all the way through their "wings are joined one to another." (But see our addendum on the four Gospels and Ezekiel's vision.)

Matthew

It is when we follow the *characteristic emphases* that we see the true parallel. The lion was the emblem of the tribe of Judah, the royal tribe, the tribe in which the Davidic dynasty ran. In Matthew our Lord is uniquely "the Lion of the tribe of Judah," "the Root of David," the "King and Lawgiver." The opening sentence at once gives the key: "The book of the generation of

Jesus Christ, the Son of *DAVID*, the Son of *ABRAHAM*." That beginning is peculiar to Matthew, as also is the genealogy which immediately follows it, in which our Lord's human lineage is traced downwards from *Abraham* through *David*. Mark has no such genealogy. Luke travels right back to *Adam*. John goes right back into *eternity*. Each has a beginning peculiar to itself and in keeping with the special emphasis which is thereafter maintained throughout. *All* expositors agree that Matthew is the Gospel in which, as in no other, our Lord is offering Himself to the Jews as their Messiah-King, performing His Messianic miracle-credentials, and uttering the "laws" and "mysteries" of the *kingdom* (as in the Sermon on the Mount, and in the kingdom parables of chapter xiii.). Did space here allow, to trace it all out would be as fascinating as it would be convincing.

Mark

The ox is the emblem of lowly service. Especially among old-time easterners it represented patient, productive labour. All students of the Gospels have noticed that *Mark* is pre-eminently "the Gospel of action" (as some have called it). No genealogy is prefixed, and there are only the briefest snatches of our Lord's discourses, where given at all (which alone is why Mark's story is the shortest of the four). The emphasis right through is on Christ as the active One, the strong but lowly Servant; and the characteristic word (which in the Greek occurs forty-three times) is "straightway."

Luke

Equally clearly in Luke it is "the face of a man." There is no obscuring of His kingship or His deity, nor is there any obtruding of His humanity, yet somehow, with artless genius, Luke has lifted up the lovely manhood and its human sympathies in a way which is unmistakably peculiar to the third Gospel. He *begins* with noticeably human touches, telling us about the parents and the birth of that wonder babe, "John the Baptist" (Matthew, Mark, and John give nothing of this). Then he narrates the birth of Jesus, telling of the pre-natal journey to Bethlehem, and of the birth in the outhouse because there was no room even in the *kataluma*, or travellers' enclosure; and instead of bringing eastern sages to Jerusalem enquiring "Where is He that is born *King*?" he tells how angels sang to local shepherds: "Unto you is born this day a *Saviour*." Thereafter he tells us how in His babyhood Jesus was presented in the temple; how when He was twelve He went with His parents to the Passover at Jerusalem; how He continued with them as an obedient Son; and how He "increased in wisdom and stature, and in favour with God and man."

All this is found *only* in Luke. He was a doctor, and perhaps Mary would feel that she could therefore speak with less reserve to him about our Lord's birth and childhood. It is not until the latter half of chapter iii. that Luke gives us a genealogy, but in it, having travelled back by a different route (i.e. by *Mary's* ancestors) to David, and linking there with the main line back to Abraham, he pushes right back to Adam, the first *man*. Did space permit, it would be pleasurable to show how all these introductory features are selected in conformity with the ruling emphasis of the whole story as written by Luke.

John

Similarly with John, all conforms to special pattern and purpose. No one would even faintly suggest that any of the four evangelists had his mind on the four cherubs of Ezekiel's vision when penning his sketch of our Lord Jesus; yet here again, in John, unmistakable as in the other three, is the aspective correspondence, this time with the eagle.

There is no human genealogy in John's prologue, but in a few profound strokes of the pen he has lifted us to a loftier and sublimer height than any of the other Gospels. What is mere *earthly* antiquity? To begin with this wonderful Christ you must go right beyond the first sunrise of time, into *eternity*! Before the world had its beginning the Word had His being. "In the beginning was the Word; and the Word was with God; and the Word was God. . . . All things were made by Him; and without Him was not anything made that was made. In Him was life; and the life was the light of men."

He is not just the "Son of David," or the "Son of Abraham" or the "Son of Adam"—He is the *Son of God*. He is the WORD, and therefore co-eternal with the eternal MIND. But lest as such He should be thought of as impersonal, He is also the SON, and therefore co-personal with the FATHER. Albeit, although He is co-eternal and co-personal with the Father, He is not personally identical with the Father: nay, as the Word He was "*with* God," and as the Son He is "*in the bosom of* the Father." Nor is even this all: for, lest He should be thought essentially subordinate to the Father—as a word is to a thought, or a son to a father— He is also the LIFE and the LIGHT. He does not merely *transmit* the life or *reflect* the light—He "*is*" the life, He "*is*" the light. The life is "*in* Him." The light shines *from* Him.

Why, all in this short exordium, John has described Him as the WORD, as the LIGHT, as the LIFE, as the SON. And who needs any telling that this is the aspect of Christ which distinguishingly recurs right through the fourth Gospel? All is adapted to show the revelation of the Divine light and life and love through Him who, at the outset, is named the Word. As the "Light" He reveals. As the "Son" He redeems. As the "Life" He renews. There is no obscuring of the manhood; but the emphasis is on the Godhead. It is the "eagle" aspect.

Fourfold Appeal and Outlook

There are other significances, too, in the number and the order and the discriminating emphases of these four Gospels.

The number *four* in Scripture is peculiarly the number of the earth and of the human race as occupying the earth. Four is the number of man as a creature, as six is the number of man as a sinner. All our earthly life seems to be encompassed and conditioned by it. We need only think of the four points of the compass —north, south, east, west; of the four dimensions—breadth, length, depth, height; of the four seasons of the year—spring, summer, autumn, winter; of the four parts of the day—morning, after-the-noon, evening, night (darkness); the four comprehensive compounds of material elements into earth, air, fire, water; of the four members which constitute the human family—father, mother, son, daughter; of the four lunar phases which intersect the calendar into months.

Away back in the first book of the Bible, three times in the tenth chapter of Genesis, the "generations of the sons of Noah," from which the earth was repeopled, are divided by the number four into "families," "tongues," "countries," "nations" (verses

5, 20, 31). In the *last* book of the Bible, as the human story comes to its end, there are no less than seven similar descriptions of the race. (Rev. v. 9, vii. 9, x. 11, xi. 9, xiii. 7 (in R.V.), xiv. 6, xvii. 15). Both in Genesis and Revelation the order varies in different verses, but the number is invariably four.

When God entered into covenant with Noah and "all flesh that is upon the earth," that there should no more be "a flood to destroy the earth," He gave the rainbow as His covenant-sign. Thereafter the rainbow always speaks of God's covenant with His earthly creatures. When Ezekiel saw his vision of the four "living beings" he also saw a *rainbow* circling the heavenly throne. It spoke at once of God's covenant faithfulness with the earth; and the four faces of the seraphs, besides expressing something in the moral nature of God, represented all earth's living creatures in the covenant, the lion representing the *wild* beasts of the earth, the ox representing the *tame* animals, the eagle representing the *birds,* and the man representing the *human* family.

Much more might be added, of course, about the number four in nature and in Scripture, but enough has been said to show that it has special reference to the terrestrial and temporal, to matter and to man.

Now in a unique way the four Gospels are earth-girdling and race-embracing. As we shall see, Matthew writes with first reference to the *Hebrew* mind. Perhaps that will have been gathered already from his repeated references to the Old Testament. Mark, the travel companion of Peter, writes with a primary applicability to the *Roman* mind, presenting our Lord more pronouncedly as the mighty Miracle-worker. Luke, the travel-physician of Paul, adapts his approach with equal appropriateness to the *Greek* mind, more prominently exhibiting the matchless manhood of the Friend and Saviour of sinners. John, whose writing occupies a unique place, being an interpretation as well as a record, and composed practically a generation after the others, writes more particularly for the *Church*, to emphasise the unqualified deity of our Lord Jesus, but also to set forth for the whole world of mankind, without racial distinction, the revelation of Divine "grace and truth" through "the Word become flesh." It has been truly observed that those three peoples of old—the Jews, the Greeks, the Romans—represent, as no others, human types which persist right through our racial history. They represent religion, culture, and administration (especially legal and commercial). The first three Gospels spoke *then* with particular adaptedness to those three, and *they still do,* complemented and crowned by John, with his one Divine "Word" for the whole human world.

Clearly Matthew must stand *first*, right at the beginning of the New Testament, for he connects the two Testaments together, showing the fulfillings of Old Testament predictions and the preparing for Christ's appearance by the promised forerunner, John the Baptist, and the offering of the long-promised "kingdom of heaven" by the miracle-working wonder-Teacher of Galilee. Of similar necessity John must come *last,* with his final review, supplementation and interpretation, after the three synoptists have long since laid down their pens, and the records of the historical Jesus are well known.

Synoptists Versus John

This leads us to mention another obvious feature of the four Gospels, namely, that Matthew, Mark and Luke cover much the same ground, whereas the record of John, besides having been written considerably later than the others, mostly deals with matter unrecorded by them. It is separated both in time and character from the others. There is a contrastive relationship between the three and the one, as set out herewith:

SYNOPTISTS	*JOHN*
The *outer* facts of the Lord's life.	The *inner* facts of the Lord's life.
The *human* aspects of the Lord's life.	The *Divine* aspects of the Lord's life.
The *public* discourses (largely).	The *private* discourses (largely).
The *Galilean* ministry (mainly).	The *Judæan* ministry (mainly).

Selective Adaptation

So then, primarily (though not exclusively), Matthew writes for the *Jew,* Mark for the *Roman,* Luke for the *Greek,* John for the *Church.* With this fourfold distinction in mind, take just a few instances which show the principle of selection and adaptation running through them.

Matthew, we have said, writes primarily for the *Jew*. What is Matthew's *first miracle*? It is the healing of the leper. Now to the Jew the diseases of the body had a symbolic significance. Leprosy, the most loathsome and dreaded of all diseases, was a walking parable of the loathsomeness of sin and Divine judgment. There was no cure for leprosy, and to touch or even go near a leper meant ceremonial defilement as well as the risk of contagion. "Here is inspiration," says Joseph Parker; "no sooner does Jesus come down from the mountain where He has been teaching the multitude than, 'behold there came a leper.' How the Jew's eyes round with wonder! This matter of leprosy has been a serious matter to him through all the ages. Matthew, therefore, instantly brings the new Teacher into contact with a leper. Nor does the inspired genius end there; Matthew proceeds, 'And Jesus put forth His hand, and'—mark his ingenuity— 'touched him'—the unheard of, the impossible miracle! Nothing could have so struck Jewish attention. Christ might have been the prince of necromancers, and have done many wonderful things, and the Jew would not have listened to any one of them; but to tell the Jews that this Man came to a leper, and touched the leper, and healed the leper, and sent him away a clean man! Oh the power of genius, the master-touch, the wisdom of God!"

What is *Luke's* first miracle? Not the cleansing of the leper. Luke wrote primarily for Gentiles, and leprosy did not speak to the Gentile as it did to the Jew. The great theme of Gentile and specially of Greek speculation was demonology, demon-worship, demon possession, how to get rid of the demon. The Greeks were interested in every aspect of demonology. It was the favourite subject. Luke says, as it were, "See, I will tell you all about that. This wonderful Man casts out the demon! This wonderful 'kingdom of God' shatters the kingdom of the devil!" So this is Luke's first miracle: "And in the synagogue there was a man which had a spirit of an unclean demon, and cried out with a loud voice. . . . And Jesus rebuked him, saying, Hold thy peace, and come out of him. And when the demon had thrown him in the midst, he came out of him and hurt him not. And they were all amazed, and spake among themselves, saying: What a word is this! for with authority and power He commandeth the unclean spirits and they come out!" (Luke iv. 33–6).

Characteristic Variation

This genius of selection and presentation by no means pertains only to the first miracle which each writer chooses. It characterises the four records throughout.

Turning to Christ's denunciation of the scribes and Pharisees as recorded by Matthew, we find the words: "Woe unto you, scribes and Pharisees, hypocrites! for ye pay tithe of mint and annise and cummin, and have omitted the weightier matters of the law, judgment, mercy and faith." That is how Matthew puts it. He was writing first for Jewish readers. The Gentiles would not have understood it as did the Jews. The "law"? *What* law? *Whose* law? The Jews knew well enough!

Now turn to Luke, who writes for a Gentile public: "Woe unto you, scribes and Pharisees, hypocrites! for ye tithe mint and rue and all manner of herbs, *and pass over judgment and the love of God.*" This is language at once understandable to the non-Jewish audience which Luke had in view. He gives the Law in substance, without employing the Jewish nomenclature.

Again, Matthew reports: "Woe unto you, scribes and Pharisees, hypocrites! for ye are like unto whited sepulchres, which indeed appear beautiful outward, but are within full of dead men's bones and of all uncleanness." Scathing language!—and it is peculiarly for Jewish ears. What did the Gentiles know about "whited sepulchres"? There was no such term in their speech. But the Jew knew! If a Jew crossed a grave he was ceremonially defiled. Even if he walked over it without knowing it was a grave, it was none the less a grave, and he was none the less defiled and must undergo the inconveniences of the prescribed purification ceremonies. The Jews therefore, we are told, resorted to the practice of whitening graves so that a man might see them clearly and keep the required distance!

Now see how Luke gives it: "Woe unto you, scribes and Pharisees, hypocrites! for ye are as *graves which appear not, and the men that walk over them are not aware of them.*" Here there is nothing that is local and Jewish. The reference is set in general and universal form. Luke is reporting for a constituency quite different from that with which Matthew is primarily concerned. These are just a couple of instances representing many.

Characteristic Discrimination

What is the subject of Christ's preaching? According to Matthew it is "the kingdom of heaven." According to Luke it is "the kingdom of God." Is there not inspired selection here? That expression "the kingdom of God" had its dangers for the Jewish mind. It occurs in Matthew's writing only three or four times. The Hebrew language had no superlatives. To express the superlative it used the word "God." What is it that is to be described? Is it that magnificent, that exceedingly great city? Then the Hebrew language calls it "the city of God." Is it the unexcelled cedars of Lebanon? Then the Hebrew calls them "the cedars of God." Had Matthew used the expression "the kingdom of God," the Jew would have been in the way of falling into his favourite error, thinking only of the kingdom in its outward aspects, as a visible kingdom of superlative material magnificence, splendour and wealth—for the Jew! "This is just what we have been waiting for," he would have said.

On the other hand, what is "the kingdom of *heaven*" to the Gentile? It is something which sounds vague and unreal to him. Luke has a different name, therefore. This kingdom that Jesus proclaimed is "the kingdom of *God*." Is not that startling? "The kingdom of *God*," mind you—nothing to do with any of the paltry, petty deities of polytheistic heathendom, but the kingdom of the one true Creator-God. Luke lived in a day when thousands of disillusioned men and women were turning from the unrealities and stupidities of Greek and Roman polytheism to seek the true Reality. It was this break-away which accounted for the increasing proselytising to the Hebrew faith. It was inspired strategy to announce this "kingdom of *God*"! This was the word needed for the Gentile.

A Problem of Inspiration

This variation of language in the four "Gospels" creates a "problem" of inspiration to some; but is it not rather an *evidence* of inspiration? Listen to Joseph Parker again: "The pedant says, Behold, Matthew says one thing, and Luke says another, yet they both profess to be reporting the same discourse. So they are, but not phonographically: they are reporting the soul of things, they are interpreting the heart of Christ. Why will men not come into the larger interpretation, the nobler construction, and see what peddling and embarrassing things words may be when they are employed to set forth the infinite, the spiritual, the Divine?"

Some minds, however, will not be satisfied with Joseph Parker's explanation. They will object: "That explanation may have a certain spiritual appeal, but it does not touch the literal problem here. If, for instance, in denouncing the scribes and Pharisees, Christ used the words given in Matthew's report, then the variations in Luke's account cannot be an accurate report: and how then can Luke truly say that those are the words which Christ spoke?"

There is a clear answer. Examination of the two passages concerned shows that they do not pertain to the same occasion. They are both chronologically and circumstantially separated from each other, the one being during the Lord's last visit to Jerusalem, and the other before it. Matthew gives the Lord's full and final denunciation of the scribes and Pharisees. Who shall say that there were no earlier and shorter outbreaks of similar though not verbally identical indignation? The genius of the two writers is seen in their selection of what to report. Each chooses that which most tellingly contributes to the distinctive viewpoint and purpose of his treatise.

A Question of Language

This matter of Christ's reported speeches also involves the complex question of the language or dialect in which He spoke. There is now no doubt about the fact that in the time of Christ the population of Palestine was largely bi-lingual. The language most in use was Aramaic. That language, although it is called Hebrew in the New Testament and in the writings of Josephus, and although similar to Hebrew, is really a different language from the Hebrew of the Old Testament, having its own peculiarities, and having undergone in Palestine a development of several centuries. The other language in use was Greek—not Greek in its pure Attic or classical form, but a vernacular enriched by the admixture of Hebrew and Aramaic words and idioms. Aramaic was the language usually spoken by the rural population or "common people" of Palestine. In Jerusalem and the larger towns, among rulers and priests, among the educated and trading classes, Greek was generally spoken.

Our Lord's Ministry probably Bi-Lingual

The population of Palestine in the time of Christ being so largely bi-lingual, it follows almost as a matter of course that our Lord Himself spoke in both languages. That He sometimes spoke in Aramaic is indicated by the fact that in some places His actual words in that language are retained for us: "Talitha cumi" (Mark v. 41); "Eli, Eli, lama sabachthani" (Matt. xxvii. 46). In the capital, specially when addressing the Jewish rulers, our Lord Jesus would mostly use Greek. That He then spoke Greek is indicated in the question which the Jews asked among themselves after His word that they should seek Him but not find Him (John vii. 34): "Then said the Jews among themselves: Whither will He go, that we shall not find Him? Will He go unto the dispersed (Jews) among the Gentiles (Greeks), and teach the Gentiles (Greeks)?" Had they not been accustomed to hear Jesus speak in Greek, such a question would never have been on their tongues.

It does not lie within our present purpose to discuss this question. We simply refer to it here (along with the fact that our Lord probably uttered different parts of His teaching on more than one occasion—with differing phraseology and perhaps in two languages) to show that there are satisfactory grounds on which the variations in Christ's reported speeches may be explained in ways which uphold the strictest views of inspiration. The four writers give us four true accounts, while yet there is this process of discrimination, selection, and presentation, which gives each of the four Gospels its unique emphasis.

Characteristic Endings

It is interesting, also, to note the characteristic way in which each of the four records ends, and the progress of thought which the four endings exhibit when taken together. Matthew ends with our Lord's *resurrection*. Mark goes further, and ends with His *Ascension*. Luke goes still further, and ends with the promise of *the Spirit*. John completes the four by ending with the promise of the *second coming*. How appropriate that Matthew, the Gospel of the mighty Messiah-King, should end with the mighty act of His resurrection, the crowning proof of Messiahship and Divine power! How perfectively fitting that

Mark, the Gospel of the lowly Servant, should end with the lowly One exalted to the place of honour! How beautifully in keeping that Luke, the Gospel of the sympathetic-hearted ideal Man, should end with the promise of the coming enduement! How fitting a completion that John, the Gospel of the Divine Son, written with special thought for the church, should end with the risen Lord's own promise of His return! Truly, the interwoven design exhibited by the four "Gospels" makes them a masterpiece of variety in unity.

AND NOW, TEST YOURSELF

1. What would you say is the dominant idea of the New Testament in relation to the Old? Give texts.

2. In what four ways does the Old Testament seem incomplete? How does Christ complete it?

3. Why may we call the four Gospels the crux of the Bible?

4. The New Testament book-groups are five, nine, four, nine: which they, and what is the main characteristic of each group?

5. What correspondences are there between the opening and closing books of the two ninefold groups?

6. Would you say that the four Gospels are in their true order? If so, give one main reason for saying so.

7. What threefold order do we find in the New Testament epistles and their three main writers?

8. Can you give reasons why there are *four* Gospels, and not just one?

9. How do the four Gospels parallel with the cherubim in Ezekiel's vision, and *why*?

10. Can you give four ways in which the Synoptists contrast with John?

11. Give instances of selective adaptation in Matthew and Luke.

12. How would you account for some of the verbal differences between Matthew's reports and those of Luke?

The Four Cherubim and the Four Gospels

We say again, and emphasise it, that the remarkable correspondence between the four cherubim of Ezekiel's opening vision and the four Gospels does not sanction the fanciful idea that the former were a *type* of the latter. The real explanation of the correspondence is that which we have given in our article on "The Four Gospels Collectively" (study number 110). Those holy seraphs symbolically express the four basic social aspects of the Divine nature; and it was inevitable that when the Divine Son Himself became incarnate the same four aspects should again conspicuously manifest themselves—as they *do* in the characteristic emphases of the four Gospels.

There are not a few expositors, however, both ancient and modern, who hold that the four "living creatures" were actually *intended* as types of the four Gospels in their aspective presentation of our Lord. But to view them as actually *types* opens the door to much fancifulness. Grotius saw them as types of four apostles—Peter (the lion) James (the ox) Matthew (the man) Paul (the eagle). Others have seen them as types of four patriarchal churches—Jerusalem, because of its constancy (the lion); Antioch, ready to obey the command of the apostles (the ox); Alexandria, famed for learning (the man); Constantinople, noted for men of elevated contemplation (the eagle).

Others have seen them as types of the four motive powers of the human soul—reason, anger, desire, conscience; and others, the four elements—earth, air, fire, water; and others, the four orders in the Church—pastoral, diaconel, doctrinal, contemplative; not to mention still others! We would say, in Paul's words to Timothy, "From all such turn away"! Such imaginative licence brings *true* Biblical typology into undeserved disrepute.

However, what we wish to settle here is that in the non-typical yet significant parallel between Ezekiel's four "living creatures" and the four Gospels the true apposites are those which we have shown, i.e. the lion aspect in Matthew, the ox aspect in Mark, the man aspect in Luke, the eagle aspect in John.

To turn away from this and adopt make-fits is to leave the obvious for the fatuous. To give just one instance, the Roman Catholic interpretation has it that "St. Matthew is likened to a man, because he beginneth with the pedigree of Christ, as He is a man; St. Mark to a lion, because he beginneth with the preaching of St. John the Baptist, as it were the roaring of a lion in the wilderness; St. Luke to a calf, because he beginneth with a priest of the Old Testament, (to wit, Zacharias, the father of John the Baptist,) which priesthood was to sacrifice calves to God; St. John to an eagle, because he beginneth with the Divinity of Christ, flying as high, as more is not possible."

Could anything be more childish? If these are the only resemblances between the faces of the seraphs and the features of the Gospels, far better say nothing about them at all!

THE GOSPEL ACCORDING TO MATTHEW (1)
Lesson Number 111

NOTE.—For this study read Matthew's Gospel at least twice.

Christ has come, the Light of the world. Long ages may yet elapse before His beams have reduced the world to order and beauty, and clothed a purified humanity with light as with a garment. But He has come: the Revealer of the snares and chasms that lurk in darkness, the Rebuker of every evil thing that prowls by night, the Stiller of the storm-winds of passion; the Quickener of all that is wholesome, the Adorner of all that is beautiful, the Reconciler of contradictions, the Harmonizer of discords, the Healer of diseases, the Saviour from sin. He has come: the Torch of truth, the Anchor of hope, the Pillar of faith, the Rock for strength, the Refuge for security, the Fountain for refreshment, the Vine for gladness, the Rose for beauty, the Lamb for tenderness, the Friend for counsel, the Brother for love. Jesus Christ has trod the world. The trace of the Divine footsteps will never be obliterated. And the Divine footsteps were the footsteps of One who is Man. The example of Christ is such as men can follow. On! until mankind wears His image. On! towards yon summit on which stands, not an angel, not a disembodied spirit, not an abstract of ideal and unattainable virtues, but THE MAN JESUS CHRIST.

—*Peter Bayne: "The Testimony of Christ to Christianity."*

THE GOSPEL ACCORDING TO MATTHEW (1)

THE FIRST book of the New Testament lies open before us—the Gospel according to Matthew. Those who know it best will praise it most. To say that it is a masterpiece of combined human genius and Divine supervention is no indulgent flattery, as we shall try to show, even though in necessarily constricted compass.

What is our right approach to it? Ought we first to browse over the latest discussions on its authorship, or gather the available data concerning Matthew himself? No; the first thing, as with all the other New Testament oracles, is to *read* it just as it lies before us, ànd read it until we are thoroughly familiar with its contents. Even at a first reading, especially if read right through at one sitting, it will yield much; but if we read it three or four, or seven or eight, or a dozen times, it becomes more revealing and rewarding each time. So is it with all parts of Holy Writ, for behind the human penmen is the directive activity of the Divine Spirit.

Assuming, then, that we have each read through Matthew several times, we can set down our preliminary findings, and then proceed to a closer study. At each reading the method and message have shaped themselves more clearly to us. One feature, of course, which has caught the eye each time is the geographical dividing-line at the beginning of chapter xix.:

"And it came to pass that when Jesus had finished these sayings, *He departed from Galilee*, and came into the coasts of Judæa beyond Jordan."

Up to that point Matthew has devoted himself to our Lord's ministry in *Galilee*, but from there onwards he describes its culmination in *Jerusalem*. That "divide" at once hooks back to chapter iv. 12, where its one and only other occurrence in Matthew marks the *beginning* of the Galilean ministry:

"Now when Jesus had heard that John was cast into prison, *He departed into Galilee*."

We mark those two "divide" points carefully, as the first indicators of Matthew's ground-plan:

HE DEPARTED *INTO* GALILEE (iv. 12).
HE DEPARTED *FROM* GALILEE (xix. 1).

Up to the first of these (iv. 12) all is introductory—and in Judæa. After the second (xix. 1) all is culminative—back again in Judæa. *Between* the two is the ministry in Galilee, which occupies the bulk of the book.

In both instances Matthew uses the boundary line with such noticeable deliberateness that it certainly seems as though he thereby indicates his main plan of treatment. Note iv. 12 again: "Now when Jesus had heard that John was cast into prison, He departed into Galilee." It was a deliberate choice of Galilee because of significant circumstances. The silencing of the forerunner's voice had given solemn signal that the voice of the King Himself should now speak with full publicity: but there was an unpropitious hostility in Jerusalem which threatened to abort the predesigned message and ministry of the King. The signal had now been given—the choice was deliberate: *"He departed into Galilee."*

Glance now at xix. 1 again: "And it came to pass that when Jesus had finished these sayings, He departed from Galilee." Observe, it was when Jesus had "finished" that He crossed the boundary line again. It was not because of any dangerous hostility in Galilee. There was still danger in Judæa; and Jesus could have lingered in Galilee; but no, He had "finished" His predesigned words and works in Galilee, and the hour had struck for the decisive presentation of Himself at Jerusalem. Therefore, with equally noticeable deliberateness, *"He departed from Galilee."*

It is useful thus to see how and why Matthew so clearly demarcates the "into" and "out of" Galilee, for it helps us to keep in mind that the whole Galilean ministry was in reality a kind of *detour*. Our Lord's objective was Jerusalem, but circumstances made an immediate approach impracticable; and the Galilean detour became a necessary strategy.

As soon as this two-fold arrangement stands out, we are ready for our further exploration. Moreover, the pattern now begins to open up with fascinating orderliness and progress. Trace out the groupings and movements in part one.

The Ministry in Galilee (iv. 12—xviii.)

Matthew is impressionist rather than particularist. He does not detail his descriptions as Mark and Luke do. He paints with a larger brush. His strategy is to present meaningful *groupings* of our Lord's sayings and doings; of the impacts which He made; and of the reactions thereby provoked. You and I are meant to catch the vivid significance of these impressionist groupings and to see the bigger, bolder lines of the picture. Matthew is thus the perfect preparation for the other three Gospels.

First, in chapters v., vi. and vii., there is a grouping of our Lord's *teachings*, in what is commonly known as the Sermon on the Mount.

Next, in chapters viii., ix. and x., there is a grouping together of our Lord's *miracles*.

Next, in chapters xi. to xviii. there is a grouping of the various *reactions* to our Lord and His ministry, accompanied by His own counter-reactions or verdicts.

Anyone can see what a commonsense plan of presentation that is. What is it that any new reader wants to know? Why, of course, first what Jesus *said*; then what Jesus *did*; then what were the *results*. In other words, we want to know what Jesus *taught*; what Jesus *wrought*; what people *thought*; and that is the order Matthew follows.

These three groupings seem to run in *tens*. The Sermon on the Mount (v.–vii.) consists of ten principal components. The next three chapters (viii.–x.) particularise ten miracles. And the next chain of chapters (xi.–xviii.) successively register ten representative reactions. Designed or undesigned, this repeated tenfold feature is arresting to the eye and helpful to the memory.

It should be realised that the Sermon on the Mount is in the widest sense a public utterance, as the occurrence of *hoi ochloi* (i.e. "the *multitudes*") both before it and after it indicates (v. 1, vii. 28). Notice, in vii. 29, that it is "the people" (lit. "the *multitudes*") who are astonished, for "He taught *THEM*. . . ."

The Tenfold Message (v.–vii.)

Here are the ten components of the Sermon on the Mount:

1. The Beatitudes (v. 3–16).
   Or the subjects of the kingdom.
2. Moral Standards (v. 17–48).
   Or Christ versus "It was said."
3. Religious Motives (vi. 1–18).
   Alms (1); prayer (5); fasting (16).
4. Mammon Worship (vi. 19–24).
   Or earthiness versus godliness.
5. Temporal Cares (vi. 25–34).
   Or anxiety versus trust in God.
6. Social Discernment (vii. 1–6).
   Censuring (1); indiscretion (6).
7. Encouragements (vii. 7–11).
   Prayer makes it all practicable.
8. Summary in a sentence (vii. 12).
   Such a life fulfils Scriptures.
9. The Alternatives (vii. 13–14).
   Two ways: broad versus narrow.
10. Final Warnings (vii. 15–27).
    False prophets (15); false profession (21); false foundation (26).

Some of these sections certainly lend themselves to further analysis, but careful rereading (so we believe) will confirm that these are the ten thought-zones which both divide and contain all the contents of the Sermon. Moreover, to see this famous discourse so dissected enables us at a glance to mark its logical orderliness. Its first three sections concern virtues, morals, motives. The next three concern things material, temporal, social. The next three give encouragement, summary, exhortation. The discourse then closes with three solemn warnings.

In the final part note the succession of solemn *alternatives*— the two ways, broad and narrow; the two gates, wide and strait; two destinations, life and destruction; two classes of travellers, many and few; two kinds of trees, good and corrupt; two sorts of fruit, good and bad; two builders, wise and foolish; two foundations, rock and sand; two houses; two storms; two results.

The Ten Miracles (viii.–x.)

Here are the ten miracles which Matthew now groups in chapters viii. to x.:

1. The cleansing of the leper (viii. 1–4).
2. Centurian's servant: palsy (viii. 5–13).
3. Peter's wife's mother: fever (viii. 14, 15).
4. The stilling of the storm (viii. 23–7).
5. Gergesene demoniacs healed (viii. 28–34).
6. The man cured of the palsy (ix. 1–8).
7. The woman with hæmorrhage (ix. 18–22).
8. The ruler's daughter raised (ix. 23–6).
9. Two blind men given sight (ix. 27–31).
10. The dumb demoniac healed (ix. 32–4).

Additionally, in these three chapters which group the miracles there are also two generalising statements that Jesus healed "all" and "every" sickness; yet it remains that only the above-noted ten are particularised. Moreover, the third of these chapters, i.e. chapter x., narrates the most comprehensive miracle of all, namely, the imparting of this miracle-working power to the twelve apostles, so that they, too, might extend the glad tidings and healing benefits of the kingdom. Yet, even so, no particular exercise of that imparted power is recorded, so that our gaze is still kept focused on the ten miracles already described.

Is there, then, something specially significant about them? There is. There is a representativeness and completeness about them. The first three belong together; then there is a break in which our Lord answers certain would-be followers who had become enthused by His mighty works. The next three also run together; then there is another break in which our Lord answers the Pharisees and John's disciples. The remaining four also belong together; after which there is the completive comment: "And Jesus went about all the cities and villages . . . healing every sickness and every disease among the people."

The first three miracles heal functional physical diseases which affect *the whole body,* i.e. leprosy, palsy, fever. The next three show our Lord's power in other spheres, i.e. in the *natural* realm (the stilling of the storm), in the *spirit* realm (the expelling of the demons), in the *moral* realm ("Thy sins be forgiven thee"). The final four concern local and organic ailments of the body, i.e. bleeding, blindness, dumbness, and the crowning power-display of raising the dead.

The effect produced by the first trio was an eager desire of some to follow "whithersoever Thou goest." The response after the second trio was that the multitude "marvelled and glorified God." The result after the third group was that "the multitudes marvelled, saying, It was never so seen in Israel."

In Scripture the number ten signifies representative completeness. That is easily understandable. Our whole system of numeration consists of so many *tens*, the first being a type of the whole, inasmuch as it is a complete and representative cycle of all the usable figures. Even so, in Scripture, the ever-present signification of the number ten is representative completeness, a marking of the entire round or cycle—as for instance in the ten generations of the antedeluvian age; the ten plagues on Egypt, representing the complete circle of Divine judgment; the ten commandments of the Law; the ten kingdoms symbolising the world-power of Antichrist; and so on. So does it seem to be with these ten miracles which Matthew has grouped for us in chapters viii. to x. They have a representative completeness.

And there is a further word to add. These ten are selected from the *many* which our Lord performed, because of some noteworthy feature attaching to each of them. In each of the first trio we are pointed to something remarkable which *Jesus Himself* did or said. In the next trio there are three remarkable utterances *about* Jesus by other speakers. In the final quartette there are four notable culminations.

Take the first trio—with the three remarkable things which *Jesus Himself* did or said. Nothing would startle the Jew like the instantaneous cure of leprosy—most dreaded and symbolic of all diseases. So Matthew puts that first. Yet even *that* marvel must be crowned by *this* lovely wonder: "Jesus put forth His hand, and *touched* him. . . ." That Jesus thus touched the loathsome untouchable made the cure as much a revelation of God-like compassion as of superhuman power. Next, in healing the palsied servant of the Gentile centurian Jesus makes the astonishing statement: "Many shall came from the east and west, and shall sit down with

Abraham and Isaac and Jacob in the kingdom of heaven; but the children of the kingdom shall be cast out into outer darkness." Next, the dispelling of the fever brings so many other sufferers that the great Healer is suddenly seen fulfilling the Old Testament Scripture as Matthew writes: "That it might be fulfilled which was spoken by Isaiah the prophet: Himself took our infirmities and bare our sicknesses."

Take now the second trio—and the three remarkable utterances *about* Jesus. The stilling of the storm evokes the wonder-struck exclamation, "What manner of man is this, that even the winds and the sea obey Him!" Next, the demons in the two Gergesene demoniacs cry out, "Jesus, Son of God! Art Thou come hither to torment us before the time?" Next, as the palsied man is cured, the Scribes mutter, "This Man blasphemeth," thus provoking the immensely revealing rejoinder: "The Son of Man hath power on earth to forgive sins."

Look now at the remaining four—four notable *culminations*. In the raising of the ruler's daughter there is the climax-miracle of recalling the dead. Next, in the cure which came through simply touching our Lord's garment there is the culminating evidence that He was no mere agent, but Himself the source and fulness of healing-power, His very presence being electrically alive with it. Next, in the giving of sight to the two blind men there is a completive exhibition that there must be faith toward Christ. The two blind men had never even seen Jesus or had eyes to witness one single cure. For the first time, therefore, Jesus prefaces His cure by asking: "Believe ye that I am able to do this?" Finally, in the curing of the dumb demoniac, the emphasis is thrown on the wicked cynicism of the Pharisees: "He casteth out demons through the prince of the demons." Their hypocritical verdict was a *culmination* of hostile prejudice. In the preceding three cures there is a culmination of *faith*—faith even though the little girl is dead; faith that even to touch the garment of Jesus will bring healing, without even a word from Himself; faith even amid blindness and apart from all visible evidence. But here, in these Pharisees, we see a culmination of *unbelief,* for they even dare to attribute our Lord's gracious cures to complicity with Satan! Yes, the ten miracles are a significant set!

The Ten Reactions (xi.–xviii.)

By this time we are wanting to know more definitely what were the various reactions to this wonder-working Preacher and His exposition of the kingdom of heaven. Matthew anticipates us, and in his new grouping (xi.–xviii.) he successively instances ten such reactions. Incidental episodes intermingle with these, giving colour and sequence to the onmoving story, but the spotlight is now on these responses which were provoked. Here are the ten:

    1. John the Baptist (xi. 2–15).
    2. "This generation" (xi. 16–19).
    3. Galilean cities (xi. 20–30).
    4. The Pharisees (xii. 2, 10, 14, 24, 38).
    5. The multitudes (xiii. See footnote).[1]
    6. The Nazarethites (xiii. 53–8).
    7. Herod the king (xiv. 1–13).
    8. Jerusalem scribes (xv. 1–20).
    9. Pharisees, Sadducees (xvi. 1–12).
  10. The twelve Apostles (xvi. 13–20).

How revealing these ten are! If we run through them again, noting the main characteristic in each, the general result of our Lord's Galilean itinerary is laid bare.

    1. John the Baptist—undecided (xi. 3).
    2. "This generation"—unresponsive (xi. 17).
    3. Galilean cities—unrepentant (xi. 20).
    4. The Pharisees—unreasonable (xii. 10, 14, 24).
    5. The multitudes—undiscerning (xiii. 13–15).
    6. The Nazarethites—unbelieving (xiii. 58).
    7. Herod the king—unintelligent (xiv. 2).
    8. Jerusalem scribes—unconciliatory (xv. 2, 12).
    9. Pharisees, Sadducees—unrelenting (xvi. 1).
  10. The Apostles—glad recognition (xvi. 16).

---

[1] It is quite clear that in the parables of chapter xiii. our Lord was summing up the results of His preaching thus far. The first of the parables shows that only a small number among the multitudes were "good ground" hearers. All through, He has the multitudes in mind; and His verdict on them is seen in verses 13–15.

The general reaction at the end of the Galilean ministry may be summed up in that prefix "un." There were the exceptions, yet that was the *general* result. Later, in the climax at Jerusalem, the passive "*un*" was to give place to the active, fateful "*anti*." But even now, it was already evident that while the long-promised kingdom was welcome enough in its material aspects (i.e. the healing of the sick and the feeding of the hungry), there was mass unwillingness to accept its ethical and spiritual standards. Jesus was not deceived by the crowds. The crowd will always abound where there is novelty, miracle, bread, physical benefit.

The change in our Lord's tone from chapter xi. onwards is too noticeable to miss. There is denunciation. There are clashes. Going with the ten reactions recorded by Matthew are our Lord's *counter*-reactions, which are equally arresting.

His reaction to the undecided John evokes an eye-opening explanation of the forerunner's prophetic identity and positional significance (see study 113, p. 168). His reaction to the unresponsiveness of "this generation" is sad resignation with the comment, "But wisdom is justified of her children"; i.e. although there had not been a worthy response either to ascetic John or to His own social friendliness, the fault lay in the hearers, not in the approach His reaction to the impenitent cities, as collective units, was to predict judgment, and turn away from them with a new message for the *individual*: "Come unto Me, all ye that labour and are heavy laden . . ." To the unreasonable Pharisees His reaction is an awesome warning against perverting the truth too far and perpetrating unpardonable insult to the Holy Spirit. To the misty-minded multitude it is that henceforth His kingdom teaching becomes mainly by parable (xiii. 10, 34). To His disdaining townsmen it is a suspension of His "mighty works." Toward Herod it is silence and avoidance. To the Jerusalem scribes it is to charge them with hypocritically nullifying the very Scriptures of which they were professedly the custodians. To the Sadducees it is rebuke and refusal. To the Twelve, who recognise and confess Him, it is, "Blessed! . . . flesh and blood hath not revealed it . . . and upon this rock I will build My church." After this, until His departure from Galilee, our Lord no more addresses the public, but devotes instruction to His disciples alone.

This, then, is the sum of all these factors and features: there is widespread, enthusiastic interest in the miracles, the message, the Man; but those who respond with spiritual sincerity and intelligence are a very small minority, while the religious and political leaders are fixedly hostile. Already, as the Galilean detour nears its end, our Lord sees Israel's implicit rejection of King and kingdom, and announces the coming new dispensational turning-point: "*I will build My CHURCH.*"

THE GOSPEL ACCORDING TO MATTHEW (2)

Lesson Number 112

NOTE.—For this study, why not set time apart to read right through Matthew at one sitting?

SHOULD MATTHEW COME FIRST?

It seems the intellectual fashion nowadays to place Mark before Matthew, on the assumption that his Gospel is of earlier date than those by Matthew and Luke, and was used by both as a main authority. For ourselves, we are unconvinced by the prior-Mark theory. We consider it a doubtful refuge, only resorted to because other theories as to the origin of the synoptists have collapsed. Some of the arguments on which it survives are pretty tenuous, and its early demise would not over-surprise us. All such critical considerations apart, however, is it not clear as noonday that Matthew properly leads our four Gospels? As none of the others, he links the New with the *Old,* showing our Lord's fulfilling of the Hebrew Scriptures. He has more Old Testament quotations and allusions than Mark and Luke together. Moreover, since Matthew (and only he) writes primarily for the *Jews,* is he not the true leader-in of the *New,* as well as the obvious link-back with the Old?—for even the New is "to the *Jew first."* Forgive us, therefore, if we keep Matthew first and stay out of fashion!

—J.S.B.

THE GOSPEL ACCORDING TO MATTHEW (2)

The Climax in Judæa (xix.-xxviii.)

LOOK NOW at the second area of Matthew's Gospel. With his pen as our guide we have retrodden the detour in Galilee; and now, in chapters xix. to xxviii., we see *the climax in Judæa*.

Chapter xix. begins: "And it came to pass that when Jesus had finished these sayings, He departed from Galilee, and came into the coasts of *Judæa*. . . ." Thereafter, Matthew's story quite naturally forms itself around the three successive developments:

1. The Presentation (xix.–xxv.).
2. The Crucifixion (xxvi.–xxvii.).
3. The Resurrection (xxviii.).

Perhaps, therefore, it may be helpful to eye and memory if we frame our analysis of the two parts of Matthew's Gospel as they open up to us thus far.

1. THE DETOUR IN GALILEE (v.–xviii.)	2. THE CLIMAX IN JUDÆA (xix.–xxviii.)
(a) What Jesus Taught— or the tenfold message (v.–vii.).	(a) The Presentation Journey, entry, clash, Olivet (xix.–xxv.).
(b) What Jesus Wrought— or the ten "mighty works" (viii.–x.).	(b) The Crucifixion Bethany, Sanhedrin, Pilate, Calvary (xxvi.–vii.)
(c) What People Thought— or the ten reactions (xi.–xviii.).	(c) The Resurrection the angel, the Lord, the lie, the Eleven (xxviii.).

We can make a fuller analysis later, as required, but this one will serve for the moment. And now let us look through the second part (xix–xxviii.).

The Presentation

By the "Presentation" we mean, of course, our Lord's public presentation of Himself at Jerusalem as Israel's Messiah-King. This part of the narrative runs in a fourfold sequence:

> The journey *to* the city (xix.–xx.).
> The entry *into* the city (xxi. 1–17).
> The clashes *in* the city (xxi. 18–xxiii.).
> The discourse on Olivet (xxiv.–xxv.).

What is it that Matthew wants us to see in these four movements? Amid various incidentals, there are four features which are evidently meant to capture our special attention, as follows:

First, in the *journey* to the city (xix.–xx.) we are to see that our Lord foreknew the outcome of His timed appearance at Jerusalem before ever He entered its gates.

> "And Jesus going up to Jerusalem took the twelve disciples apart in the way, and said to them: Behold, we go up to Jerusalem, and the Son of Man shall be betrayed unto the chief priests and the scribes, and they shall condemn Him to death, and shall deliver Him to the Gentiles, to mock and to scourge and to crucify Him; and the third day He shall rise again" (xx. 17–19).

> "Even as the Son of Man came not to be ministered unto but to minister, and to give His life a ransom for many" (xx. 28).

Second, in our Lord's triumphal *entry* (xxi. 1–17) we are meant to see that He certainly *did* thus offer Himself as Israel's Messiah-King, and that the Jewish leaders so understood. How any expositor, even "anti-dispensationalist," could write (as we have recently seen) "Jesus nowhere offered Himself to the Jews as their Messiah-King" is passing strange. Knowingly and most deliberately He fulfilled Zechariah ix. 9, as Matthew emphasises:

> "Tell ye the daughter of Zion: Behold thy King cometh unto thee, meek and sitting upon an ass, and a colt the foal of an ass" (xxi. 5).

He not only accepted from the multitude their continuous "Hosanna to the Son of David!" but, with flash of regal indignation in His eyes, cast out the money traffickers from His temple; and when the chief priests, provoked by the children's hosannas, asked, "Hearest Thou what these say?" He replied, "Yea, have ye never read: Out of the mouths of babes and sucklings Thou hast perfected praise?" Certainly those Jewish leaders understood. It was no accident that a little later there was a superscription over His Cross: "THIS IS JESUS, THE KING OF THE JEWS."

Third, in the fateful *collisions* which now ensued inside the city between Jesus and the Jewish sects (xxi. 18–xxiii) we are meant to see not only that *they* had set themselves implacably to reject *Him* but that *He* also had now rejected *them*. The barren fig tree which He cursed was His symbol of them (xxi. 18–27). From the moment of His entry, see how they contest Him (xxi. 15, 23–7). Herodians, Sadducees, Pharisees concertedly close in upon Him (xxii.). But all the way through Jesus has the upper hand. They are not only answered: they are humiliatingly silenced (xxii. 46). Moreover, He exposes them in parable after parable (xxi. 28–xxii. 14), and finalises His utter aversion in that public, deadly denunciation punctuated eight times with, *"Woe unto you, scribes and Pharisees, hypocrites!"* (xxiii. 13–36). Oh, tragedy of self-blinded religiosity and outraged love, that He who commenced His ministry in Galilee with eight "Blesseds" should have to close it in Jerusalem with those eight "Woes"! The Jewish leaders could not resist His wisdom, but they *did* resist His *witness* (Christian disciple, note that fact well, for the same thing still happens!) And so the broken-hearted royal Redeemer withdrew, with that sob which was the sudden outgushing of an infinite deep: "O Jerusalem, Jerusalem, thou that killest the prophets and stonest them which are sent unto thee, how often would I have gathered thy children together even as a hen gathereth her chickens under her wings; but ye would not! Behold, your house is left unto you desolate. For I say unto you, Ye shall not see me henceforth till ye shall say, Blessed is He that cometh in the name of the Lord."

Fourth, in our Lord's *Olivet prophecy* of things to come (xxiv.–xxv.) we are meant to see, before anything else, that it was uttered *outside* the city, by a Christ who had now withdrawn, and that

the predicted happenings were *because* of His having been rejected. The chapter break should not be allowed to obscure the
connection between the last words of chapter xxiii. and the opening words of chapter xxiv.: "Ye shall not see Me henceforth. . . .
And Jesus went out. . . . There shall not be left here one stone
upon another. . . . When shall these things be? . . . And Jesus
answered [i.e. the Olivet discourse]."

Thus did the triumphal entry end in dark anti-climax. Our
Lord's attention was now devoted exclusively to the inner circle
of His disciples. The omniscient foreknowledge which expressed
itself in His Olivet discourse must have been a steadying relief to
them, for they had doubtless been staggered by the angry dignity
with which He had now deliberately antagonised the nation's
religious leaders and flung the ruling class away. There is anger,
but no temper. Calmly, as He sits on the slopes of Olivet, He
tells of ultimate triumph beyond present tragedy and impending
troubles.

Someone may ask: "If Jesus foreknew that He would be rejected, why did He offer Himself to Jerusalem at all?" Matthew
leaves us in no doubt. Our Lord never once foretells His crucifixion apart from the coming master-stroke of His *resurrection*
(see xvi. 21, xvii. 22, 23, xx. 17-20, xxvi. 28-32). That fact
causes us to distinguish between Divine foreknowledge and Divine
foredetermination. God did not predetermine either that Judas
should betray the Lord of Glory or that the Jewish leaders should
maliciously slay Him; but He foreknew it all, anticipated it, and
sovereignly overruled it in suchwise as to display how, without
violating the freedom of the human will, He has graciously
triumphed even over the evil exercise of free-will, to the fulfilling
of still further and bigger designs for the good of His universe. The
same foreknowing and overruling goes on all the time, and covers
our time, individually, internationally, racially. That is why
many things are permitted which seem baffling enigmas to ourselves who live and see merely minute by minute. We are now
at a point of time where we can see how faithfully the Olivet forecast of this present age has unfolded and now reaches its final
descriptions. The distant ultimates which our prescient Lord
then painted for His disciples on a far horizon are to ourselves
the sunshafts of a millennial age and kingdom soon to break
upon us!

The Crucifixion

And now come to the two chapters on the crucifixion (xxvi., xxvii.). Again there is fourfold sequence. Four scenes succeed each other in pathetic and dramatic culmination. We see our Lord Jesus in four settings:

> Among His own disciples (xxvi. 1–56).
> Before the Jewish Sanhedrin (57–75).
> Before the Roman Governor (xxvii. 1–26).
> Crucified, dead and buried (27–66).

Once again we are impressed by the straightforward factualness of the narrative. There is no straining after any mere pen-effect; no emotional elaborating of harrowing detail. Yet it is equally perceivable that Matthew *does* have a purpose colouring his narrative. There are certain main significances in these four moving scenes which he is plainly concerned for us to grasp.

In the first of them, where our Lord is *withdrawn with the twelve* (xxvi. 1–56) the emphasised feature is that He perfectly *foresaw* every detail in the new turn of events. When Mary of Bethany anoints Him with the precious ointment He says, "She hath done it for my burial" (xxvi. 12). When the twelve sit at supper with Him He tells them that it is actually one of themselves who is about to betray Him, and indicates Judas (xxvi. 25). When Peter boasts, "Though all men shall be offended because of Thee, yet will I never be offended," He sadly fore-apprises him: "Before the cock crow thou shalt deny Me thrice." And it is superlatively significant how this foreknowledge now expresses itself as to the Cross. He links it with the Jewish Passover in such a way as to imply that He is the *new* Passover (xxvi. 2). He links it with Jeremiah xxxi. 31, etc., and designates His blood as "the blood of the *new* covenant" (xxvi. 28). He links it with Old Testament prophecies such as Isaiah liii., for His bloodshedding is to be *substitutionary* ("shed for many"), and *propitiatory* ("for the remission of sins"). In the Gethsemane agony the Father's sovereignty is recognised in it all, and the incarnate Son bows in sublime yieldedness.

In the second scene, where our Lord is *before the Jewish Sanhedrin* (xxvi. 57–75), the big fact is that Jesus was condemned specifically for claiming to be Israel's Messiah. His baffling silence eventually provoked the high priest to cry: "I adjure Thee by the living God, that Thou tell us whether Thou be the Christ, the Son of God." Reply to such an adjuration was incumbent, and our Lord therefore said: "Thou has said; moreover I say unto you, Hereafter shall ye see the Son of Man sitting on the right hand of power, and coming in the clouds of heaven." That was all the Sanhedrin wanted. They at once charged Him with "blasphemy" and declared Him "guilty of death" (verses 65–8). He was crucified for that, *and for nothing else.*

In the third scene, where He is before the Roman Governor (xxvii. 1–26), we are meant to note that the Jews handed Him over for claiming to be their Christ, only they had now given it just that twist which would make it tingle in Pilate's ears, namely, that Jesus had proclaimed Himself *King* of the Jews. Pilate's first question is, "Art Thou the King of the Jews?" The experienced Pilate soon knew that there was no cause of death in his prisoner (verses 23, 24), but the thing which would save his own neck if his Roman superiors should ask why Jesus was allowed to be crucified was that He had advertised Himself as "King" of the Jews in ostensible opposition to Cæsar: hence Pilate's large-written accusation over the Cross, "THIS IS JESUS, THE KING OF THE JEWS," which also served as a sarcastic slap-back at the Jews, whose motive in delivering Jesus, as Pilate well knew, was envy (xxvii. 18).

And now, that fourth scene, that awe-inspiring, soul-subduing spectacle, *the Crucifixion* (xxvii. 27–66). To those of us who love our Lord Jesus, that Cross can never be an object of coldly intellectual study. Our theology of it cannot but be continually saturated with our tears, for we have entered somewhat into "the fellowship of His sufferings." Yet even our tenderest emotion of gratitude and adoration will not obscure that there are two things which above all others Matthew would impress upon us. First, as he describes (more fully than Mark, Luke or John) the accompanying abnormalities—the midday darkness, the earthquake, the cleaving of the rocks, the disturbed graves, he would have us exclaim with the startled centurian: "Truly this was the Son of God!" (verse 54). Second, as he reports the simultaneous rending of the temple veil into the Holy of Holies, not by a human hand from below, but by a Divine "from the top," not merely part way, but completely, "from the top to the bottom," he would have us see the profound *Godward* significance of that Cross. That Sufferer is "the Son of God"; and that Cross has effected something tremendous between earth and heaven. The after-details ensure that physical life became extinct, and that the corpse was really entombed. There could be no bodily re-emergence except by miraculous resurrection.

The Resurrection

Just one short chapter of twenty verses given to the titanic super-climax—to that event which of all "Christian evidences" is the most basal and vital! Might we not have expected that Matthew would dotingly expand his narrative here, fondly lingering over the mighty triumph which had vindicated his Hero and confounded His malicious crucifiers? Perhaps so, at first sight; but on second thoughts, no. Matthew's sole concern is to *get there* —to reach that resurrection miracle as the triumphant final *fact* in his faithfully factual memoir. He is not here concerned with the theological development of the fact (which was to follow later) but with the narrating of the fact itself, and the simply stupendous pronouncement which now fell from the lips of the risen Christ in virtue of it: "All power is given unto Me, in heaven and in earth. Go ye therefore and disciple all nations, baptising them in the name of the Father, and of the Son, and of the Holy Spirit; teaching them to observe all things whatsoever I have commanded you. And, lo, I am with you alway, even unto the end of the age." The brief account falls into four paragraphs: I. The intervention of the angel (verses 1–7); 2. The reappearance of the Lord (verses 8–10); 3. The lying story of the Jews (verses 11–15); 4. The reordaining of the Eleven (verses 16–20).

How many, or how few, of those who read Matthew's last-recorded utterance of the risen Lord really catch the utter splendour of it? "All authority is given unto Me, in heaven and in earth." The word "authority" is a better translation than "power," for what is meant here is not our Lord's inherent power but His *administrative authority*. That is why He says: "All authority is *given* unto ME." But did He not always have this authority? As God the Son, yes; but not as Jesus, "Son of Man," "Son of David." Both by plain and veiled intimations the Scriptures convey that *Satan* has sustained a peculiar relationship of authority over our earth. He was not always Satan and Diabolos, but Lucifer, the "anointed cherub." There are indications that the global desolation described in Genesis i. 2 was consequent upon the vain infidelity and insurrection of this arch-prince among the angels. When earth-dominion was placed under *man* Satan at once contrived Adam's fall. He is called "the prince of this world." When he tempted our Lord, saying, "All this power will I give Thee [i.e. 'all the kingdoms of the world'] for it is delivered unto me," our Lord did not dispute the claim. Moreover, in some mysterious way he has held "the power of death" (Heb. ii. 14) and is called "the prince of the authority of the air" (Eph. ii. 2).

But his power is now broken, and his authority is forever taken away. *That* is the meaning of our Lord's resurrection, and of His words: "All authority is given unto *Me*. . . ." As the first Adam fell and forfeited his dominion, so Jesus the "second Adam" overcame by choosing the Father's will even to that costliest extreme of Calvary, by which He became not only the Redeemer of Adam's fallen race but the leader of a new humanity, the tried, tested, proven, all-worthy Executor of the Divine will, and the resurrection-attested Administrator of the Divine purposes.

That is why He now says: "All authority is given unto Me, in heaven and in earth." That is why He later said to John on lonely Patmos: "Behold, I am alive for evermore, and have the keys of death and hades." The keys are no longer in Satan's grasp; they hang at Jesus' girdle; and the sceptre of "all authority" is in the hands which bear the nail-scars!

In the Old Testament we find it plainly enough predicted that the coming Christ should be the "Son of David," that He should take the throne and reign, not only over a restored Israel but over all other nations as well. It is equally foretold that He should be a Redeemer and Saviour in a substitutionary and sin-expiating sense; that He should be a Prince and a Saviour not only to the Jews but to the Gentiles as well. But in our risen Lord's pronouncement at the end of Matthew's Gospel there is that which was *not* predicted, and which transcends all that *was* predicted; for Israel's rejected Christ, who has now become the world's Saviour, is lifted "far above all principality and power and authority, and every name that is named" (Eph. i. 21), and crowned as the *Administrator of the whole universe*!

THE GOSPEL ACCORDING TO MATTHEW

THE PROMISED KING
ATTESTED YET REJECTED: SLAIN YET RISEN

Introduction: Genealogy (i. 1–17) and Nativity (i. 18–ii. 23).
Baptism (iii. 1–17 and Temptation (iv. 1–11).

I. THE DETOUR IN GALILEE (IV.12–XVIII.).

(a) *What Jesus Taught—the tenfold message (v.–vii.).*
Beatitudes (v. 3–16). Morals (v. 17–48). Motives (vi. 1–18).
Mammon (vi. 19–24). Cares (vi. 25–34). Discernment (vii.
1–6). Encouragements (vii. 7–11). Summary (vii. 12).
Alternatives (vii. 13, 14). Warnings (vii. 15–27).

(b) *What Jesus Wrought—the ten "mighty works" (viii.–x.).*
Leper cleansed (viii. 1–4). Palsied healed (viii. 5–13). Fever
cured (viii. 14, 15). Storm calmed (viii. 23–7). Demoniacs
(viii. 28–34). Palsy cured (ix. 1–8). Haemorrhage (ix.
18–22). Girl raised (ix. 23–26). Sight given (ix. 27–31).
Demoniac (ix. 32–34).

(c) *What People Thought—the ten reactions (xi.–xviii.)*
John Baptist (xi. 2–15). "This generation" (xi. 16–19).
Galilean cities (xi. 20–30). Pharisees (xii. 2, 10, 14, 38).
Multitudes (xiii. 1–52). Nazarethites (53–8). Herod (xiv.
1–13). Scribes (xv. 1–20). Sadducees (xvi. 1–12). The
Twelve xvi. 16).

II. THE CLIMAX IN JUDÆA (XIX–XXVIII.).

(a) *The Presentation—Jesus offered as King (xix–xxv.).*

The journeying up to Jerusalem (xix.–xx.).
The triumphal entry into Jerusalem (xxi. 1–17).
The collisions inside of Jerusalem (xxi. 18–xxiii.).
The resultant prophecy on Olivet (xxiv.–xxv.).

(b) *The Crucifixion—Jesus slain as Felon (xxvi.–vii.).*
Jesus among His own disciples (xxvi. 1–56).
Jesus before the Jewish Sanhedrin (xxvi. 57–75).
Jesus before the Roman Governor (xxvii. 1–26).
Jesus crucified, dead, and buried (xxvii. 27–66).

(c) *The Resurrection—Jesus risen as Saviour (xxviii.).*
The intervention of the angel (xxviii. 1–7).
The reappearance of the risen Lord (xxviii. 8–10).
The lying invention of the Jews (xxviii. 11–15).
The new outsending of the Eleven (xxviii. 16–20).

THE GOSPEL ACCORDING TO MATTHEW (3)

Lesson Number 113

NOTE.—For this study read chapters xii. and xiii. again several times.

ABOUT MATTHEW HIMSELF

We know only four things about Matthew with certainty, but they are most revealing.

(1) *He was a "publican"* (x. 3), a Jew who had become a tax-gatherer for the hated Romans, which was regarded as deeply dis-honourable. We read of "publicans and sinners", which indicates the general moral level. We know Matthew was a publican by his own pen alone. In the three accounts of his "call" (Matt. xviii. ; Mark ii. ; Luke v.) Mark and Luke name him *Levi,* so from them only we could not have identified him as the former publican. See, too, the three accounts of the choosing of the Twelve (Matt. x. ; Mark iii. ; Luke vi.) : Mark and Luke now call him Matthew, but only Matthew has the self-humbling reminder, "Matthew *the publican;*" and he alone preserves the stinging words, "The publicans and the harlots" (xxi. 31), which words do not imply that he himself had been profligate, but *do* show how publicans in general were regarded. Matthew's reporting of them reveals his self-abasing humility.

(2) *He became a disciple of Jesus* (ix. 9). Mark and Luke tell that when he left the "receipt of custom" he hospitably opened "his own house" to our Lord ; that he gave a "great feast" for many other publicans to hear Jesus ; and (a hint of his considerable money) that *"he left all."* Not one of these things does Matthew himself tell. His omissions as well as his insertions reveal humility.

(3) *He was later appointed an apostle* (x. 3). See the three accounts again. Our Lord sent the apostles out two by two (Mark vi. 7). Their names accordingly go in pairs. Matthew and Thomas go together each time and are given in that order by Mark and Luke ; but *Matthew* puts *Thomas first*—another incidental token of humility.

(4) *He became the writer of the Gospel which bears his name*—of which that New Testament expert, A. T. Robertson, says : "The book is probably the most useful one ever written ; it comes first in the New Testament collection, and has done more than any other to create the impression of Jesus that the world has obtained."

—*J.S.B.*

THE GOSPEL ACCORDING TO MATTHEW (3)

WE HAVE seen how invitingly this first book of the New Testament opens up and tempts us to a fuller exploration. Yet if we are to keep within the intended limits of our Bible course we can spare only this and one further instalment on it. So, in this present review, we simply offer what we hope will be useful guidance on certain features of the narrative which may have halted some readers in perplexity.

The Kingdom of Heaven

It is of first importance to know what is meant by the "kingdom of heaven," for it was the main subject of our Lord's preaching. Alas, there is no little confusion about it. It is commonly supposed to be a *spiritual* kingdom, more or less identical with the *Church*: yet to confuse the two obscures one of the clearest demarcations in Holy Writ.

Both John and our Lord began by proclaiming, "The kingdom of heaven is at hand"; yet neither explained what that kingdom was. Why? Because their hearers knew, without need of explanation, that it meant the Messianic kingdom long-promised through the Old Testament prophets. But do the prophecies of that coming kingdom have any reference to the Church? None whatever! Consult a few of them, and see.

What is foretold is a visible kingdom, with Messiah reigning on the throne of David, over a reunited Israel and the Gentile nations, in world empire. There are exalted ethical and spiritual aspects forecast, but the kingdom itself is to be visible, Messianic, global—the very antithesis of a "church", which by its very name, i.e. *ecclesia*, is a called-out, exclusive minority.

That promised kingdom was announced by the forerunner, then preached by our Lord with Messianic credentials unmistakable to all but a self-blinded generation. To a people doting on the material prospects of the long-looked-for kingdom, its *moral* requirements were unacceptable. Despite popular enthusiasm aroused by His teachings and healings, our Lord had to say:

"This people's heart is waxed gross" (xiii. 15). The kingdom was rejected and the King crucified. Renewed offer was made during the suspense-period covered by the Acts, plus the tremendous new message of atonement through the now-crucified, risen, ascended Messiah Jesus, and attested by Pentecostal miracle-signs; but again there was rejection, first by the Jews of the homeland (Acts ii.–xii.), then by the Jews of the dispersion (xiii.–xxviii.).

So the kingdom is withdrawn. "His blood be upon us, and on our children!" yelled the Jewish leaders on the crucifixion morn. "How often would I! . . . Ye *would* not. . . . Ye *shall* not . . ." (Matt. xxiii. 37, 39). Israel *would* not see, and now *cannot* see. "Blindness in part is happened unto Israel, until the fulness of the Gentiles be come in" (Rom. xi. 25). The Church is not the kingdom; nor is this present age the kingdom age. When the angel preannounced to Mary the birth of Jesus, he said, "The Lord shall give unto Him the throne of His father David, and He shall reign over the house of Jacob" (Luke i. 32, 33). Thus were our Lord and the "kingdom of heaven" which He preached linked at once with the Messianic kingdom fore-promised in the Old Testament. The "throne of David" and the "house of Jacob" must not be spiritualised. Our Lord has never yet taken that throne of David, but He will do so at His second advent. The kingdom will be set up when the King returns and a repentant Israel says, "Blessed is He that cometh in the name of Jehovah!"

Turn over Matthew's pages again: look up the many references to the "kingdom of heaven" which speak of it as yet future, historical, visible. Then try to make them mean a purely spiritual kingdom identifiable with the Church—and see how difficult it is!

Our Lord's Use of Parables

How often one hears glib generalisations made from texts which are purely local in intent! Several times recently we have been told that Jesus never preached except in parables, because Matthew xiii. 34 says, "Without a parable spake He not unto them." Why, in our Lord's longest recorded discourse, i.e. the Sermon on the Mount, there is entire absence of parable, as is also true of much else in His teaching. Matthew xiii. 34 refers only to the occasion of which it speaks.

That our Lord had not hitherto used parables so fully is indicated by the surprise of the disciples: "Why speakest Thou unto them in parables?" (xiii. 10). Moreover, His fuller resort to parables from that time onwards is explained in His own reply: "Because it is given unto *you* to know the mysteries [i.e. hitherto hidden truths] of the kingdom of heaven, but to *them* [i.e. the superficial crowds] it is not given. For whosoever hath, to him shall be given, and he shall have more abundance; but whosoever hath not, from him shall be taken away even what he hath. Therefore speak I to them in parables, because they seeing see not, and hearing they hear not, neither do they understand" (xiii. 11–13).

So our Lord's change-over to a more parabolic method was most meaningful. For those people to keep on seeing and hearing without *really* seeing and hearing (i.e. without inwardly acknowledging and responding to the plainly spoken truth) was adding more and more to their responsibility and culpability. For long enough now a watching Heaven had sighed over their fathers and themselves: "This people draweth nigh unto Me with their mouth, and honoureth Me with their lips, but their heart is far from ME" (xv. 8). By a fateful process the very capability of recognising and heeding the truth had become impaired, and our Lord now sadly diagnosed: "This people's heart is waxed gross, and their ears are dull of hearing, and their eyes they have closed; lest at any time they should see with their eyes, and hear with their ears, and should understand with their heart, and should be converted, and I should heal them."

It is a law of life that what we will not *use* we eventually *lose*. That is what was happening to Israel; and that was the principle now expressed in our Lord's words, "To him that hath [i.e. to him who has sincerely received the word] to him shall be given, and he shall have abundance; but whosoever hath not [i.e. has not sincerely received the word] from him shall be taken away even what he hath" (verse 12). From now onwards our Lord would veil His kingdom teaching somewhat in parables. There was mercy in this, for it spared the unreceptive hearer from the heavier guilt of further spurning plainly stated truth. There was judgment in it too—"From him shall be taken away even what he hath."

Yet the very parables which were to *veil* the truth from some were to reveal *new truth* to sincere disciples, for "To him that hath shall be given." By this time Israel's implicit rejection of the kingdom was in evidence; and in these parables of Matthew xiii. our Lord was now going to open up hitherto hidden truth about the future of the kingdom consequent upon its present rejection. That is the meaning of verse 35: "I will open My mouth in parables: I will utter things which have been kept secret from the foundation of the world" (see also verses 16, 17). Yes, Jesus was now opening up *new* truths about the future aspects of the kingdom, following its rejection by Israel. It is that fact which guides us to their meaning.

The Seven Parables of Matthew xiii.

If the seven parables of Matthew xiii. are to speak consistently, there are two opposite extremes of interpretation which must be avoided: first, that of *spiritualising* them so that they supposedly refer to the Church and the Christian religion; second, that of *manipulating* them so as to make them fit a dispensational theory. Those who regard the kingdom as purely spiritual will naturally fall into the first error. Those who hold hyper-dispensational views are prone to the second. We should also guard against pressing every detail of a parable into meaning something. It is the main figures and features which carry the parallel. Often the details are merely incidental scenery.

What, then, is the meaning of these seven parables in Matthew xiii.? Well, first, they do *not* refer to the Church—for the Church had not yet been even mentioned. Each one of them, except the first, begins: "The kingdom of heaven is like . . ." That kingdom is *not* the Church.

Nor do they picture *Christendom* in this present age, as certain dispensationalists aver. This is where, in our own judgment, the "Scofield" Bible slips into error, propounding an artificial theory that the kingdom exists on earth today in a so-called "mystery-form." The Scofield note on Matthew xiii. 3 equates this "mystery-form" of the kingdom with "the sphere of Christian profession," and then adds, "It is Christendom." I would gratefully acknowledge much that is excellent in the Scofield notes; but this dispensational fiction that the rejected kingdom now exists on earth in "mystery-form," alias Christendom, is surely a travesty. At point

after point the Scofield notes contradict our Lord's plainest wording, as a couple of instances shall show. First: in the parable of
the wheat and the tares our Master most plainly says: "The field
is the *world*" (verse 38); but the Scofield note, although it begins
by acknowledging this, later curves round to say: "The parable
of the wheat and tares is not a description of the world, but of
that which professes to be the kingdom." Second, in the parable
of the leaven, our Lord distinctly begins: "The kingdom of
heaven is *like unto* leaven"; but the Scofield note says that the
leaven is "the principle of corruption working subtly" in the form
of "evil doctrine." Is not such contradiction of our Lord a strange
presumption?

What then is the purport of these parables? Let their *location*
be our first guide. They occur in that section of the narrative
which tells of the various reactions to our Lord's message (see
study number III). Already He has rebuked Galilee's unrepenting cities; and now, in the parable of the sower, He portrays the
results of His preaching among the multitudes. Only a fraction
had proved good-soil hearers (see xiii. 18–23). The other six
parables are designed to reveal, though in partly veiled form,
certain far-reaching truths hitherto unreleased concerning the
postponement of the kingdom, consequent upon Israel's present
imperviousness.

The Wheat and the Tares

There is the parable of the wheat and the tares, which also our
Lord afterward explained privately. Against His direct explanation, the Scofield theory of the kingdom as now existing on earth
in so-called "mystery-form" surely seems strange. The good
sower is the "Son of Man." The field is "the world." The good
seed are the "children of the kingdom." The tares are the
"children of the wicked one"; and the "enemy" who sowed
them is the "devil." The harvest is the "end of the age." The
reapers are "the angels." And the parable ends: "THEN [i.e.
at the end of the age] shall the righteous shine forth as the sun in
the kingdom of their Father."

Now this sending forth of angels when the Son of Man returns
at the end of the present age, and the setting up of the kingdom
then, is found again and again in the New Testament. Our Lord

Himself directly states it in His Olivet discourse. The kingdom comes "THEN," and not before.

What our Lord did *not* disclose in the parable was that the "THEN" was so far away, with the present dispensation of grace intervening. *That* could not very well have been revealed, else the continued offer of the kingdom to Israel by the Lord and His apostles would have become merely theatrical, whereas it was thoroughly genuine; the nation's free will was respected, and events were allowed to take their course accordingly. It is the Divine foreknowledge which speaks in these parables, divulging what was to happen in view of Israel's *foreknown* behaviour. The setting up of the kingdom was to be postponed.

Apparently the detail which suggested that the kingdom exists *now* in so-called "mystery-form" as Christendom is that the "children [i.e. inheritors] of the kingdom" and the "children of the wicked one" both grow together *until* the age-end harvest. That is where the Scofield note parts company with what is actually written and slips into mere theorising, viz.: "The parable of the wheat and tares is not a description of the world, but of that which professes to be the kingdom."

There are three big factors which decide against the Scofield idea:

(1) Although our Lord said that the "children" or inheritors of the kingdom were already in the world, and were to continue so, with the tares, to the end of the age, He was equally definite that the kingdom itself would not come *until* "then," i.e. until the end of the age; so it is egregiously wrong for Scofield to claim that this presence of the "children" on earth beforehand is the kingdom itself, already here in "mystery-form" as Christendom!

(2) Historically, the decisive fact is that from A.D. 70, when the Romans destroyed Jerusalem and disintegrated Judæan Jewry, the "kingdom of heaven" has no more been offered to the Jews. What *is* being preached in *this* dispensation, to individual Gentiles and Jews alike, is *personal salvation* through the Saviour whose Calvary death made atonement for all mankind.

(3) Inasmuch as our Lord said that He Himself was the Sower of the good seed, would not the seed-sowing seem to refer to our Lord's own ministry *then* rather than to something going on

now, in His bodily absence? Also, since our Lord as the Sower takes the Messianic title "Son of Man," would not that indicate reference to *Israel* rather than to the Church or Christendom?

The idea must be rejected that in this present dispensation the "children of the kingdom" are one and the same as regenerated Christian believers. The Spirit-born members of our Lord's body and bride are far more than "children of the kingdom" in the way our Lord meant. When the kingdom comes, *they* will enter it, not as *subjects* only, but to *reign with* Christ (as other Scriptures show).

If it should be said that the "children of the kingdom" *must* be on earth somewhere today because they were to grow together" with the tares *until* the "end of the age," we reply that the end of *that* age came long ago, when the fearful judgment of A.D. 70 ended Jewish nationality and brought "great tribulation" the like of which had never before been known. Up to that time the kingdom had been offered to the Jews, first by our Lord in person (in the Gospels), then through the Apostles (in the Acts); but Israel's double refusal had now become crystallised into unmistakable fixity. Judgment fell; that age ended; the kingdom was withdrawn; there came a suspension; and now, meanwhile, there swings into view God's further purpose, the wonderful new movement through the *Church,* in this present dispensation of *grace.*

If it should be objected that there was no sending forth of angels then, such as our Lord fore-pictured, and that therefore the judgment of A.D. 70 could not be what He meant by the "end of the age," our reply, in line with His other pronouncements on the subject, is that there is both a first and a final fulfilment of this parable arising from the suspension following Israel's rejection. In Matthew xxiv. 34 our Lord says, "This generation shall not pass till all these things be fulfilled" (see footnote[1]), and we know that all those predicted happenings *did* break upon that generation, except our Lord's own visible return with the harvesting angels to set up His kingdom—and our Lord Himself made *that* the one great exception, for He said: "But of *that* day and hour knoweth no man; no, not the angels of heaven; but My Father only" (xxiv. 36).

---

[1] Some have tried to explain the words "this generation" as meaning the Jewish race; others as meaning the generation which would be on earth at the time when the predicted age-end happenings would eventually occur. We reject both explanations as unexegetical.

This same phenomenon of nearer and further fulfilments, with the present suspension intervening, appears again and again in prophecies related to the kingdom. For instance, our Lord said (see Matt. xi. 14) that John the Baptist was a fulfilment of the prophecy in Malachi iii. 5: "Behold, I will send you Elijah the prophet. . . ." Yet after John's death He said that Elijah was *still* to come, meaning the predicted coming of Elijah at the end of this *present* age (see the excellent Scofield note on Matt. xvii. 10, 11). Similarly, the "wrath to come" which John preached had an awful first fulfilment in A.D. 70; but the ultimate fulfilment, as the epistles show, is at the end of this present age: see Revelation vi. 17—"The great day of His wrath is come; and who shall be able to stand?"

Finally, we need see no problem in our Lord's word that the "children of the kingdom" should be in the world "*until*" the "end of the age," even if He meant this *present* age. Our Lord says that they are the "*righteous*." Both the "children of the kingdom" (i.e. the penitent, upright, godly, believing) and the "children of the wicked one" are in the world all through this present age; and the former—always a minority—will certainly be the inheritors of the promised kingdom when it comes.

But let it be settled in our minds that the "kingdom of heaven" has *not yet* come; nor is it here in any so-called "mystery-form" more or less identical with Christendom or "the sphere of Christian profession."

Mustard Seed and Leaven

The third and fourth parables (mustard seed and leaven) both illustrate the present hiddenness but ultimate greatness of the kingdom. How gifted expositors can turn our Lord's lovely picture of the full-grown mustard tree into the "unsubstantial growth" of the kingdom in supposed "mystery-form" (see Scofield note) and then teach (as some do) that the "birds of the air" which gratefully "lodge in its branches" are false teachers and hypocrites who exploit the kingdom in its "mystery-form," is a sad wonder to our own mind.

It is even sadder that although our Lord so clearly says, "The kingdom of heaven is *like unto leaven*," they should insist that the kingdom is *not* the leaven but the meal, and the leaven false doctrine. The Scofield note not only explains the leaven as "the principle of corruption" or "evil doctrine" but even identifies the woman in the parable as the "apostate church!"

Is it not pathetic how prepossession with theories can lead well-meaning expositors astray! Because Scripture elsewhere uses leaven unfavourably in a symbolic sense, is it unthinkable that our Lord should here use it in a *good* sense? Adam is used both as an evil type and as a type of Christ. In Revelation xvii. a woman symbolises a vast evil; yet in chapter xii. a woman represents the covenant people. In Matthew xiii. "fowls" illustrate Satanic activity, yet in chapter vi. 26 and many other places they are referred to in the happiest ways. Why, even the serpent, repeatedly used in an evil sense, and as a name for Satan, is also used as a type of our Lord (see John iii. 14). In Numbers vi. we find that when a man undertook a Nazarite vow, anything "made from the vine tree, from the kernel even to the husk" was defilement to him; yet how often elsewhere is the vine used in a *good* sense! (John xv., etc.). Even so, leaven was used in every household; and our Lord, who loved to take the common things of home and nature for His illustrations, found in it just the illustration for His purpose.

Whatever may be said against leaven, there is no getting over our Lord's own word: "The kingdom of heaven is *like unto* leaven." In the mustard seed and the leaven—the one buried in the ground yet eventually a great tree, the other hidden in the meal yet eventually filling the whole, our Lord surely pictures the then-rejected kingdom as similarly being now hidden, or removed from view, but at last reappearing in greatness all-pervading. Instead of some supposed "mystery-form" of the kingdom now on earth, let it be realised that there is a present suspension, and that when our Lord returns all these parables will suddenly "come alive" with new activity again and be seen in their true fulfilment.

Hidden Treasure and Pearl Merchant

In the two short parables of the hidden treasure and the pearl merchant the kingdom is again represented as hidden, but with the further aspect that it is nevertheless the supreme "find" to those who are seeking the best. Instead of publicity and common offer, there is now concealment and individual discovery; there is "seeking" and "finding," and an esteeming of the coming kingdom as such treasure that it is worth selling all else to possess it.

We marvel at the naïveté with which the Scofield note assures us that the treasure is "Israel, especially Ephraim, the lost tribes hidden in 'the field,' the world," and that "the Lord is the buyer at the awful cost of His blood." But does Scripture anywhere tell us that Christ needed to "buy" the *kingdom*? To be sure "Christ loved the *Church*, and gave Himself for *it*" (Eph. v. 25), but the kingdom was already His by Divine right and Davidic descent. If we keep closely to the wording, it is the *"kingdom of heaven"* which is the "treasure," not the Israel tribes who were rejecting it. Nor is the "pearl of great price" the *Church* (an idea which is utterly extraneous), but again the "kingdom of heaven", as the wording strictly requires. Nor can our Lord very well be the "man" who makes the surprise "find" and then sells out to buy, for *He* came openly *offering* the kingdom. We need not be surprised that the easiest interpretation is the truest, namely, that the "treasure" or "pearl of great price" is the "kingdom of heaven," and that the "man" who now "finds" is the sincere seeker who "seeks first the kingdom of God and His righteousness," and, to quote Paul, "counts all things but loss" for the "excellency" of inheriting the coming kingdom.

The Drag-net

Of these seven parables in Matthew xiii. the last is the drag-net. Like the others, it has its own particular emphasis, which is the final severance of evil-doers from the upright who inherit the kingdom. We know this is its intended emphasis because it is the one point which our Lord interprets for us, viz.: "So shall it be at the end of the age: the angels shall come forth and sever the wicked from among the just, and shall cast them into the furnace of fire: there shall be wailing and gnashing of teeth."

Thus there is progress in these seven parables. In the first we are given the results of our Lord's own preaching up to that time. In the second the wheat and the tares "grow together *until* . . ." In the third and fourth the mustard seed and leaven tell the present abeyance but future triumph of the kingdom. In the fifth and sixth the treasure and the pearl express the supreme worthwhileness of counting all things but loss for that coming kingdom. In the seventh the emptying of the dragnet shows the doom-filled exclusion of the wicked from the kingdom.

It should be borne in mind all through that these seven parables have their first reference to our Lord's own time on earth. It is beyond question that in the first of them (the Sower) He is describing the reaction *then and there* to His own presenting of the kingdom. In the second the sowing of the tares is something which Satan had *already done*, for verse 39 says: "The enemy which *sowed* them is the devil." This makes it clear that the "end of the age" to which our Lord referred was primarily the end of *that* age; from which time the kingdom has been "hidden," withdrawn, postponed. The Church age now intervenes. So far as the kingdom is concerned there is suspension. But at the end of the *present* age these kingdom parables will take up again from where they were interrupted by the present suspension and will have their *final* fulfilment. The kingdom shall come. The angels shall "gather out all things that offend." Then shall the righteous inherit the kingdom.

It is in this light that all the later parables of the kingdom should be interpreted. The time of their final fulfilment is surely at hand. Even now, after two thousand years of global dispersal and recurrent spoliation such as would have extinguished any other race, the covenant people are representatively regathered in *Eretz Yisrael* again as a self-governing State. Blindness still darkens their minds toward our Lord Jesus. Both inside and outside the land there are renegades and unbelievers in the traditional faith. But there are also, as always, the "godly remnant," loyal to all that is highest and truest in Judaism, pathetically groping, devoutly hoping, for the coming of the kingdom. "He that keepeth Israel shall neither slumber nor sleep." "The eyes of Jehovah are upon the righteous, and His ears are open unto their cry." Their King is on His way! The day of His coming shall "burn as an oven, and all the proud, yea, and all that do wickedly, shall be stubble"; but to all who fear Jehovah, the "Sun of righteousness" shall then arise "with healing in His wings." Before the fire-judgments of the "wrath to come" break upon the earth, not only is the blood-bought Church translated, but the angels are sent forth to seal the "hundred and forty and four thousand" of Israel (Rev. vii.) and preserve them to "shine as the sun in the kingdom of their Father," even as our Lord foretold. "Who hath ears to hear, let him hear."

THE GOSPEL ACCORDING TO MATTHEW (4)

Lesson Number 114

NOTE.—For this study reflect again as discerningly and retentively as possible on our Lord's baptism and temptation, and His repeated "I say unto you" in chapter v.

The more we study the records of that short ministry in the flesh, the more we are impressed with the fact that all the past and all the future are gathered up in it . . . and the words of Prophets on the one side, and of Apostles on the other, are for ever justified and maintained by the words of Him who came between them.

—*T. D. Bernard.*

As we scan Matthew's story again, we find ourselves lingering at this or that or the other point, with the thought that perhaps a few explanatory remarks might help the average reader. So here they are.

The Opening Genealogy

Why that longish genealogy at the beginning? There is a very good reason. Remember that Matthew wrote primarily for Jews, who, in keeping with Old Testament prophecy, expected their Messiah to be born of a certain family. Matthew need not begin away back with Adam, but he *must* start with Abraham, the progenitor of the covenant nation, and then show the descent through David, head of Judah's royal line in which ran the covenant promise of the coming Messiah-King. Matthew must show that Jesus was truly Son of Abraham and Heir of David. That is just what he does.

Why the different *spelling* of the names from that of the Old Testament? It is because Matthew either wrote the genealogy from records written in *Greek,* or translated them from Aramaic into Greek, whereas the names had originally been written in Old Testament Hebrew. It is better to read them in the Revised Version where they are conformed to the spelling which we have in our English Old Testament.

In verse 17 Matthew writes: "So all the generations from Abraham to David are fourteen generations; and from David until the carrying away into Babylon are fourteen generations; and from the carrying away into Babylon unto Christ are fourteen generations." There certainly are fourteen from Abraham to David, and from David to Jehoiachin; but there are only thirteen in the third stretch, unless we count Jehoiachin twice. Is there an explanation? There is, as comparison with the Old Testament shows. Verse 11 says: "And Josiah begat Jeconiah *and his brethren* about the time they were carried away into Babylon." Now Josiah did *not* beget Jeconiah, nor did Jeconiah have "brethren." But Josiah *did* beget Jehoiakim, and Jehoiakim *did* have "brethren" (see 1 Chron. iii. 15). In Matthew's list (as we now have it) there is an omission of *Jehoiakim* between Josiah and Jechoniah. Indeed, some few Greek manuscripts *do* insert it, which regularises the third of Matthew's fourteens.

There may be meanings in these genealogies which do not meet the eye. For instance, we see that between Adam and Christ there are just sixty generations. These sixty seem to go in six tens, each tenth man being notably significant. From Adam onwards the first tenth man is *Noah*. In his days God sent destructive judgment on the whole race, and it looked as though Satan had aborted the Messianic line; but that line is preserved in righteous Noah, demonstrating the indestructibility of the Divine purpose.

The next tenth man is *Abraham*, with whom God entered into unconditional covenant that of his seed should come the Messiah in whom all kindreds of the earth should be blessed.

The next tenth man is *Boaz*, who married beautiful Moabitess Ruth; and through Gentile Ruth all the Gentile peoples are representatively incorporated into the Messianic hope.

The next tenth man is *Uzziah*—for the Messianic line has now become the royal line of Judah, and the coming Christ is to be King of Kings. Indeed it was "in the year that King Uzziah died" that Isaiah, greatest of all Israel's writing prophets, "saw the Lord", i.e. the Messiah (Isa. vi.), sitting on the throne which rules all thrones (for John xii. 41 tells us that it was *Christ* whom Isaiah saw!).

The next tenth man is *Zerubbabel*, one of the most monumental Old Testament characters; the Jewish prince who headed the return of the Remnant to Judæa after the Babylonian exile! Zerubbabel is a type of Christ, so Haggai shows (ii. 20–3), as the supreme Leader of Israel from age-long exile into Millennial blessing.

Ten generations later, we read: "*Joseph*, the husband of Mary of whom was born JESUS who is called CHRIST." Each tenth man is typical, prophetic, anticipative: Christ fulfils all. We will not try to "read *into*" this more than is there, though of course we are pleasantly tempted to reflect that ten is the number of completeness, and six is the number of man as a sinner. Six complete cycles of ten: then comes Christ, who is the goal of all the generations and the Saviour of sinners. In Him the line *ends*. In Him it *never* ends. It perfectly conforms, that He who is God's great *SEVEN* should immediately follow those six completed tens, bringing in the new *spiritual* generation, and the kingdom which, although at present withheld, shall crown the preceding six thousand years of human history with a seventh great thousand-year day, the Millennium of Messiah's worldwide empire, with its exact time-cycle of ten times ten times ten years of peace and glory.

Christ Versus " It Was Said "

It is fashionable today among those who would belittle the Old Testament to quote from the Sermon on the Mount our Lord's reiterated "It was said of old time . . . but *I* say unto you . . ." Jesus thereby repudiated, or at least corrected, Old Testament ethics, so we are told. But those who so argue fail to recognise the difference between the *Written* Law of the Old Testament, and the *Oral* Law which had developed prolifically during the four centuries of the inter-Testament period. Our Lord's usual mode of quoting the Old Testament is, "It is written" (iv. 4, 6, 7, 10, xi. 10, xxi. 13, xxvi. 24, 31), whereas the Sermon on the Mount has "It was *said*", indicating reference to the *Oral* Law Six times it occurs in Matthew v. (21–2, 27–8, 31–2, 33–4, 38–9, 43–4).

Perhaps it may be objected that some of the quoted items *are* in the Old Testament. None the less, our Lord cites them as they had come down per the Oral Law. For instance, the first, "Thou shalt not kill; and whosoever shall kill shall be in danger of the judgment", is the sixth command of the Decalogue plus the comment of the Oral Law. So far as His quotations actually concur with Old Testament tenets, our Lord, other than repudiating them, intensifies them, insisting on an inward and spiritual, as well as an outward and formal, compliance. The very existence of the now complicated Oral Law was an oppressive monument to Judaistic literalism and legalism; and our Lord's comments in each case purposed to lift the minds of His hearers from the mere syllables to the *spirit* of the Law. His own attitude to the Old Testament, and His total endorsement of it, are emphatically announced at the outset (v. 17–19).

Our Lord's Baptism

Why was our Lord baptised of John in Jordan? John's baptism was *"unto repentance."* The sinless Jesus therefore did not need to undergo it. Even when He came to the river John had to say: "I have need to be baptised of Thee; and comest Thou to me?" Yet there *were* reasons for that public immersion, which we should duly appreciate.

First, our Lord thereby demonstrated, at the outset of His public ministry, His oneness with John's call to the nation; and from that time, also, He took up John's cry: "Repent, for the kingdom of heaven is at hand" (iii. 2, iv. 17).

Second, He thereby crowned John's own ministry, giving the faithful forerunner the honour of baptising into public office the Messiah-King whom he had so movingly heralded (John. i. 33, 34). Just afterward John's voice was silenced by imprisonment (Matt. iv. 12).

Third, in submitting to John's baptism He showed His own self-humbling identification with the godly remnant in Israel, who were devoutly living for the coming of the kingdom. It was "becoming" for Him to do so, as now being a member of the nation which deeply needed to heed the call to repentance; hence His remark to John, "Thus it becometh us to fulfil all righteousness" (iii. 15).

Fourth, and much more deeply, He was baptised in a *representative* capacity for those whom He had come to redeem. From the moment He entered upon His public ministry He was the representative new Man, the "Second Adam," the new Champion of our fallen race. At once, therefore, He became identified with us as *sinners,* and His very first act, significantly enough, was to undergo, in a vicarious capacity, the baptism "unto *repentance.*" As, in the opening genealogy, it is our Lord's *manhood* which is connected up with the Messianic descent, so in the baptism and the temptation, it is again the *manhood* which is anointed and then tempted. That manhood has a representative and vicarious aspect all the way through our Lord's actions and experiences.

It is well worth while mentioning, also, that the attesting voice from heaven, "This is my beloved Son, in whom I am well pleased," set God's seal to the sinlessness of the silent thirty years preceding the baptism. Furthermore, at that Jordan baptism the triunity of the Godhead is for the first time objectively exhibited. The Son stands in the Jordan. The Father speaks from heaven. The Spirit descends as a dove.

The Wilderness Temptation

Why that wilderness temptation? It was because Christ, as the new representative Human, must be tested and tried. The very Spirit who had descended on Him in dove-like gentleness now "led" Him into the wilderness, where the arch-fiend waylaid Him when He was weak with fasting.

It is vital to realise that our Lord was there as *Man*. As God He could not be tempted (Jas. i. 13). It is the manhood which was solicited. With pious-sounding cunning Satan at once sought to blurr the battle-point. "If Thou be the *Son of God*"—an allusion to the voice from heaven at the Jordan—"command that these stones be made bread." But immediately Jesus brought the encounter into right focus again by His reply: "It is written: *Man* shall not live by bread alone, but by every word that proceedeth out of the mouth of God." Our Lord was there as *Man*.

As human nature is threefold—body, soul, spirit—so were Satan's three approaches successively directed at those three areas of our Lord's human nature. The first temptation concerned the body ("Command that these stones be made bread"). The second related to the soul ("Cast Thyself down," i.e. give self-display). The third went right to the spirit ("Fall down and worship me"). The first suggested something reasonable. The second suggested something questionable. The third suggested something definitely wrong. How often that is Satan's technique of temptation!— physical, psychical, spiritual; from that which seems reasonable to that which is questionable, and from that which is questionable to that which is damnable. In the first there is the disguise of sympathy. In the second there is a veneer of admiration. In the third the mask is off, all pretence is gone, and the real motive is exposed—"Worship me."

Three times the sword flashes in our Lord's hand, as He repulses the tempter with: *"It is written."* Three times we see the secret of victory—submission to the Word of God. So complete is the victory that in the final repulse Jesus flings the arch-foe back with: "*Get thee hence, Satan*; for it is written: Thou [i.e. each Israelite] shalt worship the Lord Thy God, and Him only shalt thou serve" (see Deut. vi. 13, x. 20).

Immediately thereupon "angels came and ministered unto Him," so His hunger was satisfied without need to turn stones into bread; also the Scripture was fulfilled, "He shall give His angels charge over thee," without there being any need to leap from a pinnacle of the temple! God always has His angels in attendance for those who overcome by fidelity to His Word.

The Unpardonable Sin

What is the unpardonable sin spoken of in Matthew xii. 22, 23? So solemn is our Lord's warning that it at once challenges our most serious enquiry. Startlingly enough, it was addressed to *very religious* persons, the Pharisees, which seems at once to suggest that the unpardonable sin is not some isolated sin of excessive vulgarity, impurity, criminality, or even a course of such.

It is called "*blasphemy against the Holy Spirit.*" Probably none of those who heard the words fall from our Saviour's lips would think of the Holy Spirit as we ourselves now think of Him, i.e. as a distinct Person of the Godhead, any more than they then recognised in Jesus the incarnate *second* Person of the Divine Trinity. They would think of the Holy Spirit as an influence emanating from God. Their monotheism was unitarian, not trinitarian. The full revelation of God as triune breaks on us only as the pages of the New Testament unfold.

But the fact that our Lord's hearers did not apprehend the personalness of the Holy Spirit does not lessen the solemnity of our Lord's words. Nay, it increases it, for it betokens that we may commit the unpardonable sin against the Holy Spirit without even knowing that He *is* a person.

Blasphemy is speaking in such a way as vilifies or insults or otherwise outrages God. In what way, then, were those old-time Pharisees outraging God? They were saying: "This fellow casts out demons by Beelzebub, the prince of the demons." That is, they were *ascribing the Holy Spirit's gracious and holy activities to the devil*. They may not have known, as we now do, that the Holy Spirit is a Divine person, but they *did* know that our Lord's healing miracles were manifestly beneficent intervenings of *God*; nevertheless, in jealous rebellion against clear light, and to guard their prestige among the people, they lied to their own consciences, and outspokenly averred that those gracious works of God were wrought by Satan!

Such was the blasphemy; and the factor which made it unpardonable (or which *would* have made it unpardonable if persisted in) was its being *intelligent, wilful, determined.* Such blasphemy uttered in ignorance is pardonable (see 1 Tim. i. 13) —let us grasp that gratefully and firmly; but the blasphemy which those old-time Pharisees were indulging was open-eyed, envious and malicious. Wilfully, they alleged that what the Holy Spirit was doing proceeded from hell. What awful blasphemy, then, it was!—and how fearfully unmistakable the warning against it!

(There are other aspects of the "unpardonable sin" which we cannot touch on here; but for a full treatment see chapter 10 of my book *Studies in Problem Texts*.)

The Miracle of the Tribute Money

More than a few have been puzzled by the miracle which Matthew alone records in chapter xvii. 24–7 (which please consult).

The problem-point is our Lord's comment, "Then are the children free . . ." (verse 26), which obviously implies His non-liability to pay the tribute, yet seems obscure as a *reason* for non-liability. Surely, as a member of the subject Jewish race, our Lord *was* liable to the Roman tax.

However, the problem is only seeming, not real. The Greek word here translated "tribute" does not refer to the *civil* tax at all but to the *temple* dues. Those who raised the matter were not the tax-gatherers (i.e. the so-translated "publicans") but "they who collected the *didrachmas*"; and their question would be better translated, "Doth not your Master pay the *didrachmas*?"

Now the *didrachmon* was the "half shekel" of Exodus xxx. 11–16, which all grown Israelites were to pay for the upkeep of the tabernacle. Later it became an annual payment. We find it referred to in 2 Kings xii. 4; 2 Chronicles xxiv. 9; Nehemiah x. 32. Josephus refers to it as annual. Philo tells about the loyal payment of it by Jewish communities scattered throughout the Roman empire and their sending of it at stated intervals, by consecrated messengers, to Jerusalem. Not being a government tax, it was not legally compulsory, but as an ecclesiastical levy it was morally obligatory.

As soon as we realise that the *didrachmas* were temple dues, not the civil tax, the incident in Matthew xvii. lights up with attractive new meaning. Notice where it occurs in Matthew's narrative. Peter and his fellow-apostles had made their fervent confession: "Thou art . . . the *SON* of the living God" (xvi. 13–20). This had been followed by the Transfiguration and the attesting voice from heaven itself: "This is My beloved *SON*" (xvii. 1–13). And now our Lord asks Peter: "Of whom do the kings of the earth take levy or census-tax?—of their own *SONS*, or of strangers?" Peter replies, "Of strangers"; so our Lord adds: "Then are the *SONS* free," meaning, of course, that He, as the *SON OF GOD*, whose very house the Jewish temple was, could certainly have no need to pay the *didrachmas* to His own house! Peter would get the point at once; and I hope we ourselves do.

The amount of tribute due from each person was a *didrachmon* (the prefix "*di*" meaning two or double). One *didrachmon*, therefore, was two "drachmas"—just as in English one florin is a *two*-shilling piece. So our Lord, if He was to pay for both Himself and Peter, needed *four* "drachmas," i.e. two for Himself and two for Peter. He said to Peter: "Go thou to the sea, and cast an hook, and take the fish that first cometh up; and when thou hast opened his mouth thou shalt find a *statēr*. . . ." The *statēr* was a coin equal to four "drachmas," the exact payment required. "Take that, and give unto them," says our Lord, "for Me and thee." Peter himself would be open-mouthed, as well as the fish, when he found that coin! It was a real coin from the mint. Who dropped it into the lake, in the first place, so that it was already there for the fish to pick up? That is a question which we had better not stay to discuss!

Other Interest-points

Pages and pages might be filled, of course, concerning this or that or the other point of interest. But there are so many excellent verse-by-verse commentaries which anyone can consult. Here, as we finish our brief exploring of this first Gospel, we merely touch on several other incidental matters which were jotted down for special mention but now seem almost crowded out.

Our Lord, and Peter's Confession

The Roman Catholic Church has made much for itself from our Lord's words to Peter: "Thou art Peter; and upon this rock I will build My church" (xvi. 18). Every Protestant should clearly understand that what our Lord actually said was: "Thou art *Petros*; and upon this *Petra* I will build My church." He simply uses Simon's surname, *Petros*, which means a stone, and no more, to point to the great *PETRA* or mighty rock, i.e. Himself, the now-confessed *Son of God*, on which He would found His "ecclesia." This very verse, which the Romanists use to teach that our Lord built the Church on Peter, is that which most definitely refutes the idea.

It should also be clearly appreciated that our Lord *never* gave "the keys of the Church" to Peter, as the Roman Church maintains. What our Lord actually said to Peter was: "And I will give unto thee the keys of *the kingdom of heaven*" (verse 19). That kingdom is not the Church; nor will it come until the Church age is over, when our Lord's mystic body and bride shall have become completed. When that kingdom comes, as it surely will at our Lord's return, the keys of its administration will be seen by all, in the hands of Peter and his co-apostles.

Parable of the Vineyard Labourers

The parable of the labourers in the vineyard (xx. 1–16) seems to have disturbed some readers. After all, was it right that those who had "wrought only one hour" should receive as much as those who had "borne the burden and heat of the day"? Well, let us be quick to perceive that by its very connection this parable was not intended to teach what human masters should practise toward their employees. It is meant *only* to illustrate our Lord's words which immediately precede it: "But many that are first shall be last; and the last shall be first." It was never meant to be taken as expressing a trade-union principle! When it comes to matters of capital and labour, the Bible stands firm in insisting on fair wages for fair work. But this parable is meant simply and solely to illustrate the words of chapter xix. 29, 30, and to illustrate it by the *un*usual!

The Man Without a Wedding Garment

It is almost entertaining to go through some of the well-known commentaries and see what a problem is that "man which had not on a wedding garment." Read the parable again (xxii. 1–14). There he is, by an invitation which he has accepted; yet now because he has not on a wedding garment he is "speechless," and the king orders him to be cast into the "outer darkness"! Whom does he represent? He certainly cannot represent any true believer on our Lord Jesus Christ, for all such are born anew of the Holy Spirit, and are clothed with the garment of our Lord's imputed righteousness; nor will any such be found without the "wedding garment" when sitting down at "the marriage supper of the Lamb." But neither can he represent *hypocritical professors* of salvation through Christ, for such will never be present at the coming marriage feast of the Lord and His bride, either with or without a wedding garment!

Yet there is really no problem at all about that strange figure, once we take the parable just as Jesus Himself used it, namely, to illustrate the *"kingdom of heaven"* (see verse 2), and not the salvation of believers. Look at the words which immediately precede it, and note that it was spoken primarily against the Pharisees (xxi. 45, 46, xxii. 1). The typical Pharisee, proudly cloaking inward unrighteousness by outward religiousness, was *sure* that whenever the kingdom of heaven came, he would be in it. Jesus says, No; those wicked ones who were first bidden, but refused, should be destroyed, and their city with them, i.e. the Jewry of that generation, especially the leaders. That, indeed, was what actually happened. But the marriage feast (which, remember, represents the kingdom of heaven) will none the less take place, and be furnished with guests, though it shall now be just as *in*clusive ("as many as ye shall find") as it was at first *ex*clusive (i.e. to the Jews).

Yes, that kingdom of heaven which shall yet come, that Millennium "feast" which shall yet provide peace and plenty for the meek, will include all; yet there will be no tolerance of wickedness or hypocrisy, i.e. for the man who will not wear the required "wedding garment." Let it be settled in our minds: this parable of the royal wedding feast does *not* relate to the Church but to the "kingdom of heaven"—which was offered, refused, is now withheld, and is soon to be set up on earth. The man without the "wedding garment" is *not* some faulty kind of present-day "believer," but an illustration of what will happen when that kingdom-age of righteousness is brought in, when our Lord fulfils Isaiah xi. 4, and other similar pledges: "But with righteousness shall He judge the poor, and reprove with equity for the meek of the earth; *but with the breath of His lips shall He slay the wicked.*"

Like rivers overflowing their banks in rainy seasons, this final study in Matthew is exceeding its proper limits. How many other passages we should like to have singled out for special consideration! Still, we shall feel comforted if we have said enough to lure some new student to further exploration. Perhaps we cannot do better than close this quartette of studies in Matthew by referring to those precious words of the risen Jesus with which Matthew himself closes: "Lo, I am with you alway, even unto the end of the age." Note the "I am." In the Greek it is the strongest possible form of expression—*Ego eimi*. Both *ego* and *eimi* mean "I am"; but the former puts the emphasis on the "I" while the latter puts it on the "am." Taken together they are the strongest Greek form to express the name of God as the great "*I AM*." That is how the risen Christ here refers to Himself. "Lo, *I AM* with you!" But there is a lovely feature in the Greek construction here which does not reveal itself in our English translation. It reads like this:

"And lo, *I* with you *AM.* . . ."

You and I, dear fellow-believer, are in between the "I" and the "AM." He is not only *with* us, He is *all round us*—not only now and then, but "alway," which, literally translated, is "*all the days*"—*this* day, this hour, this moment. Why, when we reflect on it, were not our Lord's sudden appearings and disappearings during the forty days between His resurrection and His ascension meant to teach those early disciples (and ourselves) this very thing, that even when He is invisible He is none-the-less present, hearing, watching, knowing, sympathising, overruling? Nor let us forget that the special promise of His presence is given in connection with our going forth as winners of others to Him!

SOME QUESTIONS ON MATTHEW

1. What are the two main parts to Matthew's Gospel?

2. What are the ten parts of the Sermon on the Mount?

3. Which are the ten miracles in chapters viii. and ix.?

4. Which (and what) are the ten reactions in chapters xi. to xviii.?

5. Which are the three sub-divisions in the second part of Matthew's Gospel?

6. If our Lord fore-knew He would be rejected in Jerusalem, why did He go? Mention one feature which casts light on this.

7. Neither John nor our Lord *explained* what the kingdom of heaven was. Why was this?

8. Did our Lord *continually* use parables? If not, when did He begin to use them more fully?

9. Can you say why the parables of Mustard Seed, Leaven, and Hid Treasure have their envisaged fulfilment when Christ returns rather than now, supposedly, in Christendom?

10. Who are the successive six tenth men in Matthew's genealogy?

11. Can you give four reasons why our Lord, although sinless, was baptised of John?

12. How would you explain the man without a "wedding garment" in Matthew xxii.?

THE GOSPEL ACCORDING TO MARK (1)

Lesson Number 115

NOTE.—For this study read right through Mark's Gospel at least twice.

Mark makes no effort to reconcile the human traits of Jesus with His deity. He draws the picture sharply and boldly, as Peter did in his preaching. . . . Mark's Gospel here at the very start proclaims Jesus as the Son of God in a sense not true of other men, in the Johannine sense of deity on a par with the Holy Spirit. In reality, the doctrine of the Trinity is contained in i. 9–11, in Mark's concrete fashion. He states the facts, and leaves us to draw our own conclusions.

—*A. T. Robinson, D.D., LL.D., Litt. D., in "The Christ of the Logia."*

THE GOSPEL ACCORDING TO MARK (1)

IT IS captivating how Nature contrives her varying artistries in different places, all from the same materials—earth, foliage, waters. Even in the small area covered by the British Isles it is conspicuously observable. How different the characteristic scenery of Scotland from that of Wales, or that in most of England from either! And how decidedly its own is the landscape of the emerald isle just over the Irish Sea! Basic identity only makes more remarkable the featuristic divergence—the rugged grandeur of Scotland's glens, straths, bens and lochs; the smooth-carpeted heights and winding valleys of Wales; those greenest of green fields and barish steeps of Ireland; the homey meadows, woody downs, greeny-brown moors and mountain-circled lakes of old England. How different the cactus artistries of the Arizona desert from Australia's Nullarbor Plain or the Sind Desert of Pakistan!— the Indian Himalayas from the Swiss Alps!—the Hawaiian Islands from the neighbouring Fijis, though washed by the same Pacific!

It is the same with the four Gospels. All deal with the same basic material, and the first three practically coincide in what they relate—hence their being called the "Synoptists," from *syn* (together) and *opsis* (a view). Yet though all four are substantially the same, each one is distinguishingly aspective and presents things in peculiarly its own purposive way to the mental eye.

Our present study brings us to the second of them. How evident is the basic identity of subject-matter in Matthew and Mark! Yet how definite is the differentiating individuality! It is intriguing how, from such closely parallel data, such featuristic differentials are sustained throughout.

The Uppermost Purpose

We only need to read Mark two or three times, and his uppermost purpose captures us. He wants us to see *Jesus at work*. It is as though he says: "Look! What Jesus *did* proves who He *was*. What he *wrought* authenticates what He *taught*. The mighty

189

works verify the startling *words*. Watch Him at work, and marvel at this supernatural Wonder-worker! *That* will convince you."

So, there is no opening genealogy as in Matthew, no introductory account of what preceded and attended and succeeded the birth of Jesus. Right away we are at the Jordan, to hear John announce that "One mightier" is at hand. Forthwith Jesus is on the scene; the miracle-ministry begins; and by eager, graphic strokes Mark reaches in chapter one what Matthew takes eight chapters to overtake. He covers in nine chapters what Matthew traverses in twice as many. Not that his account is skimpy, for, on the contrary, it is alive with vivid detail; but he focuses on what Jesus *did*, and omits much of what Jesus *said*.

In fact, it is solely the absence of our Lord's discourses which makes this the shortest of the four Gospels. The whole Sermon on the Mount belongs (but is omitted) between verses 39 and 40 of Mark's first chapter. Matthew's long chapter on the kingdom parables (xiii.) has only a shadow parallel in Mark. Our Lord's commission to the Twelve, which takes all forty-two verses of Matthew x., has a meagre seven verses here; while His denunciation of Galilee's impenitent cities finds no mention at all. The long condemnation of scribes and Pharisees which fills Matthew xxiii. is without even an echo in Mark; and the Olivet discourse is reduced to a third—not to mention other contractions or omissions.

Yes, Mark is distinctively the Gospel of what Jesus *did*. Even the "kingdom," which filled our Lord's preaching and is named over fifty times in Matthew, is on our Lord's lips only fourteen times in Mark. It is clear as can be what our evangelist intends: we are meant to look and marvel at the "mighty *works*"—and well we may!

Modus Operandi

There are no designed groupings like Matthew's. That is not Mark's policy. He wants us to catch the wonder of this Mighty-One *in action*. So, instead of specialised groupings or methodical sectioning, we have a purposely unhalting *succession* of astonishing doings. Mark is the camera-man of the four Gospel-writers, giving us shot after shot of unforgettable scenes. There *are* certain main breaks in his story, as we soon see; but even they are not allowed to interrupt these rapid, one-after-another snapshots of breath-taking marvels.

Some of us can recall the old-fashioned days when static pictures were thrown on the screen by the good old "magic lantern." Oblong glass slides, containing six or more scenes in horizontal succession, were drawn through the projector, so that the pictures were filed across the screen, sometimes with staccato jerks, one after another. Even so, in this "Gospel According to Mark" one mighty work follows another across the canvas, sometimes with abrupt transition, until by force of cumulative impact we are compelled to exclaim—just as Mark intends—"Surely this was the Son of God! This is the most tremendous episode, the most tragic anti-climax, and the most astounding Divine overruling ever known!"

Look and See!

Look through the earlier chapters and see how this is so. Right away, in the short preface, four voices startle us, one after another, by the august terms in which they announce the Wonder-worker now being introduced.

Mark—"Jesus Christ, the *SON OF GOD*" (verse 1).
Isaiah—"Prepare ye the way of *THE LORD*" (verse 3).
John—"There cometh *ONE MIGHTIER*" (verse 7).
God—"Thou art *MY BELOVED SON*" (verse 11).

Then at once the public ministry begins. Straightway we have a rapid series of astounding exploits:

A *demon* cast out in the synagogue (verse 26).
A *fever case* healed in the home (verse 31).
Crowds of invalids cured at the door (verse 34).
A *leper* cleansed by the wayside (verse 42).

All this is in chapter one. The word *euthios* ("straightway," "immediately") is everywhere. The people are "astonished" at His "doctrine," and are "amazed" at His "authority." His "fame" spreads "throughout all the region" and is "blazed abroad."

On the very heels of all this, chapter two brings a quick succession of hostile criticisms:

The Scribes—"This man speaketh blasphemy. Who can for-
    give sins but God only?" (verse 7).
The Pharisees—"How is it that He eateth and drinketh with
    publicans and sinners?" (verse 16).
John's disciples—"Why do the disciples of John and the Phari-
    sees fast, but Thy disciples fast not?" (verse 18).
The Pharisees—"Behold, why do they [His disciples] on the
    Sabbath day that which is not lawful?" (verse 24).

And in each case we are made to marvel at the sheer originality
of our Lord's replies. He moves from one encounter to another
in perfect control of every situation.

Chapter three begins with "And" (out of the sixteen chapters
twelve begin with "And," indicating the unhalting continuity of
the narrative!)—and so the quickly moving story hastes on. It
is almost a sin to read Mark only in bits and paragraphs for the
hurried "daily portion." Never in that way do we find ourselves
caught up and carried along in the glowing, vivid aliveness of the
story. Even a slow reader can travel through Mark in about two
hours. We ought therefore to read it right through at one sitting
as a kind of sacred novel, all the more wonderful because it is
actual truth and not mere fiction.

Significant Peculiarities

Such, then, are our first impressions; and further re-reading
not only confirms them but shows that the interesting peculiarities
of this second Gospel all contribute to one over-all concept of our
Lord.

We recall again the four mnemonic faces of the cherubim in
Ezekiel's vision—lion, ox, man, eagle; speaking respectively of
kingship, service, manhood, Godhead. As we noted in an earlier
study, those four are paralleled in the four Gospel memoirs. In
Mark, our Lord Jesus is uniquely transcribed as the SERVANT,
corresponding with the second of the cherubic faces; and were
it not that Mark's pen-picture was supernaturally guided, we
could only have described it as a product of superb human genius.
Perhaps the most fascinating phenomenon of all, to a closely
concentrating reader, is the seemingly artless yet exquisite way in
which the perfect balance is sustained throughout between human

servanthood and Divine lordship. The lordship is on every page, yet everywhere the Lord is the *SERVANT*—of the Divine will and of human need; the authorised and empowered Sent-One (ix. 37), expeditious, swiftly executive, dominating every situation, yet unobtrusive, compassionate, and in all things obeisant to the supreme Will; the lovely inspiration of Paul's words: "He took upon Himself the form of a *servant* . . . and became obedient unto death, even the death of the cross" (Phil. ii. 7, 8).

Nativity Omissions

Look at some of the omissions and insertions peculiar to Mark and see how they all go with this emphasis on our Lord as Jehovah's *SERVANT*.

To begin with, there is a complete absence of any *incarnation narrative*. There is nothing which answers to the introductions in the other three Gospels: no Davidic genealogy; no pointing star; no eastern sages bringing their gifts and enquiring "Where is He that is born King of the Jews?"; no angel messengers, as in Luke; no worship of shepherds; nothing about Bethlehem or Nazareth; no Benedictus of Zacharia; no Magnificat of Mary; no Nunc Dimittis of Simeon; no incident of our Lord's boyhood; no prologue on His pre-existence, as in John; no clothing of the Eternal Word in flesh; no emerging of the Eternal Son from the bosom of the Father. *Why?* Is it purely accidental that Mark omits all these, and starts right away with the active ministry in Galilee? Or is it intentional, as best according with the *Servant* emphasis? Is it usual to give the genealogy of a servant? Or is it usual to supply description of a servant's birth and infancy? It certainly was never required among the Jews or in old eastern homes.

Discourses Deleted

Then, as already mentioned, there is either outright deletion or severe abridgement of *our Lord's discourses*. In Mark there are sixteen chapters; in Matthew twenty-eight. When the length of the chapters is taken into account, Matthew is practically twice as long as Mark. Yet here is a revealing fact: if Matthew's opening genealogy and nativity record are left out, with those chapters which consist of sermons or parables Mark is by far the longer of

the two as a chronicle of doings! Is this also mere chance? Or
does it designedly fit in with the idea that *works* rather than
words are the required characteristic of a *servant*?

Absence of Indictments

There is also a complete absence of *indictments* such as occur
in the other Gospels. There is no denunciation of Galilee's impenitent cities (Matt. xi.); no flaming condemnation of scribes
and Pharisees (Matt. xxiii., Luke xi.); no awesome consigning
of Christ-rejecting Jerusalem to impending Divine judgment
(Matt. xxiii., Luke xiii.)—not to mention other instances. *Why?*
Is it just so, and nothing more? Or is it not that the *omission* of
such stern "Woes!" and kingly indictments best befits the *Servant*
aspect of our Lord which Mark is emphasising?

Incidental Omissions

Glance, too, at some of the *incidental omissions*. "Whosoever
shall be ashamed of Me and of My words in this adulterous and
sinful generation, of him also shall the Son of Man be ashamed
when He cometh in the glory of His Father with the holy angels"
(Mark viii. 38). Why does Mark omit Matthew's "And then shall
He *reward every man* according to his works"; and Luke's
"When He shall come in *His own* glory"? It is the Servant
speaking. See also the Olivet discourse: "When they shall lead
you and deliver you up, take no thought beforehand what ye
shall speak, neither do ye premeditate: but whatsoever shall be
given you in that hour, that speak ye; for it is not ye that speak,
but the Holy Spirit" (Mark xiii. 11). Why the absence of those
further words which Luke preserves: "For *I will give you* a
mouth and wisdom which all your adversaries shall not be able
to gainsay?" It is the Servant speaking. These omissions are
representative of many.

Incidental Additions

Pass on to some of the *incidental additions*. "Whosoever
receiveth one of such children in My name receiveth Me"—to
which Mark adds: "And whosoever shall receive Me, receiveth
not Me, but *Him that sent Me*." It is the Servant speaking.
Similarly in the Olivet discourse, "But of that day and that hour

knoweth no man, no, not the angels which are in heaven, *neither the Son*, but the Father." It is Mark alone who retains our Lord's insertion of "neither the Son." Why? Because it is the Servant speaking; even as our Lord Himself said: "The servant knoweth not what his Lord doeth."

It is in Mark only that the *hands* of Jesus are so conspicuous. When He healed Peter's mother-in-law He "took her *by the hand* and lifted her up." At Bethsaida He "took the blind man *by the hand*," and afterwards "put *His hands* upon him." "After that, He *put His hands* again upon his eyes." In the healing of the demoniac son "Jesus took him *by the hand*, and lifted him up." In giving hearing and speech to the deaf and dumb man He *"put His fingers* into his ears." These are all in Mark only, as also is the surprised question of the townsfolk: "From whence hath this Man these things? and what wisdom is this which is given unto Him, that even such mighty works are wrought *by His hands*?" Is the repeated prominence of those hands unintentional? Or is it yet another contribution to this *Servant* aspect of our Lord? Are not hands the very symbol of service?

Other Exclusive Features

It is Mark, also, who lays peculiar stress on our Lord's *unobtrusiveness*. "He entered into an house, and *would have no man know it*, but He could not be hid" (vii. 24). "He took him aside from the multitude" (vii. 33). "He led him *out of the town*" (viii. 23).

So also in Mark special notice is given to our Lord's *withdrawments*. "Rising up a great while before day, He went out, and departed into a solitary place, and there prayed" (i. 35). "Come ye yourselves apart into a desert place, and rest awhile. . . . And they departed into a desert place by ship privately" (vi. 31, 32).

Still further, in Mark our Lord's *looks and feelings* are adverted to more than anywhere else. "He looked round about on them with *anger*, being *grieved* for the hardness of their hearts" (iii. 5). "He looked round about, to see her that had done this thing" (v. 32). "And looking up to heaven, He *sighed*" (vii. 34). "But when He had turned about and *looked on* His disciples, He rebuked Peter" (viii. 33). "He *marvelled* because of their unbelief" (vi. 6). "When Jesus saw it, He was *much displeased*" (x. 14).

"Then Jesus, beholding him, *loved* him" (x. 21). "And He *sighed deeply* in His spirit" (viii. 12).

All these personal touches are Mark's alone, as also are others which might be cited. As they accumulate, does it not become apparent that they are strands purposely woven into a pre-designed pattern? Ponder them. They are all characteristics which blend into Mark's presentation of our Lord as the *SERVANT*.

The Title "Lord"

Even the title "Lord" seems intendedly excluded from this second Gospel. According to Matthew and Luke, the leper says, "*Lord,* if Thou wilt, Thou canst make me clean." In the storm on Galilee the disciples cry: "*Lord* [or in Luke, '*Master*'] save us; we perish!" At the last supper they ask: "*Lord*, is it I?" In each case Mark omits the title. Although "Master" occurs in Mark's account of the storm, it is not the same Greek word as Luke uses; and there is the almost rude-sounding complaint (peculiar to Mark's account): "Carest Thou not that we perish?" —as if it were blameworthy for the One who was always working ever to be found sleeping!

Although the title "Lord" is addressed to Him between seventy and eighty times in the other three Gospels, it is *never* so used in Mark—at least, not before His resurrection; except in chapter vii. 28, where the Syrophœnician woman uses it more in the sense of "Sir" (in ix. 24 the word lacks manuscript authority; and in x. 51 it is only *Rabbi*). Not until the very last paragraph of this second Gospel does Mark himself name Jesus "Lord"—not until the Servant has finished the work given Him to do on earth and is *exalted to the throne in heaven*!

Mark's Signature Word

The word which above all others featurises Mark is *eutheos*, translated as "immediately," "straightway," "forthwith," etc. It is almost like the author's recurring signature on the busy exploits which crowd the earlier phase of the story. "*Straightway* He entered into the synagogue" (i. 21). "And *immediately* His fame spread abroad throughout all the region" (i. 28). "And *forthwith* they entered into the house of Simon and Andrew" (i. 29). "And *immediately* the fever left her" (i. 31). These are but four out of the eight occurrences in the first chapter. The word occurs forty-two times in Mark; only seven in Matthew and but once in Luke. As Julius Cæsar's Gallic War records abound with the word "swiftly," so does Mark's memoir of Jesus abound with *eutheos*. And does not this again accord with the emphasis on *service*— prompt, tireless, active, expeditious *service*?

These differentiating touches are but a few selected from many. They are enough, however, to show how markedly the emphasis on our Lord as the *SERVANT* is sustained throughout this second Gospel. And, in crowning endorsement, the little scroll actually closes with the words: "So then after the Lord had spoken unto them, He was received up into heaven, and sat on the right hand of God. And they went forth, and preached everywhere, *THE LORD* WORKING *WITH THEM*, and confirming the word with signs following. Amen."

THE GOSPEL ACCORDING TO MARK (2)

Lesson Number 116

NOTE.—For this study go through this second Gospel again marking
its larger and lesser divisions as they become clear.

The moment we accept the Gospels as a Divine revelation, we have
done with that *protégé* of the critics, the "historic Jesus," and we stand
in the presence of our Divine Lord and Saviour. And from His hands
it is that we receive the Hebrew Scriptures. Three times over in the
Temptation He appealed to the Book of Deuteronomy as the Word
of God—His only defence and answer to the Devil's arguments and
claims.

—*Sir Robert Anderson.*

THE GOSPEL ACCORDING TO MARK (2)

EVEN IN our preliminary conning of this second Gospel we have found fascinating peculiarity enough to refute the undeserved yet clinging notion that it is the least important of the four.

We were saddened to find our favourite old commentator, Matthew Henry, fumbling into the half-apology: "When many witnesses are called upon to give testimony to the same facts we are not to think it tedious, but highly necessary that they should relate the facts in their own words again and again in order to establish the truth by their concurrent testimony." He sees no more in Mark than a repetition of things in Matthew "because man is apt to forget them."

Others have opined that Mark is an *abridgement* of Matthew; yet how widely mistaken they are is shown by the circumstances that in its record of our Lord's *activities* it is definitely longer than Matthew.

All such comparative disappreciations of Mark's memoir result from blindness to its specialistic rendition of our Lord in his *SERVANT* aspect.

Much to the point is E. A. Thompson's observation: "Most certainly Mark, even if later than Matthew, cannot be said to have either copied or abridged Matthew: there are such distinctive characteristics, particularly such minuteness and fulness of personally witnessed and attested detail in almost everything which he records, as irresistibly lead us to conclude that his Gospel is also in the proper sense original—the fruit of independent observation, of independent authorship." The same writer is keenly aware that these and other exclusive Markan touches all designedly cohere in the unifying purpose of projecting Christ especially as Jehovah's *Servant*, the mighty *Worker*.

Extra Details, Vivid Touches

It is well worth while that we should here note some specimens of these extra details and sharpening touches from Mark's pen.

They will help to show us how much we owe to him for the filled-out picture which we have of our Lord in "the days of His flesh." Angus's *Bible Handbook* well says: "In vividness, fulness, and picturesque detail, he often surpasses the other synoptists."

Take the following as extra touches of graphic *perspective*: "He was in the wilderness forty days, tempted of Satan; and was *with the wild beasts*" (i. 13). "And all the city was gathered together *at the door*" (i. 33). "And again He entered into Capernaum, after some days, and it was *noised that He was in the house*" (ii. 1). "And straightway many were gathered together, insomuch that there was no room to receive them, *no, not so much as about the door*" (ii. 2). "And when they could not come nigh unto Him because of the press, *they uncovered the roof* where He was; and when they *had broken it up*, they *let down the bed* wherein the sick of the palsy lay (ii. 4). "And when they had sent away the multitude, they took Him *even as He was* in the ship. And there were also with Him *other little ships*. And there arose a great storm of wind, and the waves beat into the ship *so that it was now full*. And He was in the hinder part of the ship, *asleep on a pillow*" (iv. 36–8). "Make all sit down by companies upon the *green* grass" (vi. 39). "And they sat down *in ranks, by hundreds and fifties*" (vi. 40). "He saw them *toiling in rowing*" (vi. 48). "About the fourth watch of the night He cometh unto them, walking upon the sea, *and would have passed by them*" (vi. 48).

"And when they were come out of the ship, straightway they knew Him; and ran through that whole region round about, and *began to carry about in beds those that were sick, where they heard He was*" (vi. 53–5). "And whithersoever He entered, into villages or cities or country, *they laid the sick in the streets*" (vi. 56). "The multitude have been with Me three days . . . and if I send them away fasting . . . they will faint by the way: *for divers of them came from far*" (viii. 2, 3). "Neither had they in the ship with them *more than one loaf*" (viii. 14). "Shining, exceeding white as snow, *so as no fuller on earth can white them*" (ix. 3). "He took a child, and set him in the midst of them: and when He had *taken him in His arms*" (ix. 36). "There came one *running* and *kneeled* to Him" (x. 17). "In the way going up to Jerusalem, Jesus went [i.e. walked] before them: and *they were amazed*: and as they followed, *they were afraid*" (x. 32). "And he [blind Bartimæus], *casting away his garment, sprang up* and came to Jesus (x. 50, R.V.). They found the colt tied *by the door without*" (xi. 4). "Two mites, *which make a farthing*" (xii. 42). "*Ah!*" (xv. 29). "Who shall roll us away the stone from the door of the sepulchre? . . . *for it was very great*" (xvi. 4). All these vivifying incidentals we owe to Mark.

Names, Times, Numbers, Locations

Observe also how Mark, in a way all his own, particularises *names, times, numbers, locations.* "James and John he surnamed *Boanerges*, which is, the sons of thunder" (iii. 17). "As He went out of Jericho with His disciples and a great number of people, blind *Bartimæus* . . . sat by the highway side begging" (x. 46). "And they compel one Simon a Cyrenian, who passed by, coming out of the country, *the father of Alexander and Rufus*, to bear His cross" (xv. 21).

"And *in the morning,* rising up *a great while before day*" (i. 35). "And the same day, *when the even was come*" (iv. 35). "And whenever [i.e. each day] *evening was come*, He went out of the city" (xi. 19). "It was *the third hour*, and they crucified Him" (xv. 25).

"And they come unto Him bringing one sick of the palsy, which was *borne of four*" (ii. 3). "The unclean spirits entered into the swine ; and the herd ran violently down a steep place into the sea : *they were about two thousand*" (v. 13). "And He called the twelve [apostles] and began to send them forth *by two and two*" (vi. 7). "Before the cock crow *twice* thou shalt deny Me thrice." (xiv. 30). "And the *second* time the cock crew: and Peter called to mind" (xiv. 72).

"And He went forth again *by the sea side*" (ii. 13). "In a place *where two ways met*" (xi. 4). "And Jesus sat *over against the treasury*" (xii. 41). "The centurion, which *stood over against Him*" (xv. 39). "And entering into the sepulchre, they saw a young man sitting *on the right side*" (xvi. 5).

We forbear giving further examples, for those which we have adduced are ample enough to show how much of life-like colour and vivifying detail we owe to this second Gospel; and, moreover, they serve to show how far astray is any theory which supposes Mark to have been merely an abridgement of Matthew or Luke. There is scarcely any incident which Mark gives in common with the other synoptists which he does not enrich or enliven by some exclusive contribution. Those who will make time to go into this further will find it both engrossing and enriching.

There is characteristic emphasis by repetition: "He began to *publish it much,* and to *blaze abroad* the matter" (i. 45); "It sprang up and *increased* and *brought forth*" (iv. 8); "I *know not, neither understand* I what thou sayest" (xiv. 68). There are the touches of dramatic reality supplied by Mark's retention of the very syllables which fell from our Lord's lips in the Aramaic dialect, sometimes with an interpretation, e.g. "*Talitha cumi*" (v. 41); "It is *Corban*" (vii. 11); "*Ephphatha,* that is, Be opened" (vii. 34); "*Abba,* Father" (xiv. 36); "*Eloi, Eloi*"(xv. 34). It is from this shorter Gospel that we owe almost all the snapshots of our Lord's looks, gestures, and emotional reactions. In the first three or four readings of Mark, these are the things which catch the eye of the eager reader, rather than clear divisions of the narrative; that is why we are mentioning them first. Orderly plan and progress there certainly are, but they are subordinated to the leading purpose of portraying, in the most living and graphic way, *Jesus at work;* Jesus as Jehovah's *Servant;* Jesus the *mighty Worker.*

Mark's Account of the Transfiguration

In confirmation of the foregoing, take Mark's rendering of just one complete incident which is common to all three synoptists, namely, the healing of the demoniac son, just after our Lord's transfiguration on the mount. We here submit Mark's account in full, and emphasise by italics the features which are peculiar to it. We do not italicise the variant forms of saying the same thing; but only those touches which are in Mark but not in either Matthew or Luke.

"And when He came to His disciples, He saw a great multitude about them, *and the scribes questioning with them.*

And straightway all the people, when they beheld Him, *were greatly amazed, and running up to Him saluted Him. And He asked the scribes: What question ye with them?* And one of the multitude answered and said: Master, I have brought unto Thee my son *which hath a dumb spirit*; and wheresoever he taketh him, he teareth him; and he foameth *and gnasheth with his teeth and pineth away*; and I spake to Thy disciples that they should cast him out, but they could not.

He answereth him, and saith: O faithless generation, how long shall I be with you? how long shall I suffer you? Bring him unto Me.

They brought him unto Him: *and when he saw Jesus,* straightway the spirit tare him, and he fell on the ground, *and wallowed foaming.*

And He asked his father: How long is it ago since this came unto him? And he said: Of a child. And oftimes it hath cast him into the fire and into the waters to destroy him. *But if Thou canst do anything, have compassion on us, and help us.*

Jesus said unto him: If thou canst believe, all things are possible to him that believeth.

And straightway the father of the child cried out and said with tears: Lord, I believe. Help Thou mine unbelief.

When Jesus saw that the people came running together, He rebuked the foul spirit, saying unto him: Thou dumb and deaf spirit, I charge thee, come out of him, and enter no more into him.

And the spirit cried, and rent him sore, and came out of him: and he was as one dead, insomuch that many said: He is dead.

But Jesus took him by the hand and lifted him up: and he arose [more literally: *Jesus, grasping his hand, raised him, and he stood erect!*]"

Incidentally, how tellingly again these arresting extras accord with Mark's ruling purpose of picturing Jesus to us as the mighty Worker! Over against the powerless disciples, baulked and baffled by this obstinate Satanic defiance, even though they themselves had practised and proved the conferred power of exorcising demons—over against this, behold in contrast the all-dominating power of Jesus!

Yes, we owe much to this shortest of the four Gospels, with its eager vigour of style, its cameo-sharp delineations, and its descriptive detail. We should read it often, and enjoy it the more.

It has a way of surprising us every now and then—especially if we sometimes read it in a modern version—with sudden new slants on things, and sudden new insights into the significance of Jesus. And every part of it will acquire new fascination as we keep "this same Jesus" photographically before our minds as Jehovah's *Servant,* the *mighty Worker.*

Years ago, one who is now a friend of mine was induced by a seemingly accidental circumstance to read through Mark. He had an eye for interesting "story" and became so gripped that without any other agency he was truly converted to Christ. He is now an influential minister of the Gospel; but after the lapse of twenty years and more he still avers that there is no book in all the Bible like "The Gospel according to Mark"!

And Now—the Plan

There are three questions to press in studying a book of Scripture: (1) What is its main *aim?* (2) What is its broad *plan?* (3) What are its chief *traits?* And that is the right order. Mark, however, forces us to invert the order. That is why we have not submitted any analysis until now. The other three Gospel writers plainly indicate their purpose (see Luke i. 1–4, John xx. 31, and Matthew's "That it might be fulfilled"), but in Mark it is the *traits* which guide us to both the *aim* and the *plan.*

Those traits, as we have seen, plainly betoken the main *aim* of portraying Jesus in His *Servant* aspect. They are also fingerposts to a true analysis. Mark's memoir does not lie in set sections: it runs in *movements.* Of course, it *can* be usefully sectionised in flat analysis. Either of the following would serve.

Introduction: "There cometh One" (i. 1–8).

1. THE JORDAN—
   AND MIGHTY WORKS IN GALILEE (i. 9–ix. 50).

2. THE JOURNEY—
   AND FINAL WEEK IN JERUSALEM (x. 1–xv.).

Culmination: "He is risen" (xvi.).

OR (see next page)

Introduction: The Baptist, the Baptism, the Temptation
(i. 1–13).

1. THE EARLIER MINISTRY (i. 14–ix. 50).
2. THE LATER MINISTRY (x.1–xv. 47).

Issue: Resurrection, Commission, Ascension (xvi.).

These "rightly divide" the general material, and lend them-selves to further analysis or subdivision; yet somehow they do not realistically represent Mark's energetic recital of the super-epic. Dr. Campbell Morgan's summation shows livelier imagina-tion. The introduction (i. 1–13) he calls *Sanctification*; chapters i. 14 to viii. 30 *Service*; and chapters viii. 31 to xvi. *Sacrifice*. His acute eye has caught the significant swerve of emphasis be-ginning at chapter viii. 31. Strangely, however, no prominence is given to the tremendous finale of the resurrection and ascension!

Getting inside the Story

Let us quickly go through Mark's chapters again, getting inside the story and asking all the time: What are the main significances which Mark himself intends shall arrest our minds?

Well, of course, straightway in the opening paragraphs those four voices startle us by their designation of this Jesus who now appears on the scene:

Mark—"Jesus Christ, the *SON OF GOD*."
Isaiah—"Prepare ye the way of *THE LORD*."
John—"There cometh *ONE MIGHTIER*."
GOD—"Thou art *MY BELOVED SON*."

Thereupon, the Galilean ministry begins; and Mark narrates it in suchwise that one must keep interjecting, "Yes, and *what* a ministry, too!" Miracle-exploits one after another break on us throughout chapter one. Chapters ii. and iii. pursue the march of marvels, showing also the surprising, unanswerable originality, not to say unconventionality, of the benign Miracle-worker's replies and pronouncements. Specimen parables follow briefly in chapter iv., but are quickly followed by even mightier miracles

—the quelling of the tempest; the expulsion of a whole demon "legion"; the curing of the incurable; and even the raising of the dead! Still more spectacular wonders follow in chapters vi., vii., viii.—the feeding of the five thousand by the creative multiplication of a few morsels; the nocturnal walk over the gale-swept sea; demonism, deafness and dumbness healed; and the feeding of the four thousand with the seven "loaves."

All this in so few chapters, with such energetic rapidity!—and punctuated by references to the electric effect on the populace, the ever-swelling crowds, the multiple healings, the utter discomfiture of the critical minority, and the rising tide of popularity:

"They were *astonished* at His doctrine" (i.22).

"And they were all *amazed*" (i. 27).

"His *fame spread abroad* throughout all the region" (I. 28).

"They came to Him *from every quarter*" (i. 45).

"Many were gathered together, insomuch that there *was no room to receive them*" (ii. 2).

"They were all *amazed*. . . . We never saw it *on this fashion* (ii. 12).

"All the *multitude* resorted unto Him" (ii. 13).

"A *great multitude* from Galilee followed Him, and from *Judæa*, and from *Jerusalem* and from *Idumæa*, and from *beyond Jordan*, and they about *Tyre* and *Sidon*; a great *multitude*, when they had heard what great things He did" (iii. 7, 8).

"The *multitude* . . . lest they should *throng* Him" (iii. 9).

"And unclean spirits . . . *fell down before Him*, and cried, Thou art the Son of God!" (iii. 11).

"The *multitude* cometh together again, so that they could not so much as eat bread" (iii. 20).

"He began again to teach . . . and there was gathered unto Him *a great multitude*" (iv. 1).

"What manner of Man is this, that *even the wind and the sea obey Him*? (iv. 41).

"*Much people* gathered unto Him" (v. 21).

"They were *astonished* with a *great astonishment*" (v. 42).

"The people ran afoot out of *all cities*, and came together unto Him" (vi. 33) (verse 44 shows they were thousands).

"They . . . ran through that *whole region* round about, and began to carry about in beds those that were sick, where they heard He was. And whithersoever He entered, into *villages or cities or country*, they laid the sick in the streets, and besought Him that they might touch if it were but the border of His garment: and *as many as touched Him were made whole!*" (vi. 55, 56).

"They were *beyond measure astonished*, saying, He hath done all things well!" (vii. 37).

So runs the incomparable story. The like had never been witnessed from the foundation of the world. This is truly the Son of the Blessed! This is indeed the Christ of Israel! This is at last the King long awaited! The kingdom of heaven has come! All are flocking to Him. The healed, the blessed, the grateful, the applauding are everywhere. Public acclaim has reached high-tide. Surely He will now be borne on a sheer flood of enthusiasm to the crown and sceptre which rightly belong to Him in Jerusalem!

But no; suddenly the light dims, the air chills; for at chapter viii. 31 we read (with utter surprise if we have really got "inside" the story):

"And He began to teach them that the Son of Man must *SUFFER* many things, and be *REJECTED* of the elders and of the chief priests, and scribes, and be *KILLED*."

To be sure, Matthew and Luke both record the same thing but not with the same divisive significance as Mark. It is Mark alone who comments: "And He spake that saying *OPENLY*." It was the publicity of it, accentuating the shock of it, which provoked Peter's remonstrance (verse 32); but our Lord's counter-reply was to make it even more public, for Mark adds in verse 34: "And when He had *called the PEOPLE*, with His disciples also, He said unto them: Whosoever will come after Me, let him deny himself, and take up *his* cross, and follow *Me*."

Well, there it is, right after the culminating avowal of the now convinced disciples: "Thou art the Christ." Just when it seems a peak-point is reached, hopes are dashed, and there comes this abrupt, astounding transition. Instead of a throne waiting at the capital, there is a cross! Instead of royal purple, a felon's death! That such an one as *HE* should be thus spurned, killed, shamed, and that *SUCH* a ministry of mighty works and gracious cures and super-wisdom should end in such ignominy, is an almost incredible incongruity: it is the most tragic refusal and enigma of the ages.

It is quite clear from the way Mark relates it that we are meant to see it so. The fact is, that although the disciples were deceived by appearances, and the multitudes by their own superficiality, the Prophet of Nazareth had seen right through the seeming to the real. He knew how unsubstantial was the popular clamour; how deeply influential the entrenched enmity of the Sanhedrin, leaders, scribes; and how unwilling the people were to respond in *heart* to the moral challenge of "the kingdom of God." The opposition had asserted itself from the outset; it was bitter and persistent (ii. 7, 16, 22, vii. 1, 2, viii. 11). Early in the narrative Jesus has spoken of "stony-ground" hearers, of those who become offended "when *persecution* ariseth for the word's sake," and of others in whom "the cares of this world choke the word." Already He has explained as a sad irony His use of parables: "That seeing they may see, and not perceive; and hearing they may hear, and not understand; lest at any time they should be converted, and their sins should be forgiven them" (iv. 12–19).

Nevertheless, the sudden change of aspect at chapter viii. 31 is staggering. Yet there is no mistaking it, for from that point onwards the cross is uppermost in our Lord's mind, and repeatedly on His lips (ix. 12, 31, x. 21, x. 32–4, 38, 45, xii. 7, 8, xiv. 8, 18, 22–5). In Mark's memoir it is "the great divide," so that the story falls into two vivid parts—the *MIGHTY WORKS* which He wrought (i. 14–viii. 30), and the *TRAGIC ENIGMA* of His rejection (viii. 31–xv.).

And now let us sum up. The key *idea* in Mark is that of our Lord as Jehovah's Servant, the mighty Worker. The key *verse* is chapter x. 45: "The Son of Man came not to be ministered unto, but to minister, and to give His life a ransom for many." The key *word* is "straightway." We may set the whole out as follows:

THE GOSPEL ACCORDING TO MARK

Key idea: Jesus Jehovah's Servant, the Mighty Worker.
Key verse: x. 45—"To minister . . . and give His life."
Key word: *Euthios*—"straightway," "immediately," etc.

Foreword: Four Voices Announce Him:
(i. 1–13)
"Son of God," "The Lord," "One Mightier," "My Son."

1. THE MIGHTY WORKS (i. 14–viii. 30).

First message and disciples
(i. 14–20).
First mighty works and effect
(i. 21–ii. 12).
First critics—and replies
(ii. 13–iii. 6).
Crowds flock: Twelve chosen
(iii. 7–19).
Scribes warned: reply to kin
(iii. 20–35).
Parables = few "good" hearers
(iv. 1–34).

More mighty works and effects
(iv. 35–vi. 6).
The Twelve endued and sent out
(vi. 7–13).
Herod's idea: the Twelve report
(vi. 14–31).
Still mightier mighty works
(vi. 32–56).
Critics; sighs; final signs
(vii. 1–viii. 26).
Avowal: "Thou art the Christ"
(viii. 27–30).

2. THE TRAGIC ENIGMA (viii. 31–xv.).

Strange new note: the Cross
(viii. 31–ix. 1).
Transfiguration: Cross again
(ix. 2–13).
Mighty miracle: Cross again
(ix. 14–32).
Apostles rebuked; counselled
(ix. 33–50).
Judæa again: sayings, doings
(x. 1–31).
To Jerusalem: Cross in view
(x. 32–52).

The triumphal entry: Day 1
(xi. 1–11).
Fig tree: Temple purge: ,, 2
(xi. 12–19).
Foes: Olivet prophecy: ,, 3
(xi. 20–xiii.).
Bethany—and betrayal: ,, 4
(xiv. 1–11).
Passover–Garden–Trial: ,, 5
(xiv. 12–72).
Pilate; Cross; Burial: ,, 6
(xv. 1–47).

Finale: Fourfold triumph (xvi.).
Risen (1–8). Appearing (9–18). Ascended (19). Working (20).

THE GOSPEL ACCORDING TO MARK (3)

Lesson Number 117

NOTE.—For this final instalment on Mark, look up every New Testament reference to Mark himself, with the aid of a concordance. Also read carefully again chapters i. and xvi , and Acts x.

AS TO AUTHORSHIP

It seems questionable whether any of our four Gospels originally bore either title or author's name. We are left in no doubt, however, about the authorship of this second Gospel. Right from sub-Apostolic days tradition firmly testifies three facts: (1) that a record of our Lord's words and works was written by one called Mark ; (2) that this record was what we now know as the Gospel according to Mark ; (3) that this Mark is the John Mark who figures in the Acts and the epistles of the New Testament. Such has been the view uniformly held. It is also the renewed verdict of present-day scholarship.

—J.S.B.

THE GOSPEL ACCORDING TO MARK (3)

IN THIS final contribution on the second Gospel we shall briefly advert to four matters of inherent interest: (1) its author himself; (2) its Petrine impress; (3) its first-intended readers; (4) its spiritual values.

About Mark Himself

Mark himself deservedly claims our eye. Doubtful at first, but likeable and laudable later, he is a stimulating study. See him first appear in Acts xii. 12. His mother's name, "Mary," indicates that she was Jewish. He himself had a Jewish forename and a Roman surname, "John" and "Mark"; so his father may have been a Roman. Their home was evidently large and a rendezvous for the early Christians. They were presumably well-to-do, as also Mark's uncle Barnabas seems to have been (Acts iv. 37).

In Acts xii. 25 Barnabas and Paul take Mark with them to Antioch, and later show their confidence by taking him on that first epic missionary journey (xiii. 5). Alas, when they reach Perga, on the frontiers of the great heathen world, his courage fails, and he returns home (xiii. 13). When Barnabas would take Mark again later, on a follow-up tour, Paul and he so disagree that they seperate; and Barnabas goes off with Mark to Cyprus (xv. 36–41).

From that point we hear no more of Barnabas; but Mark reappears in the epistles, and most commendably so. Nigh twenty years slip away. Paul, now a battle-scarred veteran, is in prison at Rome. He sends a letter to some Christian believers in a faraway little Phrygian town—the "Epistle to the Colossians." In chapter iv. 10 he says: "Aristarchus, my fellow-prisoner, saluteth you, *and Marcus, sister's son to Barnabas (touching whom ye received commandments: if he come unto you receive him)*." So Mark is still alive, still active for Christ, and with Paul again! Indeed, he is apparently purposing an evangelising visit to Asia Minor, the very place from which he had once turned back!

That, seemingly, is why Paul tells the Colossians, whose little town lay in Mark's possible line of travel: "If he should call on you, receive him."

But even more arresting is what Paul adds to this, in verse 11: "*These only* are my fellow-workers unto the kingdom of God, which have *been a comfort* unto me." Only three Jewish Christians in Rome have remained actively loyal to Paul, and one of those three is *Mark!*" Paul now speaks of him as a "*fellow-worker*" and "*a comfort*"! (See also Philemon 24.) So there is fullest restoration!

Again, in Paul's last letter before his martyrdom Mark is mentioned. Paul is still in prison. He has no companions now except Luke, "the beloved physician." In chapter iv. 9–11 he writes: "Do thy diligence to come shortly unto me: for Demas hath forsaken me, having loved this present world, and is departed into Thessalonica; Crescens to Galatia; Titus to Dalmatia. Only Luke is with me. *Take Mark, and bring him with thee, for he is profitable to me for the ministry.*" Yes, Paul was longing to have Mark by him again! Yes, for Mark had proved a loyal friend to him in Rome before. Yes, for Mark had now so proved his courageous devotion to Christ through the years that his early default at Perga was utterly erased!

Once again we find mention of Mark, this time by Peter. Turn to 1 Peter v. 13: "She that is elected with you at Babylon saluteth you, *and so doth Marcus, my son.*" This affectionate designation indicates that it was Peter (as might well be expected) who had begotten Mark as a convert to Christ: but it also shows that through all the years Mark had *proved* himself truly a "son" in the faith to Peter. There are clear evidences that there was a special bond between them, as we shall mention later.

But what had Mark been doing during all those years between that zero day at Perga and his reappearance in Paul's later epistles? Tradition which there is no reason to distrust tells of his remarkable ministry in Egypt, his winning many converts, and his founding the first Christian church at Alexandria. Yes, it was the once-turncoat Mark who invaded luxurious Alexandria, "glorious with marble temples to Serapis and Isis," with its renowned library and brilliant intellectuals eclipsing those of Rome itself!

Thus, not only was Mark gratefully reinstated by the greatest two apostles, but God Himself most signally attested his labours for the Lord. Nor is even that all, for the Spirit of God came specially upon this man, and by a supernatural inspiration used him as one of the four Gospel writers to whom we owe the priceless records of our Saviour's life on earth. What imperishable honour for the young man who once quailed and quaked and quit!

Moreover, this young man who once turned back is the same glorious martyr who, with deathless devotion to the dearest of all masters, gave himself to be dragged through the streets by exasperated Egyptians, flung bruised and bleeding into a dungeon, then burned to death.

Let our spirits be hushed; let our hearts be bowed; and let us give thanks to God for John Mark. How comfortingly he demonstrates that early failure can be retrieved, cancelled out, expunged, by later loyalty; that poor beginnings can give place to noble developments; that natural cowardice can be transformed to martyr-heroism through grace! "The greatest of all heroes is the coward who compels himself to be brave," says a schoolboy book of mine. "Many a ragged colt makes a noble horse," says Alexander Maclaren. Some of us would do well to take a good, long, steady look at John Mark!

> They on the heights are not the souls
> Who never erred or went astray,
> Or reached those high rewarding goals
> Along a smooth, flower-bordered way.
> Nay, they who stand where first comes dawn
> Are those who stumbled—but went on.

The Impress of Peter

As already remarked, there is a vividness of description and detail in this second Gospel which seems to betoken that the writer was actually an eye-witness of what he now records. We have given many instances and need not furnish others here. So autoptical do some of the incidental touches seem that we can only suppose them to have been related by one of the apostles or by someone directly transcribing an apostle. Who but a personal observer, an apostle, could have given us this?—

"And the same day, *when even was come,* He saith unto them: Let us pass over unto the other side. And when they had sent away the multitude, they took Him *even as He was* in the ship; and there were also with Him *other little ships.* And there arose a great storm of wind, and the waves *beat into* the ship so that it was now *being filled.* And He was in the *hinder part* of the ship, asleep *on a pillow.*"

In place after place, comparison of Mark with Matthew or Luke indicates the same first-hand familiarity with detail.

If, then, we were asked *which* of the leading apostles this Gospel reflects, what would be our reply? Would it be John, or James, or Andrew? No. Would it be Peter? Yes. Have we not sensed already how this second Gospel somehow suggests *Peter's* way of saying and doing things? There is the same forthright, intense, impulsive, sympathetic, energetic activity in Mark's *narrative* as there is in Peter's *nature.* Could this second Gospel be more accurately concentrated in a sentence than to call it an *"enlarged likeness"* of Peter's characteristic address to the household of Cornelius, in Acts x.?—

"The word . . . was published throughout all Judæa, and began from Galilee, after the baptism which John preached: how God anointed Jesus of Nazareth with the Holy Spirit and with power; who went about doing good, and healing all that were oppressed of the devil; for God was with Him," etc.

Furthermore, there is a similarity of nature between Peter and Mark which makes the latter the perfect penman of the former. In looking up the references to Mark, have we not found the same well-meaning, impulsive eagerness, offset by the same liability to sudden weakness, as in Peter? Both display earnest forwardness. Both default badly, early on, through collapse of courage: Peter denies his Lord—Mark deserts at Perga. But both recover and are restored, not only to bravest service but to outstanding leadership.

Still, if there were nothing more definite, we might dismiss these things as mere coincidences: but the fact is, that Peter's direct connection with Mark's Gospel is attested by reliable *external* witness. There is a *tradition,* going right back to sub-Apostolic days, that this second Gospel, although attributed to Mark, was, in reality, written by him as the *amanuensis of Peter*, or else as the translator and continuator of an original by Peter in Aramaic.

The most important evidence is that of Papias, bishop of Hierapolis in Phrygia, early in the second century. He wrote a book in five volumes, long since lost, *An Exposition of Oracles of the Lord*. But Eusebius, at the end of the third century, quotes three extracts from it in his *Ecclesiastical History*. Here are the first two:

Extract 1.

"Whatsover I have at any time accurately ascertained and treasured up in my memory, I have received it from the Elders, and have recorded it in order to give additional confirmation to the truth by my testimony. . . . If I met with anyone who had been a follower of the Elders anywhere, I made it a point to enquire what were the declarations of the Elders; what had been said by Andrew, Peter, or Philip; what by Thomas, James, John, Matthew, or any of the disciples of our Lord; what was said by Aristion and the presbyter John, disciples of the Lord; for I do not think that I derived so much benefit from books as by the living voice of those that were still surviving."

(It will be noted that this brings us quite close to the days of the Apostles, and gives his witness a corresponding weight.)

Extract 2.

"And John the presbyter also said this: Mark, being the interpreter of Peter, whatsover he recorded he wrote with great accuracy, but not however in the order in which it was spoken or done by our Lord; for he neither heard nor followed our Lord, but as before said, he was in company with Peter, who gave him such instruction as was necessary, but not to give a history of our Lord's discourses. Wherefore Mark has not erred in anything, by writing some things as he has recorded them; for he was carefully attentive to one thing: not to pass by anything that he heard, or to state anything falsely in these accounts."

My own view is that Mark was the compiler-translator of records already *written* by Peter, in *Aramaic*, many of them written at, or soon after, the actual times of the events and forming a kind of diary. I think, too, that others of the apostles would write similar synchronistic "memorabilia." However, whether that be so or not, Papias leaves us in no doubt as to the special impress of Peter on this "Gospel according to Mark." Indeed, Justyn Martyr in the middle of the second century quotes our Mark iii. 17 as from the *"Memoirs of Peter"*!

Now as soon as this community of production is appreciated, Mark's Gospel lives with new interests. It is *Peter's* story. Peter's quick eyes and ears and hands are everywhere in it. The narrative throbs with his energetic spirit. We see, too, why some things are *in*cluded and other things *ex*cluded about Peter himself. Run through the chapters again and see.

Chapter i. 29 says: "They entered into the house of Simon *and Andrew*." Just one of those touches peculiar to *this* Gospel and showing the hand of Peter, who knew that the house was one of joint tenancy with his brother and would have it carefully recorded so.

Matthew and Luke tell us that our Lord's Olivet discourse was in response to an inquiry by the disciples; but *this* Gospel says: *"Peter and James and John and Andrew* asked Him privately" (xiii. 3).

In chapter xi. 21 we are told that it was *Peter* who first noticed how quickly the fig tree had withered.

It is noticeable how certain incidents which reflect honour on Peter are omitted from *this* Gospel, from a motive which we can admire, knowing that this Gospel is Peter's account of things. There is no mention of his walking on the sea; no mention of the grateful benediction pronounced upon him when he avowed on behalf of the Twelve: "Thou are the Christ, the Son of the living God." In the resurrection account we do not find here, as in Luke, "The Lord is risen indeed, and hath *appeared to Simon*!" (Luke xxiv. 34). No, the honourable distinction is given to Mary Magdalene (Mark xvi. 9).

On the other hand, Peter's denial of his Lord is told most fully in Mark, with the added circumstance that it was not until "the *second* time the cock crew" that Peter suddenly "called to mind" the sad prediction of Jesus. Both Matthew and Luke say that Peter "went out and wept *bitterly*." In Mark it is only "And when he thought thereon, *he wept*," lest reference to the *bitterness* of his tears should seem an *affectation* of humility.

And, of course, there is that lovely final touch which is found only in Mark, and which the once fallen but lovingly restored Simon must have thrilled to record, namely, the first message sent from the empty sepulchre on the resurrection morning: "Go your way: tell His disciples, *and Peter*, that He goeth before you into Galilee" (xvi. 7). What those two little words "and Peter" must have meant to broken-spirited Simon, tongue could never tell; but with fond gratitude he makes sure that they are here preserved. As with other similar touches, they are like Peter's initials to the story, this time in the closing paragraph—a sort of parting reminder that this second Gospel is really "the Gospel according to Mark—*and Peter*"!

The First-intended Readers

Of equal interest is the question as to who were the first-intended readers of this second Gospel. It soon becomes plain that the writer has *Gentiles* in mind. If he had been writing for Jews, would he have used words such as in chapter vii. 3: "For the *Pharisees*, and all the *Jews*, except *they* wash their hands oft, eat not, holding the tradition of the elders"? Would he have explained that the "preparation" was "the day before the Sabbath" (xv. 42)?—or that the Mount of Olives was "over against the temple" (xiii. 3)?—or that the disciples of John and of the Pharisees "used to fast" (ii. 18)?

It has long been held that Mark wrote his Gospel in Greek, at Rome, for Gentile Christians there. This may well have been so, though our own view is somewhat otherwise. We do not doubt that he wrote it in Greek, but we incline to think that the place of writing was Palestine rather than Rome.

For one thing, the narrative seems to assume throughout that the readers are familiar with the *localities* of Palestine. There are no topographical explanations such as we find in Luke and would expect in Mark if written for readers in Rome.

Again, although the explanatory comments on *Jewish practices* indicate that the intended readers were not Jews, they seem equally to presuppose a *degree* of conversance with Jewish matters. To cite just one instance, the difference between the two closely connected feasts of Passover and Unleavened Bread is assumed known (xiv. 1). References here and there to other Jewish festivals and the Sabbath are made without any such comment as might have been expected for readers entirely strange to Jewry.

Well, *were* there such persons as hereby seem implied?—and, if so, *where* were they? The answer is: Yes, and they were in Palestine. Do not our minds immediately fly again to Acts x., to that "Gentile Pentecost," as someone has called it, when the Holy Spirit fell on the household of Cornelius, that "centurion of the Italian cohort," that "devout man which feared God with all his house"? Were there not *many* such Gentiles, Romans, in Palestine? Were there not many of them who had become proselytes to the Jewish faith—and then gone the further step of becoming Christians? Were there not those many who thus knew Palestine fairly well, who had first-hand acquaintance with Jewish religious matters, though not an intimate knowledge of them? May we not well assume that during the years following Pentecost there were many conversions among foreign residents in Palestine, both military and civil?

Was there not a need, then, to issue a "Gospel" record for *those* persons—just as much as Matthew's for the Jews, and Luke's for the Gentiles? Somehow, those Palestine non-Jewish proselytes to Judaism and converts to Christianity seem to belong *between* outright Jews and outright Gentiles; and that is where John Mark seems to fit, too, if as seems likely he was of both Jewish and Roman parenthood. He would have a dominant interest in those Palestine Gentiles, Romans, proselytes, Christians; and an aptitude to write the kind of record best adapted to them. This, incidentally, would account for the numerous Latinised expressions in Mark's Gospel.

But, even so, is it *likely* that our Jew-Gentile John Mark would write his Gospel in Palestine? It certainly is. We have already seen the close association of Mark with Peter. Well, wherever Peter may have travelled in his latest years, we know for certain that he remained in Palestine at least twenty years after Pentecost. We know, too, that Mark was there until he set out with Paul and Barnabas on that first missionary journey; that when he deserted them at Perga he "returned to Jerusalem"; and that he was apparently there until his uncle took him to Cyprus some eight years later. So for twenty years after Pentecost Palestine was Mark's abode.

Another consideration which seems to cast doubt on the tradition that Mark wrote either at Rome or Babylon, and reproduced the substance of Peter's oral teaching, is that Peter's preaching *there* would certainly be in *Greek*, whereas Mark's Gospel is manifestly a translation from *Aramaic*.

Doubtless, when his Gospel became more freely circulated, Roman Christians going back to Rome from Palestine would carry their copies of it with them, which would explain how the idea first grew that he actually wrote it in Rome. The real evidences, so we believe, are that he wrote it in Palestine for the type of persons we have described.

If so, then how appropriate that Mark's is the *"second"* Gospel! There are some who seem to think it a sign of scholarship to put Mark first and Matthew after it. No! *Matthew* must come first— "to the Jew first"—being the obvious first link-up of the New Testament with the Old. And Luke must come *third*—"also to the Gentile"—because Mark is the *between* Gospel for Gentile-Jews, i.e. those who were Gentiles by birth and Jews by faith; and because it was specially adapted to that transition period when the Gospel was moving out from Jewish exclusiveness, as in Matthew, to a racial outlook, as in Luke. Leave Mark where we now have him, please! His proper place is *between* Matthew and Luke!

Those Last Twelve Verses

Almost certainly someone asks: What about those last twelve verses of this Gospel? Are they genuine—or spurious? How we wish the question could be answered as easily as it is asked! That Mark ended at verse 8, with the words, "for they were afraid," thus breaking off with a strange anti-climax and leaving the resurrection finale patently incomplete, is unthinkable; the more so on grammatical grounds, i.e. (in the Greek) the final word is the little conjunction "for."

The "Scofield" note *in loco* rightly says: "The passage from verse 9 to the end is not found in the two most ancient manuscripts, the Sinaitic and Vatican, and others have it with partial omissions and variations. But it is quoted by Irenæus and Hyppolytus in the second or third century." It might have been added that the Vatican manuscript *does* have a *space* left after our verse 8, indicating a *known* absence of some completive portion. And, as the Angus *Bible Handbook* says: "The overwhelming mass of MSS., versions and Fathers are in favour of the verses." Moreover, doubt concerning them does not seem to have been expressed until the fourth century. But for an excellent summary of the matter see the latest edition of the Angus *Bible Handbook*.

My own view, believing as I do that the apostles made synchronistic *written* records of our Lord's sayings and doings, is that at verse 8 Mark came to the end of Peter's own written memorabilia, and that the rapid but telling summary which follows was Mark's own. There is the same quick transition from one scene to another, and the whole is notably in keeping with all that precedes. It may be that for this reason some of the early copyists omitted it; or it could be that Mark himself appended it some little time after his first transcribing had gone forth. This would account for its being in some copies and not in others.

Rich Spiritual Values

The more closely one studies this Gospel of Mark, the more fascinating it becomes. Besides quick movement and graphic detail, there is a perfect genius of saying much in fewest words. It is amazing how much is said in how little. Take chapter i. 13, as simply one instance: "He was there in the wilderness forty days, tempted of Satan; and was with the wild beasts; and the angels ministered unto Him."

This Gospel, also, is singularly rich in its spiritual lessons and illustrations. They are everywhere, but we can here give only one as a sample of the many.

Turn to the first chapter, verses 9–13. We have been saying that Mark's is the Gospel of Jesus as Jehovah's Servant, the *perfect* Servant. Let us not forget that He is to us the *pattern* Servant, the ideal Example of service, whom we ourselves are to follow. From the very first verses this significance attaches to Him. In the paragraph which we have indicated (i. 9–13) we see the *commencement* of His public ministry, or, rather, the *preparation* which was necessary immediately prior to it. How eloquently and seriously these verses speak to all of us who would truly serve the heavenly Master! They show that there are four indispensable prerequisites to all effective Christian service.

1. *A Preliminary Separation* (verse 9)

Our Lord's *baptism* was His initial, deliberate separation of Himself to His public Messianic ministry. This separation was twofold. There was (*a*) a separation *from* His former kind of life; (*b*) a separation *to* His new ministry of teaching and healing: and utter separation to God. That is also the first prerequisite for *us*.

2. *A Preliminary Anointing* (verse 10)

Our Lord (*a*) *saw* something, i.e. "the heavens opened"; (*b*) *felt* something—"the Spirit descending upon Him." That also is the second prerequisite for *us*. We must know the heavens "opened" to our praying, and the enduement with "power from on high."

3. *A Preliminary Assuring* (verse 11)

Our Lord at Jordan received a preliminary assuring (*a*) as to *sonship*—"Thou art My beloved Son"; (*b*) as to *character*—"in whom I am well pleased." That is the third prerequisite for *us*. We need the inwrought assurance of the Holy Spirit, and motives well-pleasing to God.

4. *A Preliminary Testing* (verses 11, 12)

There are two things to note about this preliminary tempting of our Lord: (*a*) It was Divinely *sanctioned*, i.e. "The Spirit driveth Him"; (*b*) it was real temptation—"of Satan." Strange though it may seem, even the entirely separated, Spirit-anointed, Heaven-attested Servant must undergo this preliminary testing, to settle it whether He will go only and utterly *God's* way—or man's.

Let all who would serve the Lord of heaven, in this sinful world, observe carefully those four prerequisites. The question of all questions for the Christian is: Am I really willing to yield myself here and now to Christ for His will alone to be done through my life?

As for Mark's Gospel, it is simply full of these compact, significant, eloquent *incidents*. Wanted!—new explorers!

TRY THESE FEW QUESTIONS

1. Can you add the final word to the following sentence?—
   "Mark's is distinctively the Gospel of what Jesus . . ."

2. What is the special aspect of our Lord in Mark? Could you
   mention certain omissions and additions which indicate it?

3. Can you recall some of the extra details and vivid touches
   supplied by Mark?

4. Four voices announce our Lord in Mark's preface. Which are
   they, and what titles do they give our Lord?

5. What are the two main parts into which Mark's account falls?
   Why does Mark's Gospel aptly fit between Matthew's and
   Luke's?

6. Can you summarise what the New Testament reveals to us
   about Mark?

7. Can you give two good reasons why it seems certain that
   Mark's Gospel bears the impress of Peter?

8. What incidental touches or omissions suggest Peter's influence?

9. Who, do you think, were Mark's first-intended readers, and
   why?

10. Where do you think Mark wrote his Gospel? Please give
    reasons for your reply.

THE GOSPEL ACCORDING TO LUKE (1)

Lesson Number 118

NOTE.—For this study read right through Luke's Gospel at least twice.

LUKE'S GENEALOGY

Much might be said about Luke's genealogy of our Lord; but perhaps even this brief note may be of use to some. *Matthew's* genealogy uses the word "begat," right down the list until "Jacob begat *Joseph* the husband of Mary." So, clearly, Matthew's genealogy is that of *Joseph*, who, besides being (only) legally the father of our Lord, was of Davidic descent. *Luke's* genealogy does not use "begat." It begins: "And Jesus himself began to be about thirty years of age, being (as was supposed) the son of Joseph which was *the son of* Heli, which was *the son of* Matthat, which was *the son of* . . .," etc. Joseph was not the *offspring* of Heli, but of Jacob (as shown by Matthew's "begat"), but he had become a son of Heli in another and very real Jewish sense by his marriage to Mary. In old-time Jewish genealogies, when a link in the chain of descent was carried on through a woman, her husband's name was inserted instead of her own, and he thereby became something more than a son-in-law, and was called "the son of . . ." Undoubtedly, in Luke we are given *Mary's* lineage. *Both* our Lord's parents were of Davidic descent. It is interesting to note how Luke's genealogy at both ends refutes the popular evolution theory. He goes right back to Adam, but stops there, for man was not before Adam. Moreover, the doctrines of the New Testament depend for their validity upon the unity of the race in and from that one man. At *this* end is Christ—millions of years before His time, if a product of evolution!—for if our race should progress for another thousand million years it could never pass beyond that perfect character of two thousand years ago!

—*J.S.B.*

THE GOSPEL ACCORDING TO LUKE (1)

As we studied our way through the second Gospel we found ourselves saying, "How different is Mark from Matthew!" In pressing on through this third Gospel, we cannot help exclaiming: "How different is Luke from either!" Though all three cover the same ground, yet other than the dullness of repetition there is the fascination of illuminating variation. Not only is the individuality of each evangelist distinguishingly stamped upon all he tells us, but we gradually become aware that "this same Jesus" on whom they all focus is being exhibited to us in different lights and shades with an exquisite subtlety which is more than human.

"Behold the Man"

In Matthew He is the *King*. In Mark He is the *Servant*. In Luke, behold the *Man*. These different emphases or aspects can be overstated, but they can scarcely be overlooked, for they are really there. We are far from suggesting that each of the four Gospel-writers wrote with a clearly formed intention of conforming our Lord to any one of the four aspects which now characterise the four Gospels respectively. Nothing truer was ever said than that those four penmen wrote with "the simplicity of men whose desire is to let their story speak for itself, and who never dream of twisting it to suit their own views." Moreover, they wrote independently of each other, and could have had no idea of the ultimate fourfold design which their memoirs would collectively comprise. Yet it seems equally true that each had a certain class of readers primarily in view, selecting and using his material accordingly; while behind and above them all was the Holy Spirit Himself, supernaturally conducing their willing pens to expedite the *Divine* pattern of their fourfold presentation.

So, then, in Matthew He is Israel's *King*; in Mark He is Jehovah's *Servant*; in Luke He is the perfect *Man*. In Matthew we have significant *groupings*. In Mark we have successive *snapshots*. In Luke we have a beautifully told *story*.

Luke's Fourfold Story

Yes, "a beautifully told story"—that is what it is. Renan described it as "the most beautiful book ever written." Luke has the pen of a gentleman and an artist. An old tradition has it that he was a painter. We doubt the tradition, but appreciate that he was an artist in words, a painter of pen-pictures which, alas, translation from one language into another inevitably blurs.

When we explored Mark we found ourselves diverted from drafting out a preliminary analysis. We soon saw that literary divisions were quite secondary to the vivid scenes and rapid transitions which were intended to hold the reader's mind. In fact it was the engrossing idiosyncrasies of that second Gospel which eventually led us to an analysis in keeping with the type and spirit of it.

How different is it with Luke! We scarcely read through the chapters once without seeing the clear arrangement into parts or movements; and a continued re-reading confirms our first impression. So, then, let us go through this third Gospel, noting down those things which first impress us, marking its main divisions, and then abstracting an analysis. In this way we shall catch the meaning and harmony of the story as a whole.

The first feature which detains us, of course, is Luke's *nativity narrative*. It has no parallel in the other Gospels. Mark and John tell nothing at all about our Lord's advent at Bethlehem. Matthew does; but although he supplies data untouched by Luke, he does not describe, as Luke does, the birth, babyhood, boyhood; and his account is only a quarter the length of Luke's.

Then comes Luke's report of our Lord's *ministry in Galilee*, noticeably shorter than either Matthew's or Mark's, and followed by a further peculiarity which none can miss, namely, the long chronicle of our Lord's *journey to Jerusalem*. In contrast with only two chapters in Matthew and one in Mark, it extends through no less than *ten* chapters in Luke, thereby forming the longest part of the story (ix. 51–xix. 44). There can be no doubt that all these chapters belong to that last journey. Seven times the writer inserts comments which imply it:

"He steadfastly set His face *to go to Jerusalem*" (ix. 51).
"He went through the cities and villages, teaching, and journeying *toward Jerusalem*" (xiii. 22).

"And it came to pass, as He went to Jerusalem" (xvii. 11).
"Behold, we go up to Jerusalem" (xviii. 31; see also
xix. 11, 28, 37).

In neither Matthew nor Mark is there any parallel to this slow, protracted trek to Jerusalem. It has been called "The Great Insertion."

Thus we see at once that whereas the Gospels by Matthew and Mark are each in two clear parts—the ministry in Galilee, and the climax in Judæa—Luke's memoir runs in *four* unmistakable movements:

1. The nativity, boyhood, manhood   (i. 5–iv. 13).
2. The itineratings in Galilee   (iv. 14–ix. 50).
3. The journey up to Jerusalem   (ix. 51–xix. 44).
4. The final tragedy and triumph (xix. 45–xxiv.).

The Characteristic Aspect

But no sooner do we see this than we begin to sense how in keeping it is with the characteristic *aspect* of Jesus in this third Gospel.

If we ask *why* Luke lingers over his nativity narrative, the reply begins already to form itself for us. Luke is peculiarly concerned with the human nature, the *manhood* of our Lord, so he must needs tell us more particularly about the wonderful birth and babyhood and boyhood. Matthew's briefer account is rather from the standpoint of how the birth fulfils prophecy, but Luke's special interest is in the actual babyhood and boyhood.

Matthew and Luke each give a long genealogy showing our Lord's ancestry, but Matthew puts his right at the beginning of his Gospel, whereas Luke does not insert it until after the baptism in Jordan. Why? It is because the first-important thing with Matthew is to establish our Lord's Davidic lineage, whereas Luke's first concern is the real human birth and the growth through boyhood to the perfect manhood.

Similarly in keeping, Matthew gives the genealogy through *Joseph,* who was legally, though not actually, the father of Jesus; whereas Luke gives it through *Mary,* who really *was* the mother of His manhood.

Again, Matthew starts the genealogy at Abraham and traces it down through David, for his purpose is to show Jesus as the fulfilment of promise and the lineal heir to the throne; whereas Luke presses right back to *Adam,* as though, even in a genealogy, he wishes to transcend any suggestion of confinement merely to Jewish connection, and to show the *racial* relationship of Jesus— exactly where and how He appeared in the race's history. Luke *could* have gone back *beyond* Adam, of course (as John does); but no, although he must needs travel away back beyond Israel's covenant king and covenant patriarch, he stops with the first *man.*

Fragmentary Galilee Chapters.

It is his special interest in our Lord's manhood which explains also why Luke's rendering of our Lord's Galilean ministry (iv. 14– ix. 50) is so much shorter than in Matthew or Mark; and why, in compensation, he gives such a long, leisurely diary of the winding journey to Jerusalem (ix. 51–xix. 44). The order (or, as some argue, *mis*order) of Luke's materials in both these sections, as compared with Matthew and Mark, is the perplexity of scholars and the despair of harmonists—from intermeddling with which let us here gratefully excuse ourselves; but certainly our third evangelist has selected and dovetailed his data in suchwise as to bring out the Master's manhood with subtle charm to those Greek or Greek-minded readers whom he seems to have had foremost in mind.

Whereas the emphasis in Matthew is on what Jesus *said,* and in Mark on what Jesus *did,* here in Luke it is rather on *Jesus Himself.* In his short record of the Galilean ministry Luke gives about equal space to our Lord's deeds and words, so that neither is emphasised above the other, and both equally reflect back on the Wonder-Man Himself. See how the marvellous ministry of message and miracle *begins,* with Jesus in the synagogue at Nazareth (recorded *only* by Luke), and with emphasis at once on the manhood of Jesus Himself:

"The Spirit of the Lord is upon *ME,* because He hath anointed *ME* to preach the Gospel to the poor. . . . And the eyes of all in the synagogue were *fastened on HIM.* . . . This day is this Scripture fulfilled in your ears. And all bare witness and wondered at the gracious words which proceeded out of His mouth. And they said: Is not this Joseph's son?"

See how, in chapter v., after the miraculous draught of fishes (again recorded *only* by Luke), Peter suddenly discerns the awful holiness of that wonderful manhood and prostrates himself before Jesus, crying out: "Depart from me, for I am a sinful man, O Lord!"

See how, in chapter vii. (recorded *only* by Luke), as the widowed mother weeps her way out through the gate of Nain to bury her only son, the compassionate sympathy at once wells up in the tender-hearted Son of Mary as He says to her, "Weep not," and restores her loved one to life.

See how, again in chapter vii. (recorded *only* by Luke), the "woman which was a sinner," perceiving in that perfect manhood not only utter purity but a human understanding and compassion for which her desolate heart had ached, bathed His feet with her tears.

All these instances are peculiar to Luke, and they serve to introduce this emphasis on the *human*, which we can only mention here but shall examine in our next study.

Journal of Jerusalem Journey.

It is the same with the extended narration of our Lord's journey to Jerusalem (ix. 51–xix. 44). In all these chapters only five miracles are reported—as against twenty-one (fifteen single, six plural) in the earlier few chapters covering the Galilee ministry; and there is not even one discourse of a set or lengthy kind (unless we so regard the tri-parable of the lost sheep, the lost coin, and the prodigal son, in chapter xv.). Instead, there is an unwinding miscellany of memorable sayings and doings, gracious replies and forthright rebukes, occasional miracles and compelling parables; yet all cohere (with a beauty unsuspected perhaps at first) in exhibiting, from different angles, and under different lights, and in different attitudes, the mind and heart of *that matchless Man*.

Whatever problems may be created for Biblical criticism by Luke's seemingly unchronological order of narration, one thing which immediately charms our grateful eyes is that in these ten or eleven chapters he has collected and preserved for us a simply priceless treasury of sayings, parables and incidents unrecorded by any of the other three Gospel writers. There are no less than thirty or more such, and here they are:

Anger of John and James rebuked	ix.	51–6.
Plough simile to would-be follower	ix.	61–2.
The seventy sent ahead of Him	x.	1–12.
Return and report of the seventy	x.	17–20.
Parable of the good Samaritan	x.	25–37.
The cumbered Martha corrected	x.	38–42.
Parable of importunate friend	xi.	5–10.
Parable of presuming rich fool	xii.	13–21.
Reply about those slain by Pilate	xiii.	1–5.
Parable of the fruitless fig tree	xiii.	6–9.
Woman loosed from her infirmity	xiii.	10–17.
Reply to Pharisees concerning Herod	xiii.	31–3.
Sabbath cure of man with dropsy	xiv.	1–6.
Parable about guests and inviters	xiv.	7–14.
Parable of the great supper	xiv.	15–24.
Simile: intending tower-builder	xiv.	28–30.
Further simile: war-making king	xiv.	31–33.
Trio-parable (2) the lost coin	xv.	8–10.
Trio-parable (3) the wayward son	xv.	11–32.
Parable of the unjust steward	xvi.	1–15.
Account of rich man and Lazarus	xvi.	19–31.
Illustration: master *v.* servant	xvii.	7–10.
The healing of the ten lepers	xvii.	11–19.
Reply concerning kingdom of God	xvii.	20–1.
Parable of unrighteous judge	xviii.	1–8.
Parable of Pharisee and publican	xviii.	9–14.
Jericho: conversion of Zacchæus	xix.	1–10.
Parable of pounds and servants	xix.	11–27.
The Saviour weeps over Jerusalem	xix.	41–4.

One only needs to glance down that list to realise at once what a wealth we have in these chapters. Why, to mention only the parables of the good Samaritan, the great supper, the prodigal son, the Pharisee and the publican, without referring to the other parables, miracles, incidents and sayings, is enough to indicate the preciousness of it all. We cannot do without Matthew. We certainly must have Mark. But, oh, with this jewel-chain of exclusive memorabilia before us, could we ever part with Luke?

It is not only the intrinsic worth of these parables, miracles, incidents, which makes them mean so much to us: it is the way they reveal *HIM*. One after another they come, like so many successive floodlights of different colour turned on an object of supreme attractiveness. We shall see more fully in our next study how all bear on the *human nature* of our Lord; but even a first survey leaves some impression of this in the mind of a thoughtful reader.

Without going into detail just here, think what human feeling, sympathy, largeness, compassion, breathes through the parables of the good Samaritan, the prodigal son, the Pharisee and the publican; the reply to James and John when they would have called down fire on the Samaritans; the rebuke which silenced the little-minded synagogue ruler when the infirm woman was healed on the Sabbath: "Doth not each one of you on the Sabbath loose his ox or his ass from the stall? And ought not this woman, being a daughter of Abraham, whom Satan hath bound, lo, these eighteen years, be loosed from *this* bond on the Sabbath day?" How startlingly brotherly and big-hearted are His words both to and about Zacchæus! How melting His human emotion and tears "when He beheld the city"!

For the moment, however, we have said enough about this characteristic aspect of our Lord in Luke's Gospel. We have willingly lingered over it as one of the first distinguishing traits which attract us, and shall gladly return to it later. Meanwhile, we have grasped enough of the general "spread" of Luke's story to be able to make a useful analysis.

Lay-out of Parts and Whole

Part One

As already noted, Luke's pre-nativity and post-nativity records (i. 5–iv. 13) are more than an introduction—they form the first phase of his fourfold story. They cover a period of thirty years; for as Luke (alone) tells us in chapter iii. 23, Jesus was about thirty years of age when He underwent His Jordan baptism. The first two chapters cover the first twelve years (see ii. 42). Then, after a break of another eighteen years, we are at the Jordan to see the baptism of Jesus by John, and in the wilderness to witness the temptation of Jesus by Satan.

The chapters are woven into an interesting pattern. Over the first two we may write: *"In the days of Herod."* Over the next two we may write: *"Thirty years later."* In the first two we have the two annunciations by the angel Gabriel—one to Zacharias concerning John, the other to Mary concerning Jesus (i. 5–38). Next, we see the two elect mothers, Elisabeth and Mary, brought together, and hear them breaking forth into inspired prophesying (i. 39–56). Then the two wonder-births are narrated—of John and Jesus (i. 57–ii. 52). The remaining chapters obviously break up into the ministry of John (iii. 1–22), the genealogy through Mary (iii. 23–38), and the onset by Satan (iv. 1–13). We may set it out thus:

"In the days of Herod"	*Thirty years later*
The two annunciations— by Gabriel (i. 5–38).	Ministry by John: baptism of Jesus (iii. 1–22).
The two elect mothers— Elisabeth, Mary (i. 39–56).	Genealogy by Mary: lineage of Jesus (iii. 23–38).
The two wonder-sons— John, Jesus (i. 57–ii. 52).	Onset by Satan: testing of Jesus (iv. 1–13).

Part Two

After the inceptive anointing and testing, the Galilean ministry begins at chapter iv. 14, with the words: "And Jesus returned in the power of the Spirit into Galilee: and there went out a fame of Him through all the region round about." This second phase of the story runs to chapter ix. 50, after which the longer narrative of the travel to Jerusalem begins.

The short account of the ministry in Galilee breaks up into *itinerations* (iv. 14–ix. 17) and *culminations* (ix. 18–50). First there are our Lord's itinerations *before* His choosing of the twelve apostles (iv. 14–vi. 11); then further ministries *after* "the twelve were with Him" (vi. 12–viii. 56); then multiplied ministry by means of *sending forth* the Twelve (ix. 1–17).

Peter's *confession* of Jesus as "The Christ of God" (ix. 18) marks a break. It was spoken representatively for all the twelve apostles, and was in reply to a direct question by the Lord, who knew that He must now turn in the direction of Jerusalem. So much depended on what those twelve men had come to believe about Him by that time. In one vital respect our Lord was now assured of them, and from then onwards He introduced—though much to their sad perplexity—the intimation of His coming rejection and inflicted death.

That confession was a culmination. So also was the *transfiguration* which now followed on the mountain height (ix. 27–36). The one was a human acknowledgement of Him as the Christ of Israel. The other was a Divine attestation of Him as the Son of God. That voice from heaven had spoken once before, at His baptism: "This is My beloved Son; in whom I am well pleased," thereby attesting the perfect sinlessness of the preceding thirty years and of the now adult manhood of Jesus. Here, at the transfiguration, that voice attests not only the continued sinlessness of His life but the infallibility of His lips. He is not only the perfect *character*; He is the perfect *Messenger*—"This is My beloved Son: *hear Him.*" Already His perfect manhood is ready for the society of heaven; Moses and Elias "appear in glory" on the mount to converse with Him. Without any need for death, that innocent and holy humanity of His could at once pass into the heavenly sphere and glory, as His transfiguring metamorphosis suddenly showed. Yes, the voice spoke at His baptism—at the end of the thirty years, as He faced His public mission; and now it gives Divine endorsement at the end of the Galilean ministry, as He sets His face toward His passion-baptism at Jerusalem.

Following the transfiguration comes the last public miracle before the journey actually begins, through Galilee, Samaria, Peræa and Judæa, to Jerusalem. It is a conclusive exhibition of invincible power over the forces of evil. Even the disciples had been defied and repulsed by the demon intelligence possessing the young demoniac (ix. 37–50) and could not dislodge it. The father appeals in very agony to Jesus: "Master, I beseech Thee, look upon my *son,* for he is mine *only child.*" Jesus says: "Bring thy son hither." The demoniac son is brought; but "even as he was yet coming, the devil threw him down, and tare him." Their eyes meet, that only-begotten Son of the *heavenly* Father, and that only-begotten son of an *earthly* father; the One fresh from a supernatural transfiguration by the indwelling *Holy* Spirit, the other even now gnashing and disfigured by an indwelling *evil* spirit! A look! A word!—and Satan's hold snaps, the demon flees, the son is healed! No wonder that "they were all amazed at the mighty power of God"!

It is noteworthy that with each of these three culminations there is a reference to *the Cross*. As soon as Peter has made his confession, our Lord says: "The Son of Man must suffer many things, and be rejected of the elders and chief priests and scribes, and be slain; and be raised the third day" (ix. 22). When Moses and Elias appeared at the transfiguration they spoke of "His decease which He should accomplish at Jerusalem" (ix. 31). And after the release of the demoniac son we read: "But while they wondered every one at all things which Jesus did, He said unto His disciples: Let these sayings sink down into your ears; for the Son of Man shall be delivered into the hands of men" (ix. 43, 44).

So, then, we may set out these chapters on the Galilean ministry thus:

Itinerations	*Culminations*
Miracles; sayings: before Twelve chosen (iv. 14–vi. 11).	Peter's confession— Cross foretold (ix. 18–26).
Teachings; miracles: after Twelve chosen (vi. 12–viii.).	The transfiguration— Cross foretold (ix. 27–36).
Multiplied operations: Twelve sent out (ix. 1–17).	Last public miracle— Cross foretold (ix. 37–50).

Part Three

Little need be added here to what we have already said about this lengthier part of Luke's story (ix. 51–xix. 44)—fewness of miracles, frequency of parables, and so on. But a further mentionable feature is that most of the memorable sayings and practically all the parables are *replies*. Look them through once again and see. Our Lord was supreme in the art of reply. How much might be learned by studying His replies as such!

Also, these chapters break into two almost equal sections— the one ending with our Lord's *first* lament over Jerusalem (xiii. 34, 35), the other with His *second* lament (xix. 41–4).

Moreover, His enigmatical *prefix* to that first lament, at the end of chapter xiii., conveys that the far longer round-about of the journey was now behind, and Jerusalem only some days ahead—"I must walk today and tomorrow and the day following; for it cannot be that a prophet perish out of Jerusalem." Chapter xvii. 11 confirms this, telling us that Jesus now travelled *between* Galilee and Samaria, i.e. to cross Jordan into Peræa, then back across into Judæa at Jericho. We know, too, that our Lord's blessing of infants, and the incident of the rich young ruler, which Luke goes on to record, happened just before the entering of Jericho (compare with Matthew and Mark). So we may now set out part three as follows:

The earlier weeks	*The last few days*
Missioners sent: answers, parables (ix. 51–xi. 12).	Galilee: dropsy cured. Sayings (xiv. 1–xvii. 10).
Pharisees warned: rebukes, parables (xi. 13–xii. 12).	Samaria: lepers cured. Sayings (xvii. 11–xviii. 34).
Covetous reproved: woman healed (xii. 13–xiii. 21).	Jericho: blind man: Zacchæus. Sayings (xviii. 35–xix. 27).
Jesus urged away: Lament over Jerusalem (xiii. 22–35).	Jerusalem: ascent: Lament over Jerusalem (xix. 28–44).

Part Four

This fourth and last movement runs from chapter xix. 45 to the end of chapter xxiii. It begins with our Lord in the temple, and ends with Him in the tomb. It breaks into two: (1) *before* the arrest; (2) *after* the arrest. In the first of these (xix. 45–xxi. 4) we see Jesus in collision with the hostile Jewish leaders; then on Olivet with His disciples, foretelling the future; then at the Last Supper, and in Gethsemane. In the second, we see Jesus before the high priest and the Sanhedrin; then before Pilate and Herod; then on the Cross and in the grave.

Such is Luke's story—all but the lovely splendour of the last chapter on the Lord's resurrection and ascension! So we may now bring together the parts and set out the whole of it in broad but useful analysis. Let us do so in such a way as suits its *story* form, heading each of the four main parts with the very words which Luke himself uses at the successive stages of his narrative.

THE GOSPEL ACCORDING TO LUKE

Explanatory foreword: i. 1–4.

1. "GOOD TIDINGS"—A SAVIOUR (i. 5–iv. 13)

In the days of Herod

The two annunciations—
by Gabriel (i. 5–38).
The two elect mothers—
Elisabeth; Mary (i. 39–56).
The two wonder-sons—
John; Jesus (i. 57–ii. 52).

Thirty years later

Ministry by John: baptism
of Jesus (iii. 1–22).
Genealogy by Mary: lineage
of Jesus (i. 23–38).
Onset by Satan: testing
of Jesus (iv. 1–13).

2. "IN THE SPIRIT"—GALILEE (iv. 14–ix. 50)

Itinerations

Miracles; sayings: before
Twelve chosen (iv. 14–vi. 11).
Teachings; miracles: after
Twelve chosen (vi. 12–viii.).
Multiplied operations: the
Twelve sent out (ix. 1–17).

Culminations

Peter's Confession: Cross
foretold (ix. 18–26).
Jesus transfigured: Cross
foretold (ix. 27–36).
Demoniac son cured: Cross
foretold (ix. 37–50).

3. "HE SET HIS FACE"—JERUSALEM (ix. 51–xix. 44)

The earlier weeks

Messengers sent on: answers,
parables (ix. 51–xi. 12).
Pharisees warned: rebukes,
parables (xi. 13–xii. 12).
Covetous reproved: woman
healed (xii. 13–xiii. 21).
Jesus urged away: Lament
over Jerusalem (xiii. 22–35).

The last few days

Galilee: dropsy cured;
sayings (xiv. 1–xvii. 10).
Samaria: lepers cured;
sayings (xvii. 11–xviii. 34).
Jericho: blind: Zacchæus;
sayings (xviii. 35–xix. 27).
Jerusalem; ascent; Lament
over Jerusalem (xix. 28–44).

4. "THIS IS THE HEIR—KILL HIM" (xix. 45–xxiii.)

Before the arrest

Jesus versus priest, scribe,
Sadducee (xix. 45–xxi. 4).
Jesus foretells the future;
Olivet address (xxi. 5–38).
Last Passover; Gethsemane;
betrayal (xxii. 1–53).

After the arrest

Jesus before high priest and
council (xxii. 54–71).
Jesus before Pilate: Herod:
mocked (xxiii. 1–12).
Jesus sentenced, crucified,
buried (xxiii. 13–56).

Resurrection!—Promise!—Ascension!

THE GOSPEL ACCORDING TO LUKE (2)

Lesson Number 119

NOTE.—For this second instalment on Luke, pick out and read carefully again all the parables and miracles.

WHAT ABOUT THEOPHILUS?

Luke addresses his Gospel and the Acts to the "most excellent Theophilus." It has been held that this Theophilus (or "friend of God") was not a real person but a fictitious artifice by which Luke covertly addressed *all* Christians. We are told that about the time Luke wrote there was inflamed Jewish hostility, and that he therefore used this cryptogram to "divert the attention of an enemy" from the real persons he had in mind, especially Mary, who was still in the danger zone. We reject the supposition as unrealistic and unnecessary. All the internal indications are that Luke did not write primarily for Palestine disciples. None can pin-point either when or where Luke's Gospel first appeared, or say with certainty whether Mary was alive or not. Moreover, the use of such fictions is foreign to the sacred writers; and in any case, to have written *no* dedication would have been safer than a *bogus* one. Why is it that Luke is so careful to explain the locality of places in Palestine if writing to Jews there?— "A city of Galilee named Nazareth"; "Capernaum, a city of Galilee"; "Arimathea, a city of the Jews"; "Emmaus, which was from Jerusalem about three-score furlongs," etc. And why is it that as soon as his narrative reaches Sicily and Italy he names places without a word about location, unless the person written to was a dweller out that way? We may take it that Theophilus was a real person, with a lovely though not uncommon name, a man of high rank in the Roman world, and a convert to our Lord Jesus. Oh, for many more such!

—*J.S.B.*

THE GOSPEL ACCORDING TO LUKE (2)

ONE OF the most enjoyable preliminaries—and one of the most necessary—in exploring a book of Scripture is the alert look-out for clues or keys. In this Gospel according to Luke they are early perceivable even to an unpractised eye.

It has *a very human beginning*. Right away we are in the hearts and homes and hopes of simple-living, godly, likeable folk —Zacharias and Elisabeth, Joseph and Mary, "neighbours and cousins," shepherds, Simeon, Anna. There is a tarrying at the unusual cradle, to see the Babe in those humble swaddling wraps. Whereas Matthew at once concerns himself with the *genealogy*, and Mark eagerly starts with the public *ministry*, Luke lingers over the *nativity*—the human birth and babyhood and boyhood of the "holy Child."

As we press on into the succeeding chapters, we soon begin to sense that this marked attention to the *human* is not only our first clue but the main *key*. There are other hints and pointers in these opening chapters, such as the recurring references to the Holy Spirit; certain supra-Jewish outreachings to the Gentiles; the inspired uprising of Godward jubilation in the hymns of Zacharias, Mary, the angels, Simeon; but this emphasis on the *human* is the "master-key" which unlocks Luke's Gospel; it is the "cipher-key" which interprets the inward meaning behind the outward story.

We touched on it in our foregoing study, but now let us look into it rather more closely. Although we cannot attempt an exhaustive exploration, we may observe enough to leave us wondering yet the more at that lovely manhood.

The Aspective Emphasis

Take those *first* concomitants of our Lord's human nature which find their *only* mention in Luke's pre-natal and post-natal records. Here alone we find, "Blessed is the fruit of thy *womb*" (i. 42). Here alone we read of the "*Babe*" (ii. 12, 16); the circumcision of the "*Male*" (ii. 23); the twelve-year-old "*Lad*" (ii. 43, R.V.).

243

Here alone we read that "the Child *grew*", and that He "increased in *wisdom* and in *stature*" (ii. 40, 52); and that at His baptism He was "about *thirty years* of age" (iii. 23).

Of course, Luke does not obscure either the deity or the royalty of the Wonder-Child. Gabriel announces: "He shall be called the Son of the Highest, and the Lord God shall give unto Him the throne of His father David" (i. 32). Yet even that is accompanied by a delicate pre-intimation of the necessary human conception (i. 34, 35). From the birth to the baptism it is the human which has the emphasis. Luke has no star signalising the birth of a King, no eastern sages bringing rich homage to the infant Majesty; no enquiry from royal Herod; but there is the anxiety of an expectant young mother far from home, the ordeal of first childbirth in an outhouse or grotto, and the hurried expedient of a fodder-rack as a baby-crib. At the Jordan baptism, thirty years later, there is no announcement by John (as in Matthew): "The *kingdom* . . . is at hand!" Instead, John comes preaching "the baptism of repentance for the remission of sins" (iii. 3).

Pass to Luke's records of the grown manhood. He alone tells how the Galilean ministry began at Nazareth; and it is at once a decidedly human touch that the little township is denoted: "Nazareth, where He had been *brought up*" (iv. 16). Here alone His first synagogue address appears, laying all the emphasis from the outset on that *Spirit-anointed manhood* (iv. 18, 19). Here alone we see Jesus emotionally broken into tearful *lamenting* over the city (xiii. 34, xix. 41); *kneeling down* in prayer (xxii. 41); being *strengthened* by an angel (xxii. 43); agonising so sorely that His *sweat* was "as drops of blood" (xxii. 44); and yielding up His spirit on the Cross: "Father, into Thy hands I commend *My spirit*" (xxiii. 46). Here alone we find Him verifying His resurrection-body to the Eleven, by asking them to "handle" Him; by partaking of the "broiled fish" and "honeycomb"; and by *eating it "before them"* (xxiv. 38–43)—all in His lovely eagerness to show that He was still humanly *one* with them.

Threefold Interplay of Emphasis

But we must mention a unique feature of this third Gospel, which, when once seen, adds new fascination. All the way through there is a *THREEFOLD INTERPLAY* of this emphasis on the human. (1) Certain traits of our Lord's humanity are shown prominently *in Himself*. (2) These, in turn, re-emphasise themselves through *His teaching*. (3) The very narrative with which Luke surrounds our Lord enhances the emphasis.

Human Dependence on Prayer

All through, we see a human dependence on God expressing itself in *prayerfulness*. Each synoptist records the Gethsemane praying, but apart from that our Lord's engagement in prayer occurs only once in Matthew and twice in Mark, whereas in Luke it occurs repeatedly. Here alone we learn that when Jesus was endued by the Holy Spirit at Jordan He was *"praying"* (iii. 21); that in His wilderness withdrawments from incessant thronging He *"prayed"* (v. 16); that before He chose the Twelve He solitarily *"continued all night in prayer"* (vi. 12); that ere He asked the Twelve "Whom say ye that I am?" He was *"alone praying"* (ix. 18); that at His transfiguration He had climbed the mountain *"to pray"* (ix. 28), and that the actual transmorphosis occurred *"as He prayed"* (ix. 29); that just before He prescribed the now-called "Lord's Prayer" He Himself was *"praying in a certain place"* (xi. 1); that He assured Peter, "I have *prayed for thee,* that thy faith fail not" (xxii. 32); that in Gethsemane He *"prayed more earnestly"* (xxii. 44); that on the Cross both His first and last utterances were *prayers* (xxiii. 34, 46).

There can be no mistaking *that* emphasis, or the appealing way it shows our Lord's human dependence. But see now how it reappears in His *teaching*. Only in Luke do we have the parable of the midnight appeal, "Friend, lend me three loaves," teaching *importunity* in prayer (xi. 5–10); the parable of the harried judge and the widow, teaching *constancy* in prayer (xviii. 1–8); the parable of the Pharisee and the publican praying in the temple, teaching *humility* in prayer (xviii. 9–14); only here "Watch ye therefore, and *pray always*" (xxi. 36); only here the second "Rise and *pray*, lest ye enter into temptation" (xxii. 46).

See also how even Luke's accompanying *narrative* enhances this emphasis. Only in Luke, of course, do we find "And the whole multitude of the people were *praying* without" (i. 10); the angel's word "Fear not, Zacharias; for thy *prayer* is heard" (i. 13); Anna serving God "with fastings *and prayers* night and day" (ii. 37); only here "Why do the disciples of John fast often and *make prayers?*" (v. 33); only here, the request, "Lord, teach us to *pray*" (xi. 1); only here, the explained aim of a parable— "that men ought *always to pray* and not to faint" (xviii. 1); and the strange circumstance which occasioned our Lord's re-assurance to Peter: "But I have *prayed* for thee." Is it surprising that some have called this the Gospel of *prayer?*

Human need of the Holy Spirit

Closely in keeping is the prominence given to the Holy Spirit. He is named more in Luke than in Matthew and Mark together, and even more than in John. With delicate reticence, yet equal definiteness, His miraculous activity is emphasised in connection with our Lord's *human nature*; then in our Lord's own *teaching*; and completively in the incidental scenery of Luke's *story*.

In both Matthew and Luke an intervening angel speaks of Mary's supernormal pregnancy as a phenomenon wrought by the Divine Spirit; but in the first Gospel it is simply stated as *fact*, with no reference to process; whereas in Luke there is a highly significant pre-conception description, with singular accent on the activity of the Spirit.

> "The Holy Spirit shall come upon thee, and the
> power of the Highest shall overshadow thee:
> therefore also that holy being which shall be
> born of thee shall be called the Son of God" (i. 35)

Note well the words: "That holy being which shall be born *of thee.*" Our Lord's manhood was begotten *entirely* from the substance of that pure virgin, and not even partly by communica-tion of the Holy Spirit, whose essence is incommunicable. As Pearson says, somewhat bluntly in his classic on the Creed, the Holy Spirit was not "the Father" of our Lord, even though our Lord "was conceived by Him." Mary was as truly a virgin after her begetting of the sinless Jesus as before. The derivation was entirely of the human mother. The miracle was entirely of *the Holy Spirit.*

All four Gospels record the descent of the Spirit upon that guile-less Man at the Jordan baptism, but only Luke goes on to say: "And Jesus, being *full of the Holy Spirit,* returned from Jordan"

(iv. 1). All three synoptists tell how the Spirit took Him into the wilderness to be tempted of Satan, but only Luke adds: "And Jesus returned *in the power of the Spirit*" (iv. 14).

Peculiar to Luke, also, is a startling word in chapter x. 21: "In that hour Jesus rejoiced in spirit." The Greek word means to leap or exult; and manuscript evidence is that the word "spirit" should be "the Holy Spirit", thus: "In that hour Jesus *exulted in the Holy Spirit.*" All such references betoken the exquisite affiliation of the Holy Spirit with that sinless manhood.

But more, that Spirit-begotten manhood needed the *enduing* of the Holy Spirit for spiritual victory and service. Our Lord became incarnate to be One of *us*—to be *like* us, *with* us, *for* us, as the new Adam, the new representative Man, the new Champion of the race, the human Challenger of usurper Apollyon. It would have been no *moral* victory for the incarnate Son of God to over-whelm Satan by some sudden release of Divine power. Our Lord was tempted as *Man*. He overcame as *Man*. In all such connection His Divine power was in abeyance. He overcame in His depen-dent, prayerful, Spirit-endued *manhood*! This human victory of His is as precious to us individually as it was crucial to the race as a whole, for it means that He who thus became our victorious Champion became also our *Example*. It means that our *own* human nature may now be endued by that same Holy Spirit for similar victory and service.

See now how this emphasis on the Holy Spirit reappears in Luke's notices of our Lord's *teaching*. All three synoptists record the beginning of the Galilean ministry, but only Luke prefixes our Lord's prelude-manifesto at Nazareth: "The *Spirit of the Lord* is upon Me, because He hath *anointed* Me to preach glad tidings" (iv. 18).

Note the featuristic difference between Matthew vii. 11 and Luke xi. 13. The former reads: "How much more shall your Father which is in heaven give good things to them that ask Him?" Luke has: "How much more shall your heavenly Father give *the Holy Spirit*?"

Luke alone records our Lord's striking allusion to the Holy Spirit as "the finger of God" (xi. 20); and closes his Gospel with the Saviour's parting *promise* of enduement by the Holy Spirit: "Behold, I send the promise of My Father upon you: but tarry

ye in Jerusalem until ye be endued [or clothed] with *power from
on high*" (xxiv. 49).

Even apart from our Lord and His teaching, Luke's very
narrative has the same impress. Right at the beginning the angel
preannounces of John: "He shall be filled with *the Holy Spirit*"
(i. 15). Next: "Elisabeth was filled with *the Holy Spirit*" (i. 41).
Again: "Zacharias was filled with *the Holy Spirit*, and prophesied"
(i. 67). A little later: "There was a man in Jerusalem whose name
was Simeon . . . and *the Holy Spirit* was upon him: and it was
revealed unto him by *the Holy Spirit* that he should not see death
before he had seen the Lord's Christ. And he came *by the Spirit*
into the temple" (ii. 25–7). All this prepares us for a distinctive
emphasis. Right at the beginning the Holy Spirit is the "power
of the Highest" (i. 35) and right at the end He is the promised
"power from on high."

Human Catholicity

Another emphasised feature of our Lord's humanity, in this
third Gospel, is its *catholicity*. This re-expresses itself in His
teaching, and persists through Luke's accompanying narrative.

The note of unconfined goodwill towards those outside the pale
of Jewry is struck early, in the nativity chapters. There is no
overlooking Israel's interests (see i. 16, 32, 33, 54, 55, 68–74,
ii. 11) but while Matthew's report is exclusively Jewish, Luke's
at once overflows to the Gentiles. The suddenly inspired Zacharias
is alluding to an Isaian prophecy on the *Gentiles* when he says:
"The Dayspring from on high hath visited us, to give light to
them that sit in darkness and in the shadow of death" (i. 79).
When the eager angels troop down into the night sky, the message
is: "Behold, I bring you good tidings of great joy, which shall
be *to all people*" (ii. 10)—connecting our Lord's human incarnation with the whole race.

Aged Simeon's words are carefully preserved: "Lord, now
lettest Thou Thy servant depart in peace, according to Thy word;
for mine eyes have seen Thy salvation which Thou hast prepared
before the face of *all people*; a light to lighten *the Gentiles*" (ii.
29–32).

Yet further, while all three synoptists link John the Baptist with
Isaiah xl. 3–5: "The voice of one crying in the wilderness,"

Luke alone continues with: "And *all flesh* shall see the salvation of God" (iii. 6).

Thus, in this third Gospel, a noticeable catholicity atmospheres our Lord's coming in human form. And this is the vestibule to spacious catholicity in our Lord's *teachings*.

How different is the uniform "headline" of our Lord's parables in Luke from that in Matthew! There are sixteen parables in Matthew (not counting minor similes) and all but four begin: "The kingdom of heaven is like." There are twenty in Luke, and all but two begin with: "There was a certain *man*" or some similar general headline.

The parables which are reported by Luke are set in the widest human terms. How familiar they are, in their broad human outreach!—"A certain *man* went down from Jerusalem to Jericho, and fell among thieves." "The ground of a certain rich *man* brought forth plentifully." "A certain *man* had two sons." We need only compare the type of parables preserved respectively by Matthew and Luke, to see the supra-Jewish catholicity of the latter. If anywhere the genius of selection is evident, it is here.

Take those two parables, the one in Matthew, the other in Luke, which are so alike in substance that some expositors assume them to be two versions of the same parable, i.e. the royal "marriage feast" (Matt. xxii.) and the "great supper" (Luke xiv.). In Matthew we have: "The kingdom of heaven is like unto a certain *king* which made a marriage for his son." In Luke we have: "A certain *man* made a great supper, and bade many"—a human instead of a royal setting, and no reference to the "kingdom." (There is no problem of inspiration created by this variation between Matthew and Luke. Our Lord was continually moving from place to place, and many of His teachings, parables, sayings, would be repeated by Him in different places, with circumstantial adaptations. Each Gospel writer exercises discriminative selection.)

Those parables which occur only in Luke are enough in themselves to indicate the broad human emphasis in this third Gospel—the two debtors (vii.), the good Samaritan (x.), the great supper (xiv.), the lost coin (xv.), the prodigal son (xv.), the importunate widow (xviii.), the Pharisee and the publican (xviii.).

The same catholicity is found even in Luke's accompanying

narrative. In the first place, his Gospel is addressed to a *Gentile,* i.e. the "most excellent Theophilus" (i. 3). When he gives our Saviour's human genealogy, he must needs travel away back beyond all merely Hebrew confines, to *Adam,* the only other man who ever had a completely racial significance, and who, like our Lord, had no father but God.

Luke alone records our Lord's Nazareth comments about the *Gentile* widow of Sidon, and the *Gentile* Syrian, Naaman (iv. 16–30). Luke alone adds the appealing detail that the *Gentile* centurian's "servant" was *"dear* unto him" (vii. 2, 5). In his account of our Lord's outsending of the Twelve he noticeably *omits* the words preserved by Matthew: "Go not into the way of the Gentiles" (Luke ix. 1–6). Luke alone tells how James and John wanted to call down fire on certain inhospitable *Samaritans,* and how Jesus rebuked them (ix. 51–6). Luke alone tells of the ten lepers who were cleansed, and of the one, a *Samaritan,* who ran back to give thanks (xvii. 11–19). Luke alone preserves for us: "Jerusalem shall be trodden down of the *Gentiles,* until the times of the *Gentiles* be fulfilled" (xxi. 24). All these references bring out the distinctive, wide human outreach of this third Gospel.

Human Poverty

Another such speciality of this Gospel is the prominence it gives to the *poor.* It appears in the usual threefold form—first in connection with our Lord's *manhood,* then in His *teaching,* and again in Luke's *narrative.*

Who does not know Luke's story of the baby Boy for whom there was "no room in the inn"; whose first night on earth was in a stable, with a manger for a cradle (ii. 7); and whose parents were so poor that when they dedicated Him in the temple they could bring only an offering of two birds instead of the regulation lamb (ii. 24)?

From the first, that sublime manhood is associated with poverty; and this in turn flavours all our Lord's teaching as recorded by Luke. Both Matthew and Mark retain several of our Lord's references to the poor, which also reappear in Luke; but all the following are found *only* in Luke.

At the very outset of His ministry Jesus announces Himself as "anointed to preach good tidings to the *poor*" (iv. 18). Next, in the "Sermon on the Plain" (vi. 17–49), which is Luke's parallel to the "Sermon on the Mount" in Matthew, instead of "Blessed are the poor in spirit," we have simply "Blessed are *ye poor*"; instead of "Blessed are they that hunger and thirst after righteousness," we have simply "Blessed are *ye that hunger*"; and instead of "Blessed are they that mourn," we have "Blessed are *ye who weep*." The beatitudes preserved by Luke address actual *physical* poverty and hunger and tears, which sharpens them into a more pointed human poignancy.

Next, in chapter xiv., we find Jesus saying: "When thou makest a feast, call the *poor*, the *maimed*, the *lame*, the *blind*" (verse 13). In the same chapter comes the parable of the "great supper," with its "Go out quickly into the streets and lanes of the city, and bring in hither the *poor*, the *maimed*, the *halt*, and the *blind*" (verse 21). A bit further on we find the story of Lazarus and Dives: "There was a certain *beggar* . . . full of sores, desiring to be fed with the *crumbs* which fell from the rich man's table. . . . And the beggar died, and was *carried by the angels* into Abraham's bosom" (xvi. 19–31). How the poor must have listened to such a story! Still further, in chapter xix. 8, we find Zacchæus, head publican of Jericho, converted and exclaiming: "Behold, Lord, the half of my goods I give to the *poor*!"

But now see how even Luke's accompanying *narrative* completes all these. When Mary sings her Magnificat, this is her first rejoicing: "He hath regarded the *low estate* of His handmaiden" (i. 48). Later she adds: "He hath put down the mighty from their seats, and exalted them of *low degree* (verse 52). And yet again: "He hath filled *the hungry* with good things" (verse 53). Luke alone tells us that as our dear Lord travelled round, He was dependent, in His human poverty, on grateful women who "ministered unto Him of their substance" (viii. 1–3). And it is Luke alone who shows us, again and again, our Lord sitting at other men's tables for His sustenance (v. 29, vii. 36, x. 38–42, xi. 37, xiv. 1, xix. 5)—"as *poor* yet making many rich."

Human Sympathies

We must end our brief round-up of these incidental emphases on the *human* aspect of our Lord in this third Gospel. They accumulate to a point where all but the dullest eyes must see that the convergence of the whole is upon Christ as *MAN*. Neither the kingship (as in Matthew) nor the servanthood (as in Mark) is obscured; while His deity (as in John) is either latent or patent all the way through; yet the distinguishing aspect is the *manhood*. We need not discuss whether or how far Luke purposely designed it so. All we say is that the fascinating peculiarity is really *there*.

In closing, then, let us notice how markedly the human *sympathies* of our Lord appear in Luke's Gospel.

Who can have failed to notice the prominence given to *women*? Right at the beginning there is a pointer in the prominence given to Elisabeth, Mary, Anna. It appears all through our Lord's teachings. It is in Luke alone that we find Jesus absolving the penitent "*woman* which was a sinner" (vii. 37, 50); sympathetically pacifying "a certain *woman*" by His unforgettable "Martha, Martha, thou art careful and troubled about many things" (x. 41); here alone that He heals the "*woman* which had an infirmity eighteen years," and then confounds the criticising Sabbatarian bigots by His rejoinder: "Ought not this *woman,* being a daughter of Abraham, be loosed from this bond on the Sabbath day?" (xiii. 10–17). It is in Luke alone that we meet the "*woman* having ten pieces of silver" (xv. 8); and here alone that we find Jesus turning about, on the via Dolorosa, to say: "Weep not for Me, *daughters* of Jerusalem" (xxiii. 28).

Luke's own narrative completes all this. It is he alone who tells us about John's *mother*, Elisabeth; and of Anna the octogenarian *prophetess* (i., ii.); of the "certain *women* . . . who ministered of their substance" (vii.); of Martha's complaint, and Mary's sitting at Jesus' feet (x.); of the "certain woman" in the company who called out: "Blessed is the womb that bare Thee!" (xi.); and of the many "*women*, which also bewailed as they followed Jesus to the cross" (xxiii.).

Women are mentioned in Luke more than in any of the other three Gospel writers; and widows more than in the other three together. Here only we meet Anna the "*widow*" (ii.); and hear Jesus speak about the "many *widows* in Israel," and the Sarepta woman who "was a *widow*" (iv.). Here only we meet the sorrowing "*widow*" of Nain (vii.) and here alone the determined "widow" who would give the judge no rest (xviii.).

Note the sympathy with *parental feeling*. All three synoptists relate the healing of Jairus's daughter, but Luke alone tells us that she was his "*only* daughter" (viii. 42). All three record the healing of the demoniac son after our Lord's transfiguration, but only in Luke do we find "for he is mine *only* child" (ix. 38). And when Luke shows us that Nain widow weeping behind the pall-bearers, he explains that the premature casualty was "the *only* son of his mother" (vii. 12).

These and other like touches in this third Gospel indicate a sympathetic entering into the sorrows and feelings of other humans. Note the very human interest in *personal* details. Prophetess Anna was a widow of "*fourscore and four*" years, and had lived with an husband "*seven years* from her virginity." Jesus was "*twelve* years old" when His parents took Him to the Passover at Jerusalem; and about "*thirty* years" when baptised of John in Jordan. The daughter of Jairus was about "*twelve* years of age." The woman with the paralysis had been bowed together "lo, these *eighteen* years." All these touches are peculiar to Luke, and underline the extra human sympathies which differentiate his Gospel.

Finally, mark the compassionate outreaching toward *outcasts*. At this point the characteristic emphasis becomes unmistakable. It is here alone that Jesus is the Babe for whom "there was *no room* in the inn"; and the young Prophet "*thrust out*" of Nazareth (iv. 29). Our sinless Lord, the "despised and rejected," knew the feelings of the outcast. In this third Gospel only we have that social outcast, the *publican*, standing "afar off" in the temple, smiting his breast, as he says: "God be merciful to me, a sinner," and going down to his house "justified" rather than the vain Pharisee (xviii.). Here alone we have the "woman in the city, which was a *sinner*," whose deep contrition evoked gracious absolution (vii.). Here alone we find publicans visiting John's baptism (iii. 12), and upholding our Lord's words (vii. 29), and "drawing near" to Him (xv. 1). Here alone we read: "This Man receiveth *sinners*" (xv. 2). Here alone we have the parable of the prodigal son (xv. 11–32); and here alone we find, at Calvary, the penitent "robber" to whom Jesus said, "Verily, I say unto thee: Today shalt thou be with Me in paradise" (xxiii. 43). Yes, this is the Gospel for outcasts!

Surely these accumulating singularities of this third Gospel are such that only the most obtuse can miss seeing the one featuristic emphasis unifying them all, namely, the large-hearted humanity, sympathy, compassion, of that perfect Man who is the ideal become actual.

And it is all with a big, vital purpose—our *salvation*. In a special sense, among the four Gospels, this is the one which rings the bells of salvation by grace through faith. It is in Luke only, among the synoptists, that we come across the word "Saviour" (i. 47, ii. 11). Here only we find the word "salvation" (six times, i. 69, 71, 77, ii. 30, iii. 6, xix. 9); and here that we find the lovely word, *evangelizo* (=to tell glad tidings: ten times—i. 19, ii. 10, iii. 18, iv. 18, 43, vii. 22, viii. 1, ix. 6, xvi. 16, xx. 1) which occurs only once in the other Gospels. Only in Luke do we find "Thy faith hath saved thee" (vii. 50, viii. 48). Luke alone of the three uses the word "grace" (eight times—i. 30, ii. 40, 52, iv. 22, vi. 32, 33, 34, xvii. 9); and here for the first time in the New Testament we meet the word "redemption" (i. 68, ii. 38, xxiv. 21). Right at the beginning the herald angel announces "To all people . . . a *Saviour*!" (ii. 11). Right at the end, the risen Saviour tells that "repentance and *remission of sins* should be preached in His name *among all nations*" (xxiv. 47). That Saviour is our Kinsman, "bone of our bone, and flesh of our flesh," in all things "made like unto His brethren"; in all points "tempted like as we are"; overcoming by the Holy Spirit; even on the Cross praying, "Father, forgive them"; and leaving us the perfect pattern for *all* human living.

Let the children look at Him, for, as the Christmas hymn says, "He is our childhood's pattern"—of respectful subjection to parents, and reverent eagerness about our *heavenly* Father's business. Let the women, the widows, the poor, the needy, the sinner, the outcast look to Him, the Saviour whose heart beats with sympathetic compassion. Let all Christian believers look again at this Man of *prayer*, and learn that "men ought always to pray, and not to faint." Yea, let all of us look again, and look often, at this wonderful Jesus of the third Gospel. Oh, that we ourselves may learn the lesson of His sympathy, gentleness, compassion; and be "kind one to another; tender-hearted, forgiving one another," even as we, through Him, have *been* forgiven!

Lovely Manhood, perfect Pattern,
Live again Thy life through mine!

THE GOSPEL ACCORDING TO LUKE (3)

Lesson Number 120

NOTE.—For this final consideration of Luke, first consult a concordance to examine every New Testament reference to Luke; then read prayerfully again chapters xix. 45 to the end of the resurrection chapter.

THE SEVEN "CRISES"

In the earthly life of our Lord there were seven supremely transcendent events. They were: (1) His birth, (2) His baptism, (3) His temptation, (4) His transfiguration, (5) His crucifixion, (6) His resurrection, (7) His ascension. We wish we could have lingered over each of them in these studies, but our self-imposed limits preclude our so doing. The finest book that the late Dr. G. Campbell Morgan ever wrote was on this very theme. He called it *The Crises of the Christ*; and we are grateful to recommend it wholeheartedly.

—J.S.B.

THE GOSPEL ACCORDING TO LUKE (3)

THE MORE we delve into this "Gospel according to Luke," the more pleasantly embarrassed we become by the many avenues of interest which invite further exploration. It is far from easy to give a satisfying impression of it in three short allotments like these.

We have seen how distinctively it is the Gospel of our Lord's *humanity*, the Gospel of prayer, of the Holy Spirit, of gracious catholicity and broad human sympathies; the Gospel of especial goodwill to the poor and the needy, to womanhood and widowhood, to the Samaritan and the Gentile, to the prodigal and the outcast. These Lukan slants and angles should not be overstressed, for there is not one of them which cannot be paralleled in some degree by correspondences in the other Gospel writers. Yet neither should they be *under*-stressed; for together they form the subtle mosaic of a Divine design which patterns itself out through the guided pens of those four writers. None of the four has a monopoly of *any* aspect, yet each of the four supremely immortalises *one* aspect; and in Luke it is our Lord's sinless, perfect, gracious, glorious *manhood*.

In this final instalment on the third Gospel we shall speak first about Luke himself, and then return, in closing, to the central theme of his Gospel, namely, the manhood of our Lord.

About Luke Himself

This third Gospel and the Acts of the Apostles are both inscribed to the same person—"Theophilus" (Luke i. 3; Acts i. 1). Both also were written by the same author; for the "former treatise" mentioned in Acts i. 1 can be none other than our Gospel according to Luke. That Luke was the penman of both is now the practically unanimous vote of scholarship, as it has also been the firm tradition right from Irenæus in the second century A.D.

Yet although we owe to Luke the first written history of the primitive Church, from its inception to its implantation throughout the Roman world, we know less of him than of any other New Testament writer. Nowhere does he refer to himself in his Gospel, nor yet in the Acts except where the plurals "we" and "us" anonymously include him in Paul's travel group.

Travel Companion

We know first, then, that he was a *travel companion of Paul*. The change from "they" to "we" in Acts xvi. 10 seems to indicate that he linked up at Troas, where Paul in a night vision saw the "man of Macedonia" beckoning them to Europe. From there onwards Luke was Paul's ever-dependable co-worker. He was with Paul through the exciting adventures in Philippi, and perhaps other places "out west" (though the resumption of "they" again instead of "we," until xx. 5, may well indicate that Luke stayed on at Philippi). Six years later he leaves Phillipi with Paul (Acts xx. 6) and thenceforth accompanies him without break. He is with him in Jerusalem at the attempted lynching by the fanatical mob, and during the two years of imprisonment in Cæsarea (xxiv. 27 with xxvii. 1); with him during the hazardous voyage and shipwreck on the way to Rome (xxvii. 1–xxviii. 16); with him through all his prison detention and the trials before Nero; with him, apparently, right to the hour of martyrdom (Col. iv. 14; 2 Tim. iv. 11; Philem. 24).

Physician

We learn, too, that *he was a physician*. In the closing salutations of the Epistle to the Colossians (written from Rome) Paul refers to him as such (iv. 14). The legend that he was also a painter dates only from the fourteenth century, and is at least dubious, having probably originated in rhetorical references to his literary gift as a painter of vivid word-pictures. When he joined Paul's travel group he would have to relinquish ordinary medical practice, though it is possible that at places of prolonged sojourn (Philippi mainly) he would resume temporary physiciancy. Later, however, he seems to have subordinated everything to attending on Paul as private physician, companion, and co-worker, though he would probably also engage in general practice during the lengthening stay in Rome.

Dear to Paul

Again, we gather that he was *very dear to Paul*. The fraternal salutation above-cited reads: "Luke, the *beloved* physician, and Demas, greet you," which indicates Paul's feelings. How much must such an one as Luke have meant to Paul! Perhaps the mutual attachment grew strong because in addition to being fellow-believers they were both persons of education, superior in a literary sense to the many. Luke's trained medical care of Paul would the more deepen the latter's appreciation and regard. It is noteworthy that the link-up at Troas synchronises with an attack of Paul's seemingly chronic ophthalmic malady (compare "Galatia," Acts xvi. 6, with "we" in xvi. 10, and Gal. iv. 13–15). It seems, too, that the natures of the two men were reciprocally congenial. They have been compared to Luther and Melanchthon at the time of the Reformation—Luther, the moving spirit, the grand actor, the public champion, admired for his intrepidity and Samsonian prowess; Melanchthon, a retiring spirit, out of view, writing his Common-places, the first "Body of Divinity" produced by the Reformation Church. Both Pauls and Lukes are needed, and usually get on well together, for there is not as much treading on one another's toes by companions whose specialities are so different. Without the Pauls there would be little to write. Without the Lukes there would be little preserved.

Luke's Loyalty

Not only was Luke dear to Paul; it is equally clear that he was *very loyal to Paul*. So far as is known, Second Timothy was Paul's last-written letter before martyrdom. In it he says: "Do thy diligence to come shortly unto me; for Demas hath forsaken me, having loved this present world, and is departed into Thessalonica; Crescens to Galatia, Titus unto Dalmatia. *Only Luke is with me*" (iv. 9–11). What emotion is in those last two words! How much Luke means to him now! The final trial at Nero's judgment seat is at hand. Like a Damocles' sword the impending "To die, or not to die?" hangs over Paul's neck. During his later days in Rome there have been drag and discouragement. Professed supporters have fallen away. Paul writes: "At my first defence, no one took my part, but all forsook me" (iv. 16, R.V.). Former travel companions and fellow-labourers have been needed elsewhere. Demas has given way to the pull of the world, and deserted. But *"Luke is with me."* How it reflects Luke's courage in the hour of disappointment and danger! How eloquently it testifies his deep affection for the great-hearted apostle lying there in his solitary dungeon, fettered and forsaken!

Widely Esteemed

It would seem, also, that among those early Christians, in general, Luke was *widely known and beloved.* Glance again at Colossians iv. 14: "Luke, the beloved physician." The words indicate not only Paul's own warm esteem, but also what was felt toward Luke by a wide circle. As most are agreed, it is Luke who is referred to in 2 Corinthians viii. 18: "The brother whose praise in the Gospel is throughout all the churches" (though we can scarcely agree with the suggested translation, "Whose *Gospel* is a subject of praise throughout the churches," i.e. Luke's written Gospel). See also verse 19. Probably at various times and places Luke had given able and kindly medical help to different saints.

A Gentile

It may further be inferred that Luke was a *Gentile.* This has been contradicted; but we think the following data are enough to establish it. In those farewell cordialities of Colossians iv. 10–14 he is distinguished from Aristarchus, Marcus and Justus, who were Jews (*v* 11), and is linked with Epaphras and Demas, who were not. His name, *Loukas,* is Greek. Both his Gospel and the Acts begin with a formal dedication in Greek and Roman style— the only New Testament books which do so. His facility in the Greek tongue, and the touch of classical finesse in his opening dedication, and the fact that the addressee, Theophilus, was a Gentile, all point the same way.

The Pre-conversion Luke

It does not seem possible to determine whether Luke was a *proselyte* to Judæism before his conversion to Christ or whether he came over directly from paganism. My own inclination is to think that his ready grasp and easy relating of Jewish matters suggest a pre-conversion familiarity. Or, it is thinkable that, like Timothy, perhaps, he had a Gentile father and a Jewish mother.

To say that he was one of the "Seventy" sent forth by our Lord (Luke x.), or the companion of Cleopas in the walk to Emmaus (xxiv.), simply because he alone of the four Gospel writers mentions these, is gratuitous fancy. In fact it is contradicted by Luke himself, who in his opening dedication plainly distinguishes himself from those who were "eye-witnesses."

The Antioch Tradition

Tradition has it that before his conversion he was a proselyte to the Jewish faith and a native of Antioch. Scholars warn us, however, that we must not confuse Luke with the Lucius of Cyrene who is mentioned as at Antioch in Acts xiii. 1, or the Lucius in Romans xvi. 21, because Luke's name, in the Greek, is *Loukas,* whereas Lucius is *Loukios*; but in 1912 Sir William Ramsay found an inscription on the wall of an old Pisidian temple, in which the two names are interchangeable of the same person. We ourselves still think that Luke must *not* be confused with that "Lucius of Cyrene" (even though, singularly enough, Cyrene was famous for its medical school!), but we *do* think that the Lucius of Acts xiii. 1 and the Lucius of Romans xvi. 21 *are* the same—a converted African Jew, whom Paul distinctly calls one of his own "kinsmen," i.e. a Jew.

That Lucius presumably was converted while visiting Jerusalem at the Pentecost when the Holy Spirit was outpoured on the Apostles (Cyrenians are mentioned as among Peter's hearers: Acts ii. 10), and was among those Cyrenians who, when the first Christians were "scattered abroad upon the persecution that arose about Stephen," travelled to Antioch (xi. 19) and preached to the *Greeks* there (not "Grecians," or Hellenist Jews, as in A.V.). And perhaps here we are touching on one of those hidden coincidences of Scripture which are as fascinating as they are elusive, for it is not improbable that our Gentile doctor *Luke* was at Antioch at that very time, and may thus have been converted. According to the manuscript *Codex Bezae* and certain Latin authorities Luke uses the first person plural in xi. 28, which would mean that he was then actually at Antioch. Eusebius and Jerome (fourth century) both speak of him as belonging to Antioch. Others would link him with Alexandria, Philippi, Troas. None can say with finality, but we ourselves think the Antioch tradition far the likeliest.

We do not think Luke was a convert of Paul. The apostle never calls him "son," as he does Timothy and Titus. But there is no doubt that he was greatly influenced by Paul—of which there are clear traces in his writings. We owe much to Luke, as Paul did. Probably Luke saved Paul from more than one serious illness, and lengthened as well as eased his days. Some of Paul's letters might never have been written but for Luke. Not only was Luke the first ecclesiastical historian, making his notes while on travel, and "writing them up" during Paul's two imprisonments (as we surmise), but he was in a real sense the Church's first "medical missionary."

Luke the Penman

It is interesting to notice how what Luke *was* betrays itself in what he *wrote*.

Was he a physician?—then see the traces of this in his Gospel. Our Lord's first text is: "He hath sent Me to *heal*" (iv. 18). It is here, too, that we find: *"Physician, heal thyself"* (iv. 23). It is here only that we have: "The power of the Lord was present to *heal*" (v. 17). There is more mention of "healing" in Luke than in Matthew and Mark together. Then, too, the diagnoses often indicate the pen of a medical. Peter's mother-in-law had a *"great* fever" (physicians used to distinguish fevers as the "great" and the "small" fevers); the leper was *"full* of leprosy" (v. 12); the paralytic was "taken with a palsy"—in the Greek a technical term, *"struck with paralysis"* (v. 18); the centurion's servant was "sick and *ready to die"* (vii. 2); the woman with an infirmity was *"bowed together"* and could *"in no wise lift up herself"* (xiii. 11)—and so on.

Was Luke a Gentile? See how *that* comes out in this third Gospel. We need not retread ground already covered, for have we not seen that Luke's is peculiarly the Gospel of glad tidings to the Gentiles?

Was Luke a companion of Paul? Equally unmistakably that leaves its impress. Perhaps that is why tradition grew up that he was little more than Paul's amanuensis. His foreword is enough in itself to crush that tradition, for he tells us that he himself was the independent compiler, from first-hand evidences by "eye-witnesses." Nonetheless, Paul's influence is discernible. Take the institution of the Lord's Supper: can any careful reader fail to notice the almost verbal correspondences between Luke's account and that of Paul? Think back over those characteristic evangelical emphases in Luke's Gospel—Jesus as Saviour; supra-Jewish catholicity; free forgiveness of sins to the believing and penitent; unmerited justification even for the publican who repented and sought God; the person and work of the Holy Spirit; the glorifying of God in holy gladness and praise and service; are not the epistles of Paul similarly featured by these very topics?

All these matters lend themselves to fuller exploration; but so far as this present study is concerned, this must be our last word.

The Great Theme

In closing we return to the controlling, unifying emphasis of this third Gospel, namely, *the sublime manhood of our Lord*. How that manhood speaks to those of us who are Christian believers—to those of us who would fain serve as *He* served and win as *He* won! We think of Luke as a Greek writing to a Greek. The Greeks were an idealistic-minded people. Their philosophers and moralists had their theoretic ideal of perfect manhood. Luke sets forth Jesus in all the simple purity, lovely naturalness, profound beauty, and moral sublimity of His sinless manhood, letting it be seen how He not only transcends the highest conceptions of Greek culture, but translates the ideal into concrete actuality. To Christian believers, however, Jesus means something nearer than that: He is our perfect *example*. His manhood is our *pattern*. We are called to live *like* Him. Let us therefore follow Him again through these precious pages of Luke's Gospel, and mark well how that pattern manhood speaks to us.

Part One: His Perfect Humanity

Run through part one again (i. 5–iv. 13). Here, at the outset, Luke shows us the threefold perfection of that wonderful Man. First he tells us about the *physical*, i.e. the birth (i. 26–ii. 20). Then about the boyhood and the *mental* development (ii. 40–52). Then the Jordan baptism and the voice from heaven which attested His *moral and spiritual* perfection when He was thirty: "Thou art My beloved Son, in whom I am well pleased" (iii. 21, 22). So at the beginning there is that threefold perfection—physical, mental, spiritual—of our Lord's real and complete humanity.

Is then that perfect Man now ready for the special purpose and service He is to fulfil? We ourselves would surely say "Yes." But no, there is something else needed (and remember all the time that we are looking at Jesus as exemplifying something which has its counterpart in ourselves). That threefold human perfection of Jesus may be called His *natural* perfection. It was an indispensable prerequisite; but even that perfect natural manhood needed a special *spiritual anointing*. That is the arresting significance of what happened in the Jordan, when from the opened heavens the Holy Spirit in visible form as a dove descended upon the approved and sanctified Jesus.

Is then that perfect Man *now* ready? We ourselves would again say "Yes." But no, besides that anointing with the Spirit there must now be temptation by Satan. What! Temptation? Yes, the sanctified and anointed One must be *tested, tried, proved*. Mark well the way Luke tells of it, showing how the temptation of Jesus did not mean that He had lost the fulness of the Spirit, but rather was under His special control: "And Jesus, being full of the Holy Spirit, returned from Jordan, and was *led by the Spirit* into the wilderness, being forty days tempted of the devil" (iv. 1). And can it be different with ourselves? There is no big spiritual blessing can come to us from God without there being the inevitable testing afterwards. In fact, almost invariably after a big blessing there is a big temptation. This is where many believers "lose the blessing"; they are stunned by surprise, and collapse through shock. They imagine that after such a blessing they will be above temptation, or that temptation will have lost its force. Thus they experience withering spiritual reactions. Yet need we fear such temptations? Nay, it is the Holy Spirit's opportunity of showing what He can be to us. We tend to forget that all the while Jesus was being tempted He was still "full of the Holy Spirit," and that the *joy of victory* must have been almost as glorious as the joy of the filling itself, through which the victory was achieved. The temptation was threefold and was successively directed against the three parts of His humanity: the physical, the spiritual, the mental; but the completeness of the assault only emphasised the completeness of the victory. Does not this, also, speak to us, if we have "ears to hear"?

Part Two: The Galilee Ministry

Look now at part two (iv. 14–ix. 50). See how it begins: "And Jesus returned *in the power of the Spirit* into Galilee." Ah, now we shall see immediate response, delight, success! Here is the sanctified, Spirit-filled, victorious Servant of God. Like the ripe corn bending before the wind, the souls of His hearers will bow before His words. But is that what we find? No, the very opposite! "And all they in the synagogue, when they heard these things, were filled with wrath; and rose up and thrust Him out of the city, and led Him unto the brow of the hill, whereon their city was built, that they might cast Him down headlong" (iv. 28, 29).

Think of it: the first experience of the Spirit-filled Minister, a deadly rebuff! Think of it: all the way through, opposition by the *religious!*—and in the end, a cross! Think of it: they could not resist His *wisdom*, but they did resist His *witness*. Yet although they rejected His love, and resisted His word, they could not destroy His *joy*, and they could not destroy His *influence*; for His cross became His throne, and from His grave He brought "life and immortality to light through the Gospel." His crucifiers are dead; but Jesus lives on in millions of hearts for ever.

Do not these things all bear on you and me as the would-be servants of Jesus? Well, all the way through Luke's Gospel this wonderful Jesus is talking to us just by what he *was* in His sublime manhood and ministry. For instance, we see how He felt the need for *fellowship* in service, hence His selecting of the Twelve, that they might continue "with Him" (viii. 1); also His realisation that there must be at least some *organisation*, hence His training and enduing and despatching of the Twelve "two by two." But from this point we must leave our readers to "follow His steps" for themselves. We would only add that the Transfiguration is all the more significant, coming, as it does, just before our Lord starts on His long, slow trek to Jerusalem. Right at the beginning of His ministry the voice from heaven had attested the perfection of His *character*. Now, as the Galilee ministry ends, the voice attests the perfection of His *ministry*: "This is My beloved Son; *hear Him*."

Yes, we may well watch His ways, and hear His words.

Part Three: The Jerusalem Journey

Now pass again through part three (ix. 51–xix. 44). This is
how it begins: "And it came to pass that when the time was come
that He should be received up, He *steadfastly set His face to go to
Jerusalem*." At the beginning of His ministry He was already
perfect; but the perfect instrument had now become perfect*ed*
through trial and service. Is not that, then, enough? No; He
who is perfect in Him*self* and perfected in *service* must be perfected "through *suffering*"! Does not that, also, speak to you
and me? Does it not suggest that perhaps the greatest contribution
we can make for God and man is not busy service but *sacrifice*?
Certainly, in the present scheme of things, the deepest fellowship
with God seems always to come that way. Again and again sacrifice is not an alternative to service, but the highest form of it.
Turn your eyes and ears to Jesus as He travels that Jerusalem
way. Even apart from the astonishing miracles and never-to-be-
forgotten parables, His incidental conversation and behaviour are
eloquent. Read the chapters again: on the way He is continually
obliged to be straightening out the wrong ideas of others; shaming
hypocrisy and softening prejudice; steadying excitement and
calming impatience; bearing with things and folks far below the
level of His own life; gently correcting and kindly instructing;
but never once Himself impatient or discomposed. See His frankness and bravery in rebuke, where it was needed. See how he
visits not only the "cities" but the *"villages"*—for every soul in
the meanest group of dwellings is precious to Him as that of a
king. See how again and again He overleaps national conceit
and racial barrier. He is continually unconventional (as with
Zacchæus) but never unnatural. He is so pure, so simple, so frank,
so natural, that His very naturalness sometimes *seems* unnatural
to the meretricious sinners and artificial religiosities around Him.
Sin has so coarsened us, and social artificialities have so un-
naturalised us, that often the really natural now seems *un*natural.
It is even more so now than it was then.

Oh, we need to go back more than ever to Luke's pictures of
Jesus on that Jerusalem road! Keep company with the Master
there. His words are wisdom. His looks are love. His tread is
sure. Every step brings Him nearer to pain, shame, suffering,
tragedy, but He goes steadily on. He knows no fear. When they

urge Him "Get Thee out, for Herod will kill Thee!" He neither tarries nor hurries. Things are in higher hands than Herod's. He is so humble that nothing can humiliate Him. He is so loving that nothing can affright Him. He is so simple that nothing can deceive Him. What is it that causes all *our* fear? There are three things which cause it—pride, lack of love and twisted motives. Where there is no pride there can be no fear of humiliation. Where there is true love there can be no fear of force. Where there is pure sincerity there can be no fear of exposure.

Yet He who had no fears had burning *tears,* for He was in a world of pride and hatred and twisted motives. See Him twice weeping over the city (xiii. 34, 35, xix. 41–4). And He could feel anger, though He never had "temper." When He reached the city His first act was to cleanse the temple—not the streets or the houses or the council chambers, but the temple, for He knew (what our leaders today are so slow to realise) that any nation which is wrong *there* cannot be right anywhere. Oh, Luke's Jesus of that long-ago journey to Jerusalem will more than repay long and careful contemplation! Was He going to pain and tragedy? Yes, and He "steadfastly set His face" toward it. But He knew, also, that truth and right and love and God always have the ultimate victory and song. He knew that beyond tragedy was triumph, that beyond the throes and the Cross were the throne and the crown, that beyond the grave was the glory, and a countless multitude of the redeemed praising before the heavenly throne! And all this mightily mirrors what is subordinately true of those who faithfully follow in the prints of His sandals.

Part Four: The Calvary Sacrifice

We add just a brief but reverent further word about part four (xix. 45–xxiii.). See that exemplary Man amid the deep, awful doings which culminated at Calvary: the murderous coalition of religious men with Satan against Him; the serpent-venom in the betrayer's kiss; the panic-struck break-up of the apostles; the denial and blasphemy of Peter; the fiendish hypocrisy of the Sanhedrin; the sarcastic mockery of Herod, and the grovelling cowardice of Pilate; Gethsemane, with its first breaking of that direst storm which ever shuddered over a soul; Calvary, where the floodgates of bitter waters were opened full upon Him, and the billows of unknowable anguish whelmed Him, and the horror of the deep darkness enveloped Him. What *now* are His reactions? Amid the first, sudden intensity of the storm as it breaks upon Him in Gethsemane, there is complete abandon to the will of God: "Nevertheless, *not My will, but Thine be done.*" When His crucifiers drive the cutting iron through His hands and feet, and prop Him up, pinioned there in public shame and torture, His first word is: "Father, forgive them." Oh, that life! That death! Wonderful Man of Galilee and Calvary! Perfect Pattern! Condemning yet alluring Example! Ever calling us; ever before us and beyond us; yet ever *with* us, too, for He has risen; and ever with*in* us, for He has come to us again in the person of the Holy Spirit to indwell us, to share His victory with us, and to enable us to follow in the shining wake of His own lovely example!

CAN YOU ANSWER THESE?

1. What is the special aspect of our Lord in Luke's Gospel?

2. What are the four main parts in Luke's story? (Sub-divisions need not be given).

3. Can you cite eight parables and three miracles which Luke alone records?

4. Where do the following occur? (1) Sending of the Seventy, (2) Conversion of Zacchæus, (3) Rich man and Lazarus?

5. In what way was the Transfiguration a culmination?

6. Give references indicating catholicity of outlook in this third Gospel.

7. What traces are there in it that Luke was a doctor, and a Gentile? What else may be gleaned about him from the New Testament?

8. There is a threefold interplay of emphasis in Luke's story. Can you exemplify this in its oft-mention of *prayer*?

THE GOSPEL ACCORDING TO JOHN (1)

Lesson Number 121

NOTE.—For this first instalment on John there should certainly be a fairly familiar grasp on the book as a whole, and we recommend that it be read through at a single sitting (easily in two hours) twice or three times.

NOTA BENE!

That brilliant scholar of New Testament Greek, the late **Dr. A. T. Robertson**, calls the Gospel according to John the "most wonderful of all books." We, too, feel much the same about it, and would say so with equal assurance were it not for our still being under the mighty spell of Matthew and Mark and Luke. Somehow, each of the four is the "greatest ever" when one gets really inside it. Certainly never was there written anything *more* wonderful than this Gospel according to John; and for that very reason we have a gloomy presentiment that the following three brief studies of it will seem hopelessly inadequate. Yet brief as they are, they can at least supply a ring of keys for the further opening up of its spacious spiritual treasures. This *nota bene,* however, is intended as a precaution. While we are just as eager to be at the spiritual riches of the book as any student of this Bible course, we have devoted our *first* instalment mainly to considering the relation of John to the synoptists, so as to obtain a correctly *consecutive full view* of our Lord's public ministry. We dread to think that this should seem tedious to any reader, for it has much more practical value than appears at first, and is of great importance to those who want a reasoned mental hold on the four Gospels. We hope the cross-references will be looked up carefully: it will be time well spent.

—*J.S.B.*

THE GOSPEL ACCORDING TO JOHN (1)

A WHOLE volume might be filled with the encomiums which scholars and saints have written on this "Gospel according to John." Is there anywhere a more exquisite compound of infinite profundity and lingual simplicity? Was there ever a sublimer subject more ingenuously interpreted?

But its priceless preciousness, of course, lies in its Divine revealings and spiritual values. Gleaming over its portal is the inscription: "No man hath seen God at any time: the only begotten Son which is in the bosom of the Father, He hath declared Him." The Greek verb-form here translated as "declared" is *exegesato*, from which comes our English word "exegesis." It means that in the visible Jesus the invisible God is *brought forth* to view. The incomprehensible concept, "GOD," is objectively elucidated before us. The very *heart* of the Eternal is livingly "exegeted," for the only begotten Son comes even from "the *bosom* of the Father."

"That ye might Believe"

John's *raison d'être,* also, flashes like a torch all the way through his Gospel and finds final expression at the end: "That ye might *believe* that Jesus is the Christ, the Son of God, and that believing ye might have life through His Name" (xx. 31). The three synoptists simply set forth the facts, and leave them to make their own impression on the reader. Not so John: all is stately selected and directed to the securing of a verdict. He is concerned not only with the facts but with the *issues*. In this is there supernatural foreplanning again? By the time anyone has gone through Matthew, Mark, Luke, John, the biggest of all decisions must be made. It may have been made before John is reached, but if not it can no longer be side-stepped. The reader is directly challenged, and must choose—to receive and be saved, or to reject and perish forever.

A Completive Necessity

The triune similarity of the other three Gospels accentuates the *dis*similarity of this fourth. As we read through it we are soon aware of its different viewpoint and atmosphere. Many a reader may not be able to explain readily just how or why this difference is there, but it *is* there; and to grasp its significance is of first importance to us in this trio of exploratory studies.

This fourth Gospel is a completive *necessity*. Have we not felt this on coming to the end of the first three? In them we have companied with Jesus, learning what He said, what He did, what He felt. We have marvelled at those seven peak-events, His supernormal birth, baptism, temptation, transfiguration, crucifixion, resurrection, ascension. We have been impelled to blend our eager hearts with Peter's avowal: "Thou art the Christ, the Son of the living God." Yet, even so, we have learned *what* He was rather than *who* He was. His words and works and ways have compelled identification of Him as somehow God-Man, but that very confession lands us at the brink of utter mystery. We know now *what* He is: somehow God as well as Man; but is there, then, duality or plurality in God? Now that we know *what* Jesus is, oh, that someone would interpret *who* He is!

That is just where John's Gospel completes the others. The earlier three are a *presentation* of Jesus; this fourth is an *interpretation*. The other three show us Jesus outwardly; this fourth interprets Him inwardly. The other three emphasise the human aspects; this fourth unveils the *Divine*. The other three correspond respectively with the lion and the ox and the man in Ezekiel's vision; this fourth parallels with the *eagle*. The other three concern themselves mainly with our Lord's public discourses; this fourth gives larger place to His *private* conversations, His verbal *conflicts* with the Jews, and His closer teachings in seclusion to His inner disciples. The other three are mainly occupied with His Galilean ministry; this fourth is almost wholly devoted to His *Judæan* ministry. The other three are purely factual; John is also *doctrinal*. The other three begin with a human genealogy and a fulfilment of Jewish prophecy; John begins with a direct Divine revelation of that which was altogether pre-mundane and eternal. All these features accord with John's interpretative purpose.

It is this interpretative emphasis on the inward and Divine which explains the different "feel" about our Gospel according to John. It also creates an interesting problem, for at certain points it is not easy to decide where reporting gives place to John's own comments or explainings. Take, for instance, that best-known text of the Bible, John iii. 16. Did Jesus Himself speak the immortal words to Nicodemus? or has John's reporting of Jesus now given place to his own reflective commenting? In the final paragraph of that same chapter, does the last testimony of the Baptist finish at verse 30 or 31 or 32, or run right to verse 36? Incidentally, John's own recurrent comments and explainings are a rewarding study all in themselves.

Flashlight on Synoptists

Another thing which strikes us right away as we read through John's Gospel is that it does not furnish us with anything like the diary of factual detail which we have in the other three. There is no account of our Lord's birth; no description of His baptism; no mention of His temptation, or of His transfiguration, or of His ascension. Over against twenty miracles in Matthew, eighteen in Mark, and twenty in Luke, there are only eight in John. Over against sixteen parables in Matthew, five in Mark, and twenty in Luke, there is scarcely one parable in John (see x. 6). There is nothing like the running succession of major and minor incidents, or the interweaving of miracle and parable which we have found in the synoptists. John himself, of course, is fully cognisant of these spacious omissions and would have us know it (xx. 30). They are not neglected areas; they are purposely by-passed for the sake of concentration on the significances of what he has selected (xx. 31).

Most of what John *has* recorded is omitted by the other three. Moreover, it throws a flood of light on them. For instance, when the synoptists tell of our Lord's "Follow Me" to Peter and Andrew, James and John, it would almost seem as though He had not met them before, which makes their immediate abandonment of all else to follow Him so surprising as to seem almost artificial; but in this fourth Gospel we find that they had not only met Jesus earlier, at John the Baptist's gatherings along the winding Jordan valley, but had companied with Him both in Judæa and in

Galilee (i. 40, 42, 43, 47). Before ever He started His preaching itineraries in Galilee there was a group called "His disciples" (ii. 2, 11), which certainly included Andrew, Peter, James, John, and others of those who later comprised the Apostolate. His sea-shore "Follow Me," recorded by the synoptists, came *later*, and was a call to *full-time* service with Him.

Again, in reading the other three Gospels we may have won-dered how such wide fame and vast crowds could have happened from the minute Jesus "began to preach" in Galilee (Matt. iv. 17). But here, in John, we find that before ever He started there He had worked miracles in Jerusalem (ii. 23), which had become big news up in Galilee. See chapter iv. 45: "Then when He was come into Galilee, the Galileans received Him, having seen all the things that He did in Jerusalem at the feast: for they also went to the feast." There had also been the turning of the water into wine at Cana in Galilee, where He thus "manifested forth His glory, and His disciples believed on Him" (ii. 11). We know for a certainty that all these things happened before our Lord com-menced His preaching circuit of Galilee, because "John [the Bap-tist] was not yet cast into prison" (iii. 24)—and it was not until *after* John was imprisoned that Jesus began in Galilee (Matt. iv. 12).

Furthermore, an observant noting of John's dates and places corrects certain misimpressions as to our Lord's movements. Not only do we now learn that after His baptism our Lord was five or six months or more in Jerusalem and Judæa, with goings to and fro between there and Galilee, before ever His main Galilean ministry began, but we find that there was also another time-break between the *end* of His Galilean ministry, and His triumphal entry into Jerusalem. Were we to go only by the synoptists we might easily assume that the triumphal entry climaxed without interruption the journey from Galilee to Jerusalem. In fact, with this further data from John before us, the sensible thing is right away to juxtapose the synoptists and this fourth Gospel so as to ensure a correct "build-up" of our Lord's main public movements. Let no new student think that such attempted correlation of John and the synoptists is needless or tedious; it is the only means whereby we can gain an accurate full view of our Lord's public ministry or see the full force of His offer to the nation.

All four make the Jordan baptism the starting-point of public action. We know, too, that the Galilean mission, on which the synoptists concentrate, did not begin until John the Baptist was imprisoned (Matt. iv. 12, 17; Mark. i. 14). So, then, let us try to co-ordinate John and the synoptists.

(1) Inceptive Judæan Ministry

The actual spot where the baptism took place cannot be known, but it was *not* in Galilee, for Matthew says that John came preaching in the "wilderness of *Judæa*" (Matt. iii. 1), i.e. the open country on the eastern side of Judæa, round about the Jordan but not stretching up as far as Galilee. Doubtless John moved up and down the Jordan valley. We find him later at a certain "Bethany beyond Jordan" (John i. 28, R.V.), and still later at Ænon, inside the border of Samaria (John iii. 23). *If* he ever travelled up Jordan as far as the Sea of Galilee, he never went further north than that. But in any case we know that our Lord was not baptised in Galilee, for Matthew iii. 13 distinctly says: "Then cometh Jesus *from* Galilee to Jordan, unto John, to be baptised of Him." The synoptists all tell us that *straightway* after His baptism our Lord underwent His lonely temptation, which also was in the "wilderness" of Judæa, and that *after* the temptation He *returned* to Galilee (Matt. iv. 1, 12; Mark i. 12, 14; Luke iv. 1, 14).

The *fourth* Gospel does not narrate either the baptism or the temptation. Many who read the first chapter of John mistakenly assume that the forerunner's words in verses 15, 26, 32, 33 were spoken *at* our Lord's baptism. But no; those verses are a record of what the Baptist said *later* to a deputation of enquiry from Jerusalem (verses 19, 24). That is why he uses the past tense each time: "This is He of whom I *spake*" (verse 15); "I *saw* the Spirit descending . . . upon Him" (verse 32); "And I *knew* Him not" (verse 33).

Glance at that first chapter again. When the Baptist says "There standeth One among you, whom ye know not" (verse 26) he so speaks because Jesus has already been among those crowds, and has been baptised there some forty days earlier. When we find in verse 29 "The next day John seeth Jesus coming unto him, and saith: Behold the Lamb of God, which taketh away the sin of the world!" we are to understand that Jesus has now returned after His forty days of temptation in the wilderness.

And when John continues "I saw the Spirit descending and remaining on Him" (verse 32) he is describing in retrospect what he had witnessed some forty days earlier. We know this because the ensuing paragraph tells us that *"The next day after"* Andrew and another "abode with Jesus"; and verse 43 adds that again *"the day following"* Jesus started for Galilee, where He called Philip; and chapter ii. tells us that "the third day" after this He was at a wedding in Cana. Now these activities could not have taken place *between* our Lord's baptism and His temptation, for, as the synoptists show, the temptation followed *"immediately."* Therefore these activities narrated in John's opening chapter must have been *subsequent* to the temptation; which means, of course, that the Baptist's witness to the descent of the Holy Spirit upon Jesus was spoken in retrospect, over forty days later, when Jesus had returned from the temptation.

Soon after the Cana wedding Jesus is in Jerusalem for the Passover—His first appearance there after His baptism. He now publicly acts as One conscious of prophetic vocation, and with resistless godly wrathfulness drives the desecrating traffickers from the temple (ii. 13–22). He also gives miraculous signs to certify His Divine authorisation (23–5). He is interviewed by Pharisee Nicodemus, and the conversation implies that our Lord must already have uttered teaching about the "kingdom of God" (iii. 3, 5), and that He must have made a deep impression on the public.

We know that all this *preceded* the Galilean ministry because (let repetition emphasise it) chapter iii. 24, now says that "John [the Baptist] was not yet cast into prison."

Chapter iv., then, tells us that Jesus returned yet again to Galilee. (We say "returned" because His home was still there; and it was still at Nazareth, for He did not remove to Capernaum until after John was imprisoned: Matt. iv. 13.) On the way back to Galilee He "must needs go through Samaria" (verse 4), where He has the memorable conversation with the woman of Sychar at Jacob's well (verses 6–42). Afterwards He performs His second miracle at Cana, i.e. the healing of the nobleman's son (verses 43–54).

Chapter v. relates a further excursion to Jerusalem for "a feast of the Jews," and the healing of the paralytic at the pool of Bethesda, followed by a powerful discourse in reply to the Jews, who now fanatically sought to kill Him for healing the paralytic on the Sabbath, and also for "making Himself equal with God."

All these things, in these first five chapters, are peculiar to John's Gospel, and all precede the Galilee preachings. *What length of time do they cover?* Verses like ii. 12, iii. 22, iv. 1–3 are revealing. When we find that "after these things came Jesus and His disciples into the land [as distinct from the capital] of Judæa; and there He *tarried* with them and was baptising" (iii. 22) we infer that an interval of weeks, if not months, is indicated; and we are confirmed in this by the further comment in iv. 1, that "Jesus made and baptised *more disciples than John*." This must have taken time.

That our Lord was exercising a preaching ministry at this time is indicated in the last testimony of John the Baptist (iii. 32, 34). Being ill-received in the capital, He turned to the less-prejudiced country people. We are to think of continued public teaching; of movement from place to place; of Jesus re-emphasising John the Baptist's call to repentance as the first preliminary to the "kingdom"; of increasing numbers being influenced. We know how quickly crowds would accumulate at such a time and in such a place; for not only had John the Baptist informed his own great audiences that Jesus was the eagerly awaited Messiah, but Jesus had now performed astonishing miracles in Jerusalem (ii. 23, iii. 2); yet, even so, we must allow weeks, possibly a few months, for this early public ministry in Judæa before ever the ministry in *Galilee* began. If only we knew for certain which "feast" it was in chapter v. 1, we could fix the time easily; but which of the "feasts" was it?

(2) The Galilean Ministry

So, then, everything up to the end of chapter v. belongs to the period (approximately five months?) which preceded the Galilean ministry. But now, *between* the end of that fifth chapter and chapter x. 22, the whole round-up of Galilee occurs as related by the synoptists, though passed over by John in silence, except for the feeding of the five thousand and the walking on the sea (vi.). We know this for three reasons: (1) Our Lord's use of the past tense when referring to John the Baptist, in v. 35, indicates that

John's imprisonment had now taken place (the event which precipitated the commencement of the Galilean ministry: see Matt. iv. 12). (2) Chapter vi. 1 tells us that our Lord now went to Galilee again. (3) John now records the feeding of the five thousand, which, of course, was in Galilee and near the end of the itineraries there. This miracle, followed by that of our Lord's walking on the sea, is John's one and only extract from our Lord's Galilean tour; and he obviously picks it out because of its tremendous significance along with the discourse which it occasioned on the "Bread of Life."

In corroboration of this it is well to note that in chapter v. 16–18, linked with chapter vii. 1, we are given the *reason* why Jesus left Judæa at that juncture for His Galilean ministry.

Perhaps, then, this is the point for a bit of Bible marking. Turning to the fourth chapter of Matthew, it might be useful to insert between verses 11 and 12: "THE FIRST FIVE CHAPTERS OF JOHN ALL FIT IN HERE." (The same between Mark i. 13 and 14, also between Luke iv. 13 and 14.) Similarly, in John, it might be well to write between chapters v. and vi.: "MOST OF GALILEE MINISTRY FITS FROM HERE UP TO VII. 1." Next, in John x., between verses 21 and 22, write: "THREE-MONTHS BREAK HERE. JESUS BACK TO GALILEE, WHICH HE NOW FINALLY LEAVES AS PER MATTHEW XIX. 1; MARK X. 1."

Can We be Sure?

But as soon as we reach this point some student is sure to interrupt: "Are you quite *certain* that Jesus went back to Galilee after x. 21, and that His final exit from Galilee was soon after that, as per Matthew xix. 1 and Mark x. 1? Do not others suggest different departure points? Does not the Scofield Bible say: 'FINAL DEPARTURE FROM GALILEE' at the tenth verse of the *seventh* chapter?" Well, let us see how John guides us.

In that tenth verse of the seventh chapter he says that Jesus went up to Jerusalem "*in secret,*" whereas Matthew (xix. 1) and Mark (x. 1) and Luke (ix. 51, x. 1, etc.) all tell us that His "final departure" from Galilee was attended by crowds and utmost publicity: so John vii. 10 simply *cannot* mark the event!

And there is another very cogent reason why John vii. 10 cannot possibly mark the "final departure from Galilee." Matthew, Mark and Luke all show us how that final departure eventually culminated in the *triumphal entry,* after which our Lord did not vacate Jerusalem and Bethany again before His crucifixion; whereas *after* John vii. 10 we find our Lord away *three times,* each for a considerable lapse (first, between x. 21 and 22, as our next paragraph shows: second, x. 39–43; third, xi. 54).

That final exit *must* have been later than John vii. 10: but *when*? Again John guides us. Chapters vii. to x. are linked so unbrokenly, that, as *all* are agreed, they all belong to that one particular visit to Jerusalem for the "feast of Tabernacles." But it is equally plain that a break occurs at chapter x. 21 because the feast of Tabernacles occurred in *October,* whereas the next verse (22) says: "Now it was at Jerusalem the feast of the Dedication, and *it was winter.*" Between the Feast of Tabernacles in October and that of the Dedication (which was in *December*) there was a full two months. Where was Jesus during that time? He must have returned to *Galilee,* because after His *next* two visits to Jerusalem and Bethany He did *not* go back there; He went no further than Peræa (x. 40) and Judæa (xi. 54); and His next visit to Jerusalem after *that* was for the triumphal entry (xii. 1–19) and the crucifixion. So His final visit *to* and exit *from* Galilee must certainly have occurred between John x. 21 and 22.

This brings us to a most intriguing poser, which, however, is far friendlier than it looks at first. How are we to interrelate those *four* goings up to Jerusalem (vii. 10, then x. 22, then xi. 17 to Bethany, then xii. 12 for the triumphal entry) with the *one and only* journey thither as reported by Matthew, Mark, and Luke? This seems to have been a headache to most expositors. Some argue that Luke's long account (ix. 51–xix. 44) in which there is so much which neither Matthew nor Mark record, is in reality not just one journey to Jerusalem but *three,* the first one (Luke ix. 51–xiii. 21) corresponding with the December visit in John x. 22–42; the second one (Luke xiii. 22–xvii. 10) corresponding with the visit to Bethany for the raising of Lazarus, in John xi. 1–54; the third one (Luke xvii. 11–xix. 44) corresponding with John xii., the triumphal entry. But the one and only blow needed to demolish such a theory is that after none of those visits in *John* does Jesus return to Galilee, whereas in Luke, even as late as xvii. 11, we are *still* in Galilee!

Is there a Solution?

Is there a solution? We think there is. To us it is the simplest and most obvious. First let us solve the lesser problem of Luke's long Jerusalem journey in relation to the other two synoptists. Both Matthew and Mark transfer our Lord right from Galilee to "the borders of Judæa" in a single sentence (Matt. xix. 1; Mark x. 1), whereas Luke tells of "messengers" and the "seventy" sent on ahead (ix. 52, x. 1), of parables and miracles, and of visits to various places *en route*. But then, at chapter xviii. 15, Luke suddenly links up again with Matthew and Mark, and thenceforth parallels with them right on through the triumphal entry into the capital. See how markedly this is so:

Jesus blesses little children	Matt. xix, 13, 15; Mark x. 13–16; Luke xviii. 15–17.
The rich young ruler—and attendant teaching	Matt. xix. 16; Mark x. 17–31; Luke xviii. 18–30.
Jesus foretells His death and resurrection	Matt. xx. 17–19; Mark x. 32–4; Luke xviii. 31–4.
Ambitious request of James and John	Matt. xx. 20–8; Mark x. 35–45; Luke, no mention.
Jericho — crowds; blind man healed; Zachæus	Matt. xx. 29–34; Mark x. 46–52; Luke xviii. 35–xix. 27.
Triumphal entry into Jerusalem	Matt. xxi. 1–11; Mark xi. 1–11; Luke xix. 28–44.

So, point by point, from chapter xviii. 15 onwards, Luke parallels with Matthew and Mark. The inference, therefore, fairly forces itself upon us, that those wonderful extra chapters in Luke (ix. 51–xviii. 14) belong to the thronged journeying *through* Galilee and Samaria and Peræa (the region east of the Jordan) to the border of Judæa. Luke joins up again with Matthew and Mark at the point where Jesus is about to cross the Jordan for Jericho and thence up to His triumphal entry into Jerusalem.

Now it was *from there*, Peræa, along the Jordan border of Judæa, that our Lord made those two short visits to Jerusalem and Bethany, which *John* records, i.e. to the December Feast of the Dedication (x. 22–39) and for the raising of Lazarus (xi. 1–46). That is why we are told after the one that Jesus "went away again *beyond Jordan*" (x. 40), and after the other that He "went thence into a country [locality] near to *the wilderness, into a city called Ephraim*" (xi. 54).

Thus, the four accounts of our Lord's public ministry, at least in its general outline, dovetail into a united, consecutive order.

Yet it may be that some perspicacious student still demurs with dogged doubt. In supposing that our Lord's last resort *to* and final exit *from* Galilee fits between John x. 21 and 22, are we allowing a sufficient interval (i.e. the two months from "Tabernacles" in *October* to "Dedication" in *December*) for all that long journey of evacuation narrated in Luke ix. 51 to xviii.? Yes, we are. A very few days would see our Lord back in Galilee from Jerusalem. A careful inspection of Luke's chapters quickly shows them to be so linked together and so considerably filled with parables that all could easily have happened in seven weeks or less. (Compare these chapters with a map and see.)

The one and only objection which can be raised is that Luke x. 38–42 says: "Now it came to pass, as they went, that He entered into a certain village; and a certain woman named Martha received Him into her house. And she had a sister called Mary." How comes it that so early in Luke's narrative of the final journey out from Galilee there could be a visit to the home of Martha and Mary at Bethany, near *Jerusalem*? An easy solution on purely critical grounds is that Luke simply got his small papyrus leaves mixed a bit, and that this incident of our Lord's kindly rebuke of Martha, "cumbered about much serving," slipped in here by mistake. That is not *our* idea of Luke or of Scripture. Where there is an insoluble problem of this sort we prefer to leave it so, rather than offer an explanation which in any way compromises the supernatural inspiration of the Scriptures. But in this particular incident is there a problem at all? Who *says* it happened at Bethany? Does Luke? No! He simply says "a certain village." Is it likely that he would thus have referred to the well-known Bethany near Jerusalem? Scarcely, since he so definitely names it in chapter xix. 29. Moreover, this incident must not be confused with the "supper" at Bethany in John xii., for *that* was in the house of "Simon the leper" (compare Matt. xxvi. 6; Mark xiv. 3). Who is to say that Martha did not have a "house," perhaps her *home*, in Galilee?

How Long was Our Lord's Public Ministry?

Now that we have before us the further data supplied by John, we can also figure out the approximate time covered by our Saviour's public ministry. It was surprisingly short. The usual assumption is three years; but was it even as long as that?

The big clue is in John's three occurrences of the Passover (ii. 13, vi. 4, xi. 55, etc.).

Take the first of them. John says, "Now the Jews' Passover was at hand, and Jesus went up to Jerusalem" (ii. 13). Before that, there had been His baptism, temptation, return to Jordan, first contacts with Andrew, Peter, and others of His future apostles, and a return to Galilee. We must allow the "forty days" for the temptation, two or three days or more back to Jordan, then one week up to the wedding in Cana (compare i. 29, 35, 43, ii. 1), say two months in all, plus whatever length of days were then spent in Capernaum (ii. 12).

Next, there was His visit to *Jerusalem* for the Passover, allowing enough days for His miracles there, and the impact on the crowds (ii. 23) and the interview of Nicodemus (iii.), followed by a ministry of teaching and baptising at the Jordan boundary of Judæa (iii. 22–4), and a further return to Galilee (iv.). For all these we must allow the minimum of eight days at the Passover (ii. 23–iii. 21), then, at a rough guess, a month or nearly so for that Jordan ministry where He "tarried" (iii. 22) long enough to make "more disciples than John" (iv. 1); then two or three days back to Galilee (iv. 4, 40). Say some six or seven weeks.

This seems confirmed by what now comes in John v. "After this there was a feast of the Jews; and Jesus went up to Jerusalem." This unnamed feast certainly could not have been the next year's Passover, for that would leave an inexplicable gap of silence for nearly a year, not only by John, but by all four Gospel writers; moreover it is no mere presumption that had it been another Passover John would have named it so, as he does in other places. No, this unnamed feast would be the feast of Pentecost, seven weeks, or "fifty days," after the Passover (Lev. xxiii. 15). If not, and if not another Passover, then which?

It *could* have been the feast of Tabernacles, but is it likely, seeing that John refers to *that* feast by *name* in chapter vii. 2? And is it likely that our Lord's wilderness ministry at Jordan (iii. 22) stretched on from the Passover (April) to Tabernacles (October)?

We ourselves feel confident that the unnamed feast in John v. was Pentecost, but we shall not dogmatise. Whether it was Pentecost or Tabernacles does not affect the total duration of our Lord's ministry. If it was Pentecost (June) then our Lord's subsequent ministry in Galilee started four months earlier than if the feast was Tabernacles (October). We cannot resist pointing out an ancillary bit of evidence in favour of its being Pentecost, namely, our Lord's remark in chapter iv. 35: "Say not ye, There are *yet four months* and then cometh harvest?"—which obviously could not fit October! So we assume the unnamed feast in John v. to have been Pentecost (April), after which the *Galilean* ministry largely fits into John's silent gap *between* chapters v. and vi., and also *includes* chapter vi. Therefore *from the Baptism to the beginning of the ministry in Galilee was about four to five months.*

Galilee and After

We know from John vi. 4 that during the *next* Passover Jesus stayed in Galilee, at which time He performed His mighty miracle, the feeding of the five thousand (vi. 5–15). We know also from the synoptists that a large part of His Galilean ministry was then over (which is yet another confirmation that the unnamed feast in John v. must have been the *earlier* one, i.e. Pentecost). He had now been in Galilee some ten months, that is, from just after the preceding feast of Pentecost (June) to this further Passover (April). The following October He went to Jerusalem for the feast of Tabernacles (vii. 2–x. 21). Between x. 21 and 22 His Galilee ministry ended, as we have shown, having lasted some eighteen months. He was back in Jerusalem for the feast of the Dedication in December; and was crucified the following Passover (April).

So, from the Jordan baptism to that first Passover was about three months; and from that Passover to the next-but-one when He was crucified covers two years. That unnamed feast in John v. could not have been another Passover. There were only *three* Passovers, not four. Therefore our Lord's public ministry lasted only two years and three months. It may be thus outlined:

Order and length of Our Lord's Ministry

1. CONTACTS IN JUDÆA (*four to five months*).

Jordan baptism and temptation in wilderness	Matt. iii. 1–iv. 11; Mark i. 4–13; Luke iii. 1–iv. 13.
At Jordan again; meets Andrew and Peter	John i. 19–42.
Return to Galilee: Cana and first miracle	John 1. 43–ii. 12.
At Jerusalem for the Passover; Nicodemus interview	John ii. 13–iii. 21.
Interval of teaching, baptising in Judæa, near Jordan	John iii. 22–36.
Galilee again: Sychar woman; second Cana miracle	John iv. 1–54.
At Jerusalem feast: Bethesda cure; Jews oppose	John v. 1–47.

2. CIRCUIT OF GALILEE (*about one year and ten months*).

The three synoptic accounts of the Galilean ministry	Matt. iv. 12–xviii; Mark i. 14–ix.; Luke iv. 14–ix. 50.
Short break—to Jerusalem for feast of Tabernacles	John vii. 2–x. 21.
Slow, final exit-journey from Galilee	Luke ix. 51–xviii. 14.
Halt in Peræa; visit to Jerusalem; feast of Dedication	John x. 22–39.
Peræa again; whence up to Bethany to raise Lazarus	John x. 40–xi. 54.
From "city called Ephraim" up to triumphal entry	Matt. xix. 1–xxi. 11; Mark x. 1–xi. 11; Luke xviii. 15–xix. 44; John xi. 54–xii. 19.

3. CLIMAX AT JERUSALEM (*about one week*).

Clashes with Jewish leaders in the capital	Matt. xxi. 12–xxiii; Mark xi.–xii.; Luke xix. 45–xxi. 4.
Prophetic forecast on the Mount of Olives	Matt. xxiv., xxv.; Mark xiii. Luke xxi. 5–38.
At Bethany: the anointing by Mary	Matt. xxvi.; Mark xiv.; John xii.
Last Passover: Discourse to the apostles	Matt. xxvi.; Mark xiv.; Luke xxii.; John xiii.–xvii.
Gethsemane; the arrest; Peter's denial	Ditto and John xviii.
Arraignment, crucifixion, and burial	Matt. xxvii.; Mark xv.; Luke xxiii.; John xviii. 28–xix.

Notes

(1) If the feast in the fifth chapter of John is the feast of Tabernacles (October) and not the feast of Pentecost as we have assumed, the pre-Galilee section will be four months more and the Galilee ministry four months less; but the total will not be affected.

(2) The anointing of our Lord by Mary of Bethany is placed after the triumphal entry and after the Olivet discourse, by the synoptists. In fact, Matthew xxvi. 2, and Mark xiv. 1 would indicate that several days had elapsed between the triumphal entry and Mary's anointing. In John xii., however, it is placed *before* the triumphal entry; and on that account there has been a ready inclination by some critical writers to pronounce Matthew and Mark in error, since John wrote later and (so it is presumed) here corrected them. But no; John here mentions the supper and anointing in advance of the actual day because of his having just said that Jesus had reached *Bethany*, and he at once associates the two. He mentions the very same anointing in advance in chapter xi. 2. Moreover, in the twelfth chapter verse 9 clearly indicates that Jesus had at the time of the anointing been at Bethany enough days for "much people of the Jews" to know that He was there, and to come "not for Jesus' sake only, but that they might see Lazarus also, whom He had raised from the dead." When verse 12 says "On the next day" it means the day after the arrival at Bethany on the way to Jerusalem, not the day after Mary's anointing.

(3) Read John xiii. 2–30 between Matthew xxvi. 20 and 21; and read John xv., xvi., and xvii. between Matthew xxvi. 30 and 31.

Perhaps to some readers or students it may not seem over-exhilarating to go into details such as the foregoing. None the less, we are persuaded that it is of utmost practical value. Those things which thrill us most at the moment are not always those which leave the most permanent or practical benefit. In our next study we shall explore some of the spiritual treasures of John's Gospel; but as we leave this present chapter we cannot resist saying again that to master the general outline of our Lord's public ministry is of underlying usefulness in all our studies of its spiritual aspects.

THE GOSPEL ACCORDING TO JOHN (2)

Lesson Number 122

NOTE.—For this study read right through John's Gospel again, picking out and listing (*a*) the miracles, (*b*) our Lord's interviews.

The prominence given in this Gospel to the *discourses* of Jesus and certain conversations is especially noteworthy. John relates none of the parables recorded by the Synoptists, but gives us the dialogue with Nicodemus (iii. 1-15) and the Samaritan woman (iv. 4-38); the discourse after the healing at Bethesda (v. 19-47), and the allegorical addresses on "the Bread of Life" (vi. 35 ff.); "the Light of the World" (viii. 12 ff.); "the Door" and "the Good Shepherd of the Sheep" (x. 1 ff.); "the Way, the Truth, and the Life" (xiv. 6-31); "the true Vine" (xv.); the mission of the Comforter (xvi.). Different in style as these discourses are from those in the Synoptists, there are many remarkable correspondences of doctrinal teaching to be found, sufficient to prove that there is no new doctrine, only a fuller expounding of truths presented by the Synoptists in a more concrete form.

Angus, Bible Handbook.

THE GOSPEL ACCORDING TO JOHN (2)

WE CANNOT possibly come with too much eagerness to learn the spiritual teachings of this "Gospel according to John." It never disappoints either the early seeker or the continuing searcher. There is no polysyllabic wording to deter the simple, and no obscurantism to puzzle the earnest. All the way through there is transparent simplicity. Yet there are interior meanings too profound for language, and depths that are deep as infinity; so that every new exploring yields new reward. Those who have studied it most would be the first to say:

> *My pail I'm often dropping*
> *Deep down into this well,*
> *It never touched the bottom,*
> *However deep it fell;*
> *And though I keep on dipping*
> *By study, faith and prayer,*
> *I have no power to measure*
> *The living water there.*

So, then, let us now examine its contents, and learn its main message. At once we are struck by the different way of saying and seeing things from that of Matthew, Mark, or Luke. In Matthew we have impressionist groupings; in Mark a rapid succession of camera-shots; in Luke a beautifully unfolding story. Here, in John, everything subserves the developing of certain *recurrent ideas*. These are assembled in the prologue, and then developed right through to the end. Not that these ideas are mere abstractions of John's own producing; they are spiritual *truths* outgrowing from fertile *facts*. From a large store of available data John selects just those which demonstrate and develop these central truths of his treatise.

Mark it well: the structural characteristic of this fourth Gospel is that of *recurrent ideas*. Even among these (some of which we shall shortly pick out for separate consideration) there is one which is centre-most, namely, *eternal life by believing on Jesus as Son of God and Saviour of men.* We miss the real genius and cumulative force of this fourth Gospel if we try to plot it out in doctrinal sections. To make out, for instance, that Christ is revealed as *Life* in the first group of chapters, as *Light* in the next group, and as *Love* in the last group, is artifice, not analysis. The three alliteratives could be transposed yet fit just as well. Or to say that in chapters i. to vi. we have *Revelation,* in chapters vii. to xii. *Rejection,* and in chapters xiii. to xxi. *Reception,* is a merely arbitrary trio of "Rs". The fact is that revelation, rejection, reception go side by side all the way through, as also do life, light, love. We do not say that there is *no* ground-plan of arrangement in John's Gospel; what we are insisting is that it is not according to doctrine or subject-matter, and that to force such analysis upon it badly blurs its cumulative *recurrence of ideas.* (We find just this same form of teaching by recurrent emphases in John's first *epistle.*)

Perhaps before we come to consider some of these progressive themes in this fourth Gospel we ought just to glance at John's own basic arrangement of his material as it really is. There is a prologue (i. 1–18) and an epilogue (xxi.). The intervening body of chapters fall thus:

    1. The public ministry of Jesus to the Jews (i. 19–xii.).
    2. The private ministry of Jesus to "His own" (xiii.–xvii.).
    3. The paschal climax of tragedy and triumph (xviii.–xx.).

The first of these chapter-groups is occupied with the miraculous "signs" which our Lord gave, of which John here records seven, culminating with the raising of Lazarus from death. Note how the early *contacts* quickly develop into later *conflicts,* and then issue in utter *cleavage.*

The second group mainly concerns our Lord's wonderful new disclosures about the coming *Paraclete.* The final chapters are the awful yet glorious outcome of the whole.

More detailed analysis is not only a burden on the memory, instead of an aid to it, but it is quite needless for our present purpose. It is well to fix the three main divisions in mind; and having done so, let us hasten to examine some of those concatenated themes which, as we have said, stretched like shining linked chains right through the book.

GROUND-PLAN OF JOHN'S GOSPEL

Prologue (i. 1–18).
"The Word became flesh."

1. PUBLIC MINISTRY OF JESUS TO THE JEWS
(i. 19–xii.).

First "signs," witness and *contacts* (i. 19–iv.).
Further "signs," witness and *conflicts* (v.–x.).
Final "sign," witness and *cleavage* (xi.–xii.).

2. PRIVATE MINISTRY OF JESUS TO "HIS OWN"
(xiii.–xvii.).

Presage of His own departure (xiii.–xiv. 15).
Promise of the coming Spirit (xiv. 16–xvi.).
Prayer for them to God the Father (xvii.).

3. PASCHAL CLIMAX: TRAGEDY AND TRIUMPH
(xviii.–xx.).

Apprehension and prosecution (xviii.–xix. 15).
Crucifixion and entombment (xix. 16–42).
Resurrection and reappearance (xx. 1–31).
Epilogue (xxi.): "Till I come."

Key Verse and Theme

Think carefully: which would *you* give as key verse and theme in John's Gospel? May we help you to a true answer? All the way through there is a gloomy background of Jewish unbelief, reminding us repeatedly of chapter i. 12: "He came unto His own; and *His own received Him not*." But in the foreground there is a compensating succession of interviews with individuals who *did* receive Him, reminding us *again* of chapter i. 12: "But *as many as received Him*, to them gave He power to become the sons of God." Closely associated with these foreground figures is a chain of eight remarkable "sign" miracles which demonstrate with never-to-be-forgotten vividness the transforming power of

Christ, reminding us yet *again* of chapter i. 12: "To them He gave *power to become* the sons of God." I know that the Greek word here translated as "power" may be appropriately rendered as "right" or "authority," but that in no wise detracts from the dynamic sense. The "right" or "authority" to become the sons of God *implies* the "power" to do so; for (mark well) it is not merely the right to "be," but to "become" (*genésthai*), implying the transforming moral *power* to become so, and to live as such. (What use, for instance, is "authority" to a king if he lacks the *power* to exercise it?)

So far as the spiritual message of John's Gospel is concerned, the key verse is undoubtedly chapter i. 12. Those of us who have now familiarised ourselves with the contents of this Gospel can scarcely miss seeing how these three centre-lines run with parallel persistence and increasing sharpness right through the chapters:

    1. "His own received Him not."
    2. "But as many as received Him."
    3. "To them He gave power to become."

The Eight Miracles

Let us look first at the eight miracles around which the narrative gathers. Certain features at once arrest the eye.

    1. The turning of the water into wine   (ii.).
    2. The healing of the nobleman's son   (iv.).
    3. The curing of the Bethesda paralytic   (v.).
    4. The feeding of the five thousand   (vi.).
    5. The walking over the sea of Galilee   (vi.).
    6. The giving of sight to the blind man   (ix.).
    7. The raising of Lazarus from death   (xi.).
    8. The miraculous draught of fishes   (xxi.).

As all musical sound is comprehended in eights or octaves, so John has comprehended the significance of all our Saviour's miracles in these eight. Musical sound, whether produced by strings as in a piano, or by columns of air as in a pipe organ, is created by minute vibrations; the higher the pitch, the minuter are the vibrations; but all these vibrations go in sets of eights. For instance, starting off with middle c, we ascend seven full consecutive notes, and then we are at another c. But *why* must we call that eighth note c again? It is because the number of vibrations is exactly double that of middle c, and therefore in exact sound-alignment with it. Thus the octave always repeats the first note of the eight.

So is it with the octave of miracles in John's Gospel. The first of them strikes the key-note: "This beginning of miracles did Jesus in Cana of Galilee, and manifested forth His glory; and His disciples *believed on Him.*" This does not occur again until we come to the eighth: "That ye might *believe that Jesus is the Christ, the Son of God;* and that *believing* ye might have life through His name." It is the same with other Bible octaves, as for instance the eight beatitudes of the Sermon on the Mount. The first, so to speak, strikes middle c: "Blessed are the poor in spirit, for *theirs is the kingdom of heaven.*" There is no recurrence of this until we come to the last, the eighth, when it sounds again: "For *theirs is the kingdom of heaven.*" Indeed, the whole of human history as revealed in Scripture conforms to this law of the octave. We start with a *new creation*, in Genesis. Then there are four thousand years B.C., followed by the present two thousand years A.D., which are to be followed by a further *one* thousand years R.D. (*Regno Domini*), making seven great days of one thousand years each, to be ended by the general judgment of mankind at the Great White Throne; after which the eighth or octave note recurs with another *new creation*—"a new heaven and a new earth"; "Behold I make all things new."

There are three features about John's eight sign-miracles which should be noted: (*a*) he numbers the first two; so there is *sequence;* (*b*) there is no duplication, as in the synoptists; so there is careful *selection;* (*c*) there is an over-all purpose (xx. 11), so there is *speciality.*

Also there is one unifying idea traceable through them all, namely that of *transformation.* Passing through them successively, we find transformation from sadness to gladness; from disease to health; from paralysis to energy; from hunger to fulness; from agitation to tranquillity; from darkness to light; from death to life; from frustration and failure to copious success. It requires no hard study to see how these eight supernatural transformations provide not only evidential "signs" of our Lord's deity but striking illustrations of that transforming "power to become" which operates in "as many as receive Him."

"As Many as Received Him"

Our Lord's private interviews with individuals or small groups has often been noted as a unique feature of this fourth Gospel. John reviews eight of them for us. These are they:

1. Peter, Nathaniel, etc.   (i. 35–51).
2. The ruler Nicodemus   (iii. 1–21).
3. The Sychar woman   (iv. 6–26).
4. The man born blind   (ix. 35–41).
5. Martha and Mary; Bethany   (xi.).
6. The eleven apostles   (xiii.–xvi.).
7. Mary Magdalene   (xx. 1–18).
8. The apostle Peter   (xxi. 15–23).

These eight representatively exemplify *"as many as received Him."* It may be thought momentarily that John the Baptist should be included; but no, there is here no recorded converse of Jesus with him; nor is there with the Bethesda paralytic in chapter v., beyond the bare words which uttered cure and warning.

The first of the eight sets the note: *"Power to become."* We are not told what passed during the leisurely interview of Andrew and John with Jesus (i. 39); the emphasis is on what Jesus said to Simon and Nathaniel: "Thou art . . . thou shalt be." "Thou shalt see greater things than these." This is the *promise* involute in that protoplasmic "power to become."

Then in the interviews which follow we see illustrated how that new life-power operates in "as many as received Him."

In the interview with Nicodemus we see that its operation begins with a being "born anew." In the interview with the Sychar woman it becomes an inner spring of life and satisfaction. In the man born blind it is an inward as well as an outward eye-opening to see Jesus as "the Son of God" (ix. 35). In the conversation with the Bethany sisters it is an energy which, in answer to faith, conquers the seemingly impossible (xi. 40). In the long and touching conversation with the Eleven (xiii.–xvi.) we learn by direct information that the executive of this new power-life is the Divine Paraclete. Next, in the pathetic yet thrilling interview with Mary Magdalene, we see how it brings individual manifestation of the risen Lord to His loved ones, transforming heart-break into joy-break. Finally, in the epilogue interview with Peter, we see it bringing restoration and new commission to ministry for the Saviour.

Incidentally, it is interesting to see how the octave charac-teristic repeats itself here, in this *eighth* interview—playing on Peter again as in the *first* of the eight. The promise still held good: "Thou art . . . thou shalt be"; but Peter was needing to learn that the higher octave of "power to *become*" is power to *overcome*.

"As many as received Him, to them gave He the power to become the children of God, even to them that believe on His name" (i. 12). Yes, that is the central spiritual message running through this Gospel according to John.

What field for closer study this provides! How wonderfully those eight sign-miracles illustrate the operation of this "power to become"! Just as a mere hint, take the four actions of our Lord in feeding the five thousand with the little laddie's lunch— (1) He took, (2) He blessed, (3) He brake, (4) He used.

A Remarkable Parallel

There is also a captivating correspondence between the struc-ture of this fourth Gospel and the furniture of the long-ago Tabernacle. We mentioned this away back among our studies in the Pentateuch, but we must briefly outline it again here, in its proper place, without the slightest apology for some repetition.

That old-time Hebrew Tabernacle was in three parts. There was the large, oblong outer court, 100 cubits long (about 150 feet) by 50 cubits wide (i.e. 75 feet); and inside this, toward one end, was the "sanctuary", which was 30 cubits long by 10 cubits wide. The sanctuary was in two parts—the Holy Place (20 × 10), and at the further end (from entrance of outer court) was the Holy of Holies (10 × 10). Both the oblong outer court and the oblong inner sanctuary were always pitched in east-west direction, with their respective entrances on the east. The entrance to the outer court was called the "gate"; that to the Holy Place the "door"; that to the Holy of Holies the "veil."

That old-time Tabernacle was furnished with *seven* most signifi-

cant objects. Entering by the "gate" of the outer court, we find
(1) the brazen altar of sacrifice. Further in, we find (2) the brazen
laver of cleansing.

Next, passing through the "door" into the Holy Place, we find
(3) the table of the showbread (on the right-hand or north side)
with its oblations and libations (Ex. xxv. 29) or food and drink
offerings, typifying Christ, the Bread of God, and nourisher of
the Christian's life as a believer-priest (Lev. xxiv. 9). On the
left-hand or south side of the Holy Place stands (4) the seven-
thonged golden candelabrum, typifying Christ our Light, shining
in the fulness of the power of the sevenfold Holy Spirit, who is
represented in the oil which feeds the light. Also, in that Holy
Place, standing just before the "veil" into the Holy of Holies, is
(5) the golden altar of incense, which speaks typically of Christ as
our Intercessor, and of the believer-priest's prayers made fragrant
by the all-perfect merits of the precious Name in which he prays.

Finally, beyond the "veil," inside the Holy of Holies, we find
(6) the ark, that most sacred gold-covered acacia chest, about
three feet nine inches long, by two feet three inches wide and
high (containing the two stone slabs of the Law, a golden pot of
manna, and Aaron's rod) typifying Christ as the all-perfect
ground and centre of covenant relationship with God. Upon this
there stood (7) the solid gold mercy seat, overarched by the outstretched wings of the two golden cherubim which stood, one at
each side of it, facing each other, the whole structure being of
equal dimensions with the ark beneath it, and having the throne,
or lengthside, facing the entrance veil. That mercy seat typified
the throne of God. Its being a throne of grace instead of a judgment seat was due to the blood of atonement which sprinkled it
on behalf of the sinning Israelites.

But there was something else in that Divinely designed tabernacle which gave those seven progressively sacred objects a consummation of mysterious glory. It was the *shekinah,* the inde-
finable, unearthly light which glowed just above the mercy seat,
between the arching wings of the two cherubim. That supernatural glory-gleam was more than a symbol, it was actually a
visible form of the Divine presence, hallowing with an utter
solemnity the precincts and articles of that ancient sanctuary.

The furniture of the Tabernacle, with its symbolical and typical
meanings, may be set out as follows:

1. Brazen altar.	Atonement through sacrifice.	The Atonement of Christ.
2. Brazen laver.	Spiritual renewal.	Regeneration by the Holy Spirit.
3. Table of showbread.	Spiritual sustenance.	Christ as Living Bread of his people.
4. Candlestand.	Spiritual illumination.	Christ the Light, especially of His people.
5. Altar of incense.	Acceptable supplication.	Prayer in Name of Jesus (John xiv. Rev. v. 8).
6. The ark.	Access through covenant relationship.	Christ as our covenant access.
7. The mercy seat.	Acceptance at the throne of God.	Acceptance with God in Christ (Rom. iii. 25).

Now, as we have said, there is a fascinating parallel between that Tabernacle furniture and the Gospel according to John. Whether John purposed it or was even cognisant of it we shall not tarry to decide, but it is certainly there. Perhaps the reason for the correspondence is the basic unity of things. The true order of approach to God is one and the same, whether in the old dispensation or the new. Anyway, in this fourth Gospel John leads us, in exactly the same order as those seven articles of Tabernacle furniture, to the great spiritual realities which they typify.

He begins by leading us to the brazen altar of sacrifice, for twice over in chapter i. he bids us "Behold the Lamb of God, which taketh away the sin of the world." Then, in chapter iii., he has us at the brazen laver of cleansing or renewal, telling us that "Except a man be born of water and of the Spirit, he cannot enter the kingdom of God."

Next, in chapters iv.–vi., he takes us to the table of the showbread, with its food and drink, recording for us our Lord's converse with the Sychar woman concerning the "living water" of which, if a man drink, he shall never thirst again; and our Lord's great discourse on Himself as the "living Bread" of which, if a man eat, he shall live for ever. Next, in chapters viii. and ix., John takes us to the golden candelabrum; for twice over we now hear our Lord saying "I am the Light of the world," and "He that followeth Me shall not walk in darkness, but shall have the light of life"—and the man born blind is given sight as a living illustration.

Then, in chapters xiv.–xvi., in that long and tender discourse to the Eleven, we find ourselves at the golden altar of incense, learning to pray in a way and by a Name unknown before, learning how to offer prayers in the name of Jesus, prayers which become as fragrant incense when perfumed by the breathing of that Name which, above all others, is dear to the heart of God.

Next, in that sublime seventeenth chapter, in that moving intercessory prayer which we are allowed to overhear as it falls from the lips of our dear High Priest, we are taken through the "veil" into the very Holy of Holies: we are permitted a glimpse into the high-priestly ministry of intercession which He exercises for us in the presence of God.

Then, in the heart-subduing climax of Calvary, we see, in chapters xviii. and xix., how He is also the very Ark of the Covenant, and the Mercy Seat sprinkled with the holy blood of His own vicarious Self-offering. And chapter xx. follows, the resurrection chapter, in which our risen Lord at once announces our new covenant-relationship with God: "I ascend unto *My* Father and *your* Father; unto *My* God and *your* God."

Thus does John travel, in parallel, from the first to the last of those seven objects which comprised the furniture of the Israelite tabernacle. Finally he discloses the reality which corresponds with that unutterably holy *shekinah*. In the evening of that wonderful day when Jesus rose He suddenly appeared to the Eleven with the tranquillising greeting, "Peace be unto you!" showing them His wounded hands and side, and speaking reassuring words. Then, before He disappeared again, He both *did* and *said* something culminatingly significant: "He *breathed* on them, and saith unto them, *Receive ye the Holy Spirit*." Yes, that is the *new* shekinah of Christian experience!

How engrossing is all this correspondence of order between Israel's long-ago tabernacle in the wilderness and John's new pen-and-ink tabernacle of testimony! Shall we put it down to accident or design? How much more wonderful still is that dear Saviour in whom we possess all these seven Divine provisions, right from the altar of atonement to the indwelling Pentecostal Shekinah!

THE GOSPEL ACCORDING TO JOHN (3)

Lesson Number 123

NOTE.—For our final review of John's Gospel, linger reflectingly again over the prologue, chapters v., vi., and xxi.

The literary relations between the Gospels are a matter of great difference of opinion between scholars, and while from time to time efforts have been made to harmonise the Gospels into one whole, none of those attempts has proved very satisfactory. Scarcely any two harmonies agree. What is known as the Synoptic problem is not only unsolved, but is perhaps insoluble. Indeed, it may be said, without much question, that a real harmony is impossible because each Gospel has its own characteristic features, which cannot be blended with others.

There are several weighty reasons for this contention. In the first place, these features, expressive of the definite purpose of each Gospel, are necessarily lost or at least ignored in the attempt to harmonise them. Then, the material is not always arranged chronologically, but is often grouped according to subject matter. Most important of all, we do not possess anything like a full and orderly record of the words and actions of the Lord Jesus (John xx. 30, 31, xxi. 25), and each writer has evidently been led to make a selection according to his specific purpose. It is not as though all four Gospels were written by one person, for then it would be possible to consider and compare the substance of each in a way that is impracticable with the works of four men. This may suggest the wisdom of giving primary attention to all the Gospels at once and not to three only. On the main points there is substantial agreement that Christ's ministry was exercised first in Judæa (John i. to iv.); then in Galilee (bulk of Matthew and Mark); then in Judæa again, closing with the last week in Jerusalem, in which all four Gospels unite.

—W. H. Griffith Thomas.

As ALREADY remarked, many pages might be filled with notable eulogies of this Gospel according to John. Dr. H. R. Reynolds, late of Cheshunt College, called it "this most wonderful of all the Biblical writings." De Wette described it as "this tender, unique, veritably supreme Gospel." Dr. A. T. Robertson's *Christ of the Logia* refers to it as "the supreme literary work of the world."

By a strange irony, that which has evoked most eulogy has provoked most controversy. The keenest contentions of New Testament criticism have raged around it—and still do. Not even the Pentateuch has been a fiercer battleground of rival scholarship. The collision of pens, brains, theories and prejudices has so developed that one can scarcely be charged with erratic imaginativeness for suspecting in it a very stratagem of Satan to obscure by the dust of debate the outshining splendour of this most precious Gospel. In this present study it is no purpose of ours to join issue among the combatants. To ourselves the fourth Gospel is a genuine document, and its human author is the apostle John.

In our last study we pointed out that everything in this Gospel of John subserves the developing of certain *recurrent* ideas. We think it will prove profitable if we take that up again here. It is interesting to see how these are assembled at the outset, in the prologue, and then developed throughout the subsequent chapters.

The Prologue

John's prologue (i. 1–18) is the primordial nucleus of the whole book. So obvious is this, to an unbiased average reader, that one can only gasp to find princes among scholars averring that "it plays no part in the rest of the volume," and a giant critic like Harnack styling it, at the turn of the century, merely a philosophic prefix meant to please a coterie of the more learned. Truly the late Sir Robert Anderson had reason for complaining that "specialists" were notoriously unreliable when it came to evaluating plain, general evidence! There is a specialised refinement of scholarship which so loses itself in technical minutiæ that in the words of the old proverb it "cannot see wood for trees." John's prologue, without a doubt, is a bunch of keys which unlock all that follows.

In the prologue there are four designations of our Lord which at once capture attention: (1) the WORD, (2) the LIFE, (3) the LIGHT, (4) the SON. Two of these declare His relationship to God the Father. The other two indicate function towards us human creatures.

In relation to God, even the Father, He is the WORD and the SON. These terms are so vastly meaningful that human thought cannot sound their depths. Yet they are illuminatingly significant as well as impenetrably mysterious. They are meant to *tell* us something—and they *do*.

Our Lord is the WORD, i.e. the *expression* of God, not only towards man, not only from pre-mundane antiquity, but before all the creation (verses 2, 3), fundamentally, eternally, indivisibly. He was not merely *from* the beginning; He already was, "*in* the beginning" (verse 1). He was not only "*with* God"; He "*was* God" (verse 1). No exegetical jugglery can really hide the force of the Greek here, especially when it is read honestly with its context. The Greek word *Logos*, here translated as "Word," is fuller than our English representative, yet even our noun "Word" is richly useful here. As a word may be distinguished from the thought which it expresses (for the two are not identical), so can the Second Person of the Godhead be distinguished from the First. Yet as there simply cannot be a word apart from the thought behind it, so also "God" and the "Word" cannot be conceived of as ever having existed without each other. They are distinguishable but inseparable.

Our Lord is also the SON. The concept of *Logos* in relation to *Theos* is warmed into that of the *SON* in relation to the *Father*. At best such human comparisons must fall short of those archetypal realities which they seek to make humanly intelligible; yet even so, they are revealingly approximate. The Logos is simply "*with*" God (verse 1), but the Son is "in the *bosom*" of the Father (verse 18). There is a reciprocal fellowship of love immanent in the Deity; and it is one of the ultimates, eternal as God, for there cannot be eternal fatherhood without eternal sonship.

These two metaphors, the "Word" and the "Son," supplement

and protect each other. Taken separately they might lead divergent thinkers to widely different and equally erroneous conceptions of our Lord; but when they are taken together, each corrects the possible misuse of the other.

To think of our Lord only as the eternal "Word" might suggest merely an impersonal quality or faculty in God. To think of Him only as the "Son" might falsely limit us to the concept of a personal yet created being. But the two terms combined ensure both aspects of the truth to us, and at the same time guard us from error. Our Lord and Saviour, the second Member of the Triunity, is both eternal and personal.

Next, in relation to us human beings, He is the *LIFE* and the *LIGHT*. From Him all creature life derives, both physical and psychical. From Him irradiates all true illumination, both intellectual and spiritual (verses 4, 9). The two terms are equally as implicative of our Lord's deity as are the figures "Word" and "Son."

Indeed, these two designations the "Life" and the "Light" *correspond* with the "Word" and the "Son." As the *Word* He is the expresser, the revealer, the illuminator, the *Light.* As the *Son* He is the personal executive, quickener, imparter, the *Life.* And again, paralleling with these, there are the two words, "grace" and "truth," in verses 14 and 16. The incarnate One is "full of grace and truth," i.e. full of "grace" to redeem *man*, and full of "truth" to reveal *God.* He is the God-Man Revealer-Redeemer.

Oh, this all-transcendent Saviour of ours! "His name shall be called *WONDERFUL*"! Why, in this first chapter alone there are no less than eight glorious titles ringed like diadems around His Divine-human brow; eight supremes which belong to Him absolutely and exclusively: the *WORD* (verse 1), the *LIFE* (verse 4), the *LIGHT* (verse 7), the *SON* (verse 18), the *LAMB* (verse 29), the *MESSIAH* (verse 41), the *KING* (verse 49), the *SON OF MAN* (verse 51)!

And, right away in the prologue, John assembles all the main aspects which he is to develop in his ensuing chapters: the "Word" (verses 1, 14), the "Life" (verses 3, 4), the "Light" (verses 5, 9), the "Son" (verses 14, 18), "darkness" (verse 5), "witness" (verses 7, 8, 15), "believe" (verse 7), "power to become" (verse 12), "born of God" (verse 13), "fulness" (verses 14,

16). How anyone can fail to see that this prologue is John's indicative ritornelle to the whole composition is surely strange. These ten emphases go right through the book, in five associated pairs, and they will most richly reward a painstaking study:

1. The Word—becoming flesh as the incarnate truth (i. 1, 14, 17, viii. 40, xiv. 6, "Verily, verily," etc.).
2. The Light—shining in the darkness; "the darkness comprehended it not"; "His own received Him not" (iii. 19, xii. 46, etc.).
3. The Life—imparting new birth and "power to become" (i. 12, 13, iii. 8, 15, x. 10, etc.).
4. The Son—coming forth "full of grace" and sharing His "fulness" (i. 14, 16, 33, iv. 10, xiv. 27, xv. 11, etc.).
5. Witness—that all "might *believe*" (i. 7, with frequent recurrence) and "have *life*."

Whole continents here invite new exploration! What can we do in this one short sketch? Let us, even though briefly, trace out the last of the five, i.e. the idea of *life by believing*. We select this because among the chain-themes which run right through the book this one carries John's main purpose (xx. 31).

Eternal Life Through Believing

John gives his practical purpose as "That ye might *believe* that Jesus is the Christ, the Son of God; and that believing ye might have *life*" (xx. 31). That word "believe" occurs in its several forms ninety-eight times; the words "life" (*zoe*) and "live" (*zaō*) fifty-five times. When we pick out the principal references to eternal life (i. 4, iii. 14–16, iii. 36, iv. 10–14, v. 24–9, vi. 35–55, viii. 12, x. 10, 28, 29, xi. 25, 26, xvii. 3, etc.) we discover an unmistakable *progress of doctrine*. Each new reference reveals a further truth in suchwise that transposition would spoil the order. We do not say that John himself knowingly patterned it so; but there was a higher guidance.

We start with chapter i. 4: "In Him was life, and the life was the light of men." So the first thing is that this life is in the Son, and that its first action upon the soul is to give *light*, the light which reveals spiritual realities, which "shineth in the darkness," revealing human sin and Divine truth.

Second, in chapter iii. 14–16 we read: "And as Moses lifted up the serpent in the wilderness, even so must the Son of Man be lifted up; that whosoever believeth in Him should not perish, but have eternal life." Here we learn that the life is imparted to us through faith in the Calvary work of the Saviour-Son, and that it is *eternal*.

Next, in chapter iii. 36 we find: "He that believeth on the Son hath everlasting life; and he that believeth not the Son shall not see life, but the wrath of God abideth on him." It is that word "hath" which leaps to the eye here, telling us that this eternal life is the *present possession* of the believer. There is nothing doubtful; it does not say *"may* have." Nor is it only future; for the word is *"hath,"* meaning here and now.

Again, in chapter iv. 14 Jesus says: "But whosoever drinketh of the water that I shall give him shall never thirst; but the water that I shall give him shall become in him a well of water springing up into everlasting life." Here the life is not only a present possession but an *inward satisfaction.* We drink, and the life-giving draught becomes a very fountain within the soul, ever springing, ever satisfying!

And now comes chapter v. 24: "Verily, verily, I say unto you: He that heareth My word, and believeth on Him that sent Me, hath everlasting life, and shall not come into condemnation; but is passed from death unto life." The word "condemnation" here is *krisis* (judgment) and refers to the final judgment of mankind, as verse 29 shows. The possession of eternal life through faith in the Saviour gives *exemption from judgment*. There has been a pass-over from "death" in sin to "life" in Christ. Once for all, Jesus bore the penalty due to the believer's sin; and once for all, therefore, eternal life in Him delivers from penal judgment.

This brings us to chapter vi. 40: "And this is the will of Him that sent Me, that every one which seeth the Son, and believeth on Him, may have everlasting life: and I will raise him up at the last day." In His great discourse here our Lord is the Bread of Life. He becomes so by giving His flesh and blood (verses 51, 53). He also indicates that feeding upon Him is *believing*, and that the sustenance is *spiritual* (verses 35, 56, 63). But the remarkable addition, which occurs like a refrain, is: "And I will raise him up at the last day" (verses 39, 40, 44, 54). This eternal life not only ensures the salvation of the soul, it includes the promise of *immortality for the body*!

Our next reference is chapter x. 27-9: "My sheep hear My voice, and I know them, and they follow Me. And I give unto them eternal life; and they shall never perish, neither shall any one pluck them out of My hand. My Father which gave them Me is greater than all; and no one is able to pluck them out of My Father's hand." This picture of our Lord's saved ones being held secure in the interlocked grasp of both the Son and the Father is the strongest possible assurance that eternal life means *eternal preservation*!

And now we encounter chapter xi. 25, 26: "I am the resurrection and the life: he that believeth in Me, though he were dead, yet shall he live; and whosoever liveth and believeth in Me shall never die." I wonder how many catch the startling meaning here. Martha has just said: "I know that he [Lazarus] shall rise again in *the resurrection at the last day*." Our Lord uses an aorist subjunctive in reply: "He that believeth in Me, though he *may have died* [i.e. at "the last day"], yet shall he live [for I am the resurrection]; and whosoever is [then] *living and believing* in Me shall never die [for I am the life]." So all the possessors of eternal life in Christ are to share in this promised *age-end transfiguration*!

Finally, in chapter xvii. we are told the inmost and utmost about this eternal life. In verse 3 our Lord says: "And this is life eternal that they might know Thee, the only true God, and Jesus Christ whom Thou hast sent." To possess Jesus Christ and be possessed *by* Him is to find *GOD*—and the true life. All who accept Christ are drawn to Him by the Father. The drawing may be resisted; but where it is responded to the believer is the Father's gift to the Son (seven times Jesus says so in this chapter). Verse 2 says that the Son imparts eternal life to "as many as" the Father has "given Him"; and this is crowned by verse 24: "Father, I will that they whom Thou hast given Me be with Me where I am, *that they may behold My glory*." So the eternal life which believers possess through the Saviour is to be consummated in a *heavenly glorification*!

Is there not in all this a superhuman progression of disclosure? First we see that this life is in the Son, and is an exposure-light on sin and darkness. Next we see that the life is received by faith on the Calvary Sinbearer. Then, successively, it is a present possession, an inward satisfaction, an exemption from judgment, a pledge of bodily immortality; it has the guarantee of eternal preservation; it awaits age-end transfiguration, and is to be consummated in heavenly glorification!

John has all this in mind when he writes at the end of his Gospel: "These are written that ye might believe that Jesus is the Christ, the Son of God; and that *believing* ye might have *life through His Name*." Who can measure all that is involved in such immensities? Yet how simple is the way *into* this eternal life—"*Believe*"!

> *Oh, how unlike the complex works of man,*
> *Heaven's easy, artless, unencumbered plan!*
> *No meretricious graces to beguile,*
> *No clustering ornaments to clog the pile;*
> *From ostentation as from weakness free,*
> *It stands like the cerulean arch we see,*
> *Majestic in its own simplicity.*
> *Inscribed above the portal, from afar*
> *Conspicuous as the brightness of a star,*
> *Legible only by the light they give,*
> *Stand the soul-quickening words—*
> *BELIEVE AND LIVE!*

Incarnate Word: Only-begotten Son

Running right through from prologue to epilogue is the developing presentation of Jesus as the incarnate Word and only-begotten Son. This is the centre-glory of John's Gospel.

Although we merely fringe the subject here, we can at least indicate features which invite further inquiry.

Twenty-three times we find our Lord's meaningful "*I am*" (iv. 26, vi. 20, 35, 41, 48, 51, viii. 12, 18, 24, 28, 58, x. 7, 9, 11, 14, xi. 25, xiii. 19, xiv. 6, xv. 1, 5, xviii. 5, 6, 8). From these we pick out those in which He successively couples His "I am" with seven tremendous metaphors expressive of His saving relationship toward mankind:

"I AM the Bread of Life" (vi. 35, 41, 48, 51).
"I AM the Light of the World" (viii. 12).
"I AM the Door of the Sheep" (x. 7, 9).
"I AM the Good Shepherd" (x. 11, 14).
"I AM the Resurrection and the Life" (xi. 25).
"I AM the Way, the Truth, the Life" (xiv. 6).
"I AM the true Vine" (xv. 1, 5).

Fundamentally, our Lord's message was Himself. He did not come merely to *preach* a Gospel; He Himself *is* the Gospel. He did not come merely to *give* bread; He said: "I *am* the bread." He did not come merely to *shed* light; He said: "I *am* the light." He did not come merely to *show* the door; He said: "I *am* the door." He did not come merely to *name* a shepherd; He said: "I *am* the shepherd." He did not come merely to *point* the way; He said: "I *am* the way, the truth, the life." He did not come merely to *plant* a vine; He said: "I *am* the vine."

But our Lord's *other* utterances of "I am," also, seem to carry a profound implication, though latently rather than apparently. In the Greek "I am" is *ego eimi*. Both *ego* and *eimi* mean "I am"; but the former emphasises "I," and the latter "am." Thus, *ego eimi* expresses personal being in the strongest possible way. It is the Greek expression for the Divine name *"I AM."* Here are the references again: iv. 26, vi. 20, viii. 18, 24, 28, 58, xiii. 19, xviii. 5, 6, 8.

Take the first of them (iv. 26). Literally, what our Lord says to the Sychar woman is not "I that speak to thee am He" (i.e. the Messiah) as translated in both Authorised and Revised Versions; but *"I AM* who am speaking to thee." In some of these verses our translators have apparently felt difficulty in knowing whether to insert the "He" or not, so they give it in italics only. We would not unduly press, yet it certainly does seem as though in some of these utterances our Lord uses that *EGO EIMI* with maximum implication. Look them up and see.

All this, of course, is given support by our Lord's august claims and assumptions which find periodic expression right through this Gospel. Take, for instance, the passage beginning at chapter v. 19. This terrific public reply to the Jewish leaders is prefaced by the explanation: "Therefore the Jews sought the more to kill Him, because He . . . said also that God was His Father, making

Himself *equal with God*" (v. 18). The question is at once provoked: Did Jesus *really* make Himself "equal with God"? Well, let us see. He here claims equality in seven particulars.

1. Equal in working	"What things soever He [the Father] doeth, these also the Son doeth likewise" (verse 19).
2. Equal in knowing	"For the Father loveth the Son, and showeth Him all things that He Himself doeth" (verse 20).
3. Equal in resurrecting	"For as the Father raiseth up the dead, so the Son quickeneth whom He will" (verse 21 with verses 28, 29).
4. Equal in judging	"For the Father judgeth no man, but hath committed all judgment unto the Son" (verse 22 with verse 27).
5. Equal in honour	"That all men should honour the Son, even as they honour the Father" (verse 23).
6. Equal in regenerating	"He that heareth My word and believeth on Him that sent Me . . . is passed from death unto life," etc. (verses 24, 25).
7. Equal in self-existence	"For as the Father hath life in Himself, so hath He given to the Son to have life in Himself" (verse 26).

Who can read claims like these without seeing in them the assumption of such oneness with the eternal Father as betokens essential equality? The Jewish leaders rightly enough understood His claims, and John would have ourselves clearly understand them, too.

"Full of Grace and Truth"

Our necessary limits will not allow us more than a few further paragraphs on this fourth Gospel; yet (much to our disappointment) we have not found place to speak of the apostle John himself, his connection with Ephesus, and the circumstances which probably occasioned the writing of this Gospel which bears his name.

In closing we turn attention to yet another of those statements in the prologue:

"And the Word became flesh and dwelt among us (and we beheld His glory, the glory as of the only begotten of the Father) full of grace and truth" (i. 14).

This "fulness" is another of John's recurrent emphases and will richly reward a follow-through study. It occurs again in the prologue: "And of His fulness have all we received" (i. 16). The fulness is *embodied* that it might be *imparted*. Two lines run through the succeeding chapters: (1) fulness of grace to *restore*; (2) fulness of truth to *reveal*. The first of these runs through His *works*; the second through His *words*.

But the feature to which we call special attention here is that the "fulness" is predicated of our Lord *after* He had become incarnate. This, therefore, is at once a Scriptural refutation of the socalled "kenosis" theory which would have us believe that our Lord "emptied Himself" (Phil. ii. 7, R.V.) practically to the degree of ordinary human fallibility.

The "kenosis" Christ of the critics is certainly not the Lord Jesus of the Gospel writers. According to the former view, our Lord's knowledge was "adequate to the delivery of the doctrines of His kingdom, but did not extend to questions of scholarship and criticism." On these latter "Jesus speaks as any other man." But according to John and the synoptists, it was utterly otherwise.

Just here we are referring only to *John's* witness, and very meagrely at that: yet even a few references will suffice. The immortal third chapter is introduced with the explanation: "Jesus . . . *knew all men*, and needed not that any should testify of men; for He *knew what was in man*" (ii. 24, 25). He not only knew "all" men individually, but "man" constitutionally. What was that but a knowledge supernaturally exceeding all human limits?

We recall His telling the Sychar woman all about her past; of His healing the nobleman's son a day's journey away; of His knowing that Lazarus had just died, fifty miles away, at Bethany; of His informing two of His disciples that at a certain place they would find a colt tied, which He required—not to mention other such incidents.

We recall some of His pronouncements concerning *Himself*: "Before Abraham was, *I AM*" (viii. 58); "I am . . . *THE TRUTH*" (xiv. 6); and prophecies which foretell the future both far and near (ii. 19, iii. 14, v. 28, xii. 32, xiv. 3, xv. 26, xvi. 1–4, etc.). We think of these, with many other evidences, and the inevitable conclusion faces us that, instead of an "emptying" down to our merely human level, there is a *supernatural FULNESS*.

That our Lord may have suspended the *activity* of His Divine attributes in some directions during His life on earth we readily concede; but that He could exist apart from them is absolutely unthinkable. To make His incarnation empty Him of His Divine attributes would mean, not that "the Word became flesh," but that the Word became defunct—an idea as insulting as it is preposterous.

John's exordium on the coming of the Word in flesh is the interpretative Scripture parallel to Paul's "kenosis" passage in Philippians. The two should be studied side by side. Not that there is any dubiety about Paul's intention in Philippians ii. 5–8. The "kenosis," or self-emptying, has to do only with "form" (*morphē*) or expression, not essence (verses 6, 7). When our Lord "emptied Himself" (*ekenōsen*) for the purpose of incarnation He separated Himself from the *pre*-incarnate expression of Himself, i.e. from *"THE GLORY"* which He had with the Father *"BEFORE THE WORLD WAS"* (John xvii. 5).

We cannot understand the mystery of that profound transition in which He disrobed Himself of that pre-cosmic "glory," but we *can* understand that He neither did nor could detach Himself from what He eternally *is*. We cannot penetrate the psychic duality of that God-Man, but with the copious evidences before us we *can* intelligently accept that the Ego was the incarnate *LOGOS*; that it was the incorporated *human* nature which was supernaturally Spirit-endued, and that thus the human part was made a perfect vehicle for the Divine Ego.

Look at the Christ of this fourth Gospel again. Instead of the merely natural there is the ever-present *super*natural. Instead of an "emptying" there is an infinite *filling*. Over against "kenosis," there is a Divine *"PLEROMA"*—One who is "the fulness of the Godhead bodily" (Col. ii. 9). See it in every miracle—"full of grace." Hear it in every message—"full of truth." Follow it right through, and you will appreciate John's words as never before—"We beheld *His glory*."

A Parting Retrospect

As we leave the four Gospels we realise acutely the inadequacy of these brief studies; yet we take comfort in the thought that they may have been usefully exploratory, and may have indicated attractive avenues for further enquiry. As we have seen, each of the four Gospels has its own distinctive aspect or emphasis in presenting our Lord Jesus. It is unwise to *over*stress the lines of demarcation; but the respective emphases are certainly there, and it is a sad fault to overlook them, for they build up a wonderful fourfold whole. So, now that we have picked our way through all four, let us glance back retrospectively and get the quadripartite delineation clearly focused:

Matthew	The promised One is here; see His credentials.
Mark	This is how He worked; see His power.
Luke	This is what He was like; see His nature.
John	This is who He really was; see His Godhead.

Oh, this wonderful Saviour! How we ought to prize Him, love Him, extol Him, witness to Him, and long for that day of days when we shall see Him! For all our need He is the "fulness" of supply. The fulness is embodied in *Him* that it may be imparted to *us*. "Of His fulness have all we received." Let us keep on receiving, for He came that we "might have life . . . more abundantly" (John x. 10).

And let us keep on *serving* Him. His parting words, at the end of John's Gospel, have given us the three vital qualifications for this. First, "Lovest thou Me?" (xxi. 15, 16, 17); second, "Feed My lambs . . . Tend My sheep" (15, 16); third, "Follow Me" (19, 22).

Yes, they are the three essentials—a deep *love* for Him, a sense of His *commission* to us, and a devoted *following* of Him, with our eyes ever on that lovely prospect of which He Himself speaks, in the very last sentence of John's Gospel:

"TILL I COME."

A FAREWELL SHEAF OF QUESTIONS

1. How is John completive to the Synoptist presentation of our Lord?

2. In what three ways especially does John cast light on the other Gospels?

3. How long elapsed between our Lord's baptism and His Galilee itinerary?

4. At the end of which chapter in John does the Galilee ministry fit?

5. Why is it unlikely that the Feast in John v. was either Passover or Tabernacles?

6. John records three Passovers. Does this bear on the length of our Lord's ministry?

7. What is the main threefold ground-plan of John's Gospel?

8. What are the key verse and theme of John's Gospel?

9. Which are the eight miracles? and what the main idea running through them?

10. How do the designations "Word" and "Son" supplement and protect each other?

11. Which are our Lord's seven "I AM" metaphors, and where are they?

12. How does John's prologue correct the mistaken so-called "kenosis" theory?

EXPLORE THE BOOK

A Basic and Broadly Interpretative Course
of Bible Study from Genesis to Revelation

J. SIDLOW BAXTER

VOLUME SIX

ACTS TO REVELATION

CONTENTS OF VOLUME SIX

	Page
THE ACTS OF THE APOSTLES	7
Studies 124 to 126	
CHURCH EPISTLES COLLECTIVELY	53
Study 127	
ROMANS, CORINTHIANS, GALATIANS	65
Studies 128 to 134	
EPHESIANS, PHILIPPIANS, COLOSSIANS	161
Studies 135 to 137	
FIRST AND SECOND THESSALONIANS	211
Studies 138 and 139	
THE PASTORAL EPISTLES	229
Studies 140 and 141	
THE EPISTLE TO THE HEBREWS	257
Study 142	
THE EPISTLE OF JAMES	281
Study 143	
THE EPISTLES OF PETER AND JUDE	295
Studies 144 and 145	
THE THREE EPISTLES OF JOHN	319
Study 146	
THE BOOK OF THE REVELATION	333
Study 147	

THE ACTS OF THE APOSTLES (1)

Lesson Number 124

NOTE: For this study read right through the Acts of the Apostles at least twice.

Notwithstanding the severe criticism to which the book has been subjected during recent decades, scholars like Professor Ramsay have shown conclusively that it is worthy of the highest credit as a first-century history. There is an atmosphere of actuality about it: no other New Testament book connects its material with the general history of the world like this work. (The great authority on all questions concerning the credibility of the Acts is Professor W. M. Ramsay, especially in his *The Church in the Roman Empire*; *St. Paul the Traveller and Roman Citizen*; *An Historical Commentary on Galatians*.)

—*W. H. G. Thomas.*

THE ACTS OF THE APOSTLES (1)

TWENTY-EIGHT thrilling chapters lie before us! Any one of them we can read a dozen times, only to find its fascination growing with each reading. Never since writing began was a more gripping record penned. If the epochal events here narrated do not electrify the imagination and stir the emotions of any serious reader, nothing ever could. Yet even the sheer interest of the book is quite eclipsed by its historical and dispensational importance. It is the sequel to the mighty events of the Gospels, and the gateway to the glorious doctrines of the Epistles. It marks, in fact, one of the greatest turning-points in history, as we shall soon see.

Author and Date

But first we must say a word about author and date. It can be affirmed with almost categorical finality that the author was Luke, the writer of the third Gospel. There are four considerations which together settle this.

First: both the "Acts of the Apostles" and the "Gospel according to Luke" are dedicated to "Theophilus" (Luke i. 3; Acts i. 1); and in commencing the "Acts" our writer refers to his "former treatise," evidently meaning the "Gospel according to Luke."

Second: there is a unanimously recognised similarity of style, phrases, and arrangement between the two books, notably a correspondence in certain medical phraseology such as befits Luke "the beloved physician" (Col. iv. 14). For more on this see *The Medical Language of St. Luke,* by W. K. Hobart, LL.D.

Third: the pronoun "we" in such verses as xvi. 10 and xx. 6 is generally agreed to indicate that the narrator, at least from chapter xvi. onwards, was one of Paul's travel companions. Silas and Timothy seem ruled out by such verses as xvi. 19 and xx. 4, 5, nor is there a shred of indication that the writer could be Titus. Who, then, could he have been but Luke? And since the style in all the chapters *preceding* that sixteenth is in every way like that which *follows* it, must not the whole book be by him?

9

Fourth: Luke's authorship, both of the Acts and of the third Gospel, is uniformly attested by Christian tradition right down from Irenæus in the second century A.D., and is conceded by critics of all or most schools today.

The *date* of the writing, like its authorship, can be clearly fixed. It was completed about the year A.D. 63 at Rome; that is, about the end of Paul's two years' imprisonment there, and presumably with the attendant guidance of that great apostle. The narrative comes right down to that point, so that the book could not have been completed earlier than then. Yet it could not well have been written much later than that, for if Paul's trial before Nero and his acquittal had taken place Luke would surely have told us. Still more, if Paul's conjectured further journeying and second trial—and most of all his martyrdom—had taken place, would not Luke most certainly have said so instead of breaking off so abruptly as he does at the end of chapter xxviii.? It is almost certain that he would, for we know from 2 Timothy iv. 6, 11 that Luke was with Paul right to the end.

Scope and Title

What is the scope, i.e. subject and aim, of the Acts? There are those who would prefer to name this book "The Acts of the Holy Spirit," because of its many references to the Holy Spirit. Others would name it "the Acts of the Ascended Christ." They refer us to Luke's opening words: "The former treatise have I made, O Theophilus, of all that Jesus *began* to do and to teach, until the day in which He was taken up . . ."; and they suggest that Luke now designs, in this new treatise, to tell what the Lord *continued* to do after His ascension. But, in our own judgment, the true name of the book is that which it has always had, "The Acts of the Apostles"; for although the ascended Christ and the infilling Spirit are operating through and above all, the seen figures are these Christ-commissioned, Spirit-controlled *men*, the apostles; and it is with the significance of what these men said and did that the book primarily challenges us. If we would interpret the ascended Christ and the phenomenon of Pentecost we must watch *these men*.

Some deny that the title "The Acts of the Apostles" is a true title to the book. For instance, Marshall's Commentary on the

Acts says: "The work cannot in any sense be regarded as a record of the doings of the apostles, inasmuch as it contains no detailed account of the work of any of the apostles except St. Peter and St. Paul. In fact it is but the record of *some* acts of *certain* apostles, and of *some who were not apostles*." The simple answer to this is that if the work is not mainly a record of the doings of the apostles, it is difficult to know *what* it is. *All* the twelve apostles are named together in the first chapter, so that we may know beyond doubt those to whom Luke is referring when he speaks of "the apostles" in the chapters which follow. The apostles are afterwards collectively referred to no less than twenty-three times! Their outstanding pronouncements, decisions, and activities as a corporate body are preserved, revealing their unanimity and recognised authority; so that although the writer has not felt it needful or possible to give the personal history of each, we may know that those who are picked out for special mention are spoken of representatively or because of leadership. And we may add that although "the Twelve" occupy a unique place, the term "apostle" is used of Barnabas and others who are either personally mentioned or are included in the narrative without being named. Yes, the book is true to its name. It is the "Acts of the Apostles." We are to catch the significance of *these men,* of what they did and said, and of what happened to them.

Key and Plan

The key-thought in the Acts is that of *witness to Christ*; and the key verse is undoubtedly chapter i. 8: "Ye shall receive power after that the Holy Ghost is come upon you, and ye shall be witnesses unto Me, both in Jerusalem and in all Judæa and in Samaria, and unto the uttermost part of the earth." In this eighth verse we have the Divine appointment, the spiritual equipment, and the geographical commitment of Christ's witnesses.

But besides this, the *geographical* development of the whole book is here anticipated: "Jerusalem and all Judæa and Samaria, and unto the uttermost part of the earth." In chapters ii. to vii. the witness is borne in Jerusalem. In chapters viii.–xii. it is borne in all Judæa and Samaria. Finally, in chapters xiii. to the end of the book it is borne to "the uttermost part of the earth."

What is it that these first witnesses were called upon to say? What was the *matter* of their witness to Christ? It is in answering that question carefully and truly that we shall find the book assuming its supreme meaning.

As for its *plan,* this book of the Acts is in two parts, the first part running to the end of chapter xii., the second part running from chapter xiii. to the end. In the first part Jerusalem is the centre. In the second part Antioch is the centre. In the first part Peter is the prominent figure. In the second part Paul is the prominent figure. In the first part there is a reaching-out move-ment from Jerusalem, through Judæa to Samaria. In the second part there is a reaching-out movement from Antioch, through the empire, to Rome. In the first part we are restricted to Palestine, where witness is borne first to the Jews of the homeland and then to Jews and Gentiles alike. In the second part we are conducted through the empire, where again witness is borne first to the Jews of the Dispersion, and then to Jews and Gentiles alike. The first part ends with the general rejection of the Word by the Jews of the homeland. The second part ends with the general rejection of the Word by the Jews of the Dispersion. The first part ends with the imprisonment of Peter. The second part ends with the imprisonment of Paul.

There is a parallel between Peter in the first part and Paul in the second which seems to be more than merely coincidental.

PETER	*PAUL*
First sermon (ii.).	First sermon (xiii.).
Lame man healed (iii.).	Lame man healed (xiv.).
Simon the sorcerer (viii.).	Elymas the sorcerer (xiii.).
Influence of shadow (v.).	Influence of handkerchief (xix.).
Laying on of hands (viii.).	Laying on of hands (xix.).
Peter worshipped (x.).	Paul worshipped (xiv.).
Tabitha raised (ix.)	Eutychus raised (xx.).
Peter imprisoned (xii.).	Paul imprisoned (xxviii.).

With these two parts thus standing out sharply, we see indeed how the book of the Acts is planned in accord with the key verse, chapter i. 8. Let us mark it well—in the first part of the Acts (i.–xii.) we have "Jerusalem, Judæa and Samaria"; in the second part (xiii.–xxviii.) we have "the uttermost part of the earth." It may be helpful to the eye to set down the facts as follows:

THE ACTS OF THE APOSTLES

Key theme: Witness to Christ.
Key Verse: chapter i. 8.

PART 1 (i.–xii.).	PART 2 (xiii.–xxviii.).
Jerusalem the centre.	Antioch the centre.
Peter the chief figure.	Paul the chief figure.
Out to Samaria	Out to Rome.
Word rejected by Jews of homeland.	Word rejected by Jews of Dispersion.
Peter imprisoned.	Paul imprisoned.
Judgment on Herod.	Judgment on Jews.

So much, then, as to "scope" and "key" and "plan." We shall also find that there are three pivotal events recorded in the Acts which give the book a quite startling dispensational significance. Before we attend to those, however, there is a preliminary question of utmost importance which we must carefully answer. What was the *nature and content* of the apostolic witness to our Lord Jesus Christ?

What was the Apostolic Witness?

The first chapter of the book covers the fifty days from the Lord's resurrection to the day of Pentecost. Those fifty days are divided into forty and ten—the forty days of the Lord's resurrection ministry, and the ten days of "tarrying" between the ascension of Christ and the effusion of the Holy Spirit. The importance of those final forty days of our Lord's ministry on earth is beyond exaggeration. What was it that was uppermost in His thoughts and words? What was the subject of His last conversations and of His final counsels to the apostles? Verse 3 tells us: "He showed Himself alive after His passion by many infallible proofs, being seen of them forty days, *and speaking of the things pertaining to the kingdom of God.*" Language could not be plainer. During those forty days the supreme and engrossing subject of conversation was "the kingdom of God." This evoked a quite natural question on the part of the apostles, which is recorded in verse

6: "When they therefore were come together, they asked of Him, saying: *Lord, wilt Thou at this time restore again the kingdom to Israel?*"

This question, we say, was the quite natural outcome of our Lord's instruction—an intelligent, pertinent question such as we ourselves would have asked if we had been in their places. Yet, strangely enough, most writers on the Acts fail to see this. Confounding the "kingdom of God" with the "Church" (and thus completely spiritualising it, to say nothing of divorcing it from Old Testament prophecy) they charge the apostles with incorrigible unintelligence and self-centred ambitions. For example, the late Rev. William Arthur thus explains it in his book *The Tongue of Fire*—a book which had an extraordinary influence some sixty years or so ago:

"Apparently more ready to interpret 'power' as referring to the hopes of their nation than to the kingdom of grace, they asked, 'Lord, wilt thou at this time restore the kingdom to Israel?' He had said nothing of a kingdom for Israel, or in Israel. . . . When, therefore, they asked if He would at this time restore again the kingdom to Israel, He shortly turned aside their curiosity. What were the Father's designs as to Israel nationally, what the times when they might again be a kingdom, were points not for them. They had better work, and nearer at hand. 'It is not for you to know the times or the seasons which the Father hath put in His own power.'"

These words, which we quote because they are representative of many other similar comments on this question which was asked by the apostles, seem to ourselves to be marked by strange contradictions. However the writer could aver that our Lord had "said nothing of a kingdom for Israel, or in Israel" seems strange indeed in view of what the four Gospels tell us. And it certainly seems strange to be told that our Lord "shortly turned aside their curiosity" in view of the fact that only a matter of days beforehand (see Matt. xxiv.) our Lord had gone into a long and detailed reply to a very similar question! Moreover, Luke, in recording the disciples' question, uses a significant "therefore." To quote the verse in the exact order of the words: "They indeed, *therefore,* having come together, asked Him, saying: Lord, at this time restorest Thou the kingdom to Israel?" Luke uses the "therefore" here obviously to show that the disciples' question was a logical result of what our Lord Himself had been saying about the "kingdom."

However, there it is—most writers take the view set forth in the quotation which we have just given from Mr. Arthur's book. When we turn to the well-known Bible commentaries, both the older and the newer, we find the same view expressed everywhere.

But is this explanation of the apostles' question true to background and context? We think not. And surely, so far as the apostles themselves are concerned, it puts an unbearable strain upon our credulity. Think of it—here are grown men, men who, although not having the intellectual finish of the schools, are men of sound common sense and judgment; they have companied for some three years with the Lord Jesus, have watched Him and listened to Him in public and in private, have seen all the miracles and heard all the parables, have received special explanations of them, have heard all the preaching and teaching about the kingdom of heaven, or kingdom of God, and although not having grasped all the far-reaching significance contained in some of the Lord's utterances, have, nevertheless, intelligently comprehended the gist of His teaching (as we see from such passages as Matthew xiii. 51, where, in reply to our Lord's question, "Have ye understood all these things?" they reply, "Yea, Lord"). And now, these specially chosen and tutored men, the Lord's confidants, having companied with Him right to the Cross, have had those wonderful forty days of culminating tuition from the lips of the risen Christ, specially pertaining to "the kingdom of God"; and if, like many of ourselves, they were previously "slow of heart to believe all that the prophets have spoken," they are not so *now*, for Luke tells us that when the risen Christ came to His disciples, "*then* opened He their understanding, that they might know the Scriptures"! Yet *after* all this, and *in spite of* all this, we are expected to believe that when the disciples asked, "Lord, wilt Thou at this time restore again the kingdom to Israel?", they were asking an irrelevant and unspiritually minded question, and were so completely without understanding that they had taken teaching about a *spiritual* kingdom (the Church) to mean a material and outward kingdom, and had therefore misconstrued the plain teaching of Christ not merely upon a minor matter but upon the central and most vital communication of all His teaching!

Surely this is too preposterous to gain thoughtful credence! If the apostles were such men, then we had better admit them half-wits outright, and have done with it! It simply will not do to say that the apostles, although normal enough mentally, were too unspiritually minded to grasp the spiritual truths which Christ had been uttering to them, for all will agree that the apostles were now regenerate men. Our Lord Himself had pronounced them "clean through the word" (John xv. 3); and all will agree that these men, although still young in spiritual experience, had been specially taught by the Holy Spirit, as we see, for instance, in our Lord's words to Peter: "Flesh and blood hath not revealed it unto thee, but My Father which is in heaven" (Matt. xvi. 17). No, it is not a question as to their being either spiritually or unspiritually minded, but of their ordinary common sense, of their either under-standing or not understanding the plain words of our Lord to them both before and after His resurrection. Put any normal men of today in their place (I do not mean necessarily "converted" men), and what should we expect of them? We know quite well. Then ought we, or dare we, expect less of these specially chosen and instructed men, the apostles? Had the apostles been making such a colossal blunder as to confound the Church, which is a spiritual organism, with an outward, material, national, Israelite kingdom when they asked, "Lord, wilt Thou at this time restore again the kingdom to Israel?", then our Lord, far from simply replying that it was not for them to know "the times or the seasons which the Father hath put in His own power", would surely have broken out into what would have been one of the most piteous utterances in the Bible—either of stinging disapproval or of compassionate disillusionment!

As for the Lord's actual reply being a rebuke, as is suggested, we judge it to be no such thing. It was the plain statement of a fact. Their being kept uninformed concerning "the times or seasons" relating to the return of the Messiah-King and the setting up of the kingdom was no rebuke at all. Had not our Lord said that He Himself did not know that day? "Of that day and that hour knoweth no man, no, not the angels which are in heaven, neither the Son, but the Father" (Mark xiii. 32). Far other than our Lord's words being a rebuke to the apostles, we shall see shortly that there was a special significance in them, for which reason Luke is careful to record them.

Now *why* should there be this misunderstanding about the apostles' question and our Lord's reply to it? It is caused simply through the mistake of confounding the kingdom of heaven, or kingdom of God, with the Church of the present dispensation.

What, then, was it that the apostles were commissioned to preach by the risen Christ? Clearly, as we have noted, it was something to do with "the kingdom of God," for that was *the* subject of consideration during the forty days.

It was in connection with two things, specially, that the risen Lord appointed the apostles as witnesses to Himself. They were to witness to Him (1) as being indeed the Messiah-King of Israel, the crucified but now risen Deliverer of His people, the predestined King of the long-promised "kingdom of heaven"; and (2) as the personal Saviour, from the guilt and power and eternal penalty of sin, of all who believe upon Him, through His atoning death and resurrection. They were to present the offer of the King and the kingdom, just as the Lord Himself had done up to the time of His crucifixion; only now there was a wonderful new factor in the message—that of the Cross, the atonement for "the sin of the world," and the good news of personal salvation by faith on the Lord Jesus, the Christ of Israel and now the Saviour of the world.

Whatever other meanings may inhere in the Acts of the Apostles, the book is primarily

THE RENEWED OFFER OF THE KINGDOM OF HEAVEN TO THE NATION ISRAEL.

Specimen Apostolic Preachings

This renewed offer of the kingdom to Israel is the key to all the recorded proclamations of the apostles to the nation at and after Pentecost. Glance at the first two public utterances of Peter—the one on the day of Pentecost, and the other in the Temple porch.

Peter's great sermon on the day of Pentecost is given in chapter ii. 14–40. It is addressed specifically to the men of Israel (verses 14, 22, 36). Next (note carefully), the Pentecostal effusion is said to be in fulfilment of Joel ii. 28–32. Peter says: "This is that which was spoken by the prophet Joel" (verse 16). What, then, does the prophecy in Joel refer to? Does it refer to the Church?

It does not. It refers to the nation Israel, and, in particular, to the Messianic kingdom (which so largely figures in Old Testament prediction), as Joel ii. and a comparison with other Old Testament prophecies will settle conclusively. Then, next, Peter charges home the responsibility for the crucifixion of the Messiah upon the nation Israel (verses 22, 23), reminding them of the "miracles and wonders and signs" which He had wrought among them. Then, at this point, Peter breaks forth in the new message of the resurrection and exaltation of the crucified Jesus, showing it to be the fulfilment of Messianic prediction (verses 24–33). It is a tremendous and triumphant passage. Note the following five grand assertions concerning "Jesus of Nazareth" (verse 22):

1. This Man, Jesus, is the subject of Old Testament prophecy— "David speaketh concerning *Him*" (verse 25).

2. This Man, Jesus, is *the Lord*—"David speaketh of Him: I foresaw *the Lord*" (verse 25).

3. This Man, Jesus, is the promised *"Holy One"*—"David speaketh concerning Him . . . the Holy One" (verse 27).

4. This Man, Jesus, is the promised *Messiah*—"He [David] seeing before . . . spake of the Christ" (verse 31).

5. This Man, Jesus, is the promised *KING*—"David, knowing . . . the Christ would . . . *sit on his throne*" (verse 30).

These tremendous assertions, accompanied by the miraculous "signs" at Pentecost, must have fallen with startling effect on the minds of Peter's Jewish hearers. But Peter has something even more startling yet to utter. Having urged the Messiahship of Jesus from the "miracles and wonders and signs" which Jesus Himself had done among them, then from the fact of His resurrection, in the light of Davidic prediction, Peter gives the crowning proof not only that this Jesus is indeed the Messiah but that He is, in the unique and transcendent sense, *the very Son of God*. This is in verse 33: "Therefore, being by the right hand of God exalted, and having received of the Father the promise of the Holy Ghost, He [*Jesus*] *hath shed forth this*, which ye now see and hear." Peter's word is unhesitating; and the implication is inescapable: this Jesus has done what only God Himself can do—He has poured forth the Divine Spirit! To have asserted that Jesus had exercised this utterly Divine prerogative would have been blasphemy if our Lord Jesus were not indeed God the Son. But He is in very truth Jehovah-Jesus; or, in Peter's double title, He is "both Lord and Christ" (verse 36).

Such, then, is Peter's sermon on the day of Pentecost. It is addressed to Israel. The supernatural phenomena are explained as fulfilling Old Testament prophecy concerning the promised Messianic kingdom. The crucified but now exalted Jesus is declared to be the promised Christ and King. Then, when the hearers ask what they shall do about it, Peter exhorts them to repentance and baptism into the Name of Jesus Christ, for the remission of their sins, and in order to their participating in the blessing of the now-outpoured Spirit. And then Peter finally adds: "For the promise [that of Joel, and the kingdom promise of Old Testament prophecy in general] is UNTO YOU AND YOUR CHILDREN, and [afterward] to all that are afar off [Gentiles], as many as the Lord our God shall call."

As for Peter's *second* public address (chapter iii. 12–26), a mere glance will be sufficient to show us its centre-point of significance. There are two striking things about it: first, the admission that there was ignorance in the crucifying of Jesus; and, second, the promise that the Lord Jesus would return *then,* if the people of Israel repented and received Him. Verses 17 and 21 read as follows:

"And now, brethren, I know that through ignorance ye did it, as did also your rulers; but those things which God before had showed by the mouth of all His prophets, that the Christ should suffer, He hath thus fulfilled. Repent ye, therefore, and be converted, that your sins may be blotted out, and the times of refreshing shall come from the presence of the Lord; and *He shall send Jesus Christ* who was proclaimed before unto you; whom the heaven must indeed receive until the times of the restoration of all things, of which God hath spoken by the mouth of all His holy prophets from of old."

What can this mean but a renewed offer of the Messiah-King Jesus and the kingdom of heaven to the Jews? And is it not equally clear that these words of Peter utter the promise that the Lord Jesus would return, and the times of restoration set in, without delay, upon the repentance and conversion of Israel? Here is the fact, clearly stated, that had there been a national repentance and acceptance of Jesus as Lord and Christ on the part of Israel, the second advent of Christ in power and glory would have taken place then and there—for never was a plainer promise given.

In emphasizing this we are not overlooking those words in verse 21 where Peter adds, "Whom [our Lord Jesus] the heaven must indeed receive until the times of the restoration of all things of which God hath spoken by the mouth of all His holy prophets from of old." It certainly must not be thought that the inspired Peter, in so speaking, had any such two-thousand-year postponement in mind as that which we twentieth-century believers now see retrospectively to have intervened between then and the still-future return of our Lord. To think that any such recondite reservation was in Peter's mind would make his preceding pledge unworthily theatrical and misleading.

The "times of *restoration*" to which Peter here referred are the same as the "times of *refreshing*" which he had just said should come without delay, along with our Lord's return, if Israel would repent and receive. The apostles themselves had been thinking of this same "restoration" when they asked, "Lord, wilt Thou at this time *restore* the kingdom to Israel?" The Old Testament prophets repeatedly foretell a restoration of dispersed Israel to the covenant land; a restoration of the theocracy under the coming Messiah; and a restoration to full privileges under the finally realised provisions of the Abrahamic covenant. The "times of restoration" *could* have set in *then*, or Peter's words are unreal.

It was no part of Divine predetermination that the Messianic reign and Israel's restoration should be delayed another two millennia after the Incarnation; but God *did* foreknow Israel's disobedience, and overruled accordingly. As ever, due scope was allowed to human free-will, and events were allowed to develop their corresponding consequences. Therefore Peter's words of renewed offer were spoken in all good faith; and our Lord's return *could* have happened *then*, without any *fundamental* necessity for postponement.

THE ACTS OF THE APOSTLES (2)

Lesson Number 125

NOTE: For this study read carefully again Stephen's address to the Sanhedrin and the account of his martyrdom, also the three missionary tours of Paul.

IMPORTANCE OF THE ACTS

The preciousness of a book may sometimes best be estimated if we consider the loss which we should experience if we did not possess it. If so, we can hardly value the Acts of the Apostles too much. If it had not come down to us there would have been a blank in our knowledge which scarcely anything else could have filled up.

—Farrar.

If the Book of the Acts were gone, there would be nothing to replace it; and we may go further, that the Christian Scriptures would then lie before us in two disjointed fragments; the complete arch would not be built.

—Howson.

THE ACTS OF THE APOSTLES (2)

THE THREE PIVOTAL EVENTS

ENOUGH has now been said, we think, to show that the message of the apostles was *primarily* a renewed offer of the Messianic kingdom to Israel (though it needs to be always borne in mind that while the promised kingdom is primarily concerned with Israel, it is not exclusively so, as is made clear by the Old Testament prophecies relating to it). This brings us to a consideration of the three pivotal events in the Acts and the final issue of the book. The three turning-points are:

The outrage against Stephen (vii. 54–60) ⎫
The outbreak against Paul   (xxii. 22) ⎬ with context.
The outgoing to the Gentiles (xxviii. 28) ⎭

The Outrage against Stephen

Take the first of these: *the outrage against Stephen*. We have pointed out that the book of the Acts is in two main parts. Everything in the first part (i.–xii.) either leads up to or results from the outbreak against Stephen. This event is the pivot around which all else swings.

It will be seen that in each of the early chapters of the Acts we have first miracle then witness. The miracles were meant to prepare the way for the message. They were the supernatural evidences, in accordance with Old Testament prophecies such as Joel's, that the long-promised kingdom was really here in its beginnings, in its incipient stage: and the message was that if the nation, welcoming these evidences, repented and accepted the renewed offer of the Lord Jesus Christ, then Christ would return, and the kingdom be brought in fully.

Thus in chapter ii. we have first the miracle of the "tongues," and then Peter's great sermon explaining the meaning. Similarly, in chapters iii. and iv., which are both about the healing of the lame man, we have first the miracle at the "Beautiful Gate," followed by the double witness of the apostles—to the people at large, then to the leaders of the nation. In chapter v. we have the supernatural warning in the case of Ananias and Sapphira, and the statement in verse 12 that "by the hands of the apostles were many signs and wonders wrought among the people," followed by a further double witness to the public and to the council. Then in chapters vi. and vii. we have the "great wonders and miracles among the people" performed by Stephen, followed by his witness before the council and his scathing indictment of the Jewish leaders. What is more, in these early chapters we see that in each case, after miracle and message, there is immediate opposition by the Jewish authorities.

Final Indictment of Nation

Now all this is brought to a head in the outrage against Stephen. First: in the miracles, message and martyrdom of Stephen we have *the final trial and indictment of the nation*. More than a few readers, perhaps, have wondered just what is the special point of Stephen's long address to the Sanhedrin. Why this long historical review? Could it not have been made shorter? Such questions reveal that the real meaning of Stephen's utterance has been missed. To begin with, his review was an indictment. It was meant to show how, again and again, right through the national history, Israel had rejected the witness of God's Spirit, until at length, under the influence of their perverted leaders, the people had gone to the ugly extreme of murdering the Messiah Himself. Stephen's sorrowful purpose is to charge home intelligent and conscious guilt for the heinous dual sin, first of crucifying the Son of God, and now of resisting still further the graciously renewed witness of the Divine Spirit. On the Cross Christ had said: "Father, forgive them, for they know not what they do"; and Peter had made allowance for this in his words to the crowd: "I know that in ignorance ye did it"; but now ignorance may be pleaded no longer—the situation shall now be so clarified that the Jewish leaders will at once be seen to be acting in the full realisation of what they are doing. No longer shall the words, "They know not what they do" be a covering for them. Wonders have been wrought. Witness has been given. Offer has been made. They have seen and heard and understood—and have resisted.

Certainly, the *miracles* had been unmistakable and unanswerable. The leaders themselves had been forced to admit it. We see both their admission of it and their attitude to it in chapters iv. 16, 17 and v. 12, 17, 18.

Similarly, the *witness* of the apostles had been clear as language could make it. There could be no mistaking such direct utterances as that in chapter iv. 9–12.

No, there could be no mistaking such plain speaking. Yet what was the result? Chapter v. 33 tells us: "When they [the leaders] heard that, they were cut to the heart, and took counsel to slay them"! Their jealous rage and opposition would stop at nothing. Their knowing and wilful resistance of the Holy Spirit was more and more uncloaked until its evil face was finally unmasked at the trial of Stephen: "Ye stiffnecked and uncircumcised in heart and ears, *ye do always resist the Holy Ghost*." The nation was tried and found guilty.

Final Rejection of Renewed Offer

Second: the martyrdom of Stephen marked the *official Jewish rejection of the renewed offer of the kingdom*. In these early chapters of the Acts there are two words used to describe the supernatural works wrought by the apostles. They are the words "signs" and "wonders." (The word "miracle" also is used in the Authorised Version in chapters iv. 16, 22 and vi. 8, but the Greek word in these places is that which is elsewhere translated as "signs.") The apostolic miracles were "signs"—signs that the kingdom, in offer, had indeed drawn nigh again in the renewed message through the lips of the apostles. As to their nature, these signs were "wonders" (lit. prodigies), works so obviously supernatural as to make it quite certain that God Himself was at work among the people. The signs were as plain as the witness was outright. Yet all the way through there was hostility on the part of the Jewish leaders.

The temperature of their passion rapidly mounted until, in the outrage against the seraphic Stephen, the steaming, scalding liquid of their uncontrollable rage flowed over in the first officially instigated public persecution of the new Christian minority. The stoning of Stephen was the signal for a general uprising against the believers. It was the spark which set ablaze the smouldering fuel of Jewish hatred against the Nazarene and His followers. Note the connection between the last verse of chapter vii. and the first verse of chapter viii.: "They stoned Stephen, calling upon God, and saying: Lord Jesus, receive my spirit; and he kneeled down, and cried with a loud voice: Lord, lay not this sin to their charge. And when he had said this he fell asleep. . . . *And at that time there was a great persecution against the assembly which was at Jerusalem; and they were all scattered abroad. . . .*" Stephen the protomartyr was quickly joined by hundreds of others who fell beneath the stroke of the persecutor. Tradition tells us that over two thousand were put to death in the Stephenic outbreak. Stephen's martyrdom was the desperate, deadly, decisive expression of the official Jewish further rejection of our Lord Jesus as Messiah-Saviour-King.

First Out-movement of Evangelism.

Third: the martyrdom of Stephen precipitated *the first outward movement of evangelism from the Jewish capital*. We turn again to chapter viii. In the first verse we are told that, consequent upon the persecution which arose around Stephen, "they were all scattered abroad throughout the regions of Judæa and Samaria, except the apostles." In verse 4 we read: "They that were scattered abroad *went everywhere preaching the word*." In verse 5 we read: "Then Philip went down to the city of *Samaria*, and preached Christ unto them." In verse 25 we read: "And they [Peter and John], when they had testified and preached the word of the Lord, returned to Jerusalem, and preached the Gospel in *many villages* of the Samaritans." Still further, in verse 40 we have it that "Philip, passing through [from Azotus], preached in *all the cities* till he came to Cæsarea."

Following the account of Stephen's death, all the remaining chapters in the first part of the Acts deal with this first outward movement. They give us the principal aspects of it, showing how witness was borne to key cities and persons, thus:

Ch. viii.	Samaria	Ethiopian chancellor.
ix.	Damascus	Saul the future Paul.
x.	Cæsarea	Cornelius the centurian.
xi.	Antioch	Ministry to Gentiles vindicated.

Fourth: the outbreak against Stephen occasioned *the trans-ference to a new centre, Antioch*. In chapter xi. 19 we read: "Now they which were scattered abroad upon the persecution that arose about Stephen travelled as far as Phenice and Cyprus and Antioch, preaching the word to none but Jews only." From this point Antioch begins to take the lead in the Acts. Jerusalem still retains nominal leadership. It is still the centre of authoritative decision and pronouncement, for the Twelve still remain there. Moreover, there is still the uniqueness of the Judæan capital arising from its sacred associations; and it remains for all time the historic cradle of the new faith: yet *in strategic importance* it is Antioch which now comes to the fore.

In a special way "the hand of the Lord" is with them at Antioch. "A great number" believe and turn to the Lord there. Jerusalem sends Barnabas down to Antioch. Barnabas brings Saul from Tarsus to Antioch. The disciples are first called "Christians" at Antioch. The base from which the great Pauline missionary campaigns are conducted through the empire is Antioch. It is Antioch which now sends relief to Jerusalem and Judæa. The whole of the second part of the Acts proceeds from what happens at Antioch.

We see, then, that the outrage against Stephen is, in a fourfold way, a pivotal event in the Acts. It marks (1) the final trial of the nation at the capital, (2) the official Jewish rejection of the renewed offer of the kingdom, (3) the first outward movement of evangelism, (4) the emerging of a new strategic centre.

Thus, the main outcome and central significance of this first part of the Acts is: THE RENEWED REJECTION OF THE KINGDOM OFFICIALLY AT THE CAPITAL.

The Outcry Against Paul

We move on now to the second pivotal crisis in the Acts, i.e. *the outcry against Paul*. As, in the first part of the book, the martyrdom of Stephen is the focus-point, the climax of what precedes it and the cause of what follows it, so here in this second half of the book the impassioned outburst of Jewish hostility described in chapter xxii. (and notably in verse 22) is that which brings things again to a head, clarifying the situation as by a sudden flash, and immediately determining the new line of action which follows.

But first we must examine chapters xiii.–xxi., which lead up to this wild outcry. The Lord's word was: "Ye shall be witnesses unto Me, both in Jerusalem and in all Judæa, and in Samaria, and unto the uttermost part of the earth." We have now seen in the first part of the book the witness borne in Jerusalem and Judæa and Samaria, the message having been taken "to the Jew first," and then, in view of Jewish opposition, carried "also to the Gentile." But it is not enough that the good news of the kingdom should be proclaimed only in the homeland. What of the millions of Jews scattered throughout the Roman world, the Jews of the Dispersion? Will *they* accept the message? This must yet be seen. They must have their chance. Hence the second part of the Acts is taken up with the witness of the kingdom to the Jews of the Dispersion, and to the "uttermost part of the earth." Here again we see strict adherence to the order, "the Jew first" and then "also to the Gentile."

First Missionary Tour

The first Pauline missionary journey is given in chapters xiii. and xiv. Among the places mentioned *en route,* these are they at which ministry is recorded:

Salamis	xiii. 5
Paphos	xiii. 6
Antioch (Pisidia)	xiii. 14
Iconium	xiii. 51
Lystra and Derbe	xiv. 6, 20
Return journey	xiv. 21, 22

Now with the exception of Lystra and Derbe we find that in every case, on this first missionary tour, the two apostles went "to the Jew first," and therefore began at the synagogue. As for Lystra and Derbe, besides the probability that there was no synagogue at either, it may be doubted whether there were Jews in those two places at all. The narrative says: "And there came thither Jews from Antioch and Iconium, who persuaded the people, and having stoned Paul, drew him out of the city, supposing he had been dead." That expression, "the people," in our New Testament is often the translation of the Greek word *laos* and is used distinctively of the Jewish nation. The Jews considered themselves in a unique way *"the* people" on account of their special covenant relation with Jehovah. We find such use of the word, for instance, in Acts xxi. 28. Here, however, it is not *laos,* but a word which means the *crowds.* The spiteful Jews who pursued Paul and Barnabas to Lystra incited *"the crowds"* (non-Jewish) against them. The likelihood, therefore, is that there were neither synagogues nor Jews at Lystra or Derbe.

What was the message which the two apostles preached on this first missionary expedition? We well realise that Luke's reports of their utterances are necessarily severe abbreviations; but the gist of the message is clearly preserved. Moreover, Luke summarises it at the end of the itinerary, in chapter xiv. 21, 22: "And when they had preached *THE GOSPEL* to that city, and had discipled many, they returned again to Lystra, and to Iconium and Antioch (in Pisidia), confirming the souls of the disciples, and exhorting them to continue in the faith, and that we must through much tribulation enter into *THE KINGDOM OF GOD."* The message was that of *JESUS AS MESSIAH-KING AND PERSONAL SAVIOUR.*

What were the *results* of this first missionary tour? Take the visited places in order. At Salamis no result is stated. At Paphos no result is given so far as the general reaction is concerned, but we find opposition from the Jewish sorcerer, and sympathetic response from a Gentile official. At Antioch in Pisidia there is an awakened interest shown by many Jews and proselytes in the synagogue (xiii. 43); but it is followed by bitter opposition from the Jewish community (verses 45, 50). The notable thing is that there is a glad acceptance of the Word by the Gentiles (verse 42, 44, 48); and it is here, in the face of Jewish hostility, that Paul says: "Lo, we turn to the Gentiles" (verse 46). Next, at Iconium, a "large number" (not a "great *multitude"* as in A.V.) in the synagogue, both of Jews and Greeks, believed (xiv. 1); but there is bitter opposition again from the Jews as a whole (verses 2, 4), who also incite Gentiles against Paul and Barnabas (verses 2, 5). Finally, at Lystra and Derbe, Jewish pursuers stir the mob against the apostles, yet many Gentiles are there discipled (verses 19, 21).

Thus we see that the Jews were more and more closing the

door against the apostolic witness, and that at the same time the "door of faith" was being opened to the Gentiles (xiv. 27). From the opening visit to Cyprus, it would seem as though the two evangelists had intended to go exclusively to the Jews. In Antioch and Iconium they are forced to recognise that they *cannot* go exclusively to the Jews, though they still go to the Jew primarily (xiii. 46). When we see them as fugitives in Lycaonia they have been fairly driven out to the Gentiles!

On returning to their home base, they "rehearsed all that God had done with them, and how He had opened the door of faith unto the Gentiles." They could bear no glad report of Jewish repentance and receptiveness. The one bright relief was this opening of the door to the Gentiles. A great transition was taking place. More and more we see those other words assuming prominence: *"And also the Gentiles."*

Second Missionary Journey

Paul's second missionary journey runs from chapter xv. 36 to xviii. 22. It may be analysed as follows:

THE SECOND MISSIONARY TOUR

Place	Method and message		Reaction and result	
Philippi	"To Jew first"	(1) The promised Messiah a Sinbearer	Unrecorded (Lydia is won)	On to Thessalonica
Thessalonica	,,		Some accept: opposition	Flight to Berea
Berea	,,	(2) That Messiah is Jesus, crucified but risen	Many accept: opposition	Flight to Athens
Athens	,,		No Jewish response	Out to the Gentiles
Corinth	,,	(3) Jesus is now offered as King, Messiah, Saviour.	Bitter opposition	"Henceforth to Gentiles"
Ephesus	,,		Not recorded till later	Back to home base at Antioch

Such was the method, message and outcome of the second Pauline missionary adventure. Although at Thessalonica the response seems very favourable at first, it is only "some" of the Jews who accept the word; the "multitude" who accept are Greeks (xvii. 4). The one cheering spot (so far as *Jewish* inclination is concerned) is Berea, though even there it is clear that the larger part did not respond. Jewish opposition seems to have reached high-water mark at Corinth (xviii. 6, 12, 17). It is in connection with this that we have the last recorded word spoken by Paul before his return journey to the home base, and it is significant: "From henceforth I will go *unto the Gentiles.*"

Third Missionary Journey

The third missionary tour covers xviii. 23–xxi. 3. The one place at which ministry is described is Ephesus, and the whole of chapter xix. is devoted to it. The *method* was again "to the Jew first" (verse 8). The *message* was "the kingdom of God" (verse 8). The *reaction* was largely unbelief and opposition on the part of the Jews (verses 9, 13), though there seems to have been some measure of response. As to the *result,* there was a turning to the Gentiles, among whom there was a widespread movement set going (verses 9, 18–20).

So, then, the Jews of the Dispersion have now had the message preached to them in these three eventful missionary tours of Paul, and in the unrecorded witness of others, such as Barnabas. What are the recorded results? One only needs to look back over the analyses of the first two itineraries, and then over this briefer third excursion which needs no analysis, to realise the sorrowful fact that the Jews of the Dispersion have exhibited the same attitude as their kinsmen in the homeland. Although appreciable numbers have responded in two or three places, the vast majority have rejected and opposed. Alas, the stubborn cry has been: "We will not have this Man to reign over us!" When Paul returns to Jerusalem after his third missionary tour what does his report consist of? Chapter xxi. 19 tells us: "And when he had saluted them [James and the elders], he declared particularly what things God had wrought *among the Gentiles* by his ministry." It is of momentous significance, especially in the light of what now follows in Jerusalem.

Paul at Jerusalem—the Outcry!

This brings us right up to the second of the three key events in this book of the Acts. Paul was at Jerusalem on the occasion of the annual Pentecost (xx. 16). There were present therefore at the Jewish capital Jews from all over the world, just as there had been when, some twenty-seven years earlier, the Holy Spirit was first outpoured on the apostolic band, and when Peter had declared to the "devout men *out of every nation under heaven*", who were then gathered for the Passover and Pentecost, that the effusion of the Spirit was a fulfilment of Joel's prophecy (ii. 5, 16). Now, in these later chapters (xxi., xxii.) where the murderous outcry is raised against Paul, the Jews of the Dispersion are well represented by the many who have come from the various parts of the Roman world to be present in Jerusalem for the celebration. Paul is now only too well known to them as a result of his three evangelistic expeditions. They are now about to utter their fierce, final repudiation of him and his message.

Mark well that it is "the Jews *which were from Asia*" (xxi. 27) who drag Paul into prominence and instigate the riot against him. Their cry is a spark to dynamite. "All the city" is soon "in an uproar"! And it is only swift intervention by the military police which averts Paul's being done to death (verses 30–32)! But the battered and bruised apostle is yet to make his momentous "defence" to the angry crowd of his fellow-nationals from the castle stairs. It is given in chapter xxii., a spirited and stirring utterance: but the apostle is not allowed to complete it. The very instant that Paul reaches a certain point, and allows a certain remark to pass his lips, the mob gives one mighty yell for his death. It is this frantic outburst at this certain point which gives the occasion its pivotal significance. Verse 22 says: "And they gave him audience unto this word, and then lifted up their voices and said: Away with such a fellow from the earth, for it is not fit that he should live. And they cried out, and cast off their clothes, and threw dust into the air . . . " What, then, was it at which they so violently stampeded? It was this:

"AND HE [JESUS] SAID UNTO ME: DEPART, FOR I WILL SEND THEE FAR HENCE UNTO THE GENTILES."

"And they gave him audience unto *this word,* and then lifted up their voices . . . !" It was the representatives of the Jews of the Dispersion, united with the unbelieving Jews of the homeland, uttering their loud and final rejection of Jesus as their Christ and of the message of salvation to the Gentiles. This latter was intolerable to them. It infuriated and maddened them in their conceited bigotry. They would not themselves receive the kingdom, but they were determined that no semblance of privilege should be accorded to the Gentiles.

Everything from the beginning of chapter xiii. has been leading up to this point; and we shall now see that all which follows it is significantly resultant from it. There is no missing this:

Chapter xxiii.	Paul before the Sanhedrin,
,, xxiv.	Paul before Governor Felix,
,, xxv.	Paul before Governor Festus,
,, xxvi.	Paul before King Agrippa,
,, xxvii.	Paul sent from Judæa to Rome.

The Outgoing to the Gentiles

The final crisis-point in this book of the Acts is reached in chapter xxviii. After a hazardous voyage (xxvii. 1–xxviii. 15) Paul at last set foot in Rome (xxviii. 16). Not being a criminal in the ordinary sense, and perhaps on the recommendation of the courteous centurion Julius, under whose custody the apostle had been brought to Rome (xxvii. 1), Paul is given a measure of privilege (xxviii. 16), as also had been the case during his imprisonment at Cæsarea (xxiv. 23), and during the voyage to Rome (xxvii. 3). Although apparently fastened by a chain to a prætorian (xxviii. 16, 20), he is allowed to live in his own rented apartment (verse 30). After the first three days in Rome, he calls together to himself the chief Jews, to explain to them his presence there and to fix a day with them when he could expound the Word of God to them concerning the Lord Jesus and the renewed offer of the kingdom of God to Israel.

When these Jewish leaders subsequently came for the interview, what was it precisely to which the apostle gave testimony? The answer is in chapter xxviii. 23: "And when they had appointed him a day, there came many to him, into his lodging; to whom he expounded and testified *the kingdom of God*, persuading [i.e. endeavouring to persuade] them concerning Jesus, both out of the law of Moses, and out of the Prophets, from morning till evening." Even after the apostle's discouraging experiences in Judæa and through the empire, his approach is still *"to the Jew first"* (verse 17), and only afterward "also to the Gentile" (verse 30); and the subject of his testimony is still *"the kingdom"* (verse 23, 31).

What was the outcome? Verses 24 and 25 tell us: "And some believed the things which were spoken, and some disbelieved. And disagreeing with one another, they departed. . . ." We get the impression that even those who "believed" (or, more literally, "were persuaded") did not receive the word with anything like enthusiasm. As the Greek word indicates, it was more a case of mental assent or credence, merely, than a glad acceptance into the heart. The others definitely rejected the word. The total result is made plain beyond any mistake in Paul's own comment: "And, disagreeing among themselves, they departed, after that Paul had spoken one word: Well spake the Holy Spirit by Esaias the prophet unto our fathers, saying: Go unto this people, and say, Hearing ye shall hear and shall not understand; and seeing ye shall see and not perceive; for the heart of this people is waxed gross, and their ears are dull of hearing, and their eyes have they closed; lest they should see with their eyes, and hear with their ears, and understand with their heart, and should be converted, and I should heal them" (verses 25–7). Then, immediately following this, the final crisis-point of the book is reached in the words:

"BE IT KNOWN THEREFORE UNTO YOU, THAT THE SALVATION OF GOD IS SENT UNTO THE GENTILES AND THAT THEY SHALL HEAR IT" (verse 28).

Having brought us to this third and most significant crisis-point, the book of the Acts closes. It has reached its tragic goal, and fulfilled its intended purpose. The renewed offer of the kingdom of heaven to Israel has been made over a period of thirty years, first to the Jews of the homeland, then to the Jews of the Dispersion throughout the Roman world, and finally to the Jews at the imperial city. With that message of the re-offered kingdom there has been coupled the wonderful Saviourhood of the Messiah Jesus, through His Calvary sacrifice, and the fact of His Resurrection. But in general the Jewish attitude has everywhere been unbelieving and hostile. The concluding episode at Rome is a final corroboration: THE JEWS HAVE SAID "NO" TO THE RENEWED OFFER OF JESUS AS ISRAEL'S CHRIST AND KING AND SAVIOUR. THE "KINGDOM" IS NOW TO BE WITHDRAWN AND HELD IN ABEYANCE. FOR THE TIME BEING (i.e. FOR THIS PRESENT AGE) THE NATION ISRAEL IS TO BE SET ASIDE AS GOD'S REPRESENTATIVE PEOPLE ON EARTH, AND A FAR-SURPASSING GOSPEL OF WORLD-EMBRACING DIVINE GRACE IS TO BE MADE KNOWN AMONG ALL THE NATIONS OF THE GENTILES.

The book has thus brought our minds to the point where they are ready to turn onward to the Christian Church Epistles (Romans to 2 Thessalonians) and to learn there of the wonderful new movement in the Divine purpose, hitherto hidden in the secret counsels of the Godhead but now revealed as heaven's sublime answer to Jewish unbelief—namely, THE CHURCH, the mystic body and bride and temple of the Son of God.

THE ACTS OF THE APOSTLES (3)

Lesson Number 126

NOTE: For this study read specially chapters iii. to xii., with xxvii. and xxviii.

THIS BOOK OF THE ACTS

Its record of facts is full of illustrations and examples of Christian doctrine. We see what the Christian teaching meant by the way the Christians lived. It is a book of teaching by example, and its facts are full of ideas and principles. We have here the germs of Christian doctrine afterwards elaborated in the epistles of the great apostles Paul, Peter and John; and the special value is that we have the doctrine exemplified by the life.

—W. H. G. Thomas.

THE ACTS OF THE APOSTLES (3)

WE HAVE now explored our way right through the Acts and have learned its first-intended significance from the three crisis-points which it records.

Because of its abrupt ending there are many who aver that it is an *unfinished* work; but to regard it as such surely misses its most momentous meaning. Admittedly there is much more which we could wish had been told us about Paul's closing days on earth, but no more was added because no more was *needed* to fulfil the purpose of the book.

Whatever may be said from a literary or historical viewpoint anent its ending, this real-life drama is tragically complete in its strategic significance (which is the vital thing). It marks a fateful dispensational turning-point. Israel has said "NO" to Jesus as Messiah-King-Saviour and to the renewed offer of the kingdom. Luke conducts us through the suspense-period of further offer, right to the point where Israel's refusal has become unmistakably firm-fixed. The very abruptness of his breaking off at that point urges our minds onward the more enquiringly to the Christian Church Epistles, to find there the glorious doctrine emerging of a *CHURCH* which is the mystic body and bride of God's dear Son.

In some senses, of course, the story is *intendedly* incomplete. It leaves us asking all sorts of questions. Was Paul liberated after his first trial at Rome? Did he, as some infer, spend further months in travel? What course did things take in Jerusalem? What happened to the Twelve? Did Peter visit Rome? These matters are left unresolved because they are outside the aim of the book.

Surprise turns and vivid incidents challenge enquiry on every page of the Acts; but our concern here is with the *main* meanings, in the light of which all the incidentals assume their true size, force, and value. The following analysis gives a photographic view of the whole book, showing its determinative crisis-points and movements.

THE ACTS OF THE APOSTLES
Renewed offer of the kingdom to the Jews

Ch. i. Apostles prepared and commissioned.

(1) RENEWED OFFER TO JEWS OF THE HOME-LAND
(ii.–xii.).

Ch. ii.   Miracle—Witness—Response.
iii., iv.   Miracle—Witness—Opposition.
v.   Miracle—Witness—Opposition.
vi., vii.   Miracle—Witness—Opposition.

First crisis-point: Outrage against Stephen (vii.).

(1) Final trial of nation at the capital.
(2) Official Jewish rejection of kingdom.
(3) First outward movement of evangelism.
(4) Transference to new centre—Antioch.

The outward movement: Key cities and persons.

viii.   Samaria—Ethiopian chancellor.
ix.   Damascus—Saul the future Paul.
x.   Cæsarea—Cornelius the Gentile.
xi.   Antioch—Gentile inclusion (verse 18).
xii.   Jerusalem—at end of part 1. Judgment on Herod, as head of nation.

(2) RENEWED OFFER TO JEWS OF THE DISPERSION
(xiii.–xxviii.).

xiii., xiv.   First Pauline missionary excursion.
xv. 36   Second Pauline missionary excursion.
xviii. 23   Third Pauline missionary excursion.
General Jewish reaction—opposition.

Second crisis-point: Outcry against Paul (xxii.).

(1) Climax of Jewish hatred against Paul.
(2) Culminating "No" by Jews of Dispersion.
(3) This causes witness to key persons.
(4) Leads to Paul's final witness at Rome.

The further witnessing before key persons.

xxiii.   Paul witnesses before the Sanhedrin.
xxiv.   Paul witnesses before Governor Felix.
xxv.   Paul witnesses before Governor Festus.
xxvi.   Paul witnesses before King Agrippa.
xxvii.   Paul goes to Rome: final witness there.

Third crisis-point: Outgoing to Gentiles (xxviii.).

"Be it known therefore unto you that the salvation of God is sent unto the Gentiles, and that
they will hear it" (xxviii. 28).

The Astonishing Overruling

In the light of our findings we affirm once again that this book, the Acts of the Apostles, is primarily an account of the renewed offer of Messiah-Jesus and the long-promised "kingdom of heaven" to the nation Israel. Certainly that people's refusal of the renewed approach was the circumstance which historically occasioned the emergence of the visible Church on earth; but that does not alter the fact that the prime subject of the Acts is this renewed offer of the Messianic kingdom to Israel, and that herein lies its first significance.

It is only when we turn on and read through the Epistles that we find revealed to us the deeper movement of Divine purpose which was operating underneath and concurrently with the renewed rejection of Jesus and the kingdom by the Jews. The second offer of the kingdom, as we have seen, was rejected first by the Jews of the homeland and then by the Jews of the Dispersion. All over the Roman world, however, groups of believers were formed, though these were largely Gentile (for while many individual Jews may have responded, the Jewish people as a whole persisted in determined refusal). As Jewish unbelief became more and more fixed, these groups of intermingled Jewish and Gentile believers came to assume a new meaning. Just as the awful deed of Calvary had been Divinely foreknown and over-ruled—inasmuch as the crucifixion of the nation's Messiah had been sublimated into the atoning self-sacrifice of the world's Saviour—so also this further failure of the Jewish people had been Divinely anticipated and overruled. Under the sovereign operation of God these groups of believers scattered throughout the Roman world now became seen and known, through inspired eyes and pens, as the first assemblies of those blood-redeemed, Spirit-born human beings who constitute the spiritual CHURCH, the mystic body and bride and temple of the eternal Son.

Paul tells us that it was to himself the "mystery" of the Church was first disclosed (see Eph. iii. 3–11). Up to this point the Church had been a secret hid in God" and concealed "throughout the ages." Clearly this means that the Church of the New Testament cannot be the subject of Old Testament prophecy. Therefore the effort to read it *into* Old Testament prophecy, whether it be into Joel ii. or any other passage, is wrong. Certainly the Church may be latent in Old Testament type and fore-shadowing; but it is nowhere the subject of direct pronouncement. Now, however, as the tragic story of Jewish unbelief unfolds itself to the last paragraph of the Acts, we see these many little groups of believers up and down the Roman world transfigured by the light which breaks on them from the Epistles. Out from the ashes of Jewish unbelief there rises up this wonderful new spiritual building, the Church, of which these little groups are the first expression. Lo, an elect bride for the heavenly Isaac! A spiritual temple for the glorified Lord! A mystic body for Him who is "Head over all things"! Behold, "the grace of God that bringeth salvation hath appeared to all men"! A new age breaks! The kingdom twice refused by unbelieving Israel is now for the time being held over; but the purpose of God moves on un-thwarted. We do not wonder that Paul himself, contemplating but one aspect of this profound "mystery," should exclaim: "Oh, the depth of the riches, both of the wisdom and the knowledge of God! How unsearchable are His judgments, and His ways past finding out!" (Rom. xi. 33).

We stress the fact again, however, that only in the light of the Epistles do we perceive this deeper significance in these newly formed assemblies of believers scattered throughout the Roman world, as recorded in the Acts. The word "church" in verses like Acts ii. 47 should be read as "assembly" lest we prematurely read meanings into the word "church" which it only acquires later. If we keep well in mind that this book is firstly the renewed offer of the Messianic kingdom to Israel, we are spared various pitfalls; moreover, seeming problems connected with present-day non-appearance of Pentecostal miracles begin to evaporate.

We do not say that it is *wrong* to date the beginning of the historic Christian Church back to Pentecost, but it should be with guarded reservations, lest we misread the miraculous accom-paniments of that abnormal manifestation as the norm for the Christian Church right through the present age. To finalise the point as sharply and clearly as possible, we may put it that the Pentecostal effusion of the Holy Spirit, which was *patently* the Divine attestation of the renewed kingdom-offer to Israel, was also *latently* the historical origination of the Church by the Spirit-wrought fusion of those first individual human units into one spiritual organism and corporate body. The meaning of the supernatural effusion was clear at once so far as *Israel* was concerned; it only emerged later in relation to the *Church*.

The Acts a Continuation

If only for the sake of re-emphasis, we ought to mention here what has often been pointed out by others, namely, that this book of the Acts is a *continuation*. Luke's opening words are: "The former treatise have I made, O Theophilus, of all that Jesus *began* both to do and teach, until the day in which He was taken up. . . ." As he *ends* his Gospel at our Lord's ascension, he here *begins* from it; so that his second "treatise" is a continuation of his first.

But there is far more in it than that. The arrangement of the words in the Greek purposely throws the emphasis on that word "began." The implication is tremendous. The Acts is no mere chronicle of witness to an absent Christ. His ascension did not rob His followers of His presence. The lovely paradox is that He was never so really *with* them as after He had *left* them! All the way through Acts Jesus is chief Actor, even *more* present now because physically invisible. This is the wonder-epic of what the crucified, risen, ascended *Jesus Himself* CONTINUED to do by His Spirit through His chosen witnesses!

All the way through, we repeat, He is the dominating Mover. What a study this makes! Trace it through just a little here, then complete the study later. It is *HE* who pours forth the glorious Holy Spirit (ii. 33). It is *HE* who makes the lame man whole (iii. 16, iv. 10). It is *HE* who "adds to the assembly" those who are being "saved" (ii. 47). It is *HE* who is seen "standing at the right hand of God" (vii. 55). It is *HE* who directly intervenes to convert Saul on the Damascus Road (ix. 5). It is *HE* who cures the sick Æneas (ix. 34). It is *HE* who comforts Paul in the castle at Jerusalem (xxiii. 11). And so it is right through the story. During the days of visible, bodily, localised presence, He was "straitened," but now in fuller degree He works and speaks by the Holy Spirit. See Luke xii. 50; John xvi. 12, 13.

Let all Christian workers gratefully and graphically appreciate this. We do not merely work *for* Jesus; He Himself is on the spot, in control, working *with* us. What we have in the Acts is the thrilling demonstration of Mark xvi. 20.

The Spiritual Key

As we have said, the key to the Acts considered structurally is chapter i. 8: "Jerusalem and all Judæa, and in Samaria, and unto the uttermost part of the earth." That is the order in which the witness-bearing expands and the book takes shape; and correspondingly the door of faith is opened successively to Jews, Romans, Greeks—as in the successive Gospels. But the *spiritual* key is that expression in chapter i. 2—"*Through the Holy Spirit.*" One only needs to glance through the opening chapters to see what spiritual treasures open up to *this* key:

Chapter　i.　"Through the Holy Spirit"—Power
　　　　　　　　　　　　　　　　　　(verses 5, 8).
　　,,　　ii.　"Through the Holy Spirit"—Utterance
　　　　　　　　　　　　　　　　　　(verses 3, 4, 6).
　　,,　iii., iv.　"Through the Holy Spirit"—Boldness
　　　　　　　　　　　　　　　　　　(iv. 8, 19–31).
　　,,　　v.　"Through the Holy Spirit"—"Signs, wonders"
　　　　　　　　　　　　　　　　　　(verses 7, 12, 25, 32).
　　,,　　vi.　"Through the Holy Spirit"—Wisdom
　　　　　　　　　　　　　　　　　　(verses 3, 10).

What about pursuing and completing that line of enquiry? It would fill too much space here; but we have barked the first few trees and urge the young Bible explorer to "blaze the trail" right through to the end. He who studies, ponders and understands the ways of the Holy Spirit as disclosed in the Acts of the Apostles will be wise with the wisest of all wisdom in serving God and witnessing to Christ. Perhaps the saddest of all the references to the Holy Spirit is that which comes in the last paragraph of.the book. God save us and those around us from that obtusity and obduracy which cursed the old-time Jews and grieved away the Spirit of the Lord!

Spiritual Patterns

How largely can the Church of today learn from those first assemblies of believers which figure in the Acts! We do well to turn back again and again to those Spirit-wrought originals and test ourselves by them, both individually and corporately. How far, alas, from that Christian communion of the *first* days have many so-called "churches" fallen away in *these* days! "See that thou make all things according to the pattern showed to thee in the mount," was the Divine admonition to Moses. The Holy Spirit says the same to the churches through the Acts of the Apostles. "He that hath an ear, let him hear what the Spirit saith unto the churches."

We are here touching on an aspect which might well fill a book by itself. The time is much overdue for a re-study of those first Christian groups. By way of illustration, we alight on just *one* glimpse in chapter v. 12–17, 18, 42. Observe the three features which distinguished *that* "church."

First, there was power to *repel*. Verse 13 says: "Of the rest durst no man join himself to them." That holy band had the power to create fear. See verse 11. Most people today think that the only power needed by the churches is the power to attract. They are wrong. The local church needs also the power to repel— to repel the hypocritical fraterniser, the worldly compromiser, the intriguing insinuator. Oh, the curse of the "mixed multitude" in our churches, whose appetite is for the leeks and garlics of Egypt! In that *first* Church the Spirit-charged atmosphere was life to holiness and death to pretence.

Second, there was power to *attract*. Verse 14 says: "And believers were the more added to the Lord, multitudes both of men and women." There were two classes attracted: (*a*) "believers"; (*b*) "the sick." The believers came for *fellowship*. The sick ones came for *healing*. How do the churches of today measure up to that? Why are the churches so largely disregarded today, even by the sin-sick and the lonely?

Third, there was power to *surmount*. Verse 17 begins: "Then the high priest rose up, and all they that were with him . . ." The pot boils over with scalding hatred against the Nazarenes! There is prison, scourging, interdict. But how does the chapter end? "And daily in the temple and in every house, they ceased not to teach and preach Jesus Christ."

When the Holy Spirit is really in control that is always the story. Opposition is not eliminated, but it is overruled. Trouble is turned to triumph. Present suffering for the Name may be permitted; but there is exuberant grace, and eventual victory for the cause.

Divine Purpose, yet Permitted Opposition

This seeming enigma of permitted opposition and trouble intertwines itself with the narrative all the way through the Acts. The wise-hearted will take it duly into account. Pentecostal Christianity provides no immunity from Satanic retaliation in one form or another. Right at the end, in Luke's travelogue of Paul's deportation from Cæsarea to Rome (xxvii., xxviii.) it appears with persisting and culminating ferocity. As G. Campbell Morgan says: "On the one hand, difficulties and dangers multiplied and seemed to conspire to thwart and prevent a Divine purpose. On the other hand, steadily, surely, if slowly, that purpose was carried out. It would seem as though the power of God should be equal to the fulfilment of His purposes through more peaceful processes. Yet at last it is manifest that through these very difficulties and oppositions that purpose is served in the fullest and largest measure." When Satan has done his last and worst, however, Luke is still able to write: *"So we came to Rome"* (xxviii. 16, R.V.); and the purpose of God moves on with irresistible tread. Let tried and troubled saints learn this securely!

Vivid spiritual patterns are everywhere in the Acts. It is a regret that we cannot here linger over them, especially the more conspicuous, such as that immortal first "day of Pentecost" in chapter ii., and the Spirit's later invasion of Cornelius's household in chapter x. In our present brief enquiries we are more concerned to silhouette the significance of the epochal transition as a whole. So for the present we must reluctantly leave even the larger incidentals or else find that we have far overshot our intended boundary-line.

New Light on Our Lord's Return

There is one further matter, however, which we feel duty-bound to discuss before leaving this article. Involved in the Acts is the tremendous truth of our Saviour's future return to this earth. When once we realise that this book is primarily the renewed offer of the Messianic kingdom to Israel, we come into new intelligence concerning that "blessed hope."

If we rightly read the Scriptures, the second coming of Christ to this earth is not, so to speak, an event fixed by calendar for a certain date, but rather an event which is *contingent upon* certain other events. Our Lord said: "Of that day and hour knoweth no man." No man *could* have been given to know it in advance, for it was contingent upon Israel's reaction to the renewed offer of Jesus as Christ and Saviour. If the "day and hour" had been a date-fixture revealed to any man, or to any set of men, how could a *bona fide* offer have been made to the Jews, such as we have in the Acts of the Apostles, that if they would now accept the renewed offer of Jesus as their Messiah-Saviour-King, then He would forthwith return from heaven to bring in the promised "times of refreshing" and set up His reign? As we have seen, such a promise was clearly given through the lips of the apostles. We turn back again to chapter iii. 17–21:

"And now, brethren, I know that through ignorance ye did it, as did also your rulers; but those things which God before had showed by the mouth of all His prophets, that the Christ should suffer, He hath thus fulfilled. Repent ye, therefore, and be converted, that your sins may be blotted out, and the times of refreshing shall come from the presence of the Lord; AND HE SHALL SEND JESUS CHRIST WHO WAS PROCLAIMED BEFORE UNTO YOU, Whom the heaven must indeed receive until the times of the restoration of all things which God hath spoken by the mouth of all His prophets from of old."

Such plain speaking cannot be misunderstood. Had there been a national repentance and acceptance of Jesus as indeed Israel's Messiah-Saviour-King, the return of our Lord in public glory would have happened without further postponement. In other words, the second coming of Christ was contingent upon Israel's reaction to the new message through the apostles. Very clearly, then, we can see why, when the disciples asked, "Lord, wilt Thou at this time restore again the kingdom to Israel?" (Acts i. 6), He replied, "It is not for you to know the times or the seasons which the Father hath put in His own power." To have known the day and hour in advance would have been to know Israel's reaction before ever the renewed offer of the kingdom was made. Truly, in the words of James: "Known unto God are all His works from the beginning of the world" (Acts xv. 18); and it is in the light of His perfect foreknowledge that He preadapts and prearranges and predetermines. Thus, while He never leaves His ultimate purposes at the mercy of human uncertainty, in the out-working of things to the predetermined end He recognises the free-will of man all through, and prearranges according to His foreknowledge of what man will do. Thus it is that events are allowed in the main to take their natural course, while at the same time God foreknows and overrules all to the fulfilment of His ultimate purpose. Thus, in all genuineness, the renewed offer of the Messianic kingdom was made to the Jews, as recorded in the Acts; and the return of Christ was for the time being contingent upon their reaction.

This has a bearing upon *the Epistles*. In those to the Thessa-lonians the second coming of Christ is represented as though it might have burst into sudden occurrence in the imminent future. In some of the other Pauline epistles there is a noticeable shift of emphasis: the wondrous hope still gleams ahead, but there is not the same impression of impending fulfilment. This has been a problem to thoughtful readers; but once again, when we see the Acts as distinctively the renewed offer of the kingdom to Israel the problem evaporates.

The period covered by the Acts, we repeat, was a suspense-period. So long as the kingdom was being re-offered to the nation the return of the Lord could have happened without any delay upon the fulfilment of the conditions. The offer was real; the promise was true; the crucified but ascended Son of Man was indeed "standing at the right hand of God," ready to descend again in kingdom blessing. Would Israel respond, repent, receive? That was the suspense-point. Now it is in those epistles which were written during this suspense-period of the Acts, when there was still hope of Israel's repentance, that we find the seeming imminence of the Lord's return. Of those epistles, the earliest were 1 and 2 Thessalonians (written A.D. 53). 1 and 2 Corin-thians, Galatians, Romans, were written four or five years later, when Jewish antipathy was becoming more firmly crystallised, but when to assemblies of believers all over the Roman world the hope of Christ's return was still that which filled the im-mediate horizon (hence such words as Rom. xiii. 11, 12; 1 Cor. vii. 26, 29, xv. 52, 58, xvi. 22; 2 Cor. iv. 14). When we turn over to Ephesians, Philippians, Colossians, 1 and 2 Timothy and Titus, however, there is a noticeable new emphasis. The grand prospect of the Lord's return is still there, and still as bright: but there is not just the same sense of impendence. A great new conception swings into commanding prominence, taking the precedence for the time being, and claiming the soul's wonder—that is, the CHURCH as the mystic body and bride and temple of the eternal Son. *These* epistles were not written until A.D. 64 (or possibly even later), i.e. after the culminating pronouncement of Acts xxviii. 28.

We do not say that there is a hard-and-fast division between these two groups of epistles. The hope of the Lord's return is found in both; but there is modification as the later developments recorded in the Acts clarify the situation. Similarly, the Church is found in both; but there is profounder conception of it as the wonderful Divine "mystery" is more fully revealed. We do not say there is a rigid demarcation between the two groups; yet the difference of emphasis is distinctly there; and the explanation is found in a true understanding of the Acts as the further offer of the kingdom to Israel.

Another point on which it is well to be precise is that the two Thessalonian epistles, although they certainly give the impression that the Lord's return was expected in the very near future, do not anywhere actually state that it was thus impending. With that more-than-human genius which everywhere characterises the Scriptures a fine point of balance is maintained, so that while the sense of expectancy is stressed and even encouraged, there is no actual commitment as to the "day" or the "hour." In this connection it is important to distinguish between what Paul *thought* and what Paul *taught*. Maybe Paul himself thought that the Lord's return was close at hand; but he never actually wrote so. We do not claim inspiration and infallibility for all that the apostles *thought*; but we do claim it for all that they *taught*.

Thus, these two Second Advent letters to the Thessalonians preserve a kind of sensitive poise between an encouraged expectancy on the one hand and a careful indefiniteness as to time on the other. Does this seem unfair to those early believers? Actually it was the very opposite. Looking at things from the human side, our Lord's return *might* have happened then; for as we have seen, it was a *contingent* prospect. Looking at things from the Divine side (which the now-completed Scriptures permit us to do) there could have been no renewed offer of the kingdom without this contingent promise. Certainly, the further Jewish refusal lay in the foreknowledge of God, but so did His larger purpose through the Church and the eventual return of Christ after the calling in of the Church's elect members. In keeping with this, the great hope was set before those early believers so that they might have—along with all who have followed them—this sanctifying intelligence concerning the eventual consummation.

Nor is this all. The more we reflect on it, the more do we discern the wisdom of a controlling Divine inspiration in the fine poise which these Thessalonian epistles maintain between seeming to imply the imminence of the Lord's return and yet carefully withholding any actual time-commitment. It was necessary that those early believers should live in expectancy of our Lord's return, that they should have their queries about believers who fell asleep before the great day came, and that an inspired pen should write them about such points, so that *we* today, upon whom the end of the age is closing, might possess God-given light and guidance as well as they.

This leads us to our final remark on our Lord's return. As we have seen, during the suspense-period of the Acts the Lord's return was contingent upon Israel's reaction to the renewed offer of the kingdom. Is there not a real sense, also, in which it is *still* a contingent event? It is no longer contingent upon Israel's response to the apostolic message, nor has it been so since the hour of that solemn, final pronouncement in Acts xxviii. 28:

"BE IT KNOWN THEREFORE UNTO YOU, THAT THE SALVATION OF GOD IS SENT UNTO THE GENTILES, AND THAT THEY WILL HEAR IT."

No; *that* contingency has forever passed. Yet it certainly seems as though the promised Coming is now, in some real sense, made contingent upon a *further* historical development. In Romans xi. 25 (R.V.) we read:

"For I would not, brethren, have you ignorant of this mystery, lest ye be wise in your own conceits; that a hardening in part hath befallen Israel, until the fulness of the Gentiles be come in."

"UNTIL THE FULNESS OF THE GENTILES BE COME IN"! How, then, is that "fulness" of the Gentiles to be completed? Is it not by our own co-operation? It is in this same passage that Paul asks: "How shall they call on Him in whom they have not believed? And how shall they believe in Him of whom they have not heard? And how shall they hear without a preacher?" (Rom. x. 14).

But there is another New Testament reference to which we call attention. In 2 Peter iii. 11, 12 we read:

"Seeing then that all these things shall be dissolved, what manner of persons ought ye to be in all holy conversation and godliness? Looking for and hasting unto the coming of the day of God."

Note specially the words "Looking for and *hasting unto* the day of God." That word "unto"—here is an interloper. It does not come in the Greek. The translators of our Authorised Version seem to have been nervous about letting Peter's word slip through without this softening "unto", lest it might appear too strange that *we* could have any influence either to advance or to retard that august "day." Our Revised Version replaces "hasting unto" by "earnestly desiring" (apparently from a touch of the same nervousness!—for the margin confesses that the Greek word is simply "hastening"). Peter's word really reads: "LOOKING FOR AND HASTENING THE DAY OF GOD."

So there it is: *we* may hasten that day! How? By striving, as Paul did, to bring in "the fulness of the Gentiles"! That great "day," in some mysterious but real sense, has been made again contingent!

How this should startle us! We often think hard thoughts against the Jews of old, who were "slow to believe all that the prophets have spoken," and who would not respond to the renewed offer of the kingdom through the lips of the apostles; but when our own days are viewed in retrospect, shall we ourselves appear in somewhat similar blameworthiness? How slow *we* are to believe all that our Lord and His inspired apostles have spoken!

We have just quoted from 2 Peter iii. 12. See how Peter follows it up in verse 14: "Wherefore, beloved, seeing that ye look for such things *be diligent* . . ." Yes, that is our true watchword:

"BE DILIGENT"!

TWELVE QUESTIONS ON THE ACTS

1. Can you recall four factors which indicate Luke as the author of the Acts?

2. Do you think that "The Acts of the Apostles" is a true title to the book? If so, why?

3. Which are the key verse and theme? Which are the two halves of the book?—and in what six features do the two parts parallel?

4. In what ways do Peter (in the first half) and Paul (in the second) parallel with each other?

5. When the apostles asked: "Lord, dost Thou at this time restore again the kingdom to Israel?" were they unspiritual, or mistaken as to the nature of the kingdom? Please explain.

6. Whatever other meanings the book may have, it is primarily a . . . (what?)

7. What are the three pivotal events which give the book its tremendous significance?

8. There were four significant features involved in the outrage against Stephen. Which were they?

9. Which were the places visited on Paul's second missionary tour?

10. In what sense was the period covered by the Acts a "suspense-period"?

11. In what sense does the book of the Acts (in the light of the epistles) mark an astonishing Divine overruling?

12. Can you suggest a reason why the strange-seeming abrupt ending of the Acts may have been supernaturally intended?

THE CHRISTIAN CHURCH EPISTLES

INTRODUCTORY

Lesson Number 127

I think it is good that among English translations of the Bible there should be one which is the acknowledged standard version for general public use. To have one such version uniformly in use is obviously advantageous in the public reading, quoting, and citing of Scripture. I think, too, that in this connection we are wise in preferring our venerable old Authorised Version. Yet in *private* reading of the Bible I would be the first to recommend a free use of *modern* translations. We should welcome all new rays and slants on the inspired original. Some of the recent translations cause many a passage to flash with new beauty or comfort or challenge. We do not advocate them as *substitutes* for the Authorised Version, but as *companions* to it; for their new renderings are all the more vivid and forcible against a background of familiarity with the *old* version. We make these remarks here because they are particularly relevant to the epistolary area of the New Testament which we are now to explore.

—J.S.B.

THE CHRISTIAN CHURCH EPISTLES

WE HAVE now left the Gospels and the Acts, and are at the Epistles. There are twenty-two of these, if we include the Book of the Revelation as an epistle (which it really is, according to the opening verses); and they break up into three groups. First there are the nine *Christian Church Epistles* (Romans to 2 Thessalonians). Next there are the four *Pastoral and Personal Epistles* (1 Timothy to Philemon). Finally, there are the nine *Hebrew Christian Epistles* (Hebrews to Revelation).

There are noteworthy correspondences between the two ninefold groups, as we have pointed out earlier in this course of studies. Each group begins with a great doctrinal treatise—in the one case Romans, in the other case Hebrews. Each ends with an "apocalypse" or unveiling of the future in relation to the return of our Lord Jesus—in the one case Thessalonians, in the other case the Book of the Revelation. All the nine "Church" epistles, as the name implies, are written to Christian *churches*. Not one of the nine "Hebrew Christian" epistles is written to a church. Those nine are Christian epistles, but their aspect and atmosphere are peculiarly Hebrew. We shall consider them in due course; but for the present we occupy ourselves with the nine "Church" epistles.

Their Special Importance to Us

We wonder whether few or many Christians today discern the concentrated importance of these nine "Christian Church" epistles and of the four "Pastoral and Personal" epistles for this present age. All Scripture, from Genesis to Revelation, is written *for* us, and is profitable to us in many ways; but not all Scripture is written *about* us or directly *to* us as Christian believers of the present dispensation. The one part of the Bible which is specifically written *to* us and *about* us, as members of the mystic body and bride of Christ, is that part which consists of the nine "Christian Church" epistles and the four "Pastoral" epistles. Therefore, if there is any part of Scripture which Christian believers ought to know thoroughly, it is this part.

55

Among a certain class of preachers and theologians today there is much talk about "getting back" to the four Gospels and the Jesus of history. This in part springs from a serious misconception concerning the unity and progress of Scripture doctrine as a whole. Certainly, we dare not underrate the foundational importance of the four "Gospels"—they are the historical basis of everything Christian; but if we would know the Divine interpretation, the doctrinal meaning, and the wonderful spiritual implications of those basic historical records, *we must turn to the Epistles*. Nowadays among our churches there is a pathetic deficiency in the grasp of Christian *doctrine*, and it is largely due to this comparative over-emphasis on the Gospels at the expense of the Epistles. We would say to all Christians: Get to know the Christian Church Epistles well; they are that part of the Scriptures with which, in the very nature of the case, we ought to be specially concerned.

Their Uniqueness and Appropriateness

The fact that so large a part of our New Testament is in the form of *letters* should not be lost upon us. In this respect the foundation documents of Christianity are unique among the world's religions. But, besides this, these epistles have a marked appropriateness for the mission which they were meant to fulfil. What is the Divine purpose behind their composition and preservation?

As we have seen, during the suspense-period covered by the Acts of the Apostles our Lord's return was contingent upon the reaction of Israel to the renewed offer of our Lord Jesus as Messiah-Saviour-King. Had there been a national response, the Lord would have returned in kingdom glory without further postponement (Acts iii. 17–21); but as Israel's refusal became more and more deep-set, the promised return became unrealisable. Side by side with Israel's failure, however, it became gradually revealed that a new movement of God was taking shape in history. Although the nation Israel as a whole had refused the renewed offer of the true Messiah-Saviour-King, there had come into being throughout the Roman world groups or "churches" of believers, acknowledging Jesus as Divine Saviour and living in the hope of His return. These were the first expression on earth of that spiritual organism, the *Church*, the mystic body and bride of God the Son.

It was necessary that these communities should now be given instruction in a more permanent form than the merely oral teaching by which they had been called into existence. How then should this be done? The Epistles are the answer. They preserve in permanent form those inspired teachings which are specially provided for Christian believers during the present age. Paul and his co-writers little guessed that they were writing for twenty centuries ahead as well as for their own day! But the Holy Spirit knew; and they were so guided in what they wrote that their letters have become the Church's doctrine for all time.

As we have said, there is a marked appropriateness about these letters for the purpose which they were to serve. We may well be grateful that the truths which are unfolded in them were committed to us in the form of these letters rather than in cut-and-dried theological theses or catechisms! Coming to us in the form of these heart-moving letters, they have a warmth, a passion, an energy, a freshness and a personal touch which they could never have had otherwise.

Further, this form of communicating truth was peculiarly appropriate to a nature like Paul's. "It suited that impetuosity of feeling, that warm emotional nature which modern cynicism would have sneered at as 'gushing' or 'hysterical,' which could not have been fettered down to the composition of formal treatises. It permitted a freedom of expression far more vigorous and far more natural to the apostle than the regular syllogisms and rounded periods of a formal book."

Moreover, Paul's style as a writer is so full and complex that it provides a unique vehicle of expression for the Holy Spirit; so that while the great truths concerning salvation and the Church and the Christian life are written plain for all to read, there are also hidden depths and concealed treasures which are forever rewarding those who dig to discover them! Thus these letters not only give permanence to the Holy Spirit's teaching for the Christian Church; they clothe it with an interest which becomes greater and greater the more we study them.

Their Number and Arrangement

Although there are nine of these "Church" epistles, there are only seven churches addressed, since in two instances there are two letters addressed to the same church. It is noteworthy, there-fore, that the Holy Spirit through Paul here addresses the same mystic number as did the Lord Jesus Himself when from the glory He later addressed "the seven churches" as recorded in Revela-tion ii. and iii. The number seven in Scripture has the idea of completeness. In the epistles addressed by the Holy Spirit through Paul to these seven Christian churches we have the complete em-bodiment of the Holy Spirit's teaching for us Christian believers as such during the present dispensation. They contain the "all truth" into which our Lord pre-announced that the Holy Spirit would guide us.

The Scripture *order* of these "Church" epistles, also, is of particular interest to us. In 2 Timothy iii. 16 Paul writes: "All Scripture is given by inspiration of God, and is profitable for *doctrine*, for *reproof*, for *correction*." Now it would seem as though the Holy Spirit, in addressing these seven churches through Paul, has divided them into three and four, in a way which corres-ponds with Paul's words just quoted. We find that the letters addressed to three of these churches are more in the nature of *doctrinal elaborations*, each occupied with one commanding sub-ject. These are the Epistles to the Romans, the Ephesians, the Thessalonians. In these, quite distinctively, we have *"doctrine."* In the epistles to the other four churches, while of course there is instruction all the way through, in one way or another, we do not find any one commanding subject being set forth in treatise form. They are *epistolary* rather than doctrinal treatises. These are the epistles to the Corinthians, the Galatians, the Philippians, the Colossians. In these, quite distinctively, we have *"reproof"* and *"correction."* Thus:

ROMANS ("Doctrine")
CORINTHIANS ("Reproof")
GALATIANS ("Correction")
EPHESIANS ("Doctrine")
PHILIPPIANS ("Reproof")
COLOSSIANS ("Correction")
THESSALONIANS ("Doctrine").

Take the three churches to which were written the doctrinal treatises—Romans, Ephesians, Thessalonians. The letters to these three are the norms on the subjects with which they deal: Justification by faith (Romans), the doctrine of the Church (Ephesians), the Second Coming of Christ (Thessalonians).

As for Corinthians and Galatians, they follow Romans (the head of their quartette) because they exhibit departure from its special teaching, and evoke, respectively, "reproof" (Corinthians) and "correction" (Galatians)—"reproof" referring rather to wrong *conduct* and "correction" to wrong *doctrine*.

As for Philippians and Colossians, they follow Ephesians (the head of their trio) because they, in turn, exhibit departure from its special teaching, and evoke, respectively, "reproof" (Philippians) and "correction" (Colossians).

1 and 2 Thessalonians put the crown on this seven-fold "instruction" by the Holy Spirit. In Romans the believing sinner is shown as dead in sin and then "risen with Christ." In Ephesians he is "seated with Christ in the heavenlies," in a spiritual sense. In Thessalonians he is "caught up" to be for ever in the glory with the Lord! And even in the two short Thessalonian letters there is the same order of (1) "doctrine," (2) "reproof," (3) "correction." That *first* letter to the Thessalonians gives the true "doctrine" and sets the norm of second-advent doctrine. The *second* follows it with "reproof" of wrong behaviour in view of the expected return, and "correction" of wrong ideas.

Their Chronological Order

Perhaps we ought to add that their canonical order, to which we have just been referring, is not their *chronological* order. As to the approximate dates and places of composition, the consensus of opinion seems to be as follows:

1 Thessalonians	Corinth	A.D.	52–3.
2 Thessalonians	Corinth		53.
1 Corinthians	Ephesus		57.
2 Corinthians	Macedonia		57.
Galatians	Corinth		57–8.
Romans	Corinth		58.
Colossians	Rome		63.
Ephesians	Rome		63.
Philippians	Rome		64.

As for Paul's other epistles, with the exception of Philemon (which was written about the same time as Colossians) they were written later, i.e. about A.D. 66 or 67. We have not included the Epistle to the Hebrews, as its Pauline authorship is controverted; and in any case the date of its composition is a matter of uncertainty.

Their Threefold Grouping

But while it is good thus to see the "Church" epistles in their chronological order, their true *spiritual* order is undoubtedly that in which we now find them in our New Testament. It is a noteworthy fact that this order of these "Church" epistles never varies in any of the manuscripts. It is the same everywhere, without exception. It would seem as though the Holy Spirit was just as careful about the arrangement of these precious letters as about their original inclusion in the sacred canon. Observe their threefold group-development. We have already shown how the Corinthian and Galatian epistles go with that to the Romans and supplement it. We have seen also how Ephesians and Philippians and Colossians similarly belong together. Thus, these "Church" epistles fall into three groups: (1) Romans to Galatians, (2) Ephesians, Philippians, Colossians, (3) 1 and 2 Thessalonians. In the first group the distinctive emphasis is on *CHRIST AND THE CROSS.* In the middle three the distinctive emphasis is on *CHRIST AND THE CHURCH.* In the final pair the distinctive emphasis is on *CHRIST AND THE COMING.* We may therefore call the three parts respectively, evangelical, mystical, eschatological.

Is it without significance that 1 and 2 Thessalonians, which were written *first,* now stand *last?* And is it without significance that Romans, which was written *last* of the so-called "evangelical" epistles, now stands *first?* These "Church" epistles, in their three groups, form just the order in which the Holy Spirit would have us learn and then teach them. First, in the Romans group, we learn those great evangelical truths by which we are saved. Then, in the Ephesians group, we pass to those deeper depths concerning the "Mystery," and of our indissoluble oneness with the Son of God as elect members of His mystic body and bride. Finally, in 1 and 2 Thessalonians our gaze is turned onward to the coming consummation of rapture and glory at the reappearing of our Saviour. Thus, these three groups of the "Church" epistles are a trinity in unity. Having regard to their respective emphases, we may say that in the first group faith looks back to the Cross and is strengthened. Then in the second group love looks up to the Bridegroom and is deepened. Finally, in the two Thessalonian epistles hope looks on to the Coming and is brightened. In the words of 1 Corinthians xiii. 13: "And now abideth faith, hope, love, these three; and the greatest of these is love."

Their Authorship

No discussion is needed here as to the Pauline authorship of these "Church" epistles. The stop-at-nothing Biblical criticism of the past century has now resolved itself into clear issues so far as the genuineness of these epistles is concerned. Of 1 and 2 Corinthians, Galatians and Romans we may say, in the words of Professor G. G. Findlay, that their Pauline authorship is now "beyond all dispute." The same may be said of 1 and 2 Thessalonians. Paul's authorship of these has only been called into question by a few critics of the most extreme school; and even in that school others have been compelled to admit the Pauline authorship. Philippians is so obviously from Paul's pen that it has remained practically unquestioned. Objections have been raised by some modern scholars against the Pauline authorship of Ephesians and Colossians; but most of these objections belong to what even that cautious scholar, Dean Alford, once called them—"the insanity of hyper-criticism."

So far as *external* evidence goes, such as the uniform tradition of the Church and the corroboration of early writers, the case for the Pauline authorship of *all* the epistles which bear his name is about as strong as could be. It is only on grounds of supposed *internal* indications that the apostle's authorship has been impugned—supposedly un-Pauline style and doubtful allusions in various passages. These objections are not over-difficult to refute. It would be useful to consult the introduction to Ephesians in the *Pulpit Commentary,* which is still up to date enough.

So, then, the human author of these "Church" epistles is Paul. Let us express gratitude to God for all that Paul has meant to the Christian Church. The Scofield Bible aptly says:

"Through Paul alone we know that the Church is not an organisation, but an organism, the body of Christ; instinct with His life, and heavenly in calling, promise, and destiny. Through him alone we know the nature, purpose, and form of organisation of local churches, and the right conduct of such gatherings. Through him alone do we know that "we shall not all sleep," that "the dead in Christ shall rise first," and that living saints shall be "changed" and caught up to meet the Lord in the air at His return.

"Paul converted by the personal ministry of the Lord in glory, is distinctively the witness to a glorified Christ, Head over all things to the Church which is His body, as the Eleven were to Christ in the flesh, the Son of Abraham and of David."

It does not fall within our scope here to give even the briefest outline of Paul's life and labours after his conversion; but there are many well-written books of modest size and price which do that; and we refer the student to those, notably to Dr. James Stalker's *Life of St. Paul*. Undoubtedly Paul is one of the greatest minds in history; and no time will be ill-spent in studying him. But there is one interesting phenomenon in the ministry of the great apostle to which we would here call special attention. It is the fact that there are two periods in Paul's life after his conversion which are passed over in complete silence. These are commonly known as "the two silences." The Scofield Bible has an excellent further note on these:

"Two periods in the life of Paul after his conversion are passed over in a silence which is itself significant—the journey into Arabia, from which the Apostle returned in full possession of the Gospel explanation as set forth in Galatians and Romans; and the two silent years in prison in Cæsarea, between his arrest in the temple at Jerusalem and his deportation to Rome.

"It was inevitable that a trained intellect like that of Paul, a convinced believer in Mosaism and, until his conversion on the Damascus road, an eager opposer of Christianity, must seek the underlying principles of the Gospel. Immediately after his conversion he preached Jesus as the Messiah; but the relation of the Gospel to the Law, and, in a lesser degree, to the great Jewish promises, needed clear adjustment if Christianity was to be a reasonable faith, and not a mere dogma. In Arabia Paul sought and found that adjustment through revelation by the Spirit. Out of it came the doctrinal explanation of salvation by grace through faith, wholly apart from the law, embodied in Galatians and Romans.

"But the Gospel brings the believer into great relationships —to the Father, to other believers, to Christ, and to the future purposes of God. It is not only a salvation from sin and the consequences of sin, but into an amazing place in the Divine counsels. Furthermore, the new thing, the Church in its various aspects and functions, demanded clear revelation. And these are the chief themes of the Epistles written by Paul from Rome, and commonly called the "Prison" epistles—Ephesians, Philippians, Colossians. It is contrary to the method of inspiration, as explained by Paul himself, to suppose that these crowning revelations were made apart from deep meditation, demanding quietness, and earnest seeking. It seems most congruous with the events of Paul's life to suppose that these great revelations came during the silent years at Cæsarea— often spoken of as wasted."

Their Distinctive Emphases

Finally, before we come to the study of these epistles each in turn, we ought to see them all together as constituting a progressive series. Nothing is more fascinating than to see them thus, each with its distinctive emphasis and distinguishing contribution. Take, for instance, the successive emphases on our Lord Jesus:

Romans	Christ the *power* of God to us.
1 Corinthians	Christ the *wisdom* of God to us.
2 Corinthians	Christ the *comfort* of God to us.
Galatians	Christ the *righteousness* of God.
Ephesians	Christ the *riches* of God to us.
Philippians	Christ the *sufficiency* of God to us.
Colossians	Christ the *fulness* of God to us.
1 Thessalonians	Christ the *promise* of God to us.
2 Thessalonians	Christ the *reward* of God to us.

Or, if we take these same nine epistles from the standpoint of *the Gospel message*, we find again that each has its own unmistakable viewpoint and aspect:

Romans	The Gospel and its message.
1 Corinthians	The Gospel and its ministry.
2 Corinthians	The Gospel and its ministers.
Galatians	The Gospel and its mutilators.
Ephesians	The Gospel and the heavenlies.
Philippians	The Gospel and the earthlies.
Colossians	The Gospel and the philosophies.
1 Thessalonians	The Gospel and the Church's future.
2 Thessalonians	The Gospel and the Antichrist.

Or, still further, take these nine "Church" epistles in their successive teaching concerning the believer's union with Christ. Once again we find a distinctive emphasis or prominent aspect peculiar to each of them. Thus:

Romans	In Christ — justification.
1 Corinthians	In Christ — sanctification.
2 Corinthians	In Christ — consolation.
Galatians	In Christ — liberation.
Ephesians	In Christ — exaltation.
Philippians	In Christ — exultation.
Colossians	In Christ — completion.
1 Thessalonians	In Christ — translation.
2 Thessalonians	In Christ — compensation.

Nor is even this all. If we may anticipate our coming studies for a moment, we shall find that each of these nine "Church" epistles has its own unmistakable *"key" word*. In Romans the key word is "righteousness." In 1 Corinthians it is "wisdom." In 2 Corinthians it is "comfort." In Galatians it is "faith." In Ephesians it is "blessed." In Philippians it is "gain." In Colossians it is "filled." In 1 Thessalonians it is "working." In 2 Thessalonians it is "waiting."

Much more might be said along this line, but we have used the appropriate space for our introduction to these nine precious letters. As we now turn on to examine them each in turn, may the Holy Spirit who inspired them give us illumination!

THE EPISTLE TO THE ROMANS (1)

Lesson Number 128

NOTE.—For this study read Romans through at a single sitting ; then once or twice again as time allows.

The profoundest piece of writing in existence.

—Coleridge.

The chief book of the New Testament. . . . It deserves to be known by heart, word for word, by every Christian.

—Luther.

In studying it we find ourselves, at every word, face to face with the unfathomable.

—Godet.

Chrysostom used to have it read over to him twice every week by his own express order. . . . Unquestionably the fullest, deepest compendium of all sacred foundation truths.

—C. A. Fox.

THE EPISTLE TO THE ROMANS (1)

"This is St. Paul's *magnum opus*. Here we see him at his greatest as a constructive thinker and theologian. The Epistle to the Romans is the complete and mature expression of the apostle's main doctrines, which it unfolds in due order and proportion and combines into an organic whole. For the purposes of systematic theology it is the most important book in the Bible. More than any other, it has determined the course of Christian thought."

If Professor Findlay's words are true, then every Christian ought thoroughly to digest this Epistle to the Romans. It is both the alphabet and the charter of evangelical Christianity. To master its contents is to be "grounded and settled" in the faith, and to acquire a life-long enrichment.

The need for such a treatise is clear. When Paul wrote it the Gospel had been preached through the Roman world for a quarter of a century, and many communities of Christians had come into being. It was inevitable that the wide-spreading new faith should evoke momentous questions. What about the doctrine of God's righteousness if, as this new preaching says, sinners everywhere may be freely pardoned through grace? What about the relation of this "Gospel" to the Law of Moses? Does it not repudiate Moses? And what about the Abrahamic covenant? How can the admission of Gentiles to equal privilege with the Jews be reconciled with that? And what is going to become of morals if God is now going to deal with men on the ground of grace instead of holding them accountable to a righteous law? Will not people sin more than ever, that grace may abound? And what about Israel's special covenant-relation with God? Does not the new "Gospel" imply that God has now cast off His people? To many a pious Jew it would seem as though the new doctrine was flinging to the winds those heritages which were dearest and most vital. So, too, many a new Christian convert, whether Jew or Gentile, would be perplexed by such questions.

"There was only one man equal to this crisis, capable of grasping in all its breadth the situation," says Professor Findlay. "With his Pharisaic training, with his strict and delicate conscience, and his intense faith in the religion of Israel, St. Paul realised, even more than his opponents, the force and the difficulty of these questions; and we can see that it cost him, both before and during the controversy, a prolonged struggle and the most strenuous mental effort to arrive at the solution he has given us. We must not suppose that inspiration superseded study on the part of the teachers of Scripture, that the gifts of the Holy Spirit served as a contrivance for saving labour. On the contrary, it was with severe toil and by the unsparing exertion of his spiritual and intellectual powers that St. Paul composed his great doctrinal epistles; and the Holy Spirit prompted, sustained, and crowned the travail of his human will and reason." Thus was this Epistle to the Romans written; and its composition was so overruled as to make it the foundation-document of evangelical Christianity ever after.

Structure and Message of the Epistle

Let us now traverse the epistle together, and "take the measure" of its goodly territory. We read it once, twice, three times; and one thing becomes clear as noonday—it is a progressively constructed treatise, arranged in three main parts. There is no major break in chapters i. to viii. ; but as soon as we reach chapters ix., x. and xi. we realise that Paul has passed from his general application of the Gospel to a particular consideration of its relation to the nation Israel. Then when we come to chapter xii. we are just as clearly aware that Paul passes on again from this to a consideration of the Gospel in its bearing upon individual character and conduct.

This threefold structure of the epistle is made the plainer by the fact that Paul winds up each of the three parts with a form of doxology (viii. 38, 39, xi. 33–6, xvi. 25–7).

There is no doubt as to the subject in part 1 (i.–viii.). After a brief introduction (i. 1–15), Paul plunges into an elucidative discussion as to *how the Gospel saves the sinner*. In fact he epitomises his whole subject beforehand in the formal proposition with which he begins (verses 16, 17):

"I am not ashamed of the Gospel; for it is the power of God unto salvation to everyone that believeth; to the Jew

first, and also to the Greek. For therein is revealed the righteousness of God from faith to faith."

This is the seed-plot of the whole treatise. Here are gathered up in advance all the great ideas which are to be expanded in the ensuing chapters: THE GOSPEL—POWER OF GOD—SALVATION—EVERYONE—BELIEVETH—RIGHTEOUSNESS.

The first eight chapters are throughout *doctrinal.* They expound the basic doctrines of the Gospel. The next three chapters (ix.–xi.) are *national,* in the sense that they answer questions as to the relationship of the Gospel to Israel. The remaining chapters (xii.–xvi.) are *practical,* inasmuch as they apply the doctrines of the Gospel to individual conduct.

These, then, are the three main movements of Romans. In the first we have *exposition;* in the second, *explanation;* in the third, *application.* The first part is *racial;* the second, *Israelite;* the third, *individual.* The first part deals with the *sin*-problem; the second, with the *Jew*-problem; the third, with the *life*-problem. The three parts may be set out thus:

1. DOCTRINAL: HOW THE GOSPEL SAVES THE SINNER (i.–viii.).
2. NATIONAL: HOW THE GOSPEL RELATES TO ISRAEL (ix.–xi.).
3. PRACTICAL: HOW THE GOSPEL BEARS ON CONDUCT (xii.–xvi.).

And now, with this triform lay-out of the epistle in mind, we must track through these three parts again and pick out the sub-breaks in the apostle's handling of his subject. If we do this observantly, we soon find that each of the three main parts opens up with clear and logical progressiveness.

Part I (i.-viii.): Doctrinal

Take the first part, in which the subject is: How the Gospel saves the sinner. Clearly from i. 18 to iii. 20 Paul is showing man's desperate *need* of the Gospel. First he shows the plight of the *Gentiles* (i. 18–32). Then he exposes the fallacy of supposed Israelite superiority, and shows that the *Jews* are stricken with the same sin-plague (ii. 1–iii. 20). Although Paul does not at first actually name the Jew (ii. 1), the ensuing verses make clear that the Jew is intended. Paul begins in such a way as not needlessly to arouse the prejudices of any Jewish reader. He states his principles so generally and simply that they would force the assent of the Jew almost before he was aware of their special application to himself.

Notice, in this section (i. 18–iii. 20), that the racial plight is twofold. First, both Jew and Gentile have *"sinned"* (ii. 12)— which refers to *acts of transgression*. Second both Jew and Gentile are in *"sin"* (iii. 9, 10)—which refers to an *inward condition.* Transgression is the *legal* aspect of man's plight. The inward condition is the *moral* aspect of it. As to his acts of transgression, man is legally "guilty" and is brought under condemnation. As to his inward condition, man is morally "corrupt" and is perishing. This, then, is the racial plight—"sins" and "sin" (i. 18–iii. 20).

But now from chapter iii. 21 onwards, Paul shows how God deals with this double problem, through the Gospel. First he shows us the Gospel answer as to *"SINS"* (iii. 21–v. 11). Thoughtful readers are bound to notice the break which occurs in that fifth chapter, at the end of verse 11. Up to that point the subject is *"SINS"*; but after that it is *"SIN."* The late E. W. Bullinger wrote: "No commentary or exposition is worthy of the slightest attention which does not mark this distinction and division between verses 11 and 12." Bullinger's words are too severe— though the break between those two verses is certainly important to note. Up to that point the word "sin" occurs only three times; but from there to the end of chapter viii. it comes thirty-nine times!

So then from iii. 21 to the end of chapter viii. the theme is the Gospel answer concerning "sins" and "sin." The section concerning "sins" (plural) is iii. 21–v. 11. The section concerning "sin" (singular) is v. 12–viii. 39, where the first main part of the epistle ends.

See the Gospel answer concerning *"sins"* (iii. 21–v. 11). First Paul shows how God deals with the "sins" problem *judicially* (iii. 21–iv. 25). God sets forth Christ as the all-sufficient Propitiation. Through Him He can justly justify the believing sinner (iii. 21– 31); and this principle of justification by faith has its root in the Old Testament Scriptures (iv.). Second Paul shows how the

Gospel answers the "sins" problem *experimentally,* i.e. in the experience of the believer (v. 1–11). "Being justified by faith, we have peace with God . . . the love of God is shed abroad in our hearts by the Holy Spirit . . ." etc. Thus we are shown the Gospel answer as to "sins"—judicially (iii. 21–iv. 25) and experientially (v. 1–11).

And now, from v. 12 to viii. 39, comes the Gospel answer as to *"SIN."* Paul's method is the same as in the former section. First he shows how God deals with "sin" *judicially* (v. 12–vii. 6); then how it is dealt with *experientially* (vii. 7–viii. 39). It will be plain to any reader that from chapter v. 12 to the end of that chapter Paul is showing how God deals with sin and salvation in the judicial sense, on the principle of the federal headship of Adam and of Christ, respectively: "As through one man" condemnation and death come upon the many, so "through the obedience of One" righteousness and life come to the many.

Chapter vi. carries further this treatment of the subject from the judicial standpoint. A reading of it in the Revised Version will make this the clearer. The verb tenses are all in the past, indicating something which God *did* once-for-all, judicially and historically, in connection with sin, through the Cross of Christ; not something which God is *now doing* in the hearts of believers (as expositors commonly say). Verse 6, instead of being in the present tense, should read: "Our old man *was* crucified with Him [Christ], that the body of sin might be destroyed." The expressions "our old man" and "the body of sin" refer to the Adam race as a whole; and this chapter teaches that in the *judicial* reckoning of God the Adam race was put away once for all in and by the Cross of Christ.

Chapter vii., up to verse 6, completes this judicial section, showing that in the death of Christ the believer also *died to the Law,* thus becoming judicially free to be "married" to Another, even to "Him who is raised from the dead."

Finally, in one of the grandest passages of all Holy Writ (vii. 7–viii. 39), Paul shows us how the Gospel deals with the sin-problem in the actual *experience* of the believer. In the foregoing chapters Paul has shown how the Gospel deals with sins (plural) both judicially and experientially, and with sin itself (singular) judicially; yet the acutest problem of all still remains—*"sin that dwelleth in me"* (vii. 17, 20). The very commandment of the Law against an evil evokes in my depraved nature precisely that which it forbids! The Law is all right, but *I* am all wrong! "Oh, wretched man that I am!—who shall deliver me?"

Chapter viii. gives the glorious answer. Attention has often been called to the fact that the Holy Spirit is mentioned in this chapter no less than nineteen times, whereas He is mentioned only once in all the earlier chapters; but the *significance* of this does not seem to have been appreciated. It confirms what we have been saying, namely, that up to now Paul has been dealing only with the *judicial* aspect of the "sin" problem (v. 12–vii. 6). *Now,* in this culminating *eighth* chapter, Paul shows how the new life and law and liberty of the Spirit in the believer, along with the other inward ministries of the Spirit, are the ample answer to the cry, "Who shall deliver me?" We shall revert to this chapter again later. Here we simply note its significance in the structure of the epistle. The apostle has now shown us how the Gospel deals with *"SINS"* (iii. 21–v. 11)—the judicial aspect (iii. 21–iv. 25), the experiential aspect (v. 1–11); and how the Gospel deals with *"SIN"* (v. 12–viii. 29)—the judicial aspect (v. 12–vii. 6), the experiential aspect (vii. 7–viii. 39). This, then, is the first of the three main parts of the epistle.

Part 2 (ix.-xi.): National

There is a solemn grandeur and profundity about these three chapters. We are not surprised that the inspired writer, having contemplated the mystery and sovereignty of the Divine purpose in human history, should end with, "Oh, the depth of the riches both of the wisdom and the knowledge of God!" (xi. 33). But what is the essential point of the apostle's reasoning here? He is showing us how the Gospel relates, in a dispensational and historical sense, to the nation Israel: and there are three movements in his argument, which accord with the three chapters in our English version.

First, in chapter ix., his point is that this wonderful Gospel to the whole world *does not annul God's special purpose with Israel.* Note the words in verse 6: "Not as though the word of God hath come to nought: for they are not all Israel which are of Israel." The word of God could not *then* be fulfilled to the nation because so many who were Abraham's *"seed"* (his natural descendants) were not Abraham's *"children"* (in a moral and spiritual sense)— see verse 7. But there was an elect "remnant" who were being saved and through whom the purpose would eventually be realised (verses 27–9). Note: verses 14–26 are a kind of parenthesis, justifying the sovereign acts of God. Read verses 27–9 in the Revised Version.

Second, in chapter x. (which should perhaps begin at ix. 30), the point is that the Gospel, other than annulling the special purpose of God with Israel, *fulfils the promise made to that people.* The main part of this chapter is given to showing that this Messiah-Saviour of Paul's Gospel is the subject of the Hebrew Scriptures ("For Moses writeth," "For the Scripture saith," "For Isaiah saith"—verses 5, 11, 16, etc.). But, alas, despite the Scripture promise of salvation through faith, Israel is bent on justification by works (verses 1–4), and so stumbles through unbelief (verses 18–21).

Third, in chapter xi., the point is that the Gospel, besides fulfilling the promise to Israel, *confirms the great prospect before Israel,* namely, that all Israel shall yet be saved (verses 25–9); and meanwhile, tragic as Israel's present fall is, it is overruled to bless the Gentiles (11, 12). There is much more in these three chapters, of course; but it is not within our scope to go into them in detail here. With a view to drafting out a true analysis of the epistle, we have simply tried to get the focus-point of the case which Paul here makes out on the relation of the Gospel to the nation Israel. And what *is* the focal truth here? It is this: The Gospel does not conflict with the purpose and promise and prospect pertaining to Israel as shown in their Scriptures, but confirms them.

Part 3 (xii.-xv. 13): Practical

In chapters xii.–xv. we have the practical application of the Gospel to life and behaviour. As might be expected, therefore, we do not find in them the intricacy which we have encountered in some of the earlier and more argumentative paragraphs. In fact they are so straightforward that we scarcely need to do more than simply point out the way in which the exhortations are grouped together.

Take chapter xii. Here, plainly, we have the Christian life as to *social aspects*. In the first two verses there is the appeal for consecration with a view to inward transformation, for this is the root of all Christian godliness. Then, right to the end of the chapter, we see the fruit of this in humble and loving service *toward others*. This, then, is the social aspect.

Now take chapter xiii. Here, plainly, it is the Christian life as to *civil aspects*. The chapter begins: "Let every soul be subject to the higher powers"; and of course the higher powers here spoken of are the civil authorities. In verses 1–7 we are told that the true expression of the Christian life, so far as civil duties go, is conscientious submission. Then, in verses 8–14, we see that this way of behaviour has its foundation in love to one's neighbour.

Finally, take chapters xiv. and xv. Here is the Christian life as to certain *mutual aspects*. We are told what is to be the reciprocal relation between the "weak" and the "strong," between those who are over-scrupulous and those who are seemingly under-scrupulous as regards certain debatable practices. First, in xiv. 1–23 the principle of mutual considerateness is enjoined; and then in xv. 1–13 this is reinforced by a reference to the example of Christ and the teaching of the Scriptures. The remainder of the epistle (xv. 14–xvi. 27) is simply a brief supplement containing personal references and greetings, with a benediction and doxology in conclusion.

Such, then, is this epistle to the Romans; and it will be helpful if we now set out our findings in flat analysis. Our analysis, of course, is interpretative, not exhaustive. We have gone through the epistle to get at its central meaning and message, not to conduct a dissection of all its component parts!

It almost seems as though Paul had difficulty in ending this mighty epistle, for there are four "amens" before he finally tears himself away! "Now the God of peace be with you all. *Amen*" (xv. 33). "The grace of our Lord Jesus be with you. *Amen*" (xvi. 20). "The grace of our Lord Jesus be with you all. *Amen*" (xvi. 24). "To God only wise, be glory for ever. *AMEN*" (xvi. 27).

THE EPISTLE TO THE ROMANS
The Gospel, the power of God to Salvation.

Introductory i. 1–15.
1. DOCTRINAL: HOW THE GOSPEL SAVES THE SINNER
(i. 16–viii.).

THE RACIAL PLIGHT—"SINS" AND "SIN" (i. 18–iii. 20).
The Gentile guilty and sinful (i. 18–32).
The Jew guilty and sinful (ii. 1–iii. 20).

THE GOSPEL ANSWER—(*a*) AS TO "SINS" (iii. 21–v. 11).
Judicially (iii. 21–iv. 25).
In experience (v. 1–11).

THE GOSPEL ANSWER—(*b*) AS TO "SIN" (v. 12–viii. 39).
Judicially (v. 12–vii. 6).
In experience (vii. 7–viii. 39).

2. NATIONAL: HOW THE GOSPEL RELATES TO ISRAEL
(ix.–xi.).

DOES NOT ANNUL THE PURPOSE WITH ISRAEL (ix.).
Because not all Israel true Israel (verses 7–13).
And an elect remnant being saved (verses 27–9).

RATHER, IT FULFILS THE PROMISE TO ISRAEL (x.).
But Israel bent on salvation by works (verses 1–4).
And stumbles (ix. 32) *through unbelief* (verses 18–21).

AND CONFIRMS THE PROSPECT BEFORE ISRAEL (xi.).
Israel's fall made to bless Gentiles (verses 1–24).
And all Israel shall yet be saved (verses 25–9).

3. PRACTICAL: HOW THE GOSPEL BEARS ON CONDUCT
(xii.–xv. 13).

THE CHRISTIAN LIFE AS TO SOCIAL ASPECTS (xii.).
The root—consecration and renewal (verses 1–2).
The fruit—service and love to others (verses 3–21).

THE CHRISTIAN LIFE AS TO CIVIL ASPECTS (xiii.).
Its expression—conscientious submission (verses 1–7).
Its foundation—love to one's neighbour (verses 8–14).

THE CHRISTIAN LIFE AS TO MUTUAL ASPECTS (xiv., xv.).
The principle—mutual considerateness (verses 1–23).
The incentive—the example of Christ (xv. 1–13).
Supplementary xv. 14–xvi.

THE EPISTLE TO THE ROMANS (2)

Lesson Number 129

NOTE.—For this study read several times chapters v.–vii. and ix.–xi.

The Epistles stand in relation to the Gospels somewhat as Leviticus to Exodus. In the Gospels we are *set free* through the blood of the Lamb. In the Epistles we are *indwelt* by the Spirit of God. In the Gospels, as in Exodus, God speaks to us from *without*. In the Epistles, as in Leviticus, God speaks to us from *within*. In the Gospels we have the *ground* of fellowship with God, i.e. redemption. In the Epistles we have the *walk* of fellowship with God, i.e. sanctification. As in Leviticus, so in the Epistles there is exhibited to us the *many-sidedness* of our Lord's atonement as it bears on those who are already redeemed.

—*J.S.B.*

THE EPISTLE TO THE ROMANS (2)

OUR EXPLORATION of this epistle thus far will have reinforced the verdict in our minds that it is Paul's *magnum opus*. Luther called it "The masterpiece of the New Testament." So important is it as a manifesto of evangelical doctrine that Protestant believers should regularly reread it to confirm themselves in the basic truths of the real Gospel.

It is a superlative irony and tragedy that the church to which it was originally written is that which has erred most grievously from it. What a difference there is between the church of Rome today and that first church at Rome to which Paul wrote! An honest facing up to the teachings of this apostolic letter would do more than anything else to cure papal Rome of its dark heresies and fond superstitions!

In fact, this Romans epistle should be given priority treatment by all of us. It stands first among these "Church" epistles because the Holy Spirit designed that it should be the first to be digested.

Having seen its structure and main import, let us now retread its three main areas, pausing here and there at its more salient features. All sorts of incidental points and questions must be reluctantly by-passed in a constricted survey like this; but we shall have fulfilled our purpose if we supply reliable *general* guidance and direction for closer study. First, however, we ought to say a word about that long-ago Roman *church* to which the epistle was sent.

The Church at Rome

When Paul wrote this epistle he had not been to Rome (i. 15), but had often wished to go (i. 13, xv. 23), and now purposed to do so (xv. 24, 28). How, then, was the church there brought into being? That it had originated early we deduce from the fact that when Paul wrote this epistle, the faith of those Roman believers was already "spoken of throughout the world" (i. 8). Doubtless the planting of the Gospel in Rome would be facilitated by the large settlement of Jews there. Angus's *Bible Handbook* has a note that Ovid speaks of the Jewish synagogues there as places of general resort; and Juvenal later ridicules his countrymen for becoming Jews. Turning back to Acts ii., we find in Peter's audience on the never-to-be-forgotten day of Pentecost "devout men" who were "sojourners from *Rome,* both Jews and proselytes." Before they returned to Rome they would learn much more than simply what they heard in that first sermon by Peter. Some of them would return to Rome as true converts and disseminators of the new faith. Moreover, the ever-busy intercourse between Rome and the provinces would almost certainly bring Christian converts to the capital, not only from Judæa, but from other parts as well.

It is clear, also, that the congregation at Rome was a thorough mixture of Jews and Gentiles. Paul addresses its members as Jews (ii. 17–29, iv. 1, vii. 1, etc.), yet equally as Gentiles (i. 13, xi. 13–32, xv. 15, 16, etc.). An interesting light is thrown on this by the salutations in the last chapter of the epistle. Twenty-six persons are greeted, and two-thirds of the names are Greek.

It may be objected that the epistle assumes a knowledge of the Old Testament and the Jewish religion which Gentile converts would not have: but we should remember that many of the earliest Gentile converts to Christianity were those who had already become proselytes to Judaism and whose concern in the problem arising from the relating of the new "Gospel" to the old religion would be almost as acute as that of the Jewish Christians themselves.

It seems most likely that Paul wrote his epistle to Rome from Corinth during his three months' stay in Achaia (i.e. Greece) after his uproarious ejection from Ephesus (Acts xx. 3), and that he took opportunity of sending it by the hand of Phœbe, a sister in the church at Cenchrea (the port of Corinth) who was going to Rome (xvi. 1–2).

Paul—a Strategic Figure

Moreover, as Romans stands *first* among the Pauline epistles, we ought here to say at least a brief word about Paul himself. But who can say a *"brief"* word about Paul? We cannot do better than let the following paragraph, from the late C. A. Fox, snapshot the great apostle for us just as we need to see him at this point.

"Many apparently opposite qualities went to make up the special fitness of St. Paul for his great life-work. He combined in his own unique experience a personal connection of the closest kind with the three principal social spheres of his age. He was called out of the very heart of Judaism. *Jewish legalism* he knew from end to end. He was called out of the very heart of *Greek culture,* for he lived his early life from infancy in one of the great centres of Hellenic life, and was familiarised with all that was great and noble in Greek literature. He had, moreover, enjoyed from birth all the varied privileges of *Roman citizenship.* He was thus a Hebrew to the backbone; he was a Greek in the fullest sense of the term; and he was a Roman citizen freeborn. But besides all this, he united in his rare personality an unusual vigour of intellect, strength of will, depth of feeling and sympathy. Intensity was the mark of his character, whether intellectually or morally. Yet the one thing which surpassed all else in preparing him for his apostleship has yet to be mentioned. His sudden and miraculous conversion and call by the direct interposition of Christ Himself, beyond all else, fitted him to compare together Judaism and Christianity with perfect fairness, and enabled him to set the two systems side by side in vivid, startling contrast, as well as empowered him to testify how that Christianity, instead of being a violent antagonism and outrage upon pure Judaism, was the legitimate outcome, development and completion of Old Testament truth."

Leading Doctrines

Look through those first eight chapters again, in which the subject is: How the Gospel saves the sinner. They may all be summed up in the phrase: Present righteousness and final salvation through Christ by faith.

The cry of sin-burdened but God-seeking hearts all through the centuries has been: Oh, for a right relationship with God! Oh, for a way of righteousness before Him! Oh, for an acceptable access to Him!

"Where shall righteousness be found?" This was the pathetic cry of serious minds everywhere in those far-gone days when Paul penned the true answer. Even more pathetic is the way this native concern of sinning man is crushed down or crowded out by our own mechanically advanced but spiritually deteriorated

civilisation of today. In the older, simpler days, men at least had time to ponder the deep things of the soul; but nowadays, in our commercialised, industrialised, urbanised, mechanised civilisation, when we live by the clock rather than by the calendar, our complicated set-up fastens men's thoughts down more and more on the ever-pressing secondary problems of things temporal and material. Yet still, today, despite all the whirring wheels and breakneck tempo and loud clash of our twentieth-century bedlam, there are haunted hearts and uneasy consciences, seeking, groping, yearning for a right relationship with God, and wistfully sighing: "Oh, to know how I might find a way of salvation and a way of true righteousness before God!"

"Where shall righteousness be found?" Paul is going to tell us how his "Good News" answers that question. He is going to tell it all the more eagerly and urgently because the very Gospel which tells of a God-provided righteousness for the repentant and believing brings with it a new revelation of the wrath of God against all *un*righteousness:

"For the wrath of God is revealed [i.e. in a new way now] against all *un*godliness and *un*righteousness" (i. 18).

The wrath of God is revealed against idolatry and sensuality (i. 21–32); against hypocritical self-superiority (ii. 1–16); against religious pretence and externalism (ii. 17–29); against evil abuse of spiritual privilege (iii. 1–19).

"Where shall righteousness be found?" Yes, Paul is going to tell us; but first he shows us where it is *vain* to look for righteousness:

1. Not in natural religion (i. 19, 20).
　　(*a*) Corrupted to vile idolatry (i. 21–32).
　　(*b*) Perverted too by hypocrisy (ii. 1–16).

2. Not in revealed religion (iii. 1, 2).
　　(*a*) Jews do not keep God's Law (ii. 17–29).
　　(*b*) Jews guilty under the Law (iii. 1–20).

"Where shall righteousness be found?" Yes, Paul is going to tell us; but he would first have us mark well a fourfold truth and tragedy. The *world* says: "It is not in me" (i. 20). The *self* says: "It is not in me" (ii. 15). And *religion* says: "It is not in me" (ii. 17, 21). And the *Law* says: "It is not in me" (iii. 20).

"Where shall righteousness be found?" The Gospel has the answer, or rather *is* the answer; and that is what we have in Romans i.–viii. There are two aspects: the judicial, and the dynamic; or the legal and the moral. Man needs a new *standing* before God—that is the judicial aspect. Man also needs a new *power* which can make a practical, daily righteousness achievable—that is the dynamic or regenerative aspect. The Gospel provides both. There is righteousness *IMPUTED* (iii. 21–vii. 6) —that is a righteousness reckoned to us judicially through the meritorious propitiation of Christ. There is also righteousness *IMPARTED* (vii. 7–viii. 39)—that is a righteousness wrought in us and through us by the renewing *Spirit* of Christ. Mark it well: judicial righteousness by the *Cross*; practical righteousness by the *Spirit*.

Paul begins with the great, basal declaration in chapter iii. 21–6, which (slightly paraphrased) reads thus:

"But now a righteousness of God apart from the Law is revealed, to which the Scriptures [i.e. the Old Testament Law and the Prophets] bear witness; a righteousness of God which comes through faith on Jesus Christ to all who believe, without any distinction. For all alike have sinned, and all fall short of God's ideal, but are now given a new standing of legal righteousness quite freely by His unmerited favour which comes to us through the redemption provided in Christ Jesus. For God hath set Him forth as a propitiation appropriable to faith by virtue of His blood-shedding. This was to demonstrate His [God's] justice in forbearingly passing over men's sins committed aforetime; so that His justice in so doing might be made clear at this present time, and that it might be clear that He can justly be the justifier of anyone who believes on Jesus."

Paul then goes on to show that the imputing or reckoning of righteousness to members of Adam's fallen race, in response to faith, is not an altogether novel idea. God had always had the Cross of Christ in view (as in the above quotation) and had dealt with Abraham and David on this principle of justification by faith (chapter iv.). Paul develops this aspect of his subject up to chapter vii. 6.

Then, from chapter vii. 7 onwards, he shows how the Gospel, in addition to having provided this new standing of imputed *judicial* righteousness, also makes possible *practical* righteousness of heart and life. This is "good news" indeed!

In chapter vii. 15–24 he gives us his graphic pen-picture of the "wretched man" who continually enacts the tantalising self-contradiction of wanting to do the good but *not* doing it, and wanting *not* to do the evil but *doing* it, until in his exasperating self-frustration he exclaims: "Oh, wretched man that I am! Who shall deliver me?"

That "wretched man" has been a problem to expositors. Does he represent a Christian believer, "born again" but not fully liberated? Or does he represent the unregenerated sinner? Some say the former; but if, as is usually taught, chapter vi. teaches the believer's sanctification and death to sin (verse 11, etc.), why does Paul suddenly slip back in chapter vii. to this pitiful bondage of the "wretched man"? Yet there is equal difficulty if we regard this "wretched man" as representing the unregenerated. If *that* is how he must be regarded, why bring him in *here*? Does he not rather belong to the first half of chapter iii.?

I remember how a renowned old Calvinistic Methodist preacher once threw out a challenge on this seventh chapter of Romans. He had been brought up in the old Puritan school, and would have none of your "second blessing" or "sinless perfection" ideas! According to him, Romans *seven* was inserted to save us from inferring too much from Romans *six*! There was no real deliverance from the wicked old "self" in each of us! He must plague us to the bitter end! I remember how the grand old preacher quoted bits from this "wretched man" paragraph, and then triumphantly wheeled round on us with: "There, now; there's no going beyond *that*, is there?" Well, of course, the answer is: "Yes; it is quite easy to go beyond *that*: you simply go beyond it to the next chapter (viii.), where you learn that the 'wretched man' finds full deliverance!"

The fact is that the "wretched man" in Romans vii. is not meant to represent either the believer or the unbeliever in distinction from each other: he is simply the representative *human being*, exhibiting one of the fundamental needs of our fallen human nature. Take him just where he comes in the epistle, and you soon see *why* Paul puts him *there*. In the preceding chapters we have learned how the Gospel saves us from *SINS* (plural)— first by bringing us imputed judicial righteousness (iii. 21–iv. 25), and then confirming it to us inwardly, inasmuch as "the love of God is shed abroad *in our hearts* by the Holy Spirit who is given unto us" (v. 1–11). Next, Paul shows how the Gospel deals with *SIN* (singular) racially and hereditarily (v. 12–vii. 6). We need to be shown this, because even when we have become "justified" in Christ we are still sinners in our *nature*. So Paul shows us that what we inherit justifyingly in Christ our *new* Adam, more than covers all that we inherit condemningly from the *first* Adam.

Yet there is still a dismaying problem which I need the Gospel to solve for me. What I *now* crave, along with judicial righteousness, is to achieve *practical* righteousness of motive and conduct in my daily living, through a power which shall liberate me from slavery to this tyrant *"sin which dwelleth in me"* (vii. 17, 20, 23). Until *that* problem is solved, I am still left moaning: "Oh, wretched man that I am!"

That is why the "wretched man" comes in chapter vii. He has found *three* deliverances but needs a *fourth*. He has found *judicial* righteousness, but still lacks the power to achieve *practical* righteousness. The transforming answer is given in that climactic *eighth* chapter. Nineteen times the Holy Spirit is now named, the first thirteen occurrences showing successively how He gives power over "sin," power over the "flesh," power over the "body." The great practical result is enunciated in verse 4:

> "That the requirements of the Law might
> be fulfilled by us who walk not after the
> flesh, but after the SPIRIT."

How wonderful, then, is this Gospel of "justification by faith," with its twofold message of God-provided righteousness, i.e. righteousness *imputed* through the Cross, and righteousness *imparted* by the Spirit! And how wonderful is that God-Man Saviour who effects it all for us! He voluntarily becomes chief Partner in the bankrupt, condemned firm, contracts upon Himself all its liabilities, debts and penalties, and then transforms shameful bankruptcy into riches by pouring through it His own inexhaustible credits! He fulfils the *law* of God for us (v. 19).

He sets free the *love* of God to us (v. 5). He implants the very *life* of God in us (viii. 9). It is because of all this that chapters vii. and viii. end so differently from each other. Chapter vii. ends: "Oh, wretched man that I am! Who shall deliver me?" Chapter viii. ends: "We are *more than conquerors* through Him that loved us!"

"Therefore, being justified . . ."

Note gratefully the seven products of our justification by faith, as summed up in chapter v. 1–11. "Being justified by faith . . .":

1. "We have peace with God. . . ."
2. "We have access by faith. . . ."
3. "We rejoice in hope of glory. . . ."
4. "We glory in tribulations. . . ."
5. "The love of God is shed in our hearts. . . ."
6. "We shall be saved from the wrath. . . ."
7. "We joy in God" (having received "atonement"
   i.e. *reconciliation*, although
   formerly condemned rebels!)

The Three Deaths

Note further the three deaths predicated of the Christian believer in chapters vi., vii. and viii.

vi. Dead to sin . . . . . . alive unto God (verse 11)
vii. Dead to the Law . . . married to Christ (verse 4)
viii. Dead to the flesh . . . led by the Spirit (verse 13).

Chapters ix., x., xi.

Would it be an exaggeration to say that these three chapters have been almost if not quite the most problematical passage in all the Scriptures? They grapple with the titanic and awesome reality of an absolutely sovereign Divine will operating throughout the sin-cursed history of humanity. To my own mind, Romans ix. 18 has been the most disturbing verse in the Bible. Linked with its context, it easily seems to suggest that what we call the sovereignty of God is an unspeakably awful Divine *despotism*.

What are we to say about it? It is wrong to evade it. It is wrong to soften down (supposedly) the meaning of the words which Paul uses. It is wrong to force an artificial "explanation" which does not really explain at all. It is equally wrong, also (as we shall soon see), to infer, with a sort of gloating hyper-Calvinism, more than is actually said.

The apostle has now completed his main argument (i.–viii.), showing how the Gospel saves the individual human sinner. Glorious though this Gospel is, however, he simply cannot leave off there and affect blindness to the acute problem which it raises in relation to the nation Israel. If Gentiles are now accepted, justified, given sonship and promise, on equal footing with the Jews, what about Israel's special covenant relationship with God? Does not this new "Gospel" imply that God has now "cast away His people which He foreknew" (xi. 2)?

If the new "Gospel" *does* mean that, are not God's dealings with Israel the most hypocritical enigma and irony of history? Were not the covenant people the repository of most wonderful Messianic promises? Were not the godly among them right in anticipating Messiah's coming as that which would end the sufferings of their people, when the scattered tribes should be regathered as one purified Israel, and the nation, so long ruled by the Gentiles, should at last be exalted *over* them? Yet now that Messiah had come, instead of consummation for Israel there was the most reactionary of all paradoxes—those to whom the covenant promises were given were apparently shut out, and all the long-looked-for benefits were going to Gentile outsiders!

Well, that is the background problem of Romans ix.–xi., and it is vital to realise it in considering any of the foreground statements separately. But besides this, if we are going to interpret truly *any* of these Pauline statements on the Divine sovereignty, we must keep to the *point* and the *scope* of the passage. As to the former, Paul's purpose is to show that (*a*) the present by-passing of Israel nationally is not inconsistent with the Divine promises (see ix. 6–13); (*b*) because Israel's present sin and blindness nationally is overruled in blessing to both Jews and Gentiles as individuals (see ix. 23–xi. 25); (*c*) and because "all Israel *shall* yet be saved" at a postponed climax, inasmuch as "the gifts and calling of God are irreversible" (see xi. 26–36).

As to the *scope* of the passage, it will by now have become obvious that it is all about God's dealings with men and nations historically and dispensationally, and is *not* about individual salvation and destiny beyond the grave. Now *that* is the absolutely *vital* fact to remember in reading the problem-verses of these chapters, especially the paragraph ix. 14–22.

John Calvin is wrong when he reads into these verses election either to salvation or to damnation in the eternal sense. That is not their scope. They belong only to a Divine economy of *history*. Paul opens the paragraph by asking: "Is there then unrighteousness with God?"—and the rest of the paragraph is meant to show that the answer is "No"; but if these verses referred to *eternal* life and death, there *would* be unrighteousness with God; and that which is implanted deepest in our moral nature by God Himself would protest that even God has no honourable right to create human beings whose destiny is a predetermined damnation.

No, this passage does not comprehend the *eternal* aspects of human destiny: Paul has already dealt with those in chapters i–viii. It is concerned (let us emphasise it again) with *the historical and dispensational*. Once that is seen, there is no need to "soften down" its terms or to "explain away" one syllable of it. Even the awesome words to Pharaoh (verse 17) can be faced in their full force—"Even for this same purpose have I raised thee up, that I might show My power in thee, and that My name might be declared throughout all the earth." The words "raised thee up" do not mean that God had raised him up from *birth* for this purpose: they refer to his elevation to the highest throne on earth. Nay, as they occur in Exodus ix. 16, they scarce mean even *that,* but only that God had kept Pharaoh from dying in the preceding plague, so as to be made the more fully an object lesson to all men.

Moreover, when Paul (still alluding to Pharaoh) says, "And whom He [God] will, He *hardeneth*" (verse 18), we need not try to soften the word. God did not override Pharaoh's own will. The hardening was a reciprocal process. Eighteen times we are told that Pharaoh's heart was "hardened" in refusal. In about half of these the hardening is attributed to Pharaoh himself; in the others, to God. But the whole contest between God and

Pharaoh must be interpreted by what God said to Moses before ever the contest started: "The king of Egypt *will not* . . ." (Exod. iii. 19). The will was already set. The heart was already hard. God *overruled* Pharaoh's will, but did not *override* it. The hardening process developed inasmuch as the plagues forced Pharaoh to an issue which *crystallised* his sin.

Thus Pharaoh was made an object-lesson to all the earth (Rom. ix. 17). But Pharaoh's *eternal* destiny is not the thing in question; and moreover in thus making an example of this "vessel of wrath" who was "fit for [such] destruction" (verse 22), God was working out a vast purpose which was not only righteous, but overrulingly *gracious* towards many millions of "vessels of mercy which He had afore prepared unto glory," as we learn in verse 23!

It is always important to distinguish between Divine fore-knowledge and Divine predestination. God foreknows every-thing that every man will do; but He does not *predetermine* everything that every man does. Nay, that would make God the author of sin!

God foreknew that Esau would despise his birthright; that Pharaoh would be wicked; that Moses would sin in anger at Meribah; that the Israelites would rebel at Kadesh-Barnea; that Judas would betray our Lord; that the Jews would crucify their Messiah: but not one of these things did God *predetermine*. To say that He did would involve Him in the libellous contradiction of predetermining men to commit what He Himself declared to be *sin*. God did *not* predetermine these sinful acts of men; but He *did* foreknow them, and anticipate them, and overrule them to the fulfilling of His further purposes.

We mention this because it involves Esau, Pharaoh, and Moses, all of whom Paul cites in Romans ix. Let us say two things emphatically of Paraoh in particular: (1) God did not create him to be a wicked man; (2) God did not create him to be a damned soul. And, with mental relief, let us further say that God could never create *any* man either to be wicked or to be eternally damned. "Is there unrighteousness with God? God forbid!" In Romans ix. we simply must *not* read an after-death signifi-cance into what is solely historical. Moses, because of his sin at Meribah, was denied entrance into the promised land; but would we argue that this punishment extended in anyway to the salvation of his soul beyond the grave? Thousands upon thousands of Israelites died in the wilderness because of that grievous sin at Kadesh-Barnea ; but were they all lost souls beyond the grave? Look up some of the generous offerings and acts of devotion mentioned earlier in connection with some of them!

Chapters xii. to xvi.

It is a regret to us that we cannot here linger over the final group of chapters, which show us how the Gospel bears on conduct. In keeping with their practical subject, however, they are quite straightforward, and scarcely need comment here. We recommend a reading of them in Weymouth's *New Testament in Modern Speech,* with a careful tracing out of the sections which we have indicated in our analysis at the end of study 128.

AND NOW—A FEW QUESTIONS

1. Which are the two ninefold groups of Epistles, and why are they so named?

2. What is the special relation of the first nine to us as Christian believers?

3. What is the threefold order of the first nine, corresponding with a certain text in 2 Timothy?

4. Can you give the nine distinctive aspects of Christ in the nine Church Epistles respectively?

5. What are the three main parts of the Romans epistle, and the three sub-divisions in each?

6. What is the key verse in Romans? What the leading doctrine? and (briefly) the developing truth in chapters i. to viii.?

7. What are the seven results of justification by faith as given in the early verses of chapter v.?

8. Do chapters ix., x., xi. teach an election to damnation? Give reasons for your reply.

THE FIRST EPISTLE TO THE CORINTHIANS (1)

Lesson Number 130

NOTE.—For this study read the whole epistle through twice.

THE FALLIBILITY OF MINISTERS

Paul versus Peter at Antioch

The first great lesson we learn from Antioch is that *great ministers may make great mistakes.* Peter without doubt was one of the greatest in the company of the apostles. And yet here this very Peter, this same apostle, plainly falls into a great mistake. The Apostle Paul tells us: "I withstood him to the face." He tells us that "he was to be blamed." He says "he feared them of the circumcision." He says of him and his companions, that "they walked not uprightly according to the truth of the Gospel." He speaks of their "dissimulation." He tells us that by this dissimulation even Barnabas, his old companion in missionary labours, "was carried away."

But it is all meant to teach us that even the apostles themselves, when not writing under the inspiration of the Holy Ghost, were at times liable to err. It is meant to teach us that the best men are weak and fallible so long as they are in the body. Unless the grace of God holds them up, any one of them may go astray at any time. It is very humbling, but it is very true. True Christians are converted, justified, and sanctified. They are living members of Christ, beloved children of God, and heirs of eternal life. They are elect, chosen, called, and kept unto salvation. They have the Spirit. But they are *not infallible.*

—*J. C. Ryle, D.D.*

THE FIRST EPISTLE TO THE CORINTHIANS (1)

It seems like trying to hold an ocean in a teacup to deal with these two Corinthian letters in a couple of short studies. Yet if we are to respect our self-imposed proscriptions in this present series that is all the space we can allow. However, although we cannot plot out a complete navigation map of these two seas, we can arrow the main currents, and enring the fertile fishing grounds, and chart the chief treasure islands with their rich pearl beds.

In our ritornelle to the nine Christian Church Epistles (see study 127) we pointed out that they consist of a quartette, a trio, and a pair. The first four cohere; so do the middle three; so do the final two. In the first four the emphasis is on Christ and the *Cross*. In the middle three it is on Christ and the *Church*. In the final two it is on Christ and the *Coming*. And in each case the order in which truth is presented corresponds with the order of the wording in 2 Timothy iii. 16: "All Scripture is given by inspiration of God, and is profitable [1] for doctrine, [2] for reproof, [3] for correction. . . ."

Thus is it with the first four, where we find *doctrine* in Romans; *reproof* in Corinthians; *correction* in Galatians. Reproof always has to do with wrong practice. Correction always has to do with wrong doctrine. The Romans epistle sets the *norm*. The Corinthian epistles expose *fault*. The Galatian epistle counters *error*.

Of course the distinction into "doctrine" and "reproof" and "correction" is characteristic, not absolute. We readily concede that there is "doctrine" in *all* the epistles, inasmuch as they all teach Christian truth. Yet the distinction which we have mentioned is really there, and should be duly appreciated. For instance, in Romans one subject is developed thesis-like from beginning to end, whereas in Corinthians there is a variety of topics provoked by way of reproof or reply. In Romans the doctrinal pronouncements are formal and didactic; in Corinthians they are only incidental to the replies which Paul is writing to

93

requests and reports from Corinth. The Romans epistle is dogmatic; the Corinthian epistles are apologetic.

For instance, in Romans iii. 27 we find it explained doctrinally that all "boasting" is excluded from the economy of salvation in Christ; whereas in 1 Corinthians i. 29, 31 this reappears purely incidentally, but *reprovingly*, to those who were "glorying in men."

Again, in Romans v. 13 and vii. 7–13 we have it stated and shown in doctrinal form that "the strength of sin is the law"; whereas in 1 Corinthians xv. 56 this slips in quite incidentally to enhance the prospect of the coming resurrection-victory.

In Romans v. 12–21 there is a notable passage doctrinally deliberating the contrast between the *first* Adam and the *new* Adam (Christ). In 1 Corinthians xv. 21, 22, 45 the same contrast recurs but only now as incidental to the great resurrection argument and exhortation.

Or again, in Romans xiv. 1–xv. 7 we have a whole section given to a general discussion of Christian liberty in things debatable, gathering round the principle "that no man put a stumbling-block in his brother's way"; whereas in 1 Corinthians viii. we find the same, but only as related to one particular aspect, and applied reprovingly: "But when ye sin so against the brethren and wound their weak conscience, ye sin against Christ."

And so we might go on; but we will not take page-space for further illustrations. Why, even that classic chapter on love, 1 Corinthians xiii., is in reality purely incidental to Paul's treatment of local Corinthian disadjustments in the matter of "speaking with tongues"; and that magnificent chapter on the subject of resurrection is appended in reproof to some who were gainsaying it (1 Cor. xv. 12, 35).

Of course, just as there is something solidly satisfying about the way things are doctrinally *stated* in Romans, there is something thrillingly stirring about the way they are *related* in Corinthians. All that we stress here is that the distinction between the epistles should be usefully borne in mind all the while. In Romans evangelical truth is stated as doctrine to be learned and received. In Corinthians it is rather seen as truth already taught and departed from. In Romans we have the *norm*; in Corinthians the *sub*-norm; in Galatians the *ab*-norm.

We need only read this first Corinthian epistle once to see that it is largely full of reproof for practical errors in life and walk. There is reproof for divisions, envyings, contentions (i.–iv.); unjudged sexual sin (v.); selfish litigation between Christian and Christian (vi.); inconsiderate liberties in doubtful practices (viii.); querulous querying of Paul's apostleship (ix.); social and ritual disorders in the public meeting (xi.); errors in the use of spiritual gifts (xiv.); wrong attitudes toward the coming resurrection (xv.).

Contents and Analysis

Let us now go through the epistle together with a view to drafting out an analysis.

After the introduction (i. 1–9) the first feature, unhappily, is an exposure of man-exalting *schisms* in the assembly—Paulinians, Apollonians, Cephasites (i. 10–17). The Pauline loyalists doubtless championed Gospel freedom and would claim primacy for Paul as the founder of their church. The Apollos clique were the intellectuals, carried away by the eloquence and seeming superiority of the brilliant Alexandrine expositor who had made such a flash among them since Paul's first visit. The Cephas block were presumably the Judaistically inclined, whose boast would be in Peter as the authoritative voice of the apostles and the mother church at Jerusalem. There was even a "Christ" party invidiously arrogating the Name, and saying, "I am of Christ" in a factious way which implied the inferiority of all others. Thus were the names of the Lord's public servants and of the Lord Himself disputatiously played off against each other, until the silly but serious rivalries threatened a fatal disruption of the church.

In the earlier chapters, therefore, we find Paul reproving them for this and showing how wrong it all was. In chapter i. 18–31 he shows that man-exalting schisms are wrong because salvation by the *Cross* sets aside human wisdom altogether. Next, in chapter ii., he shows that they are wrong because the true wisdom is imparted by the *Spirit*, not by man. Then, in chapters iii. and iv., he further shows that they are wrong because human teachers, after all, are only "stewards" and the real power is of *God* (see especially iii. 5, 6, 21, iv. 1). Finally, in chapters v. and vi., he brings the matter to a most humiliating issue for the Corinthians, showing that such "gloryings" were a sheer mockery while flagrant evils were condoned—incest, law-suits, impurity! "Ye are puffed up," he exclaims, "and have not rather mourned!" (v. 2). "Your boasting is unseemly; clean out the evil dough" (verses 6, 7). "I speak to your shame" (vi. 5). "There is utterly a lapse among you" (vi. 7).

Without a doubt, then, the subject of these first six chapters is *REPROOF—CONCERNING SCHISMS.*

Chapters vii.–xv.

Quite clearly chapter vii. indicates a new departure. It begins: "Now concerning the things *whereof ye wrote me* . . ." So from this point Paul is answering written questions. We may well be grateful to God that ever the Corinthians wrote that letter of questions because of these inspired replies which it evoked. Three well-known members of the Corinthian church had travelled to *Ephesus,* where Paul was labouring at the time, and from where he wrote his reply to Corinth (see xvi. 8, 9). They were Stephanas, Fortunatus, and Achaicus (verses 17, 18); and it seems inferable that they were a delegation entrusted to bear the sheaf of queries.

In chapter vii. we have Paul's reply concerning marriage matters and celibacy. Then, in chapters viii.–x., comes his counsel on certain meats considered doubtful because of association with idols. Paul's handling is masterly, so that there is neither compromise nor needless provocativeness. He expands his reply somewhat because delicate social considerations are involved. Thus, in chapter viii., we are shown the *principle* which is to determine conduct (verses 9–13); in chapter ix., Paul's own *example*; in chapter x., a Scripture *warning* (verses 1–22), and *the issue* of the matter (x. 23–xi. 1).

This brings us to chapter xi., where we have reply as to sex propriety in the assembly (verses 2–16) and general behaviour at the Lord's table (verses 17–34). And next we find a trio of chapters (xii., xiii., xiv.) on "spiritual gifts." The orderly treatment teaches that these gifts are dispensed by the Spirit (xii.); that they are poor without love (xiii.); and that prophecy is the best (xiv.).

Chapter xv. crowns the whole with the eye-opening reply on the age-end resurrection of the saints. Verses 1–19 relate it to *Christ's* resurrection. Verses 20–34 describe the *order and outcome* of it. Verses 35–49 deal with the *physiological* aspect of it. Verses 50–58 fore-depict the actual transition affected by it.

We may now frame all this in flat analysis, as follows. We purposely avoid making a more elaborate analysis, so that the main shape and drive of the epistle may be the more readily seen and easily remembered.

FIRST EPISTLE TO THE CORINTHIANS

JESUS CHRIST MADE UNTO US WISDOM.

Introductory i. 1–9.

I. REPROOF—CONCERNING SCHISMS (i.–vi.).

(The Corinthians were factiously glorying in men—i. 12.)

Ch. i. Man-exalting schisms (verses 10–17) wrong because salvation by the *Cross* sets aside man's wisdom altogether (verses 18–31).

ii. Man-exalting schisms wrong because the true wisdom imparted by the *Spirit*, not by man (verses 5–13).

iii.–iv. Man-exalting schisms wrong because human teachers only stewards: power is of God (iii. 5, 6, 21, iv. 1).

v.–vi. Such "gloryings" (v. 2) a mockery (v. 6) while flagrant evils condoned—incest, law-suits, impurity!

II. REPLIES—CONCERNING PROBLEMS (vii.–xv.).

(The Corinthians had written Paul about problems—vii. 1.)

Ch. vii. Reply concerning marriage and celibacy.

viii.–x. Reply re meats. The principle (viii); Paul's example (ix.); Scripture warning (x.); issue (x. 23–xi. 1.).

xi. Reply on sex propriety in the assembly (verses 2–16) and general behaviour at the Lord's Table (verses 17–34).

xii.–xiv. Reply re spiritual gifts. Dispensed by the Spirit (xii.); poor without love (xiii.); prophecy the best (xiv.).

xv. Reply concerning resurrection of Saints. Relation to Christ's (verses 1–19); the prospect (verses 20–34); the body (verses 35–49); the "mystery" (verses 50–8).

Supplementary xvi.

At this point our embarrassment becomes acute; for having thus surveyed the epistle, how shall we now deal in half a dozen pages with such a spread of treasures? We shall limit ourselves to observations and elucidations here and there, which may usefully contribute to further exploration.

Human Leaders and Labels

Let us learn at once and forever the fatal folly of factious denominationalism, and of leaning wrongly on human leaders. Think—four full chapters regretting and reproving it! See how unmistakably Paul keeps human leaders and teachers at the lowly level which alone is proper or allowable. In chapter iii. 5 they are but "servants"; it is "the *Lord*" who "gives to every man." In verse 6 they are but farm-hands; it is *God* who giveth the growth." In verses 10–15 they are "builders"; but *Jesus* is the "foundation." In chapter iv. 1 they are merely "subordinates" (or attendants); while *Christ* is the Director. Again, in that same verse, they are only "stewards"; the real treasure is "of *God*."

Apparently it was the Apollos "fans" who were the most "puffed up" of the several Corinthian "splits", for which reason Paul here says more about Apollos than Peter. But notice that in all his reproof of the Apollos *party* he does not pen the slightest criticism of Apollos himself; nor is there even the subtlest suggestion of reflection upon him anywhere. The references are all appreciative; and it is lovely to see, in chapter xvi. 12, that Paul was not *jealous* because so many of his converts had become keen admirers of Apollos, nor was Apollos over-eager to exploit his popularity there by a return visit. See how in chapter iii. 8, 9 Paul says that he and Apollos are *"one,"* and then adds: "For *we* [i.e. Paul and Apollos] are *fellow-workers.*"

What wickedness it is today, the way that soundly evangelical preachers criticise each other! It does nothing but harm, besides leaving a bitter taste in the disparager's mouth. It is a poisonous weed which springs from jealousy. It is a dishonour to Christ and a grief to the Spirit. Let our motto be "Kill that weed"! And let those of us who are ministers, missionaries, preachers, public workers, learn how fickle audiences can be! Paul, beware— Apollos is going to spell-bind your converts! Apollos, beware— a deeper teacher than thou art is soon coming to Corinth! God save us from being mere men-pleasers! God save us from being carried away by congregational applause! God save us from being jealous of another's gifts! "For who maketh thee to differ from another? And what hast *thou* that thou didst not receive?"

Let the Christian rank and file, also, learn to appreciate the Lord's gifted human servants without idolising them. Doubtless even in the first days of the Christian era preachers and teachers had their differing excellences, emphases and ways of putting things, so that different men appealed to different minds. Equally doubtless, now as then, immoderate adulation of such "ministers" is a mark of spiritual immaturity. It is worst of all when they are put on such pedestals that Paul and Apollos and Peter are played off against each other; yet this is usually what develops from infatuation with the human.

We do not say there is no place for "denominations" such as we have in modern Protestantism. Each of our main bodies came into existence to ensure emphasis on certain important components of the full truth. We much prefer the outward diversity and free spiritual *unity* of evangelical Protestantism to the compulsory *uniformity* of Roman Catholicism. But when denominationalism becomes inflated bigotry, would that denominations had never been born!

Let even the simplest among us learn not lean unwisely on human leaders. They were meant to be *learned* from, not *leaned* on! Mark well Paul's word in chapter iv. 6: "Learn in us [i.e. in Paul and Apollos] not to think excessively [of men], that no one of you be puffed-up champions of one teacher against another."

Paul as an Example

It is a superb apologetic when a Christian leader lives so close to His Lord that he can counsel his hearers not only to "Do as I say" but "Do as I *do*." Let the ideal of every Christian evangelist and teacher be that preaching and practice shall maintain an equally high level. In this Paul is an illustrious example. Again and again he refers to himself in this first Corinthian letter, never obtrusively, always incidentally, to illustrate or press home some truth; and oh, how some of these personal touches challenge us! He was writing to persons who knew him well and had watched him closely; yet in chapter iv. 16 he writes: "Wherefore I exhort you be ye *imitators of me*"; and again in chapter xi. 1: "Be ye *imitators of me*, even as I also am of Christ." Paul the pattern is a rewarding study right through the epistle. Turn over the leaves again, lingering at each of the ten places where his exemplariness gleams out most gloriously. See his exemplary:

1. Loyalty in message, method and motive, ii. 1–5
2. Soundness in founding and building, iii. 10–23.
3. Fidelity as a trustee of saving truth, iv. 1–6.
4. Endurance of tribulations for Christ, iv. 9–16.
5. Considerateness of weaker brethren, vi. 12, viii. 13
6. Foregoing of proper rights and dues, ix. 12–18.
7. Self-denial for the saving of souls, ix. 19–23.
8. Self-discipline in body and behaviour, ix. 27, x. 33.
9. Self-restraint in public assemblies, xiv. 18–20.
10. Self-abnegation and active gratitude, xv. 9–10.

Paul the Pattern Preacher

All these are photographs which may well hold our eyes for a long, steady appreciation. Why, simply to look more closely at the first of them, how revealing and alluring, how provoking and perhaps rebuking it is to all of us who are public teachers of the Word! There are two crises through which we must each pass, in one way or another, if we would be powerful and prevailing preachers. The first crisis is intellectual; the other is spiritual. They both appear in those first five verses of chapter ii., where we see Paul as the pattern preacher.

Here is the *intellectual* crisis: "And I, brethren, when I came to you, came not with excellency of speech or of wisdom, declaring unto you the testimony of God; for I determined not to know anything among you, save Jesus Christ, and Him crucified." *Why* did Paul renounce oratory and philosophy just at the place where they might have seemed most useful? It was because he was declaring "the testimony of *GOD*." Either the Gospel *is* or is *not* a testimony of *GOD*. If it is, then to enhance it (supposedly) by display of human art or learning is like holding a candle aloft to help the sun. It is like trying to silver the stars, or presuming to paint the petals of the polyanthus! Is the Gospel really Divine

in origin and authority? If it *is*, then human intellect and eloquence must be utterly subordinated. The Divine message itself
must be allowed to do its own work and prove its own power.
That is where the intellectual crisis arises. Notice Paul's word: "I
determined." It indicates cogitation, mental wrestling, emergent
resolution. Others of us need a similar inward struggle and iron-
willed decision. Thus Paul puts himself completely out of the
picture: "I came *not* with oratory or learning." Then he puts
Christ right in the forefront to *fill* the picture: "Nothing, save
Jesus Christ, and Him crucified." Nor is even the Christ of
Galilee enough: it must be the Christ of Calvary.

Here is the *spiritual* crisis: "And I was with you in weakness,
and in fear, and in much trembling; and my speech and my
preaching was not with persuasive words of man's wisdom, but
in demonstration of the Spirit and of power." So it is not enough
even to have the *message* right—with all display excluded and
Jesus supreme; the *method* must be right as well. The Christ of
Calvary must be preached in the power of Pentecost. No matter
how true the sermon or how earnest the speaker, there is no spiritual effect in the hearer except by the Holy Spirit. That is where
the *spiritual* crisis arises. Many a preacher who preaches Christ,
and is bravely prepared to preach even "the offence of the Cross,"
is not prepared to give up his own way of doing it. There is to be
absolutely no reliance on anything of self, or anything human.
This is a delicate point, and not too easy perhaps to express with
fine exactness, yet it is vital to spiritual effectiveness. There may
be a place for cultivated speech, organising, advertising and other
means; but the minute they are relied on for *spiritual* results they
are fatal. There must be utter abandonment to the Holy Spirit.
It is this which brings what Paul calls the "demonstration of
the Spirit and of power." The "power" is in the preacher. The
"demonstration" is in the hearer. The Holy Spirit is the invisible
connection between the two; and that alone is how vital spiritual
effects are wrought.

Paul had come through both these crises—the intellectual and
the spiritual. The one message was Christ. The one power was
the Holy Spirit. Mark well those frank and rather astounding
words: "And I was with you in weakness, and in fear, and in
much trembling"! Is that indeed the lion-like Paul speaking?
"Weakness"—"fear"—"trembling"! What a trinity of surprises!

Was that the kind of preacher who would impress the flashy, display-loving Corinthians? Is that the kind who would impress you or me? Well, it was just because Paul had come to the end of himself that the Holy Spirit could really use all that he *was*! Oh, for more such weakness and fear and trembling in our modern pulpit—and more of the same results!

And what was the *motive* behind it all? It was this: "That your faith should not stand in the wisdom of men, but in the power of God." This was the man whom God so mightily used. Brother preacher, Christian worker, read that paragraph again—chapter ii. 1–5. Learn more carefully what apostolic and Pentecostal preaching really is. Mark well the true message, method and motive. Then ask yourself: "How do *I* compare with this snapshot of Paul the pattern preacher?"

THE FIRST EPISTLE TO THE CORINTHIANS (2)

Lesson Number 131

NOTE.—For this study read carefully through the epistle again, checking off the analysis given in the preceding study.

The ministry demands *superhuman self-abasement* (iv. 9–13), for Christ's workers in the arena of time are conscious of a mysterious background of unseen spectators, "for we are made a spectacle unto the world, and to angels, and to men." The arena of earth, where this wondrous drama of life and death is being played out amid natural and supernatural machinery, is like some city theatre in broad daylight ("theatre" is the very Greek word for "spectacle" used here) ; all seems indeed dusty, grimy, and disappointing to the last degree ; but above it are arrayed tier above tier, rank above rank, a sublime host of unseen witnesses, bending down their awful forms with earnest gaze, and intent upon the life-struggle between light and darkness, sin and holiness, faith and falsehood, suffering and triumph ; "which things the angels desire to look into."

What a contrast between the celestial spectators and the poor players in the arena ! "We are made the filth of the world and the off-scouring of all things unto this day."

—*C. A. Fox.*

This mysterious background of invisible spectators seems largely ignored by public Christian workers nowadays ; and reference thereto is often taken as sentimental or imaginative. But *Paul* was keenly alive to the reality of it.

—*J.S.B.*

THE FIRST EPISTLE TO THE
CORINTHIANS (2)

THE RIVER has overflowed its banks! Our intent to assign only *one* study to First Corinthians is broken down! Yet can we begrudge the pages expended on Paul himself as Christian exemplar and pattern preacher? This epistle is certainly a "lively oracle" against deadly errors. Every part of it pulsates with energy, sympathy, concern, and relevance for our own days. Having seen its general plan and aim, we ought now to scan the *parts,* halting at each to make sure of its salient significance.

The Gospel and its Ministry

In *form,* the first six chapters are a rebuke of schism; but in *substance* they are a heart-stirring explication of true Gospel ministry, particularly in relation to the local Christian assembly. What *is* this message and ministry of the Gospel? Paul's answer takes a five-fold course, as follows:

1. Its foolishness to the worldly-wise (i. 18–31).
  Foolishness of message (verses 18–25).
  Foolishness of advocates (verses 19–31).

2. Its operation in preacher and hearer (ii. 1–16).
  Power through the preacher (verses 1–8).
  Revelation in the hearer (verses 9–16).

3. Its teachers and the local assembly (iii. 1–23).
  Are fellow-workers for God (verses 5–15).
  Are gifts to the assembly (verses 16–23).

4. Its ministers as responsible to God (iv. 1–21).
  The true will be vindicated (verses 1–7).
  Some make costly sacrifice (verses 8–21).

5. Its demand of sanctity in believers (v.–vi.).
  The assembly must expel impurity (v.).
  No defrauding! No unchastity! (vi.).

The whole movement is gripping to those who have eyes for vital truths. Paul readily admits the seeming foolishness of the *message* (i. 18–25): "For the preaching of the Cross is to them that perish foolishness. . . . It pleased God by the foolishness of what we preach to save them that believe." So the centre-point is the *Cross*, which to human pride (Greek) and prejudice (Jew) is "foolishness." The truths of this Gospel *still* seem foolishness to the warped minds of the worldly-wise. They are foolishness because of their very simplicity; because they are equally free to the unlearned as to the highly sophisticated; because they abase self-righteous merit-works, thus offending religious pride; and because a shameful cross is such a sign of helpless weakness that it seems impossible for it to be the organ of Divine saving-power.

Equally "foolishness" to the worldly-wise are the Gospel *personnel*. "God hath chosen the foolish things of the world to confound the wise; the weak things to confound the mighty; and base things, and things which are despised, yea, and things which are not, to bring to nought things that are." Such are the five ranks of the Gospel army: the foolish, the weak, the base, the despised, the nonentities! This is not because God has no other choice. He *prefers* these; for thus all human boasting is excluded, and all the glory is Christ's. The "fools" are the first rank. Paul gladly became one (ii. 2, iv. 10), though naturally brilliant. The "weak" are the second rank. Have you been thinking you were too weak for Christian service and witness? You are just the recruit for this army! Step in here, behind the "fools"—who are such fools that they are not ashamed to be in the front rank! Or, if you are not good enough for this second rank, fall in with the "base" or the "despised" or the "nobodies"!

What! Is *this* the laughable army which is ordered up to charge and break the enemy line? And is the Cross their only weapon? Yes! for hidden within their contemptible exterior is the all-victorious presence of Christ and the irresistible power of the Holy Spirit. There is not a Midian's host can withstand this Gideon's handful in their Pentecostal panoply. Goliaths galore go down before this strange young David as the Christian era overpowers the world's calendars. It is no mere instance of "diamond cutting diamond"; it is the lamb slaying the lion, and the dove proving wiser than the serpent. The weak ones are the indomitable conquerors, and the "chief of sinners" the foremost of the apostles! Christ is everything—"wisdom" to the fools, "power" to the weak, "righteousness, sanctification and redemption" to the base, the despised, and the nobodies.

Chapter iii.

We lingered over chapter ii. in our preceding study, so we pass over it here; but note in chapter iii. how factions frustrate the full operation of the truth (verses 1–4). Observe also that true Christian evangelists and teachers are but *servants* of the Lord and His Church (verses 5–7); they are *co-workers* for God, not competitors (verses 8–11); their work will be *finally tested*, and either rewarded or exposed as reprobate (verses 12–17); they are therefore not to be factiously gloried in, for all are *the Church's possession*, not its possessors (verses 18–23).

Mark carefully that the words in verse 15—"If any man's work shall be burned, he shall suffer loss: but he himself shall be saved; yet so as by fire"—are part of the paragraph concerning Christian *workers*. Personal salvation is not the matter in question, as many unobservant readers have wrongly supposed, but a final testing of *service* (verse 13).

Verse 17 may seem a sudden shock: "If any man defile the temple of God, *him shall God destroy*." In the Greek, however, the word translated "destroy" is the same as "defile" in the earlier clause. That it does not mean destruction in the sense of damnation seems clear from other occurrences (1 Cor. xv. 33; 2 Cor. vii. 2, xi. 3). The continuing subject is teachers and workers inside the Church, not outsiders. Read the verse: "If any man spoil the sanctuary of God [i.e. the local church—verse 16] God shall cause *this* [i.e. either this *work*, or this *man*] to be spoiled."

Chapter v. 5.

Someone is sure to ask about Paul's words in chapter v. 5: "To deliver such an one unto Satan for the destruction of the flesh, that the spirit may be saved in the day of the Lord Jesus."

This verse is the direct grammatical continuation of the words "I have judged" in verse 3. Paul was not asking *them* to judge but simply to carry out what he himself, an inspired apostle, had judged. The apostles were a group of authoritatively inspired men in a category all by themselves, required for a special epoch (see first chapter in my book *Studies in Problem Texts*). They were no more intended to have "successors" than the now completed New Testament writings were meant to have apochryphal additions. They were uniquely authorised teachers with a conferred authority strictly peculiar to themselves. What Paul the apostle could do by that invested authority and supernatural insight, *we cannot*. Yet the incident shows what our *attitude* ought to be toward such sin among believers.

Furthermore, it was the *body* which was to be handed over— and for a mercifully corrective purpose, namely, "that the *spirit* may be saved," i.e. savingly disciplined through physical chastisement. The Greek word here translated as "destroyed" nowhere means annihilation. The same kind of handing over occurs in I Timothy i. 20. (See also Luke xiii. 16 and 2 Cor. xii. 7.)

We have actually read the suggestion that the verse gives sanction to the Roman Catholic "Inquisition"! Nay! That iniquitous inquisition was for so-called *heresy* (which in reality was the pure truth of the Gospel), whereas in I Corinthians v. 5 the discipline is for patently culpable immorality. Furthermore, the handing over was to *Satan* as the inflicting agent, which makes a most awkward parallel with the Roman Church and her diabolical torture chambers!

We must not forget to relate this verse to its context. Note how the chapter begins: "It is actually *reported*." The word "reported" here indicates that Paul is still occupied with what had been verbally passed on to him (i. 11). He has not yet started answering the written questions which the Corinthians had sent him (vii. 1). Before ever he can come to their questions he must rebuke their frictions and shameful lapses. So chapters v. and vi. belong to the first four. They were meant to show how deeply ridiculous (as well as unspiritual) all partisan boastings were while domestic immorality (v.), business defraudings (vi. 1–8) and social unchastity (vi. 9–18) disfigured the fellowship. But the two chapters (as we have shown) also form part of Paul's exposition of the Gospel and its ministry, their purpose being to emphasise that the Gospel of Christ tolerates absolutely no compromise with what is immoral or unworthy. Corinth was not an easy place in which to learn such lessons.

Corinth the Corrupt

It is only fair to remember that those Corinthian converts had been born and bred in surroundings which were about as vile and vicious as could be imagined. Take the following description of Corinth. "Amongst the great provincial cities of the Empire, Corinth was the most central, and was affected by all the various currents of the age. Standing on Grecian soil, it was a Roman colony, refounded by Julius Cæsar in 46 B.C., the seat of Roman government and of Greek commerce. For profligacy the city had an infamous notoriety. Here vice was raised into a religion; and the 'idolators' of Corinth are fitly set between 'fornicators' and 'adulterers' (vi. 9). From the filthiest slough of sin Paul's converts at Corinth were extracted (vi. 9–11). Not even at Antioch had he seen the condition of the Gentile world—its pride and power, its fancied wisdom, its utter depravity—displayed so vividly." We can well imagine how staggered and sickened Paul must have been by this huge quagmire of refined voluptuousness and gross sensualism; the filthy rituals of idolatry, and the soul-debasing "religions" which made animal indulgence meritorious; the swaggering pride of (supposed) Greek "wisdom," and the utter corruption of it all. In all the Bible there is not a more awful description of human sin and degradation than the first chapter of Paul's epistle to the Romans—and it was written from *Corinth*!

We say, then, that it is only fair to remember the upbringing and environment of those first Corinthian converts. They had been truly won for Christ, and formed into a local church. They had indeed broken from their idolatries, to worship the living and true God. But they could not break free in ten minutes from all that was ingrained *in* them, or from the social conditions and seductions *around* them. Missionaries tell of the same problem among Christian converts in heathen areas today. Yet those converts must learn right away that the Gospel will not tolerate compromise. There must be a clean break. This is the thrust of 1 Corinthians v. and vi. The Holy Spirit is grieved and thwarted in the assembly where sin is allowed a footing. "The temple of God is holy, which temple ye are" (iii. 17). We twentieth-century Christians may think ourselves far removed from those early Corinthian brethren; yet again and again, just below the surface in many Christian assemblies today, there are goings-on equally grieving in their own way as those for which Paul flagellated the Corinthians. The Holy Spirit is grieved; His supernatural grace-ministries are frustrated; there is spiritual impotency and deadness.

Some Problem-Points (vii.)

Chapter vii. presents a sheaf of posers to many a new reader. There are several verses which seem to cast doubt on Paul's supernatural inspiration; and others which refer to wedlock in a rather puzzling way. A comment or two on these may be useful.

In verse 6, according to the Authorised Version, Paul says: "But I speak this by permission and not of commandment"—as though *he himself* had no more than a bare permission to write so. The verse should read: "But this I say by way of *concession* . . ." that is, he leaves the *details* of their lives, whether married or unmarried, to their individual consciences as Christians and will not *command* them this way or that.

In verse 10 he says: "And unto the married I command, yet not I, *but the Lord* . . ." Two verses later he adds: "But to the rest speak I, *not* the Lord." He simply means that in the first case the rule for *married* persons had been uttered by our Lord Jesus Himself (Matt. v. 31, 32, xix. 5–9; Mark x. 11; Luke xvi. 18), whereas in the latter case, i.e. Christian husbands and wives whose partners were still heathen, no such word had been spoken. A similar instance occurs in verse 25. Obviously there were many such incidentals which our Lord could not touch upon but for which He made provision in the sending of the Holy Spirit who should afterward guide His followers. The very way in which Paul speaks in verse 12 reveals his consciousness of apostolic inspiration and authority. As the Christian faith overflowed the boundaries of Jewry, many such cases inevitably arose in Gentile connections which required authoritative guidance such as only an inspired apostle could give.

That Paul was conscious of such supernatural inspiration is confirmed by the last sentence of the chapter, which, unfortunately, reads rather hesitatingly in our Authorised Version. Transpose the "also," then read the verse: "And I hold that I *also* have the Spirit of God" (i.e. as well as others who may claim so). Paul was confident of it. Incidentally, this verse is remarkable as showing how Divine inspiration blends with rational human reasoning, guiding it, guarding it, yet never swamping individuality.

What, now, about those seemingly discomposing references to wedlock in such verses as 8, 9, 14, 28, 32–4, 37–40? The answer is that the whole passage must be read in the light of verse 26: "This is good for *the present distress*." Perhaps, with some of the more recent translators, we ought to read it: "the *impending* distress." The apostle had doubtless warned them of trouble ahead. The first of the awful anti-Christian persecutions under Nero was almost on them. Also, our Lord's prediction of the "great tribulation" precursory to His own second advent would be in Paul's mind—for the return was believed to be imminent. Paul did not know that the Lord's return was centuries away; but in no wise does that detract from his words; for the Holy Spirit who inspired him knew it, and knew also that there certainly *was* impending "distress" for those early Christians. Thus, Paul's words were just as cogent and timely as if the Lord's return *had* been about to happen then; while at the same time they give guidance to *us* on whom the end of the age is soon to break.

In this seventh chapter, then, we must be careful to distinguish between the temporary and the permanent, between the local and the general. *All* of the apostle's counsels here are *sympathetic* in view of the "imminent distress", but *some* of them belong to the circumstances of a place and a time now gone. This does not mean that they have no voice to us today, for running through all of them there are *principles* which are of lasting application.

Meats, Liberties, Stumbling-Blocks, Weaker Brethren!

Chapters viii., ix. and x. belong together and are a reply to the enquiry of the Corinthians concerning the permissibility of eating meats which had been offered to idols. In fact, all the different reply-sections are marked off by the little conjunction "Now."

vii. 1: "*Now* concerning the things . . ." (wedlock).
viii. 1: "*Now* concerning things offered unto idols . . ."
xi. 2: "*Now* I praise you, brethren . . ." (ordinances).
xii. 1: "*Now* concerning spiritual gifts . . ."
xv. 1: "*Now* I declare to you . . ." (resurrection).
xvi. 1: "*Now* concerning the collection . . ."

Does this matter of meats offered to idols seem far removed from our own circumstances? Nay, it affects us very closely, for it involves the whole question of *Christian liberty* in things doubtful and the next-door subject of *self-subjugation*.

The *Jews* had known this meat problem long before it cropped up for Gentile *Christians*. Wherever the Jews lived they had to have their own butchers, trained in all the regulations which decided between clean and unclean flesh. They could eat only that which was certified by an affixed leaden seal marked "Lawful." On the basis of Scriptures like Exodus xxxiv. 15 and Numbers xxv. 2 they were most severely interdicted from meats offered to idols. One rabbinical teaching forbade the Jew even to attend a Gentile funeral, though he took his own food with him, lest inadvertently he should drink from a cask of which even a goblet had been drawn for the pouring out of a little to Gentile gods.

But now the Gentile *Christians* had a kindred problem. Much of the meat in their markets was the residue (i.e. after the priests had taken their share) of animals killed as sacrifices. So much was this so that it was generally impracticable to distinguish with certainty between offered and non-offered meats. If, then, it was wrong to buy the former, now mixed up with all the other meat stocks of the markets, a complicated problem indeed was created. Besides the problem in buying for one's own family, what about social meals with friends or relatives who were not Christians and who served meats which had perhaps been first offered to idols? What about Christians who were poor, to whom the public feasts associated with the gods were perhaps the only chance of eating meats at all?

Other than being niggling, the question was big and touchy. It was made the more so because that historic first Christian synod in Jerusalem a few years earlier had issued the resolution:

"For it seemed good to the Holy Spirit, and to us, to lay upon you [Gentiles] no greater burden than these necessary things: That ye abstain from *meats offered to idols*; and from blood; and from things strangled; and from fornication; from which if ye keep yourselves ye shall do well" (Acts xv. 28, 29).

Paul handles the question with obvious sympathy, sincerity and sagacity. At once he shows (viii. 1) the need to distinguish between "knowledge" and "love" in deciding one's conduct: "Knowledge *puffeth* up [ourselves], but love *buildeth* up [our brethren]." With those who have now come to see that there is "none other God but one," that "an idol is nothing," and that meat is neither affected one way nor another by ceremonial associations, Paul at once agrees (verses 4–6). Yet while he assumes the Christian *right* of such, thus to view meats indifferently (and plainly recommends it later—x. 25), he also guards this liberty from *abuse,* lest it should become a stumbling-block to weaker believers who, having been idolators all their lives hitherto, had not yet managed sufficiently to break free from their mental association of meats with idols (verses 7–9); and he certainly draws the line at feasting *in* idol temples (verses 9–12). To be seen reclining at banquets in the temples of Aphrodite or Poseidon, was a "bowing in the house of Rimmon" (2 Kings v. 18) which stretched Christian liberty too far, and was certain to be misunderstood. In thus "wounding" weaker Christian consciences they committed "sin" against the Lord Himself (verse 12).

Thereupon, in verse 13, Paul enunciates the basic principle: "*Wherefore, if what I eat stumbles my brother, I will not eat flesh while the age lasts, so that I do not cause my brother to stumble.*" Instead of a superior "I-know-better-than-you" attitude, which puffs up one's own self, *love* triumphs in sympathetic considerateness and helps to build up the weaker brother or sister in the faith.

Five times in these three chapters the principle of considerateness for the weaker brother finds expression (viii. 9, 13, ix. 19–23, x. 24, x. 29). Paul's own example is given in chapter ix. What an example—self-*denial* (verses 1–18), self-*effacement* (verses 19–23), self-*discipline* (verses 24–7)! All these were for the sake of *others* (verses 18, 22, 27). By lovely paradox this self-subjugation becomes self-*realisation*. It purifies and simplifies and unifies and amplifies and glorifies life! It richly proves the Master's words: "Whosoever will save his life shall lose it; and whosover will *lose* his life for My sake shall *find* it"!

Note ix. 24: "They which run in the stadium run all, but only one receiveth the prize. So run that *ye* may win." It might seem to suggest an each-for-himself competitiveness rather than considerateness for the weaker brother. But no—the pronoun "ye" is plural. "So run, that *ye all* may obtain"! Chapter x. gives a warning example from old-time Israel (verses 1–22); then the *issue* of the whole discussion (verses 23–33); and the section is *finalised* by an admonitory reiteration of the general principle:

> Whether therefore ye eat or drink or whatsoever ye do, do all to the glory of God. Give no offence to the Jews, nor to the Gentiles, nor to the Church of God."

Woman: The Lord's Table (xi.)

How grievously misconstrued have been Paul's words concerning woman in relation to her husband and to the public assembly of Christian believers! Let us learn once and for all, from this eleventh chapter, verse 5, that women certainly did "prophesy" (i.e. preach or teach, to edify, exhort, comfort, under impulse from the Holy Spirit) in that church of the first days. The words *"every* woman praying or prophesying" indicate that it was general. In this passage Paul's concern is solely that what they *wear* in thus taking public part should conform to the preservation of true womanly dignity. The very "authority" (verse 10) which she was to wear on her head (some form of head-dress then in vogue as the proper thing), other than being meant to advertise inferiority and subjection, was that which protected her *right* to speak. To refer to it as a "veil" is not warranted by the context; though even the veil worn by women in some eastern parts can tell us the meaning of the head-dress to which Paul refers. Sir W. M. Ramsay, in his book *The Cities of St. Paul*, says: "In the Oriental lands the veil is the power and honour and dignity of the woman. With the veil on her head she can go anywhere in security and profound respect. She is not seen; it is the mark of thoroughly bad manners to observe a veiled woman in the street. She is alone. The rest of the people around her are non-existent to her as she is to them. She is supreme in the crowd. She passes at her own free choice and a space must be left for her. The man who did anything to molest or annoy her would have a bad time of it in an Oriental town, and might easily lose his life. But without the veil the woman is a thing of nought, whom anyone may insult." Professor Ramsay then adds: "The teaching of the verse, 1 Corinthians xi. 10, is that the wearing of the veil was the woman's sign of authority in the church at Corinth to pray and prophesy."

But what, then, about chapter xiv. 34–7: "Let your women keep silence in the churches"? Well, is it thinkable that Paul could so soon and so seriously contradict himself? Remember, he is here answering questions which the Corinthians had asked him by letter. Why had they raised the matter? The reason is not far to seek. In the early Church there was a Judaising party agitating to graft rites and rules of Judaism upon the Christian faith. Ever since Paul's victorious collision with Peter at Antioch (Gal. ii. 11–21) his lonely but mighty struggle for the freedom of the Gospel from Jewish legalism had been contested by these Judaisers. They followed Paul in the churches which he founded and did all they could to undermine his authority, professing to represent a superior form of Christianity with the authority of the Jerusalem apostolate behind it.

They held the usual Judaistic view of woman; and it is to *their statements* that Paul is replying in 1 Corinthians xiv. The component sentences of verses 34 and 35 are all from the Oral Law, or Tradition of the Elders, which was the armoury of Judaisers. Paul quotes them to *repudiate* them. That is why he adds, "What! Did the word of God come from *you*? Or did it come only to *you*?" Would they set *that* teaching above his own? "If any man think himself to be a prophet, or spiritual, let him acknowledge that the things which *I* write unto you are the *commandments of the Lord*" (verse 37).

Paul is the champion of woman's liberation, and it is tragic that he has been so misinterpreted. His handling of *the husband's headship* in chapter xi. is as masterly as it is commonly misunderstood. He does *not* teach that the man is head of the woman but that the *husband* is head of the *wife*—for that is what is meant by the words "man" and "woman" in verse 3. The headship is matrimonial, domestic, economic, but *not in nature*; for as verse 11 adds: "Neither is the man without the woman, nor the woman without the man, in the Lord." The headship here parallels with that of the Father and Christ, who are co-equal in nature. All Paul's counsels in this chapter are *safeguards* of Christian womanhood, not prison-chains! We write these words with deep feeling because we know what problem and pain have been inflicted on godly women through misunderstanding.

Concerning Spiritual Gifts (xii.-xiv).

In recent times certain enthusiastic evangelical movements have given such prominence to "speaking in tongues" that we ought to look again with a sharp eye at these chapters on "spiritual gifts." There are those who teach that all these gifts are meant for all believers, and that they should all be in full manifestation today. Believers are urged to seek until they receive the "baptism of the Holy Spirit," which brings (so it is urged) these supernatural gifts. We ourselves have several times heard it preached to large and eager audiences that the *sign* of having received the "baptism" is this speaking in tongues; and the hearers have been exhorted not to rest content until, by speaking in tongues, they had the *evidence* of their "baptism."

This going in for the gifts, especially tongues and healings, is looked on as a superior spirituality, a "going all the way with God's word." There are many earnestly spiritual and lovely characters in these movements; but on the other hand thousands of Christians have been brought into pitiful bondage or bewilderment, and there have been many cases (some of which we have seen and heard for ourselves) where the speaking with tongues was of demons and not of the Holy Spirit at all. So, then, with these three chapters now before us, let us duly observe the following factors:

(1) This short tract of Scripture is the only place in all the epistles, from Romans to Revelation, where the gift of tongues is mentioned—which indicates its *relative* value!

(2) The only church to which Paul has to say "Ye are yet carnal" and "babes in Christ" (iii. 1–4) is that which was making the much ado about these more demonstrative efflorescences—which means that speaking in tongues can go with a *poor spiritual condition*!

(3) Each time in his three lists of the gifts (xii. 8–10, 27–8, 29–30) Paul puts speaking in tongues right at the end, even though the order of the others is varied—which points to its *lesser importance* among the gifts.

(4) Chapter xii. 8–10 says: "For to one is given by the Spirit the word of wisdom; to another the word of knowledge . . . to another faith . . . to another divers kinds of tongues"—which, with verse 30, shows that "tongues" are *not meant for all*.

(5) In the passage where Paul *particularly* deals with speaking in tongues (xiv. 1–28) it is remarkable that every single mention either compares it unfavourably with "prophecy" (i.e. speaking to edification in one's own tongue) or attaches a cautionary word!

(6) To the hankerers after speaking in tongues he says: "Brethren, be not children" (verse 20). Even when he agrees that it is for a "sign" to unbelievers (verse 22) he warns of its impotency (verse 21). In verse after verse he shows that it is of little or no benefit in the assembly (verses 2, 4, 5, 6, 9, 16, 19, 22, 23, 28). His highest commendation is a merely negative one, where, at the very end of the section, he concludes: "Wherefore, brethren, *covet* to prophesy; and do not *forbid* to speak with tongues" (verse 40) —i.e. so long as the aforementioned regulations are observed.

The movement of the three chapters is as follows:

"CONCERNING SPIRITUAL GIFTS."

1. The Spirit divides them as He will (xii.).
> Diversity of gifts but one Spirit (verses 4–11).
> Diversity of members but one body (verses 12–27).
> Diversity of service but one Church (verses 28–31).

2. They are valueless without love (xiii.).
> The utter necessity of love (verses 1–3).
> The moral excellency of love (verses 4–7).
> The abiding supremacy of love (verses 8–13).

3. The greatest of them is prophecy (xiv).
> It most edifies the Church (verses 1–22).
> It most convinces outsiders (verses 23–8).
> Its use should be orderly (verses 29–40).

The Resurrection Chapter

At the end of this engrossing epistle, the longest chapter of all is devoted to the subject of the coming resurrection. It is, in fact, the longest passage on the subject in the Bible, and may well be called the Church's resurrection *Magnificat*. It mounts up, step by step, like the glorious stairs of ascent to Solomon's temple of Jehovah, which when Sheba's queen beheld it, "there was no more spirit left in her." Step by step it rises, until in the very skies it unveils the "mystery" of that consummating translation of the saints in which death has forever lost its sting and the grave is forever robbed of its victory!

We have so overshot our apportioned limits in this study that we cannot linger over this climax chapter. We simply pick out the following points as worthy of particular mention.

First: notice that Paul's Gospel begins with the *Cross* (verses 3, 4). It is not Christ the perfect *Example,* merely, but a crucified Christ who alone is the *SAVIOUR.*

Second: let verses 35–42 show us that there is no *physiological difficulty* about the resurrection. "Thou sowest not that body which shall be, but the bare kernel." What comes up is not the actual seed, yet it is something inseparably related to the seed which was buried. Our resurrection bodies will be similar in structure, but *not identical in texture* with these mortal bodies which we now possess. Neither burial nor cremation, neither severance of limbs nor complete disintegration of parts can present any problem to the all-knowing, almighty Lord who will then clothe His redeemed people with their resurrection bodies.

Third: mark the seven transition-features of that coming resurrection:

1. It is sown in "corruption"; it is raised in "incorruption."
2. It is sown in "dishonour"; it is raised in "glory."
3. It is sown in "weakness"; it is raised in "power."
4. It is sown a "physical" body; raised a "pneumatical" body.
5. It is sown an "earthy" body; it is raised a "heavenly" body.
6. It is sown a "flesh-and-blood" body; raised a "changed" body.
7. It is sown a "mortal" body; it is raised an "immortal" body.

Fourth: notice the two "alls" in verse 51. The second of the two surely cuts out the idea of a partial rapture. We believe that in this coming consummation *all* the blood-bought, Spirit-born members of Christ will have their part.

How characteristic of Paul that he should immediately turn towering doctrine into spiritual challenge! "Therefore, my beloved brethren, be ye steadfast, unmovable, always abounding in the work of the Lord, forasmuch as ye know that your labour is not in vain in the Lord."

THE SECOND EPISTLE TO THE CORINTHIANS

Lesson Number 132

NOTE.—For this study read through the epistle twice.

ABOUT THE JUDAISERS
Paul's rebuke of Peter at Antioch

This was a momentous epoch in apostolic history. The whole future of Christianity was involved in it. The fact that the contention broke out at Antioch, the centre and mother city of the Gentile churches, where Barnabas and Paul, their two great founders, had for seven years laboured side by side ; and that the entire body of the liberal Jewish Christians there and "even Barnabas" were "carried away" by Judaistic agitation ; and, above all, that "Cephas" lent his name to it, who was far and away the most revered and influential man in the whole Church,—all this made the occasion one of extreme gravity and peril. Single as he stood, Paul resisted the entire force and weight of Jewish opinion. His remonstrance convicted St. Peter of "dissimulation," and recalled him to his own better principles. But the error of the Jewish apostle, so openly committed and so well calculated to encourage the legalistic party, could not fail to have disastrous consequences.

They proceeded now to carry the war into the enemy's country. They made their way to the Pauline churches, where doubtless they found sympathisers amongst their countrymen ; and they brought into play all the arts they could command to undermine the authority of the Gentile apostle, to poison the minds of his converts, and to graft the principles of their own Judaism upon the faith that Gentile believers had received from his lips. Added to all his other dangers and trials, the apostle was now "in perils among *false brethren*" (2 Cor. xi. 26).

—*G. G. Findlay.*

THE SECOND EPISTLE TO THE CORINTHIANS

WHILE others of Paul's epistles may be more profound, scarcely any could be more precious than this second heart-outpouring to the Corinthians. It was written with a quill dipped in tears, from the apostle's "anguish of heart," and contains more of human pathos than any other of his letters. Yet there is a lovely rainbow shining through it all, for in his dire distress and deep disappointments he is discovering more than ever before that "the Father of mercies" is the "God of all comfort," and that the heavenly Master's strength is made perfect in His servant's weakness.

If the full force of such a letter is to register itself in our minds, we must see it in the context of the agitations and cogitations which precipitated it.

As we have seen, Paul's earlier letter to Corinth was written at Ephesus (1 Cor. xvi. 8). Soon afterward he was compelled to flee because of the fanatical uprising instigated by the shrine-makers of Artemis (Diana). From Ephesus he made his way up to Troas, thence across the north-eastern end of the Ægean Sea, to revisit churches which he had founded in Macedonia, and then travel south again to Corinth, in Achaia (Acts xx. 1, 2). He eventually *did* reach Corinth, and stayed there three months (Acts xx. 3), but in the *interval* between leaving Ephesus and reaching Corinth he wrote this further letter, presumably from Philippi, and under deeply affecting circumstances.

Paul's Hour of Darkness

His valued helper, Titus, was to have met him at Troas, with an anxiously awaited report on developments at Corinth, but he did not turn up (2 Cor. ii. 13), which accentuated the apostle's concern. Disappointment, apprehensiveness, and physical illness now swooped in concerted attack upon Paul to make this perhaps the darkest hour in his heroic but costly struggle for the propagation and preservation of the true Gospel. "When we were come into Macedonia," he writes, "our flesh had no rest, but we were troubled on every side. Without were fightings; within were fears" (vii. 5). As G. G. Findlay says: "Corinth appeared to be in full revolt against him. Galatia was falling away to 'another Gospel.' He had narrowly escaped from the enraged populace of Ephesus— 'wild beasts' with whom he had long been fighting, and at whose mercy he had left his flock in that turbulent city. Under this continued strain of excitement and anxiety, his strength succumbed; he was seized with an attack of sickness which threatened to terminate his life."

The apostle's own comment is: "We were pressed out of measure, above strength, insomuch that we despaired even of life. . . . We had the sentence of death in ourselves" (i. 8, 9). In chapter iv. he tells of "bearing about in the body the dying of the Lord Jesus" and of "the outward man perishing" (verses 10, 16). These and other expressions leave no doubt as to the mental distress and physical prostration of our wonderful hero. "He had been at death's door. His life and work, to all appearance, were coming to an end, and under circumstances of the most ominous nature. Together with his life, the fate of his mission and of Gentile Christianity trembled in the balance. Never had he felt himself so helpless, so beaten down and discomfited, as on that melancholy journey from Ephesus to Macedonia, and while he lay upon his sick-bed (perhaps at Philippi), not knowing whether Titus or the messenger of death would reach him first."

Incidentally, how characteristic of the man it is, that, although so apprehensive and fagged while anxiously awaiting Titus at Troas, he discovers "a door opened of the Lord (ii. 12) and preaches the Gospel so effectively as to form a church there, which he revisits some months later on his return journey to Palestine (Acts xx. 6–12).

The Report of Titus

Titus *did* eventually reach Paul in Macedonia (vii. 6)—whither Paul had hasted forward, unable to check his restless anxiety any longer at Troas. Tension was relieved. There was much to comfort and cheer the apostle (vii. 7–16). In response to the earlier epistle his Corinthians had dealt with the grievous offender (1 Cor. v.). There had been an upsurge of grief, and a flaming-out of new zeal, and a new expression of affection for Paul. So consoled was the poorly apostle that he purposed to dictate this further letter and send it by the hand of Titus, who should return to Corinth and finish the good work which he had started there (vii. 15, 16, viii. 6).

But, alas, there were other and darker aspects of the situation at Corinth, which perhaps Titus disclosed only bit by bit, out of consideration for the apostle's physical affliction and weariness. "His change of plan about the double visit had given rise to a charge of levity, and many remarks most injurious to his character had been industriously disseminated, especially, it would seem, by some Jewish emissary. His opponents hinted at his cowardice in not coming; his vacillation and insincerity in changing his mind; the conscious inferiority which made him abstain from any claim to maintenance; the meanness of his aspect; the baldness and simplicity of his speech; the fact that he had no commendatory letters from Jerusalem; his dubious position as regards the Law. They insinuated doubts about his perfect honesty. They charged him with underhand guile, and fraudulent or self-interested designs with regard to the collection. They even ventured to hint at their doubt as to his perfect sanity. Such charges would have been hard to endure at any time. They were so especially at a time when the apostle was suffering overwhelming distress— a combination of fears without and fightings within, which produced a mental and physical prostration. It became a duty and a necessity, however distasteful, to defend himself. Personally he neither required nor cared for any self-defence. But before God in Christ he felt bound to clear his character from these detestable innuendoes, because they were liable, if unnoticed, to hinder his work both in Corinth and in other churches; and his work had on him a sacred claim. Hence, though nothing was more repellent to his sensitive humility than any semblance of egotism or boasting, he is driven by the unscrupulosity of his opponents to adopt such a tone of self-defence that the word 'boasting' occurs no less than twenty-nine times. He neither could nor would appeal to any letters of commendation or to any certificate from his brother apostles, because he had received his own apostolate direct from God; and hence he is forced to appeal, on the one hand to his visions and revelations, and on the other hand to the seal of approval which in every way God had set to his unparalleled activity and devotion."

The Shifted Battle-centre

A comparison of this epistle and its predecessor certainly does seem to show, however, that there had been a psychological shift at Corinth in favour of Paul. The first epistle deplores *four* factions, and deals prominently with the Apollos party. *That* breach, being one merely of personal admiration rather than of doctrine, seems now to have been ironed out, and the *majority* at Corinth seem loyally behind Paul again as their spiritual father (1 Cor. iv. 15). In this second epistle it is the Petrine party, the "I am of Cephas" set, who are the much bigger danger. Most modern translators use the word "majority" in chapter ii. 6: "Sufficient to such a man is this censure by the *majority*"; and the very word emphasises the presence of a hostile *minority,* who doubtless dissented on the ground of Paul's supposed lack of real apostolic authority. This Petrine schism was becoming more determined in its hostility to Paul as it developed its Judaistic tendencies; and a point was now reached where a still-unsettled majority was imperilled by this strong, impressive minority.

It would appear that representatives of the Judaising element in Jerusalem had latterly visited Corinth, carrying "letters of commendation" (iii. 1). From chapter x. onwards, where Paul turns his attention more particularly to the Judaisers, we can gather, in verse after verse, the things which they were saying about him. He was bold only from a distance (x. 1, 2). His outward appearance was base, and his speech contemptible (x. 1, 10, 11). Compared with themselves he was inferior, despite his pretensions (x. 12–15); and what he preached was a poor edition of the Gospel (xi. 4); and the Corinthian church was a poor-grade church in so far as it was Pauline (xii. 13, xi. 7–9). He was not truly an apostle (xi. 5, xii. 11, 12). He did not have the qualifications or credentials which *they* (from Jerusalem) could boast (xi. 22–8). Even in his refusing financial support there was a hidden simulation and an admission of inferiority (xii. 16–19).

Paul is not slow to expose these fine-feathered birds as in reality birds of prey. *They* were dignified enough to take all the material benefit they could extract (xi. 20)! *They* were the Gospel aristocracy indeed, but as "ministers of Christ" what had they been prepared to suffer? (xi. 22–3). *They* spoke of visions and revelations, but what if Paul tells them that *he* had been lifted up to

the third heaven and had been given abundance of such apoca-
lypses as it would be profanation to divulge? (xii. 1–7). It is plain
that throughout "Paul is combating a systematic and cunning
attempt to overthrow his authority at Corinth, in which the Judæan
emissaries took the lead, supported by a minority in the Church.
By these men he was attacked openly, and with the most malicious
weapons. They aimed at nothing short of his deposition from the
apostleship and at bringing the churches founded by Paul under
the direction of Jerusalem." Painful as the personal slurs upon
himself must have been to the generous-hearted Paul, the more
deadly hurt was that under cover of the *personal* there was an
insinuating perversion of the *doctrinal*. In the words of chapter
xi. 3, 4, "*Another* Jesus . . . *another* spirit . . . *another* gospel"
were being speciously substituted for "the simplicity that is in
Christ."

Contents and Analysis

There seems to be an idea that while the first Corinthian letter
is the most systematic of all Paul's writings, this second is least
so: yet surely an observant exploring of its contents reveals otherwise. The first is deliberative, objective, practical, and answers
the Corinthians with an almost sermonic firstly, secondly, thirdly;
whereas this second is sensitively subjective, and has been well
described as "the impassioned self-defence of a wounded spirit to
erring and ungrateful children." Just because it is the most emotional of the epistles, it is the least formal; yet even *that* remark
applies only to its subsidiary sections and not to its main contour.
This is no unguided torrent. Even the rapids rush along a planned
course.

To begin with, it is plain as can be that in the opening chapters
Paul is giving an *account of his ministry,* and in such a way as
to clear himself against cruel misrepresentations. As indicative of
this, see chapters i. 6, 12, 17, 23, ii. 4, 17, in all of which he is
laying bare the genuineness of his *motive.* See also chapters iii.
6, 12, iv. 1, 3, 5, 18, v. 14–21, in all of which he is defending the
genuineness of his *message.*

It is equally clear that at chapter vi. there is a change; for,
beginning with the words "We then, as workers together with
Him, beseech you . . .", Paul launches out on an appeal to his
converts at Corinth, which continues to the end of chapter ix. See

chapters vi. 1, 11–17, vii. 1–4, in all of which the appeal concerns things *spiritual*. See also viii. 7, 11, 24, ix. 5–7, 13, in all of which the appeal concerns things *material*.

The further break at chapter x. is patent to all. Here is Paul's all-out *answer to his critics*. See chapters x. 2, 7, 10, 12, 15, 16, 18, xi. 3–5, 12–15, in all of which he hits at his critics' *pretensions*. See also the passage xi. 16–xiii. 10, throughout which he shows and uses his own *credentials*.

We may say that the first part (i.–v.) is *explanation*; the second part (vi.–ix.) *exhortation*; and the third part (x.–xiii.) *vindication*. In the first part we have Paul the *minister* (iii. 6, iv. 1); in the second part Paul the *father* (vi. 13); and in the third part Paul the *apostle* (xi. 5, xii. 11, 12). So, then, we can now set the epistle out in framed analysis. We purposely avoid a more detailed analysis, for the sake of seeing at a glance the main form and force of the epistle.

THE SECOND EPISTLE TO THE CORINTHIANS

Key i. 3.   CHRIST OUR COMFORT AMID TRIAL

Introduction, i. 1, 2.
1. PAUL'S ACCOUNT OF HIS MINISTRY (i.–v.).
(Explanation: Paul the Minister.)

(A) As to the motive (i.–ii.).
(B) As to the message (iii.–v.).

2. PAUL'S APPEAL TO HIS CONVERTS (vi.–ix.).
(Exhortation: Paul the Father.)

(A) Concerning things spiritual (vi., vii.).
(B) Concerning things material (viii., ix.).

3. PAUL'S ANSWER TO HIS CRITICS (x.–xiii.).
(Vindication: Paul the Apostle.)

(A) The critics and their pretensions.
(B) The apostle and his credentials.
Conclusion, xiii. 11–14.

Doctrine through the Crucible of Experience

Our leader-article on these Christian Church Epistles drew attention to the *order* in which the Holy Spirit here teaches evangelical truth. It is the order of the wording in 2 Timothy iii. 16: "Doctrine . . . reproof . . . correction." Distinctively in Romans we have doctrine; in Corinthians reproof; in Galatians correction. The "doctrine" inculcates the *norm*. The "reproof" reprehends wrong *practice*. The "correction" objurgates wrong *teaching*. Now that we have travelled through both these Corinthian letters we can see how truly they conform to *their* part of the pattern, the second equally with the first. The bulk of both is reproof. Precious "doctrine" there is in both, as we said before; but whereas in Romans doctrine is delivered didactically, in these Corinthian letters it occurs only *incidentally* to the build-up of reproof, appeal, defence, exhortation.

We gave samples of this in the first Corinthian epistle. Take just a few from the second. Whereas in Romans the "righteousness of God" is discussed doctrinally as a basic subject of Christian theology, here in 2 Corinthians it appears incidentally as a reason for Paul's urgency (v. 21). Whereas the believer's death judicially with Christ is argued out doctrinally in Romans v. and vi., here it suddenly reappears as one of Paul's constraining incentives in preaching the Gospel (v. 14, R.V.). Whereas in Romans viii. we are taught, quite independently of any personal reference, how "the sufferings of this present time" are to be overwhelmingly compensated in the ultimate consummation, here in 2 Corinthians iv. 17 it slips in as a supporting consolation to the Christian evangelist amid his distresses. We have not space here to give other instances, but we recommend further pursuance of these Romans-versus-Corinthians parallels as being spiritually profitable. They show us how to relate the great doctrines of our Christian faith to individual experience and circumstances.

The Two Covenants and Ministries (iii.-iv.)

Such an array of spiritual treasures as we have in 2 Corinthians baffles any hope of ever summarising them worthily in the few pages here left to us. Each of the three parts is rich and full and fascinating. Take, for example, the contrast between the two covenants or ministries, the old versus the new, in chapters iii.

and iv. The key to the passage is chapter iii. 6: "God hath made us sufficient as ministers of a new covenant" (R.V.). Thereupon follows a seven-point contrast between the "ministration" of the *Law* and that of *Grace*.

1. The old covenant was that of the *"letter"* (the "letter engraven on stones"—verse 7, R.V.); the new covenant is that of the *Spirit* (iii. 6).
2. The old covenant was a ministration of *death*; the new is a ministration of *life*. "The letter killeth, but the Spirit giveth life" (iii. 6).
3. The old covenant was one of *condemnation*; the new is a ministration of *righteousness* (iii. 9).
4. The old covenant was *transitory*; the new is *permanent*— "that which remaineth" (iii. 11).
5. The old gathers round the face of *Moses*; the new shines from the face of *Jesus Christ* (iv. 6).
6. The symbol of the old covenant was a *veil*; that of the new covenant is a *mirror* (iii. 13–18).
7. The old could not change *heart-hardness* (iii. 14, R.V.); under the new we are "changed into the same image [of the Lord] by the Spirit" (iii. 18).

Running through this series of contrasts between the old covenant and the new, we find the "veil" mentioned again and again. The symbol of the old ministry is a "veil" hiding the face of *Moses*. The symbol of the new is a "mirror" reflecting the face of *Jesus* (iii. 18, R.V.).

Now in this passage Moses' veil has four remarkable significances. First, it is a sign of *transitoriness*: "Moses put a veil upon his face, that the children of Israel should not look stedfastly on the end of that which was passing away" (iii. 13, R.V.). The usual idea is that Moses wore that veil because the shining from his face was too bright for the Israelites to look upon; but here Paul says that he wore it so that they should not see its *passing away*! The common misunderstanding is due to the insertion of *"till"* in Exodus xxxiv. 33 by our Authorised Version. The word is italicised because it does not occur in the Hebrew. It should be replaced by "when," as in the Revised Version. The veil betokened something which was *passing*.

Second; that veil becomes a symbol of *Jewish unbelief*: "Their minds were hardened: for until this day the same veil remaineth untaken away in the reading of the old covenant" (iii. 14). It is astonishing that both our standard English versions complete this fourteenth verse by adding: "Which *veil* is done away in Christ." But if it still "remaineth," how can it at the same time be "done away"? Fortunately both versions put the word "veil" in italics, which tells us that it does not occur in the Greek. Obviously the clause should read: "Which *covenant* [i.e. the old] is done away in Christ." The old covenant *is* done away; but, alas, the blinding veil remains. See verse 15: "But even unto to this day, when Moses is read, the veil is upon their heart."

Third, and tragic beyond words, Moses' veil becomes a figure of *Satanic deception*: "But if our Gospel be veiled, it is veiled to them that are perishing, in whom the god of this age hath blinded the minds of the unbelieving" (iv. 5, R.V.). Here the veil is over the millions of unconverted, unregenerate, unsaved souls in Christendom, and is in the hand of Satan! That is why preaching is not enough, however faithful it may be; there must be wrestling in *prayer*!

Fourth, Moses' veil, by very contrast, sets off the transforming *glory-light of the Gospel*: "But we all, with *unveiled* face, reflecting as a mirror the glory of the Lord, are transformed into the same image" (iii. 18, R.V.). Here the veil is taken away "by the Spirit of the Lord." See also iv. 6: "God, who told light to shine out of darkness, hath shined into our hearts to irradiate [others through us] with the knowledge of the glory of God in the face of Jesus Christ." What an unveiling—"by the Spirit"! What an outshining—from "the face of Jesus Christ"! What a transfiguration—"reflecting as a mirror"! What a ministry—the "irradiation" of others with the "knowledge" which saves! The receivers become reflectors. God shines *in* that *we* may shine *out*!

Treasure in Earthen Vessels

Yes, what a message! Yet the writer is just up from a sick bed, and cannot help thinking how frail is the poor, earthen vessel which conveys such treasure: "But we have this treasure in earthen vessels" (iv. 7). See the sharp contrasts which now become vivid to his mind—"earthen vessels," yet the "power of

God" (verse 7); "troubled" yet "not distressed" (verse 8); "perplexed" yet "not in despair" (verse 8); "persecuted" yet "not forsaken" (verse 9); "struck down" but "not destroyed" (verse 9); the "outward man" perishing, the inward man daily "renewed" (verse 16); present "affliction," but a coming compensation of "glory" (verse 17); visible things evanescent, but the invisible ever-abiding (verse 18); this mortal body (only a "tabernacle") being taken down, but an imperishable "house in heaven" (v. 1); "absent" from the body, "at home" with the Lord (verse 8).

There can be no doubt that Paul's inward crisis and bodily sickness in the interval between leaving Ephesus and reaching Corinth left a deep mark on his thinking and subsequent ministry. It had been suddenly forced upon his mind that he himself would probably die before the Lord's return occurred. He talks of being "absent from the body" and *thus* being "present with the Lord." At first he shrinks from this thought of dying; "We do not want to be unclothed" (v. 4); but as he muses that to be "absent from the body" is to be "present with the Lord," even death is so robbed of gloom and robed in glory that he says: "We should be better pleased to leave our home in the body, and make our home with the Lord" (verse 8, Weymouth). It marks an epoch in his ministry. Hitherto the *parousia* had been expected as imminent, but now an extended vista is seen stretching ahead, which affects all the apostle's future teaching.

The various relations of the Gospel, and of the Church, and of the individual Christian, to domestic and civil and other earthly concerns are discussed in suchwise as they could not have been while Paul lived in the daily expectation of our Lord's return.

Yes, there was a struggle and a turning-point; but a chastened and enriched Paul rose from that sick-bed "with a serene and lofty spirit, master of the fears within, and assured that he would prevail in the fightings which had well-nigh overwhelmed him from without." Is there not here a spiritual lesson for ourselves? How much we owe to those terrifying cyclones of trouble and problem and suffering which have sometimes swirled around us, yet have brought us our deepest discoveries of truth and our richest revelations of God! Let past experience teach us to trust and rest and not be afraid!

The Heart of Pauline Theology

Paul completes this first part of his epistle by unveiling that which lay at the very heart of his ministry and message. It occupies chapter v. 14–21, and its centre-point is: "One died for all . . . and rose again" (verses 14, 15). But we call attention here to the "wherefore" which arises out of this, in verse 16:

"Wherefore, henceforth know we no man after the flesh: yea, though we have known Christ after the flesh, yet now henceforth know we Him [thus] no more."

It shows us at once that a true view of the Cross gives us a true view of *men*.

"We know no man after the flesh." Why? Because *"One died for all."* If the One died for all, then all must be of equal fundamental value. This has been revolutionary in history. This is the driving conviction behind all the world-girdling missionary activity of our Christian era. "One died for all"; Paul no longer asks whether a man is Jew or Gentile, slave or free, rich or poor, scholar or illiterate; these are earthly and superficial classifications. "One died for all"; we need to see humanity in the light of that Cross again today. Fierce nationalisms exalt rival bloods. Heartless totalitarianisms obliterate individual human worth and dignity. The Cross levels all yet preserves each. It dignifies even while it humbles. When we see our human species in the light of Calvary, each member is a *soul* made in the image of God, and worth redeeming even though it costs the blood and passion of Heaven's incarnate Son.

"We know no man after the flesh." Why? Because "If One died for all, *then all died*" (verse 14, R.V.). In His incarnation Christ became identified with the Adam creation, for He was made "in the likeness of sinful flesh"; yet He was sinless and separate, the representative Man of a new order which must ultimately prevail. In Him the old order is positionally done away. When He died, *all* men died in the judicial reckoning of God; for the death penalty already overhanging the sinful Adamic creation was then executed. By the threefold law of identification, representation and substitution, all men died in the death of Christ, so far as involuntary guilt and condemnation through

Adam are concerned. God now deals with the race on a new basis. It swings round a new Centre-Man. Paul thus sees humanity in a new way; and so must we. Everything is determined in relation to *HIM*. We know no man "after the flesh," as merely a member of the Adamic race, or as filling this or that place in the visible and temporal order; we see everything and every man in relation to Christ. What does it now matter ultimately what a man's place is in the Adamic scheme of things, since that basis of reckoning is done away? What matter whether a man be rich or poor or anything else? The vital thing is his relation to Christ. That is the deciding factor by which men are either saved or lost. "Therefore, henceforth know we no man after the flesh."

"We know no man after the flesh." Why? Because the One who died for all *"rose again,"* and if any man be in Him "he is a new creation" (verse 17). In both the Authorised and the Revised Versions the words "he is" are put in italics, indicating that they do not occur in the original. The verse simply says, "Therefore, if any man be in Christ—new creation," meaning that *there* is the new creation, seen through that person; "old things are passed away; behold all things are become new!" How can we any longer view him according to the values of the old when he is now in the new?

"We know no man after the flesh." Why? Because we no longer know even Christ Himself in that way (verse 16). What though some of us remembered the face, the voice, the dress? To us, who have died with Him and risen again in newness of life, no longer is He first of all a fellow-countryman, or even an historically fixable figure; He is the eternal Son of God. We know Him now, not in the weakness of the flesh, but in the limitless dimensions of His resurrection and the new creation! During the past half-century there has been a marked revival of interest in *the Jesus of history*. It has high value. We prize all new light which can be thrown upon "the days of His flesh." Yet if our ruling concept of Christ is merely that of an historical Figure, we know Him only "after the flesh," which is rudimentary and inadequate. Nor is He any more the pinioned Christ of the crucifix; for He is no longer on the Cross or shedding His blood. He is neither on the Cross nor in the grave, for atonement is complete and death is conquered. We are to know Christ, not simply as an august and pathetic Figure of tradition, but as the living contemporary of all generations. A merely historic Christ can be but the object of *memory*; whereas the risen Lord of the new creation is the object of *faith* and the communicator of new spiritual *life*.

"We know no man after the flesh." Why? Because as Christian believers we are now (or should be) living among the eternal things. Look back over the larger context here. See how Paul views everything from a spiritual and eternal standpoint—iv. 16, 17, 18, v. 1, 8, 9, 10. Already, even while still labouring on earth, he is moving in mind and heart and spirit among the invisible and eternal things; that is his true home—and ours.

The Apostle Paul Autobiographically

In devoting the foregoing pages to the first part of this epistle, we have been fully aware that there would not be space left for us to deal similarly with the other two parts. It was necessary, however, to make selection; and we hope that these "findings" from the earlier chapters may usefully preface the student's own further study of the remainder. The simple analysis which we have given of this epistle will serve to point out the main pathways.

Every section has its own unique interest and treasures. Even when Paul is talking about a collection he must utter, though quite incidentally, great pronouncements like viii. 9 and ix. 8, and the very thought of a gift from Corinth reminds him of the "unspeakable gift" from heaven.

But especially in this epistle should those passages be explored where Paul in his enforced "boasting" speaks about himself. Oh, what a servant of the Lord! How poor, mean, selfish, lazy some of us feel, by contrast! Yet what comfort, also, his reminiscences bring to us! We revert to just one of them here, before ending this present study. And what an eye-opener it is as to the inner life of this great-hearted champion! It is the passage in which he tells about his "thorn in the flesh" (xii. 1–10).

See how the chapter begins: "Fourteen years ago . . . caught up to Paradise . . . abundance of revelations . . . Lest I should be exalted above measure . . . a thorn in the flesh, the messenger of Satan to buffet me. . . ." The Greek word translated "thorn" comes from a verb which means to impale or crucify. Paul's thorn was not the sort with which we prick a finger. It was a *stake*

(see R.V. margin) on which, so to speak, he was transfixed, even
as his Lord had been transfixed to that beam and crossbar on
Golgotha. More, as Paul was pinioned to this stake there was
an *angel* of Satan (not just "messenger") continually buffeting
him! Satan has his angels! There are harassing spirits as well
as ministering spirits. Need we be surprised that the arch-fiend
should set apart one of his subordinates solely to concentrate on
Paul? This is how Weymouth translates it:

"Lest I should be over-elated there has been sent to me, like
the agony of an impalement, Satan's angel dealing blow after
blow."

What depth of *agony* here!—and dragging on for *fourteen
years* up to the time of Paul's writing! Three times he had pleaded
with his Lord to end it, but the reply had been otherwise; so it
seemed as if the inward crucifixion must continue to life's end!

Well, what can Paul do about it? Shall he complain to Christ
that He is cruelly unfair? Shall he give up the unequal struggle,
and escape from such penalised apostleship into restful retirement? This is his own reply: "He said unto me: My grace is
sufficient for thee; for My strength is made perfect in [thy] weakness. Most gladly therefore will I rather *GLORY IN MY IN-
FIRMITIES THAT THE POWER OF CHRIST MAY REST
UPON ME.*"

The whole paragraph is *full* of the most precious and moving
spiritual lessons, but we cannot linger over them here. Rather,
we must close this study by quoting and praying the threefold
benediction (the fullest in the New Testament) with which Paul
closes this most moving epistle:

"The grace of the Lord Jesus Christ, and the love of God, and
the communion of the Holy Spirit, be with you *ALL*."

How small in size, how big in meaning is that little word "all,"
here! Hundreds of those long-ago Achaian believers owed their
salvation to Paul, though some of them had later criticized him
cruelly. His benediction includes them all.

Yes, "with you *ALL*"—even with those who have spoken most
bitterly against him. God give *us* a like spirit!

NOTE ON PAUL'S TRINITARIAN BENEDICTION

The last verse of 2 Corinthians has become the best-known benediction in Christendom, and well merits reflection. Whether, as some expositors aver, it is "alone sufficient to prove the Biblical doctrine of the Trinity" is open to question; but taken with all the other cognate intimations of Scripture, it certainly "completes the evidence". We may fairly claim that it indicates three ultimate truths as to the plurality of the Deity, as follows.

Trinity

Surely beyond all cavil, *three* distinct personal Entities are differentiated in the phraseology. All will agree that "the Lord Jesus Christ" is a real person, and that here, as elsewhere, He is personally distinguished from the One who is here called "God". All will agree that the One who is here called "God" is also meant to be understood as personal, and is called "the Father" in corresponding passages. All must agree that "the Holy Spirit" is here mentioned in exactly the same way, as though similarly personal and similarly distinguishable. If this be not the intended meaning here, then these interlinked phrases are blameworthily misleading. We know, however, from comparison with other passages, that this is precisely what Paul *did* mean: the Deity is tripartite, subsisting as three personal Beings, the Father, the Son, the Holy Spirit.

Equality

But does not this benediction also imply that these Three are *equal*? If not, then again the grammatical form is strangely deceiving. If, as the various unitarian sects say, Christ is but a creature, and the Holy Spirit only an impersonal emanation, then does it not border on blasphemous confusion for this benediction to associate them so closely, so co-actively, so supremely, with the One who alone is God? And if, as even some Trinitarians hold, the Son and the Holy Spirit are essentially subordinate to the Father, why, in such a formal, measured benediction, is the Son mentioned before the Father? Would not the Father most certainly have been given priority of mention here if there were eternal priority of status? In various other passages the Father *is* given priority of mention; but the very inversion of that order, in this benediction, shows that there is no rigid uniformity, and that the order of mention is determined simply by sequence of thought. That there is *functional* subordination of the Son and Holy Spirit to the Father, in the economy of creation and redemption, we do not deny. But the Trinity considered economically must be distinguished from the Trinity considered essentially. Subordination must not be confused with inequality. Any such subordination is volitional and operational, not fundamental. It is functional, not essential. Father, Son, and Holy Spirit are co-equal.

Unity

Still further, this benediction implies that the Father, the Son, and the Holy Spirit, besides being three and being equal, are *one*. They are not only a trinity; they are a tri*unity*; and the old hymn puts it truly—"Three in One, and One in Three". Nothing less than that is required by this Pauline benediction; for if, as we have seen, the phrasing implies that the Three are equally Divine, then although we ourselves cannot grasp the mystery of it, They simply *must* somehow be one; there cannot possibly be three separate Infinites; even infinity itself can hold only one Infinite. If the Scriptures assign Divine attributes to each of the Three, then the Three *must* be one in essence, for there can be only one absolute God.

Finalizing proof

But the finalizing proof of all this lies in the fact that this benediction is in reality a *prayer*. The words, "I pray that", are to be understood at the beginning of it, just as really as if Paul had written them with pen and ink. Who would deny that? Who would say that this benediction was a mere optative wish? Its supreme attractiveness lies in the fact that it is a prayer with an expected answer. But prayer is to be offered to God alone. Why then is it offered to the Lord Jesus Christ and the Holy Spirit equally with God the Father? If They are not equally God, why are They also and equally invoked in such a prayer? How strange for an inspired apostle to pray to a mere creature, and an impersonal influence along with the one true God!

If Christ be but exalted man or angel, how strange for Paul to solicit the "grace" of that man or angel as on the same level with the "love" of God Himself! How strange that in such a considered and deliberate farewell-prayer Paul should place the name of mere man or even angel before that of the eternal God! And how strange, if Christ be a mere creature, that Paul should here pray to him as having the God-like prerogative of conferring spiritual qualities! Yes, it is indeed strange, if Christ be not "very God of very God"!

And if the Holy Spirit is merely an effluence or attribute, how strange that Paul should pray to such an impersonal concept in abstraction from the living Deity Himself, in and of whom are *all* such attributes and emanations! How *could* prayer be prayed to an attribute or influence? Yet here, in this benediction, the Holy Spirit is not only prayed to, but presumably is expected, as an intelligent, self-acting agent, to impart blessing distinct from that which the Father and the Lord Jesus confer. There is the same distinction here indicated as that which exists between Christ and the Father.

Surely, then, this parting pen-prayer furnishes clear proofs of personal tripartition in the Godhead—proofs which, so far as we know, have never been satisfactorily countered by unitarian authorities, and which, so far as we can see, cannot possibly be overthrown.

THE EPISTLE TO THE GALATIANS (1)

Lesson Number 133

NOTE.—For this study read the whole of this short epistle through at least twice, in the Revised Version, and at a single sitting.

Galatia, like Corinth, had been disturbed by "troublers" imported from Judæa; and a considerable interval must be allowed for their coming and the dissemination of their views, and, again, for full information of their disastrous success reaching the apostle. . . . The apostle's adversaries, while sparing him (in Galatia) the indignities cast upon him at Corinth, did not fail to intimate that his ministry was of an inferior and secondary order. His knowledge of the Gospel, so they said, and his authority to preach it, came from Peter and the Twelve, against whom he now dares to measure himself! "James and Cephas and John," they exclaimed—these are the "pillars" of the faith, "the men in repute" everywhere through the Church! This Paul, with his excessive pretensions, is an upstart—a mere novice compared with the others. And besides, he is inconsistent with himself: it is well known that he formerly "preached" the rite of "circumcision," which in Galatia he so bitterly opposes (v. 11). In Galatia, therefore, as in Corinth, the personal and the doctrinal matters under discussion are involved in each other. But here the theological question, which in 2 Corinthians was lying in the shade, comes to the front and presents itself in its full breadth and its momentous import. It occupies the central and largest part of the letter, being pursued through three chapters of the most profound, condensed, and powerful argument ever expressed in writing.

—*G. G. Findlay.*

THE EPISTLE TO THE GALATIANS (1)

THE PAULINE POLEMIC AGAINST GOSPEL PERVERSION

THIS epistle to "the churches of Galatia" is a kind of polemic pamphlet rather than an ordinary letter. Yet it *is* a letter, atmosphered in the warm emotion and personal concern of the writer for those to whom he wrote. The specious and ever-recurring error which it counters and corrects, and the masterly case which it presents with equal passion and logic, make it an arresting little document to all who sense what is at stake in the struggle to preserve the purity of the Gospel in the earth. It is an altogether remarkable blend of Divine inspiration with human skill and fervour.

As we have noted, the nine "Church" epistles (Romans to 2 Thessalonians) fall into a triform grouping. This Galatian epistle completes the first group (Romans, 1 and 2 Corinthians, and Galatians), which we have called the four *evangelical* epistles. In an earlier study we drew attention to 2 Timothy iii. 16: "All scripture is given by inspiration of God, and is profitable for doctrine, for reproof, for correction"; and we pointed out that the groups of epistles observe the order there indicated, i.e. "doctrine . . . reproof . . . correction." Thus, in this first group we have, distinctively, "doctrine" in Romans; "reproof" of wrong practice in Corinthians; "correction" of wrong doctrine in Galatians. We may well say, especially to young converts: Read Romans to be *grounded* in Christian doctrine; read Corinthians to be *guided* in Christian practice; read Galatians to be *guarded* against deceptive error.

C. H. Spurgeon once said: "No man can be a Christian in these days without being a controversialist." If that was true in Spurgeon's days, it is even truer now. But it was true right at the beginning, in Paul's day, as this Galatian letter bears witness. One of the mighty ways in which Paul fought "the good fight of the faith" was the writing of his epistles. What gallant contending for "the truth of the Gospel" they reveal! We may well thank God for those of them which have been providentially preserved to us in our dear old Bible. What mighty argument, what exalted contending, what nobleness of motive, and what costly devotion to truth they exhibit! Every one of them marks a battle fought by the grand apostle on behalf of Gospel faith and freedom, and this is pre-eminently true of the Epistle to the Galatians.

In Paul's time the name "Galatia" had two different usages. More commonly it meant the strip of country (to the north of Asia Minor) inhabited by the Galatai, or Galatians (an offshoot of the Gauls); but in a Roman and imperial sense it was the name of a whole Roman province, of which the little *country* of Galatia was but a part. So the question has arisen as to which Galatia Paul addresses in his letter. The matter is too complicated to discuss here. For our own part, after carefully weighing the pros and cons, we incline to think that the epistle was sent to the actual *country* of Galatia.

Paul's Visits to Galatia

It is generally agreed, from Paul's words in chapter iv. 13— "I preached the Gospel unto you the first [or former] time"— that he had visited Galatia *twice* before he wrote there. The record in the Acts of the Apostles corresponds with this. We are there told that Paul went to Galatia on his second missionary tour (Acts xvi. 6); and that he paid a second visit there during his third missionary tour, some three years later (xviii. 23).

The First Visit

About the earlier of these two visits we are told two notable facts. First, it was occasioned through bodily illness. The Revised Version brings this out clearly: "Ye know that *because of an infirmity of the flesh* I preached unto you the *first* time" (Gal. iv. 13). Paul apparently had not intended preaching in Galatia, but he was suddenly smitten by a violent attack of some malady which evidently affected his appearance, and which might easily have caused the Galatians to "despise" him (iv. 14). It was to this sickness that the Galatians owed their knowledge of the Gospel. (How God overrules seeming setbacks!) Second, despite this bodily sickness and disfigurement, the Galatians had welcomed him with a warmth and responsiveness which were remarkable, even allowing for their naturally demonstrative Gallic temperament. "That which was a temptation to you in my flesh ye despised not, nor rejected; but ye received me as an angel of God, as Christ Jesus. . . . I bear you witness that if possible ye would have plucked out your eyes and given them to me" (iv. 14, 15, R.V.). The melting fervency of the homeless, stricken preacher, and the sympathetic responsiveness of the hearers, had outmatched all physical discouragements. Amid their hearty hospitality the convalescing apostle-evangelist had lingered probably for several months.

The Second Visit

But Paul's *second* visit there had been far less reassuring to him. He had sensed a changed atmosphere. He had detected unhealthy symptoms among the Galatian believers which caused him uneasiness. References to this second visit are not difficult to detect in the epistle. He had found it needful at that time to charge them that they should hold as "accursed" any who perverted the Gospel as it had come to them from his own lips (i. 9). He asks: "Am I become your enemy because of my speaking the truth to you?" (iv. 16)—and these words must refer to his second visit, for there had been no enmity on his first visit, and the enmity could not have been occasioned by the epistle, which they had not yet read! Then again, he reminds them in his epistle that he had already needed to warn them—evidently on his second visit—against excesses and errors (v. 21). But it is evident all through the epistle that Paul is combating some deadly mischief among the Galatians which he had detected and denounced, in its beginnings, during his second visit, and which, alas, had further developed up to the time of his now writing to them.

The Galatian Error

And *what* was the main Galatian error? Paul calls it *"another gospel,* which is *not another"* (i. 6, 7), and then adds: "There be some that trouble you and would *pervert* the Gospel of Christ." It is unfortunate that our Authorised Version puts the word "another" twice here, for Paul uses two different Greek adjectives (as the R.V. indicates). The first adjective (*heteros*) means "another of a *different* kind"; whereas the second adjective (*allos*) means "another of the *same* kind." Paul would have the Galatians definitely to understand that they were being drawn away, not to a superior form of the same Gospel (as they gullibly supposed), but to something which was essentially different. And then, to make his meaning finally clear, he adds that the real bent of these troublers was to "*pervert*" the "Gospel of Christ." The Greek verb here translated as "pervert" means, literally, to twist a thing round, or reverse it. In reality these troublers of the Galatians were not giving them merely "another Gospel of the same kind," with supposedly superior features: they were twisting the *one and only* "Gospel of Christ," and reversing its meaning into something which it never meant at all.

Paul does not leave us in any doubt as to the *nature* of the Galatian defection. After his opening salutation, his very first word is: "I marvel that ye are so quickly removing from Him that called you into the *GRACE OF CHRIST*, unto a different gospel." Speaking summarily, that was both the first and the final thing about the Galatian failure—they were erring from that *absolutely distinctive* doctrine of the one true Gospel, that the eternal salvation of the soul is altogether of Divine *grace* in Christ, apart from religious observances and human merit-works of every kind. And what was it to which they were turning? Glance through the epistle. They were seeking to be "justified by the law" (v. 4). They were toying with the observance of "days and months and seasons and years" (iv. 10). They were yielding to the idea that the rite of circumcision was necessary (v. 2, vi. 12, 13). They were seeking to supplement the work of the Holy Spirit by law-works of the flesh (iii. 3). They were overlaying the simplicity and spirituality of the Gospel with Judaistic observances; and, indeed, it would seem that a fairly thorough conformity to the Law of Moses was becoming insisted on among them (iv. 21). It was not that the Gospel was being directly denied; but their minds were becoming inoculated with legalistic and ritualistic ideas which destroyed its vital doctrines.

Who were the mischief-makers in Galatia? At the time when Paul wrote his letter they appear to have been a group of Galatian believers themselves. Chapter vi. 13 speaks of them, in the present tense, as even then "undergoing" the Jewish rite of circumcision; which implies that this had not happened to them before, and that they were Gentiles. Chapter v. 12 perhaps points the same way: "I would that they which confuse you would even *mutilate themselves*" (i.e. Why do they stop at circumcision if they are so keen on sign-marks in the flesh? Why not mutilate themselves, as your own heathen priests of Cybele?). By native temperament these Gallic people were prone to a demonstrative and ritualistic type of religion. Nor must we forget that there was a nucleus of Jews among the Galatian believers; and these would not find it easy to *unlearn* all at once their hitherto bigoted Judaism.

But it seems equally clear that the movement had been *originated* by outside interference. The epistle as a whole leaves us in no doubt that the minds of the Galatians had been definitely influenced against Paul; and this could only have come, in the first place, from outside. It had happened too suddenly and too emotionally (i. 6, iv. 14–20) to be the product of a slow growth from within. When Paul asks, "O foolish Galatians, *who did bewitch you?*" (iii. 1), he clearly has in mind some definite time and some agency outside the Galatians themselves which marked the beginning of the changed attitude toward himself. The same applies to chapter v. 7: "Ye [all of you] were running well: *who did hinder you?*" And the same applies to chapter iv. 17: "*They* [as distinct from the 'ye' of verse 21] zealously seek you in no good way."

The Judaisers from Jerusalem

There was a group in Jerusalem who were set on spreading a Judaistic form of Christianity. Acts xv. tells of the trouble they caused at Antioch. Paul mentions such in this very epistle (ii. 12, etc.). He speaks of the "false brethren" of this sort in Jerusalem (ii. 4). We know how grievous was the influence of such "false apostles" upon the church at Corinth (see 2 Cor.). Some, apparently, carried "letters of commendation" (2 Cor. iii. 1). When actual emissaries from Jerusalem were not sent, contact would be made with leading Jews in the places where Christian churches had been formed; and these in turn would get their influence into the churches through the Jewish converts there. These Judaisers were the party whose representatives followed everywhere in the wake of Paul, undermining his work (Satan's ministers as "angels of light"!). It was these who from time to time nearly broke the apostle's heart, yet at the same time roused his intensest indignation. At Corinth the attack was mainly on Paul's apostleship: it was against Paul in a personal sense. In Galatia the attack was rather on Paul's *doctrine*, as the epistle shows by implication all through; though in Galatia too there had been no hesitation to disparage the apostle himself (see forenote to this present study).

To Paul the issue was as vivid as it was absolutely vital—the very Cross of Christ itself was imperilled by this plausible legalism of the Judaisers: for "IF RIGHTEOUSNESS COME BY THE LAW, THEN CHRIST IS DEAD IN VAIN" (Gal. ii. 21).

The Epistle Itself

We pass now from these preliminary considerations, to the epistle itself. It has been said with some truth that "in a writer like Paul," any analysing of his epistles into "systematic arrangement" must be "more or less artificial," especially where (as in Galatians) he is "stirred by deep feelings." Yet although Paul's epistles are a closely woven whole, their main thought-movements are always distinct and orderly. This is so with the Epistle to the Galatians. It runs in three clear movements of two chapters each. This is noticeable almost at a first reading. The first two chapters are a *narrative* (pertaining to Paul himself). The next two chapters are a *discussion* (pertaining to the Gospel). The remaining two chapters are an *exhortation* (pertaining to the Galatian believers). In other words, the first two chapters are *personal*; the middle two are *doctrinal*; the last two are *practical*.

But what is the *purpose* in each of these three parts? That is what we are after every time in these present studies. We are not concerned with analysis for its own sake, however minute and careful, but only from an *interpretative* point of view. It is the drift, the point, the significance, which we are after, in any given passage.

Chapters i. and ii.

Look, then, through the first two chapters of Galatians—the part where we have personal narrative. *Why* does Paul give this account of his movements? The usual idea is that he is here defending his apostleship: but if we are to be strictly exact, that rather misses the real purpose here. Read the chapters carefully again: Paul is here proving the genuineness, the *authenticity* of the *Gospel* which he preached.

He begins by saying that his apostleship was neither from nor through man, but of God (i. 1). His Gospel was "not after men," for he had neither received it nor been taught it of men—it had come by direct Divine revelation (verses 11, 12). And after he had received this direct revelation and commission he had "conferred *not* with flesh and blood" (verse 16). He certainly could not have got his Gospel second-hand from the other apostles (as his detractors were apparently alleging), for he had not gone up to Jerusalem at that time to see them (verse 17); and even when later, after the expiry of three years, he *had* gone up on a short visit, he had seen only Peter and James (verse 19). And, even after that, he had remained *still* unknown by face to the churches in Judæa (verses 22, 23). So there can be no doubt as to Paul's purpose here. It is to show that the Gospel which he preached was *genuine as to its origin*.

Chapter ii. continues this same authentication, but with a different emphasis. This Gospel which in all genuineness (i. 20) Paul had received direct from God he had later compared and checked off among the other apostles. Fourteen years after his first visit to Jerusalem he had gone there again for that very purpose (ii. 1, 2); and there had been thorough concurrence between them and himself (verses 6–10). So complete had been their agreement and mutual understanding as regards the central doctrine of salvation solely and wholly by *grace*, that when Peter and others, on a later occasion at Antioch, had lapsed into Judaistic behaviour Paul had been able to rebuke him on the very basis of that common understanding (ii. 11–21); so that the *circumstantial* "difference" between them had really been turned into another evidence of the *underlying agreement* which existed as to the true nature of the Gospel. Thus both by *comparing* (ii. 1–10) and by *contesting* (11–21) Paul had proved his Gospel to be identical in nature with what the other apostles preached.

Here, then, in chapters i. and ii., we have the AUTHENTICITY of the Gospel: (*a*) as to its *origin*, in chapter i.; and (*b*) as to its *nature,* in chapter ii. Moreover, these two chapters are important as showing the basic identity of the Gospel preached by Paul, Peter, and the other apostles. Beware of some today who play off "Pauline" versus "Petrine" versus "Johanine"!

Chapters iii. and iv.

We turn on to chapters iii. and iv. What is the real point of the theological argument here? Well, to begin with, we cannot but observe that Paul's attitude throughout is that of sheer surprise. He speaks as though it is almost incredible to him that anyone should turn back from the glorious liberty and superiority of the Gospel to the bondage and beggarliness of legalism. His first words are: "O foolish Galatians, who did bewitch you?"—as though he could only attribute it to some strange hypnotic spell. He picks up that word "foolish" again in verse 3: "Are ye so foolish?—having begun in the Spirit, do ye now attempt perfection through the flesh?" And again, in iv. 9, he asks: "How turn ye back again to the weak and beggarly elements whereunto ye desire to be in bondage again?" It is as though Paul feels almost nonplussed. Indeed, he actually says as much in iv. 20 (R.V.): "I am perplexed about you."

All through these two chapters Paul is showing the *superiority* of the Gospel over Judaism; of "the Spirit" over "the flesh" (iii. 3); of "faith" over "works" (iii. 2); of being "justified" over being held by law (verses 8, 11); of being "blessed" over being "cursed" (verses 9, 10); of the "promise" in Abraham over the command through Moses (verses 12–14); of the Abrahamic covenant over the Mosaic covenant (verses 16–22); of maturity over tutelage (verses 25, 26); of sonship over bondmanship (iii. 26, iv. 6); of "adoption," i.e. of adult-sonship status and privilege, over legal infancy, with its inability to inherit (iv. 1, 3, 5); of liberty over bondage (iv. 8, 21–31). What superiority indeed is all this! And what strange folly to lapse into legalism again!

Note, also, that while this one theme, the superiority of the Gospel, unites both these chapters, each strikes its own emphasis. A careful reading of chapter iii. will disclose that the focus-point is in the words of verse 7: "Know, therefore, that they which be of faith, the same are *the sons of Abraham*." The "therefore" denotes inference from what precedes. What do the earlier verses say? It was by *faith* that the *Holy Spirit* had been received; and that was the unarguable *evidence of sonship*. The rest of the chapter expands this: (*a*) Christ redeemed us from the curse of the Law that the promise of the Spirit might be fulfilled to us through faith (see verses 10–14). (*b*) The giving of the Law did not override the Abrahamic promise (verses 15–29). The chapter closes with a reiteration of its special emphasis: "Ye are all *sons of God* through faith in Jesus Christ" (verse 26); "If ye are Christ's, then are ye *Abraham's seed*" (verse 29). So the emphasis in this third chapter is on "sonship." In other words, here is the superiority of the Gospel demonstrated by the superior new *relationship* into which it brings us.

In chapter iv. the emphasis is on the *privileges* of this sonship. Taking up from that word "heir" in the last sentence of chapter iii., Paul now stresses that to be a son is also to be an *heir* (see verses 1, 7, 30). Two words here sum up the believer's sonship privileges—"adoption" (verse 5) and "inheritance" (verse 30, R.V.). The Greek word here rendered "adoption" (as elsewhere in Paul's epistles) does not mean adoption in the common English sense of taking some orphan child to be one's own. It refers rather to adult sonship, to the coming of legal age, and the privileges which this confers. In Paul's day the reaching of adult sonship and legal heirship was commonly attested by public ceremony. The *public attestation* of the sonship of believers is yet to be (see the word "adoption" in Romans viii. 18–23); but already we enter into the privileges of adult sonship in a *spiritual* sense, because (as here, in Galatians iv. 6, 7) "God hath sent forth the Spirit of His Son into our hearts, crying, Abba Father: so that thou art no longer a bondservant, but a son; and if a son, then an heir through God" (R.V.).

Paul is amazed that the Galatians could listen to a "different" Gospel which would *cheat* them of these privileges; and he would have them realise sharply that their bewitching new teachers were playing that very trick on them: "They zealously seek you in no good way; nay, they desire to shut you out" (verse 17).

Finally he expounds the allegory of Isaac and Ishmael (verses 21–31). Believers, so to speak, are Isaac, to whom the inheritance in Abraham belongs; whereas to be under the Law is to be Ishmael, the son of the bondwoman, and rejected from the inheritance (verse 30). The inheritance here spoken of is that of the *promises* (iii. 14, 16–22, 29, etc.).

So, then, in chapters iii. and iv. we have the SUPERIORITY of the Gospel: (*a*) in the new *relation* which it effects, as in chapter iii., and (*b*) in the *privileges* which it confers, as in chapter iv.

Chapters v. and vi.

In the last two chapters we have Paul's *exhortation* to the Galatians. What is the gist of it? The opening verse tells us: "Stand fast, therefore, in *the liberty wherewith Christ hath made us free*." These two chapters concern our liberty in Christ in its practical application to life and conduct. There is nothing intricate about the passage. A few comments will suffice. Any careful eye will notice that *two aspects* of this liberty are spoken of here.

First, in chapter v. 1–15, it is the liberty of a *love-service* instead of a law-bondage. In verses 2 to 12, which are practically a parenthesis, Paul shows with a new drastic finality the alternative to this liberty in Christ: it is to be "debtors to the whole law" and to be "fallen away from grace." Then, at verse 13, connecting up again with verse 1, he shows that the true liberty of the Gospel is the liberty of love, not of licence (in answer, probably, to the insinuations of the false teachers, that Paul's doctrine of so-called liberty gave licence for sin).

Second, this liberty of the Gospel is the liberty of "*the Spirit*" in the place of bondage to "the flesh." This is brought out in the passage v. 16–vi. 10. No comment is needed here on these verses. At the end of chapter vi. verses 11 to 18 are really a postscript. Thus in chapters v. and vi. we have the LIBERTY of the Gospel: (*a*) the liberty of *love-service* instead of bondage to the law, as in v. 1–15; and (*b*) the liberty of *the Spirit* instead of bondage to the flesh, as in v. 16–vi. 10.

We may now set out our results in a brief analysis; but before doing so we ought to ask ourselves: What is the key idea running through this Galatians epistle? There can be only one answer. It is LIBERATION THROUGH THE GOSPEL. The word "liberty" in different grammatical forms (sometimes translated as "free") comes some ten times in the epistle. The *basis* of our liberty is given in chapters i. and ii., which demonstrate the *genuineness* of the Gospel and prepare for the doctrinal discussion which follows. Then the *truth* of our liberty is thrashed out in chapters iii. and iv. And, finally, the true effect of our liberty is shown in chapters v. and vi. The climax-note is struck at chapter v. 1: "STAND FAST, THEREFORE, IN THE LIBERTY WHEREWITH CHRIST HATH LIBERATED US."

(*For analysis see flyleaf to next study*)

THE EPISTLE TO THE GALATIANS (2)

Lesson Number 134

NOTE.—For this study go carefully through the epistle again, checking it off with the analysis given on this flyleaf.

> Whence but from Heaven could men unskilled in arts,
> In different ages born, in different parts,
> Weave such agreeing truths? Or how, or why,
> Should all conspire to cheat us with a lie?
> Unasked their pains, ungrateful their advice,
> Starving their gains, and martyrdom their price.
>
> — *Dryden.*

THE EPISTLE TO THE GALATIANS
Liberation through the Gospel

Salutation i. 1–5.

1. THE AUTHENTICITY OF THE GOSPEL (i. ii)

    (*Personal narrative*).

    Genuine as to its origin (i.).
    Genuine as to its nature (ii.).

2. THE SUPERIORITY OF THE GOSPEL (iii., iv.)

    (*Doctrinal argument*).

    In the new relation it effects (iii.).
    In the privileges it releases (iv.).

3. THE TRUE LIBERTY OF THE GOSPEL (v., vi.)

    (*Practical application*).

    Love-service ends law-bondage (v. 1–15).
    The Spirit ends flesh-bondage (v. 16–vi. 10)

Postscript vi. 11–18.

THE EPISTLE TO THE GALATIANS (2)

UP TO DATE AND URGENTLY NEEDED

LET NO one think that the issue raised in this epistle is one which belongs to a bygone day merely. It is as up to date as when it set Paul's pen in motion. The struggle between the true Gospel and its legalistic mutilators is a perpetual crisis. The outer circumstances may vary, but it is always the same vital truths which are at stake. The present-day apostles of the linsey-woolsey mixture of law and grace which Paul denounced are no longer Judaisers from Jerusalem; but their perversion of the Gospel is practically the same, and they inherit the same anathema. Who, in these days, thinks of observing Jewish rites and ordinances and holy-days as the way of acquiring justification before God? Yet that evil bewitchment, that "different" gospel which is anathematised in Galatians, is in substance the very religion which one hears preached up and down Christendom today.

Present-day Ritualism

Look at the Galatianism of the Roman Catholic Church! For deceptive ingenuity and imposing display it puts the "troublers" of Paul's day in the shade! See how that harlot of the seven hills mixes masses and crucifixes and confessionals and penances and ordinances and Mary-worship and saint-worship and all sorts of merit-works with the true Gospel of the grace of God in Christ, until "grace is no more grace" (Rom. xi. 6), and the real "truth of the Gospel" is sacrificed on the altar of superstition.

Look at the recrudescence of ritualism in the Church of England today! See how that church's cassocked clerics and mitred bishops turn the Lord's table into a priest's altar again! See how the Anglo-Catholic party are insisting on ritualistic forms and ceremonies which are as alien to the New Testament as darkness to light, or as disease to health. See with what airs of Galatianist superiority these gowned and frilled "high" churchmen look down on those of us who stick to the simple Gospel. We could laugh when we see what dressed-up sillies they make of themselves were it not for the deadly harm which they do because of their position as religious leaders. These high-blown Galatianists of the Anglican and other communities are tricking our people into the downgrade process which ends in kissing Peter's toe at Rome. The "troublers" in Paul's day exalted Peter at the expense of Paul, and Moses at the expense of Christ; and that is just what Romanism does today. Rome hates Paul. The Roman Church dare not allow its people to study the epistles of Paul for themselves: if it did, there would be awkward Luthers and Calvins springing up everywhere! The Galatian "mixing" process is seen in fully-developed presentation in the history of Romanism: it is the progressive mixing of faith and works, grace and law, Spirit and flesh, truth and error, Church and State, Christianity and Paganism, Christ and pseudo-Christ, God and the devil.

Present-day Radicalism

But it is not only in Romanism and ritualism that we see modern Galatianism. It comes to us with the bland smile of so-called "Modernism." Look at the Modernists, with their glorification of human scholarship, and their "gospel" of salvation by good character. This is just another expression of the same old evil which Paul attacked. It is the attempt to establish justification before God by the mixing of self-effort and human merit with Divine grace. The Cross alone is not sufficient: salvation must be partly, at least, by good character.

Up to date? There is no more up-to-date writing in the world than this little polemic to the Galatians! The force of the Reformation has largely spent itself. Protestantism has become leavened in great degree with the evil leaven of legalism. Law is mixed with grace again. The fatal error is rife, that merit-works and religious observances are part of the Christian message. This is found in all the so-called Protestant denominations: and the result is the same as was the result of the legalism in Paul's day, i.e. ironically enough, instead of making people really more godly, the insistence on human merit-works and outward ceremonial feeds the dangerous vanities in human nature, and engenders a deteriorated morality. Despite the supposedly superior form of Christianity which the Galatians were embracing, we find the apostle having to rebuke them for the most flagrant ill-behaviour (v. 19–21).

There is good cause today why we should read this epistle to the Galatians again and again, until its urgent truths have become thoroughly ingrained in our thinking. From first to last faith is the condition of salvation, and the Cross the all-sufficient ground of it. From first to last it is faith apart from works, grace apart from merit, Christ apart from Moses, and the Cross apart from ordinances. This Galatians epistle is Paul's most impassioned defence of the true Gospel. His supreme purpose, in his own words, is "THAT THE TRUTH OF THE GOSPEL MIGHT CONTINUE WITH YOU" (ii. 5). May God renew in our own hearts that same purpose and that same passion! The very life and soul of Christianity are at stake! God help us to fight this "good fight of the faith"!—for the fight goes on unslacked today, and will go on until Christ Himself returns and casts the arch-deceiver of mankind into the bottomless pit.

Treasure-trove in Galatians

But now we turn to some pleasanter considerations. This epistle, besides being a red lamp of warning against legalism, is a treasure-find of edifying truths. We could occupy much space exhibiting the good things in it which invite further study; but a few examples must suffice.

Turn again to the last of the three main parts of the epistle (chapters v. and vi.), where Paul's theme is the *true liberty of the Gospel*. We have seen that this liberty is shown in two aspects: (*a*) it is the liberty of a love-service in place of a law-bondage (v. 1–15); and (*b*) it is the liberty of "the Spirit" in place of bondage to "the flesh" (v. 16–vi. 10). In this latter section, where Paul speaks of the liberty of "the Spirit," he exhibits in a beautiful, fourfold way what the true expression of that liberty is. This Galatian epistle was written to groups of believers scattered through a rural area, in which most of the people were agricultural workers of one sort or another. In keeping with the mentality and circumstances of the Galatians, Paul uses language and metaphors which are specially appropriate to them. There were four kinds of "bearing" with which the Galatians were familiar above all else. These were: fruit-bearing, burden-bearing, seed-bearing, and brand-bearing (for, as many of the agricultural labourers were slaves, they were branded to indicate whose property they were). See now how Paul makes use of these things in expounding the true liberty of the Spirit:

FRUIT-BEARING: "The fruit of the Spirit is love, joy, peace, long-suffering, etc." (v. 22, 23).

BURDEN-BEARING: "Bear ye one another's burdens, and so fulfil the law of Christ" (vi. 2).

SEED-BEARING: "Whatsoever a man soweth, etc." (vi. 7). "Let us not be weary in well-doing, for . . . we shall reap" (verse 9).

BRAND-BEARING: "I bear in my body the marks [or brands] of the Lord Jesus" (vi. 17).

We have here a study as beautiful as it is practical. Many lessons are suggested, as, for instance, that in making contact with souls for Christ, we should stand on their own ground with them, as far as possible, talking to them in terms which are familiar and appropriate to them. Paul was a master of this art, as his epistles reveal.

But, of course, the great lesson to take to heart is that we ourselves are to be fruit-bearers, burden-bearers, seed-bearers, brand-bearers for our dear Lord's sake.

The fruit of the Spirit (v. 22, 23)

While we are in this section of the epistle, we ought to notice the way in which Paul speaks of the graces which the Holy Spirit produces in the life of the consecrated believer. He calls them the "fruit" of the Spirit. There are nine virtues enumerated; and at a first glance they seem to be written without any reference to order; but when they are more carefully examined they reveal a most significant progress. These nine go in three groups of three each. The first three—"love, joy, peace"—are states which I experience in my own heart; i.e. they directly concern myself. The next three—"longsuffering, gentleness, goodness"—are dispositions which I am to reveal toward others; i.e. they look out toward my neighbour. The third three—"faith, meekness (or humility), temperance (or self-control)"—are attitudes which I am to maintain as the very first essentials of godliness; they have special reference toward God. So these three trios respectively express the Christian life as concerns myself, my neighbour, and my Maker; or in other words, the first three look *inward,* the next three look *outward,* and the third three look *upward.*

These three trios cover all the relationships of life. They tell us that a life under the control of the Holy Spirit is one of full-orbed beauty. They indicate, also, that the true beauty of the Christian life consists in qualities of the heart rather than in outward doings. They stress the fact that what we *are* determines the value of what we *do.* Only the Holy Spirit can produce these qualities in the heart and life. There are close imitations; but in reality this love-life can only be the product of the indwelling and sanctifying Spirit. Nor ought we to miss the comfort of the truth that these inward, outward, and upward attitudes of the heart are spoken of as "fruit", i.e. they come by growth, not merely self-effort. Moreover, fruit comes gradually. Here is hope for some of us who have to lament many failures in the past and much weakness in the present! Christian virtues are "fruit"; they are growth from an inward life; and this growth is progressive. Would we know in experience this "fruit of the Spirit"? Then the secret is *utter monopoly of the heart* by the Spirit.

This is not all. These nine virtues or graces of the Spirit, besides going in three trios, are found to possess further beauties of arrangement. Each of the trios reveals a perfect order. Take the *first*: "love, joy, peace." Here, the first-mentioned of the three virtues is the foundation of the other two. So, first comes "love"; then comes "joy," which is love *exulting*; and then comes "peace," which is love *reposing.* Take the *second* trio: "longsuffering, gentleness, goodness." Here, again, the first-mentioned is the foundation of the other two. So, first comes "longsuffering"; then comes "gentleness," which is longsuffering in its *passive* expression; and then comes "goodness," which is longsuffering in its *active* expression. Take the *third* trio: "faith, meekness, self-control." Here, again, the first-mentioned is the foundation of the other two. So, first comes "faith"; then comes "meekness," which is the expression of faith *toward God*; and then comes "self-control," which is the expression of faith *in the life.* Perhaps there are still other hidden beauties in this fruit-cluster of graces!

Vivid Contrasts, Metaphors and Ideas

This Galatian epistle is remarkable for its vivid contrasts: grace versus law; faith versus works; the Spirit versus the flesh; circumcision versus new creation; the Cross versus the world; freedom versus bondage; the natural (Ishmael) versus the spiritual (Isaac); Christ versus Moses; and others. By means of such contrasts truth is made the more vivid and forceful; and the epistle is well worth careful study in its use of these contrasts.

But besides these there are some of the most memorable metaphors and ideas and sayings of the New Testament to be found in these six chapters. What about that awful anathema in chapter i. 8, 9? If there is one word more than another in the New Testament which the ritualists and modernists of our day need to ponder it is that anathema! What about those precious words in chapter ii. 20? What about that vital paragraph which defines the relationship of the Law as a pedagogue?

And what about that allegory of Ishmael and Isaac? What a commentary history has furnished on those two sons! Never were two more remarkable sons born. They were both covered in advance by notable prophecies. It was the Ishmaelites who bought and sold Joseph, long ago; and they have been connected with the slave business ever since. From this line came Mohammed, who chose as his ensign the moon at its darkest point, and took as his weapon the sword, and founded a religion which more than any other has oppressed woman and opposed Christ. On the other hand, from Isaac's line have come those blessings which have enriched the world beyond measure: the Scriptures of the Old and New Testaments, the world's Saviour, and the Gospel of the grace of God to men. Is it asked how two such strangely different sons could come from one father—the one to blight and the other to bless? The answer is found in Galatians iv. 21–31. These two sons were born of two different principles which struggled for the mastery in one man, Abraham. Ishmael was born of the flesh, and in unbelief. Isaac was born of "promise" in response to faith. What a study is the life of Abraham, as recorded in the Scriptures, and as showing the struggle between the two principles which struggled against each other, with faith ever gaining strength until it triumphed absolutely in the offering up of Isaac!

Note the two admonitions concerning the *liberty* of the Gospel (in v. 1, 13), expressing divergent aspects, yet both necessary and each balancing the other. We are to hold it fast and never let it go (1), yet to use it in love and never to abuse it (13).

Note the two admonitions concerning our Christian *"walk"* in chapter v. 16 and 25. In verse 16 the Greek word means our walk in general, our demeanour, settled habits and general conduct. But in verse 26 Paul uses a word with a military connection. It has to do with a rank of soldiers, and means that in all the *details* of our life we are to *"keep step"* with the Holy Spirit!

Note that arresting metaphor in chapter vi. 10, *"The household of the faith."* The Christian Church is the household of "the faith." This cannot be too strongly emphasised today, for the present breakdown in Christian faith is deplorable. One of the gravest misconceptions just now is that a Christian church is merely an association of persons brought together by similarity of humanitarian ideals, or by any other purely human sympathies, instead of its being a fellowship of faith, of *the* faith, of that faith which is based on certain unique facts and centred in certain great Divine truths. Nor let us forget that the true Church is a *"household."* The true Church is a *family*, with family relationships, and family affinities, and family privileges, and family obligations. Nor let us forget the separative implication of this metaphor. This "household of the faith" is clearly marked off from the rest of men and women. "As we have opportunity" we are to "do good unto all men," but *"especially* to them who are of the household of the faith." What joyous places our churches would be if this idea of the "household" and the family were really lived out among the Lord's people!

These are but a few of the thought-provoking, mind-enriching things which catch the eye in this epistle to the Galatians; but we think they are enough to show what fertile soil it is to those who have a mind to farm it.

Postscript

Even the postscript which Paul adds to this epistle is packed with striking sayings (vi. 11–18); but we call attention simply to the closing words: "From henceforth let no man trouble me; for I bear in my body the brands of the Lord Jesus." There were five classes of persons who were branded, i.e. *slaves* (as a mark of ownership), *soldiers* (as a mark of allegiance), *devotees* (as a mark of consecration), *criminals* (as a mark of exposure), and *the abhorred* (as a mark of reproach). The "marks" of the Lord Jesus in the body of Paul were all these five in one! And *what* were they? For part of the answer read 2 Corinthians xi. 23–8. (What a record!) Paul had been battered and bruised in ways which could not but leave permanent memorials in his poor body. Could he, for instance, have undergone that stoning at Lystra, after which he was dragged outside the city and left for dead, without bearing life-long effects? We do not know whether the five Jewish whippings would leave any abiding marks; but the three floggings by the Roman soldiers would plough lines which would remain for life. And besides these, there were those more barbarous violences which he suffered by the brutality of mobs, the ambush of enemies, and the assaults of robbers. Such had been his bodily hardships, and such must have been the effects, that by his appearance he would easily be taken for some deservedly wretched outcast, paying the penalty of his criminality. Indeed, in 1 Corinthians iv. 9–13 the apostle actually speaks of himself as being thus treated.

But *why* does the apostle mention these brands at the end of his Galatian letter? One reason is indicated by the fact that the "I" is emphatic: "*I* bear in my body the brands of the Lord Jesus." Paul here draws a contrast between himself and the Judaising teachers who were subverting the Galatian believers. These men were mouthing big pretensions; but did *they* bear the brand-marks of the Lord Jesus in their persons as Paul did? No; like most shouters, they were shirkers. They were swell preachers but poor sufferers. They were fine platform figures, but they had a profound regard for the safety of their own skin.

A second reason why Paul mentions these brand-marks here is found in his emphasis on the fact that they are "the brand-marks of *the Lord Jesus*." He is drawing a contrast between the marks of Jesus, and the mark of Moses (circumcision: see verses 12–15). Circumcision is the mark of Moses and speaks of servitude to a legal system. "The marks of the Lord Jesus" are those of a glad, free, voluntary self-sacrificing service.

A third reason why Paul here speaks of these brand-marks is

found in the words, "From henceforth let no man trouble me." This Galatian epistle, as we have seen, is full of trouble. And all the trouble had come from the Judaistic fifth-columnists who were bent on perverting the young faith of Paul's converts. But these false teachers were also attacking Paul himself, were discrediting his apostleship and even questioning his sincerity. The one trouble was bad enough; but that the battle-scarred hero should himself still be thus personally maligned and doubted was more than he could endure. In the words "From henceforth let no man trouble me, for I bear in my body the brand-marks of the Lord Jesus" there is something of touching appeal, that if these subversive teachers have any sense of honour or honesty at all they will at least drop this dastardly trick of destroying faith in Paul's own sincerity, seeing that he has now suffered so much for the sake of his message. Paul felt, and rightly so, that he had received enough scars to place his loyalty as Christ's servant and apostle beyond doubt. The very name of Jesus, so to speak, had become branded up and down his bruised and buffeted body.

And what do these brand-marks of Paul say to ourselves? They say three things: first, let us never be ashamed of bearing suffering or reproach for Jesus' sake; second, let us not be afraid of bearing such marks on our bodies; and, third, let it be our daily prayer that we may bear the marks of the Lord Jesus on our *character*.

> *Captain beloved, battle-wounds were Thine,*
> *Let me not wonder if some hurt be mine;*
> *Rather, O Lord, let my deep wonder be*
> *That I may share a battle-wound with Thee.*

The victories of Christianity, wherever they have been won, have been won by distinct doctrinal theology; by telling men of Christ's vicarious death and sacrifice; by showing them Christ's substitution on the Cross and His precious Blood; by teaching them justification by faith and bidding them believe on a crucified Saviour; by preaching ruin by sin, redemption by Christ, regeneration by the Spirit; by lifting up the Brazen Serpent; by telling men to look and live, to believe; repent and be converted. This is the only teaching which for eighteen centuries God has honoured with success, and is honouring at the present day both at home and abroad.

—*J. C. Ryle, D.D.*

TEST YOURSELF ON CORINTHIANS AND GALATIANS

1. How far can you reproduce the analysis which we have given of 1 Corinthians?

2. The opening verses of 1 Corinthians ii. suggests both an intellectual and a spiritual crisis in Paul as a preacher. What were they?

3. Mention a couple of ways in which, according to 1 Corinthians, the Gospel is foolish to the worldly-wise.

4. What was the "meats" problem of the Jews and later of the Christians in places like Corinth?

5. How would you explain Paul's words, "But to the rest speak I, *not* the Lord"? also his words, "But this I speak by permission and not of commandment"?

6. Could you reproduce our analysis of 1 Corinthians xii., xiii., xiv., the passage about "spiritual gifts"?

7. Who (briefly) were the Judaisers who so maligned Paul and damaged his work?

8. Can you reproduce our analysis of 2 Corinthians?

9. Can you give the seven points of contrast between the old and new covenants as delineated in 2 Corinthians iii. and iv.?

10. What was the Galatian error? What the key idea, and threefold structure of the epistle?

11. What four kinds of "bearing" does Paul speak of in Galatians iv.–v., and what is their peculiar applicability to the Galatians?

12. Give three reasons why Paul mentions his "brand-marks" as he closes his Galatian epistle.

THE EPISTLE TO THE EPHESIANS

Lesson Number 135

ABOUT EPHESIANS, PHILIPPIANS, COLOSSIANS

The Galatian and Roman Epistles (as the history of the Reformation of the sixteenth century showed) are the treasure-house of the truths of personal Christianity; for the very thought of justification, dominant in them, brings each soul face to face with its own sin and its own salvation, in that supreme crisis of life and death in which it is conscious of but two existences—God and itself. These *later* epistles are equally the storehouse of the less vivid, yet grander conception of the Holy Catholic Church. The central idea is of Christ the Head, and the whole collective Christianity of the Church as His Body. He is conceived not solely or mainly as the Saviour of each individual soul but rather as "gathering up" all humanity, or even all created being, "in Himself." The two conceptions are, of course, inseparable. In the *earlier* epistles the Church is constantly recognised; in these later the individual relationship to God in Christ is never for a moment ignored. But the proportion (so to speak) of the two truths is changed. What is primary in the one case is secondary in the other.

—C. J. Ellicott, D.D.

THE EPISTLE TO THE EPHESIANS

ALTHOUGH not nearly the longest of Paul's epistles, Ephesians is generally conceded to be the profoundest. There is a grandeur of conception about it, a majesty and dignity, a richness and fulness which are peculiar to it.

Two Main Parts and Ideas

If we read the epistle observantly, just as it lies before us, and without forcing any artificial analysis upon it, we shall find that it opens up with clearness and beauty. Even a first or second reading will show us that its six chapters fall into two equal parts. The climactic doxology at the end of chapter iii. at once indicates to any reflective reader that the apostle is thereby marking off a main division of his treatise.

The first half of the epistle, covering chapters i., ii. and iii., is *doctrinal*. The second half, covering chapters iv., v. and vi., is *practical*. Part one, the doctrinal part, is about the believer's *wealth* in Christ. Part two, the practical part, is about the believer's *walk* in Christ.

Any of us can easily verify this by carefully rereading the two trios of chapters. In both instances the apostle has hung the key, so to speak, right in front of the door which is to be unlocked, for the key-verse in both parts is the *first* verse. In part one, which describes the believer's *wealth* in Christ, the opening verse after the salutation reads: "Blessed be the God and Father of our Lord Jesus Christ, who hath *blessed us with all spiritual blessings in heavenly places in Christ.*" Then, in part two, which describes the believer's true *walk* in Christ, the opening verse (iv. 1) reads: "I therefore, the prisoner of the Lord, beseech you that ye *walk worthy of the vocation wherewith ye are called.*" So, then, we see at once that Ephesians is the epistle of *OUR WEALTH AND OUR WALK IN CHRIST*.

In the first half of the epistle the chapter divisions are very helpful. They mark off the true breaks in the apostle's treatment of his subject. Each of these three chapters is in a sense complete in itself; yet the three together are a trinity in unity.

In the second half of the epistle the chapter breaks must be ignored. The successive aspects of the believer's true walk in Christ occur as follows: in relation to the Church *corporately* (iv. 1–16); believers *individually* (iv. 17–v. 2); sensual-living *outsiders* (v. 3–21); wives, husbands, children, parents, servants, masters (v. 22–vi. 9); Satanic spirit-powers (vi. 10–20). It will best serve us if at the outset we delineate the whole epistle in a framed analysis.

THE EPISTLE TO THE EPHESIANS

SALUTATION (i. 1, 2).

1. OUR WEALTH IN CHRIST (i.–iii.).

Ch. 1 { Praise for spiritual possession (verses 3–14).
        { Prayer for spiritual perception (verses 15–23).

Ch. 2 { Our new condition in Christ (verses 1–10).
        { Our new relation in Christ (verses 11–22).

Ch. 3 { Revealing of the Divine mystery (verses 1–12).
        { Receiving of the Divine fulness (verses 13–21).

2. OUR WALK IN CHRIST (iv.–vi.).

As regards the Church corporately (iv. 1–16).
As regards believers individually (iv. 17–v. 2).
As regards sensual-living outsiders (v. 3–21).
As regards special relationships (v. 22–vi. 9).
As regards Satanic spirit-powers (vi. 10–20).

CONCLUSION (vi. 21–4).

PART 1: OUR WEALTH IN CHRIST (i.–iii.).

Let us now look briefly through part one, which covers the first three chapters. Here we shall see something of the wonderful, spiritual, heavenly, eternal riches which are ours, through grace, in our Lord Jesus Christ. Although in such a short survey as this we cannot linger over any one passage in particular, we can point out the comprehensive *assortments* of these immense treasures.

Praise for Spiritual Possession (i. 3-14)

Each of the three chapters in the doctrinal half of Ephesians subdivides into two parts. This is obviously so in the opening chapter. Immediately after the salutation the apostle leads off in verse 3 with the key-doxology: "Blessed be the God and Father of our Lord Jesus Christ, who hath blessed us with all spiritual blessings in the heavenlies, in Christ." With this there begins a sublime *outflowing of PRAISE* which runs right on to the end of verse 14—the longest sustained outflowing of praise anywhere in Paul's epistles.

Then at verse 15 there is a transition (marked by the "Wherefore") to an equally great *outpouring of PRAYER*: "Wherefore I also, after I heard of your faith in the Lord Jesus, and love unto all the saints, cease not to give thanks for you, making mention of you in my prayers; that . . ." Here follows the prayer which unfolds to the end of the chapter. Note that the "praise" (verses 3–14) is for spiritual *POSSESSION*, and that the "prayer" (verses 15–23) is for spiritual *PERCEPTION*.

Travel quickly through the *praise for spiritual possession*, in verses 3 to 14. Pick out the six tremendous items in this catalogue of wonders.

Pre-mundane Election

"He [God] hath *chosen* us in Him [Christ] before the foundation of the earth, that we should be holy and without blame before Him in love" (verse 4). The Greek verb translated "chose" is in the aorist tense, meaning "once for all." It has the preposition *ek* prefixed, which equals "out of." It is the middle voice of the verb which adds the sense of choosing for one's own self. So then, think of it—chosen *out of* the world, *once for all*, to be God's *own* as a peculiar treasure! And we were chosen before the earth was! And we were chosen to be holy; not *because* we were holy, but *to be* holy. Note also that the holiness to which we are called here and now is "without blame before Him in love." We cannot yet have faultless powers, but we may have blameless *motives*, if our hearts are filled with His love.

Predestination

"Having *predestinated* us to the adoption of children by Jesus Christ to Himself" (verses 5, 6). The Greek word here rendered "adoption" does *not* mean adoption in our modern Western sense, i.e. the taking of an orphan to be one's own child; it means the public attestation of adult sonship and the conferment of the privileges belonging to sons who have come to be of legal age. (So it is whenever that word "adoption" comes in our New Testament.) Already we *are* the "sons of God" by a new birth, though as such "the world knoweth us not" (1 John iii. 1); but at the reappearing of Christ in glory the "adoption" or public attestation of our sonship will be given, and we shall enter upon its full privileges and heavenly blessedness. What a promise! What a prospect!

Redemption

"In whom [Christ] we have *redemption* through His blood" (verses 7, 8). Blessed be His name, He not only fore-chose us and fore-fixed our destiny; He *bought* us, oh, at what cost to Himself! To "redeem" is to buy back, to release by ransom. Not that God paid a ransom-price to the devil, a queer theory propounded in the early years of the Church's history! No, the redemption price was paid in respect of the eternal principles of righteousness which govern the universe, to the holy law of God which human sin has outraged. We have been "redeemed from the curse of the law" (Gal. iii. 13), from the death penalty due to our guilt. We have been "bought with a price" (1 Cor. vi. 20) from the slavery of inherited bondage through hereditary depravity. We are now HIS, by costliest payment, even "through His *blood*."

Revelation

"He hath abounded toward us in all wisdom and prudence, having *made known unto us the mystery of His will,* according to His good pleasure which He hath purposed in Himself; that in the dispensation of the fulness of times He might gather together in one, all things in Christ, both which are in the heavens and which are on the earth." This expression "the fulness of times" looks not only beyond the present age but even beyond the Millennium and the Great White Throne, to the "ages to come" (Eph. ii. 7) when there shall be one "throne of God and the Lamb" (Rev.

xxii. 3) and a sinless glory which shall never end. What a revelation! Well may we long for that ineffable daybreak!

Inheritance

"In whom [Christ] also we have obtained an *inheritance*, being predestinated according to the purpose of Him who worketh all things after the counsel of His own will." Never was such an endowment heard of before! It is those two little words "in whom" which give it such limitless significance. It is "in HIM" who is heir to the whole universe that we have *our* inheritance! And note that we are "*predestinated*" to it by "Him who worketh *all* things after the counsel of *His own will*"; so that not all the powers of darkness can overthrow the Divine purpose or rob us of our inheritance!

Sealing by the Spirit

"After ye believed, ye were sealed with that Holy Spirit of promise, which is the earnest of our inheritance until the redemption of the purchased possession" (verses 13, 14). So first the inheritance is made sure to God's elect, and then the elect are sealed secure for the inheritance. The two predominant ideas in sealing are ownership and security. We are *His,* and we are *safe.* Many seals have been broken as was Pilate's, but who shall break *this* one?

Look back now on these six towering marvels, these "spiritual blessings" which are ours in Christ—election, predestination, redemption, revelation, inheritance, sealing by the Spirit. Can we wonder that these breadths and lengths and depths and heights of Divine grace and power and wisdom drove the apostle to his knees in a devout intensity of prayer? And should there not be a similar impact upon ourselves?

Prayer for Spiritual Perception (i. 15-23)

This brings us to the second half of chapter one. It is a prayer that we may "*know*"; and there are three things which Paul prays we may know: (1) "what is the hope of His calling"; (2) "the riches of His inheritance in the saints"; (3) "the exceeding greatness of His power to usward who believe."

The Hope of the Divine Calling

See verse 18: "The hope of His calling." Careful examination of the many places where the word "calling" occurs in this connection in our New Testament shows that it means the effectual work of God's grace in our hearts whereby we were brought into saving union with the Son of God. In other words, it refers to our *conversion*. "Election" and "predestination" refer to what was in the mind of God away back in eternity; but this word "called" refers to something which has happened since we ourselves were born, something that has taken place in our own experience. (See Acts ii. 39, Rom. viii. 29, 30, 1 Cor. i. 9, and follow up other references for confirmation.)

But what is this *"hope"* of His calling? The word carries our minds away into the future. There is a prize, an ultimate fulfilment of our heavenly calling. A collation of New Testament references reveals that there are four superlative prospects in it: (1) resurrection and immortality (see 1 Cor. xv. 19, 20); (2) joint-reign with Christ in His coming kingdom (see Rom. xv. 4–13; Rev. iii. 21); (3) eternal inheritance in heaven (see Col. i. 5; 1 Pet. i. 4); (4) perfect transformation into the image of Christ (see Rom. viii. 29; 1 John iii. 2; Rev. xxii. 3–5). This fourfold hope centres in Christ and will burst into fulfilment at His return. What a hope! It baffles the imagination and overwhelms the mind. It thrills and yet humbles the heart. It sanctifies the life. It prostrates us before God in adoring gratitude.

God's Inheritance in the Saints

Paul's prayer that we may "know" now moves on to "the riches of the glory of *His* [God's] inheritance in the saints" (verse 18). Does this seem rather staggering? Does it seem surpassingly strange that the infinite One should find an inheritance in *us*? One or two expositors try their best to make the verse mean that *God* is the inheritance, and the saints the inheritors; but no, the Greek here means just what our English translation of it says.

So there it is—"the riches of the glory of His inheritance in the saints." It is pretty staggering; yet the idea is not altogether new. In the Old Testament Scriptures we find that the nation Israel was constituted an "inheritance" to Jehovah (Deut. iv. 20; 1 Kings viii. 53; Ps. xxxiii. 12; Isa. xix. 25). But in a far sublimer sense the blood-bought members of the true Church are constituted an inheritance to God by virtue of the supreme covenant in Christ.

What are the greatest values in God's universe? Are they stars or souls? The biggest of the stars is blind. It can be seen but cannot see. It can be weighed and analysed, but it cannot know or feel. It may be admired, but it cannot love. What are the immensest stellar systems compared with a soul which has the capacity for God, for holiness and fellowship and worship and service and adoration and love? And are there any intelligent beings throughout the universe who can mean more to God by way of gratitude, adoration, love and fellowship, than those whom He has redeemed by the precious blood of His own Son, whom He has sanctified and glorified and lifted up into the highest of all intimacies with Himself? Oh, what adoring gratitude, what fellow-ship of worshipping *love* will God inherit in the "saints" through the coming ages!

The Divine Power to Us-ward

But still further Paul prays that we may "know" what is the *"exceeding greatness of His power to us-ward who believe"*(verses 19–23). Notice carefully that the gauge of this power is *"accord-ing to"* what God wrought in Christ. Then observe that this power did not only raise Christ from the dead; there are *three* things all going together, namely: resurrection, transformation, exaltation. It is in the three together that we see the full display of this "mighty power" which God "wrought in Christ." First God showed this power by raising that dead body to life again. Then He further showed it by transubstantiating it into one of super-mundane superiority. Then, having fitted that resurrected body for heavenly as well as earthly habitation, He lifted it away from the earth, through the terrestrial air-space, through the stellar spaces, to that place which Solomon calls "the heaven of heavens," and Paul calls "the third heaven," and our Lord calls the "Father's house," that place, whatever and wherever it is, in which the presence of God is localised as nowhere else in the universe. And God did all this over against all the exhausted weight of Satanic opposition and resistance, against the full combine of "principality and power and might and dominion" (verse 21). *That* is the New Testament standard of God's "power to us-ward who believe"!

In chapter ii., as we shall now see, Paul shows us the operation of that power in believers—quickening us, raising us, and making us to "sit together in heavenly places," sharing our Lord's victory over all the power of the enemy. But let each of us ask at this point: How much or how little do *I* know of this power in my own daily prayer, service, experience? Does someone reply, "Ah, that is just the point. This passage about God's power to us-ward who believe is all very wonderful, but how far removed it seems from the actual experience of most Christians!" Well, that is just why Paul prays that we might "*know*" these things. It is possible to know them merely with the *mind*, but that is not to know them in the inmost and vital sense. They must be known by a *spiritual knowing*; and it is the special function of the Holy Spirit to make them luminously significant within us, so that we inwardly *see* them and live in the power of them. Think this over prayerfully. When the Holy Spirit is really given chance to monopolise us, then all these things become alive in a new way.

Our New Condition in Christ (ii. 1-10)

Look now through the first ten verses of chapter ii., which tell of our *new condition* in Christ. In verses 1 to 3 we see the four unhappy characteristics of our condition before we were brought into saving union with Him.

Spiritual Death

"Dead in trespasses and sins" (verse 1). The fundamental idea in death is not cessation, but *separation*. Physical death is the separation of the body from the soul. Spiritual death is the separation of the spirit from God. It means the absence of that highest life which was originally in man before sin divorced man's spirit from God who is its life-giving environment. To pass from time into eternity thus dead toward God, alienated and separated from Him, is surely a dread enough thought to send us out with renewed concern for the saving of the Christless souls around us.

Subjection to Satan

"Ye walked according to the course of this world, according to the prince of the power of the air, the spirit that now worketh in the children of disobedience" (verse 2). This "power of the air" is Satan's combine of subordinate demon-accomplices who exercise a deadly influence on human hearts and in human affairs. Think of it—that evil power, as Paul here says, *"now worketh"* in unbelievers. The fact that most men and women are so blind to it only makes it the more pitiable.

Flesh-bound affections

"We all had our way of living in time past, in . . . the desires of the flesh and of the mind" (verse 3). The "desires of the *flesh*" are earth-bound appetites. The "desires of the *mind*" are earth-bound ambitions. This was our pre-conversion condition. We did not realise it until the Holy Spirit broke through the thick encrustments of our depravity with the regenerating light of the Gospel.

Under Divine Condemnation

"And we were by nature the *children of wrath*, even as others" (verse 3). According to Hebrew idiom the expression means under *sentence* of wrath, as when Saul said of David, "He is a son of death" (1 Sam. xx. 31), meaning that he should surely die (see also 2 Pet. ii. 14; Matt. xxiii. 15; John xvii. 12). How can we read such words without our hearts being gripped with new concern for the Christless?

But now, thank God, at verse 4 there comes an emphatic break —"*BUT GOD*"—and from this point there is a grandly different story to tell. Verses 4–10 express what we now are through our saving union with Christ. Our new condition is set forth in four particulars which stand out in marked contrast over against the four unhappy characteristics of our former life apart from Christ.

Quickened

First, over against "dead in trespasses and sins" we now have: "Even when we were dead in sins, He hath *quickened* us together with Christ" (verse 5). It is a marvel of Divine *power*, for when our condition was such who *could* have done it but God? And it is a marvel of Divine grace, for when our condition was such who *would* have done it but God? This is the *first* operation of God's power "to us-ward" who believe, namely, renewal to spiritual aliveness in Christ.

Raised

Second, over against subjection to Satan we now read that God has *"raised us up together"* with Christ (verse 6). Our Lord Jesus Himself was not merely "quickened"; He was *"raised"* and visibly brought forth from the grave, which demonstrated His victory over Satan and His entrance upon a higher form of life. So is it with ourselves. We are not only given new life; we are freed from bondage! We are "raised" with One who has Satan beneath His feet!

In the Heavenlies

Third, over against flesh-bound affections we now find: "And made us to *sit together in heavenly places, in Christ Jesus"* (verse 6). Our eyes are opened to heavenly realities, and our minds moved by heavenly desires, and our hearts satisfied with heavenly joys. That is where we are *now* in the sense of spiritual privilege. We ought to be living there daily in spiritual experience.

Objects of Superlative Favour

Fourth, over against "children of wrath" we now find: "That in the ages to come, He [God] might show the exceeding riches of His grace in His *kindness toward us* through Christ Jesus" (verse 7). What language—"exceeding riches of grace" . . . ."ages to come"! Who shall even faintly sense the plethora of pure blessedness which the words pledge to us? No wonder Paul twice in this passage exclaims: "By grace are ye saved!" and emphasises it by: "Not of works, lest any man should boast." Divine grace, not human merit, must have all the praise.

Our New Relation in Christ (ii. 11-22)

Just as verses 1 to 10 draw a contrast between our new *condition* in Christ and what we were before, so these further twelve verses draw a contrast between our new *relation* in Christ and what it was before. The passage turns on three pivotal expressions:

> "At that time ye were . . ." (verses 11, 12).
> "But now in Christ Jesus . . ." (verses 13–18).
> "Now therefore ye are . . ." (verses 19–22).

"At that time ye were . . ." (*verses 11, 12*).

Five things are here said of our past: (1) at that time we were *"without Christ,"* having no title-right as Gentiles to the Messianic expectations of Israel; (2) we were *"aliens* from the common-wealth of Israel," having no part or lot in the inheritance of the chosen people; (3) we were *"strangers* from the covenants of [the] promise," having no share by birth in the provisions of the covenant with Israel; (4) we had *"no hope,"* for apart from this Messiah-Saviour there was no hope either for man in general or men as individuals; and (5) we were *"without God* in the world," being without the true knowledge of God.

"But now in Christ Jesus . . ." (*verses 13–18*).

The "But now" marks a break. Verses 13–18 show how the situation has been completely transformed by the Calvary work of our Lord. The five big barriers between Jew and Gentile have been swept away: (1) He has destroyed *distance,* for in verse 13 the "far off are made *nigh"*; (2) He has destroyed disunion, for in verse 14 "He is our peace, who hath made both [Jew and Gentile] *one"*; (3) He has destroyed *division,* for in verse 15 down goes the "middle wall of partition"; (4) He has destroyed *dissension,* for in verse 15 He has "abolished the enmity . . . so making *peace"*; and (5) He has destroyed all *distinction,* for, as verse 15 again says, He makes "of the twain [Jew and Gentile] *one new man."*

"Now therefore ye are . . ." (*verses 19–22*).

Finally, at verse 19 comes the further break, marked by the words: "Now therefore ye are . . ." Here, in verses 19 to 22, the contrast between what we were and what we now are is consummated; and our new relationship is set forth in five striking particulars. First, we are all "fellow-citizens" of the one heavenly city (verse 19). Second, we are all members of the one heavenly household (verse 19). Third, we are all built on the one imperishable foundation (verse 20). Fourth, we are all living stones in the one spiritual building (verse 21). Fifth, we are all indwelt by the one renewing Spirit (verse 22). Now see the whole movement at a glance: marvel at the wonder of this salvation as seen in the total structure of the passage.

THE OLD RELATIONSHIP

"At that time ye were ..." (verses 11–12).

"Without Christ."
"Aliens."
"Strangers."
"Having no hope."
"Without God."

THE NEW RELATIONSHIP

"Now therefore ye are ..." (verses 19–22).

Citizens of the one city (verse 19).
Members of the one family (verse 19).
Built on the one foundation (verse 20).
Parts of the one building (verse 21).
Indwelt by the one Spirit (verse 22).

HOW THE CHANGE WAS WROUGHT

"But now in Christ Jesus ..." (verses 13–18)

Distance done away
　　("Ye are made nigh").
Disunion done away
　　("He hath made both one").
Division done away
　　("Broken middle wall").
Dissension done away
　　("He abolished enmity").
Distinction done away
　　("Of twain one new man").

Both Jew and Gentile are now—

Reconciled to God
　　("reconciled both to God").
Have peace with God
　　("peace to you ... and them").
Have access to God
　　("we both have access").

What beauty and wonder there is in the paragraph when thus viewed in its complete structure! And what a salvation it is which has brought us from such plight to such privilege, from such poverty to such riches, from such shame to such honour, from such ruin to such glory!

The Revealing of the Divine Mystery (iii. 1-12)

This third chapter brings the doctrinal part of Ephesians to its climax. There is not a profounder passage in the Bible. Here we view the topmost peaks and sound the deepmost depths. The first part of the chapter is all about *the revealing of the Divine mystery* (verses 1–12); the second part is all about *the receiving of the Divine fulness* (verses 13–21).

What *is* the "mystery" (or previously hidden Divine secret) which is now divulged (verses 1–12)? Let us be quite clear that it is not the Gospel, though the Gospel includes it. It was no hidden secret that Christ was to come, was to bear the sins of the many, was to be a Prince and a Saviour to both Jews and Gentiles; nor that the Holy Spirit was to be outpoured, that remission of sins was to be preached, and that Christ should take the throne of David. All these are foretold in the Old Testament. As the Scofield Bible note aptly says on verse 6: "The mystery 'hid in God' was the Divine purpose to make of Jew and Gentile a wholly new thing—'the Church, which is His [Christ's] body,' formed by the baptism with the Holy Spirit (1 Cor. xii. 12, 13) and in which the earthly distinction of Jew and Gentile disappears (Eph. ii. 14, 15; Col. iii. 10, 11). The revelation of this mystery, which was foretold but not explained by Christ (Matt. xvi. 18), was committed to Paul. In his writings alone we find the doctrine, position, walk, and destiny of the Church."

To put it rather more fully, the "mystery" or revealed secret is that Christ, instead of immediately taking over the "kingdom" when He came to this earth—the kingdom foretold by Old Testament prophets—should, after His rejection, crucifixion and resurrection, completely disappear from this earthly scene, should be exalted in heaven to the right hand of God, high over every power and sphere, should be given the administration of the entire universe both now and in the age to come (not merely "the throne of David" and "the kingdom under the whole heaven" as promised in the Old Testament); and that during the present age an elect people, the Church, should be gathered out, irrespective of nationality—an elect people who should be brought collectively into such an intimate union of life and love and eternal glory with Him as can only be expressed by saying that the Church is His "body," and His "bride," and His "temple" (three metaphors which, respectively, express union in *life,* and in *love,* and in *glory*)! Such is the "mystery" in Ephesians iii. 4–10. See how Paul exults in it (verses 8, 9). Is it not as wings of joy to our *own* hearts?

The Receiving of the Divine Fulness (iii. 13-21)

Note again the "Wherefore" at verse 13, indicating both the connection and the division between what precedes and what follows. Note also how this second great prayer in Ephesians is occasioned: "Wherefore I desire that *ye faint not* at my tribulations for you, which is your glory; for this cause I bow my knees unto the Father of our Lord Jesus Christ." It would seem as though those to whom Paul wrote *had* been tending to faint in their minds on account of Paul's tribulations. If Paul was indeed a Divinely commissioned apostle, why did such adversities overtake him? They were tempted to doubt.

Read now through the prayer again. What rush of spiritual desire! What reaching out to lay hold on the highest and fullest that is ours in Christ! The prayer in chapter i. was that we might *KNOW.* This prayer in chapter iii. is that we may *HAVE,* and it is threefold: (1) that we may be "strengthened with power by His Spirit"; (2) that we may be "rooted and grounded in love"; and (3) that we may be "filled with all the fulness of God." This threefold division is marked by three occurrences of the conjunction "that," in verses 16, 17 (second "that") and 19. These represent the three occurrences of the Greek conjunction *hina,* "in order that."

The climax of the prayer is: "That ye might be *filled with all the fulness of God.*" But does that sound absurdly impossible? Can the universe be held on the point of a pin? Shall an egg-cup hold the Atlantic? Well, we need to understand what is meant here by "the fulness of God." The vital thing to grasp is that *CHRIST* is the fulness. Colossians i. 19 and ii. 9 settle that. We have the same truth in Ephesians i. 22, though as it appears in our English translation it would seem to make the *Church* the fulness. Taken with the immediate context and with Pauline doctrine elsewhere, the force of the words surely is: "[God] put all things under *HIS* [Christ's] feet, and gave *HIM* to be head over all things to the Church which is His body, even *HIM* who is the fulness of Him that filleth all in all." Yes, indeed, *CHRIST* is the fulness, and to be "filled with all the fulness of God" is to be filled with *Christ*. The conclusive commentary on this is Paul's own word in Colossians ii. 9, 10: "In Him dwelleth all the fulness of the Godhead bodily; and *ye are FILLED FULL in Him*."

The preposition "with" should be "unto," as in the Revised Version. We are to be "filled *unto*"—a certain point indicated by the little word "all" which follows and signifies entirety or completeness. So, of course, it is not a question at all as to whether these poor little selves of ours can hold all the fulness of God; the reference is simply to our *capacity to hold*. We are to be filled *"unto"* our utmost capacity—completely possessed, pervaded, permeated by Him who is "the fulness of God" and "Head over all things to the Church." What a prayer! What an ideal! This is entire sanctification in its highest, purest, richest, deepest aspect —utter absorption of and into the love-life of Christ. Oh, that we may more fully prove it in our own experience! Does it seem an unscaleable height? Then listen to the closing doxology:

"Now unto Him that is able to do exceeding abundantly above all that we ask or think, according to the power that worketh in us, unto Him be glory in the Church, by Christ Jesus throughout all ages, age without end. Amen."

Part 2. Our Walk in Christ. (iv.-vi.)

We cannot regret the space given to the first three chapters of this epistle, for it was our main intention to set forth by preference its *doctrinal* aspects; yet we do regret that on this account we cannot similarly travel together through chapters iv., v. and vi. However, we find comfort in this, that our analytical exposition of the earlier chapters makes useful preparation for the student's own exploration of the latter. We call attention to the analysis which we supplied at the outset. Most of the sections are so self-evident in their meaning that no comment is required here. We must content ourselves with making what we hope may be useful suggestions in closing.

An attentive reader soon discerns that this second half of the epistle answers like an *echo* to the first. The doctrines in part one now echo back on us in exhortations to corresponding *practice*. In passage after passage this ethical rebound meets us; and it is highly profitable to match up the counterparts. For instance, in part one we are told doctrinally of the "good *works* which God hath before ordained that we should *walk* in them" (ii. 10); and now, in part two, we are told in detail *what* the walk and works are. In chapter i. 13 we are taught doctrinally that the Holy Spirit *seals* believers; and now, in chapter iv. 30, we are exhorted, "*Grieve not* the Holy Spirit of God whereby ye are sealed." And so on.

Another feature which is sure to catch the eye is that after *wealth* in the first three chapters, and *walk* in the ensuing chapters, the end bit is about spiritual *war* (vi. 10–20). "We wrestle . . . against principalities." "Take unto you the whole armour of God. . . ." Do you think Satan is going to let such wealth and walk go uncontested? Nay, there is a need to "wrestle." The centre-point of the struggle, and of prevailing, is *prayer* (verse 10) —"Praying always . . . and sticking at it with *steady tenacity*."

Then again, we certainly ought to pursue the *chain-themes* running through Ephesians. There is that of the believer's *walk*. "Walk worthy of the vocation . . ." (iv. 1). "Walk in love" (v. 2). "Walk as children of light" (v. 8). "See that ye walk circumspectly" (v. 17). Look up the other "walk" verses, and complete the chain.

Pick out the twelve references to the Holy Spirit, noting that all those in part one tell us what the Holy Spirit is and does toward the believer, while all those in part two tell us what *we* are to be and do toward *Him*.

Last but not least, there are the wonderful passages which unfold to us the "mystery" of the true, spiritual *Church*. Follow them through to their climax in chapter v. 25–33. See the three tenses of our Lord's love-work for the Church: (past) "Christ *loved* the Church"; (present) "That He might *sanctify* it"; (future) "That He might present it to Himself. . . ." But there we must break away . . . !

THE EPISTLE TO THE PHILIPPIANS

Lesson Number 136

NOTE.—For this study read twice through Philippians at one sitting.

The Epistle to the Philippians was written about thirty years after the Ascension, about ten years after the first preaching of the Gospel by St. Paul at Philippi. Christianity was still young, in all the freshness of its first youth. It had come suddenly into the world. The world seemed growing old: the old religions had lost whatever power they once possessed; the old philosophies were worn out; the energies of political life had been weakened or suppressed by the all-pervading despotism of Rome. Avarice, uncleanness, cruelty, were rampant in the earth. There was little faith in God, in goodness, in immortality. "What is truth?" was the despairing question of the age. The Gospel flashed upon this scene of moral confusion like, what it is in truth, a revelation from heaven. It brought before the eyes of men a life and a Person. The world saw for the first time a perfect life; not a mere ideal, but a real life that had been really lived upon the earth; a life that stands alone, separate from all other lives; unique in its solitary majesty, in its unearthly loveliness, in its absolute purity, in its entire unselfishness. The world saw for the first time the beauty of complete self-sacrifice. And this life was not merely a thing past and gone. It was still living, it *is* still living in the Church. The life of Christ lived in His saints.

—B. C. Caffin.

THE EPISTLE TO THE PHILIPPIANS

AN IMMORTAL interest attaches to this little Philippian epistle, for it was sent to the first Christian church ever planted in Europe. Few events of history have had deeper or wider repercussions than the unostentatious visit of Paul and his few helpers to that colonial township of long ago. The letter was written about ten years later.

The City of Philippi

The ancient name of Philippi had been Datos, afterwards Krenides, which means the springs or wells. It was later renamed Philippi by Philip, the father of Alexander the Great, who extracted a great revenue from its gold mines. It was located in a region of exceptionally fertile soil and mineral riches. But even more than its local gold and silver mines, that which gave Philippi its importance was its situation as a kind of toll-gate on one of the main routes between Asia and Europe. Near it the mountain range separating East from West flattens down into a wide pass, a feature which prompted the victorious Cæsar Augustus to make Philippi a Roman *colony*.

We are told that the settlers planted there by Augustus were "mainly Italians, discharged Antonian soldiers," and that there co-existed a large proportion of Grecian Macedonians. In its social set-up Philippi was a kind of Rome in miniature. Its inhabitants called themselves Romans (Acts xvi. 21). The official language was Latin, but the everyday tongue was Greek. "Romans and Macedonians were mingled together at Philippi, and the Macedonian character seems to have resembled the Roman more nearly, perhaps, than that of any other of the subject races. The Macedonians, like the old Romans, were manly, straightforward and affectionate. They were not sceptical like the philosophers of Athens, nor voluptuous like the Greeks of Corinth." Few Jews lived at Philippi, doubtless because it was a "military colony" rather than a "mercantile city." That is why there was no synagogue, but only the *proseuche*, or legally-proper "Prayer-Place," outside the walls, by the river Gangites (Acts xvi. 13). When Luke tells us that Philippi was "the first city of that part of Macedonia" (Acts xvi. 12) we are to understand it as first geographically rather than commercially or dimensionally, though of course it probably *was* the chief city of its own *district*.

The Church at Philippi

That first Christian church at Philippi has an interest all its own. The at-first peaceful and then suddenly stormy experiences which attended its inception are narrated in Acts xvi. 12–40. The first convert in Europe was a woman, though she was an Asiatic, from Thyatira, and was then visiting Philippi as a seller of crimson fabrics. (Thyatira was famed for its crimson dyes, in those days called "purple.") Paul's only-recorded miracle, also at Philippi, was upon another female, the expelling of a demon— supposedly a "spirit of Python," the Delphi serpent—from a slave-girl clairvoyant. This rescued young fortune-teller, and commercial-traveller Lydia, along with any of those riverside "women" who believed, and the Roman gaoler converted in the midnight earthquake, were the first potential of that church which soon afterwards became the dearest to Paul of all his children in the faith.

See Paul's references to them in this epistle. His relationship with them had never been hurt by distrusts and defaults like those of some other groups. "From the first day until now" their fellowship with him in his mighty enterprise had been undeviating, co-operative, sympathetic (i. 3–9). They had made his labours and afflictions their own, sending sustenance to him at different places. They were the first, so it seems, to seize the privilege of supporting Paul in his apostolic labours. They did not wait to see what others would give—they set the example; they gave what they could, and that at once. Twice at least they had sent support to him at Thessalonica (iv. 16). When he had left Macedonia on further itineraries they had sent again (iv. 15). They had sent yet again when he was down south in Greece, at Corinth, and Paul had gratefully received it when he would accept nothing at all from the different-natured Corinthians (2 Cor. xi. 9). They had "abounded" in their "liberality" toward the poor brethren at Jerusalem, though at the time they themselves were suffering "deep poverty" (2 Cor. viii. 1–5). And now, once more, their affectionate considerateness had "flourished" toward Paul (iv.

10), and they had sent to him in his prison "affliction" (verse 14) a further bounty (verse 18). In full measure their love (i. 9) was reciprocated (i. 7, 8). Three times in four chapters that adjective "beloved" flows from Paul's pen. But see chapter iv. 1, where they are Paul's "brethren dearly beloved," his "longed for," his "joy and crown," and again his "dearly beloved." These are no mere fulsome endearments, but the deep, real, joyous reciprocities of sanctified hearts united for ever in Christ.

We learn also from the epistle that the church at Philippi was already an organised society (two orders of ministry are mentioned by name, i.e. "bishops" or overseers, and "deacons"); that the believers there were undergoing persecution; that there was a tendency to discord, particularly in an antipathy between two of the women members. There is no indication of other moral failure or of wrong doctrine, though Paul's warnings in chapter iii. 1–9 and 17–19 seems to imply that the Judaisers had not altogether left the Philippi believers alone, even though few Jews were there. There is no evidence that the Philippians had succumbed to their wiles, however, and it is with praiseful joy that the apostle reviews their growth in grace (i. 6, iv. 1, 18).

The Occasion of the Epistle

Where and why did Paul pen this letter? Some have said that he wrote it during his imprisonment at Cæsarea (Acts xxiii. 23, xxiv. 27), but the large majority of commentators say during his imprisonment at Rome. It is of no basic importance, though there is much of background interest. We ourselves are convinced that it was written from Rome. The reference to the prætorium in chapter i. 13 could apply equally to Cæsarea or Rome (as also to Jerusalem: Matt. xxvii. 27); but the reference to "Cæsar's household" in chapter iv. 22 surely indicates Rome, as also does the account of the "preaching" (i. 14–18) and Paul's expectation of a speedy release (i. 19, ii. 24).

Learning of Paul's imprisonment, they had sent Epaphroditus, who may well have been their chief pastor, to convey their gifts to him, with assurances of their unchanged love and pledges of prayer (iv. 18). They had wanted to send earlier but had "lacked opportunity" (i.e. through their own poverty and persecutions: iv. 10, i. 29). Paul was greatly cheered by the gift and the thought behind it (iv. 10). His sorrow, however, was keen that Epaphroditus had been taken seriously ill on the journey to Rome (ii. 27), though he was relieved at his recovery, through the mercy of God (verse 27), and was therefore sending him back "the more carefully," i.e. without delay, both for *his* sake and *theirs* (how beautiful this love between Epaphroditus and his flock at Philippi!). In sending Epaphroditus back he takes occasion to send this epistle with him. We may well be glad, then, that those dear Philippians sent their love-gift to prisoner Paul, for as a result this priceless little epistle came to them—and to *us*!

The Epistle Itself

This short epistle is simply and naturally a *letter*, not a formal treatise. Bishop Lightfoot calls it "the least dogmatic of the apostle's letters." It is practical rather than theological; corrective rather than formative; a letter of Christian appreciation and exhortation. Of course, the whole of it is *interpenetrated* with Christian doctrine, but any theological teaching occurs only *incidentally*, and always to press home practical Christian godliness. The faults which it corrects were, fortunately, only incipient rather than developed—strife, vainglory, wrong self-esteem, disunity, murmurings, disputings—all of which are very human besetments. Paul knows how hard the lessons are; the Philippians need more than precept; they need a high, constraining example —and so there threads its way into the letter that "unique and splendid theological paragraph" beginning: "Let this mind be in you, which was also in Christ Jesus" (ii. 5–11).

Recurrent Ideas

There are prominent *ideas,* too, running through the letter. One is that of Christian joy and rejoicing (i. 4, 18, 25, ii. 16, 17, 18, 28, iii. 1, 3, iv. 1, 4). Another is that of *gain* in Christ (i. 21, 23, iii. 7, 8. R.V., 14, iv. 19). Also, a feature is that of teaching by *example*—i.e. of Christ (ii. 5–11), of Timothy (ii. 19–24), of Epaphroditus (ii. 25–30), of Paul (iii. 1–iv. 9). Over against certain who say there is an "absence of plan in the epistle" we would point out that there is an introversion-structure which is as clear as it is effective:

Salutation: "Grace be unto you" (i. 1, 2).
Paul's concern for the Philippians (i. 3–26).
EXHORTATION: EXAMPLE OF CHRIST (i. 27–ii. 16).
EXAMPLE OF TIMOTHY (ii. 19–24).
EXAMPLE OF EPAPHRAS (ii. 25–30).
EXHORTATION: EXAMPLE OF PAUL (iii. 1–iv. 9).
The Philippians' concern for Paul (iv. 10–20).
Salutation: "Grace be with you" (iv. 21–23).

The Fourfold Christ

But we miss everything in this epistle if we fail to perceive and appreciate its wonderful fourfold presentation of Christ in relation to the experience of the individual believer. Once this fourfold Christ of Philippians is seen, the little epistle gleams and flashes with an altogether new lustre—it becomes a gem precious beyond all words.

Fortunately, in Philippians the four chapters accurately represent the four movements of this main theme (except that the first verse of chapter iv. obviously ends chapter iii.).

We find a key verse, expressing a key idea in each chapter. In the first chapter the key thought is expressed in verse 21: "To me to live is Christ." Everything in this first chapter centres in the thought that Christ is the believer's *life*.

In the second chapter the key thought is expressed in verse 5: "Let this mind be in you which was also in Christ Jesus." The whole of this second chapter gathers round the thought that Christ is the believer's *mind*.

In the third chapter the key thought is expressed in verse 10: "That I may know Him." Here everything centres in the truth that Christ is the believer's *goal*.

In the fourth chapter the key thought is the enabling power of Christ, as expressed in verse 13: "I can do all things through Christ which strengtheneth me." In this last chapter the apostle's thought is gathered up in the truth that Christ is the believer's *strength*.

Thus we see in the progress of this epistle a fourfold truth as rich with suggestion as it is vital to Christian experience. Let us get it photographed clearly in our minds:

Chapter 1: Christ our life.
Chapter 2: Christ our mind.
Chapter 3: Christ our goal.
Chapter 4: Christ our strength.

The sequence here will be at once obvious. If Christ be truly our life, as in chapter one, His life will express itself in and through our mental activity, as in chapter two. Then, the mind being thus suffused with His life, the desires will become more and more toward Christ as the perfect ideal, the sum of objective perfection and subjective satisfaction, the supreme goal of desire, as in chapter three; while finally, as in chapter four, Christ Himself is the strength by which the ideal becomes the actual, and by which the objective reality becomes subjectively realised in experience. In these four Philippian chapters, therefore, we observe clear progress and completeness.

Chapter I: Christ our Life

"To me to live is Christ" (i. 21). In this first chapter we find seven remarkable expressions of the truth that Christ is the believer's true life. If He be really so, what is the first evidence of it which we shall naturally expect to find? It is surely this: that the Christ-filled believer has *the feelings of Christ*. This is what we *do* find. Turn to verse 8. Here the apostle says: "I long after you all in the very affections of Christ." Ellicott renders it: "I long after you all in the very heart of Jesus Christ," and says that the phrase here is striking and even startling. Christ's heart had, as it were, become Paul's, and was beating anew in the apostle's bosom. The very feelings of Christ were moving within the consciousness of His servant. Even so, as Dean Alford says, "The great love wherewith He loved us lives and yearns in all who are vitally united to Him"—though our consciousness of it is determined by the depth of our consecration to Him.

What is the second thing which we expect to find if Christ be the believer's life? Is it not this: that the believer has *the same interests as Christ*? This also is just what we find in this chapter. Look at verses 12 to 18, in which Paul speaks of the things that have happened to him. He is at Rome, imprisoned, fettered, suffering unjustly, and surrounded by circumstances which would make it easy for any man to chafe and complain.

But no—Christ is the life within his life, and there is such community and identity of interest that Paul's own personal concerns are lost in his concern for the interests of his Lord. We need not quote the whole passage; the first and last words are enough to show this: "The things which happened to me have fallen out rather unto the furtherance of the Gospel . . . Christ is preached, and therein I do rejoice."

So, if we ourselves are filled and swayed by the life of Christ, personal ambitions will be sublimated into sanctifying union with the interests of Christ. We shall say with General Gordon: "The last and only thing I value in this life I have given over to Jesus Christ."

What is the third thing which we find resulting from this great truth that Christ is the believer's life? It is that the very *Spirit of Christ* is imparted to the believer. See verse 19. Paul says: "I know that this shall turn to my salvation through your prayer, and the supply of the Spirit of Jesus Christ." The word "spirit" is here spelt with a capital "S" in the Authorised Version; and quite rightly it is so. But the essential thing to note is that Paul here speaks of "the Spirit of *Jesus Christ*." As in human nature, the spirit is the inmost and deepest, so the supply of the spirit of Jesus Christ" implies the imparting of His inmost life, His own motives and aims becoming ours!

What is the next thing that follows if Christ be the believer's life? It is that Christ Himself becomes the believer's *supreme concern*. As a man will give up friends, wealth and all things rather than life itself, because life is the supreme possession, so, because Christ is the very *life* of the believer, He will be the supreme possession and concern. This, again, is what we find in this first chapter of Philippians. Turn to verse 20. Paul's one concern is: "Christ shall be magnified in my body, whether it be by life or by death."

Following naturally upon all this, we find that to the consecrated Christian Christ is *unspeakably dear*. He becomes the object of longing desire. Read verse 23: "I am in a strait betwixt two, having a desire [a strong desire or longing] to depart and to be with Christ which is far better." The words translated "far better" should be "by much very far better." Paul piles up comparatives as if unable to seize on terms adequate to express the rapture of the anticipated consummation. Christ has become unspeakably dear to him; and so will He be to ourselves if our hearts are inbreathed by His life and love.

And now, in the sixth place, if Christ is the believer's life, this will clearly *determine conduct*. We find this emphasised in verse 27: "Let your manner of life be worthy of the Gospel of Christ" (R.V.). If Christ be our life, He will express Himself in the way we live. Christ in us and through us is the secret of that one type and quality of living which is fully worthy of Himself. When our hearts are held and swayed by the indwelling Son of God our personalities become His living pulpits and our lives incarnate sermons.

Finally, it follows that if Christ is our life, suffusing the heart and revealing Himself through the whole of our activity, this will greatly affect *the attitude of others towards us;* for the kind of life we live inevitably determines the reaction of those around us—whether friendly or hostile. This is what we find in verses 27–30. Here we read of "adversaries," and of "suffering" for Christ's sake, while the believers are exhorted to show their affectionate affinity with each other by standing together in "one spirit and one soul."

Here, then, in this first chapter of Philippians, we see *Christ the believer's life,* re-expressing Himself through all the inward and outward activity of the consecrated personality. By a spiritual absorption the believer shares His feelings, His interests, His Spirit, finding in Christ his supreme concern and dearest possession, while the outward life, with all its relationships, is determined from a new centre.

What shall we then say to these things? Are we not yearning to be able to say with Paul: "I live, yet not I, but Christ liveth in me"?

Chapter ii.: Christ our Mind

This whole chapter centres in the words, "Let this mind be in you which was also in Christ Jesus" (verse 5), and amplifies the thought that Christ is the believer's *mind*—the true mind *within* his mind.

First, in verses 1 and 2 we find Paul's *exhortation* to the believer to have the mind of Christ: "If there be therefore any *exhortation* [as the Greek word means] in Christ, if any comfort of love, if any fellowship of the Spirit, if any tender emotions and compassions, fulfil ye my joy that ye be *likeminded* [i.e. with HIM], having the same love [as HIS], being of one accord, of one mind [with each other]."

Second, in verses 3 and 4 Paul shows the true *exhibition* of the mind of Christ through the believer. These two verses (see R.V.) simply run on from verses 1 and 2 as the natural exhibition of the Christ-mind, thus, ". . . *nothing being done through strife or vainglory, but in lowliness of mind each counting other better than himself, not looking each of you to his own interests, but also to the interests of others.*" Such is the natural, inevitable expression of the mind of Christ through the believer in whom His life is not obstructed. Mark well these qualities of Christ-mindedness—peaceableness, guilelessness, lowliness, unselfishness. This is the lovely cure for faction and friction in the churches!

Third, in verses 5 to 8 Paul gives an *exposition* of the mind of Christ. This sublime paragraph is commonly spoken of as the classic passage on our Lord's "humiliation." What it teaches, however, is not humiliation but *self-humbling,* which is greatly different. That which gives our Lord's condescending identification with us its supreme moral glory is its gracious voluntariness. The key-word is "He humbled Himself" (verse 8). The seven steps in our Lord's vast, self-effacing descent have often been pointed out; but to linger over them again is always moving and edifying: (1) "Being in the form of God He deemed it not to be selfishly clung to"; (2) "but emptied Himself"; (3) "and took the form of a bondman"; (4) "becoming in the likeness of men"; (5) "He humbled Himself"; (6) "and became obedient unto death"; (7) "even the death of the Cross." Marvel again at the wonder of it—God . . . Man . . . Slave . . . Criminal! In time or eternity, on earth or throughout the universe, this is the supreme expression of self-sacrificing *otherism.* Here is the supreme example. "Let *this* mind be in *you.*"

See how Paul *applies* this exposition in verses 12 to 15. "So, then, my beloved, even as *ye* have always obeyed [i.e. have become obedient to God as Christ became so], work out [as Christ worked out by obedience] your *own* salvation [in the sense of similar final vindication] with fear and trembling; for [while *you* are working it all *out*] it is *God* which worketh *in* you, both to will and to work His good pleasure [as He willed and worked out His good pleasure in Christ]. Do all things without murmuring [against God] and disputings [with men], that ye may be blameless [before God] and harmless [among men] the *sons of God* [as Christ in the supreme sense was the Son of God]."

Finally, in verses 19 to 30 Paul gives an *exemplification* of Christ-mindedness in Timothy and Epaphroditus. Look at Timothy: "likeminded" (verse 20); "care truly" for others (verse 20, R.V.); faithful, lowly service (verse 22). Look at Epaphroditus: self-humbling by ministering (verse 25); concerned for others (verse 26); self-forgetting (verse 30). Thus the second chapter is all about the mind of Christ in and expressed through the believer.

Chapter iii.: Christ our Goal

If Christ be our new *life,* as in chapter i., and our true *mind,* as in chapter ii., then it follows that the inmost desirings and aspirings of all who are truly His must correspondingly be towards Him as the objective embodiment of saving righteousness, of Divine love, and of future bliss. This is what we now find in chapter iii., the key to which is verse 10: *"That I may know Him."* Christ is the goal of all our faith and love and hope.

See how the chapter begins with a renunciation of all *other* glorying but in Him: "We glory in Christ Jesus, and have no confidence in the flesh" (verse 3, R.V.). Now if ever a man had any seeming reason to glory in things of the flesh, Paul had. In verse 4 he says: "If any other man thinketh that he hath whereof he might trust in the flesh, I more." Then in verses 5 and 6 he lists the things which had been his former glory, and which he had once for all renounced at his conversion to the Lord Jesus Christ. They were things which must have meant more to a zealous Jew than we today can readily realise.

 1. *"Circumcised the eighth day."* Paul was no mere proselyte, but an Israelite by birth, having, by heredity and the sign of the covenant, his part in the covenant promises of Israel; and like many another, he was proud of this.

2. *"Of the stock of Israel."* Paul's parents, also, were not merely proselytes, but were themselves Hebrews by birth. Paul was of Israelite descent through and through; and he was proud of his unblemished pedigree.

3. *"Of the tribe of Benjamin."* The tribe which gave the first king to Israel; which remained true to the Davidic throne when the other tribes broke away; which had helped Judah and Levi to restore the temple; and within the boundary of which stood the Holy City.

4. *"An Hebrew of the Hebrews."* Although living at Tarsus, Paul's parents adhered to the Hebrew language and customs. Paul was no Hellenist by upbringing, but was educated at Jerusalem under the famous Gamaliel. He was proficient in the Hebrew language and Scriptures, and adhered to Hebrew customs.

5. *"As touching the law, a Pharisee."* By birth an Israelite, by upbringing a Hebrew, he was also, by his own choice, a Pharisee. He had embraced the straitest sect, the one which took the strictest view of the Law.

6. *"Concerning zeal, persecuting the Church."* Paul was not satisfied even with being a Pharisee. He was a zealous Pharisee, the conscientious and relentless persecutor of all heretics and heretical sects.

7. *"Touching the righteousness which is in the law, blameless."* So far as the observance of all the formal rules, precepts and practices of the Law were concerned, Paul measured up to the last requirement.

In outward ground of confidence no man could surpass Paul. Yet all confidence in these things, and any supposed merit accruing from them, had been once for all thrown overboard when his suddenly floundering vessel had struggled through troubled waters to its new haven in the encircling arms of the risen Christ Jesus; and now, looking back, he writes—using the *past* tense— "What things were gains to me, those I *counted* loss for Christ."

Those things, however, were far from being the only things which Paul renounced for his Lord's sake. His renunciation increased as time elapsed, until now, at the time of his writing, he says—using now the *present* tense—"I count *ALL* things but loss for the excellency of the knowledge of Christ Jesus my Lord."

Nor is Paul's sweeping abandonment anything of a merely theoretical nature, for he adds: *"have suffered* the loss of all things" (v. 8).

Now *why* all this renunciation? Here is the answer: "That I may gain *Christ"* ("win" in the A.V. should be "gain"). Thus these two verses are all about loss and gain.

"What things were GAINS to me, those I counted LOSS for Christ. Yea, verily, and I count all things to be LOSS for the excellency of the knowledge of Christ Jesus my Lord, for whom I have suffered the LOSS of all things, and do count them refuse that I may GAIN Christ, and be found in Him."

So Paul puts down loss after loss on the one side, while on the other there is but the one solitary item: "CHRIST JESUS MY LORD." How much Paul has given up for his Lord! He has parted with the things dear to him as life itself. But now he has found more than all he has lost, and thrills to know that, having given up so much, he is the more fully Christ's, and Christ is the more fully his own. How true it is that those who give up most for Christ love Him most dearly and possess Him most satisfyingly!

Mark the focal passage in this chapter, with its recurrent expression "that I may":

"That I may gain . . ."   (verse 8).
"That I may know . . ."   (verse 10).
"That I may attain . . ."   (verse 11).
"That I may apprehend . . ."   (verse 12).

The recurrence of this expression shows the outreaching of the apostle's soul towards the great goal on which his desire was eagerly set. The whole of the man is gathered up in this one all-absorbing quest; and the focus-point of all is in the words of verse 10: "THAT I MAY KNOW *HIM."* Christ Himself is the supreme object of the believer's desire, the true goal of our whole life and being.

See how in this third chapter Christ is the believer's goal in a threefold way:

The goal of our *faith* — verse 9.
The goal of our *love* — verse 10.
The goal of our *hope* — verses 11–14, etc.

He is the goal of our faith for a heavenly *righteousness*. He is the goal of our love for a heavenly *fellowship*. He is the goal of our hope for a heavenly *blessedness*. All these will richly reward a closer study than we can linger to enjoy just here. Dig deeply into them. The deeper the spade the richer the "finds"! With what glad anticipation in these days should we be on the *qui vive* for that super-event which is the goal and fulfilment of all our dearest hopes—His return! Then He will be our "joy and *crown*," as we shall be His.

Chapter iv.: Christ our Strength

Here the prevailing emphasis is that Christ is the believer's *strength*, as in verse 13: "I can do all things *through Christ which strengtheneth me.*"

As we have said, the first verse of this chapter rightly belongs to chapter iii. Perhaps it is even truer to say that the section beginning at chapter iii. 1, with "Finally, my brethren, *rejoice,*" runs right on to verse 4 of this fourth chapter, ending: "*Rejoice in the Lord alway; and again I say, Rejoice.*"

The short final section begins then at verse 5: "Let your forbearance be known unto all men" (however much they persecute you) for "*the Lord is at hand*" (i.e. with you to strengthen you).

Next we find: "In nothing be anxious." Does it seem beyond realisation? Well, in answer to prayerfulness even "the peace of God shall garrison your hearts and minds *through Christ Jesus*" (verse 7).

Crowningly, in verse 13, we have: "I can do all things *through Christ which strengtheneth me.*" Strictly, the word "do" does not occur in the Greek. The verb *ischuo* means, "I am able"; but whether it means able to *be*, or to *bear*, or to *do*, or to *dare*, must be decided by the context. Ferrar Fenton perfectly hits the sense in translating it, "I am equal to anything. . . ." Take it with its context: "I know both how to be abased, and I know how to abound; everywhere and in all circumstances I have learned the secret both to be filled and to be hungry, both to abound and to suffer want: I can . . . all things through Christ which strengtheneth me." Well, shall we insert "do"—or "be" —or "bear"? Taken with the immediate context, I think that perhaps it should be "I can *bear* all things," but when read in its larger context it holds all three.

There it is, then, as Weymouth renders it: "I have strength for anything . . ." See now the secret: *"through Christ."* The Greek preposition is *"in,"* which expresses our oneness with Christ even more than our English translation "through." It is when we are most truly living *in Him* that He can most fully realise Himself in and through *us*. Note that the word "strengtheneth" is in the present tense, indicating a continuing inward replenishment moment by moment and hour by hour, unseen by human eyes but sustaining indeed in the secret consciousness of the believer.

Here then in chapter iv. is Christ our strength; Christ the believer's companion, guardian, indweller; Christ the Christian's secret of quiet forbearance (verse 5), confident tranquillity (verses 6, 7) and victorious enablement for "all things" (verses 12, 13).

Such are the four chapters of Philippians. And such is the wonderful fourfold Christ Who is ours—always and evermore sufficient! They who trust Him wholly find Him never-failing. If we really let Him, He will change every plaintive "I can't" into a gladsome "I can!"

What a triumphant little document this Philippian epistle is! Chains are clanking on the writer's wrists and ankles, but he makes them sound like bells of heaven! In the very first paragraph he speaks of "grace," "peace," "joy," "love," "glory," "praise"! And the bells ring right through all four chapters until they give a triumphant final peal in the last paragraph: "But my God shall supply all your need according to His riches in glory by Christ Jesus." What more need be said after *that*? All that is needed is a doxology; and that is just what Paul adds, in verse 20:

"NOW UNTO OUR GOD AND FATHER BE
THE GLORY UNTO THE AGES OF THE
AGES. AMEN."

THE EPISTLE TO THE COLOSSIANS

Lesson Number 137

NOTE.—For this study read twice through this epistle at one sitting.

ABOUT GNOSTICISM

Gnosticism may be provisionally described as a number of schools of philosophy, oriental in general character, but taking in the idea of a redemption through Christ, and further modified in different sects by a third element, which may be Judaism, Hellenism, or Christianity . . . the Gnostics took over only the idea of a redemption through Christ, not the full Christian doctrine, for they made it rather a redemption of the philosophers from matter, than a redemption of mankind from sin.

—Gwatkin: "Early Church History."

The intellectual pride of the Gnostics refined away the Gospel into a philosophy. The clue to the understanding of Gnosticism is given in the word from which it is derived—*gnosis*, "knowledge." Gnosticism puts knowledge in the place which can only rightly be occupied by Christian faith. To the Gnostic the great question was not the intensely practical one, "What must I do to be saved from sin?" but "What is the origin of evil?" "How is the primitive order of the universe to be restored?" In the knowledge of these and similar questions, and in the answers given to these questions, there was redemption, as the Gnostic understood it.

—Rev. John Rutherfurd: "Int. Stand. Bible Encyclopædia."

These little Gnostic sects and groups all lived in the conviction that they possessed a secret and mysterious knowledge, in no way accessible to those outside, which was not to be proved or propagated, but believed in by the initiated, and anxiously guarded as a secret. This knowledge of theirs was not based on reflection or scientific inquiry and proof, but on revelation. It was derived directly from the times of primitive Christianity, from the Saviour Himself and His disciples and friends, with whom they claim to be connected by a secret tradition, or else from later prophets, of whom many sects boasted. It was laid down in wonderful mystic writings, which were in the possession of the various circles.

—Bousset: "Encylopædia Britannica."

THE EPISTLE TO THE COLOSSIANS

IF the full cogency and urgency of this short but rich Colossian epistle are to register in our minds, we need to remember again the arrangement of these nine Christian Church Epistles as a group. The first four belong together; so do the middle three; so do the final two. In the first four the emphasis is on Christ and the *Cross*; in the middle three, Christ and the *Church*; in the final two, Christ and the *Coming*. In each case the order in which the Holy Spirit teaches truth is that of 2 Timothy iii. 16: "Doctrine . . . reproof . . . correction." "Doctrine" fixes the *norm* or canon. "Reproof" concerns deviation in *practice*. "Correction" counters deviation in *doctrine*. Thus in the first four, as already shown, we have, distinctively, doctrine in Romans, reproof in Corinthians, correction in Galatians. Similarly, in the middle trio, we have doctrine in Ephesians, reproof in Philippians, correction in Colossians.

The distinction, of course, is relative, not absolute, but it is really there. Accordingly in the middle trio, while doctrine interpenetrates all three, in Ephesians it is presented normally and formally, whereas in Philippians and Colossians it reappears only *incidentally* to reproof or correction. This does not mean that Philippians and Colossians are necessarily less important to us than Ephesians. Nay, they fill a vital place. We need to see truth not only statedly but *relatedly*. It often becomes best defined when it is being *defended*. Especially do we need to see cardinal evangelical doctrine sharply silhouetted against its specious counterfeit; and *that is what we have in Colossians*.

It is this which explains both the likeness and the *un*likeness of Colossians to Ephesians. Only the other day we heard a lady remark, "Colossians is so like Ephesians that the one seems to repeat the other." The remark was about equally discerning and *un*discerning. Colossians stands in the same relation to Ephesians as Galatians to Romans. The special characteristic in both Colossians and Galatians is "correction" of serious doctrinal deviation from the already-given standard. The affinity of Colossians with

Ephesians is so close that, if E. W. Bullinger's comparison is exact, 78 out of the 95 verses in Colossians have a "marked resemblance" to verses in Ephesians; which means that, although Ephesians is two chapters longer, more than half its verses speak again here in Colossians, only *now* they speak with a new pointedness against perilous deviation from the Ephesian norm.

This middle trio of epistles, Ephesians, Philippians, Colossians, belong together in *date* as well as in aspect. They all emanate from Paul's first imprisonment at Rome. Ellicott comments that Ephesians "does not appear to have been called forth by any particular circumstances," but is "more general in treatment." The same is true of the other "norm" epistles, i.e. Romans and Thessalonians. But the letters to the Corinthians, the Galatians, the Philippians and the Colossians were all precipitated by some pressing consideration, and all reveal a corresponding solicitude, especially the two which correct doctrinal error, i.e. Galatians and Colossians.

Ephesians sets forth the glorious *mystery*, even "the Church which is His body." Christ is the Head (i. 22, iv. 15, v. 23); the Church is the body (i. 23, iv. 16); individual believers are "members of His body" (v. 30), and therefore "members one of another" (iv. 25). The incipient fault at Philippi was disjointedness of the *members* (Phil. i. 27, ii. 3, 14, iv. 2). The incipient Gnosticism at Colosse was a "not holding the *Head*" (Col. ii. 19), which was a default far more serious.

City and Church of the Colossians

But before we say more about the doctrinal danger-signal at Colosse we ought to glance at the *city* and the *church* there.

Colosse was a Græco-Phrygian city in the Roman proconsular "Province of Asia." This province covered the western area of the large peninsula which nowadays is known as Asia Minor. The capital of this "Asia" was Ephesus, situated near the middle of the western coast of the peninsula. Some hundred and twenty miles inland from Ephesus were the three cities, Laodicea, Hierapolis, and Colosse, in the valley of the river Lycus. Laodicea and Hierapolis stood on opposite sides of the valley, some six miles apart. Colosse was ten or twelve miles farther north, on the river itself.

Like Thyatira (much farther north again) these three cities were noted for their manufacture of dyes, especially crimson (then called purple). Another source of prosperity lay in the excellent pasturage for sheep and the resultant trade in wool. The population was heterogeneous but basically Phrygian; there seems also to have been a large and wealthy Jewish community. Colosse had earlier been "a great city of Phrygia" (Herodotus), and "a populous city, prosperous and great" (Xenophon), but at the time when Paul's epistle was written it had fallen behind Laodicea and Hierapolis. It was in decline. Not long afterward, so it would seem, the city became finally disintegrated in a violent earthquake which shook those parts.

So far as we know, Paul never visited Colosse. Certainly at the time of his writing this epistle he had not been there, but had only *"heard"* (i. 4, 9, ii. 1) about the faith and love of the Colossians to whom he wrote. How and by whom, then, was the church formed there? Our first answer is found in the mighty impact of Paul's three years at Ephesus (Acts xx. 31). Of Paul's daily discussions in the lecture-room of Tyrannus we read: "And this continued by the space of two years; so that *all they which dwelt in Asia heard the word of the Lord Jesus, both Jews and Greeks*" (Acts xix. 10).

We know that there was a mighty movement of conversion in Ephesus itself (Acts xix. 17–20). There must also have been a wide outspreading of testimony; for the enraged Demetrius exclaimed, "Moreover, ye see and hear that not alone at Ephesus, *but almost throughout all Asia,* this Paul hath persuaded and turned away much people" (xix. 26). This certainly includes Colosse! (Wonderful Paul!)

But the prime evangelist to Colosse had been a certain Epaphras (i. 7), who was himself a Colossian (iv. 12), and who seems to have carried the witness to Laodicea and Hierapolis as well (iv. 13). Presumably he had been converted while visiting Ephesus. Thereafter he had carried on his testimony under Paul's guidance, and had proved "faithful" ever since in his message and ministering (i. 7). After a lapse of years, his prayerful zeal was increased rather than abated (iv. 12, 13).

It is probable that the new church at Colosse first met in the house of Philemon, for it was to Colosse that Paul returned

Philemon's runaway slave Onesimus (iv. 9); and the little epistle to Philemon speaks of "the church in thy house" (verse 2). Paul has nothing but grateful endorsement for the teaching and labours of Epaphras (i. 5–7, 23, ii. 6, 7, iv. 12, 13).

Now, however, about six years later, Epaphras has travelled to Rome to visit Paul in his imprisonment; and although he brings a good report in general, with warm assurance of love (i. 8), he has to confess anxiously that certain heresiarchs, evidently of eloquence and influence, had appeared among them, propagating a specious and deceptively attractive false doctrine (ii. 8–23) which was gravely endangering the fellowship. Paul at once enters into this apprehensiveness of his loyal Epaphras, and sends back this "Epistle to the Colossians" by the hand of Tychicus (iv. 7).

The Error of the Colossians

What, then, was the heterodox teaching which was ensnaring the Colossians? It bore the name of a "philosophy" (ii. 8), and had a "show of wisdom" (ii. 23), thus appealing to the higher intellectual tastes. It paid regard to "tradition" (ii. 8), which gave it further attractiveness to those who reverenced the past. It also practised asceticism and affected a humility (ii. 23) which gave it the appearance of a superior sanctity. This strange mixture of Jewish traditionalism and Greek philosophy stressed two things: reverence for angelic powers (ii. 18), and contempt for the body (ii. 20–3).

Dr. Alexander Maclaren gives a vivid impressionist idea of this new Colossian cultus in the following quotation:

"The tidings were that a strange disease, hatched in that hot-bed of religious fancies, the dreamy East, was threatening the faith of the Colossian Christians. A peculiar form of heresy, singularly compounded of Jewish ritualism and Oriental mysticism—two elements as hard to blend in the foundation of a system as the heterogeneous iron and clay on which the image in Nebuchadnezzar's dream stood unstably—had appeared among them, and though at present confined to a few, was being vigorously preached. The characteristic Eastern dogma, that matter is evil and the source evil, which underlies so much Oriental religion, and crept in so early to corrupt Christianity, and crops up today in so many strange places and unexpected ways, had begun to infect them. The conclusion was quickly drawn: 'Well, if matter be the source of all evil, then of course God and matter must be antagonistic'; and so the creation and government of this material universe could not be supposed to have come *directly* from Him. The endeavour to keep the pure Divinity and the gross world as far apart as possible, while yet an intellectual necessity forbad the entire breaking of the bond between them, led to the busy working of the imagination, which spanned the void gulf between God who is good, and matter which is evil, with a bridge of cobwebs—a çhain of intermediate beings, emanations, abstractions, each approaching more nearly to the material than his precursor, till at last the intangible and infinite was confined and curdled into actual earthly matter, and the pure was darkened thereby into evil.

"Such notions, fantastic and remote from daily life as they look, really led by a very short cut to making wild work with the plainest moral teachings both of the natural conscience and of Christianity. For if matter be the source of all evil, then the fountain of each man's sin is to be found, not in his own perverted will, but in his body, and the cure of it is to be reached, not by faith which plants a new life in a sinful spirit, but simply by ascetic mortification of the flesh.

"Strangely united with these mystical Eastern teachings, which might so easily be perverted to the coursest sensuality, and had their heads in the clouds and their feet in the mud, were the narrowest doctrines of Jewish ritualism, insisting on circumcision, laws regulating food, the observance of feast days, and the whole cumbrous apparatus of a ceremonial religion. It is a monstrous combination, a cross between a Talmudical rabbi and a Buddhist priest, and yet it is not unnatural that, after soaring in these lofty regions of speculation where the air is too thin to support life, men should be glad to get hold of the externals of an elaborate ritual. It is not the first nor the last time that a misplaced philosophical religion has got close to a religion of outward observances, to keep it from shivering itself to death. Extremes meet. If you go far enough east you are west."

Let no one think that this "disease" which was symptomatic at long-ago Colosse has no meaning for our own days, that there is no fear of our being "haunted by the ghosts of dead heresies." In every generation one or another reappears in fresh garb and

with new deceptiveness. We are needing the corrective of this
Colossian epistle today as much as ever. To mention only one
instance; what about Roman Catholicism, with its supposedly
meritorious asceticism and its elaborate interposing of saint-and-
angel worship? Oh, there is much need today to preach the Christ
of this Colossian letter, the Christ who is the one and only but
all-sufficient incarnate manifestation of the Creator; in whom
alone is effected true union of the Divine Spirit with the material
creation; the one God-Man who spans the gulf between a holy
God and sinful man, laying His hand on both, so that there is
neither need nor place for "a misty crowd of angelic beings or
shadowy abstractions" to graduate the measureless vast across
which His incarnation "flings its single solid arch"; the Christ
whose coming in flesh and blood has dignified the human body
into a temple of the Highest, and whose mighty work of reconciliation on the Cross excludes all further need either for "ascetic
mortification" or "Jewish scrupulosities."

The Letter to Colosse

The Epistle to the Colossians is a profound and priceless little
document. The first two of its four chapters are doctrinal; the
other two are practical. In its doctrinal half the tone is polemic,
for Paul is combating the semi-Judaistic mysticism and asceticism
which we have described, with its false cosmogony, angel-
worship, and supposedly penetrative insight into spiritual secrets.
It is a quite methodical composition, as our simple analysis shows.
Its dominant theme is the fulness and pre-eminence of Christ,
and the full completeness of Christian believers in Him, as against
the mysticisms and asceticisms enjoined by the philosophies and
traditions of men. There is no need for us in this instance to go
through the letter together, paragraph by paragraph, picking out
its main features and different sections. The epistle is so short
and clear that we may set out our analysis at once. Both of its
main parts are anticipated in the apostle's opening words. In
chapter i. 9 he prays that they "may be *filled*" with spiritual
knowledge—which is his subject in the first half of the epistle.
In verse 10 he prays that they might *"walk worthily"* of the Lord
—which is his subject in the second half of the epistle. Here it is,
then, in simple outline, at a glance:

THE EPISTLE TO THE COLOSSIANS

CHRIST THE FULNESS OF GOD TO US

Introductory thanksgiving (i. 1–8).

Opening prayer for "fulness" and "worthy walk" (i. 9–14).

I. DOCTRINAL—"THAT YE MAY BE FILLED"
(i.–ii.).

Christ the fulness of God in the creation (i. 15–18)
Christ the fulness of God in redemption (i. 19–23)
Christ the fulness of God in the Church (i. 24–ii. 7)
Christ the fulness of God versus heresy (ii. 8–23)

II. PRACTICAL—"THAT YE WALK WORTHILY"
(iii.–iv.).

The new life—and believers individually   (iii. 1–11)
The new life—and believers reciprocally   (iii. 12–17)
The new life—and domestic relationships   (iii. 18–21)
The new life—and employment obligations (iii. 22–iv. 1)
The new life—and "them that are without"   (iv. 1–6)

Personal addenda (iv. 7–18).

The Christology of Colossians

However spiritually superior the heretical compound of incipient theosophy and Judaism and asceticism may have seemed outwardly, its actual effect was to depose Christ from His solitary all-supremacy and all-sufficiency as Lord and Saviour. It was this which called forth, in our Colossian epistle, its superlative presentation of the all-pre-eminent God-Man Saviour who is the very "fulness of the Godhead bodily."

The Person of Christ (i. 15–18)

See, first, how in chapter i. 15–18 Paul gives his glorious full-length portrait of the *real* Christ who became our Saviour. It is well to set out separately again the seven super-glorious features:

1. "The visible form of the invisible God."
2. "The Prior-Heir of all creation."
3. "In Him the universe was created."
4. "He *IS* before the universe."
5. "In Him the universe coheres."
6. "The Head of the body, the Church."
7. "The Firstborn from among the dead."

That is the *real* Christ who had been preached to the Colossians. How then could they exchange *HIM* for any of the fanciful inferior angel-powers of the specious philosophisers who were now trying to talk them over? Where are His equals or rivals? Why, all the others were made *by* Him and *for* Him—"thrones, angelic lords, celestial powers and rulers" (verse 16)! Who else could even *pretend* this absolute sovereignty over the whole universe? He alone, with mysterious obviousness and unassuming ease, unites in Himself God and man, nature and super-nature, eternity and time, heaven and earth, past and future, all worlds and our world, all-transcending sovereignty and all-sufficient saviourhood—"that in *all* things *He* might have the *pre-eminence*"!

The Fulness, the Cross, the Mystery (i. 19–27)

See now how this magnificent sevenfold identification of the true Christ is followed up by three simply tremendous *aspects* of His person and passion and purpose.

Verse 19 says: "For in Him *the whole fulness* of the Godhead was pleased to dwell." There is no vague distribution of it among numberless shadowy spirit-beings such as the new mystics were presuming to have discerned by their secret insight! Nor is it distributed among those historical religious geniuses, originators, and teachers of whom Christ is (supposedly) merely the greatest— as is all too often taught today. This wonderful Christ, the *real* Christ, is the one concentrated Pleroma, the infinite Pleni- potentiary!

Next, verse 20 adds: "And having made peace through the blood of His Cross, by Him to reconcile all things unto Himself . . . whether things on the earth or *things in the heavens*." So His Cross has both a cosmic and a *universal* comprehensiveness!

Sin was in the universe before ever it entered the human race through Adam. It may have cursed other life-zones besides our own; but as all the universe centres in the eternal Son, so the peace-making of His cross has a universal circumference. Why then toy about with recondite notions of secretly finding some mysterious peace through prying into the unseen realm of spirits?

Next, see verses 24 to 27: "His body . . . the Church . . . the mystery which hath been hid from ages and generations, but is now made manifest to His saints . . . the riches of the glory of this mystery among the Gentiles, which is Christ in you, the hope of glory." What were all the petty "mysteries" and clandestine draperies of the new theosophisers compared with *this* glorious mystery which spans all the ages and generations?

Mark well, then, these three titanic aspects. First, the *"fulness"* of Christ comprehends the whole Godhead (verse 19). Second, the *"Cross"* of Christ comprehends the whole universe (verse 20). Third, the *"mystery"* of Christ comprehends all the ages (verse 26).

See now the surpassingly wonderful sevenfold salvation which the FATHER has effected for us through this incomparable One, the "Son of His love" (verse 13):

1. INHERITANCE—"Partakers of the inheritance of the saints in light" (verse 12).

2. DELIVERANCE—"Who hath delivered us from the power of darkness" (verse 13).

3. TRANSLATION—"And hath translated us into the kingdom of the Son of His love" (verse 13).

4. REDEMPTION—"In whom we have redemption through His blood" (verse 14).

5. FORGIVENESS—"Even the forgiveness of sins" (verse 14).

6. RECONCILIATION—"And you hath He reconciled" (verse 21).

7. TRANSFIGURATION—"To present you holy and unblameable in His sight" (verse 22).

Oh, how could those Colossians ever turn away from, or try to add to, such a full, Divine, eternal salvation as *that*? Or how can enlightened minds in our own times be dazzled away from it by the vain vagaries of human philosophy—"ever learning, and never able to come to the knowledge of the truth" (2 Tim. iii. 7)? Yet still today, alas, there are the superior intellectuals, ritualists, traditionalists, who insist on holding up their paltry little tapers to help the glorious sun to shine! What fools are the wise! How wise are the simple!

The Doctrine of the Fulness

It will scarcely need more than stating that the core of this Colossian letter is its doctrine of the *pleroma* or "fulness." There are two sides to this: the Divine and the human. The two great truths which the Colossians (and ourselves) were meant to learn are: (1) all the fulness of God is in Christ; (2) all the fulness of Christ is for us.

As we have shown in our analysis, the first eight verses of chapter i. are introductory. The letter properly begins at verse 9, with a prayer which gives the key to all that follows:

"For this cause we also, since the day we heard it, do not cease to pray for you, and to desire that ye might be *FILLED* with the knowledge of His will in all wisdom and spiritual understanding."

The Gnostic bewitchers at Colosse were insinuating that their own new inner knowledge added completion to the Gospel (the name "Gnostic" is from the Greek *gnosis*, "knowledge"), and affected to give (*a*) a fulness or completion to the truth as it is in Christ; (*b*) a completive inner knowing of Divine realities; (*c*) a superior "wisdom" or "spiritual understanding." Paul is using the favourite words when he prays that the Colossian believers "might be '*FILLED*' with the '*epignosis*' of His will in all '*wisdom*' and '*spiritual understanding.*' "

How, then, was this filling to become real in experience? The first need is to see the fulness of Christ Himself. So in chapter i. 19 we find: "It was the good pleasure [i.e. of God the Father] that in Him *all* the fulness should dwell." Next, in chapter ii. 3, we read: "In whom [Christ as the 'mystery' of God] are *all* the treasures of wisdom and knowledge *hidden*." Next, in chapter ii. 9: "In Him dwelleth *all* the fulness of the Godhead *bodily*."

The undivided pleroma of chapter i. 19 is here unmistakably defined as the fulness of "the Godhead." The very nature and attributes of God in all their plenitude reside in Christ. Moreover, whereas in chapter i. 19 the dwelling of the pleroma in Christ is seen rather as the *economic* "good pleasure" of the Father in relation to the stupendous Divine scheme of reconciliation, here in chapter ii. 9 it is seen as an *abiding fact*. Still further, all the fulness now and forever dwells in Him *"bodily"*—a clear reference to Him as the *incarnate* One, our own dear Lord and Saviour, *JESUS!*

In the first of these three statements the fulness *"dwells"* in Him; in the second it is *"hidden"* in Him; in the third it abides in Him *"bodily."* In the first it "dwells"-in Him as the qualification for all-sufficient Saviourhood. In the second it is "hidden" in Him that we may have the intellectual pleasure of ever-growing search and new discovery. In the third it resides in Him "bodily" that it may come to us spiritually through the Divine-human love and Spirit of One whom we can see and know and trust and love and lay hold of as *JESUS*.

Now comes the statement which lies at the very heart of this epistle, in chapter ii. 10. Verses 9 and 10 together read:

"In Him dwelleth all the *FULNESS* of the Godhead bodily;
and ye are *FILLED-FULL* in Him."

That is the one, straight, final reply which was needed. If He is the very fulness of the Godhead bodily, then nothing can be added to Him; and if the believer is "in Him," what can be added which the believer does not already possess in Him?

This finds echoes all through the epistle: "We pray . . . that ye might be *filled*" (i. 9). "I was made a minister according to the stewardship of God given me towards you, to *fulfil* [i.e. expound in its *fulness*] the word of God, the mystery" (i. 25). "That their hearts might be comforted, being knit together in . . . the *full*-assurance of understanding" (ii. 2). "That ye may stand perfect and *filled to completeness* in all the will of God" (iv. 12).

See now in chapter ii. how Paul turns all this against the subtle troublers of the Colosse assembly. "And this I say [i.e. 'all treasures of wisdom and knowledge hid in Him'] *lest any man should beguile you* with plausible sophistry" (ii. 4). "Beware lest any man makes prey of you through philosophy and empty make-believe after the tradition of men, after elementary notions of the world [i.e. the idea that harmful spirits tenant material things] and not after Christ; for in Him dwelleth all the fulness of the Godhead bodily" (ii. 8, 9). "Let no man therefore sit in judgment on you [as though you were any longer under traditional obligation] as to what you should eat or drink, or as regards festivals, new moons, or sabbaths, which are but a shadow of the things which are to come, whereas the substance is of Christ" (ii. 16). *"Let no man beguile you* of your reward in a voluntary humility and worship of angels, presuming on those things which he has supposedly seen, inflated in his fleshly mind instead of keeping in union with the HEAD" (ii. 18, 19).

It is quite clear that in verses 3–10 Paul is countering the *philosophy* glitter of the errorists. In verses 11–17 he is rebutting the *tradition* veneration which went with it. His answer to the former is the fulness of our Lord. His answer to the latter is the finality of the Cross. Lastly, in verses 18–23 he reproves them both together as a false duality of mysticism and legalism which (instead of bringing the supposed enlargement) engenders bondage. Moffatt's rendering certainly gives the force and spirit of verses 20–3: "If you died with Christ to the elemental spirits of the world, why live as if you still belonged to the world? Why submit to rules and regulations like 'Hands off this!' 'Taste not that!' 'Touch not this!'—referring to things that perish by being used? These rules are determined by *human precepts and tenets*; they get the name of 'wisdom' with their self-imposed devotions, with their fasting, with their rigorous discipline of the body, but they are of no value, they simply pamper the flesh!"

"If ye then be risen with Christ"

As our analysis indicates, the second part of this epistle is practical. Such is always the order of teaching in the New Testament—doctrine first, then practice. The Oxford Group slogan "Never mind what you believe; the only thing that matters is how you live" sounds breezy and practical enough; but in reality it is utterly fallacious. "How you live" is always determined by "what you believe." Doctrine is the basis of practice.

There was good reason, too, why Paul should add the further
two chapters on the Christian *walk*, for, as is often the case, going
with the big pretensions and hyper-spirituality of the supposedly
superior form of Christianity there was apparently a slump in
practical Christian godliness.

We cannot go through the several sections separately here:
they are demarcated in our analysis, and we can but recommend
a close follow-up study of them.

The only observation we shall make here is that Paul characteristically begins by lifting up CHRIST again as the highest of all
inspirations to sanctity of CONDUCT: "If ye then be risen with
Christ, seek the things which are *above* . . . mortify your members
on earth." Notice the three tenses of the believer's union with
Christ, in the opening paragraph of this third chapter:

Past tense   — "If ye then were *raised* with Christ."
Present tense — "Your life *is hid* with Christ in God."
Future tense — "When Christ, who is our life, shall
                appear, then shall ye also appear *with
                Him in glory*."

Going with these three tenses are two admonitions: "Seek those
things which are above"; "set your mind on things above, not
on things on the earth." Oh, that increasingly we may become
heavenly-minded, not in any dreamy, merely mystical sense, but
in the sense of prayerful, practical Christlike godliness—until we
"appear with Him in glory"! Remember, our dear Lord Himself
once said: "Where your treasure is, *there will your heart be also*."

> Our risen Lord is there,
>   Amid those mansions bright;
> He said He would our place prepare
>   In that fair land of light.
> A heaven of perfect love
>   Is ours through saving grace;
> We yet shall drink of joys above,
>   Before our Saviour's face.
> Our wistful hearts oft steal away,
> And wish forever there to stay.

TRY THESE, ON EPHESIANS, PHILIPPIANS, AND COLOSSIANS

1. Ephesians is distinctively the epistle of . . . (please say what).

2. Write out from memory our outline of Ephesians.

3. What are the six great "spiritual blessings" in Ephesians i. 3–14? and the three great truths Paul prays we may "know" in verses 15–23?

4. What are the five negative and three positive aspects of our Lord's Calvary work as shown in Ephesians ii. 13–18?

5. What is the fourfold presentation of Christ in Philippians? Give the key verse of each chapter.

6. Which are the four great personal *examples* set before the Philippians?

7. Can you give the seven steps in our Lord's descent (Phil. ii. 5–8), and show why it is not exact to call it His *"humiliation"*?

8. What (briefly) was the error of the Colossians?

9. Can you reproduce our brief analysis of Colossians?

10. What are the seven features in Paul's portrait of the *real* Christ in Colossians i. 15–18? And what (in the same chapter) are the seven wonderful blessings which are ours in the great salvation which the Father has effected for us through Christ?

THE FIRST EPISTLE TO THE THESSALONIANS

Lesson Number 138

Lesson Number 138

NOTE.—For this study read this short epistle through at least two or three times beforehand.

The apostle wrote to these people because he could not go to see them. This was due, indeed, to Jewish persecution and the "hindering of Satan" (ii. 18). At the same time, it marks a new juncture in St. Paul's career as Apostle of the Gentiles. The churches founded upon his first tour lay comparatively near to Antioch, his original head-quarters, and could all be visited from that centre in the course of a few months. It was otherwise when his mission-field extended to Europe, and included two continents. From this time it was impossible for him to superintend the churches he had founded, without the aid of messengers and letters. He is obliged to *write*, and to have a staff of helpers whom he may send backwards and forwards between himself and distant Christian societies. To this growth and enlargement of the field of his labours we owe the apostolic letters.

—*G. G. Findlay.*

THE FIRST EPISTLE TO THE THESSALONIANS

BOTH THE internal and the external evidences are such as to leave no doubt that the two epistles to the Thessalonians are genuine epistles of Paul. Also, it is generally agreed that they were the earliest-written of Paul's epistles. In fact, they and the Epistle of James seem to be the earliest-written documents of the New Testament. Most probably they were written from Corinth in A.D. 53. Their historical background is given in Acts xvii. 1–14. Paul's movements and feelings about that time may be traced and appreciated by comparing Acts xvii. 13–16 and xviii. 1–5 with 1 Thessalonians iii. 1–8. These passages should be looked up again and sympathetically re-read.

The occasion of Paul's writing the first of these two little epistles is given in chapter iii. 6. His brief but wonderfully fruitful visit to Thessalonica had been abruptly aborted by violent opposition from unbelieving Jews, who, by using "vile fellows of the rabble," set the whole city in an uproar, charging Paul and his attendants with sedition because they preached "another king, one Jesus" (Acts xvii. 7). Paul had been compelled to flee, and had gone to Berea, only to be pursued by Thessalonian Jews, and obliged to move on again, this time to Athens. From there (iii. 2), and with a heart full of longing solicitude for his beloved Thessalonian converts, he had sent Timothy to Thessalonica to enquire concerning their well-being and to confirm them in their faith. Timothy had returned to Paul (now in Corinth) a little later with a most heartening report (iii. 6), whereupon Paul wrote his first letter to them.

The two epistles naturally link themselves together, as they are alike in their main subject, which is the second coming of Christ, and their significance as a *pair* should be duly appreciated. How anyone can read them with an open mind and yet not see that our New Testament teaches a personal, visible return of Christ in great glory is an enigma to my own mind.

1 and 2 Thessalonians a Culmination

As we have said earlier, the nine Christian Church Epistles consist of a quartette, a trio, and a pair. The first four belong together, and their distinctive emphasis is Christ and the *Cross*. The middle three belong together, with distinctive emphasis on Christ and the *Church*. The final two belong together, putting a culminative emphasis on Christ and the *Coming*. In the first four *faith* looks back to the Cross and is strengthened. In the middle three *love* looks up to the heavenly Bridegroom and is deepened. In the final two *hope* looks on to the consummation and is brightened. "And now abideth faith, hope, love, these three."

This threefold order of the nine Christian Church Epistles is the Holy Spirit's way of indicating the order in which we are to teach Christian truth. The sinner's first need is neither the doctrine of the Church nor that of the Second Advent, but the Christ of Calvary, as in the four *evangelical* epistles (Romans, 1 and 2 Corinthians, Galatians). Next we are to show how individual salvation through Christ the Saviour introduces the blood-bought, Spirit-regenerated believer into a wonderful fellowship, an indissoluble spiritual oneness with all other true believers, in heaven and on earth, who in their totality compose the mystic body and bride and temple of God's eternal Son. Then we are to crown the instruction by pointing on to the sublime climax when the glorious Lord shall return for His completed Church, and the resurrected saints, translated into His likeness, shall together be "forever with the Lord."

As C. J. Ellicott says, in his introduction to the later Pauline epistles: "The Galatian and Roman epistles (as the history of the Reformation of the sixteenth century showed) are the treasure-house of the truths of *personal* (or individual) Christianity; for the very thought of justification, dominant in them, brings each soul face to face with its own sin and its own salvation, in that supreme crisis of life and death in which it is conscious of but two existences—God and itself. These later epistles (Ephesians, Philippians, Colossians) are equally the storehouse of the less vivid, yet grander conception of the holy catholic *Church*. The central idea is of Christ the Head, and the whole collective Christianity of the Church as His body." What else is needed? Just 1 and 2 Thessalonians to tell us of the Church's ultimate historical and heavenly consummation. In these two Thessalonian letters the doctrine of the Cross and of the Church is seen at its very simplest; but the wonderful prospect of the Lord's return is elucidated in relation to His Church as nowhere else in the New Testament.

First Thessalonians

Let us look now through the first of the two. There is a pleasing, straightforward orderliness about it. Our English version breaks it into five short chapters, each of which ends with a reference to the Lord's return. This tells us at once that everything here is being viewed in the light of that coming climax.

Next, we find that although everything is thus viewed futuristically, the first three chapters are *reminiscent*. The first word after the introduction is "Remembering"; and all ten verses of chapter one look back to the *conversion* of those Thessalonian believers. We see that it was an exemplary conversion, too. They had really felt the *"power"* of the Gospel (verse 5). They had quickly become *"ensamples"* to others (verses 6, 7). They had also become eager *"sounders out"* of the saving Word to others (verses 8–10).

Chapter ii. continues this backward look, only now the reminiscence fixes, not upon the converts, but upon the *evangelists*. It begins: "For yourselves, brethren, know *our entrance* in unto you." Paul thinks back gratefully over the brief, disturbed mission which he and his little team had conducted at Thessalonica. As we read of their *motive* in verses 1 to 6, of their *conduct* in verses 7 to 12, of their *message* and unselfish concern for souls in verses 13 to 16, we cannot help feeling that the exemplary evangelism in chapter ii. had much to do with the exemplary conversion in chapter i.

Chapter iii. follows on with recollections of Paul's *after-care* for his beloved new children in the faith. Verses 1 to 5 tell about his deep *concern* for them. Verses 6–8 tell of Timothy's *follow-up* work among them. Verses 9–13 tell of Paul's own "night-and-day" *praying* for them.

Chapter iv. marks a turn. Paul turns from looking backward to looking forward. His subject is characteristically practical. If in the first three chapters he has been usefully reminding them how they had been *saved*, in these additional two chapters he tells them how they should *live*. There can be no mistaking the three sub-sections. First, in chapter iv. 1–12 he speaks of *conduct and calling* (verses 1, 7). Next, in chapter iv. 13 to v. 11 he shows how the prospect of the Lord's return is one of *comfort* (iv. 13–18) and *challenge* (v. 1–11). Finally, in chapter v. 12–24 he exhorts to *concord* (verses 12–15) and *constancy* (verses 16–24). We may therefore set out the whole structure as follows:

FIRST THESSALONIANS

Key Truth: CHRIST OUR HOPE.

Salutation i. 1.

LOOKING BACK: HOW THEY WERE SAVED (i.–iii.).

(a) EXEMPLARY CONVERSION (i.).
   Knew Gospel power (5), Examples (6, 7), Witnesses (8–10).

(b) EXEMPLARY EVANGELISM (ii.).
   In motive (1–6), in conduct (7–12), in message (13–16).

(c) EXEMPLARY AFTER-CARE (iii.).
   Concern (1–5), Follow-up (6–8), Fervent prayer (9–13).

LOOKING ON: HOW THEY SHOULD LIVE (iv., v.).

(a) CONDUCT AND CALLING (iv. 1–12).
   In the light of the Father's will.

(b) COMFORT AND CHALLENGE (iv. 13–v. 11).
   In prospect of the Lord's return.

(c) CONCORD AND CONSTANCY (v. 12–24).
   In keeping with Christian fellowship.

Requests and benediction (v. 25–8).

The Glorious Hope

As Paul opens this first letter to his beloved Thessalonians he is "remembering without ceasing" their "work of faith, and labour of love, and patience of hope, in our Lord Jesus Christ." He soon defines these terms, as a comparison of verse 3 with verses 9 and 10 shows:

Verse 3.	Verses 9, 10.
"Your work of faith."	"Ye turned to God from idols."
"And labour of love."	"To serve the living and true God."
"And patience of hope."	"And to wait for His Son from heaven."

This comparison also confirms that the letter was sent to a church mainly Gentile, in which most of the converts had been only recently won from idolatry. Although strong in enthusiasm, it was young in experience. It is a significant fact, all in itself, that to such a church, and to such young converts, Paul unhesitatingly unfolded the splendid truth of our Lord's future coming and kingdom. Some present-day preachers might do well to "read, mark, learn, and inwardly digest" that fact.

Another unmistakable evidence that the Thessalonian church was in its youngest infancy shows itself in chapter iv. 13, where Paul says: "But I would not have you ignorant, brethren, concerning them which are asleep [or rather, *are falling asleep*: see R.V.], that ye sorrow not, even as others which have no hope." It is plain that Paul is here replying to misapprehensions which had arisen in their minds. The ever-busy, unsparing scythe of the great black reaper had brought bereavements to the brotherhood. A strange fear had struck at the faith of the mourners. Had their deceased Christian loved ones forfeited their participation in the hoped-for golden daybreak? The question had evidently arisen among them *for the first time*; and it evoked a reply which, more than any other passage in First Thessalonians, has stamped its special distinguishment upon this epistle (iv. 13–18).

The comparative study of Scripture is always useful in determining the true interpretation of controverted passages. Only recently we heard one of our ablest evangelical preachers declare that in John xiv. 3 our Lord had no thought of a second and visible coming to earth when He said, "I will come again, and receive you unto Myself; that where I am, there ye may be also." The words, said our recent preacher, referred to our Lord's coming in the person of the Holy Spirit at Pentecost. We ourselves need no support from elsewhere to convince us that in John xiv. 3 our

Lord *did* refer to a second and visible coming to this earth for His own; but in any case it is good to turn the light of 1 Thessalonians iv. 16, 17 on John xiv. 3 just for the sake of confirmation by comparison.

John xiv. 3.	1 Thessalonians iv. 16, 17.
"I will come again."	"The Lord Himself shall descend from heaven."
"And receive you unto Myself."	"Then we . . . shall be caught up . . . to meet the Lord in the air."
"That where I am, there ye may be also."	"And so shall we ever be with the Lord."

Just as this Thessalonian passage flashes backwards on John xiv. 3, so there is a passage in Matthew xxiv. which flashes forward upon this Thessalonian passage, lighting it up by comparison and deciding whether it is a *"secret* rapture" of the Church or not. Our very use of that phrase "secret rapture" calls for a cautionary word. Ten thousand pities that the glorious future event which is the Church's dearest hope should ever have been allowed to cause acrid heartburning among those who differ in their interpretation of its subsidiary aspects! But so it has. Why cannot those who agree on fundamentals disagree lovingly on the incidentals? There are those who claim that there will be two phases to our Lord's return—a first descent into the air *for* the saints, and then a later coming to the earth *with* them. A necessary corollary of this theory is that the first phase must be *secret.* All are agreed that the New Testament teaches a return in spectacular splendour. All are agreed that there are *not two* returns predicted. So, if there is a *preceding* descent for believers, it must necessarily be *secret.* And this indeed is what is commonly assumed. Where then does the New Testament teach this "secret rapture"? Strange as it seems to some of us, the classic proof-text is supposed to be 1 Thessalonians iv. 15–18. But *does* this passage teach a *secret* translation? Well, that is just where a comparison with Matthew xxiv. can help to decide for us.

We refer, of course, to our Lord's Olivet discourse. The particular part which bears on our Thessalonian passage is that where our Lord says:

"And then shall appear the sign of the Son of Man in heaven; and then shall all the tribes of the earth mourn; and they shall see the Son of Man coming in the clouds of heaven, with power and great glory. And He shall send His angels with a great sound [lit. *voice*] of a trumpet, and they shall gather together his elect from the four winds, from one end of heaven to the other" (Matt. xxiv. 30, 31).

Without dissent (except among those who disbelieve altogether in our Lord's second coming) it is agreed that these words, spoken by our Lord Himself, pre-describe a return which in the most glorious, overawing and spectacular sense is *visible and public*. Yet the remarkable feature, which must surely impress all but those who simply will not see, is the singular correspondence between the phraseology here, and that which is used in 1 Thessalonians iv. 15–18, to teach (supposedly) a *secret* coming. See the passages side by side.

Matthew xxiv.	1 Thessalonians iv.
"They shall see the Son of man coming."	"The Lord Himself shall descend from heaven."
"His *angels*, with a great *voice*."	"With the *voice* of the archangel."
"With a great *trumpet*."	"With the *trumpet* of God."
"They shall *gather together* His elect.	"Caught up *together* with them."
"In the *clouds* of heaven."	"In the *clouds* to meet the Lord."

Mark well the parallels here—angels, voice, trumpet, congregating, clouds. All are agreed that Matthew xxiv. teaches the splendid, outward, public coming. Then what kind of Bible interpretation is it which can take *exactly the same phrases and symbols* in 1 Thessalonians iv. 15–18 and say that *there* they teach a *secret* coming!

Of course, there are details in the Thessalonian paragraph which do not occur in Matthew xxiv., simply because our Lord could not divulge such *Church* doctrine beforehand (John xvi. 12, 13); and in any case no one passage has a monopoly of all the details about any given topic. Nothing can disguise to an honest eye the parallel between Matthew xxiv. 30, 31, and I Thessalonians

iv. 15–18, which surely settles it that the latter does *not* teach a supposedly secret coming.

I shall probably be asked forthwith: "What, then, do *you* believe about the two phases to the Lord's return?" My tantalising rejoinder is that at this point I purposely evade answer! The foregoing comparison serves its end if it only shows some younger students how important it is not to accept theories without duly testing them with Scripture revelation as a whole. Remember, in this matter of a suggested two phases of our Lord's return I have not committed *myself* either way—at least not *here*. I intentionally refrain from doing so here if only to take a further chance of appealing for Christian love and considerateness wherever there is divergence of view concerning such supplemental aspects of our Christian faith and hope.

One further comment must suffice. Note again the three arresting features in this Thessalonian passage: "shout"—"voice"—"trumpet." Each has its special relevance. The "shout" is given by "the *Lord*." The "voice" is that of the *"archangel."* The "trumpet" is "the trumpet of *God*." The Lord's shout is His resurrection-call to the *Church* (only once elsewhere do we read of His giving a shout, i.e. in John xi., where He raises Lazarus). The "archangel" is Michael (Scripture reveals many angels, but only the one *arch*angel) who has special connection with *Israel* (Dan. x. 21, xii. 1). The "trumpet" has to do with judgment, and that relates to the *nations* (Rev. viii.). Thus the "shout," the "voice," the "trumpet" have reference respectively to the Church, to Israel, to the nations. The "shout" brings resurrection; the "voice" effects regathering; the "trumpet" sounds for judgment. Such a dramatic, stupendous, Divine interruption of history utterly baffles imagination. It will end the present age, and introduce our Lord's millennial empire over all nations. Here in 1 Thessalonians, however, it is the Lord's coming in relation to the *Church* which is specially in view. Oh, what a precious hope and peerless prospect it is! Even so, come, Lord Jesus.

> With the archangel's cry,
>   And a loud trumpet-blast,
> With a shout from the sky,
>   He is coming at last!
> Yea, come Lord; for the bride
> And the kingdom are waiting!

THE SECOND EPISTLE TO THE THESSALONIANS

Lesson Number 139

NOTE.—For this study read carefully through the epistle three times, specially chapter ii., which should be read in the Revised Version.

Not long after the apostolic times the golden calves of idolatry were set up by the Church of Rome. What the effect of the captivity was to the Jews, that of the Reformation has been to Christendom. The first evil spirit has been cast out. But by the growth of hypocrisy, secularity and rationalism the house has become empty, swept and garnished: swept and garnished by the decencies of civilisation and discoveries of secular knowledge, but empty of living and earnest faith. And he must read prophecy but ill who does not see under all these seeming improvements the preparation for the final development of the man of sin, the great repossession, when idolatry and the seven worse spirits shall bring the outward frame of so-called Christendom to a fearful end.

—Henry Alford, D.D.

SECOND THESSALONIANS

Patient waiting, watching and working.

Salutation i. 1, 2.

COMFORT—FROM THE HOPE OF CHRIST'S RETURN

(i.).

The consolation of it in the present (verses 3–7).
The compensation by it in the future (verses 8–12).

CAUTION—ON THE TIME OF CHRIST'S RETURN

(ii.).

The when and the how of the coming (verses 1–12).
The why and the how of the waiting (verses 13–17).

COMMAND—IN THE LIGHT OF CHRIST'S RETURN

(iii.).

Basis of command: appeal, confidence (verses 1–5).
Nature of command: must work as we wait (verses 6–15).

Benediction and Signature iii. 16–18.

THE SECOND EPISTLE TO THE THESSALONIANS

It is generally agreed that this second letter to the Thessalonians was written within a few months of the first, while Paul was still at Corinth. Its main purpose is made quite clear by its contents. Certain evils mentioned in the first letter had further developed by the time of the second. We gather, also, that there had arisen some misunderstanding or even misrepresentation of the apostle's teaching about the Lord's return. Notwithstanding the admonitions of the first letter, there were those, apparently, who presumed to declare that "the day of the Lord" was "at hand" or even then "present" (R.V.); and there is a hint that some spurious letter or message, purporting to come from Paul himself (ii. 2) had found its way among them, by which they had been "shaken in mind." The agitation which had resulted was showing rather fanatical tendencies in some. Assuming that the Lord's return was almost immediately upon them, they were leaving their employment, thus bringing the burden of their maintenance on the fellowship. It was not surprising, either, that such misguided ones were falling prey to the temptation to become "busy-bodies" (iii. 11), and that thus the peace of the Christian brotherhood was being impaired (iii. 6, 12, 16). The gentler and more guarded reproof of the first letter, therefore, now gives place to sterner words.

But we must not overstate that side of things, for there was far more on the other side of the scale, calling for overflowing gratitude and praise to God. Speaking of the Thessalonian assembly in the main, their faith was "growing exceedingly," their mutual love "abounded," their "faith and patience" amid persecutions was an example to the Lord's people everywhere (i. 3–5). This second letter is one of exultation, explanation and exhortation.

It is a very short letter, and we must not try to over-analyse it. Yet it is well to pick out and see clearly its threefold progress.

In chapter i. the Lord's return is held up as the great *COMFORT* of the saints amid persecutions and distresses. In verses 4–7 it gives consolation in the *present*. In verses 8–12 it means compensation in the *future*.

Next, in chapter ii. comfort gives place to *CAUTION*, for there were wrong ideas afloat concerning the Lord's return and certain matters connected with it. In verses 1–12 Paul guides and corrects as to the "when" and the "how" of the coming. In verses 13–17 he tells them why (verses 13, 14) and how (verse 15) to *wait*.

Finally in chapter iii. Paul passes on to *COMMAND* (not, however, as a military general—but as an apostle of the Lord). Four times that word "command" occurs (verses 4, 6, 10, 12), and the section ends with: "And if any man *obey* not our word in this epistle, note that man." Verses 1–5 give us Paul's kindly prelude to his "commanding," namely, an appeal (verses 1, 2) and an expression of confidence (verse 4). The remaining verses (verses 6–15) give Paul's apostolic commands, which in this case seem all to concern practical behaviour.

So, then, the contents of this little epistle fall into clear order and division. In chapter i. the great hope of the Lord's second coming is set before the Thessalonians as their great *consolation* amid the tribulations which they were having to endure for Christ's sake. Next, in chapter ii. the apostle furnishes them with authoritative *correction* concerning the time and the way of Christ's return. Finally, in chapter iii. there is the apostle's *counteraction* of practical error concerning present duty in the waiting-time till Christ returns. The epistle may be set out as follows: (*See flyleaf of present study.*)

That Second Chapter

We cannot here discuss with anything like thoroughness the rather obscure apocalyptic passage in chapter ii. (we have just read many pages on it and have been surprised at the numerous variety of interpretations from earliest Christian times until now —not any of which entirely convinces at least one obstinate mind!). But the following comments may be of useful guidance to some. First, read the verses as follows:

"But we beseech you, brethren, concerning the coming of our Lord Jesus Christ, and our assembling together unto Him, that you be not soon shaken from your sober mind, nor be troubled, neither by spirit, nor by word, nor by epistle as from us, to the effect that the day of the Lord is upon us. Let no man deceive you by any means, because that day shall not come, except there come the apostasy first, and the man of sin be revealed, the son of perdition, who opposeth and exalteth himself against all that is called God, or is an object of worship; so that he sits in the temple of God, showing himself that he is God. Remember you not that when I was with you, I told you these things? And now you know what restraineth, that he might be revealed in his time. For the mystery of lawlessness is already working, yet only until he that restraineth be gone; and then shall the lawless one be revealed, whom the Lord Jesus will slay with the breath of his mouth, and annihilate by the appearance of his coming; even him whose coming is after the working of Satan, in all power and signs and wonders of falsehood, and in all deceit of unrighteousness for them that perish, because they receive not the love of the truth, that they might be saved. And for this cause God sends to them the working of error, that they might believe the lie; that they might be judged who believed not the truth, but had pleasure in unrighteousness."

Now, unless we start tinkering with plain wordings and meanings, the first plain intention is that the "man of sin" is one individual *person*—not a *system*, such as Judaism or Romanism, and not a *succession* of men, such as the Cæsars or the popes. It is the "man," "who," "he," "himself," "whom," "son of perdition". Over against Bishop Lightfoot's remark that the man of sin here need not be an individual man because in figurative passages personification does not always mean an actual person, we reply that *this* passage is clearly *not* merely figurative. The man of sin is directly and repeatedly referred to in the singular, in such a way as makes him as really a person as the Lord who destroys him.

The second thing which stands out plainly (verse 3) is that "the day of the Lord" does not come until two things happen: (1) the "apostasy," and (2) the revealing of the "man of sin." These two things are the signs and precursors of the great day. Over against the artificial suggestion that perhaps between these two occurrences and the Lord's return a long period could intervene we reply: "No, for if so there would have been absolutely no point in Paul's giving them as indicators for the Thessalonians. Moreover, the "then" and the "whom" of verse 8 *complete* the impression that the revealing of the "man of sin" *precipitates* the Lord's "coming."

The third thing which stands out unmistakably is that the Lord's "coming" here spoken of is His coming in visible splendour and power, to bring in "the day of the Lord." By no stretch can it be referred to His coming at Pentecost in the outshedding of the Holy Spirit; nor can it possibly be so utterly contracted as to mean only the fall of Jerusalem in A.D. 70. Except to those who altogether disbelieve in such a second coming of Christ the "coming" and the "day" here mean most definitely the *still-future* return of our Lord. *That* being so, the "man of sin," also, must be still future, for he appears just ahead of it. Therefore he cannot be Nero, or Mohammed, or any of the popes or other figures of the past, though some of these behaved like advance adumbrations of him!

The preceding three observations are made finally secure because equally clearly they correspond with *other* Scriptures. The Old Testament type of the "man of sin" is Antiochus Epiphanes (Dan. xi. 21–45), and he was an individual man. The corresponding figure in John's Apocalypse is the "beast," of which it is written: "Let him that hath understanding count the number of the beast, for it is the number of a man; and his number is six hundred threescore and six." That the "apostasy" and the "lawless one" appear shortly before our Lord's return is corroborated by various passages, notably Matthew xxiv. and 2 Timothy iii., where we see an intense heading-up of evil just beforehand.

But perhaps the point of keenest perplexity is the words: "And now you know what *restraineth* that he [the man of sin] may be revealed in his [appointed] time. For the mystery of lawlessness is already working, but only until *he that restraineth* is gone; and *then* shall the lawless one be revealed." The vast majority of interpreters believe the restraining power to have been the Roman empire which for so long maintained law and order; but if the passage relates to what is yet future, imperial Rome must be ruled out as having been removed long ago. Does not the personal pronoun "until *he* be gone" suggest the Holy Spirit— the Holy Spirit operating through the truth and power of the Gospel, through the presence and witness of the Church, and through a certain present direct restraint of Satan? None can say dogmatically, though it is evident from verse 6 that Paul had earlier told the Thessalonians quite openly what the "restraint" was. For my own part, believing as I do in the supernatural inspiration of the Bible, I am sure that Paul was withheld by the Holy Spirit from being more explicit, so that his written words here might have a far reach into the future which his spoken words to the Thessalonians perhaps did *not* have.

Let us not be so occupied with the problem here that we lose sight of the tremendous fact which is disclosed, namely, that there is in this present age *a restraint upon Satan*. Thank God, the devil cannot do just as he likes: the strong man's house has been spoiled by a Stronger! What this sin-cursed world would have been like by now if Jesus had not come, and if Satan were not so greatly restrained in consequence, imagination cannot picture.

During the Millennium, Satan will be completely bound, out of action, and in the abyss of Hades; but during the end-epoch of this *present* age the restraint upon him is to be relaxed; and then: "Woe to the inhabitants of the earth and of the sea! for the devil is come down unto you, having great wrath because he knoweth that he hath but a short time" (Rev. xii. 12). It is then that he will fling off all disguise, and appear as the morally ugly archfiend that he really is, no longer going about only as "an angel of light" cunningly seeking whom he may deceive (2 Cor. xi. 14), but "as a roaring lion, seeking whom he may devour" (1 Pet. v. 8)! It is then that he will appear as "the beast out of the sea" and the "other beast out of the earth," which latter is the *"man"* whose number is 666 (Rev. xiii.). He will enter and possess this human being in a way never known before, and with wide powers he will exercise an awful tyranny over millions—first deceiving and then enslaving them.

But *why* should this have to happen? It is because this is the only way that Christ-rejecting men and nations will learn. They shall be allowed a final and culminating lesson in which to learn by bitterest experience what is the ultimate alternative to the grace and government of "our God and His Christ." But just when it looks as though 666 is to dominate all flesh, God's great SEVEN, the glorious Prince and Saviour, shall suddenly appear in flaming splendour from the skies, and shall utterly consume "that wicked one" with the breath of His mouth!

We write these words with deep and solemn emotion, for the occurrence of these things is almost certainly "at hand." We have seen pre-editions of the final anti-Christ in Hitler and Stalin, both of whom claimed worship and enslaved millions. Today the nations of the earth range themselves under either one or the other of two political and economic ideologies, and our atomic age is heading up to the titanic struggle between them. As we write these lines, more millions than can be counted are behind Communist curtains and in Communist slavery. All but blind eyes can see that "the scene is set" for the coming of 666. Yet it was in this very connection that our omniscient Lord said: "When these things begin to come to pass, then look up and lift up your heads, for your redemption draweth nigh." What a hope! What a Saviour!

EIGHT QUESTIONS ON I AND II THESSALONIANS

1. Can you reproduce our framed analysis of 1 Thessalonians?

2. Can you quote any verse showing that the Thessalonian church was mainly Gentile?

3. In 1 Thessalonians ii. Paul's evangelism is exemplary in three ways. Which are they?

4. Can you give argument why 1 Thessalonians iv. 15–18 does *not* teach a "secret rapture"?

5. What are the three parts of the short second epistle?

6. What two things are to happen before the Day of the Lord comes?

7. How would you explain the "restraint" on the "lawless one" in 2 Thessalonians?

8. Why would you say that the "man of sin" is neither a *system* nor a *succession* of men?

THE EPISTLES OF PAUL TO TIMOTHY

Lesson Number 140

NOTE.—For this study read twice through 1 Timothy then twice through 2 Timothy, mentally comparing the two.

These Pastoral Epistles—1 and 2 Timothy and Titus, to which is conjoined the short letter to Philemon—are so named and grouped because they are addressed to Christian pastors. (Even Philemon was a church elder with perhaps considerable pastoral engagement; for in addressing him Paul adds, "and to the *church in thy house*.")

They have a positional significance which should not be overlooked, fitting, as they do, between the two cohesive main groups of New Testament epistles, i.e. the nine Christian Church Epistles (Romans to Thessalonians) and the nine Hebrew Christian Epistles (Hebrews to Revelation). The two ninefold groups noticeably differ from each other in viewpoint and emphasis. The pastoral Epistles, coming between them, fulfil a meaningful function. As the book of the Acts marks the transition from the distinctive message of the Gospels to that of the Epistles, so these Pastoral Epistles, both by their nature and their position, mark the transition from the special doctrinal contribution of the Church Epistles to the new emphasis and aspects of the Hebrew Christian Epistles. We shall touch on this again later, but it is well to mention it here beforehand.

—*J.S.B.*

THE EPISTLES OF PAUL TO TIMOTHY

IN AN earlier instalment of our Study Course we remarked that if there is one part of the Bible more than another which Christian believers should thoroughly study it is that part which is specifically written *to* Christian believers, namely, the nine Christian Church Epistles (Romans to 2 Thessalonians). We would now add that if there is any part of the Bible which Christian *ministers* should study it is that part which particularly addresses *them,* namely, the Pastoral Epistles (1 and 2 Timothy and Titus, to which, quite fittingly as we shall see, is added the letter to Philemon). These Pastoral Epistles are known as such because they have to do with the organised church from the *pastor's* point of view. They are full of instruction for *all* Christian believers, of course; yet their message in a special sense concerns those who have the oversight of local Christian assemblies or churches.

We need not stay here to discuss the *authorship* of these epistles. From earliest times they have been generally accepted as genuine Pauline writings; and although some of our modern "higher critics" have questioned them, as they have questioned practically everything else in the Bible, they have been so roundly rebutted by other scholars, equally able, that there is no need to halt here on that score.

These Pastoral Epistles have a special interest in three ways: (1) in their subject-matter; (2) in their leading ideas; (3) in their positional significance. So, let us first take a "look round" at the *contents* of these two Timothy epistles and see if they lend themselves to orderly analysis.

THE FIRST LETTER TO TIMOTHY

Timothy was pastor of the Christian "assembly" at Ephesus (1 Tim. i. 3). That he was a comparatively young man is made clear by expressions in both letters to him and by references in the Acts of the Apostles. Paul's references also leave us in no doubt that Timothy was very dear to him. A following up of these, in their chronological order, makes an interesting and profitable study.

The two epistles to Timothy are a "charge" from Paul to Timothy. We are told this no less than ten times in the two letters. And *what* is the charge? The first epistle (i. 18 and vi. 20) and the second epistle (i. 12, 14, ii. 2) make the answer plain—if read in the wording given in the margin of the Revised Version. The "charge" is that Timothy shall *"guard"* something which Paul is committing to him. Paul calls it "the deposit" in the verses just cited. In 2 Timothy i. 12 Paul says: "I know whom I have believed, and am persuaded that He is able to guard *the deposit* until that day." Here the "deposit" is not something which Paul had committed to Christ (as our Authorised Version gives it) but a trust which *Christ* had committed to *Paul*. Paul's two letters to Timothy, written by the apostle in the knowledge that soon he himself must pass beyond, are a charge that the younger man shall bravely and faithfully "guard" the sacred "deposit" in the days to come. Paul specifically states the *nature* of the "deposit" in 1 Timothy i. 11 as "the glorious Gospel of the blessed God, which was committed to my trust."

Looking particularly into the *first* of these two epistles we soon see that its over-all subject is the local "church" or "assembly" of Christian believers and the pastor-in-charge. It turns out to be a quite methodical little document.

The first seventeen verses of chapter i. give a preliminary *explanation* why the letter was being written, and end with a doxology: "Now unto the King eternal, immortal, invisible, the only wise God, be honour and glory for ever and ever, Amen." Thereupon, in the remaining three verses (18–20), with a touch of solemn formality, the great apostle introduces his *"charge"* to "son Timothy."

The "charge" itself begins at the first verse of chapter ii., and thereafter the letter breaks into two clear parts. Chapters ii. and iii. concern the *assembly* and its conduct. Chapters iv., v. and vi. concern the *minister* and his conduct.

Glance again through the chapters and verify this. In chapter ii. the first eight verses are about the *men* and their public praying; the remaining verses are about the *women* and their public mien. In chapter iii. the first seven verses give the qualifications of *elders*; the ensuing verses give the qualifications of *deacons*. So, then, chapters ii. and iii. concern public order and public office in the assembly.

Chapters iv., v. and vi. now follow, with their emphasis upon the *minister* and his conduct. In chapter iv. he is shown how to be "a good minister of Jesus Christ" toward the assembly as a whole, i.e. faithful *teaching* (verses 1–11), and exemplary *living* (verses 12–16). In chapters v. and vi. he is shown his true conduct toward particular *classes* in the assembly, i.e. toward older and younger (verses 1, 2), widows (verses 3–16), elders (verses 17–25), servants (vi. 1–8), the rich (verses 9–19). The epistle then ends with: "O Timothy, guard that which is committed to thy trust." It may be set out in flat analysis, as follows:

FIRST EPISTLE TO TIMOTHY

The local "Church" and its "Minister."

A CHARGE, i. 18, vi. 13, 20,—"Guard the deposit."

Preliminary explanation i. 1–17.
The "charge" introduced i. 18–20.

I. THE ASSEMBLY AND ITS CONDUCT (ii.–iii.).

(*a*) CONCERNING ORDER (ii.).
The men and public prayer (1–8).
The women and public mien (9–15).

(*b*) CONCERNING OFFICE (iii.).
Qualifications of elders (1–7).
Qualifications of deacons (8–14).

II. THE MINISTER AND HIS CONDUCT (iv.–vi.).

(*a*) TO THE ASSEMBLY IN GENERAL (iv.).
A "good minister" in faithful teaching (1–11).
A "good minister" in exemplary living (12–16).

(*b*) TOWARD PARTICULAR CLASSES (v., vi.).
Older and younger (v. 1, 2), *widows* (3–16).
Elders (17–25), *Servants* (vi. 1–8), *Rich* (9–19).

Closing appeal vi. 20, 21.

It seems clear from chapter i. 3, 4 that the letter was a follow-up of oral advice already given by Paul to Timothy. Perhaps it was deemed wise that the younger man should have such a letter in his possession to which he could appeal if challenged on any point of action. We may well be grateful that it was penned. Good had it been for our churches if they had neither added to nor taken from the simple administrative guides left for us in these Pastoral Epistles!

THE SECOND LETTER TO TIMOTHY

This second letter to Timothy, like the first, is occupied with the exercise of the ministry within the local church. It was written soon after the first letter. Paul was in prison at Rome; and he did not expect (as he did in the earlier letter) to be freed again (except by his "departure" to be with Christ). This second letter to Timothy is the last writing of Paul preserved to us. As such it has a peculiar and touching interest. In it we see Paul's final attitudes. These are a study all in themselves. Never does the apostle shine in nobler light. His passion for the great work to which his whole energy has been devoted is strong as ever upon him. This parting letter should often be read, especially by ministers and other Christian workers. Never was its message more needed than today.

If as we have seen, the first epistle to Timothy is a *"charge,"* this second one develops it into a *challenge*. It is a challenge to fortitude and faithfulness in face of *present* testings and of *further* testings which were yet to come. It is equally orderly as the first. The four chapters break into two pairs. Chapters i. and ii. are about the Christian pastor and his true reactions to *present* testings. Chapters iii. and iv., commencing "This know, also, that in the last days perilous times shall come," concern the pastor's reaction to *age-end* troubles.

Take the first two chapters. Running from i. 3 to ii. 13, the aspect is that of the pastor's *personal* reactions; while in the remaining verses of chapter ii. it is that of his *pastoral* reactions. In each section there is challenge and incentive. In the personal section see the *challenge* in such expressions as "Stir up" (i. 6), "Be not ashamed" (i. 8), "Be strong" (ii. 1), "Endure" (ii. 3);

and the *incentive* in "Remember" (i. 6, ii. 8), and in Paul's own moving example (i. 12, ii. 9, 10).

Then in the pastoral section (ii. 14–26) see again *challenge* in such words as "Charge" (verse 14), "Study" (verse 15), "Shun" (verse 16), "Refuse" (verse 23); and the *incentive* in "Nevertheless the foundation of God standeth sure" (verse 19), and "That they may recover themselves out of the snare of the devil" (verse 26).

Take now the last two chapters, which forewarn of age-end troubles. Chapter iii. gives the true *personal* reaction, and chapter iv. the true *pastoral* reaction. Running through both parts there is again both challenge and incentive. But see the whole epistle now in framed outline:

SECOND EPISTLE TO TIMOTHY
The True Minister and His Reactions.

A CHALLENGE TO FORTITUDE AND FAITHFULNESS.

Salutation i. 1, 2.

THE TRUE PASTOR AND PRESENT TESTINGS (i., ii.).

THE TRUE PERSONAL REACTION (i. 3–ii. 13).

Challenge—"stir up," "Be not ashamed," "endure," etc.
Incentive—"Remember" (i. 6, ii. 8), *Paul's example*
(i. 12, ii. 9), *etc.*

THE TRUE PASTORAL REACTION (ii. 14–26).

Challenge—"charge," "study," "shun," "refuse," etc.
Incentive—"foundation sure" (19), souls rescued (26).

THE TRUE PASTOR AND AGE-END TROUBLES (iii., iv.).

THE TRUE PERSONAL REACTION (iii.).

Challenge—"Perilous times" (1–9) "continue thou" (14).
Incentive—Paul's example (10, 11) Scripture (15, 16).

THE TRUE PASTORAL REACTION (iv.).

Challenge—"Preach the Word," "do work of evangelist."
Incentive—the coming kingdom (1), the coming crown (8).

For the moment we make no comment on any of the component sections. Having seen the two epistles in separate analysis, we ought next to review them as a pair, tracing out their leading ideas; for it is when thus surveyed that they assume an arresting, irresistible significance which, when once seen and felt, can never be forgotten.

A Charge, a Challenge, a Forecast

1 and 2 Timothy a "Charge"

We emphasise again that in form and force these two Timothy letters are a *"charge."* Paul is reinforcing, clarifying and amplifying a charge already given verbally to Timothy (see 1 Tim. i. 4, R.V.). See how this idea of a charge persists right through. (Where necessary we quote from R.V.)

"That thou mightest *CHARGE* some that they teach no other doctrine" (1 Tim. i. 3).

"Now the end [or aim] of the *CHARGE* is love, out of a pure heart and a good conscience" (i. 5).

"This *CHARGE* I commit unto thee, son Timothy . . . that thou mightest war the good warfare" (i. 18).

"These things *CHARGE*, and teach" (iv. 11).

"These things also *CHARGE*, that they may be blameless (v. 7).

"I *CHARGE* thee before God and the Lord Jesus Christ and the elect angels" (v. 21).

"I *CHARGE* thee in the sight of God who quickeneth all things" (vi. 13).

"*CHARGE* them that are rich in this present age that they be not high minded" (vi. 17).

"I *CHARGE* (or solemnly testify) thee in the sight of God and of Christ Jesus" (2 Tim. iv. 1).

What is the Charge?

As we have said, the gist of this charge is that Timothy shall *"guard"* something which Paul is *"committing"* to him. This something is called *"the deposit."* Trace this through the two letters.

"This charge I *DEPOSIT* with thee, son Timothy" (1 Tim. i. 18).

"I charge thee . . . *GUARD* these things without prejudice" (v. 21).

"O Timothy, *GUARD* the *DEPOSIT*" (vi. 20, R.V. margin).

"I know whom I have believed, and am persuaded that He is able to *GUARD* the *DEPOSIT* against that day" (2 Tim. i. 12).

"The good *DEPOSIT* do thou *GUARD* through the Holy Spirit which dwelleth in us" (i. 14).

"The things which thou hast heard from me . . . *DEPOSIT* with faithful men" (ii. 2).

We recall that Paul clearly defines the "deposit" in the first epistle, chapter i. 11: "The glorious Gospel of the blessed God, which was committed to my trust." The "deposit" is the Christian faith, "the truth as it is in Christ Jesus." The time of Paul's own "departure" is now at hand. As he looks back over the years, he can say: "I have fought the good fight; I have finished the course; I have *held intact* the faith." But what of the future? He must give this solemn, written "charge" to his dearest son in the faith. With a new sense of responsibility Timothy is now to "guard" this priceless, vital "deposit" of Christian truth: he is to preserve it, protect it, proclaim it.

This, then, is the order:

(1) The "glorious Gospel of the blessed God" is entrusted to Paul (1 Tim. i. 11).

(2) Paul now "deposits" it in (and as) a special "charge" to Timothy (i. 18).

(3) Paul exhorts Timothy: "O Timothy, *guard* the *deposit*" (vi. 20).

(4) Paul knows whom he has believed, and is persuaded *HE* will "guard the deposit" (2 Tim. i. 12).

(5) Timothy is further to "deposit" the treasure of truth to other faithful trustees who are "able to teach others also" (ii. 2).

"The Faith"

Now it is because these two epistles are a charge concerning the guardianship of this sacred deposit of truth that we find in them certain expressions occurring in almost every paragraph. One such is *"the faith."* In many of the verses where the expression occurs the definite article is omitted by our Authorised Version, but the Greek has it in all the following references—which should be noted because this expression, "the faith," seems to have been commonly used to sum up Christian truth and practice viewed together as a *religion*.

"Some have made shipwreck as regards *the faith*" (1 Tim. i. 19).

"Holding the mystery of *the faith* in a pure conscience" (iii. 9).

"A good standing and great boldness in *the faith*" (iii. 13).

"In the latter times some shall depart from *the faith*" (iv. 1).

"A good minister of Jesus Christ, nourished in the words of *the faith*" (iv. 6).

"If any provide not for . . . his own house, he hath denied *the faith*" (v. 8).

"Some reaching after [money] have erred from *the faith*" (vi. 10).

"Fight the good fight of *the faith*; lay hold on the life eternal" (vi. 12).

"Science, falsely so called, which some professing have erred from *the faith*" (vi. 21).

"Men of corrupt minds, reprobate as regards *the faith*" (2 Tim. iii. 8).

"Wise unto salvation through *the faith* which is in Christ Jesus" (iii. 15).

"I have fought the good fight; I have finished the course; I have kept *the faith*" (v. 7).

"The Doctrine"

We find, also, a lot about "teaching," "teachers," "doctrine," in these two Timothy epistles. "Teaching" and "doctrine" are the same word in the Greek, which turns up about fourteen times here, carrying with it the solemn implication that the sacred "deposit" is to be guarded *doctrinally*.

Again and again we meet here the expression *"the doctrine,"* which sums up the whole Christian system from a doctrinal standpoint.

"Law is made . . . for the lawless . . . any other thing contrary to sound *doctrine*" (1 Tim. i. 9, 10).

"Nourished in the words of the faith and of the good *doctrine*" (iv. 6).

"Give heed to reading, to exhortation, to the *doctrine*" (iv. 13).

"Take heed to thyself and to the *doctrine*" (iv. 16).

"That the name of God and the *doctrine* be not blasphemed" (vi. 1).

"The words of our Lord Jesus Christ, and the according-to-piety *doctrine*" (vi. 3).

"But thou hast closely followed the *doctrine* of mine" (2 Tim. iii. 10).

"Teachers" Wanted!

The leaders whom Timothy is to gather around him must be men who are "apt to *teach*." See on this the following references:

"The overseer, therefore, must be without reproach . . . apt to *teach*" (1 Tim. iii. 2).

"Let the elders that rule well be counted worthy of double honour, especially those who labour in the word and in *teaching*" (v. 17).

"And the things which thou hast heard from me . . . commit thou to faithful men, who shall be able to *teach* others also" (2 Tim. ii. 2).

"Every Scripture is God-inspired and profitable for *teaching*" (iii. 16).

"Preach the word; be instant in season, out of season; reprove, rebuke, exhort, with all longsuffering and *teaching*" (iv. 2).

But *why* all this emphasis on "the doctrine" and the urgent necessity of "teaching" it? A further glance through the two letters soon answers that for us.

"That thou mightest charge certain men not to teach a *different* doctrine" (1 Tim. i. 3).

"Some having turned aside unto *vain talking*, desiring to be teachers of the law" (i. 7).

"In the later times some shall fall away from the faith, giving heed to seducing spirits and *teachings of demons*" (iv. 1).

"If any man teacheth *heterodox* doctrine, and consenteth not to sound words" (vi. 3).

"For the time will come when they *will not endure* the sound teaching" (2 Tim. iv. 3).

"But having itching ears will heap to themselves teachers after their own lusts . . . and *turn aside unto fables*" (iv. 3, 4).

"The Godliness"

Once again we find the word "godliness" noticeably recurring (see 1 Tim. ii. 2, 10, iii. 16, iv. 7, 8, vi. 3, 5, 6, 11; and 2 Tim. iii. 5). Not only so, but it occurs with the definite article—"*the* godliness," which may sound strange to us who speak English, but has a significance not to be missed in the Greek. Just as those other two expressions, "the faith" and "the doctrine," sum up the Christian Gospel in its religious and doctrinal aspects, so this one, "the godliness," sums it up on the *practical* side. This seems certain from comparing "the mystery of the faith" in iii. 9 with "the mystery of the godliness" in iii. 16. The three terms were evidently "current coinage" in the phraseology of original Christianity and should be duly noted. They sum up the Christian system, respectively, as (1) a religious *worship*, (2) a body of *truth*, (3) a way of *life*.

"And without controversy, great is the mystery of *the godliness*" (1 Tim. iii. 16).

"Bodily exercise is profitable for a little, but *the godliness* is profitable for all things" (iv. 8).

"Men corrupted in mind and bereft of the truth, supposing that *the godliness* is a way of gain" (vi. 5).

"But *the godliness* with contentment is great gain" (vi. 6).

But *why* this emphasis on "the godliness"? The answer is found in the second epistle, chapter iii. 5: ". . . holding a [mere] *form* of godliness, but having denied the *power* thereof."

The Crucial Significance

Now all our foregoing quotations about "the charge," and "the deposit," and "the faith," and "the doctrine," and "the godliness," lead us up to the crucial significance of these two Timothy epistles. When we perceive clearly what that significance really is we realise at once what a solemn voice these two letters have for our own time.

Think back for a moment to the opening paragraph of the first letter, where we find the primary purpose of Paul's charge to Timothy, i.e.: "That thou mightest charge SOME not to teach heterodox doctrine" (i. 3). Remember, too, the word in chapter iv. 1: "But the Spirit saith expressly that in later times SOME shall fall away from the faith." Then, with that repeated "SOME" in mind, recall the five sad, disturbing instances in this first epistle where it tells of apostasy:

> "SOME have turned aside" (i. 6).
> "SOME have made shipwreck" (i. 19).
> "SOME are turned after Satan" (v. 15).
> "SOME have been led astray" (vi. 10).
> "SOME have missed the mark" (vi. 21 margin).

In the *second* epistle the "SOME" has become "ALL." At the beginning of it we find:

"This thou knowest, that ALL that are in Asia have turned away from me" (i. 15).

Then again, at the end we find:

"At my first defence, no one took my part, but ALL forsook me" (iv. 16).

That is why these two letters were written so urgently to Timothy. They strike a crisis-point. They are a critical challenge. The first of them marks a break-*away*. The second marks a break-*down*.

In this, are these two Timothy epistles latently prophetic? Coming, as they do, just at the end of the nine Christian Church Epistles, do they throw on the screen an advance picture of tragic break-away and break-down which are to characterise organised Christianity at the end of this present Church-age? We know, of course, that the end-times certainly were in Paul's mind as he wrote, even though he apparently had no knowledge that a long trail of twenty centuries would unwind before the Lord's return. In referring to the end-times which he thought were *then* drawing on, was not Paul so guided that his words, like prophetic arrows, find their Divinely intended distant target in our twentieth century, when at long last the final days really *are* upon us? In the first letter, chapter i. 16, he speaks of himself and his ministry as a "pattern" or "delineation" (or "intimation to posterity" as Ferrar Fenton translates it). In chapter iv. 1 he tells us what the Holy Spirit says "expressly" about the latter days; and again, in the second letter his pen returns to these "last days," speaking of them as "grievous times" (iii. 1).

Yes, undoubtedly Paul is directly thinking about these eventualities; but the further point which we are here making is that perhaps in a way which he himself did not suspect, his two Timothy letters *as a whole* (not just their occasional direct references to the latter days) give a *prophetic photograph* of our own twentieth-century Christendom. If this is so, how carefully ought the Lord's Timothies to be studying them, and praying over them again today! Of course, quite apart from that, they have an intrinsic value which makes them precious at *any* time; yet their peculiar reference to these age-end days of ours gives them an urgent interest and significance such as they can scarcely ever have had before.

> Jesus, my Lord, Thou art coming!
>   The signs are around us today.
> Coming, dear Lord, Thou art coming;
>   The times are preparing Thy way.
> World-wide conditions portentous,
>   Undreamed by our fathers appear;
> Happenings vast and momentous
>   Proclaim that Thy coming is near.
> Coming, coming, Jesus my Lord!
>   Even so, come, Lord Jesus.

THE EPISTLES TO TITUS AND PHILEMON

Lesson Number 141

NOTE.—For this study read the two short epistles through several times each, preferably in the Revised Version.

Judging from the allusions to Titus in Paul's epistles he seems to have been the ablest and most reliable of all the friends and coadjutors whom the apostle had about him in his later years. As an uncircumcised Gentile who had been converted by Paul, he represented in his own person the breadth and freedom of the Gospel, for which the apostle had so zealously and successfully contended.

The conversion of Titus had taken place at a comparatively early period in the apostle's ministry, for he accompanied Paul and Barnabas on their visit from Antioch to Jerusalem to vindicate the freedom of the Gentiles from the ceremonial law of the Jews (Gal. ii. 1–4). We find him figuring prominently at another crisis in the apostle's ministry, when the strife and confusion in the Corinthian Church threatened to destroy St. Paul's influence. His remarkable success in the difficult mission then assigned to him, which called for the exercise of combined firmness and tact, and from which Apollos appears to have shrunk (1 Cor. xvi. 12), marked him out as an able and trustworthy delegate, and explains his selection ten years later for the important and difficult position which he temporarily held in Crete when this letter was addressed to him.

J. A. McClymont, D.D.

THE EPISTLES TO TITUS AND PHILEMON

THE LETTER TO TITUS

THE SAME kind of urgent interest clings around this letter to Titus as we have found in the two letters to Timothy. The Lord's return is in view (ii. 11–15). Paul's sense of responsibility is strong upon him as his own ministry nears its end (i. 3). The progress of the Gospel is endangered by "unruly men, vain talkers and deceivers" (i. 10).

Titus was a Greek, and one of Paul's own converts. He had proved himself a loyal and zealous co-worker, and was very dear to the apostle (Gal. ii. 3; Titus i. 4; 2 Cor. ii. 13, vii. 6, viii. 1–6, 16, 17). At the time when Paul wrote this epistle to him Titus was in the island of Crete. No account of Paul's own visit has been preserved for us; but he had evidently gone there, taking Titus, whom he afterward left there to consolidate the work, and constitute the Christian "assemblies" there on an orderly basis.

The little epistle was written about the same time as 1 Timothy. It has much in common with the two epistles to Timothy, but it strikes a different emphasis. In 1 and 2 Timothy the emphasis is on *doctrine*: in Titus it is on *good works*. First Timothy is a *charge*. Second Timothy is a *challenge*. The epistle to Titus is a *caution*—a strong and urgent reminder that sound faith must be accompanied by good works. The *doctrine* must be adorned by *doing*. These three "Pastoral" epistles are really a trinity in unity, exhorting us to "guard" the precious "deposit" of the Gospel. In 1 Timothy we are to *protect* it. In 2 Timothy we are to *proclaim* it. In Titus we are to *practise* it.

Read Titus again, noting the emphasis, all through, on good works as the necessary evidence of salvation. It will leave no doubt as to the key theme here. Perhaps we may say that the key verse is chapter iii. 8: "Be careful to maintain good works"; though we might also say the same about chapter ii. 14 and one or two other verses. The very last word before the parting salutation is again, "Maintain good works" (iii. 14).

We have come across some very ambitious and elaborate "analyses" of this simple little epistle. Chapter i. is said to set forth Church government, and the last chapter, Church and State. As a matter of fact, chapter i. is simply about the appointment of *elders* over the several little Christian groups in Crete; and the last chapter has nothing whatever to say about the Church and the State, except it be in the first verse only, which, however, simply exhorts believers as individuals to respect the civil powers! It is a pity to becloud the simple directness of emphasis and appeal in this way. The little epistle runs as follows.

THE EPISTLE TO TITUS
The True Local Church—Its Leaders and Members

A CAUTION—"MAINTAIN GOOD WORKS" (iii. 8, 14).

Opening benediction i. 1–4.

1. AS TO ELDERS IN THE ASSEMBLY (i.).

As to the office—eldership (verse 5).
As to the men—blameless (verses 6–9).
As to the need—gainsayers (verses 10–16).

2. AS TO CLASSES IN PARTICULAR (ii.).

The older men and women (verses 2–3).
The younger men and women (verses 4–8).
Those in service to Masters (verses 9–14).

3. AS TO THE MEMBERS IN GENERAL (iii.).

Good works of every kind (verses 1–2).
The supreme inspiration (verses 3–8).
Avoid the unprofitable (verses 9–11).

Parting remarks—iii. 12–15.

Chapter i.: "Put things in order"

It is a significant fact that although the New Testament gives counsels and directions as to the organising of local Christian assemblies or "churches" (1 Cor.; 1 and 2 Tim.; Titus), it nowhere even hints at any central board of administration such as those which have since developed and which exist with such wide powers today. The argument of expediency may be used to vindicate these latter, but they certainly have no Scriptural warrant. So far as New Testament indications go, each local church was meant to be autonomous. If it should be said that in the first days there was the authoritative word of apostles in central command, then it must be replied that so is it substantially today; for we have the apostolic directions in our New Testament, and they go no further than prescribing for each local church, leaving each directly responsible thereto. Such an elaborate hierarchical pyramid as the Roman Catholic system is utterly foreign to the New Testament; so also are *all* central executives which exercise a *governmental* control over combines of churches. There may well be voluntary unions of churches which do not infringe local autonomy; but there must be no governing executives, for these, while seeming to accomplish a useful *outward* unity, almost invariably violate and often destroy that vital *inward* unity which comes of free and direct loyalty to the apostolic word.

We may also learn from this letter to Titus that there is meant to be *adequate*, even though *simple*, organisation. Titus was to "set in order" the things which were lacking in the local assemblies of Crete (i. 5). Local autonomy is never meant to be haphazard disorderliness. There is to be pastoral oversight, such as that of Timothy and Titus. There are to be elders and deacons to oversee, respectively, the spiritual and economic aspects of the fellowship. In the very nature of things there must be leadership as well as membership in such corporate fellowships; yet good had it been for our Protestant churches if they had never moved from the simple originals to such complicated organisation as we have today.

Another thing which must surely catch our eye is that in the appointment of office-bearers spiritual *character* takes precedence over natural gifts. The elder must have a threefold blamelessness: first, domestically (i. 6); second, personally (verses 7, 8); third, doctrinally (verse 9). "He that hath an ear, let him hear what the Spirit saith to the churches." Many churches today need to learn that the absence of the first two qualifications is not compensated for by the presence of the third. Other churches need to learn it *vice versa*.

Chapter ii.: "Adorn the doctrine"

Whereas chapter i. concerns the elders, chapter ii. widens out to different classes of members. The *ideal* set before them is to "adorn the doctrine" in all things (verse 10). The *incentives* given are three, i.e. "the grace of God (verse 11), the Lord's "appearing" (verse 13), His death to "redeem" (verse 14).

Shining like a resplendent alpha-star in this second chapter is "the blessed hope" of the "glorious appearing." The reference to it occurs quite incidentally, yet it is set in one of the most notable little epitomes of saving truth anywhere in the New Testament. Glance again at verses 11–14. See the three tenses of salvation:

> Past: "The grace of God which bringeth salvation appeared" (verse 11).
>
> Present: "Teaching us that denying ungodliness and worldly lusts" (verse 12).
>
> Future: "The blessed hope . . . the appearing of our great God and Saviour" (verse 13).

The word "appearing" in verses 11 and 13 is the Greek *epiphany*: a shining forth. The first is the epiphany of grace. The other is the epiphany of glory. Between the two, we are to live "*soberly* . . . looking for the blessed hope"—so to be looking for that second "appearing" is one of the *sober* things! It is rather comforting to some of us to have an apostle's word for *that*!

Chapter iii.: "Maintain good works"

After "*appoint*" in chapter i., and "*adorn*" in chapter ii., comes "*maintain*" in chapter iii. "Be careful to maintain good works" (verse 8). "Learn to maintain good works" (verse 14). How noticeable it is, all through these epistles, that Christian doctrine comes to us linked with highest ideals of conduct. High doctrine with low conduct is intolerable to New Testament Christianity. Notice the threefold incentive in this chapter—first a reminder of what we once were (verse 3), second, the wonder of our conversion (verses 4–6), third, our now being "heirs of eternal life" (verse 7).

Somehow, as we ponder this short but weighty note to Titus, we have an uneasy feeling that all too many of us modern Christians live far below its simply worded but searching standards. Although there is a transparent courtesy about it, there is a plain-spoken directness which goes straight to inner motives, and a simple forthrightness concerning Christian conduct which shames our polite modern evasions.

Oh, we have much need to linger often among the purifying paragraphs of this little letter. We may well spill tears of joy over some, and tears of contrition over others. Remember again, our Saviour "gave *Himself* for us" on awful Calvary, "that He might redeem us from all iniquity, and purify unto Himself a people for His own possession, *zealous of good* works." How the sinnings of Christians, then, must hurt Him! Read Titus again for a lesson in practical Christlikeness. Thank God, if its final injunction is "Maintain good works" (verse 14), its final benediction shows how to do it: *"Grace* be with you all."

THE LETTER TO PHILEMON

Even in the best art galleries there is always a space for choice miniatures. This personal note from Paul to Philemon is such a graceful little masterpiece of "fine courtesy, exquisite tact, and even playfulness of wit," and withal it has such distinct spiritual values, that one can only wonder sadly at those who have be-grudged it the little niche which it adorns. As G. G. Findlay says: "In every line and syllable this note betrays Paul's personality. Nothing more genuine was ever written."

Does it seem almost unworthy of mention that from the fourth century, when it was questioned as being supposedly beneath the dignity of apostolic authorship, there *have* been those who have doubted it? We need not linger over these. The late scholarly Dean Alford's comment will suffice: "It (the letter) was preserved in the family to which it was addressed, and read first, no doubt, as a precious apostolic message of love and blessing, in the church which assembled in Philemon's house. Then copies of it became multiplied, and from Colosse it spread through the church universal. It is quoted as early as the second century, and has ever, except with some few who question everything, remained an undoubted portion of the writings of St. Paul."

We may well be grateful for its preservation to us.

Points of Interest

Though so short, this note to Philemon has points of unique interest. When one reflects, Paul must have written numerous short letters, besides his "epistles." This is the only private letter which has survived to us. It attempts no grandiloquent phraseology, but it is a perfect model of "tact, delicacy, and good feeling" in connection with a sensitive, master-versus-slave situation. It is a revealing little window into the more private contacts and disposition of the apostle. It provides a unique practical illustration of Christian principle applied to social relationship. It says by *example* what Galatians and Colossians say in precept, as to the "nullity of worldly rank" in the Church, i.e. "There is neither slave nor freeman in Christ Jesus." One only needs to know the helpless abjection of slaves under Roman law to realise the height which Paul scales when he asks the slave-owner to receive back the runaway thief-slave as a *"brother beloved"* (verse 16).

The Persons Concerned

The letter to Philemon is about a certain Onesimus. Who then was Philemon? And who was Onesimus?

Paul addresses the former as "Philemon our dearly beloved, and fellow-labourer." This seems at once to imply not only first-hand contact, but an already formed friendship; and this is confirmed by verses 19 to 21, which imply that he was one of Paul's own converts. A comparison of the letter with Colossians iv. 9 shows that Philemon lived at Colosse, to which city Onesimus was now being returned. Philemon was a freeman; a slave-owner; presumably of the higher class socially; and a local Christian leader, for Paul speaks of "the church in thy house" (verse 2). The "beloved Apphia" and "Archippus our fellow-soldier" (verse 2) are assumed to have been, respectively, his wife and son. As Paul had not visited Colosse, it would seem that Philemon had come under his influence at Ephesus (some hundred and twenty miles west) during Paul's memorable three years there; for there was much coming and going between Ephesus, the capital, and cities such as Colosse. Archippus, Philemon's son, seems to have been pastor either at Colosse or at Laodicea (Col. iv. 17).

As for *Onesimus,* he was one of Philemon's slaves, as the letter soon makes clear. When the epistle to the Colossians was despatched from Rome, per the hand of Tychicus, Onesimus accompanied him (Col. iv. 7–9). The two of them also carried this private note to Philemon.

The Background Story

Onesimus, who was probably a *domestic* slave of Philemon, had absconded; and verse 18 would seem to indicate that he had stolen money from his master, by which to effect his get-away. He made his flight right out of "Asia," away west, overseas across the Ægean and Adriatic, to Rome, that populous haven of concealment to which many another such fugitive had fled. He little thought that he would ever see Colosse again; but there, in Rome, he came under the influence of Paul, was truly converted, and later returned to Colosse a changed man. As Paul was then in prison at Rome, it seems the more remarkable that they met. But at that very time, as it happened, Epaphras had come all the way from Colosse, on a visit to Paul; and it seems a likely coincidence, as well as an overruling providence, that *he* saw and recognised Onesimus in Rome.

Onesimus quickly "grew in grace," and endeared himself to Paul (verses 11, 12), proving so serviceable that Paul would gratefully have detained him in Rome (verse 13). But no, Onesimus belonged to Philemon; so the apostle took opportunity to send him back along with Tychicus, bearing the Colossian epistle, and the private note to Philemon.

The Letter

But what shall Paul say to a master who has been so outraged? Terrible punishments were sanctioned by Roman law for such offences, even to the inflicting of death. Bishop Lightfoot comments: "The slave was absolutely at his master's disposal: for the smallest offence he might be scourged, mutilated, crucified, thrown to the wild beasts." But Philemon was himself a Christian brother, which fact put a kindlier complexion on the situation and gave Paul his basis of appeal. So the little letter was composed and sent on its delicate errand.

And what a little masterpiece of guileless diplomacy it is! Read the following eulogy from Smith's Bible Dictionary.

"The Epistle to Philemon . . . has been admired deservedly as a model of delicacy and skill in the department of composition to which it belongs. The writer had peculiar difficulties to overcome. He was the common friend of the parties at variance. He must conciliate a man who supposed that he had good reason to be offended. He must commend the offender, and yet neither deny nor aggravate the imputed fault. He must assert the new ideas of Christian equality in the face of a system which hardly recognised the humanity of the enslaved. He could have placed the question on the ground of his own personal rights, and yet must waive them in order to secure an act of spontaneous kindness. His success must be a triumph of love, and nothing be demanded for the sake of the justice which could have claimed everything. He limits his request to a forgiveness of the alleged wrong, and a restoration to favour and the enjoyment of future sympathy and affection, and yet would so guard his words as to leave scope for all the generosity which benevolence might prompt towards one whose condition admitted of so much alleviation. These are contrarieties not easy to harmonise; but Paul, it is confessed, has shown a degree of self-denial and a tact in dealing with them, which in being equal to the occasion could hardly be greater."

Paul little dreamed, as he sat and wrote to Philemon, that his little note would undergo centuries of expository and homiletical vivisection! That, however, is a penalty of writing something which lives! Who bothers about mere "dead letter"? Still, anything more than simplest analysis of this Philemon note defeats its own purpose. It is like dissecting heart-beats! All we need to see is that verses 1–7 are about *Philemon*; verses 8–17 are about *Onesimus*; and verses 18–22 are about *Paul*. In the first group of verses Paul's affectionately diplomatic approach to his intercession for Onesimus consists of sincere *praise* for Philemon. In the next group of verses Paul deftly presents his lovely *plea* on behalf of thief-runaway but now converted Onesimus. In the third group Paul gives his solemn *pledge* to repay whatever amount Onesimus has stolen. Thus:

Salutation (verses 1–3).

PAUL'S *PRAISE* OF PHILEMON (verses 4–7).

PAUL'S *PLEA* FOR ONESIMUS (verses 8–17).

PAUL'S PLEDGE AND ASSURANCE (18–22).

Salutations: Benediction (verses 23–5).

As has often been pointed out, Paul plays on the name "Onesimus," which means *profitable*. See verse 11: *"Onesimus . . . who was aforetime unprofitable to thee but, now is profitable* both to thee and to me."

There is a lovely touch in verse 19, where Paul, in giving his "I.O.U." to Philemon, quickly adds his "U.O.Me." Is there a guileless, sly humour in the deliberately adopted solemnity: *"I, Paul,* write it *with my own hand,* I will repay it"?

This short letter can preach powerful truths to us, if we will let it. Here is the first: *Social evils are soonest changed by transformed lives.* How simple was this Philemon-Onesimus matter compared with the complicated master-versus-worker problems of modern industry! Yet here is the open secret which can solve every social and industrial dispute, to the wellbeing of men and the honour of God, i.e. the application of Christian principles by Christian men.

Again, true conversion to Christ will always cause a man to put *principle before mere expediency.* To some it would have been a question as to whether Onesimus really *needed* to go back now. His conversion more than made up for his having stolen and run away. Philemon would appreciate this and excuse Onesimus for what he had done in his "unconverted days." But is that how Paul reasoned? Did he say, "Perhaps the best thing now is just to say nothing about it"? Is that how Onesimus himself viewed it? No; Onesimus just as much as Paul knew what was the right thing, the Christian thing, and resolved to do it, cost what it might, for the Saviour's sake.

And again, see in this letter *the value of a thieving, runaway slave!* There was a providential overruling in the life of Onesimus just as truly as we see in the Book of Esther. God was watching, loving, guiding. See the dignity which Christianity puts on the brow of a slave, making him a "brother" and spiritual equal in Christ! Need we marvel that such teaching eventually *abolished* slavery, emancipated woman, and claimed social justice for all men as human equals?

Just once more, we cannot help seeing a kind of profile analogy between this Philemon letter and *the Gospel way of salvation.* Under Roman law, a slave had no right of asylum. If he absconded and was caught, his owner had full right to disfigure or

lame or even kill him. But the slave was conceded at least one
right, namely, that of appeal to his master's friend, to whom he
could flee, not for concealment, but for advocacy. The slave-
owner was still absolute master, but he might be pleaded with
through his friend to whom the slave had appealed, and would
listen for his friend-and-equal's sake if not for the poor slave's.
This was the more likely if the friend was a *partner* of the slave-
owner. Moreover, the slave who thus fled to such an intercessor
did not incur the guilt and penalty of an ordinary escapado. Moreover, a slave could be freed, as faithful slaves sometimes were, by
adoption into the owner's family.

With these things in mind, and this Philemon note lying open,
see what a parallel we have with the Gospel way of salvation. As
human beings you and I are God's property; but as sinners we
have robbed Him and are fugitives. Our guilt is great, and our
penalty heavy. The Law condemns us. Conscience hunts us down.
But if the Law condemns us, grace concedes us the right of appeal.
As Onesimus found refuge with Paul, so *we* find refuge with *Jesus*,
who, besides being the sinner's Friend, is the co-equal Friend and
Partner of the One whose property we are. In Jesus we find both
a *precator* (intercessor) and a *genitor* (or begetting father), just as
Onesimus found in Paul the one who not only interceded for him
to Philemon but led him into the secret of a new life (verse 10).
Moreover, just as Paul contracted Onesimus's debt, saying to
Philemon, "Put that to mine account," so has our Lord Jesus
graciously contracted upon Himself all *our* debt and demerit,
wiping it out once for all. And now, just as Onesimus became
reconciled in heart to Philemon and voluntarily returned to his
owner, so have *we* become "reconciled to God" and of our own
free-will have gratefully returned to Him, no longer rebels, or
even servile slaves, but gladly to be "received" by Him "for ever"
(verse 15).

> Free from the Law; oh, happy condition!
> Jesus hath bled, and *there* is remission!
> Cursed by the Law, and bruised by the Fall,
> Grace hath redeemed us—once for all!

THINK BACK, AND TEST YOURSELF
ON THE PASTORAL EPISTLES

1. Can you show by quotation that 1 Timothy was a "charge", also what the charge *was*?

2. Can you reproduce our framed outline of the first epistle?

3. Which are the two main divisions of 2 Timothy?

4. How do the three expressions, "The faith", "The doctrine", "The godliness" respectively sum up the Christian system?

5. Which are the five sadly significant occurrences of "SOME" in 1 Timothy?

6. In 2 Timothy i. 12, what do you think is meant by, "He is able to keep that which I have committed unto Him"?

7. What is the cautionary emphasis of the Epistle to Titus?

8. Which are the three groups addressed, respectively, in the three chapters of Paul's letter to Titus?

9. How is the paragraph on the "blessed hope" a notable little epitome of Christian truth, and where does it occur?

10. Who were Philemon and Onesimus?

11. Why was the little letter to Philemon written, and from where?

12. How does the little letter divide itself up? and how does it suggest a parallel with the Gospel way of salvation?

THE EPISTLE TO THE HEBREWS

Lesson Number 142

NOTE.—For this study, the Hebrews epistle, although long, should
be unhurriedly read through at least twice. The Revised
Version is preferable.

(1) We wish to make it clear that in these studies we knowingly use
the terms "Hebrews," "Israelites," "Jews," as practically interchangeable. After looking carefully into the matter, we cannot
make any such distinction as our British-Israel theorists do.

(2) Our rather long approach to this Hebrews epistle should be read
with patient care; for more than any other epistle this one has
suffered through misunderstanding of its standpoint and of its
first-century readers.

(3) The much-disputed authorship of Hebrews, although not affecting
the interpretation of the epistle, has a peculiar interest, into which,
Moses-like, we may well "turn aside and see." We hope our
addendum on it may be useful.

—*J.S.B.*

THE EPISTLE TO THE HEBREWS

I SHALL not forget my first sight of Mont Blanc, towering up beyond the Chamonix Valley, king among Alpine giants, crowned with a sun-transfigured majesty. One may well feel a similar, reverential wonder with this transcendent "Epistle to the Hebrews" opening up to view. It is one of the greatest two theological treatises in the New Testament. Moreover, it is king and leader to a new range of heights, the last group of books in our New Testament, namely, the Hebrew Christian Epistles.

The Hebrew Christian Epistles

As we have noted in a former study, these final nine (Hebrews to Revelation) are distinguished from the earlier epistles by their distinctively Hebrew standpoint and atmosphere. Unlike the *first* nine (Romans to 2 Thessalonians), which are all addressed to Christian *churches,* not one of these last nine is so addressed. The first of them is clearly to Hebrews, as the opening words show (i.e. "fathers" and "us"). The epistle of James is sent to "the twelve tribes scattered abroad" (i. 1). Peter's two epistles are to "the sojourners of the Dispersion" (1 Pet. i. 1; 2 Pet. iii. 1). Not all of them so specifically address Jewish readers, but they all carry incidental indications of their Jewish direction (see "synagogue" in Jas. ii. 2; "Gentiles" in 1 Pet. ii. 12, iv. 3; 3 John 7; Rev. xi. 2). The Jewish cast of Jude and Revelation are clear to all.

Again, unlike the Christian Church Epistles, which open up to us the wonderful "mystery" of the Church as the mystic "body" and "bride" and "temple" of Christ, these nine Hebrew Christian Epistles have nothing whatever of such teaching. There is nothing here about the members having died and risen with Christ; nothing of Jews and Gentiles being one new spiritual organism; nothing of sitting together "in the heavenlies in Christ."

Then again, there is a provocative contrast (either seeming or real) between the two groups in their attitude to the final preservation of believers. What a difference between the out-and-out guarantee of Romans viii. 29, 30, 38, 39 and the disturbing warning of Hebrews vi. 4–6, x. 26–9!—or between the lovely reassurances of Ephesians ii. 7–10, Philippians i. 6, and 2 Peter i. 10, Revelation ii. 5, iii. 5!

Now because of these differentiæ, i.e. their Hebrew standpoint, their silence on the Church as the "mystery," and their apparent retrogression as to the ultimate security of the believer, these Hebrew Christian Epistles have been thought to mark a backward rather than a forward step in the unfolding revelation of Divine truth. But to regard them as such is to misunderstand and misappreciate them.

Think again: Israel had now twice rejected Jesus as Messiah-King: first when He offered Himself in the flesh, next when He drew near again through the Pentecostally endued witnesses of His resurrection and Saviourhood. But the crucifixion of Israel's Messiah had been Divinely overruled to provide salvation for the whole race. "The grace of God that bringeth salvation had appeared to all men" (Titus ii. 11). It was first of all necessary, therefore, that the meaning of the Cross should be expounded for Jew and Gentile alike; and this we have in the first four Christian Church Epistles. Then, it was time to release the hitherto hidden "mystery" of the Church, uniting Jew and Gentile in the one spiritual organism; and this we have in the next three Church Epistles. Then, to complete the revelation concerning the Church, the two Thessalonian letters devote themselves to the Lord's return and the Church's translation. But there is a whole area of vitally related truth still requiring to be unfolded, and this is what we have in these Hebrew Christian Epistles.

Once this "whosover" Gospel is propagated among men in general, and the "mystery" of the Church divulged among believers, the question inevitably arises: How does all this relate to Judaism, the religion of the Jews, the one and only authentically Divine religion ever given to men? This question is the more acute because the Saviour Himself as a Jew honoured the covenant observances; the first believers on Him were Jews; and the Gospel itself is "to the Jew first" (Rom. i. 16). The Apostle Paul has already shown the relation of the Gospel to Israel *dispensationally* (Rom. ix.–xi.); but what of its relation to the ordinances, the offerings, the priesthood, the temple? Is it thinkable that all these

Divine institutions are now done away? So the first of these nine Hebrew Christian Epistles takes this up. How instructively it opens the subject and how conclusively it closes the question are best appreciated by those who have explored it most attentively. But that is not all; the Holy Spirit has overruled the discussion to give us (what has nowhere earlier been developed) a most wonderful revelation of *our Lord's heavenly priesthood and intercessory ministry*.

Furthermore, although these Hebrew Christian Epistles have nothing of "Church" doctrine in them, there is one sense in which they carry us beyond the Church Epistles to *the utmost goal of Christian experience*. What is it, beyond all else, that our creation and redemption as human beings is meant to actualise? Why did God create us? Was it just to preserve us alive? Was it merely to govern us, judge us, punish or reward us? No; mysterious as it may seem, He created us for *individual fellowship* with Himself, a pure fellowship of *perfect love*. Sin aborted that fellowship and estranged human nature; but the ultimate purpose of both our creation and our redemption is *fellowship with God*. That is what all else leads to; and that is what we have in *the First Epistle of John*.

Still further, now that there have been disclosed all these successive truths and aspects of the Gospel, the Church, the Rapture, the heavenly Priesthood, and the way of heart-to-heart fellowship with God, the last of these nine Hebrew Christian writings sweeps us on to the end of the present age, to the Lord's return in relation to the whole world, to the millennial kingdom, the Great White Throne, and even the ultimate "new heaven and new earth," thus completing the continually progressive revelation of the most wonderful volume ever written.

Hebrews: The Special Aspect

If we are to catch the focal significance of this Hebrews epistle, we must duly appreciate its *standpoint*. It corresponds with that of Leviticus in relation to Exodus. All the sweet savour and non-sweet savour offerings enjoined and particularised in Leviticus typify aspects of our Lord's sacrifice on the Cross, but they are all aspects of the benefits which it provides for those who are already redeemed and in covenant relationship with God. The

Israelites were already redeemed from Egypt and brought into covenant relationship at Sinai, as recorded in Exodus. In virtue of that covenant God had now come to "dwell among them" (Exod. xxv. 8); hence Leviticus commences: "And the Lord called unto Moses, and spake unto him *out of the tabernacle.*" Correspondingly, this Hebrews epistle, although it is a wonderful interpretation of the Pentateuchal sacrifices and priesthood, does not say so much as a single word about the *Passover* lamb. Its object is to show how already-redeemed sinners may be confirmed as "holy brethren, partakers of a heavenly calling" (iii. 1), in their participation of covenant privileges.

Going with this are some startling implications. Our Lord's priesthood did not begin on earth when He offered Himself on the Cross, but only when He entered "into heaven itself, now to appear in the presence of God for us" (ix. 24). How often have we heard it taught that when our Lord sacrificed Himself upon the Cross He did so as our great Priest. No; He was not then our Priest. "If He were on earth, He would not be a priest at all" (viii. 4). Everywhere in Christendom today the idea obtains that a priest means a *sacrificing* priest, yet Scripture does not say so. On the contrary, we find in Leviticus that the priests were only to offer what had already *been* sacrificed. See how explicit are the opening words of Leviticus: "Speak unto the children of Israel, and say unto them: If any man of you bring an offering unto the Lord . . . he [i.e. the man himself, not the priest] shall kill the bullock before the Lord" (Lev. i. 2–5). So was it with *all* the offerings (see iv. 24, 29, 33). Not until *after* the blood-shedding did the ministry of the priests begin. So was it with our Lord and *His* sacrifice, and *His* priestly ministry.

But someone may object: Was not Aaron, the high priest, a type of Christ? And did not Aaron actually "kill the goat of the sin-offering" on the annual day of national atonement (Lev. xvi. 15)? Yes, the entire ritual of that day necessarily fell upon Aaron as the appointed representative of the people; but (oh, the Divine exactness of Scripture typology!) until all the *sacrificial* rites were accomplished he was *not to wear his high-priestly garments*—not until the already-slain burnt offering was on the altar (xvi. 23, 24).

For centuries before the time of Aaron men had been offering sacrifices without intervention or any mention of priests. On that never-to-be-forgotten night of the exodus from Egypt, the Passover lamb—one for each family—was slain, not by a priest, but by the head of the household. Mark it well: all this was before Aaron was appointed to the priestly office. When our Lord gathered His apostles to the upper room, just before going to the Cross, with what did He connect His death?—with the Leviticus offerings? No; He connected it with the *Passover*. There was nothing priestly about it. This distinction is vital. The Leviticus offerings were to continue day in, day out; but the Passover was *once for all*; it was to be annually memorialised but not re-enacted. The annual Paschal supper was a memorial, but not a repetition; nor was the memorial in any way connected with the priesthood. So, with the Sinai *covenant* which followed the Passover; the sacrifices were offered, not by the priests, but by "*young men* of the children of Israel*" (Exod. xxiv. 5). "And Moses took the blood and sprinkled it on the people, and said: Behold the blood of the covenant which the Lord hath made with you" (verse 8). Therefore, when our Lord said to His disciples in the upper room, "This is my body . . . this is my blood of the *new covenant*" He was obviously alluding to the Passover and the covenant blood-sprinkling which was the *complement* of the Passover, both of which were once-for-all, never-to-be-repeated redemption sacrifices. What a *sheer* blunder it is, then, as stupid as it is baneful, for the Roman Church not only to connect it all with priests, but through the supposedly mystical endowments of her priests to turn the once-for-all broken body and shed blood of our Lord into a continuing priestly sacrifice, and even say that the blood must be drunk—a procedure utterly forbidden with *any* sacrifice!

Why, even our Lord Himself is not still offering in heaven. That is why, in Hebrews x. 11, 12, a contrast is made between the Aaronic priests, who are daily "*standing*" (their work never finished), and our Lord Jesus, who, "after He had offered one sacrifice for sins for ever, *sat down* on the right hand of God."

Now this Hebrews epistle is alive to the once-for-all finality of our Lord's Passover sacrifice and covenant blood-shedding. It is talking to those who have believed on Him and are in the covenant, and its purpose is now to show them how our wonderful JESUS completely fulfils (and thereby supersedes) the Leviticus priesthood and sacrifices. We should keep this standpoint continually in mind as we study our way through Hebrews.

For Whom Intended

It is easy enough for *us*—twentieth-century Gentiles—to appreciate that the Jewish religion of types and figures was both consummated and abrogated in our Lord Jesus; but for many of those first-century Jewish believers the break-away must have been a razor-edged problem. The very fact that Judaism was an authenticatedly *Divine* religion, and its observance a national covenant obligation, made their problem the sorer.

As the late Sir Robert Anderson says: "Surely we can sympathise with the feelings of a Hebrew Christian as, standing in the temple courts thronged with worshippers at the hour of the daily sacrifice, he watched the Divinely appointed priests accomplishing the Divinely ordered service which, during all the ages of his nation's history, had been the most ennobling influence in the national life. Every element of pious emotion, of national sentiment—of superstition, if you will—must have combined to attract and fascinate him, as with reverence and awe he gazed upon that splendid shrine which had been raised by Divine command upon the very spot which their Jehovah God had chosen for His sanctuary, the place where kings and prophets and generation after generation of holy Israelites had worshipped for more than a thousand years."

Yes, we can sympathise, as also we can well appreciate how, with such associations and venerations filling the mind and heart of any Hebrew Christian, "nothing but the revelation of something higher and more glorious could ever wean him from his devotion to the national religion." To give it all up for One branded with infamy, and "go forth unto Him without the camp, bearing His reproach," was not easy. The temple, rich with sacred appeal, was still standing. The way back was ever open and was a subtle snare.

Furthermore, those first-intended readers must be connected back with certain peculiar phenomena in the Acts of the Apostles, for this has an important bearing on the interpretation of several controverted passages in the epistle. In Acts vi. 7 we read: "And the word of God increased, and the number of the disciples multiplied in Jerusalem greatly; and a great company of the *priests* were obedient to the faith." But how could those priests be Christian believers and yet continue as priests of the altar and ordinances which were now done away in Christ? In chapter xv. 5 we find: "But there rose up certain of the sect of the *Pharisees* which believed . . ." But how could they remain Pharisees now that they were believers on the Lord Jesus? In chapter xxi. 20 the Christian leaders at Jerusalem say to Paul: "Thou seest, brother, how many thousands of Jews there are which *believe,* and they are all *zealous of the Law.*" But if they were really "believers" on the Lord Jesus as their personal Saviour, how could they thus be "zealous of the Law"? Is it not the very first implicate of the Gospel that grace and law are sheer opposites, that salvation by faith and salvation by law-works are mutually exclusive ideas? Acts xxi. 20–6 would seem to indicate that many of those "thousands" who had been led to "believe" on Jesus as Messiah knew little of Him yet as personal Saviour. They were still so "zealous of the Law" that they had not forsaken Moses, nor given up circumcision, but were walking after "customs," and still offering "sacrifices" (verse 26), and (being "thousands") were presumably among the crowd which were desirous to slay Paul for his contrary teaching! In fact this hostility was exactly what "James and all the elders" had expressly feared (not just from Jews, but from those "thousands which *believe*")!

We cannot encounter such abnormalities without being reminded again that the thirty years covered by the Acts were an unresolved suspense-period. A second offer of the "kingdom of heaven," and of Jesus as Messiah-King, was being made to Israel, accompanied by Pentecostal credentials, and the message of individual salvation through the now crucified, risen and exalted "Jesus of Nazareth" (consult again our studies in the Acts). Apparently the thorough-going *personal* implications of the new message had neither been fully apprehended nor clearly defined at that time by the apostles. But as Israel's official and general rejection of it became deep-set and firm-fixed, a fateful choice was forced upon individual Jewish believers. It was the Jewish *religious* world which had crucified Jesus; and now, so it seemed, the Divine religion itself of which Jesus was the fulfilment and consummation was repudiating Him! The point had come where to "go on" with Jesus meant nothing less than a going to Him "outside the camp" and a bearing of "reproach."

This immediately throws light upon those two keenly debated passages, Hebrews vi. 4–6, and x. 26–9. There is no need to go into hyper-exact Lexicon meanings of the words used in order to decide their main reference. They refer to a particular class, in a situation which has forever passed away. All of us who *now* believe upon the Lord Jesus Christ for salvation accept Him as the Saviour who is fully made known in our completed New Testament. Whether we come to Him from Jewry, Mohammedanism, Roman Catholicism, or any other system, if our faith is according to the New Testament we make *at the outset* a choice which breaks us away from all dependence on legalistic self-righteousness, or religious merit-works, and brings us to One who is the fulfiller of all Judaism's ritual, the solitary but all-sufficient Saviour, and the finality of Divine revelation. That is, at our conversion *we* make a choice which those early Hebrew believers had *not* made, and had not seen the *need* of making, when *they* first believed.

Why, one can easily see from chapters like Acts viii. the abnormality of that period. We are told that the Samaritans "believed" (verse 12). Now today, when a person really "believes" in Jesus as Saviour there is a being "born anew" of the Holy Spirit. This we preach, and this we prove. Yet of those Samaritan "believers" verse 16 says that "as yet" the Holy Spirit "was fallen on none of them." Some would try to make out that they *must* have been regenerate, only the Spirit had not yet fallen upon them in the sense of the "second blessing" or the "baptism" of the Spirit. But that will not do. One of those "believers" was Simon the sorcerer. He is plainly said to have "believed" and then been "baptised" in water (verse 13). Yet Peter later declares him to be in a state of awful estrangement from God (verses 20–3)—a baptised believer, yet *not* regenerate! It is clear that neither this "believing" nor this extraordinary "falling of the Spirit" on people at that time must necessarily be identified with true conversion and regeneration as *now* preached and experienced. The Holy Spirit, be it remembered, once fell even on that old hypocrite Balaam and prophesied through him (Num. xxiv. 2)—but without regenerating him! It is at least open to question how *far* many of those long-ago Jewish "believers" on Jesus as Messiah had penetrated into a clear faith upon Him as personal Saviour from the guilt and power of individual sin.

The spectacular Pentecostal whelmings and workings of the Holy Spirit were supernatural sensory seals to the Divine genuineness of the apostolic message. The writer of our Hebrews epistle

THE EPISTLE TO THE HEBREWS 267

has these in mind when, in the sixth chapter, he speaks of "those who were once enlightened," who had "tasted of the heavenly gift," and had become "partakers of the Holy Spirit," and had "tasted the good word of God" and "the powers of the coming age" (i.e. the millennial reign). When we read that "if *they* shall fall away" it is impossible to "renew *them* to repentance" we must immediately connect them up with those chapters in the Acts. We need not start either minifying or magnifying the phraseology, either to prove that the once saved are saved for ever, or that they can fall away and be lost again. The words refer exclusively to a special class, in special circumstances, at a special historical crisis-point which has forever passed away. Let no sincere Christian ever think that anything in this Hebrews epistle contradicts that glorious guarantee of eternal preservation in Romans viii. 28, 29! If those of us who are the blood-bought, Spirit-born members of the true spiritual Church of Christ would know what the Spirit says specifically to *us* on this matter, we must turn—obviously—to the *Church* Epistles. The *Hebrews* epistle was directed to *Hebrews,* of whom some at least were "believers" after the sort we have described, and its first interpretation belongs to *them.*

Fulfilment and Finality.

This does not mean that the Hebrews epistle has no message for *us.* Nay, on the contrary, the Holy Spirit has overruled the writing of it to reveal great and precious truths, such as that of our Lord's heavenly priesthood, which *all* believers need to know. Although its standpoint is primarily Hebrew, it expounds some of the profoundest fundamentals of the Christian revelation, and should be mastered by all who would know with fulness the provisions which are ours in the new covenant. More particularly, those Hebrew believers of long ago needed to learn the measureless superiority of the Gospel over all the forms and rites and provisions of the *old* covenant; but not only so; they needed to be shown, by vivid comparisons and contrasts, that this superiority of the Gospel was the superiority of superlative fulfilment, of absolute perfection and of Divine finality; that there could be no going beyond it, no adding to it, and no mixing with it. That is what we ourselves need to learn ever more firmly and fully; and that is what this magnificent epistle expounds to us.

Leading Ideas and Analysis

This epistle, then, being written primarily to Hebrew Christians, and especially to such as were tempted to lapse into Judaism, is concerned throughout to exhibit the superiority of the Gospel over the covenant and system connected with Moses. This it does, not by minimising the old covenant but by showing the *perfection* and *finality* of the new. Other than belittling Judaism, the new covenant transfigures it, and honours it by finally fulfilling it. Hence the keyword here is "better," which occurs thirteen times (i. 4, vi. 9, vii. 7, 19, 22, viii. 6 (twice), ix. 23, x. 34, xi. 16, 35, 40, xii. 24); and besides the actual *word* "better," the *idea* recurs right through. In the first part of the epistle our Lord Jesus is better than *angels* (i. ii.); better than *Moses* (iii.); better than *Joshua* (iv); better than *Aaron* (v.–vii.). In the next part there is the "better" *covenant* (viii. 6), based upon "better" *promises* (viii. 6), opening up a better *sanctuary* (ix. 11), sealed by a better *sacrifice* (ix. 23). In the third part faith fixes on the "better" *substance* in heaven (x. 34), and looks for a "better" *country* (xi. 16), and a "better" *resurrection* (xi. 35), and inherits God's "better" *thing* (xi. 40).

The runner-up idea is that of *finality*—the finality of Christ, and of the Cross, and of the new covenant. Look up the occurrences of the word "once" (with the meaning of *once for all*): see vi. 4, vii. 27, ix. 12, 26, 28, x. 2, 10, xii. 26, 27. A further prominent feature of the epistle is its punctuation with solemn admonitions. Look up the oft-recurring challenge *"Let us . . ."*

The epistle is a methodical and progressive treatise, more regular in structure and rhetorical in form than any of its predecessors. It has suffered much, we think, at the hands of writers who have worked out clever analyses rather than perceiving the real hinges on which its argument turns, and the focal truths in each of its three main parts. Quite clearly chapter x. 19 marks a break. Up to that point the treatise is almost wholly *doctrinal*, whereas from there onwards it is almost wholly *hortatory*. It will be noticed, also, by any careful reader, that in chapters i.–vii. the emphasis is upon the *person* of Christ; that in chapters viii.–x. 18 it is upon the mediatorial *work* of Christ; and that from chapter x. 19 to the end of the epistle it is upon *faith* as the true response toward the person and work of Christ. Mark the main contour and ideas:

THE EPISTLE TO THE HEBREWS
CHRIST THE "NEW AND LIVING WAY."

Key words, "better" and "perfect." Focal passage x. 19–22.

1. JESUS—THE NEW AND "BETTER" DELIVERER
(i.–vii.).

Jesus the God-Man—better than angels (i., ii.).
Jesus the new Apostle—better than Moses (iii.).
Jesus the new Leader—better than Joshua (iv. 1–13).
Jesus the new Priest—better than Aaron (iv. 14–vii.).

2. CALVARY—THE NEW AND "BETTER" COVENANT
(viii.–x. 18)

New covenant has better promises (viii. 6–13).
And it opens up a better sanctuary (ix. 1–14).
And is sealed by a better sacrifice (ix. 15–28).
And it achieves far better results (x. 1–18).

3. FAITH—THE TRUE AND "BETTER" PRINCIPLE
(x. 19–xiii.)

Faith the true response to these "better" things (x. 19–39)
It has always been vindicated as such: examples (xi.).
Is now to endure, patiently looking to Jesus (xii. 1–13).
Is to express itself in practical sanctity (xii. 14–xiii. 21).

Parting words xiii. 22–5.

Each of the above-indicated subdivisions lends itself to further analysis, of course; each richly rewards closer study; and we could almost envy newer students the joyous discoveries which accompany a first enthusiastic exploration.

The New and Better Deliverer (i.-vii.)

If those Jewish believers of long-ago were to be rescued from their danger of viewing the new Christ-faith as merely supplementing Judaism without abrogating it, they must first be made vividly to see the all-eclipsing Divine glory of *the God-Man Saviour Himself*, which gives absolute finality to all His redemptive and mediatorial work, thereby completely excluding all other saviours and sacrifices. So, this is the opening subject, in chapters i.–vii. "God, having of old time spoken unto the fathers in the prophets

. . . hath at the end of these days spoken unto us in His SON."
All others point to Him, but there cannot be any going beyond
Him. Then why go back to *them*, since He to whom they all
pointed has Himself appeared? *They* have now served and ended
their function in pointing to Him who now fulfils all. "The sun
has risen; the stars retire."

Messiah Jesus is far above *angels* (i., ii). He is the *SON*;
they are but servants (i. 5–9). He is the *Creator*; they are but
creatures (verses 10–12). He is the *Sovereign*; they are but subjects (verses 13–14). He is the glorified *God-Man Saviour*, who is
not only Himself above angels, but brings many sons into glory,
lifting *them* also above the angels (ii. 5, 9, 10).

He is correspondingly "better" than *Moses*, Israel's great
apostle, greatest of all merely human mediators and law-givers
(iii.). Moses was merely the human *agent* of the old economy;
Christ is the Divine *Founder* of the new (verses 3, 4). Moses was
faithful as a *steward* of God's house; but Christ is faithful as *Son*
over His house (verses 5, 6). Moses was a *witness* to something
better to come; Christ is the *fulfiller* (verses 5, 6).

He is "better" than *Joshua*, captain of Israel's Canaan conquest
(iv. 1–13). Joshua led the people into the earthly Canaan, but
could not lead them into the true rest, whereas Jesus brings us
into the true rest of "ceasing from works" to enjoy a spiritual
sabbath-keeping with God (verses 8, 3, 9).

He is "better" than *Aaron*, Israel's representative high priest
(iv. 14–vii. 28). He ministers in a better *sanctuary,* i.e. heavenly
versus earthly (iv. 14). He maintains a better *priesthood,* i.e.
Melchizedechan versus Aaronic (v. 6, 10, vii. 3, 17, 18–25). He
is of better *qualification,* i.e. sinless, never-dying, perfect, versus
sinning, ever-dying, infirm (vii. 26, 27, 23–5, 28). He offers a
better *offering,* i.e. Himself versus animals; once-for-all versus
daily and ever-incomplete (verse 27).

Note the order: angels, Moses, Joshua, Aaron. All here leads
to the contrast between Christ and Aaron, because the *main* objective is to demonstrate the transcendent and abrogating superiority
of the Gospel economy to the whole sacerdotal system of Judaism
and the old covenant.

Note, too, that from chapter v. 11 to vi. 20 is certainly parenthetical. The alignment of our Lord's priesthood with that of

Melchizedek is resumed at chapter vii. 1. Over this whole group of chapters we may write: "Wherefore, holy brethren, partakers of a heavenly calling, *CONSIDER THE APOSTLE AND HIGH PRIEST OF OUR CONFESSION, EVEN JESUS*" (iii. 1).

The New and Better Covenant (viii.-x. 18)

Following on, as developments of the foregoing, the further superiorities and finalities of the new covenant now break into full view: better promises (viii. 6–13); better sanctuary (ix. 1–14); better sacrifice (ix. 15–28); better results (x. 1–18).

Note how the writer sums up thus far as he commences this new section (viii. 1–5). Then see how he follows by showing the *need* for a new covenant, owing to the defectiveness of the old (verses 6–13). At chapter ix. 1 he opens out a series of contrasts: earthly versus heavenly (verses 1–5, 11, 24); fleshly versus spiritual (verses 10, 11–14); temporary versus eternal (verses 9, 10, 12, 15); animals versus Son of God (verses 12–14); patterns versus realities (verses 23, 24); incompletive repetition versus once-for-all finality (verses 25, 26); promise versus fulfilment (x. 1, ix. 11); inability to remove sins versus true sanctification (x. 4, 10); year-by-year remembrance versus "no more" remembrance (x. 3, 17); never-finished sacrificing and ever-*standing* priests versus one sacrifice and one Priest who has "*sat down* on the right hand of God" (x. 11, 12). This last-mentioned contrast precipitates the great affirmation to which everything else in the epistle has been leading:

"FOR BY ONE OFFERING HE HATH PERFECTED FOR EVER THEM THAT ARE SANCTIFIED . . . THERE IS NO MORE OFFERING FOR SIN" (x. 14, 18).

Think of it!—worshippers for ever perfected; sins and iniquities remembered no more; neither need nor possibility of any further such offering for sin! This is not only the writer's climax of exposition; it was the *crisis-point* for those Hebrew believers of the first days. The whole case was now set before them, with the issues graphically emphasised, and the alternatives solemnly presented. Inevitably this triumphant culmination, "perfected for ever," becomes an implicit ultimatum to the waverers between going "on" in the new and going "back" to the old—"*No more offering for sin*"!

They must choose. The writer would fain help them; and so from this point the epistle becomes hortatory, with appeal, reminder, warning, encouragement, incentive all interwoven in one great *"THEREFORE, LET US . . ."*

Faith, the True and Better Way (x. 18-xiii.)

"Having therefore, brethren, boldness to enter into the holiest by the blood of Jesus, by a new and living way, which He hath consecrated for us, through the veil, that is to say, His flesh, and having a high priest over the house of God, *let us draw near* with a true heart in full assurance of *faith.*" But "if we sin wilfully [i.e. apostasy: drawing back] after that we have received the knowlege of the truth, there remaineth *no more sacrifice for sins,* but a certain fearful looking for of *judgment*" (x. 19–22, 26, 27). Yes, they are the alternatives! But oh, how *can* they refuse, and "draw back"? (verses 32–9). Let them remember how faith has been honoured in the past (xi.)—*righteousness* by faith (verses 1–7); *promises* by faith (verses 8–22); *exploits* by faith (verses 23–38). How much more efficacious, then, is *"looking unto Jesus,"* who is both "the pioneer and the *perfecter* of faith," and is "set down at the right hand of the throne of God"! (xii. 1, 2).

In such strain does the final part of the epistle relate itself to the arguments which have preceded. We cannot linger over it, much as we could wish to do so. Indeed, as we leave this stately, magnificent, heart-moving epistle, after this one short study, we are humblingly conscious how utterly inadequate is such a constricted review of it. All we shall attempt now is to make a few retrospective observations which we hope may be useful.

Think again how wonderful is this Hebrews doctrine of our *access* to God by this "new and living way"—the new way of the Cross, and the living way of the ever-interceding One on high. The epistle to the Romans tells us how a sinner may stand before a righteous God; but this epistle to the Hebrews opens up the even more astonishing truth that the justified sinner may approach a God who in His holiness is "a consuming fire." And, even more than that, it shows how the justified sinner may draw near with utmost confidence, "having *boldness* to enter the *holiest*"! We would recommend students to study carefully the whole teaching of the epistle on this subject of access. It is wonderful. How clearly it expresses that our boldness of access arises from no vain esteeming the dignity of man, nor from any under-reverencing the majesty of God. Our "boldness to enter" is *by the blood of Jesus*" (x. 19), and because we have a "great Priest over the house of God" (verse 21). In other words, our access to God is on the ground of what Jesus did for *us*, and what He means to *God* for us.

This exalted privilege of access to God, remember, is a spiritual and practical *culmination*. All else leads to it. The fact that the new covenant actually effects it shows at once its transcendent superiority to the old. Judaism never effected it, for the "veil" ever hung between the worshippers and the Holy of Holies, the Holy Spirit thereby "signifying that the way into the holiest of all was not yet made manifest while the first tabernacle as yet had its standing" (ix. 8). Now the very veil which kept the people out let the high priest in, on the ground of covenant blood; and it therefore becomes a type of our Lord's body—for Hebrews x. 20 says that our Lord Jesus has made the "new and living way" of entrance for us "through the veil, that is to say, His *flesh*." The first thing that happened as our Lord died on Calvary was that "the veil of the temple was rent in twain from the top to the bottom" (Matt. xxvii. 51). Thank God for that rent veil!

The "therefores" and "wherefores" of this Hebrews epistle should be duly pondered; so should the "more excellents" and "more perfects," and all the references to the "covenant." The admonitions and exhortations are a rich study indeed: there is one such homily or practical application appended to each new doctrinal argument (a procedure which should not be lost on us preachers!). The repeated occurrence of "Let us . . ." is another feature which invites a follow-up study. But above all else, the *glorious heavenly priesthood* of our wonderful JESUS should be unhurriedly studied, passage by passage. It will make Him dearer than ever to our grateful hearts. It will lift the mind into heavenly surroundings, bring "full assurance" to the heart, and embolden our faith toward God.

One Sunday evening a young man came to me with the question: "If, as you say, our Lord's death on Calvary was a full and final atonement for sin, how is it that He needs now to be ever interceding for us as our Priest in heaven?" The answer, of course, is that although the finished work of Calvary brings us a full and free forgiveness, we still remain *sinners*, pathetically disqualified from fellowship with a holy God. The heavenly ministry of our Lord answers the further need. Through His sacrifice on earth we have our *forgiveness*; through His priesthood in heaven we are kept in *fellowship*.

Our Lord was not born of Aaron's family, nor even of the tribe of Levi. He never was an Aaronic priest. His is the *royal* priesthood of Melchizedek (vii. 1). It is the *new* priesthood (verse 11); the *true* priesthood (verse 16); the *everlasting* priesthood (verse 17); the perfect priesthood (verses 26-8); the "able-to-the-uttermost" priesthood (verse 25).

"WHEREFORE HE IS ABLE TO SAVE THEM TO THE UTTERMOST THAT COME UNTO GOD BY HIM, SEEING HE EVER LIVETH TO MAKE INTERCESSION FOR THEM."

> There is a way for man to rise
>   To that sublime abode;
> An offering and a sacrifice,
> A Holy Spirit's energies,
>   An Advocate with God.

WHO WROTE HEBREWS?

MATTERS of literary criticism scarcely belong to the orbit of a study-series such as this; yet here and there orbit lines cross, so that purely critical questions swing in, because of their peculiar bearing on our own studies. To settle who wrote this Epistle to the Hebrews is really no more necessary to our edifying study of its contents than to a recognition of its supernatural inspiration. The early Christian scholars did not allow its *anonymity* to debar it from *canonicity*; they recognised in it, as we ourselves do, the imprimatur of unique and authoritative inspiration. None the less, there is an intriguing halo continually clinging about this question as to who wrote it; and someone is sure to ask us, "What do *you* think about it? *Was* Paul the author? Or did someone else write it?"

We wish we knew some secret source of information which would settle the question once for all! Alas, we neither know of such nor possess the scholarship to reply as we could desire. Still, we will bravely hazard our considered opinion, because the scholars themselves greatly disagree—and "when the doctors disagree, what shall the plain man do?"

To show how scholars *do* disagree as to the authorship of Hebrews, take the following. The late learned Dean Alford waxes so emphatic on its grammatical and literary differences from the usual Pauline epistles that he says: "Well might Origen pronounce the man void of the power of distinguishing character, who could imagine that one and the same person could, even by the most artificial disguise, have produced both." Yet the eminent Greek scholar, Dr. Bloomfield, says in his *Greek Testament*: "After a study of the Greek language as diligent, and an acquaintance with its writers of every age, as extensive probably as any person at least of my own country now living, I must maintain my decided opinion that the Greek is, except as regards the *structure of sentences*, not so decidedly superior to the Greek of St. Paul as to make it even improbable that the epistle was written by him."

There seems similar disagreement as to *date*. Dean Alford inclines to date it as late as the sub-apostolic period, whereas J. Barmby in the *Pulpit Commentary* avers that "internal evidence" precludes "any date later that A.D. 70," and suggests years earlier.

Equally contradictory are the evaluations of the early *tradition* that Paul was the author. Sometimes scholars seem to contradict their own deductions, as for instance the last-mentioned, who in one place says, "This distinct early tradition is plainly of *great importance* in the argument as to authorship," yet later questions it thus: "But what does this [tradition] amount to? All we know accurately is that at Alexandria, in the second century, the epistle, being itself anonymous, had been handed down, and was generally received, as one of St. Paul's."

So what? Well, our own considered opinion is that the human author was *Paul*. We have come to this conclusion not because of any predilection or prejudice in his favour. On the contrary, if it could be convincingly shown that someone else was the author we should rather be gratified, for it would provide a useful reply to those who still prattle that the Pauline form of Christianity is Paulinism, and not the pure, basic Christianity of Christ, or of the apostles other than Paul. We believe that Paul was the author for the following reasons mainly.

First, we believe that the Pauline *tradition* is much weightier than is generally allowed. Think of it: by about A.D. 150 Pantænus, the then leading teacher of Alexandria, was referring to it as a generally accredited epistle of Paul—which means that in only seventy years after Paul's death it was generally accepted as his! The point is not merely that Pantænus himself believed it to be Pauline, but that at so early a date it was *generally* viewed as such. How could it so quickly and altogether uncontradictedly have been thus generally received as Paul's if it were someone else's? The belief that it was Paul's must obviously have been handed down from years earlier, i.e. practically from the date of the epistle itself; and indeed that this was the case is confirmed by Origen, who followed Clement as leader of the Alexandrian school, for he adds that "*the men of old* handed it down as Paul's," which means, of course, that decades *before* Pantænus those who immediately followed the apostles regarded it as truly Paul's.

Now it seems to us that whatever the difference of literary form and style may be between this Hebrews epistle and the uncontroverted epistles of Paul, those differences should be viewed subordinately to this all-but-final tradition, and not *it* subordinately to *them*. We agree that in the third century other authors began to be suggested as alternatives to Paul, but there is surely cogency in the following interrogation put by the *Speaker's Commentary*: "Shall the positive testimony of men, who, knowing St. Paul intimately, were qualified to give witness on such a point, be outweighed by the doubts of those who lived some hundred years later, and therefore were not so qualified?"

Furthermore, it seems to us that the very early attribution of the authorship to Paul receives unmistakable endorsement from the apostle Peter, who says in his second epistle (iii. 15): "And account that the longsuffering of our Lord is salvation; even as our beloved brother *Paul* also according to the wisdom given unto him *hath written unto you*." So Paul *did* at least write *an* epistle to the same *Jewish* constituency as Peter was then addressing! If not the Epistle to the Hebrews, which was it? Where is it? What *trace* of any other?

But now, secondly, we believe in its Pauline authorship because of *internal* indications. It is remarkable, sometimes even amusing, how even those who most sharply repudiate the Pauline authorship admit the presence of Pauline characteristics in it. Origen, in the third century, whose words first suggested an alternative to Paul, has to admit that "the *thoughts* are the apostle's." And in recent times the scholarly Dean Alford, who would fain use Origen's words to lessen the force of the early Pauline *tradition,* is obliged to agree that "the *general cast* of thought is Pauline." The learned Franz Delitzsch, who prefers Luke as the writer, and discounts, as far as is reasonable, the Pauline traits of the epistle, must needs say: "It produces throughout the impression of the presence of the original and creative force of apostolic spirit. And if written by an apostle, who could have been its author but St. Paul? True, till towards the end it does not make the impression upon us of being his authorship; its form is not Pauline, and the thoughts, though never un-Pauline, yet often go beyond the Pauline type of doctrine as made known to us in the other epistles; but towards the close, when the epistle takes the epistolary form, we seem to hear St. Paul himself, and no one else." To my own mind it has at least *some* evidential significance that even those who argue the dictional *differences* between Hebrews and the acknowledged epistles of Paul should thus have to admit the basic *similarities* between them.

One thing which impresses itself on my own mind all the way through Hebrews is the tone of apostolic *teaching-authority*. The form of expression is kindly, but there is no concealing the underlying composure of Spirit-given certitude and finality. Although there is a marked courtesy, the way of speech brooks no reply. It does not merely word the *thinking* of a disciple; it delivers the firm *dicta* of an apostle. Even the arguments in it nowhere merely present the author's reasoned *conclusions,* but simply make plainer what is being laid down with apostolic *uncontradictableness*. Delitzsch feels the same when he says that the epistle "produces throughout the impression of the presence of the original and creative force of the *apostolic spirit*." But if it was written by an apostle, then, as Delitzsch asks: "Who could have been its author but St. Paul?"

Another thing which strikes us is the author's use of the pronoun "we" in addressing his readers, as though he speaks representatively for a group (v. 11; vi. 9, 11; xiii. 18, 23). This associative use of the plural pronoun is never found in John, Peter, James, Jude. It often occurs, of course, in verses where the writer includes himself with his readers in some large class, as for instance in 1 John i. 7, "If *we* walk in the light," where the writer includes himself with *all* Christian believers; but not once is it used by the writer as associating others co-operatively with himself. Yet it is found everywhere in *Paul's* epistles, and again in *Hebrews*. Moreover, in this Hebrews epistle it is assumed that the group embraced in the plural pronoun is well-known to the readers. So, if Paul was not its author, where, in this sense, is there a *parallel alternative* to him? Certainly not in any of the names ever yet suggested.

Again, although the epistle is always said to be "anonymous," it is only superficially so, for, plainly as can be, the last chapter shows that the writer was well known to his readers and that he was not in the least degree attempting anonymity. Who, then, is it who freely "gives away" his identity in that last chapter? Well, even Delitzsch agrees that here, at least, we "seem to hear Paul himself, and no one else." Who is it but Paul who writes (in verses 18, 19): "Pray for us; for we are persuaded that we have a good conscience, desiring to live honestly in all things: and I exhort you the more exceedingly to do this, that I may be restored to you the sooner"? Who is it but Paul who adds: "Know ye that our brother Timothy has been set at liberty, with whom, if he come shortly, I will see you"?—and then ends with the characteristic: "Grace be with you all"?

Why, as we come to these parting verses, we suddenly seem to realise that they must surely have been added in the very *handwriting* of Paul himself, for verse 22 says, "I have written you in a *few words*," which simply cannot refer to the whole epistle, with its *eight thousand* words! Nay, we begin to see that the last chapter, or part of it, is really a covering note to the treatise—which at the same time explains what so many have noticed, namely, that the book is a *treatise* rather than a letter, yet becomes quite epistolary just at the end. And if the covering note is so clearly Pauline, then the formal *treatise* (which by its very form and style and idiom as such has caused its Pauline authorship to be doubted) must also be by Paul.

Unconvincing Objections

Thirdly, our belief in Paul's authorship of Hebrews is confirmed inasmuch as the objections to it leave us unconvinced. Some of the objections, indeed, seem to us rather unworthy of the scholars who press them. For instance, Dean Alford is certain that chapter ii. 3 excludes Paul. He says: "The writer speaks of himself as among those who had received the Gospel from the apostles and those who had heard the Lord." This stands "directly against" Paul's authorship, for Paul "always upholds his independence of man's teaching." The verse can only be "explained away" by those who hold Paul's authorship, which they commonly do "by supposing the writer to be for the moment putting himself in the same category as his readers." But although such a practice is common among authors, it is scarcely thinkable that *Paul*, of all men, writing to *Jews* would adopt it. "Compare with any such idea his abrupt and energetic protests in Galatians i., ii. ; and if the idea be not abandoned, all we can say is that some minds must be very differently constituted to our own."

Well, our *own* must be among those minds which are "very differently constituted" from the dean's, for to us the very verse (ii. 3) which he says refutes Paul's authorship *confirms* it! He is quite inaccurate when he says: "The writer speaks of himself as among those who had 'received' the 'Gospel' from the 'apostles'. . . ." The writer neither mentions the "apostles" nor the "Gospel"; nor does he use the word "received"! Read the verse: "How shall we escape if we neglect so great salvation? which having at first been spoken through the Lord was *confirmed unto us by them that had heard.*" Now without needing to make capital out of the dean's inaccuracies we would simply ask: Does not that verse *indicate* Paul? So far as we have any knowledge, he never heard one of the Lord's parables, never saw one of the miracles; never once met, and never even saw the Lord, during His days on earth. Did the ascended Lord, whom Paul first met on the Damascus road, supernaturally re-enact the whole of His earthly ministry for Paul, or was it "confirmed" to Paul by "them that had heard"? Surely, then, chapter ii. 3, other than excluding Paul, *indicates* him!

But of course the chief objection is that "the whole Greek style of the epistle is different from that of St. Paul's acknowledged writings —more classical in its idiom, as well as more finished and rhetorical; and also that the studied arrangements of the thoughts and arguments, the systematic plan of the whole work, is so unlike the way of writing so characteristic of the great apostle." Against this, the late Sir Robert Anderson asks: "Will any student of literature maintain that so great a master of the literary art as the apostle Paul might not, in penning a treatise such as Hebrews, display peculiarities and elegancies of style which do not appear in his epistolary writings?"

Personally, I do not wish to underrate the grammatical and literary difficulty, but I think its advocates tend to overstate it. What a difference between the Greek of the Gospel according to John and that of the Apocalypse!—yet on weighty evidence, both external and internal, John is accepted by first-rank scholars as the author of both. Remember, too, most of Paul's epistles to the "churches" were written *earlier*; were written in the thick of busy, adventurous ministry, movement and travel; were provoked by sudden emergencies of false doctrine or other peril; were written with that emotion which a spiritual father felt for his own children in the faith, and churches which he himself had founded; and, moreover, were written to *Gentiles*: whereas Hebrews was one of the latest, written perhaps during imprisonment, amid quiet, unhurried broodings, with ample leisure for meditative planning and well-chosen sentences; was a set treatise to his countrymen, not a letter to his own children in the faith; was not to Gentiles, but to *Jews*.

To me, such considerations, especially in relation to a versatile genius like Paul, adequately cover the literary objection to his authorship of Hebrews. I am the more persuaded of this because of an admission by Dr. Barmby in his *Pulpit Commentary* article on Hebrews. He himself is one of those who reject the Pauline authorship on literary grounds, yet he says: "This consideration [i.e. that Paul *could* have written it under such circumstances as we have mentioned] would have decided weight in the way of explanation if there were any really valid *external* evidence of his having been the actual writer." But then there *is* most definitely "external evidence" of Paul's authorship in the *tradition* handed down right from Paul's own time!

If still further answer is required to the literary difficulty, we ourselves are not at all averse to believing that probably all over the Hebrews epistle there are welcomed touches of Greek "finish" and style from the pen of Luke, who, as we know, was with Paul in Rome, right to the end (2 Tim. iv. 11). This must not be taken as suggesting that we have Paul's thoughts in Luke's words. Both the thoughts and their expression are Paul's, but given a certain literary finish by the concurrent grammatical collaboration of companion Luke. We can illustrate the likelihood of this from our own experience. Some time ago we were asked to write an "epistle" for a poorly old lady to her daughter in another town. We conscientiously wrote down all that she told us, almost entirely in her own words, improved the construction of various sentences (though carefully preserving her own words), gave it grammatical finish, and posted it. It began: "Dear Margaret, I am having this letter typewritten, to spare you another struggle with my shaky old handwriting. . . ." A while later her daughter said of it,

"It was just mother's own way of seeing and saying things, just her own characteristic reactions and pawky comments, though of course the form of many sentences and the grammatical carefulness were clearly not hers."

Unconvincing Alternatives

Who are the alternatives actually suggested? There are four only who could be taken seriously. They are Luke, Barnabas, Clement of Rome, Apollos.

But surely it could not be Luke, for he was almost certainly a Gentile. In the farewell cordialities of Colossians iv. 10–14 he is distinguished from Aristarchus, Marcus, and Justus, who were Jews (verse 11), and is linked with Epaphras and Demas, who were not. His name, *Loukas,* is Greek. Both his Gospel and the Acts begin with a formal dedication in Greek and Roman style. But then the author of Hebrews was a Hebrew of the Hebrews, as clearly as can be.

As for Barnabas, he was just as certainly a Hebrew, a Levite, and in very definite ways could be the *possible* author; but is there anything to make him the *probable* author? No; the only writer of antiquity to assert him as such was Tertullian (A.D. 160–230), and he found no real support. There is an epistle supposed by early Church Fathers to have been written by Barnabas. Its genuineness is doubtful. If Barnabas *did* write it, then that settles the matter; he certainly did *not* write Hebrews; for the two are so *utterly* unlike both in style and sentiment as to make one author for both unthinkable. But if the supposed Barnabas epistle is spurious, then we have no knowledge that Barnabas *ever* wrote an epistle: why then attribute *Hebrews* to him?

Could the author have been Clement, one of the earliest bishops of Rome? If so, why was there never the slightest tradition of it in Rome? Why did that church for so long reject the Hebrews epistle? Why is the epistle which Clement wrote to the Corinthians so unlike the Hebrews epistle in ways which seem altogether to preclude a common authorship?

What of Apollos? He was never even thought of until Martin Luther suggested him! He is certainly a most tempting candidate. Dean Alford makes out a strong case for him. But there are two strong objections: (1) *None* of the ancients (who *must* have known more of the probabilities than moderns do) ever even suggested him; (2) Apollos was an *Alexandrian* Jew; but does not the Hebrews epistle require a Jew of long and intimate acquaintance with *Jerusalem* and the temple—and with the Jewish Christians there (xiii. 23)?

On the whole, therefore, we ourselves incline the more confidently to believe that Paul, and no other, was the human author of the Epistle to the Hebrews.

THE EPISTLE OF JAMES

Lesson Number 143

NOTE.—For this study read the epistle through twice, then see if, in a third reading, you can pick out the breaks and parts.

Tradition fixes the martyrdom of James in the year 62, but his epistle shows no trace of the larger revelations concerning the Church and the distinctive doctrines of grace made through the Apostle Paul, nor even of the discussions concerning the relation of Gentile converts to the law of Moses, which culminated in the first council (Acts xv.), over which James presided. This presumes the very early date of James, which may confidently be set down as "the first Epistle to Christians."

—*Weston.*

By the "twelve tribes scattered abroad" we are to understand, not Jews, but Christian Jews of the Dispersion. The Church began with such (Acts ii. 5–11), and James, who seems not to have left Jerusalem, would feel a particular pastoral responsibility for these scattered sheep. They still resorted to the synagogues, or called their own assemblies by that name (Jas. ii. 2, where "assembly" is "synagogue" in the Greek). It appears from James ii. 1–8 that they still held the synagogue courts for the trial of causes arising amongst themselves. The epistle, then, is elementary in the extreme. To suppose that James ii. 14–26 is a polemic against Paul's doctrine of justification is absurd. Neither Galatians nor Romans was yet written.

—*Scofield Bible Note.*

THE EPISTLE OF JAMES

WHAT A difference there is between the long, rhetorical epistle to the Hebrews and this short, staccato epistle of James! And how intriguing is the subtle miracle by which supernatural inspiration blends itself with the differing mentalities of our New Testament writers, suffusing yet never suppressing the traits of human personality!

How interesting, too, is the *order* in which these nine Hebrew Christian writings occur! Right through the group they strike a careful balance in their respective aspects. Is there not a significant appropriateness that Hebrews, which stresses *faith,* should be seconded by James, insisting on good *works?*—that First Peter, the epistle of future *hope,* should be followed by Second Peter, which is all about present *growth* in grace?—that the epistles of John, with their emphasis on *love,* should be balanced by Jude, with its call to *contend* for the faith? And is it not an obviously perfective finale, that this progressive lesson in matching faith by good works, future hope by present growth, and brotherly love by contending for the faith, should be crowned by the characteristic promise of the Apocalypse—*"To him that overcometh"?*

About James Himself

The name "James" occurs forty times in our New Testament. Collation restricts these to (1) James the "son of Zebedee," and brother of the Apostle John; (2) James the "son of Alphæus"; (3) James the "brother" of our Lord (Matt. xiii. 55; Mark vi. 3). The first of these was martyred by Herod (Acts xii. 2) about A.D. 42 and was *not* the writer of this epistle. It is a point of keen debate whether (2) and (3) are the same person. Our own view is that they are *not,* and we have given our reasons in a brief addendum to this study. There is far more of interest than of actual importance in the enquiry. The practical issue is that the writer of our epistle was that James who figures so largely in the Acts of the Apostles as a kind of chairman or leader of the Christian elders and assembly in Jerusalem.

Prominence

There is such a correspondence between what we see of him in the Acts and what we read *from* him in the epistle that each endorses the genuineness of the other. In Acts xii. 17 we find that on the night when Peter was miraculously delivered from Herod's prison his instruction to the prayer-group was: "Go, show these things to *James* and the brethren"—which is a first clue to the latter's prominence among the leaders. Later, in chapter xv., at that first historic Christian synod, we find him clearly occupying a position of chairmanship, summing up (verses 13–18), giving a president's judgment (verses 19–21: *ego krino*, I judge), and his advice from the chair being implemented (22–31). Still later, in chapter xxi., we find that when Paul came to Jerusalem after his third missionary tour he "went in . . . unto *James*; and all the elders were present" (verse 18), which indicates again a recognised primacy.

Outlook

What is this apostle's *outlook* in the Acts? It is exactly that which we find again in his epistle. There is what might seem to *us* a strange mixture of true faith in Christ, with ardent veneration of the Mosaic law. Both in the Acts and in his epistle the Gospel bell rings clearly, that individual salvation is by faith in Christ; that the Gentiles are under no obligation to "keep the Law" (Acts xv. 24); but there is no demarcation between *Jewish* Christian faith and the observance of the Mosaic economy. This, presumably, arises from the peculiarity of the transition-period covered by the book of the Acts (see our lead-up to the Hebrews epistle). There is a being "zealous for the Law," and a tender considerateness not to offend "the many thousands of Jews which believe" (xxi. 20). There seems to have been in James a clear-thinking astuteness blended with a strong tendency to religious rigidity. There may not be the dash and originality about such types, but they often make strong, wise chairmen, guiding with practical good sense, and often restraining from rashness. It is characteristic that in the Jerusalem council (xv.) it is Peter who stands up and *proposes* Gentile freedom from the legal yoke (verses 7–11) and chairman James who shapes the *restrictive* clauses (verses 20, 29).

Character

Eusebius preserves an interesting sketch of James by Hegesippus, a writer of the early second century. "James, the brother of our Lord, who, as there were many of this name, was surnamed the Just by all from the days of our Lord until now, received the government of the Church with the apostles. He drank neither wine nor strong drink, and abstained from animal food. A razor never came upon his head; he never anointed himself with oil; and never used a bath. He never wore woollen, but only fine linen garments. He was in the habit of entering into the temple alone, and was often found upon his bended knees, asking for the forgiveness of the people; so that his knees became hard like a camel's knees in consequence of his habitual supplication and kneeling before God. And, indeed, on account of his exceeding righteousness he was called the Just, also Oblias, which in the Greek is 'Bulwark of the people,' as the prophets declare concerning him." Bishop Lightfoot, in his Galatians commentary, warns us that there are reasons for not accepting this account too literally; but that it has a true *basis* is undoubted.

Martyrdom

James was martyred. Josephus the historian places the event between the death of governor Festus (see Acts xxv.) and the coming of his successor, Albinus, which by our calendar was A.D. 62. He thus recounts it: "Caesar, upon hearing of the death of Festus, sent Albinus into Judæa as procurator. . . . Ananus (the high priest at Jerusalem) thought he had now a proper opportunity . . . so he assembled the sanhedrin of judges, and brought before them the brother of Jesus called Christ, whose name was James, and some others; and when he had formed an accusation against them as breakers of the law, he delivered them to be stoned. . . ." Hegesippus's melodramatic variation, that James was hurled from the temple pinacle by scribes and Pharisees, and then clubbed to death, seems far-fetched and improbable.

First-intended Readers

Before we now explore the little epistle itself we call attention to the following excerpts from an article by the late Principal E. C. S. Gibson. "We cannot understand the epistle aright unless we remember that those to whom it is addressed, in becoming Christians, *had not ceased to be Jews*. We are probably prone to exaggerate the gulf which existed between Jews and Christians in the early days of the Church. At first the preaching of the apostles was 'rather a purification than a contradiction of the popular doctrine.' Those who were present in Jerusalem on the day of Pentecost must have carried home little more than the fact of the Messiahship of Jesus and the barest rudiments of Christianity. The Gospel preached by those 'who were scattered abroad upon the persecution which arose about Stephen' would be somewhat fuller, though still incomplete. It was preached 'to none but Jews only,' but it spread the new faith over a wide region—'as far as Phenice and Cyprus and Antioch.' Thus Christian communities would be founded in the Jewish quarters in most large cities; but it must have been years before they ceased to be 'Jews' and were entirely separated from the synagogues, with a definite and complete organisation of their own.

"It is to such as these that he [James] is writing; not perhaps to a definitely organised and *mixed* Christian Church, consisting of Jews and Gentiles, but rather to those synagogues which, like that at Berea, had embraced Christianity. To these he writes in the style of one of the old prophets. Their synagogue was still open to all Jews. . . . These communities of Jewish Christians, in the mind of St. James, stood in the position of Israel of old, and required just the same treatment at the hands of Christian teachers and prophets as Judæa and Samaria had received from the prophets of the old covenant."

About the Epistle Itself

The epistle is addressed *"to the twelve tribes scattered abroad"*. This at once will show how necessary are our foregoing preparatory paragraphs about its first-intended readers. Only an informed idea of those early Jewish Christians can give the key to certain strange-seeming paragraphs and make some of the allusions in the epistle fully intelligible to us. The "twelve tribes scattered abroad" were Jews of the Dispersion, Jews in places other than Palestine. James writes to them as president of the Christian assembly at Jerusalem.

The main purpose of the epistle may be gathered from its opening and closing words. It begins: "Count it all joy, my brethren, when ye fall into manifold temptations [or trials]." The closing paragraph says: "Be ye also patient; stablish your hearts: for the coming of the Lord is at hand." It was written to exhort and comfort Christian brethren undergoing trials—testings and penalties which were already coming because of their Christian faith.

The Early Date

The probable *date* of this epistle is of peculiar importance. The indications are that it was the earliest-written of *all* the New Testament documents. The "very slight line" which appears to exist between Judaism and Christianity; the "absence of definite Christian phraseology"; the sparseness of "specifically *Christian* doctrine"; the non-reference to *Gentile* Christianity—all these considerations are suggested as indicating its very early date. According with this is the circumstance that in the oldest manuscripts it stands first of these Hebrew Christian epistles, which *precede* the Pauline group. Assuming, then, this early date, how empty is the suggestion of some, that the epistle of James is an adverse reply to *Paul's* writings—which writings were not yet written!

Argument and Theme

The *argument* of the epistle is that true Christian faith must express itself in practical goodness. Hence, all the way through, the emphasis is on good works. And this is surely a very necessary emphasis. There is no contradiction between Paul, with his primary emphasis on faith, and James, with his insistence on good works. James is not arguing for good works as a *means* to salvation, but as the *product* of salvation. To argue therefore (as some have tried) that this epistle is a kind of polemic against Paul's doctrine of justification by faith (we say it again for emphasis) is *absurd*; for even if the epistle is not absolutely the earliest article of the New Testament, there can scarcely be a doubt that neither Romans nor Galatians had been penned when James wrote.

We may say that the theme of this epistle is *the proofs of true faith*. Many of us would do well to face up to these proofs again and again. They are expressed here and there in severe tones, yet always there is a warm brotherliness atmosphering them (the address, "my brothers" or "my *beloved* brothers," occurs more frequently here than in any other epistle except First Thessalonians). We ought also to add that besides stern admonitions there are in this epistle some of the most precious promises to Christ's people ever written by the pen of inspiration. We recommend a prayerful familiarity with it.

Analysis and Comments

We can scarcely agree with those who say that the epistle is "almost impossible to analyse." It is not simply a chain of one-after-another thoughts; there are easily distinguishable areas. Chapter i. is decidedly about *temptation* and considerations associated with it (see verses 2, 12, 13, 14; then verse 17, which assures us that, other than temptation, only *good* comes from above). The *first* proof of true faith, says James, is *endurance of temptation*.

Chapter ii. is equally clearly devoted to *impartial benevolence,* as a further proof of true faith (see specially verses 1–4, 14–18)

Chapter iii. follows with its unsparing, graphic deliverance on *control of the tongue,* as another proof of true Christian faith. It has been truly said that there is scarcely a more "burning and scorching" paragraph in the New Testament.

The remainder of the letter (iv. 1–v. 6) exhorts us to *godliness* in all things—in a series of flashlights on successive aspects.

There is no need here for a closer analysis. Let us clearly see the central stem and its main outreachings:

THE EPISTLE OF JAMES

Theme: The Proofs of Faith

Proof 1—ENDURANCE OF TEMPTATION (i.).

Proof 2—IMPARTIAL BENEVOLENCE (ii.).

Proof 3—CONTROL OF THE TONGUE (iii.).

Proof 4—GODLINESS IN ALL THINGS (iv.–v. 6).

Final encouragements, v. 7–20.

Each of these sections opens up in response to further study, like a flower opening its petals to the sun. Take the first chapter, with its wise and weighty words on temptation. Verses 2–12 show us the right *reaction* to it. Verses 13–20 tell us the true *origin* of it. Verses 21–7 give us the best *antidote* to it. Ponder these a moment or two.

(1) The *right reaction* to temptation. If we had not grown so familiar with the phraseology we should realise at once what a lovely new "slant" James gives on the subject when he begins, "My brothers, count it all joy."

In its way it is an almost breath-taking paradox. How many of us Christian believers, even in this advanced twentieth century of our Christian era, really count our trials and testings as joyous? Is it not still the natural and usual thing to regard them dolefully as much-to-be-lamented misfortunes? Perhaps even *we* are needing more doses of James's tonic!

But *why* would James have us "count it all joy"? His answer is: Because temptation may be transfigured into a ministry of spiritual blessing: "The trying of your faith worketh *patience*; and let patience have its perfect work, that ye may be perfect and complete, *lacking in nothing*."

Then, *how* can temptation be transformed? The answer is: (*a*) go to God in prayer—see verses 5–8; (*b*) accept providential orderings gratefully—see verses 9–11; (*c*) be assured that for patient enduring there is a final *crowning*—see verse 12.

(2) The *real origin* of temptation. It is good to have an apostle's word on this, for in a time of acute temptation or tribulation it is easy to get distorted ideas of God. James would have us settle three things firmly in our minds: (1) temptation in the sense of solicitation to evil is never from God—see verse 13; (2) it comes by our allowing inward desire to draw us into enticement—see verses 14 and 15; (3) other than temptation coming from God, only "good and perfect" things come to us "from above"—see verses 16 and 17. Nay, how *could* God tempt us when "of His own will He *brought us forth* by the word of *truth*, that we should be a kind of firstfruits of His creatures" (verse 18)?

(3) The *best antidote* to temptation. We should be quick to perceive how the remaining verses of the chapter grow out of what has preceded. James has just said that God "begat" us, or

"brought us forth," by the *word of truth* (verse 18) and that therefore every man should be "swift to *hear*" (verse 19). He now
follows this with : "Wherefore . . . receive with meekness the
implanted *word* which is able to save your souls" (verse 21).
"Be ye doers of the *word,* and not hearers only, deluding your
own selves. For if any one is a hearer of the *word,* and not a
doer . . ." Ah, this is the safest build-up against temptation—
God's *word* within, enlightening the mind, purifying the heart,
checking the inclinations, and bracing the will! It is this which,
when honestly received and faithfully obeyed, proves to be "the
perfect law of *LIBERTY*" (verse 25)!

James and Paul

We will not attempt to discuss chapter ii. 21–6, that battle-
centre of the supposed (but non-existent) conflict between James
and Paul. Ringing in our ears is James's "our beloved Barnabas
and Paul" (Acts xv. 25), and the ageing Peter's "our beloved
brother Paul" (2 Pet. iii. 15). We know well enough that in
Romans iv. Paul says that Abraham was justified by *faith,*
whereas James asks: "Was not Abraham our father justified by
works, when he had offered Isaac his son upon the altar?" But
the very reference to Isaac should guard us from any misunderstanding. Abraham's justification by *faith* was even before the
seal of circumcision. His offering up of Isaac was *twenty years
later*; so that the man who was now justified by *works* had already
been justified by *faith* for twenty years! If James had been
conscious of the slightest contradiction, would he have quoted
just afterwards the very verse (Gen. xv. 6) which tells of Abraham's justification by *faith*?—"Abraham believed God, and it
was imputed unto him for righteousness" (Jas. ii. 23). Surely
the twofold position is: Faith justifies the man; works justify
the faith.

Parting Words

Every part of the epistle is of tireless interest, but the closing
references to the Lord's return, to Job and Elijah, to sickness
and soul-winning, are specially so. The reference to supernatural
healing of the body claims comment. There is often a gracious
ministry in suffering. Before ever we think of "claiming" healing

we should ascertain whether it is an ordinary sickness, brought about by natural causes, or an "affliction," i.e. some Divinely imposed measure of correction, with which we are dealing. James makes this distinction. "Is any *sick* among you? let him call for the elders of the assembly; and let them pray over him, anointing him with oil in the name of the Lord; and the prayer of faith shall save the sick." "Is any among you *afflicted*? let him pray" (v. 14, 15, 13). Healing is not promised for "affliction." The only prescription is: "Pray." To be "claiming" deliverance from something which God Himself has purposively imposed or permitted is to be at cross-purposes with the will of God.

With the last few strokes of his pen James has a parting encouragement for soul-winners. It is noteworthy that this was the last thing in his mind. "Let him know that he which converteth the sinner from the error of his way shall save a soul from death, and shall hide a multitude of sins." There is a tender considerateness in the words "Let him know." Mark it well: the Holy Spirit would have the soul-winner "know." But is that surprising when we consider the fateful issues—"shall save a soul from death"? Oh, the ghastly depth of that word "death"! As used here, it means that deeper death in the Beyond, which the Bible calls "the second death." The tenses of the verb indicate so; for whereas the word "converteth" is a present tense, denoting something which happens here and now, the verb "shall save" is future, indicating a salvation which extends away forward into eternity. Note that James speaks in the singular—"a sinner," "a soul." See here the importance of one soul, of *any* soul! To save one soul from such a "death" is more than a whole life given to outward "social reform." The soul-winner is both anonymous and singular—"he which converteth"; no mention of theologians, preachers, evangelists. Despite the most circumscribed circumstances, need any of us be entirely debarred from witnessing to others with a view to their salvation in Christ? Oh, to win more living gems for His crown! It fulfils the highest of all functions to our fellow-creatures; it obeys our Saviour's last command; it receives the highest reward.

"LET HIM KNOW THAT HE WHICH CONVERTETH THE SINNER FROM THE ERROR OF HIS WAY SHALL SAVE A SOUL FROM DEATH, AND SHALL HIDE A MULTITUDE OF SINS."

Addendum: Who was James?

As we have said, the forty occurrences of the name "James" in our New Testament distribute themselves to (1) James the "son of Zebedee", and brother of John; (2) James the "son of Alphæus"; (3) James the "brother of our Lord" (Matt. xiii. 55). The first of these was martyred by Herod (Acts xii. 2). There has been much controversy as to whether (2) and (3) were identical. Our reason for touching on such questions in this study-series is that *investigation* always yields useful *information*. To our own mind, the pointers seem to be as follows.

1. John xix. 25 plainly says that Mary, the wife of Cleophas, was "sister" of our Lord's mother.
2. By clear parallel, Matthew xxvii. 56 gives this Mary as "the mother of *James* and Joses."
3. By further parallel, Mark xv. 40 calls this James "James the less" (i.e. in stature).
4. This James, son of Cleophas or Alphæus (and therefore our Lord's *cousin*), was one of the twelve apostles (Matt. x. 3; Mark iii. 18; Luke vi. 15).
5. This apostle-cousin James reappears with the apostles in Acts i. 13, and (surely, with no hint otherwise) in xii. 17, xv. 13, xxi. 18.
6. We conclude, therefore, that the James whom Paul calls our Lord's "brother" and an *"apostle"* in Galatians i. 19, ii. 9, 12, must be the *same* James.

So far, all seems straightforward; but controversy begins as soon as the question is raised: Was this apostle James the same person as the James who in Matthew xiii. 55 and Mark vi. 3 is actually called one of our Lord's brothers?—"Is not this the carpenter's son? Is not His mother called Mary? And His brethren, *James* and Joses and Simon and Judas? And His sisters, are they not all with us?"

Our own reply is that the two are not to be confused, for the following reasons: (1) These "brethren" of our Lord are connected with the *"carpenter"* (i.e. Joseph) and Mary; *not* with Alphæus and Mary, the parents of the *other* James. (2) In the Gospels these "brethren" of our Lord are kept markedly distinct from His apostles and even from His disciples generally (Matt. xii. 46; Mark iii. 31; John ii. 12, vii. 3), and we are told that as a *whole* they did not believe on Him: see John vii. 5. (3) In Acts i. 13, 14 *"Mary*, the mother of Jesus, and His *brethren,"* are *still* markedly separate from the Twelve, even though now His brethren *did* believe on Him. There is not a scintilla of evidence that these "brethren" who are each time mentioned with our Lord's own mother were only His *cousins* (as is made out by those who would identify this "brother" James with the *cousin* James who was an apostle); but there is ample evidence that the *cousin* James (son of Alphæus and the other Mary) was the apostle who became chairman or president among the Christian leaders in Jerusalem. This was the James who wrote our epistle. He was our Lord's *cousin*.

As for James, Joses, Simon and Judas, who were our Lord's "brothers" in Joseph's family, tradition and likelihood unite to make them children of Joseph by a former marriage. They were thus step-sons of Mary, and legally (though not really) half-brother to our Lord. Their seniority, perhaps, explains their attitude of restraint and critic-ism toward Jesus (Mark iii. 21, with verse 31; John vii. 3, 4) and perhaps underlay their disbelief (John vii. 5); and suggests a reason why Jesus, on the Cross, committed Mary to the care of John rather than to His unsympathetic half-brothers, Mary's stepsons.

J. A. McClymont in his *The New Testament and Its Writers* says: "According to a tradition, which we have no reason to disbelieve, their conversion was due to the appearance of the risen Lord to James, which is mentioned in 1 Corinthians xv. 7." But *was* that the James to whom our Lord appeared? Was it not the *apostle* James? It seems strange to us to find such an one as Dr. McClymont gratuitously adding: "Among the Christians at Jerusalem James soon took a prominent place, being, indeed, the recognised head of the Church there after the death of James, the brother of John (A.D. 44), and the dispersion of the other apostles. This commanding position he owed partly to the special relation in which he stood to Jesus. . . ." Thus, Dr. McClymont assumes, as do others, that the James of our epistle, who became leader of the Jerusalem assembly, was *not* the apostle-cousin James, but our Lord's half-brother. Yet surely we cannot accept this, for it would mean that in the Acts of the Apostles Luke, having mentioned the *apostle* James at the outset (i. 13), quietly drops him and without a word of explanation means *another* James in chapters xii. 17, xv. 13–21, xxi. 18–25—a James who had not com-panied with our Lord in His earthly ministry, had not heard His teachings to the inner circle, and was *not an apostle*! No; that will not do. It only serves the more to convince us that the James who became leader in Jerusalem and wrote our New Testament epistle was James the son of Alphæus and Mary, our Lord's *cousin*, and quite distinct from James the half-brother. That Paul refers to our *apostle* James years afterwards as our Lord's brother (Gal. i. 19, ii. 9) holds no real difficulty. There was a stricter (legal) way, and a quite common freer (kinship) way of using that word "brother." As one in the inner ring of our Lord's family relatives, the apostle-cousin could be properly called our Lord's brother. In any case, when Paul referred to James as one the the "apostles" (Gal. i. 19) he could not very well have meant the *other* James, our Lord's half-brother, for so far as we have any knowledge at all *he never became an apostle*.

We do not wish to appear needlessly over-confident, but frankly, to our own mind, the data are so clear and united that we are sur-prised at there having been such doubt as to the identity of the James who wrote the epistle.

SOME QUESTIONS ON HEBREWS AND JAMES

1. The spread of the Gospel raised not only the question: How does this relate to Israel as the covenant nation? but the further question: How does all this relate to . . . ? . . . ? Can you fill this in?

2. The discussion of this in Hebrews has been overruled to give us a wonderful revelation of our Lord's. . . . Well, what?

3. Who were the first-intended readers? Can you elaborate this by references to the Acts of the Apostles?

4. Which are the two key *words*, and which the focal passage of the epistle?

5. Which are the three main divisions of the epistle?

6. In chapters viii. to x. 18, which are the four ways in which the new covenant is "better" than the old?

7. How, would you say, does the last chapter of Hebrews specially bear on the authorship of the epistle?

8. Who are the four suggested alternatives to Paul as the author of Hebrews? Do you think any of them likely? . . . Why?

9. Who was the James who wrote the epistle bearing that name?

10. Can you give a brief comment on (1) the prominence, (2) the outlook, (3) the character, of this James?

11. What is the main theme of his epistle, and what are the four parts or aspects (corresponding with the four chapters)?

12. Can you give two good reasons why James ii. 26 could not possibly be a counter-argument to Paul's doctrine that Abraham was justified by faith?

THE FIRST EPISTLE OF PETER

Lesson Number 144

NOTE.—For this study read First Peter through at least twice, making notes of special emphases.

The floorway inside the main entrance to a beautiful European cathedral consists of three large marble slabs, the first being inscribed *CREDO,* the second *SPEIRO,* the third *AMO.* That is the order, also, in which the three main epistle-writers of our New Testament occur. First comes Paul, who is distinctively the apostle of *faith.* Next comes Peter, with his emphasis on *hope.* Finally comes John, with his emphasis on *love.* "I believe." "I hope." "I love." This would seem also to be the usual order of progress in the spiritual experience of believers.

—*J.S.B.*

THE FIRST EPISTLE OF PETER

THIS First Epistle of Peter stands third in the nine Hebrew Christian Epistles which constitute the final group of books in our New Testament. That the apostle Peter was indeed its author is substantiated, as most scholars agree, both by internal and external evidence. It seems likely that *both* his epistles were written towards the close of his days on earth.

The first epistle was written to "the sojourners of the Dispersion" (i. 1, R.V.). That expression, "the Dispersion," was the common Jewish term for those many thousands of Jews who from the time of the Assyrian and Babylonian captivities recorded in the Old Testament had been scattered throughout the regions over which the Assyrian and Babylonian powers had once reigned. Clearly, then, Peter is writing primarily, even though not exclusively, to *Hebrew* Christians. There does not seem to be any indication in the epistle that Peter had made first-hand contact with many of those to whom he now wrote; nor is there anything in it of a controversial nature. Its evident purpose is that of encouraging and strengthening those Jewish believers during a time of acute trial. I think we shall find, however, that it lights up with peculiar significance for our own time, and the age-end days which seem to be coming upon us.

So, then, let us now inspect the epistle, just as it lies before us. Let us avoid forcing any prefabricated analysis upon it and see if the little document will yield up its own precious secret to us (for I believe that the Holy Spirit has set some special jewel of truth in each component part of Holy Writ).

The only preliminary observation I would make about the arrangement or structure of the little epistle is that the doxology and "amen" in chapter iv. 11 obviously mark an intended major break—i.e. "That God in all things may be glorified through Jesus Christ, to whom be praise and dominion for ever and ever. Amen." Up to that point Peter has been speaking about trials which were already present; but after that "amen" he speaks of a "fiery trial" yet to come—i.e. "Beloved, think it not strange concerning the fiery trial which is [yet] to try you." Incidentally, notice that form of address—"Beloved." Its only other occurrence is in chapter ii. 11, where, similarly, it seems to mark the beginning of a new section. However, we shall "check up" on that as we read the epistle through together.

Let us read through chapter i. together, noting its special features.

Immediately after his opening salutation Peter commences with a grateful doxology (verse 3) for the great mercy of God in having "begotten us again unto a *LIVING HOPE*, by the resurrection of Jesus Christ from the dead, to an inheritance . . ." The thought of this wonderful hope is expanded in the ensuing verses (verses 5, 7, 8, 11, 13, 21). In fact, a further glance will show that all the verses up to the twelfth *declare* the hope, and verses 13–21 show the right *reaction* to it: "Wherefore, gird up the loins of your mind," etc.

How interesting it now is to find that at verse 22 Peter slants off to talk about the *"LIVING WORD"*!—"Seeing ye have purified your souls in obeying the truth through the Spirit . . . love one another with a pure heart fervently; being born again, not of corruptible seed, but of incorruptible, by the word of God, which liveth and abideth for ever." The "wherefore" with which chapter ii. opens shows us our true reaction to that "living word" (ii. 1–3).

Still more interesting is it to find that the *next* sub-section (ii. 4–10) is all about the *"LIVING STONE"*!—"To whom [Christ] coming, a *living Stone*, rejected indeed of men, but elect of God, and precious" (verse 4). Verses 5–10 tell us our relation thereto: "Ye also, as living stones, are built up a spiritual house, an holy priesthood, to offer up spiritual sacrifices."

So, then, in this first part of the epistle we find Peter speaking about three "living" realities of our Christian faith and life:

> The "living hope" (i. 3).
> The "living Word" (i. 23).
> The "living Stone" (ii. 4).

It is not just that these things are incidentally mentioned; the whole section is about them. In chapter i. 3–21 everything is about the "living hope" and *our reaction* to it. In i. 22–ii. 3

everything is about the "living Word" and again *our reaction* to it. In chapter ii. 4–10 everything is about the "living Stone" and our *relation* thereto.

The Living Hope

But that which is pre-eminent throughout this first section is the "living *hope*" which is ours in Christ. It is that to which we are immediately directed in the opening verse: "Blessed be the God and Father of our Lord Jesus Christ, who, according to His abundant mercy hath begotten us again unto a LIVING HOPE by the resurrection of Jesus Christ from the dead; to an inheritance, flawless, faultless, and fadeless, reserved in heaven for you." The "living Word" and the "living Stone" are the pledge and base which make our "living hope" imperishable and indestructible.

The Pilgrim Life

And now let us continue our observant reading of the epistle. We resume at chapter ii. 11 with that "Dearly beloved." At once we realise that a different note is now being sounded. There is a transition from explanation to *exhortation*. Peter is telling us about *the pilgrim life and how to live it*. We can easily verify this if we read slowly onwards from that eleventh verse: "Dearly beloved, I beseech you as strangers and pilgrims, abstain from fleshly lusts which was against the soul."

How methodical and progressive it all is! Consecutively we are told how to live the pilgrim life as *citizens* (ii. 12–17), as *employees* (ii. 18–25), as *married persons* (iii. 1–7); next in relation to *outsiders* and the enduring of *suffering* (iii. 8–iv. 6), then finally in relation to other *believers* and the rendering of mutual service (iv. 7–11).

Quite obviously Peter's own intended boundary-line to this part of his letter is the inclusive final doxology and "amen" in chapter iv. 11: "That God in all things may be glorified, through Jesus Christ, to whom be praise and dominion for ever and ever. Amen."

Observation of modern trends persuades me that there is accentuated reason today why we should linger thoughtfully and frequently over Peter's paragraphs on the pilgrim life. There is not much of the pilgrim pattern about many professing Christians. The strong tendency today is to live as settlers rather than pilgrims, as owners rather than stewards, and according to human standards of citizenship, employment, and wedlock, rather than according to the Divine ideals here set forth.

The constant and supreme purpose of the true pilgrim life is to glorify God in all things—as subjects, as employees, as wives, as husbands, in our social contacts, in suffering, in our fellowship with other believers.

The Fiery Trial

As we have said, the doxology and "amen" in chapter iv. 11 obviously indicate a major break in Peter's treatise. To my own mind it is difficult to understand how anyone can miss seeing this, especially in the light of what follows. Peter is evidently much concerned about a tribulation which was yet future but which was surely coming for Christian believers. He begins: "Beloved, think it not strange concerning the fiery trial which is to try you, as though some strange thing had happened unto you" (iv. 12, etc).

What, then, are we to suppose that Peter had in mind when he thus spoke about the yet future "fiery trial"? Undoubtedly, as the succeeding verses confirm, he was thinking of what is often called "the great tribulation," which is predicted to occur at the end of the present age. The passage on the "fiery trial" is Peter's parallel with the teaching of Paul and John, that the second coming of Christ is to be preceded by a brief but fiery period of excessive tribulation for godly souls on earth.

See how prominently the second coming of Christ is here in Peter's mind.

"Rejoice inasmuch as ye are partakers of Christ's sufferings, that when His glory shall be revealed, ye may be glad also with exceeding joy" (iv. 13).

"The elders which are among you I exhort, who am also an elder, and a witness of the sufferings of Christ, and also a partaker of the glory which shall be revealed" (v. 1).

"When the chief Shepherd shall appear, ye shall receive the crown of glory that fadeth not away" (v. 4).

Notice, too, how certain other features of this "fiery trial" section now assume new significance. Mark that age-end picture of Satan, in v. 8: "Be sober, be vigilant, because your adversary, the devil, as a roaring lion, walketh about, seeking whom he may devour." How surely it parallels with Revelation xii. 12, and its apocalyptic representation of Satan at the same latter-day crisis-epoch: "Woe to the inhabiters of the earth and of the sea! for the devil is come down unto you, having great wrath, because he knoweth that he hath but a short time"! The masquerading "angel of light" will then fling away all disguise and appear as the soul-murdering fiend that he really is, clawing and tearing and savagely ravaging as the "roaring lion" and the "great red dragon."

Yes, that is the coming "fiery trial" period which Peter pre-envisages. Ponder the passage again with that in mind. It flashes with new meaning in its prophetic relevance to the end-times which are even now drawing upon us.

But look at that lovely encouragement in verse 7: *"Casting all your care upon Him, for He careth for you."* That pledge and promise has always been precious to the people of Christ. How often, when we have gone to the Saviour's feet with our burden of anxiety, we have found unspeakable comfort in the reassurance "He careth for you!" Think of it—He who carries the universe on His shoulders carries you and me continually on His heart. Underneath all our seemingly big but comparatively tiny burden of care are the strong arms and tender upholding of an infinite wisdom, an infinite power, and an infinite love, which will never let us down, and never give us up, and never let us go! Yes, the promise has always been precious. It has been a seven-hued rainbow in many a weeping sky. It has turned weights into wings, burdens into benedictions, and sighings into singings. Yet it is when taken in its setting that it becomes most wonderful of all. Muse on it again in relation to its context. It is when the troubles of the "fiery trial," the "great tribulation," begin to break loose at the end of this age that godly hearts will most fully prove the triumphant thrill of this advance-reassurance, "Cast all your care upon Him, for He careth for you."

There has been much argument as to whether the Church will escape the so-called "great tribulation" or go through it. Sometimes, alas, the arguing has been badly disfigured by headstrong dogmatism, fanatical extravagance, and regrettable recrimination, so that the Church's rapturous prospect of the Lord's return has been brought into disrepute. May the Lord save *us* from such unchristlike contention on the matter! With my eye gratefully

scanning the Petrine passage about the coming "fiery trial," all
I would say is this, that *whatever* may be coming to us in the
days ahead, we need have no fear. He has anticipated it all.
"Cast all your care upon Him, for He careth for you"! If you
had gone to Shadrach, Meschach and Abed-nego after their
"burning fiery furnace" exploit, and had expressed sympathy
that they should ever have had to endure such an ordeal, what do
you think they would have replied? They would have politely
disclaimed all right to your sympathy and have assured you that
the trial by fire was the grandest experience of their lives; for it
was there, in the seven-times-heated furnace, that they suddenly
found Christ Himself walking with them amid the flames and
transforming the "burning fiery furnace" into a dew-kissed garden
of Eden!

Have no fear about the future, Christian believer. "He careth
for you." He has pledged Himself to you in advance. "Cast all
your care upon Him." This is the message which comes to you
from Peter's final section about the "fiery trial."

And thereafter Peter brings his letter to a close with a final
assurance and doxology: "But the God of all grace, who hath
called us unto His eternal glory, by Christ Jesus, *after that you
have suffered awhile*, make you perfect, stablish, strengthen,
settle you. To Him be glory and dominion unto the ages of the
ages. Amen."

There, also, I myself must leave you. But glance back just once
again over the little epistle, and catch the glory of its triple
message:

> The Living Hope.
> The Pilgrim Life.
> The Fiery Trial.

What a lovely little letter from Peter's pen this is! What
comfort and challenge and cheer it must have brought to those
first believers! What robust reassurance it brings, right down the
centuries, to ourselves, on whom history's climaxes are beginning
to break! Somehow these eschatological forepicturings of the New
Testament have "come alive" in a new way during the last few
decades. The unleashed powers of the material world, since the
splitting of the atom; the development of a vast, international
anti-godism; the considerable regathering in Palestine of still-

unbelieving Israel—these and other pointers, all coming simultaneously into focus, can surely mean only one thing, namely, that the golden daybreak which brings back our dear King is near. "Even so, come, Lord Jesus"!

This is how the epistle looks in block-analysis:

FIRST EPISTLE OF PETER

CHRIST OUR HOPE AND EXAMPLE AMID TRIAL

Address i. 1–2.

THE LIVING HOPE—AND WHAT GOES WITH IT

(i. 3–ii. 10).

The "living hope" (i. 3–12) and our reaction thereto (13–21).
The "living word" (22–5) and our reaction thereto (ii. 1–3).
The "living stone" (ii. 4) and our relation thereto (ii. 5–10).

THE PILGRIM LIFE—AND HOW TO LIVE IT

(ii. 11–iv. 11).

As citizens (ii. 12–17) servants (18–25) married (iii. 1–7).
As regards outsiders, and enduring suffering (iii. 8–iv. 6).
As regards other believers, and mutual service (iv. 7–11).

THE "FIERY TRIAL" AND HOW TO BEAR IT

(iv. 12–v. 11).

"Rejoice" and "commit": the Lord's return near (iv. 12–19).
Elders are to be examples in view of His return (v. 1–4).
All are to be humble and vigilant—glory beyond! (v. 5–11).

Farewell v. 12–14.

Let us evermore rejoice in that living hope. Let us daily seek grace to live that pilgrim life. Let us banish all dread of the "fiery trial," for even the "fiery trial" leads to the final triumph.

> Oh, blessed hope! with this elate,
> Let not our hearts be desolate;
> But, strong in faith and patience, wait
> Until He come!

THE SECOND EPISTLE OF PETER AND THE EPISTLE OF JUDE

Lesson Number 145

NOTE.—For this study read both these short epistles through two or three times.

ABOUT SECOND PETER

The majesty of the Spirit of Christ exhibits itself in every part of the epistle.

—*John Calvin.*

There is a strong probability that it was written before the destruction of Jerusalem. Otherwise such an impressive instance of Divine judgment could scarcely have been left unnoticed in alluding to the retributive justice of God.

At the same time the errors and dangers described in this epistle, which bear a strong resemblance, in some respects, to those referred to in the pastoral epistles (1 Tim. iv. 1, 2, vi. 5, 20, 21; 2 Tim. ii. 18, iii. 1–7), prove that it could not have been written much sooner than A.D. 70. The allusion to Paul's epistles as known to his readers (iii. 15, 16) leads to the same conclusion, as does also the frequency of the expression "put in remembrance" and kindred words (i. 12, 13, 15, iii. 1, 2), which indicate an advanced period in the apostolic age, as well as in the life of Peter—assuming that he was the writer.

—*J. A. McClymont, D.D.*

THE SECOND EPISTLE OF PETER AND THE EPISTLE OF JUDE

IT SEEMS advantageous to couple these epistles in this one study, because they are both short, and are noticeably similar to each other. In fact, there is such a close resemblance between Jude's letter and the second chapter of Second Peter, that (as many suppose) one of them must surely have given rise to the other, or else both were strongly impressed from a common original.

The balance of opinion gives priority of date to Jude. His denunciation and invective are the more scorchingly indignant against the wicked doers whose false doctrine and evil lives he describes, as though he had come into direct collision with them; whereas the forceful but calmer wording in Second Peter could suggest by comparison, a less direct contact, and an impact from the startling exposures made by Jude.

Then again, there is a good deal more in Second Peter than this one passage which is so like Jude, which suggests that the latter was made use of in this one place only; whereas if *Jude* were the borrower from Second Peter, would he have omitted all reference to the other parts of it? However, we must leave this without being able to bring the scales down firmly on either one side or the other!

THE SECOND EPISTLE OF PETER

Scholarship speaks with practically united voice on the genuineness of *First* Peter; but it is the opposite with this second epistle. It has been perhaps the most controverted epistle of the New Testament. We have no thought of dragging in a wearying discussion of it here; but a few useful comments may not be out of place.

First: its delayed recognition as canonical seems to have been mainly due to absence of direct quotations from it in the Christian writings of the first two centuries (though there are apparent allusions to it here and there).

Second: it was accepted as genuine and canonical, by the councils of Laodicea (about A.D. 366), Hippo (393), Carthage (397); and it should be remembered that those early councils and leaders possessed far more original data in deciding than has survived to ourselves.

Third: its not having been accepted until after prolonged and suspicious scrutiny reflects the cautiousness of those early Christian leaders, and makes their decided recognition of it later an underlined endorsement of its genuineness.

Fourth: despite objections, the *internal* evidences of the epistle betoken its apostolic date and Petrine origin. For instance, who can read the predictive parts of Second Peter without hearing an echo of our Lord's Olivet forecast, in which that fearful catastrophe, the destruction of Jerusalem, figures so graphically? Yet it is well nigh impossible, in reading Second Peter, to think that the awful overthrow had already happened. Similarly, if some falsarius of a later generation had been dealing, as this epistle does, with false teachers, could he possibly have done so without accidentally betraying *some* slight evidence of the more developed forms of Gnostic heresy?

However, for those who would follow all this further, we recommend Professor B. C. Caffin's excellent article on Second Peter in the *Pulpit Commentary*, from which we cull the following:

"Another important element in the evidence for the authenticity of this epistle is its own intrinsic power and beauty. We have several Christian writings of the second century; they are precious for many reasons; we should be very sorry to be without any one of them. But the value of them all put together is as nothing compared with that of this epistle. They are such books as good men might write now; full of piety and holiness, but not beyond the reach of men endued with the ordinary gifts of the Holy Spirit. But is there any man living, however wise and holy, who could write an epistle like this? Could any of the sub-apostolic Fathers whose writings have come down to us have produced anything to be compared with it? The books of Holy Scripture and human compositions lie in different planes; they do not bear comparison. There is an indescribable something in the Word of God which appeals to the human nature which God created, to the conscience which bears witness of Him—something which tells us that the message comes from God. The Second Epistle of St. Peter possesses that authority, that holy beauty, those notes of inspiration which differentiate the sacred writings from the works of men."

To Whom Written, Why, and When

Chapter iii. begins: "This second epistle, beloved, I now write unto you, in both of which I stir up your pure minds by way of remembrance." So it would seem that it was addressed to the same people as the first. A comparison of the opening salutation of the first epistle with that of the second, suggests that perhaps Peter may have had a rather wider range in mind when he wrote the second—and for a very real reason, namely, the appearance of a new peril to believers, in the form of *false doctrine*.

In his first epistle he has written to hearten them and encourage patient hope amid the trials which were coming to them by way of persecution for their faith; but these *spiritual* perils to which they were now exposed were far more to be dreaded, and called far more for warning than any merely physical tribulation! There is no mention in the first epistle of any such doctrinal apostasy and libertinism among believers themselves; but here, in this second letter, the deep concern is to rescue those early Jewish Christian assemblies and their members from the wily errors and corrupting influence of false teachers who were bringing in "destructive heresies" (ii. 1).

There must have been deep sadness in Peter's heart about this disturbing development, increased no doubt by his having apparently been apprised that his own martyrdom was near at hand: "I must shortly put off this tabernacle, even as our Lord Jesus Christ hath showed me" (i. 14). His martyrdom took place about A.D. 68. Whether he was at Babylon (1 Pet. v. 13) or not when he wrote this short second circular letter cannot be decided.

The Epistle Itself

So, then, the purpose of this short epistle is, by *reminder* and *re-emphasis*, to ground its readers more firmly in the *epignosis* or "full-knowledge" of saving truth as it is in Christ Jesus; and thereby to reinforce their faith against the imperilling counterfeits of that time. Trace this in chapters i. 12, 13, iii. 1, 2, 17, 18. But the warning also reaches down through the centuries, to our own times, to the "scoffers" at the end-days of this present age who deride the "promise" of our Lord's return. The tone is much graver than that of the first epistle; yet throughout it there is the same note of triumphant certainty and hope in Christ. The primal facts are well attested (i. 16–21). The final outcome is sure (iii. 9–13).

Whereas the emphasis in the first epistle is on *hope* amid trial, the emphasis running through this second one is on *growth* in the true knowledge; though here again the Lord's return is also prominent. Peter is distinctively the apostle of hope, as is Paul of faith, James of works, and John of love.

This second epistle is in three parts, corresponding with the three chapters into which it is divided in our English version. It will be seen that chapter i. is all about the true "knowledge" (verses 2, 3, 5, 8). In the first half of the chapter (verses 2–11) we are told how the truths of this knowledge are to be increased in. The second half of the chapter (verses 12–21) then tells us why "these things" are to be always "held in remembrance." Next, chapter ii. is all about "false teachers" who, alas, were to come among the Lord's flock, and cause great harm. Finally, chapter iii. is wholly given to the supreme "promise" (notice how "promise" recurs) of the Lord's return. The epistle may be briefly represented as follows:

SECOND EPISTLE OF PETER

THE TRUE KNOWLEDGE AND THE SURE HOPE

THE TRUE "KNOWLEDGE"—IN WHICH TO GROW (i.)

How "these things" are to be "abounded" in (verses 2–11).
Why "these things" are to be "remembered" (verses 12–21)

THE FALSE "TEACHERS"—WHO WERE TO COME (ii.)

Their havoc and their own destruction (verses 1–9).
Their excesses and peril to believers (verses 10–22).

THE SURE "PROMISE"—FOR AGE-END DAYS (iii.).

The promise upheld against scoffers (verses 1–9).
The promise a challenge to believers (verses 10–18).

The very seriousness of this epistle gives a keen edge to its teachings. Here is no mere doctrine for doctrine's sake, but for the vital issues at stake between the false and the true. As above shown, the dual emphasis of the epistle is, the "true knowledge" and the "sure hope"; but clinging to this there is a momentous significance which may well startle every eye, namely, that just as true knowledge and sure hope are inseparably linked together, so are false doctrine and final destruction! What is more, just as true doctrine and holy living are linked together (i. 5–10, iii. 14, 17, 18), so are false doctrine and unholy living (ii. 1, 10, 14, 19)! All of which shows how important is sound evangelical doctrine. How often in recent days have we heard the breezy aphorism, "Never mind what you believe; the thing which matters is how you live"! It seems to smack of such liberty from bondage to dusty creeds (just as in 2 Peter ii. 19), but it is fatally wrong; for how we live is most of all determined by "what we *believe*." This shows itself in individual lives the world over. It is also showing itself very grimly nowadays in governments and international relationships. Beliefs go far deeper than politics and economics. How important indeed is sound *"doctrine"*! Most of all is it so inside the Church. Second Peter rings the warning: "Danger inside the Church!" There are always two tests of Christian genuineness. The doctrinal test is: "What is the attitude to the person and work of Christ?" The practical test is: "What is the resultant character and conduct?" Both tests appear in Second Peter.

Chapter i.

Note the two dangers indicated in that first chapter. There is the danger of life without *growth* (verses 3–8); and there is the danger of knowledge without *practice* (verses 9–14). Life never remains static: it either goes forward or backward. Life without growth becomes atrophy. Similarly knowledge without practice becomes blindness instead of vision (verse 9). It is vital to be members of the *"progressive* party"! On the latter verses of chapter i., concerning the origin and "private interpretation" of Scripture, may we refer to our treatment of it in the book *Studies in Problem Texts*? The Roman Catholic Church has made much capital out of that misunderstood twentieth verse; and all evangelicals should be clear as to its real meaning.

Chapter ii.

To be forewarned is to be forearmed, says the old proverb. Study carefully Peter's forewarning in chapter ii. It is a point of incidental interest that in verses 14 and 18 the word translated as "beguiling" and "allure" ("entice" in R.V.) in the Greek is literally to *take with a bait*—a relic from Peter's fishing days. "Beware," says Peter in effect, "your most dangerous deceivers are those who come with a tasty bait and a concealed hook!" Let this second chapter convince us that wherever there is a Divine truth which saves, there will be a Satanic counterfeit which damns: so will it be until the arch-deceiver is flung into the abyss.

What a *scathing* exposure is this second chapter! There is no "mincing of words" or "beating about the bush." There can be no tolerance of that which, inside the very Church itself, dishonours Christ and ruins souls! There can be no "dainty handling" of false teachers! A viper can be a gorgeous creature to look at, but once let its poison fang get you, or its strangle-coils enwrap you . . . ! Peter sees the issue with Spirit-anointed clearness. There can be no compromise. Remember, this second chapter is not merely Peter speaking; it is the Spirit of God. It may well make some of us think deeply. When easy-going kindness lounges in the place of righteous indignation, and allows Christ-dishonouring false doctrine to play havoc inside the Church, kindness has ceased to be Christian, it has become disguised disloyalty, camouflaged cowardice, or a moral wasting-disease.

Chapter iii.

The third chapter might have been written for this very hour. Indeed, it *was* written long in advance for us today, though Peter little guessed so. How up to date does the brag and pooh-poohing of these third-chapter "scoffers" sound! What titanic cosmic upheavals are on the way! We cannot linger over the individual verses, for this is a Bible course, not a commentary. We mention only one, in closing. Verse 12 runs on: "Looking for and hasting unto the coming of the day of God." But the preposition "unto" does not occur here in the Greek. Leave it out, and read it just as Peter wrote it: "Looking for and *hastening* the coming of the day." There is a co-operativeness between God's purposes and His people's responses. There is a certain contingency about our

Lord's return. Paul mentions one aspect of this in Romans xi. 25, when he uses the expression "until the fulness of the Gentiles be come in." But how can *we* hasten that day? There are three ways: (1) by daily longing for His appearing, remembering that He is coming to them who, according to 2 Timothy iv. 8, *"love His appearing"*; (2) by daily *praying* for His appearing, remembering that the last prayer of the Bible, in Revelation xxii. 20, is, "Even so, come, Lord Jesus"; (3) by daily seeking to win souls, until "the election of grace" and "the fulness of the Gentiles" complete the bride of the coming Bridegroom. Thus may future hope and present growth go hand in hand!

THE EPISTLE OF JUDE

The writer of this short but intense letter calls himself a "bond-servant of Jesus Christ, and brother of James." By common consent, the James here referred to is the James who wrote the Epistle of James. If our brief enquiry into the identity of *that* James be sound (see our addendum to that epistle), then both he and Jude were sons of Alphæus and Mary, and were the *cousins* of our dear Lord. Jude's being so closely related to our Saviour after the flesh lends lustre to his designation of himself as the *"bond-servant* of Jesus Christ." Our Lord's human kinsmen recognised His Divine nature and glory, though some of them had disbelieved at first, and were now His adoring servants.

As to the *genuineness* of this powerful fragment, we quote the late principal Salmond: "No doubt appears to have been entertained by the early church as to the genuineness of the epistle. Opinions might waver for a time as to the position assignable to it in the church, and as to the particular Jude who wrote it. But there was no dispute about its being the work of a Jude, the genuine work of the man from whom it professed to proceed. Even in later times few have been found to pronounce it fictitious or spurious. It is true that some recent critics have attempted to make it out to be a product of the post-apostolic age, and that several scholars of considerable authority have regarded it as a protest against the Gnosticism of the second century. But its direct and unaffected style, the witness which it bears to the life of the church, the type of doctrine which it exhibits, and, above all, the improbability that any forger would have selected a name comparatively so obscure as that of Jude under which to shelter himself, or indeed would have thought of constructing an epistle of this kind at all, have won for it general acceptance as genuine. 'Whatever may be our opinion as to Second Peter,' it is justly remarked by Dr. Plummer, 'sober criticism requires us to believe that Jude was written by the man whose name it bears. To suppose that Jude is an assumed name is gratuitous.' "

Contents and Analysis

This little epistle of Jude was written under special constraint, as the writer himself tells us in verse 3 (see R.V.). The constraint arose from a disturbing consideration of the apostasy which was blighting Christian assemblies through the subversive teachings of false brethren. It speaks with special force to our own times.

There is a clear orderliness of thought running through it. Its central idea is that of *contending for the faith*, in accord with verse 3, which gives the key. The first sixteen verses tell us *why* to contend, i.e. because of apostate teachers. The remaining verses tell *how* to contend, showing our true resources.

First, then, in verses 3 and 4 we find that the subtle perverters were culpable of *two basic denials*: (1) denying grace by "turning" it into lasciviousness; (2) "denying our only Master and Lord, Jesus Christ."

Next, in verses 5–7 we find their certain doom foretold and illustrated by three historic examples of a like Divine vengeance on such, i.e. Egypt, angels, Sodom.

Next, in verses 8–11 Jude describes in scathing terms the character and conduct of these false teachers whom he combats, comparing them with three historic figures infamous for their impiousness, i.e. Cain, Balaam, Korah.

Next, in verses 12–16 he exposes their utter falsity, dragging away all their deceiving draperies, in six awful metaphors, i.e. (1) "hidden rocks"; (2) exploiting "shepherds"; (3) "clouds without water"; (4) "trees without fruit"; (5) "wild waves of the sea"; (6) "wandering stars." Then this section ends with the Enoch prophecy of coming destruction upon all such.

The remaining verses of the letter, which show us *how* to contend for the faith, break up equally clearly. First, we are to realise that such apostasy has been foretold (verses 17-19). Second, there is to be a "building up of yourselves on your most holy faith, praying in the Holy Spirit" so as to "keep yourselves in the love of God, looking for the mercy of our Lord Jesus Christ" (verses 20, 21). Third, we are to "show compassion" to certain who "doubt" or, more literally, "contend" (verse 22). Fourth, we are urgently to seek the rescue of others, but to keep our separation and purity in doing so, "hating even the garment spotted by the flesh" (verse 23).

The little epistle then ends with a prophetic doxology envisaging an ultimate heavenly consummation (verses 24, 25). The following framed analysis will put it all in one convenient view.

THE EPISTLE OF JUDE

CONTEND FOR THE FAITH

KEY VERSE—3

Greeting, verses 1, 2.

WHY TO CONTEND—APOSTATE TEACHERS (3-16).

Their subtle perversions: two basic denials (3-4).
Their certain doom: three historic examples (5-7).
Their impious ways: three historic examples (8-11).
Their utter falsity: six awful metaphors (12-13, R.V.).
Enoch's prophecy: Coming destruction (14-16).

HOW TO CONTEND—OUR TRUE RESOURCES (17-23).

Realise that the apostasy has been foretold (17-19).
"Build," "pray in the Spirit," "keep," "look" (20, 21).
Show compassion towards certain who contend (22).
Others seek urgently to rescue: but keep pure (23).
Jude's doxology: Coming consummation.

Perhaps the language of this short but sharply severe epistle may seem *too* scalding to some readers. We ourselves have been tempted at times to think so. But when one honestly, realistically reflects on the life-and-death issues involved, on the awful majesty and marvellous grace of God, on the costliness and preciousness of the salvation purchased on Calvary, on the measureless sin of knowingly distorting grace, dishonouring Christ, deceiving souls, and thus "doing despite" to the Holy Spirit—NO, it is not Jude who is too severe but our own perception which is blurred.

Of course, in all contending for the faith we must "keep ourselves in the love of God," the counterpart of which is that the love of God must be *in us*. We must love, even while we contend against the errors of apostatisers. We must love their *souls* even while we oppose their *words* and deplore their *ways*. Sometimes it is delicately difficult to keep these separate, but the love of Christ in our hearts will put wisdom in our lips. Also, we must make a distinction between different *kinds* of errorists, as verses 22 and 23 tell us. Read those verses in the Revised Version. Even in the Revised Version the word "doubt" in verse 22 should be "contend." There are some who "contend" against *us*. Endless counter-contention with them is useless. But there are others who need "snatching out of the fire"; they have been deceived, and in one sense or another, i.e. by bewilderment, remorse, doubt, or danger, are in the fire. And there are still others on whom we are to "have mercy with fear," i.e. being cautious lest in seeking to bring them back we should defile our own garments.

Yes, we must make distinction. Let this letter of Jude's show us that there is urgent need for contending to preserve the purity of the true Gospel; but let it show us at the same time that in such contending, more than in anything else, we need the love of Christ in our hearts, and the wisdom of the Spirit in our minds.

The closing doxology—one of the sublimest in the New Testament—begins: "Now unto Him . . ."; but in the Greek the "Now" is really *"But"*, marking a contrast with what has just preceded, i.e. the "garment spotted by the flesh." Over against that metaphor of defilement comes this:

"But unto Him who is able to guard you from stumbling, and to set you *WITHOUT BLEMISH* before the presence of His glory, in exceeding joy; to the only God our Saviour, through Jesus Christ our Lord, be glory, majesty, dominion and power, before all time, and now, and unto all the ages.
Amen."

TEN QUESTIONS ON 1 AND 2 PETER, AND JUDE

1. What are the three main parts in the First Epistle of Peter, and what are the three "living" realities in part one?

2. How do the doxology in chapter iv. 11, and the structure of the epistle guide us to view the "fiery trial" as yet future?

3. What was it which provoked Peter's second epistle?

4. What are the three parts of Second Peter? (Sub-divisions need not be given.)

5. To whom were Peter's two epistles addressed?

6. Can you quote 1 Peter v. 7, and say why it has an increased preciousness today?

7. Why would you say Jude was a cousin of our Lord?

8. What is the key emphasis of Jude's letter? Which are its two parts? What three examples of doom, and six metaphors of falsity, does Jude use?

9. Who were the "sojourners of the Dispersion," or the "strangers scattered throughout Pontus, Galatia," etc.?

10. What part of Second Peter suggests either that Peter had seen Jude's epistle, or that both Peter and Jude had been influenced by a common original?—and why?

THE EPISTLES OF JOHN

Lesson Number 146

NOTE.—For this study read First John *several* times. Its recurrent ideas only in that way become fixed in the memory, but the time is well spent.

I JOHN

This is probably the last apostolic message to the whole Church. If the second and third epistles were written later, they were to individuals. This letter is catholic in the fullest sense of the word, being addressed to no particular church or district, and dealing with the fundamental question of the life which is the true bond of the Church's unity.

A comparison of John xx. 31 and I John v. 13 will show the Gospel and epistle to be complementary. The Gospel was written that men might have life, the epistle that believers might know they had life. In the former we have Divine life as revealed in Christ; in the latter the same life as realised in the Christian. The Gospel declares the way of life through the incarnate Son; the epistle unfolds the nature of that life as possessed by the children of God.

—*G. Campbell Morgan.*

THE EPISTLES OF JOHN

How much we owe to the pen of John! Try to imagine the deprivation if *his* writings were deleted from our New Testament. We take his three epistles together here, because they naturally cohere. The first of them opens up some of the deepest realities of the spiritual life, while the second and third *illustrate* the truths which it teaches. The first, also, has a spacious catholic outlook, though it rightly belongs here, in this ninefold group of Hebrew Christian Epistles, for its approach and implicit background are kindred with the others. Verse 7 in the *third* epistle, of course, clearly indicates a Hebrew standpoint.

The First Epistle

It seems to be the general opinion of scholars that this first epistle of John was written about A.D. 90. At that time John would be the only surviving apostle, and would be a great age. In keeping with this, the tone of the epistle is *paternal* both in the fatherly affection and in the fatherly authority which characterise it.

It is a wonderful epistle. The words are very simple, but the thoughts are rich and deep. The style is direct and plain, yet there is a subtle, mystic depth in the way that truths are stated and in the way they are developed from one sentence to another.

How different is John's form of thought and expression from that of Paul! There is a certain vivacity and liveliness about Paul's way of presenting things which we do not find here in John. Yet somehow there is here a ring of finality and persuasive confidence which is equally distinctive and impressive. John is contemplative rather than argumentative. He presents truths as they come by intuitive perception rather than by reasoned conclusion. He is mystical rather than logical. He sees the confirmation of truth in one's *experience* of it rather than in demonstration by argument.

This should be duly borne in mind as we now take up a closer study of this first epistle of John. It will be both a guide and a guard to us in analysing and interpreting the epistle. In the epistles of Paul and Peter we have generally found the different parts so clearly distinguishable from each other that it has been fairly easy to sectionise them, but it is not quite like that with this first epistle of John. It is an epistle of recurrent ideas rather than of hard-and-fast divisions. If we try to set out this epistle too rigidly or squarely in analysis we shall obscure its sustained lines of emphasis. There certainly are distinguishable breaks and sections in it (for instance, the words "light" and "darkness" which noticeably recur in the first twenty-one verses never once occur afterwards; or again, the Holy Spirit, who is not once named before chapter iii. 24, is thereafter mentioned seven times along with five references to other spirits); but these divisions are not such as to break certain *chains* of thought which run *right through* the epistle. Of these chain-themes the main ones are:

> MUTUAL CHRISTIAN LOVE.
> ABIDING IN CHRIST AND GOD.
> HOW TO KNOW TRUTH FROM ERROR.
> THE TRAITS OF THE BORN-AGAIN.
> THE BELIEVER AND THE WORLD.

These chain-themes should be traced through and carefully marked. They make rich and edifying studies.

The usual way in which this first epistle of John is analysed is to make out that all in chapters i. and ii. relates to the truth that God is *Light*, all in chapters iii. and iv. to the truth that God is *Love*, and all in chapter v. to the truth that God is *Life*. This, of course, makes its appeal to the eye and to the mind, but surely it is somewhat artificial, as (we think) a careful rereading of the epistle will show. We would not seem to press our objection unkindly, but, after all, we are dealing with Divinely inspired writings, in each part of which the Holy Spirit has invested some special significance; and the pity, in fastening the above-mentioned analysis, or others similar to it, on this first epistle of John, is that it tends to blur the really focal emphasis and significance of the epistle.

Seven Successive Contrasts

The fact is, that this first epistle of John runs in a series of *seven successive contrasts* which throw up into sharp relief the central idea of the epistle, and the dominant concern in the aged apostle's mind. These seven successive contrasts are too striking to miss. They set off, in vivid antagonism, truth and error in their most vital aspects, and in relation to the Christian believer. They are accompanied all the way through, by the significantly recurrent little clause, "Hereby ye know," or "Hereby shall we know," or "By this we know." These recurrent clauses in this epistle are like the traffic-lights at the corners of our city thorough-fares, with their red for "Stop," and their green for "Go." They should be picked out and underscored and linked together right through the epistle. Moreover, the seven striking contrasts which make up this epistle, and these significantly recurring clauses, leave us in no doubt as to the dominant, urgent, intense and unspeakably vital *purpose* of the epistle. It is written in order that we may *"know" and distinguish, in their most vital aspects, Christian truth from error, and Christian love from its counterfeits,* and that thus being able to *"know"* the true we may *"abide"* in it. Here, then, in this epistle, are the criteria of "the truth" exhibited in seven vivid contrasts:

THE FIRST EPISTLE OF JOHN

TRUTH VERSUS ERROR: HOW TO "KNOW" AND "ABIDE."

Key Clause—"Hereby we know."

SEVEN CONTRASTS.

1. THE LIGHT VERSUS THE DARKNESS (i. 5–ii. 11).
2. THE FATHER VERSUS THE WORLD (ii. 12–ii. 17).
3. CHRIST VERSUS THE ANTICHRIST (ii. 18–ii. 28).
4. GOOD WORKS VERSUS EVIL WORKS (ii. 29–iii. 24).
5. THE HOLY SPIRIT VERSUS ERROR (iv. 1–iv. 6).
6. LOVE VERSUS PIOUS PRETENCE (iv. 7–iv. 21).
7. THE GOD-BORN VERSUS OTHERS (v. 1–v. 21).

Much might be written under each of these seven contrast-titles, but we have not space here. We recommend a thorough re-study of these contrasts in the light of what we have said about them. We would simply point out here that in these seven contrasts we have seven searching *tests*. Taking them in their order, we have the acid "test" (1) of profession, (2) of desire, (3) of doctrine, (4) of conduct, (5) of discernment, (6) of motive, (7) of new birth.

There seems to be no good reason why we should reject the common tradition that all the apostles were martyred except the Apostle John. God had special purposes in preserving John alive upon the earth. One of these purposes finds its expression in the apocalyptic visions which were given to him on the lonely isle of Patmos, and which have been transmitted to us by pen in the last book of the Bible. But another purpose we may well suppose was that John should live long enough to see not only the Satanic innoculation of Christian doctrine with the virus of "antichrist" heresy but its process and principal characteristics, so that he might write this First Epistle of John for the future guidance of the Lord's people. Let us be deeply grateful for this epistle of the seven contrasts. May we learn it thoroughly and heed it constantly!

A Noteworthy Significance

All the way through this epistle there is a clear-seeing demarcation between the true and the false, and a clean-cutting incisiveness in dealing with them. John's pen is a surgeon's knife, not a philosopher's quill. There is a downright spiritual simplicity which sees things as they really are. White is white, and black is black; and they cannot be compromised into a middle grey. This moral clear-sightedness is always a mark of real spiritual maturity. No need for circuitous windings of arguments; the Spirit-illuminated inward eye sees vital moral distinctions immediately—often causing much annoyance to those who profess more loudly but see more dimly. What hazy seeing and pious parleyings with questionable practices there are among Christian believers today! Look through this first epistle of John again, and mark well the significant fact that this epistle which is distinctively that of Christian *love* is at the same time the epistle of *NO COMPROMISE*! This is something which needs special consideration today.

Spiritual Fundamentals

Then again, all the way through this epistle we are meeting with pronouncements on profound spiritual fundamentals. If we are after the evidential or argumentative bases of the Christian religion, we must look elsewhere, but the *spiritual* ultimates are here in First John. Think of only a few of them:

The all-inclusive commandments are two: that we believe on Jesus Christ; and that we love one another (iii. 23).

A profession of love for others, without active ministry to their needs is false (iii. 17, 18).

The Father's sacrificing the Son is Love's last word: and that, if nothing else, should move us to "love one another" (iv. 10, 11).

The true blessedness is a heart at rest before God. The secret is: "Perfect love casteth out fear" (iv. 18).

Such are found from beginning to end of the epistle; and they ceaselessly insist that we face up to the simple ultimates, to the really decisive choices and issues. In these five short chapters God's Isaacs may find spacious fields for sanctifying meditation.

Incipient Gnosticism—and today.

There can be little doubt that throughout this epistle John is combating certain errorists, even though he leaves them unnamed. He so writes that his expounding of truth is an exposing of its counterfeit. Whether the errorists were early Gnostics, or Cerinthus and his school, cannot be conclusively deduced. Gnosticism (see fly-leaf to our study on Colossians) did not reach full bloom until the second century, but it existed in its earlier forms for two or three decades before John's demise. The usual sect or local group of Gnostics supposedly possessed some special "revelation" superior to that of normal Christianity, handed down mystically from Christ or other great ones but known only to the inner circle of the initiated.

This invariably led to a *seriously defective view of Christ.* In Gnosticism the old Greek philosophical dualism had assumed a religious form. The philosophical distinction between the realm of reality and that of sense-appearance now took a new form as *God* (the light) and *matter* (the evil) in ceaseless antagonism. Therefore Jesus as pure Spirit could not really have had a material body. He had not really "come in the *flesh*" (1 John iv. 3). His body was only "docetic," or phantasmal. Or, if the body was real, then it was only the body of *Jesus* the man, but not of the pure Christ-Spirit: the Christ entered Jesus at his water-baptism, but left him just before his crucifixion, as it was impossible for the Christ-Spirit to undergo crucifixion in an evil material body. In other words, He "came by *water*" (the baptism)—but *not* also by "*blood*" (the Cross) as John says in chapter v. 6. On either of these views the Calvary work of our Lord is utterly nullified.

John strikes back at this, swiftly and powerfully, though without naming it, in the very first sentence of his epistle. "That which was from the beginning, which we have *HEARD*, which we have *SEEN WITH OUR OWN EYES*, which we have *CLOSELY OBSERVED*, and which *OUR OWN HANDS HAVE HANDLED*, of the Word of Life: for the Life was manifested, and *WE HAVE SEEN* . . . That which we have *SEEN AND HEARD* declare we unto you."

Here is no recondite, clandestine mystery-mongering, with its head in the clouds and its feet swinging in space, but first-hand witness to well-proven facts! Jesus was no mere phantom. Nor was He merely human. He was the "Word" and the "Life"— as John had testified to them in his earlier writing (i.e. the Gospel according to John) and as he now testifies again: "We have *SEEN* and do *TESTIFY* that the Father sent the *SON* to be the *SAVIOUR* of the world" (iv. 14).

But besides this, those early Gnostic subtleties led to *lowered standards of conduct*. There was an idea that the secret super-revelation possessed by the initiated élite lifted them above obligation to Gospel standards of conduct into a superior "liberty." John also answers *that*. Over against the very idea of inner circles and secret divinings he proclaims at the outset: "God is *light*, and in Him is no darkness at all" (i. 5). Everything about the real Gospel is frank and open. There are no dark rooms or curtains of mystery. The real truth is a light which shines out upon all. Over against the idea of some secret "illumination" he says: "These things have I written unto you concerning them that would lead you astray. And as for you, the *ANOINTING* which ye have received of Him (i.e. the Holy Spirit) *abideth* in you, and ye *need not that anyone teach you*; but His anointing teacheth you concerning all things, and is true, and is no lie" (ii. 27). "Ye have an *ANOINTING* from the Holy One, and ye know all things" (ii. 20). Over against the proud imagining of a superior "liberty" in conduct, he writes: "If we say we have fellowship with Him [the Light], and walk in the darkness, we lie, and do not the truth" (i. 6). Indeed, all through the epistle this last-mentioned error is counteracted. Profession without practical godliness of conduct is either hypocrisy or self-delusion.

How true it is that although John was writing guidance for those first-century believers the Holy Spirit was so guiding *him* that his words have provided guiding tests of doctrine and conduct ever since! Heretical break-aways have always been either one or the other of two kinds: (*a*) those which have said that Christ was too Divine to be really human; or (*b*) those which have said He was too human to be really Divine. Christian Science today ranks with the first; Unitarian cults rank with the second. Let us learn deeply and firmly that any tampering with the *person* of Christ at once jeopardises the true doctrine of His atoning death. Let us learn, too, that false doctrine, however superior-sounding, always results, sooner or later, in lowered standards of conduct.

The Seven Tests

Following up our remark that this is an epistle of guiding *tests,* we would urge again that its several chain-themes be carefully traced and studied—the seven distinguishing traits of the born-again (ii. 29, iii. 9, iv. 7, v. 1 (twice), v. 4, v. 18); the seven reasons why the epistle was written (i. 3, i. 4, ii. 1, ii. 13–17, ii. 21–24, ii. 26, v. 13); the seven *tests* of Christian genuineness (i. 6, i. 8, i. 10, ii. 4, ii. 6, ii. 9, iv. 20). Perhaps it may be useful to set out the last mentioned a little more fully. Seven times there is an "If we say," or "He that saith"; and each time it marks a test by which falsity is exposed. They are seven tests of honesty and reality. They search us. They penetrate like a white flame. They expose hypocrisy. Here they are:

i. 6: "If we say
    that we have fellowship with Him, and walk
    in darkness, we lie."   False fellowship.

i. 8: "If we say
    that we have no sin, we deceive ourselves
    and the truth is not in us."   False sanctity.

i. 10: "If we say
    we have not sinned, we make Him a liar,
    and His word is not in us."   False righteousness.

ii. 4: "He that saith
    I know Him, and keepeth not His command-
    ments, is a liar."   False allegiance.

ii. 6: "He that saith
    he abideth in Him ought to walk even as
    He walked."   False behaviour.

ii. 9: "He that saith
    he is in the light, and hateth his brother, is
    in the darkness."   False spirituality.

iv. 20: If a man say
    I love God; and hateth his brother, he is a
    liar."   False love to God.

Look back over the seven. In the first the religious profession-
alist is not honest with *others*. In the second he is not honest with
himself. In the third he is not honest with *God*. In the fourth
he is not honest with *Christ*. In the fifth he is not honest with
the *world*. In the sixth he is not honest with his Christian
brother. In the seventh he is by implication (ponder it and
see) false to *all*. We have already mentioned the seven places
in this epistle where John states his purpose in writing. The
first of these, chapter i. 3, casts its significance, of course, over
the whole epistle: "That which we have seen and heard declare
we unto you, that ye also may have *fellowship* with us: and truly
our *fellowship* is with the Father, and with His Son, Jesus Christ."
We cannot strictly call this verse the "key" to the epistle, or say
that "fellowship" is John's uppermost subject (seeing that after
chapter i. 7 the word does not once occur again); yet who can
help but realise that the underlying purpose all through is that by
avoiding the false and abiding in the truth we should know the

pure joy of an unclouded *fellowship with God*? It would not be inappropriate to write over this epistle as a whole,

THE GATEWAY TO FELLOWSHIP WITH GOD

These are just a few of the "seams" in this wonderful mine of spiritual values; but just as we are getting into it we must now leave it—comforting ourselves with the thought that at least we may have encouraged someone else to "mine" it more thoroughly.

> Oh, gift of gifts! oh, grace of grace!
> That God should condescend
> To make my heart His dwelling-place,
> And be my closest Friend!

THE SECOND EPISTLE

An Apostle's Letter to a Mother

This second epistle of John is addressed to an "elect lady and her children." Some would have us believe that this lady and her children were really a *church and its members*; but verses 5, 10 and 12 convince us that such an idea is far-fetched and artificially imported. We are glad that at least one little epistle in our New Testament is addressed to a Christian *mother*.

What is the little letter about? Well, look at the opening lines and note that the word *"truth"* comes no less than five times. Next, read again the exhortation which begins at verse 4 and note that John is not writing any new commandment but is emphasising the need of *continuing* in what had been commanded *"from the beginning."* Twice we have that expression, "from the beginning" (verses 5, 6). Quite clearly John is here exhorting continuance in "truth" which had been "received" (verse 4) right "from the beginning" (verses 5, 6). Here, then, is the *raison d'être* of this little personal letter to the elect mother and her house. It is an exhortation to *continuance in the truth*.

The exhortation occupies verses 4–11 and is in two parts. In verses 4–6 we have the *practical* aspect of continuing in the truth: we are to "walk" in "love." Then in verses 7–11 we have the *doctrinal* aspect of continuing in the truth: we are to "look," or watch, against error. We may set this out as follows:

THE SECOND EPISTLE OF JOHN

CONTINUANCE IN THE TRUTH

Greeting, verses 1– 3.

PRACTICAL ASPECT: WALK IN LOVE (4–6).

(*Love to the brethren is the centre-test of Christian practice.*)
The Divine insistence on love (verse 5).
The human expression of love (verse 6).

DOCTRINAL ASPECT: WATCH AGAINST ERROR (7–11).

(*The person of Christ is the centre-test of Christian doctrine.*)
Warning against false teaching (verses 7–9).
Warning against false charity (verses 10, 11).

Parting, verses 12–13.

That which directly *evoked* this brief but concentrated note of affectionate greeting and warning was the unhappy circumstance referred to in verse 7: "Many deceivers are gone forth into the world." All that precedes in the letter is quite plainly a lead-up to this.

The particular seducers before John's mind are certain who "confess not that Jesus Christ cometh in the flesh." Just as the expression "love not" in 1 John iii. 10, 14 is the practical equivalent of "hate" in iii. 15, iv. 20, so here the expression "confess not" equals "deny". Of such denial John does not hesitate to say: "This is the deceiver and the antichrist"—very plain speaking which should not be lost on us. These misleaders are here said to have denied "Jesus Christ *as coming* in the flesh"; or (as the Greek could mean) "Jesus *as Christ coming* in the flesh." The Jew denied that the Christ *had* come in the flesh. The Gnostic denied that Christ *could* come in the flesh. (Some in the present-day church deny that He ever can or will come *again* in the flesh.)

It is the incipient Gnostic position which John thinks of in this letter to the elect lady, with its denial that the Divine Spirit *could* come in material form. Our remarks in connection with John's *first* epistle will have indicated how specious this superior-sounding religious philosophy could be, especially when plausible lips and clever reverence were allied with it.

"*Look to yourselves!*" That is the concentration-point of the letter (verse 8). The deceivers are beckoning you on; but the red light is against you! Pull up! "Whosoever abideth not in the doctrine of Christ, *hath not God*" (verse 9). It is this which brings John to write: "If there come any unto you and bring not this [the true, apostolic] doctrine, receive him not into your house, neither bid him God speed" (verse 10). There is a superficial sentimentalism today which recoils from John's words as uncharitable. But do we castigate the doctor for being intolerant with *disease*? Ask any of his patients! Would any of us knowingly welcome deadly virus into our bodies? We all have to mix up with people of different views and beliefs, and as Christian believers we are truly to love their souls; but to *fellowship co-operatively* with them in Christ-dishonouring propaganda of any kind is a betrayal of our love to the Lord who bought us.

THE THIRD EPISTLE OF JOHN

TRUTH AND LOVE VERSUS PRIDE AND STRIFE.

"HOSPITALITY—A FAITHFUL WORK" (verse 5, R.V.).

Address—verse 1.

GAIUS—SERVICE IN TRUTH AND LOVE (2–8).

"Brethren . . . witness to thy truth" (verse 3, R.V.).
"Brethren . . . witness to thy love" (verse 6, R.V.).

DIOTREPHES—EVIL BY PRIDE AND STRIFE (9–11).

"Who loveth to have the pre-eminence" (verse 9).
"And casteth them out of the church (verse 10).
Commendation of one, Demetrius—(verse 12).

Parting words—verses 13, 14.

This third epistle of John is addressed to "Gaius." As this name was just about as common in the Roman world as the name John Smith is in the British Isles today, it would be rather rash without any further data to infer that the Gaius whom John here addresses is the same as others of that name who are mentioned elsewhere in the New Testament (Acts xix. 29, xx. 4; Rom. xvi. 23; 1 Cor. i. 14).

Let all who open their homes and give hospitality to our Lord's ministering servants see from this letter to the hospitable Gaius how the Lord Himself regards their kindliness. They are *"fellow-helpers of the truth"* (verse 8). The providing of such hospitality can sometimes be very tiring. Had Gaius been generously over-doing it? Had he overtaxed himself, giving cause for John's solicitous concern as to his health (verse 2)?

Alas, over against the unselfish Gaius was the selfish Diotrephes, who cuts a sorry contrast. His tongue and temper are deplored in verse 10. Dr. Campbell Morgan well says: "The whole truth about this man is seen in one of those illuminative sentences in which the character of a man is so often revealed in the Scriptures. 'Diotrephes, who loveth to have the pre-eminence.' That is the essential violation of love, for 'love . . . seeketh not her own.' This is an instance of heterodoxy of spirit or temper, rather than of intellect. There is no evidence that this man was teaching false doctrine, but he was not submissive to authority. As is always the case, the unsubmissive one becomes the greatest tyrant, and thus by disobedience he manifests his lack of love."

Glance again at verse 7: "They went forth for the sake of *THE NAME*." It is arresting. To Christian hearts it is thrilling. Just as "the Name" to a Jew always meant Jehovah, so now to the Christian—whether Jew or Gentile—"the Name" means the One which is dear and glorious above all others. Ignatius, later writing to the Ephesians, says: "I am in bonds for *the Name's sake*"; and, "Some are wont of malicious guile to hawk about *the Name*." In Acts v. 41 the whipped apostles left the council chambers, not chafed and humiliated, but "rejoicing that they were counted worthy to suffer dishonour for THE NAME"! Oh, for a like humility, loyalty and love!

> Oh, let my love be such to Thee,
> That I may ever grateful be
> To suffer stigma, brand or shame,
> And count it honour for Thy Name
>   Who didst so much for me!

THE REVELATION OF SAINT JOHN

Lesson Number 147

NOTE.—For this study a ready general idea of Revelation is required. If several readings through it are necessary for newer readers, the time taken in getting familiar with it will be well worth while.

It is true of all parts of the Bible that they study it best who come feeling that they are on holy ground; that it were fitting, like Moses before the burning bush, to take off one's shoes and to cover the head, and to bend with reverence and godly fear to hear the voice that speaks. If this which we are about to study is God's word, then happy is he who receives it, "not as the word of men, but, as it is in truth, the word of God" (1 Thess. ii. 13) in all lowliness. For "to this man will I look" saith the Lord, "even to him that is poor and of a contrite spirit, and that trembleth at my word" (Isa. lxvi. 2).

Of all the books of the Bible none other is so solemnly introduced to us; none so specially urged upon our attention; and, we must add, none so generally disregarded, so shunned, and so neglected. Yet no other book opens with a gracious promise of blessing on him that readeth, on those who hear and keep the things written therein. And to no other book is attached such a warning lest anyone should take from or add to its message. It is a message therefore of the very highest importance, though by men often lightly esteemed and treated as though it were superfluous, and could be dispensed with without material loss. In God's estimate, at least, this book is of supreme value. In it we behold the end and consummation of all God's work and plan, the climax and outcome of all His dispensations and dealings with men; and in it every prophecy and promise, every purpose and covenant finds its ultimate goal and fulfilment. In Genesis we have the beginning of all, in Revelation we have the end and goal of all.

—*R. H. Boll.*

THE REVELATION OF SAINT JOHN

ON ONE occasion that prince of preachers, C. H. Spurgeon, was accosted by a critic with a poser from the Bible. "There now, can you tell me what *that* means?" flaunted his would-be tripper-up. With a well-known twinkle in his eye Spurgeon replied: "Why, of course I can tell you what it means. *It means just what it says.*" We ourselves have sometimes felt how appropriate that reply might be when eager individuals have come to us, usually at the close of public meetings, and with a look of innocent trustfulness have asked: "Would you please tell me what the Book of Revelation means?" We have also thought of the wise words: "A question may be asked in a sentence; the reply may take a century."

Still, to our own mind, there always seems a touch of incongruity about the fact that this book which seems the most mystifying is the one book of the Bible which is named a *"Revelation."* It is the very opposite of a dark concealment: it is an *apocalypse,* or "unveiling," as the Greek title signifies. Will it seem like stupid effrontery if we dare to say here that the book is one of the *easiest* to understand? Well, we say it, and we mean it. This is far from saying, however, that we can unlock all the (often intendedly enigmatical) symbolism of the book. Who on earth can? Yet we *do* mean that in its *total* significance and in its *focal* message it is surely such as the plain man can understand. We hope that the analysis which we submit will make this clear. Meanwhile, so far as the *predictive* interpretation of the book is concerned, everything depends on a right *approach* to it.

Four Different Approaches

Speaking broadly, there are four schools of interpretation which would elucidate this Book of Revelation for us. These are: the Præterist, the Historist, the Idealist, the Futurist.

The *Præterists* see the greater part of the book as already fulfilled in the early history of the Church. The words "Write the things which thou hast seen, and the things which are, and the things which shall come to pass hereafter" (i. 19) are taken as referring to "the contemporary state of things in the Church and the world, and the events which were to follow in immediate sequence." On this theory much of the book pictorially represents "the Neronian persecution and the Jewish rebellion." The seven kings of Revelation xvii. 10, are interpreted as the emperors Augustus, Tiberias, Gaius (Caligula), Claudius, Nero, Galba, Otho. The number of the beast—666—is the total numerical value of Neron Cæsar spelled in Hebrew letters—and so on.

The *Historists* (or Presentists, as they are sometimes called) see in the book a prophetic programme covering the whole of history from apostolic days to the end of time. Dr. Grattan Guinness was the well-known chief populariser of this view in recent years. Vision after vision, seal after seal, vial after vial, are seen to have successive correspondence with successive history, leaving only the end-part of the book to be yet fulfilled in immediate connection with our Lord's return. As one writer puts it: "The Book of Revelation is divinely pre-depicted history, from about A.D. 96 to the present time and beyond; the economic, political and ecclesiastical events of which are written in cipher, figure, or code." Thus, on this theory, the book is unfolding itself all through this present age.

The Idealists take the book as simply setting forth great spiritual realities under various symbols and not as depicting actual events of history at all, either past or future. It is "the pictorial unfolding of great *principles* in constant conflict, though under various forms, and eclectic in its character." Dr. J. A. McClymont, for instance, tells us that the "safest and probably the truest interpretation of the book is to regard it as a symbolic representation of great principles rather than a collection of definite predictions."

The Futurists understand the major part of the book as referring to what is still future, that is, to the end-epoch of the present age, and then onwards. Many futurists would concur that the letters to the seven churches in chapters ii. and iii. *do* cover successive stages of church history; but either from chapter iv. or from chapter vi. all the vision-developments up to chapter xix. fore-picture events which will break into occurrence shortly before (and some actually at) the second coming of Christ; while chapter

xx. leads through the Millennium to the final general judgment of mankind; and the last two chapters (xxi., xxii.) bring us into the "new heaven and new earth."

Which of the four?

Which of the four, then, really interprets the book? Impressive names are associated with each. We will give our own view, frankly and briefly; but let not our frankness be mistaken as either dogmatism or disrespect.

Quite definitely we must reject the *Idealist* theory. The more we read the book, the more are we compelled to believe that what is unveiled is in the main definitely prophetic. The correspondences between it and other plainly prophetic passages of both Old and New Testaments are too clear to admit of doubt. Unless all those other passages are also to be idealised or spiritualised, we simply cannot so treat the parallel visions in our Book of Revelation.

Nor can we accept the *Præterist* view. Those who argue that all was fulfilled during the first age of the Church land themselves in insuperable difficulties when they come to certain parts of the book, parts telling of things which most definitely have *never yet* happened. Also, on their theory, it would certainly seem as though some of the seer's forecasts soon became falsified by events—leaving us wondering why the book continued to be so highly esteemed by the early Church. Even though some of the Præterist school allow an historical fulfilment up to the fall of the Roman empire in the fifth century, it still remains that on this theory our Book of Revelation is of no more than a merely historical interest today.

Nor can we think that the endlessly variable *Historist* or Presentist interpretation is right. The knowledge of history which it necessitates before anyone can understand the book at all seems plainly to disqualify it. According to some, the *seals* release history down to the fall of the Roman empire; the *trumpets* sound the Barbarian and Mohammedan invasions down to the eleventh century. The *beast* is the Papacy in the sixteenth century. The *vials* are judgments on the Papacy and Mohammedanism in the nineteenth century. There is no lack of ingenuity in hooking symbols to events, but there is much lack of real likelihood. Many of the events which they fit as fulfilments are scarcely worthy of the predictions they supposedly fulfil, while really major determinative events are left completely ignored both by God and man!

Dr. Joseph Angus's note on the Historist theory is too forceful to leave unquoted: "While agreeing, however, in this general view, the historical interpreters display the utmost diversity of opinion as to the application of the different symbols in numbers, animated forms, forces of nature, colours, etc.; some extending them more or less to the events of secular history, while others restrict them entirely to the affairs of the Church. It would be wrong to ridicule the mistakes and contradictions of interpreters whose solemn pursuit was that of truth, in their calculations of times and seasons and their interpretations of apocalyptic symbols; but in the fact that authorities of such reputation as Bengel, Wordsworth, Elliott, and others are at hopeless variance, this system breaks down. Where one interpreter (Elliott) sees in the sixth seal a reference to Constantine, another (Faber) sees allusion to the first French Revolution; where one sees in the star fallen from heaven a good angel (Bengel), another (Elliott) discerns Mohammed: the scorpion locusts that have power for five months mean to Mede one hundred and fifty years of the dominion of the Saracens, but to Vitringa they mean Goths, and to Scherzer Jesuits. All this seems to be arbitrary and hazardous in the extreme."

The Futurist Interpretation

To our own mind, the true interpretation is that known as the *Futurist*. This does not mean that we would agree in detail with all that marches forth as supposed interpretation under the Futurist banner; but the view in general we believe to be the true one. Of course, the very fact that it makes the body of the book refer to what is still future means that it cannot yet be tested as to historical *results*, as the other theories can (unfortunately for them!); but the Futurist interpretation can be tested in other ways, specially by *comparison with other Scriptures*—which to ourselves is the most important test of all. I believe the Futurist interpretation to be true because it interprets the disclosures of John's Revelation in parallel correspondence with *the whole scheme of Biblical prediction*.

What *is* that "whole scheme"? Is it not briefly as follows? The Old Testament prophecies repeatedly foretell the coming of a royal Christ who should reign on David's throne, in Jerusalem, over a regathered, regenerated Israel, and rule in beneficent empire over all the Gentile peoples. These prophecies are so many and so worded that to *spiritualise away* their plain meaning seems to us a deep irreverence to the Holy Spirit. But there is also a strain in Messianic prediction which shows the coming Messiah as a suffering Saviour whose death brings salvation from sin. The New Testament floodlights all this, showing that there is but the one Messiah, with two comings—first as suffering Saviour, second as Davidic sovereign, and that between the two comings the present age intervenes. The New Testament also makes plain that the second coming is to be preceded, and in fact precipitated, by age-end troubles surpassing in intensity and magnitude anything known before, and that there will follow it the long-promised reign of Christ. The New Testament does not disclose the duration of this intervening age, for in the very nature of things our Lord's second coming is meant to have a continuing *imminence*; but it does tell, again and again, that just beforehand there will be unprecedented developments which will serve as recognisable precursors (Matt. xxiv. 27–31; 2 Thess. ii. 1–12; 2 Tim. iii., etc.).

Now it seems to me that the Futurist interpretation of John's Revelation clearly fits in with this general pattern of Scripture prophecy. If not, who will show us otherwise? We have just read a pamphlet, *Some Errors of Futurism*, in which the author condemns the Futurist interpretation as a sixteenth-century invention of Ribera, a Jesuit priest of Salamanca, in order to save papal Rome from being identified as Antichrist (as in the Reformers' historist interpretation). So far as I myself am concerned, there was a time when I decided to consult no other writings on the matter until I had independently "searched the Scriptures" for myself; and that is how *I* came to my persuasion. The pamphlet also says that the Futurist interpretation depends upon the "gap" theory, i.e. a supposed long interval (the present age) between the sixty-ninth and seventieth weeks of Daniel's prophecy; but no—so far as I am concerned no gap theory is needed; the New Testament alone satisfies me as to the end-epoch of this present age and our Lord's return. The pamphlet criticises the writings of certain Futurists; but that is very different from disproving the interpretation in general. I myself do not agree with all that Futurists say on subsidiary aspects: but neither can I find one real, Scriptural argument against the Futurist view in all the fourteen large pages of the said booklet.

Of course, I am only too eager to make certain concessions. With the *Idealists* I am willing enough to see, in the apocalyptic visions and symbols, vivid illustrations of spiritual principles, struggles, and issues, even though these are not the first *interpretation* of the book. With the *Præterists* I readily see in the precursors and crash which ended the apostolic era a fulfilment, a kind of *advance* fulfilment, even though not *the final* fulfilment; just as our Lord's predictions in Matthew xxiv. 4–31 all had a fulfilment *then* except the actual return of our Lord Himself. With the *Historists* I can see recurrent correspondences and fulfilments all through the present age, inasmuch as "history repeats itself," and God has overruled events to adumbrate and lead onward to the *ultimate* fulfilment. Thus my Futurism can find some accommodation for all the other three, though none of them can possibly allow a place for *it*!

A Guiding Principle

We must content ourselves here by submitting only one of the guiding principles which we think should be observed in interpreting the symbols of the book. It is this: Beware of that false exegesis which says, "If any part of Scripture is symbolical, *all* is symbolical: if any part is literal, *all* is literal." The very first vision in this Book of Revelation should guard us against any such sweeping assumption. Our Lord appears as—

1. "One like unto the Son of Man."
2. "Clothed with a garment down to the foot."
3. "Girt about the bosom with a golden girdle."
4. "His head and hair as white wool, as snow."
5. "His eyes were as a flame of fire."
6. "And His feet like unto burnished brass."
7. "His voice as the sound of many waters."
8. "He had in His right hand seven stars."
9. "Out of His mouth a sharp two-edged sword."
10. "His countenance as the sun shineth."

Here, certainly, is symbolism. Dignity, power, office, character, all are garbed in symbol. But, note it well, although *much* is symbolic, not all is so. It was in all reality *the Lord Himself* whom John saw, not just a symbolic representation of Him. Again and again all through the Book of Revelation we find symbolism thus grouped round central literal truth and realities.

Main Movements and Analysis

So then let us now go through the book together, writing down our findings and drafting out an analysis as a basis for further study. No book of Scripture is built upon a clearer plan. It runs in three movements, each issuing in a transcendent climax. The first covers the first five chapters. The second covers chapters vi.–xx. The third runs through chapters xxi. and xxii.

In the first movement, covering the first five chapters, the goal is the enthronement of Christ *in heaven*. In the central movement, covering chapters vi.–xx., the goal is the enthronement of Christ *on earth*. In the final movement the lovely climax is the enthrone-ment of Christ *in the new creation*. Let us get hold of this, first of all, then, that the Book of Revelation is the unveiling of our Lord's *three enthronements*.

Next, let it be realised that the main body of the book (chapters vi.–xix.) runs in two parallel series of chapters ; i.e. chapters vi.–xi. and chapters xii.–xix., run parallel with each other, both chapter-groups depicting the same series of happenings but from two different aspects. Both run through two awful epochs: (1) "The Great Tribulation," and (2) "The Wrath of God." Note that the seven *seals* in the first member of the parallel (vi.–xi.) are matched by the seven *personages* in the second member (xii.–xix.) also that in both there is the sealing of an Israel remnant on earth and the blessedness of the saints in heaven ; that the seven *trumpets* of the one part exactly parallel with the seven *vials* of the other part. In the first member (vi.–xi.) we have the earthly view of these things ; in the second member (xii.–xix.) we have the heavenly view of them.

Thus the book may be preliminarily summed up in brief, as follows:

1. *FIRST MOVEMENT (i.–v.).*

The entronement of Christ in heaven.

2. *SECOND MOVEMENT (vi.–xx.).*

The Great Tribulation.
The Wrath of God.
The entronement of Christ on earth.

3. *THIRD MOVEMENT (xxi.–xxii.).*

The entronement of Christ in
the new creation.

To begin with, look again through those first five chapters. Who can fail to see that the fifth is climactic to the others? Observe the order and progress running through them.

The First Chapter Group

In chapter i. we have the vision of the Son of Man amid the lampstands. What is the central truth thereby symbolised? Surely we are meant to get a vivid, moving impression of *the Christ in heaven operating through the Church on earth.*

Then come chapters ii. and iii., with their seven letters of commendation, instruction, exhortation and correction, to those "seven churches" of Christ on earth. What is the prevailing thought in these? Equally clearly it is that of *the Church on earth functioning for the Christ in heaven.*

Thus the vision of the Son of Man amid the lampstands, and the letters to the seven churches, are the converse sides of the one truth. In the one case we have the heavenly aspect—the Lord in heaven operating through the Church on earth; in the other case, the Church on earth functioning for the Christ in heaven. Naturally, we would like to linger over details, but that is outside our purpose here. What we want is to capture the central or crucial ideas.

Christ, then, is risen, living, ascended; robed in awful holiness and overwhelming heavenly splendour. Although at present invisible to the earth, He is more active on earth than ever. He is moving amid the lampstands; He is operating through the Church on earth; and the Church (singular) on earth is functioning for Him through the *churches* (plural).

What is His last word to the Church? It is this: "To him that overcometh will I grant to sit with Me in My throne, even as I also overcame, and am set down with My Father in His throne" (iii. 21). This reference to our Lord's joint-occupancy of the Father's throne opens the door to the *vision of that throne* which now follows in chapters iv. and v. Chapter iv. spends itself in describing the throne of the Deity and the worship of heaven. In it we are shown *the place of supreme authority—the throne*. Then chapter v. follows—the chapter of the Lamb and the seven-sealed book, in which we see the Lamb Himself "set down" amid the throne. Grasp it firmly: the ruling purpose in this first movement of the Apocalypse is to put the Lamb amid the throne. The book cannot go forward *until He is there*. Thus this first movement reaches its climax: *CHRIST, THE LAMB, IN THE PLACE OF SUPREME CONTROL.*

Again we must reluctantly by-pass the intriguing incidentals of the wonderful symbolism so as to emphasise the controlling ideas. The one pendant which we would hook on to chapters iv. and v. is: to insist that they describe something which has *already happened*. Their enthronement of the Lamb in heaven is not something which is yet to happen. He is there *now*. Recall chapter iii. 21: "Even as I also overcame, and *sat down* with My Father in His throne" (R.V.). This agrees with the uniform teaching of the New Testament (Mark xvi. 19; Acts ii. 33; Rom. viii. 34; Eph. i. 20, 21; Heb. i. 13 with ii. 9, x. 12, 13). That enthronement in heaven has already taken place. See, then, at a glance the course and climax of these first five chapters:

THE FIRST CHAPTER-GROUP (*i.–v.*).

ch. i. The Son of Man amid the Lampstands.
   —Christ in heaven operating by Church on earth.

ii.–iii. The Letters to the Seven Churches.
   —Church on earth functioning for Christ in heaven.

iv. The Heavenly Throne and the Worship.
   —The place of supreme authority.

v. The Lamb and the Seven-sealed Book.
   —Christ, the Lamb, in supreme control.

The Second Movement (vi.–xx.)

As soon as the Lamb is put in the throne, the Apocalypse moves on through the two shock-epochs of the "Great Tribulation" and the "Wrath of God." In this middle and longest part many readers find themselves in a chaotic mix-up simply because they fail to see that chapters xii.–xix, are a parallel *"repeat"* of chapters vi.–xi. We can easily exhibit the parallel as follows:

Chapters vi.–xi.	*Chapters xii.–xix.*
Ch. vi. The seven seals.	The seven persons (xii., xiii.).
vii. Parenthetical:	Parenthetical (xiv.):
(1) Israel remnant sealed	(1) Israel remnant sealed.
(2) Blessedness of saints in heaven.	(2) Blessedness of the saints.
viii., ix. SEVEN TRUMPETS.	SEVEN VIALS (xv., xvi.).
1. On the earth.	1. On the earth.
2. On the sea.	2. On the sea.
3. On the rivers.	3. On the rivers.
4. Sun, moon, stars.	4. Sun.
5. Darkness, scourge.	5. Darkness, scourge.
6. Euphrates: army.	6. Euphrates: kings
7. "Nations angry"; "Wrath"; "Great voices"; "Time no more."	7. "Nations fell"; "Wrath"; "Voices"; "Thunderings"; "It is done."
x. xi. Parenthetical: Jerusalem in the "Great Tribulation".	Parenthetical (xvii.–xviii.): Babylon in "Wrath of God."
xi. 15 End of seventh trumpet.	After seventh vial (xix.)
1. "Kingdom of the Lord."	1. "Lord God reigneth."
2. The 24 elders worship.	2. The 24 elders worship.
3. "Wrath" is come.	3. "Armageddon."

This concurrent parallel can easily be looked up and verified, for which purpose it is better to use the Revised Version. There can surely be no mistaking it. It is really there; and the interpretation of the book hangs upon it.

"Great Tribulation" versus "Wrath of God"

In this parallel there is one feature which is peculiarly arresting when once it is perceived, namely, the solemn pause between the seven seals and the seven trumpets in column one, and the correspondingly solemn break between the seven personages and the seven vials in column two. (See in the one case vi. 17–viii. 1, and in the other case xiii. 18–xv. 1). *Why*, then, this break between seals and trumpets, and before the vials? It is to mark a distinction between the two stages of the age-end crisis, i.e. between the oft-called "Great Tribulation" and the "Wrath of God." We cannot recall having seen this distinction pointed out before in expositions of New Testament eschatology, yet it is certainly *there* (not only in the Apocalypse, but in other Scriptures too: see Matt. xxiv. 29–31), and has an illuminating bearing upon the question as to whether the Church will or will not go through the "Great Tribulation."

With what acrimoniousness that sensitive question has often been discussed by opposite-thinking parties! Yet there seems to be considerable confusion of thought by some who are severely dogmatic. Again and again we meet persons who hold the common idea that the Church will have been transplanted to heaven before the "Great Tribulation" develops on earth, yet to us their main reason for so believing seems doubtful. They say: "We cannot think that the Church could possibly be left on earth during those awful few years which end the present age, because that will be the time when the judgments and wrath of God are poured down upon the earth; and how could the Church be allowed on earth to undergo all *that*, since the cross of Christ has *saved* believers from such judgment?"

Yet there are passages in the New Testament which to our own mind certainly seem to show that believers of the last days (there is only one small part of the total Church on earth at any given moment) *will* be on earth during the so-called "Great Tribulation." 2 Thessalonians ii. is one such.

We know what a touchy point this has been, and do not purpose to develop discussion of it here; but we do suggest that there is one fact which has hitherto been overlooked, namely, that the "Great Tribulation" and the "Wrath of God" are not identical. When Christians say they cannot think that the Church could be left on earth during the "Great Tribulation" because it is then that the "wrath to come" is poured out, they are confusing things which differ. That "Wrath of God" is the last, awful end-bit which "immediately *follows*" (Matt. xxiv. 29) the "Great Tribulation." Now certainly no blood-bought, Spirit-sealed member of our Lord's mystic body can be thought of as left on earth and undergoing *that*. Yet it is quite possible—and from some passages in the New Testament seems (to us) necessarily implied—that believers will still be here during the "Great Tribulation" when the "man of sin" is here.

We do not here dogmatically affirm either one way or the other; but we think that the distinction which we have made—or, rather, which we believe the *Scripture* makes—between the "Great Tribulation" and the "Wrath of God" is important. Remember, the "Great Tribulation" is largely of Satanic instigation through the "man of sin," whereas the "Wrath of God" is entirely an affliction from God Himself. Certainly the Book of Revelation (compare also Matthew xxiv.) seems to observe this distinction, as our framed analysis will show; and when once this necessary distinction is duly recognised the central stretch of the book (vi.–xix.) unfolds its remarkable parallel far more intelligibly. When the "Great Tribulation" and the "Wrath of God" are treated as identical, confusion results, as one may see from some of the varying analyses and explanations of the book.

The Final Movement (xxi.-xxii.)

The apocalypse reaches its sublime climax in the "all things new" of chapters xxi. and xxii. Reflect a moment on what leads up to this. The first movement of the book (i.–v.) finds its climax in the enthronement of the Lamb in *heaven*. Both of the parallel chapter-series which comprise the middle area issue in the enthronement of our Lord on *earth* (xi. 15–17 and xx.). The climax-point of this final unveiling in chapters xxi. and xxii. is the enthronement of the Lamb in "the new heaven and new earth" for evermore. Seven times the Lamb is mentioned; and this is what the seventh mention says:

"And there shall be no more curse, but the *throne of God and of the Lamb* shall be in it [i.e. in the new Jerusalem]."

Not Heaven

These last two chapters of the Bible must not be thought of as a description of *heaven*; they describe something which is to be on *earth* (though of course in that new order of things there will be open traffic between earth and heaven). In chapter xxi. 2 John says: "And I, John, saw the holy city, new Jerusalem, coming *down* from God out of heaven," i.e. to *earth*. See also verse 24, which says: "And the *nations* shall walk in the light of it" (R.V.). Yes, this is the ultimate golden prospect for this old earth of ours! Indeed, it will not be "this old earth" any longer; it will be a "new earth"; and the "new heaven" will mean that the invisible environs of the earth have been forever freed from "the prince of the power of the air."

Nor the Millennium

Again, the glorious new era which breaks on our view in these last two chapters must not be taken as an additional description of the *Millennium*. No; the Millennium is the subject of the *twentieth* chapter, where we find the saints "reigning with Christ a thousand years" (verses 4–6). During that thousand years Satan is interned in the abyss (verses 1–3); but at the end he is released; whereupon he immediately goes forth to deceive the nations, and there is a swift, last, violent insurrection (verses 7–10). The purpose of this is finally to demonstrate the utter incorrigibility of Satan, and the irremediable failure of Adamic human nature—even after a thousand years of perfect government; thus immediately preparing for the final, general judgment at the "Great White Throne" (verses 11–15) and the winding up of the present order. During the Millennium the *old* Jerusalem is built up; but in these last two chapters (xxi., xxii.) the "*new* Jerusalem" comes "down" from heaven.

Such, then, is the contour and main import of this Book of Revelation; and we may set it out in flat analysis.

Our framed outline, of course, gives merely a general conspectus of the book; but it may serve as a basis for more detailed analysis. We are sorry that it does not show more prominently our Lord's three enthronements, but, in lieu, it does bring out the distinction between the "Great Tribulation" and the "Wrath of God."

THE RISEN CHRIST ENTHRONED

Ch. i. THE SON OF MAN AMID THE LAMPSTANDS.
(Christ in heaven, operating through the assemblies on earth.)

ii.–iii. THE LETTERS TO THE SEVEN ASSEMBLIES.
(The assemblies on earth, functioning for Christ in heaven.)

iv. THE HEAVENLY THRONE AND THE WORSHIP.
(The place of supreme authority and control.)

v. THE LAMB AND THE SEVEN-SEALED BOOK.
(Christ put in the place of supreme control.)

THE "GREAT TRIBULATION"

Ch. vi.—**The seven seals.**
vii.—Parenthetical.

(1) Israel remnant sealed on earth before "Wrath".
(2) Blessedness of saints **in heaven.**

Ch. xii.–xiii.—The seven personages.
xiv.—Parenthetical.

(1) Israel remnant sealed before "Wrath" comes.
(2) Blessedness of saints.
(3) Warning: "Wrath" coming.
(4) Vision: reason for Armageddon.

THE "WRATH OF GOD"

SEVEN TRUMPETS (viii.)	SEVEN BOWLS (xv., xvi.)
1. On the earth.	1. On the earth.
2. On the sea.	2. On the sea.
3. On the rivers.	3. On the rivers.
4. Sun, moon, stars.	4. Sun.
5. Darkness, scourge.	5. Darkness, scourge.
6. Euphrates: army.	6. Euphrates: kings.
7. "Nations angry"; "Wrath"; "Great voices"; "Time no **longer.**"	7. "Nations fell"; "Wrath"; "Voices, thunderings"; "It is done."

NOTE: x., xi, parenthetical (Jerusalem in "Great Tribulation").

NOTE: End of seventh trumpet (end of xi.):

1. "Kingdom of Lord and Christ."
2. The 24 elders worship.
3. "Time of dead to be judged."
4. "WRATH" come.

NOTE: xvii.–xviii. parenthetical (Babylon in "Wrath of God").

NOTE: End of seventh bowl (end of xvi., and xix.):

1. "Lord God reigneth."
2. The 24 elders worship.
3. "He hath judged."
4. Armageddon.

Ch. xx. 1–6 THE MILLENNIAL REIGN OF CHRIST.
xx. 7–10 THE FINAL OUTRAGE AND DOOM OF SATAN.
xx. 11–15 THE FINAL JUDGMENT OF MANKIND.
xxi.–xxii. THE NEW HEAVEN AND THE NEW EARTH.

This, also, brings us to the end of these studies. In a kind of preliminary reconnoitre we have explored the whole land, "from Dan even to Beer-sheba"; and have we not found it "a goodly land, and a large"? We have gathered "grapes of Eshcol" from its verdant valleys, and refreshed ourselves at its streams from the clefts of the rocks. We have stood with the majestic Moses, to see the moving panorama of history's beginnings; and we have stood with the seraphic John, on Patmos, to watch the dramatic unveiling of history's consummations; while between the two— oh, what treasures of truth beyond all price! This is a land to *live* in! This is our "*goodly* heritage." Let us really possess it and prize it as beyond all price.

Can we do better than finish this series of studies where the Bible itself finishes? Look again at its final picture of our Lord and His redeemed ones in the glory of the coming "new heaven and new earth":

"And there shall be no more curse: but the throne of God and of the Lamb shall be in it; and His servants shall serve Him; and they shall see His face; and His name shall be in their foreheads. And there shall be no night there, and they need no candle, neither light of the sun; for the Lord God giveth them light; and they shall reign unto the ages of the ages" (Rev. xxii. 3–5).

Ineffable consummation! Described, yet in its full meaning utterly indescribable! Pick out the seven elements which together constitute its supernal sublimity:

"There shall be no more curse" — i.e. perfect sinlessness.

"The throne of God and the Lamb" — i.e. perfect government.

"His servants shall serve Him" — i.e. perfect service.

"They shall see His face" — i.e. perfect vision.

"His name in their foreheads" — i.e. perfect likeness.

"The Lord God giveth them light" — i.e. perfect illumination.

"They reign for ever and ever" —i.e. perfect blessedness.

And now, with this Divinely unveiled, soul-thrilling consummation in view, let us close, praying the last, yearning prayer of the Bible:

"EVEN SO, COME, LORD JESUS.

The grace of our Lord Jesus Christ be with you all.
Amen."

A PARTING SHEAF OF QUESTIONS

1. Which are the five main chain-themes in 1 John?

2. Which are the seven "contrasts" in 1 John?

3. 1 John is the epistle of "Truth versus . . .". It shows how to "know" and how to ". . ." Can you fill these in?

4. Which are the seven tests (beginning, "If we say", or "He that saith") which occur in 1 John?

5. To whom did John address his second letter? It is in two parts: which are they? The two parts give the centre-test of . . . What?

6. To whom did John write his third epistle? Though short, it breaks into two parts: which are they?

7. Which are the four *approaches* (or schools of interpretation) to the Book of Revelation? Add just a word in explanation of each.

8. Which of the four do *you* think right, and why?

9. The first chapter-group (i.–v.) is progressive and culminative. Can you show how?

10. Which are the three enthronements of our Lord in the Book of Revelation?

11. What indications are there that chapters vi. to xi., and chapters xii. to xix. run parallel with each other?

12. Can you outline the main structure of the book?